CIVIL PROCEDURE
A MODERN APPROACH

Seventh Edition

■ ■ ■

Richard L. Marcus
Horace O. Coil ('57) Chair in Litigation,
University of California,
Hastings College of the Law

Martin H. Redish
Louis and Harriet Ancel Professor of Law and Public Policy,
Northwestern University School of Law

Edward F. Sherman
David Boies Distinguished Chair in Law Emeritus,
Tulane Law School

James E. Pfander
Owen L. Coon Professor of Law,
Northwestern University School of Law

AMERICAN CASEBOOK SERIES®

WEST
ACADEMIC
PUBLISHING

American Casebook Series is a trademark registered in the U.S. Patent and Trademark Office.

COPYRIGHT © 1989, 1995 WEST PUBLISHING CO.
© West, a Thomson business, 2000, 2005, 2008
© 2009 Thomson Reuters
© 2013 LEG, Inc. d/b/a West Academic Publishing
© 2018 LEG, Inc. d/b/a West Academic
    444 Cedar Street, Suite 700
    St. Paul, MN 55101
    1-877-888-1330

West, West Academic Publishing, and West Academic are trademarks of West Publishing Corporation, used under license.

Printed in the United States of America

ISBN: 978-1-64020-185-9

PREFACE TO THE SEVENTH EDITION

It's been nearly 30 years since the first edition of this casebook was published. Although the basic structure has stood the test of time well, the materials relevant to the various topics have evolved. With each new edition, therefore, we find different parts of the book changing significantly. In the sixth edition, for example, the tumult about pleading produced considerable revisions in Chapter 3 to take account of a new aggressiveness of the Supreme Court in that field.

Although the pleading front has hardly been tranquil, other topics have experienced more change during the past five years. The 2015 amendments to the Federal Rules of Civil Procedure have received much attention in the academy and the courts, and they are featured prominently in Chapter 5. The Supreme Court's recent personal jurisdiction decisions have continued an evolution generally toward stricter standards for exercise of jurisdiction. Though a perusal of the Table of Contents for those chapters shows largely the same principal cases, teachers will find that the new textual material uses those cases to highlight and explore the recent developments. A number of important Supreme Court decisions about appellate jurisdiction have been added to Chapter 12, and older cases have been replaced with more recent decisions in Chapter 13. In addition, it is worth noting that several intellectual property cases have been added as principal cases, permitting teachers to highlight this increasingly important area.

All in all, we believe that the new edition provides an entirely up-to-date treatment of civil procedure. And we intend to continue our tradition of providing annual Teachers' Updates to ensure that users of the book remain up-to-date on developments after publication.

An enduring reality for civil procedure teachers is the fact that many students perceive this to be the most difficult and least comprehensible course in their first-year curriculum. To a considerable extent, students' difficulty stems from the fact they have not encountered these issues before even though some civil procedure topics (e.g., class actions and large damage awards) have begun to surface in more general political discourse. By way of contrast, students often have personal experience dealing with the subject matter covered in torts, contracts, and even property courses, and most have some attitudes about criminal law and constitutional law. Few, however, have been personally involved with the intricacies of court rules and procedures. Although issues in substantive law courses relate to "real life" situations, issues of procedure may seem to involve only technical matters that students just beginning the study of law may find difficult to appreciate. For many, developing a taste for procedure is a gradual process; the reality that it will become second nature to many when they are in practice is likely to provide cold comfort at the outset.

This book is premised on the belief that a taste for civil procedure is worth cultivating and that students will find the study of civil procedure more challenging and rewarding than they might have expected. The procedure governing a trial or other dispute resolution process provides the ultimate context for enforcing substantive rights in our society, and it is a common-place that bears repeating that procedure is often critical to the outcome of a case. The initial impression of some law students that civil procedure is a rote-like study of precise rules should give way to an appreciation that procedure, no less than substantive law, is a complex subject that defies a simplistic approach. The perpetual tension between certainty and flexibility in the law is no less important in matters of procedure, and problems of generality and ambiguity are as insistent in procedure as they are in substantive law. Similarly, the impression that procedure does not go the "heart" of the law needs to be tempered with the realization that procedural rules reflect fundamental value judgments and social policies. The manner in which society chooses to resolve its disputes, and its notion of what constitutes procedural fairness, bear directly on social choices about the conduct we want to encourage or discourage and on the allocation and distribution of resources.

We have chosen the subtitle "A Modern Approach" in the belief that this casebook has a focus that puts a distinctive cast on the subject of civil procedure. Recent and ongoing developments have had a significant impact on the way we resolve disputes in this country. It is not so much that the basic procedural rules and mechanisms have been materially altered as that the way they are applied in dispute resolution processes has been affected. To mention only a few of the developments and their impacts on procedure:

- New and often more complex causes of action created by courts and legislatures continue to demand more satisfactory ways to reach a resolution of the dispute;

- New causes of action and our strong societal impulse towards resolving disputes through litigation have resulted in serious court crowding and delay;

- For decades, the high cost of legal services has prompted experiments with ways to cut costs and time in lawsuits through resort to alternative dispute resolution methods;

- Broader standards of legal responsibility and liability have enlarged the number of parties in suits and, to some extent, have also complicated the procedural posture and prompted counterpressures favoring early disposition of claims;

- The class action, in particular, has emerged as a prominent vehicle for "wholesale" redress and as the object of concerns about a variety of perceived abuses, a development furthered by the large recent growth in the dockets of multidistrict proceedings in the federal courts;

- The influence of such disciplines as economics, sociology, and psychology has resulted in a more sophisticated approach to such procedural issues as resource allocation, fundamental fairness, and analysis of competing considerations in dispute resolution;

- Technological developments such as electronic discovery increasingly challenge traditional methods of gathering and presenting evidence at trials, and could alter the form of dispute resolution in ways that depart markedly from the traditional Anglo-American trial format.

- Comparative material has become increasingly prominent; in the globalized economy of the 21st century, American litigation increasingly will be measured by international as well as domestic standards.

This book attempts to reflect the impact of these kinds of contemporary developments without losing sight of the fact that much of civil procedure still concerns traditional rules and mechanisms and time-honored policies. The Seventh Amendment, for example, still relies largely on the "historical" test to determine when parties have a right to jury trial. Modern civil procedure has fortunately not been called upon to reinvent the wheel. In order to understand the contemporary "system" of civil procedure, students must still acquire a sense of its historical development, the traditional interrelationship of procedural devices, and the proper interaction of doctrine and policy. Thus history, doctrine, and key precedents remain an important part of this casebook.

The book roughly follows the chronological order of a lawsuit— proceeding from the initial complaint and pleadings to appeal and the binding effect of a judgment. The first two chapters, however, deviate from the generally-chronological order of presentation, providing an overview of the policies and features of our adversary system (Chapter 1) and of the remedies available in civil litigation (Chapter 2). The chapters on jurisdiction and the choice between state and federal law (the *Erie* problem) follow the chapters on trial preparation and trial in the belief that students are better able to handle the conceptual complexities of these matters once they have an appreciation of the adjudication process. The book concludes with chapters on appellate review and preclusion that not only address the question "What happens after judgment is entered in the trial court?" but also provide an important opportunity to reinforce students' understanding of topics covered earlier.

We think this book offers some distinctive approaches that are not as comprehensively treated in other civil procedure casebooks. These include:

- A continuing reexamination of the policies and mechanisms of our American adversary system, including criticisms of the system and of the procedural innovations (such as sanctions and early-decision devices) that attempt to remedy its shortcomings;

- A reflection, through choice of cases and regularly updated descriptive material, of the impact that the development of public law and complex litigation has had on procedure;

- Treatment, both in an introductory chapter on remedies (Chapter 2) and in a separate chapter on judicial supervision of pretrial and promotion of settlement (Chapter 7) of the developing processes and techniques of alternative dispute resolution;

- Examination of the new management techniques of trial courts, including the devices (such as docket and trial-preparation trial control, discovery, and use of surrogate judicial personnel) and the strengths and weaknesses of such responses;

- Use of interdisciplinary and comparative materials reflecting practices in other countries and various states to introduce the student to alternative ways of dealing with various procedural issues.

We hope that a student will come away from this course with a sense of the process called civil procedure, and with an appreciation of both its strengths and weaknesses and the range of other solutions that are possible in particular situations. We have put some emphasis on practice materials in the belief that one must be able to work effectively with the Federal Rules of Civil Procedure and the various doctrines to claim a mastery of civil procedure. But we also try to ensure that the practice materials force the student to think about the policies underlying the practice and to relate it to the general process themes of the book.

Finally, some comments on format: We have tried to make this text accessible to students by editing out unimportant materials and by minimizing the use of asterisks to indicate those omissions. Whenever we have deleted material from a case or other source, we have indicated that omission either by a bracketed summary of the omitted material or by asterisks. Where quoted material includes deletions by the court or other primary source, there is a conventional ellipse rather than asterisks. We have not indicated the deletion of case and source citations, and have made some effort to remove unimportant citations. We have omitted footnotes from cases and source materials unless they seemed to add something of use, but have retained their original numbering for footnotes we have not deleted.

Throughout the book, we have included substantial notes and questions because we believe they shed light on the principal cases and provide important backup information and citations for those who wish to pursue a matter further. Indeed, even where the primary case remains unchanged we have often modified and updated the notes and questions to ensure that the discussion is up-to-date. In this edition, that sort of updating is particularly prominent in Chapters 5 (on discovery) and 9 (on personal jurisdiction), as rule changes on discovery and Supreme Court decisions on jurisdiction point up new issues while, to some extent, resolving old issues.

The questions we have asked fall basically into three categories: (1) questions that ask the student to ascertain the answer either from what the case says or from the applicable rule or statute; (2) questions, often leading questions, that challenge or provide new perspectives on the assertions made in the principal cases; and (3) questions that invite reflection on the underlying process issues we have tried to raise throughout the book. We hope students will quickly learn to identify the different types of questions and to appreciate the different mental activity called for by them.

We are indebted to many people for their help and guidance during the years we have been working on this book and the previous editions. Most of all, we want to thank our families for their understanding of the demands of the project, and particularly our spouses, Laurie Mikva, Caren Redish, Andrea Saltzman, and Alice Sherman, for their advice, help, and (most of all) their patience. We also want to thank the research assistants who have helped out prepare this edition: Tyler Keefe and Olivia Molodanof of Hastings and Adam Alexander, Samantha Fidler, and Julio Pereyra of Northwestern.

We are also indebted to the copyright holders for permission to reprint excerpts from copyrighted materials listed in the footnote.[1]

RICHARD MARCUS
MARTIN REDISH
EDWARD SHERMAN
JAMES PFANDER

May 2018

---

[1] The following materials are listed in the order in which they appear in the book:

L. Fuller, The Problems of Jurisprudence (1949), copyright © 1949, by Lon Fuller, reprinted by permission of Marjorie D. Fuller.

Zeidler, Evaluation of the Adversary System: As Comparison, Some Remarks on the Investigatory System of Procedure, 55 Australian L.J. 390 (1981), copyright © 1981, by The Law Book Company Ltd.

Frankel, The Search for Truth: An Umpireal View, 123 U.Pa.L.Rev. 1031 (1975), copyright © 1975, Marvin E. Frankel.

Ely, The Irrepressible Myth of Erie, 87 Harv.L.Rev. 693 (1974), copyright © 1974, by the Harvard Law Review Association.

SUMMARY OF CONTENTS

TABLE OF CONTENTS

TABLE OF CASES

The principal cases are in bold type.

TABLE OF AUTHORITIES

CIVIL PROCEDURE

A MODERN APPROACH

Seventh Edition

CHAPTER 1

CHOOSING A SYSTEM OF PROCEDURE

■ ■ ■

Law can be conveniently divided into two categories, substance and procedure. Substantive law defines legal rights and duties in everyday conduct. Thus, it is a rule of substantive law that an individual will be liable in damages for injuring another person through negligence. Procedural law sets out the rules for enforcing substantive rights in the courts. It is a rule of procedure that a complaint filed in a federal court must contain "a short and plain statement of the claim showing that the pleader is entitled to relief" (Federal Rule of Civil Procedure 8(a)(2)). The line between substance and procedure is sometimes difficult to draw, but the basic distinction is central to the theory of procedure.

A procedural system provides the mechanism for applying substantive law rules to concrete disputes. Without rules of procedure there would be no guidelines as to what information is received by the decision-maker (that is, the judge or jury in the American system), how the information is to be presented, or what standards of proof or scope of review apply. In short, without procedure there would be no standardized method of litigation, all cases would be decided *ad hoc,* and there would be no assurance that the same kinds of information and same standards of examination would be applied in similar cases.

The American legal system falls within the family of the "common law," that process, originating in England, by which many rules of law are derived from court cases arising out of disputes between adverse parties. In terms of procedure, the "common law" is often referred to as an "adversary system," with the courts providing an impartial forum for resolution of private disputes in civil cases (and of prosecutions by the state in criminal cases). The moving party (called the plaintiff) is expected to take the initiative in filing a civil suit in the proper manner, and the parties (both plaintiff and defendant) are expected to prepare their cases and present them at trial with a minimum of judicial interference.

Of course, this is not the only plausible way for a court system to operate. In the European "civil law" system, for instance, the judge plays a much more active role in litigation. The "Continental" model, as we shall refer to it, actually is not uniform and has evolved over time. During the 19th century the influential French code, for example, reflected a laissez faire attitude giving the parties much control over the presentation of the

1

case, but late 19th century developments reemphasized the active role of the judge.[1] In the mid 20th century, a Soviet model emerged emphasizing more control by judicial officials in what might be called an "inquisitorial" process in which the officials had the main responsibility for ensuring a correct outcome.[2] But the American model remained distinctive.[3] "The concept that the judiciary properly controls the quest for evidence in civil litigation is * * * fundamental in the civil law,"[4] with the result that the American idea that the parties themselves can use discovery and investigation to obtain evidence (to be covered in Chapter 5) offends against a fundamental precept of that system. In the U.S., the parties' latitude to litigate is often relied upon as a desirable method to enforce the substantive law.[5]

This chapter is entitled "Choosing a System of Procedure" to emphasize that rules of procedure reflect important policy values and that one must approach procedure with some appreciation of the objectives sought to be achieved through litigation. In it, we focus on the roles of the parties and the judge because "[t]he problem of the reciprocal roles of the judge and the parties [is] the central problem of any system of civil procedure."[6]

Most people would list "truth" and "justice" as primary objectives of a good system of dispute resolution. If the only question were one of determining objective facts (as is usually the case in scientific inquiry), then "truth" would be the appropriate standard for decision-making. But the legal process is concerned, for the most part, with the resolution of conflicts of interests between competing parties. Although scientific inquiry may also involve disputes—as when there is disagreement over opposing theories—this is a purely "cognitive conflict," and once the true facts are determined, it is in the interest of all concerned to adopt the solution supported by the facts. Determining the facts, however, is often insufficient to resolve a law suit. A law suit is ordinarily a zero-sum game because it presents competing claims to rights or assets, and a decision that favors one party necessarily disfavors the other. It thus requires a determination of how rights, assets, or losses will be apportioned, and necessitates resort to policy values which we loosely attempt to describe by the term "justice." Inquiry into the "truth," of course, is a necessary aspect

---

[1]   See C.H. van Rhee, European Traditions in Civil Procedure 3–14 (2005).

[2]   See M. Damaska, The Faces of Justice and State Authority 154–73 (1986).

[3]   See Marcus, Putting American Procedural Exceptionalism in Globalized Context, 53 Am. J. Comp. L. 709, 723–24 (2005).

[4]   Hazard, Discovery and the Role of the Judge in Civil Law Jurisdictions, 73 Notre Dame L. Rev. 1017, 1025 (1998).

[5]   See S. Farhang, The Litigation State (2010) (explaining reliance of Title VII employment anti-discrimination statute and many other statutes on enforcement by private plaintiffs rather than public authorities).

[6]   M. Capelletti, The Judicial Process in Comparative Perspective 252 (1989).

of the legal process, but much of what a court does is to go beyond the facts to decide which party has a "just" claim.

Apart from assuring that the outcome is consistent with the rules of substantive law, procedure has a function in making even an unsatisfactory outcome palatable to the parties by making them feel they have had their "day in court." We must recognize that the outcome of every case will not always be consistent with abstract substantive law rules, or with the outcomes in similar cases, and that at least one party is often unhappy with the outcome. There is reason to believe that litigants tend to judge the justness of dispute proceedings without reference to the outcome if they deem the process itself to have been fair.[7] Thus, procedure serves to validate the integrity of the legal system as a whole by providing a remedial process that replaces much more destructive motivations like self-help and personal retribution.

If truth, justice, and fair process are all valid objectives of a legal system, what system of procedure is best suited to accomplishing them? It has been suggested that the manner of distributing control over the process and the decision between the decision-maker and the parties is the most significant factor in characterizing a procedural system.[8] Since procedure largely governs what information will be provided to the decision-maker, the degree of control over the selection and presentation of information given to litigants is a critical feature of any procedural system. The role of attorneys is to exercise the control that is given to the parties. Although procedural systems exist which do not involve lawyers, attorneys play a vital role in our procedural system in ensuring that each party is able to take advantage of the degree of control accorded it. These themes will resurface later as we consider whether particular procedural rules should limit or enhance the control of various participants in particular situations.

It may now be useful to consider a concrete case in an attempt to discern the policies underlying our procedural system.

BAND'S REFUSE REMOVAL, INC. V. BOROUGH OF FAIR LAWN

Superior Court of New Jersey, Appellate Division, 1960
163 A.2d 465

GOLDMANN, S.J.A.D.

Defendants Capasso appeal from a Law Division judgment declaring void *ab initio* and setting aside their garbage removal contract with the Borough of Fair Lawn; declaring illegal and void *ab initio* all payments made to them under the contract; setting aside as illegal and void *ab initio*

---

[7]   Walker, Lind & Thibaut, The Relation Between Procedural and Distributive Justice, 65 Va.L.Rev. 1401, 1412–1414 (1979).

[8]   Thibaut & Walker, A Theory of Procedure, 66 Calif.L.Rev. 541, 548–552 (1978).

Fair Lawn ordinance No. 688, a supplement to the borough sanitary code; and awarding $303,052.62 in favor of the borough against them.

[In February 1957, the Borough of Fair Lawn advertised for bids for collection of garbage in town. After considering bids, the borough council unanimously voted to award the contract to the Capassos, the lowest qualifying bidder, at a base price of $18,260 per month. The contract was signed in May, the Capassos promptly began garbage collection, and they continued to do so in a satisfactory manner through the trial and ensuing appeal.

In August 1957, the borough adopted ordinance 688, which required a permit to collect garbage and provided that only a person who held a contract with the town could be granted a permit. In effect, this meant that only the Capassos could collect garbage in Fair Lawn. Plaintiff Band's Refuse then had a contract to collect garbage from the Western Electric plant in town, so it applied for a permit. The borough denied the application pursuant to the ordinance.

On November 25, 1957, Band's Refuse filed a complaint alleging that ordinance 688 was arbitrary, discriminatory, unconstitutional, and ultra vires. It asked the court to declare the ordinance void and order the borough to renew its previous permit or issue a new one. Plaintiff sued the borough and a number of its officials, and all these defendants filed an answer alleging their action was proper since the contract had been awarded to the Capassos under proper competitive bidding as required by state statute. On motion, the Capassos themselves were allowed to intervene in the suit as defendants and filed an answer that was identical with the borough's. They also filed a counterclaim asking that the borough be restrained from issuing a permit to plaintiff during the term of their contract, restraining plaintiff from collecting garbage in the town and adjudging ordinance 688 and the contract valid.

Meanwhile, a grand jury investigation into scavenger (garbage collection) contracts in the county disclosed allegations of improprieties in the bidding for the Fair Lawn contract and led to indictments of numerous Fair Lawn officials. On May 15, 1958, plaintiff was allowed (over defendants' objections) to file an amended complaint which added a third count alleging that the Fair Lawn-Capasso contract was not the result of open competitive bidding but of "secret agreements and understandings * * * which tainted the bidding with fraud." Both the municipal defendants and the Capassos filed answers denying fraud and claiming compliance with the bidding statutes.

At the same time the complaint was amended, the case was pretried by the trial judge who later presided at trial. Although the amendment expanded the issues involved, the pretrial order limited the fraud contentions to two discrete concerns. The trial was projected to take one day. In fact, it took 21 days.

Before turning to the Capassos' objections to the conduct of the trial, the appellate court held that ordinance 688 was valid and that Band's Refuse could not challenge the legality of the bidding procedure because it lacked "standing" to sue, because it had not bid and was not a resident of Fair Lawn.][a]

The Capassos next contend that the judgment must be reversed because of the manner in which the trial judge conducted the proceedings. On the very first day of the trial, June 19, 1958, counsel for these defendants moved that the judge disqualify himself because his activities before trial demonstrated that he had prejudged the issues and exhibited a plan to use the litigation as a vehicle for a broad municipal investigation. Additionally, counsel during the trial objected repeatedly to the participation in the prosecution of the action by both the trial judge and the *amicus curiae* whom he had appointed. There were also several motions for mistrial because of the allegedly prejudicial actions of the court. All of these were overruled or denied.

The Capassos charge—and it is conceded by the trial judge and plaintiff's attorney, Mr. Zimel—that the judge communicated with Mr. Zimel before the trial began and discussed with him the production of various witnesses. It is also an admitted fact that when, during the course of a telephone conversation, Mr. Zimel informed the judge of the possibility of discontinuing the third count of the complaint, the judge said that if that were done he would immediately declare the contract void.[b] When this was subsequently revealed in the course of a colloquy shortly to be mentioned, the trial judge sought to justify what he said on the ground that this was his sole means of controlling the case, since a very important issue involving the public welfare would be eliminated. We find the justification without merit. What the trial court said suggests a possible prejudging of the issues before a single word of testimony had been adduced. Indeed, it foreshadows what later became manifest—an attitude on the part of the court that a complete exploration into everything that might possibly touch upon the contract was his personal responsibility.

In discharge of his duty, as he conceived it, the trial judge addressed letters to various counsel demanding the production of certain witnesses and records, thus reflecting a prior partisan analysis and preparation of the case normally considered the exclusive function and legitimate interest of counsel representing the respective parties.

---

[a]   Bracketed material was inserted by the editors to summarize portions of the opinion that were deleted. Asterisks indicate deletions of material by the editors.—Eds.

[b]   Presumably this refers to the contract between plaintiff and Western Electric.—Eds.

* * *

Six days before the opening of the trial—on June 13, 1958—the trial judge requested counsel to appear before him. The attorney for the Capassos could not attend because he was engaged in another trial. Nevertheless, the court proceeded to question counsel for plaintiff and the borough, requesting that they produce and subpoena certain named witnesses. As to some of these, plaintiff's attorney said that he had had no intention of calling them. It was during this court appearance that mention was made of the telephone conversation between the trial judge and Mr. Zimel, in the course of which the possibility of discontinuing the third count of the amended complaint was discussed. Mr. Zimel told the court on June 13 that he had amended the complaint because the grand jury had indicted Health Officer Begyn and made a presentment. He frankly admitted, "I have no information other than was contained in the indictment and in the newspapers . . . I have no further proof on that than is contained in the presentment." He went on to explain that the reason he had mentioned dropping the third count when he spoke to the judge on the phone was that "In the recent trial of Mr. Begyn, that part of the indictment which involves him with Capasso Brothers was dismissed by the Court. Since that was dismissed by the Court and there was no ruling on it by any jury or otherwise, I felt that perhaps under those circumstances I might drop the third count and proceed on the illegality of the ordinance itself, feeling now very confident, in my mind anyway, that I would be successful on that point."

After further colloquy, the trial judge proceeded to read a statement obviously prepared in advance for public presentation at the June 13 court session. He reviewed the contents of the pleadings, their filing dates, and the similarity of the positions taken by the borough and the Capassos. He observed that "the fact that the Borough appears unwilling to inquire into the validity of the contract under the present circumstances is most unusual," and then went on to refer to such obviously extra-judicial and legally inadmissible materials as the grand jury investigation, its presentment, and the indictment of two Fair Lawn officials for an offense unrelated to the litigation. "These facts," he said, "together with the newspaper accounts of fraud connected with the collection of garbage under the contract involved in this suit, makes it imperative in the public interest that the matter be investigated. . . ." He concluded this part of his statement with the remark that the apparent neglect of the borough to undertake and adequately protect the public interest and welfare involved in the suit "borders on criminal nonfeasance."

The trial judge then proceeded to appoint an *amicus curiae,* whose duty it would be "to present evidence, subpoena witnesses, examine all witnesses, and submit to the court briefs on the law and facts."

* * *

Even a casual reading of the record, covering some 2,000 pages of printed appendix, reveals an extraordinary participation by the judge in the trial of the cause. He obviously had devoted much time in preparing for the questioning of witnesses and the offering of exhibits. This preparation on the part of the court extended to the issuance of subpoenas by the court itself and by its *amicus curiae,* and the contacting of witnesses for their appearance. The trial judge secured files and documents from the prosecutor's office and sifted them in advance, in preparation of having such of them as he deemed relevant offered as exhibits.

At the hearings the judge called witnesses on his own motion or had the *amicus* do so, and examined and cross-examined them at length. He offered exhibits he had called for. He ruled upon the propriety of his own questions and upon the admissibility of his own exhibits. On occasion he attacked the credibility of witnesses called by him.

In all, there were 32 witnesses who took the stand during the 21 trial days. Of these, the parties produced five; the trial judge, by his own subpoena, direction or arrangement, called 27. Of the latter, 24 were permitted to testify upon questioning by the court or *amicus curiae,* and this over the objection of counsel for the Capassos that their names had not been supplied in answer to interrogatories.

* * *

Defendants Capasso do not question the right of a judge to interrogate a witness in order to qualify testimony or elicit additional information, or his right under special circumstances to summon a witness on his own initiative. Generally, a court's interrogation of witnesses, where not excessive, has been sustained. As was pointed out by our Supreme Court, the power to take an active part in the trial of a case must be exercised by the judge with the greatest restraint. "There is a point at which the judge may cross that fine line that separates advocacy from impartiality. When that occurs there may be substantial prejudice to the rights of one of the litigants."

The motivation of the trial judge may be found in what he said in his opinion in justification of his appointment of *amicus curiae*; he felt that the court was "faced with a grave situation testing its ability and will to use its powers, if necessary, to prevent fraud, preserve justice, and protect the public interest." He also observed that he had the power to investigate as auxiliary to his power to decide, and "the power to investigate implies necessarily the power to summon and to question witnesses."

What is called for here is a balancing of judicial power against the interests of a litigant. On the one hand, there is the recognized power of a trial judge to call witnesses. Balanced against this power of a trial judge must be the necessity of judicial self-restraint and the maintenance of an atmosphere of impartiality. Courts must not only be impartial; they must give the appearance of impartiality.

The power of a trial judge to call and examine witnesses is not unlimited. His conduct of a trial contrary to traditional rules and concepts which have been established for the protection of private rights constitutes a denial of due process. The limitations upon the activities and remarks of a trial judge have usually been considered within the frame of reference of a jury trial. However, the necessity of judicial self-restraint is no less important where the judge sits alone; if he participates to an unreasonable degree in the conduct of the trial, even to the point of assuming the role of an advocate, what he does may be just as prejudicial to a defendant's rights as if the case were tried to a jury. * * *

It is our conclusion that the trial judge overstepped the permissible bounds of judicial inquiry in this case. In effect, he took on the role of advocate, his activities extending from investigation and preparation to the actual presentation of testimony and exhibits at the trial. He converted the action into what amounted to a municipal investigation. Cf. Canons of Judicial Ethics, Canon 15, dealing with a judge's interference in the conduct of a trial.

We agree with defendants Capasso that the trial court committed prejudicial error by producing a large number of witnesses and admitting their testimony in evidence.

Defendants Capasso served supplemental interrogatories upon plaintiff on May 20, 1958 requesting the names and addresses of all witnesses to the facts alleged in the third count of the amended complaint. The answer [contained the names of only seven witnesses]. This answer was not supplemented or amended before trial.

The court, as noted, produced 27 witnesses on its own motion; 24 had not been named in the answer to interrogatories. Counsel for the Capassos had no advance notice of the identity of these witnesses and no opportunity to conduct adequate pretrial investigation. He made proper objection as each witness was called, but to no avail. The testimony they gave, as a reading of the trial judge's lengthy opinion and supplemental opinion will demonstrate, played an important part in the factual conclusions he reached.

Under R.R. 4:23–12 of our interrogatory rules, the penalty for failure to name a witness in answer to interrogatories is the exclusion of the testimony of that witness at the trial. * * *

It would seem anomalous to give a party protection from surprise witnesses when they are called by the opposition, but not when called by the court itself. The potential for harm is identical in either case. In addition, the testimony of the witnesses here called by the court brought entirely new issues into the case which were in no wise comprehended by the pretrial order. These issues found their way into the court's opinions and will be mentioned hereinafter.

* * *

Prejudicial error also resulted from the creation of new issues by the court—issues never mentioned or suggested in the pretrial order.

On September 10, 1958, the eleventh day of the trial and four months after the pretrial conference was held, the trial judge on his own motion, and without prior notice, stated that he was adding new issues, and this over the most strenuous objection of counsel for the Capassos. [The new issues alleged noncompliance with the bidding process required by various state statutes.]

The five added issues provided a substantial foundation for the court's conclusion that the Capasso contract was invalid. Although the trial judge in his original opinion made the bare statement that "There was no justifiable reason to allege surprise on any new issue raised during the trial," we cannot agree. The issues were injected into the case without notice or warning. There was no reason for the Capassos or their counsel to anticipate that these questions were issues to be tried until the judge, against a background of testimony he was largely responsible for adducing, brought them into the trial picture.

As in the case of the judge's other activities before and during trial, so here—he apparently considered it his duty to introduce new issues because of the public character of the case, in disregard of those which had been defined by the parties, and in disregard of the rules and precedents applicable in civil cases.

The function of a trial judge is to serve litigants by determining their disputes and the issues implicated therein in accordance with applicable rules and law. Established procedures lie at the heart of due process and are as important to the attainment of ultimate justice as the factual merits of a cause. A judge may not initiate or inspire litigation and, by the same token, he may not expand a case before him by adding new issues which come to mind during the trial, without giving the parties affected a full and fair opportunity to meet those issues.

* * *

On September 11, 1958, the twelfth day of the trial, the recently substituted counsel for the borough and its officials applied for permission to change the position theretofore taken by them, as set forth in their original answer and amended answer and as repeated on a number of occasions during the preceding trial days. Up to that moment the borough and its officials had insisted that the ordinance and the contract were valid.

These defendants were now allowed to file a second amended answer alleging fraud and the invalidity of the contract, and a cross-claim seeking recovery against the Capassos of all monies paid them under the contract. This change of position was permitted over the vigorous and extended objection of the Capassos' attorney. Counsel's request for adequate time to protect the interests of his client by investigation and discovery proceedings was promptly denied.

The Capassos insist that this sudden shift came as a shock and a surprise and amounted to a substantial deprivation of their fundamental rights. They quote from Grobart v. Society for Establishing Useful Manufactures, 2 N.J. 136, 149, 65 A.2d 833 (1949), where former Chief Justice Vanderbilt said:

> ". . . It is not a mere matter of formal logic that leads the courts to insist that litigants shall not shift their position in *successive* pleadings.
>
> . . . [S]hifting causes of action in successive pleading will completely block the purpose of all pleading, i.e., getting to an issue or issues where one party asserts the affirmative and the other the negative on a question or questions of law or of fact."

It seems inappropriate to extend the *Grobart* rule in the present case. When the original answer was filed by the borough and borough officials—and so with the amended answer to plaintiff's amended complaint—the officials apparently had the honest belief that the Capasso contract was in all respects valid. What came out in the course of the trial, mostly through witnesses and exhibits brought into the case by the court and its *amicus curiae*, must have changed their minds. It is also possible that they had a second thought in the light of the impact of the grand jury's action upon the public and the newspapers, and the impending legislative investigation into the scavenger business.

If the Capasso contract was not in fact the result of *bona fide* competitive bidding, it was important and proper from the point of view of the paramount public right and interest to allow the amended answer. However, fairness to defendants dictated that they be allowed a reasonable time for discovery and investigation, in order that the facts in support of their claim that the contract was valid might be developed and presented. They had up to that moment been dealing with a situation where the borough and its officials had stoutly affirmed the validity of the contract. The municipality had taken no steps to rescind the agreement, but had accepted scavenger service and made monthly payments thereunder even during the period of the hearings. Its position had been affirmed and reaffirmed, in its pleadings, in the pretrial order, and during the trial. Fundamental fairness required that the court allow the Capassos sufficient time to meet the radically new situation facing them. The denial of that opportunity was the denial of due process.

* * *

The judgment is reversed and the matter remanded for a full trial to determine the validity of the scavenger contract. Substituted pleadings should be filed, reasonable discovery allowed and a new pretrial conference held, in order that the exact position of the several parties will be manifest, their respective contentions clearly defined, and the issues sharply drawn. In view of the fact that the borough, mayor and council, and borough manager now challenge the validity of the Capasso contract, there would appear to be no need for the services of an *amicus curiae*. The parties can be relied upon to develop fully what are patently the issues of the case, including such questions as compliance with the bidding, appropriation and prequalification statutes, and the charges of collusion and connivance among the bidders and between the Capassos and the borough officials.

NOTES AND QUESTIONS

1.　This suit, filed in a New Jersey trial court, was subject to the New Jersey rules of civil procedure, rather than the Federal Rules of Civil Procedure that apply in federal courts. Today many states' rules of civil procedure are directly modelled on the Federal Rules. The New Jersey rules applicable at the time of this case had a number of significant variations from the Federal Rules, but many of the basic steps in the litigation chronology are the same. Note the various pretrial procedural steps followed in this case (with the analogous Federal Rule shown in parentheses):

— complaint filed by plaintiff Band's Refuse Removal, Inc. (Fed.R.Civ.P. 8(a));

— answer filed by defendant Borough of Fair Lawn, containing five separate defenses (Fed.R.Civ.P. 8(b)–(c));

— motion of the Capassos to intervene as defendants granted (Fed. R.Civ.P. 24);

— answer and counterclaims filed by defendants Capasso (Fed.R.Civ.P. 8, 13);

— plaintiff permitted to file an amended complaint after Grand Jury issued indictments (Fed.R.Civ.P. 15);

— discovery conducted by the parties, including interrogatories requesting identity of witnesses (cf. Fed.R.Civ.P. 26, 33);

— judge held pre-trial hearing (cf. Fed.R.Civ.P. 16);

— judge appointed *amicus curiae* to present evidence, subpoena and examine witnesses, and submit briefs (cf. Fed.R.Civ.P. 53);

— trial held (cf. Fed.R.Civ.P. 38–52);

— judgment entered (cf. Fed.R.Civ.P. 54(a); 58);

— appeal taken (cf. Fed.R.App.P. 3; 4).

2.   If the trial judge had reason to believe that the Capassos had influence over the borough, was he powerless to do anything about it? Cf. Haitian Refugee Ctr. v. Civiletti, 503 F.Supp. 442, 461 (S.D.Fla.1980) ("Federal Courts are not roving engines of justice careening about the land in search of wrongs to right.") Does his claim that the public welfare was at stake justify a more activist role? If so, how did he err in carrying out that role? Does the fact that the borough eventually switched sides show that the trial judge was right to do as he did? If it had not switched sides, what would the appellate court have done with the case?

In *Band's Refuse* the judge justified his activism by saying that his investigation was integral to his responsibility to decide the case correctly. Should the judge's responsibility extend this far? Consider the following description of the role of judges in 19th century Japan in Goodman, Justice and Civil Procedure in Japan (2004) at 68:

> Since the responsibility for clarifying issues was a responsibility of the judge and since the judge was also responsible for reaching a correct decision in the matter, the process was judge centered. Judges could on their own call witnesses and could question witnesses before the parties were permitted to examine. The parties did not have ultimate responsibility for either fact gathering and fact production or for legal contention presentation. As the judge was responsible for arriving at a "correct" decision, these matters were part of the court's responsibility. If the judge failed to properly clarify the case (i.e., if the judge failed to address legal issues that might change the decision or failed to investigate into factual matters that might change the result—even if such legal or factual matters had not been raised by the parties) the court's decision could be reversed on appeal.

It bears emphasis that this "self-starter" role is not the norm for judges in other systems. Instead, the judge in the Continental system usually investigates according to "suggestions" from the parties, not as a self-starter. Should judges be self-starters? In France, there have since Napoleonic times been officials called "investigating magistrates" who wield great authority. Balzac, for example, said in the 19th century that "No human authority can encroach upon the power of an investigating judge; nothing can stop him; no one can control him." But that sort of judicial behavior is not countenanced in the rest of Western Europe. In the U.K., for example, the Court of Appeal denounced intervention by trial judges in pending cases, saying it involved "a quasi-inquisitorial role" that is "entirely at odds with the adversarial system." Southwark LBC v. Maamefowaa Kofiadu [2006] EWCA Civ. 281 at [148].

3.   *Band's Refuse* says an American trial judge can call witnesses in civil cases "under limited circumstances." What are those circumstances? Consider the following views regarding the judge's questioning of witnesses: "A trial

judge may not advocate on behalf of a plaintiff or a defendant, nor may he betray even a hint of favoritism toward either side. This scrupulous impartiality is not inconsistent with asking a question of a witness in an effort to make the testimony crystal clear for the jury. The trial judge need not sit on the bench like a mummy when his intervention would serve to clarify an issue for the jurors." Ross v. Black & Decker, Inc., 977 F.2d 1178, 1187 (7th Cir.1992). How could the trial judge in *Band's Refuse* have exercised that power properly?

In Williams v. Warner, 731 F.3d 731 (7th Cir. 2013), the district judge responded to a pro se prisoner complaint (filed without a lawyer) by convening a telephonic "merit-review hearing" with plaintiff. On that basis, the judge dismissed, but the court of appeals found this practice improper (id. at 732–33):

> The procedure employed by the judge was inquisitorial. It resembles the procedure employed by a French *juge d'instruction*, who doubles as judge and investigator, and by other similar officials in other Continental judicial systems. The practice has no basis in American law other than in proceedings before some administrative agencies, and was conducted in this case without any of the safeguards that attend the Continental practice, such as the right to assistance of counsel.

4.   With these issues in mind, let us reflect on whether the American adversary model is inevitable, or even desirable.

Lon Fuller, The Problems of Jurisprudence
706–07 (1949)

Adjudication involves a complex of factors that may appear in various combinations and that may be present in varying degrees. We may, however, say that the moral force of a judgment or decision will be at a maximum when the following conditions are satisfied: 1) The judge does not act on his own initiative, but on the application of one or both of the disputants. 2) The judge has no direct or indirect interest (even emotional) in the outcome of the case. 3) The judge confines his decision to the controversy before him and attempts no regulation of the parties' relations going beyond that controversy. 4) The case presented to the judge involves an existing controversy, and not merely the prospect of some future disagreement. 5) The judge decides the case solely on the basis of the evidence and arguments presented to him by the parties. 6) Each disputant is given ample opportunity to present his case.

It is seldom that all of these conditions can be realized in practice, and it is not here asserted that it is always wise to observe all of them. What is asserted is merely that adjudication as a principle of order achieves its maximum force when all of these conditions are satisfied. Some of this moral or persuasive force may wisely be sacrificed when other considerations dictate a departure from the conditions enumerated above, and where the tribunal, as an agent of legitimated power, has the capacity to compel respect for its decision.

The connection between the conditions enumerated above and the moral force of the judgment rendered is not something irrational and fortuitous. The key to it is found in the fact that men instinctively seek to surround the process of adjudication with those conditions that will tend to insure that the decision rendered is the closest possible approximation of the common need. This obviously explains the conditions of disinterestedness on the part of the judge and the opportunity for a full hearing of both sides, that is, conditions 2 and 6 in the enumeration above. Underlying the other four conditions is a single insight, namely, that men's interests and desires form a complex network, and that to discover the most effective and least disruptive pattern of order within this network requires an intimate acquaintance with the network itself and the interests and desires of which it is composed. In other words, these conditions are designed to obviate an evil that may be broadly called "absentee management." The judge must stick to the case before him (condition 3), because if he ventures beyond it he may attempt to regulate affairs on which he is inadequately informed. The judge must work within the framework of the parties' arguments and proof (condition 5), because if he goes beyond these he will lack the guidance given him by the parties and may not understand the interests that are affected by a decision rendered outside that framework. The case must involve a present controversy (condition 4), because neither the parties nor the judge can be sure that they fully understand the implications of a possible, future controversy or the precise interests that may be affected by it when it arises. The first condition (that the judge should act on the application of the parties) is perhaps the most difficult to justify. It arises from the fact that the judge who calls the parties in and himself sets the framework of the hearing lays himself open to the suspicion of planning a general regulation in which the controversy on which he hears evidence and arguments appears as a mere detail. Thus a violation of condition 1 tends to carry with it a strong suspicion that condition 3 is being violated.

W. ZEIDLER, EVALUATION OF THE ADVERSARY SYSTEM: AS COMPARISON, SOME REMARKS ON THE INVESTIGATORY SYSTEM OF PROCEDURE
55 Australian L.J. 390, 394–97 (1981)

While the English judge is an umpire sitting at the sidelines watching the lawyers fight it out and afterwards declaring one of them the winner, the German judge is the director of an improvised play, the outcome of which is not known to him at first but depends heavily on his mode of directing.

Thus to our English colleague the German judge will seem highly vocal and dominant whereas counsel will appear to act with somewhat subdued adversary zeal. * * *

It is the task of the Continental lawyers to determine through the facts which they introduce and by the applications which they make what the specific question in issue in the litigation is. The parties, therefore, do draw the perimeters of the dispute and within these the court must determine the issues raised by the parties. But most of the rest is, it is true, then up to the judge. It is he who advances the course of the proceedings and conducts the hearings at the trial. He has the duty of finding out the law including the foreign law and to some extent even the facts of the case. To allow the examination of the witnesses and experts to be placed in the hands of the attorneys has always been thought to be incompatible with the most important rule, namely that it is the chief function of a court of law to find out the truth and not merely to decide which party has adduced better evidence. * * *

As a result, the judge interrogates the witnesses and experts, while the attorneys only put supplementary questions. * * *

The German judge is not * * * limited only to consideration of the probative value of the material put forward by the parties. The judge can, for example, appoint ex officio an independent expert even if neither of the parties requested this to be done. The judge may of his own motion make an order that a view be taken of a locus quo such as the scene of a traffic accident, and he may also request public authorities to transmit documents or to furnish official information. He may also order a litigant to produce any documents to which he has referred as a means of proof and which are in his possession. In the words of Kaplan, von Mehren and Schaefer: "Always examining the case as it progresses with understanding of the probably applicable norms, the court puts questions intended to mark out areas of agreement and disagreement, to elucidate allegations and proof offers and the meaning of matters elicited in proof-takings. In this way the court enlightens itself about the issues, and at the same time broadens the understanding of counsel and the parties. The court leads the parties by suggestion to strengthen their respective positions, to improve upon, change, and amplify their allegations and proof offers and to take other steps." [See "Kaplan, von Mehren and Schaefer, Phases of German Civil Procedure, 71 Harv.L.Rev. 1193, 1225 (1958)].

The leading part played by the court both in deciding on the nature of the evidence to be examined and in taking it explains why the lawyers are generally not allowed to examine the witnesses privately before this is done by the court. It is feared that this could unduly influence their testimony.

* * * It is the court who asks for the witness' name, age, occupation and residence and who warns him that he must tell the truth. The witness is then invited by the judge to tell in narrative form and without undue interruption what he knows about the matter. After he has told his story it is the court which asks questions designed to test, clarify and amplify it. When the lawyers' and the parties' turn comes to formulate pertinent questions, very little use is normally made of this opportunity, at least by English standards, perhaps because extensive questioning by them might appear to be critical of the court itself.

MARVIN FRANKEL, THE SEARCH FOR TRUTH: AN UMPIREAL VIEW
123 U.Pa.L.Rev. 1031, 1042–43 (1975)*

The fact is that our system does not allow much room for effective or just intervention by the trial judge in the adversary fight about the facts. The judge views the case from a peak of Olympian ignorance. His intrusions will in too many cases result from partial or skewed insights. He may expose the secrets one side chooses to keep while never becoming aware of the other's. He runs a good chance of pursuing inspirations that better informed counsel have considered, explored, and abandoned after fuller study. He risks at a minimum the supplying of more confusion than guidance by his sporadic intrusions.

The ignorance and unpreparedness of the judge are intended axioms of the system. The "facts" are to be found and asserted by the contestants. The judge is not to have investigated or explored the evidence before trial. No one is to have done it for him. The judicial counterpart in civil law countries, with the file of the investigating magistrate before him, is a deeply "alien" conception. * * * Without an investigative file, the American trial judge is a blind and blundering intruder, acting in spasms as sudden flashes of seeming light may lead or mislead him at odd times.

The ignorant and unprepared judge is, ideally, the properly bland figurehead in the adversary scheme of things. Because the parties and counsel control the gathering and presentation of evidence, we have made no fixed, routine, expected place for the judge's contributions. It is not a regular thing for the trial judge to present or meaningfully to "comment upon" the evidence. As a result, his interruptions are just that— interruptions; occasional, unexpected, sporadic, unprogrammed, and unduly dramatic because they are dissonant and out of character. The result—to focus upon the jury trial, the model for our system including, of course, its rules of evidence—is that the judge's participation, whether in the form of questions or of comments, is likely to have a disproportionate and distorting impact. The jury is likely to discern hints, a point of view, a

---

*   At the time he wrote this article, Marvin Frankel was a U.S. District Judge.

suggested direction, even if none is intended and quite without regard to the judge's efforts to modulate and minimize his role. Whether the jury follows the seeming lead or recoils from it is not critical. The point is that there has been a deviant influence, justified neither in adversary principles nor in the rational competence of the trial judge to exert it.

We should be candid, moreover, in recognizing that juries are probably correct most of the time if they glean a point of view from the judge's interpolations. Introspecting, I think I have usually put my penetrating questions to witnesses I thought were lying, exaggerating, or obscuring the facts. Less frequently, I have intruded to rescue a witness from questions that seemed unfairly to put the testimony in a bad light or to confuse its import. Similar things appear in the reported decisions. The trial judge who takes over cross-examination seems to be hot on the scent after truth. Even the cold page conveys notes not wholly austere or detached. This would all be agreeable for a rational system of justice if there were grounds to suppose that the judge was always, or nearly always, on the right track. But there are not such grounds. The apparatus is organized to equip the judge poorly for the position of attempted leadership. Within the confines of the adversary framework, the trial judge probably serves best as relatively passive moderator.

NOTES AND QUESTIONS

1.   Professor Fuller speaks in rather general terms of the attributes of adjudication. Do both the American and the Continental models embody the characteristics he endorses? Has he emphasized the wrong things?

2.   According to Professor Kessler, in the early 19th century American judges regularly exerted much more control over evidence-gathering, and the lawyers were largely shut out of that activity. But during the mid 19th century American lawyers "embraced adversrialism * * * because they were eager to exercise more procedural control," and they succeeded in gaining control. See A. Kessler, Inventing American Exceptionalism 151 (2017).

3.   Some have argued that the American approach should be revised more radically to resemble the Continental model. Professor Langbein, for example, contends that it would be possible to preserve the adversary nature of adjudication while leaving fact development to the judge. See Langbein, The German Advantage in Civil Procedure, 52 U.Chi.L.Rev. 823 (1985). Does this argument disregard important differences between the two systems? For example, in the American system much of the law is derived from previous cases, while the Continental approach, influenced by the Napoleonic Code, relies more heavily on statutes. More significantly, the American commitment to the jury trial seems incompatible with the Continental emphasis on fact development by the judiciary.

Sherman, Transnational Perspectives Regarding the Federal Rules of Civil Procedure, 57 J. Legal Ed. 510 (2006), notes that American practice under the Federal Rules differs from traditional civil law procedure as to such features as notice pleading, single-event trials with live testimony, broad discovery, a central role for counsel and correspondingly reduced role for the judge, liberal joinder and aggregation devices, and promotion of settlement. But in recent decades, "the two systems have increasingly influenced each other" and have moved closer in their methods. The American Law Institute, in conjunction with the International Institute for the Unification of Private Law (UNIDROIT), has published Principles of Transnational Civil Procedure (Cambridge U. Press, 2006), which attempts to identify "fundamental principles for transnational commercial litigation" that sometimes deviate from those used in American courts. As to the role of the judge in calling and examining witnesses in civil law countries versus examination by counsel in common law countries, they comment (Principles at 145):

> The chief deficiency in the common-law procedure is excessive partisanship in cross-examination, with the danger of abuses and distorting the truth. In the civil law the chief deficiency is passivity and lack of interest of the court while conducting an examination, with the danger of not reaching relevant information. Both procedures require efficient technique, on the part of the judge in civil-law systems and the lawyers in common-law systems.

4.   What impact would emphasizing judicial control have on the parties' willingness to accept the outcome? Would litigants be reluctant to turn over factual investigation to judges? How would plaintiffs suing the government be likely to view such a process?

5.   The American judge's role has also been expanded pursuant to amendments to the Federal Rules. Fed.R.Civ.P. 16 now provides for two kinds of pretrial conferences—"scheduling and planning" and "final." A judge must enter a "scheduling order" limiting the parties' time to complete various pretrial tasks within 90 days after the complaint is served. A "final" conference should be held "as close to the time of trial as is reasonable" and result in a pretrial order that "control[s] the course of the action." Some see a shift in the role of judges: "Judges began to see themselves less as neutral adjudicators—deciding what the parties brought to them for decision and proceeding at a pace to be determined by the parties—and more as managers of a costly and complicated process." Shapiro, Federal Rule 16: A Look at the Theory and Practice of Rulemaking, 137 U.Pa.L.Rev. 1969, 1983 (1989); see also Marcus, Reining in the American Lawyer: The New Role of American Judges, 27 Hast. Int'l & Compar. L. Rev. 3 (2003).

Judicial management has been criticized as making judges meddling, bureaucratic administrators who lose their basic sense of judging. See Resnik, Managerial Judges, 96 Harv.L.Rev. 374, 445 (1982) ("Seduced by controlled calendars, disposition statistics, and other trappings of the efficiency era and the high-tech age, managerial judges are changing the nature of their work.") But the case management movement has nevertheless spread to other common law countries, and England adopted similar techniques in 1999. "Certainly, the new [English procedural] code has reshaped the relationship between the parties, their lawyers, and the courts. Already, it is clear that there has been an important shift of procedural control from the parties to the court." N. Andrews, English Civil Procedure 29–30 (2003).

KOTHE V. SMITH

United States Court of Appeals, Second Circuit, 1985
771 F.2d 667

Before LUMBARD, VAN GRAAFEILAND and PIERCE, CIRCUIT JUDGES.

VAN GRAAFEILAND, CIRCUIT JUDGE:

Dr. James Smith appeals from a judgment of the United States District Court for the Southern District of New York (Sweet, J.), which directed him to pay $1,000 to plaintiff-appellee's attorney, $1,000 to plaintiff-appellee's medical witness, and $480 to the Clerk of the Court. For the reasons hereinafter discussed, we direct the judgment be vacated.

Patricia Kothe brought this suit for medical malpractice against four defendants, Dr. Smith, Dr. Andrew Kerr, Dr. Kerr's professional corporation, and Doctors Hospital, seeking $2 million in damages. She discontinued her action against the hospital four months prior to trial. She discontinued against Dr. Kerr and his corporation on the opening day of the trial.

Three weeks prior thereto, Judge Sweet held a pretrial conference, during which he directed counsel for the parties to conduct settlement negotiations. Although it is not clear from the record, it appears that Judge Sweet recommended that the case be settled for between $20,000 and $30,000. He also warned the parties that, if they settled for a comparable figure after trial had begun, he would impose sanctions against the dilatory party. Smith, whose defense has been conducted throughout this litigation by his malpractice insurer, offered $5,000 on the day before trial, but it was rejected.

Although Kothe's attorney had indicated to Judge Sweet that his client would settle for $20,000, he had requested that the figure not be disclosed to Smith. Kothe's counsel conceded at oral argument that the lowest pretrial settlement demand communicated to Smith was $50,000. Nevertheless, when the case was settled for $20,000 after one day of trial, the district court proceeded to penalize Smith alone. In imposing the penalty, the court stated that it was "determined to get the attention of the carrier" and that "the carriers are going to have to wake up when a judge tells them that they want to settle a case and they don't want to settle it." Under the circumstances of this case, we believe that the district court's imposition of a penalty against Smith was an abuse of the sanction power given it by Fed.R.Civ.P. 16(f).

Although the law favors the voluntary settlement of civil suits, it does not sanction efforts by trial judges to effect settlements through coercion. Del Rio v. Northern Blower Co., 574 F.2d 23, 26 (1st Cir.1978) (citing Wolff v. Laverne, Inc., 17 A.D.2d 213, 233 N.Y.S.2d 555 (1962)). In the *Wolff* case, cited with approval in *Del Rio,* supra, the Court said:

> We view with disfavor all pressure tactics whether directly or obliquely, to coerce settlement by litigants and their counsel. Failure to concur in what the Justice presiding may consider an adequate settlement should not result in an imposition upon a litigant or his counsel, who reject it, of any retributive sanction not specifically authorized by law.

In short, pressure tactics to coerce settlement simply are not permissible. "The judge must not compel agreement by arbitrary use of his power and the attorney must not meekly submit to a judge's suggestion, though it be strongly urged." Brooks v. Great Atlantic & Pacific Tea Co., 92 F.2d 794, 796 (9th Cir.1937).

Rule 16 of the Fed.R.Civ.P. was not designed as a means for clubbing the parties—or one of them—into an involuntary compromise. Although subsection (c)[(2)(I)] of Rule 16, added in the 1983 amendments of the Rule, was designed to encourage pretrial settlement discussion, it was not its purpose to "impose settlement negotiations on unwilling litigants." See Advisory Committee Note, 1983, 97 F.R.D. 205, 210.

We find the coercion in the instant case especially troublesome because the district court imposed sanctions on Smith alone. Offers to settle a claim are not made in a vacuum. They are part of a more complex process which includes "conferences, informal discussions, offers, counterdemands, more discussions, more haggling, and finally, in the great majority of cases, a compromise." J. & D. Sindell, Let's Talk Settlement 300 (1963). In other words, the process of settlement is a two-way street and a defendant should not be expected to bid against himself. In the instant case, Smith never received a demand of less than $50,000. Having received no indication from Kothe that an offer somewhere in the vicinity of $20,000 would at least be given careful consideration, Smith should not have been required to make an offer in this amount simply because the court wanted him to.

Smith's attorney should not be condemned for changing his evaluation of the case after listening to Kothe's testimony during the first day of the trial. As every experienced trial lawyer knows, the personalities of the parties and their witnesses play an important role in litigation. It is one thing to have a valid claim; it is quite another to convince a jury of this fact. It is not at all unusual, therefore, for a defendant to change his perception of a case based on the plaintiff's performance on the witness stand. We see nothing about that occurrence in the instant case that warranted the imposition of sanctions against the defendant alone.

Although we commend Judge Sweet for his efforts to encourage settlement negotiations, his excessive zeal leaves us no recourse but to remand the matter with instructions to vacate the judgment.

NOTES AND QUESTIONS

1. If the plaintiff's offer to settle for $20,000 had been communicated to the defendant, would sanctions still not have been appropriate? Given the court's comment that an attorney should not be condemned for changing her evaluation of the case after hearing the evidence, would it ever be fair to impose sanctions on one who thought that the case was stronger than it actually appeared at trial? Does the court's comment that the law does not support efforts "to effect settlements through coercion" mean that a judge can never sanction a party for refusal to settle? A district judge with a large number of asbestos personal injury cases set a time limit for settling cases set for trial, and the appellate court held that this was permissible under Rule 16: "[I]mposing sanctions for unjustified failure to comply with the court's schedule for settlement is entirely consistent with the spirit of Rule 16. The purpose of Rule 16 is to maximize the efficiency of the court system by insisting that attorneys and clients cooperate with the court and abandon practices which unreasonably interfere with the expeditious management of cases." Newton v. A.C. & S., 918 F.2d 1121 (3d Cir.1990).

2. The judge in *Kothe* ordered the parties to conduct settlement negotiations, and that Rule 16 authorizes settlement conferences with the judge. For some time, there was a debate about whether Rule 16 permitted judges to require parties represented by counsel to attend settlement conferences. (This is discussed fully in G. Heileman Brewing Co. v. Joseph Oat Corp., infra p. 490.) In 1993 this rule was amended to permit the judge to "require that a party or its representative be present or reasonably available by telephone in order to consider possible settlement of the dispute." How should judges use this authority? Consider U.S. v. U.S. District Court for the Northern Mariana Islands, 694 F.3d 1051 (9th Cir. 2012) (holding that the district court abused its discretion by ordering that the Assistant Attorney General attend the initial settlement conference in a tax refund suit filed in the Northern Mariana Islands).

An additional complicating factor is the role of insurance companies in settlement. In *Kothe* the judge said he wanted to "get the attention" of insurance companies. Should the judge be allowed to compel their attendance? The reality is that insurers may play a critical role in controlling settlements. See Syverud, The Duty to Settle, 76 Va.L.Rev. 1113, 1115–17 (1990). Nevertheless, there is doubt about whether courts can require their participation in settlement conferences. Compare In re Novak, 932 F.2d 1397 (11th Cir.1991) (court may not compel attendance by representative of insurer) with Lockhart v. Patel, 115 F.R.D. 44 (E.D.Ky.1987) (court sanctioned defendant because his insurer did not send representative with authority to settle rather than "some flunky who has no authority to negotiate").

3. If a judge can require parties and counsel to attend a settlement conference, what can they be required to do there? In G. Heileman Brewing Co. v. Joseph Oat Corp., 871 F.2d 648 (7th Cir.1989), the court found that a district judge did not have authority to require attendance by a person "willing to settle on someone else's terms," but only a person with authority to speak definitively and to commit the corporation in the litigation. What does "authority to settle" mean? If the defendant's representative only has authority to settle the case for $100 "nuisance value," is that sufficient authority to settle? Does it suffice if the representative has been instructed "not to pay one cent" because the company believes the suit is without merit? Court orders to mediate sometimes require that the parties "participate in good faith." Is it possible to have a "good faith participation" standard that does not improperly interfere with the parties' right not to yield or settle? For discussion, see Sherman, Court-Mandated Alternative Dispute Resolution, 46 S.M.U.L.Rev. 2079, 2089–94 (1993).

In Shedden v. Wal-Mart Stores, Inc., 196 F.R.D. 484 (E.D. Mich. 2000), Wal-Mart sent one of its store managers to the final pretrial settlement conference, but the store manager reiterated Wal-Mart's policy that it would not settle suits brought by customers. According to Wal-Mart, there was accordingly nothing more to say. The judge reacted as follows (id. at 486):

> Because Wal-Mart's asserted "no settlement" litigation policy will require the Court to expend substantial judicial time and resources in a trial which might have been avoided if Wal-Mart had been willing to engage in meaningful settlement negotiations, the Court finds that it would be just to require the attendance at trial of Wal-Mart's general counsel or some other Wal-Mart corporate officer with litigation policy authority.

> The Court recognizes that a party has the right to refuse to offer any money for settlement in a given case and the court cannot require a party to make a monetary settlement offer in any given case. (Indeed, one might find it refreshing for a party to take a "principled stand" against settlement in a given case.) However, in the Court's view, an across-the-board policy of refusing to negotiate frustrates both the letter and spirit of both the Federal Rules of Civil Procedure and this Court's Local Rules, which encourage good faith settlement efforts in order to preserve scarce judicial resources. Here, the Court is, in fact, not even requiring Wal-Mart to engage in settlement negotiations. It is simply requiring Wal-Mart's General Counsel, or other responsible corporate officer, to be present for trial, as the Court believes that requiring the attendance of such a Wal-Mart official during trial could have a salutary effect in that the responsible officer would have an opportunity to observe first-hand the effect of the company's policy both on the Court in general and in a particular case. Certainly, if this policy is important enough for Wal-Mart to persist in, then it is not asking too much for a responsible corporate officer to be present for trial.

Compare Koehn v. Tobias, 866 F.3d 750 (7th Cir. 2017), in which there was a settlement conference with the court that was unsuccessful when plaintiff rejected defendants' offer. Nearly a year later, during a telephonic status conference, new counsel for defendants said he believed that defendants' insurer had proposed a settlement in the range of $150,000. Plaintiff's counsel responded that she had never heard that figure and, in light of it, thought a settlement conference would be productive. But at the ensuing settlement conference, defendants renewed their earlier offer, which was for less than half the amount mentioned by its new lawyer. Plaintiff again rejected the offer. After trial (in which defendant won), the district judge ordered defendants to pay plaintiff over $4,000 in attorney fees and costs incurred by plaintiff's attorney to prepare for the abortive settlement conference. The court of appeals affirmed, finding a violation of Rule 16(f)(1)(B) on the assumption that the conference would have been called off had the mistake by defendants' new lawyer been corrected before the settlement conference (id. at 753):

> Defendants were free to change that posture before the settlement conference. However, we cannot say that the district court abused its discretion in finding that, by changing their positions so drastically without any indication that they intended to do so, Defendants did not participate in the settlement conference in good faith.

4.   Whatever the judicial role, the reality is that far more lawsuits are settled than tried. In different jurisdictions, the rate of trial varies, but it is everywhere a small and declining percentage of civil filings. See Galanter, The Vanishing Trial: An Examination of Trials and Related Matters in State and Federal Courts, 1 J. Empir. Legal Studies 439 (2004) (finding a large decline in trials between 1962 and 2002); compare Hadfield, Where Have All the Trials Gone?, 1 J. Empir. Legal Stud. 705 (2004) (suggesting that the decline has not been so large). Indeed, most grievances in our society never enter the litigation system at all. Does that reality argue in favor of promoting settlement of suits that would not settle without such pressure? See Kiser, Asher & McShane, Let's Not Make a Deal: An Empirical Study of Decision Making in Unsuccessful Settlement Negotiations, 3 J. Empir. Legal Stud. 551 (2008) (analyzing frequency of parties' "mistaken" rejection of settlements followed by less favorable outcome from adjudication).

5.   How should an American judge approach the question of settlement amount? One possibility is to try to find an amount both parties will accept. In Kothe, for example, the judge seems to have selected a figure this way. Should the judge instead try to identify a figure that is "right"? What would make a figure "right"? Would a judge who is more familiar with the evidence be in a better position to identify such a figure? Alternatively, should a judge avoid giving any indication of the amount of settlement she considers fair?

At least in some cases, American judges do become deeply involved. For example, consider the much-celebrated settlement achieved by District Judge Weinstein in the Agent Orange class action brought against several chemical companies on behalf of Vietnam veterans who were exposed to the herbicide in

Southeast Asia and claimed that it caused a variety of illnesses, including cancer. See P. Schuck, Agent Orange on Trial: Mass Toxic Disasters in the Courts (1986). Throughout the pretrial preparation of the case after he took it over from Judge Pratt, Judge Weinstein involved himself intensely in the details of the dispute about whether Agent Orange actually caused the types of harms plaintiffs claimed. Throughout, he also pressed for a settlement.

Over the weekend before trial was to begin, the lawyers for both sides were directed to report to the courthouse for around-the-clock settlement negotiations supervised by David Shapiro, an experienced lawyer whom the judge had appointed as a special settlement master (see Rule 53). Shapiro concluded at one point that the defendants would be willing to agree to plaintiffs' pending demand of $200 million. Believing he had a deal, he reported to the judge and received a rude shock: The judge refused to allow a settlement that high because he felt the veterans' case was extremely shaky and that he had an obligation to the legal system not to encourage groundless mass toxic tort litigation by allowing a settlement that would signal that the case was stronger than it actually was. When later informed of this, one of the lawyers for defendant Dow Chemical Co. said that the judge was "too much of an idealist." In any event, eventually a settlement at the judge's preferred figure of $180 million was reached at three o'clock on the morning that trial was to begin.

How does Judge Weinstein's role in Agent Orange compare with the behavior of the judges in *Band's Refuse* and *Kothe*? Consider Marcus, Apocalypse Now?, 85 Mich.L.Rev. 1267, 1293–94 (1987):

> Is this judging? It is far from the classical view of the judge as an inactive figure who decides according to announced rules of law. Yet that vision has long since given way to a more flexible view of the judicial function, and promoting settlement is now an accepted part of the picture. It is surely troubling to picture judges as unprincipled settlement promoters who only care about achieving settlement, and not about the terms, particularly when they are armed with the variety of persuasive tools Judge Weinstein employed in the Agent Orange litigation. Better, perhaps, that they should be idealists whose settlement posture is informed by a vision of what is right. Indeed, that may make them superior in the settlement arena as well.

> The Agent Orange case illustrates this point. A primary impediment to settlement, from defendants' perspective, was allocation of any global settlement figure among defendants. Despite long efforts to resolve the problem among themselves, defendants failed. The defendants' solution? "Let's let the judge do it; he's fair." And so Judge Weinstein devised a formula that "brought squeals of pain and shrieks of delight from the [defendants'] lawyers," but which even the unhappy accepted. Similarly, when the ability of one of the small defendants to pay threatened to derail the settlement later, the

judge was again recruited to decide the issue. In each instance, "the settlement hinged on the lawyers' perception that Weinstein was scrupulously fair and their willingness to be guided by his decision when internal negotiations reached an impasse." An unscrupulous pursuer of a deal, any deal, would probably not be able to perform this function.

But is this judging? What standards did Judge Weinstein use in fashioning the critical allocation formula? Were they "legal"? In a sense, these episodes suggest a model of judging that depends more on the personality of the judge than on his position in the institutional hierarchy. Judge Weinstein could do it but Judge Pratt [who had presided over the case earlier in the litigation], perhaps, could not. It is nice to have charismatic judges, but this is hardly a trend to be embraced; as Max Weber observed long ago, in a complex society it is necessary to shift authority from a charismatic to an institutionalized leadership. Of all governmental officials, this should be most true of judges, and our system therefore resolutely opposes judge shopping while permitting forum shopping. Although *Agent Orange* thus affords an intriguing glimpse into the Brave New World of judging, the judge's resolution of defendants' internal disputes is institutionally troubling.

The judge's settlement figure, however, is more problematical. At least the defense lawyers submitted their internal disputes to the judge for his disposition with their eyes open. The [plaintiffs' lawyers] did not, so far as we are told. To the contrary, after he failed to persuade the judge to press for a $200 million settlement Special Master Shapiro told the [plaintiffs' lawyers] that "they would never get the *defendants* to go above $180 million" even though he had by then concluded that defendants could easily be convinced to pay more. No doubt the [plaintiffs'] lawyers did not, like Dow's lawyer, call the judge an "idealist" when they found out what really happened.

6.   Is the kind of intervention performed by Judge Weinstein an appropriate role for a judge in the American system? In any system? In Against Settlement, 93 Yale L.J. 1073 (1984), Professor Fiss argues that "[t]o be against settlement is only to suggest that when the parties settle, society gets less than what appears, and for a price it does not know it is paying. Parties might settle while leaving justice undone." He explains:

I do not believe that settlement as a generic practice is preferable to judgment or should be institutionalized on a wholesale and indiscriminate basis. It should be treated instead as a highly problematic technique for streamlining dockets. Settlement is for me the civil analogue of plea bargaining. * * * Like plea bargaining, settlement is a capitulation to the conditions of a mass society and should be neither encouraged nor praised.

How persuasive are these arguments? So long as settlements accurately reflect forecasts about likely outcomes at trial, why should they not be favored and promoted by judges? Cf. McCoy & Mirra, Plea Bargaining as Due Process in Determining Guilt, 32 Stan.L.Rev. 887, 921–22 (1980) (arguing that the only due process concern with plea bargaining is that the innocent will plead guilty). Is justice advanced by judicial promotion of settlements?

7.   We will return to issues raised by increasing enthusiasm for settlement at the end of Chapter 2 and in Chapter 7. Since settlement is the outcome of more litigated cases than judicial resolution, you should have the question of the relation between formal litigation and settlement in the back of your mind throughout the course.

PROCEDURAL CHALLENGES OF OUR FEDERAL SYSTEM

In the chapters that follow, we will focus on adjudication in the federal courts, deferring until later detailed consideration of the complications that can arise because this is a large country with many state court systems and a somewhat parallel federal court system. For background purposes, however, it is helpful to describe in a general fashion the rules that govern these problems.

Subject matter jurisdiction: One of the cases we have read in this chapter was decided in state court and the other was decided in federal court. Federal courts are courts of "limited jurisdiction" because they can decide only certain types of claims. In civil cases, there are basically two situations in which federal courts have such jurisdiction. First, there are cases in which there is a federal question (see § 28 U.S.C.A. § 1331), which usually means that the plaintiff is asserting a claim created by federal law. Examples include claims for violation of civil rights, the federal antitrust laws, or federal rules against securities fraud. Second, federal courts have jurisdiction of cases in which all plaintiffs come from different states than the defendants, and diversity of citizenship therefore exists (see § 28 U.S.C.A. § 1332). In Kothe v. Smith, for example, the ground for jurisdiction in federal court was diversity of citizenship because the malpractice action did not involve any federal question. Where a case cannot be brought in federal court, there will be a state court of "general jurisdiction" in which it can be brought, as was done in Band's Refuse v. Borough of Fair Lawn. We examine the rules governing these problems in Chapter 10.

Personal jurisdiction: Defending a lawsuit is a burdensome undertaking. It can become much more burdensome if the suit is filed in a court a great distance from the defendant's residence. Accordingly, entirely separate from the question of subject matter jurisdiction is the question whether the defendant can be compelled to travel to the geographical location chosen by the plaintiff for the suit. The limitations on plaintiff's power to make defendant travel a great distance to defend the suit usually apply whether the case is in federal court or state court. The Supreme Court has held that the due process clause of the Constitution forbids assertion of personal jurisdiction unless the defendant has voluntarily established a contact with the state in which the court sits so that it is fair to require a defense there. We explore these problems in Chapter 9.

Federal v. state law: When cases like Kothe v. Smith are in federal court on grounds of diversity of citizenship, the judge must usually look to state law to decide them because they do not involve federal claims. Thus, you will find that in many of the cases that are covered in the coming chapters federal judges will be applying state substantive law to determine whether plaintiff has a valid claim against defendant. In general terms, federal judges in such cases are to apply state substantive law, but they should also apply federal procedural law. Thus, you will find that in such cases the federal judges apply the Federal Rules of Civil Procedure. We will examine the complexities of this subject (often called the Erie problem, after a famous case) in Chapter 11.

CHAPTER 2

THE REWARDS AND COSTS OF LITIGATION—OF REMEDIES AND RELATED MATTERS

■ ■ ■

Before they file lawsuits, people should stop and think about what they can obtain from the courts in order to decide whether litigation is worth the trouble. The relief that a court could grant may not be sufficient to warrant the investment involved in getting it; in any event, some other method may be a better way of seeking redress. Litigation is society's preferred substitute for private self-help; for that purpose the remedies it offers (using the assistance of the government) need to be sufficiently attractive to induce citizens to forgo other (possibly even more primitive) means.

The law of remedies exists uneasily in the area between "substantive" rules and "procedural" rules. Our interest in beginning with consideration of remedies is to explore the interaction between substance and procedure with a view to developing a thesis about when (and how) a court should mete out judicial relief. In your other courses (particularly torts and contracts, and later remedies) you should be able to explore remedial issues in more detail.

A. PREJUDGMENT SEIZURE

A party cannot expect, of course, to obtain the relief it seeks until the case is tried on the merits. However, there are a number of procedural devices which permit some form of interim relief before the case goes to trial. Their purpose is generally to preserve the status quo so that any relief obtained after a trial is really meaningful. Temporary restraining orders and preliminary injunctions (which we will consider in connection with Carey v. Piphus, infra p. 69) particularly serve this purpose by allowing the court to order the parties to do certain acts (or refrain from certain acts) that would change the status quo. Prejudgment seizure of the defendant's property is a means of ensuring that property will be available for execution in case the plaintiff prevails. We consider this device here to examine some considerations that infuse the subject of remedies, and to reflect further on the policies underlying procedure.

At common law, plaintiff usually had to wait until the end of the case to get judicial relief, although sometimes it was possible to have property of the defendant seized before trial to coerce the defendant to appear at the trial. In Chapter 9, we will examine the continuing validity of this method of securing jurisdiction over a defendant. See Shaffer v. Heitner, infra p. 801.

Over time, pretrial seizure of defendant's property came to serve another function—assuring plaintiff that there would be sufficient assets available to satisfy any judgment that might later be entered. This device could be especially important where the dispute was about possession of the very property that was seized at the beginning of the lawsuit. All states developed statutory procedures for some prejudgment seizure of assets under a variety of names—replevin, garnishment, attachment and sequestration. Although there were differences between states and among different types of prejudgment relief, there were many common features. Ordinarily the remedy was available only for certain kinds of claims, most often commercial obligations or claims to certain specific property. But once plaintiff asserted a claim of the correct type, it could easily have the sheriff or a similar officer seize the property either physically, or symbolically by serving an order on the custodian directing certain disposition of the property.

For our purposes, the principal concern is the procedure that attends use of these prejudgment remedies. Initially, these procedures were extremely casual. Arguably as a result, there were abuses. As one Congressman put it with regard to garnishment of wages: "What we know from our study of this problem is that in a vast number of cases the debt is a fraudulent one, saddled on a poor ignorant person who is trapped in an easy credit nightmare, in which he is charged double for something he could not pay for even if the proper price was called for, and then hounded into giving up his pound of flesh, and being fired besides." Remarks of Rep. Sullivan, Chairman of House Subcommittee on Consumer Affairs, 114 Cong.Rec. 1832. These preliminary remedies could, therefore, become the only remedies.

In Sniadach v. Family Finance Corp., 395 U.S. 337 (1969), the Court held that the due process clause of the 14th Amendment* requires some procedural protections in connection with such remedies. In that case, a lender sued claiming that defendant had failed to pay $420 she owed on a promissory note and, without notice to her, obtained an order of garnishment directed at her employer. Under the order, the employer retained half of defendant's salary for disposition after trial according to the outcome, and paid her only the other half. Evidently there was no way for defendant to release the garnishment until the end of the trial. Stressing the "tremendous hardship" that seizure of this "special type of property" presented, the Court held that the state attachment law was

---

*   "[N]or shall any State deprive any person of life, liberty, or property, without due process of law * * *."

unconstitutional for failure to provide notice and an opportunity to be heard before garnishment was issued.

The following cases try to work out the due process requirements for such immediate remedies. As you analyze their holdings reflect on the considerations identified in Chapter 1. If due process sets an absolute minimum for procedure, is it being sensibly applied?

FUENTES V. SHEVIN

Supreme Court of the United States, 1972
407 U.S. 67

JUSTICE STEWART delivered the opinion of the Court.

We here review the decisions of two three-judge federal District Courts** that upheld the constitutionality of Florida and Pennsylvania laws authorizing the summary seizure of goods or chattels in a person's possession under a writ of replevin. Both statutes provide for the issuance of writs ordering state agents to seize a person's possessions, simply upon the ex parte application of any other person who claims a right to them and posts a security bond. Neither statute provides for notice to be given to the possessor of the property, and neither statute gives the possessor an opportunity to challenge the seizure at any kind of prior hearing. The question is whether these statutory procedures violate the Fourteenth Amendment's guarantee that no State shall deprive any person of property without due process of law.

I

The appellant in No. 5039, Margarita Fuentes, is a resident of Florida. She purchased a gas stove and service policy from the Firestone Tire and Rubber Co. (Firestone) under a conditional sales contract calling for monthly payments over a period of time. A few months later, she purchased a stereophonic phonograph from the same company under the same sort of contract. The total cost of the stove and stereo was about $500, plus an additional financing charge of over $100. Under the contracts, Firestone retained title to the merchandise, but Mrs. Fuentes was entitled to possession unless and until she should default on her installment payments.

For more than a year, Mrs. Fuentes made her installment payments. But then, with only about $200 remaining to be paid, a dispute developed between her and Firestone over the servicing of the stove. Firestone instituted an action in a small-claims court for repossession of both the stove and the stereo, claiming that Mrs. Fuentes had refused to make her remaining payments. Simultaneously with the filing of that action and

---

** A three-judge federal court was a special device used in cases involving constitutional challenges to state statutes. For a variety of reasons the practice was largely abandoned in 1976.— Eds.

before Mrs. Fuentes had even received a summons to answer its complaint, Firestone obtained a writ of replevin ordering a sheriff to seize the disputed goods at once.

In conformance with Florida procedure, Firestone had only to fill in the blanks on the appropriate form documents and submit them to the clerk of the small-claims court. The clerk signed and stamped the documents and issued a writ of replevin. Later the same day, a local deputy sheriff and an agent of Firestone went to Mrs. Fuentes' home and seized the stove and stereo.

Shortly thereafter, Mrs. Fuentes instituted the present action in a federal district court, challenging the constitutionality of the Florida prejudgment replevin procedures under the Due Process Clause of the Fourteenth Amendment. She sought declaratory and injunctive relief against continued enforcement of the procedural provisions of the state statutes that authorize prejudgment replevin.

The appellants in No. 5138 filed a very similar action in a federal district court in Pennsylvania, challenging the constitutionality of that State's prejudgment replevin process. Like Mrs. Fuentes, they had had possessions seized under writs of replevin. Three of the appellants had purchased personal property—a bed, a table, and other household goods— under installment sales contracts like the one signed by Mrs. Fuentes; and the sellers of the property had obtained and executed summary writs of replevin, claiming that the appellants had fallen behind in their installment payments. The experience of the fourth appellant, Rosa Washington, had been more bizarre. She had been divorced from a local deputy sheriff and was engaged in a dispute with him over the custody of their son. Her former husband, being familiar with the routine forms used in the replevin process, had obtained a writ that ordered the seizure of the boy's clothes, furniture, and toys.[4]

In both No. 5039 and No. 5138, three-judge District Courts were convened to consider the appellants' challenges to the constitutional validity of the Florida and Pennsylvania statutes. The courts in both cases upheld the constitutionality of the statutes. We noted probable jurisdiction of both appeals.

II

Under the Florida statute challenged here, "[a]ny person whose goods or chattels are wrongfully detained by any other person . . . may have a writ of replevin to recover them. . . ." There is no requirement that the applicant make a convincing showing before the seizure that the goods are, in fact, "wrongfully detained." Rather, Florida law automatically relies on the bare assertion of the party seeking the writ that he is entitled to one

---

4   Unlike Mrs. Fuentes in No. 5039, none of the appellants in No. 5138 was ever sued in any court by the party who initiated seizure of the property.

and allows a court clerk to issue the writ summarily. It requires only that the applicant file a complaint, initiating a court action for repossession and reciting in conclusory fashion that he is "lawfully entitled to the possession" of the property, and that he file a security bond

> "in at least double the value of the property to be replevied conditioned that plaintiff will prosecute his action to effect and without delay and that if defendant recovers judgment against him in the action, he will return the property, if return thereof is adjudged, and will pay defendant all sums of money recovered against plaintiff by defendant in the action."

On the sole basis of the complaint and bond, a writ is issued "command[ing] the officer to whom it may be directed to replevy the goods and chattels in possession of defendant . . . and to summon the defendant to answer the complaint." If the goods are "in any dwelling house or other building or enclosure," the officer is required to demand their delivery; but if they are not delivered, "he shall cause such house, building or enclosure to be broken open and shall make replevin according to the writ. . . ."

[handwritten margin note: Sheriff is entitled to use violence]

Thus, at the same moment that the defendant receives the complaint seeking repossession of property through court action, the property is seized from him. He is provided no prior notice and allowed no opportunity whatever to challenge the issuance of the writ. After the property has been seized, he will eventually have an opportunity for a hearing, as the defendant in the trial of the court action for repossession, which the plaintiff is required to pursue. And he is also not wholly without recourse in the meantime. For under the Florida statute, the officer who seizes the property must keep it for three days, and during that period the defendant may reclaim possession of the property by posting his own security bond in double its value. But if he does not post such a bond, the property is transferred to the party who sought the writ, pending a final judgment in the underlying action for repossession.

The Pennsylvania law differs, though not in its essential nature, from that of Florida. * * * Unlike the Florida statute, however, the Pennsylvania law does not require that there ever be opportunity for a hearing on the merits of the conflicting claims to possession of the replevied property. The party seeking the writ is not obliged to initiate a court action for repossession. Indeed, he need not even formally allege that he is lawfully entitled to the property. The most that is required is that he file an "affidavit of the value of the property to be replevied." If the party who loses property through replevin seizure is to get even a post-seizure hearing, he must initiate a lawsuit himself.[9] He may also, as under Florida law, post

---

9   None of the appellants in No. 70—5138 attempted to initiate the process to require the filing of a post-seizure complaint * * *.

his own counterbond within three days after the seizure to regain possession.

III

* * *

Prejudgment replevin statutes like those of Florida and Pennsylvania are most commonly used by creditors to seize goods allegedly wrongfully detained—not wrongfully taken—by debtors. At common law, if a creditor wished to invoke state power to recover goods wrongfully detained, he had to proceed through the action of debt or detinue. These actions, however, did not provide for a return of property before final judgment.[12] And, more importantly, on the occasions when the common law did allow prejudgment seizure by state power, it provided some kind of notice and opportunity to be heard to the party then in possession of the property, and a state official made at least a summary determination of the relative rights of the disputing parties before stepping into the dispute and taking goods from one of them.

IV

For more than a century the central meaning of procedural due process has been clear: "Parties whose rights are to be affected are entitled to be heard; and in order that they may enjoy that right they must first be notified." It is equally fundamental that the right to notice and an opportunity to be heard "must be granted at a meaningful time and in a meaningful manner."

* * *

The constitutional right to be heard is a basic aspect of the duty of government to follow a fair process of decisionmaking when it acts to deprive a person of his possessions. The purpose of this requirement is not only to ensure abstract fair play to the individual. Its purpose, more particularly, is to protect his use and possession of property from arbitrary encroachment—to minimize substantively unfair or mistaken deprivations of property, a danger that is especially great when the State seizes goods simply upon the application of and for the benefit of a private party. So viewed the prohibition against the deprivation of property without due process of law reflects the high value, embedded in our constitutional and political history, that we place on a person's right to enjoy what is his, free of government interference.

The requirement of notice and an opportunity to be heard raises no impenetrable barrier to the taking of a person's possessions. But the fair process of decisionmaking that it guarantees works, by itself, to protect against arbitrary deprivation of property. For when a person has an

---

[12] The creditor could, of course, proceed without the use of state power, through self-help, by "distraining" the property before a judgment.

[handwritten margin note: State must listen]

opportunity to speak up in his own defense, and when the State must listen to what he has to say, substantively unfair and simply mistaken deprivations of property interests can be prevented.

* * *

If the right to notice and a hearing is to serve its full purpose, then, it is clear that it must be granted at a time when the deprivation can still be prevented. At a later hearing, an individual's possessions can be returned to him if they were unfairly or mistakenly taken in the first place. Damages may even be awarded to him for the wrongful deprivation. But no later hearing and no damage award can undo the fact that the arbitrary taking that was subject to the right of procedural due process has already occurred. "This Court has not . . . embraced the general proposition that a wrong may be done if it can be undone." Stanley v. Illinois, 405 U.S. 645, 647.

* * *

The Florida and Pennsylvania prejudgment replevin statutes fly in the face of this principle. To be sure, the requirements that a party seeking a writ must first post a bond, allege conclusorily that he is entitled to specific goods, and open himself to possible liability in damages if he is wrong, serve to deter wholly unfounded applications for a writ. But those requirements are hardly a substitute for a prior hearing, for they test no more than the strength of the applicant's own belief in his rights.[13] Since his private gain is at stake, the danger is all too great that his confidence in his cause will be misplaced. Lawyers and judges are familiar with the phenomenon of a party mistakenly but firmly convinced that his view of the facts and law will prevail, and therefore quite willing to risk the costs of litigation. Because of the understandable, self-interested fallibility of litigants, a court does not decide a dispute until it has had an opportunity to hear both sides—and does not generally take even tentative action until it has itself examined the support for the plaintiff's position. The Florida and Pennsylvania statutes do not even require the official issuing a writ of replevin to do that much.

The minimal deterrent effect of a bond requirement is, in a practical sense, no substitute for an informed evaluation by a neutral official. More specifically, as a matter of constitutional principle, it is no replacement for the right to a prior hearing that is the only truly effective safeguard against arbitrary deprivation of property. While the existence of these other, less effective, safeguards may be among the considerations that affect the form

---

[13] They may not even test that much. For if an applicant for the writ knows that he is dealing with an uneducated, uninformed consumer with little access to legal help and little familiarity with legal procedures, there may be a substantial possibility that a summary seizure of property—however unwarranted—may go unchallenged, and the applicant may feel that he can act with impunity.

of hearing demanded by due process, they are far from enough by themselves to obviate the right to a prior hearing of some kind.

V

The right to a prior hearing, of course, attaches only to the deprivation of an interest encompassed within the Fourteenth Amendment's protection. In the present cases, the Florida and Pennsylvania statutes were applied to replevy chattels in the appellants' possession. The replevin was not cast as a final judgment; most, if not all, of the appellants lacked full title to the chattels; and their claim even to continued possession was a matter in dispute. Moreover, the chattels at stake were nothing more than an assortment of household goods. Nonetheless, it is clear that the appellants were deprived of possessory interests in those chattels that were within the protection of the Fourteenth Amendment.

A

A deprivation of a person's possessions under a prejudgment writ of replevin, at least in theory, may be only temporary. The Florida and Pennsylvania statutes do not require a person to wait until a post-seizure hearing and final judgment to recover what has been replevied. Within three days after the seizure, the statutes allow him to recover the goods if he, in return, surrenders other property—a payment necessary to secure a bond in double the value of the goods seized from him.[14] But it is now well settled that a temporary, nonfinal deprivation of property is nonetheless a "deprivation" in the terms of the Fourteenth Amendment. Sniadach v. Family Finance Corp., 395 U.S. 337 (1969).

* * *

The Fourteenth Amendment draws no bright lines around three-day, 10-day or 50-day deprivations of property. Any significant taking of property by the State is within the purview of the Due Process Clause. While the length and consequent severity of a deprivation may be another factor to weigh in determining the appropriate form of hearing, it is not decisive of the basic right to a prior hearing of some kind.

B

The appellants who signed conditional sales contracts lacked full legal title to the replevied goods. The Fourteenth Amendment's protection of "property," however, has never been interpreted to safeguard only the rights of undisputed ownership. Rather, it has been read broadly to extend

---

14   The appellants argue that this opportunity for quick recovery exists only in theory. They allege that very few people in their position are able to obtain a recovery bond, even if they know of the possibility. Appellant Fuentes says that in her case she was never told that she could recover the stove and stereo and that the deputy sheriff seizing them gave them at once to the Firestone agent, rather than holding them for three days. She further asserts that of 442 cases of prejudgment replevin in small-claims courts in Dade County, Florida, in 1969, there was not one case in which the defendant took advantage of the recovery provision.

protection to "any significant property interest," including statutory entitlements. See Goldberg v. Kelly, 397 U.S., at 262.

The appellants were deprived of such an interest in the replevied goods—the interest in continued possession and use of the goods. They had acquired this interest under the conditional sales contracts that entitled them to possession and use of the chattels before transfer of title. In exchange for immediate possession, the appellants had agreed to pay a major financing charge beyond the basic price of the merchandise. Moreover, by the time the goods were summarily repossessed, they had made substantial installment payments. Clearly, their possessory interest in the goods, dearly bought and protected by contract, was sufficient to invoke the protection of the Due Process Clause.

Their ultimate right to continued possession was, of course, in dispute. If it were shown at a hearing that the appellants had defaulted on their contractual obligations, it might well be that the sellers of the goods would be entitled to repossession. But even assuming that the appellants had fallen behind in their installment payments, and that they had no other valid defenses,[17] that is immaterial here. The right to be heard does not depend upon an advance showing that one will surely prevail at the hearing. "To one who protests against the taking of his property without due process of law, it is no answer to say that in his particular case due process of law would have led to the same result because he had no adequate defense upon the merits." Coe v. Armour Fertilizer Works, 237 U.S. 413, 424 [(1915)]. It is enough to invoke the procedural safeguards of the Fourteenth Amendment that a significant property interest is at stake, whatever the ultimate outcome of a hearing on the contractual right to continued possession and use of the goods.[18]

C

Nevertheless, the District Courts rejected the appellants' constitutional claim on the ground that the goods seized from them—a stove, a stereo, a table, a bed, and so forth—were not deserving of due process protection, since they were not absolute necessities of life. * * *

No doubt, there may be many gradations in the "importance" or "necessity" of various consumer goods. Stoves could be compared to television sets, or beds could be compared to tables. But if the root principle of procedural due process is to be applied with objectivity, it cannot rest on

---

[17] Mrs. Fuentes argues that Florida law allows her to defend on the ground that Firestone breached its obligations under the sales contract by failing to repair serious defects in the stove it sold her. We need not consider this issue here. It is enough that the right to continued possession of the goods was open to some dispute at a hearing since the sellers of the goods had to show, at the least, that the appellants had defaulted in their payments.

[18] The issues decisive of the ultimate right to continued possession, of course, may be quite simple. The simplicity of the issues might be relevant to the formality or scheduling of a prior hearing. But it certainly cannot undercut the right to a prior hearing of some kind.

such distinctions. The Fourteenth Amendment speaks of "property" generally. And, under our free-enterprise system, an individual's choices in the marketplace are respected, however unwise they may seem to someone else. It is not the business of a court adjudicating due process rights to make its own critical evaluation of those choices and protect only the ones that, by its own lights, are "necessary."[21]

VI

There are "extraordinary situations" that justify postponing notice and opportunity for a hearing. Boddie v. Connecticut, 401 U.S., at 379. These situations, however, must be truly unusual.[22] Only in a few limited situations has this Court allowed outright seizure[23] without opportunity for a prior hearing. First, in each case, the seizure has been directly necessary to secure an important governmental or general public interest. Second, there has been a special need for very prompt action. Third, the State has kept strict control over its monopoly of legitimate force; the person initiating the seizure has been a government official responsible for determining, under the standards of a narrowly drawn statute, that it was necessary and justified in the particular instance. Thus, the Court has allowed summary seizure of property to collect the internal revenue of the United States,[24] to meet the needs of a national war effort, to protect against the economic disaster of a bank failure, and to protect the public from misbranded drugs and contaminated food.

The Florida and Pennsylvania prejudgment replevin statutes serve no such important governmental or general public interest. They allow

---

[21] The relative weight of liberty or property interests is relevant, of course, to the form of notice and hearing required by due process. But some form of notice and hearing—formal or informal—is required before deprivation of a property interest that "cannot be characterized as de minimis." Sniadach v. Family Finance Corp., supra, 395 U.S., at 342 (Harlan, J., concurring).

[22] A prior hearing always imposes some costs in time, effort, and expense, and it is often more efficient to dispense with the opportunity for such a hearing. But these rather ordinary costs cannot outweigh the constitutional right. Procedural due process is not intended to promote efficiency or accommodate all possible interests: it is intended to protect the particular interests of the person whose possessions are about to be taken. "The establishment of prompt efficacious procedures to achieve legitimate state ends is a proper state interest worthy of cognizance in constitutional adjudication. But the Constitution recognizes higher values than speed and efficiency. Indeed, one might fairly say of the Bill of Rights in general, and the Due Process Clause in particular, that they were designed to protect the fragile values of a vulnerable citizenry from the overbearing concern for efficiency and efficacy that may characterize praiseworthy government officials no less, and perhaps more, than mediocre ones." Stanley v. Illinois, 405 U.S. 645, 656.

[23] In three cases, the Court has allowed the attachment of property without a prior hearing. In one, the attachment was necessary to protect the public against the same sort of immediate harm involved in the seizure cases—a bank failure. Coffin Bros. & Co. v. Bennett, 277 U.S. 29. Another case involved attachment necessary to secure jurisdiction in state court—clearly a most basic and important public interest. Ownbey v. Morgan, 256 U.S. 94. * * * Seizure under a search warrant is quite a different matter, see n. 30, infra.

[24] Phillips v. Commissioner of Internal Revenue, 283 U.S. 589. The Court stated that "[d]elay in the judicial determination of property rights is not uncommon where it is essential that governmental needs be immediately satisfied." (emphasis supplied). The Court, then relied on "the need of the government promptly to secure its revenues."

summary seizure of a person's possessions when no more than private gain is directly at stake.[29] The replevin of chattels, as in the present cases, may satisfy a debt or settle a score. But state intervention in a private dispute hardly compares to state action furthering a war effort or protecting the public health.

Nor do the broadly drawn Florida and Pennsylvania statutes limit the summary seizure of goods to special situations demanding prompt action. There may be cases in which a creditor could make a showing of immediate danger that a debtor will destroy or conceal disputed goods. But the statutes before us are not "narrowly drawn to meet any such unusual condition." Sniadach v. Family Finance Corp., supra, 395 U.S. at 339. And no such unusual situation is presented by the facts of these cases.

The statutes, moreover, abdicate effective state control over state power. Private parties, serving their own private advantage, may unilaterally invoke state power to replevy goods from another. No state official participates in the decision to seek a writ; no state official reviews the basis for the claim to repossession; and no state official evaluates the need for immediate seizure. There is not even a requirement that the plaintiff provide any information to the court on these matters. The State acts largely in the dark.[30]

[The Court held that appellants had not waived their right to a hearing by signing form contracts authorizing repossession.]

* * *

---

[29] By allowing repossession without an opportunity for a prior hearing, the Florida and Pennsylvania statutes may be intended specifically to reduce the costs for the private party seeking to seize goods in another party's possession. Even if the private gain at stake in repossession actions were equal to the great public interests recognized in this Court's past decisions, the Court has made clear that the avoidance of the ordinary costs imposed by the opportunity for a hearing is not sufficient to override the constitutional right. See n. 22, supra. The appellees argue that the cost of holding hearings may be especially onerous in the context of the creditor-debtor relationship. But the Court's holding in Sniadach v. Family Finance Corp., supra, indisputably demonstrates that ordinary hearing costs are no more able to override due process rights in the creditor-debtor context than in other contexts.

In any event, the aggregate cost of an opportunity to be heard before repossession should not be exaggerated. For we deal here only with the right to an opportunity to be heard. Since the issues and facts decisive of rights in repossession suits may very often be quite simple, there is a likelihood that many defendants would forgo their opportunity, sensing the futility of the exercise in the particular case. And, of course, no hearing need be held unless the defendant, having received notice of his opportunity, takes advantage of it.

[30] The seizure of possessions under a writ of replevin is entirely different from the seizure of possessions under a search warrant. First, a search warrant is generally issued to serve a highly important governmental need—e.g., the apprehension and conviction of criminals—rather than the mere private advantage of a private party in an economic transaction. Second, a search warrant is generally issued in situations demanding prompt action. The danger is all too obvious that a criminal will destroy or hide evidence or fruits of his crime if given any prior notice. Third, the Fourth Amendment guarantees that the State will not issue search warrants merely upon the conclusory application of a private party. It guarantees that the State will not abdicate control over the issuance of warrants and that no warrant will be issued without a prior showing of probable cause. Thus, our decision today in no way implies that there must be opportunity for an adversary hearing before a search warrant is issued.

Prox. Comment
— This Florida law was written in relationship to "poor ppl" and their need for installment payments
— They are "judgement proof" to have no $ to give if they lose a case

This case has a clean rule but through a number of exceptions

VIII

We hold that the Florida and Pennsylvania prejudgment replevin provisions work a deprivation of property without due process of law insofar as they deny the right to a prior opportunity to be heard before chattels are taken from their possessor. Our holding, however, is a narrow one. We do not question the power of a State to seize goods before a final judgment in order to protect the security interests of creditors so long as those creditors have tested their claim to the goods through the process of a fair prior hearing. The nature and form of such prior hearings, more-over, are legitimately open to many potential variations and are a subject, at this point, for legislation—not adjudication. Since the essential reason for the requirement of a prior hearing is to prevent unfair and mistaken deprivations of property, however, it is axiomatic that the hearing must provide a real test. "[D]ue process is afforded only by the kinds of 'notice' and 'hearing' that are aimed at establishing the validity, or at least the probable validity, of the underlying claim against the alleged debtor before he can be deprived of his property. . . ." Sniadach v. Family Finance Corp., supra, 395 U.S. at 343 (Harlan, J., concurring).

For the foregoing reasons, the judgments of the District Courts are vacated and these cases are remanded for further proceedings consistent with this opinion.

JUSTICE POWELL and JUSTICE REHNQUIST did not participate in the consideration or decision of these cases.

JUSTICE WHITE, with whom THE CHIEF JUSTICE and JUSTICE BLACKMUN join, dissenting.

Because the Court's opinion and judgment improvidently, in my view, call into question important aspects of the statutes of almost all the States governing secured transactions and the procedure for repossessing personal property, I must dissent for the reasons that follow.

* * *

It goes without saying that in the typical installment sale of personal property both seller and buyer have interests in the property until the purchase price is fully paid, the seller early in the transaction often having more at stake than the buyer. Nor is it disputed that the buyer's right to possession is conditioned upon his making the stipulated payments and that upon default the seller is entitled to possession. Finally, there is no question in these cases that if default is disputed by the buyer he has the opportunity for a full hearing, and that if he prevails he may have the property or its full value as damages.

The narrow issue, as the Court notes, is whether it comports with due process to permit the seller, pending final judgment, to take possession of the property through a writ of replevin served by the sheriff without affording the buyer opportunity to insist that the seller establish at a hearing that there is reasonable basis for his claim of default. The interests of the buyer and seller are obviously antagonistic during this interim period: the buyer wants the use of the property pending final judgment; the seller's interest is to prevent further use and deterioration of his security. By the Florida and Pennsylvania laws the property is to all intents and purposes placed in custody and immobilized during this time. The buyer loses use of the property temporarily but is protected against loss; the seller is protected against deterioration of the property but must undertake by bond to make the buyer whole in the event the latter prevails.

In considering whether this resolution of conflicting interests is unconstitutional, much depends on one's perceptions of the practical considerations involved. The Court holds it constitutionally essential to afford opportunity for a probable-cause hearing prior to repossession. Its stated purpose is "to prevent unfair and mistaken deprivations of property." But in these typical situations, the buyer-debtor has either defaulted or he has not. If there is a default, it would seem not only "fair," but essential, that the creditor be allowed to repossess; and I cannot say that the likelihood of a mistaken claim of default is sufficiently real or recurring to justify a broad constitutional requirement that a creditor do more than the typical state law requires and permits him to do. Sellers are normally in the business of selling and collecting the price for their merchandise. I could be quite wrong, but it would not seem in the creditor's interest for a default occasioning repossession to occur; as a practical matter it would much better serve his interests if the transaction goes forward and is completed as planned. Dollar-and-cents considerations weigh heavily against false claims of default as well as against precipitate action that would allow no opportunity for mistakes to surface and be corrected. Nor does it seem to me that creditors would lightly undertake the expense of instituting replevin actions and putting up bonds.

The Court's rhetoric is seductive, but in end analysis, the result it reaches will have little impact and represents no more than ideological tinkering with state law. It would appear that creditors could withstand attack under today's opinion simply by making clear in the controlling credit instruments that they may retake possession without a hearing, or, for that matter, without resort to judicial process at all. Alternatively, they need only give a few days' notice of a hearing, take possession if hearing is waived or if there is default; and if hearing is necessary merely establish probable cause for asserting that default has occurred. It is very doubtful in my mind that such a hearing would in fact result in protections for the debtor substantially different from those the present laws provide. On the contrary, the availability of credit may well be diminished or, in any event, the expense of securing it increased.

None of this seems worth the candle to me.

⌐ To him sellers can contract around this or pull out of the market

Question? In who's interest are you acting? You're only raising costs for the poor.

NOTES AND QUESTIONS

1.   In the Court's view, what is the purpose for holding the hearing? If the creditor establishes at the hearing that a prejudgment remedy is appropriate, does that mean that the hearing was a waste of time?

2.   The Court downplays the costs associated with the hearing requirement. Has it properly appreciated those costs? What proportion of people subjected to replevin have, like Ms. Fuentes, potential defenses or other grounds for retaining the goods? What will lenders and merchants do in response to this added wrinkle in the debt remedies procedure? See White, The Abolition of Self-Help Repossession: The Poor Pay More, 1973 Wis.L.Rev. 503, 504, estimating that only 6 out of 1,000 people whose cars are repossessed have defenses on the merits and that interfering with this self-help alternative to judicial relief would significantly increase the cost of auto purchases, at least for the poor. On the basis of these estimates, Professor White concluded that "Fuentes v. Shevin is probably an undesirable outcome, and that the application of the same doctrine to self-help repossession is certainly undesirable and would constitute due process gone berserk." Would the added costs be equally significant where plaintiffs resort to judicial prejudgment remedies instead of self-help? Do added procedures always lead to added costs? How do we decide if the costs are justified?

3.   To what extent will imposition of more procedures drive people to employ self-help? In *Fuentes*, what would have happened if the creditors had simply hired thugs to seize the property involved? Acting independently, people do not have the assistance of the sheriff or another state officer, and they may be prosecuted for a breach of the peace or something more significant if they try to do the same kinds of things themselves. Moreover, certain remedies, such as garnishment, probably do not have a self-help analogue. Hence many people will still use the judicial procedure even if it is costly and cumbersome.

For those who have workable self-help alternatives, the Court seemed to have removed any due process obstacles in their path in Flagg Brothers, Inc. v. Brooks, 436 U.S. 149 (1978). Brooks was evicted by the city marshall who arranged to store her belongings in Flagg Brothers' warehouse. Two months later, when Brooks refused to pay the storage charges because she disputed them, Flagg Brothers threatened to sell her goods to satisfy the debt, as permitted by the Uniform Commercial Code. Brooks sued in federal court to prevent the sale on the ground that due process forbade this self-help without a prior hearing to decide the dispute about the storage charges.

Despite the initial role of the city marshall in evicting Brooks and arranging to store the goods with Flagg Brothers, the Supreme Court upheld dismissal of the suit on the ground that there was no "state action" (a requirement of the 14th Amendment) involved in the sale. As Justice Rehnquist explained, "[t]his total absence of overt official involvement plainly distinguishes this case from earlier decisions imposing procedural restrictions on creditors' remedies." The complex application of the "state action" concept must await fuller development in courses on constitutional law. For our purposes, the basic focus is on the effect of this limitation of due process on the incentives confronting claimants. *Flagg Brothers* appears to eliminate Professor White's worry about "due process gone berserk" with regard to auto repossession. Are you comfortable with the result? If not, what different result might be prescribed? What costs might that generate?

4. Besides cost, does the creditor have other interests that are threatened by requiring a hearing before seizure? Note that the Court acknowledges in *Fuentes* that in "extraordinary" situations pre-seizure notice and hearing are not required. In Calero-Toledo v. Pearson Yacht Leasing Co., 416 U.S. 663 (1974), the Court provided a further explanation of this concept. Plaintiff's yacht, which it had leased to two Puerto Rican residents, was seized by Puerto Rico when found to contain marijuana, and it was later forfeited to the government. The Court rejected plaintiff's claim that the seizure was improper because there was no prior notice to them and hearing:

> First, seizure under the Puerto Rican statutes serves significant governmental purposes: Seizure permits Puerto Rico to assert in rem jurisdiction over the property in order to conduct forfeiture proceedings, thereby fostering the public interest in preventing continued illicit use of the property and in enforcing criminal sanctions. Second, preseizure notice and hearing might frustrate the interests served by the statutes, since the property seized—as here, a yacht—will often be of a sort that could be removed to another jurisdiction, destroyed, or concealed, if advance warning of confiscation were given. And finally, unlike the situation in Fuentes, seizure is not initiated by self-interested private parties; rather, Commonwealth officials determine whether seizure is appropriate under the provisions of the Puerto Rican statutes. In these circumstances, we hold that this case presents an "extraordinary" situation in which postponement of notice and hearing until after seizure did not deny due process.

5. *Fuentes* is quite vague about the procedure for the actual hearing itself. Some insight on this subject can be gleaned from Goldberg v. Kelly, 397 U.S. 254 (1970), in which the Court held that before welfare payments could be cut off the recipient was entitled to notice and a hearing. It went on to explain that the agency's practice of deciding questions about eligibility on written submissions was inadequate, at least where there were factual disputes:

> It is not enough that a welfare recipient may present his position to the decision maker in writing or secondhand through his caseworker. Written submissions are an unrealistic option for most recipients, who lack the educational attainment to write effectively and who cannot obtain professional assistance. Moreover, written submissions do not afford the flexibility of oral presentations; they do not permit the recipient to mold his argument to the issues the decision maker appears to regard as important. Particularly where credibility and

veracity are at issue, as they must be in many termination proceedings, written submissions are a wholly unsatisfactory basis for decision. * * * Informal procedures will suffice; in this context due process does not require a particular order of proof or mode of offering evidence.

In almost every setting where important decisions turn on questions of fact, due process requires an opportunity to confront and cross-examine adverse witnesses. What we said in Greene v. McElroy, 360 U.S. 474 (1959), is particularly pertinent here:

> Certain principles have remained relatively immutable in our jurisprudence. One of these is that where governmental action seriously injures an individual, and the reasonableness of the action depends on fact findings, the evidence used to prove the Government's case must be disclosed to the individual so that he has an opportunity to show that it is untrue. While this is important in the case of documentary evidence, it is even more important where the evidence consists of the testimony of individuals whose memory might be faulty or who, in fact, might be perjurers or persons motivated by malice, vindictiveness, intolerance, prejudice, or jealousy. * * *

Welfare recipients must therefore be given an opportunity to confront and cross-examine the witnesses relied on by the department.

"The right to be heard would be, in many cases, of little avail if it did not comprehend the right to be heard by counsel." We do not say that counsel must be provided at the pre-termination hearing, but only that the recipient must be allowed to retain an attorney if he so desires. Counsel can help delineate the issues, present the factual contentions in an orderly manner, conduct cross-examination, and generally safeguard the interests of the recipient. We do not anticipate that this assistance will unduly encumber the hearing. Finally, the decisionmaker's conclusion as to a recipient's eligibility must rest solely on the legal rules and evidence adduced at the hearing. To demonstrate compliance with this elementary requirement, the decision maker should state the reasons for his determination and indicate the evidence he relied on, though his statement need not amount to a full opinion or even formal findings of fact and conclusions of law. And, of course, an impartial decision maker is essential. We agree with the District Court that a prior involvement in some aspects of a case will not necessarily bar a welfare official from acting as a decision maker. He should not, however, have participated in the determination under review.

Mitchell v. W.T. Grant Co., 416 U.S. 600 (1974):

JUSTICE WHITE delivered the opinion of the Court.

[Grant sold a refrigerator, range, stereo and washing machine to Mitchell on credit and later filed suit in Louisiana state court claiming some $574 was overdue and unpaid. Louisiana statutes provided for sequestration where "one claims the ownership or right to possession of property * * * if it is within the power of the defendant to conceal, dispose of, or waste the property or the revenues therefrom, or remove the property from the parish, during the pendency of the action." Grant submitted the affidavit of its credit manager, which attested to the debt and added that Grant "had reason to believe" Mitchell would encumber, alienate or otherwise dispose of the merchandise described in the foregoing petition during the pendency of these proceedings. Under Louisiana law, the vendor's lien would expire if the buyer transferred possession. Based on the affidavit, without notice to Mitchell, a judge then signed an order of sequestration, directing a constable to take possession of the items after Grant posted $1,125 bond.

The Supreme Court held that the procedure was constitutional. It stressed that "[t]he question is not whether a debtor's property may be seized by his creditors, pendente lite, where they hold no present interest in the property sought to be seized. The reality is that both seller and buyer had current, real interests in the property." Finding that resolution of the due process challenge must therefore take account of the interests of the buyer and the seller in the property, the Court concluded further that "*Fuentes* was decided against a factual and legal background sufficiently different from that now before us and that it does not require the invalidation of the Louisiana sequestration statute."]

The Louisiana sequestration statute followed in this case mandates a considerably different procedure [from that in *Fuentes*]. A writ of sequestration is available to a mortgage or lien holder to forestall waste or alienation of the property, but, different from the Florida and Pennsylvania systems, bare conclusory claims of ownership or lien will not suffice under the Louisiana statute. Article 3501 authorizes the writ "only when the nature of the claim and the amount thereof, if any, and the grounds relied upon for the issuance of the writ clearly appear from specific facts" shown by verified petition or affidavit. Moreover, in the parish where this case arose, the requisite showing must be made to a judge, and judicial authorization obtained. Mitchell was not at the unsupervised mercy of the creditor and court functionaries. The Louisiana law provides for judicial control of the process from the beginning to the end.[12] This control is one of

---

12 The approval of a writ of sequestration is not, as petitioner contends, a mere ministerial act. "Since a writ of sequestration issues without a hearing, specific facts as to the grounds relied upon for issuance must be contained in the verified petition in order that the issuing judge can

the measures adopted by the State to minimize the risk that the ex parte procedure will lead to a wrongful taking. It is buttressed by the provision that should the writ be dissolved there are "damages for the wrongful issuance of a writ" and for attorney's fees "whether the writ is dissolved on motion or after trial on the merits."

The risk of wrongful use of the procedure must also be judged in the context of the issues which are to be determined at that proceeding. In Florida and Pennsylvania [whose statutes were invalidated in *Fuentes*] property was only to be replevied in accord with state policy if it had been "wrongfully detained." This broad "fault" standard is inherently subject to factual determination and adversarial input. * * * In Louisiana, on the other hand, the facts relevant to obtaining a writ of sequestration are narrowly confined. As we have indicated, documentary proof is particularly suited for questions of the existence of a vendor's lien and the issue of default. There is thus far less danger here that the seizure will be mistaken and a corresponding decrease in the utility of an adversary hearing which will be immediately available in any event.

Of course, as in *Fuentes*, consideration of the impact on the debtor remains. Under Louisiana procedure, however, the debtor, Mitchell, was not left in limbo to await a hearing that might or might not "eventually" occur, as the debtors were under the statutory schemes before the Court in *Fuentes*. Louisiana law expressly provides for an immediate hearing and dissolution of the writ [upon defendant's filing a "contradictory motion"] "unless the plaintiff proves the grounds upon which the writ was issued."

To summarize, the Louisiana system seeks to minimize the risk of error of a wrongful interim possession by the creditor. The system protects the debtor's interest in every conceivable way, except allowing him to have the property to start with, and this is done in pursuit of what we deem an acceptable arrangement *pendente lite* to put the property in the possession of the party who furnishes protection against loss or damage to the other pending trial on the merits.

JUSTICE POWELL, concurring.

In sweeping language, Fuentes v. Shevin, 407 U.S. 67 (1972), enunciated the principle that the constitutional guarantee of procedural due process requires an adversary hearing before an individual may be temporarily deprived of any possessory interest in tangible personal property, however brief the dispossession and however slight his monetary interest in the property. The Court's decision today withdraws significantly from the full reach of that principle, and to this extent I think it fair to say that the *Fuentes* opinion is overruled.

---

properly evaluate the grounds." Wright v. Hughes, 254 So.2d 293, 296–297 (La.Ct.App.1971) (on rehearing).

I could have agreed that the Florida and Pennsylvania statutes in *Fuentes* were violative of due process because of their arbitrary and unreasonable provisions. It seems to me, however, that it was unnecessary for the *Fuentes* opinion to have adopted so broad and inflexible a rule, especially one that considerably altered settled law with respect to commercial transactions and basic creditor-debtor understandings. Narrower grounds existed for invalidating the replevin statutes in that case.

[JUSTICE STEWART dissented, joined by JUSTICES DOUGLAS and MARSHALL. He accused the majority of overruling *Fuentes* without admitting it, concluding that "this case is constitutionally indistinguishable from Fuentes v. Shevin, and the Court today has simply rejected the reasoning of that case and adopted instead the analysis of the *Fuentes* dissent." JUSTICE BRENNAN wrote separately that he agreed *Fuentes* required invalidation of the Louisiana procedure.]

(original def.)

North Georgia Finishing, Inc. v. Di-Chem, Inc., 419 U.S. 601 (1975):

(original Plaintiff)

JUSTICE WHITE delivered the opinion of the Court.

[Plaintiff sued defendant in a Georgia state court alleging that defendant owed over $51,000 for goods it bought from plaintiff. Georgia statutes authorized a writ of garnishment if plaintiff or its attorney submitted an affidavit "stating the amount claimed to be due" and asserting "that he has reason to apprehend the loss of the same or some part thereof unless process of garnishment shall issue." Plaintiff therefore filed an affidavit of its president (seemingly on a printed form) asserting the defendant owed over $51,000 and that plaintiff "has reason to apprehend the loss of said sum or some part thereof unless process of Garnishment issues." The clerk of the court issued a summons of garnishment to defendant's bank, in effect freezing defendant's bank account. The Georgia courts rejected defendant's constitutional objections to the procedure.

The Supreme Court held that the Georgia courts had failed to take account of *Fuentes*. Justice White explained the import of *Fuentes* as follows: "Because the official seizures [in Fuentes] had been carried out without notice and without opportunity for a hearing or other safeguard against mistaken repossession they were held to be in violation of the Fourteenth Amendment."]

The Georgia statute is vulnerable for the same reasons [as the statutes in Fuentes]. Here, a bank account, surely a form of property, was impounded and, absent a bond, put totally beyond use during the pendency of the litigation on the alleged debt, all by a writ of garnishment issued by a court clerk without notice or opportunity for an early hearing and without participation by a judicial officer.

Nor is the statute saved by the more recent decision in Mitchell v. W.T. Grant Co., 416 U.S. 600 (1974). That case upheld the Louisiana sequestration statute which permitted the seller-creditor holding a vendor's lien to secure a writ of sequestration and, having filed a bond, to cause the sheriff to take possession of the property at issue. The writ, however, was issuable only by a judge upon the filing of an affidavit going beyond mere conclusory allegations and clearly setting out the facts entitling the creditor to sequestration. The Louisiana law also expressly entitled the debtor to an immediate hearing after seizure and to dissolution of the writ absent proof by the creditor of the grounds on which the writ was issued.

The Georgia garnishment statute has none of the saving characteristics of the Louisiana statute. The writ of garnishment is issuable on the affidavit of the creditor or his attorney, and the latter need not have personal knowledge of the facts. The affidavit, like the one filed in this case, need contain only conclusory allegations. The writ is issuable, as this one was, by the court clerk, without participation by a judge. Upon service of the writ, the debtor is deprived of the use of the property in the hands of the garnishee. Here a sizable bank account was frozen and the only method discernable on the face of the statute to dissolve the garnishment was to file a bond to protect the plaintiff creditor. There is no provision for an early hearing at which the creditor would be required to demonstrate at least probable cause for the garnishment. Indeed, it would appear that without the filing of a bond the defendant debtor's challenge to the garnishment will not be entertained, whatever the grounds may be.

JUSTICE STEWART, concurring.

It is gratifying to note that my report of the demise of Fuentes v. Shevin, see Mitchell v. W.T. Grant Co., 416 U.S. 600, 629–36 (1974) (dissenting opinion) seems to have been greatly exaggerated. Cf. S. Clemens, cable from Europe to the Associated Press, quoted in 2 A. Paine, Mark Twain, A Biography 1039 (1912).

JUSTICE POWELL, concurring in the judgment.

* * * The Court's opinion in this case, relying substantially on *Fuentes*, suggests that decision will again be read as calling into question much of the previously settled law governing commercial transactions. I continue to doubt whether *Fuentes* strikes a proper balance, especially in cases where the creditor's interest in the property may be as significant or even greater than that of the debtor. Nor do I find it necessary to relegate *Mitchell* to its narrow factual setting in order to determine that the Georgia garnishment statutes fail to satisfy the requirements of procedural due process. * * *

In my view, procedural due process would be satisfied where state law requires that the garnishment be preceded by the garnishor's provision of adequate security and by his establishment before a neutral officer[3] of a factual basis of the need to resort to the remedy as a means of preventing removal or dissipation of assets required to satisfy the claim. Due process further requires that the State afford an opportunity for a prompt postgarnishment judicial hearing in which the garnishor has the burden of showing probable cause to believe there is a need to continue the garnishment for a sufficient period of time to allow proof and satisfaction of the alleged debt. Since the garnished assets may bear no relation to the controversy giving rise to the alleged debt, the State also should provide the debtor with an opportunity to free those assets by posting adequate security in their place.

The Georgia provisions fall short of these requirements. Garnishment may issue on the basis of a simple and conclusory affidavit that the garnishor has reason to apprehend the loss of money already owed. As shown by the affidavit filed in this case, an unrevealing assertion of apprehension of loss suffices to invoke the issuance of garnishment. This is insufficient to enable a neutral officer to make even the most superficial preliminary assessment of the creditor's asserted need.

The most compelling deficiency in the Georgia procedure is its failure to provide a prompt and adequate postgarnishment hearing. * * * [T]he Georgia statute contains no provision enabling the debtor to obtain prompt dissolution of the garnishment upon a showing of fact, nor any indication that the garnishor bears the burden of proving entitlement to the garnishment.

Prompt Postgarnishment hearing

JUSTICE BLACKMUN, with whom JUSTICE REHNQUIST joins, dissenting.

* * *

Fuentes, a constitutional decision, obviously should not have been brought down and decided by a 4–3 vote when there were two vacancies on the court at the time of argument. It particularly should not have been decided by a 4–3 vote when Justices filling the vacant seats had qualified and were on hand and available to participate on reargument.[1]

* * *

[T]he Court now has embarked on a case-by-case analysis (weighted heavily in favor of *Fuentes* and with little hope under *Mitchell*) of the respective state statutes in this area. That road is a long and unrewarding

---

[3] I am not in accord with the Court's suggestion that the Due Process Clause might require that a *judicial* officer issue the writ of garnishment. The basic protection required for the debtor is the assurance of a prompt postgarnishment hearing before a judge.

[1] *Fuentes* was decided June 12, 1972. Mr. Justice Powell and Mr. Justice Rehnquist had taken their respective seats as Members of the Court five months before, on January 7. *Fuentes* had been argued November 9, 1971.

one, and provides no satisfactory answers to issues of constitutional magnitude.

[CHIEF JUSTICE BURGER also dissented.]

NOTES AND QUESTIONS

1.   Did *Mitchell* overrule *Fuentes*, as Justices Stewart and Powell contended? What would you emphasize in support of the argument that *Fuentes* was overruled? Does Justice White's characterization of *Fuentes*' rule in *Di-Chem* accurately reflect the decision in *Fuentes*? Recall that Fuentes noted that "[t]here may be cases in which a creditor could make a showing of immediate danger that a debtor will destroy or conceal disputed goods." See *supra* p. 39. Does that observation invite a reconciliation of the two cases?

2.   Note Justice White's efforts to distinguish *Fuentes* in *Mitchell*:

(a)   *Mitchell* stresses Louisiana's emphasis on specificity instead of "conclusory claims." What is the value of specificity? What should the plaintiff be specific about? Are more specific claims inherently more trustworthy? Keep these issues in mind for the discussion of pleading in Chapter 3.

(b)   *Mitchell* also says that the basis for obtaining a writ under the Louisiana procedure—with the nature and amount of the claim and grounds relied upon appearing from specific facts—is significantly different from the "broad fault" standard involved in *Fuentes*. Would the Louisiana standard require consideration of contentions like those made by Ms. Fuentes about Firestone's failure to perform its servicing obligations? Would it be fair to require creditor plaintiffs to identify and provide specifics about the debtor's possible defenses?

(c)   *Mitchell* stresses the involvement of the judge in issuance of the writ. Why are judges to be preferred to other state employees? Is the need for the judge related to the specificity requirement? Recall the interventionist behavior of the judge in *Band's Refuse*, supra p. 3. Is a more activist approach what the *Mitchell* Court has in mind? Compare the role of the judge in issuing a search warrant (see n. 30 in *Fuentes*): "It is almost as if the *Mitchell* Court is carrying into the due process clause the very special requirements of the fourth amendment [for a search warrant]." Catz & Robinson, Due Process and Creditor's Remedies, 28 Rutgers L.Rev. 541, 559–60 (1975).

(d)   Finally, *Mitchell* relies on Louisiana's provision of a post-seizure hearing at which plaintiff has the burden of proving grounds for issuance of the writ. Would this alternative suffice under *Fuentes*? Does *Mitchell* place as much emphasis as does *Fuentes* on participation by the defendant to assure an accurate decision?

3.   Is *Mitchell* of continuing importance after *Di-Chem*? Courts have continued to rely upon it in some circumstances. See McLaughlin v. Weathers, 170 F.3d 577, 581 (6th Cir.1999) ("Under the *Mitchell* rationale, we deem the Tennessee prejudgment statute not to be facially invalid as lacking due process.").

4. In *Di-Chem*, Justice Blackmun protests that *Fuentes* should not have been decided by a Court with positions unfilled. After *Di-Chem*, does *Fuentes* have any lasting importance? Is Justice White's position in Di-Chem consistent with his position in *Fuentes*?

5. What was the "rule" regarding the need for preseizure notice after *Di-Chem*? Leading constitutional scholars opined at that time that a statute authorizing seizure without a hearing "must have the following features: (1) the creditor must post a bond to safeguard the interest of the debtor; (2) the creditor or someone with personal knowledge of the facts must file an affidavit which sets out a prima facie claim for prejudgment attachment of the property; (3) a neutral magistrate must determine that the affidavit is sufficient before issuing the writ of attachment or replevin; (4) there must be a provision for a reasonably prompt post-attachment hearing for the debtor." J. Nowak, R. Rotunda & J. Young, Constitutional Law § 13.9 at 504 (1986). Based on your reading of the cases, would you add considerations to this list? Why should provision of these factors make a pre-seizure hearing unnecessary? Note that in *Di-Chem* Justice White says that *Fuentes* required either a hearing "or other safeguard against mistaken repossession."

6. *Mathews v. Eldridge*: The Court's procedural due process analysis was further clarified in Mathews v. Eldridge, 424 U.S. 319 (1976), which cut back on the 1970 holding in Goldberg v. Kelly (supra pp. 43–44 n. 5) that a trial-type evidentiary hearing was always required before termination of welfare benefits. In *Mathews* the question was whether Social Security disability benefits could be terminated based on an administrative finding that the disability had ceased. The Social Security administrative process afforded what the Court called "elaborate" opportunities for claimants to contest the conclusion that their disability had ended, but allowed a full evidentiary hearing only after actual cessation of benefits. Noting that due process is a flexible concept in the administrative arena, the Court explained that the due process decision calls for consideration of three factors:

> First, the private interest that will be affected by the official action; second, the risk of an erroneous deprivation of such interest through the procedures used, and the probable value, if any, of additional or substitute procedural safeguards; and finally, the Government's interest, including the function involved and the fiscal and administrative burdens that additional or substitute procedural requirement would entail.

Examining the Social Security disability situation, the Court found that a pre-termination hearing should not be required. Since disability benefits are not based on financial need, the likelihood of serious loss due to an erroneous termination is less than in the welfare situation. Because the question of disability ordinarily turns on review of routine medical reports, the potential value of an evidentiary hearing is less than with the question of welfare eligibility. Finally, considerable burdens would result from a requirement for a pre-termination evidentiary hearing because continuance of benefits will prompt many who might not otherwise demand such a hearing to ask for one, and there will be few opportunities for the Government to recoup the additional payments if the initial decision is found correct.

This approach can be challenged. Mashaw, The Supreme Court's Due Process Calculus for Administrative Adjudication in Mathews v. Eldridge: Three Factors in Search of a Theory of Value, 44 U. Chi. L. Rev. 28 (1976), asserts that the Court's embrace of utilitarianism fails to credit "process values" that might be served by oral hearings, and that it tends to undermine individual dignity by denying a right to be heard before the sensitive judgment whether the person is entitled to continued support is made. See also R. Dworkin, Principle, Policy, Procedure, in A Matter of Principle (1985) at 72, 102 (the "psychological fact that people generally mind an adverse decision more if it is taken facelessly, without their participation, * * * is the sort of harm that figures in any decent utilitarian calculation"). Moreover, it has been said that, "by including the recipient's substantive interests in the balance, the Court signalled just how tenuous the distinction between procedure and substance really was," and that *Mathews* suggested "that adversary process was not always optimal." Bone, The Process of Making Process: Court Rulemaking, Democratic Legitimacy, and Procedural Efficacy, 87 Geo.L.J. 887, 902 (1999).

Mathews did not directly address procedure in formal courts, however. We turn now to its implications for prejudgment remedies.

CONNECTICUT V. DOEHR
Supreme Court of the United States, 1991
501 U.S. 1

JUSTICE WHITE delivered an opinion, Parts I, II, and III of which are the opinion of the Court.*

This case requires us to determine whether a state statute that authorizes prejudgment attachment of real estate without prior notice or hearing, without a showing of extraordinary circumstances, and without a requirement that the person seeking the attachment post a bond, satisfies the Due Process Clause of the Fourteenth Amendment. We hold that, as applied to this case, it does not.

I

On March 15, 1988, Petitioner John F. DiGiovanni submitted an application to the Connecticut Superior Court for an attachment in the amount of $75,000 on respondent Brian K. Doehr's home in Meridan, Connecticut. DiGiovanni took this step in conjunction with a civil action for assault and battery that he was seeking to institute against Doehr in the same court. The suit did not involve Doehr's real estate nor did DiGiovanni

---

* The Chief Justice, Justice Blackmun, Justice Kennedy, and Justice Souter join Parts I, II, and III of this opinion, and Justice Scalia joins Parts I and III.

have any pre-existing interest either in Doehr's home or any of his other property.

Connecticut law authorizes prejudgment attachment of real estate without affording prior notice or the opportunity for a prior hearing to the individual whose property is subject to the attachment. The State's prejudgment remedy statute provides, in relevant part:

> "The court or a judge of the court may allow the prejudgment remedy to be issued by an attorney without hearing as provided in sections 52–278c and 52–278d upon verification by oath of the plaintiff or of some competent affiant, that there is probable cause to sustain the validity of the plaintiff's claims and (1) that the prejudgment remedy requested is for an attachment of real property. . . ." Conn.Gen.Stat. § 52–278e (1991).

The statute does not require the plaintiff to post a bond to insure the payment of damages that the defendant may suffer should the attachment prove wrongfully issued or the claim prove unsuccessful.

As required, DiGiovanni submitted an affidavit in support of his application. In five one-sentence paragraphs, DiGiovanni stated that the facts set forth in his previously submitted complaint were true; that "I was willfully, wantonly and maliciously assaulted by the defendant, Brian K. Doehr"; that "said assault and battery broke my left wrist and further caused an ecchymosis to my right eye, as well as other injuries"; and that "I have further expended sums of money for medical care and treatment." The affidavit concluded with the statement, "In my opinion, the foregoing facts are sufficient to show that there is probable cause that judgment will be rendered for the plaintiff."

On the strength of these submissions the Superior Court judge, by an order dated March 17, found "probable cause to sustain the validity of the plaintiff's claim" and ordered the attachment on Doehr's home "to the value of $75,000." The sheriff attached the property four days later, on March 21. Only after this did Doehr receive notice of the attachment. He also had yet to be served with the complaint, which is ordinarily necessary for an action to commence in Connecticut. As the statute further required, the attachment notice informed Doehr that he had the right to a hearing: (1) to claim that no probable cause existed to sustain the claim; (2) to request that the attachment be vacated, modified, or that a bond be substituted; or (3) to claim that some portion of the property was exempt from execution. Conn.Gen.Stat. § 52–278e(b) (1991).

Rather than pursue these options, Doehr filed suit against DiGiovanni in Federal District Court, claiming that § 52–278e(a)(1) was unconstitutional under the Due Process Clause of the Fourteenth Amendment. The District Court upheld the statute and granted summary judgment in favor of DiGiovanni. Pinsky v. Duncan, 716 F.Supp. 58

(D.Conn.1989). On appeal, a divided panel of the United States Court of Appeals for the Second Circuit reversed. Pinsky v. Duncan, 898 F.2d 852 (1990).[3] Judge Pratt, who wrote the opinion for the court, concluded that the Connecticut statute violated due process in permitting ex parte attachment absent a showing of extraordinary circumstances. "The rule to be derived from *Sniadach* and its progeny, therefore, is not that post attachment hearings are generally acceptable provided that the plaintiff files a factual affidavit and that a judicial officer supervises the process, but that a prior hearing may be postponed where exceptional circumstances justify such a delay, and where sufficient additional safeguards are present." This conclusion was deemed to be consistent with our decision in Mitchell v. W.T. Grant Co., 416 U.S. 600 (1974), because the absence of a preattachment hearing was approved in that case based on the presence of extraordinary circumstances.

Highly factual nature of case

A further reason to invalidate the statute, the court ruled, was the highly factual nature of the issues in this case. In *Mitchell*, there were "uncomplicated matters that lent themselves to documentary proof" and "the nature of the issues at stake minimized the risk that the writ [would] be wrongfully issued by a judge." Similarly, in Mathews v. Eldridge, 424 U.S. 319, 343–344 (1976), where an evidentiary hearing was not required prior to the termination of disability benefits, the determination of disability was "sharply focused and easily documented." Judge Pratt observed that in contrast the present case involved the fact-specific event of a fist fight and the issue of assault. He doubted that the judge could *only 1 side heard.* reliably determine probable cause when presented with only the plaintiff's version of the altercation. "Because the risk of a wrongful attachment is considerable under these circumstances, we conclude that dispensing with notice and opportunity for a hearing until after the attachment, without a showing of extraordinary circumstances, violates the requirements of due process." Judge Pratt went on to conclude that in his view, the statute was also constitutionally infirm for its failure to require the plaintiff to post a bond for the protection of the defendant in the event the attachment was ultimately found to have been improvident.

Judge Mahoney was also of the opinion that the statutory provision for attaching real property in civil actions, without a prior hearing and in the absence of extraordinary circumstances, was unconstitutional. He disagreed with Judge Pratt's opinion that a bond was constitutionally required. Judge Newman dissented from the holding that a hearing prior to attachment was constitutionally required and, like Judge Mahoney, disagreed with Judge Pratt on the necessity for a bond.

---

[3]   The Court of Appeals invited Connecticut to intervene pursuant to 28 U.S.C. § 2403(b) after oral argument. The State elected to intervene in the appeal, and has fully participated in the proceedings before this Court.

The dissent's conclusion accorded with the views of the Connecticut Supreme Court, which had previously upheld § 52–278e(b) in Fermont Division, Dynamics Corp. of America v. Smith, 423 A.2d 80 (Conn. 1979). We granted certiorari to resolve the conflict of authority.

II

With this case we return to the question of what process must be afforded by a state statute enabling an individual to enlist the aid of the State to deprive another of his or her property by means of the prejudgment attachment or similar procedure. Our cases reflect the numerous variations this type of remedy can entail. In Sniadach v. Family Finance Corp. of Bay View, 395 U.S. 337 (1969), the Court struck down a Wisconsin statute that permitted a creditor to effect prejudgment garnishment of wages without notice and prior hearing to the wage earner. In Fuentes v. Shevin, 407 U.S. 67 (1972), the Court likewise found a Due Process violation in state replevin provisions that permitted vendors to have goods seized through an ex parte application to a court clerk and the posting of a bond. Conversely, the Court upheld a Louisiana ex parte procedure allowing a lienholder to have disputed goods sequestered in Mitchell v. W.T. Grant Co., 416 U.S. 600 (1974). Mitchell, however, carefully noted that Fuentes was decided against "a factual and legal background sufficiently different . . . that it does not require the invalidation of the Louisiana sequestration statute." Those differences included Louisiana's provision of an immediate postdeprivation hearing along with the option of damages; the requirement that a judge rather than a clerk determine that there is a clear showing of entitlement to the writ; the necessity for a detailed affidavit; and an emphasis on the lien-holder's interest in preventing waste or alienation of the encumbered property. In North Georgia Finishing, Inc. v. Di-Chem, Inc., 419 U.S. 601 (1975), the Court again invalidated an ex parte garnishment statute that not only failed to provide for notice and prior hearing but that also failed to require a bond, a detailed affidavit setting out the claim, the determination of a neutral magistrate, or a prompt postdeprivation hearing.

These cases "underscore the truism that 'due process unlike some legal rules, is not a technical conception with a fixed content unrelated to time, place and circumstances.'" Mathews v. Eldridge, supra, [424 U.S.] at 334. In Mathews, we drew upon our prejudgment remedy decisions to determine what process is due when the government itself seeks to effect a deprivation on its own initiative. That analysis resulted in the now familiar threefold inquiry requiring consideration of "the private interest that will be affected by the official action"; "the risk of an erroneous deprivation of such interest through the procedures used, and the probable value, if any, of additional or substitute safeguards"; and lastly "the Government's interest, including the function involved and the fiscal and administrative burdens that the additional or substitute procedural requirement would entail."

Here the inquiry is similar but the focus is different. Prejudgment remedy statutes ordinarily apply to disputes between private parties rather than between an individual and the government. Such enactments are designed to enable one of the parties to "make use of state procedures with the overt, significant assistance of state officials," and they undoubtedly involve state action "substantial enough to implicate the Due Process Clause." Tulsa Professional Collection Services, Inc. v. Pope, 485 U.S. 478, 486 (1988). Nonetheless, any burden that increasing procedural safeguards entails primarily affects not the government, but the party seeking control of the other's property. See Fuentes v. Shevin, supra, at 99– 101 (White, J., dissenting). For this type of case, therefore, the relevant inquiry requires, as in *Mathews*, first, consideration of the private interest that will be affected by the prejudgment measure; second, an examination of the risk of erroneous deprivation through the procedures under attack and the probable value of additional or alternative safeguards; and third, in contrast to *Mathews*, principal attention to the interest of the party seeking the prejudgment remedy, with, nonetheless, due regard for any ancillary interest the government may have in providing the procedure or forgoing the added burden of providing greater protections.

We now consider the *Mathews* factors in determining the adequacy of the procedures before us, first with regard to the safeguards of notice and a prior hearing, and then in relation to the protection of a bond.

III

We agree with the Court of Appeals that the property interests that attachment affects are significant. For a property owner like Doehr, attachment ordinarily clouds title; impairs the ability to sell or otherwise alienate the property; taints any credit rating; reduces the chance of obtaining a home equity loan or additional mortgage; and can even place an existing mortgage in technical default where there is an insecurity clause. Nor does Connecticut deny that any of these consequences occurs.

Instead, the State correctly points out that these effects do not amount to a complete, physical, or permanent deprivation of real property; their impact is less than the perhaps temporary total deprivation of household goods or wages. But the Court has never held that only such extreme deprivations trigger due process concern. To the contrary, our cases show that even the temporary or partial impairments to property rights that attachments, liens, and similar encumbrances entail are sufficient to merit due process protection. Without doubt, state procedures for creating and enforcing attachments, as with liens, "are subject to the strictures of due process."[4]

We also agree with the Court of Appeals that the risk of erroneous deprivation that the State permits here is substantial. By definition, attachment statutes premise a deprivation of property on one ultimate factual contingency—the award of damages to the plaintiff which the defendant may not be able to satisfy. For attachments before judgment, Connecticut mandates that this determination be made by means of a procedural inquiry that asks whether "there is probable cause to sustain the validity of the plaintiff's claim." Conn.Gen.Stat. § 52–278e(a). The statute elsewhere defines the validity of the claim in terms of the likelihood "that judgment will be rendered in the matter in favor of the plaintiff." Conn.Gen.Stat. § 52–278c(a)(2) (1991). What probable cause means in this context, however, remains obscure. The State initially took the position, as did the dissent below, that the statute requires a plaintiff to show the objective likelihood of the suit's success. DiGiovanni, citing ambiguous state cases, reads the provision as requiring no more than that a plaintiff demonstrate a subjective good faith belief that the suit will succeed. At oral argument, the State shifted its position to argue that the statute requires something akin to the plaintiff stating a claim with sufficient facts to survive a motion to dismiss.

We need not resolve this confusion since the statute presents too great a risk of erroneous deprivation under any of these interpretations. If the statute demands inquiry into the sufficiency of the complaint, or, still less, the plaintiff's good-faith belief that the complaint is sufficient, requirement of a complaint and a factual affidavit would permit a court to make these minimal determinations. But neither inquiry adequately reduces the risk of erroneous deprivation. Permitting a court to authorize attachment merely because the plaintiff believes the defendant is liable, or because the plaintiff can make out a facially valid complaint, would permit the deprivation of the defendant's property when the claim would fail to convince a jury, when it rested on factual allegations that were sufficient to state a cause of action but which the defendant would dispute, or in the case of a mere good-faith standard, even when the complaint failed to state a claim upon which relief could be granted. The potential for unwarranted attachment in these situations is self-evident and too great to satisfy the requirements of due process absent any countervailing consideration.

Reduce Risk of erroneous deprivation

---

[4] Our summary affirmance in Spielman-Fond, Inc. v. Hanson's, Inc., 417 U.S. 901 (1974), does not control. In *Spielman-Fond*, the District Court held that the filing of a mechanic's lien did not amount to the taking of a significant property interest. 379 F.Supp. 997, 999 (Ariz.1973) (three-judge court) (per curiam). A summary disposition does not enjoy the full precedential value of a case argued on the merits and disposed of by a written opinion. The facts of *Spielman-Fond* presented an alternative basis for affirmance in any event. Unlike the case before us, the mechanic's lien statute in *Spielman-Fond* required the creditor to have a pre-existing interest in the property at issue. As we explain below, a heightened plaintiff interest in certain circumstances can provide a ground for upholding procedures that are otherwise suspect.

Even if the provision requires the plaintiff to demonstrate, and the judge to find, probable cause to believe that judgment will be rendered in favor of the plaintiff, the risk of error was substantial in this case. As the record shows, and as the State concedes, only a skeletal affidavit need be and was filed. The State urges that the reviewing judge normally reviews the complaint as well, but concedes that the complaint may also be conclusory. It is self-evident that the judge could make no realistic assessment concerning the likelihood of an action's success based upon these one-sided, self-serving, and conclusory submissions. And as the Court of Appeals said, in a case like this involving an alleged assault, even a detailed affidavit would give only the plaintiff's version of the confrontation. Unlike determining the existence of a debt or delinquent payments, the issue does not concern "ordinarily uncomplicated matters that lend themselves to documentary proof." *Mitchell*, 416 U.S., at 609. The likelihood of error that results illustrates that "fairness can rarely be obtained by secret, one-sided determination of facts decisive of rights. . . . [And no] better instrument has been devised for arriving at truth than to give a person in jeopardy of serious loss notice of the case against him and an opportunity to meet it." Joint Anti-Fascist Refugee Committee v. McGrath, 341 U.S. 123, 170–172 (1951) (Frankfurter, J., concurring).

What safeguards the State does afford do not adequately reduce this risk. Connecticut points out that the statute also provides an "expeditious" postattachment adversary hearing, § 52–278e(c);[5] notice for such a hearing, § 52–278e(b); judicial review of an adverse decision, § 52–278l(a); and a double damages action if the original suit is commenced without probable cause, § 52–568(a)(1). Similar considerations were present in *Mitchell* where we upheld Louisiana's sequestration statute despite the lack of predeprivation notice and hearing. But in *Mitchell*, the plaintiff had a vendor's lien to protect, the risk of error was minimal because the likelihood of recovery involved uncomplicated matters that lent themselves to documentary proof, and plaintiff was required to put up a bond. None of these factors diminishing the need for a predeprivation hearing is present in this case. It is true that a later hearing might negate the presence of probable cause, but this would not cure the temporary deprivation that an earlier hearing might have prevented. "The Fourteenth Amendment draws no bright lines around three-day, 10-day or 50-day deprivations of property. Any significant taking of property by the State is within the purview of the Due Process Clause." *Fuentes*, 407 U.S., at 86.

---

[5]   The parties vigorously dispute whether a defendant can in fact receive a prompt hearing. Doehr contends that the State's rules of practice prevent the filing of any motion—including a motion for the mandated post attachment hearing—until the return date on the complaint, which in this case was 30 days after service. Under state law at least 12 days must elapse between service on the defendant and the return date. The State counters that the postattachment hearing is available upon request. Even on this assumption, the State's procedures fail to provide adequate safeguards against the erroneous deprivation of the property interest at stake.

Finally, we conclude that the interests in favor of an ex parte attachment, particularly the interests of the plaintiff, are too minimal to supply such a consideration here. Plaintiff had no existing interest in Doehr's real estate when he sought the attachment. His only interest in attaching the property was to ensure the availability of assets to satisfy his judgment if he prevailed on the merits of his action. Yet there was no allegation that Doehr was about to transfer or encumber his real estate or take any other action during the pendency of the action that would render his real estate unavailable to satisfy a judgment. Our cases have recognized such a properly supported claim would be an exigent circumstance permitting postponing any notice or hearing until after the attachment is effected. Absent such allegations, however, the plaintiff's interest in attaching the property does not justify the burdening of Doehr's ownership rights without a hearing to determine the likelihood of recovery.

No interest the government may have affects the analysis. The State's substantive interest in protecting any rights of the plaintiff cannot be any more weighty than those rights themselves. Here the plaintiff's interest is de minimis. Moreover, the State cannot seriously plead additional financial or administrative burdens involving predeprivation hearings when it already claims to provide an immediate post deprivation hearing.

Historical and contemporary practice support our analysis. Prejudgment attachment is a remedy unknown at common law. Instead, "it traces its origin to the Custom of London, under which a creditor might attach money or goods of the defendant either in the plaintiff's own hands or in the custody of a third person, by proceedings in the mayor's court or in the sheriff's court." Ownbey [v. Morgan], 256 U.S., at 104. Generally speaking, attachment measures in both England and this country had several limitations that reduced the risk of erroneous deprivation which Connecticut permits. Although attachments ordinarily did not require prior notice or a hearing, they were usually authorized only where the defendant had taken or threatened to take some action that would place the satisfaction of the plaintiff's potential award in jeopardy. Attachments, moreover, were generally confined to claims by creditors. As we and the Court of Appeals have noted, disputes between debtors and creditors more readily lend themselves to accurate ex parte assessments of the merits. Tort actions, like the assault and battery claim at issue here, do not. Finally, as we will discuss below, attachment statutes historically required that the plaintiff post a bond.

Connecticut's statute appears even more suspect in light of current practice. A survey of state attachment provisions reveals that nearly every State requires either a preattachment hearing, a showing of some exigent circumstance, or both, before permitting an attachment to take place. Twenty-seven States, as well as the District of Columbia, permit attachments only when some extraordinary circumstance is present. In such cases, preattachment hearings are not required but postattachment hearings are provided. Ten States permit attachment without the presence of such factors but require prewrit hearings unless one of those factors is shown. Six States limit attachments to extraordinary circumstance cases but the writ will not issue prior to a hearing unless there is a showing of some even more compelling condition. Three States always require a preattachment hearing. Only Washington, Connecticut, and Rhode Island authorize attachments without a prior hearing in situations that do not involve any purportedly heightened threat to the plaintiff's interests. Even those States permit ex parte deprivations only in certain types of cases: Rhode Island does so only when the claim is equitable; Connecticut and Washington do so only when real estate is to be attached, and even Washington requires a bond. Conversely, the States for the most part no longer confine attachments to creditor claims. This development, however, only increases the importance of the other limitations.

We do not mean to imply that any given exigency requirement protects an attachment from constitutional attack. Nor do we suggest that the statutory measures we have surveyed are necessarily free of due process problems or other constitutional infirmities in general. We do believe, however, that the procedures of almost all the States confirm our view that the Connecticut provision before us, by failing to provide a preattachment hearing without at least requiring a showing of some exigent circumstance, clearly falls short of the demands of due process.

IV

[Justice White, joined by Justices Marshall, Stevens and O'Connor but not a majority of the Court, proceeded to consider whether due process also requires the plaintiff to post a bond in addition to requiring a hearing or showing of some exigency.

These four Justices concluded that a bond should be required. "A defendant's property rights remain at undue risk even when there has been an adversarial hearing to determine the plaintiff's likelihood of recovery. At best, a court's initial assessment of each party's case cannot produce more than an educated guess as to who will win. This is especially true when, as here, the nature of the claim makes any accurate prediction elusive. In consequence, even a full hearing under a proper probable-cause standard would not prevent many defendants from having title to their homes impaired during the pendency of suits that never result in the contingency that ultimately justifies such impairment, namely, an award to the plaintiff."

Having so concluded, the four Justices proceeded to consider whether provision of a bond sufficiently protects the defendant so that other procedural safeguards would not be necessary. But they concluded that a prompt postattachment hearing would remain necessary to avoid continuing harm to defendant due to a wrongful attachment. "An individual with an immediate need or opportunity to sell a property can neither do so, nor otherwise satisfy that need or recreate the opportunity. The same applies to a parent in need of a home equity loan for a child's education, an entrepreneur seeking to start a business on the strength of an otherwise strong credit rating, or simply a homeowner who might face the disruption of having a mortgage placed in technical default. * * * Reliance on a bond does not sufficiently account for the harms that flow from an erroneous attachment to excuse a State from reducing that risk by means of a timely [postattachment] hearing." For the same reasons, requiring a bond would not justify forgoing a pre-seizure hearing in cases where exigent circumstances are not shown.]

V

Because Connecticut's prejudgment remedy provision, Conn.Gen.Stat. § 52–278e(a)(1), violates the requirements of due process by authorizing prejudgment attachment without prior notice or a hearing, the judgment of the Court of Appeals is affirmed, and the case is remanded to that court for further proceedings consistent with this opinion.

CHIEF JUSTICE REHNQUIST with whom JUSTICE BLACKMUN Joins, concurring.

I agree with the Court that the Connecticut attachment statute, "as applied in this case," fails to satisfy the Due Process Clause of the Fourteenth Amendment. I therefore join Parts I, II and III of its opinion. Unfortunately, the remainder of the Court's opinion does not confine itself to the facts of this case, but enters upon a lengthy disquisition as to what combination of safeguards are required to satisfy Due Process in hypothetical cases not before the Court. I therefore do not join Part IV.

As the Court's opinion points out, the Connecticut statute allows attachment not merely for a creditor's claim, but for a tort claim of assault and battery; it affords no opportunity for a pre-deprivation hearing; it contains no requirement that there be "exigent circumstances," such as an effort on the part of the defendant to conceal assets; no bond is required from the plaintiff; and the property attached is one in which the plaintiff has no pre-existing interest. The Court's opinion is, in my view, ultimately correct when it bases its holding of unconstitutionality of the Connecticut statute as applied here on our cases of Sniadach v. Family Finance Corp., 395 U.S. 337 (1969); Fuentes v. Shevin, 407 U.S. 67 (1972), Mitchell v. W.T. Grant Co., 416 U.S. 600 (1974), and North Georgia Finishing v. Di-Chem, Inc., 419 U.S. 601 (1975). But I do not believe that the result follows so inexorably as the Court's opinion suggests. All of the cited cases dealt with personalty—bank deposits or chattels—and each involved the physical seizure of the property itself, so that the defendant was deprived of its use. These cases, which represented something of a revolution in the jurisprudence of procedural due process, placed substantial limits on the methods by which creditors could obtain a lien on the assets of a debtor

[handwritten margin note: My thoughts: It does deprive of use. It deprives of full use of the credit aspects of owning land.]

prior to judgment. But in all of them the debtor was deprived of the use and possession of the property. In the present case, on the other hand, Connecticut's pre-judgment attachment on real property statute, which secures an incipient lien for the plaintiff, does not deprive the defendant of the use or possession of the property.

The Court's opinion therefore breaks new ground, and I would point out, more emphatically than the Court does, the limits of today's holding. In Spielman-Fond, Inc. v. Hanson's, Inc., 379 F.Supp. 997, 999 (D.Ariz. 1973), the District Court held that the filing of a mechanics' lien did not cause the deprivation of a significant property interest of the owner. We summarily affirmed that decision. 417 U.S. 901 (1974). Other courts have read this summary affirmance to mean that the mere imposition of a lien on real property, which does not disturb the owner's use or enjoyment of the property, is not a deprivation of property calling for procedural due process safeguards. I agree with the Court, however, that upon analysis the deprivation here is a significant one, even though the owner remains in undisturbed possession. "For a property owner like Doehr, attachment ordinarily clouds title; impairs the ability to sell or otherwise alienate the property; taints any credit rating; reduces the chance of obtaining a home equity loan or additional mortgage; and can even place an existing mortgage in technical default when there is an insecurity clause." Given the elaborate system of title records relating to real property which prevails in all of our states, a lienor need not obtain possession or use of real property belonging to a debtor in order to significantly impair its value to him.

But in *Spielman-Fond, Inc.*, supra, there was, as the Court points out in fn. 4, ante, an alternate basis available to this Court for affirmance of that decision. Arizona recognized a pre-existing lien in favor of unpaid mechanics and materialmen who had contributed labor or supplies which were incorporated in improvements to real property. The existence of such a lien upon the very property ultimately posted or noticed distinguishes those cases from the present one, where the plaintiff had no pre-existing interest in the real property which he sought to attach. Materialman's and mechanic's lien statutes award an interest in real property to workers who have contributed their labor, and to suppliers who have furnished material, for the improvement of the real property. Since neither the labor nor the material can be reclaimed once it has become a part of the realty, this is the only method by which workmen or small businessmen who have contributed to the improvement of the property may be given a remedy against a property owner who has defaulted on his promise to pay for the labor and the materials. To require any sort of a contested court hearing or bond before the notice of lien takes effect would largely defeat the purpose of these statutes.

Petitioner in its brief relies in part on our summary affirmance in Bartlett v. Williams, 464 U.S. 801 (1983). That case involved a lis pendens, in which the question presented to this Court was whether such a procedure could be valid when the only protection afforded to the owner of land affected by the lis pendens was a post-sequestration hearing. A notice of lis pendens is a well established traditional remedy whereby a plaintiff (usually a judgment creditor) who brings an action to enforce an interest in property to which the defendant has title gives notice of the pendency of such action to third parties; the notice causes the interest which he establishes, if successful, to relate back to the date of the filing of the lis pendens. The filing of such notice will have an effect upon the defendant's ability to alienate the property, or to obtain additional security on the basis of title to the property, but the effect of the lis pendens is simply to give notice to the world of the remedy being sought in the lawsuit itself. The lis pendens itself creates no additional right in the property on the part of the plaintiff, but simply allows third parties to know that a lawsuit is pending in which the plaintiff is seeking to establish such a right. Here, too, the fact that the plaintiff already claims an interest in the property which he seeks to enforce by a lawsuit distinguishes this class of cases from the Connecticut attachment employed in the present case.

Today's holding is a significant development in the law * * *. The change is dramatically reflected when we compare today's decision with the almost casual statement of Justice Holmes, writing for a unanimous Court in Coffin Brothers v. Bennett, 277 U.S. 29, 31 (1928):

> "Nothing is more common than to allow parties alleging themselves to be creditors to establish in advance by attachment a lien dependent for its effect upon the result of the suit."

The only protection accorded to the debtor in that case was the right to contest his liability in a post-deprivation proceeding.

It is both unwise and unnecessary, I believe, for the Court to proceed, as it does in Part IV, from its decision of the case before it to discuss abstract and hypothetical situations not before it. This is especially so where we are dealing with the Due Process Clause which, as the Court recognizes, "unlike some legal rules, is not a technical conception with a fixed content unrelated to time, place and circumstances," and it is even more true in a case involving constitutional limits on the methods by which the states may transfer or create interests in real property; in other areas of the law, dicta may do little damage, but those who insure titles or write title opinions often do not enjoy the luxury of distinguishing between dicta and holding.

The two elements of due process with which the Court concerns itself in Part IV—the requirement of a bond, and of "exigent circumstances"— prove to be upon analysis so vague that the discussion is not only unnecessary, but not particularly useful. Unless one knows what the terms and conditions of a bond are to be, the requirement of a "bond" in the abstract means little. The amount to be secured by the bond and the conditions of the bond are left unaddressed—is there to be liability on the part of a plaintiff if he is ultimately unsuccessful in the underlying lawsuit, or is it instead to be conditioned on some sort of good faith test? The "exigent circumstances" referred to by the Court are admittedly equally vague; non-residency appears to be enough in some states, an attempt to conceal assets is required in others, an effort to flee the jurisdiction in still others. We should await concrete cases which present questions involving bonds and exigent circumstances before we attempt to decide when and if the Due Process Clause of the Fourteenth Amendment requires them as prerequisites for a lawful attachment.

[Opinion of JUSTICE SCALIA, concurring in part and concurring in the judgment, omitted.]

NOTES AND QUESTIONS

1.   *Postscript*: Eventually, a jury awarded DiGiovanni $5,600 in damages in his state-court suit against Doehr. In the federal case, the district court rendered summary judgment in Doehr's favor on the constitutional deprivation issue, but found that no damages should be awarded against DiGiovanni. See Pinsky v. Duncan, 79 F.3d 306 (2d Cir.1996). For further details, see Bone, The Story of Connecticut v. Doehr: Balancing Costs and Benefits in Defining Procedural Rights, in Civil Procedure Stories (2d ed. 2008), at 159.

2.   In United States v. James Daniel Good Real Property, 510 U.S. 43 (1993), the Court held, 5–4, that seizure of Good's house without notice and a prior hearing pursuant to drug trafficking forfeiture laws violated Fifth Amendment due process under *Fuentes* and *Doehr*. Good had pleaded guilty to "promoting a harmful drug" after 89 pounds of marijuana were seized at his Hawaii home in a search pursuant to a search warrant. More than four years later, the United States obtained an ex parte writ of arrest in rem from a Magistrate Judge on the basis that it had made a prima facie showing that the house was subject to forfeiture under 21 U.S.C.A. § 881(a) because it had been used in drug trafficking. The government did not dispossess Good's tenants, but ordered them to pay their rent to it rather than to Good.

Writing for the Court, Justice Kennedy found Good's case distinguishable from the seizure of a yacht in Calero-Toledo v. Pearson Yacht Leasing Co. (supra p. 43 n. 4) because real property like Good's house "can be neither moved nor concealed." Invoking *Fuentes* for the proposition that "[w]e tolerate some exceptions to the general rules requiring predeprivation notice and hearing, but only in 'extraordinary situations where some valid governmental interest is at stake,'" the Court concluded that the governmental interest at stake was not "some general interest in forfeiting property but the specific interest in seizing real property before the forfeiture hearing," noting that lesser measures such as a lis pendens would protect the government's interest in that interregnum. The Court also found that there was an unacceptable risk of error because the statute allows a defense of innocent ownership but the government is not required to put on evidence on that subject. The Court stated that its decision applied to all real property.

Chief Justice Rehnquist dissented from the majority's "expansive readings" of *Fuentes* and *Doehr*, noting that *Fuentes* appeared to approve summary seizure of property to collect taxes, which he considered analogous to the seizure of Good's house, and argued that "the seizure of respondent Good's real estate serves important governmental purposes in combatting illegal drugs." Justice O'Connor, also dissenting, added that "it is difficult to see what advantage a preseizure hearing would have had in this case. There was already an ex parte hearing before a magistrate to determine whether there was proper cause to believe that Good's property had been used in connection with a drug trafficking offense." On this point, see also Kaley v. United States, 134 S.Ct. 1980 (2014) (holding that a grand jury indictment sufficed to support an order freezing defendants' assets in anticipation of forfeiture after their convictions even though defendants had no opportunity to participate in grand jury proceedings and claimed to need the money to pay their lawyer in the criminal case).

3.   Note that the Court in *Doehr* says at the outset that the Connecticut statute violates due process "as applied in this case." In Shaumyan v. O'Neill, 987 F.2d 122 (2d Cir.1993), the court held that attachment under the same statute was constitutional because the facts were different. Shaumyan, a Yale professor, had contracted for painting and repairs on his house in New Haven but refused to pay when the work was not done to his satisfaction. The contractor sued in a Connecticut state court and obtained an attachment on the home without a hearing or a bond, and Shaumyan responded with a class action in federal court on due process grounds. The court distinguished *Doehr* as an intentional tort case and limited its attention to whether the statute was unconstitutional as applied to Shaumyan. Although the same property interests were involved, the court found that the risk of an erroneous deprivation was not high. The contractor had submitted an affidavit detailing the contract and plaintiff's failure to pay the amount due. The Second Circuit found the facts "easily documented" regarding liability in a sum certain and concluded that the safeguards of the statute were similar to those upheld in Mitchell v. W.T. Grant Co. (supra p. 45). In addition, unlike plaintiff in Doehr, the contractor had a preexisting interest in the property that the attachment protected.

Despite the possibility that its statute could still be constitutionally applied, Connecticut amended its § 52–278e(a) in 1991 and 1993 to require the plaintiff to file an affidavit setting forth facts sufficient to show probable cause that a judgment would be rendered in its favor and showing exigent circumstances including defendant's likely removal of property from the state or fraudulent hiding or disposition of property that would be available to satisfy a judgment. Defendant may request that a bond be posted. See § 52–278e(b).

4.   In *Doehr*, the Court applies the three-part analysis of Mathews v. Eldridge to prejudgment remedies. Is this preferable to the approach adopted in the Court's earlier cases? Consider the following endorsement of this approach by the leading proponent of law and economics analysis:

> Of course, * * * it is rarely possible (or at least efforts are rarely made) to quantify the terms. But the formula is valuable even when used qualitatively rather than quantitatively. Suppose, for example, the question is whether the owner of an apparently abandoned car should be notified, and given an opportunity for a hearing, before the car is towed away and sold for scrap. The probability that the car wasn't really abandoned, but broke down or was stolen, is not trivial, and the cost of a hearing is modest relative to the value of the car; so maybe, as most courts have held, the owner should be entitled to the hearing. But suppose we are speaking not of abandoned but of illegally parked cars. Since the cars are not about to be destroyed, the deprivation is much less than in the case of the abandoned car. The probability of error is also much lower, because ordinarily the determination of whether a car is illegally parked is cut and dried. And the cost of a predeprivation hearing is very high; if the owner has to be notified before the car is towed, he'll remove it and the deterrent effect will be eliminated. So courts hold that due process does not require a predeprivation hearing in the case of illegally parked cars.

R. Posner, Economic Analysis of Law 594 (7th ed. 2007); compare Propert v. District of Columbia, 948 F.2d 1327 (D.C.Cir.1991) (due process violated by towing and destruction without a hearing of plaintiff's 1969 Volkswagen Karmann Ghia, which was parked near his house, removed on basis of determination of officer that due to its physical appearance it was "junk") with Oberhausen v. Louisville-Jefferson County Metro Gov't, 527 F.Supp.2d 713 (W.D. Ky. 2007) (due process not violated by application of Denver boot to plaintiff's car without prior hearing for failure to pay outstanding parking tickets).

In Van Harken v. City of Chicago, 103 F.3d 1346 (7th Cir. 1997), Judge Posner applied this analysis to a challenge to the City's parking ticket procedure, which treated the ticket as prima facie evidence of a parking violation and relied on private attorneys hired as hearing officers to determine challenges to tickets. Plaintiffs contended that due process required that the police officer appear at every hearing, rather than permitting the hearing officer to rely on the ticket as prima facie evidence of a parking violation. "The due process clause is not a straitjacket," said the judge. The City issues 4 million parking tickets a year, with an average fine of $55. Approximately 67,000 people demand an oral hearing each year. Assuming that attending those hearings would require an average of two hours' time for the officer involved, and that officers work 40 hours per week (2,000 hours per year), that would mean the City would have to commit the equivalent of 67 officers' full-time work to attending hearings. And if those who receive tickets know that the citation will be dismissed if the officer does not appear, there probably would be more demands for oral hearing, not only diverting police resources but also undermining the City's interest in deterring illegal parking. On the other side of the balance, Judge Posner noted, the benefit in increased accuracy of requiring the officer to appear is harder to estimate (id. at 1352):

> Suppose that in [the officer's] absence the probability of an erroneous determination that the respondent really did commit a parking violation is 5 percent, and the officers' presence would cut that probability in half, to 2.5 percent. Then the average saving to the innocent respondent from this additional procedural safeguard would be only $1.38 ($55 × .025)—a trivial amount.

> These calculations are inexact, to say the least; but they help to show, what is pretty obvious without them, that the benefits of requiring the police officer to appear at every hearing are unlikely to exceed the costs.

In City of Los Angeles v. David, 538 U.S. 715 (2003), the Supreme Court faced a similar question. Plaintiff's car was towed from a no parking zone, but plaintiff claimed that the no parking sign was obscured by trees and insisted on a hearing to contest the $134.50 he had to pay to recover the car. The hearing was held 30 days later, and after he lost at the hearing plaintiff sued in federal court insisting that due process entitled him to a hearing within five days. The Supreme Court rejected his arguments, using the Mathews v. Eldredge three-part test. First, the private interest was merely a monetary interest, which could be compensated by an interest payment. Second, concern for accuracy does not require a hearing within five days because a delay of less than 30 days is unlikely to affect the accuracy of the decision. "[T]he straightforward nature of the issue—whether the car was illegally parked— indicates that initial towing errors, while they may occur, are unlikely." Finally, the governmental interest argues strongly for allowing the city more time, because scheduling hearings that quickly would pose severe administrative burdens on the city. See also Krimstock v. Kelly, 306 F.3d 40 (2d Cir.2002) (time lag of one or two months in initiating proceedings to forfeit a seized vehicle, during which owner could not challenge seizure, did not violate due process, particularly in light of the government's direct interest in the vehicle it claimed was subject to forfeiture).

5.   Are the *Mathews* factors correctly applied in *Doehr*?

(a)   Regarding the deprivation suffered by Doehr, note that the issue seems to be the effect of an attachment during the delay until a hearing is held. Given the depressed state of the Connecticut housing market in 1988, how likely is it that a lender would take any action against Doehr during that time due to the attachment if he had been making his mortgage payments on time? Wouldn't Doehr's only real deprivation during that interim occur if he were in the process of selling or refinancing his house? In fact, Doehr was in the process of putting his house on the market. Bone, supra note 1, at 156.

(b) Regarding the risk of error found by the Court, consider whether it was due to the type of issue presented in this tort suit or to the fact that there was no adversary proceeding.

(c) Regarding the plaintiff's interest, does the Court hold that attachment without notice is only permitted when the plaintiff has a preexisting interest in the property? Recall the suggestion above that the only significant deprivation Doehr would be likely to suffer would occur if he were about to sell or refinance his house. How would those circumstances bear on the question whether exigent circumstances warranting immediate action were present?

6. Recall the factors emphasized in the Court's decisions in *Mitchell* (supra p. 45) and *Di-Chem* (supra p. 47) such as (1) that there be a showing under oath by the plaintiff of a prima facie right to relief (2) presented to a judge, who should (3) require posting of a bond if attachment issues and (4) afford defendant an opportunity for a prompt post-deprivation hearing, and perhaps that (5) plaintiff have a pre-existing interest in the property such as a vendor's lien and/or (6) show exigent circumstances and/or (7) assert a claim readily resolved on documentary evidence. Which of the *Mathews* factors do these various considerations address? In *Doehr* the Court discussed the expeditious postattachment hearing as an element of the risk of error. Does that seem to be the proper factor under *Mathews* for analysis of this consideration?

7. The Court emphasizes the current practice of other states in evaluating the constitutionality of Connecticut's prejudgment seizure statute. In some instances, the Court treats the prevalence of a practice among the states as important evidence that the practice satisfies due process. See Burnham v. Superior Court, infra p. 813 (upholding constitutionality of basing personal jurisdiction solely on personal service in state). But the practices condemned in *Fuentes* were widespread. Ironically, the current strictness exhibited by many states toward prejudgment seizure and relied upon by the Court in *Doehr* can be traced to the decision in *Fuentes*, which made it necessary for states to revise their attachment statutes. Connecticut itself had revised its attachment statutes based on *Mitchell*. See Bone, supra note 1, at 159.

B. POST JUDGMENT REMEDIES

The centerpiece of a law suit—indeed, the very reason it was filed—is the remedy sought by the claimant. A remedy, in the form of a judgment, may be awarded after a full trial, or, in certain circumstances, after a final determination short of trial (such as default judgment or summary judgment). The usual remedy in our legal system is money damages. "Actual damages are the bottom line in most lawsuits." Frey & Orr, Litigating Damages: Actual and Punitive, 29 Litigation 33, 33 (Winter 2003). However, other remedies such as equitable relief (for example, an injunction or specific performance) or declaratory relief (a court order declaring the respective rights of the parties) may be available. We will consider here certain aspects of the remedies of damages and injunctive relief in an attempt to give you an early insight into the nature of the judicial remedies that are the ultimate objective of the litigation process.

At the outset, however, it is useful to emphasize that you probably have the impression that huge recoveries in court are more frequent than really occurs. The "holler of the dollar" prompts stories in the media that emphasize big-dollar jury verdicts out of all proportion with actual awards in normal cases. See W. Haltom & M. McCann, Distorting the Law: Politics, Media, and the Litigation Crisis 167 (2004) (explaining that "multimillion-dollar winners of state lotteries are covered far more than those who win only thousands," and that big-money awards similarly enable the press to present court cases in dramatic form). Thus, the authors find that the great majority of awards and settlements reported in the media far exceed ordinary outcomes. See id. at 166.

1. DAMAGES

CAREY v. PIPHUS

Supreme Court of the United States, 1978
435 U.S. 247

JUSTICE POWELL delivered the opinion of the Court.

In this case, brought under 42 U.S.C. § 1983, we consider the elements and prerequisites for recovery of damages by students who were suspended from public elementary and secondary schools without procedural due process. The Court of Appeals for the Seventh Circuit held that the students are entitled to recover substantial nonpunitive damages even if their suspensions were justified, and even if they do not prove that any other actual injury was caused by the denial of procedural due process. We disagree, and hold that in the absence of proof of actual injury, the students are entitled to recover only nominal damages.

I

Respondent Jarius Piphus was a freshman at Chicago Vocational High School during the 1973–1974 school year. On January 23, 1974, during school hours, the school principal saw Piphus and another student standing outdoors on school property passing back and forth what the principal described as an irregularly shaped cigarette. The principal approached the students unnoticed and smelled what he believed was the strong odor of burning marijuana. He also saw Piphus try to pass a packet of cigarette papers to the other student. When the students became aware of the principal's presence, they threw the cigarette into a nearby hedge.

The principal took the students to the school's disciplinary office and directed the assistant principal to impose the "usual" 20-day suspension for violation of the school rule against the use of drugs. The students protested that they had not been smoking marijuana, but to no avail. Piphus was allowed to remain at school, although not in class, for the remainder of the school day while the assistant principal tried, without success, to reach his mother.

A suspension notice was sent to Piphus' mother, and a few days later two meetings were arranged among Piphus, his mother, his sister, school officials, and representatives from a legal aid clinic. The purpose of the meetings was not to determine whether Piphus had been smoking marijuana, but rather to explain the reasons for the suspension. Following an unfruitful exchange of views, Piphus and his mother, as guardian ad litem, filed suit against petitioners in Federal District Court under 42 U.S.C. § 1983 and its jurisdictional counterpart, 28 U.S.C. § 1343, charging that Piphus had been suspended without due process of law in violation of the Fourteenth Amendment. The complaint sought declaratory and injunctive relief, together with actual and punitive damages in the amount of $3,000. Piphus was readmitted to school under a temporary restraining order after eight days of his suspension.

Respondent Silas Brisco was in the sixth grade at Clara Barton Elementary School in Chicago during the 1973–1974 school year. On September 11, 1973, Brisco came to school wearing one small earring. The previous school year the school principal had issued a rule against the wearing of earrings by male students because he believed that this practice denoted membership in certain street gangs and increased the likelihood that gang members would terrorize other students. Brisco was reminded of this rule, but he refused to remove the earring, asserting that it was a symbol of black pride, not of gang membership.

The assistant principal talked to Brisco's mother, advising her that her son would be suspended for 20 days if he did not remove the earring. Brisco's mother supported her son's position, and a 20-day suspension was imposed. Brisco and his mother, as guardian ad litem, filed suit in Federal District Court under 42 U.S.C. § 1983 and 28 U.S.C. § 1343, charging that Brisco had been suspended without due process of law in violation of the Fourteenth Amendment. The complaint sought declaratory and injunctive relief, together with actual and punitive damages in the amount of $5,000. Brisco was readmitted to school during the pendency of proceedings for a preliminary injunction after 17 days of his suspension.

Piphus' and Brisco's cases were consolidated for trial and submitted on stipulated records. The District Court held that both students had been suspended without procedural due process.[5] * * * Despite these holdings, the District Court declined to award damages because:

---

5   The District Court read Goss v. Lopez, [419 U.S. 565 (1975)], as requiring "more formal procedures" for suspensions of more than 10 days than for suspensions of less than 10 days, and it

> "Plaintiffs put no evidence in the record to quantify their damages, and the record is completely devoid of any evidence which could even form the basis of a speculative inference measuring the extent of their injuries. Plaintiffs' claims for damages therefore fail for complete lack of proof."

The court also stated that the students were entitled to declaratory relief and to deletion of the suspensions from their school records, but for reasons that are not apparent the court failed to enter an order to that effect. Instead, it simply dismissed the complaints. No finding was made as to whether respondents would have been suspended if they had received procedural due process.

On respondents' appeal, the Court of Appeals reversed and remanded. It first held that the District Court erred in not granting declaratory and injunctive relief. It also held that the District Court should have considered evidence submitted by respondents after judgment that tended to prove the pecuniary value of each day of school that they missed while suspended. The court said, however, that respondents would not be entitled to recover damages representing the value of missed school time if petitioners showed on remand "that there was just cause for the suspension[s] and that therefore [respondents] would have been suspended even if a proper hearing had been held."

Finally, the Court of Appeals held that even if the District Court found on remand that respondents' suspensions were justified, they would be entitled to recover substantial "nonpunitive" damages simply because they had been denied procedural due process. Relying on its earlier decision in Hostrop v. Board of Junior College Dist. No. 515, 523 F.2d 569 (C.A.7 1975), cert. denied, 425 U.S. 963 (1976), the court stated that such damages should be awarded "even if, as in the case at bar, there is no proof of individualized injury to the plaintiff, such as mental distress. . . ." We granted certiorari to consider whether, in an action under § 1983 for the deprivation of procedural due process, a plaintiff must prove that he actually was injured by the deprivation before he may recover substantial "nonpunitive" damages.

II

Title 42 U.S.C. § 1983, derived from § 1 of the Civil Rights Act of 1871, provides:

> "Every person who, under color of any statute, ordinance, regulation, custom, or usage, of any State or Territory, subjects, or causes to be subjected, any citizen of the United States or other person within the jurisdiction thereof to the deprivation of any

---

set forth a detailed list of procedural requirements. Petitioners have not challenged either the holding that respondents were denied procedural due process, or the listing of rights that must be granted.

rights, privileges, or immunities secured by the Constitution and laws, shall be liable to the party injured in an action at law, suit in equity, or other proper proceeding for redress."

The legislative history of § 1983, elsewhere detailed, demonstrates that it was intended to "[create] a species of tort liability" in favor of persons who are deprived of "rights, privileges, or immunities secured" to them by the Constitution.

Petitioners contend that the elements and prerequisites for recovery of damages under this "species of tort liability" should parallel those for recovery of damages under the common law of torts. In particular, they urge that the purpose of an award of damages under § 1983 should be to compensate persons for injuries that are caused by the deprivation of constitutional rights; and, further, that plaintiffs should be required to prove not only that their rights were violated, but also that injury was caused by the violation, in order to recover substantial damages. Unless respondents prove that they actually were injured by the deprivation of procedural due process, petitioners argue, they are entitled at most to nominal damages.

Respondents seem to make two different arguments in support of the holding below. First, they contend that substantial damages should be awarded under § 1983 for the deprivation of a constitutional right *whether* or *not* any injury was caused by the deprivation. This, they say, is appropriate both because constitutional rights are valuable in and of themselves, and because of the need to deter violations of constitutional rights. Respondents believe that this view reflects accurately that of the Congress that enacted § 1983. Second, respondents argue that even if the purpose of a § 1983 damages award is, as petitioners contend, primarily to compensate persons for injuries that are caused by the deprivation of constitutional rights, every deprivation of procedural due process may be presumed to cause some injury. This presumption, they say, should relieve them from the necessity of proving that injury actually was caused.

A

Insofar as petitioners contend that the basic purpose of a § 1983 damages award should be to compensate persons for injuries caused by the deprivation of constitutional rights, they have the better of the argument. Rights, constitutional and otherwise, do not exist in a vacuum. Their purpose is to protect persons from injuries to particular interests, and their contours are shaped by the interests they protect.

Our legal system's concept of damages reflects this view of legal rights. "The cardinal principle of damages in Anglo-American law is that of *compensation* for the injury caused to plaintiff by defendant's breach of duty." 2 F. Harper & F. James, Law of Torts § 25.1, p. 1299 (1956) (emphasis in original). The Court implicitly has recognized the applicability of this principle to actions under § 1983 by stating that damages are available under that section for actions "found . . . to have been violative of . . . constitutional rights *and to have caused compensable injury*. . . ." Wood v. Strickland, 420 U.S., at 319 (emphasis supplied). The lower federal courts appear generally to agree that damages awards under § 1983 should be determined by the compensation principle.

The Members of the Congress that enacted § 1983 did not address directly the question of damages, but the principle that damages are designed to compensate persons for injuries caused by the deprivation of rights hardly could have been foreign to the many lawyers in Congress in 1871. Two other sections of the Civil Rights Act of 1871 appear to incorporate this principle, and no reason suggests itself for reading § 1983 differently. To the extent that Congress intended that awards under § 1983 should deter the deprivation of constitutional rights, there is no evidence that it meant to establish a deterrent more formidable than that inherent in the award of compensatory damages.[11]

B

It is less difficult to conclude that damages awards under § 1983 should be governed by the principle of compensation than it is to apply this principle to concrete cases. But over the centuries the common law of torts has developed a set of rules to implement the principle that a person should be compensated fairly for injuries caused by the violation of his legal rights. These rules, defining the elements of damages and the prerequisites for their recovery, provide the appropriate starting point for the inquiry under § 1983 as well.

It is not clear, however, that common-law tort rules of damages will provide a complete solution to the damages issue in every § 1983 case. In some cases, the interests protected by a particular branch of the common law of torts may parallel closely the interests protected by a particular constitutional right. In such cases, it may be appropriate to apply the tort rules of damages directly to the § 1983 action. In other cases, the interests protected by a particular constitutional right may not also be protected by an analogous branch of the common law of torts. In those cases, the task will be the more difficult one of adapting common-law rules of damages to

---

[11] This is not to say that exemplary or punitive damages might not be awarded in a proper case under § 1983 with the specific purpose of deterring or punishing violations of constitutional rights. [The Court cited several lower court decisions upholding punitive awards in § 1983 cases.] Although we imply no approval or disapproval of any of these cases, we note that there is no basis for such an award in this case. The District Court specifically found that petitioners did not act with malicious intention to deprive respondents of their rights or to do them other injury, and the Court of Appeals approved only the award of "non-punitive" damages.

We also note that the potential liability of § 1983 defendants for attorney's fees, see Civil Rights Attorney's Fees Awards Act of 1976, 42 U.S.C. § 1988, provides additional—and by no means inconsequential—assurance that agents of the State will not deliberately ignore due process rights.

provide fair compensation for injuries caused by the deprivation of a constitutional right.

Although this task of adaptation will be one of some delicacy—as this case demonstrates—it must be undertaken. The purpose of § 1983 would be defeated if injuries caused by the deprivation of constitutional rights went uncompensated simply because the common law does not recognize an analogous cause of action. In order to further the purpose of § 1983, the rules governing compensation for injuries caused by the deprivation of constitutional rights should be tailored to the interests protected by the particular right in question—just as the common-law rules of damages themselves were defined by the interests protected in the various branches of tort law. We agree with Mr. Justice Harlan that "the experience of judges in dealing with private [tort] claims supports the conclusion that courts of law are capable of making the types of judgment concerning causation and magnitude of injury necessary to accord meaningful compensation for invasion of [constitutional] rights." With these principles in mind, we now turn to the problem of compensation in the case at hand.

C

The Due Process Clause of the Fourteenth Amendment provides:

"[N]or shall any State deprive any person of life, liberty, or property, without due process of law. . . ."

This Clause "raises no impenetrable barrier to the taking of a person's possessions," or liberty, or life. Fuentes v. Shevin, 407 U.S. 67, 81 (1972). Procedural due process rules are meant to protect persons not from the deprivation, but from the mistaken or unjustified deprivation of life, liberty, or property. Thus, in deciding what process constitutionally is due in various contexts, the Court repeatedly has emphasized that "procedural due process rules are shaped by the risk of error inherent in the truth-finding process. . . ." Mathews v. Eldridge, 424 U.S. 319, 344 (1976). Such rules "minimize substantively unfair or mistaken deprivations of" life, liberty, or property by enabling persons to contest the basis upon which a State proposes to deprive them of protected interests. Fuentes v. Shevin, supra, 407 U.S., at 81.

In this case, the Court of Appeals held that if petitioners can prove on remand that "[respondents] would have been suspended even if a proper hearing had been held," then respondents will not be entitled to recover damages to compensate them for injuries caused by the suspensions. The court thought that in such a case, the failure to accord procedural due process could not properly be viewed as the cause of the suspensions. The court suggested that in such circumstances, an award of damages for injuries caused by the suspensions would constitute a windfall, rather than compensation, to respondents. We do not understand the parties to disagree with this conclusion. Nor do we.

The parties do disagree as to the further holding of the Court of Appeals that respondents are entitled to recover substantial—although unspecified—damages to compensate them for "the injury which is 'inherent in the nature of the wrong,' " even if their suspensions were justified and even if they fail to prove that the denial of procedural due process actually caused them some real, if intangible, injury. Respondents, elaborating on this theme, submit that the holding is correct because injury fairly may be "presumed" to flow from every denial of procedural due process. Their argument is that in addition to protecting against unjustified deprivations, the Due Process Clause also guarantees the "feeling of just treatment" by the government. They contend that the deprivation of protected interests without procedural due process, even where the premise for the deprivation is not erroneous, inevitably arouses strong feelings of mental and emotional distress in the individual who is denied this "feeling of just treatment." They analogize their case to that of defamation per se, in which "the plaintiff is relieved from the necessity of producing any proof whatsoever that he has been injured" in order to recover substantial compensatory damages.[16]

Petitioners do not deny that a purpose of procedural due process is to convey to the individual a feeling that the government has dealt with him fairly, as well as to minimize the risk of mistaken deprivations of protected interests. They go so far as to concede that, in a proper case, persons in respondents' position might well recover damages for mental and emotional distress caused by the denial of procedural due process. Petitioners' argument is the more limited one that such injury cannot be presumed to occur, and that plaintiffs at least should be put to their proof on the issue, as plaintiffs are in most tort actions.

We agree with petitioners in this respect. As we have observed in another context, the doctrine of presumed damages in the common law of defamation *per se* "is an oddity of tort law, for it allows recovery of purportedly compensatory damages without evidence of actual loss." Gertz v. Robert Welch, Inc., 418 U.S. 323, 349 (1974). The doctrine has been defended on the grounds that those forms of defamation that are actionable per se are virtually certain to cause serious injury to reputation, and that this kind of injury is extremely difficult to prove. Moreover, statements

---

[16] Respondents also contend that injury should be presumed because, even if they were guilty of the conduct charged, they were deprived of the chance to present facts or arguments in mitigation to the initial decisionmaker. They claim that "[i]t can never be known . . . what, if anything, the exercise of such an opportunity to plead one's cause on judgmental or discretionary grounds would have availed." But, as previously indicated, the Court of Appeals held that respondents cannot recover damages for injuries caused by their suspensions if the District Court determines that "[respondents] would have been suspended even if a proper hearing had been held." This holding, which respondents do not challenge, necessarily assumes that the District Court can determine what the outcome would have been if respondents had received their hearing. We presume that this determination will include consideration of the likelihood that any mitigating circumstances to which respondents can point would have swayed the initial decisionmakers.

that are defamatory per se by their very nature are likely to cause mental and emotional distress, as well as injury to reputation, so there arguably is little reason to require proof of this kind of injury either.[18] But these considerations do not support respondents' contention that damages should be presumed to flow from every deprivation of procedural due process.

First, it is not reasonable to assume that every departure from procedural due process, no matter what the circumstances or how minor, inherently is as likely to cause distress as the publication of defamation *per se* is to cause injury to reputation and distress. Where the deprivation of a protected interest is substantively justified but procedures are deficient in some respect, there may well be those who suffer no distress over the procedural irregularities. Indeed, in contrast to the immediately distressing effect of defamation *per se*, a person may not even know that procedures were deficient until he enlists the aid of counsel to challenge a perceived substantive deprivation.

Moreover, where a deprivation is justified but procedures are deficient, whatever distress a person feels may be attributable to the justified deprivation rather than to deficiencies in procedure. But as the Court of Appeals held, the injury caused by a justified deprivation, including distress, is not properly compensable under § 1983.[19] This ambiguity in causation, which is absent in the case of defamation per se, provides additional need for requiring the plaintiff to convince the trier of fact that he actually suffered distress because of the denial of procedural due process itself.

Finally, we foresee no particular difficulty in producing evidence that mental and emotional distress actually was caused by the denial of procedural due process itself. Distress is a personal injury familiar to the law, customarily proved by showing the nature and circumstances of the wrong and its effect on the plaintiff.[20] In sum, then, although mental and emotional distress caused by the denial of procedural due process itself is compensable under § 1983, we hold that neither the likelihood of such injury nor the difficulty of proving it is so great as to justify awarding compensatory damages without proof that such injury actually was caused.

---

[18] The essence of libel *per se* is the publication in writing of false statements that tend to injure a person's reputation. The essence of slander per se is the publication by spoken words of false statements imputing to a person a criminal offense; a loathsome disease; matter affecting adversely a person's fitness for trade, business, or profession; or serious sexual misconduct.

[19] In this case, for example, respondents denied the allegations against them. They may well have been distressed that their denials were not believed. They might have been equally distressed if they had been disbelieved only after a full-dress hearing, but in that instance they would have no cause of action against petitioners.

[20] We use the term "distress" to include mental suffering or emotional anguish. Although essentially subjective, genuine injury in this respect may be evidenced by one's conduct and observed by others. Juries must be guided by appropriate instructions, and an award of damages must be supported by competent evidence concerning the injury.

D

The Court of Appeals believed, and respondents urge, that cases dealing with awards of damages for racial discrimination, the denial of voting rights and the denial of Fourth Amendment rights, support a presumption of damages where procedural due process is denied. Many of the cases relied upon do not help respondents because they held or implied that some actual, if intangible, injury must be proved before compensatory damages may be recovered. Others simply did not address the issue.[22] More importantly, the elements and prerequisites for recovery of damages appropriate to compensate injuries caused by the deprivation of one constitutional right are not necessarily appropriate to compensate injuries caused by the deprivation of another. As we have said, these issues must be considered with reference to the nature of the interests protected by the particular constitutional right in question. For this reason, and without intimating an opinion as to their merits, we do not deem the cases relied upon to be controlling.

III

Even if respondents' suspensions were justified, and even if they did not suffer any other actual injury, the fact remains that they were deprived of their right to procedural due process. "It is enough to invoke the procedural safeguards of the Fourteenth Amendment that a significant property interest is at stake, whatever the ultimate outcome of a hearing. . . ." Fuentes v. Shevin, 407 U.S., at 87.

---

[22] In Jeanty v. McKey & Poague, Inc., 496 F.2d 1119 (C.A.7 1974), and Seaton v. Sky Realty Co., 491 F.2d 634 (C.A.7 1974), the court held that damages may be awarded for humiliation and distress caused by discriminatory refusals to lease housing to plaintiffs. The court's comment in Seaton that "[h]umiliation can be inferred from the circumstances as well as established by the testimony," suggests that the court considered the question of actual injury to be one of fact.

In Basista v. Weir, 340 F.2d 74 (C.A.3 1965); Sexton v. Gibbs, 327 F.Supp. 134 (N.D.Tex.1970), aff'd, 446 F.2d 904 (C.A.5 1971), cert. denied, 404 U.S. 1062 (1972); and Rhoads v. Horvat, 270 F.Supp. 307 (Colo.1967), the courts indicated that damages may be awarded for humiliation and distress caused by unlawful arrests, searches, and seizures. In Basista v. Weir, the court held that nominal damages could be awarded for an illegal arrest even if compensatory damages were waived; and that such nominal damages would, in an appropriate case, support an award of punitive damages. Because it was unclear whether the plaintiff had waived his claim for compensatory damages, that issue was left open upon remand. In Sexton v. Gibbs, where the court found "that Plaintiff suffered humiliation, embarrassment and discomfort," substantial compensatory damages were awarded. In Rhoads v. Horvat, the court allowed a jury award of $5,000 in compensatory damages for an illegal arrest to stand, stating that it did "not doubt that the plaintiff was outraged by the arrest."

Wayne v. Venable, 260 F. 64 (C.A.8 1919), and Ashby v. White, 1 Bro.P.C. 62, 1 Eng.Rep. 417 (H.L.1703), rev'd 2 Ld.Raym. 938, 92 Eng.Rep. 126 (K.B.1703), do appear to support the award of substantial damages simply upon a showing that a plaintiff was wrongfully deprived of the right to vote. Citing Ashby v. White, this Court has held that actions for damages may be maintained for wrongful deprivations of the right to vote, but it has not considered the prerequisites for recovery. Nixon v. Herndon, 273 U.S. 536, 540 (1927). The common-law rule of damages for wrongful deprivations of voting rights embodied in Ashby v. White would, of course, be quite relevant to the analogous question under § 1983.

Common-law courts traditionally have vindicated deprivations of certain "absolute" rights that are not shown to have caused actual injury through the award of a nominal sum of money. By making the deprivation of such rights actionable for nominal damages without proof of actual injury, the law recognizes the importance to organized society that those rights be scrupulously observed; but at the same time, it remains true to the principle that substantial damages should be awarded only to compensate actual injury or, in the case of exemplary or punitive damages, to deter or punish malicious deprivations of rights.

Because the right to procedural due process is "absolute" in the sense that it does not depend upon the merits of a claimant's substantive assertions, and because of the importance to organized society that procedural due process be observed, we believe that the denial of procedural due process should be actionable for nominal damages without proof of actual injury. We therefore hold that if, upon remand, the District Court determines that respondents' suspensions were justified, respondents nevertheless will be entitled to recover nominal damages not to exceed one dollar from petitioners.[25]

The judgment of the Court of Appeals is reversed, and the case is remanded for further proceedings consistent with this opinion.

JUSTICE MARSHALL concurs in the result.

JUSTICE BLACKMUN took no part in the consideration or decision of this case.

NOTES AND QUESTIONS

1.   *Preliminary injunction*: Piphus was readmitted after eight days of suspension pursuant to a temporary restraining order. This operates like an injunction by directing a party to do, or cease doing, something. The procedures for issuing a temporary restraining order (TRO) and a preliminary injunction are found in Rule 65. The primary difference between them is that a TRO may be granted without notice to the adverse party but cannot remain in effect for more than fourteen days while a preliminary injunction can be issued only after notice (and opportunity to be heard) to the adverse party and can last indefinitely. See Four Seasons Hotels & Resorts, B.V. v. Consorcio Barr, S.A., 320 F.3d 1205 (11th Cir.2003) (two days' notice provided insufficient time to respond to preliminary injunction motion).

---

[25] Respondents contend that the Court of Appeals' holding could be affirmed on the ground that the District Court held them to too high a standard of proof of the amount of damages appropriate to compensate intangible injuries that are proved to have been suffered. It is true that plaintiffs ordinarily are not required to prove with exactitude the amount of damages that should be awarded to compensate intangible injury. But, as the Court of Appeals said, "in the case at bar, there is no proof of individualized injury to [respondents], such as mental distress. . . ." With the case in this posture, there is no occasion to consider the quantum of proof required to support a particular damages award where actual injury is proved.

In general, it is said that courts should grant such relief only where plaintiff has shown (a) a strong likelihood of success on the merits, (b) irreparable harm should preliminary relief be denied; (c) that the balance of hardships strongly favors plaintiff; and (d) that issuing the injunction will advance the public interest. How should this analysis have been done in Carey v. Piphus? For a criticism of the requirement that the judge find that plaintiff is likely to prevail in the end, asserting that it tends to lock that ultimate outcome into the judge's mind, see Lynch, The Lock-in Effect of Preliminary Injunctions, 66 Fla.L.Rev. 779 (2014).

2.   Does *Carey* provide further insights into the purpose of procedural due process? Is the sole concern accuracy of outcome? Plaintiffs argued that, whatever the ultimate outcome, they were denied the opportunity to participate in the decisionmaking process. Does the Court conclude that concern is unimportant? Would it matter if the decision turned not only on resolution of a factual dispute but also on a discretionary evaluation of the facts found to be true?

3.   What sort of hearing would suffice? In Goss v. Lopez, 419 U.S. 565 (1975), the Court spelled out what it had in mind for a student faced with suspension: "There need be no delay between the time 'notice' is given and the time of the hearing. In the great majority of cases the disciplinarian may informally discuss the alleged misconduct with the student minutes after it has occurred. We hold only that, in being given an opportunity to explain his version of the facts at this discussion, the student first be told what he is accused of doing and what the basis of the accusation is." What would be the value of even so abbreviated a "hearing" in the case of plaintiff Brisco? Isn't his real objection to the rule that forbids earrings? See the Court's footnote 16.

4.   In *Carey*, the Court draws on the general law of tort remedies to handle a constitutional tort. The basic idea of tort remedies is that money damages should be sufficient to make up to plaintiff for what he or she wrongfully lost due to defendant's actions. See generally D. Dobbs, Remedies §§ 3.1; 3.2 (2d ed. 1993). How should that approach be applied here?

(a)   Lost time at school: If it is determined that the plaintiffs would not have been suspended if they had been given a hearing, they may be compensated for the days of schooling lost due to their suspension without a hearing. How much is a day of schooling in the Chicago Public Schools worth? Should the court look to the tuition costs of private schools? Should the court try to value the extent to which schooling increases the future earning power of the plaintiffs? If so, how can it determine the shrinkage in earning power due to loss of a few weeks of high school?

(b)   Lost procedural right: Whether or not they would have avoided suspension had they been granted hearings, plaintiffs are entitled to prove that they suffered damages because they were denied procedural due process, but such damages may not be presumed. What sort of showing should suffice to justify such damages? See Laje v. R. E. Thomason General Hosp., 665 F.2d 724 (5th Cir.1982) ("Dr. Laje and his wife both testified specifically that the summary proceedings surrounding his dismissal caused severe anxiety and distress, and that these feelings were not relieved until after the full hearing on his discharge.").

In defamation cases, plaintiffs need not put on such specific proof to recover "general" damages for mental distress. Should the denial of procedural due process be treated differently? In terms of plaintiffs' showing regarding distress, would it matter if the court concluded that they would not have been suspended had they been afforded a hearing? Would it be natural to assume that temporary exclusion from school (like defamation) would cause substantial mental distress?

Should the fact that we are dealing with the denial of basic constitutional rights affect the measure of damages? In Memphis Community School Dist. v. Stachura, 477 U.S. 299 (1986), the Court found that Carey represents a "straightforward" application of compensatory principles, and therefore held invalid a jury instruction that allowed the jury to consider, in computing damages in a case involving denial of a constitutional right, "the importance of the right in our system of government."

5.   In personal injury cases, a similar damages analysis prevails. See generally D. Dobbs, Remedies § 8.1 (1973). Thus, plaintiffs who are injured can recover for medical costs and lost earning capacity (including lost wages) by proving with reasonable certainty the amount of these losses. In addition, under the heading of "pain and suffering," plaintiffs can recover money to compensate them for the discomfort they have endured and (where applicable) for the discomfort they will endure in the future. How easily do these damages fit under the compensation idea described in Carey? "It is sometimes suggested that these damages can be used by an injured plaintiff to purchase distractions, but it is clear that the price of distractions is not the measure of these damages and it is equally clear that no plaintiff's attorney has ever argued to the jury that he only wanted $500 to buy a new TV set. * * * Because pain and suffering damages are not compensatory, at least in the ordinary sense, there is no clear method of measuring them; indeed, there is almost no method at all." Dobbs, supra, at 550; 545; see also Cusimano, By the Numbers, Trial Mag., Sept. 2016 (jurors find it more difficult to decide on the amount of damages than on liability "because there is no yardstick, method, or formula").

Nonetheless, personal injury plaintiffs are routinely allowed to recover for pain and suffering, often based largely on their testimony about the pain and dislocation caused by their injuries. Sometimes their lawyers are allowed to urge the jurors to estimate an amount they would consider sufficient to compensate them for enduring for a day what plaintiff must endure every day, and then use that amount as a guideline in setting damages. In Foradori v. Harris, 523 F.3d 477 (5th Cir. 2008), plaintiff recovered $10 million for pain and suffering after his lawyer made a "transparent per-diem argument," but the appellate court upheld the award because the lawyer did not "mislead the jury into believing that the determination of a proper award of legal damages for pain and suffering is a matter of precise and accurate determination," and there was no indication the jury had in fact adopted the unit-of-time method.

Note, Modernizing the Critique of Per Diem Pain and Suffering Damages, 92 Va. L. Rev. 289 (2006), urges that breakthroughs in medical treatment for pain undermine the assumption that a plaintiff will continue to suffer as much as presently. See also Niemeyer, Awards for Pain and Suffering: The Irrational Centerpiece of Our Tort System, 90 Va. L. Rev. 1401 (2004).

6.   It would seem that the task of measuring damages should be straightforward when the plaintiff's loss consists of items obtainable in the marketplace, but even there problems may arise. Consider the venerable case of Wall v. Platt, 48 N.E. 270 (Mass. 1897), in which a railroad started a fire that destroyed plaintiff's house and the contents of the house. The problem was that although the house would cost $5,250 to rebuild, rebuilding it would only add $3,250 to the value of the lot without the house. The trial court adopted the higher figure, and the appellate court affirmed on the ground that it reflected the "real value" of the buildings destroyed by the fire. Similarly, although defendant attempted to prove regarding the contents of the house that second-hand items could be obtained very cheaply, the court upheld a significantly higher amount as proper for the "intrinsic value of the articles," looking to the cost of new replacement articles and then determining their "worth to the owner" in light of their condition at the time of the fire.

Do you see any problems with the court's measure of damages? The court explained that the objective was "to restore [the plaintiff] to as good a position as he was in before the fire occurred." Should that include paying more than it would cost to replace the used clothing and furniture in the house with other furniture? Although the damages for loss of the house reflected the cost of rebuilding, plaintiff need not rebuild to receive that amount. Will this result in a windfall for plaintiff? The court did say that it was "excluding any fanciful or sentimental considerations." Should it do so? Compare Mieske v. Bartell Drug Co., 593 P.2d 1308 (Wash. 1979), in which plaintiffs recovered $7,500 for loss of their home movies, which included their wedding, honeymoon, vacations and their children growing up. The jury was instructed not to compensate for sentimental value, but did it really follow its instructions? Should it be so instructed?

7.   *Punitive damages*: The Court also mentioned punitive damages in Carey v. Piphus, but found them inapplicable. These damages are not designed to compensate, but to deter wrongful conduct or vindicate an important right that was violated. In a later case, the Court held that they could be recovered in a civil rights action "when the defendant's conduct is motivated by evil motive or intent, or when it involves reckless or callous indifference to the federally protected rights of others." Smith v. Wade, 461 U.S. 30 (1983).

Traditionally, the measure of punitive damages has taken account of the outrageousness of defendant's conduct and also focused on defendant's wealth (so that the award is large enough to prompt a change in behavior). This analysis has sometimes led to remarkable punitive damage jury awards. See, e.g., Liggett Group, Inc. v. Engle, 853 So.2d 434 (Fla.Ct.App.2003) ($145 billion in punitive damages in class action on behalf of 700,000 smokers overturned); compare Bankhead v. ArvinMeritor, Inc., 139 Cal.Rptr.3d 849 (Cal.Ct.App.

2012) ($4.5 million punitive damage award upheld even though defendant's accountants gave it a negative net worth, where it had $343 million in cash assets). Although such awards are controversial (and often overturned) they may be very rare: "Contrary to public belief, juries rarely award such damages, and award them especially rarely in products liability and medical malpractice cases. Rather, juries tend to award punitive damages in intentional misconduct cases. When juries do award punitive damages, they do so in ways that relate strongly to compensatory awards." Eisenberg, LaFountain, Ostrom, Rottman & Wells, Juries, Judges, and Punitive Damages, 87 Cornell L. Rev. 743, 745 (2002); compare Hersch & Viscusi, Punitive Damages: How Judges and Juries Perform, 33 J. Legal Stud. 1 (2004) (reporting that juries award punitive damages more frequently than judges, and that jury awards correlate less with compensatory damages).

There are both common law and constitutional limitations on juries' punitive damages awards, and courts have often said that appellate courts should scrutinize such awards more closely than compensatory awards. In a series of cases, the Supreme Court has found punitive damage awards excessive in violation of due process. In BMW of North America, Inc. v. Gore, 517 U.S. 559 (1996), punitive damages of $2 million awarded against a car dealer for representing a car that had been previously painted as new were found excessive where compensatory damages were only $4,000. In State Farm Mut. Auto Ins. Co. v. Campbell, 538 U.S. 408 (2003), the Court endorsed a 4 to 1 ratio of punitive to compensatory damages as "instructive" for purposes of due process. In Exxon Shipping Co. v. Baker, 554 U.S. 471 (2008), arising out of the oil spill caused by the Exxon Valdez, the Court dealt with the common law limitation on punitive damages because the claim was based on admiralty law, which is federal. It adopted a ratio of 1:1. Although that justified a punitive damages award equal to the compensatory award of $507.5 million, it greatly reduced the jury verdict of $5 billion in punitive damages. The court did note that in cases of "exceptional blameworthiness" combined with "modest economic harm or odds of detection" or "serious constitutional issues" a higher award might be upheld.

Punitive awards that do not violate due process or common law limits may nonetheless be windfalls for the plaintiffs who obtain them. In some states, statutes provide that plaintiffs should get only part of the punitive award. See, e.g., Mo. Ann. Stat. § 537.675; Ga. Code Ann. § 51–12–5.1. In Dardinger v. Anthem Blue Cross & Blue Shield, 781 N.E.2d 121 (Ohio S.Ct. 2002), the court itself ordered that two thirds of a $30 million punitive award not be paid to the plaintiff but instead "go to a place that will achieve a societal good, a good that can rationally offset the harm done by the defendants in this case" (a cancer research fund at the state university). Should jurors be advised that the awards will go to good purposes? See Ford v. Uniroyal Goodrich Tire Co., 476 S.E.2d 565 (Ga. 1996) (holding that it was improper to inform jurors that 75% of the punitive damages award would go into the state treasury); Honeywell v. Sterling Furniture Co., 797 P.2d 1019 (Ore. 1990) (improper to tell jurors that part of a punitive damages award would go to the state's Criminal Injuries Compensation Account).

Should punitive damages be employed for such purposes? See Redish & Mathews, Why Punitive Damages are Unconstitutional, 53 Emory L.J. 1 (2004) (arguing that allowing private plaintiffs to seek punitive damages is "the legal version of vigilantism and blood feuds," and that "the power to do no more than punish is a power that is reserved exclusively to the state"). Compare Sharkey, Punitive Damages as Societal Damages, 113 Yale L.J. 347 (2003) (arguing that punitive damages should be understood and justified as compensating society, which would legitimate diverting a portion to social purposes); Colby, Clearing the Smoke From *Philip Morris v. Williams*: The Past, Present, and Future of Punitive Damages, 118 Yale L.J. 392 (2008) (arguing that punitive damages are allowed for private revenge, but not to redress public harms).

8. In *Carey* the Court holds that plaintiffs can recover nominal damages of a dollar for the deprivation of procedural due process. Does this recovery have any real value to them? See Farrar v. Hobby, 506 U.S. 103 (1992) (party who obtains only nominal damages ordinarily may not recover attorneys' fees even if covered by a fee-shifting statute). But see Lucas v. Guyton, 901 F.Supp. 1047 (D.S.C.1995) (fees of $30,000 awarded where verdict of ten cents returned in suit by prisoner because counsel had a difficult time overcoming antipathy toward the prisoner and showing that he too had constitutional rights).

9. By now you should realize that the measurement of damages is often a difficult task, and that there are situations in which the amount a plaintiff can recover will not be nearly as substantial as hoped. We cannot canvass the whole law of remedies here, but you should keep this reality in mind as we examine other issues.

ENFORCING MONEY JUDGMENTS

Obtaining a money judgment may not end a case but merely move it into another stage of the litigation process. Although detailed examination of the problems of enforcing money judgments must await a course on creditors' remedies, it is worthwhile to pause now to sketch the available devices.

A money judgment "is not an *order* to the defendant; it is an adjudication of his rights or liabilities. No one may be held in contempt for failing to pay some debt as adjudicated by the law court." D. Dobbs, Remedies 94 (1973). See Baxter State Bank v. Bernhardt, 186 F.R.D. 621 (D.Kan.1999) (judgment creditor could not obtain court order requiring judgment debtor to satisfy judgment). So even successful suits for money damages may be fraught with peril. See In the Judgment Trade, ABA Journ., Nov. 2011, at 33 (reporting claim that "[n]early 80 percent of judgments in the U.S. aren't collected").

Of course, defendant may pay promptly anyhow. If not, plaintiff, now known as the judgment creditor, must take further action to enforce the judgment against defendant, now known as the judgment debtor. Some actions may be rather simple. Thus, by recording the judgment plaintiff may obtain a lien (called a judgment lien) against all defendant's real property. Most states allow a similar filing procedure to give the judgment creditor a lien on personal property of the judgment debtor that is subject to other security interests filed with the state pursuant to the Uniform Commercial Code. But these liens are not worth a great deal unless the judgment debtor wants to sell the property.

Before we turn to methods of forcing sale of property, it is important to note another problem. Ordinarily, judgments can be enforced against assets, as opposed to income. Garnishment, which we examined in the first section of this chapter, affords a limited opportunity to reach the judgment debtor's earnings. See Sniadach v. Family Fin. Corp., supra p. 30. To enforce a money judgment, the plaintiff may often have to find other assets. Many people have few assets of significant value, and most people are reluctant to turn their assets over to people who have sued them. Accordingly, judgment creditors are afforded discovery to compel judgment debtors to reveal where their assets are located. Debtors are naturally reluctant to answer these questions, but courts can sometimes apply substantial pressure to force them to do so. You should reconsider the difficulties that might attend this process when you reach the discovery materials in Chapter 5.

Once the judgment creditor has located the assets, she can obtain a writ of execution from the court directing the sheriff or similar officer to "levy" on the asset. This may take the form of physical seizure of the asset, or service of an order on a debtor of the judgment debtor (such as the judgment debtor's bank or employer) directing it to pay the money over to the court. If the physical seizure of the asset is accomplished, the sheriff may thereafter sell it at auction and (after deducting the costs of the sale) pay the balance over to the judgment creditor up to the amount of the judgment. But there may be other persons with an interest in the asset. The debtor's car, for example, may be subject to a lien in favor of the bank that loaned him the money to buy it. Those "secured" creditors, like the sheriff, stand in front of the judgment creditor seeking to collect. That special status, indeed, explains much of the concern about limiting the prejudgment remedies available to secured creditors under Fuentes.

Yet another problem for the judgment creditor is that all states exempt certain assets from execution. Thus, even if there are unencumbered assets, the judgment creditor may be unable to realize against them because the debtor has a right to keep them and, in essence, disregard the debt to plaintiff. These rules vary from state to state, but commonly include clothing, furniture and other household possessions, food, fuel, automobiles and tools of the debtor's trade. In addition, if the debtor owns a house, there may be a "homestead" exemption that protects it against execution.

Finally, the judgment creditor must worry about bankruptcy. A judgment debtor who cannot pay one bill may be unable to pay other bills. Such persons often seek protection against their creditors under the

Bankruptcy Act, which automatically interdicts enforcement of existing judgments and pursuit of others. Then the debtor's non-exempt property is pooled by the court, and all the creditors are allowed to make claims against that property (which may be worth far less than the total of the claims). Meanwhile, the debtor may obtain a "discharge" from his prior debts, precluding his creditors from pursuing him.

This paints an overly pessimistic picture of the prospects for plaintiffs. The prospects of enforcing a money judgment against many defendants are very good. Large businesses are usually easy targets for collection, which may explain in part why they are such frequent targets for suits. Insurance companies will pay judgments, so plaintiff can recover if the defendant is insured.

Moreover, there are important policy reasons for affording many judgment debtors protection against overbearing collection activities. Long ago there actually were debtors' prisons. Should those be revived? Consider the following report about bad check writers, people who have not even been the subject of a court proceeding:

> The letters are sent by the thousands to people across the country who have written bad checks, threatening them with jail if they do not pay up.

> They bear the seal and signature of the local district attorney's office. But there is a catch: the letters are from debt-collection companies, which the prosecutors allow to use their letterhead. In return, the companies try to collect not only the unpaid check, but also high fees from debtors for a class on budgeting and financial responsibility, some of which goes back to the district attorney's offices.

Silver-Greenberg, In Prosecutors, Debt Collectors Find a Partner, N.Y. Times, Sept. 16, 2012, at A1; see also Silver-Greenberg, Debtor Arrests Criticized, Wall St.J., Nov. 22, 2011, at C3; Silver-Greenberg, Cowley & Kitroef, Price of Unpaid Student Debt: The Very Job Needed to Pay It, N.Y. Times, Nov. 19, 2017, at A1 ("in 19 states, government agencies can seize state-issued professional licenses from residents who default on their educational debts"). The point is that many judgment debtors are not large companies with deep pockets, and that enthusiasm for enforcement of money judgments must be balanced against concern for the judgment debtor.

2. EQUITABLE REMEDIES

Until now, we have focused on suits for money damages, and one might well conclude that this remedy is sometimes not sufficient to protect the plaintiff's rights. Money damages were the traditional remedy in England "at law." Alongside remedies at law, there developed "equitable" remedies that directly ordered defendant to take or cease certain specified action. To appreciate some of the limitations on equitable relief, it is important to provide a brief canvas for the gradual development of the English system of adjudication because that history had a profound impact on the way in which adjudication was organized in this country. Unfortunately, the English organization resulted as much from coincidence and politics as from rational examination of the sensible handling of disputes.

Courts as we know them now began to develop in England over a millennium ago as dispute resolution devices. Local disputes in those feudal times could be resolved by the local lord; when he "held court" this was one of the things he would do. Resolving other disputes required royal intervention. Royal authority was invoked by a "writ," which a complaining subject could obtain at the office of the Lord Chancellor. The writ empowered the King's courts at Westminster to decide the dispute. Unfortunately, some complainants had disputes that didn't fit into the traditional writs. At first, the Chancellor felt free to invent new writs to fit new situations. The nobles, however, feared royal intrusion into areas where they had traditionally held sway. As a result, in 1258 the Chancellor was forbidden to invent new writs, but this was softened by the Statute of Westminster in 1285, which authorized the Chancellor to adapt existing writs to new situations that were similar (*in consimili casu*).

Over the centuries, the established writs gradually evolved into what were known as the "forms of action." As their requirements were clarified, they gave birth to legal rules which we have come to call the common law. Thus, much of the legal doctrine that you will study in your substantive courses has its roots in the common law forms of action: trespass, debt, detinue, replevin, covenant, account, trespass on the case, trover, assumpsit and ejectment. Because this history bears on current practice only distantly, we will not try to master the special requirements of these different forms of action, but they will never be entirely forgotten. (For further discussion, see infra pp. 124–125.)

For present purposes, the point is that even though the writs could be adapted there still arose cases in which they did not suffice either because the common law offered no relief to a certain claimant, or because the relief that the common law courts would accord such a litigant was insufficient for some reason. In such cases, the Chancellor might intercede personally. For political reasons (if not a desire to limit his own workload), the Chancellor would not do so except where necessary because of some deficiency in the relief available to the claimant at law. (Common law judges, like local lords, could be jealous of their power.) This is the source of the current idea that equitable remedies are only available when plaintiff is faced with "irreparable" harm, i.e., when money damages would not be a sufficient remedy. When the Chancellor did intervene, however, he did more than issue the sort of judgment that the common law judges offered. Rather than making plaintiff pursue defendant's assets, the Chancellor would act "in personam" by issuing a personal order directing or forbidding specified action by defendant.

There thus developed two parallel systems of adjudication in England. The law courts administered the gradually evolving forms of action. Equity, as the Chancellor's court came to be called, had jurisdiction of cases falling generally into three categories: (1) cases in which the common law did not prescribe the legal rules, most notably the administration of trusts, so that equity's jurisdiction in such cases was "exclusive," (2) cases in which jurisdiction was "concurrent" in that the "substantive" legal rules governing plaintiff's right to relief were based on common law but equity would also entertain the suit because of some deficiency in the relief afforded at law, and (3) cases in which the equity action was "ancillary" to an action at law, most notably an action at equity for a bill of discovery which might be useful for a suit for damages in the law courts.

As the third type of equitable jurisdiction suggests, the two systems had different procedures. Four types of differences will concern us in this book. First, the rules surrounding the way in which plaintiff and defendant had to state their positions—pleading—were very strict at law, with the result that the outcome often turned not on the merits but on who won a stylized pleading contest. The Chancellor was much less interested in the formalities of pleading, so that petitions in equity tended to be more straightforward descriptions of the facts on which the plaintiff's claim was based. We shall examine the contemporary handling of these problems in Chapter 3. Second, the common law courts severely limited a plaintiff's opportunity to combine claims or parties in one action. Plaintiff could not combine claims under different writs in a single action, and could very rarely sue more than one defendant at a time. The rules concerning joinder are examined in Chapter 4. Third, equity afforded assistance to parties in collecting information, while law did not; hence the "ancillary" action at equity for a bill of discovery. In Chapter 5 we shall see how discovery is currently handled. Finally, the manner of trial was markedly different. At law, factual disputes were resolved by a jury trial. At equity, however, there was no jury, and in some senses there was no trial. Instead, the decision was based on the material developed through the discovery process without a single presentation of evidence in a courtroom. For better or worse, this difference was written into the Seventh Amendment of our Constitution, which "preserves" the right to jury trial in "suits at common law." We shall deal with these problems in Chapter 8.

The reason these ancient problems are still with us today is that the American Colonies modeled their legal system (like so much else) on the English system. But over time the system was changed. The English tinkered with their judicial system for much of the nineteenth century, eventually abandoning the forms of action in the Judicature Acts of the

1870s and merging the law and equity courts. Similar efforts were afoot in this country, and in the Field Code, adopted in New York in 1848, the forms of action were abandoned and the two systems merged. The federal courts had law and equity "sides" from 1789, when they were created, until 1938, when the federal rules were adopted. See Fed.R.Civ.P. 2 ("There is one form of action—the civil action.") Most states have similarly changed their systems, although some still have separate equity courts. Procedure, meanwhile, has been modelled on the more flexible practices of equity rather than the rigid procedures of the common law, a choice that involves tradeoffs in simplicity and predictability of outcomes. See Subrin, How Equity Conquered Common Law: The Federal Rules of Civil Procedure in Historical Perspective, 135 U.Pa.L.Rev. 909 (1987). For purposes of this chapter, however, this historical background is a necessary introduction to the handling of equitable remedies.

SMITH V. WESTERN ELECTRIC CO.

Missouri Court of Appeals, 1982
643 S.W.2d 10

DOWD, PRESIDING JUDGE.

Plaintiff appeals from an order dismissing his petition on the ground that it fails to state a claim upon which relief can be granted.

The petition seeks an injunction to prevent plaintiff's employer from exposing him to tobacco smoke in the workplace and from affecting his pay or employment conditions because of his medical reaction to tobacco smoke. The petition alleges that by allowing smoking in the work area, defendant permits its employees to be exposed to a health hazard and thereby breaches its duty to provide a safe place in which to work.

The petition includes the following allegations. Plaintiff has been employed by defendant since 1950 and has worked in defendant's Missouri branch since 1967. He is a nonsmoker sharing an open office area with other employees, many of whom smoke tobacco products as they work. In 1975 plaintiff began to experience serious respiratory tract discomfort as a result of inhaling tobacco smoke in the workplace. A subsequent medical evaluation determined that plaintiff suffers a severe adverse reaction to tobacco smoke. His symptoms include sore throat, nausea, dizziness, headache, blackouts, loss of memory, difficulty in concentration, aches and pains in joints, sensitivity to noise and light, cold sweat, gagging, choking sensations, and lightheadedness. After a sufficient period of non-exposure to smoke, plaintiff's symptoms abate somewhat. The symptoms have become increasingly severe over the years, however. Doctors evaluating and treating plaintiff have advised him to avoid contact with tobacco smoke whenever possible.

The petition further alleges that plaintiff first complained to defendant about the tobacco smoke in the workplace in 1975. Defendant thereafter moved plaintiff to different locations within the plant, but no improvement resulted because each location contained significant amounts of tobacco smoke. In 1978 plaintiff was informed that he should no longer submit complaints about the smoke through defendant's anonymous complaint procedure since defendant would not process them. In response to recommendations of the National Institute for Occupational Safety and Health,[1] defendant adopted a smoking policy in April 1980. The declared policy was to protect the rights of both smokers and nonsmokers by providing accommodations for both groups and by making a reasonable effort to separate the groups in work areas. Because defendant has failed to implement its policy by making such a reasonable effort, improvement of the air in the workplace has not resulted.

According to the petition, in August 1980 plaintiff filed with defendant a Handicapped Declaration Statement that he was handicapped by his susceptibility to tobacco smoke. Refusing to segregate smokers or to limit smoking to non-work areas, defendant informed plaintiff he could either continue to work in the same location and wear a respirator or apply for a job in the computer room (where smoking is prohibited). The latter option would entail a pay decrease of about $500 per month. Defendant thereafter provided plaintiff with a respirator that has proven ineffective in protecting plaintiff from tobacco smoke.

The petition states that plaintiff has exhausted all avenues of relief through defendant; he has no adequate remedy at law; he is suffering and will continue to suffer irreparable physical injuries and financial losses unless defendant improves working conditions. The petition alleges that defendant is breaching its common law duty as an employer to provide plaintiff a safe place to work, and that defendant has available reasonable alternatives to avoid the continuing breach of duty, as demonstrated by defendant's ability to protect its computer equipment from tobacco smoke. The petition further states that, although "second-hand smoke" is harmful to the health of all employees, defendant is permitting them to be exposed in the workplace to this health hazard which is neither related to nor a necessary by-product of defendant's business.

Construing these allegations favorably to plaintiff, we must determine whether they invoke principles of law entitling him to relief.

It is well-settled in Missouri that an employer owes a duty to the employee to use all reasonable care to provide a reasonably safe workplace, and to protect the employee from avoidable perils. Whether the employer has fulfilled its duty depends upon the facts of each case. For example, in

---

[1]   The Occupational Safety and Health Act of 1970, 29 U.S.C. §§ 651–678, established the National Institute for Occupational Safety and Health, § 671, to develop safety standards and implement sections 669 and 670 of the Act.

McDaniel v. Kerr, 258 S.W.2d 629 (Mo.1953), the employer had failed to provide a safe workplace where the employee's inhalation of dust on the job caused damage requiring removal of his lung. In DeMarco v. United States, 204 F.Supp. 290 (E.D.N.Y.1962), the court found a negligent failure to provide a safe working environment where the plaintiff was injured when he fainted and fell after complaining about gasoline fumes in an unventilated work area.

The allegations of the instant case, taken as true, show that the tobacco smoke of co-workers smoking in the work area is hazardous to the health of employees in general and plaintiff in particular. The allegations also show that defendant knows the tobacco smoke is harmful to plaintiff's health and that defendant has the authority, ability, and reasonable means to control smoking in areas requiring a smoke-free environment. Therefore, by failing to exercise its control and assume its responsibility to eliminate the hazardous condition caused by tobacco smoke, defendant has breached and is breaching its duty to provide a reasonably safe workplace. As stated in Thompson v. Kroeger, 380 S.W.2d 339, 343–44 (Mo.1964):

> the exercise of due care requires precautions which a reasonably prudent employer would have taken in given circumstances, even though other employers may not have taken such commensurate precautions. What usually is done may be evidence of what ought to be done, but what ought to be done is fixed by a standard of reasonable prudence, whether it usually is complied with or not.

If plaintiff's petition establishes defendant's failure to provide a safe place for plaintiff to work, we must next consider whether injunctive relief would be an appropriate remedy. An injunction may issue "to prevent the doing of any legal wrong whatever, whenever in the opinion of the court an adequate remedy cannot be afforded by an action for damages." § 526.030 RSMo 1978. Injunctive relief is unavailable unless irreparable harm is otherwise likely to result, and plaintiff has no adequate remedy at law.

The petition alleges that plaintiff's continuing exposure to smoke in the workplace is increasingly deleterious to his health and is causing irreparable harm. Assuming the allegations and reasonable inferences therefrom to be true, we think it is fair to characterize deterioration of plaintiff's health as "irreparable" and as a harm for which money damages cannot adequately compensate. This is particularly true where the harm has not yet resulted in full-blown disease or injury. Money damages, even though inadequate, are the best possible remedy once physical damage is done, but they are certainly inadequate to compensate permanent injury which could have been prevented. Plaintiff should not be required to await the harm's fruition before he is entitled to seek an inadequate remedy. Moreover, the nature of plaintiff's unsafe work environment represents a recurrent risk of harm that would necessitate a multiplicity of lawsuits. Finally, the petition states that plaintiff has no adequate remedy at law and alleges facts indicating that prior to this action plaintiff unsuccessfully pursued relief, both through his employer's in-house channels and through administrative agencies. Viewing the petition favorably, as we must to determine its sufficiency, we find that injunction would be an appropriate remedy.

Defendant contends the trial court lacks jurisdiction to provide relief, and therefore the petition fails to state a claim upon which relief can be granted, because the subject matter of this case is preempted by the Occupational Safety and Health Act (OSHA), 29 U.S.C. §§ 651–678 (1970). The Act specifically states, however, that it does not affect the common law regarding "injuries, diseases, or death of employees arising out of . . . employment." § 653(b)(4). The Act also declares that it does not prevent a state court from asserting jurisdiction over an occupational safety or health issue for which no OSHA standard is in effect. § 667(a). We are unpersuaded by defendant's argument that § 653(b)(4) refers only to the common law pertaining to workers' compensation laws. In addition, defendant has not directed our attention to any OSHA standard which would appear to cover tobacco smoke. No such standard figured in the opinions of other courts considering OSHA and tobacco smoke. Furthermore, defendant conceded in oral argument that a court may retain jurisdiction in the absence of an OSHA standard.

We conclude that plaintiff has stated a claim upon which relief can be granted and that the trial court therefore erred in dismissing the petition. Plaintiff should be allowed the opportunity to prove his allegations.

NOTES AND QUESTIONS

1.   The court does not hold that plaintiff is entitled to an injunction, but only that he may be. What will plaintiff have to prove to obtain one? On remand, there was a three-day trial after which the judge ruled that plaintiff had not proved that second-hand smoke was dangerous, resulting in judgment for defendant.

The criteria for granting a permanent injunction resemble those for granting a preliminary injunction. Thus, the court is to ask (1) whether plaintiff has actually succeeded on the merits, (2) whether he has an adequate remedy at law, (3) whether he risks imminent irreparable harm, (4) whether the balance of hardships weighs against issuance of an injunction, (5) whether an injunction would serve the public interest, and (6) whether the court can, as a practical matter, administer the injunction. As might be expected, it is easier for a plaintiff who has won to obtain final injunctive relief than for a plaintiff who only hopes to win to obtain preliminary injunctive relief. At the same time, it is important to appreciate that courts are often reluctant to issue permanent injunctions. Does *Smith* suggest reasons why this reluctance makes sense?

The second and third criteria above state what has become known as the irreparable injury rule, derived in part from the historical unwillingness of the English Chancellor to intervene in a dispute unless the complainant showed that there was something wrong with the relief afforded by the law courts. Laycock, The Death of the Irreparable Injury Rule, 103 Harv. L. Rev. 687 (1990), argues on the basis of a review of over 1,400 cases that there really is no such rule, and that "our law embodies a preference for specific relief if plaintiff wants it. The principal doctrinal expression for this preference is the rule that damages are inadequate unless they can be used to replace the specific thing that plaintiff lost." He adds that "[d]amages are the standard remedy for personal injury only because personal injuries can rarely be anticipated in time to prevent them by injunction." He concludes, however, that the rule still serves a purpose at the preliminary injunction stage. There, "it is still possible that plaintiff will not get any remedy at all. Defendant has a legitimate interest in a full hearing and in freedom to act in ways not yet shown to be unlawful. These interests coincide with the court's interest in avoiding error and being fair to both sides."

It is usually said, however, that the court has substantial discretion to refuse a request for an injunction after considering the above factors. See Winter v. Natural Resources Defense Council, Inc., 555 U.S. 7 (2008) ("An injunction is a matter of equitable discretion; it does not follow from success on the merits as a matter of course."); eBay, Inc. v. MercExchange, L.L.C., 547 U.S. 388 (2006) (rejecting lower court's "general rule that courts will issue permanent injunctions against patent infringement"). See also Gergen, Golden & Smith, The Supreme Court's Accidental Revolution? The Test for Permanent Injunctions, 112 Colum. L. Rev. 203 (2012) (objecting that the irreparable injury rule threatened the presumption that an injunction would issue for violation of certain rights, such as patents). As you review the further questions below, consider whether you might hesitate to grant Smith's request if you were the judge in his case.

2.   Is plaintiff's legal remedy inadequate in *Smith* because damages are an inadequate substitute for health? The court emphasizes that the exposure "has not yet resulted in full-blown disease or injury." Should courts be receptive to injunctive suits by plaintiffs whose damages claims are not ripe? Ordinarily our legal system limits remedies to those who have actually suffered harm. For example, in Metro-North Commuter R.R. Co. v. Buckley, 521 U.S. 424 (1997), plaintiff was a pipefitter for defendant whose job involved working with asbestos dust, a known carcinogen. Pipefitters were known as "the snowmen of Grand Central" because they would emerge from their work covered with asbestos dust. Although plaintiff regularly received medical checkups for cancer and asbestosis, no evidence of either disease had shown up. Plaintiff nonetheless sued under the Federal Employers' Liability Act (FELA) to recover emotional distress damages for his fear of contracting cancer. Defendant admitted negligently exposing plaintiff to asbestos dust, but denied he could sue until he manifested actual injury. The Court held that exposure that poses a risk of future disease should not support a present claim for emotional distress damages. It emphasized the difficulty of separating valid claims from

trivial ones, and the threat of unlimited and unpredictable liability and a flood of trivial claims. The Court reasoned that "the physical contact at issue here— a simple (though extensive) contact with a carcinogenic substance—does not seem to offer much help in separating valid from invalid emotional distress claims. That is because contacts, even extensive contacts, with serious carcinogens are common."

3.   If plaintiff in *Smith* was entitled to injunctive relief when he sued, how much sooner could he have sought it? Presumably smoking in the workplace was as much a hazard to workers in 1950 as it is now. Could plaintiff have obtained an injunction in 1950 (assuming that the health hazards of smoking could have been shown at that time)? Could he have obtained one in 1975, when he first developed symptoms? In 1980, when the defendant refused to segregate smokers and non-smokers? Generally, courts refuse to issue injunctions unless the plaintiff's claim is "ripe" because irreparable harm is imminent. When did plaintiff reach that point?

Obviously few would favor subjecting people to personal injuries that could be avoided. Should that fact prompt courts to favor preventive injunctive relief over compensatory relief? How about an injunction ordering a taxicab company not to allow its drivers to drive negligently? Would it be better to enjoin individual cab drivers from driving hazardously? Are injunctions a good way to deal with the problem of injuries inflicted by cabs? Are they better suited to a case like Smith?

4.   *Justiciability*: Under Art. III § 2 of the Constitution, federal courts may decide only "cases" or "controversies." This directive has produced various justiciability doctrines that prove challenging to apply. Since they raise issues like those presented by requests for equitable remedies, some mention of them is appropriate. One requirement is "ripeness," which means that plaintiff must show that a legal controversy has actually erupted between plaintiff and defendant, not that one may arise in the future. A second is "standing to sue," meaning that the plaintiff must demonstrate an injury to a legally protected interest to seek relief in court. Recall that plaintiff in Band's Refuse Removal, Inc. v. Borough of Fair Lawn, supra p. 3, was held to lack standing to challenge the bidding process used for scavenger contracts. A third is "mootness," which directs that even if plaintiff had standing at the beginning of the suit the case should be dismissed if a later development shows that plaintiff no longer has a personal stake in the controversy.

Sometimes plaintiff may have standing to seek one remedy but not another. In City of Los Angeles v. Lyons, 461 U.S. 95 (1983), plaintiff was injured when a police officer subdued him with a choke hold. He sued for damages and an injunction against future use of the choke hold, alleging that the police had a practice of using it on unresisting people. The Court held that the allegation of routine use of the hold provided no reason for believing that plaintiff would himself again be subjected to it, and that he therefore lacked standing to sue for an injunction even though he could sue for damages. In the alternative, it reasoned that "the equitable remedy is unavailable absent a showing of irreparable injury, a requirement that cannot be met where there is no showing of any real or immediate threat that the plaintiff will be wronged again. * * * Lyons is no more entitled to an injunction than any other citizen of Los Angeles; and a federal court may not entertain a claim by any or all citizens who no more than assert that certain practices of law enforcement officers are unconstitutional."

5.   What injunction should the court issue to solve plaintiff's smoke exposure problem? The court cites two cases in support of the idea that noxious fumes can make the workplace unsafe within the meaning of the common law employer's duty on which it relies. But McDaniel v. Kerr and DeMarco v. United States were both suits for damages by workers who claimed compensable injuries, and in measuring relief those courts could refer to traditional remedial guidelines for personal injury cases. What guidelines should the court use in fashioning a decree for plaintiff in Smith? Would it be sufficient to order defendant not to expose plaintiff to smoke, or should it adopt a more specific decree? See Rule 65(d)(1) (stating that the injunction order must "state its terms specifically" and "describe in reasonable detail * * * the act or acts restrained or required"). If it should be more specific, where does it look for the specifics that it will use? Should it begin to monitor the conditions at defendant's plant on a regular basis? Are regulatory agencies like the National Institute for Occupational Safety and Health better equipped for this task? Courts trying to desegregate schools or improve conditions in prisons are regularly faced with such problems of designing appropriate injunctions. See Chayes, The Role of the Judge in Public Law Litigation, 89 Harv.L.Rev. 1281, 1298–1302 (1976). Does Smith's claim justify a similar effort by the court? Wouldn't an injunction have been easier to fashion in Carey v. Piphus, supra p. 69?

6.   If the court is going to design an injunction, should the smokers in defendant's workforce have a say about the terms of the decree? See Nowaczyk v. Shaheen, 49 Fed.R.Serv.3d 107 (D.N.H. 2001) (rejecting prisoners' claim that prison's tobacco-free policy violated the constitutional rights of prisoners who smoke). We will deal with problems of required parties in Chapter 4, but it is important to note now that injunctive relief may widen the circle of affected parties greatly. Is that a reason for favoring monetary relief? Would the smokers at the Western Electric plant be similarly affected by a judgment for money damages?

7.   Should the cost of complying with the court's decree matter? In Boomer v. Atlantic Cement Co., 257 N.E.2d 870 (N.Y.1970), the trial court found that defendant's cement plant was a nuisance because it was so noisy and made so much dust that it interfered with the dairy farms operated by plaintiffs (seven farmers whose land abutted defendant's factory). Noting that no existing technology would eliminate either the noise or the dust, however, the trial court refused to order defendant to stop operating its $45 million plant, thereby putting defendant's 300 employees out of work, instead awarding plaintiffs $185,000 for the diminution in value of their farms. Should similar cost considerations bear on plaintiff's request for injunctive relief against Western Electric?

8.   Injunctions are not the only equitable remedies. Courts also use their equitable powers when they order parties to perform their contractual commitments (specific performance), appoint receivers to take control of businesses or other institutions and run them, or intervene in other ways in out-of-court activities.

ENFORCING EQUITABLE DECREES—CONTEMPT

Unlike money judgments, equitable decrees such as injunctions often order defendant to take some action. Because the court itself has ordered defendant to act, it cannot accept defendant's failure to do so with the kind of indifference that may attend defendant's failure to pay plaintiff the amount of a money judgment. Instead, defendant may be cited for contempt, which has been described as a "civil-criminal hodgepodge." United States v. United Mine Workers, 330 U.S. 258, 364 (1947) (Rutledge, J., dissenting). See generally Dobbs, Contempt of Court: A Survey, 56 Cornell L.Q. 183 (1971). Basically, the hodgepodge falls into three categories:

Criminal Contempt: Violation of a court's order can be prosecuted as a crime. Usually, the initiator in such a prosecution is the plaintiff, but the plaintiff does not control the case and cannot "settle" for a payment of money in return for dropping the prosecution. The distinguishing feature of criminal contempt is that the penalty imposed is not designed either to compensate the plaintiff or to prompt compliance in the future. Because it is a criminal case, the prosecution must prove guilt beyond a reasonable doubt. In addition, defendant has a right to a jury trial unless the contempt is a "petty offense," one involving imprisonment for less than six months. If a fine is involved, the outside limit of petty offenses is less clear, but it is generally felt to be $500 with individuals.

Compensatory Civil Contempt: The court may direct defendant to pay plaintiff an amount that will compensate plaintiff for the harm caused by violation of the decree. This resolution of the problem is rather odd, however, in that the court presumably determined that money damages were an inadequate remedy when it decided to issue the injunction in the first place. And the award is limited to the harm resulting from the violation of the court's order. Cf. Goodyear Tire & Rubber Co. v. Haeger, 137 S.Ct. 1178 (2017) (court may not impose an additional amount as punishment; for that purpose "a court would need to provide procedural guarantees applicable in a criminal case"). Nevertheless, an inadequate monetary payment is better for plaintiff than no relief at all.

Coercive Civil Contempt: This approach is a genuine addition to the criminal law features of criminal contempt and the civil damages features of compensatory civil contempt. Using this type of contempt, the court may impose a penalty on defendant in order to prompt future compliance with the decree (rather than punishing defendant for past violations). In general, the penalty must be contingent in that it applies only if defendant does not obey the order. If that is so, defendants "carry the keys to their prison in their own pockets." In re Nevitt, 117 Fed. 448, 461 (8th Cir.1902). But the penalty may be quite severe, including imprisonment for an indefinite period or rather hefty fines. See, e.g., Chadwick v. Janecka, 312 F.3d 597 (3d Cir.2002) (former husband who had refused to reveal where he had hidden marital assets continued in custody after seven years); International Business Mach. Corp. v. United States, 493 F.2d 112 (2d Cir.1973) (IBM fined $150,000 per day until it turned over documents).

NOTES AND QUESTIONS

1.   If the court in Smith v. Western Electric Co., supra p. 88, enjoined defendant to provide smoke-free areas for nonsmoking workers and the company failed to do so, which type of contempt should plaintiff seek? How should the court fashion an appropriate contempt sanction?

2.   Whatever its utility in litigation between private parties, contempt may prove to be a blunt instrument against public officers. For example, assume that in Carey v. Piphus, supra p. 69, the court had ordered defendant not to suspend students without a hearing, but that defendant continued suspending them on the spot as before. How should the court use contempt to enforce its decree? By putting the school officials in jail? By fining the school system?

Contempt sanctions against elected officials can present great difficulties. For example, in Spallone v. United States, 493 U.S. 265 (1990), the city council of Yonkers, New York, voted 4–3 not to comply with an injunction requiring the city to build low-cost housing to remedy years of racial discrimination in the location of such housing. Besides imposing escalating and substantial fines on the city, the district court also imposed fines on the four recalcitrant members of the city council. The Supreme Court held that this was improper under "traditional equitable principles" because the court should limit its use of the contempt power to "the least power adequate to the end proposed." The large fines against the city should have sufficed, and the individual fines against members of the city council risked "a much greater perversion of the normal legislative process" by influencing councilmembers' votes on personal grounds.

3.   Fed. R. Civ. P. 65(d)(2) provides that an injunction binds only those who receive actual notice and who are parties, parties' officers, agents, servants, employees, and attorneys, or "other persons who are in active concert or participation" with the parties or their agents or employees. These limitations become important when someone who is not obviously a party is cited for contempt. Should Rule 65(d) be interpreted broadly? Could a fellow employee of plaintiff Smith be held in contempt for smoking at the Western Electric plant? Could the court put the employee in jail until he kicks the smoking habit? See United States v. Hall, 472 F.2d 261 (5th Cir.1972) (nonparty held in contempt of order from court supervising integration of

school that forbade anyone except teachers and students to go on school grounds); Note, Binding Nonparties to Injunctive Decrees, 49 Minn.L.Rev. 719 (1965).

4.   *The collateral bar rule*: As should be apparent by now, contempt shows how serious courts are about enforcing injunctions. This resolve is further emphasized by the collateral bar rule, which precludes the defendant from challenging the validity of the injunction in the "collateral" contempt proceeding. See United States v. United Mine Workers, 330 U.S. 258 (1947); Cox, The Void Order and the Duty to Obey, 16 U.Chi.L.Rev. 86 (1948). Perhaps the most controversial application of this rule was in Walker v. City of Birmingham, 388 U.S. 307 (1967), in which Rev. Martin Luther King, Jr., and a group of local Birmingham, Alabama, ministers planned a parade to protest racial segregation during the Easter holidays. The protesters attempted unsuccessfully to obtain a permit to march, as required by a local ordinance. Local authorities obtained an ex parte temporary restraining order in state court against the demonstrations, but Dr. King and others marched anyway and were held in contempt.

The Supreme Court upheld the contempt convictions despite very serious questions about the constitutional validity of the ordinance. (Indeed, the Court held this very ordinance unconstitutional two years later.) But the possible invalidity of the ordinance was irrelevant, said the Court, because "in the fair administration of justice no man can be judge in his own case." Instead, the validity of a court order should be challenged through the appeals process even though this particular order was obtained ex parte only a week before the scheduled march. The Court did suggest that a different result might obtain if the injunction were "transparently invalid" or "had only a frivolous pretense to validity."

Curiously, the same principle is not used when a person is prosecuted for violating a statute she claims is unconstitutional. Indeed, that is how the Birmingham ordinance was eventually held invalid. See Shuttlesworth v. City of Birmingham, 394 U.S. 147 (1969) (reversing conviction for marching without a permit on ground that permit requirement was unconstitutional). Should court orders receive greater respect than statutes? Consider the arguments of Chief Justice Warren, dissenting in Walker v. City of Birmingham, 388 U.S. at 327:

> It has never been thought that violation of a statute indicated such a disrespect for the legislature that the violator always must be punished even if the statute was unconstitutional. On the contrary, some cases have required that persons seeking to challenge the constitutionality of a statute first violate it to establish their standing to sue. Indeed, it shows no disrespect for law to violate a statute on the ground that it is unconstitutional and then to submit one's case to the courts with the willingness to accept the penalty if the statute is held constitutional.

Is the collateral bar doctrine necessary to orderly operation of the courts? What would happen if parties routinely disregarded orders they believed to be invalid even though the judge has rejected their arguments? If the doctrine is generally justified, should it apply to a case like *Walker* where the injunction was obtained ex parte and the defendants had no opportunity to be heard before it was entered? Note that the Court in *Walker* suggested that there might be an exception to the doctrine if the order was "transparently invalid." Could that idea subvert the doctrine? For a discussion of the collateral bar rule, see M. Redish, Freedom of Expression: A Critical Analysis 164–70 (1984).

Whatever your reaction to the collateral bar doctrine, it is worthwhile noting the consequence of its operation in Birmingham, as chronicled in Oppenheimer, Martin Luther King, Walker v. City of Birmingham, and the Letter From the Birmingham Jail, 26 U.C. Davis L.Rev. 791 (1993). Dr. King had earlier seen an effort to fight segregation in Albany, Ga., fail because of a similar injunction that was reversed on appeal, but only after resistance to segregation in the city had withered under the effect of the injunction. Moreover, by the time he decided to march in Birmingham, Dr. King knew that if he were arrested for violating the injunction there would not be funds to bail him out. But rather than see another challenge to segregation die during the appeals process, Dr. King marched, was arrested and jailed. While in the jail he wrote the *Letter From the Birmingham Jail*, which "has come to be widely recognized as the most important single document of the civil rights era." Id. at 816. King eventually spent eight days in jail before being bailed out by singer Harry Belafonte.

C. COST OF LITIGATION

VENEGAS V. MITCHELL
Supreme Court of the United States, 1990
495 U.S. 82

JUSTICE WHITE delivered the opinion of the Court.

Under 42 U.S.C. § 1988, a court may award a reasonable attorney's fee to the prevailing party in civil rights cases. We granted certiorari to resolve a conflict among the Courts of Appeals as to whether § 1988 invalidates contingent-fee contracts that would require a prevailing civil rights plaintiff to pay his attorney more than the statutory award against the defendant.

I

This dispute arises out of an action brought by petitioner Venegas under 42 U.S.C. § 1983 in the United States District Court for the Central District of California, alleging that police officers of the city of Long Beach, California, falsely arrested Venegas and conspired to deny him a fair trial through the knowing presentation of perjured testimony. After an order of the District Court dismissing Venegas' complaint as barred by the statute of limitations was reversed by the Court of Appeals, Venegas retained respondent Mitchell as his attorney. Venegas and Mitchell signed a contingent-fee contract providing that Mitchell would represent Venegas at trial for a fee of 40% of the gross amount of any recovery. The contract gave Mitchell "the right to apply for and collect any attorney fee award made by a court," prohibited Venegas from waiving Mitchell's right to court-awarded attorney's fees, and allowed Mitchell's intervention to protect his interest in the fee award. The contract also provided that any fee awarded by the court would be applied, dollar for dollar, to offset the contingent fee. The contract obligated Mitchell to provide his services for one trial only and stated that "[i]n the event there is a mistrial or an appeal, the parties may mutually agree upon terms and conditions of [Mitchell's] employment, but are not obligated to do so." Venegas subsequently consented to the association of co-counsel with the understanding that co-counsel would share any contingent fee equally with Mitchell.

Venegas obtained a judgment in his favor of $2.08 million. Mitchell then moved for attorney's fees under § 1988, and on August 15, 1986, the District Court entered an order awarding Venegas $117,000 in attorney's fees, of which $75,000 was attributable to work done by Mitchell. The District Court calculated the award for Mitchell's work by multiplying a reasonable hourly rate by the number of hours Mitchell expended on the case, and then doubling this lodestar figure to reflect Mitchell's competent performance. Negotiations between attorney and client about the possibility of Mitchell's representing Venegas on appeal broke down, and on September 14, 1986, Mitchell signed a stipulation withdrawing as counsel of record. Venegas obtained different counsel for the appeal.

[Mitchell then asserted a $406,000 attorney's lien against the judgment proceeds, representing his half of the 40% fee. Venegas objected that the fee was excessive, arguing that Mitchell should be limited to the $75,000 found to be reasonable on the motion for attorney's fees. The district court refused to disallow or reduce the fee, finding it reasonable and not a windfall for Mitchell. The court of appeals affirmed the district court with regard to the fee dispute. Venegas v. Mitchell, 867 F.2d 527 (9th Cir.1989).]

II

Section 1988 states in pertinent part that "[i]n any action or proceeding to enforce a provision of sections 1981, 1982, 1983, 1985, and 1986 of this title, . . . the court, in its discretion, may allow the prevailing party, other than the United States, a reasonable attorney's fee as part of the costs." The section by its terms authorized the trial court in this case to order the defendants to pay to Venegas, the prevailing party, a reasonable attorney's fee. The aim of the section, as our cases have explained, is to enable civil rights plaintiffs to employ reasonably competent lawyers without cost to themselves if they prevail. It is likely that in many, if not most, cases a lawyer will undertake a civil rights case on the express or implied promise of the plaintiff to pay the lawyer the statutory award, i.e., a reasonable fee, if the case is won. But there is nothing in the section to regulate what plaintiffs may or may not promise to pay their attorneys if they lose or if they win. Certainly § 1988 does not on its face prevent the plaintiff from promising an attorney a percentage of any money judgment that may be recovered. Nor has Venegas pointed to anything in the legislative history that persuades us that Congress intended § 1988 to limit civil rights plaintiffs' freedom to contract with their attorneys.

It is true that in construing § 1988, we have generally turned away from the contingent-fee model to the lodestar model of hours reasonably expended compensated at reasonable rates. See Blanchard v. Bergeron, 489 U.S. 87, 94 (1989); Riverside v. Rivera, 477 U.S. 561, 574 (1986) (plurality opinion); Blum v. Stenson, 465 U.S. 886, 897 (1984). We may also assume for the purposes of deciding this case that § 1988 would not have authorized the District Court to enhance the statutory award upward from the lodestar figure based on the contingency of nonrecovery in this particular litigation. But it is a mighty leap from these propositions to the conclusion that § 1988 also requires the District Court to invalidate a contingent-fee agreement arrived at privately between attorney and client. We have never held that § 1988 constrains the freedom of the civil rights plaintiff to become contractually and personally bound to pay an attorney a percentage of the recovery, if any, even though such a fee is larger than the statutory fee that the defendant must pay to the plaintiff.

Indeed, our cases look the other way. Section 1988 makes the prevailing party eligible for a discretionary award of attorney's fees. Evans v. Jeff D., 475 U.S. 717, 730 (1986). Because it is the party, rather than the lawyer, who is so eligible, we have consistently maintained that fees may be awarded under § 1988 even to those plaintiffs who did not need them to maintain their litigation, either because they were fortunate enough to be able to retain counsel on a fee-paying basis, Blanchard v. Bergeron, supra, at 94–95, or because they were represented free of charge by nonprofit legal aid organizations, Blum v. Stenson, supra, 465 U.S., at 894–95. We have therefore accepted, at least implicitly, that statutory awards of fees can coexist with private fee arrangements. And just as we have recognized that it is the party's entitlement to receive the fees in the appropriate case, so have we recognized that as far as § 1988 is concerned, it is the party's right to waive, settle, or negotiate that eligibility. See Evans v. Jeff D., supra, 475 U.S., at 730–731.

Much the same is true of the substance of a money judgment recovered under § 1983 (exclusive of fees awarded under § 1988), of which the contingent fee in this case is a part. A cause of action under § 1983 belongs "to the injured individua[l]," Newton v. Rumery, 480 U.S. 386, 395 (1987) (plurality opinion), and in at least some circumstances that individual's voluntary waiver of a § 1983 cause of action may be valid. If § 1983 plaintiffs may waive their causes of action entirely, there is little reason to believe that they may not assign part of their recovery to an attorney if they believe that the contingency arrangement will increase their likelihood of recovery. A contrary decision would place § 1983 plaintiffs in the peculiar position of being freer to negotiate with their adversaries than with their own attorneys.

Relying heavily on Blanchard v. Bergeron, supra, Venegas argues that if a contingent-fee agreement does not impose a ceiling on the amount of a "court awarded fee which would go to the attorney" (as he understands the holding of *Blanchard*), such a fee agreement should also be ignored for the benefit of the client so that he need pay only the statutory award. There are two difficulties with this argument. First, *Blanchard* did not address contractual obligations of plaintiffs to their attorneys; it dealt only with what the losing defendant must pay the plaintiff, whatever might be the substance of the contract between the plaintiff and the attorney. Second, we have already rejected the argument that the entitlement to a § 1988 award belongs to the attorney rather than the plaintiff. See Evans v. Jeff D., supra, 475 U.S., at 731–732.

Venegas also argues that because Congress provided for a reasonable fee to be paid by the defendant so that "a plaintiff's recovery will not be reduced by what he must pay his counsel," *Blanchard*, supra, 489 U.S., at 94, the plaintiff should be protected from paying the attorney any more than the reasonable fee awarded by the trial court. Otherwise, Venegas contends, paying the contingent fee in full would greatly reduce his recovery and would impose a cost on him for enforcing the civil rights laws, a cost that the defendant should pay. This argument, too, is wide of the mark. *Blanchard* also noted that "[p]laintiffs who can afford to hire their own lawyers, as well as impecunious litigants, may take advantage" of § 1988. Civil rights plaintiffs, if they prevail, will be entitled to an attorney's fee that Congress anticipated would enable them to secure reasonably competent counsel. If they take advantage of the system as Congress established it, they will avoid having their recovery reduced by contingent-fee agreements. But neither *Blanchard* nor any other of our cases has indicated that § 1988, by its own force, protects plaintiffs from having to pay what they have contracted to pay, even though their contractual liability is greater than the statutory award that they may collect from losing opponents. Indeed, depriving plaintiffs of the option of promising to pay more than the statutory fee if that is necessary to secure counsel of their choice would not further § 1988's general purpose of enabling such plaintiffs in civil rights cases to secure competent counsel.

* * *

Venegas also argues that even if contingent fees exceeding statutory awards are not prohibited per se by § 1988, nonetheless the contingent fee in this case is unreasonable under federal and state law. Venegas made this contention to both lower courts, and both courts rejected it. We find no reason in the record or briefs to disturb their conclusion on this issue. We therefore have no occasion to address the extent of the federal courts' authority to supervise contingent fees.

NOTES AND QUESTIONS

1.   As almost everyone seems to recognize, litigation is expensive. Fed. R. Civ. P. 54(d)(1) provides that the prevailing party usually can recover its costs of suit. See Marx v. General Revenue Corp., 133 S.Ct. 1166 (2013) (Rule 54(d) required a losing plaintiff in a Fair Labor Standards Act case to reimburse defendant for more than $4,000 in costs). But these costs are ordinarily limited to the items listed in 28 U.S.C. § 1920—filing fees and certain out-of-pocket expenditures. See Taniguchi v. Kan Pacific Saipan, Ltd., 132 S.Ct. 1997 (2012) (§ 1920 does not cover costs for document translation); Race Tires America v. Hoosier Racing Tire Corp., 674 F.3d 158 (3d Cir. 2012) ($365,000 in electronic discovery costs not recoverable under statute).

In most cases the recoverable costs are much smaller than attorneys' fees, but they can be considerable. See Depasquale v. International Business Mach. Corp., 40 Fed.R.Serv.3d 425 (E.D.Pa.1998) (in product liability action, defendant sought to recover over $50,000 in costs from plaintiff). In Moore v. Citgo Ref. & Chem. Co., 735 F.3d 309, 319–20 (5th Cir. 2013), the court of appeals held that the district judge acted improperly in reducing the cost award to defendant due to its wealth. "The court errred as a matter of law in relying in CITGO's 'enormous wealth'—or the comparative wealth of the parties as a basis for reducing the cost award." See also Quan v. Computer Sciences Corp., 623 F.3d 870 (9th Cir. 2010) (Rule 54(d)(1) creates a "presumption for awarding costs").

From an early date, however, American courts refused to make the loser pay the winner's attorneys' fees. The requirement that each party bear its own attorneys' fees has become known as the "American rule." But a damage recovery that is depleted by attorneys' fees would seem incomplete. A defendant who is exonerated arguably should not be impoverished by the cost of the successful defense. That seems to be the idea behind routine shifting of ordinary costs. Beyond the compensation rationale, routine fee-shifting might have desirable effects on behavior of litigants by deterring the assertion of groundless claims and defenses because those would increase the cost of litigation without improving the chance of winning. For reasons like these, almost all other countries allow the winning party to recover attorneys' fees, and some urge that this country should do the same. Would plaintiffs with good claims but moderate means be willing to sue large organizations and risk liability for the defendant's attorneys' fees? How sure would plaintiff have to feel about success before filing suit? Would the risk of liability for plaintiff's added fees really deter defendants from asserting groundless defenses?

In terms of incentives, shifting away from the American rule might prompt higher expenditure on litigation. If the parties must pay their own lawyers, win or lose, it makes sense for them to be frugal. If they can collect from their opponents if they win, they may be willing to spend more lavishly. Consider the following description of the consequences of the English full indemnity rule:

> [O]nce it is clear that a dispute is destined to go all the way to trial, the indemnity principle tends to erode resistance to costs. * * * Indeed, a point may come where the parties would have reason to persist with investment in litigation, not so much for the sake of a favorable judgment on the merits as for the purpose of recovering the money already expended in the dispute, which may well outstrip the value of the subject matter in issue.

Zuckerman, Lord Woolf's Access to Justice: Plus ça Change . . ., 59 Mod. L.Rev. 773, 778 (1996). Similarly, the American rule may prompt even parties confident of victory in court to settle because settlement relieves them of paying attorneys' fees.

2.   Whatever your reaction to the policy debate about the American rule, the reality in this country is that fees are recoverable only if there is an exception to that rule. In Alyeska Pipeline Serv. Co. v. Wilderness Society, 421 U.S. 240 (1975), the Court held that Congress had not "extended any roving authority to the Judiciary to allow counsel fees as costs or otherwise whenever the courts might deem them warranted." In response, Congress amended 42 U.S.C.A. § 1988 the following year to add the fee-shifting provisions involved in Venegas v. Mitchell, providing that the court "may allow the prevailing party * * * a reasonable attorney's fee as part of the costs."

Although it appears bilateral, like Rule 54(d)(1), this provision has been interpreted in the same way as Title VII of the 1964 Civil Rights Act, which has been held to authorize recovery of fees by defendants only when plaintiff's suit is "frivolous, unreasonable, or without foundation." Christiansburg Garment Co. v. EEOC, 434 U.S. 412 (1978). But when civil rights plaintiffs prevail, defendants must usually pay their fees whether or not the defenses were groundless. Newman v. Piggie Park Enter., Inc., 390 U.S. 400 (1968). Compare Fogerty v. Fantasy, Inc., 510 U.S. 517 (1994) (refusing to read a similar pro-plaintiff intention into the fee-shifting provisions of the Copyright Act, 17 U.S.C.A. § 505 even though it is "virtually identical" to § 1988 because "in the civil rights context, impecunious 'private attorney general' plaintiffs can ill afford to litigate their claims against defendants with more resources. Congress sought to redress this balance in part, and to provide incentives for the bringing of meritorious lawsuits, by treating successful plaintiffs more favorably than successful defendants.").

Besides § 1988 and the copyright act, there are more than 100 other federal statutes that provide for fee shifting. See Marek v. Chesny, 473 U.S. 1, 44–51 (1985) (Brennan, J., dissenting, listing statutes). See further discussion in Chapter 7.

3.   Ordinarily, as in § 1988, fee-shifting statutes authorize the award of a "reasonable" fee. In Venegas v. Mitchell, this fee award is calculated by what is called the "lodestar" method—multiplying the hours worked by the lawyer times the lawyer's hourly rate. In deciding whether the fee award is reasonable, the court may disallow hours that were spent on unsuccessful claims or inefficiently used. Regarding billing rate, ordinarily the court will use the attorney's customary rate for paying clients. In *Venegas*, the court doubled the lodestar fee award because Mitchell performed "competently." But the Supreme Court has frowned on such enhancements of the lodestar amount. Thus, it is likely that under current law Mitchell's work would result in a fee award half the size approved by the district court—$37,500.

4.   In Blanchard v. Bergeron, 489 U.S. 87 (1989), plaintiff had a contract with his attorney providing that the lawyer would accept 40% of the award as payment, but the district court awarded more using the lodestar method. Defendant argued that the contract should set a ceiling for the fee award, but the Court disagreed, holding that the lodestar approach is "the centerpiece of attorney's fee awards" and that fees so calculated "by definition will represent the reasonable worth of the services rendered in vindication of a plaintiff's civil rights claim." It found this result consistent with the purpose of Congress that "a plaintiff's recovery will not be reduced by what he must pay his counsel."

If under the lodestar Mitchell's fee of $37,500 was by definition reasonable in *Venegas*, how could a fee of 20% of the recovery, over ten times that large, also be reasonable? See Model Rules of Professional Conduct 1.5(a) ("A lawyer's fee shall be reasonable."). Note that there is an inherent tension between the lawyer and the client in the negotiation of a fee. At some point a court may disallow a fee as too high. Do you think that it should have been trimmed in this case?

Some additional facts revealed in the lower courts' decisions and the oral arguments may shed light on this question. Mitchell was hired three months before the trial of Venegas' suit, after the bulk of discovery had been done. A state court suit by Venegas had already resulted in a $1,000,000 verdict that was overturned on grounds not applicable to the federal claim. Mitchell insisted on a $10,000 nonrefundable retainer and took the case to trial. After trial, defendants moved to have the judgment set aside and, when those motions were denied, appealed. Mitchell then offered to handle the appeal for an additional 10% of the recovery ($200,000 more, as things turned out). The appellate court affirmed in all respects. See Venegas v. Wagner, 831 F.2d 1514 (9th Cir.1987); Venegas v. Mitchell, 867 F.2d 527 (9th Cir.1989). Should Mitchell have offered Venegas the alternative of paying by the hour? Can you think of a reason why Venegas might not have taken this option?

In many personal injury cases, American lawyers have long worked for a share of the recovery, an arrangement with little parallel in the rest of the world. For civil rights suits, that model may not work because ordinarily "the risks plaintiffs face in § 1983 litigation are greater and the rewards are smaller" than in typical personal injury suits. Kirchoff v. Flynn, 786 F.2d 320, 323–34 (7th Cir. 1986). But in personal injury cases it may be objected that lawyers screen cases to "cherry pick" strong ones promising large recoveries. See Kritzer, Seven Dogged Myths Concerning Contingency Fees, 80 Wash. U. L. Rev. 739 (2002) (reporting that contingency fee lawyers actively screen cases and, as a result, run only a small risk of nonrecovery). Some criticize the percentage measurement of attorney fees for overcompensating lawyers, see Brickman, Contingent Fees Without Contingencies: Hamlet Without the Prince of Denmark, 37 U.C.L.A. L. Rev. 29 (1989) (arguing that percentage fee arrangements overcompensate lawyers who actually are taking no risk). Do these concerns affect the propriety of Mitchell's insistence on being paid another 10% to take the appeal in *Venegas*?

5. If percentage fees can overcompensate counsel in some large-recovery cases, lodestar computations can present that risk when the recovery is small. In Riverside v. Rivera, 477 U.S. 561 (1986), plaintiffs sued a variety of police officers for illegal arrest and ultimately obtained judgments against some of them totalling $33,000. The district court awarded $245,000 in fees, noting that the police misconduct "had to be stopped and * * * nothing short of having a lawsuit like this would have stopped it." Justice Rehnquist argued that "billing judgment" should have prevented the lawyers from seeking such a large fee, but the Court affirmed the award because Justice Powell decided the findings regarding the larger public importance of the suit were not clearly erroneous. Justice Brennan, writing for a plurality, asserted that "[w]e reject the notion that a civil rights action for damages constitutes nothing more than a private tort suit benefitting only the individual plaintiffs whose rights were violated. Unlike most private tort litigants, a civil rights plaintiff seeks to vindicate important civil and constitutional rights that cannot be valued solely in monetary terms." Should this mean that in civil rights cases the size of the claim is no constraint on the amount of lawyer time invested in the case?

6. Mitchell's contract with Venegas forbade Venegas from waiving court-awarded attorneys' fees. In Evans v. Jeff D., 475 U.S. 717 (1986), defendants in a class action brought on behalf of handicapped children regarding health-care treatment offered plaintiffs "virtually all the injunctive relief" they had sought provided that plaintiffs would waive attorneys' fees. The Court rejected the argument that this was improper:

> Although respondents contend that Johnson, as counsel for the class, was faced with an "ethical dilemma" when petitioners offered him relief greater than that which he could reasonably have expected to obtain for his clients at trial (if only he would stipulate to a waiver of the statutory fee award), * * * we do not believe that the "dilemma" was an "ethical" one in the sense that Johnson had to choose between conflicting duties under the prevailing norms of professional conduct. Plainly Johnson had no ethical obligation to seek a statutory fee award. His ethical duty was to serve his clients loyally and competently. Since the proposal to settle the merits was more favorable than the probable outcome of the trial, Johnson's decision to recommend acceptance was consistent with the highest standards of our profession.

Given that defendants in *Jeff D.* seem almost to have conceded that they violated plaintiffs' rights, does this decision unduly erode the value of the fee-shifting statute? Will the risk that defendants may insist on a fee waiver in return for favorable relief on the merits affect the willingness of attorneys to accept such cases? Does a provision like the one used by Mitchell solve that problem? Does it raise an ethical problem?

7.   *Publicly subsidized attorneys*: Some countries have tried to assure legal representation for all by subsidizing lawyers for the poor, but many such programs have been cut back. See A. Zuckerman, Civil Procedure 949–51 (2003) (describing "radical reform" to cut the costs of English scheme for government to pay for privately-retained lawyers). In the 1960s, the federal government in this country created a network of legal services offices that provided lawyers on the government payroll for eligible poor people. In the 1980s, however, funding for this program was cut.

8.   *Third-party funding*: Although government funding has receded, for some lawsuits private, profit-seeking entities offer a source of litigation funding. "Large banks, hedge funds and private investors hungry for new and lucrative opportunities are bankrolling other people's lawsuits, pumping hundreds of millions of dollars into medical malpractice claims, divorce battles and class actions against corporations—all in the hope of sharing the potential winnings." Appelbaum, Putting Money on Lawsuits, Investors Share in the Payouts, N.Y. Times, Nov. 15, 2010; see also Sahani, Judging Third-Party Funding, 63 UCLA L. Rev. 388 (2016); Comment, Revolution in Progress: Third-Party Funding of American Litigation, 58 UCLA L. Rev. 571 (2010).

9.   *Filing fees*: Besides paying lawyers, litigants must initially pay filing fees and the like even if they are ultimately able to recoup them. Federal courts will excuse payment of those fees by people eligible to file in forma pauperis, 28 U.S.C.A. § 1915, but that option is not always available. The Supreme Court has sometimes found the imposition of these fees to violate due process when a "fundamental right" is involved and a litigant cannot afford the fees. See Boddie v. Connecticut, 401 U.S. 371 (1971) (holding that state could not impose a filing fee for obtaining a divorce); compare United States v. Kras, 409 U.S. 434 (1973) ($50 filing fee for bankruptcy petition could be imposed because bankruptcy discharge is not a fundamental right like dissolving a marriage); Ortwein v. Schwab, 410 U.S. 656 (1973) (upholding $25 fee for court review of reduction of welfare allowance for the aged on ground that no fundamental right was involved). See also M.L.B. v. S.L.J., 519 U.S. 102 (1996) (due process violated by state requirement that party seeking to appeal termination of parental rights post over $2,300 to cover the cost of preparing a transcript of the proceedings from which the appeal was taken).

D. PRIVATE ORDERING THROUGH ALTERNATIVES TO LITIGATION

Now that we have examined some of the difficulties in fashioning judicial remedies for disputes, and before we turn to the litigation process itself, it is useful to consider alternative means of resolving disputes. Until the late 20th century, discussion of alternative processes would not be found in a first-year civil procedure casebook. But developments since the 1980s have contributed to a new awareness of the close interrelationship between litigation and other means of resolving disputes. First, the movement referred to as "Alternative Dispute Resolution" or "ADR" has generated both a new philosophy and new processes for resolving disputes short of trial. Second, courts have embraced settlement as a principal objective in every case, shaping settlement conferences and other devices for use in case administration. We have already encountered this phenomenon in Kothe v. Smith, supra p. 19. Third, creative experimentation by both dispute resolution professionals and judges has resulted in a cornucopia of new methods for aiding disputants to find solutions to their disputes. We will address many of these developments in much greater detail in Chapter 7 entitled Judicial Supervision of Pretrial and Promotion of Settlement.

For our purposes here of providing an overview of the remedies offered by our court system, it is useful to consider three of the principal alternatives to a full trial—negotiation and settlement promotion; third-party intervention; and arbitration. Adjudication in a court involves an ultimate decision on the rights of the parties by a public officer, the judge, or by a jury sworn to uphold the law and instructed in the applicable legal principles by the judge. The decision is made after a public trial at which the parties have the right to present evidence they have obtained through pretrial efforts assisted by the court (as in allowing discovery, see Chapter 5). The decision of the case is supposed to conform to legal rules of substantive law, and can therefore be scrutinized by another group of public officials, judges of an appellate court, who determine whether it was correct under that law.

A central difference between adjudication and the three alternatives is that they are conducted privately and extrajudicially (although increasingly they may be "court-annexed" and serve as a step in the litigation process, as will be discussed more fully in Chapter 7). Thus, these alternatives can be viewed as a form of "private ordering" of disputes. Legal standards still provide a guide for resolution of the dispute under these alternatives, but there is greater latitude than in litigation to reach a solution that does not mirror the rights and remedies that would be applied in a court.

Another difference is in the degree of formality. The alternative processes vary in formality, from negotiation, which is an essentially unstructured process, through mediation and other forms of third-party intervention which involve certain formalities, to arbitration which follows formal procedures for the presentation of the case. But they are not bound by court procedures nor strict standards of evidence, and they lack the stuffiness (or majesty, depending on your point of view) of the courtroom with its robed judge and ritual. These differences may be viewed as either advantages or disadvantages depending on one's philosophy of dispute resolution.

NEGOTIATION AND SETTLEMENT PROMOTION

Negotiation is as old as social interaction. It occurs when one person attempts to persuade another to agree to his or her terms. Consciously or not, each of us has engaged in negotiation, often over such insignificant details as selecting a movie to see, or a restaurant to go to. Some may have negotiated in more "official" circumstances as, for example, trying to persuade a police officer not to issue a speeding ticket.

Negotiation is a common first reaction to a dispute. If a neighbor is playing loud music, negotiation may lead to a reduction in the noise level. The potential value of negotiation may explain why such a small percentage of disputes actually lead to litigation, although calculating that percentage with precision is difficult. Researchers who tried to measure the winnowing effect of pre-litigation factors on pursuit of disputes found that, among people who had grievances, negotiated agreements before litigation were much more frequent than actual commencement of litigation.[1]

Once lawyers do get involved, the negotiation process usually continues, often both before and after formal litigation is commenced. This reality is confirmed by the fact that many more lawsuits are settled rather than decided by a court or jury. Indeed, some suggest that the process might better be called "litigotiation" than litigation.[1] At this point, however, the negotiation is usually done by the lawyers, and not by the parties themselves.

Negotiation is a tool of the trade for lawyers, but sometimes outside assistance is needed to encourage them to employ it effectively. Wariness over appearing too anxious to settle or over making the first offer can be overcome by court promotion of settlement. Rule 16(c)(2)(I) authorizes the court to take "appropriate action" regarding "settling the case and using special procedures to assist in resolving the dispute when authorized by statute or local rule." Settlement conferences can be held with or without the judge being present. The judge's active involvement can sometimes be effective but also runs the risk of coercion, as was seen in the *Kothe* case, supra p. 19. Suffice it to say that today judges are very much involved in

---

[1]   See Miller & Sarat, Grievances, Claims and Disputes: Assessing the Adversary Culture, 15 Law & Soc'y Rev. 525, 537 (1981); see generally Galanter, Reading the Landscape of Disputes: What We Know and Don't Know (and Think We Know) About Our Allegedly Contentious and Litigious Society, 31 U.C.L.A.L.Rev. 4, 11–18 (1983) (examining the attrition rate among potential disputes before a third party—such as a lawyer—is called upon).

[1]   See Galanter, Worlds of Deals: Using Negotiation to Teach About Legal Process, 34 J.Legal Ed. 268, 269 (1984).

the promotion of settlement, whether through informal jaw-boning, mandated conferences, or more formal ADR devices.

THIRD-PARTY INTERVENTION

Settlement negotiations can often be assisted by the intervention of a third party, as suggested by the frequent role of judges in promoting settlement. The role of the third party can vary considerably, ranging from facilitating discussion and generating options (in the traditional "mediation") to providing an evaluation of the strengths of the parties' cases on the law or facts (found in "neutral evaluation" programs that have been adopted by some federal courts), to more formal "trial runs" in which the third party or parties give a nonbinding opinion after hearing the parties summarize their cases (for example, in a "summary jury trial" before a representative jury, a "court-annexed arbitration" before volunteer attorneys, or a "mini-trial" before the decision-makers of the parties). We will consider these methods in more detail in Chapter 7, but something more might be said here about the most frequently used form of third-party intervention, mediation.

MEDIATION

Mediation is a step away from negotiation because the parties turn to a third person to help them make a deal to end their dispute. Like negotiation, it has existed since humans began to develop social organization because people seem to have a natural instinct to seek the guidance of others in settling their differences. Mediation is widely used in the United States in divorce and related family law cases, and is increasingly being used in labor law employee grievances, low-level disputes taken to neighborhood dispute resolution centers, public law disputes such as civil rights and environmental cases, and personal injury and commercial suits.

The function of the mediator is quite different from that of a judge. Rather than applying legal rules to the parties' behavior, the mediator lacks any authority to decide who is right. One view is that the parties are not bound by legal rules about behavior. "[I]n mediation—as distinguished from adjudication and, usually, arbitration—the ultimate authority resides with the disputants. The conflict is seen as unique and therefore less subject to solution by application of some general principle. The case is neither to be governed by a precedent nor to set one. Thus, all sorts of facts, needs, and interests that would be excluded from consideration in an adversary, rule-oriented proceeding become relevant in a mediation. Indeed, whatever a party deems relevant is relevant."[2]

While mediation allows the parties to disregard the law as to their rights and obligations if they chose to do so, legal standards still provide a

---

[2] Riskin, Mediation and Lawyers, 43 Ohio St.L.J. 29, 34 (1982).

framework for resolution of a dispute. If the mediation fails, the dispute will be resolved in a trial through formal application of legal rules. Thus the parties in a mediation do not bargain "in a vacuum: they bargain in the shadow of the law," as Professors Mnookin and Kornhauser described in the context of divorce.[3] "The legal rules governing alimony, child support, marital property, and custody give each parent certain claims based on what each would get if the case went to trial. In other words, the outcome that the law will impose if no agreement is reached gives each parent certain bargaining chips—an endowment of sorts." Thus the function of the law is "not as imposing order from above, but rather as providing a framework within which divorcing couples can themselves determine their post-dissolution rights and responsibilities." If the law is relevant in family law mediations where continuing relationships may be the most critical factor, it can be even more important in more impersonal forms of litigation like personal injury, product liability, antitrust, or business transactions.

Although without power to enforce rules, the mediator can perform important tasks.[4] One is to reduce the level of antagonism between the parties to persuade them to trust each other. "The adversary process—the engine of the adjudicatory system—operates on a theory of fundamental distrust: Never put faith in the adversary. Litigation thus becomes formal, tricky, divisive, time-consuming, and distorting. * * * In contrast, the creation of trust is central to the design of many ADR processes."[5] To avoid these disruptive effects of litigation, mediators have sometimes insisted that the parties leave their lawyers (if they have any) behind and handle the mediation sessions alone. Disputes involving ongoing personal relationships may be more suitable for mediations without lawyers. However, when they have lawyers the parties would normally be briefed in advance by them to understand the legal framework and the benefits and risks of certain kinds of settlements. As mediation is increasingly used as a pretrial settlement device, lawyers generally participate, contributing legal expertise and advice. A study of mediation involving divorce with minor children found it a "myth" that lawyers do not participate (93% did) and that lawyers spoiled the process by arguing the law and pursuing adversarial tactics (most of the parties found their participation helpful).[6]

---

[3] Mnookin & Kornhauser, Bargaining in the Shadow of the Law: The Case for Divorce, 88 Yale L.J. 950, 968 (1979). See also Mnookin, Bargaining in the Shadow of the Law: A Testable Model of Strategic Behavior, 11 J Legal Stud 225 (1982).

[4] A great deal has been written about mediation techniques in treatises, ADR course materials, training manuals, and legal literature, e.g., ABA Section of Dispute Resolution Task Force on Improving Mediation Quality, Final Report, April 2006–Feb. 2008; Riskin, Understanding Mediators' Orientations, Strategies, and Techniques, 1 Harv. Nego. L. Rev. 7 (1994), 12 Alternatives 111 (1994).

[5] Lieberman & Henry, Lessons From the Alternative Dispute Resolution Movement, 53 U.Chi.L.Rev. 424, 427 (1986).

[6] McEwen & Rogers, Bring the Lawyers Into Divorce Mediation, Disp. Resol. Mag. 8–10 (1994).

Another task for the mediator is creativity. The parties may have turned to the mediator not only because of mistrust but also because they are at loggerheads. Here again, the absence of legal limitations on the mediator's actions can prove helpful because "participants in ADR are free to go beyond the legal definition of the scope of their dispute. They can search for creative solutions to the problem that gave rise to the dispute, and those solutions may be far more novel than any remedy a court has the power to provide."[7] Thus, "the mediator employs two fundamental principles of effective mediation: creating doubt in the minds of the parties as to the validity of their positions on issues; and suggesting alternative approaches which may facilitate agreement. These are two functions which parties to a dispute are very often unable to perform by themselves. To carry out these functions, the mediator has the parties separately 'brainstorm' to produce alternatives or options; discusses the workability of each option; encourages the parties by noting the probability of success, where appropriate; suggests alternatives not raised by the parties and then repeats the three previous steps."[8]

The most used form of mediation is often called "non-directive" or "facilitative," in which the mediator seeks to facilitate communication but not to impose her values or solutions on the parties. However, there is a variety of other approaches, depending on the mediator, such as a "therapeutic" approach (more often taken in family law cases) in which the mediator plays a more active role in helping the parties resolve their differences and an "evaluative" approach (more often used by former judges) in which the mediator is more inclined to give her opinion as to how the case might be resolved in the courts.[9] There has also been considerable discussion of a "transformative" approach in which the mediator seeks to engender "moral growth" in the parties through "empowerment" and "recognition"[10] and to understand and appreciate the position of the opponent. The U.S. Post Office Department has trained mediators in this approach to mediate its internal personnel disputes. In recent years, another approach, the "collaborative law" movement, has had a significant impact on divorce mediation. The parties and their lawyers must agree in advance to avoid adversary aspects of litigation including threats and strategic tactics, to fully disclose relevant information, and to negotiate all

---

[7] Lieberman & Henry, 53 U.Ch.L.Rev. at 429.

[8] Cooley, Arbitration vs. Mediation—Explaining the Differences, 69 Judicature 263, 267 (1986).

[9] See Riskin, Mediator Orientations, Strategies, and Techniques, 12 Alternatives 111 (1994).

[10] See R. Bush & J. Folger, The Promise of Mediation: Responding to Conflict Through Empowerment and Recognition (1994). The U.S. Postal Service adopted an ambitious dispute resolution program called "Redress" that uses a "transformative" approach to mediation of employee grievance and disciplinary disputes. See Advanced Mediation Skills for Postal Service Mediators: Practice Within A Transformative Framework (A Course Prepared for the U.S. Postal Service by Robert A. Baruch Bush, Joseph P. Folger, Dorothy J. Della Noce, & Sally Ganong Pope, 2000).

matters that require the approval of the court. If a settlement is not reached, the lawyers will resign, and the parties can hire litigation counsel.[11]

The goal of mediation is that the parties ultimately agree voluntarily to a specific solution to their dispute. Once they do, the mediator will ordinarily put the agreement in writing and have the parties sign the agreement. Mediation agreements are legally binding, if they satisfy the requirements of contract law. It is said that they are actually followed more often than decrees by judges: "The internal and interactional dynamics of consensual settlement processes combine to create pressures toward compliance that are largely lacking in adjudication. * * * Consent, unlike command, brings with it an assumption of responsibility for the settlement and for its implementation. This sense of responsibility, along with general normative pressures to live up to commitments, can weigh heavily on disputants, even those who may regret having given consent in the heat of negotiation or mediation. The more explicit these pressures, the more effective they are. Our data suggest that the personal and immediate commitments generated by consensual processes bind people more strongly to compliance than the relatively distant, impersonal obligations imposed by authorities."[12]

Since the 1980s, mediation has become "court-annexed" in many jurisdictions. Statutes and court rules now often either encourage or require the parties to a law suit to mediate as an integral part of the litigation process.[13]

NOTES AND QUESTIONS

1.   There has been a long-standing debate over the virtues of adjudication versus settlement. Concerns have been expressed that judicial encouragement of settlement could deny parties the protection of courts, which are best suited to preserving constitutional and public law rights, and could undermine the rights-oriented litigation process which provides binding precedents applicable to others similarly situated. Although these criticisms are generally leveled at mediation, they may also apply to arbitration since arbitrator awards in non-labor cases are generally without an opinion which provides a precedent.

---

[11] See Rau, Sherman & Peppet, Processes of Dispute Resolution: The Role of Lawyers 403 (2006); Tesler, Collaborative Law: Achieving Effective Resolution in Divorce Without Litigation (ABA 2001).

[12] McEwen & Maiman, Mediation in Small Claims Court: Achieving Compliance Through Consent, 18 Law & Soc'y Rev. 11, 42, 44–45 (1984).

[13] See Sherman, Court-Mandated Alternative Dispute Resolution: What Form of Participation Should be Required?, 46 S.M.U.L.Rev. 2079 (1993); Plapinger & Stienstra, ADR and Settlement in the Federal District Courts: A Sourcebook for Judges and Lawyers (2000); Welsh, Making Deals in Court-Connected Mediation: What's Justice Got to Do With It?, 79 Wash.U.L.Q. 787 (2001) (observing that bargaining in court-ordered mediation is similar to that in private mediation).

Professor Owen Fiss, in his article Against Settlement, 93 Yale L.J. 1073, 1085 (1984), argued that "[a]djudication uses public resources, and employs [public officials whose] job is not to maximize the ends of private parties, nor simply to secure the peace, but to explicate and give force to the values embodied in authoritative texts such as the Constitution and statutes: to interpret those values and to bring reality into accord with them."

Judge Harry Edwards added: "one essential function of law is to reflect the public resolution of such irreconcilable differences; lawmakers are forced to choose among these differing visions of the public good. A potential danger of ADR is that disputants who seek only understanding and reconciliation may treat as irrelevant the choices made by our lawmakers and may, as a result, ignore public values reflected in rules of law. We must also be concerned lest ADR becomes a tool for diminishing the judicial development of legal rights for the disadvantaged. * * * Inexpensive, expeditious, and informal adjudication is not always synonymous with fair and just adjudication." Edwards, Alternative Dispute Resolution: Panacea or Anathema, 99 Harv. L. Rev. 668, 676–77 (1986).

Professor Edward Brunet observed that "the output of conventional litigation should be viewed as a public good": "Litigation guides third parties. Litigation results in written opinions that apply necessarily vague positive law to concrete fact situations." Private ordering devices and ADR erode the guidance function of law, he argued: "In the worst case scenario, widespread ADR independent of substantive law could increase disputes since third parties would lack the incentive to perform in accordance with custom crafted legal norms. For example, a rational polluter would be foolish to comply with a published regulation permitting a low amount of emissions when it could probably pollute at a substantially greater amount through environmental mediation." Brunet, Questioning The Quality of Alternate Dispute Resolution, 62 Tulane L.Rev. 1, 19–20 (1987).

Is there a response to these concerns of the ADR critics? There is a risk of overstating the case. Professor Fiss has challenged the idea that courts should be concerned with dispute resolution at all: "To my mind courts exist to give meaning to our public values, not to resolve disputes." As to disputes that do not involve public values, he suggests that having courts resolve them is "an extravagant use of public resources, and thus it seems quite appropriate for those disputes to be handled not by courts, but by arbitrators." Fiss, Foreword: The Forms of Justice, 93 Harv.L.Rev. 1, 29–30 (1979). Although it must be noted that Fiss defines "public value" broadly, doesn't this attitude underestimate the importance of courts as devices for resolving a whole range of disputes?

2. For many clients, the greater flexibility represented by private ordering devices and ADR approaches may be more important than litigation opportunities. Lawyers are not social workers, but they should be alert to the possibility that creative compromises may be more useful to their clients in many instances than insisting on litigation to the end. Where the parties to the dispute expect to have a long-term relationship with one another, there may

be particular reasons to think seriously about something short of full adjudication. At the same time, it is important to realize that the anti-litigation sentiment prevalent in some quarters is not universally shared, and that the grounds for it are subject to serious question. The existence of a litigation "boom," for example, is highly debated. Those who claim it has occurred point to dramatic increases in court filings. Others, however, look closely at the statistics and report that the increase is not so dramatic as is claimed. See Galanter, Reading the Landscape of Disputes: What We Know And Don't Know (And Think We Know) About Our Allegedly Contentious and Litigious Society, 31 U.C.L.A.L.Rev. 4 (1983) (arguing that the patterns in litigation relate to other changes in society). Galanter, The Vanishing Trial: An Examination of Trials and Related Matters in Federal and State Courts, 1 J. Empir. Legal Studies 459 (2004).

3.   A prevalent attitude in the ADR movement has been that litigation is bad. One ADR organization, for example, asks its members to sign a pledge: "In the event of a business dispute between our company and another which has made or shall make a similar statement, we are prepared to explore with that other party resolution of the dispute through negotiation or ADR techniques before pursuing full-scale litigation." Center For Public Resources, Corporate Policy Statement: Alternative Dispute Resolution. Except for considerations of cost and delay, are there reasons to shun litigation in this way?

4.   Another common ADR theme is that lawyers and litigation are too adversarial. In place of what is perceived as a cult of adversariness, ADR advocates cooperative solutions in which parties are not riveted on notions of their "rights." This is reflected in the idea that ADR produces better outcomes than litigation.

Some advocates of ADR consider it a "self-empowering process." The argument is that because the parties participate voluntarily, the less powerful party is able to confront the other with commonly-accepted standards and thus to achieve basic fairness that might not be possible in a formal legal proceeding. Critics, however, doubt the efficacy of mediation, any more than litigation, in getting disputing parties to recognize and accept higher values not in their immediate self interest. ADR advocates respond that mediation is better able to make them appreciate that those values are in their ultimate self interest.

Critics also argue that, without an advocate in mediation, the less powerful party is more likely to surrender rights that would be protected in a court. This disagreement recalls our discussion in Chapter 1 of the adversary versus other forms of justice. The amorphous, informal procedures of ADR have been faulted for putting the less powerful party at risk. ADR has been especially criticized as disadvantaging women, poor people, and minorities. Grillo, The Mediation Alternative: Process Dangers for Women, 100 Yale L.J. 1545 (1991); Delgado et al., Fairness and Formality: Minimizing the Risks of Prejudice in Alternative Dispute Resolution, 1985 Wis. L. Rev. 1359.

In family law disputes, it has been argued that mediation enables the spouse with greater social and financial power (often the man) to dominate the other. "The claim that people have common interests can be a way of misleading the less powerful into collaborating with more powerful in schemes that mainly benefit the latter." J. Mansbridge, Beyond Adversarial Democracy 5 (1983). But does litigation effectively protect against the effects of such imbalance? Note that the American courts usually do not appoint counsel for civil litigants who cannot afford to hire their own lawyers. Could a careful mediator be more likely to equalize power imbalances? At least in theory, the mediator is to pursue a fair outcome, and thereby to keep one disputant from taking advantage of the other by virtue of greater power. The process referred to as "collaborative divorce" involves an agreement among the parties and counsel not to seek contested hearings or discovery, to make full disclosure of all relevant financial information, and to refrain from acting in a manner detrimental to the future relationship of the parties. Herman, Collaborative Divorce: A Short Overview, 4 Divorce Litig. 68 (April 2001). Does this assuage concerns over gender-based power disparities?

ARBITRATION

Arbitration has long been an alternative to litigation. One of the purposes behind the creation of the Chambers of Commerce in the colonial period was to arbitrate disputes among their members.[14] George Washington himself put an arbitration clause in his will to resolve any disputes among his heirs.

Arbitration resembles adjudication more closely than mediation because the third person, the arbitrator, has the authority to decide the dispute, not merely to try to get the parties to agree on a decision. This power is conferred on the arbitrator by the parties' agreement to submit their dispute to arbitration. Although arbitration produces a decision, it is still an example of private ordering. An agreement to arbitrate can occur after the dispute arises, but ordinarily it is part of an agreement on some other subject between the parties that is made before there was any dispute (as was the clause inserted in George Washington's will and as in many contracts today). Clauses requiring arbitration of any dispute are commonplace today in collective bargaining agreements and commercial contracts (particularly those of certain industries such as construction, or those involving parties from different countries).

To initiate the arbitration process, one of the parties demands arbitration of a specified dispute. If the other party refuses, it is possible to get a court order to arbitrate pursuant to the agreement. Or, if an opposing party has already filed suit on the matter, to stay the trial of the action pending arbitration. Federal Arbitration Act (FAA), 9 U.S.C.A. §§ 3 & 4. The FAA was passed in 1925 to provide that federal courts would enforce arbitration clauses and awards at a time when many states would not. It

---

[14] Mentschikoff, Commercial Arbitration, 61 Colum.L.Rev. 846, 854–55 (1961).

applies to any contract "evidencing a transaction involving commerce" (which today covers almost all contracts), and it has been interpreted to require that both federal and state courts enforce arbitration clauses.

The FAA also provides some procedural rules for the conduct of arbitrations. However, most of the procedures governing an arbitration come from whatever the parties put in the arbitration clause of their contract, or, more typically, the rules of an institution that they chose to administer the arbitration (such as the American Arbitration Association (AAA)). The first step is selection of the arbitrator. Typically that task is delegated to the administering institution. For example, the AAA would provide the parties a list or lists of persons on its panel whom it deems to be qualified arbitrators for that kind of case, and the parties can strike names until there is someone to whom there is no objection. Domestic arbitrations in the U.S. usually have only one arbitrator, but international arbitrations have three, with each party appointing one and these two selecting the third. If the parties cannot agree on an arbitrator, it is possible to have a court appoint one for them. See 9 U.S.C.A. § 5.

The procedures specified by the parties (or by the rules of the administering institution they have selected), concern such matters as timing and place of the hearings, calling of witnesses, receipt of documents, etc. Traditionally there was no discovery because the arbitrator and parties came together for the first time when the arbitration was scheduled. However, today the arbitrator has discretion to allow advance discovery, and pre-arbitration hearings and some discovery (though not necessarily as extensive as in a court) may be permitted. After a hearing at which the parties present their cases (usually through lawyers), the arbitrator(s) render a decision, called an award, which, in American practice, usually does not contain the reasons for the result (labor arbitration is an exception). One of the advantages claimed for arbitration is greater finality than a court judgment where extensive appeals are possible. There is no direct appeal from an arbitration award to a court, although a party may seek an order from a federal court to vacate an award. Under the FAA an award may not be vacated for error as to the law or the facts. It may only be vacated on the limited grounds stated in the FAA such as being procured by corruption, fraud, or undue means; misconduct by the arbitrators in refusing to hear evidence pertinent and material or misbehavior prejudicing the rights of a party; or the arbitrators exceeding their authority.[15] FAA, § 10.

---

[15] See Hall Street Associates, L.L.C. v. Mattel, Inc., 555 U.S. 576 (2008) (the FAA precludes enforcement of an arbitration agreement that required the court to vacate or correct any award if the arbitrator's conclusions of law were erroneous). Thus parties may not contract for expanded court review which Hall Street saw as undermining "arbitration's essential virtue of resolving disputes straightaway."

MANDATORY ARBITRATION IN ADHESION CONTRACTS

One of the most significant developments in the field of dispute resolution in recent years is the explosive growth of contractual arbitration, particularly in adhesion contracts. The effect of an arbitration clause is to deny the customer the right to a jury trial as to any dispute arising out of the contract. Arbitration has been embraced by various institutions for numerous reasons—perceived quicker and less costly resolution than litigation, finality because of limited review, resort to a decision-maker with more experience and expertise in the subject matter than the average jury member, and avoidance of high damage awards associated with jury trials.

There are many legal issues attending this growth of contractual arbitration. The Supreme Court has applied the FAA broadly, holding that it "declared a national policy favoring arbitration and withdrew the power of the states to require a judicial forum for the resolution of claims which the contracting parties agreed to resolve by arbitration."[16] Supreme Court decisions have found that a variety of state laws imposing restrictions on arbitrations are preempted by the FAA.[17] In recent years, the Court has also rejected exceptions for claims brought under certain federal statutes that had been previously thought to require a trial by jury.[18]

In the wake of expanded resort to arbitration clauses in adhesion contracts, courts often scrutinize the circumstances to ensure that there was knowing waiver of the right to sue, and that it does not involve fundamental unfairness. For example, in Kummetz v. Tech Mold, Inc., 152 F.3d 1153 (9th Cir.1998), the court found that an employee's signed acknowledgement that he was covered by the company's Employment Information Booklet (that contained an arbitration provision) did not bar him from suing under the ADEA because the acknowledgement did not specifically notify him that arbitration was required.

Although the FAA preempts state laws considered to disadvantage the enforcement of arbitration, it must be applied against the backdrop of state contract law.[19] The FAA's guarantee that arbitration clauses are enforceable specifically states "save upon such grounds as exist at law or in equity for the revocation of any contract." FAA, § 2. Thus all the usual

---

[16] Southland Corp. v. Keating, 465 U.S. 1, 10 (1984).

[17] See Southland Corp. v. Keating, 465 U.S. 1 (1984) (state statute prohibiting arbitration in franchise agreements); Allied-Bruce Terminix Cos., Inc. v. Dobson, 513 U.S. 265 (1995) (state statute invalidating pre-dispute arbitration agreements).

[18] See Gilmer v. Interstate/Johnson Lane Corp., 500 U.S. 20, 111 S.Ct. 1647, 114 L.Ed.2d 26 (1991); Rodriguez de Quijas v. Shearson/American Express, Inc., 490 U.S. 477, 109 S.Ct. 1917, 104 L.Ed.2d 526 (1989); Mitsubishi Motors Corp. v. Soler Chrysler-Plymouth, Inc., 473 U.S. 614 (1985) (antitrust).

[19] The Federal Arbitration Act, 9 U.S.C.A. § 2, provides that "arbitration agreements shall be valid, irrevocable, and enforceable, save upon such grounds as exist at law or in equity for the revocation of any contract."

defenses under state law to a breach of contract suit—such as failure of meeting of the minds, lack of consideration, mistake, duress and coercion, fraud, and unconscionability—may be raised in challenging the enforcement of an arbitration clause.[20] Unconscionability has become a principal ground for challenging arbitration clauses in adhesion contracts as banks, credit card issuers, service industries, product manufacturers, employers, and the health care industry have increasingly added such clauses to their contracts. The California Supreme Court, for example, held that to overcome a challenge of unconscionability, an arbitration clause must: 1) allow all remedies available in court 2) provide for adequate discovery 3) require a written arbitration award and judicial review, and 4) not require the claimant to pay the arbitration costs.[21] Other courts differ as to the exact standards necessary to avoid unconscionability, and, as a result, there is a wide variety in court outcomes.

CLASS ACTION BANS IN ARBITRATION CLAUSES

One of the most controversial issues concerning arbitration is the inclusion in an arbitration clause of a prohibition on class actions or class treatment. The issue is whether, when there is an arbitration clause in a contract, the arbitration can be conducted on behalf of a class of persons similarly situated, or must be limited to the individual who is a party to the contract and arbitration clause. Prohibitions on class treatment often arise in adhesion contracts involving consumers, employees, or others who lack the bargaining power to question the clause. Some courts have found such a ban to be unconscionable by preventing those with small dollar claims from seeking a class action in order to obtain a lawyer and prosecute their claims effectively. Other courts disagreed.[22]

The Supreme Court Weighs in: AnimalFeeds, Concepcion, and Italian Colors

The Supreme Court, in a trilogy of decisions over a three-year period, severely curtailed challenges to class-action waivers in arbitration clauses.

In 2010, in Stolt-Nielsen S.A. v. AnimalFeeds International Corp.,[23] the Supreme Court addressed whether parties could be compelled to arbitrate on a class-wide basis where an arbitration provision was silent on the issue. The opinion by Justice Alito reflected the triumph of the contract and of the parties' intent as central to arbitration law: "Whether enforcing an agreement to arbitrate or construing an arbitration clause," it stated, "courts and arbitrators must 'give effect to the contractual rights

---

[20] See Rau, Sherman & Peppet, Processes of Dispute Resolution: The Role of Lawyers 695–712 (3d ed. 2002).

[21] Armendariz v. Foundation Health Psychcare Services, Inc., 6 P.3d 669 (Cal.2000).

[22] Zawikowski v. Beneficial Nat. Bank, 1999 WL 35304, at *1 (N.D. Ill. 1999) ("nothing prevents the Plaintiffs from contracting away their right to a class action").

[23] 559 U.S. 662 (2010).

and expectations of the parties.'" The Court held that "a party may not be compelled under the FAA to submit to class arbitration unless there is a contractual basis for concluding that the party agreed to do so." This was a reversal of what seemed to many to be the Court's prior view that allowed class arbitration when the contract was silent on the matter, if the arbitrator so ordered.

Justice Alito's opinion reflects a low regard for class arbitration. Noting the "commercial stakes" of class arbitration, he cited "fundamental changes" that are brought about by a shift from bilateral arbitrations to class arbitration. These included the absence of privacy and confidentiality protections, adjudication of the rights of absent parties, a high-value stakes in the case before the Court (a maritime contract for the shipment of goods and not the typical low value consumer action), and resolution of "many disputes between hundreds or perhaps even thousands of parties." Describing the benefits of arbitration as lower costs, greater efficiency and speed, as well as expert adjudicators, Justice Alito concluded that "the relative benefits of class-action arbitration are much less assured, given reason to doubt the parties' mutual consent to resolve disputes through class-wide arbitration."

The contrast in attitude toward class actions in Justice Ginsburg's dissent is striking: "When adjudication is costly and individual claims are no more than modest in size, class proceedings may be 'the thing,' i.e., without them, potential claimants will have little, if any, incentive to seek vindication of their rights." The usual justification for class actions—access to the courts where individual litigation or arbitration is too expensive or burdensome and as a deterrent to wrongful conduct by defendants—would also apply to class arbitrations.

Although *AnimalFeeds* made clear that class arbitration could not be imposed absent agreement by the parties, it did not decide whether express prohibitions on class treatment in an arbitration agreement would be allowed to stand against a challenge of unconscionability under state law. The Court turned to that question in AT&T Mobility LLC v. Concepcion.[24] In a 5–4 decision written by Justice Scalia, it held that the FAA preempted the California precedents that class treatment waivers are unconscionable. Recognizing that the "saving" clause in section 2 of the FAA preserves applicable state contract defenses, Justice Scalia nevertheless found "nothing in it [that] suggests an intent to preserve state-law rules that stand as an obstacle to the accomplishment of the FAA's objectives." Because the FAA embodies a strong policy in favor of arbitration, state public policies that disfavor arbitration cannot supplant the parties' agreed-upon terms for arbitration. *Concepcion* reiterated the dim view of class arbitration expressed in *AnimalFeeds*. It viewed class arbitration as sacrificing the advantages of informality, making the process slower and

---

[24] 563 U.S. 333 (2012).

more costly, and requiring all the procedural formalities attendant to class actions. In addition, it increases the risk for defendants from liability for an individual claim to that of thousands of aggregated cases, with the absence of multilayered review, making it "more likely that errors will go uncorrected."

Justice Breyer, dissenting, found class arbitration to be "consistent with the use of arbitration" and "well known in California and followed elsewhere." Class arbitrations had been held satisfactorily in California for twenty years.[25] He noted: "When Congress enacted the [FAA], arbitration procedures had not yet been fully developed," and Congress "may well have thought that arbitration would be used primarily where merchants sought to resolve disputes of fact, not law, under the customs of their industries, where the parties possessed roughly equivalent bargaining power." By requiring equivalent bargaining power, the California rule is "consistent with, and indeed may help to further, the objectives that Congress had in mind."

Addressing the dissent's concern that small-dollar claims would not be prosecuted without the possibility of class arbitration, the majority opinion pointed to a number of "consumer-friendly" provisions in the arbitration agreement before the Court. For example, AT&T promised to pay claimants a minimum of $7,500 and twice their attorneys' fees if they obtained an arbitration award greater than AT&T's last settlement offer.[26]

American Express Co. v. Italian Colors Restaurant,[27] was a suit by merchants alleging antitrust violations. They had entered into an agreement with American Express to accept its credit cards that forbade class, as opposed to individual, suits against it. The Court addressed the question whether the arbitration clause prohibiting class action suits was enforceable, even though it would compel arbitration of federal statutory antitrust claims.

The opinion, by Justice Scalia for the 5–3 majority, held that the prohibitively high cost of arbitration is not a sufficient reason for a court to overrule an arbitration clause that forbids class action suits. Federal law does not guarantee that a claim will be resolved affordably. The fact that it can be more expensive to litigate individual arbitrations than they are

---

[25] Southland Corp. v. Keating, 465 U.S. 1, 10 (1984), found a California law that denied enforcement of arbitration clauses in suits by franchisees was preempted by the FAA, but remanded so the arbitration could proceed.

[26] The Ninth Circuit, whose decision striking down the class waiver was reversed by the Supreme Court, saw little benefit in these provisions: "The $7,500 premium payment is available only if AT&T does not make a settlement offer to the aggrieved customer in a sum equal to or higher than is ultimately awarded in arbitration, and before an arbitrator is selected. This means that if a customer files for arbitration against AT&T, predictably AT&T will simply pay the face value of the claim before the selection of an arbitrator to avoid potentially paying $7,500. Thus, the maximum gain to a consumer for the hassle of arbitrating a $30.22 dispute is still just $30.22."

[27] 570 U.S. 228 (2013).

worth does not negate the right to pursue a statutory remedy. Therefore, it found no exception to the Federal Arbitration Act can be applied.

Justice Kagan wrote a dissent that argued that the purpose of the FAA is to resolve disputes and facilitate compensation of injuries. By barring any means of sharing or shrinking of arbitration costs, the arbitration clause in this form of contract functioned to confer immunity from potentially meritorious federal claims, which runs counter to the purpose of the FAA. The contract also violated the Sherman Act by depriving parties of a chance to challenge allegedly monopolistic conduct. Justices Ginsburg and Breyer joined in the dissent (Justice Sotomayor did not participate in the decision).

The spectacular growth in the use of arbitration in recent years has led to calls for revising the Federal Arbitration Act and the various state arbitration acts. A revised Uniform Arbitration Act, adopted in ten states by the end of 2004, made changes in such procedures as the availability of discovery (making arbitration more like litigation), remedies such as attorneys' fees and punitive damages, and disclosure requirements by arbitrators. Consumer groups have also given support to federal legislation that would confine arbitration to more traditional business-type transactions. The Arbitration Fairness Act of 2007 would have prohibited pre-dispute arbitration clauses in all consumer, employment, medical, securities, and franchise contracts.[28] A number of bills designed to overturn *AnimalFeeds* and *Concepcion* have been filed in Congress.

It appears that binding arbitration is becoming a primary mode of dispute resolution for many contractual disputes in our society. Lawyers are likely to find in the future that a larger part of their litigation practices involves arbitration, requiring them to adapt to different procedures and decision-makers than exist in a jury trial. At the same time, there seems to be some adaptation of both trial and arbitration procedures that bring them closer together. Arbitrators are increasingly ordering discovery and holding pre-arbitration hearings to resolve case management issues. On the litigation side, judges are increasingly limiting the scope of oral testimony and requiring expert testimony to be presented in affidavit form, which is closer to arbitration practice. Significant differences, however, remain in the respective remedies provided by litigation and arbitration. A court, whether acting on its own in a bench trial or instructing the jury in a jury trial, is limited by what the law of remedies provides and may be reversed if it strays from those standards. An arbitrator possesses greater flexibility of remedy to achieve the essential purposes of the contract and can only be overturned under the limited court review for gross misconduct. This has its good side (in allowing greater flexibility to achieve raw justice)

---

[28] S. 1782 (110th Cong. 1st Sess. 2007); H.R. 3010 (110th Cong., 1st Sess. 2007).

and its bad side (in the often-made charge that arbitrators tend to "split the difference" in violation of the contract terms).

NOTES AND QUESTIONS

1. Several large businesses introduced arbitration provisions after *Concepcion*. However, Microsoft Corp. eliminated a requirement that employees pursue sexual harassment and gender bias claims through arbitration instead of in court, after revelations this year of improper behavior across technology, entertainment and other industries. Microsoft also endorsed a bill introduced by Democratic Senator Kirsten Gillibrand and Republican Senator Lindsey Graham that would prevent companies from contractually requiring employees to settle these kinds of cases behind closed doors. Jing Cao, Microsoft Eliminates Arbitration in Sexual Harassment Cases, 18 Class (Bloomberg) 1177 (2017).

2. The impact of the three Supreme Court cases on plaintiffs attempting to avoid class action waivers in arbitration clauses has enhanced the ability of companies to contract out of class procedures and potentially reduced the availability of the class-action device. These cases have generally been applied to prevent customers, employees, clients and other constituents of corporate America from utilizing class actions where a contract only provides for individual arbitration. The cases have been viewed as rejecting the "effective vindication" doctrine by which some lower courts and state courts had refused to enforce class action bans in arbitration clauses However, the Tenth Circuit affirmed its use as a defense to a motion to compel arbitration in Nesbitt v. FCNH, Inc., 811 F.3d 371 (10th Cir. 2016), class action plaintiffs in a Fair Labor Standards Act case defeated a motion to compel individual arbitrations by asserting that under the AAA Commercial Rules, each plaintiff would have to pay between \$2,300 and \$12,500 in arbitrator fees and could not recover attorneys' fee.

3. The Supreme Court heard oral argument in October 2017 on an issue that had embroiled the NLRB and circuit courts for some time: "Whether arbitration agreements with individual employees that bar them from pursuing work-related claims on a collective or class basis in any forum are prohibited as an unfair labor practice under 29 U.S.C. § 158(a)(1), because they limit the employees' right under the National Labor Relations Act to engage in "concerted activities" in pursuit of their "mutual aid or protection," 29 U.S.C. § 157, and are therefore unenforceable under the savings clause of the Federal Arbitration Act, 9 U.S.C. § 2." National Labor Relations Board v. Murphy Oil of America, 808 F.3d 1013 (5th Cir. 2015) (5th Circuit 2017). See also D.R. Horton, Inc. v. NLRB, 737 F.3d 344 (5th Cir. 2013) (the NLRA does not "override" the FAA and the "use of class action procedures * * * is not a substantive right" under Section 157).

CHAPTER 3

DESCRIBING AND DEFINING
THE DISPUTE

■ ■ ■

A central function of a system of civil procedure is to describe and define the dispute between the parties. It is preferable if this can be accomplished early in the litigation because the nature of the dispute affects both the substantive law that will be applied to the facts and the procedural course to be taken. It is not always possible, however, to define a dispute comprehensively from the start. All the facts may not yet be known, and the exact structure of the suit may not take shape until various moves are made by each side. Thus the objective of assuring certainty through early definition of disputes, and perhaps of deciding disputes early in the litigation, can clash with the objective of allowing flexibility to take account of unforeseen developments. We will examine in this chapter the procedural devices that seek to achieve early definition of disputes and to weed out groundless claims, while attempting to retain flexibility and fairness.

A. THE HISTORICAL EVOLUTION OF PLEADING

Under English common law, the issues in a suit were defined by pleadings. The word *pleading* derives from the practice that developed after the Norman Conquest (1066) by which persons filed *pleas* in the emerging royal courts for a remedy against one who had wronged them. The pleas were originally addressed only to violations of the king's peace, but in course of time, as the historian Maitland has written, "the king's peace devours all other peaces."[1] The royal courts thus came to accept a wide range of disputes between private individuals that did not directly affect the monarch. The courts responded by issuing a *writ*—an order to the sheriff to bring the person complained of before the judge on a certain day to answer the allegations. These writs gradually became standardized as it became established that courts would hear particular kinds of complaints.[2]

---

[1]   F. Maitland, The Constitutional History of England 107 (1908).

[2]   By the 14th century, the royal courts included the King's (Queen's) Bench for criminal cases, Common Pleas for civil cases, Exchequer for matters involving royal revenues, and Chancery for equitable actions.

1. THE FORMS OF ACTION

The standardization of writs resulted in the development of *forms of action* as each writ came to embody an action which included both the substantive theory of recovery and the procedures for obtaining a remedy. A suit had to be cast in terms of the "procedural pigeon-hole" of one of the forms of action which a court would recognize.[3] The forms of action had different procedures as to such matters as the form of bond required to avoid arrest or seizure of goods and the type of trial. The allegations that had to be made for each form were stylized and sometimes fictional. For example, the writ of ejectment could only be used by a freeholder to recover land wrongfully withheld by alleging the fiction that the plaintiff had demised the land to a fictional John Doe, who was ejected, and then bringing the action in John Doe's name. The writ of trover, a means of recovering goods which had been lost, could be used for any conversion of property by alleging the fiction that the property had been lost and that the defendant had found it but refused to return it.[4]

Over the years, the number and complexity of the forms of action grew. By the early 19th century, there were 60 forms of action just dealing with real property and dozens more for personal actions. The forms of action had also leaped the ocean and were firmly ensconced in pleading practices in many American states. Among the commonly used forms of personal actions (the names of which we sometimes still find in American common law and statutes) were:

Trespass—An action for damages for unlawful injury to plaintiff's person, property, or rights. It was necessary that the act be done with force and that the injury be immediate as opposed to consequential. The modern notion of trespass as an unlawful entry upon the plaintiff's land was only one of a number of applications of this form of action.

Trespass on the Case (or simply *Case*)—An action that developed for the situation in which the injury did not result from direct or immediate force, but as an indirect consequence of defendant's act. It is hard for us today, used to the notion of "negligence," to fully appreciate the conceptual development that was required for common law courts to move from allowing recovery for injuries resulting from direct force under trespass (as in hitting someone with a stick) to allowing recovery for the injuries resulting from indirect action under *case* (as in leaving a log on the highway where a passer-by is injured by driving over it).

---

[3] F. Maitland, The Forms of Action at Common Law 3 (1909, reprinted 1971). See also Milsom, Historical Foundations of the Common Law 28–40 (1969).

[4] Cooper v. Chitty, 97 Eng.Rep. 166, 172 (K.B. 1756) ("in form it is a fiction"). For a demonstration of the useful role that fictions can serve in the law, see L. Fuller, Legal Fictions (1967).

Covenant—An action for damages for breach of a contract under seal. Other contract-remedy forms of action obviously had to develop to cover the much more common situation of contracts not under seal.

Debt—An action to recover a specific sum of money, or a claim that could be reduced to a certainty, due under an express agreement. Debt, however, carried with it various unattractive procedural features (such as the right to invoke "wager of law"[5]). This form has only a vague relationship to what we today loosely refer to as a "debt."

Assumpsit—An action for damages for non-performance of a parol contract not under seal. It was based on the premise that the defendant had undertaken to do something and had injured the plaintiff in his person or goods by failing to perform. *Special Assumpsit* ultimately developed as a remedy for breach of promise even if the breach had no element of misfeasance but was simply a failure to perform. Pleaders developed "common counts" as simplified forms for various situations. *General Assumpsit*, which did not arise until the 18th century, was based on the sophisticated concept that an implied promise arises from unjust enrichment. It allowed recovery on contracts implied in fact even though all the elements of a contract claim could not be satisfied.

Detinue—An action to recover personal chattels in specie from one who acquired them lawfully, but retained them without right (for example, a bailment). An ancient writ, it had procedural disadvantages (such as trial by wager of law) that led to the development of other actions for recovery of property.

Replevin—An action to recover possession of goods unlawfully taken. The remedy was recovery of the goods in specie, and thus if the goods had been injured or destroyed, a different action that provided damages would be necessary. Cf. Fuentes v. Shevin, supra p. 31.

Trover—An action, originally a sub-category of case, for damages against a defendant who had found another's goods and wrongfully converted them. It was broadened to provide a remedy for any wrongful interference with or detention of another's goods by fictionalizing the allegation that the goods had been lost and then found.

2.   COMMON LAW PLEADING

For a long time, pleading in the English courts was oral, but gradually oral pleas were replaced by written ones. The plaintiff initiated suit and caused a writ to issue by invoking an appropriate form of action in a *declaration*. This was the beginning of a complicated process of pleading

---

[5]   Wager of law was an ancient procedure whereby the defendant could disprove a claim by taking an oath in open court that he did not owe the debt and bring with him eleven neighbors (called "compurgators") who would swear that they believed he told the truth. It is considered by some to be a forerunner of the jury trial.

designed to reduce the dispute to a single issue. The defendant had three choices in responding (called *pleas*). Defendant could file a plea in bar that either denied one or more of the essential allegations (a *traverse*) or admitted them, but stated that some legal right, such as being a minor, protected against liability for the conduct (*confession and avoidance*). Second, defendant could file a *dilatory plea* challenging the jurisdiction of the court (plea to jurisdiction) or alleging some procedural defect in the structure of the suit, such as improper joinder of parties or lack of capacity (*plea in abatement*). Third, defendant could file a *demurrer*, which claimed that even if the facts were as stated by the plaintiff, they did not state a claim for which the law provided a remedy (*general demurrer*) or that there were defects in the form of the pleading (*special demurrer*).

The defendant's pleas did not generally end the pleading process at common law. The plaintiff could file a *replication* designed to join issue with the defendant's pleas, for example, by either traversing the defendant's confession and avoidance or further confessing and avoiding it. Then the defendant could file a *rejoinder*, joining issue with any issues raised by the replication which had not been specifically responded to. Further pleadings, termed *surrejoinder*, *rebutter*, and *surrebutter*, were available to insure that issue was joined as to all matters.

All this made for an arduous process which, by the 19th century, had taken on an extraordinary degree of complexity in the belief that precision could be achieved in an almost scientific manner. The result was that pleading was the central focus of law suits, and cases were often won or lost on the pleading skills of the attorneys. "Half the labor of the bar," wrote a commentator about the persistence of common law pleading practices in the U.S. in the 19th century, "was bestowed upon questions of pleading, and the lawyer who mistook his form of action sometimes lost his case from that cause alone. The merits of the case were often wholly lost sight of and never brought to trial."[6]

This frustration of the merits resulted in large measure from two features of the system. First, the single issue idea mentioned above meant that once the parties were "at issue" the court might decide the case in favor of the winner on that issue. If defendant filed a general demurrer, for example, that might put the case at issue; if the demurrer were not sustained plaintiff could win the case because the defendant chose the wrong point to fight. Second, the pigeon-hole strictness of the forms of action could prevent relief for a plaintiff clearly entitled to relief who had chosen the wrong writ due to uncertainty about what the evidence would show. For example, if plaintiff chose to proceed under *case* (claiming negligence), defendant's evidence that the injury was inflicted on purpose

---

[6] Eastman, Chief Justice Charles Doe, 9 Green Bag 245, 246 (1897). Charles Doe (not to be confused with the fictitious John Doe) was an ardent reformer of procedures on pragmatic grounds who served on the New Hampshire Supreme Court in the 19th century.

(and therefore that the proper form of action was *trespass*) could defeat the action on the case. Plaintiff would then have to start over in trespass (if the statute of limitations had not run); there was no opportunity to switch writs in a given proceeding or to combine them in one proceeding.

The forms of action and rules of pleading just described applied to law, as opposed to equity, courts. A grievance was brought to a court of equity by filing a *bill* which contained a narrative section describing the complaint, a charging section that rebutted anticipated defenses, and an interrogative section designed to demonstrate that relief was equitable and fair. Recall the discussion of the emergence of equity in Chapter 2, supra pp. 85–88. The defendant had to file a detailed reply, but further pleadings were unnecessary. One of the procedures available at equity was the *bill of discovery* which is the forerunner of our modern discovery procedures. Equity pleading procedures were far less technical than those at law, but over the years they took on their own refinements and complexities.

3. THE AMERICAN REFORM EXPERIENCE

Reform and simplification of common-law pleading began in England in the 1820s and were largely completed by 1873 with the passage of the Judicature Act. The American colonies, and then the states, varied in the degree of acceptance of the English model. Over the years, conflicting movements—democratic impulses directed at diminishing the role of lawyers and legalisms versus attempts to impose more professionalism and procedural regularity on courts—had their impact on American pleading rules.

By the 1830s the reforms taking place in England had spread to the United States. The most important American attack on the common-law pleading system was the development of "code pleading" with the passage of the Code of Civil Procedure in New York in 1848. Often referred to as the "Field Code" for David Dudley Field (1805–94), the renowned New York practitioner who spearheaded the reform effort, it abolished the existing forms of action and mandated that there be "but one form of action." The complaint only had to contain "a statement of the facts constituting the cause of action, in ordinary and concise language, without repetition, and in such a manner as to enable a person of common understanding to know what is intended." The answer should contain "a specific denial of each material allegation of the complaint controverted by the defendant" and "a plain and concise statement of any new matter constituting a defense or set-off without unnecessary repetition." Pleadings were limited to complaint, answer, reply, and demurrers.

The Field Code ultimately served as the model for some half of the states, primarily in the west, and its impact on the Federal Rules of Civil Procedure was considerable. Today some states, notably New York and California, still retain features of code pleading. The code played an important role in accustoming courts and attorneys to non-technical "fact pleading." But pleading problems remained. In part this was because human institutions have a way of developing beyond the intentions of their creators, but it also reflected some intractable difficulties with refining pleading practice that have not disappeared under the Federal Rules. Hence we begin with a code pleading case.

GILLISPIE V. GOODYEAR SERVICE STORES

Supreme Court of North Carolina, 1963
128 S.E.2d 762

BOBBITT, J.

The hearing below was on demurrers to the complaint.

Plaintiff alleges she and each of the four individual defendants are citizens and residents of Alamance County, North Carolina; that defendant Goodyear Tire & Rubber Company is a corporation doing business in North Carolina and having a place of business and store in Burlington, North Carolina; and that Goodyear Service Stores is a division of defendant Goodyear Tire & Rubber Company.

The remaining allegations of the complaint and the prayer for relief are as follows:

"4. On or about May 5, 1959, and May 6, 1959, the defendants, without cause or just excuse and maliciously came upon and trespassed upon the premises occupied by the plaintiff as a residence, and by the use of harsh and threatening language and physical force directed against the plaintiff assaulted the plaintiff and placed her in great fear, and humiliated and embarrassed her by subjecting her to public scorn and ridicule, and caused her to be seized and exhibited to the public as a prisoner, and to be confined in a public jail, all to her great humiliation, embarrassment and harm.

"5. By reason of the defendants' malicious and intentional assault against and humiliation of the plaintiff, the plaintiff was and has been damaged and injured in the amount of $25,000.00.

"6. The acts of the defendants as aforesaid were deliberate, malicious, and with the deliberate intention of harming the plaintiff, and the plaintiff is entitled to recover her actual damages as well as punitive damages from the defendants and each of them.

"THEREFORE, the plaintiff prays that she have and recover of the defendants the sum of $25,000.00 as damages and $10,000.00 in addition thereto as punitive damages, and that she have such other and further relief as may be just and proper."

[The trial court sustained defendants' demurrers. Plaintiff appealed.]

* * *

The judgments now under consideration do not specify the ground on which the demurrers were sustained. However, the fact the court did not dismiss the action but granted plaintiff leave to file an amended complaint indicates the court sustained the demurrers on the ground the complaint did not state facts sufficient to constitute a cause of action. * * *

Does the complaint state *facts* sufficient to constitute *any* cause of action?

A complaint must contain "(a) plain and concise statement of the facts constituting a cause of action. . . ." G.S. § 1–122. "The cardinal requirement of this statute . . . is that the facts constituting a cause of action, rather than the conclusions of the pleader, must be set out in the complaint, so as to disclose the issuable facts determinative of the plaintiff's right to relief." Shives v. Sample, 79 S.E.2d 193. The cause of action consists of the facts alleged. The statutory requirement is that a complaint must allege the material, essential and ultimate facts upon which plaintiff's right of action is based. "The law is presumed to be known, but the facts to which the law is to be applied are not known until properly presented by the pleading and established by evidence." McIntosh, North Carolina Practice and Procedure, § 379.

The facts alleged, but not the pleader's legal conclusions, are deemed admitted when the sufficiency of the complaint is tested by demurrer. "Where the complaint merely alleges conclusions and not facts, it fails to state a cause of action and is demurrable. G.S. § 1–127(6)." However, it is well settled that a complaint must be fatally defective before it will be rejected as insufficient, and "if in any portion of it or to any extent it presents *facts* sufficient to constitute a cause of action the pleading will stand."

When a complaint alleges defendant is indebted to plaintiff in a certain amount and such debt is due, but does not allege in what manner or for what cause defendant became indebted to plaintiff, it is demurrable for failure to state facts sufficient to constitute a cause of action.

"The liability for tort grows out of the violation of some legal duty by the defendant, not arising out of contract, and the complaint should state facts sufficient to show such legal duty and its violation, resulting in injury to the plaintiff. What these facts are must depend upon the elements which go to make up the particular tort complained of, under the substantive law." McIntosh, North Carolina Practice and Procedure, § 388.

"In an action or defense based upon negligence, it is not sufficient to allege the mere happening of an event of an injurious nature and call it negligence on the part of the party sought to be charged. This is necessarily so because negligence is not a fact in itself, but is the legal result of certain facts. Therefore, the facts which constitute the negligence charged and also the facts which establish such negligence as the proximate cause, or as one of the proximate causes, of the injury must be alleged." Shives v. Sample, supra.

* * *

As stated by Barnhill, J., in Parker v. White, 75 S.E.2d 615, 617: "The competency of evidence, the form of the issues, and the charge of the court are all controlled in very large measure by the nature of the cause of action alleged by plaintiff. Hence, the trial judge, as well as the defendant, must know the exact right plaintiff seeks to assert or the legal wrong for which he seeks redress before there can be any intelligent trial under the rules of procedure which govern our system of jurisprudence."

Plaintiff alleges, in a single sentence, that defendant, "without cause or just excuse and maliciously," trespassed upon premises occupied by her as a residence, assaulted her and caused her to be seized and confined as a prisoner. The complaint states no facts upon which these legal conclusions may be predicated. Plaintiff's allegations do not disclose *what* occurred, *when* it occurred, *where* it occurred, *who* did what, the relationships between defendants and plaintiff or of defendants *inter se*, or any other factual data that might identify the occasion or describe the circumstances of the alleged wrongful conduct of defendants.

A plaintiff must make out his case *secundum allegata*. There can be no recovery except on the case made by his pleadings. Here, there is no factual basis to which the court could apply the law. When considered in the light most favorable to plaintiff, this complaint, in our opinion, falls short of minimum requirements.

In Stivers v. Baker, 9 S.W. 491, it was held that a petition alleging the defendant unlawfully assaulted the plaintiff, thereby putting him in great fear, but not stating how the assault was made, stated a mere conclusion of law and was demurrable as not stating facts constituting a cause of action as required by the Kentucky statute. The court, in opinion by Holt, J., points out that a statement of the facts constituting a cause of action "is not only necessary to enable the opposite party to form an issue, and to inform him of what his adversary intends to prove, but to enable the court to declare the law upon the facts stated. It cannot do so if a mere legal conclusion is stated. The term 'assault' has a legal meaning; as much so as the word 'trespass.'" In Shapiro v. Michelson, 47 S.W. 746, the Court of Civil Appeals of Texas, in opinion by Fisher, C.J., said: "The use of the expression 'assaulted' is not the averment of a fact, but is simply a statement which expresses the conclusion of the pleader."

The judgments sustaining the demurrers are affirmed on the ground the complaint does not state facts sufficient to constitute any cause of action. It would seem appropriate that plaintiff, in accordance with leave granted in the judgments from which she appealed, now file an amended complaint and therein allege the facts upon which she bases her right to recover.

NOTES AND QUESTIONS

1.   Besides giving plaintiff's lawyer a lesson in pleading, why should the court be concerned with the content of the complaint? One can discern at least three general purposes for pleading requirements:

(a)   *Notice to defendant*: It seems intuitively fair that defendant be given notice of what plaintiff is upset about since the suit is likely to impose noncompensable litigation costs on defendant. But why insist that this be in the complaint? Shouldn't there be better ways for defendant to find out what plaintiff claims occurred? (Reconsider this concern in connection with discovery in Chapter 5.) Does defendant need to know the details of plaintiff's claim at the outset? (Reconsider this concern in connection with the materials later in this chapter regarding the answer.)

(b)   *Notice to the court*: A related objective is giving the court guidelines for determining whether discovery sought, or evidence offered at trial, is relevant to the case. Should we depend on the pleadings to accomplish this objective?

(c)   *Deciding the merits*: As the court suggests in *Gillispie*, the complaint may supply the "factual basis to which the court could apply the law." That legal analysis may sometimes show that plaintiff has no right to relief against defendant, even on the complaint's version of the facts, permitting the termination of the suit at this early stage. Would encouraging early merits decisions be consistent with the objections that the framers of the Codes had to the common-law pleading system?

2.   With regard to the third objective of pleadings, the court will ask whether the plaintiff has adequately pled the elements of the claim, which are defined by the substantive law. For purposes of assessing plaintiff's complaint in *Gillispie*, you may wish to refer to the following summaries of the elements of various possible claims from the Restatement (Second) of Torts:

Assault: "An actor is subject to liability to another for assault if (a) he acts intending to cause a harmful or offensive contact with the person of the other or a third person, or an imminent apprehension of such a contact, and (b) the other is thereby put in such imminent apprehension." (Restatement § 21(1).)

False arrest or imprisonment: "An actor is subject to liability to another for false imprisonment if (a) he acts intending to confine the other or a third person within boundaries fixed by the actor, and (b) his act directly or indirectly results in such a confinement of the other, and (c) the other is conscious of the confinement or is harmed by it." (Restatement § 35(1).)

Intentional infliction of emotional distress: "One who by extreme and outrageous conduct intentionally or recklessly causes severe emotional distress to another is subject to liability for such emotional distress." (Restatement § 46(1).)

Trespass to land: "One is subject to liability to another for trespass, irrespective of whether he thereby causes harm to any legally protected interest of the other, if he intentionally (a) enters land in the possession of the other, or (b) remains on the land." (Restatement § 158.)

In *Gillispie*, the court states that the complaint should stand if it presents facts sufficient to constitute any cause of action. Assuming that the law of North Carolina was the same as the Restatement of Torts provisions above, are there facts in the complaint sufficient to constitute any of those causes of action? Is plaintiff's problem one of the substance or the form of her allegations? Cf. Fed.R.Civ.P. 10(b). Using the allegations given, could you redraft the complaint to state a claim on one of the grounds enumerated above?

3.   The court criticizes the complaint for relying on conclusions rather than facts. What is wrong with conclusions? The court suggests, for example, that it would not be sufficient for a plaintiff merely to allege that defendant is indebted to him in a certain amount. Why not? Does the same reasoning apply to plaintiff's complaint in *Gillispie*?

4.   In general, code pleading states came to insist, as does the court in *Gillispie*, on "ultimate facts." These ultimate facts were derived from the elements of the substantive claim and were distinguished from unacceptable allegations characterized as "conclusions," on the one hand, and "mere evidence," on the other. See Cal. Code Civ. Proc. § 431.10(a) (requiring allegations that are "essential to the claim"). How precisely can these categories be applied? For example, was it too conclusory for plaintiff in *Gillispie* to allege that defendants used "harsh and threatening language and physical force"? Should she have repeated the exact words they used and described in detail each physical action taken by defendants? Would it be sufficient for her to allege that one defendant "walked angrily toward plaintiff"? For an argument that the distinctions relied upon by code pleading are ultimately meaningless, see Cook, Statements of Fact in Pleading Under the Codes, 21 Colum.L.Rev. 416 (1921).

5.   In *Gillispie*, the court uses as an example of unduly conclusory allegations a complaint for personal injuries that merely labels defendant's actions negligent because "negligence is not a fact in itself, but is the legal result of certain facts." In an auto collision case, what more should plaintiff have to allege? Would it be sufficient to say that defendant "failed to keep a proper lookout"? Should this specification foreclose inquiry during discovery into whether defendant properly maintained the brakes on his car? If so, would plaintiff be allowed to pursue discovery on maintenance of the car by alleging as well that defendant "failed to maintain his automobile in proper condition"? How is plaintiff to determine which line to pursue before discovery? Do the suggested specifications serve any of the purposes of pleading mentioned in note 1 any better than a simple allegation that defendant negligently injured plaintiff?

Consider how these issues were addressed in Form 9 to the original Federal Rules of Civil Procedure:

Form 9. Complaint for Negligence

1.   Allegation of jurisdiction.

2.   On June 1, 1936, in a public highway called Boylston Street in Boston, Massachusetts, defendant negligently drove a motor vehicle against plaintiff who was then crossing said highway.

3.   As a result, plaintiff was thrown down and had his leg broken and was otherwise injured, was prevented from transacting his business, suffered great pain of body and mind, and incurred expenses for medical attention and hospitalization in the sum of one thousand dollars.

Wherefore plaintiff demands judgment against defendant in the sum of _____ dollars and costs.

As you will see in Swierkiewicz v. Sorema, N.A., infra p. 177, the Supreme Court continued to cite Form 9 into the 21st century as an example of the simplified pleading called for by the Federal Rules. Are there reasons to prefer this simplicity over the fact pleading requirements of the court in *Gillispie*? Consider Thornburg, Detailed Fact Pleading: The Lessons of Scottish Civil Procedure, 36 Int'l Lawyer 1185, 1194 (2002) ("A pleading that a [defendant] was negligent in driving at an excessive rate of speed provides far more significant limits on evidence than does a pleading that a [defendant] drove negligently.").

6.   *Leave to amend*: Even if the complaint is deficient, courts will usually dismiss without prejudice, and grant the plaintiff an opportunity to file an amended complaint before dismissing the suit. In the federal system, it is sometimes said that courts must provide such a chance to replead. E.g., Thinket Ink Info. Res., Inc. v. Sun Microsystems, Inc., 368 F.3d 1053, 1061 (9th Cir.2004) ("Dismissal without leave to amend is improper unless it is clear, upon de novo review, that the complaint could not be saved by any amendment."); compare Bradley v. Val-Mejias, 379 F.3d 892 (10th Cir.2004) (it is proper to deny leave to amend if the amendment would be futile because it would be subject to dismissal). This liberal rule means that the courts will usually treat dismissal on the pleadings as a decision on the merits for purposes of res judicata unless dismissal is without prejudice (and thus not on the merits). See Rinehart v. Locke, infra p. 1188.

7.   What if one of the defendants in *Gillispie* had been in jail on the dates of the incidents referred to in plaintiff's complaint, and that he was therefore demonstrably innocent of plaintiff's charges? Could he base a demurrer on that ground? Could he submit the jailer's affidavit attesting that he was in custody? Ordinarily a defendant was said to admit plaintiff's well-pleaded allegations by demurring, and the court would not consider anything beyond the face of the complaint. On that point, see Fed.R.Civ.P. 12(d). But these rules can be relaxed on occasion:

When ruling on a Rule 12(b)(6) motion to dismiss, if a district court considers evidence outside the pleadings, it must normally convert the 12(b)(6) motion into a Rule 56 motion for summary judgment, and it must give the nonmoving party an opportunity to respond. A court may, however, consider certain materials— documents attached to the complaint, documents incorporated by reference in the complaint, or matters of judicial notice—without converting the motion to dismiss into a motion for summary judgment. * * *

Certain written instruments attached to pleadings may be considered part of the pleading. See Fed.R.Civ.P. 10(c). Even if a document is not attached to a complaint, it may be incorporated by reference into a complaint if the plaintiff refers extensively to the document or the document forms the basis of the plaintiff's claim. The defendant may offer such a document, and the district court may treat such a document as part of the complaint, and thus assume that its contents are true for purposes of a motion to dismiss under Rule 12(b)(6). The doctrine of incorporation by reference may apply, for example, when a plaintiff's claim about insurance coverage is based on the contents of a coverage plan, or when a plaintiff's claim about stock fraud is based on the contents of SEC filings.

United States v. Ritchie, 342 F.3d 903, 907–08 (9th Cir.2003); see also Tellabs, Inc. v. Makor Issues & Rights, Ltd., 551 U.S. 308 (2007) (infra p. 161) (referring to "other sources courts ordinarily examine when ruling on Rule 12(b)(6) motions, in particular, documents incorporated into the complaint by reference, and matters of which a court may take judicial notice"); Bogie v. Rosenberg, 705 F.3d 603, 609 (7th Cir.2013) ("When an exhibit incontrovertibly contradicts the allegations in the complaint, the exhibit ordinarily controls, even when considering a motion to dismiss."). Compare Hoefling v. City of Miami, 811 F.3d 1271 (11th Cir. 2016) (holding that it was error to consider, on a motion to dismiss, exhibits plaintiff had attached to an earlier complaint but not to the amended complaint before the court because plaintiff had disavowed them as untrue). See generally, Comment, Pleading in Technicolor: When Can Litigants Incorporate Audiovisual Works Into Their Complaints?, 80 U.Chi.L.Rev. 1269 (2013).

B. DESCRIBING AND TESTING THE PLAINTIFF'S CLAIM

The Federal Rules of Civil Procedure were drafted by a committee headed by Charles Clark, then Dean of Yale Law School. They installed what has been described as the "liberal ethos," in which the preferred disposition of cases is on the merits, by jury trial, after full disclosure through discovery. See Marcus, The Revival of Fact Pleading Under the Federal Rules of Civil Procedure, 86 Colum.L.Rev. 433, 439 (1986). A central ingredient to this shift in focus was reliance on generalized pleading.

To get away from the charged terms "facts" and "cause of action," therefore, Rule 8(a)(2) requires only that the plaintiff provide "a short and plain statement of the claim showing that the pleader is entitled to relief." Moreover, Clark at first favored eliminating pleading motions altogether, but eventually they were retained in Rule 12, including the Rule 12(b)(6) motion to dismiss for "failure to state a claim upon which relief can be granted." Other pleading motions are authorized by Rules 12(c) (motion for judgment on the pleadings), 12(e) (motion for a more definite statement), and 12(f) (motion to strike).

Changing the rules did not change the habits of lawyers and judges, and the old Code pleading attitudes persisted for some time after the rules were adopted in 1938. Clark himself (appointed to the Second Circuit Court of Appeals in 1939) continued to view the Rule 12(b)(6) motion as "a mere formal motion, directed only to the face of the complaint" which too often led to "judicial haste which in the long run makes waste." Dioguardi v. Durning, 139 F.2d 774 (2d Cir.1944). In *Dioguardi*, the court reversed dismissal of an "obviously home drawn" complaint against the Collector of Customs for mishandling imported merchandise because, "however inarticulately they may be stated, the plaintiff has disclosed his claims" and "we do not see how the plaintiff may properly be deprived of his day in court to show what he obviously so firmly believes."

The Supreme Court, meanwhile, observed in 1947 that the Federal Rules "restrict the pleadings to the task of general notice-giving." Hickman v. Taylor, 329 U.S. 495, 501 (1947). But resistance to relaxed pleadings continued. The Judicial Conference of the Ninth Circuit Court of Appeals in 1952 passed a resolution urging that Rule 8(a)(2) be amended to require "a short and plain statement of the claim showing that the pleader is entitled to relief, *which statement shall contain the facts constituting a cause of action.*" See Claim or Cause of Action, 13 F.R.D. 253 (1952). Other lower court judges pressed for more demanding pleadings, at least in some "big" cases, urging that the costs of embarking on such cases without more detailed pleadings were too great. See Dawson, The Place of the Pleading in the Proper Definition of Issues in the "Big Case," 23 F.R.D. 430 (1958). Meanwhile, the rules committee in 1956 rejected calls for changing Rule 8(a)(2).

The Supreme Court weighed in firmly on the side of relaxed pleading in Conley v. Gibson, 355 U.S. 41 (1957). Plaintiffs there were African-American members of a union who alleged that their union maintained two separate locals, one for white members and the other for black members, "for the purpose of affording to plaintiffs a representation inferior and different to that offered to members of the white race." Their particular complaint was that the union had agreed to the "abolition" of 45 jobs formerly held by plaintiffs, and the hiring of white union members to replace them. Plaintiffs claimed that this discriminatory action violated their rights under the federal Railway Labor Act, a hotly debated issue at the time. See Sherwin, The Story of *Conley*: Precedent by Accident, in Civil Procedure Stories 295 (2d ed. 2008). Besides contending that the courts lacked jurisdiction over such claims, defendants also moved to dismiss for failure to state a claim. The Supreme Court rejected defendants' argument that the complaint was insufficient, explaining in what became a famous passage that "we follow, of course, the accepted rule that a complaint should not be dismissed for failure to state a claim unless it appears beyond doubt that the plaintiff can prove no set of facts to support his claim which would entitle him to relief." 355 U.S. at 45. It added (id. at 47–48):

> The respondents also argue that the complaint failed to set forth specific facts to support its general allegations of discrimination and that its dismissal is therefore proper. The decisive answer to this is that the Federal Rules of Civil Procedure do not require a claimant to set out in detail the facts upon which he bases his claim. To the contrary, all the Rules require is a "short and plain statement of the claim" that will give the defendant fair notice of what the plaintiff's claim is and the grounds upon which it rests. The illustrative forms appended to the Rules plainly demonstrate this. Such simplified "notice pleading" is made possible by the liberal opportunity for discovery and the other pretrial procedures established by the Rules to disclose more precisely the basis of both claim and defense and to define more narrowly the disputed facts and issues.

In a footnote, the Court elaborated on the "pretrial procedures" that could disclose more precisely the basis for the claim: "See, e.g., Rule 12(e) (motion for a more definite statement); Rule 12(f) (motion to strike portions of the pleading); Rule 16 (pre-trial procedure and formulation of issues); Rules 26–37 (depositions and discovery); Rule 56 (motion for summary judgment); Rule 15 (right to amend)."

Many took Conley v. Gibson to demonstrate that "notice pleading" was all that Rule 8(a)(2) required, particularly since the Court seemed to say that dismissal was forbidden unless the complaint itself demonstrated that plaintiff could not prove any facts justifying relief. But Rule 8(a)(2) has always said that the short and plain statement must be one "showing that the pleader was entitled to relief." See Hazard, From Whom No Secrets Are Hid, 76 Tex. L. Rev. 1665, 1685 (1998) (asserting that "Conley v. Gibson turned Rule 8 on its head by holding that a claim is insufficient only if the insufficiency appears from the pleading itself"). Was such a strong statement needed to uphold the complaint in *Conley* itself, given the specifics that were included about separate local unions and displacement of African-American workers in favor of white workers? Assuming discrimination by the union was actionable (as the Court held in other parts of the case), what reason would there be to require more specifics to "show that the pleader is entitled to relief" within the meaning of Rule 8(a)(2)? Wouldn't such a pleading requirement threaten to undercut the protection of the anti-discrimination law?

Is there a risk that relaxing pleading requirements too much could undermine protections for *defendants*? As we shall see, modern litigation—particularly broad discovery—sometimes seems to impose a heavy burden on defendants. Should there be some requirement that plaintiffs justify that court-imposed burden? See Elliott, *Twombly* in Context: Why Federal Rule 4(b) is Unconstitutional, 64 Fla.L.Rev. 895 (2012) (arguing that, under Fuentes v. Shevin (supra p. 31), due process requires that the court scrutinize the sufficiency of the complaint before defendant must shoulder the burden of responding to discovery). Compare with *Conley* a suit in which a prospective employee alleged that she applied for a job with defendant and that "I was turned down for this job because of my race and gender." Should that allegation, standing alone, support broad discovery concerning the prospective employer's hiring practices?

In a pair of decisions in 2007 and 2009, the Supreme Court announced that it was "retiring" the portion of Conley v. Gibson that said dismissal is permitted only if "it appears beyond doubt that plaintiff can prove no set of facts to support his claim which entitle him to relief." Among other things, it cited the costs of discovery as a reason. These decisions have provoked widespread controversy, to which we will return later in this chapter. See infra pp. 184–205. As you examine the intervening materials, keep the question whether American pleading has been too lax in the back of your mind.

(2nd Day of Discussion: 9/11/18)

1. THE PROBLEM OF SPECIFICITY

UNITED STATES V. BOARD OF HARBOR COMMISSIONERS

United States District Court, District of Delaware, 1977
73 F.R.D. 460

This sort of complaint could not be brought under old system.

LATCHUM, CHIEF JUDGE.

Defendants The SICO Company ("SICO") and North American Smelting Company ("NASCO") have moved pursuant to Rule 12(e), F.R.Civ.P., for a more definite statement on the ground that the complaint filed against them by the government is so vague and ambiguous that they are unable to frame a responsive pleading as required by Rule 7, F.R.Civ.P. * * *

The complaint, filed by the government on November 23, 1976, alleges in paragraph 11 that

> "The defendants, and each of them, own and operate onshore facilities located on or near Wilmington Marine Terminal from which oil was discharged into the Delaware River during the period June 25 through November 27, 1973, or the defendants, and each of them, took actions which caused such oil to be discharged."

The discharge of oil into navigable waters of the United States is expressly prohibited by the [Federal Water Pollution Control Act], 33 U.S.C. § 1321(b)(3),[a] and the owner or operator of a facility responsible for the discharge of oil in or upon any navigable waterway can be held liable to the United States in the amount of any actual costs incurred for the removal of such oil. 33 U.S.C. § 1321(f)(2).[b]

Defendants SICO and NASCO contend that paragraph 11 is deceptively vague because it fails to specify (1) which defendants are responsible for the alleged discharge of oil, (2) the amount of oil discharged and the removal costs incurred, and (3) the "actions" which are alleged to have caused the discharge. Therefore, before filing a responsive pleading, SICO and NASCO want the government to clarify paragraph 11 by including the foregoing details.

A motion for a more definite statement under Rule 12(e) is ordinarily restricted to situations where a pleading suffers from "unintelligibility rather than the want of detail." 2A Moore's Federal Practice ¶ 12.18[1] at 2389 (2nd ed. 1975). If the requirements of Rule 8 are satisfied and the opposing party is fairly notified of the nature of the claim, a Rule 12(e) motion is inappropriate. Id.; 5 Wright & Miller, Federal Practice & Procedure: Civil § 1376.

In this case, the complaint on its face can be fairly read to charge each of the defendants with owning or operating on-shore facilities which discharged oil into the Delaware River, or that each of the defendants took actions causing such oil to be discharged. This allegation, together with the other averments in the complaint, fairly notifies defendants of the nature of the claim against them. Defendants' motion for a more definite statement is really an effort to "flesh out" the government's case;[2] as such

---

[a] "The discharge of oil or hazardous substances into or upon the navigable waters of the United States * * * is prohibited * * *."—Eds.

[b] "Except where an owner or operator of an onshore facility can prove that a discharge was caused solely by (A) an act of God, (B) an act of war, (C) negligence on the part of the United States Government, or (D) an act or omission of a third party without regard to whether any such act or omission was or was not negligent, or any combination of the foregoing causes, such owner or operator of any such facility from which oil or a hazardous substance is discharged in violation of subsection (b)(3) of this section shall be liable to the United States Government for the actual costs incurred * * * for the removal of such oil or substance by the United States in an amount not to exceed $50,000,000 * * *."—Eds.

[2] Defendants' 12(e) motion might also be viewed as preparatory to a motion to dismiss. The majority of cases, however, have held this to be an improper use of Rule 12(e), which is designed to enable a litigant to answer, not to move for dismissal. See, e.g., 5 Wright & Miller, Federal Practice & Procedure: Civil § 1376 at 746.

it is a misuse of Rule 12(e). The evidentiary information they seek is more properly the subject of discovery under Rules 26 through 36. Accordingly, the SICO and NASCO motions for a more definite statement will be denied.

NOTES AND QUESTIONS

1. Are the allegations in *Board of Harbor Commissioners* sufficient to state a claim for relief? What are the elements that must be pleaded? Examine the statutory sections quoted in footnotes a and b. Should paragraph 11 be considered sufficient? In what way does it show that defendants are liable to plaintiff?

Recall the Supreme Court's attitude toward pleadings in Conley v. Gibson, supra pp. 135–136. Arguably the willingness of the court in the *Harbor Commissioners* case to treat paragraph 11 as sufficient is an example of that attitude. But should this complaint suffice even under Conley v. Gibson? Assume that, besides the two defendants who moved for more definite statements, there were quite a few other defendants. Would you say that paragraph 11 really gives each of them fair notice of the claims against them? Defendants haven't been told which of them is supposed to have discharged the oil or when the discharges were supposed to have occurred within a five-month period, yet the court says that the complaint "fairly notifies defendants of the nature of the claim against them." Is there any incentive for plaintiff to be more informative in the complaint? How much discovery should plaintiff be permitted in regard to these claims? Should plaintiff be allowed carte blanche for discovery regarding any handling of pollutants by any defendant? Assume plaintiff finds out thereby that a given defendant has mishandled another pollutant. Should plaintiff be able to sue about that? What incentive does a relaxed attitude about pleadings create for a plaintiff uncertain who was responsible for a given harm—to sue many or only a few?

2. Why shouldn't the plaintiff have been required to be more specific about *which* defendants discharged the oil, *what amounts* were discharged, and what caused the discharge? Is it because it couldn't reasonably have known these details until it obtained information from the defendants through discovery? Or is it because, even if it knew these details, it need not "flesh out" the essential allegations of the complaint? How do we differentiate between essential allegations and unnecessary fleshing out? In this regard, contrast the analysis in *Board of Harbor Commissioners* with that in *Gillispie*, supra p. 128. Though *Gillispie* was decided under a considerably more stringent pleading standard, might a persuasive argument be made that the complaint in *Gillispie* lacked sufficient detail, even under a "notice pleading" standard? Is it reasonable, under a notice-pleading standard, to expect greater detail in the *Gillispie* complaint than in cases like *Board of Harbor Commissioners* and Conley v. Gibson, supra pp. 135–136? Should the degree of specificity required depend on whether the plaintiff has access to necessary sources of information?

3. Can a complaint be too long, prolix, or detailed so as to run afoul of the "short and plain statement of the claim" requirement of Rule 8(a) or the "simple, concise, and direct" requirement as to averments in Rule 8(d)(1)? See

Belanger v. BNY Mellon Asset Management, LLC, 307 F.R.D. 55 (D.Minn.2015) (holding that a 462-page complaint with 393 exhibits did not comply with Rule 8(a)(2)'s requirement that a complaint be "short and plain"). See also Mendez v. Draham, 182 F.Supp.2d 430 (D.N.J.2002), striking a similarly long complaint and explaining (id. at 433):

> It is this very prolixity that makes the Complaint unclear and incomprehensible. Only through superhuman patience, effort, and insight, could any attorney review the allegations of the Complaint and make paragraph-by-paragraph responses. * * * [I]f [defendants' attorneys] fail to notice that one or two words have been varied, with meaningful import, in one of the Complaint's thousand-odd paragraphs, and inadvertently admit that allegation, they face the risk of malpractice.

But ordinarily a court cannot dismiss a complaint so long as it states some claim for relief, no matter how cumbersome and complicated it may otherwise be. See Hearns v. San Bernardino Police Dep't, 530 F.3d 1124 (9th Cir. 2008) (asserting that "verbosity or length is not a basis by itself for dismissing a complaint under Rule 8(a)"); Davis v. Ruby Foods, Inc., 269 F.3d 818 (7th Cir. 2001) (rejecting dismissal of a cluttered complaint, and holding that the most that could be done would be to strike the surplusage).

4.   The court in *Board of Harbor Commissioners* says that a motion for a more definite statement should not be used to prepare for a motion to dismiss, citing Wright & Miller. Consider the views expressed in the current edition in the same section (5C C. Wright & A. Miller, Federal Practice and Procedure § 1376 at 335–36 (3d ed. 2004)):

> [S]ome cases state that it always is improper to use a Rule 12(e) motion to obtain admissions from the claimant in the hopes of clearing the way for a later Rule 12(b)(6) motion to dismiss. Although judicial statements of this type arguably are consistent with the wording of Rule 12(e), they probably go too far in limiting the availability of the motion. The courts need not completely refrain from using Rule 12(e) as an aid in achieving the summary adjudication of certain cases; it merely is necessary to act with caution to keep its use within proper bounds.
>
> Consequently, there should be a bias against use of the Rule 12(e) motion as a precursor to a Rule 12(b)(6) motion or as a method for seeking out a threshold defense. * * * A request for a more definite statement for either of these purposes should not be granted unless the movant shows that there actually is a substantial threshold question that may be dispositive, such as a critical date. In the absence of some restraint, the motions undoubtedly will be used by litigants as a vehicle for a fishing expedition at the pleading stage.

5.   Could the court in *Board of Harbor Commissioners* have required more details pursuant to Rule 16? In Acuna v. Brown & Root, Inc., 200 F.3d 335 (5th Cir.2000), approximately 1,600 plaintiffs sued over 100 defendants in

related cases before the district court, alleging injuries due to defendants' uranium mining activities. Before allowing discovery, the district court ordered plaintiffs to submit affidavits specifying the injuries or illnesses they suffered due to alleged uranium exposure and the materials or substances causing the injury, and identifying the facility thought to be the source of the uranium materials in question and dates of exposure. After plaintiffs responded with a form affidavit from a single expert that generally identified a series of maladies that can be caused by exposure to uranium and asserted that the expert had reviewed plaintiffs' medical data and come to the conclusion that each of them had received clinically significant doses of radiation, the district court dismissed, and the appellate court affirmed, relying on the authority of the court to manage the cases under Rule 16 (id. at 340):

> The scheduling orders issued below essentially required that information which plaintiffs should have had before filing their claims pursuant to Fed. R. Civ. P. 11(b)(3) [be supplied]. Each plaintiff should have had at least some information regarding the nature of his injuries, the circumstances under which he could have been exposed to harmful substances, and the basis for believing that the named defendants were responsible for his injuries.

6. Most other countries insist on much more detailed and focused pleadings than American courts. For example, consider the following requirements specified in a set of proposed rules for commercial disputes involving litigants from different countries: "The plaintiff must state the facts on which the claim is based, describe the evidence to support those statements, and refer to the legal grounds that support the claim, including foreign law, if applicable." Rule 12.1, ALI/UNIDROIT Principles of Transnational Civil Procedure (2004). The Comment to this rule explains that it "calls for particularity of statement, such as that required in most civil-law and most common-law jurisdictions. In contrast, some American systems, notably those employing 'notice pleading' as under the Federal Rules of Civil Procedure, permit very general allegations." Should American rules move toward the approach of other countries? Consider Thornburg, Detailed Fact Pleading: The Lessons of Scottish Civil Procedure, 36 Int'l Lawyer 1185, 1186 (2002):

> Scotland's pleading requirements serve as the enforcers of an underlying requirement that a plaintiff must have pre-suit access to detailed facts and evidence sufficient to prove a claim or that claim should not be filed. This predictably skews the procedural system in favor of repeat institutional defendants and against individual plaintiffs in ways that can both prevent suits from being filed and prevent persons with legitimate claims from winning at trial.

7. Rule 12(f) authorizes a motion to strike portions of a pleading that are "redundant, immaterial, impertinent, or scandalous." How often might that be useful? See Atraqchi v. Williams, 220 F.R.D. 1 (D.D.C.2004) (court strikes complaint "that contains the wildly immaterial, delusional, and quite possibly pathological allegations that these [pro se] plaintiffs have made about a world-wide religious inquisition, illegal wire-tapping by the U.S. Government

and others to 'homosexualize them and convert them to this cult,' and conspiracy against them by Black people"). Motions to strike are sometimes used to attack an insufficient defense, or a part of a prayer for relief that is not justified by the law (such as a request for punitive damages in a breach of contract case). But see Whittlestone, Inc. v. Handi-Craft Co., 618 F.3d 970 (9th Cir. 2010) (holding that Rule 12(b)(6) motion, rather than Rule 12(f) motion, is the proper method to challenge a request for lost profits on the ground such a claim is barred by the parties' contract).

8.   *The making of a motion*: It seems useful to say a few words about how lawyers make motions, which applies not only to the motions covered by Chapter 3, but all the other motions addressed in this book. Ordinarily the moving party files a notice of motion supported by a memorandum of points and authorities with written legal argument in favor of the motion. If there are factual assertions in the motion, they usually must be supported by affidavits under oath. The opposing party then is allowed to file an opposing memorandum (and possibly affidavits), and in some places the moving party can then file a reply. After the moving papers are submitted, the court usually holds a hearing during which the judge can ask questions and the lawyers can make any clarifying points that seem useful. Sometimes the judge issues a tentative decision before the hearing. The motion will either be decided at the end of the hearing or taken under submission for later decision.

2.   CONSISTENCY AND HONESTY IN PLEADING

A.   Inconsistent Allegations

MCCORMICK V. KOPMANN
Appellate Court of Illinois, Third District, 1959
23 Ill.App.2d 189, 161 N.E.2d 720

REYNOLDS, PRESIDING JUSTICE.

[Lewis McCormick was killed when a truck operated by defendant Kopmann collided with his automobile. McCormick's widow sued Kopmann and the Huls, owners of a tavern where McCormick had drunk beer before the accident. Count I, for damages under the Illinois Wrongful Death Act, alleged that Kopmann negligently drove his truck across the center line and collided with McCormick's automobile and that "the said decedent was in the exercise of ordinary care for his own safety and that of his property." Count IV, brought "in the alternative to Count I," sought damages under the Illinois Dram Shop Act. It alleged that the Huls sold alcoholic beverages to McCormick which rendered him intoxicated and that "as a result of such intoxication" he drove his automobile "in such a manner as to cause a collision" with Kopmann's truck.

Before trial, Kopmann moved to dismiss the complaint on the theory that the contradictions between Count I and Count IV were fatal. The trial court denied his motion. There was conflicting testimony at trial concerning whether McCormick or Kopmann had driven over the center line. There was also testimony that McCormick had drunk several beers at the Huls' tavern. Defendants' motions for directed verdict were denied, and the jury returned a verdict against Kopmann for $15,500 under Count I and for the Huls under Count IV.]

* * *

Kopmann has appealed. His first contention is that the trial court erred in denying his pre-trial motion to dismiss the complaint. Kopmann is correct in asserting that the complaint contains inconsistent allegations. The allegation of Count I that McCormick was free from contributory negligence, cannot be reconciled with the allegation of Count IV that McCormick's intoxication was the proximate cause of his death. Freedom from contributory negligence is a prerequisite to recovery under the Wrongful Death Act. If the jury had found that McCormick was intoxicated and that his intoxication caused the accident, it could not at the same time have found that McCormick was not contributorily negligent. The Illinois Supreme Court has held that "voluntary intoxication will not excuse a person from exercising such care as may reasonably be expected from one who is sober." Keeshan v. Elgin A. & S. Traction Co., 229 Ill. 533, 537, 82 N.E. 360, 362.

* * *

Counts I and IV, therefore, are mutually exclusive; plaintiff may not recover upon both counts. It does not follow, however, that these counts may not be pleaded together.

* * *

[The Illinois Civil Practice Act contains provisions, similar to F.R.Civ. Pro. 8(d)(2), that claims may be made in the alternative "regardless of consistency." Urnest v. Sabre Metal Products, Inc., 22 Ill.App.2d 172, 159 N.E.2d 512 (1959), stated:]

> The theory is that on the trial the proof will determine on which set of facts, if any, the plaintiff is entitled to recover. Where the pleading is in the alternative in different counts, each count stands alone and the inconsistent statements contained in a count cannot be used to contradict statements in another count. The intent of the cited section of the Practice Act is that counts can be pleaded in the alternative regardless of inconsistency.

* * *

Sound policy weighs in favor of alternative pleading, so that controversies may be settled and complete justice accomplished in a single action. If the right is abused, as where the pleader has knowledge of the true facts (viz., he knows that the facts belie the alternative), pleading in

Consider: What are strategic implications of new rules vs. old common law rules.

144   DESCRIBING AND DEFINING THE DISPUTE   CH. 3

The most important info. is missing an autopsy). It seems the widow would seem to gain from this.

the alternative is not justified. Thus in Church v. Adler, 350 Ill.App. 471 at page 483, 113 N.E.2d 327 at page 332, we said:

> ". . . alternative pleading is not permitted when in the nature of things the pleader must know which of the inconsistent averments is true and which is false. Plaintiff must know whether she will be sick, sore, lame and disordered for the rest of her life or whether on the contrary she has regained her health, as alleged in Count II. She must make up her mind which is the fact, and strike the inconsistent allegation from her pleading on remand."

There is nothing in the record before us to indicate that plaintiff knew in advance of the trial that the averments of Count I, and not Count IV, were true. In fact, at the trial, Kopmann attempted to establish the truth of the allegations of Count IV that McCormick was intoxicated at the time of the collision and that his intoxication caused his death. He can hardly be heard now to say that before the trial, plaintiff should have known that these were not the facts. Where, as in the *Church* case, the injured party is still living and able to recollect the events surrounding the accident, pleading in the alternative may not be justified, but where, as in the case at bar, the key witness is deceased, pleading alternative sets of facts is often the only feasible way to proceed.

Key witness being dead makes a difference.

We hold that, in the absence of a severance, plaintiff had the right to go to trial on both Counts I and IV, and to adduce all the proof she had under both Count I and Count IV.

* * *

Here, either of two defendants may be liable to plaintiff, depending upon what the jury finds the facts to be. It has been aptly said that "truth cannot be stated until known, and, for purposes of judicial administration, cannot be known until the trier of facts decides the fact issues." Plaintiff need not choose between the alternative counts. Such a requirement would, to a large extent, nullify the salutary purposes of alternative pleading. Since she could bring actions against the defendants seriatim, or at the same time in separate suits, she is entitled to join them in a single action, introduce all her proof, and submit the entire case to the jury under appropriate instructions.

NOTES AND QUESTIONS

1. As the court says, plaintiff could have solved the inconsistent allegations problem by filing two lawsuits, one against the truck driver and the other against the bar owners. Is it important that the truck driver might win the suit against him by blaming the bar owners, while the bar owners might similarly escape liability by blaming the truck driver in the suit against them? As we will see when we deal with joinder of parties, modern rules permit plaintiffs to sue numerous defendants in order to avoid this possibility. Recall

United States v. Board of Harbor Comm'rs, supra p. 137. This combination avoids the risk of inconsistent results in the two cases and saves the court the effort of trying the same matters twice (since a trial against either the truck driver or the bar owners would be likely to involve examination into the events at the bar and the circumstances surrounding the accident).

2.   The court speaks of whether plaintiff knew the "truth" of her claim against the truck driver before trial. In what sense are we talking about the truth? If there is a risk of inconsistent results in separate suits against the truck driver and the bar owners, does that suggest that there is a difference between litigation outcomes and the truth? Are we bringing litigation outcomes closer to the "truth" by allowing the combination of the claims?

3.   Besides avoiding inconsistent outcomes, plaintiff may derive other tactical advantages from suing the truck driver and the bar owners in the same case because there is a substantial likelihood that each defendant will help the plaintiff make out a case against the other. For example, the truck driver attempted at trial to prove plaintiff's claim against the bar owners. Does this effect of combined treatment make it unfair to allow a single trial as to both defendants? Is there any way that a jury could consistently deny plaintiff's claim against both the truck driver and the bar owners? Is that likelihood reduced if the cases are combined?

4.   How can plaintiff make any allegations against either the truck driver or the bar owners, assuming that she was not in the bar or the car on the night of the accident? Under Code practice, it was often required that pleadings be "verified," which compels the party to swear under oath that the allegations in the pleading are true. How can somebody who lacks personal knowledge do that? The answer has been to make allegations on *"information and belief*," asserting that the pleader is not claiming personal knowledge as to these matters although they are believed to be true. The Federal Rules generally do not require verification, but rely instead on the lawyer's signature on a complaint to show that it is justified.

5.   How much uncertainty is necessary to justify alternative allegations? Had plaintiff's husband survived the accident could he have sued the truck driver and the bar owners in the alternative? Would he be foreclosed from doing so if he genuinely believed he could hold his liquor?

6.   The court in PAE Government Serv., Inc. v. MPRI, Inc., 514 F.3d 856 (9th Cir. 2007), explained the courts' general receptiveness to inconsistent allegations (id. at 858–59):

> At the time a complaint is filed, the parties are often uncertain about the facts and the law; and yet, prompt filing is encouraged and often required by a statute of limitations, laches, the need to preserve evidence and other such concerns. In recognition, we do not require complaints to be verified, see Fed. R. Civ. P. 11(a), and we allow pleadings in the alternative—even if the alternatives are mutually exclusive. As the litigation progresses, and each party learns more about its case and that of its opponents, some allegations fall by the

wayside as legally or factually unsupported. This rarely means that these allegations were brought in bad faith or the pleading that contained them was a sham.

Can this latitude be abused? Consider the following reasoning:

> Courts allow a pleading of the sort "I never borrowed the lawn mower, it was broken when I borrowed it, and I returned it in perfect condition" because pleadings precede discovery and trial. Until the last minute it may be hard to tell what the evidence will show, and inconsistent pleadings allow a party to preserve its options.

Astor Chauffeured Limousine Co. v. Runnfeldt Invest. Corp., 910 F.2d 1540, 1548 (7th Cir.1990). Is this attitude consistent with the view in many other countries that pleadings should set forth claims and defenses (and evidence) with specificity? See supra p. 141 n. 6.

7. Alternative pleading can be extremely important in many product liability suits. Consider, for example, the possibility that the accident in McCormick v. Kopmann resulted from the failure of the brakes on the truck. Plaintiff might sue the truck driver, the manufacturer, the dealer who sold the truck, the current owner and every prior owner of the truck, and every truck-service mechanic who had ever worked on the truck. Plaintiff would do so because she could not tell who was responsible for the defective condition of the brakes, and she would therefore allege alternatively, on information and belief, that each was in some way responsible. Should the law look with favor on such complexities? Should the plaintiff be allowed to file a suit that assumes that most of the defendants are not liable?

B. Certification by Signing—Rule 11

ZUK v. EASTERN PENNSYLVANIA PSYCHIATRIC INSTITUTE OF THE MEDICAL COLLEGE OF PENNSYLVANIA

United States Court of Appeals, Third Circuit, 1996
103 F.3d 294

Before SLOVITER CHIEF JUDGE, MCKEE and ROSENN, CIRCUIT JUDGES.

ROSENN, CIRCUIT JUDGE.

This appeal brings into focus difficult questions relating to the evolving uses and purposes of Federal Rules of Civil Procedure Rule 11 sanctions, the more narrow statutory function of sanctions permitted under 28 U.S.C.A. § 1927, and differences between the two. The sanctions here stem from a suit filed in the United States District Court for the Eastern District of Pennsylvania by Benjamin Lipman, the appellant, in behalf of Dr. Gerald Zuk for copyright infringement against the Eastern Pennsylvania Psychiatric Institute (EPPI). The district court dismissed the action on a Rule 12(b)(6) motion filed by the defendant, and appellant and his client thereafter were subjected to joint and several liability in the sum of $15,000 for sanctions and defendant's counsel fees. Dr. Zuk settled his liability and Lipman appealed. We affirm in part and vacate in part.

I.

Dr. Zuk, a psychologist on the faculty [of] EPPI, early in the 1970s had an EPPI technician film two of Dr. Zuk's family therapy sessions. As academic demand for the films developed, Zuk had EPPI duplicate the films and make them available for rental through [its] library. Zuk subsequently wrote a book which, among other things, contained transcripts of the therapy sessions. He registered the book in 1975 with the United States Copyright Office.

In 1980, upon a change in its ownership, EPPI furloughed Zuk. He thereupon requested that all copies of the films be returned to him; EPPI ignored the request. It would appear that EPPI continued to rent out the films for at least some time thereafter. For reasons which have not been made clear, after a long hiatus, Zuk renewed his attempts to recover the films in 1994. In 1995, appellant filed a suit in Zuk's behalf, alleging that EPPI was renting out the films and thereby infringed his copyright.

On June 19, 1995, EPPI moved for dismissal under Rule 12(b), and appellant filed a memorandum in opposition. While the motion was pending, EPPI mailed to Lipman a notice of its intention to move for sanctions under Rule 11(c)([(2)]) on the grounds essentially that appellant had failed to conduct an inquiry into the facts reasonable under the circumstances and into the law. The district court entered an order granting the motion to dismiss. The court found that the copyright of the book afforded no protection to the films, that EPPI owned the copies of the films in its possession and that their use was not an infringement, and that in any event, Zuk's claims were barred by the statute of limitations.

On August 16, EPPI filed a motion for attorney's fees pursuant to 17 U.S.C.A. § 505 which appellant opposed by a memorandum in opposition on August 31. On September 15, EPPI also filed a Rule 11 motion for sanctions, and appellant filed a memorandum in opposition. On November 1, the court entered an order to "show cause why Rule 11 sanctions should not be imposed for (a) filing the complaint, and failing to withdraw it; and (b) signing and filing each and every document presented." Appellant responded on December 1 with a declaration reiterating the facts of the case as he viewed them.

On February 1, 1996, the court, upon consideration of defendant's motion for attorney's fees and sanctions, ordered: "That plaintiff, Gerald Zuk, Ph.D., and plaintiff's counsel, Benjamin G. Lipman, Esq. are jointly and severally liable to the defendant for counsel fees in the sum of $15,000." We must ascertain the underpinnings for the Order. It appears that Dr. Zuk subsequently settled his liability with EPPI in the amount of $6,250, leaving appellant liable for $8,750. Appellant timely appealed.

II.

[The Copyright Act provides that the court may award a reasonable attorney's fee to the prevailing party. Fee awards are at the discretion of the district court, and do not depend on a showing of bad faith by the losing party. The district court recognized that the award should not be automatic in this case, but believed that an award was justified. A fee award on this ground can only be entered against a party, however, and the fee-shifting provisions provided no basis for an award against the lawyer. That would have to be justified under 28 U.S.C.A. § 1927 or Rule 11.]

We turn first to the propriety of the district court's imposition of sanctions under 28 U.S.C.A. § 1927. We review a district court's decision to impose sanctions for abuse of discretion. Cooter & Gell v. Hartmarx Corp., 496 U.S. 384, 385 (1990).

Section 1927 provides in pertinent part: "Any attorney or person admitted to conduct cases who so multiplies the proceedings in any case unreasonably and vexatiously may be required by the court to satisfy personally the excess costs, expenses and attorney's fees reasonably incurred because of such conduct." Although a trial court has broad discretion in managing litigation before it, the principal purpose of imposing sanctions under 28 U.S.C.A. § 1927 is "the deterrence of intentional and unnecessary delay in the proceedings." In this case, the trial court imposed sanctions on plaintiff and his counsel, not because of any multiplicity of the proceedings or delaying tactics, but for failure to make a reasonably adequate inquiry into the facts and law before filing the lawsuit. Thus, the statute does not apply to the set of facts before us. Furthermore, the statute is designed to discipline counsel only and does not authorize imposition of sanctions on the attorney's client.

Finally, this court has stated that "before a court can order the imposition of attorneys' fees under § 1927, it must find wilful bad faith on the part of the offending attorney." Although the court need not "make an express finding of bad faith in so many words," there must at least be statements on the record which this court can construe as an implicit finding of bad faith.

At oral argument before us, counsel for EPPI conceded that the district court had made no express finding of bad faith. Our review of the record, which in relevant part consists only of a two-page Memorandum and Order, reveals no statements which we can interpret as an implicit finding of willful bad faith. At most, the court's statements might be interpreted to indicate a finding of negligence on appellant's part.

[The appellate court concluded that the sanctions order against the attorney had to be vacated because the district court did not subdivide the sanctions between the supposed § 1927 violation and Rule 11.]

IV.

Because the order imposing sanctions on appellant must be vacated and the matter remanded, we conclude that certain issues will probably arise on the remand and should, in the interest of justice, be addressed. We refer here specifically to the question of the proper type and amount of sanctions to be imposed pursuant to Rule 11 under the particular circumstances of this case.

A.

We note at the outset that we find no error in the district court's decision to impose sanctions pursuant to Fed.R.Civ.P. 11.[3] As noted above, we review a district court's decision to impose sanctions for abuse of discretion. An abuse of discretion in this context would occur if the court "based its ruling on an erroneous view of the law or a clearly erroneous assessment of the evidence."

Prior to a significant amendment in 1983, Rule 11 stated that an attorney might be subjected to disciplinary action only for a "wilful" violation of the rule. The Advisory Committee Notes to the 1983 amendment make clear that the wilfulness prerequisite has been deleted. Rather, the amended rule imposes a duty on counsel to make an inquiry into both the facts and the law which is "reasonable under the circumstances." This is a more stringent standard than the original good-faith formula, and it was expected that a greater range of circumstances would trigger its violation. The district court did not abuse its discretion in determining that appellant had not sufficiently investigated the facts of the case nor had he educated himself well enough as to copyright law. We therefore see no error in the court's decision to impose sanctions.

1. THE INQUIRY INTO THE FACTS

In dismissing the complaint, the court found that "[i]t . . . seems highly probable that plaintiff's claims are barred by the three-year statute of limitations." Later, in the Memorandum and Order imposing sanctions, the court noted that the "obvious" statute of limitations issue would have been resolved and no lawsuit filed, had appellant conducted an adequate investigation.

Dr. Zuk left EPPI in 1980, and it is undisputed that EPPI continued to rent out the films in question for some time thereafter. Appellant,

---

[3] Appellant contended that he was not given the benefit of Rule 11's 21-day safe harbor, because the court dismissed the action before he had had the full opportunity to withdraw it. He thus claimed that sanctions were improper under Rule 11(c)[(2)] (upon motion by other party). EPPI maintained that the sanctions actually were imposed under Rule 11(c)[(3)] (on the court's initiative), which has no safe harbor provision. The court issued an order to show cause, which is required only under 11(c)[(3)], but stated that it was "in consideration of defendant's motion for sanctions." In its accompanying memorandum, the district court did not address this apparent inconsistency. At oral argument before this court, appellant acknowledged that he would not have withdrawn the complaint even if he had been given the full 21-day safe harbor. Thus, we need not address this contention.

however, had no evidence whatsoever, other than conjecture, to prove that the films were being rented in the three years preceding the commencement of this action. The Advisory Committee Notes to the 1993 amendments to Rule 11 explain:

> "Tolerance of factual contentions in initial pleadings . . . when specifically identified as made on information and belief does not relieve litigants from the obligation to conduct an appropriate investigation into the facts that is reasonable under the circumstances; it is not a license to . . . make claims . . . without any factual basis or justification."

Appellant's assertions in ¶¶ 36 and 37 of the complaint (in regard to EPPI's ongoing use of the films) are based purely upon Dr. Zuk's beliefs.[4] What little investigation appellant actually conducted did not reveal any information that the films were being rented out during the relevant period. Indeed, certain pre-filing correspondence with EPPI indicated that, pursuant to Dr. Zuk's earlier instructions, the library staff was cautioned not to rent any of Dr. Zuk's films. Nor are we persuaded by appellant's contention that further information would have been obtained during discovery. The [Advisory Committee] Note cited above observes that discovery is not intended as a fishing expedition permitting the speculative pleading of a case first and then pursuing discovery to support it; the plaintiff must have some basis in fact for the action. The need for a reasonable investigation with respect to distribution of the film during the three-year period prior to the filing of the lawsuit is evident because of the long period allegedly spanned by the distribution.

2. THE INQUIRY INTO THE LAW

Rule 11(b)(2) requires that all "claims, defenses, and other legal contentions [be] warranted by existing law or by a nonfrivolous argument for the extension, modification, or reversal of existing law or the establishment of new law."[*] Appellant does not contend that any of the latter justifications apply, and so we must ascertain whether his legal arguments are "warranted by existing law." For reasons that follow, we conclude that they are not, and that sanctions therefore were within the sound discretion of the district court.

Appellant's legal research was faulty primarily in two particular areas: copyright law (pertaining to what the parties call the "registration issue") and the law of personal property (the "ownership issue"). Turning to the registration issue, appellant states that this was the first copyright case which he had handled, and points out that a practitioner has to begin somewhere. While we are sympathetic to this argument, its thrust is more

---

4   EPPI emphasizes that while ¶¶ 36 and 37 should have been pleaded on information and belief, they were instead phrased as "Dr. Zuk believes, and therefore avers, ..." In light of liberal federal pleading practice, we do not find this to be an important distinction.

*   This rule language has been revised slightly.—Eds.

toward the nature of the sanctions to be imposed rather than to the initial decision whether sanctions should be imposed. Regrettably, the reality of appellant's weak grasp of copyright law is that it caused him to pursue a course of conduct which was not warranted by existing law and compelled the defendant to expend time and money in needless litigation.

Appellant's primary contention is that by registering a copyright in his book, Dr. Zuk had somehow also protected the films reproduced in them. The logical progression is that because the book contained transcripts of the films, the words spoken in the films were protected, and thus so were the films. Although perhaps logical, this argument runs contrary to copyright law. "The copyright in [a derivative] work . . . does not affect or enlarge the scope, duration, ownership, or subsistence of, any copyright protection in the preexisting material." 17 U.S.C.A. § 103(b).

In all fairness to appellant, we should note that the cases and commentary interpreting this provision focus on derivative works which incorporate the preexisting work of a different author. Had appellant presented his argument as a matter of first impression, and argued for a new interpretation of the statute where the same individual authored both works, he might have stood upon a more solid footing. Instead, appellant's brief evidences what strikes us as a cursory reading of the copyright laws, and a strained analysis of what appears to be an inapposite case.

We now focus on the ownership issue. The parties agree that if EPPI owns the copies of the film in its possession, then 17 U.S.C.A. § 109[5] permits EPPI to rent out the films. Appellant maintains, however, that EPPI does not own the copies, because they were made specifically for Dr. Zuk at his behest, and as a perquisite of his faculty position at EPPI. This question raises reasonable issues as to the rights of an employer in the work product of an employee, and its resolution is not so clear as to itself warrant the sanctioning of appellant for advancing this claim.

EPPI contends, however, that it is too late in the day to raise this argument. The Pennsylvania statute of limitations on replevin is two years. Dr. Zuk demanded the return of the copies in 1980, and EPPI refused to comply, based upon a claim of ownership. EPPI's possession thereafter was open, notorious, and under claim of right, and yet Dr. Zuk did not institute an action to replevy. It would therefore appear that EPPI now holds superior title, and that an inquiry into Pennsylvania personal property law would have revealed that appellant's claim was far too stale. However, EPPI raises its argument too late in this proceeding. It did not rely upon, or even mention, the adverse possession theory before the district court. Because the court could not have relied upon this aspect of the ownership

---

[5] This section states in pertinent part that a nonprofit library (such as that operated by EPPI) is free to rent, lease, or lend copywritten material without authority of the copyright owner, so long as the library owns a lawfully made copy of such material.

issue in imposing sanctions, it is inappropriate for us to consider it at this time.

B.

Having concluded that there is no error in the district court's decision to impose sanctions upon appellant under Rule 11, we turn now to the type and amount of sanctions imposed. We review the appropriateness of the sanctions imposed for abuse of discretion. As the courts have undergone experience with the application of Rule 11 sanctions, its scope has broadened and the emphasis of the Rule has changed.

According to Wright & Miller:

> The 1993 revision . . . makes clear that the main purpose of Rule 11 is to deter, not to compensate. Accordingly, it changes the emphasis in the types of sanctions to be ordered. It envisions as the norm public interest remedies such as fines and reprimands, as opposed to the prior emphasis on private interest remedies. Thus, the Advisory Committee Notes state that any monetary penalty "should ordinarily be paid into the court" except "under unusual circumstances" when they should be given to the opposing party. Any sanction imposed should be calibrated to the least severe level necessary to serve the deterrent purpose of the Rule. In addition, the new Rule 11 contemplates greater use of nonmonetary sanctions, including reprimands, orders to undergo continuing education, and referrals to disciplinary authorities.

5A Charles Alan Wright & Arthur R. Miller, Federal Practice & Procedure § 1336 (2d ed. Supp.1996).

This court has instructed the district courts that "[f]ee-shifting is but one of several methods of achieving the various goals of Rule 11," that they should "consider a wide range of alternative possible sanctions for violation of the rule," and that the "district court's choice of deterrent is appropriate when it is the minimum that will serve to adequately deter the undesirable behavior." Doering v. Union County Bd. of Chosen Freeholders, 857 F.2d 191, 194 (3d Cir.1988).

Thus, the district courts have been encouraged to consider mitigating factors in fashioning sanctions, most particularly the sanctioned party's ability to pay. Courts were also given examples of other factors they might consider, including whether the attorney has a history of this sort of behavior, the defendant's need for compensation, the degree of frivolousness, and the "willfulness" of the violation.

In *Doering*, a $25,000 sanction was imposed on a sole practitioner with less than $40,000 gross income per annum. We affirmed the district court's decision to impose sanctions, but vacated and remanded as to the amount. We noted that "in order for the district court to exercise properly its discretion in setting the amount of fees to be assessed against counsel, further evidence must be developed upon the issue of his ability to pay."

Although money sanctions are not encouraged under Rule 11, they are not forbidden. Under the circumstances of this case, we see no error in the district court's imposition of fee sanctions upon the appellant, although the amount may be contrary to the current spirit of Rule 11. The present case differs from *Doering* in that appellant did not request that the district court mitigate the sanctions. Appellant also faces a lesser financial burden in that he is liable for only $8,750, his client having paid the difference. Nonetheless, when we look to the list of mitigating factors, and consider the non-punitive purpose of Rule 11, we conclude that it was error to invoke without comment a very severe penalty. On remand, the district court should apply the principles announced by this court in Doering.

NOTES AND QUESTIONS

1.   As the court notes in *Zuk*, Rule 11 was extensively amended in 1993 to change features of a previous amendment in 1983 that strengthened the rule's provisions. Many objected that the 1983 version of the rule resulted in too much sanctions activity, and actually deterred litigants from dropping weak contentions for fear that they would be sanctioned for doing so. In particular, many objected that the rule impeded the assertion of civil rights claims. Among the concerns were the mandatory nature of sanctions under the 1983 version of the rule, and the inclination of some courts to use the rule as a fee-shifting device to compensate victims of violations. The "fang-drawing 1993 amendments," Stove Builder International, Inc. v. GHP Group, Inc., 280 F.R.D. 402, 403 (N.D.Ill.2012), made the imposition of sanctions discretionary, introduced the "safe harbor" in Rule 11(c)(2), and reoriented the choice of sanction toward deterrence and away from compensation. Some opposed these changes in the rule, and there have been proposals in Congress to restore the 1983 provisions. See Lawsuit Abuse Reduction Act of 2017, H.R. 720 (115th Cong.) (passed by House of Representatives in March, 2017).

Distinctive features of American litigation partly explain the importance of Rule 11, as explained in Northern Illinois Telecom, Inc. v. PNC Bank, N.A., 850 F.3d 880, 883–84 (7th Cir. 2017):

> In civil cases within our jurisdiction, federal courts exercise considerable discretion and great power. The proper exercise of that power can be essential in preserving the rule of law and the rights and liberties of the American people, in cases large and small, landmark and mundane. When a plaintiff invokes those powers in a civil case, it puts machinery in gear that can be powerful, intimidating, and often expensive. Those powers and machinery can be abused by litigants. Federal Rule of Civil Procedure 11 seeks to ensure that those powers and machinery are engaged only to address claims that have a reasonable basis in fact and law and that are asserted only for a proper purpose.

Are sanctions, particularly against lawyers, a suitable way for dealing with perceived problems of lawsuit abuse? Consider the views of the court in In re Pennie & Edmonds LLP, 323 F.3d 86, 90–91 (2d Cir.2003):

> Any regime of sanctions for a lawyer's role in the course of representing a client inevitably has implications for the functioning of the adversary process. If the sanction regime is too severe, lawyers will sometimes be deterred from making legitimate submissions on behalf of clients out of apprehension that their conduct will erroneously be deemed improper. On the other hand, if the sanction regime is too lenient, lawyers will sometimes be emboldened to make improper submissions on behalf of clients, confident that their misconduct will either be undetected or dealt with too leniently to matter.

2.   The district court in *Zuk* ordered plaintiff and his lawyer to justify filing the suit, failing to withdraw it, and signing and filing each subsequent document they submitted in the case. Review Rule 11 and consider how it operates:

(a)   *Signature requirement*: The rule applies to the person who signs the document submitted to the court, ordinarily a lawyer, and authorizes sanctions against the lawyer's firm. Except for discovery, Rule 11 applies to all papers filed in court, so you should keep it in mind in connection with the other matters covered in this course.

(b)   *Factual inquiry*: By signing and submitting a document, the lawyer represents that there has been a reasonable inquiry, and that the claim has evidentiary support. This calls for an "objective" inquiry; "[a]n empty head but a pure heart is no defense." Thornton v. Wahl, 787 F.2d 1151, 1154 (7th Cir.1986). What more should the plaintiff's lawyer have done in *Zuk* to comply with the rule? After filing suit, wouldn't it be easier to find out about the defendant's lending practices? What if defendant refused to answer any questions about its practices before suit was filed? See Q-Pharma, Inc. v. Andrew Jergens Co., 360 F.3d 1295 (Fed.Cir.2004) (even after suit was filed, defendant refused to provide information about the contents of its hand lotion that would have permitted plaintiff to determine that its patent was not infringed; sanctions were therefore denied even though plaintiff could have conducted its own chemical analysis of defendant's product before filing suit).

Lawyers frequently must decide whether to file suit when there is factual uncertainty, and Rule 11 may mean they must act at their peril. Consider Uy v. Bronx Municipal Hospital Center, 182 F.3d 152 (2d Cir.1999), a suit charging discriminatory discharge based on national origin in which plaintiff claimed he was told he could be fired because he was a foreigner. After defendant's witnesses contradicted that assertion, the district court found plaintiff's lawyer guilty of violating Rule 11, but the Court of Appeals reversed: "[The attorney] had no way of ascertaining before he entered into the representation whether the defendants' witnesses would corroborate or contradict the plaintiff's assertion. The defendant's employees are unlikely to make themselves available to be interviewed by an attorney who is contemplating representing the plaintiff. As a practical matter, in the usual case, the only way the attorney can discover what adverse witnesses will say is by taking their deposition, and that cannot be done until the attorney assumes the representation."

Can the lawyer usually rely on the client, or must she make her own investigation? Recall Fuentes v. Shevin, supra p. 31: "Lawyers and judges are familiar with the phenomenon of a party mistakenly but firmly convinced that his view of the facts and law will prevail and therefore quite willing to risk the costs of litigation." An experienced judge cautioned that "attorneys can be conned by devious clients." He added: "Clients come to them with stories that are, at the very least, slanted and, at the very worst, outright lies. Often clients convince themselves of the truth of their story—they fervently believe things that simply are not true. That is the difficult circumstance in which trial attorneys operate. It is the nature of our adversary system of justice. Clients feel that they have to color their story to win their case." Ward, Lawyer Beware, Calif. Lawyer, Feb., 2005, at 80.

Thus Rule 11 presents lawyers with challenges. Consider In re Taylor, 655 F.3d 274, 284 (3d Cir. 2011): "It is difficult to imagine how attorneys might function were they required to conduct an independent investigation of every factual representation made by a client before it could be included in a court filing." When the lawyer properly relies on the client, the client can be sanctioned even if the lawyer committed no violation of the rule. See Business Guides, Inc. v. Chromatic Communications Ent., Inc., 498 U.S. 533 (1991) ("The Magistrate did not recommend that [the law firm] be sanctioned for the initial application [for a temporary restraining order], however, as the firm had been led to believe that there was an urgent need to act quickly and thus relied on the information supplied by its sophisticated corporate client.").

Affirmative defenses present additional challenges of both a factual and legal variety. In *Zuk*, for example, defendant relied in part on the statute of limitations. Rule 8(c) says that the statute of limitations is an affirmative defense, which only applies if defendant raises it. Should this have a bearing on whether plaintiff's lawyer is required to investigate whether it applies? Consider Kane, The Lawyer as Litigator in the 1980's, 14 No.Ky. L.Rev. 311, 330–31 (1988):

> [D]ifficult questions are presented for plaintiff's counsel when the facts as revealed indicate a clear defense, but the defense is waivable. Is it consistent with the obligations of Rule 11 to file the pleading knowing it can be destroyed? Some courts have said yes, some no. The problem is an important one. Insofar as courts imposing sanctions in these circumstances do so because the plaintiff's lawyer did not even inquire as to whether the statute of limitations had run or jurisdiction was proper, those rulings are consistent with the purpose of the rule and serve as a needed reminder to counsel to prepare adequately before filing suit.

But the notion that some matters constitute defenses, easily waived, at least traditionally has meant that the plaintiff has no obligation to raise the matter. Consistent with that view, then, Rule 11 requirements would mean only that plaintiff had an obligation to desist from objecting if the defendant raised the defense because any resistance would be frivolous. Yet some courts now seem to be suggesting that when the plaintiff files an action knowing there is an ironclad defense, that constitutes the filing of an objectively frivolous pleading. * * * [T]he impact of this interpretation is far-reaching because it effectively transforms a defense into an element of plaintiff's case.

(c) *Legal inquiry*: The court in *Zuk* holds that the lawyer did not do a sufficient legal inquiry even though this was the first copyright case he had filed. Does this mean that a lawyer can be sanctioned for failing to recognize what an expert in copyright law would recognize? The problem seems rather basic. Under 17 U.S.C.A. § 411(b), "no action for infringement of the copyright in any United States work shall be instituted until registration of the copyright claim has been made." But Zuk had never registered his copyright in the films. Although he had registered the copyright in his book, which included transcriptions of the films, this did not satisfy the § 411(b) requirement that the films themselves be registered prior to filing a claim that the film copyrights had been infringed. 17 U.S.C.A. § 103(b) says that "[t]he copyright in a compilation of derivative work extends only to the material contributed by the author of such work, as distinguished from the preexisting material employed in the work, and does not imply any exclusive right in the preexisting material." The court understood this provision to mean that the copyright in the book (a derivative work or compilation) did not extend to the films, which were "preexisting material employed in" the book.

The court recognizes that there might be an argument that § 103(b) does not apply to Zuk's situation because § 103(b) contemplates cases in which the derivative work or compilation incorporates material created by a different author. Here, Zuk was the author of both the registered derivative work or compilation (the book) and the unregistered films. Why isn't that sufficient to satisfy Rule 11(b)(2), which permits an argument that is not based on existing law so long as it is a "nonfrivolous argument for extending, modifying, or reversing existing law or for establishing new law"? Compare Thornton v. Wahl, 787 F.2d 1151 (7th Cir.1986) (failure to clarify that argument was not based on existing law can be sanctioned) with Golden Eagle Distrib. Corp. v. Burroughs Corp., 801 F.2d 1531 (9th Cir.1986) (no need to explain that argument is for an extension of law rather than based on existing law). What arguments could be made for the Ninth Circuit approach? The Advisory Committee did not explicitly resolve this question in the 1993 amendments, but noted that "[a]lthough arguments for a change of law are not required to be so identified, a contention that is so identified should be viewed with greater tolerance under the rule." 146 F.R.D. at 53.

(d) *Harassment*: Sanctions are also warranted under Rule 11(b)(1) for actions that harass or needlessly increase the cost of litigation. Could filing a valid claim violate this portion of the rule? Consider National Association of Government Employees, Inc. v. National Fed. of Federal Employees, 844 F.2d 216, 223 (5th Cir.1988): "We do not condone litigation instituted for ulterior purposes rather than to secure judgment on a well-grounded complaint the plaintiff sincerely believes. Yet the Rule 11 injunction against harassment does not exact of those who file pleadings an undiluted desire for just deserts. * * * [I]f an initial complaint passes the test of non-frivolousness, its filing does not constitute harassment for the purposes of Rule 11."

If this is correct, what is left of the prohibition against harassment as an independent Rule 11 consideration? In Sneller v. City of Bainbridge Island, 606 F.3d 636 (9th Cir. 2010), plaintiff landowners sued the city when it denied them permission to develop land within a recognized wetland, and they also sued individual city employees. Defendants served a Rule 11 motion demanding dismissal of the claims against the individual employees on the ground they could not be sued for what the city did, and plaintiffs dropped those claims but immediately filed new and different claims against the individual employees. The majority of the court of appeals held that this was not sanctionable under the safe harbor (discussed below), but a dissenting judge argued that plaintiffs were guilty of "a tactical maneuver designed to harass and intimidate public employees," so that sanctions should be allowed under Rule 11(b)(1). The dissenting judge cited a speech given by one of the plaintiffs and broadcast on community public television, in which he explained why he sued the individual employees (id. at 641–42):

> These staff members apply for credit cards just like all of us. They apply for home loans and they apply for car loans. And when they have a lawsuit pending, every time you fill out that application, it says, "Are you a defendant in a lawsuit?" They better check that box, because it's going to be checked in any event by the company issuing the credit.
>
> If you have a two or three-million-dollar lawsuit pending against you as a defendant, you're not going to get a cell phone. So that was the approach we took.

Should this suffice to prove harassment?

(e) *Later advocating*: Before the 1993 amendment, courts were divided on whether sanctions could be imposed where a party had a legitimate basis for a filing when it was made, but later learned it was unjustified. Rule 11(b) now provides that a sanction may be imposed on a lawyer for "later advocating" a position taken in a paper even though no violation occurred when that paper was filed. For example, in Phonometrics, Inc. v. Economy Inns of America, 349 F.3d 1356 (Fed.Cir.2003), plaintiff sued for patent infringement in 1997, and the district court stayed proceedings pending a decision by the Federal Circuit (which hears appeals in patent infringement cases from across the country) on the construction of the patent in issue. After the Federal Circuit construed the patent in a way that undermined the claims, plaintiff's counsel told the district court it would nevertheless continue to pursue the claims. Defendants served a Rule 11 motion demanding dismissal, and counsel responded that the Federal Circuit's decision was "mistaken." The appellate court affirmed the imposition of sanctions on counsel for persisting in the litigation. In *Zuk*, how should this "later advocating" provision be applied? Should it matter that during the argument on the appeal plaintiff's lawyer said that he would not have withdrawn the complaint?

(f)   *Safe harbor*: Even if there has been a violation, the court may impose sanctions on motion only if the violator has been warned and invited to desist. See Rule 11(c)(2). Is this a good idea? Justice Scalia thought it was not and dissented from the 1993 amendment: "The Rules should be solicitous of the abused (the courts and the opposing party), and not of the abuser. Under the revised Rule, parties will be able to file thoughtless, reckless, and harassing pleadings, secure in the knowledge that they have nothing to lose: If objection is raised, they can retreat without penalty." 146 F.R.D. at 508 (Scalia, J., dissenting from amendments).

How should the safe harbor provision be applied in *Zuk*? The appellate court declines to address the question because counsel said he would not have withdrawn the complaint anyway. Is this a sensible application of the rule? Isn't Rule 11(c)(3) the applicable provision? The Advisory Committee Notes say that "[t]he power of the court to act on its own initiative is retained, but with the condition that this be done through a show cause order. * * * Since show cause orders will ordinarily be issued only in situations akin to a contempt of court, the rule does not provide a 'safe harbor.'" 146 F.R.D. at 591–92.

The courts have generally applied the safe harbor requirement vigorously. For example, in Penn, LLC v. Prosper Business Devel. Corp., 773 F.3d 764 (6th Cir. 2014), defense counsel wrote to plaintiff counsel upon service of the complaint, asserting that it violated Rule 11 and that sanctions would be sought unless the case were dismissed voluntarily. When dismissal did not follow, defendants moved to dismiss and the court granted the motion. After that, defendants served a motion for sanctions. The court held that defendants had not satisfied the safe harbor requirements because they only sent a letter rather than preparing and serving a full motion for sanctions. "Permitting litigants to substitute warning letters, or other types of informal notice, for a motion timely served * * * undermines these goals. Whereas a properly served motion unambiguously alerts the recipient that he must withdraw the contention within twenty-one days or defend it against the arguments raised in the motion, a letter prompts the recipient to guess at his opponent's seriousness." Id. at 767–68. Compare Matrix IV, Inc. v. American National Bank & Trust Co., 649 F.3d 539, 552 (7th Cir. 2011) ("a letter informing the opposing party of the intent to seek sanctions and the basis for the imposition of sanctions * * * is sufficient for Rule 11 purposes").

3.   If the court does decide to sanction, Rules 11(c)(4) and (5) provide directions on what the sanction should be. Sanctions need not be monetary. See In re Pennie & Edmonds LLP, 323 F.3d 86 (2d Cir.2003) (sanctioned firm

required to send copies of the court's sanction opinion to every lawyer in the firm). Could the sanction imposed in *Zuk* be justified under these provisions?

4.   In *Zuk*, plaintiff's lawyer explained that this was his first copyright case, but the court was not sympathetic, a judicial attitude that is common. For example, in Rentz v. Dynasty Apparel Industries, Inc., 556 F.3d 389 (6th Cir. 2009), one of the sanctioned lawyers was in his first job after law school, and had been following directions from the partner for whom he worked, a former mayor and Lieutenant Governor, when he signed the offending document. The court was not moved (id. at 401): "[W]e do not see how Roach's experience level or the fact that he was essentially an associate under Leonard's supervision are relevant to determining the amount of sanctions sufficient to serve the deterrent purpose of Rule 11. All attorneys, regardless of experience level or position, are equally subject to Rule 11's obligation to conduct a reasonable inquiry into the law and facts before signing papers filed with the court."

5.   *28 U.S.C. § 1927:* 28 U.S.C. § 1927 authorizes sanctions for willful "multiplication" of proceedings. What does this mean? Why should it be wrong for lawyers to do that? Why should sanctions be warranted only when the lawyer acted in bad faith? According to commentators, the limitations on Rule 11 adopted in 1993 have prompted some litigants and courts to resort more frequently to § 1927 as a ground for sanctions "to circumvent the procedural requirements of Rule 11." Hart, And the Chill Goes On—Federal Civil Rights Plaintiffs Beware: Rule 11 Vis-a-Vis 28 U.S.C. § 1927 and the Court's Inherent Power, 37 Loyola L.Rev. 645, 656–57 (2004). It has also been reported that the federal courts of appeals are split on whether § 1927 requires a showing of subjective bad faith or only recklessness. See id. at 653.

6.   *Other grounds for sanctions*: Besides Rule 11 and 28 U.S.C.A. § 1927, the Supreme Court held in Chambers v. NASCO, Inc., 501 U.S. 32 (1991), that federal courts have "inherent power" to sanction a litigant for bad-faith conduct that has not been displaced by the more specific provisions of Rule 11 and § 1927, but said that this power should be used rarely. "The imposition of sanctions using inherent powers must be accompanied by a specific finding of bad faith." Goldin v. Bartholow, 166 F.3d 710, 722 (5th Cir.1999). Even then, the sanction must be limited to the costs actually imposed by the misconduct; a court "may not impose an additional amount as punishment for the sanctioned party's misbehavior. To level that kind of separate penalty, a court would need to provide procedural guarantees applicable in criminal cases, such as a 'beyond reasonable doubt' standard of proof." Goodyear Tire & Rubber Co. v. Haeger, 137 S.Ct. 1178, 1186 (2017).

7.   Another possibility is that the victim of litigation misconduct of the sort that may justify Rule 11 sanctions may file a separate lawsuit against the lawyer for this misconduct. For examples, see General Refractories Co. v. Fireman's Fund Ins. Co., 337 F.3d 297 (3d Cir.2003) (holding that using legal process primarily to harass an adversary could constitute "perversion" of that process actionable as abuse of process under Pennsylvania law); Zamos v. Stroud, 1 Cal. Rptr. 3d 484 (Cal. Ct. App. 2003) (holding that a lawyer could be

sued for malicious prosecution if he continued to pursue a suit after learning that it was groundless).

3. HEIGHTENED REQUIREMENTS FOR SPECIFICITY

In the next sub-section, we will examine the emergence of what may be a more demanding "plausibility" standard for complaints. Although Rule 8(a)(2) prescribes the general pleading requirements, in some instances there is a requirement for greater specificity. A prominent example is Rule 9(b), which states that "[i]n alleging fraud or mistake, a party must state with particularity the circumstances constituting fraud or mistake." The rule adds, however, that "[m]alice, intent, knowledge, and other conditions of a person's mind may be alleged generally." Charles Clark, who drafted the Federal Rules' pleading provisions, viewed the rule as reflecting judges' habits, explaining that it "probably states only what courts would do anyhow." Clark, Simplified Pleading, 2 F.R.D. 456, 463 (1942).

The "mistake" referred to in Rule 9(b) is not negligence, and the main application of the Rule has been in fraud cases. The most important category of such cases has been securities fraud cases, in which the Second Circuit imposed strict pleading requirements.

In Ross v. A.H. Robins Co., 607 F.2d 545 (2d Cir. 1979), cert. denied, 446 U.S. 946 (1980), plaintiffs made a securities fraud claim asserting that defendants Robins Co. and several of its officers failed to disclose the risk to the company of marketing the Dalkon Shield, a contraceptive product the company touted as good for its business, which plaintiffs alleged was early found to be harmful to many users, putting the company at risk of massive tort liability. Plaintiffs, who bought Robins stock and saw the value of their shares decline as the tort litigation gained momentum, asserted securities fraud claims. Even though the court recognized that "[t]here is no question that the plaintiffs in this instance adequately identified the alleged 'misrepresentations,'" id. at 558, it found their allegations that defendants knew the true facts insufficient despite the rule's second sentence permitting allegations of knowledge to be made generally. It held (id.):

> [A]t this stage of the litigation, we cannot realistically expect plaintiffs to be able to plead defendants' actual knowledge. On the other hand, plaintiffs can be required to supply a factual basis for their conclusory allegations regarding that knowledge. It is reasonable to require that the plaintiffs specifically plead those events which they assert give rise to a strong inference that the defendants had knowledge of the facts contained in * * * the complaint or recklessly disregarded their existence.

The Second Circuit explained its strict interpretation of Rule 9(b) as follows (id. at 557):

[Rule 9(b)] "is a special pleading requirement and contrary to the general approach of simplified pleading adopted by the federal rules," [which] generally serves two important purposes. First, it assures the defendant of " 'fair notice of what the plaintiff's claim is and the grounds upon which it rests.' " Denny v. Barber, 576 F.2d 465, 469 (2d Cir.1978). Secondly, the specificity requirement grows out of "the desire to protect defendants from the harm that comes to their reputations or to their goodwill when they are charged with serious wrongdoing. . . ." Segal v. Gordon, 467 F.2d 602, 607 (2d Cir.1972). In the context of securities litigation Rule 9(b) serves an additional important purpose. It operates to diminish the possibility that " 'a plaintiff with a largely groundless claim [will be able] to simply take up the time of a number of other people [by extensive discovery], with the right to do so representing an *in terrorem* increment of the settlement value, rather than a reasonably founded hope that the process will reveal relevant evidence. . . .' " Denny v. Barber, supra, 576 F.2d at 470 (quoting Blue Chip Stamps v. Manor Drug Stores, 421 U.S. 723, 741 (1975)).

Securities fraud suits continued to be the most important category of litigation subject to Rule 9(b), but lower courts did not all agree on how the rule should be applied in such cases. In 1995, Congress adopted the Private Securities Litigation Reform Act, which included pleading provisions modeled on the Second Circuit's interpretation of the rule.

TELLABS, INC. V. MAKOR ISSUES & RIGHTS, LTD.

Supreme Court of the United States, 2007
551 U.S. 308

JUSTICE GINSBURG delivered the opinion of the Court.

This Court has long recognized that meritorious private actions to enforce federal antifraud securities laws are an essential supplement to criminal prosecutions and civil enforcement actions brought, respectively, by the Department of Justice and the Securities and Exchange Commission (SEC). Private securities fraud actions, however, if not adequately contained, can be employed abusively to impose substantial costs on companies and individuals whose conduct conforms to the law. As a check against abusive litigation by private parties, Congress enacted the Private Securities Litigation Reform Act of 1995 (PSLRA), 109 Stat. 737.

Exacting pleading requirements are among the control measures Congress included in the PSLRA. The Act requires plaintiffs to state with particularity both the facts constituting the alleged violation, and the facts evidencing scienter, i.e., the defendant's intention "to deceive, manipulate, or defraud." This case concerns the latter requirement. As set out in § 21D(b)(2) of the PSLRA, plaintiffs must "state with particularity facts giving rise to a strong inference that the defendant acted with the required state of mind." 15 U.S.C. § 78u–4(b)(2).

Congress left the key term "strong inference" undefined, and Courts of Appeals have divided on its meaning. In the case before us, the Court of Appeals for the Seventh Circuit held that the "strong inference" standard would be met if the complaint "allege[d] facts from which, if true, a reasonable person could infer that the defendant acted with the required intent." [Makor Issues & Rights, Ltd. v. Tellabs, Inc.,] 437 F.3d 588, 602 (2006). That formulation, we conclude, does not capture the stricter demand Congress sought to convey in § 21D(b)(2). It does not suffice that a reasonable factfinder plausibly could infer from the complaint's allegations the requisite state of mind. Rather, to determine whether a complaint's scienter allegations can survive threshold inspection for sufficiency, a court governed by § 21D(b)(2) must engage in a comparative evaluation; it must consider, not only inferences urged by the plaintiff, as the Seventh Circuit did, but also competing inferences rationally drawn from the facts alleged. An inference of fraudulent intent may be plausible, yet less cogent than other, nonculpable explanations for the defendant's conduct. To qualify as "strong" within the intendment of § 21D(b)(2), we hold, an inference of scienter must be more than merely plausible or reasonable—it must be cogent and at least as compelling as any opposing inference of nonfraudulent intent.

21D(b)(2)

§78A

I

Petitioner Tellabs, Inc., manufactures specialized equipment used in fiber optic networks. During the time period relevant to this case, petitioner Richard Notebaert was Tellabs' chief executive officer and president. Respondents (Shareholders) are persons who purchased Tellabs stock between December 11, 2000, and June 19, 2001. They accuse Tellabs and Notebaert (as well as several other Tellabs executives) of engaging in a scheme to deceive the investing public about the true value of Tellabs' stock.

Beginning on December 11, 2000, the Shareholders allege, Notebaert (and by imputation Tellabs) "falsely reassured public investors, in a series of statements . . . that Tellabs was continuing to enjoy strong demand for its products and earning record revenues," when, in fact, Notebaert knew the opposite was true. From December 2000 until the spring of 2001, the Shareholders claim, Notebaert knowingly misled the public in four ways. First, he made statements indicating that demand for Tellabs' flagship networking device, the TITAN 5500, was continuing to grow, when in fact demand for that product was waning. Second, Notebaert made statements indicating that the TITAN 6500, Tellabs' next-generation networking device, was available for delivery, and that demand for that product was strong and growing, when in truth the product was not ready for delivery and demand was weak. Third, he falsely represented Tellabs' financial results for the fourth quarter of 2000 (and, in connection with those results, condoned the practice of "channel stuffing," under which Tellabs flooded its customers with unwanted products). Fourth, Notebaert made a series of overstated revenue projections, when demand for the TITAN 5500 was drying up and production of the TITAN 6500 was behind schedule. Based on Notebaert's sunny assessments, the Shareholders contend, market analysts recommended that investors buy Tellabs' stock.

The first public glimmer that business was not so healthy came in March 2001 when Tellabs modestly reduced its first quarter sales projections. In the next months, Tellabs made progressively more cautious statements about its projected sales. On June 19, 2001, the last day of the class period, Tellabs disclosed that demand for the TITAN 5500 had significantly dropped. Simultaneously, the company substantially lowered its revenue projections for the second quarter of 2001. The next day, the price of Tellabs stock, which had reached a high of $67 during the period, plunged to a low of $15.87.

On December 3, 2002, the Shareholders filed a class action in the District Court for the Northern District of Illinois. Their complaint stated, inter alia, that Tellabs and Notebaert had engaged in securities fraud in violation of § 10(b) of the Securities Exchange Act of 1934, 48 Stat. 891, 15 U.S.C. § 78j(b), and SEC Rule 10b–5, 17 CFR § 240.10b–5 (2006), also that Notebaert was a "controlling person" under § 20(a) of the 1934 Act, 15 U.S.C. § 78t(a), and therefore derivatively liable for the company's fraudulent acts. Tellabs moved to dismiss the complaint on the ground that the Shareholders had failed to plead their case with the particularity the PSLRA requires. The District Court agreed, and therefore dismissed the complaint without prejudice.

The Shareholders then amended their complaint, adding references to 27 confidential sources and making further, more specific, allegations concerning Notebaert's mental state. The District Court again dismissed, this time with prejudice. The Shareholders had sufficiently pleaded that Notebaert's statements were misleading, the court determined, but they had insufficiently alleged that he acted with scienter. → intent/knowledge of wrongdoing

The Court of Appeals for the Seventh Circuit reversed in relevant part. Like the District Court, the Court of Appeals found that the Shareholders had pleaded the misleading character of Notebaert's statements with sufficient particularity. Unlike the District Court, however, the Seventh Circuit concluded that the Shareholders had sufficiently alleged that Notebaert acted with the requisite state of mind.

The Court of Appeals recognized that the PSLRA "unequivocally raise[d] the bar for pleading scienter" by requiring plaintiffs to "plea[d] sufficient facts to create a strong inference of scienter." In evaluating whether that pleading standard is met, the Seventh Circuit said, "courts [should] examine all of the allegations in the complaint and then . . . decide

For fraud, plaintiff is the cheapest cost providor of information. This is why plaintiffs need to be particular.

164   DESCRIBING AND DEFINING THE DISPUTE   CH. 3

whether collectively they establish such an inference." "[W]e will allow the complaint to survive," the court next and critically stated, "if it alleges facts from which, if true, a reasonable person could infer that the defendant acted with the required intent. . . . If a reasonable person could not draw such an inference from the alleged facts, the defendants are entitled to dismissal."

Scalia's Source

7th Amd.

In adopting its standard for the survival of a complaint, the Seventh Circuit explicitly rejected a stiffer standard adopted by the Sixth Circuit, i.e., that "plaintiffs are entitled only to the most plausible of competing inferences." [437 F.3d] at 601, 602 (quoting Fidel v. Farley, 392 F.3d 220, 227 (C.A.6 2004)). The Sixth Circuit's standard, the court observed, because it involved an assessment of competing inferences, "could potentially infringe upon plaintiffs' Seventh Amendment rights." We granted certiorari to resolve the disagreement among the Circuits on whether, and to what extent, a court must consider competing inferences in determining whether a securities fraud complaint gives rise to a "strong inference" of scienter.

II

Section 10(b) of the Securities Exchange Act of 1934 forbids the "use or employ[ment], in connection with the purchase or sale of any security . . ., [of] any manipulative or deceptive device or contrivance in contravention of such rules and regulations as the [SEC] may prescribe as necessary or appropriate in the public interest or for the protection of investors." 15 U.S.C. § 78j(b). SEC Rule 10b–5 implements § 10(b) by declaring it unlawful:

"(a) To employ any device, scheme, or artifice to defraud,

"(b) To make any untrue statement of a material fact or to omit to state a material fact necessary in order to make the statements made . . . not misleading, or

"(c) To engage in any act, practice, or course of business which operates or would operate as a fraud or deceit upon any person, in connection with the purchase or sale of any security." 17 CFR § 240.10b–5.

Section 10(b), this Court has implied from the statute's text and purpose, affords a right of action to purchasers or sellers of securities injured by its violation. See, e.g., [J.I. Case Co. v.] Borak, 377 U.S., at 432 [(1964)] (private securities fraud actions provide "a most effective weapon in the enforcement" of securities laws and are "a necessary supplement to Commission action"). To establish liability under § 10(b) and Rule 10b–5, a private plaintiff must prove that the defendant acted with scienter, "a mental state embracing intent to deceive, manipulate, or defraud."

In an ordinary civil action, the Federal Rules of Civil Procedure require only "a short and plain statement of the claim showing that the pleader is entitled to relief." Fed. Rule Civ. Proc. 8(a)(2). Although the rule encourages brevity, the complaint must say enough to give the defendant "fair notice of what the plaintiff's claim is and the grounds upon which it rests." Dura Pharmaceuticals[, Inc. v. Broudo], 544 U.S. [336], at 346 [(2005)]. Prior to the enactment of the PSLRA, the sufficiency of a complaint for securities fraud was governed not by Rule 8, but by the heightened pleading standard set forth in Rule 9(b). Rule 9(b) applies to "all averments of fraud or mistake"; it requires that "the circumstances constituting fraud . . . be stated with particularity" but provides that "[m]alice, intent, knowledge, and other condition of mind of a person, may be averred generally."

Courts of Appeals diverged on the character of the Rule 9(b) inquiry in § 10(b) cases: Could securities fraud plaintiffs allege the requisite mental state "simply by stating that scienter existed," or were they required to allege with particularity facts giving rise to an inference of scienter? * * * The Second Circuit's formulation was the most stringent. Securities fraud plaintiffs in that Circuit were required to "specifically plead those [facts] which they assert give rise to a *strong inference* that the defendants had" the requisite state of mind. Ross v. A.H. Robins Co., 607 F.2d 545, 558 (1979) (emphasis added). The "strong inference" formulation was appropriate, the Second Circuit said, to ward off allegations of "fraud by hindsight."

Setting a uniform pleading standard for § 10(b) actions was among Congress' objectives when it enacted the PSLRA. Designed to curb perceived abuses of the § 10(b) private action—"nuisance filings, targeting of deep-pocket defendants, vexatious discovery requests and manipulation by class action lawyers,"—the PSLRA installed both substantive and procedural controls. * * *

Under the PSLRA's heightened pleading instructions, any private securities complaint alleging that the defendant made a false or misleading statement must: (1) "specify each statement alleged to have been misleading [and] the reason or reasons why the statement is misleading," 15 U.S.C. § 78u–4(b)(1); and (2) "state with particularity facts giving rise to a strong inference that the defendant acted with the required state of mind," § 78u–4(b)(2). In the instant case, as earlier stated, the District Court and the Seventh Circuit agreed that the Shareholders met the first of the two requirements: The complaint sufficiently specified Notebaert's alleged misleading statements and the reasons why the statements were misleading. But those courts disagreed on whether the Shareholders, as required by § 21D(b)(2), "state[d] with particularity facts giving rise to a strong inference that [Notebaert] acted with [scienter]," § 78u–4(b)(2).

The "strong inference" standard "unequivocally raise[d] the bar for pleading scienter," 437 F.3d, at 601, and signaled Congress' purpose to promote greater uniformity among the Circuits. But "Congress did not . . . throw much light on what facts . . . suffice to create [a strong] inference," or on what "degree of imagination courts can use in divining whether" the requisite inference exists. While adopting the Second Circuit's "strong inference" standard, Congress did not codify that Circuit's case law interpreting the standard. With no clear guide from Congress other than its "inten[tion] to strengthen existing pleading requirements," Courts of Appeals have diverged again, this time in construing the term "strong inference." Among the uncertainties, should courts consider competing inferences in determining whether an inference of scienter is "strong"? Our task is to prescribe a workable construction of the "strong inference" standard, a reading geared to the PSLRA's twin goals: to curb frivolous, lawyer-driven litigation, while preserving investors' ability to recover on meritorious claims.

III

A

We establish the following prescriptions: *First*, faced with a Rule 12(b)(6) motion to dismiss a § 10(b) action, courts must, as with any motion to dismiss for failure to plead a claim on which relief can be granted, accept all factual allegations in the complaint as true. On this point, the parties agree.

Second, courts must consider the complaint in its entirety, as well as other sources courts ordinarily examine when ruling on Rule 12(b)(6) motions to dismiss, in particular, documents incorporated into the complaint by reference, and matters of which a court may take judicial notice. The inquiry, as several Courts of Appeals have recognized, is whether all of the facts alleged, taken collectively, give rise to a strong inference of scienter, not whether any individual allegation, scrutinized in isolation, meets that standard.

Third, in determining whether the pleaded facts give rise to a "strong" inference of scienter, the court must take into account plausible opposing inferences. The Seventh Circuit expressly declined to engage in such a comparative inquiry. A complaint could survive, that court said, as long as it "alleges facts from which, if true, a reasonable person could infer that the defendant acted with the required intent"; in other words, only "[i]f a reasonable person could not draw such an inference from the alleged facts" would the defendant prevail on a motion to dismiss. But in § 21D(b)(2), Congress did not merely require plaintiffs to "provide a factual basis for [their] scienter allegations," i.e., to allege facts from which an inference of scienter rationally could be drawn. Instead, Congress required plaintiffs to plead with particularity facts that give rise to a "strong"—i.e., a powerful or cogent—inference.

Priest–Klein theory → Cases should go to trial when...

1) sufficient legal uncertainty

2) They are making erroneous or irrational choices

These are non-directional situations, towards → neither plaintiffs or defendants (either side should win about 50% of the time)

[Handwritten top margin:] $EV_\pi = P \times A - Costs_\pi$ $-[EV_\Delta = P \times A + Costs_\Delta]$

Example $(.5) \times (200k) - 30k = \$70k$

The strength of an inference cannot be decided in a vacuum. The inquiry is inherently comparative: How likely is it that one conclusion, as compared to others, follows from the underlying facts? To determine whether the plaintiff has alleged facts that give rise to the requisite "strong inference" of scienter, a court must consider plausible nonculpable explanations for the defendant's conduct, as well as inferences favoring the plaintiff. The inference that the defendant acted with scienter need not be irrefutable, i.e., of the "smoking-gun" genre, or even the "most plausible of competing inferences." * * * A complaint will survive, we hold, only if a reasonable person would deem the inference of scienter cogent and at least as compelling as any opposing inference one could draw from the facts alleged.[5]

[Handwritten margin right:] Plaintiff's indifference point is equal to the EV_π.

[Handwritten margin right:] Defendant indifference point is any val. below EV_Δ.

[Handwritten margin right:] Diff b/w EV_π and EV_Δ is the Settlement zone.

[Handwritten below paragraph:] ↳ It's "possible" to not explicitly state other possibilities in the 12(b)(6) but in practice it's better to explicitly state your opposing inferences.

B

Tellabs contends that when competing inferences are considered, Notebaert's evident lack of pecuniary motive will be dispositive. The Shareholders, Tellabs stresses, did not allege that Notebaert sold any shares during the class period. While it is true that motive can be a relevant consideration, and personal financial gain may weigh heavily in favor of a scienter inference, we agree with the Seventh Circuit that the absence of a motive allegation is not fatal. As earlier stated, allegations must be considered collectively; the significance that can be ascribed to an allegation of motive, or lack thereof, depends on the entirety of the complaint.

Tellabs also maintains that several of the Shareholders' allegations are too vague or ambiguous to contribute to a strong inference of scienter. For example, the Shareholders alleged that Tellabs flooded its customers with unwanted products, a practice known as "channel stuffing." But they failed, Tellabs argues, to specify whether the channel stuffing allegedly known to Notebaert was the illegitimate kind (e.g., writing orders for products customers had not requested) or the legitimate kind (e.g., offering customers discounts as an incentive to buy). We agree that omissions and

---

[5] Justice Scalia objects to this standard on the ground that "[i]f a jade falcon were stolen from a room to which only A and B had access," it could not "possibly be said there was a 'strong inference' that B was the thief." I suspect, however, that law enforcement officials as well as the owner of the precious falcon would find the inference of guilt as to B quite strong—certainly strong enough to warrant further investigation. Indeed, an inference at least as likely as competing inferences can, in some cases, warrant recovery. See Summers v. Tice, 199 P.2d 1, 3–5 (Cal.1948) (plaintiff wounded by gunshot could recover from two defendants, even though the most he could prove was that each defendant was at least as likely to have injured him as the other). In any event, we disagree with Justice Scalia that the hardly stock term "strong inference" has only one invariably right ("natural" or "normal") reading—his. Justice Alito agrees with Justice Scalia, and would transpose to the pleading stage "the test that is used at the summary-judgment and judgment-as-a-matter-of-law stages." But the test at each stage is measured against a different backdrop. It is improbable that Congress, without so stating, intended courts to test pleadings, unaided by discovery, to determine whether there is "no genuine issue as to any material fact." See Fed. Rule Civ. Proc. 56[(a)]. And judgment as a matter of law is a post-trial device, turning on the question whether a party has produced evidence "legally sufficient" to warrant a jury determination in that party's favor. See Rule 50(a)(1).

[Handwritten bottom margin:] $P =$ Prob. plaintiff will win $A =$ Award to plaintiff

Handwritten margin notes: "Very high standard → Rdical departure from Rule 8 + Rule 9(b)" and "you essentially need a whistleblow"

ambiguities count against inferring scienter, for plaintiffs must "state with particularity facts giving rise to a strong inference that the defendant acted with the required state of mind." § 78u–4(b)(2). We reiterate, however, that the court's job is not to scrutinize each allegation in isolation but to assess all the allegations holistically. In sum, the reviewing court must ask: When the allegations are accepted as true and taken collectively, would a reasonable person deem the inference of scienter at least as strong as any opposing inference?

IV

Accounting for its construction of § 21D(b)(2), the Seventh Circuit explained that the court "th[ought] it wis[e] to adopt an approach that [could not] be misunderstood as a usurpation of the jury's role." In our view, the Seventh Circuit's concern was undue. A court's comparative assessment of plausible inferences, while constantly assuming the plaintiff's allegations to be true, we think it plain, does not impinge upon the Seventh Amendment right to jury trial.[8]

Congress, as creator of federal statutory claims, has power to prescribe what must be pleaded to state the claim, just as it has power to determine what must be proved to prevail on the merits. It is the federal lawmaker's prerogative, therefore, to allow, disallow, or shape the contours of— including the pleading and proof requirements for—§ 10(b) private actions. No decision of this Court questions that authority in general, or suggests, in particular, that the Seventh Amendment inhibits Congress from establishing whatever pleading requirements it finds appropriate for federal statutory claims. Cf. Swierkiewicz v. Sorema N. A., 534 U.S. 506, 512–513 (2002); Leatherman [v. Tarrant County Narcotics and Coordination Unit], 507 U.S. [163], at 168 [(1993)] (both recognizing that heightened pleading requirements can be established by Federal Rule, citing Fed. Rule Civ. Proc. 9(b), which requires that fraud or mistake be pleaded with particularity).[9]

* * * We emphasize * * * that under our construction of the "strong inference" standard, a plaintiff is not forced to plead more than she would be required to prove at trial. A plaintiff alleging fraud in a § 10(b) action, we hold today, must plead facts rendering an inference of scienter at least as likely as any plausible opposing inference. At trial, she must then prove

---

8 In numerous contexts, gatekeeping judicial determinations prevent submission of claims to a jury's judgment without violating the Seventh Amendment. See, e.g., Daubert v. Merrell Dow Pharmaceuticals, Inc., 509 U.S. 579, 589 (1993) (expert testimony can be excluded based on judicial determination of reliability); Neely v. Martin K. Eby Constr. Co., 386 U.S. 317, 321 (1967) (judgment as a matter of law); Pease v. Rathbun-Jones Engineering Co., 243 U.S. 273, 278 (1917) (summary judgment).

9 Any heightened pleading rule, including Fed. Rule Civ. Proc. 9(b), could have the effect of preventing a plaintiff from getting discovery on a claim that might have gone to a jury, had discovery occurred and yielded substantial evidence. In recognizing Congress' or the Federal Rule makers' authority to adopt special pleading rules, we have detected no Seventh Amendment impediment.

her case by a "preponderance of the evidence." Stated otherwise, she must demonstrate that it is more likely than not that the defendant acted with scienter.

* * *

While we reject the Seventh Circuit's approach to § 21D(b)(2), we do not decide whether, under the standard we have described, the Shareholders' allegations warrant "a strong inference that [Notebaert and Tellabs] acted with the required state of mind," 15 U.S.C. § 78u–4(b)(2). Neither the District Court nor the Court of Appeals had the opportunity to consider the matter in light of the prescriptions we announce today. We therefore vacate the Seventh Circuit's judgment so that the case may be reexamined in accord with our construction of § 21D(b)(2).

JUSTICE SCALIA, concurring in the judgment.

I fail to see how an inference that is merely "at least as compelling as any opposing inference," can conceivably be called what the statute here at issue requires: a "strong inference," 15 U.S.C. § 78u–4(b)(2). If a jade falcon were stolen from a room to which only A and B had access, could it possibly be said there was a "strong inference" that B was the thief? I think not, and I therefore think that the Court's test must fail. In my view, the test should be whether the inference of scienter (if any) is more plausible than the inference of innocence.

The Court's explicit rejection of this reading rests on two assertions. The first (doubtless true) is that the statute does not require that "[t]he inference that the defendant acted with scienter . . . be irrefutable, i.e., of the 'smoking-gun' genre." It is up to Congress, however, and not to us, to determine what pleading standard would avoid those extremities while yet effectively deterring baseless actions. Congress has expressed its determination in the phrase "strong inference"; it is our job to give that phrase its normal meaning. And if we are to abandon text in favor of unexpressed purpose, as the Court does, it is inconceivable that Congress's enactment of stringent pleading requirements in the Private Securities Litigation Reform Act of 1995 somehow manifests the purpose of giving plaintiffs the edge in close cases.

The Court's second assertion (also true) is that "an inference at least as likely as competing inferences can, in some cases, warrant recovery." Ante, n. 5 (citing Summers v. Tice, 199 P.2d 1, 3–5 (Cal.1948), Summers is a famous case, however, because it sticks out of the ordinary body of tort law like a sore thumb. It represented "a relaxation" of "such proof as is ordinarily required" to succeed in a negligence action. There is no indication that the statute at issue here was meant to relax the ordinary rule under which a tie goes to the defendant. To the contrary, it explicitly strengthens that rule by extending it to the pleading stage of a case.

* * * We must be content to give "strong inference" its normal meaning. I hasten to add that, while precision of interpretation should always be pursued for its own sake, I doubt that in this instance what I deem to be the correct test will produce results much different from the Court's. How often is it that inferences are precisely in equipoise? All the more reason, I think, to read the language for what it says.

* * *

JUSTICE ALITO, concurring in the judgment.

1st time we see collapse b/w motion to dismiss and summary judgment

[Justice Alito argued that the statutory language requiring plaintiffs to plead "with particularity facts giving rise to a strong inference that the defendant acted with the required state of mind" limited consideration to the facts alleged with particularity, and he therefore took issue with the majority's statement that the complaint's "omissions and ambiguities" only "count against" inferring scienter. He argued that "the Court's interpretation of the particularity requirement in no way distinguishes it from normal pleading review, under which a court naturally gives less weight to allegations containing 'omissions and ambiguities' and more weight to allegations stating particularized facts."

He also endorsed Justice Scalia's approach because it "would align the pleading test under [the PSLRA] with the test that is used at the summary-judgment and judgment-as-matter-of-law stages, whereas the Court's test would introduce a test previously unknown in civil litigation. It seems more likely that Congress meant to adopt a known quantity and thus to adopt Justice Scalia's approach."]

JUSTICE STEVENS, dissenting.

* * * Today the majority crafts a perfectly workable definition of the term, but I am persuaded that a different interpretation would be both easier to apply and more consistent with the statute.

The basic purpose of the heightened pleading requirement in the context of securities fraud litigation is to protect defendants from the costs of discovery and trial in unmeritorious cases. Because of its intrusive nature, discovery may also invade the privacy interests of the defendants and their executives. Like citizens suspected of having engaged in criminal activity, those defendants should not be required to produce their private effects unless there is probable cause to believe them guilty of misconduct. Admittedly, the probable-cause standard is not capable of precise measurement, but it is a concept that is familiar to judges. As a matter of normal English usage, its meaning is roughly the same as "strong inference." Moreover, it is most unlikely that Congress intended us to adopt a standard that makes it more difficult to commence a civil case than a criminal case.

Good point, but we are talking about money.

Plus, criminal cases have a much higher conviction bar than civil cases have liability bar.

[handwritten margin note: He's jus making up law finding]

In addition to the benefit of its grounding in an already familiar legal concept, using a probable-cause standard would avoid the unnecessary conclusion that "in determining whether the pleaded facts give rise to a 'strong' inference of scienter, the court must take into account plausible opposing inferences." (emphasis added) There are times when an inference can easily be deemed strong without any need to weigh competing inferences. For example, if a known drug dealer exits a building immediately after a confirmed drug transaction, carrying a suspicious looking package, a judge could draw a strong inference that the individual was involved in the aforementioned drug transaction without debating whether the suspect might have been leaving the building at that exact time for another unrelated reason.

[handwritten margin note: Congress did not say "probable cause"]

If, using that same methodology, we assume the truth of the detailed factual allegations attributed to 27 different confidential informants described in the complaint, and view those allegations collectively, I think it clear that they establish probable cause to believe that Tellabs' chief executive officer "acted with the required intent," as the Seventh Circuit held.

NOTES AND QUESTIONS

1.   On remand, the Seventh Circuit ruled that the allegations satisfied the PSLRA requirements. Makor Issues & Rights, Ltd. v. Tellabs, Inc., 513 F.3d 702 (7th Cir. 2008). Judge Posner began by noting that "[t]o judges raised on notice pleading, the idea of drawing a 'strong inference' from factual allegations is mysterious. Even when a plaintiff is required by Rule 9(b) to plead facts (such as the when and where of an alleged fraudulent statement), the court must treat the pleaded facts as true and 'draw all reasonable inferences in favor of the plaintiff.'" Id. at 705.

But the Supreme Court had not disturbed the lower court's earlier holding that plaintiffs had alleged that materially false statements were made about Tellabs' sales of its 5500 and new 6500 systems. The lower court then analyzed the scienter issue as follows (id. at 709):

> The critical question, therefore, is how likely it is that the allegedly false statements that we quoted earlier in this opinion were the result of merely careless mistakes at the management level based on false information fed it from below, rather than of an intent to deceive or a reckless indifference to whether the statements were misleading. It is exceedingly unlikely. The 5500 and the 6500 were Tellabs's most important products. The 5500 was described by the company as its "flagship" product and the 6500 was the 5500's heralded successor. They were to Tellabs as Windows XP and Vista are to Microsoft. That no member of the company's senior management who was involved in authorizing or making public statements about the demand for the 5500 or 6500 knew that they were false is very hard to credit, and no

plausible story has yet been told by defendants that might dispel our incredulity.

Regarding defendant Notebaert, the court found the fact he did not personally profit from the statements by selling any of his shares not particularly important, since he might knowingly have made false assertions in hopes the results would reverse themselves before corrections were necessary. "Almost all the false statements that we quoted emanated directly from him. Is it conceivable that he was unaware of the problems of his company's two major products and merely repeating lies fed to him by other executives of the company? It is conceivable, yes, but it is exceedingly unlikely." Id. at 711.

On remand from the Seventh Circuit, substantial additional litigation occurred in the district court, leading to a 73-page ruling by the district judge granting defendants summary judgment, ruling that Tellabs had not inflated sales by "channel stuffing" and that the Notebart did not have actual knowledge his statements were false. But she also held that disputed fact issues remained on some questions about whether the CEO knowingly misled investors. See Makor Issues & Rights, Ltd. v. Tellabs, Inc., 735 F.Supp.2d 856 (N.D. Ill. 2010).

2.   Justice Alito argues that the standard for scrutinizing the adequacy of plaintiff's factual allegations should mirror the standard used when a court decides whether to grant summary judgment or to grant judgment as a matter of law at trial. We will study those motions in Chapters 6 and 8. They ordinarily focus on the evidence that the party with the burden of proof (usually the plaintiff) has produced, and ask whether that evidence reasonably supports a finding in that party's favor. They do not require that the judge find that she is persuaded by plaintiff's evidence, but only that a reasonable jury could be persuaded. Does the PSLRA's "strong inference" requirement seem to focus on the same thing? Would it be proper to apply the same standard to a plaintiff before discovery? Consider Mizzaro v. Home Depot, Inc., 544 F.3d 1230 (11th Cir. 2008), which explains that the *Tellabs* test "is not the same as the standard we employ for summary judgment under Fed. R. Civ. P. 56, because [the *Tellabs* test] asks what a reasonable person would think, not what a reasonable person could think [which is the Rule 56 summary judgment standard]." If the Eleventh Circuit is correct, does this distinction make sense?

The PSLRA certainly does not contemplate that plaintiffs may utilize discovery to satisfy its pleading requirements. Instead, it provides that "all discovery and other proceedings shall be stayed during the pendency of any motion to dismiss, unless the court finds upon the motion of any party that particularized discovery is necessary to preserve evidence or to prevent undue prejudice to that party." 15 U.S.C.A. § 78u–4(b)(3)(B). The lower courts have generally applied this discovery stay vigorously. See, e.g., SG Cowen Securities Corp. v. U.S. Dist. Ct., 189 F.3d 909 (9th Cir.1999) (district court may not permit discovery that will enable plaintiffs to uncover facts sufficient to satisfy the Act's pleading requirements); Medhekar v. U.S. District Court, 99 F.3d 325 (9th Cir.1996) (discovery stay applies to initial disclosure under Fed.R.Civ.P. 26(a)(1) as well as to formal discovery). In some instances, however, lower courts have allowed limited discovery before ruling on motions to dismiss. See, e.g., In re WorldCom, Inc. Securities Litigation, 234 F.Supp.2d 301 (S.D.N.Y.2002) (plaintiffs could obtain copies of documents previously provided to public agencies in related proceedings); de la Fuente v. DCI Telecommunications, Inc., 206 F.R.D. 369 (S.D.N.Y.2002) (plaintiffs could have discovery to respond to defendants' motion for summary judgment even though the stay had applied to defendants' motion to dismiss). Does the discovery stay shed light on whether the PSLRA pleading standard should mirror the summary judgment standard? As Judge Posner noted on remand in Tellabs, the customary inclination of judges on pleading motions is to indulge all reasonable inferences in favor of plaintiff.

3. As quoted supra at p. 161, the Second Circuit offered three explanations for adopting its demanding interpretation of Rule 9(b). Are those explanations persuasive? Consider:

(a) *Notice*: Certainly some fraud cases may involve more complicated transactions and numerous parties so that more detail could be important in providing notice. Is that not true of other kinds of cases? Recall United States v. Board of Harbor Comm'rs, supra p. 137.

(b) *Injury to reputation*: Is a charge of fraud especially threatening to reputations? Consider the views of Judge Cardamone, dissenting from dismissal of claims brought under the Racketeer Influenced Corrupt Organizations statute (RICO):

> Today, defendants in civil suits are labelled as violators of environmental laws when pumping coal byproducts into the atmosphere, despoilers of our rivers when emptying oil from their tankers' bilges, adulterers in state divorce actions, and killers in vehicular wrongful death actions. The allegations of the civil complaint do not make these citizens criminals, although their conduct may well subject them to criminal prosecutions. Why the outcry over RICO?

Sedima, S.P.R.L. v. Imrex Co., Inc., 741 F.2d 482, 508 (2d Cir.1984). In reversing the dismissal of the case, the Supreme Court noted that "[a]s for stigma, a civil RICO proceeding leaves no greater stain than do a number of other civil proceedings." Sedima, S.P.R.L. v. Imrex Co., Inc., 473 U.S. 479 (1985).

(c) Limiting *in terrorem* value of suit: In Blue Chip Stamps v. Manor Drug Stores, 421 U.S. 723 (1975), the Court (dealing with an unrelated issue) warned that "in this type of litigation * * * the mere existence of an unresolved lawsuit has settlement value to the plaintiff not only because of the possibility that he may prevail on the merits, an entirely legitimate component of settlement value, but because of the threat of extensive discovery and disruption of normal business activities which may accompany a lawsuit which is groundless in any event, but cannot be proved so before trial." Are securities fraud lawsuits really different in this respect? See Ackerman v. Northwestern Mut. Life Ins. Co., 172 F.3d 467, 469 (7th Cir.1999) ("charges of fraud (and also mistake, the other charge that Rule 9(b) requires to be pleaded with particularity) frequently ask courts in effect to rewrite the parties' contract or otherwise disrupt established relationships").

Which of these concerns explains the requirements of the PSLRA? The *Tellabs* Court cites "nuisance filings, targeting of deep-pocket defendants, vexatious discovery requests and manipulation by class action lawyers."

Research by Professor Alexander suggested that in securities fraud suits the merits appear to have no substantial bearing on the amount of settlements because these cases are routinely settled for a relatively small consistent percentage of the prospective damages, seemingly without any emphasis on the strength of the case. She explains that a number of factors combine to cause this result—risk aversion among defendants when cases threaten a substantial portion of the company's assets or personal ruin, availability of insurance to fund settlements, and unwillingness of plaintiffs' lawyers to risk a trial (which might lead to a loss and no payment for them as opposed to a settlement) in order to assure that they will be paid for their efforts in the case. Another factor is the impossibility of obtaining a judicial decision before trial: "With adjudication before trial unavailable as a practical matter and adjudication at trial a virtually unthinkable alternative, settlement becomes a foregone conclusion." Alexander, Do the Merits Matter? A Study of Settlements in Securities Class Actions, 43 Stan.L.Rev. 497, 567 (1991); compare Seligman, The Merits Do Matter, 108 Harv.L.Rev. 438 (1994) (questioning Alexander's conclusions). See also Baker & Griffith, How the Merits Matter: Directors' and Officers' Insurance and Securities Settlements, 157 U.Pa.L.Rev. 755 (2009) (finding that "merits" issues seem to have some effect on settlement amounts, but so do the amount and provisions of directors' insurance); Curtis & Myers, Do the Merits Matter? Empirical Evidence From Shareholder Suits From Options Backdating, 164 U.Pa.L.Rev. 291 (2016) (finding that plaintiff attorneys appear to target the most egregious offenders).

4.   Are the concerns about abusive litigation limited to securities fraud cases? Consider Cash Energy, Inc. v. Weiner, 768 F.Supp. 892 (D. Mass. 1991), a toxic cleanup case in which plaintiffs asserted claims under the federal Comprehensive Environmental Response, Compensation and Liability Act (CERCLA) against not only the corporations alleged to have dumped toxic materials that contaminated plaintiffs' properties but also officers of those companies. The individual defendants moved to dismiss because the claims against them were based on the "bald assertion" that they had personally participated in the discharge of toxics. The judge considered the possible application of Rule 9(b), observing (id. at 897):

> Over time, the exception for fraud has been extended to a number of analogous areas involving statutory causes of action, where the original concern about opportunities for abuse inherent in the freedom to plead conclusions rather than facts applied with like force. New exceptions also have been created independently in areas where reasons for requiring particularity are especially compelling.

"Although the analogy to fraud is strained," the court acknowledged, CERCLA did involve considerations that had prompted courts to require more specificity because the cost of defense could be very great. He therefore required specific pleading for the claims against the individual defendants.

Should courts extend Rule 9(b) in this manner? Reconsider this question in connection with Swierkiewicz v. Sorema, S.A., infra p. 177, and Leatherman v. Tarrant County Narcotics and Coordination Unit, infra p. 181, n. 1, which criticize expansive judicial interpretation of that rule. Rule 9(b) clearly does apply beyond the securities fraud context (and therefore more broadly than the PSLRA). For example, in Pirelli Armstrong Tire Armstrong Tire Corp. v. Walgreen Co., 631 F.3d 436 (7th Cir. 2011). Pirelli sued Walgreens to recoup amounts it had reimbursed the pharmacy company for purchases by its retirees of two commonly prescribed drugs, claiming that Walgreens had routinely disregarded doctors' prescriptions for inexpensive generics and substituted more expensive name-brand drugs. Defendant argued that Rule 9(b) applied, and Pirelli countered that the rule should not apply because it had sued under an Illinois statute that provided recovery for "unfair practices" falling short of deception. The court disagreed (id. at 446–47):

> However, the practices alleged in Pirelli's complaint constitute fraudulent activity, and the dictates of Rule 9(b) apply to allegations of fraud, not claims of fraud. Here, the complaint alleges that Walgreens unlawfully and intentionally concealed from [Pirelli], or misrepresented to it, the form of the drug that was prescribed and that Pirelli suffered damages as a result. That is fraud predicated on either a misrepresentation or an omission. The district court correctly concluded both that Rule 9(b) applied and that its dictates were not satisfied.

Contrast Pelman v. McDonald's Corp., 396 F.3d 508 (2d Cir. 2005), where the court reversed dismissal of a suit claiming that McDonald's had violated the New York Consumer Protection Act by creating a false impression that its food products were part of a healthy diet even if consumed daily, resulting in obesity and other health problems for plaintiffs and the class they sought to represent. Because the pertinent New York law "extends beyond common-law fraud to cover a broad range of deceptive practices," the court ruled, the claim was not subject to Rule 9(b) but only the requirements of Rule 8(a). Should courts take a narrow or broad view of Rule 9(b)? On remand in *Pelman*, the district court granted defendant's motion for a more definite statement requiring plaintiffs to be more specific about the advertisements they claimed were false or misleading, but permitted the case to continue, eventually denying class-action status on the ground that individualized inquiries would be required to decide the case. Pelman v. McDonald's Corp., 272 F.R.D. 82 (S.D.N.Y.2010).

5. How much should Rule 9(b) require? Look at the second sentence of the rule. In McQueen v. Woodstream Corp., 248 F.R.D. 73 (D.D.C. 2008), the court held that the rule was satisfied, noting that "Rule 9(b) is a net designed

to catch intrinsically faulty claims, not a trap designed to ensnare claims that merely lack a Zolaesque rigor of detail." Id. at 79.

6.   In *Tellabs* the Court repeatedly emphasizes the need for private suits to enforce the securities laws. But the private right to sue was not provided explicitly in the securities laws adopted by Congress. Instead, it was "implied" by the courts as a necessary enforcement device. The PSLRA was actually the first time that Congress explicitly endorsed the courts' "implication" of a private right to sue for securities fraud. Could it be argued that the PSLRA's limitations on such suits actually undercut the very private enforcement effort the courts fostered? Consider Friedenthal, A Divided Supreme Court Adopts Discovery Amendments to the Federal Rules of Civil Procedure, 69 Calif.L.Rev. 806, 815–16 (1981): "It is always to a defendant's advantage to require the plaintiff to pinpoint its case specifically and in detail. First, if the case is based primarily on speculation, the plaintiff may be unable to allege sufficient facts to sustain the complaint and the action can be dismissed immediately. Second, even if the complaint is sufficient, it necessarily narrows the range of facts that the plaintiff will be allowed to discover and to prove at trial. If plaintiff's attorney has erred at the pleading stage as to the specific facts by which a valid case for his client could be established, defendant can thwart successful prosecution of the action by keeping out vital facts on the ground that they were not pleaded and, hence, are not relevant."

Is the PSLRA a desirable response to the problems that worried Congress? Consider Sale, Heightened Pleading and Discovery Stays: An Analysis of the Effect of the PSLRA's Internal-Information Standard on '33 and '34 Act Claims, 76 Wash. U. L. Rev. 537, 564 (1998):

> [T]he Reform Act is likely to allow only the more flagrant and obvious cases of securities fraud to proceed past a motion to dismiss, while being overinclusive in its elimination of cases where it is more difficult to identify, and therefore to plead, fraud. Presumably, the SEC, with its limited resources, pursues the flagrant and obvious cases of securities fraud. Arguably, however, the more difficult to identify frauds are precisely the ones that the plaintiffs, who function as private attorneys general, pursue. Indeed, the Commissioner of the SEC has stressed that private mechanisms are important to the enforcement of the Acts. Because the plaintiffs lack access to the information the Reform Act requires them to plead at the motion-to-dismiss stage, however, the strict application of the heightened-pleading standard is likely to result in unredressed fraud.

Could some plaintiffs actually benefit from the stricter pleading? Consider Cox, Making Securities Fraud Class Actions Virtuous, 39 Ariz. L. Rev. 497, 520 (1997):

> Though lax pleading requirements made the nuisance value of a suit much more difficult to address through pretrial motions, it must also be understood that the Reform Act's heightened pleading standard credentials suits that survive pretrial motions so that [they] will have

a greater settlement value than such suits had on average before the Reform Act. * * * [C]ounsel should feel more confident in the case after satisfying the new pleading requirements than the counsel who had previously had to know less and plead less to withstand a challenge to the pleadings.

7.   Justice Scalia invokes "normal pleading review, under which a court naturally gives * * * more weight to allegations stating particularized facts." Is that the proper attitude of normal pleading review? Recall Mitchell v. W.T. Grant Co., supra p. 45, where the Court upheld the constitutionality of a Louisiana procedure permitting attachment without prior notice and a right for defendant to be heard because it required pleading of "specific facts" rather than "conclusory allegations."

8.   If the basic goal of heightened pleading scrutiny is to ensure that plaintiff has done an investigation and has a legitimate basis for the claims asserted, why doesn't Rule 11 adequately serve that purpose? In the PSLRA, Congress indicated that it was not satisfied with that reassurance and also sought to undo some of the changes to Rule 11 effected by the 1993 amendments to the rule. Accordingly, the PSLRA requires the court to make findings about compliance with Rule 11(b) in every case and to impose sanctions on any party or attorney found to have violated the rule. 15 U.S.C.A. § 78u–4(c). This change "eliminates the [Rule 11(c)(2)] safe harbor for federal securities litigation." Smith v. Smith, 184 F.R.D. 420, 422 (S.D.Fla. 1998). Would fortifying Rule 11 for all cases be a desirable response to the concerns that have prompted more demanding pleading requirements?

4.   THE CURRENT APPLICATION OF RULE 8(a)(2) PLEADING REQUIREMENTS

SWIERKIEWICZ V. SOREMA, N. A.

Supreme Court of the United States, 2002
534 U.S. 506

JUSTICE THOMAS delivered the opinion of the Court.

This case presents the question whether a complaint in an employment discrimination lawsuit must contain specific facts establishing a prima facie case of discrimination under the framework set forth by this Court in McDonnell Douglas Corp. v. Green, 411 U.S. 792 (1973). We hold that an employment discrimination complaint need not include such facts and instead must contain only "a short and plain statement of the claim showing that the pleader is entitled to relief." Fed. Rule Civ. Proc. 8(a)(2).

I

Petitioner Akos Swierkiewicz is a native of Hungary, who at the time of his complaint was 53 years old.[1] In April 1989, petitioner began working for respondent Sorema N. A., a reinsurance company headquartered in New York and principally owned and controlled by a French parent corporation. Petitioner was initially employed in the position of senior vice president and chief underwriting officer (CUO). Nearly six years later, François M. Chavel, respondent's Chief Executive Officer, demoted petitioner to a marketing and services position and transferred the bulk of his underwriting responsibilities to Nicholas Papadopoulo, a 32-year-old who, like Mr. Chavel, is a French national. About a year later, Mr. Chavel stated that he wanted to "energize" the underwriting department and appointed Mr. Papadopoulo as CUO. Petitioner claims that Mr. Papadopoulo had only one year of underwriting experience at the time he was promoted, and therefore was less experienced and less qualified to be CUO than he, since at that point he had 26 years of experience in the insurance industry.

Following his demotion, petitioner contends that he "was isolated by Mr. Chavel . . . excluded from business decisions and meetings and denied the opportunity to reach his true potential at SOREMA." Petitioner unsuccessfully attempted to meet with Mr. Chavel to discuss his discontent. Finally, in April 1997, petitioner sent a memo to Mr. Chavel outlining his grievances and requesting a severance package. Two weeks later, respondent's general counsel presented petitioner with two options: He could either resign without a severance package or be dismissed. Mr. Chavel fired petitioner after he refused to resign.

Petitioner filed a lawsuit alleging that he had been terminated on account of his national origin in violation of Title VII of the Civil Rights Act of 1964, 42 U.S.C. § 2000e *et seq.*, and on account of his age in violation of the Age Discrimination in Employment Act of 1967 (ADEA), 29 U.S.C. § 621 *et seq.* The United States District Court for the Southern District of New York dismissed petitioner's complaint because it found that he "ha[d] not adequately alleged a prima facie case, in that he ha[d] not adequately alleged circumstances that support an inference of discrimination." The United States Court of Appeals for the Second Circuit affirmed the dismissal, relying on its settled precedent, which requires a plaintiff in an employment discrimination complaint to allege facts constituting a prima facie case of discrimination under the framework set forth by this Court in *McDonnell Douglas*, supra, at 802. The Court of Appeals held that petitioner had failed to meet his burden because his allegations were "insufficient as a matter of law to raise an inference of discrimination." 5 Fed.Appx. 63, 65 (C.A.2 2001). We granted certiorari to resolve a split

---

[1] Because we review here a decision granting respondent's motion to dismiss, we must accept as true all of the factual allegations contained in the complaint.

among the Courts of Appeals concerning the proper pleading standard for employment discrimination cases, and now reverse.

II

Applying Circuit precedent, the Court of Appeals required petitioner to plead a prima facie case of discrimination in order to survive respondent's motion to dismiss. In the Court of Appeals' view, petitioner was thus required to allege in his complaint: (1) membership in a protected group; (2) qualification for the job in question; (3) an adverse employment action; and (4) circumstances that support an inference of discrimination.

The prima facie case under *McDonnell Douglas*, however, is an evidentiary standard, not a pleading requirement. In *McDonnell Douglas*, this Court made clear that "[t]he critical issue before us concern[ed] the order and allocation *of proof* in a private, non-class action challenging employment discrimination." In subsequent cases, this Court has reiterated that the prima facie case relates to the employee's burden of presenting evidence that raises an inference of discrimination.

"Proof"

This Court has never indicated that the requirements for establishing a prima facie case under *McDonnell Douglas* also apply to the pleading standard that plaintiffs must satisfy in order to survive a motion to dismiss. For instance, we have rejected the argument that a Title VII complaint requires greater "particularity," because this would "too narrowly constric[t] the role of the pleadings." McDonald v. Santa Fe Trail Transp. Co., 427 U.S. 273, 283, n. 11 (1976). Consequently, the ordinary rules for assessing the sufficiency of a complaint apply.

Rule 8 (a)

In addition, under a notice pleading system, it is not appropriate to require a plaintiff to plead facts establishing a prima facie case because the *McDonnell Douglas* framework does not apply in every employment discrimination case. For instance, if a plaintiff is able to produce direct evidence of discrimination, he may prevail without proving all the elements of a prima facie case. See Trans World Airlines, Inc. v. Thurston, 469 U.S. 111, 121 (1985) ("[T]he *McDonnell Douglas* test is inapplicable where the plaintiff presents direct evidence of discrimination"). Under the Second Circuit's heightened pleading standard, a plaintiff without direct evidence of discrimination at the time of his complaint must plead a prima facie case of discrimination, even though discovery might uncover such direct evidence. It thus seems incongruous to require a plaintiff, in order to survive a motion to dismiss, to plead more facts than he may ultimately need to prove to succeed on the merits if direct evidence of discrimination is discovered.

"discovery"

Moreover, the precise requirements of a prima facie case can vary depending on the context and were "never intended to be rigid, mechanized, or ritualistic." Before discovery has unearthed relevant facts and evidence, it may be difficult to define the precise formulation of the required prima facie case in a particular case. Given that the prima facie case operates as a flexible evidentiary standard, it should not be transposed into a rigid pleading standard for discrimination cases.

Furthermore, imposing the Court of Appeals' heightened pleading standard in employment discrimination cases conflicts with Federal Rule of Civil Procedure 8(a)(2), which provides that a complaint must include only "a short and plain statement of the claim showing that the pleader is entitled to relief." Such a statement must simply "give the defendant fair notice of what the plaintiff's claim is and the grounds upon which it rests." Conley v. Gibson, 355 U.S. 41, 47 (1957). This simplified notice pleading standard relies on liberal discovery rules and summary judgment motions to define disputed facts and issues and to dispose of unmeritorious claims. See id., at 47–48, 78 S.Ct. 99; Leatherman v. Tarrant County Narcotics Intelligence and Coordination Unit, 507 U.S. 163, 168–169 (1993). "The provisions for discovery are so flexible and the provisions for pretrial procedure and summary judgment so effective, that attempted surprise in federal practice is aborted very easily, synthetic issues detected, and the gravamen of the dispute brought frankly into the open for the inspection of the court." 5 C. Wright & A. Miller, Federal Practice and Procedure § 1202, p. 76 (2d ed. 1990).

Rule 8(a)'s simplified pleading standard applies to all civil actions, with limited exceptions. Rule 9(b), for example, provides for greater particularity in all averments of fraud or mistake. This Court, however, has declined to extend such exceptions to other contexts. In *Leatherman* we stated: "[T]he Federal Rules do address in Rule 9(b) the question of the need for greater particularity in pleading certain actions, but do not include among the enumerated actions any reference to complaints alleging municipal liability under § 1983. *Expressio unius est exclusio alterius.*" Just as Rule 9(b) makes no mention of municipal liability under 42 U.S.C. § 1983, neither does it refer to employment discrimination. Thus, complaints in these cases, as in most others, must satisfy only the simple requirements of Rule 8(a).[4]

Other provisions of the Federal Rules of Civil Procedure are inextricably linked to Rule 8(a)'s simplified notice pleading standard. Rule 8(e)(1) [now Rule 8(d)(1)] states that "[n]o technical forms of pleading or motions are required," and Rule 8(f) [now Rule 8(e)] provides that "[a]ll pleadings shall be so construed as to do substantial justice." Given the Federal Rules' simplified standard for pleading, "[a] court may dismiss a complaint only if it is clear that no relief could be granted under any set of

---

[4]   These requirements are exemplified by the Federal Rules of Civil Procedure Forms, which "are sufficient under the rules and are intended to indicate the simplicity and brevity of statement which the rules contemplate." Fed. Rule Civ. Proc. 84 [abrogated 2015]. For example, Form 9 [see supra, p. 133 n. 5] sets forth a complaint for negligence in which plaintiff simply states in relevant part: "On June 1, 1936, in a public highway called Boylston Street in Boston, Massachusetts, defendant negligently drove a motor vehicle against plaintiff who was then crossing said highway."

This is what they tried in the oil spill case

facts that could be proved consistent with the allegations." If a pleading fails to specify the allegations in a manner that provides sufficient notice, a defendant can move for a more definite statement under Rule 12(e) before responding. Moreover, claims lacking merit may be dealt with through summary judgment under Rule 56. The liberal notice pleading of Rule 8(a) is the starting point of a simplified pleading system, which was adopted to focus litigation on the merits of a claim.

"Motion for a more def. statement"

Applying the relevant standard, petitioner's complaint easily satisfies the requirements of Rule 8(a) because it gives respondent fair notice of the basis for petitioner's claims. Petitioner alleged that he had been terminated on account of his national origin in violation of Title VII and on account of his age in violation of the ADEA. His complaint detailed the events leading to his termination, provided relevant dates, and included the ages and nationalities of at least some of the relevant persons involved with his termination. These allegations give respondent fair notice of what petitioner's claims are and the grounds upon which they rest. In addition, they state claims upon which relief could be granted under Title VII and the ADEA.

Respondent argues that allowing lawsuits based on conclusory allegations of discrimination to go forward will burden the courts and encourage disgruntled employees to bring unsubstantiated suits. Whatever the practical merits of this argument, the Federal Rules do not contain a heightened pleading standard for employment discrimination suits. A requirement of greater specificity for particular claims is a result that "must be obtained by the process of amending the Federal Rules, and not by judicial interpretation." *Leatherman*, supra, [507 U.S.] at 168. Furthermore, Rule 8(a) establishes a pleading standard without regard to whether a claim will succeed on the merits. "Indeed it may appear on the face of the pleadings that a recovery is very remote and unlikely but that is not the test."

For the foregoing reasons, we hold that an employment discrimination plaintiff need not plead a prima facie case of discrimination and that petitioner's complaint is sufficient to survive respondent's motion to dismiss. Accordingly, the judgment of the Court of Appeals is reversed, and the case is remanded for further proceedings consistent with this opinion.

NOTES AND QUESTIONS

Unanimous ruling that rule 8 means exactly what it says.

1. In Leatherman v. Tarrant County Narcotics and Coordination Unit, 507 U.S. 163 (1993), plaintiffs sued under 42 U.S.C.A. § 1983, claiming that local law enforcement officers had violated their constitutional rights. Because they were suing a county and two municipal corporations that employed the officers who took the actions leading to the suit, prevailing law required that they prove that the incidents resulted from official policy, custom, or practice. But plaintiffs did not allege that there had been multiple incidents of the sort

of which they complained, which the district court held undermined their claim that there was such a policy or practice. The Fifth Circuit upheld dismissal under its "heightened pleading standard" for such claims.

The Supreme Court held that dismissal was wrong because the rules provided no ground for heightened pleading requirements. The Court acknowledged defendants' arguments that "the degree of factual specificity required of a complaint by the Federal Rules of Civil Procedure varies according to the complexity of the underlying substantive law." But it found that the lower court's requirement that plaintiffs "state with factual detail and particularity the basis for the claim" could not be squared with the "liberal system of 'notice pleading' set up by the Federal Rules." It noted that Rule 9(b) requires greater particularity in pleading of certain claims, but that rule did not apply to this case. It concluded: "Perhaps if Rules 8 and 9 were rewritten today, claims against municipalities under § 1983 might be subjected to the added specificity requirement of Rule 9(b). But that is a result which must be obtained by the process of amending the Federal Rules, and not by judicial interpretation. In the absence of such an amendment, federal courts and litigants must rely on summary judgment and control of discovery to weed out unmeritorious claims sooner rather than later."

2.   In *Swierkiewicz*, the Court notes that plaintiff "detailed the events leading up to his termination." The Second Circuit had found plaintiff's allegations insufficient: "With respect to national origin, the only circumstances Swierkiewicz pled are that he is Hungarian, others at Sorema are French, and the conclusory allegation that his termination was motivated by national origin discrimination. * * * [Regarding age discrimination,] [t]he only circumstance that Swierkiewicz alleges gives rise to an inference of age discrimination is Chavel's comment in 1995 that Chavel wanted to 'energize' the underwriting department." Swierkiewicz v. Sorema, N.A., 5 Fed.Appx. 63, 64–65 (2d Cir.2001). In the Supreme Court's view, were these allegations essential to support plaintiff's claim? One lower court had opined that all an employment discrimination plaintiff need allege is "I was turned down for a job because of my race." Bennett v. Schmidt, 153 F.3d 516, 518 (7th Cir.1998). Did *Swierkiewicz* prove that this view was correct?

3.   As we will shortly see, the Supreme Court's stated views about Rule 8(a)(2) have shifted, but the rule has always said that a pleading "must show that the pleader is entitled to relief." Comments by the Court before *Swierkiewicz* indicated that courts had some latitude to demand more specificity in certain cases. In Crawford-El v. Britton, 523 U.S. 574 (1998), the Court emphasized that the district court "must exercise its discretion so that officials are not subjected to unnecessary and burdensome discovery or trial proceedings." It explained that there are "two primary options" available to accomplish this objective at the pleading stage:

> [T]he court may order a reply to the defendant's or a third party's answer under Federal Rule of Civil Procedure 7(a), or grant the defendant's motion for a more definite statement under Rule 12(e). Thus, the court may insist that the plaintiff "put forward specific,

nonconclusory factual allegations" that establish improper motive causing cognizable injury in order to survive a prediscovery motion for dismissal or summary judgment. Siegert v. Gilley, 500 U.S. 226, 236 (1991) (Kennedy, J., concurring).

See also Associated General Contractors, Inc. v. California State Council of Carpenters, 459 U.S. 519, 528 n. 17 (1983) ("Certainly in a case of this magnitude, a district court must retain the power to insist upon some specificity in pleading before allowing a potentially massive factual controversy to proceed.").

After *Swierkiewicz*, in Dura Pharmaceuticals, Inc. v. Broudo, 544 U.S. 336 (2005), a securities fraud action not subject to the PSLRA, the Court again seemed to embrace a more demanding attitude toward pleading requirements, albeit for purposes of notice. Plaintiffs claimed that when they bought defendant's stock in 1997–98 its value was inflated due to misrepresentations about the company's financial condition and prospects. As plaintiffs' "detailed amended (181 paragraph) complaint" alleged, the company later announced that its earnings would be lower than expected, and on the following day its shares lost almost half their value, falling from $39 per share to $21 per share. Defendants moved to dismiss on the ground that plaintiffs had not adequately alleged "loss causation"—that the decline in their share price was due to defendants' misrepresentations as opposed, for example, to the earnings forecast. The Court upheld dismissal. Proving that the price was inflated on the date of purchase does not necessarily show that a securities buyer suffered a loss as a result of a misrepresentation. Instead, the Court explained, a "tangle of factors" such as changes in the overall securities market or in the industry affect price at any given time. Securities law claims are not designed "to provide investors with broad insurance against market losses." At least, the Court suggested, plaintiffs must prove that they suffered a loss because the price fell after the truth became known.

Against that background of what plaintiffs must prove, the Court held that under Rule 8(a)(2) plaintiffs' complaint failed to provide "fair notice of what the plaintiff's claim is and the grounds on which it rests. * * * The complaint's failure to claim that Dura's share price fell significantly after the truth became known suggests that plaintiffs considered the allegation of purchase price inflation alone sufficient * * * [a]nd the complaint nowhere else provides the defendants with notice of what the relevant economic loss might be or of what the causal connection might be between that loss and the misrepresentation." "We concede that ordinary pleading rules are not meant to impose a great burden upon a plaintiff. But it should not prove burdensome for a plaintiff who has suffered an economic loss to provide a defendant with some indication of the loss and the causal connection that the plaintiff has in mind."

4. Some time ago, a commentator complained that the Court approached pleading issues with "appalling casualness." Roberts, Fact Pleading, Notice Pleading, and Standing, 65 Cornell L. Rev. 390, 399 (1980). More recently, Fairman, The Myth of Notice Pleading, 45 Az. L. Rev. 987

(2003), found that "notice pleading as a universal standard is a myth," and that "the reality of federal court practice—using all manner of fact-based particularity requirements—is shocking." Id. at 989; 997. For examples, consider Goad v. Mitchell, 297 F.3d 497, 504 (6th Cir.2002) (permitting district courts "to require plaintiffs to produce specific, nonconclusory factual allegations of improper motive before discovery in cases in which the plaintiff must prove wrongful motive"); Browning v. Clinton, 292 F.3d 235, 242 (D.C.Cir.2002) ("we accept neither inferences drawn by plaintiffs if such inferences are unsupported by the facts set out in the complaint, nor legal conclusions cast in the form of factual allegations"). Was there any justification for the lower courts' persistence in demanding details? Regarding civil rights suits, for example, it has been argued that "these situations present particularly difficult problems involving the potential abuse of litigation because they often involve outwardly innocent or admitted behavior that can, depending on the defendant's state of mind, result in very substantial liability." Marcus, The Revival of Fact Pleading Under the Federal Rules of Civil Procedure, 86 Colum.L.Rev. 433, 450 (1986).

5.   How should *Swierkiewicz* be applied in the following situation: Plaintiff sues in federal court claiming that she has received a number of parking citations over the past year because of her religious beliefs. Religious discrimination would violate plaintiff's constitutional rights, but should the court be required to credit her claim that this is why she received the tickets without an indication of the basis for this conclusion?

The next two cases introduce the Supreme Court's emphasis on "plausibility" as an important factor in applying Rule 8(a)(2). As you examine them, keep in mind the issues introduced with regard to *Swierkiewicz.*

BELL ATLANTIC CORP. v. TWOMBLY
Supreme Court of the United States, 2007
550 U.S. 544

JUSTICE SOUTER delivered the opinion of the Court.

Liability under § 1 of the Sherman Act, 15 U.S.C. § 1, requires a "contract, combination . . ., or conspiracy, in restraint of trade or commerce." The question in this putative class action is whether a § 1 complaint can survive a motion to dismiss when it alleges that major telecommunications providers engaged in certain parallel conduct unfavorable to competition, absent some factual context suggesting agreement, as distinct from identical, independent action. We hold that such a complaint should be dismissed.

I

[In 1984, the American Telephone & Telegraph Co. was divested of local telephone business, and the "Baby Bells," or Incumbent Local Exchange Carriers (ILECs) were installed as regional monopolies providing local telephone service in their respective service areas. In 1996,

Congress enacted the Telecommunications Act of 1996, which imposed a variety of duties on ILECs to facilitate the provision of local telephone service by Competitive Local Exchange Carriers (CLECs). The new Act permitted CLECs to use an ILEC's network to provide local service. The goal of the 1996 Act was to foster competition in provision of local telephone service. The ILECs resisted sharing their networks with competitors.

In this case, plaintiffs sued on behalf of a proposed class consisting of all subscribers of local telephone service from 1996 to the present, seeking treble damages and declaratory and injunctive relief. The defendants included the successors of all the Baby Bells—BellSouth Corp., Qwest Commun., Int'l, SBC Commun., Inc. and Verizon Commun., Inc. Plaintiffs asserted that defendants had conspired to restrain trade in two ways. First, each "engaged in parallel conduct" in its respective service area to inhibit the growth of competing CLECs, thereby adopting practices designed to sabotage such competition. Second, plaintiffs alleged that the ILECs had agreed not to compete with each other in providing local telephone service in another ILEC's service area. The ILECs' alleged agreement not to compete with each other, plaintiffs asserted, was shown by the failures of various ILECs to pursue their "substantial competitive advantages" in certain adjacent areas even though those advantages made entering these markets for local telephone service "attractive business opportunities." In addition, plaintiffs invoked a reported statement from Richard Notebaert,* the chief executive officer of Qwest, who was quoted as saying that competing in the territory of another ILEC "might be a good way to turn a quick dollar, but that doesn't make it right."]

The complaint couches its ultimate allegations this way:

"In the absence of any meaningful competition between the [ILECs] in one another's markets, and in light of the parallel course of conduct that each engaged in to prevent competition from CLECs within their respective local telephone and/or high speed internet services markets and the other facts and market circumstances alleged above, Plaintiffs allege upon information and belief that [the ILECs] have entered into a contract, combination or conspiracy to prevent competitive entry in their respective local telephone and/or high speed internet services markets and have agreed not to compete with one another and otherwise allocated customers and markets to one another."

[The District Court dismissed for failure to state a claim, reasoning that parallel conduct alone could not be a basis for alleging an antitrust conspiracy, so that the complaint must contain additional facts that "ten[d] to exclude independent self-interested conduct as an explanation of parallel behavior." The Court of Appeals reversed, holding that "plus factors" are

---

* This Richard Notebaert is the same person who was mentioned in Tellabs v. Makor Issues & Rights, Ltd., supra p. 161, when he was chief executive officer of Tellabs.—Eds.

not required, so long as plaintiffs plead facts that "include conspiracy among the realm of 'plausible' possibilities," adding that "to rule that allegations of parallel anticompetitive conduct fail to support a plausible conspiracy claim, a court would have to conclude that there is no set of facts that would permit a plaintiff to demonstrate that the particular parallelism asserted was the product of collusion rather than coincidence."]

We granted certiorari to address the proper standard for pleading an antitrust conspiracy through allegations of parallel conduct, and now reverse.

II

A

Because § 1 of the Sherman Act "does not prohibit [all] unreasonable restraints of trade . . . but only restraints effected by a contract, combination, or conspiracy," "[t]he crucial question" is whether the challenged anticompetitive conduct "stem[s] from independent decision or from an agreement, tacit or express." While a showing of parallel "business behavior is admissible circumstantial evidence from which the fact finder may infer agreement," it falls short of "conclusively establish[ing] agreement or . . . itself constitut[ing] a Sherman Act offense." Even "conscious parallelism," a common reaction of "firms in a concentrated market [that] recogniz[e] their shared economic interests and their interdependence with respect to price and output decisions" is "not in itself unlawful."

* * *

B

This case presents the antecedent question of what a plaintiff must plead in order to state a claim under § 1 of the Sherman Act. Federal Rule of Civil Procedure 8(a)(2) requires only "a short and plain statement of the claim showing that the pleader is entitled to relief," in order to "give the defendant fair notice of what the . . . claim is and the grounds upon which it rests," Conley v. Gibson, 355 U.S. 41, 47 (1957). While a complaint attacked by a Rule 12(b)(6) motion to dismiss does not need detailed factual allegations, a plaintiff's obligation to provide the "grounds" of his "entitle[ment] to relief" requires more than labels and conclusions, and a formulaic recitation of the elements of a cause of action will not do, see Papasan v. Allain, 478 U.S. 265, 286 (1986) (on a motion to dismiss, courts "are not bound to accept as true a legal conclusion couched as a factual allegation"). Factual allegations must be enough to raise a right to relief above the speculative level, see 5 C. Wright & A. Miller, Federal Practice and Procedure § 1216, pp. 235–236 (3d ed. 2004) (hereinafter Wright & Miller) ("[T]he pleading must contain something more . . . than . . . a statement of facts that merely creates a suspicion [of] a legally cognizable right of action"),[3] on the assumption that all the allegations in the complaint are true (even if doubtful in fact), see, e.g., Swierkiewicz v. Sorema N. A., 534 U.S. 506, 508, n. 1 (2002); Neitzke v. Williams, 490 U.S. 319, 327 (1989) ("Rule 12(b)(6) does not countenance . . . dismissals based on a judge's disbelief of a complaint's factual allegations"); Scheuer v. Rhodes, 416 U.S. 232, 236 (1974) (a well-pleaded complaint may proceed even if it appears "that a recovery is very remote and unlikely").

In applying these general standards to a § 1 claim, we hold that stating such a claim requires a complaint with enough factual matter (taken as true) to suggest that an agreement was made. Asking for plausible grounds to infer an agreement does not impose a probability requirement at the pleading stage; it simply calls for enough fact to raise a reasonable expectation that discovery will reveal evidence of illegal agreement.[4] And, of course, a well-pleaded complaint may proceed even if it strikes a savvy judge that actual proof of those facts is improbable, and "that a recovery is very remote and unlikely." In identifying facts that are suggestive enough to render a § 1 conspiracy plausible, we have the benefit of the prior rulings and considered views of leading commentators, already quoted, that lawful parallel conduct fails to bespeak unlawful agreement. It makes sense to say, therefore, that an allegation of parallel conduct and a bare assertion of conspiracy will not suffice. Without more, parallel conduct does not suggest conspiracy, and a conclusory allegation of agreement at some unidentified point does not supply facts adequate to show illegality. Hence, when allegations of parallel conduct are set out in order to make a § 1 claim, they must be placed in a context that raises a suggestion of a preceding agreement, not merely parallel conduct that could just as well be independent action.

* * *

Thus, it is one thing to be cautious before dismissing an antitrust complaint in advance of discovery, but quite another to forget that proceeding to antitrust discovery can be expensive. As we indicated over 20 years ago in Associated Gen. Contractors of Cal., Inc. v. Carpenters, 459 U.S. 519, 528, n. 17 (1983), "a district court must retain the power to insist upon some specificity in pleading before allowing a potentially massive

---

[3] The dissent greatly oversimplifies matters by suggesting that the Federal Rules somehow dispensed with the pleading of facts altogether. While, for most types of cases, the Federal Rules eliminated the cumbersome requirement that a claimant "set out *in detail* the facts upon which he bases his claim," Conley v. Gibson, 355 U.S. 41, 47 (1957) (emphasis added), Rule 8(a)(2) still requires a "showing," rather than a blanket assertion, of entitlement to relief. Without some factual allegation in the complaint, it is hard to see how a claimant could satisfy the requirement of providing not only "fair notice" of the nature of the claim, but also "grounds" on which the claim rests.

[4] Commentators have offered several examples of parallel conduct allegations that would state a § 1 claim under this standard. See, e.g., 6 Areeda & Hovenkamp ¶ 1425, at 167–185 (discussing "parallel behavior that would probably not result from chance, coincidence, independent responses to common stimuli, or mere interdependence unaided by an advance understanding among the parties").

factual controversy to proceed." That potential expense is obvious enough in the present case: plaintiffs represent a putative class of at least 90 percent of all subscribers to local telephone or high-speed Internet service in the continental United States, in an action against America's largest telecommunications firms (with many thousands of employees generating reams and gigabytes of business records) for unspecified (if any) instances of antitrust violations that allegedly occurred over a period of seven years.

It is no answer to say that a claim just shy of a plausible entitlement to relief can, if groundless, be weeded out early in the discovery process through "careful case management," given the common lament that the success of judicial supervision in checking discovery abuse has been on the modest side. And it is self-evident that the problem of discovery abuse cannot be solved by "careful scrutiny of evidence at the summary judgment stage," much less "lucid instructions to juries;" the threat of discovery expense will push cost-conscious defendants to settle even anemic cases before reaching those proceedings. Probably, then, it is only by taking care to require allegations that reach the level suggesting conspiracy that we can hope to avoid the potentially enormous expense of discovery in cases with no " 'reasonably founded hope that the [discovery] process will reveal relevant evidence' " to support a § 1 claim.

Plaintiffs do not, of course, dispute the requirement of plausibility and the need for something more than merely parallel behavior * * *, and their main argument against the plausibility standard at the pleading stage is its ostensible conflict with an early statement of ours construing Rule 8. Justice Black's opinion for the Court in Conley v. Gibson spoke not only of the need for fair notice of the grounds for entitlement to relief but of "the accepted rule that a complaint should not be dismissed for failure to state a claim unless it appears beyond doubt that the plaintiff can prove no set of facts in support of his claim which would entitle him to relief." This "no set of facts" language can be read in isolation as saying that any statement revealing the theory of the claim will suffice unless its factual impossibility may be shown from the face of the pleadings; and the Court of Appeals appears to have read *Conley* in some such way when formulating its understanding of the proper pleading standard.

On such a focused and literal reading of *Conley's* "no set of facts," a wholly conclusory statement of claim would survive a motion to dismiss whenever the pleadings left open the possibility that a plaintiff might later establish some "set of [undisclosed] facts" to support recovery. So here, the Court of Appeals specifically found the prospect of unearthing direct evidence of conspiracy sufficient to preclude dismissal, even though the complaint does not set forth a single fact in a context that suggests an agreement. It seems fair to say that this approach to pleading would dispense with any showing of a " 'reasonably founded hope' " that a plaintiff would be able to make a case; Mr. Micawber's optimism would be enough.

Seeing this, a good many judges and commentators have balked at taking the literal terms of the *Conley* passage as a pleading standard. See, e.g., Car Carriers [Inc. v. Ford Motor Co.], 745 F.2d, at 1106 [(CA7 1984)] ("*Conley* has never been interpreted literally") and, "[i]n practice, a complaint . . . must contain either direct or inferential allegations respecting all the material elements necessary to sustain recovery under some viable legal theory"; Ascon Properties, Inc. v. Mobil Oil Co., 866 F.2d 1149, 1155 (C.A.9 1989) (tension between *Conley*'s "no set of facts" language and its acknowledgment that a plaintiff must provide the "grounds" on which his claim rests); O'Brien v. DiGrazia, 544 F.2d 543, 546, n. 3 (C.A.1 1976) ("[W]hen a plaintiff . . . supplies facts to support his claim, we do not think that *Conley* imposes a duty on the courts to conjure up unpleaded facts that might turn a frivolous claim of unconstitutional . . . action into a substantial one"); Hazard, From Whom No Secrets Are Hid, 76 Tex. L. Rev. 1665, 1685 (1998) (describing *Conley* as having "turned Rule 8 on its head"); Marcus, The Revival of Fact Pleading Under the Federal Rules of Civil Procedure, 86 Colum. L. Rev. 433, 463–465 (1986) (noting tension between *Conley* and subsequent understandings of Rule 8).

We could go on, but there is no need to pile up further citations to show that *Conley*'s "no set of facts" language has been questioned, criticized, and explained away long enough. To be fair to the *Conley* Court, the passage should be understood in light of the opinion's preceding summary of the complaint's concrete allegations, which the Court quite reasonably understood as amply stating a claim for relief. But the passage so often quoted fails to mention this understanding on the part of the Court, and after puzzling the profession for 50 years, this famous observation has earned its retirement. The phrase is best forgotten as an incomplete, negative gloss on an accepted pleading standard: once a claim has been stated adequately, it may be supported by showing any set of facts consistent with the allegations in the complaint. *Conley*, then, described the breadth of opportunity to prove what an adequate complaint claims, not the minimum standard of adequate pleading to govern a complaint's survival.

III

When we look for plausibility in this complaint, we agree with the District Court that plaintiffs' claim of conspiracy in restraint of trade comes up short. To begin with, the complaint leaves no doubt that plaintiffs rest their § 1 claim on descriptions of parallel conduct and not on any independent allegation of actual agreement among the ILECs. Although in form a few stray statements speak directly of agreement, on fair reading these are merely legal conclusions resting on the prior allegations. Thus, the complaint first takes account of the alleged "absence of any meaningful competition between [the ILECs] in one another's markets," "the parallel course of conduct that each [ILEC] engaged in to prevent competition from

CLECs," "and the other facts and market circumstances alleged [earlier]"; "in light of" these, the complaint concludes "that [the ILECs] have entered into a contract, combination or conspiracy to prevent competitive entry into their . . . markets and have agreed not to compete with one another."[10] The nub of the complaint, then, is the ILECs' parallel behavior, consisting of steps to keep the CLECs out and manifest disinterest in becoming CLECs themselves, and its sufficiency turns on the suggestions raised by this conduct when viewed in light of common economic experience.

[The Court concluded that plaintiffs' allegations about efforts by each ILEC to exclude competition in its area involved "doing what was only natural anyway," and provided no basis for inferring agreement among them to behave in this manner. Regarding the ILECs' failure to try to break into one another's market areas, the Court said that it was "not suggestive of conspiracy" since "monopoly was the norm in telecommunications" and "[t]he ILECs were born in that world, doubtless liked the world the way it was, and surely knew the adage about him who lives by the sword." Indeed, they would know that if they tried to compete in the area of another ILEC, they "faced nearly insurmountable barriers to profitability owing to the ILECs' flagrant resistance to the network sharing requirements of the 1996 Act."

The comment by Qwest's CEO Notebaert that competing against other ILECs "might be a good way to turn a quick dollar" did not supply the needed support for conspiracy allegations. "This was only part of what he reportedly said, however, and the District Court was entitled to take notice of the full contents of the published articles referenced in the complaint, from which the truncated quotations were drawn. See Fed. R. Evid. 201. Notebaert was also quoted as saying that entering new markets as a CLEC would not be 'a sustainable economic model' because the CLEC pricing model is 'just . . . nuts.' "]

Congress may have expected some ILECs to become CLECs in the legacy territories of other ILECs, but the disappointment does not make conspiracy plausible. We agree with the District Court's assessment that

---

[10] If the complaint had not explained that the claim of agreement rested on the parallel conduct described, we doubt that the complaint's references to an agreement among the ILECs would have given the notice required by Rule 8. Apart from identifying a seven-year span in which the § 1 violations were supposed to have occurred (i.e., "[b]etween at least as early as February 6, 1996, and continuing to the present,"), the pleadings mentioned no specific time, place, or person involved in the alleged conspiracies. The lack of notice contrasts sharply with the model form for pleading negligence, Form 9 [now Form 11], which the dissent says exemplifies the king of "bare allegation" that survives a motion to dismiss. Whereas the model form alleges that the defendant struck the plaintiff with his car while plaintiff was crossing a particular highway at a specified date and time, the complaint here furnishes no clue as to which of the four ILECs (much less which of their employees) supposedly agreed, or when and where the illicit agreement took place. A defendant wishing to prepare an answer to the simple fact pattern laid out in Form [11] would know what to answer; a defendant seeking to respond to plaintiffs' conclusory allegations in the § 1 context would have little idea where to begin.

antitrust conspiracy was not suggested by the facts adduced under either theory of the complaint, which thus fails to state a valid § 1 claim.[14]

Plaintiffs say that our analysis runs counter to Swierkiewicz v. Sorema N. A., 534 U.S. 506, 508 (2002). * * * As the District Court correctly understood, however, "*Swierkiewicz* did not change the law of pleading, but simply re-emphasized . . . that the Second Circuit's use of a heightened pleading standard for Title VII cases was contrary to the Federal Rules' structure of liberal pleading requirements." Even though Swierkiewicz's pleadings "detailed the events leading to his termination, provided relevant dates, and included the ages and nationalities of at least some of the relevant persons involved with his termination," the Court of Appeals dismissed his complaint for failing to allege certain additional facts that Swierkiewicz would need at the trial stage to support his claim in the absence of direct evidence of discrimination. We reversed on the ground that the Court of Appeals had impermissibly applied what amounted to a heightened pleading requirement by insisting that Swierkiewicz allege "specific facts" beyond those necessary to state his claim and the grounds showing entitlement to relief.

Here, in contrast, we do not require heightened fact pleading of specifics, but only enough facts to state a claim to relief that is plausible on its face. Because the plaintiffs here have not nudged their claims across the line from conceivable to plausible, their complaint must be dismissed.

[handwritten margin note: Famous. Quote]

JUSTICE STEVENS, with whom JUSTICE GINSBURG joins, * * * dissenting.

[Justice Stevens stressed that plaintiffs did allege that defendants entered into a conspiracy, and said he would find that allegation plausible in light of the circumstantial evidence identified in the complaint. Besides Mr. Notebaert's statement, plaintiffs alleged that defendants "communicate amongst themselves" through numerous industry associations. And it was not proper for the District Court to review and interpret the article quoting Notebeart because that court "was required at this stage of the proceedings to construe Notebaert's ambiguous statement in the plaintiffs' favor." Nonetheless, "without so much as requiring petitioners to file an answer denying that they entered into any agreement," the Court upheld dismissal.

He also objected that abandoning the "no set of facts" language in Conley v. Gibson would "rewrite the Nation's civil procedure textbooks" by

---

[14] In reaching this conclusion, we do not apply any "heightened" pleading standard, nor do we seek to broaden the scope of Federal Rule of Civil Procedure 9, which can only be accomplished " 'by the process of amending the Federal Rules, and not by judicial interpretation.' " Swierkiewicz v. Sorema N. A., 534 U.S. 506, 515, 122 S.Ct. 992, 152 L.Ed.2d 1 (2002). On certain subjects understood to raise a high risk of abusive litigation, a plaintiff must state factual allegations with greater particularity than Rule 8 requires. Fed. Rules Civ. Proc. 9(b)–(c). Here, our concern is not that the allegations in the complaint were insufficiently "particular[ized]"; rather, the complaint warranted dismissal because it failed in toto to render plaintiffs' entitlement to relief plausible.

judicial decision. "Congress has established a process—a rulemaking process—for revisions of that order." *Conley*'s language had been repeatedly invoked in the Supreme Court's decisions and in the decisions of lower courts. The majority's decision seems to require the pleading of facts even though the Federal Rules clearly do not so require. That was central to Swierkiewicz v. Sorema, S.A., which was "a case more similar to the present one than the majority will allow." This ruling is more like a summary judgment ruling than a pleadings decision.

"Under the relaxed pleading standards of the Federal Rules, the idea was not to keep litigants out of court but rather to keep them in." But "if I had been the trial judge in this case, I would not have permitted the plaintiffs to engage in massive discovery based solely on the allegations of this complaint." Instead, there should be "careful case management, including strict control of discovery," but not "the dismissal of an adequately pleaded complaint without even requiring the defendants to file answers denying a charge that they in fact engaged in collective decisionmaking."]

ASHCROFT V. IQBAL

Supreme Court of the United States, 2009
556 U.S. 662

JUSTICE KENNEDY delivered the opinion of the Court.

Respondent Javaid Iqbal is a citizen of Pakistan and a Muslim. In the wake of the September 11, 2001, terrorist attacks he was arrested in the United States on criminal charges and detained by federal officials. Respondent claims he was deprived of various constitutional protections while in federal custody. To redress the alleged deprivations, respondent filed a complaint against numerous federal officials, including John Ashcroft, the former Attorney General of the United States, and Robert Mueller, the Director of the Federal Bureau of Investigation (FBI). Ashcroft and Mueller are the petitioners in the case now before us. As to these two petitioners, the complaint alleges that they adopted an unconstitutional policy that subjected respondent to harsh conditions of confinement on account of his race, religion, or national origin.

* * *

Respondent's account of his prison ordeal could, if proved, demonstrate unconstitutional misconduct by some governmental actors. But the allegations and pleadings with respect to these actors are not before us here. This case instead turns on a narrower question: Did respondent, as the plaintiff in the District Court, plead factual matter that, if taken as true, states a claim that petitioners deprived him of his clearly established constitutional rights. We hold respondent's pleadings are insufficient.

[Following the September 11, 2011, attacks, the FBI and other Department of Justice entities began a vast investigation involving more than 4,000 special agents and 3,000 support personnel to investigate more than 96,000 tips or potential leads. Some 762 people were held on immigration charges as a result of this effort, and 184 of them were held under restrictive conditions because they were "of high interest." Plaintiff was one of those arrested on immigration charges. He was held under maximum security conditions, and sued 34 current or former federal officials ranging from correctional officers who had day-to-day contact with him to Ashcroft and Mueller. His complaint did not challenge his arrest or confinement, but instead alleged that other defendants abused him while he was in custody.

As to Ashcroft and Mueller, plaintiff alleged that they designated him a person of high interest due to his race, religion, or national origin, and that they "knew of, condoned, and willfully and maliciously agreed" to subjecting him to harsh conditions of confinement solely on grounds of his religion, race or national origin. The lower courts denied defendants' motions to dismiss even though the Supreme Court had granted high officials like them broad immunity to suit for their official actions, in part to protect them against pretrial discovery.

Under earlier precedents, Ashcroft and Mueller could not be held liable for unconstitutional conduct of their subordinates under a theory of respondeat superior; instead "the plaintiff must plead and prove that the defendant acted with discriminatory purpose." Accordingly, plaintiff "must plead sufficient factual matter to show that petitioners adopted and implemented the detention policies at issue not for a neutral investigative reason but for purposes of discriminating on account of race, religion, or national origin." Mere knowledge of subordinates' discriminatory purposes is not sufficient; supervisory liability does not extend so far.]

To survive a motion to dismiss [under *Twombly*], a complaint must contain sufficient factual matter, accepted as true, to "state a claim to relief that is plausible on its face." A claim has facial plausibility when the plaintiff pleads factual content that allows the court to draw the reasonable inference that the defendant is liable for the misconduct alleged. The plausibility standard is not akin to a "probability requirement," but it asks for more than a sheer possibility that a defendant has acted unlawfully. Where a complaint pleads facts that are "merely consistent with" a defendant's liability, it "stops short of the line between possibility and plausibility of 'entitlement to relief.' "

Two working principles underlie our decision in *Twombly*. First, the tenet that a court must accept as true all of the allegations contained in a complaint is inapplicable to legal conclusions. Threadbare recitals of the elements of a cause of action, supported by mere conclusory statements, do not suffice. Rule 8 marks a notable and generous departure from the hypertechnical, code-pleading regime of a prior era, but it does not unlock the doors of discovery for a plaintiff armed with nothing more than conclusions. Second, only a complaint that states a plausible claim for relief survives a motion to dismiss. Determining whether a complaint states a plausible claim for relief will * * * be a context-specific task that requires the reviewing court to draw on its judicial experience and common sense. But where the well-pleaded facts do not permit the court to infer more than the mere possibility of misconduct, the complaint has alleged—but it has not "show[n]"—"that the pleader is entitled to relief." Fed. Rule Civ. Proc. 8(a)(2).

In keeping with these principles a court considering a motion to dismiss can choose to begin by identifying pleadings that, because they are no more than conclusions, are not entitled to the assumption of truth. While legal conclusions can provide the framework of a complaint, they must be supported by factual allegations. When there are well-pleaded factual allegations, a court should assume their veracity and then determine whether they plausibly give rise to an entitlement to relief.

* * *

Under *Twombly*'s construction of Rule 8, we conclude that respondent's complaint has not "nudged [his] claims" of invidious discrimination "across the line from conceivable to plausible."

[The complaint alleged that Ashcroft and Mueller "knew of, and condoned, and willfully and maliciously agreed" to subject him to harsh conditions of confinement "solely" on account his race, religion, or national origin, and that Ashcroft was the "chief architect" of this program, while Mueller was "instrumental" in executing it. These "bare assertions * * * amount to nothing more than a 'formulaic recitation of the elements' of a constitutional discrimination claim. * * * [W]e do not reject these bald allegations on the ground that they are unrealistic or nonsensical. * * * It is the conclusory nature of respondent's allegations, rather than their extravagantly fanciful nature, that disentitles them to the presumption of truth."

Neither did plaintiff's allegations that defendants directed the detention of thousands of Arab Muslim men suffice to survive a motion to dismiss. These allegations "are consistent with petitioners' purposefully designating detainees 'of high interest' because of their race, religion, or national origin. But given more likely explanations, they do not plausibly establish this purpose." The September 11 attacks were perpetrated by 19 Arab Muslim hijackers. "It should come as no surprise that a legitimate policy directing law enforcement to arrest and detail individuals because of their suspected link to the attacks would produce a disparate, incidental impact on Arab Muslims." Discrimination is not a plausible conclusion given the "obvious alternative explanation" that the detentions were focused on people illegally present in this country and who had potential connections with the terrorists. And plaintiff's constitutional claims do not challenge his arrest, but only his subsequent treatment; to state a claim plaintiff would have to allege facts showing that Ashcroft and Mueller "purposefully adopted a policy of classifying post-September-11 detainees as 'of high interest' because of their race, religion, or national origin."]

This the complaint fails to do. * * * [H]is only factual allegation against petitioners accuses them of adopting a policy approving "restrictive conditions of confinement" for post-September-11 detainees until they were " 'cleared' by the FBI." Accepting the truth of that allegation, the complaint does not show, or even intimate, that petitioners purposefully housed detainees in the [a high-security facility] due to their race, religion, or national origin. All it plausibly suggests is that the Nation's top law enforcement officers, in the aftermath of a devastating terrorist attack, sought to keep suspected terrorists in the most secure conditions available until the suspects could be cleared of terrorist activity. Respondent does not argue, nor can he, that such a motive would violate petitioners' constitutional obligations. He would need to allege more by way of factual content to "nudg[e]" his claim of purposeful discrimination "across the line from conceivable to plausible."

[Respondent's argument that *Twombly* is limited to antitrust cases is wrong. "Though *Twombly* determined the sufficiency of a complaint sounding in antitrust, the decision was based on our interpretation and application of Rule 8. That Rule in turn governs the pleading standard 'in all civil actions and proceedings in the United States district courts.' Fed. Rule Civ. Proc. 1." The lower courts' willingness to try to limit discovery does not justify a broader reading of Rule 8. "Our rejection of the careful-case-management approach is especially important in suits where Government-official defendants are entitled to assert the defense of qualified immunity. The basic thrust of the qualified-immunity doctrine is to free officials from the concerns of litigation, including "avoidance of disruptive discovery."] There are serious and legitimate reasons for this. If a Government official is to devote time to his or her duties, and to the formulation of sound and responsible policies, it is counterproductive to require the substantial diversion that is attendant to participating in litigation and making informed decisions as to how it should proceed. * * *

Respondent finally maintains that the Federal Rules expressly allow him [in Rule 9(b)] to allege petitioners' discriminatory intent "generally," which he equates with a conclusory allegation. It follows, respondent says, that his complaint is sufficiently well pleaded because it claims that petitioners discriminated against him "on account of [his] religion, race, and/or national origin and for no legitimate penological interest." Were we required to accept this allegation as true, respondent's complaint would survive petitioners' motion to dismiss. But the Federal Rules do not require courts to credit a complaint's conclusory statements without reference to its factual context.

It is true that Rule 9(b) requires particularity when pleading "fraud or mistake," while allowing "[m]alice, intent, knowledge, and other conditions of a person's mind [to] be alleged generally." But "generally" is a relative term. In the context of Rule 9, it is to be compared to the particularity requirement applicable to fraud or mistake. Rule 9 merely excuses a party from pleading discriminatory intent under an elevated pleading standard. It does not give him license to evade the less rigid—though still operative—strictures of Rule 8. And Rule 8 does not empower respondent to plead the bare elements of his cause of action, affix the label "general allegation," and expect his complaint to survive a motion to dismiss.

JUSTICE SOUTER, with whom JUSTICE STEVENS, JUSTICE GINSBURG, and JUSTICE BREYER join, dissenting.

[Justice Souter argued that the Court "misapplies the pleading standard under Bell Atlantic v. Twombly." He also objected that the Court's decision unduly narrowed the grounds for supervisor liability for constitutional violations. He contended that Ashcroft and Mueller had conceded that a supervisor's knowledge of a subordinate's unconstitutional conduct and deliberate indifference to that conduct would support a constitutional claim against them, but that the Court "rejects this concession." Further, "the majority is not narrowing the scope of supervisory liability; it is eliminating * * * supervisory liability entirely."]

Given petitioners' concession, the complaint satisfies Rule 8(a)(2). Ashcroft and Mueller admit they are liable for their subordinates' conduct if they "had actual knowledge of the assertedly discriminatory nature of the classification of suspects as being 'of high interest' and they were deliberately indifferent to that discrimination." * * * The complaint * * * alleges, at a bare minimum, that Ashcroft and Mueller knew of and condoned the discriminatory policy their subordinates carried out. Actually, the complaint goes further in alleging that Ashcroft and Muller affirmatively acted to create the discriminatory detention policy. If these factual allegations are true, Ashcroft and Mueller were, at the very least, aware of the discriminatory policy being implemented and deliberately indifferent to it.

Ashcroft and Mueller argue that these allegations fail to satisfy the "plausibility standard" of *Twombly*. They contend that Iqbal's claims are implausible because such high-ranking officials "tend not to be personally involved in the specific actions of lower-level officers down the bureaucratic chain of command." But this response bespeaks a fundamental misunderstanding of the enquiry that *Twombly* demands. *Twombly* does not require a court at the motion-to-dismiss stage to consider whether the factual allegations are probably true. We made it clear, on the contrary, that a court must take the allegations as true, no matter how skeptical the court may be. The sole exception to this rule lies with allegations that are sufficiently fantastic to defy reality as we know it: claims about little green men, or the plaintiff's recent trip to Pluto, or experiences in time travel. That is not what we have here.

Under *Twombly*, the relevant question is whether, assuming the factual allegations are true, the plaintiff has stated a ground for relief that is plausible. * * * Here, by contrast [to *Twombly*], the allegations in the complaint are neither confined to naked legal conclusions nor consistent with legal conduct. The complaint alleges that FBI officials discriminated against Iqbal solely on account of his race, religion, and national origin, and it alleges the knowledge and deliberate indifference that, by Ashcroft and Mueller's own admission, are sufficient to make them liable for the illegal action. Iqbal's complaint therefore contains "enough facts to state a claim to relief that is plausible on its face."

I do not understand the majority to disagree with this understanding of "plausibility" under *Twombly*. Rather, the majority discards the allegations discussed above with regard to Ashcroft and Mueller as conclusory, and is left considering only two statements in the complaint: [that the FBI arrested thousands of Arab Muslim men, and that the policy of holding them in highly restrictive conditions until they were "cleared" by the FBI was approved by Ashcroft and Mueller.] I agree that the two allegations selected by the majority, standing alone, do not state a plausible entitlement to relief for unconstitutional discrimination.

But these allegations do not stand alone as the only significant, nonconclusory statements in the complaint, for the complaint contains many allegations linking Ashcroft and Mueller to the discriminatory practices of their subordinates. See Complaint ¶ 10 (Ashcroft was the "principal architect" of the discriminatory policy); ¶ 11 (Mueller was "instrumental" in adopting and executing the discriminatory policy); ¶ 96 (Ashcroft and Mueller "knew of, condoned, and willfully and maliciously agreed to subject" Iqbal to harsh conditions "as a matter of policy, solely on account of [his] religion, race, and/or national origin and for no legitimate penological interest").

The majority says that these are "bare assertions" that, "much like the pleading of conspiracy in *Twombly*, amount to nothing more than a 'formulaic recitation of the elements' of a constitutional discrimination claim" and therefore are "not entitled to be assumed true." The fallacy of the majority's position, however, lies in looking at the relevant assertions in isolation. The complaint contains specific allegations that, in the aftermath of the September 11 attacks, the Chief of the FBI's International Terrorism Operations Section and the Assistant Special Agent in Charge for the FBI's New York Field Office implemented a policy that discriminated against Arab Muslim men, including Iqbal, solely on account of their race, religion, or national origin. Viewed in light of these subsidiary allegations, the allegations singled out by the majority as "conclusory" are no such thing. Iqbal's claim is not that Ashcroft and Mueller "knew of, condoned, and willfully and maliciously agreed to subject" him to a discriminatory practice that is left undefined; his allegation is that "they knew of, condoned, and willfully and maliciously agreed to subject" him to a particular, discrete, discriminatory policy detailed in the complaint. Iqbal does not say merely that Ashcroft was the architect of some amorphous discrimination, or that Mueller was instrumental in an ill-defined constitutional violation; he alleges that they helped to create the discriminatory policy he has described. Taking the complaint as a whole, it gives Ashcroft and Mueller " 'fair notice of what the . . . claim is and the grounds upon which it rests.' "

JUSTICE BREYER, dissenting.

[Justice Breyer joined Justice Souter's dissent. He added that he agreed with the goal of preventing unwarranted litigation from interfering with the work of government, but believed that the district court "can structure discovery in ways that diminish the risk of imposing unwarranted burdens upon public officials. * * * Neither the briefs nor the Court's opinion provides convincing grounds for finding these alternative case-management tools inadequate, either in general or in the case before us."]

NOTES AND QUESTIONS

1. *Debate about the effect of these decisions:* Shortly after *Twombly* was decided, Justice Ginsburg (a former civil procedure professor) predicted that it would "give procedure professors cause to write prolifically." Ginsburg, Annual Remarks, Judicial Conference of the Second Circuit, 278 F.R.D. 268, 272 (June 9, 2007). She underestimated. As a Ninth Circuit judge put it. "*Twombly* and *Iqbal* ignited a firestorm that within months reached all the way to Congress." O'Scannlain, Access to Justice Within the Federal Courts—A Ninth Circuit Perspective, 90 Ore. L. Rev. 1033, 1035 (2012). Shortly after *Iqbal* was decided, a New York Times article said the two cases were "the most significant * * * in a decade for day-to-day litigation in the federal courts." Liptak, Case About 9/11 Could Lead to Broad Shift in Civil Lawsuits, N.Y. Times, July 21, 2009, at A10. In 2010, one prediction was that *Twombly* would become the most cited Supreme Court case of all time, unless surpassed by *Iqbal*. Clermont, Three Myths About *Twombly-Iqbal*, 45 Wake Forest L. Rev. 1337, 1337 n. 4 (2010). The volume of law review articles about the "new pleading" has become a gusher. For some thoughtful examples, see Bone, Plausibility Pleading Revisited and Revised: A Comment on Ashcroft v. Iqbal, 85 Notre Dame L. Rev. 849 (2010); Steinman, The Pleading Problem, 62 Stan. L. Rev. 1293 (2010). Meanwhile, legislation was introduced to undo *Twombly* and *Iqbal*, see Notice Pleading Restoration Act of 2009, S. 1504, 111th Cong. (2009), and proposals were made for a rule amendment to address the issues. Neither legislation nor rule changes has been adopted, however.

In terms of lawyer behavior, the academic concern seems to have been warranted. For example, a magazine for corporate general counsel reported that "many in the defense bar think it almost malpractice not to bring a motion to dismiss." Cross, Motions To Dismiss Under *Twombly*, Today's General Counsel, Oct/Nov 2016, at 52. Nonetheless, the article concluded that "it has become apparent that the issue is more nuanced." Some academic voices have said the same. Consider Steinman, The Rise and Fall of Plausibility Pleading, 69 Vand. L. Rev. 333, 335 (2016): "[T]he Supreme Court has applied *Twombly* and *Iqbal* in ways that confirm and reinvigorate the simplified notice-pleading approach that the Federal Rules' original drafters put into place." See also Cavanaugh, Making Sense of *Twombly*, 63 S.Car.L.Rev. 97, 103 (2011): "[I]t has become increasingly apparent that the parade of horribles feared by critics of [of the Court's decisions] has not materialized."

A study by the Federal Judicial Center concluded that the frequency of motions to dismiss had increased, but that there was no statistically significant increase in the frequency of granting such motions. J. Cecil, G. Cort, M. Williams & J. Bataillon, Motions to Dismiss for Failure to State a Claim After *Iqbal*, Report to the Judicial Conference Advisory Committee on Civil Rules (2011). But these conclusions were challenged as too cautious in applying standards of statistical significance. Hoffman, *Twombly* and *Iqbal*'s Measure: An Assessment of the Federal Judicial Center's Study of Motions to Dismiss, 6 Fed. Cts. L. Rev. 1 (2011). Dodson, A New Look at Dismissal Rates of Federal Civil Claims, 96 Judicature 127 (2012), found a statistically significant increase in the rate of dismissals after *Iqbal* compared to the rate before *Twombly*, but also found that dismissal was quite common before *Twombly*, a finding that "undermines the contention that the pre-*Twombly* standard for testing pleadings was a toothless one." For a general discussion, see S. Dodson, New Pleading in the Twenty-First Century: Slamming the Courthouse Doors? (2013).

Another way of looking at lawyer behavior is to focus on plaintiff lawyers. Another Federal Judicial Center report, E. Lee, Early Stages of Litigation Attorney Survey (FJC 2012), based on interviews with lawyers, includes the following (id. at 1):

> Attorneys representing plaintiffs at least half of the time were asked whether their pleading practices have changed since the Twombly and Iqbal decisions. Half said yes, half said no. The most common change in pleading practices reported was including more factual detail in complaints, reported by 92% of those with changed practices.

In somewhat the same vein, a prominent plaintiffs' lawyer, writing in a magazine for the largest organization of the plaintiffs' bar, warned that "if trial lawyers proclaim that the sky has already fallen and concede that *Iqbal* is as broad and catastrophic as their defense brethren claim, they risk making *Iqbal*'s potential for disaster a self-fulfilling prophecy." Peddie, Let's All Play Iqbal, Trial, Aug. 2010, at 54. She predicted that plaintiffs' lawyers could offer "a construction of *Iqbal* that can be reconciled with existing law and the rights to jury trial and due process can prevail." See also Hubbard, A Fresh Look at

Plausibility Pleading, 83 U.Chi.L.Rev. 693 (2016) (arguing that plaintiff lawyers will include detail in their complaints to signal merit without regard to whether pleading rules require that they do so); Hoffman, Plausible Theory, Implausible Conclusions, 83 U.Chi.L.Rev.Online 143 (2016) (rebutting Hubbard).

2. *Subsequent Supreme Court decisions:* The Supreme Court itself has sent somewhat mixed signals. In Erickson v. Pardus, 551 U.S. 89 (2007), decided less than two weeks after *Twombly*, it summarily reversed dismissal of a prisoner's pro se complaint, emphasizing that "[s]pecific facts are not necessary" and that "when ruling on a defendant's motion to dismiss, a judge must accept as true all of the factual allegations." Then, in Skinner v. Switzer, 131 S.Ct. 1289 (2011), the Court reversed a dismissal on the pleadings, though "the complaint is not a model of the careful drafter's art, [because] a complaint need not pin plaintiff's claim for relief to a precise legal theory." In 2014, in Johnson v. City of Shelby, 135 S.Ct. 346 (2014), the Court summarily reversed after the lower courts had dismissed for plaintiffs' failure to invoke 42 U.S.C. § 1983 in their complaint. It explained that *Twombly* and *Iqbal* "concern the *factual* allegations a complaint must contain to survive a motion to dismiss" because plaintiff "must plead facts sufficient to show that her claim has substantive plausibility." Because plaintiffs did that, their failure to invoke the correct legal theory did not defeat their claims.

In *Twombly* itself, the Court reaffirmed *Swierkiewicz* and asserted that it was not endorsing a "heightened pleading" rule. See Chapman v. Yellow Cab Cooperative, 875 F.3d 846, 848 (7th Cir. 2017) ("*Twombly* cited *Schwerkiewicz* with approval," and rejected contentions that fact pleading is required). As noted by Judge William Fletcher (another former civil procedure professor) in Starr v. Baca, 633 F.3d 1191, 1204 (9th Cir. 2011):

> The juxtaposition of *Swierkiewicz* and *Erickson*, on the one hand, and *Dura*, *Twombly*, and *Iqbal*, on the other, is perplexing. Even though the Court stated in all five cases that it was applying Rule 8(a), it is hard to avoid the conclusion that, in fact, the Court applied a higher pleading standard in *Dura*, *Twombly*, and *Iqbal*. The Court in *Dura* and *Twombly* appeared concerned that in some complex commercial cases the usual lenient pleading standard under Rule 8(a) gave too much settlement leverage to plaintiffs. That is, if a non-specific complaint was enough to survive a motion to dismiss, plaintiffs would be able to extract undeservedly high settlements from deep-pocket companies. In *Iqbal*, by contrast, the Court was concerned that the usual lenient standard under Rule 8(a) would provide too little protection for high-level executive branch officials who allegedly engaged in misconduct in the aftermath of September 11, 2001. To the extent that we perceive a difference in the application of Rule 8(a) in the two groups of cases, it is difficult to know in cases that come before us whether we should apply the more lenient or the more demanding standard.

3.   *Abrogation of the forms:* In 2015, Rule 84 and the official forms were abrogated. Rule 84 said that the forms "suffice under these rules." Recall that in *Swierkiewicz*, the Court invoked Form 9's simple negligence complaint (quoted on p. 133 n. 5). Some academics read this move as a further effort to weaken the notice pleading idea. See Coleman, Abrogating Magic: The Rules Enabling Act Process, Civil Rule 84, and the Forms, 15 Nev.L.J. 1093 (2015); Spencer, The Forms Had a Function: Rule 84 and the Appendix of Forms as Guardians of the Liberal Ethos in Civil Procedure, 15 Nev.L.J. 111 (2015). But the Committee Note accompanying the abrogation of the forms noted that it "does not alter existing pleading standards or otherwise change the requirements of Civil Rule 8."

Cantone, Cecil & Jani, Whither Notice Pleading? Pleading Practice Before *Twombly* (Fed. Jud. Ctr., July 15, 2013), offers a report on the actual pleading practice before the *Twombly* decision. These researchers examined complaints in auto accident cases in which the U.S. was a party, cases that should have been subject to Form 9 as well as the relaxed attitude of *Conley v. Gibson*. Their conclusion:

> [C]omplaints before *Twombly* departed from the bare bones notice pleading requirements of Form 11. Even before *Twombly*, the level of specificity of the factual allegations contained in the complaint far exceeded the requirement expressed in the language of Rule 8(a)(2), the liberal standards expressed in *Conley*, and the example delineated in Form [9]. Pleading facts to demonstrate the plausibility of a claim was a common practice prior to *Twombly*. Attributing *Twombly* and *Iqbal* for a federal shift from notice pleading to a heightened standard denies that the notice pleading standard in *Conley* was already heading toward retirement before these decisions.

4.   Is the "plausibility" standard sometimes an improvement? Does the Court's invitation to judges to rely on "common sense" in applying this standard place too much emphasis on their personal experiences? A contrast is a jury decision, which involves multiple perspectives and lay deciders. Some argue that the invitation to "common sense" judgments invites judges to indulge their world views, even though they are, by definition, not average citizens. But others argue that the plausibility standard is not only desirable but constitutionally compelled. See Elliott, *Twombly* in Context: Why Federal Rule of Civil Procedure 4(b) is Unconstitutional, 64 Fla.L.Rev. 895 (2012) (arguing that the due process clause requires that there be some official scrutiny of the adequacy of a complaint before a defendant should be put to the expense and trouble of having to respond to it).

Redish, Pleading, Discovery, and the Federal Rules: Exploring the Foundations of Modern Procedure, 64 Fla.L.Rev. 845 (2012), concludes that "the *Twombly-Iqbal* plausibility standard represents the fairest and most efficient resolution of the conflicting interests." Id. at 850. The choice between easy access to discovery and growing costs of discovery—particularly electronic discovery (discussed in Chapter 5)—has thrown off the balance struck by the framers of the Federal Rules as they sought to "walk this procedural tightrope" (id. at 856):

> If one begins with a strong presumption in favor of the value of wealth redistribution and an overriding concern that laws regulating corporate or governmental behavior be enforced, then one is likely to choose a pleading system that demands less of plaintiffs, thereby placing a risk of over-enforcement on defendants. If, on the other hand, one were to begin with an overriding substantive concern about the costs and harms of over-deterrence and the possible waste of litigation resources and believe that courts should not transfer wealth absent a strong and clear reason to do so, then one is far more likely to adopt a more demanding pleading standard.

As one approaches these issues, it is worth noting that the American balance is starkly different from the balance struck in the rest of the world, where pleading requirements are much more demanding and discovery is either nonexistent or extremely limited. For discussion see Marcus, Bomb-Throwing, Democratic Theory, and Basic Values—A New Path to Procedural Harmonization?, 107 Nw. L. Rev. 475 (2013) (exploring political theory justifications for balance struck in U.S.).

5.   At least some lower court decisions say the new standard has made a difference. In New Albany Tractor, Inc. v. Louisville Tractor, Inc., 650 F.3d 1046 (6th Cir. 2011), the court concluded that plaintiff could not state its proposed antitrust claim adequately without discovery, but that the Supreme Court's decisions forbade permitting it to have that discovery (id. at 1050–51):

> The new "plausibility" pleading standard causes a considerable problem for plaintiff here because defendants Scag and Louisville Tractor are apparently the only entities with the information about the price at which Scag sells its equipment to Louisville Tractor. This pricing information is necessary for [plaintiff] to allege that it pays a discriminatory price for the same Scag equipment, as required by the language of the [antitrust] Act. * * *

> Before *Twombly* and *Iqbal*, courts would probably have allowed the case to proceed so that plaintiff could conduct discovery in order to gather the pricing information that is solely retained within the accounting system of Scag and Louisville Tractor. * * * The plaintiff apparently can no longer obtain the factual detail necessary because the language of Iqbal specifically directs that no discovery may be conducted in cases such as this, even when the information needed to establish a claim of discriminatory pricing is solely within the purview of the defendant or a third party, as it is here.

But a number of appellate cases reverse district court dismissals based on the new standard. For example, in Hamilton v. Palm, 621 F.3d 816 (9th Cir. 2010), defendants persuaded the district court to dismiss on the ground plaintiff did not adequately allege that he was "employed" by them when he was injured because he "merely alleges generally that he was employed by defendants and has not alleged facts to plausibly support such a conclusion." The appellate court said that "this was an unwarranted extension of the pleading standards" in *Twombly* and *Iqbal*, and that those decisions "did not abrogate the notice pleading standard of Rule 8(a)(2)." See also El-Hallani v. Huntington Nat. Bank, 623 Fed.Appx 730 (6th Cir.2015) ("Although *Twombly* and *Iqbal* have raised the bar for pleading, it is still low.").

6. If the problem is weighing the burden of discovery against the importance of discovery as a method for plaintiffs to obtain what they need to make "plausible" claims, is the solution to permit limited or targeted discovery before ruling on motions to dismiss? See Dodson, New Pleading, New Discovery, 109 Mich. L. Rev. 53 (2010), urging "[a] carefully limited and structured framework of 'pre-discovery discovery,' either before suit or before a motion to dismiss is decided." Id. at 56. Others think that allowing more discovery would be a move in the wrong direction. See Shepherd, Failed Experiment: *Twombly*, *Iqbal*, and Why Broad Pretrial Discovery Should Be Further Eliminated, 49 Ind.L.Rev. 465 (2016).

7. Justice Souter says in *Iqbal* that the plausibility standard permits rejection of "allegations that are sufficiently fantastic to deny reality as we know it." A case decided shortly after *Twombly* may be an example. In Richards v. Duke University, 480 F.Supp.2d 222 (D.C.D.C. 2007), plaintiff, a graduate of Georgetown University Law Center who had transferred there from Duke University Law School, sued various officials of both law schools, as well as the U.S. Attorney General and FBI, and Bill Gates, Melinda Gates and others associated with Microsoft Corporation. Plaintiff alleged that the various defendants illegally engaged in surveillance of her, that law professors entered her apartment to see whether she was completing her assignments, that an article she wrote for a Georgetown journal was altered to imply that she was a homosexual, and that a Georgetown professor added coverage of homosexual civil rights to his syllabus for the first time while she was a student in his class. Microsoft got involved, plaintiff alleged, because Bill Gates became physically attracted to her and the Microsoft defendants feared he would leave his wife as a result. Microsoft stole plaintiff's ideas about generating revenue through wireless email, and also circulated suggestions that she was pregnant with Bill Gates' child. Although recognizing that it had to construe plaintiff's allegations in the light most favorable to plaintiff, the court said that it "does not have to accept asserted inferences or conclusory allegations that are unsupported by facts set forth in plaintiff's complaint." Id. at 235. Employing this standard, the court dismissed all claims against all defendants. How often will complaints run afoul of this rule?

8. How does the "plausibility" standard compare to the PSLRA standard under Tellabs, Inc. v. Makor Issues & Rights, Ltd., supra p. 161? Note that the PSLRA imposes what sounds like a more demanding pleading standard than Rule 8(a)(2) ("state with particularity facts giving rise to a strong inference that the defendant acted with the required state of mind") and also imposes a "discovery stay" pending resolution of a motion to dismiss. Should there be such a stay in all cases? See Rule 26(d) (postponing discovery until after the

parties confer about a discovery plan, and compare the suggestion in note 5 above for discovery before the ruling on the motion to dismiss). Would it make sense for the Rule 8(a)(2) standard to be the same as the PSLRA standard? Consider Burbank, Pleading and the Dilemmas of "General Rules," 2009 Wis. L. Rev. 535, 552:

> [C]ertain language in *Twombly* can be read to mean that the Court's standard—by hypothesis, generally applicable—is more demanding than the standard under the PSLRA. The language in question can be read to require that inferences—or to the extent that a complaint does not rely on inferences, direct allegations—grounding liability not just be plausible in the Tellabs sense (reasonable), and not just as strong (cogent or compelling) as any competing account, but stronger than any account of nonliability. Of course, that would be ridiculous.

9.   Should we leave the calibration of discovery to district judges? As we will see in Chapter 5 (see Proportionality and the 2015 Rule Amendments, infra p. 354), Rule 26(b)(1) and 26(b)(2)(C) direct them to calibrate discovery to make certain that it is proportional to the stakes and importance of the litigation. Can they really do that? In *Twombly*, Justice Souter seemed to think they could not, and in *Iqbal* the majority rejected case management powers as an important protection for defendants. But in *Iqbal*, Justice Breyer (who joined the Court's decision in *Twombly*) seemed receptive to individual case regulation by district judges, even in cases against high government officials like Ashcroft and Mueller. Is that response preferable to making decisions on the pleadings?

10.   In *Iqbal*, Justice Souter does not urge that the *Twombly* standard should be abandoned (he wrote the Court's opinion in *Twombly*), but he does argue that the majority gutted constitutional claims for supervisory liability and improperly rejected a concession by defendants about what would suffice to impose such liability. To what extent is his dissent dependent on his disagreement with the majority about the terms for supervisory liability? If one accepts the majority's view on the grounds for liability, is its pleading decision justified? For another decision rejecting constitutional claims very similar to the claims in *Iqbal* on the merits, see Ziglar v. Abbasi, 137 S.Ct. 1843 (2017).

11.   *The Rules Amendment Process*: *Swierkiewicz* emphasized that changes to the pleading rules should be sought through the rule-amendment process, and many have asserted that Twombly and Iqbal improperly changed the rules outside that process. Indeed, Justice Stevens suggested in his dissent in Twombly that the decision unjustifiably effected a rule change by judicial decree. Is that a proper criticism of the decision? Could the same criticism be made of the Court's decision in Conley v. Gibson? Given these issues, this seems an appropriate point to provide some background on that process. We will return to this subject in Chapter 11.

Pursuant to the Rules Enabling Act of 1934, the entire set of Federal Rules was drafted by a blue ribbon committee in about a year and a half in the 1930s. In recent years, however, the amendment process has become quite public and takes much more time. Initially, rule proposals are generated by Advisory Committees, whose meetings must be public. See 28 U.S.C.A. § 2073(c). Any proposals to change the rules must be published for public comment and hearings. Based on the public input, the Advisory Committee considers modifications, and then approved proposals are forwarded to the Judicial Conference and, if further approved, to the Supreme Court. If the Court adopts them, they are submitted to Congress, which has seven months to act before proposals take effect. Altogether, it normally takes about three years for a rule change to become effective. For an overview, see Marcus, Reform Through Rulemaking?, 80 Wash.U.L.Rev. 901 (2002). The process has become more political than it was in the 1930s. "Participatory democracy now is emerging in the rulemaking process." Mullenix, Hope Over Experience: Mandatory Informal Discovery and the Politics of Rulemaking, 69 N.C.L.Rev. 795, 800 (1991).

Who should design court procedures? Congress can do so by statute, as it did in the Private Securities Litigation Act. See Burbank, Procedure, Politics and Power: The Role of Congress, 79 Notre Dame L. Rev. 1677 (2004). But the idea behind the Rules Enabling Act is that the rules committee should have primary authority for devising procedural changes. The rules process is dominated by judges, however, and some predict that they would try to further their own interests in drafting rules. See Macey, Judicial Preferences, Public Choice, and the Rules of Procedure, 23 J. Legal Stud. 627 (1994); compare Alexander, Judges' Self-interest and Procedural Rules, 23 J. Legal Stud. 647 (1994) (questioning assertion that judges will significantly favor their own interests in rulemaking). Both rulemaking and action by Congress remain possible with regard to any controversial topic.

12. Many states adopted procedure rules that were modeled on the Federal Rules. Not all state courts have adhered, in interpreting their Rule 8(a)(2) in their states, to the standard in *Twombly* and *Iqbal*. See Walsh v. U.S. Bank, 851 N.W.2d 598 (Minn.2014) (declining "to engraft the plausibility standard from *Twombly* and *Iqbal* onto our traditional interpretation of Minn. R. Civ. P. 8(a)(2)"). Similarly, in Colby v. Umbrella, Inc., 955 A.2d 1082 (Vt. 2008), the Vermont Supreme Court reaffirmed its reliance on Conley v. Gibson. Compare Iannacchino v. Ford Motor Co., 888 N.E. 2d 879 (Mass. 2008) (adopting *Twombly* approach).

13. Keep these issues in mind as we turn to discovery (Chapter 5), and later to the standards by which a court may decide to grant summary judgment (Chapter 6) or "take the case from the jury" (Chapter 8). These various topics are all connected in terms both of who should make decisions about the outcome of cases (judges or juries) and how much time, effort and money the parties must spend on litigation before the merits are decided.

C. DEFENDANT'S RESPONSE

1. PRE-ANSWER MOTIONS UNDER RULE 12

We have already considered the Rule 12(b)(6) motion in some detail and compared it to the Rule 12(e) motion for a more definite statement. In addition, there is a Rule 12(f) motion to strike "redundant, immaterial, impertinent, or scandalous matter" or "an insufficient defense." Before we turn to the usual method of asserting defenses—the answer—we need to reflect a bit longer on some of the practical concerns surrounding Rule 12 motions.

The seven defenses set out in Rule 12(b), except for failure to state a claim, are all objections of a procedural nature—that the court is not empowered to exercise jurisdiction over the subject matter of the suit (Rule 12(b)(1)); that the court lacks personal jurisdiction over the defendant (Rule 12(b)(2)); that this particular court is not the proper location (venue) for the suit (Rule 12(b)(3)); that the circumstances or method for serving process were incorrect (Rule 12(b)(4) & (5)); or that the suit shouldn't go forward without a required party (Rule 12(b)(7)). The one exception is Rule 12(b)(6)—failure to state a claim upon which relief can be granted—which challenges the legal sufficiency of the allegations in the complaint.

The filing of a pre-answer motion under Rule 12 affects the time periods for filing responsive pleadings. If the defendant files a pre-answer motion within the 21-day period following service of the summons and complaint, the deadline for filing an answer is extended. Rule 12(a)(4). If the court denies the motion or postpones its disposition, the defendant has until 14 days after notice of the court's action to file an answer. If the court grants the motion, plaintiff will usually be granted leave to amend (which starts the process again) or the suit will be dismissed; however, if a motion for a more definite statement is granted, the defendant has until 14 days after service of an amended complaint containing a more definite statement in which to file its answer.

Rules 12(g) and (h) set out consolidation and waiver provisions concerning the Rule 12 motions. Their purpose is to prevent the pleader from using multiple pre-answer motions for different defenses and from omitting certain defenses from motions or answers. Rule 12(g) provides that if a party makes a pre-answer motion, but omits one of the Rule 12 defenses then available, it cannot make any further pre-answer motions. Rule 12(h)(1) provides that four *disfavored defenses*—lack of jurisdiction over the person, improper venue, insufficiency of process, or insufficiency of service of process—will be waived forever if omitted from a pre-answer motion or, if no motion is made, from the answer. Rule 12(h)(2) provides that three *favored defenses*—failure to state a claim upon which relief can be granted, failure to join an indispensable party, and failure to state a legal defense to a claim—can be made in any pleading, or by motion for judgment on the pleadings, or at trial on the merits. Finally Rule 12(h)(3) states that the *most favored defense*—lack of jurisdiction of the subject matter—may be made at any time.

NOTES AND QUESTIONS

1.   Why would a defendant want to raise one of the Rule 12(b) defenses in a pre-answer motion instead of just including it in the answer? The fact that a pre-answer motion extends the time for filing an answer should provide a hint as to one of the reasons. What advantages might a defendant obtain by putting off having to answer immediately?

2.   Might there be tactical advantages that could prompt a defendant to raise defenses by answer rather than by motion?

(a)   Would the plaintiff ever prefer to have the issues resolved at the outset of the case? Cf. Rule 12(i) (providing that any party can insist on determination before trial of any defenses specified in Rule 12(b), even if they are only raised in the answer). Why might a plaintiff want to force pretrial resolution of such defenses?

(b)   With the defense of failure to state a claim, would there be any advantage for a defendant not to move to dismiss when plaintiff has omitted allegations regarding an essential element of his case? What does that omission suggest about whether plaintiff has paid attention to that aspect of his case? Does plaintiff's inattention create an opportunity for defendant?

[handwritten margin note: If U mot to dismiss they can amend. If you let it slide, they may not notice]

3.   Consider the following problems:

(a)   Within 20 days after service of the complaint and summons, defendant files a pre-answer motion alleging the defense of *insufficiency of service of process*. 15 days later, when the court has not yet ruled on the motion and no answer has yet been filed, defendant realizes that (1) *venue was improper* and (2) there has been a *failure to join an indispensable party*. Can these defenses be made in another pre-answer motion? Can they be made in the answer when it is filed? Would it matter whether, at the time of the filing of the pre-answer motion, the defendant was aware of the facts on which it would base the additional defenses of improper venue and indispensable party?

(b)   Defendant filed a pre-answer motion asserting the defense of *improper venue* and, when it was denied, filed an answer responding on the merits. Six months later, defendant's counsel realizes that there is a defense of *lack of jurisdiction over the subject matter*. Can this defense be raised as the basis for a motion to dismiss? Can it be raised for the first time on appeal after judgment for the plaintiff?

(c)   Defendant did not file a pre-answer motion, but timely filed an answer responding on the merits to the allegations of the complaint. Four weeks after filing the answer, he realizes that there is a defense of *insufficiency of service of process* and of *failure to state a claim upon which relief can be granted*. Can he raise these defenses? See Doe v. Columbia-Brazeria Indep. School Dist., 855 F.3d 681, 686 (5th Cir. 2017) ("Rule 12(h)(2) explicitly excepts from its consolidation requirement motions based on the defense of failure to state a claim upon which relief can be granted."). If one of these defenses can be raised, in what manner?

2. FAILURE TO ANSWER—DEFAULT

SHEPARD CLAIMS SERVICE, INC. v. WILLIAM DARRAH & ASSOCIATES

United States Court of Appeals, Sixth Circuit, 1986
796 F.2d 190

Before LIVELY, CHIEF JUDGE; WELLFORD and NELSON, CIRCUIT JUDGES.

LIVELY, CHIEF JUDGE.

On August 21, 1984, Shepard Claims Services, Inc. (Shepard) filed this contract action in the district court against William Darrah & Associates (Darrah), with jurisdiction based on diversity of citizenship. The complaint alleged essentially that Darrah, a South Carolina-based insurance broker, failed to pay Shepard, a Michigan independent claims adjuster, for services rendered. Following some difficulty in service by mail, service in person was carried out on February 7, 1985.

On February 22, 1985 Darrah's attorney's secretary secured by telephone an extension of time for filing an answer. A confirmation letter from defense counsel, drafted and signed by the secretary with the vacationing counsel's permission, stated:

> This letter will confirm my secretary's conversation with your secretary of February 22, 1985, to the effect that you have granted my office *45 days from February 22, 1985,* to answer the Complaint in the above captioned cause of action against my client, Will Darrah.

(Emphasis added). By April 10 defendant had filed no answer, so plaintiff Shepard requested that the clerk enter Darrah's default. On April 19 Darrah filed a "Notice of Retention," following on April 26 with an answer and then on April 29 with a notice of affirmative defenses, a counterclaim, interrogatories and a request for production of documents. On May 1 defendant filed a response to plaintiff's motion for default judgment (which had not been filed as of that time) and a motion to set aside entry of default pursuant to Rule 55(c), Fed.R.Civ.P. On May 8 plaintiff filed its motion for default judgment and response to defendant's motion to set aside entry of default. Along with the motion to set aside entry of default defendant filed two affidavits, from defense counsel and his secretary, in which they stated their understanding of the extension to run 45 days in addition to the normal period of 30 days under Rule 4(e), Fed.R.Civ.P.,* rather than from

---

* Now a defendant has 21 days to answer. See Rule 12(a)(1)(A).—Eds.

*We Know the Ct. didn't issue an order since there's ambiguity in when the reply was due.

SEC. C   DEFENDANT'S RESPONSE   209

February 22. Under this interpretation the answer would have been due on April 23. The confirming letter, according to the secretary, "contained a misstatement" of what she believed was the arrangement and what she informed her employer. Defense counsel did not review the confirming letter upon his return and apparently did not examine the file until the day he filed his "appearance." Defense counsel insists that he did not learn of the April 10 entry of default until April 29, by letter from opposing counsel.

The district court held a hearing on pending motions on May 28, after which the court denied defendant's motion to set aside entry of default. In its order the district court found that defendant's attorney engaged in culpable conduct when he permitted his secretary to make arrangements for the extension and then failed to review the secretary's letter upon returning from vacation.

The district court denied the defendant's motion for reconsideration and certified the case for an interlocutory appeal pursuant to 28 U.S.C. § 1292(b) upon finding that "a substantial basis exists for a difference of opinion on the question of setting aside the default in this matter, and that an immediate appeal may materially advance the termination of this litigation."

In United Coin Meter Co. v. Seaboard Coastline R.R., 705 F.2d 839 (6th Cir.1983), this court considered a set of circumstances quite similar to those recorded in the present case. After the parties were unable to go forward with a scheduled hearing on the defendant's motion to dismiss, opposing counsel agreed to a 20-day period for the defendant to file an answer. Plaintiff's counsel construed the agreement as running from April 28, while defendant's counsel believed the time ran from May 5. When no answer was filed by April 28, plaintiff's counsel caused a default to be entered by the clerk. The only matter in dispute was the date from which the 20-day period was to run.

Following a hearing the district court found no "excusable neglect" on the part of the defendant. The court also concluded that the affidavits of the defendant failed to establish the existence of a meritorious defense. The district court refused to set aside the default and entered a default judgment for the full amount sought in the complaint. A hearing was held on the defendant's motion for reconsideration. The district court denied reconsideration, finding that there was no "good cause" for setting aside entry of default or the default judgment.

This court reversed the district court in *United Coin*, finding that the criteria controlling the court's decision on a Rule 55(c) motion had not been satisfied. In agreement with other courts, we concluded that three factors determine the outcome of such a motion:

1.   Whether the plaintiff will be prejudiced; (inability to act on your complaint)

2.   Whether the defendant has a meritorious defense; and

interlocutory appeal—

*Prof. Q:
Where do parties get authority to use letter or agreement to delay Reply or ans.

↳ They were making an agreement with eachother.

☆ Nothing is self-executing

3.   Whether culpable conduct of the defendant led to the default.

In *United Coin* the plaintiff did not claim prejudice and this court found that the defendant had established a meritorious defense, one "good at law" without reference to the likelihood of success. The decisive issue was whether the default resulted from the defendant's "culpable conduct." In determining that the third requirement had not been met, we repeatedly stated that the defendant's conduct had not been "willful."

The present case differs from *United Coin* in at least one material respect. In *United Coin*, a default judgment was entered, whereas this interlocutory appeal was taken before entry of judgment. If the only issue relates to entry of default, Rule 55(c), Fed.R.Civ.P., provides the standard—"good cause shown." After entry of a default judgment, the court may set the judgment aside "in accordance with Rule 60(b)," which lists several grounds for relief from judgment. Despite this difference the district court and the parties in the present case recognized United Coin as the controlling decision. However, the district court found the *United Coin* opinion "ambiguous as to the precise definition of culpable conduct." On appeal Darrah argues that *United Coin* is not ambiguous, that it clearly adopted the "willful conduct" definition by citing with approval cases from other circuits that equated culpable conduct with willfulness. The sole reference to negligence in the *United Coin* opinion is contained in a discussion of the standards applicable to a Rule 60(b) motion, under which "excusable neglect" is a ground for relief. Darrah asserts that nothing in the opinion indicates that the "good cause" standard of Rule 55(c) is satisfied by a showing of counsel's negligence.

Shepard contends that the district court correctly found that counsel for the defendant was the "designer" of the agreement for additional time to plead, and that his failure to comply with the agreed limitations was "culpable negligence." Shepard argues that the failure of Darrah and its counsel to abide by the time limits they "designed" could properly be found willful, and therefore culpable, conduct.

Rule 55(c) leaves to the discretion of the trial judge the decision whether to set aside an entry of default. However, a strong preference for trials on the merits in federal courts has led to the adoption of a somewhat modified standard of review where defaults are involved. * * *

Since entry of default is just the first procedural step on the road to obtaining a default judgment, the same policy of favoring trials on the merits applies whether considering a motion under Rule 55(c) or Rule 60(b). In practice a somewhat more lenient standard is applied to Rule 55(c) motions where there has only been an entry of default than to Rule 60(b) motions where judgment has been entered. * * * The distinction between the two standards was discussed in Jackson v. Beech, 636 F.2d 831, 835 (D.C.Cir.1980):

* * * Once a defendant fails to file a responsive answer, he is in default, and an entry of default may be made by either the clerk or the judge. A default judgment can be entered by a clerk only if a claim is liquidated or, if a claim is unliquidated, by the judge after a hearing on damages. A default can be set aside under rule 55(c) for "good cause shown," but a default that has become final as a judgment can be set aside only under the stricter rule 60(b) standards for setting aside final, appealable orders.

In a different setting the district judge's orders in the present case might not constitute an abuse of discretion. However, we must consider the fact that the plaintiff suffered no prejudice by reason of the tardy pleadings and the defendant did present a meritorious defense in its answer. These findings of the district court are clearly supported by the record. All three factors must be considered in ruling on a motion to set aside entry of default. However, when the first two factors militate in favor of setting aside the entry, it is an abuse of discretion for a district court to deny a Rule 55(c) motion in the absence of a willful failure of the moving party to appear and plead.

The conduct of Darrah's counsel, Mark Shreve, was careless and inexcusable. Nevertheless, it is not necessary that conduct be excusable to qualify for relief under the "good cause" standard of Rule 55(c). * * *

The district court stated that defense counsel's conduct, "if not intentional, is certainly 'culpable conduct.'" In making this finding the district court apparently relied on the negligence of the defendant's lawyer in not reviewing the work of his secretary.

To be treated as culpable, the conduct of a defendant must display either an intent to thwart judicial proceedings or a reckless disregard for the effect of its conduct on those proceedings. As in *United Coin*, the delay in the present case resulted from a dispute over the date from which an agreed extension was to run. Darrah's attorney filed an entry of appearance and an answer shortly after learning that default had been entered on the basis of Shepard's interpretation of the agreement. The delay was not lengthy and there was no pattern of disregard for court orders or rules. Under these circumstances the strong policy in favor of deciding cases on their merits outweighs any inconvenience to the court or Shepard resulting from the relatively short delay in answering. We agree with the summary of court holdings in 6 Moore's Federal Practice ¶ 55.01[2] at 55–61, 62 (1985 ed.):

> Where the defaulting party and counsel have not shown disrespect for the court, or have given evidence of respect for the court's process by their haste in acting to set aside the default, the courts have been inclined towards leniency. . . . Clearly, however, the court may refuse to set aside a default, where the defaulting party has no meritorious defense, where the default is due to

willfulness or bad faith, or where the defendant offers no excuse at all for the default.

We do not believe it appropriate to attempt a precise definition of "culpable conduct." Where the party in default satisfies the first two requirements for relief and moves promptly to set aside the default before a judgment is entered, the district court should grant the motion if the party offers a credible explanation for the delay that does not exhibit disregard for the judicial proceedings.

A default judgment deprives the client of his day in court, and should not be used as a vehicle for disciplining attorneys. Although Shepard has made unverified claims that Darrah encouraged its attorney's conduct, there is no basis in the record for finding that the present case involved a deliberate attempt by Darrah to delay the proceedings. Although a party who chooses an attorney takes the risk of suffering from the attorney's incompetence, we do not believe that this record exhibits circumstances in which a client should suffer the ultimate sanction of losing his case without any consideration of the merits because of his attorney's neglect and inattention.

We can understand and sympathize with the reaction of the district court to Shreve's conduct and his explanations or excuses. The "Notice of Retention" indicated that someone in Shreve's office recognized that the time for pleading might be near, or past. Yet another week went by before Shreve filed his answer. The secretary's affidavit ascribed the misunderstanding to a "misstatement" in the letter that the affiant herself wrote. The misunderstanding could have been cured if Shreve had examined the correspondence upon his return from vacation and contacted Shepard's attorney for confirmation. Despite this evidence of inattention and disarray in defense counsel's office, the fact remains that Shepard suffered no prejudice and Darrah would be deprived of an opportunity to present its defense at a trial if the default were not set aside.

Our disposition of the case does not preclude the district court from assessing or determining some appropriate penalty or sanction against the defendant or his counsel for the delay occasioned by the careless and inexcusable conduct of defendant's counsel herein discussed.

The judgment of the district court is reversed, and the cause is remanded for further proceedings. No costs are allowed.

NOTES AND QUESTIONS

1.   The idea behind default derives from the premises of the adversary system; if one side does not want to contest the other side's case, the court is not obliged to inquire further. "New York does not require civil litigants to show up in court only to fall on their swords. If a defendant does not contest his liability as set out in the complaint, he need not appear in the action."

Connecticut Bank of Commerce v. Republic of Congo, 309 F.3d 240, 251 (5th Cir.2002).

2.   Rule 55(b)(1) sets out the only situation in which the clerk, rather than the judge, may enter a default judgment. It provides that if a defendant has been defaulted for failure to appear (and isn't a minor or incompetent), the clerk, upon plaintiff's request and filing an affidavit as to the amount due, must enter judgment if the claim is "for a sum certain or a sum that can be made certain by computation." A claim for damages for a liquidated amount meets this requirement, but not a generalized statement of the amount due. Plaintiff must also show that the sum certain is reasonable under the circumstances. The defendant must have completely failed to appear, and not merely have defaulted after an initial appearance, for the clerk to be allowed to enter judgment.

3.   The entry of default, on the other hand, may be fairly routine; unless defendant has filed an answer, the clerk may enter default when the time to answer expires. At that point, the defendant is entitled to notice of further hearings only if it has entered an "appearance." In cases like *Shepard*, should the defendant's request for additional time to respond be treated as an appearance? See Rogers v. Hartford Life & Accident Ins. Co., 167 F.3d 933 (5th Cir.1999) (waiver of service was not an appearance despite prior informal contacts between parties about the dispute); compare H.F. Livermore Corp. v. Aktiengesellschaft Gebruder Loepfe, 432 F.2d 689 (D.C.Cir.1970) (informal settlement negotiations sufficient to constitute appearance where defendant indicated intent to defend on merits). Why should the law ever dispense with notice? Is this result consistent with the Supreme Court's handling of due process requirements for prejudgment remedies?

4.   A more basic problem yet is to determine what should be treated as an answer. Consider Wheat v. Eakin, 491 So.2d 523 (Miss.1986). Acting pro se, defendant responded to the complaint with a handwritten document addressed to the clerk that stated in its entirety: "Not only do I deny all the allegations in the above styled suit, I contend, with all due respect, that the plaintiff must be suffering from a condition of brown eyeballs since he is full of so much bullshit." Id. at 527 (reproducing handwritten document). The appellate court held that it was error to enter default: "While the form and language of the appellant's response are less than desirable and more frank than customary, the appellant did state in short and plain terms his general denial of appellees' claims. A motion to strike the answer would have been appropriate, but none was filed." Is there a reason for taking such a lenient view of the requisites for an answer in the default context? Compare Interscope Records v. Benavides, 241 F.R.D. 458 (W.D.Tex.2006) (pro se defendant's letter to the court denying plaintiff's charges did not constitute an appearance because it was not sent also to plaintiff's counsel).

5.   Once default is properly entered, what impact should that action have on the court's evaluation of the merits of the case? At a minimum, it appears that the court may refuse to grant a judgment for plaintiff if the complaint fails to state a claim for relief. Beyond that, the court may insist that

plaintiff make some showing of factual support for his allegations. See 10A Wright, Miller & Kane, Federal Practice & Procedure § 2688. And the question of the amount of damages remains open for full scale litigation. Why should defendant's right to have the court probe the merits of plaintiff's case be curtailed by entry of default?

Troublesome questions may emerge where plaintiff seeks equitable relief rather than money damages. For example, in United States v. Di Mucci, 879 F.2d 1488 (7th Cir.1989), defendants were charged with discriminating against black applicants for apartments in their apartment complexes, in violation of the Fair Housing Act. After their default was entered for failure to comply with discovery, the government requested an injunction directing them to undertake a variety of curative measures, which the district court granted after a hearing.

On appeal, defendants argued that the government had to prove a continuing pattern and practice of discrimination to support an injunction even though they were in default. The appellate court upheld the injunction, noting that ordinarily no showing of violation need be made at the remedy stage. In a default case, however, proper practice would be different:

> As a general rule, a default judgment establishes, as a matter of law, that defendants are liable to plaintiff as to each cause of action alleged in the complaint. Thus, entry of the default judgment established that defendant violated the Fair Housing Act.
>
> In this case, however, the fact that the government generally does not have to introduce evidence of a pattern or practice of discrimination at the relief stage of a case such as this is of little moment. Because the DiMuccis' liability was established by default, the law in this circuit indicates that in a case such as this an evidentiary hearing may be required to establish what type of relief is necessary. Although upon default, the well-pleaded allegations of a complaint relating to liability are taken as true, allegations of a complaint relating to the amount of damages suffered ordinarily are not. * * * A judgment by default may not be entered without a hearing on damages unless the amount claimed is liquidated or capable of ascertainment from definite figures contained in the documentary evidence or in detailed affidavits.
>
> The magistrate treated this case as if it were a case presenting unliquidated damages required to be determined by hearing. She noted, however, that unlike an unliquidated damages case, where the issue of damages is separate from the facts decided by the default, the facts establishing the necessity for affirmative injunctive relief are not likely to be different from the facts already legally determined by the entry of the default judgment. In any event, it was proper for the magistrate first to determine whether an injunction was necessary, and if so, what that decree should provide. Thus, it was

necessary, in effect, for the government to show in this case that defendants engaged in a pattern or practice of discrimination.

Id. at 1497–98. The court then found that the government had made the required showing; in cases seeking injunctions, plaintiff may, in effect, have to prove the case on the merits even though there has been a default.

6.   In order to have a properly entered default set aside, defendant must make a motion and show a meritorious defense. In *Shepard*, the court suggests that, to support a motion to set aside a default, defendant need only show that its defense is "good at law," and not that it is likely to succeed. But couldn't defendant always do that by indicating its intention to deny some of plaintiff's allegations? How can the court disregard such denials? In general, courts tend to say they want more than conclusory statements about defenses in support of motions to set aside defaults, insisting instead on some factual showing of a basis for defense. Could this approach be adapted to all cases to permit judges to scrutinize defenses on the pleadings? Cf. Bell Atlantic Corp. v. Twombly, supra p. 184.

In at least one instance, the good defense requirement cannot be imposed on a defendant moving to set aside a default. In *Peralta v. Heights Medical Center, Inc.,* 485 U.S. 80 (1988), the Court held that, where defendant has not been served, the resulting default must be set aside even though defendant cannot cite a good defense. Although defendant's inability to identify a valid defense may mean that plaintiff will win the suit, the Court reasoned that "it is no answer to say that in his particular case due process of law would have led to the same result because he had no adequate defense upon the merits."

[handwritten margin note: Due Process Required]

7.   The court in *Shepard* also says that plaintiff must show some prejudice to preserve the default. How could plaintiff do that?

8.   Should it matter in *Shepard* that the mistake was made by the lawyer, not the client? Some courts say that difference is critical to the assessment of the culpable conduct issue: "The focus on the source of the default represents an equitable balance between our preference for trials on the merits and the judicial system's need for finality and efficiency in litigation. When the party is blameless and the attorney is at fault, the former interests control and a default judgment should ordinarily be set aside. When the party is at fault, the latter interests dominate and the party must adequately defend its conduct in order to show excusable neglect." Augusta Fiberglass Coatings, Inc. v. Fodor Contracting Corp., 843 F.2d 808 (4th Cir.1988).

9.   Filing an answer is not absolute protection against being held in default; a defendant who fails to participate in the lawsuit after filing the answer may find his answer stricken and his default entered. Cf. Rule 37(b)(2)(A)(vi) regarding discovery sanctions, discussed in Chapter 5. Should the court approach a motion to set aside such a default with a similarly lenient attitude?

3.   THE ANSWER

A.   Admitting or Denying the Averments

Rule 8(b)(1) requires a defendant, in the answer, to "admit or deny the allegations asserted against it by an opposing party." This is usually done by going down each paragraph in the complaint and stating that it is either admitted or denied. However, a paragraph, and even a sentence, may contain a number of different allegations (although ideally this should be avoided, see Rule 10(b)). If so, the answer should indicate which portions are admitted and which denied, if they cannot be admitted or denied in toto.

At common law it was permissible to make a general denial, which was a way of saying to the plaintiff: "I don't admit anything. You prove it." This is still permissible in a number of states. Note the limited circumstances under which a general denial may be made under Rule 8(b)(3).

If the defendant "lacks knowledge or information sufficient to form a belief as to the truth of an allegation," it may so state in its answer, which has the effect of a denial. (Rule 8(b)(5)).

DAVID v. CROMPTON & KNOWLES CORP.

United States District Court, Eastern District of Pennsylvania, 1973
58 F.R.D. 444

9/25/18

HUYETT, DISTRICT JUDGE.

The present case is a products liability action involving a serious personal injury. Defendant, Crompton & Knowles Corporation (Crompton), seeks to amend its answer to Paragraph 5 of the complaint which alleges that Crompton designed, manufactured and sold a shredding machine, 600 AAZ Series 11, to Crown Products Corporation (Crown) [plaintiff's employer]. In its answer to the complaint Crompton averred that it was without sufficient knowledge or information to admit or deny the allegation and demanded proof. It now seeks to deny that it designed, manufactured and sold the machine in question.

Crompton bases its proffered denial upon information which it claims it discovered during 1972. It alleges that the machine was designed, manufactured and sold by James Hunter Corporation (Hunter) prior to its purchase of Hunter, and that it did not assume liabilities for the negligent design, manufacture or sale of machines by Hunter prior to its purchase of Hunter's assets in 1961.

An answer to an averment in a complaint which states that the party lacks sufficient information or knowledge to admit or deny the averments is permitted by Fed.R.Civ.P. 8(b) and it has the effect of a denial. A party, however, may not deny sufficient information or knowledge with impunity, but is subject to the requirements of honesty in pleading. An averment will be deemed admitted when the matter is obviously one as to which defendant has knowledge or information. Mesirow v. Duggan, 240 F.2d 751 (8 Cir.1957), cert. denied sub nom. Duggan v. Green, 355 U.S. 864 (1957). Crompton claims that it only recently discovered the information which it now uses as a basis to deny the allegations of Paragraph 5. Plaintiff contends that Crompton's denial of knowledge or information was patently false and should be treated as an admission.

The request for leave to amend assumes significance if Crompton's original answer to Paragraph 5 is deemed an admission. If it is considered an admission, then it is necessary to decide whether an amendment which might greatly affect plaintiff's right to recovery should be allowed, but if it is not deemed admitted and is considered denied in the original answer then the amendment will only serve as a clarification.

The machine which was involved in the accident was designed, manufactured and sold by Hunter to Crown in 1961.[2] Crompton admits that it was aware that the machine was a Hunter product at the time it answered the complaint or very shortly thereafter.[3] Nevertheless, in answers to interrogatories and in a third-party complaint Crompton indicated that it was responsible for the design, manufacture and sale of the machine which was made prior to its purchase of Hunter. Crompton relies entirely on its claim that it has only recently discovered that the contract by which it purchased Hunter did not make it responsible for liabilities of this kind.

In Mesirow v. Duggan, supra, the court held that if the matter alleged in the averment was a matter of record peculiarly within the control and knowledge of the defendant, an answer that defendant was without knowledge or information sufficient to form a belief did not constitute a denial under Fed.R.Civ.P. 8(b)[(5)]. In the present case Crompton admits knowledge of Hunter's role in the design, manufacture and sale of the machine. Its assertion of lack of knowledge or information, therefore, must have been in relation to responsibility which it assumed for such a claim. Any responsibility, of course, arises from the agreement of sale between Crompton and Hunter. The terms of this agreement are certainly peculiarly within the control and knowledge of Crompton, one of the parties to the agreement. It does not seem too burdensome to hold Crompton to knowledge of the terms of its purchase agreement and their effect on its rights and liabilities more than nine years after the sale of Hunter was completed. The averment of lack of knowledge or information sufficient to

---

[2]   The shredding machine denominated in the complaint is not the correct machine. The proper machine was a Model F-4000 Garnett machine which Crompton referred to in answers to interrogatories filed October 1, 1971. This machine was sold by Hunter to Crown as was the shredding machine mentioned in the complaint.

[3]   In answers to interrogatories Crompton asserted that it learned of the action from Hunter, which is now a division of Crompton.

admit or deny the allegations of Paragraph 5 is not proper under these circumstances and plaintiff's allegation should be deemed admitted.

[The portion of the opinion discussing the question whether Crompton will be allowed to amend its answer appears infra at p. 232].

NOTES AND QUESTIONS

1.   The starting point in assessing rules governing denials is the effect of an admission. When defendant admits an allegation of the complaint, that allegation is taken as true for purposes of the litigation whether or not it is accurate in fact. See Rule 8(b)(6). Why should courts thus confine the pursuit for objective truth? Is such acquiescence in the parties' willingness to treat fiction as fact inherent in the adversary system? Given the effect of an admission, why should the law pressure a defendant into admitting anything?

2.   What should a defendant do if it is not absolutely certain as to the truth of a fact alleged in the complaint? Crompton indicates that pleading lack of knowledge may be taken as an admission when the matter is one as to which the defendant has knowledge or information. Rule 11(b)(4) explicitly addresses the legitimate grounds for denials. See Profile Pub. & Manag. Corp. v. Musicmaker.com, Inc., 242 F.Supp.2d 363 (S.D.N.Y.2003) (defendant sanctioned after refusing to withdraw defenses). In connection with allegations about which a party is ignorant, the Committee Note to Rule 11(b) explains that "a denial is permissible because, after an appropriate investigation, a party has no information concerning the matter or, indeed, has a reasonable basis for doubting the credibility of the only evidence relevant to the matter. A party should not deny an allegation it knows to be true; but it is not required, simply because it lacks contradictory evidence, to admit an allegation that it believes is not true. * * * If, after further investigation or discovery, a denial is no longer warranted, the defendant should not continue to insist on that denial." 146 F.R.D. at 586. Does this help? As shown by the remainder of the case, infra p. 232, defendant appeared to acknowledge responsibility during discovery. Should that bear on whether the answer was sufficient? Do statements in discovery supersede pleadings?

3.   In *Crompton*, the court stresses that the pertinent information was "peculiarly within the control and knowledge of Crompton." How should courts approach the duty to make admissions where this is not true? Consider the well-known case of Zielinski v. Philadelphia Piers, Inc., 139 F.Supp. 408 (E.D.Pa.1956), which points up a risk in making a denial of a multi-faceted allegation. Plaintiff sued defendant (PPI) for personal injuries he alleged he sustained in an accident on Pier 96 in Philadelphia. In paragraph 5 of his complaint, plaintiff alleged that, on the date of the accident, "a forklift or chisel, owned, operated and controlled by the defendant, its agents, servants and employees, was so carelessly managed . . . that the same . . . did come into contact with the plaintiff causing him to sustain the injuries more fully hereinafter set forth." The answer stated that "Defendant . . . denies the averments of paragraph 5." The problem was that PPI, which had once operated the pier involved, had transferred this operation to Carload Carriers,

Inc. (CCI) before the date of plaintiff's alleged injury. Moreover, this fact did not surface until it was too late for plaintiff to substitute CCI as defendant because the statute of limitations had run, a problem that would probably not exist today under the revised provisions of Rule 15(c) (see infra pp. 236–250).

Under the circumstances, the court held that PPI would be estopped to deny that it had operated Pier 96 on the date of plaintiff's accident. In part, this ruling was based on PPI's discovery responses, which failed to alert plaintiff to the problem. But the court also held that PPI had failed to comply with Rule 8(b)'s direction at that time that "[w]hen a pleader intends in good faith to deny only a part or a qualification of an averment, the pleader shall specify so much of it as is true and material and shall deny only the remainder." The court reasoned that PPI had not complied with the rule because it was aware of a report stating that there had been an accident in which plaintiff had been injured. Accordingly, "[a] specific denial of parts of this paragraph and specific admission of other parts would have warned plaintiff that he had sued the wrong defendant." The court declined, however, to find that PPI had been guilty of any bad faith in answering as it did. See Rule 8(b)(4) for the current provision.

Given the binding nature of admissions, should defendants be required to rely on reports they receive from others in answering allegations about matters discussed in those reports? Given that PPI did not in fact operate Pier 96, was there anything in paragraph 5 of the complaint that it could not have denied in good faith? If it were acting in good faith, however, wouldn't it have volunteered that plaintiff had sued the wrong party?

4.   Should defendant's obligation to admit parts of a paragraph of the complaint pursuant to Rule 8(b) be relaxed where the complaint itself is ambiguously or confusingly drafted? See Rule 10(b). Some courts have said that the existence of a poorly drawn complaint gives defendant no excuse unless defendant has objected to the complaint under Rule 12. See Winslow v. National Elec. Products Corp., 5 F.R.D. 126, 129 (W.D.Pa.1946). Is this fair to defendants? Could the complaint in *Zielinski* (note 3 above) have been drafted in a more precise way that would have isolated the problem that later arose when it was revealed that PPI no longer operated the pier? Assuming that defendant generally may not excuse defects in the answer by relying on defects in the complaint, should an exception be made in Crompton, where it appears that plaintiff's complaint identified the wrong machine?

5.   Is there any legitimate reason why plaintiffs may incline toward vague allegations? Consider Willinger v. Mercy Catholic Medical Center, 362 A.2d 280 (Pa.Super.1976), in which plaintiffs' healthy five year old son checked into the hospital on June 2, 1969, for a tonsillectomy and died shortly after the operation. Plaintiffs alleged as follows in paragraph 3 of their complaint:

3.   On or about June 3, 1969, defendant through its agents, servants and employees, acting within the course and scope of their employment, did so carelessly and negligently treat said Leonard

Willinger . . . that he developed a serious and permanent injury resulting in his death.

Assume that the hospital denied all allegations of this paragraph. Should it later be allowed to contend that while it admits the operation was negligently done, it claims that the persons responsible for the negligence were not its agents, servants or employees? Is there anything in paragraph 3 that the hospital should have admitted? Can you see any reason why plaintiff was so vague?

B. Affirmative Defenses

As we have seen, a responsive pleading must admit or deny each averment upon which the adverse party relies (Rule 8(b)). However, there are times when admitting or denying is inadequate: for example, a responding party may be willing to admit a factual allegation but still contend that she had a justifiable reason for her action. At common law, this was called pleading in "confession and avoidance." It was a way of saying that even if the allegation is proven, there is an excuse that is recognized under the law. It is different from a denial because it does not seek to deny an element of the opposing party's case, but rather sets out affirmatively a new issue that goes beyond disproving that element.

Affirmative defenses are the modern equivalent of the common-law plea in confession and avoidance, and Rule 8(c) requires that a responding party "affirmatively state" them in the answer. Eighteen affirmative defenses are listed in Rule 8(c), but this is not a comprehensive list, and any other "avoidance or affirmative defense" must also be pleaded affirmatively.

It is not always easy to determine whether a matter is an affirmative defense that must be pleaded by the responding party or simply relates to an element of the claim. Statutory language can sometimes determine who has pleading responsibility. Recall, for example, United States v. Board of Harbor Commissioners, supra p. 137. There a federal statute provided that the owner or operator of a facility from which a hazardous substance is discharged is liable to the U.S. government, *except* when the owner or operator can prove the discharge was caused solely by an act of God, act of war, negligence of the U.S., or act of a third party. The "except" language indicates that the owner of the facility has the burden of pleading and proving one of the four circumstances that will negate liability, and thus that they are affirmative defenses.

Another example is Gomez v. Toledo, 446 U.S. 635 (1980). Plaintiff there was a former police officer who sued the Superintendent of Police for firing him without a hearing (based on the officer's alleged use of illegal wiretapping). The district court dismissed the case on the ground that the defendant superintendent was entitled to qualified immunity for acts done in good faith within the scope of his official duties and that the plaintiff had failed to plead as part of his claim for relief that defendant was motivated by bad faith.

The suit was brought under 42 U.S.C.A. § 1983, which provides a cause of action for "the deprivation of any rights, privileges, or immunities secured by the Constitution and laws" by any person acting "under color of any statute, ordinance, regulation, custom, or usage, of any State or Territory." The Supreme Court read § 1983 as only requiring two allegations—that the defendant deprived plaintiff of a federal right and that this was done under color of law. "Since qualified immunity is a defense," the court said, "the burden of pleading it rests with the defendant." It went on to note that whether the defendant had acted in good faith "depends on facts peculiarly within the knowledge of the defendant" and that "[t]here may be no way for a plaintiff to know in advance whether the official has such a belief or, indeed, whether he will even claim that he does." For that reason, it makes sense that defendant have the burden of raising the issue affirmatively. See also Winforge, Inc. v. Coachmen Industries, Inc., 691 F.3d 856, 872 (7th Cir. 2012) (defenses not enumerated in Rule 8(c) are affirmative defenses if defendant bears the burden of proof or if the defense does not controvert plaintiff's proof).

Policies affecting burden allocation: As indicated in *Gomez*, statutory language may be helpful or even determinative as to whether a matter is an affirmative defense, but there are also policies that help to allocate pleading burdens when the language is not so clear. In a classic article, Professor Cleary found three types of concerns in the decisions, although he also observed that none affords a complete working rule. Cleary, Presuming and Pleading: An Essay on Judicial Immaturity, 12 Stan. L.Rev. 5, 11–13 (1959):

> (1) *Policy.* As Judge Clark remarks, "One who must bear the risk of getting the matter properly set before the court, if it is to be considered at all, has to that extent the dice loaded against him." While policy more obviously predominates at the stage of determining what elements are material, its influence may nevertheless extend into the stage of allocating those elements by way of favoring one or the other party to a particular kind of litigation. Thus a court which is willing to permit a recovery for negligence may still choose to exercise restraints by imposing on plaintiff the burden of freedom from contributory negligence, as a theoretical, though perhaps not a practical, handicap. Or the bringing of actions for defamation may in some measure be discouraged by allocating untruth to plaintiff as an element of his prima facie case, rather than by treating truth as an affirmative defense. * * *

> (2) *Fairness.* The nature of a particular element may indicate that evidence relating to it lies more within the control of

one party, which suggests the fairness of allocating that element to him. Examples are payment, discharge in bankruptcy, and license, all of which are commonly treated as affirmative defenses. However, caution in making any extensive generalization is indicated by the classification of contributory negligence, illegality, and failure of consideration also as affirmative defenses, despite the fact that knowledge more probably lies with plaintiff. Certainly in the usual tort cases, knowledge of his own wrongdoing rests more intimately in defendant, though the accepted general pattern imposes this burden on plaintiff.

(3) *Probability.* A further factor which seems to enter into many decisions as to allocation is a judicial, i.e., wholly nonstatistical, estimate of the probabilities of the situation, with the burden being put on the party who will be benefited by a departure from the supposed norm.

The probabilities may relate to the type of situation out of which the litigation arises or they may relate to the type of litigation itself. The standards are quite different and may produce differences in result. To illustrate: If it be assumed that most people pay their bills, the probabilities are that any bill selected at random has been paid; therefore, a plaintiff suing to collect a bill would be responsible for [alleging and proving] nonpayment as an element of his prima facie case. If, however, attention is limited to bills upon which suit is brought, a contrary conclusion is reached. Plaintiffs are not prone to sue for paid bills, and the probabilities are that the bill is unpaid. Hence payment would be an affirmative defense.

The burden of proving an affirmative defense at trial usually follows the burden of pleading, but that this result does not always follow. In his concurring opinion in *Gomez*, for example, Justice Rehnquist stated that he left open the question whether the defendant superintendent would have the burden of proving qualified immunity at trial. (Burden of proof at trial will be considered in Chapter 8.)

Relation to motion to dismiss under Rule 12(b)(6): As Gomez v. Toledo, supra, suggests, plaintiff usually need not include allegations dealing with possible affirmative defenses in the complaint. But affirmative defenses may sometimes be raised by a Rule 12(b)(6) motion to dismiss for failure to state a claim:

Affirmative defenses, such as the statute of limitations, may be raised in a motion to dismiss under Federal Rule of Civil Procedure 12(b)(6), provided that "the facts establishing the defense [are] clear 'on the face of the plaintiff's pleading.'" Where the dates included in the complaint show that the limitations period has been exceeded and the complaint fails to "sketch the factual predicate" that would warrant the application of either a different statute of limitations period or equitable estoppel, dismissal is appropriate.

Trans-Spec Truck Serv., Inc. v. Caterpillar, Inc., 524 F.3d 315, 320 (1st Cir. 2008); see also Jones v. Bock, 549 U.S. 199 (2007) ("If the allegations, for example, show that relief is barred by the applicable statute of limitations, the complaint is subject to dismissal for failure to state a claim"); Zean v. Fairview Health Services, Inc., 858 F.3d 520, 526 (8th Cir. 2017) (an affirmative defense "apparent on the face of the complaint" is a basis for dismissal under Rule 12(b)(6)).

Owing to the possibility of dismissal on limitations grounds, plaintiffs sometimes plead excuses for their failure to sue in time. In Richards v. Mitcheff, 696 F.3d 635 (7th Cir. 2012), a prisoner who complained of deficient medical treatment delayed more than two years (the limitations period) in filing his suit against the prison doctors. The district court dismissed even though plaintiff alleged the time to sue should have been tolled because he was disabled by his injuries. The court of appeals reversed, noting that "[t]hese allegations may not be true, but they are plausible—and no more is required of a pleading [citing *Iqbal*, supra p. 192, and *Twombly*, supra p. 184]. Actually not even that much is required of a pleading on the subject of the statute of limitations. What a complaint must plead is enough to show that the claim for relief is plausible. Complaints need not anticipate defenses and attempt to defeat them." Id. at 637.

Relation to motion for judgment on the pleadings: From the perspective of the defendant, a Rule 12(c) motion for a judgment on the pleadings is essentially the same as a Rule 12(b)(6) motion to dismiss. Katz-Crank v. Haskett, 843 F.3d 641, 646 (7th Cir. 2016) ("A motion for judgment on the pleadings * * * is subject to the same standard as a Rule 12(b)(6) motion to dismiss."). But for the plaintiff, the contents of the answer may make such a motion possible. If defendant has admitted the essential allegations of plaintiff's case and has not pleaded an affirmative defense, plaintiff could file a motion for judgment on the pleadings, which tests the legal sufficiency of all the pleadings (just as a Rule 12(b)(6) motion tests the legal sufficiency of the complaint). But what if the defendant has pleaded an affirmative defense? Assume, for example, that the complaint alleges that the defendant assaulted and battered the plaintiff, and the answer admits the acts but raises the affirmative defense that the defendant has blue eyes. The plaintiff, by making a motion for judgment on the pleadings, asks the court to determine that the complaint makes out a prima facie case of assault, that the defendant has admitted the essential facts, and that the defendant's purported affirmative defense is legally insufficient. Assume the defense that the defendant has blue eyes is not legally sufficient. If the court determines that the defense is not legally sufficient, it may strike it (Rule 12(f)) and, with the defense gone, grant the plaintiff judgment on the pleadings. If matters outside the pleadings are presented, the court may treat the motion as one for summary judgment.

Effect of failure to plead an affirmative defense: If an affirmative defense is not pleaded, the issue is not in the case, and evidence relating to it is not admissible at trial (unless such evidence is independently relevant to an essential element of the case). Because there usually need not be a reply to an answer even if it contains affirmative defenses, the allegations supporting them are taken as denied by the opposing party. If an affirmative defense is not pleaded, the defendant may not rely upon it. See Harris v. Secretary, U.S. Department of Veterans Affairs, 126 F.3d 339 (D.C.Cir. 1997) (holding it was improper to grant defendant's motion for summary judgement on the ground plaintiff delayed too long in filing suit even though the district court could grant defendant leave to amend the answer to add that affirmative defense); compare Lafreniere Park Foundation v. Broussard, 221 F.3d 804 (5th Cir.2000) (defendant could raise res judicata by summary judgment motion even though it was not asserted in the answer); Motion Medical Tech. v. Thermotek, Inc., 875 F.3d 765 (5th Cir.2017) (Rule 8(c) permits defendant to raise an affirmative defense not included in the answer so long as there is no unfair surprise). In any event, this is not the same as the waiver effected by Rule 12(h)(1), which is designed to force parties to raise certain kinds of objections early or lose them. An amendment to add an omitted affirmative defense would be governed by Rule 15(a), which states that leave to amend "shall be freely granted when justice so requires."

Pleading standards for affirmative defenses: We have seen that the Supreme Court seems to have upgraded pleading requirements for complaints. See supra pp. 184–205. Should those standards apply to affirmative defenses? The courts are divided. The decisions are reviewed in Hayne v. Green Ford Sales, 263 F.R.D. 647 (D.Kan.2009), where the court ultimately concludes that "[i]t makes no sense to find that a heightened pleading standard applies to claims but not to affirmative defenses. In both instances, the purpose of pleading requirements is to provide enough notice to the opposing party that indeed there is some plausible, factual basis for the assertion and not simply a suggestion of possibility that it may apply in the case." Compare Baron v. DirecTV, LLC, 233 F.Supp.3d 441 (D.Md.2017) (holding that *Twombly/Iqbal* standards do not apply to affirmative defenses); see Rand, Why Plausibility Must Be Confined to the Complaint, 9 Fed.Cts.L.Rev. 79 (2016).

C. Counterclaims

WIGGLESWORTH V. TEAMSTERS LOCAL UNION NO. 592

United States District Court, Eastern District of Virginia, 1975
68 F.R.D. 609

WARRINER, DISTRICT JUDGE.

Plaintiff Welford Wigglesworth, Jr., a member of Teamsters Local Union No. 592, has filed a complaint under the Labor Management Reporting Disclosures Act, "Act," 29 U.S.C. § 401 et seq., alleging that the union and its president have violated certain of his rights as protected by the Act. Specifically, the complaint avers that during meetings of defendant Local No. 592 held on 8 September 1974 and 13 October 1974, plaintiff was prevented from exercising his right to freedom of speech, and was denied his request to have the union membership informed of their rights as required by the Act.

In addition to denying generally the allegations in the complaint, defendants asserted a counterclaim alleging the following: On 3 December 1974, the day on which the complaint was filed, plaintiff called a press conference at which he accused the union of being dominated by the "Mafia" and that a certain past local union election had been "fixed." Defendants claim that these remarks constituted libel and slander. The counterclaim further alleges that plaintiff maliciously misused and abused the processes of law by maintaining the instant lawsuit for wholly vindictive and wrongful purposes.

The matter is now before the Court on plaintiff's motion to dismiss the counterclaim, inter alia, for lack of subject matter jurisdiction. There is no diversity of citizenship between the parties, and jurisdiction is founded solely on 29 U.S.C. § 412.

Defendants' initial contention is that the motion to dismiss for lack of subject matter jurisdiction is untimely and should therefore be denied. However, Rule 12(h)(3), Fed.R.Civ.P., plainly states that challenges to the Court's subject matter jurisdiction may be raised at any time, and the cases have consistently so held. Therefore, the defendants' claim of untimeliness is without merit.

Defendants' counterclaim was filed pursuant to Rule 13, Fed.R.Civ.P. which distinguishes between "compulsory" and "permissive" counterclaims. If the defendants' claim arises out of the transaction or occurrence that is the subject matter of the opposing party's claim, then, if certain other requisites not here pertinent are met, it is compulsory. By definition, compulsory claims are "ancillary to the claim asserted in the complaint and [sic] no independent basis of [f]ederal jurisdiction is required." Alternatively, if the counterclaim is unconnected with the transaction out of which the primary claim arose, it is permissive, and independent jurisdictional grounds are required.

The threshold question to be decided is whether defendants' counterclaims arise out of the same transaction or occurrence that is the subject matter of the plaintiff's claim. If so, then the counterclaims are compulsory, and are properly before the Court. Thus, the definition of "transaction or occurrence" is critical to this determination.

There is a substantial body of law which liberally defines the test of compulsoriness as requiring that there be not so much "an absolute identity of factual backgrounds for the two claims, but only a logical relationship between them." United Artists Corp. v. Masterpiece Productions, 221 F.2d 213, 216 (2d Cir.1955). In Moore v. New York Cotton Exchange, 270 U.S. 593, 610 (1926), the Supreme Court explained that " '[t]ransaction' is a word of flexible meaning. It may comprehend a series of many occurrences, depending not so much upon the immediateness of their connection as upon their logical relationship."

Defendants maintain that under this liberal test, their counterclaims meet the criteria set forth for compulsoriness, and therefore are properly within the Court's ancillary jurisdiction. We must disagree.

The gravamen of plaintiff's claim is that he was denied his right to free speech and expression at certain past union meetings. Thus, the claim arises solely from the alleged wrongful conduct on the part of the union at the specific union meetings in question. Determination of the validity of that claim is limited to ascertaining whether the challenged union meetings were conducted in conformity with the mandates of the Act. However, defendants' counterclaim for libel and slander is predicated on events which are in no wise part of the transactions or occurrences which gave rise to plaintiff's claim. This aspect of the counterclaim is grounded on words allegedly spoken by plaintiff many months after the union meetings in question. There is no indication that the alleged remarks at the press conference on 3 December 1974 had any relationship, logical or otherwise, to the events which transpired at certain past union meetings.

On issues of law almost identical to those presented here, the Court in Bose Corp. v. Consumers Union of the United States, Inc., 384 F.Supp. 600 (D.C.Mass.1974),* found defendant's counterclaims to be permissive. In Bose, the complaint alleged unfair competition and violations of the Lanham Act. The defendant filed a counterclaim for malicious abuse of process and for defamation arising out of the filing of the complaint and the issuance of a press release on the same day. Although the issue to be decided was whether the counterclaims were barred by the statute of limitations, the resolution necessarily turned on whether the claims were compulsory or permissive. After an extensive analysis of the various

---

*   A different decision in the same *Bose* case is reproduced infra p. 1142.—Eds.

standards which have been employed to ascertain the nature of a counterclaim, the Court based its determination on whether the same evidence would support or refute the opposing claims. If the same evidence would substantially dispose of the issues raised by the opposing claims, then the counterclaims were compulsory; if not, then they were permissive.

After observing that the issues of law and fact raised by the opposing claims were significantly dissimilar, the Court in Bose determined that application of the "same evidence" standard revealed that the counterclaims for libel and malicious abuse of process were permissive.

Applying the *Bose* standard to the facts of this case, a like conclusion seems inescapable. The evidence necessary for the union to prevail on its libel and slander claims is not relevant to plaintiff's case. Alternatively, the proof of violations by the union under the L.M.R.D.A. varies substantially from that necessary to recover for libel and slander. Similarly, proof of plaintiff's willful abuse of process with resulting damage to the union is quite distinct from that necessary to establish an infringement of plaintiff's rights under the federal statute.

There being no connection between the events giving rise to the counterclaims asserted by defendants, and the transaction or occurrence upon which plaintiff's claim is based, the Court holds that the counterclaims are permissive. Noting that such claims are between non-diverse parties, and are grounded solely in state law, the Court observed that they are without independent jurisdictional support, and must therefore be dismissed unless falling within an exception to the jurisdictional requirement.

* * *

Accordingly, plaintiff's motion to dismiss the counterclaims will be granted.

NOTES AND QUESTIONS

1.   This is the first case we have seen involving the question of the number of events that can properly be grouped together as part of a common "transaction or occurrence" or "series of transactions or occurrences" in a given litigation. For purposes of reference at the outset, various situations dealing with this general question are:

—   Compulsory counterclaims (Rule 13(a))

—   Relation back of amendments (Rule 15(c))

—   Permissive joinder of parties (Rule 20) (see Chapter 4)

—   Supplemental jurisdiction (see Chapter 10)

—   Res judicata (see Chapter 13)

For a review of interpretations of the various contexts in which the "transaction" is important, see Kane, Original Sin and the Transaction in Federal Civil Procedure, 76 Tex. L. Rev. 1723 (1998).

2. What test does the court in *Wigglesworth* adopt to determine whether the counterclaim is compulsory? Professors Wright, Miller and Kane distill the following four tests from the cases, while noting that "the courts have refrained from making any serious attempt to define the transaction or occurrence concept in a highly explicit fashion":

    (a) Are the issues of fact and law raised by the claim and counterclaim largely the same?

    (b) Would res judicata bar a subsequent suit on defendant's claim absent the compulsory counterclaim rule?

    (c) Will substantially the same evidence support or refute plaintiff's claim as well as defendant's counterclaim?

    (d) Is there any logical relation between the claim and the counterclaim?

6 Federal Practice & Procedure § 1410. Do these tests (except (b), which we address in Chapter 13) lead to the same result in Wigglesworth?

3. *Ancillary (now supplemental) jurisdiction*: Why was it necessary for the court in Wigglesworth to determine whether the counterclaim for libel and abuse of process was compulsory or permissive? The answer has to do with subject matter jurisdiction. Note that this was a suit based on a federal statute, 29 U.S.C.A. § 412. In general, a plaintiff asserting a federal claim invokes "federal question" jurisdiction under 28 U.S.C.A. § 1331. But the counterclaim for libel and abuse of process arose under state law and would not independently satisfy federal jurisdictional requirements. This is where what was called ancillary jurisdiction (now called supplemental jurisdiction) comes in. Because it seems unfair to make a defendant respond to suit in a federal court without allowing it to counterclaim as to matters arising out of the same transaction or occurrence, the courts have jurisdiction over compulsory counterclaims. As with Rule 13(a), the question whether ancillary jurisdiction existed depended on the connection between the grounds for plaintiff's claim and the grounds for defendant's counterclaim. The application of these jurisdictional principles is considered in detail in Chapter 10.

4. How does the counterclaim in *Wigglesworth* differ from a defense that plaintiff's claims lack merit? Didn't plaintiff's decision to call a press conference suggest that he viewed the claims in the lawsuit to be related to the charges made at the press conference?

5. Rule 13(a) says that counterclaims arising out of the same transaction or occurrence are "compulsory." Should the court refuse to let the defendant defend the case unless it asserts such counterclaims? It does not do so, and, in reality, the effect of the rule is principally to forbid a later suit on the claim that should have been asserted as a counterclaim. Is it likely that defendants are often reluctant to assert claims against those who sue them?

Cf. Rule 13(b). Why might a defendant decline to assert a claim against a plaintiff that it had a right to assert? Note that the rule does not make compulsory any claims that are already the subject of pending litigation. Why should these be exempted?

6.   Rule 13(g) permits a party to state a cross-claim against a co-party (i.e., one defendant may assert a claim against another defendant) if it arises out of the same transaction or occurrence. But such claims are never compulsory. Should they be compulsory in the same way as claims against an opposing party? Are there stronger reasons for giving co-defendants the option not to sue one another? Would making them compulsory sometimes help plaintiffs? Recall McCormick v. Kopmann, supra p. 142, where the defendant truck driver tried to prove that the accident was caused by the defendant bar owners.

D. Voluntary Dismissal

Plaintiffs sometimes want to dismiss a suit they have brought. This can occur when a plaintiff realizes that it does not have a winning suit and wants to end it without further expenditure of time and money. But a plaintiff may also want only to end the particular suit in the particular court, with the freedom to file it again, or to file it in a modified form, in another court. This may happen if the plaintiff is persuaded that it can get a more favorable result in another forum. Examples include cases in which defendant has pleaded a statute of limitations defense that seems likely to be upheld in the court in which the suit is pending but might not be in another forum, or cases in which preliminary rulings of the judge lead the plaintiff to believe that the judge is unfavorable to the claim.

At common law, a plaintiff's right to a voluntary dismissal or "nonsuit" without prejudice was absolute at any time before judgment. Ex parte Skinner & Eddy Corp., 265 U.S. 86 (1924). "State practices permitted a plaintiff to dismiss the action up to various points in the proceeding ranging from before the issue had been joined, just before the trial began, before the case was submitted to the jury, to before the verdict was returned." 9 C. Wright & A. Miller, Fed. Prac. & Pro. § 2363, at 416 (3d ed. 2008).

Today, however, we recognize that a liberal voluntary dismissal rule can cause needless expenditure of judicial resources and impose burdens on the defendant in defending against a suit that is ultimately withdrawn. Although some states still accord plaintiffs a broad right to dismiss or nonsuit, in federal court Rule 41(a)(1) reflects a policy that voluntary dismissal should be limited to the early stages of the litigation. But within those limitations, the rule does permit unilateral action by plaintiff:

Three key aspects of Rule 41(a)(1)(A)(i) control our analysis. First, a filing under the Rule is a notice, not a motion. Its effect is automatic: the defendant does not file a response, and no order of the district court is needed to end the action. Second, the notice results in a dismissal without prejudice (unless it states otherwise), as long as the plaintiff has never dismissed an action based on or including the same claim in a prior case. Third, the defendant has only two options for cutting off the plaintiff's right to end the case by notice: serving on the plaintiff an answer or a motion for summary judgment.

In re Bath and Kitchen Fixtures Antitrust Lit., 535 F.3d 161, 165 (3d Cir. 2008) (holding that a Rule 12(b)(6) motion does not cut off plaintiff's right to dismiss without prejudice unless the court converts it to summary judgment under Rule 12(d)). Compare ISC Holding AG v. Nobel Biocare Finance AG, 688 F.3d 98 (2d Cir.2012) (holding that voluntary dismissal of a petition to compel arbitration is not allowed because the petition is heard as a motion, precluding the filing of an answer that would cut off the right to dismissal under Rule 41(a)). For an analysis of the policy issues involved, see Solimine & Lippert, Deregulating Voluntary Dismissals, 36 U.Mich.J. of Law Ref. 367 (2003).

Rule 41(a)(1)(A)(i) provides a very specific time period for allowing a voluntary dismissal without court order—it must be filed before service of an answer or motion for summary judgment. However, even when voluntary dismissal is sought before an answer or motion for summary judgment, some courts have been unwilling to allow it if the merits of the case have already been addressed. Although it may be that defendants often don't incur substantial costs before filing an answer or a motion for summary judgment, sometimes they do. For example, consider the effort that may be involved in resisting a motion for a preliminary injunction, which could entail a full evidentiary hearing. Should plaintiffs be given an unfettered right to dismiss if the judge then concludes that they have not shown a likelihood of success? Recall the standards for a preliminary injunction, supra p. 78 n. 1. At least some cases have suggested that "the merits" might have been reached at such a hearing, with the result that unilateral dismissal is no longer allowed. See Harvey Aluminum, Inc. v. American Cyanamid Co., 203 F.2d 105 (2d Cir. 1953); compare D.C. Electronics, Inc. v. Narton Corp., 511 F.2d 294 (6th Cir.1975) (questioning validity of this approach and noting: "The defendant can protect himself by merely filing an answer or motion for summary judgment.").

Once plaintiff has filed a notice of dismissal, it may not unilaterally withdraw or amend the notice. However, it may move to vacate it under Rule 60(b) (see infra pp. 664–669) for mistake, surprise, inadvertence, or excusable neglect, or on a showing of good cause. See Noland v. Flohr Metal Fabricators, 104 F.R.D. 83, 87 (D.Alaska.1984) (permitting amendment to limit dismissal to one defendant, and not the entire action, where plaintiff's mistake had been inadvertent).

Once defendant's answer or motion for summary judgment has been served, the plaintiff can dismiss only upon stipulation of all the parties or by order of court upon such terms and conditions as it deems proper. Courts usually allow dismissal without imposing conditions unless the defendant has suffered prejudice. The mere prospect of having to defend against a suit in another forum is not prejudice. D'Alto v. Dahon Cal., Inc., 100 F.3d 281, 283 (2d Cir.1996) (fact that plaintiff could refile the suit is not "legal prejudice"). Compare Paulucci v. City of Duluth, 826 F.2d 780 (8th Cir.1987) (refusing dismissal where continuing uncertainty as to title to land would prejudice defendant). Court-imposed conditions on dismissal can reduce the likelihood of prejudice. For example, requiring plaintiff to pay the opposing party's costs in defending the case might be such a condition. But would that be appropriate in light of the American rule that a winning defendant cannot usually recover its attorneys' fees? See Marlow v. Winston & Strawn, 19 F.3d 300, 306 (7th Cir.1994) ("Typically, a court imposes as a term and condition of dismissal that plaintiff pay the defendant the expenses he has incurred in defending the suit, which usually includes reasonable attorneys' fees").

If the court has the power to condition a dismissal, can it make the dismissal with prejudice? See Gravatt v. Columbia University, 845 F.2d 54 (2d Cir.1988) (dismissal without prejudice can be converted into dismissal with prejudice). If the plaintiff does not like the conditions imposed, can it change its mind about dismissing? See Michigan Surgery Investment LLC v. Arman, 627 F.3d 572 (6th Cir. 2010) (holding that the district court erroneously converted to dismissal with prejudice without allowing plaintiffs to withdraw their request to dismiss). If the plaintiff moves to dismiss with prejudice, can the court refuse to grant dismissal because defendant wants to obtain vindication at trial? See Smoot v. Fox, 340 F.2d 301 (6th Cir.1964) (plaintiff has absolute right to obtain dismissal with prejudice).

A plaintiff may want a voluntary dismissal to attempt to avoid Rule 11 sanctions (see supra pp. 146–159). Cooter & Gell v. Hartmarx Corp., 496 U.S. 384 (1990), held that a voluntary dismissal did not deprive the court of jurisdiction to consider Rule 11 sanctions. The 1993 amendments to Rule 11 preclude sanctions, however, if the complaint is dismissed within 21 days after service of a motion for sanctions. See Rule 11(c)(2).

E. Amendments to Pleadings

Attorneys are often rushed for time in filing pleadings. The plaintiff's attorney might only be brought into the case a short time before the statute of limitations runs and, absent an extension of time, the defendant's attorney has only 21 days after service of the complaint to file an answer. Depending on the complexity of the case and difficulty of access to information, pleadings sometimes have to be filed when very little is known about the events. It would, therefore, be contrary to the interests of justice not to permit amendments to pleadings as the case is investigated and prepared for trial. This liberal approach to amendments is reflected in Rule 15. Rule 15(a)(1) thus permits amendments as a matter of course under some circumstances, and Rule 15(a)(2) says amendment should be allowed "freely." See Bjorgung v. Whitetail Resort, LP, 550 F.3d 263 (3d Cir. 2008)(delay alone not a sufficient ground for denying leave to amend); compare Kassner v. 2d Ave. Delicatessen, Inc., 496 F.3d 229 (2d Cir. 2007) (holding that Rule 16(b) order requiring amended pleadings to be filed by a certain date cuts off absolute right to amend.

A liberal approach to amendments, however, has its own costs. Parties may rely on the pleadings of their opponents, believing that they are facing only the claims alleged and therefore may forgo investigation into matters that are not pleaded. Thus, even a liberal pleading rule like Rule 15 must contain some limitations.

1. Permission to Amend

DAVID V. CROMPTON & KNOWLES CORP. (9/26/18)
United States District Court, Eastern District of Pennsylvania, 1973
58 F.R.D. 444

[The facts and the first portion of this opinion appear supra p. 216. The court there decided that defendant Crompton's denial, on grounds of lack of knowledge, of plaintiff's allegation that it designed, manufactured and sold the machine that injured plaintiff was ineffective, and constituted an admission.]

The next question is whether Crompton should now be permitted to amend its answer to deny the allegation in Paragraph 5. Crompton relies upon Fed.R.Civ.P. 15(a) which provides that leave to amend an answer should be freely given when justice requires. The Federal Rules clearly favor a liberal attitude towards amendments. The purpose of a permissive attitude is to encourage decision of the case on the merits by allowing parties to present the real issues of the case.

A court may deny a request to amend if it bases such denial upon a valid ground. Among the reasons commonly cited for denying permission to amend are that the amendment will result in undue prejudice to the other party, or that it has been unduly delayed. Plaintiff claims that Crompton should be denied leave to amend because of undue delay by defendant and prejudice to plaintiff if Crompton's motion is granted.

Crompton, as indicated above, knew the basic facts surrounding the manufacture and delivery of the machine no later than October 1, 1971 when it filed answers to interrogatories. It almost certainly knew the essential facts much earlier. Crompton had examined the machinery in question by June, 1971. It had received information concerning the machine from plaintiff's counsel in March, 1971. The proffered reason for this delay, Crompton's recent discovery that it was not liable for such liabilities of Hunter, cannot be considered good cause for the reasons discussed above.

The effect of this delay could be highly prejudicial to the plaintiff. The action arose on November 27, 1969. The two-year statute of limitation expired on November 27, 1971. Plaintiff is now barred from instituting this action against another party. The running of the statute is the serious type of prejudice which may justify a denial of defendant's motion to amend his answer.

In the present case the action was filed more than 11 months prior to the running of the statute. In its answer to interrogatories and in its third-party complaint Crompton gave a clear indication that it had assumed Hunter's liabilities in cases such as this. It referred to Hunter's agent as "defendant's sales representative" and averred that the machine "was received from defendant". Plaintiff cannot be considered negligent for not discovering Crompton's alleged defense. Crompton never gave any indication prior to June, 1972 that it was asserting such a defense. If plaintiff had received timely notice of this alleged defense he would have had sufficient time to investigate the relationship between Crompton and Hunter and determine which is the proper party. That possibility was denied to him by defendant's long delay.

Crompton cites Jacobs v. McCloskey & Co., 40 F.R.D. 486 (E.D.Pa. 1966) to support its motion to amend. In that case the district court permitted a defendant to amend its answer to deny ownership of a building which belonged to its wholly owned subsidiary. The effect of the amendment was to deny recovery from one defendant since the statute had run. The action, however, had been filed only nine days prior to the expiration of the statute and the answer was not filed until after the statute had run. In granting leave to amend the court stated:

> Had the Defendant answered within the nine day period remaining before the expiration of the statute, thus lulling Plaintiff into believing that his action had been properly brought, this Court would be more sympathetic to the Plaintiff's appeal. However, the Defendant was entitled to forbear responding for the twenty day period [now 21 days] specified in the summons. Moreover, it is questionable whether the plaintiff suffered any prejudice by virtue of the erroneous admission after the statute had expired. The Defendant could have denied ownership at that time, and the Plaintiff's amended complaint against First Penco Realty, Inc., would still have been subject to the defense of the statute of limitations.

Plaintiff in the present case was certainly lulled by defendant during the period between the filing of the complaint and the running of the statute, and it is unquestionable that he has been prejudiced by the delay.

Under the circumstances of this case defendant's motion to amend will be denied. This may be burdensome to defendant and may deny to it an otherwise valid defense, but that is a situation of its own making. To allow the amendment would be to penalize the plaintiff who is without fault and leave him without a possible remedy for very severe injuries.

NOTES AND QUESTIONS

1.   The court in *Crompton* found prejudice justifying denial of the right to amend where the defendant's incorrect answer gave the plaintiff no reason to believe that it had sued the wrong defendant, and therefore that it needed to bring in the right defendant before the statute of limitations had run. What other situations would demonstrate prejudice? See Rule 16(b)(3)(A) (requiring that the scheduling order "limit the time to * * * amend the pleadings"). What if a party waits until the eve of trial to amend, adding a new claim or defense to which the opponent is not prepared to respond? Would the possibility of a continuance remove the prejudice? Would the opponent have to show that evidence or witnesses were no longer available, so that even if he were granted a continuance he would still be prejudiced? If it could not do so, would the expense and delay inherent in a continuance be enough to demonstrate prejudice? Would conditioning a continuance on the amending party's paying the opponent's expenses resulting from the continuance remove the prejudice?

2.   The effect of the *Jacobs* case, cited in Crompton, is to allow a defendant to amend where the plaintiff filed just before the statute of limitations had run even though the statute of limitations has run and plaintiff cannot join the right party. Would it make a difference in Crompton whether the defendant knew (or should have known) at the time it filed its answer that its failure to deny that it designed the machine was incorrect?

Compare Beeck v. Aquaslide 'N' Dive Corp., 562 F.2d 537 (8th Cir. 1977). Plaintiff there was injured on a water slide and sued Aquaslide, alleging that it had manufactured the slide on which he was injured. Defendant's insurance adjuster made an on-site inspection of the slide on which plaintiff was injured, and reported that it was manufactured by Aquaslide. So did the insurance company representing plaintiff's employer (which had held the event at which he was injured), and the insurance company for the operators of the facility at which plaintiff was injured. Defendant admitted in its answer that it manufactured the slide, but about six months later its president visited the site of the accident and determined that the slide was not made by defendant. Aquaslide then moved for leave to amend its answer to deny manufacture of the slide. Plaintiff objected on the ground that the statute of limitations had run. The district court nonetheless allowed the amendment, noting that defendant had "relied upon the conclusions of three different insurance companies," and the court of appeals held that this decision was not an abuse of discretion.

3.   *Futility of amendment:* Recall that ordinarily the court must allow the plaintiff at least one chance to amend if it grants a motion to dismiss. See supra p. 133 n. 6. " 'Dismissal without leave to amend is improper unless it is clear, upon *de novo* review, that the complaint could not be saved by any amendment.' But a 'district court does not err in denying leave to amend where the amendment would be futile.' An amendment is futile when 'no set of facts can be proved under the amendment to the pleadings that would constitute a valid and sufficient claim or defense.' " Missouri ex rel. Koster v, Harris, 842 F.3d 658 (9th Cir. 2016).

4.   If a party seeks to amend only after it is clear it has no cause of action under the existing pleading, should a judge be less willing to grant the amendment?

5.   In ruling on a motion to amend, should the judge consider judicial efficiency and economy? For example, is it relevant whether the amendment will take the preparation and trial in a new direction or whether the discovery and preparation already done would be sufficient?

6.   *The role of discretion*: Review of decisions whether to allow amendments is governed by an abuse of discretion standard; an appellate court will reverse only if the trial court's decision is outside the bounds of reason. Thus, there will be many cases in which the judge could, without risking reversal, decide to allow or deny amendment. Would it have been an abuse of discretion for the court in *Crompton* to allow the amendment? The abuse of discretion standard lends itself to decisions tailored to the unique facts of the given case. It also may reward good lawyering, for the judge's reaction often depends on counsel's ability to emphasize certain facts and make others seem unimportant. For an analysis, see Marcus, Slouching Toward Discretion, 78 Notre Dame L. Rev. 1561 (2003).

AMENDMENTS AT TRIAL

Rule 15(b)(2) provides for an automatic amendment of the pleadings "when an issue not raised by the pleadings is tried by the parties' express or implied consent." Thus, once evidence is admitted without objection as to a claim not pleaded in the complaint, that claim will be treated as though it were raised in the complaint. What if evidence could reasonably relate to both an issue that is pleaded and one that is not? What degree of awareness should a party have in order to be considered to consent to the trial of an issue by failing to object?

Rule 15(b)(2) also provides that amendment of the pleadings may be made to conform them to the evidence, but "failure to amend does not affect the result of the trial of that issue." Why would a party seek a formal amendment?

Even if the opposing party objects, Rule 15(b)(1) directs that the court should "freely permit an amendment when doing so will aid in presenting the merits and the objecting party fails to satisfy the court that the evidence would prejudice that party's action or defense on the merits." How does this standard compare to the standard in Rule 15(a) for pretrial amendments? Should the court be more amenable to amendments at trial than before trial?

Contrast the provisions of Rule 16(e) relating to amendment of final pretrial orders. Such orders are to be entered after the final pretrial conference and may be amended "only to prevent manifest injustice." When would amendments be necessary to present the merits of the action but not to prevent manifest injustice?

Probably the actual behavior of courts is to become more restrictive about amendments as the trial date draws near, at least where the proposed change may disrupt preparation for, or conduct of, the trial. In the same vein, the court in *Crompton* seemed to stress the position defendant had taken in discovery in denying leave to amend. Should judges be less willing to permit parties to change positions they take later in litigation, when they presumably know more about the case?

SUPPLEMENTAL PLEADINGS

What if events relevant to a claim or defense arise after the pleading is filed? Rule 15(d) provides for "supplemental pleadings" for after-occurring transactions, occurrences, or events. An obvious use of supplemental pleadings would be for injuries that become manifest after filing the complaint. Would the same be true as to issues that become apparent only after discovery? Note that supplemental pleadings have been interpreted as intended to be in aid of the claim already made and not to allege a new claim. See Giglio v. Konold, 214 N.E.2d 806, 808 (Ohio App.1965) (new action, rather than supplemental pleading, should be used to allege defendant's refusal to obey court order pending appeal). Should parties be encouraged to add new disputes to existing lawsuits rather than filing new ones?

2.   *Relation Back of Amendments*

KRUPSKI V. COSTA CROCIERE S.P.A.
Supreme Court of the United States, 2010
560 U.S. 538

JUSTICE SOTOMAYOR delivered the opinion of the Court.

Rule 15(c) of the Federal Rules of Civil Procedure governs when an amended pleading "relates back" to the date of a timely filed original pleading and is thus itself timely even though it was filed outside an applicable statute of limitations. Where an amended pleading changes a party or a party's name, the Rule requires, among other things, that "the party to be brought in by amendment . . . knew or should have known that the action would have been brought against it, but for a mistake concerning the proper party's identity." Rule 15(c)(1)(C). In this case, the Court of Appeals held that Rule 15(c) was not satisfied because the plaintiff knew or should have known of the proper defendant before filing her original complaint. The court also held that relation back was not appropriate because the plaintiff had unduly delayed in seeking to amend. We hold that relation back under Rule 15(c)(1)(C) depends on what the party to be added knew or should have known, not on the amending party's knowledge or its timeliness in seeking to amend the pleading. Accordingly, we reverse the judgment of the Court of Appeals.

I

On February 21, 2007, petitioner, Wanda Krupski, tripped over a cable and fractured her femur while she was on board the cruise ship Costa Magica. Upon her return home, she acquired counsel and began the process of seeking compensation for her injuries. Krupski's passenger ticket—which explained that it was the sole contract between each passenger and the carrier—included a variety of requirements for obtaining damages for an injury suffered on board one of the carrier's ships. The ticket identified the carrier as

> "Costa Crociere S.p.A., an Italian corporation, and all Vessels and other ships owned, chartered, operated, marketed or provided by Costa Crociere, S.p.A., and all officers, staff members, crew members, independent contractors, medical providers, concessionaires, pilots, suppliers, agents and assigns onboard said Vessels, and the manufacturers of said Vessels and all their component parts."

The ticket required an injured party to submit "written notice of the claim with full particulars . . . to the carrier or its duly authorized agent within 185 days after the date of injury." The ticket further required any lawsuit to be "filed within one year after the date of injury" and to be "served upon the carrier within 120 days after filing." For cases arising from voyages departing from or returning to a United States port in which the amount in controversy exceeded $75,000, the ticket designated the United States District Court for the Southern District of Florida in Broward County, Florida, as the exclusive forum for a lawsuit. The ticket extended the "defenses, limitations and exceptions . . . that may be invoked by the CARRIER" to "all persons who may act on behalf of the CARRIER or on whose behalf the CARRIER may act," including "the CARRIER's parents, subsidiaries, affiliates, successors, assigns, representatives, agents, employees, servants, concessionaires and contractors" as well as "Costa Cruise Lines N.V.," identified as the "sales and marketing agent for the CARRIER and the issuer of this Passage Ticket Contract." The front of the ticket listed Costa Cruise Lines' address in Florida and stated that an entity called "Costa Cruises" was "the first cruise company in the world" to obtain a certain certification of quality.

On July 2, 2007, Krupski's counsel notified Costa Cruise Lines of Krupski's claims. On July 9, 2007, the claims administrator for Costa Cruise requested additional information from Krupski "[i]n order to facilitate our future attempts to achieve a pre-litigation settlement." The parties were unable to reach a settlement, however, and on February 1, 2008—three weeks before the 1-year limitations period expired—Krupski filed a negligence action against Costa Cruise, invoking the diversity jurisdiction of the Federal District Court for the Southern District of Florida. The complaint alleged that Costa Cruise "owned, operated, managed, supervised and controlled" the ship on which Krupski had injured herself; that Costa Cruise had extended to its passengers an invitation to enter onto the ship; and that Costa Cruise owed Krupski a duty of care, which it breached by failing to take steps that would have prevented her accident. The complaint further stated that venue was proper under the passenger ticket's forum selection clause and averred that, by the July 2007 notice of her claims, Krupski had complied with the ticket's presuit requirements. Krupski served Costa Cruise on February 4, 2008.

Over the next several months—after the limitations period had expired—Costa Cruise brought Costa Crociere's existence to Krupski's attention three times. First, on February 25, 2008, Costa Cruise filed its answer, asserting that it was not the proper defendant, as it was merely the North American sales and marketing agent for Costa Crociere, which was the actual carrier and vessel operator. Second, on March 20, 2008, Costa Cruise listed Costa Crociere as an interested party in its corporate disclosure statement. Finally, on May 6, 2008, Costa Cruise moved for summary judgment, again stating that Costa Crociere was the proper defendant.

On June 13, 2008, Krupski responded to Costa Cruise's motion for summary judgment, arguing for limited discovery to determine whether Costa Cruise should be dismissed. According to Krupski, the following sources of information led her to believe Costa Cruise was the responsible party: The travel documents prominently identified Costa Cruise and gave its Florida address; Costa Cruise's Web site listed Costa Cruise in Florida as the United States office for the Italian company Costa Crociere; and the Web site of the Florida Department of State listed Costa Cruise as the only "Costa" company registered to do business in that State. Krupski also observed that Costa Cruise's claims administrator had responded to her claims notification without indicating that Costa Cruise was not a responsible party. With her response, Krupski simultaneously moved to amend her complaint to add Costa Crociere as a defendant.

On July 2, 2008, after oral argument, the District Court denied Costa Cruise's motion for summary judgment without prejudice and granted Krupski leave to amend, ordering that Krupski effect proper service on Costa Crociere by September 16, 2008. Complying with the court's deadline, Krupski filed an amended complaint on July 11, 2008, and served Costa Crociere on August 21, 2008. On that same date, the District Court issued an order dismissing Costa Cruise from the case pursuant to the parties' joint stipulation, Krupski apparently having concluded that Costa Cruise was correct that it bore no responsibility for her injuries.

Shortly thereafter, Costa Crociere—represented by the same counsel who had represented Costa Cruise—moved to dismiss, contending that the amended complaint did not relate back under Rule 15(c) and was therefore untimely. The District Court agreed. Rule 15(c), the court explained, imposes three requirements before an amended complaint against a newly named defendant can relate back to the original complaint. First, the claim against the newly named defendant must have arisen "out of the conduct, transaction, or occurrence set out—or attempted to be set out—in the original pleading." Fed. Rules Civ. Proc. 15(c)(1)(B), (C). Second, "within the period provided by Rule 4(m) for serving the summons and complaint" (which is ordinarily 120 days from when the complaint is filed, see Rule 4(m)), the newly named defendant must have "received such notice of the action that it will not be prejudiced in defending on the merits." Rule 15(c)(1)(C)(i). Finally, the plaintiff must show that, within the Rule 4(m) period, the newly named defendant "knew or should have known that the action would have been brought against it, but for a mistake concerning the proper party's identity." Rule 15(c)(1)(C)(ii).

The first two conditions posed no problem, the court explained: The claim against Costa Crociere clearly involved the same occurrence as the original claim against Costa Cruise, and Costa Crociere had constructive notice of the action and had not shown that any unfair prejudice would result from relation back. But the court found the third condition fatal to Krupski's attempt to relate back, concluding that Krupski had not made a mistake concerning the identity of the proper party. Relying on Eleventh Circuit precedent, the court explained that the word "mistake" should not be construed to encompass a deliberate decision not to sue a party whose identity the plaintiff knew before the statute of limitations had run. Because Costa Cruise informed Krupski that Costa Crociere was the proper defendant in its answer, corporate disclosure statement, and motion for summary judgment, and yet Krupski delayed for months in moving to amend and then in filing an amended complaint, the court concluded that Krupski knew of the proper defendant and made no mistake.

The Eleventh Circuit affirmed in an unpublished per curiam opinion. Krupski v. Costa Cruise Lines, N. V., LLC, 330 Fed.Appx. 892 (2009). Rather than relying on the information contained in Costa Cruise's filings, all of which were made after the statute of limitations had expired, as evidence that Krupski did not make a mistake, the Court of Appeals noted that the relevant information was located within Krupski's passenger ticket, which she had furnished to her counsel well before the end of the limitations period. Because the ticket clearly identified Costa Crociere as the carrier, the court stated, Krupski either knew or should have known of Costa Crociere's identity as a potential party. It was therefore appropriate to treat Krupski as having chosen to sue one potential party over another. Alternatively, even assuming that she first learned of Costa Crociere's identity as the correct party from Costa Cruise's answer, the Court of Appeals observed that Krupski waited 133 days from the time she filed her original complaint to seek leave to amend and did not file an amended complaint for another month after that. In light of this delay, the Court of Appeals concluded that the District Court did not abuse its discretion in denying relation back.

We granted certiorari to resolve tension among the Circuits over the breadth of Rule 15(c)(1)(C)(ii),[2] and we now reverse.

II

Under the Federal Rules of Civil Procedure, an amendment to a pleading relates back to the date of the original pleading when:

"(A) the law that provides the applicable statute of limitations allows relation back;

"(B) the amendment asserts a claim or defense that arose out of the conduct, transaction, or occurrence set out—or attempted to be set out—in the original pleading; or

"(C) the amendment changes the party or the naming of the party against whom a claim is asserted, if Rule 15(c)(1)(B) is satisfied and if, within the period provided by Rule 4(m) for serving the summons and complaint, the party to be brought in by amendment:

---

[2]   See, e.g., Krupski v. Costa Cruise Lines, N. V., LLC, 330 Fed.Appx. 892, 895 (C.A.11 2009) (per curiam) (case below); Rendall-Speranza v. Nassim, 107 F.3d 913, 918 (C.A.D.C.1997) (provision does not authorize relation back where plaintiff "was fully aware of the potential defendant's identity but not of its responsibility for the harm alleged"); Cornwell v. Robinson, 23 F.3d 694, 705 (C.A.2 1994) (no relation back where plaintiff knew the identities of the responsible defendants and failed to name them); Goodman v. Praxair, Inc., 494 F.3d 458, 469–470 (C.A.4 2007) (en banc) (rejecting argument that plaintiff's knowledge of proper corporate defendant's existence and name meant that no mistake had been made); Arthur v. Maersk, Inc., 434 F.3d 196, 208 (C.A.3 2006) ("A 'mistake' is no less a 'mistake' when it flows from lack of knowledge as opposed to inaccurate description"); Leonard v. Parry, 219 F.3d 25, 28–29 (C.A.1 2000) (plaintiff's knowledge of proper defendant's identity was not relevant to whether she made a " 'mistake concerning the identity of the proper party' "). We express no view on whether these decisions may be reconciled with each other in light of their specific facts and the interpretation of Rule 15(c)(1)(C)(ii) we adopt today.

"(i) received such notice of the action that it will not be prejudiced in defending on the merits; and

"(ii) knew or should have known that the action would have been brought against it, but for a mistake concerning the proper party's identity." Rule 15(c)(1).

In our view, neither of the Court of Appeals' reasons for denying relation back under Rule 15(c)(1)(C)(ii) finds support in the text of the Rule. We consider each reason in turn.

A

The Court of Appeals first decided that Krupski either knew or should have known of the proper party's identity and thus determined that she had made a deliberate choice instead of a mistake in not naming Costa Crociere as a party in her original pleading. By focusing on Krupski's knowledge, the Court of Appeals chose the wrong starting point. The question under Rule 15(c)(1)(C)(ii) is not whether Krupski knew or should have known the identity of Costa Crociere as the proper defendant, but whether Costa Crociere knew or should have known that it would have been named as a defendant but for an error. Rule 15(c)(1)(C)(ii) asks what the prospective defendant knew or should have known during the Rule 4(m) period, not what the plaintiff knew or should have known at the time of filing her original complaint.[3]

Information in the plaintiff's possession is relevant only if it bears on the defendant's understanding of whether the plaintiff made a mistake regarding the proper party's identity. For purposes of that inquiry, it would be error to conflate knowledge of a party's existence with the absence of mistake. A mistake is "[a]n error, misconception, or misunderstanding; an erroneous belief." Black's Law Dictionary 1092 (9th ed.2009); see also Webster's Third New International Dictionary 1446 (2002) (defining "mistake" as "a misunderstanding of the meaning or implications of something"; "a wrong action or statement proceeding from faulty judgment, inadequate knowledge, or inattention"; "an erroneous belief"; or "a state of mind not in accordance with the facts"). That a plaintiff knows of a party's existence does not preclude her from making a mistake with respect to that party's identity. A plaintiff may know that a prospective defendant—call him party A—exists, while erroneously believing him to have the status of party B. Similarly, a plaintiff may know generally what party A does while misunderstanding the roles that party A and party B played in the "conduct, transaction, or occurrence" giving rise to her claim. If the plaintiff sues party B instead of party A under these circumstances, she has made

---

[3] Rule 15(c)(1)(C) speaks generally of an amendment to a "pleading" that changes "the party against whom a claim is asserted," and it therefore is not limited to the circumstance of a plaintiff filing an amended complaint seeking to bring in a new defendant. Nevertheless, because the latter is the "typical case" of Rule 15(c)(1)(C)'s applicability, we use this circumstance as a shorthand throughout this opinion.

a "mistake concerning the proper party's identity" notwithstanding her knowledge of the existence of both parties. The only question under Rule 15(c)(1)(C)(ii), then, is whether party A knew or should have known that, absent some mistake, the action would have been brought against him.

Respondent urges that the key issue under Rule 15(c)(1)(C)(ii) is whether the plaintiff made a deliberate choice to sue one party over another. We agree that making a deliberate choice to sue one party instead of another while fully understanding the factual and legal differences between the two parties is the antithesis of making a mistake concerning the proper party's identity. We disagree, however, with respondent's position that any time a plaintiff is aware of the existence of two parties and chooses to sue the wrong one, the proper defendant could reasonably believe that the plaintiff made no mistake. The reasonableness of the mistake is not itself at issue. As noted, a plaintiff might know that the prospective defendant exists but nonetheless harbor a misunderstanding about his status or role in the events giving rise to the claim at issue, and she may mistakenly choose to sue a different defendant based on that misimpression. That kind of deliberate but mistaken choice does not foreclose a finding that Rule 15(c)(1)(C)(ii) has been satisfied.

This reading is consistent with the purpose of relation back: to balance the interests of the defendant protected by the statute of limitations with the preference expressed in the Federal Rules of Civil Procedure in general, and Rule 15 in particular, for resolving disputes on their merits. A prospective defendant who legitimately believed that the limitations period had passed without any attempt to sue him has a strong interest in repose. But repose would be a windfall for a prospective defendant who understood, or who should have understood, that he escaped suit during the limitations period only because the plaintiff misunderstood a crucial fact about his identity. Because a plaintiff's knowledge of the existence of a party does not foreclose the possibility that she has made a mistake of identity about which that party should have been aware, such knowledge does not support that party's interest in repose.

* * *

B

The Court of Appeals offered a second reason why Krupski's amended complaint did not relate back: Krupski had unduly delayed in seeking to file, and in eventually filing, an amended complaint. The Court of Appeals offered no support for its view that a plaintiff's dilatory conduct can justify the denial of relation back under Rule 15(c)(1)(C), and we find none. The Rule plainly sets forth an exclusive list of requirements for relation back, and the amending party's diligence is not among them. Moreover, the Rule mandates relation back once the Rule's requirements are satisfied; it does not leave the decision whether to grant relation back to the district court's equitable discretion. See Rule 15(c)(1) ("An amendment . . . relates back . . . when" the three listed requirements are met (emphasis added)).

The mandatory nature of the inquiry for relation back under Rule 15(c) is particularly striking in contrast to the inquiry under Rule 15(a), which sets forth the circumstances in which a party may amend its pleading before trial. By its terms, Rule 15(a) gives discretion to the district court in deciding whether to grant a motion to amend a pleading to add a party or a claim. Following an initial period after filing a pleading during which a party may amend once "as a matter of course," "a party may amend its pleading only with the opposing party's written consent or the court's leave," which the court "should freely give . . . when justice so requires." Rules 15(a)(1)–(2). We have previously explained that a court may consider a movant's "undue delay" or "dilatory motive" in deciding whether to grant leave to amend under Rule 15(a). Foman v. Davis, 371 U.S. 178, 182 (1962). As the contrast between Rule 15(a) and Rule 15(c) makes clear, however, the speed with which a plaintiff moves to amend her complaint or files an amended complaint after obtaining leave to do so has no bearing on whether the amended complaint relates back.

Rule 15(c)(1)(C) does permit a court to examine a plaintiff's conduct during the Rule 4(m) period, but not in the way or for the purpose respondent or the Court of Appeals suggests. As we have explained, the question under Rule 15(c)(1)(C)(ii) is what the prospective defendant reasonably should have understood about the plaintiff's intent in filing the original complaint against the first defendant. To the extent the plaintiff's postfiling conduct informs the prospective defendant's understanding of whether the plaintiff initially made a "mistake concerning the proper party's identity," a court may consider the conduct. Cf. Leonard v. Parry, 219 F.3d 25, 29 (C.A.1 2000) ("[P]ost-filing events occasionally can shed light on the plaintiff's state of mind at an earlier time" and "can inform a defendant's reasonable beliefs concerning whether her omission from the original complaint represented a mistake (as opposed to a conscious choice)"). The plaintiff's postfiling conduct is otherwise immaterial to the question whether an amended complaint relates back.[5]

C

Applying these principles to the facts of this case, we think it clear that the courts below erred in denying relation back under Rule 15(c)(1)(C)(ii). The District Court held that Costa Crociere had "constructive notice" of Krupski's complaint within the Rule 4(m) period. Costa Crociere has not challenged this finding. Because the complaint made clear that Krupski

---

[5]   Similarly, we reject respondent's suggestion that Rule 15(c) requires a plaintiff to move to amend her complaint or to file and serve an amended complaint within the Rule 4(m) period. Rule 15(c)(1)(C)(i) simply requires that the prospective defendant has received sufficient "notice of the action" within the Rule 4(m) period that he will not be prejudiced in defending the case on the merits. The Advisory Committee Notes to the 1966 Amendment clarify that "the notice need not be formal."

meant to sue the company that "owned, operated, managed, supervised and controlled" the ship on which she was injured, and also indicated (mistakenly) that Costa Cruise performed those roles, Costa Crociere should have known, within the Rule 4(m) period, that it was not named as a defendant in that complaint only because of Krupski's misunderstanding about which "Costa" entity was in charge of the ship-clearly a "mistake concerning the proper party's identity."

Respondent contends that because the original complaint referred to the ticket's forum requirement and presuit claims notification procedure, Krupski was clearly aware of the contents of the ticket, and because the ticket identified Costa Crociere as the carrier and proper party for a lawsuit, respondent was entitled to think that she made a deliberate choice to sue Costa Cruise instead of Costa Crociere. As we have explained, however, that Krupski may have known the contents of the ticket does not foreclose the possibility that she nonetheless misunderstood crucial facts regarding the two companies' identities. Especially because the face of the complaint plainly indicated such a misunderstanding, respondent's contention is not persuasive. Moreover, respondent has articulated no strategy that it could reasonably have thought Krupski was pursuing in suing a defendant that was legally unable to provide relief.

Respondent also argues that Krupski's failure to move to amend her complaint during the Rule 4(m) period shows that she made no mistake in that period. But as discussed, any delay on Krupski's part is relevant only to the extent it may have informed Costa Crociere's understanding during the Rule 4(m) period of whether she made a mistake originally. Krupski's failure to add Costa Crociere during the Rule 4(m) period is not sufficient to make reasonable any belief that she had made a deliberate and informed decision not to sue Costa Crociere in the first instance.[6] Nothing in Krupski's conduct during the Rule 4(m) period suggests that she failed to name Costa Crociere because of anything other than a mistake.

It is also worth noting that Costa Cruise and Costa Crociere are related corporate entities with very similar names; "crociera" even means "cruise" in Italian. This interrelationship and similarity heighten the expectation that Costa Crociere should suspect a mistake has been made when Costa Cruise is named in a complaint that actually describes Costa Crociere's activities. Cf. Morel v. DaimlerChrysler AG, 565 F.3d 20, 27 (C.A.1 2009) (where complaint conveyed plaintiffs' attempt to sue automobile manufacturer and erroneously named the manufacturer as Daimler-Chrysler Corporation instead of the actual manufacturer, a

---

[6] The Court of Appeals concluded that Krupski was not diligent merely because she did not seek leave to add Costa Crociere until 133 days after she filed her original complaint and did not actually file an amended complaint for another a month after that. It is not clear why Krupski should have been found dilatory for not accepting at face value the unproven allegations in Costa Cruise's answer and corporate disclosure form. In fact, Krupski moved to amend her complaint to add Costa Crociere within the time period prescribed by the District Court's scheduling order.

legally distinct but related entity named DaimlerChrysler AG, the latter should have realized it had not been named because of plaintiffs' mistake); Goodman v. Praxair, Inc., 494 F.3d 458, 473–475 (C.A.4 2007) (en banc) (where complaint named parent company Praxair, Inc., but described status of subsidiary company Praxair Services, Inc., subsidiary company knew or should have known it had not been named because of plaintiff's mistake). In addition, Costa Crociere's own actions contributed to passenger confusion over "the proper party" for a lawsuit. The front of the ticket advertises that "Costa Cruises" has achieved a certification of quality, without clarifying whether "Costa Cruises" is Costa Cruise Lines, Costa Crociere, or some other related "Costa" company. Indeed, Costa Crociere is evidently aware that the difference between Costa Cruise and Costa Crociere can be confusing for cruise ship passengers. See, e.g., Suppa v. Costa Crociere, S.p.A., No. 07-60526-CIV, 2007 WL 4287508, *1 (S.D.Fla., Dec.4, 2007) (denying Costa Crociere's motion to dismiss the amended complaint where the original complaint had named Costa Cruise as a defendant after "find[ing] it simply inconceivable that Defendant Costa Crociere was not on notice . . . that . . . but for the mistake in the original Complaint, Costa Crociere was the appropriate party to be named in the action").

In light of these facts, Costa Crociere should have known that Krupski's failure to name it as a defendant in her original complaint was due to a mistake concerning the proper party's identity. We therefore reverse the judgment of the Court of Appeals for the Eleventh Circuit and remand the case for further proceedings consistent with this opinion.

[Concurring opinion by Justice Scalia omitted.]

NOTES AND QUESTIONS

1.   Why do we have statutes of limitations? "Statutes of limitation are vital to the welfare of society and are favored in the law. They are found and approved in all systems of enlightened jurisprudence. They promote repose by giving security and stability to human affairs." Wood v. Carpenter, 101 U.S. 135, 139 (1879). Besides giving defendants peace of mind, they can serve additional purposes, as summarized in Marcus, Fraudulent Concealment in Federal Court: Toward a More Disparate Standard?, 71 Geo.L.J. 829, 837 (1983):

> [T]he passage of time could seriously impair a defendant's ability to defend himself. Coping with stale claims also poses substantial logistical difficulties for courts. At trial, factfinders would be presented with mountains of moldy evidence resulting from discovery relating to events that occurred, perhaps, decades ago. In addition, it may be necessary to contrive alternatives to live testimony when important witnesses are unavailable or cannot recall events. These logistical difficulties are not mere inconveniences that vex judges. To

the extent that overburdened courts are entangled in such problems, they may be unable to attend to timely claims.

At their heart, statutes of limitations insist that lawsuits be commenced within a certain time. The "relation back" problem cannot arise unless that occurs; relation back looks to whether later amendments in the lawsuit should treated, for limitations purposes, as though they were included in the party's original pleading. What should a defendant who is sued do in response to the suit? Should those actions by defendant be sufficient to protect it against prejudice resulting from the belated amendment to the complaint? Consider, for instance, the role of Rule 15(c)(1)(B) in relation to the policies underlying statutes of limitations. How should courts address situations in which plaintiffs seek to amend to assert claims originally asserted against one original defendant against another original defendant instead? See the Court's footnote 3.

In *Krupski*, suppose the plaintiff later seeks to amend her complaint to assert an additional claim against Costa Crociere for faulty medical treatment provided by the ship's doctor the day after her accident. Assuming the doctor is an employee of the defendant, should that new claim relate back? See Rule 15(c)(1)(B) and Rule 15(c)(1)(C)(i). Would it be different if plaintiff sought to add a claim for food poisoning during dinner the day before the accident giving rise to the original claim?

2.   In *Krupski*, plaintiff served the original defendant three days after she filed suit, and before the statute of limitations ran out. Would it have made a difference if plaintiff had delayed serving the original defendant until Feb. 22, the day after the one-year statute of limitations expired? It has long been recognized that plaintiff usually "tolls" (suspends the running of) the limitations period simply by filing suit, and that a reasonable time is allowed for service thereafter. Rule 4(m) provides that plaintiffs should serve defendants within 90 days of filing suit. Providing plaintiff serves defendant within that time, there is no limitations defense.

What if plaintiff amends the complaint to substitute the right defendant after the limitations period expires and then serves the right defendant? In *Krupski*, for example, suppose plaintiff had realized her mistake a month after filing her complaint and before she served the original defendant. Under Rule 15(a)(1)(A), she would then be permitted to amend her complaint as a matter of right to substitute the correct defendant. Suppose that she then served the correct defendant. Would it have a valid limitations defense? In Schiavone v. Fortune, 477 U.S. 21 (1986), the Court held that Rule 15(c) as then written required that the added party must be notified before the expiration of the limitations period even though there was no corresponding requirement for to notify a properly named defendant. How is the problem handled under Rule 15(c) now? Note the role played there by Rule 4(m). How would current Rule 15(c) apply if the applicable limitations period in Krupski's case were two years, and she sought to amend after learning of the additional defendant's involvement six months after filing suit?

3.   Should the filing of a suit have any effect on the protection limitations provides for those *not* sued? At least the plaintiff has, by filing the suit, made a sort of public announcement that she believes she is entitled to relief for the event that prompted the suit. But she may not yet have acquired the necessary information to appreciate whom she should sue. Should wrongdoers who have escaped plaintiff's attention be protected once she has made the decision to sue? Under California procedure, a plaintiff may name "Doe defendants" if ignorant of their identities, and substitute their true identity once those become known. See Cal. Code Civ. Proc. § 474. California does not require that these added defendants have notice of the suit within the limitations period. For discussion, see Hogan, California's Unique Doe Defendant Practice: A Fiction Stranger Than Truth, 30 Stan. L. Rev. 51 (1977). Is Rule 15(c)(1)(C) a better way of handling the belated assertion of claims against those not initially sued?

In *Krupski*, the Court says that "making a deliberate choice to sue one party instead of another while fully understanding he factual and legal differences between the two parties is the antithesis of making a mistake concerning the proper party's identity." Should an actual deliberate choice (a subjective test looking to plaintiff's actual motivation) or an apparent one (an objective test looking to what the defendant should have concluded) be the critical question?

Consider In re Bernard L. Madoff Investment Securities LLC, 468 B.R. 620 (Bkrptcy.S.D.N.Y.2012), arising out of the spectacular fraud of Bernard Madoff. The trustee in bankruptcy, seeking to recover assets for Madoff's creditors, challenged certain intra-family transfers of millions of dollars. After limitations had expired, he sought to add claims against the spouses of Madoff and his sons, but the court refused to allow relation back because the trustee was "a sophisticated party who had access to extensive documentation" regarding the transactions involved. "Under these circumstances, * * * it would not be unreasonable for the Spouse Defendants to infer that their omission from the original complaint was the result of a strategic decision on the part of the Trustee and not a mistake." Id. at 624. See also In re Indymac Mortgage-Backed Securities Litig., 793 F.Supp.2d 637 (S.D.N.Y.2011) (State of Wyoming was "quite aware" of the involvement of Merrill Lynch but did not sue it, precluding relation back for amendment adding claims against Merrill Lynch). For a discussion of whether the possibility plaintiff made a deliberate choice not to sue the added defendant forecloses relation back, see Sherman, Amending Complaints to Sue Previously Unnamed Defendants After the Statute of Limitations Has Run: Questions Remaining From the *Krupski* Decision, 15 Nev.L.Rev. 1329, 1342–47 (2015).

4.   Does Rule 15(c)(1)(C)(i) adequately protect the interests of those not originally sued? On whom should the burden rest to show that its requirements are satisfied? How were they satisfied in *Krupski*? If the burden to prove that this rule is satisfied rests on the plaintiff, is there a reason to require that plaintiff satisfy Rule 15(c)(1)(C)(ii) also?

5.   In *Krupski*, plaintiff sought discovery to identify the proper defendant after the original defendant raised the problem. Should a plaintiff who sues the wrong person be allowed discovery to identify the right one? Although Rule 27 authorizes pre-litigation discovery in exceptional circumstances, the courts have rejected the idea that it may be generally be used to determine whether a claim exists or who should be sued. See In re I-35W Bridge Collapse Site, 243 F.R.D. 349 (D. Minn. 2007) (Rule 27 may not be used for pre-litigation discovery to determine whether a cause of action exists or against whom it should be initiated). Should plaintiff obtain the right to do discovery because she has filed a suit against the wrong defendant?

6.   How should a court handle a situation in which plaintiff knows there are additional potential defendants but does not know who they are? In Worthington v. Wilson, 8 F.3d 1253 (7th Cir. 1993), plaintiff was arrested by three police officers and sued the village that employed them for violating his rights, adding that he wanted also to sue "three unknown police officers." When plaintiff later sought to amend the complaint to add claims against two of the officers, the court ruled that relation back would not be allowed because plaintiff had been aware from the outset that he did not know the identities of these officers: "[A]mendment with relation back is generally permitted in order to correct a misnomer of a defendant where the proper defendant is already before the court and the effect is merely to correct the name under which he is sued. But a new defendant cannot normally be substituted or added by amendment after the statute of limitations has run." Could this analysis be used after *Krupski*? See Joseph v. Elan Motorsports Technologies Racing Corp., 638 F.3d 555, 559–60 (7th Cir.2011) (reasoning that the *Krupski* decision "has cut the ground out from under" this sort of analysis); Archibald v. City of Hartford, 274 F.R.D. 371 (D.Conn.2011) (refusing to apply pre-*Krupski* Second Circuit decision that said ignorance of the identity of additional defendants sued as Doe defendants defeated relation back because plaintiff had made timely efforts to identify them and they surely knew plaintiff wanted to sue them). But see Heglund v. Aitkin County, 871 F.3d 572 (8th Cir.2017) (holding that plaintiffs did not make a "mistake" within the meaning of the rule when they named "hundreds of John and Jane Does" because they knew they did not know the identity of the Doe defendants, and refusing to allow relation back).

7.   In *Krupski*, plaintiff initially sought to add a defendant without dropping her claim against the defendant she originally sued. Should that be allowed? In Goodman v. Praxair, Inc., 494 F.3d 458 (4th Cir. 2007), plaintiff initially asserted a breach of contract claim against a parent company and later concluded that claim should have been asserted against a subsidiary company. He then sought to amend to assert the breach of contract claim against the subsidiary, but wanted to continue asserting a claim against the parent company as well. Defendants urged that Rule 15(c) allows relation back only for an amendment that "changes the party or the naming of the party against whom the claim is asserted." The court rejected this argument:

[W]e can discern no policy that would be served by the Praxair defendants' restrictive reading of "changes," which would force the amending party to drop a defendant for each defendant he adds. Praxair, Inc. [the original defendant], was placed on notice within the limitations period of the claims relating to the transactions alleged in the original complaint, and no unfairness to it resulted from leaving it as a defendant in the amended complaint. Any unfairness caused by the amendment could only be claimed by Praxair Services, Inc., the new party. But the protections for Praxair Services are addressed by considering the requirements of Rule 15(c)[(1)(B)] and [(C)], not from reading the term "changes" narrowly.

Is this ruling consistent with the Supreme Court's definition of "mistake"?

8. In *Krupski*, the lower courts emphasized plaintiff's delay in moving to amend. Could the original defendant have moved for sanctions under Rule 11 when plaintiff failed to dismiss even though notified of the problem in the answer? Could the court have denied plaintiff's motion to amend under Rule 15(a) due to this delay? Note that the Court contrasts the "mandatory" nature of relation back under Rule 15(c) with the "discretionary" authority conferred by Rule 15(a). At least some judges fear that a liberal interpretation of Rule 15(c) will have undesirable effects. In Goodman v. Praxair, Inc., 494 F.3d 458 (4th Cir. 2007) (supra note 7), a dissenting judge objected that the majority's ruling upholding relation back abandoned prior circuit precedent and would have undesirable effects:

> I see no reason to abandon our precedent of almost twenty years in favor of a policy that will decrease the incentives for plaintiffs to investigate their cases fully before filing a lawsuit. I think it good that our former interpretation of the Rule limited the mistakes courts would forgive to the clerical and inconsequential. Rule 15(c)([(1)(c)]) is not intended to excuse errant lawyering, but to forgive technical, clerical errors. It is reasonable to expect plaintiffs properly to identify those whom they hale into court. It is likewise reasonable to penalize careless plaintiffs who tarry too long by forbidding them to substitute the correct defendant after the limitations period has expired.

Id. at 477–78 (Gregory, J. dissenting). Judge Gregory also worried that "a future plaintiff will be free to file suit against a placeholder defendant while continuing to search for the proper one any time the plaintiff can make a plausible claim that he believed the originally named defendant was the correct one."

9. *Krupski* places considerable weight on the protections defendants get from the notice requirement of Rule 15(c)(1)(C)(ii). What sort of notice should suffice? Some courts treat informal notice of the commencement of litigation as sufficient. See Loveall v. Employer Health Servs., Inc., 196 F.R.D. 399, 403 (D. Kan. 2000) (letter from corporation named as defendant to the company that had sold the allegedly defective product advising that, in the view of its attorneys, the other company would likely be drawn into the action was

sufficient notice). But, some courts have stated that "only service constitutes notice," Williams v. Army & Air Force Exchange Serv., 830 F.2d 27, 30 n. 2 (3d Cir.1987), and others have required more than mere awareness of the suit. See Gardner v. Gartman, 880 F.2d 797, 799 (4th Cir.1989) (suits against the U.S. and certain officials did not constitute notice to the head of the U.S. department where plaintiff worked); Bell v. Veterans Administration Hospital, 826 F.2d 357 (5th Cir.1987) (relation back not allowed even though administrative hearings put the party to be joined on notice of the suit). However, the better practice seems to be otherwise. "The conclusion of a growing number of courts and commentators is that sufficient notice may be deemed to have occurred where a party who has some reason to expect his potential involvement as a defendant hears of the commencement of the litigation through some informal means." Kinnally v. Bell of Pennsylvania, 748 F.Supp. 1136, 1141 (E.D.Pa.1990). Does *Krupski* shed light on this question? See the Court's footnote 5.

CHAPTER 4

ESTABLISHING THE STRUCTURE AND SIZE OF THE DISPUTE

■ ■ ■

When the Federal Rules were adopted, a suit by a single plaintiff against a single defendant was a fairly representative model of litigation in American courts. But that has changed dramatically with more complex business and social arrangements and new theories of liability. Today the multi-party suit is the usual form of litigation. This development has required an evolution of court procedures to accommodate the demand for resolution of disputes involving many parties and for disposition of grievances in the aggregate. This evolution was not easily accomplished. Common-law procedures developed in a very different legal landscape, and a certain amount of shaping and jettisoning of traditional forms has been required to satisfy modern needs. Because these procedural reforms have been largely accomplished through incremental changes, some review of the old forms and their history is necessary to an understanding of the modern devices for establishing the structure and size of disputes.

A. PROPER PARTIES TO A SUIT

A proper party to a suit should have a sufficient relationship to the dispute that it may appropriately be brought into the litigation. Today we normally look to substantive law, as found, for example, in state statutes, or to the principles of "standing" to determine whether a particular person or entity is a proper party. However, there are some distinctive federal procedural applications involving proper parties that will be explored in this section.

1. REAL PARTY IN INTEREST (RULE 17(a))

Rule 17(a) provides that "[a]n action must be prosecuted in the name of the real party in interest." The reason for this rule is essentially historical. At common law, an action had to be brought in the name of the person who had legal title to the right being asserted. Thus persons who had only an equitable interest, such as assignees, could not sue in their own name. Such equitable-interest owners would be dependent upon the willingness of the person with the legal interest to bring suit for their use. Courts of equity, however, allowed persons with equitable interests to sue in their own name (with the owner of the legal interest typically joined so as to bind him by the decree).

The Field Code, in merging law and equity, rejected the common-law rule and, in language later borrowed for Rule 17(a), provided that actions should be prosecuted in the name of the real party in interest. The purpose was to alter the common-law requirement that suit must be brought by the party who, under substantive law, possessed the right sought to be enforced, and who was not necessarily the person who would ultimately benefit from the recovery. Rule 17(a) adds that the following may sue in their own names without joining the person for whose benefit the action is brought: an executor, administrator, guardian, bailee, trustee of an express trust, a party with whom or in whose name a contract has been made for another's benefit, or a party authorized by statute. This makes explicit the fact that the real party in interest need not have a beneficial interest in order to sue so long as it has sufficient interest in the outcome.

One objective of Rule 17(a) is to protect the legitimate interests of the defendant. "Rule 17 now serves primarily a negative function. It is to enable the defendant to present defenses he has against the real party in interest, to protect the defendant against a subsequent action by the party actually entitled to relief, and to ensure that the judgment will have proper res judicata effect." Virginia Elec. & Power Co. v. Westinghouse Elec. Corp., 485 F.2d 78 (4th Cir.1973). These objectives are also served by Rule 19 joinder (see infra pp. 266–277) and the doctrine of res judicata (considered in Chapter 13), leading some commentators to consider the rule unnecessary. See Entman, More Reasons For Abolishing Federal Rule of Civil Procedure 17(a): The Problem of the Proper Plaintiff and Insurance Subrogation, 68 N.C.L.Rev. 893, 920–22 (1990); Kennedy, Federal Rule 17(a): Will the Real Party in Interest Please Stand?, 51 Minn.L.Rev. 675, 724 (1967).

The real party in interest rule is relevant to subrogation. Subrogation involves the substitution of one person (or entity) in the place of another with the substituted person succeeding to the rights of the other. It includes the situation in which one person pays the debt of another and is substituted to the other's rights, and the debt is treated in equity as existing for the substitute person's benefit.

Subrogation often takes place in the context of insurance whereby an insurer's payment to the insured for a harm inflicted by a third party subrogates the insurer to the insured's rights against the third party. If the insurer pays all the insured's losses, the insured no longer has a pecuniary interest in the case, and only the insurer is the real party in interest in a suit to recover against the third party. However, partial subrogation can occur when, because the loss exceeds the coverage, the insured is only paid the amount of the coverage, or when an insurance policy had a deductible that the insurer subtracted from its payment to the insured. Then both the insured subrogor and the insurer subrogee are real parties in interest and may sue in their own names. United States v. Aetna Cas. & Sur. Co., 338

U.S. 366 (1949). If either sues alone, the other may intervene to protect its interest. If the other does not intervene, the defendant may protect itself from multiple suits by having the missing party joined. See 6A C. Wright, A. Miller & M. Kane, Fed. Prac. & Pro. § 1546 at 363.

Whether there has been a subrogation is not always clear. For example, insurers sometimes enter into a "loan receipt" arrangement whereby they lend the insured the amount due on the policy and the insured is only required to pay it back to the extent that it recovers from the defendant. Some courts have treated this as a loan that does not result in subrogation, and thus the insured is still the real party in interest who must bring the suit. R.J. Enstrom Corp. v. Interceptor Corp., 520 F.2d 1217 (10th Cir.1975). Other courts have viewed it as a sham loan that actually constitutes payment, thus resulting in subrogation that makes the insurer the real party in interest. City Stores Co. v. Lerner Shops of District of Columbia, Inc., 410 F.2d 1010 (D.C.Cir.1969). Why might an insurer want to have the insured named as the only party in a suit against a third person to recover for injuries for which the insured has been compensated by the insurer? Cf. Fed. R. Evid. 411 (evidence that defendant was insured is not admissible on the issue whether defendant was negligent).

A liberal definition of "real party in interest" raises the possibility that the named plaintiff may be chosen solely to satisfy the requirements of federal court diversity jurisdiction. Thus a person from a state different from the defendants may be assigned a claim, or may be appointed as a fiduciary (such as an executor, administrator, trustee, or guardian) in order to be named as the plaintiff and invoke diversity jurisdiction to get into federal court. The limitations on such jurisdiction-motivated assignment will be considered in Chapter 10.

2.   FICTITIOUS NAMES

SOUTHERN METHODIST UNIVERSITY ASSOCIATION OF WOMEN LAW STUDENTS V. WYNNE AND JAFFE

United State Court of Appeals, Fifth Circuit, 1979
599 F.2d 707

Before AINSWORTH and VANCE, CIRCUIT JUDGES, and BOTTLE, DISTRICT JUDGE.

AINSWORTH, CIRCUIT JUDGE.

In these companion Title VII [42 U.S.C. §§ 2000e–2000e–17] sex discrimination suits, the Southern Methodist University (SMU) Association of Women Law Students (Association) and Lawyers A, B, C and D (A–D), four female lawyers seeking to proceed anonymously, allege that defendants, two Dallas law firms, discriminated against women in hiring summer law clerks and associates and request injunctive relief. Plaintiffs appeal from various pretrial orders of the district court requiring the Association to reveal by proper pleadings the true identities of lawyers A–D.

[Defendants served interrogatories asking the true identities of plaintiffs A–D. Plaintiffs objected to disclosure, proposing that if some disclosure were required it be available only to defendants' attorney. The trial court directed that the identities of these plaintiffs be disclosed "for all further purposes."]

Plaintiffs have not cited, nor have we found, any prior decisions which recognize or even discuss the right of Title VII plaintiffs to proceed anonymously. Neither the Federal Rules of Civil Procedure nor Title VII itself makes provision for anonymous plaintiffs. The rules require that "[i]n the complaint the title of the action shall include the names of all the parties." Fed.R.Civ.P. 10(a), and the language of Title VII establishes no exception to the general principle that "the identity of the parties to a lawsuit should not be concealed." Doe v. Deschamps, D. Montana, 1974, 64 F.R.D. 652, 653.

Under certain special circumstances, however, courts have allowed plaintiffs to use fictitious names. "[W]here the issues involved are matters of a sensitive and highly personal nature," such as birth control, abortion, homosexuality or the welfare rights of illegitimate children or abandoned families, the normal practice of disclosing the parties' identities yields "to a policy of protecting privacy in a very private matter." However, the cases affording plaintiffs anonymity all share several characteristics missing here. The plaintiffs in those actions, at the least, divulged personal information of the utmost intimacy; many also had to admit that they either had violated state laws or government regulations or wished to engage in prohibited conduct. Here, by contrast, to prove their case A–D need not reveal facts of a highly personal nature or express a desire to participate in proscribed activities. Furthermore, all of the plaintiffs previously allowed in other cases to proceed anonymously were challenging the constitutional, statutory or regulatory validity of government activity. While such suits involve no injury to the Government's "reputation," the mere filing of a civil action against other private parties may cause damage to their good names and reputation and may also result in economic harm. Defendant law firms stand publicly accused of serious violations of federal law. Basic fairness dictates that those among the defendants' accusers who wish to participate in this suit as individual party plaintiffs must do so under their real names.

Plaintiffs argue that disclosure of A–D's identities will leave them vulnerable to retaliation from their current employers, prospective future employers and an organized bar that does "not like lawyers who sue lawyers." In our view, A–D face no greater threat of retaliation than the typical plaintiff alleging Title VII violations, including the other women who, under their real names and not anonymously, have filed sex discrimination suits against large law firms.

Because we find neither an express congressional grant of the right to proceed anonymously nor a compelling need to "protect privacy in a very private matter," Doe v. Deschamps, supra, 64 F.R.D. at 653, we hold that these Title VII plaintiffs may not sue under fictitious names and therefore affirm the district court's order requiring disclosure of A–D's identities by proper pleadings.

NOTES AND QUESTIONS

1.   Why shouldn't the plaintiffs' concern in *SMU*—that they would be stigmatized in the legal community if they were identified as suing law firms— be given the same protection of anonymity accorded to plaintiffs in cases where facts of a highly personal nature would be revealed? In Doe v. City of New York, 201 F.R.D. 100 (S.D.N.Y.2001), a lawyer suing two police officers for violating her constitutional rights sought to proceed anonymously because otherwise a computer search of court records would turn up her name. The judge agreed that, due to computer searches of court records, "the privacy that litigants once enjoyed as a practical matter has been diminished greatly," but declined plaintiff's request. See also Doe v. Merten, 219 F.R.D. 387 (E.D.Va.2004) (plaintiff challenging policy of various colleges to deny admission to illegal immigrants would not be allowed to proceed anonymously); Doe v. Federal Bureau of Investigation, 218 F.R.D. 256 (D. Colo.2003) (state-court judge would not be allowed to proceed anonymously in Freedom of Information Act suit against the FBI). But see Plaintiff B v. Francis, 631 F.3d 1310 (11th Cir. 2011) (district court improperly denied anonymity to plaintiffs depicted in porn film "Girls Gone Wild" in their suit against marketers of the film); Doe v. Archdiocese of Portland, 249 F.R.D. 358 (D. Ore. 2008)(plaintiff alleging sexual abuse could proceed anonymously due to risk of embarrassment and further harm, but ruling would be revisited if case went to trial); Doe v. Barrow County, 219 F.R.D. 189 (N.D.Ga.2003) (plaintiff challenging the display of the Ten Commandments could proceed anonymously; opponents to the suit had even tried to intimidate the district court). In Carhart v. Ashcroft, 300 F.Supp.2d 921 (D.Neb.2004), the court allowed an expert witness to act anonymously in a suit to enjoin enforcement of the Partial-Birth Abortion Ban Act of 2003. The witness was a doctor who had performed the forbidden procedure, and the judge was persuaded that the witness's life would be in danger otherwise: "In 17 years of dealing with questions like this in both criminal and civil cases, I have never seen a more compelling showing for the need to protect the identity of a witness."

2.   Should "John Doe (or Roe, Coe, etc.)" or "Jane Doe" pleading ever be used against a private defendant given the *SMU* court's rationale that fairness dictates that the accusers use their real names? Even in suits challenging governmental activity, isn't there a potential injury to officials' good names and reputations akin to the effect on private defendants? Fairness concerns may also arise if a defendant has reason to doubt the capacity or standing of the

plaintiff, but cannot investigate it because the identity is not known. If the identity is never known, it may also be difficult to apply the standards of res judicata to know who is bound by the judgment. See discussion in Note, *Anonymity in Civil Litigation: The Doe Plaintiff*, 57 Notre Dame Lawyer 580 (1982). Should the identities at least be made available to the court and opposing parties through sealed pleadings?

3.   *SMU* makes the point that the plaintiffs face no greater threat of retaliation than the typical plaintiff alleging Title VII violations. But just because Title VII does not accord anonymity for sex discrimination complaints, should there be no such right in a court suit? Some regulatory schemes do recognize the need for anonymity by allowing the agency to sue on behalf of unnamed persons. See Gomez v. Buckeye Sugars, 60 F.R.D. 106 (N.D.Ohio 1973) (allowing migrant farm workers to use fictitious names in suing employers for wage and hour violations, noting that the Fair Labor Standards Act allows the Secretary of Labor to bring such suits for unnamed persons).

4.   In Doe v. Shakur, 164 F.R.D. 359 (S.D.N.Y. 1996), a prominent rapper, who had been convicted of sexual abuse, was sued for damages by the victim who sought to remain anonymous. The court noted that courts have considered the following factors: (1) whether the plaintiff is challenging governmental activity; (2) whether the plaintiff would be required to disclose information of the utmost intimacy; (3) whether the plaintiff would be compelled to admit his or her intention to engage in illegal conduct, thereby risking criminal prosecution; (4) whether the plaintiff would risk suffering injury if identified; and (5) whether the party defending against a suit brought under a pseudonym would be prejudiced. The court found plaintiff's fear of being "publicly humiliated and embarrassed" insufficient to overcome the fact that "this is a private suit for damages, where plaintiff is seeking to vindicate primarily her own interests." Defendant would be "at a serious disadvantage in being required to defend himself publicly while plaintiff could make her accusations from behind a cloak of anonymity," and "the public has a right of access to the courts." The court noted that the plaintiff's allegation of death threats would provide a legitimate basis, but said she had provided no details to support this claim and that if she had been threatened, her identity must already be known to those who would do her harm. But see Javier H. v. Garcia-Botello, 211 F.R.D. 194 (W.D.N.Y. 2002) (finding, in a suit for wages by migrant farm worker, that although "fairness usually requires that a plaintiff stand behind its charges publicly" in a civil suit, threats of violence to plaintiff had been substantiated by previous indictments of defendants).

5.   At least seven courts of appeals have adopted tests with multifactors like those listed in *Shakur*. The Second Circuit, in Sealed Plaintiff v. Sealed Defendant, 537 F.3d 185 (2d Cir. 2008), adopted a balancing approach in overturning the district court's dismissal of plaintiff's sealed pro se complaint using a pseudonym against state and municipal entities and officers alleging physical and sexual assault in violation of her civil and constitutional rights. It found that the lower court had not balanced plaintiff's interest in proceeding anonymously against the interests of defendants and the public and remanded.

Doe v. Pennsylvania County, Virginia, 844 F.Supp.2d 724 (W.D.Va. 2012) was a suit challenging the Board of Supervisors opening of meetings with Christian prayer. The court found that although the plaintiff had a privacy interest in her religious beliefs and there was little risk to the board in allowing her to proceed anonymously, the fact that she had not previously made an effort to hide her identity when asking the board to cease using prayer prevented her from proceeding anonymously.

6. A number of courts have reached different conclusions than did the SMU decision. The issue of anonymity has increasingly arisen in whistleblower suits. In Whistleblower 14106–10W v. C.I.R., 183 TC 183 (Tax Court) (2011), plaintiff, a senior executive in a company, sought a whistleblower award based on her information that the company had substantially underpaid its income tax. The Tax Court noted that there are 36 federal statutes with explicit provisions to protect employees who report violations of law. Although the whistleblower statute was not one of them, the court accorded plaintiff anonymity because, although she was no longer employed by the company, she was subject to retaliation, professional ostracism, and economic duress "no less severe than the harm posed to attorneys and doctors suing to enjoin disciplinary proceedings, unsuccessful job applicants suing to protect their reputation, public aid recipients, or Native Americans joining in a lawsuit pitting their personal interests against those of their communities—all cases in which plaintiffs have been allowed to proceed anonymously."

7. Fictitious names are sometimes used for defendants when plaintiffs do not know their names. This arises often in cases against police officers or governmental officials whose identities are unknown, resulting in suits against "Police Officer John Doe 1," "Jailer John Doe 2," "Detective Mary Doe," etc. This practice has been tacitly approved by the Supreme Court. Bivens v. Six Unknown Named Agents of the Federal Bureau of Narcotics, 403 U.S. 388 (1971). But an amendment to add the correct names after the Statute of Limitations has run may not relate back, and thus the "Doe" designation could fail to preserve the claim.

8. Note that the named plaintiff in the SMU suit is an association. How can it file a suit for sex discrimination? While the matter is not always clear, associations are often allowed to sue to assert the rights of their members. Thus, dealing with problems of standing, the Supreme Court has said that "the association may assert the rights of its members, at least so long as the challenged infractions adversely affect its members' associational ties." Warth v. Seldin, 422 U.S. 490, 511 (1975).

Related to the standing question is the problem of capacity to sue, which is covered by Rule 17(b). The association would have capacity in this case because it sued to enforce a substantive right under the laws of the United States. More generally, concern with capacity is designed to ensure that the party litigating has a sufficient legal right to litigate so that the outcome will be binding, a concern reflected in Rule 17(c) (dealing with incompetent persons) as well.

9.   For further discussion, see Rice, Meet John Doe: Is it Time for Federal Civil Procedure to Recognize John Doe Parties?, 57 U. Pitt. L. Rev. 883 (1996); Steinman, Public Trial, Pseudonymous Parties: When Should Litigants be Permitted to Keep Their Identities Confidential?, 37 Hast. L.J. 1 (1985).

B. JOINDER OF CLAIMS (RULE 18(A))

At common law, a plaintiff was usually prohibited from joining two different claims against the same defendant unless both claims involved the same form of action. Thus a plaintiff could not join claims for breach of contract and tort even though they arose out of the same transaction, but could join claims for two unrelated assaults because they did arise out of the same form of action. This was a good example of the formalism of the common law that viewed the rigid forms of action as the organizing principle for a law suit. Even equity was somewhat restrictive, generally limiting joinder to claims that involved common issues or the same transaction.

Rule 18(a), in contrast, is completely permissive as to joinder of claims against the same party in a single suit. (Rule 13(a) and (b) are similarly permissive regarding counterclaims.) It allows a party to join "as any claims it has against an opposing party. The claims need not even be related, the theory being that there is no point in requiring multiple law suits once parties are in court against each other. This liberal rule of joinder of claims does not, however, mean that unrelated claims will necessarily be tried together. Rule 18(a) is only a pleading rule, and the Advisory Committee Notes observe that "a claim properly joined as a matter of pleading need not be proceeded with together with the other claims if fairness or convenience justifies separate treatment." Under Rule 42(b), a court may sever unrelated claims and order separate trials when it would be "for convenience, to avoid prejudice, or to expedite and economize."

C. PERMISSIVE JOINDER OF PARTIES (RULE 20)

At common law, joinder of parties was extremely difficult. Multiple plaintiffs could join in one suit only if they had a "joint" interest. This was found where they were joint promisees on the same obligation or instrument, partners at the time of a contract, or joint owners of property that was allegedly injured by defendant. In such situations, joinder of plaintiffs was not only permitted but required. With regard to joinder of defendants, things were a bit more complicated. "Joint obligors" had to be joined, and joinder was not permitted if defendants were "several obligors," but plaintiff had the choice whether to join where defendants were joint and several obligors.

In general, the focus on the nature of the rights or obligations being asserted has less importance in modern procedure. Joinder of parties is more restricted under the Federal Rules than joinder of claims. The rules distinguish between permissive joinder (Rule 20) and mandatory joinder (Rule 19), with rather different standards and policies applying to each.

Rule 20(a) allows joinder of multiple persons as parties if they assert any right to relief jointly, severally, or in the alternative (or such a right is asserted against them) "with respect to or arising out of the same transaction, occurrence, or series of transactions or occurrences" and "if any question of law or fact common to all plaintiffs [or defendants] will arise in the action." This rule originated in English practice and spread to this country in the 1820s. Similar rules have now been adopted by most states.

KEDRA v. CITY OF PHILADELPHIA

United States District Court, Eastern District of Pennsylvania, 1978
454 F.Supp. 652

LUONGO, DISTRICT JUDGE.

This civil rights action arises out of an alleged series of brutal acts committed by Philadelphia policemen against the plaintiffs. The events set forth in the complaint span one and one-half years, from December 1975 to February or March 1977.

[The plaintiffs are Delores Kedra and her eight children, three of them minors, and a son-in-law. The defendants are the City of Philadelphia, the Police Commissioner, and various police officials and officers. The complaint alleges that two of the Kedra children and the husband of another were arrested without probable cause on December 22, 1975 and beaten and illegally interrogated at the police station. Seven days later, other police officers conducted an unlawful search of the Kedra home, unlawfully detained members of the family in the house, and took certain of them to the police station where they were beaten. Thereafter it is alleged that the police engaged "in a systematic pattern of harassment, threats and coercion" of the Kedra family. As part of this pattern, one Kedra son was arrested in June 1976 and beaten, and another son was "harassed and threatened without cause" by police in February or March 1977. Suit was filed under civil rights statutes, 42 U.S.C. §§ 1983, 1985, 1986, for deprivation of constitutional rights, seeking compensatory and punitive damages.]

Defendants contend that there has been an improper joinder of parties under Federal Rule of Civil Procedure 20(a). * * * Defendants argue that plaintiffs' claims against them do not "aris[e] out of the same transaction, occurrence, or series of transactions or occurrences" because they stem from events spanning a fourteen or fifteen month period.[1]

---

[1] The Federal Rules permit unlimited joinder of claims against an opposing party (Fed. R.Civ.P. 18(a)), but in multiparty cases joinder is limited by the requirement of Rule 20(a) that

The joinder provisions of the Federal Rules are very liberal. As the Supreme Court noted in United Mine Workers v. Gibbs, 383 U.S. 715 (1966),

> "Under the Rules, the impulse is toward entertaining the broadest possible scope of action consistent with fairness to the parties: joinder of claims, parties and remedies is strongly encouraged."

The reason for the liberality is that unification of claims in a single action is more convenient and less expensive and time-consuming for the parties and the court. Mosley v. General Motors Corp., 497 F.2d 1330, 1332 (8th Cir.1974). In recognition of this attitude, the "transaction or occurrence" language of Rule 20 has been interpreted to "permit all reasonably related claims for relief by or against different parties to be tried in a single proceeding. Absolute identity of all events is unnecessary." Id. at 1333.

Although the events giving rise to plaintiffs' claims in this case occurred over a lengthy time period, they all are "reasonably related." The complaint sets forth a series of alleged unlawful detentions, searches, beatings and similar occurrences and charges defendants with "engag[ing] in a systematic pattern of harassment, threats and coercion with the intention of . . . depriving plaintiffs of [their] rights"; each of the incidents set forth is encompassed within the "systematic pattern." There is no logical reason why the systematic conduct alleged could not extend over a lengthy time period and, on the face of these allegations, there is nothing about the extended time span that attenuates the factual relationship among all of these events. The claims against the defendants "aris[e] out of the same transaction, occurrence, or series of transactions or occurrences" for purposes of Rule 20(a), and therefore joinder of defendants in this case is proper.

Apart from the procedural propriety of the joinder under Rule 20(a), however, there is a question whether a single trial of all claims against all defendants will prejudice some of the defendants. Some of the defendants were involved in only one of the several incidents alleged, and lumping them together with other defendants who were involved in more than one incident may be unfair. This problem is of particular concern with respect to the December 29, 1975 incident, which, apart from the allegations of direction, supervision, and control, appears to involve different actors than the other incidents alleged. Federal Rule 20(b) provides the court with power to remedy this situation:

---

plaintiffs or defendants may not be joined in the same case unless some of the claims by or against each party arise out of common events and contain common factual or legal questions. Defendants have not argued that common factual and legal questions are not present in this case; the similarity of the claims against each defendant makes it abundantly clear that there are common issues. Once parties are joined under Rule 20(a), Rule 18(a)'s allowance of unlimited joinder of claims against those parties is fully applicable.

"The court may make such orders as will prevent a party from being embarrassed, delayed, or put to expense by the inclusion of a party against whom he asserts no claim and who asserts no claim against him and may order separate trials or make other orders to prevent delay or prejudice."

At oral argument, counsel for both sides recognized the potential prejudicial effect of the joinder in this case and suggested formulation of a stipulation which would attempt to remedy the problem. It appears, however, that it will be better to deal with the problem after discovery has been completed and the case is ready for trial. At that time, the degree of involvement of each of the defendants will be more clear and potential prejudice will be easier to assess. I therefore shall defer decision of this aspect of the case. I shall retain flexibility to sever portions of it or to take other remedial actions, if necessary, once the prejudice issue is more clearly focused.

INSOLIA v. PHILIP MORRIS, INC.

United States District Court, Eastern District of Wisconsin, 1999
186 F.R.D. 547

CRABB, DISTRICT JUDGE.

This is a civil action for money damages brought by three former smokers and their spouses against the country's major cigarette manufacturers and two tobacco industry trade organizations. In an order dated December 17, 1998, I denied plaintiffs' motion for class certification. [Insolia v. Philip Morris, Inc., 186 F.R.D. 535 (E.D.Wis.1998)] The case is back before the court on defendants' motion to sever the claims of the three sets of plaintiffs into three separate actions pursuant to Fed.R.Civ.P. 21. According to defendants, these claims have been joined improperly under Rule 20 because they do not arise from the same transaction or series of transactions and because they do not share a common question of fact or law. Plaintiffs contend that their claims arise from an industry-wide conspiracy to deceive consumers about the addictive, deadly characteristics of cigarettes. * * * Even under the less stringent requirements of Rule 20, plaintiffs' claims are not sufficiently similar to warrant joining them in a single proceeding.

[The complaint alleged claims for fraud and civil conspiracy to commit fraud. To prevail, the plaintiffs would have to prove that false statements were made by defendants on which the plaintiffs had relied. The three plaintiffs, who were recently diagnosed as suffering from lung cancer, had each smoked a pack a day for many years. Insolia began smoking at the age of 12 in 1934, but quit in 1974. Mays and Lovejoy each began smoking at 16 in 1953 and quit about 42 years later.

Evidence presented by the plaintiffs in support of a class action showed that the tobacco companies had worked together for many years to counteract emerging scientific evidence that smoking was harmful and tobacco was addictive. See 186 F.R.D. at 539–41. In 1958, the companies formed a trade association, the defendant Tobacco Institute, whose strategy was, among other things, to create doubt about the health effects of smoking through advertising, research reports, and lobbying. Although a tobacco industry researcher commented in 1953 that "It's fortunate for us that cigarettes are a habit they can't break," the industry actively promoted the view over the next forty years that smoking was not addictive.

The plaintiffs' motion to certify a class of all Wisconsin residents who had smoked for 20 years and had been diagnosed with lung cancer was denied by the court on the ground that common questions did not "predominate" as is required by Rule 23(b)(3). Class actions are considered in the last section of this chapter.]

I conclude that plaintiffs' claims do not arise from the same transaction or series of transactions, as they must in order to satisfy Rule 20. On an abstract level, dissimilarities in the claims brought by plaintiffs suggest that these claims are not related logically to one another. Plaintiffs began smoking at different ages; they bought different brands throughout their years as smokers; and they quit for different reasons and under different circumstances. As already mentioned, the only thread holding these disparate factual scenarios together is the allegation of an industry-wide conspiracy but this theory does not hold up on its terms much less under the weight of the individual issues associated with each plaintiff. * * * Plaintiffs' depositions revealed that tobacco industry propaganda regarding the health effects of smoking reached them, if at all, through a variety of different channels and with varying degrees of success. Complicating matters further, defendants allegedly unleashed the stream of misrepresentations in furtherance of the conspiracy over the course of a 30-year period. As emphasized by defendants, plaintiff Vincent Insolia began smoking almost two decades before the industry hatched its scheme and has not smoked for more than a quarter of a century. By contrast, plaintiffs Billy Mays and Maureen Lovejoy took up the habit in the early '50s and continued to smoke well into [the] '90s. Even if the conspiracy charged held together, serious questions exist regarding medical causation. * * * For example, medical evidence suggests that the cancer contracted by Mays may be attributable to a work-related accident, not smoking, and that Insolia's risk of developing lung cancer returned to that of a nonsmoker ten years after he quit. With this motion, defendants have submitted the report of a pathologist that casts into doubt whether plaintiff Maureen Lovejoy ever had cancer. In the face of this evidence, plaintiffs' argument that causation and other medical issues can be resolved without engaging in highly individualized inquiries is even less persuasive here than it was in their briefs in support of class certification.

The practical implications of allowing these claims to go forward suggest that joinder would not serve the policies underlying rule 20. Plaintiffs disagree, maintaining that joinder would promote efficiency. In doing so, plaintiffs rely heavily on * * * Hohlbein v. Heritage Mutual Ins. Co., 106 F.R.D. 73 (E.D.Wis.1985). * * * *Hohlbein* arose out of a series of fraudulent statements and omissions made by a defendant to more than one plaintiff—in this case, during the recruitment and employment of four executives by an insurance company. The district court acknowledged that some factual dissimilarities existed between these claims but held that they satisfied Rule 20 because each sprung "from a consistent pattern or practice of employment behavior on the part of a single defendant. . . ." Specifically, the circumstances under which the company hired, employed and fired each plaintiff bore sufficient similarity to one another, even if they were not identical; the company engaged in all of the fraudulent conduct within a discrete two and one-half year time period; at least one material aspect of this conduct applied uniformly to all of the plaintiffs; and the plaintiffs had sustained similar damages. Taken together, these considerations persuaded the court that the additional burden imposed upon the defendant and the risk of jury confusion would be "far outweighed by the practical benefits likely to accrue to all players in the conservation of judicial, prosecutorial, and defensive resources."

* * *

In contrast to the misrepresentations at issue in *Hohlbein*, the life span of the alleged conspiracy perpetrated by defendants is measured in decades, not years. Many of the facts needed to prove the existence of the conspiracy and its effect on plaintiffs Lovejoy and Mays would be irrelevant to the smoking history of plaintiff Insolia, who reached the age of majority before defendants launched the plan and who quit long before it petered out. Rather than the single employer implicated in *Hohlbein*, this case involves five tobacco companies who have manufactured hundreds of brands of cigarettes. It is unlikely that a jury could keep track of which plaintiff smoked which brand and for how long while also retaining a coherent grasp of the minutiae associated with addiction, medical causation and legal causation. But this is not simply a matter of jury confusion. Judicial resources are wasted, not conserved, when a jury is subjected to a welter of evidence relevant to some parties but not others. Confusion can lead to prejudice when there are inadequate assurances that evidence will be weighed against the appropriate party and in the proper context. Defendants are correct that the trial plan proposed by plaintiffs not only fails to address this concern effectively but may actually compound it. Under the plan, a jury would be allowed to decide whether a conspiracy existed, whether cigarettes are unreasonably dangerous and whether defendants intentionally disregarded the rights of plaintiffs—all without regard to reliance, contributory negligence, assumption of risk, addiction and medical causation. These issues, which are normally linked inextricably with a final determination on liability, would be litigated in a subsequent phase. I share defendants' concern that partitioning the trial in such an unorthodox manner would prejudice their ability to protect their rights effectively.

NOTES AND QUESTIONS

1.   We have encountered the "same transaction or occurrence" language in other federal rules: Rule 13(a) uses that standard to determine when a counterclaim is compulsory [see Wigglesworth v. Teamsters Local Union No. 592, supra p. 225], as does Rule 15(c) to determine when an amended pleading relates back for purposes of the statute of limitations [see Krupsi v. Costa Crociere S.p.A, supra p. 236]. The test for applying the standard differs in those two rules according to the policy they serve: Rule 13(a) looks to whether the matters would make a convenient trial package, while Rule 15(c) looks to whether there was adequate notice at the time of filing so that the defendant can be said to have been aware that the suit included the amended matters. Which of these policies is closest to the Rule 20 standard?

2.   Why were the actions of different police officers, occurring at different places and under different circumstances over a one and a half-year period, considered in *Kedra* to arise out of the same transaction or occurrence (or series thereof), while the actions of the tobacco defendants' collaborative propaganda activities in *Insolia* were not? Is it because a pattern of harassment was alleged in *Kedra*? Why wouldn't the allegation of conspiracy have had the same effect in *Insolia*?

3.   In Poleon v. General Motors Corp., 1999 WL 1289473 (D.Virgin Islands), five police officers who were injured in three different accidents involving different police vehicles sued the common manufacturer of their vehicles, alleging that the Antilocking Brake System and air bags malfunctioned. The court rejected defendant's claim that these were three different transactions, stating that "the controlling consideration is the extent of any product defects, and absolute identity of all events is not necessary."

4.   *Kedra* stated that "unification of claims in a single action is more convenient and less expensive and time-consuming for the parties and court." See also Thomas v. Chestnut Hill Apartments, 2010 WL 4806990 (E.D.Wis.) (allowing joinder of *city* police who conducted later raids in a suit against *county* drug enforcement officers for earlier illegal searches and seizures. It criticized a "narrow view" of "same transaction" because "joinder should be analyzed in light the overarching purpose of Rule 20, which is to 'promote trial convenience and expedite the final determination of disputes, thereby preventing multiple lawsuits.' "). The judge in *Insolia* concluded that convenience and economy would not be served by joinder, citing differing individual experiences of the various plaintiffs. Is the Rule 20 "same

transaction or occurrence" test essentially one of efficiency and economy? The plaintiffs in *Kedra* also had very different experiences in relation to defendants. Would a joint trial in *Kedra* be more efficient than in *Insolia*?

5.   In *Insolia*, plaintiffs proposed a trial plan by which common issues (whether there was a conspiracy, whether cigarettes were unreasonably dangerous, and whether defendants intentionally disregarded plaintiffs' rights) would be tried to a jury, and then individual issues (such as reliance, contributory negligence, assumption of risk, addiction, and medical causation) would be "litigated in a subsequent phase." Why would the latter issues require individual, as opposed to common, evidence? Why does the court say this trial sequence would prejudice the defendants' ability "to protect their rights effectively?" In *Kedra*, the judge reserved ruling on whether, even though joinder was appropriate, there would be a joint trial. Would "phased trials" be appropriate there?

6.   Mosley v. General Motors Corp., 497 F.2d 1330 (8th Cir.1974), cited in *Kedra*, upheld the joinder of race discrimination claims by ten employees from two different divisions of General Motors because of their "logical relationship." The court emphasized the plaintiffs' allegations of a company-wide policy of discrimination. United States v. Mississippi, 380 U.S. 128 (1965), similarly permitted joinder of claims against six county registrars who were alleged to have acted "as part of a state-wide system" designed to discriminate on the basis of race in voter registration.

The claims in *Mosley* and U.S. v. Mississippi made a convenient, efficient, and economical trial package because the same evidence could be used to show a common discriminatory policy. But if there were no such common policy— and thus the claims of discrimination would have to be proven with individual evidence as to each of the employees in *Mosley* or as to each of the county registrars in U.S. v. Mississippi—would joinder under Rule 20 have been proper? How does a court determine what the evidence will be when it must rule on a motion for misjoinder before discovery is even undertaken? Should the court rely entirely on the plaintiffs' allegations or should it go beyond them to assess whether, in fact, it is likely that the different claims will involve similar evidence? Is an evidentiary hearing necessary or can a misjoinder motion be decided on briefs?

7.   Notice that the remedy for misjoinder under Rule 21 is not to dismiss the action, but to drop or add parties by order of the court or to sever and proceed with claims separately.

8.   Would joinder be proper under Rule 20 in the following cases:

a.   Fifty home owners from the neighborhood join in the same suit against a large restaurant and night club for damages resulting from its customers taking up all available parking on the streets and blocking their driveways. What if the suit were for an injunction to abate a nuisance?

b.   Twenty purchasers of vacuum cleaners purchased from different door-to-door salesmen of the same manufacturer join in the same suit against the manufacturer for fraudulent misrepresentations as to the product. What if the suit were for breach of contract or strict liability due to various design and manufacturing defects?

c.   A bank that has five hundred notes on which payments are overdue sues the five hundred makers of the notes in a single suit. Joinder of this sort has generated controversy when copyright holders seek to sue hundreds or thousands of Doe defendants for downloading copyrighted material, and then use discovery to identify these users. Joinder issues have divided the courts in such cases. Compare Liberty Media Holdings, LLC v. BitTorrent Swarm, 277 F.R.D. 669 (S.D.Fla.2011) (holding joinder of John Doe users of peer-to-peer file sharing improper) with Call of the Wild Movie, LLC v. Smith, 274 F.R.D. 334 (N.D.Ill.2011) (upholding joinder of putative users of peer-to-peer file-sharing with regard to specific movie); see generally, Marcus, Still Confronting the Consolidation Conundrum, 88 Notre Dame L. Rev. 557 (2012) (discussing general problem).

9.   Even if joinder is permissible under Rule 20, it could create problems with federal-court jurisdiction when jurisdiction is based on "diversity of citizenship." If a party who is a citizen of the same state as an opposing party is joined, there would be no diversity of citizenship. 28 U.S.C.A. § 1367 (examined in Chapter 10, infra p. 909) accords "supplemental jurisdiction" over the claim of a non-diverse party that is "so related to claims in the action within such original jurisdiction that they form part of the same case or controversy under Article III of the United States Constitution." Supplemental jurisdiction will also be discussed in the next section on compulsory joinder.

D. COMPULSORY JOINDER OF
PARTIES (RULE 19)

Compulsory joinder of parties raises the issue whether certain persons not joined as parties have sufficient interests in the suit that they must be joined and whether, if they cannot be joined, the suit will be allowed to proceed without them or must be dismissed. The history of the legal rules governing compulsory joinder of parties is complicated, indeed one might even say byzantine, in nature. Concerns over joinder of missing parties were addressed by equity courts in the seventeenth and eighteenth centuries, resulting at that time in what Professor Hazard has referred to as "fairly workable necessary party rules":

1.   All persons who are interested in a controversy are necessary parties to a suit involving that controversy, so that a complete disposition of the dispute may be made.

2.   Joinder of necessary parties is excused when it is impossible, impractical, or involves undue complications.

3.   A person who is not a party, unless represented by one who is a party, is not bound by a decree.

Hazard, Indispensable Party: The Historical Origin of a Procedural Phantom, 61 Colum.L.Rev. 1254, 1255 (1961).

It was after these developments that what has come to be known as the "indispensable party" rule was invented. That rule was based on the premise that a court should do "complete justice or none at all" and that if a party found to be necessary could not be joined, the suit had to be dismissed. This doctrine contained the fallacy, as pointed out by Professor Reed, that because a court does not have jurisdiction over the absentee, it cannot act with respect to others that are properly before it. Reed, Compulsory Joinder of Parties in Civil Actions, 55 Mich.L.Rev. 327, 330 (1957). The Supreme Court's decision in Shields v. Barrow, 58 U.S. (17 How.) 130 (1854), had embedded this fallacy in American procedural law by categorizing parties as "necessary" and "indispensable" according to the nature of their rights ("common," "joint," or "united in interest") and applying them in a rigid and non-functional manner.

"The sonorous generalities of Shields v. Barrow," Professors Wright and Kane wrote, "led, perhaps inevitably, to a jurisprudence of labels" that became "treacherous and misleading [when] applied as a substitute for reasoning." C. Wright & M. Kane, Law of Federal Courts § 70, at 95 (7th ed. 2011). The *Shields* approach, dominant as it had been for almost a century, was continued in the new Federal Rules in 1938. Rule 19 made the possession of a "joint interest" the dividing line between permissive and compulsory joinder and, without providing guidelines, went on to state that an action could not proceed if persons with "joint interests" were not joined unless they were not "indispensable." That approach was altered in 1966 amendments to Rule 19, and you are fortunate in being spared the necessity of studying the tortured precedents under the former rule that tried to make the term "joint interest" into a workable distinction and to define the hazy line between "necessary" and "indispensable" parties.

Rule 19, as amended in 1966 and "restyled" in 2007, describes, in subsection (a), those "required" persons who are needed for just adjudication and provides that they will be joined if feasible. Sometimes, however, an absentee found to satisfy the criteria in subsection (a) cannot be joined. The usual reasons in a federal court are that the absentee comes from the same state as an opposing party and his joinder would therefore destroy diversity jurisdiction; the absentee has insufficient contacts with the forum to permit personal jurisdiction; or venue would be improper. In that case, subsection (b) requires an analysis of four factors to determine whether "equity and good conscience" permit the action to proceed without the absent party.

Under Rule 19 the terms "necessary" and "indispensable" have been loosely employed to refer to the parties identified in subsection (a) ("necessary") and subsection (b) ("indispensable"), but Rule 19(a) now uses "required," and in any event these are inexact terms and do not convey the meanings they carried under the old rules. Rule 19 uses functional and pragmatic tests for determining who falls under (a) and (b). This means that whole categories of missing parties can no longer be said in the abstract to fall within a certain category (for example, joint obligors, subrogees, or co-owners), and a case-by-case analysis must often be made to determine the requirements of compulsory joinder.

CAMACHO V. MAJOR LEAGUE BASEBALL
United States District Court, Southern District of California, 2013
297 F.R.D. 457

10/9/18 *10/10/18*

JAMES LORENZ, DISTRICT JUDGE.

On November 30, 2012, Plaintiffs David Gonzalez Camacho and Daniel Arrellano Pesqueira commenced this tort action against multiple defendants.[1] This action arises from allegations that Major League Baseball conspired with the Mexican Major Leagues to prevent baseball prospect Daniel Pesqueira from playing baseball in the United States. Pending before the Court is the Office of the Commissioner of Baseball (d/b/a Major League Baseball), Major League Baseball Enterprises, Inc., and Major League Baseball Properties, Inc.'s motion to dismiss pursuant to Federal Rule of Civil Procedure 12(b)(7). Plaintiffs oppose the motion.

Failure to join a party under Rule 19

[Plaintiff Gonzalez is a citizen of Mexico, living in San Diego, California, but doing business in Tijuana, Mexico, representing prospective Major League baseball players from Mexico. In 2010, he entered into a contract with the parents of a Mexican player named Pesqueira, who had proved himself a formidable pitcher in the Mexican leagues through only 17 years old. Through Gonzalez's efforts, in February, 2012, the Boston Red Sox invited Pesqueira to train with the Red Sox at their spring training facility in Fort Myers, Florida. But a month later, the Red Sox notified Gonzalez that Pesqueira would be returned to Mexico "based upon the direction of Major League Baseball" because Pesqueira "belonged to a Mexican league team and could not play in the major leagues without the consent of the Mexican team."

Gonzalez and Pesqueira investigated the issue, and alleged that the copies of the "contracts" with the Diablos Rojos (Red Devils), the Mexican team, had forged signatures. In their complaint in this action, Gonzalez and Pesqueira alleged that, at their urging, Major League Baseball confirmed that Pesqueira was not committed to any Mexican team, but nonetheless continued to refuse to permit him to play for the Red Sox.

---

[1] The defendants in this action are Major League Baseball, Major League Baseball Enterprises, Inc., Major League Baseball Properties, Inc., Office of the Commissioner of Baseball, National Association of Professional Baseball Leagues, National Association of Professional Baseball Leagues, Inc., and Minor League Baseball.

Plaintiffs then filed this suit, making the following claims against all defendants: (1) intentional interference with economic relations; (2) intentional interference with prospective economic advantage; (3) negligent interference with economic relations; (4) negligent interference with prospective economic relations; (5) declaratory relief; (6) negligence; and (7) unfair business practices. Defendants made a Rule 19 motion to dismiss for failure to join the Red Devils and the Mexican baseball league as parties.]

II. LEGAL STANDARD

A party may move to dismiss a case for "failure to join a party under Rule 19." Fed.R.Civ.P. 12(b)(7). Rule 19 imposes a three-step inquiry: (1) Is the absent party necessary (i.e., required to be joined if feasible) under Rule 19(a)(1)(B)(2). If so, is it feasible to order that absent party to be joined?; and (3) If joinder is not feasible, can the case proceed without the absent party, or is the absent party indispensable such that the action must be dismissed? Salt River Project Agric. Improvement & Power Dist. v. Lee, 672 F.3d 1176, 1179 (9th Cir. 2012). The terms "necessary" and "feasible" are "terms of art in Rule 19 jurisprudence": "Necessary" refers to a party who should be joined if feasible; and "indispensable" refers to "a party whose participation is so important to the resolution of the case that, if the joinder of the party is not feasible, the suit must be dismissed." Disabled Rights Action Comm. v. Las Vegas Events, Inc., 375 F.3d 861, 867 n. 5 (9th Cir. 2004). The failure to join a party under Rule 19 can only lead to dismissal of a suit where the court cannot obtain jurisdiction over the necessary party and that party is determined to be indispensable to the action. See Fed.R.Civ.P. 19(a).

* * *

III. DISCUSSION

Defendants argue that both the Red Devils and the Mexican League are necessary parties that cannot be feasibly joined to this action because (1) a determination of the validity of Mr. Pesqueira's alleged contracts with the Red Devils is necessary, and (2) joining the parties would vitiate this Court's subject-matter jurisdiction and Plaintiffs cannot establish personal jurisdiction over these absent parties in this Court. * * *

Upon reviewing the allegations in the complaint, it is clear that the threshold issue in this action is the validity of the alleged contracts entered into between Mr. Pesqueira and the Red Devils. Plaintiffs proceed with their action under the presumption that those contracts are invalid— because Mr. Pesqueira was a minor at the time the contracts were executed, or because the signatures were fraudulently lifted from another document and transferred onto these documents. These allegations in the complaint overwhelmingly demonstrate that this entire action hinges on one game-winning issue—the validity of the Red Devils contracts. * * *

A.   The Red Devils and the Mexican League Are Necessary Parties.

A party is necessary if: (1) complete relief cannot be granted in the party's absence; or (2) the district court determines that "the absent party's participation is necessary to protect its legally cognizable interests or to protect other parties from a substantial risk of incurring multiple or inconsistent obligations because of those interests." Disabled Rights Action Comm., 375 F.3d at 878. Such a legally cognizable interest must be more than a financial stake in the outcome of the litigation. Makah Indians Tribe [v. Verity], 910 F.2d [555] at 558 [(9th Cir. 1990)]. Defendants demonstrate that the Red Devils and the Mexican League are necessary parties under the latter of the two aforementioned definitions.

Under Rule 19(a)(1)(B)(i), an absent party is necessary if it "has a *legally protected interest* in the suit" and "that interest will be *impaired* or *impeded* by the suit." Makah Indian Tribe, 910 F.2d at 558. "Impairment may be minimized if the absent party is adequately represented in the suit." It is also a "fundamental principle" that "a party to a contract is necessary, and if not susceptible to joinder, indispensable to litigation seeking to decimate that contract."

Plaintiffs unequivocally seek a judicial determination of their rights and duties under the alleged contracts between Mr. Pesqueira and the Red Devils. In the complaint, Plaintiffs explicitly state that they desire "a declaration as to whether or not Pesqueira is bound to the Red Devils of Mexico." They even go as far as to state that a "judicial declaration is *necessary* and appropriate at this time under the circumstances" because without the declaration, they are "financially burdened by the wrongful position taken by defendants Major League Baseball, and unable to work in their chosen professions." In other words, determining the validity of the Red Devils contracts is necessary to resolve essentially all of the wrongful conduct alleged in this action. The same applies to the Mexican League because of its bylaws and regulations that require disputes between players and member teams to be resolved by binding arbitration before the Executive President of the Mexican League.

Neither the Red Devils nor the Mexican League are represented in this action, and a determination by this Court regarding the validity of the Red Devils contracts may impair and impede the Red Devils' and the Mexican League's legally protected interest in this suit. See Makah Indian Tribe, 910 F.2d at 558. Keeping with the baseball theme, a batter cannot record a base hit or a home run against an absent pitcher; that pitcher needs to be in the game before that happens. In this circumstance, the absent pitchers are the Red Devils and the Mexican League. Therefore, as a party to the Red Devils contracts, the Red Devils, and by extension the Mexican League, are necessary parties.

Alternatively, under Rule 19(a)(1)(B)(ii), an absent party is also necessary if there is a potential risk that adjudicating an action without the absent party could leave an existing party open to "incurring double, multiple, or otherwise "inconsistent obligations." Fed.R.Civ.P. 19(a)(1)(B)(ii).

The Ninth Circuit has stated that:

inconsistent obligations" are not . . . the same as inconsistent adjudications or results. Inconsistent obligations occur when a party is unable to comply with one court's order without breaching another court's order concerning the same incident. Inconsistent adjudications or results, by contrast, occur when a defendant successfully defends a claim in one forum, yet loses on another claim arising from the same incident in another forum.

Cachil Dehe Band of Wintun Indians of the Colusa Indian Cmty. v. California, 547 F.3d 962, 976 (9th Cir.2008).

Defendants argue that "the Red Devils could still sue others in the Mexican courts and elsewhere for wrongfully interfering with its contract with Mr. Pesqueira[,]" and "[t]his action will not have any binding effect on the Red Devils unless the team is made a party to this case." The concern that Defendants suggest is important, but for the purposes of Rule 19, the paramount concern is a Mexican court or another in the United States determining that the Red Devils contracts are valid if this Court finds that they are not, or vice versa. That would produce inconsistent obligations for all of the parties in this action in addition to the Red Devils because operating under one court's determination would then necessarily cause the parties to breach another court's determination regarding the same issue, i.e., the validity of the Red Devils contracts. Therefore, because of the risk of inconsistent obligations, the Red Devils are a necessary party to this action.

Swing and a miss—strike one.

B.   Joining the Red Devils and the Mexican League Is Not Feasible.

"If an absentee is a necessary party under Rule 19(a), the second stage is for the court to determine whether it is feasible to order that the absentee be joined. Rule 19(a) sets forth three circumstances in which joinder is not feasible: (1) when venue is improper; (2) when the absentee is not subject to personal jurisdiction; and (3) when joinder would destroy subject matter jurisdiction.

Defendants argue that "A[t]he Red Devils and the Mexican League cannot be joined both because their joinder would destroy this Court's subject-matter jurisdiction, and because Plaintiffs cannot establish personal jurisdiction over them in this Court. * * * Plaintiffs concede that joining the Red Devils and the Mexican League is not feasible under the second and third circumstances that Rule 19 enumerates. They took this pitch and it went right down the middle—strike two.

C.   The Red Devils and Mexican League Are Indispensable Parties.

If the necessary party cannot be joined, the court must then determine whether the party is indispensable. Under Rule 19(b), indispensable parties are Apersons who not only have an interest in the controversy, but an interest of such a nature that a final decree cannot be made without either affecting that interest, or leaving the controversy in such a condition that its final termination may be wholly inconsistent with equity and good conscience. Shields v. Barrow, 58 U.S. 130, 139 (1854). Rule 19(b) provides the factors that courts should consider in determining if an action should be dismissed because an absent party is indispensable: (1) prejudice to any party or to the absent party; (2) whether relief can be shaped to lessen prejudice; (3) whether an adequate remedy, even if not complete, can be awarded without the absent party; and (4) whether there exists an alternative forum. Fed.R.Civ.P. 19(b). Furthermore, "[n]o procedural principle is more deeply imbedded in the common law than that, in an action to set aside a lease or a contract, all parties who may be affected by the determination of the action are indispensable."

Plaintiffs [argue that] in equity and good conscience, this case should be allowed to proceed regardless of whether the Red Devils and the Mexican League are indispensable. The Court rejects these arguments. Plaintiffs either misread or misunderstand the cited case law, and they also fail to provide any law themselves that provides an avenue for this Court to bypass Rules 12(b)(7) and 19 and all of the related case law as they implore the Court do.

Rather, in seeking a determination that the Red Devils contracts are invalid, Plaintiffs are, for all practical purposes, attempting to set aside a contract. And it is evident from the allegations in the complaint that the Red Devils, as a party to the alleged contracts, and by extension the Mexican League, are parties that will be affected by any determination regarding the validity of the contracts. If Plaintiffs want to record an earned run against the absent pitchers, Plaintiffs need to face them. Thus, * * * the Red Devils and the Mexican League are indispensable parties to this action. Consequently, all four of the Rule 19(b) factors weigh in favor of dismissal. See Fed.R.Civ.P. 19(b). And finally, strike three—out.

IV. CONCLUSION & ORDER

In light of the foregoing, the Court GRANTS Defendants' motion to dismiss under Rule 12(b)(7) and DISMISSES this action in its entirety.

NOTES AND QUESTIONS

1.   Recall that Fuentes v. Shevin (supra p. 31) said that the "central meaning" of procedural due process is that persons whose rights are to be affected are entitled to be heard. Is Rule 19 a good way to ensure protection? The rule authorizes the defendant, not the absent party, to seek relief. See

Freer, Rethinking Compulsory Joinder: A Proposal To Restructure Federal Rule 19, 60 N.Y.U.L.Rev. 1061, 1085–86 (1985) (arguing that relying on defendant gives the absentee "sporadic, limited protection"). And note what can happen when a Rule 19 motion is successful—the suit is dismissed. It may be that defendants making Rule 19 motions are not particularly focused on protecting the interests of nonparties so much as ending or complicating suits against them.

As a court observed, perfect protection for the interests of nonparties "might be so in 'the best of all possible worlds,' as Dr. Pangloss would say, but Dr. Pangloss does not rule the legal system and in it judges and juries, not Candide, are the arbiters of lawsuits." Janney Montgomery Scott, Inc. v. Shepard Niles, Inc., 11 F.3d 399, 411 (3d Cir. 1993). And the Supreme Court has declared that Rule 19 should be given a pragmatic interpretation, attuned to the circumstances of the individual case. Provident Tradesmens Bank & Trust Co. v. Patterson, 390 U.S. 102, 118–19 (1968).

2.   *Applying Rule 19(a):* In making this pragmatic judgment, the court is required to make determinations about the reported interests of parties not before the court, and forecasts about the likely consequences of the case before the court. Focus on the claims asserted by plaintiffs against these defendants. Are the harms Rule 19 guards against at significant risk in this lawsuit?

(a)   *Complete relief*: One ground for finding a nonparty required under Rule 19(a) is that "in that person's absence, the court cannot grant complete relief among existing parties." Could it be said that plaintiffs in *Camacho* could not obtain the relief they sought without joining the Mexican defendants? If plaintiffs were seeking an award of damages, would the Mexican defendants be necessary to afford that relief? If they sought to force defendants to afford Pesqueira a chance to play in the majors, would that be possible without the joinder of the Mexican teams?

Some suggest that this ground for required party status really is derivative from the other two. The goal is to avoid hamstringing the court as it tries to fashion a remedy. For that reason, it is almost impossible to imagine a situation in which a damages action would invoke this standard.

When plaintiff wants injunctive relief, however, this ground may apply. Disabled Rights Action Committee v. Las Vegas Events, Inc., 375 F.3d 861 (9th Cir. 2004), presents a possible example. Plaintiff sued the operators of a rodeo event held annually in Las Vegas, asserting that the accommodations for people using wheelchairs did not comply with the Americans With Disabilities Act. They sought an injunction requiring compliance with the Act.

The problem was that defendants were merely renting the stadium for the rodeo from the University of Nevada, which owned it and could not be added as a party. The district court concluded that it could not really order changes to the stadium to comply with the Act unless it had before it the owner of the stadium. The Ninth Circuit disagreed, emphasizing that these defendants were only using the stadium on a short term basis (id. at 880):

Accordingly, the private defendants' [ADA] obligations would be determined with respect to the short-term nature of its relationship with the [stadium], among other considerations, and "complete relief" under the statute may not necessarily mean the achievement of a fully accessible stadium.

Meaningful relief could thus be granted by enjoining [defendants] from making certain kinds of operational decisions regarding conditions over which they have control—e.g., enjoining them from removing accessible floor seating, or requiring the erection of temporary ramps.

Is "meaningful relief" the same as "complete relief"?

Similar problems might seem to be presented if plaintiff makes monetary claims too large for a defendant with limited funds to pay. Should plaintiff be required to join all defendants potentially liable so as to maximize the likelihood of collection if the suit is successful? Remember that Rule 20 makes joinder of all potentially liable easy. In Temple v. Synthes Corp., 498 U.S. 5 (1990), however, the Court held that Rule 19 does not go so far. "It has long been the rule that it is not necessary for all joint tortfeasors to be named as defendants in a single lawsuit."

(b) *Prejudice to nonparty:* When a nonparty "claims an interest" in the action and deciding in its absence "may as a practical matter" impair its ability to protect its interest, that party should be joined. Of course, there is a somewhat hypothetical aspect to this inquiry, because it does not depend on the nonparty taking some action to "claim" an interest; the parties and the courts are left to determine whether the nonparty actually does or would claim this interest.

An initial question is what kind of interest suffices. It may often be true that people are interested in the outcome of litigation, but that does not mean that they must be joined before it proceeds. Consider the following analysis in Cachil Dehe Band of Wintun Indians v. California, 547 F.3d 962, 970–71 (9th Cir. 2008):

> We have developed few categorical rules informing this inquiry. At one end of the spectrum, we have held that the interest at stake need not be "property in the sense of the due process clause." At the other end of the spectrum, we have recognized that the "interest must be more than a financial stake, and more than speculation about a future event." Makah [Indian Tribe v. Verity], 910 F.2d [555,] 558 [(9th Cir. 1990)]; see also N. Alaska Envtl. Ctr. v. Hodel, 803 F.2d 466, 468–89 (9th Cir. 1986) (holding that miners who had submitted mining plans to National Park Service were not necessary parties to an action to enjoin mining in parks until environmental impact statements were prepared). Within the wide boundaries set by these general principles, we have emphasized the "practical" and "fact-specific" nature of the inquiry. * * * An interest in a fixed fund or

limited resource that the court is asked to allocate may also be protected.

When such an interest appears, the question for the court under Rule 19(a) is whether the nonparty risks prejudice unless joined as a party. An assumption here is that the participation of the nonparty may bear significantly on the outcome of the suit; as we saw in Bands Refuse Removal v. Borough of Fair Lawn (supra p. 3), participation by affected parties is regarded as crucial to protecting their interests.

Makah Indian Tribe v. Verity, 910 F.2d 555 (9th Cir. 1990), provides an example. Plaintiff Indian tribe sued a federal agency, challenging the federal "harvest" limits on fishing in the tribe's traditional fishing territory. The goal of the limits was to preserve the supply of fish against exhaustion that might otherwise occur. In context, then, plaintiff's request was that the court allocate a larger share to it for the coming fishing season. The district court dismissed because the other tribes allocated fishing rights were not parties to the suit. The court held that the other tribes were required parties because "any share that goes the Makah must come from the other tribes." The court of appeals agreed that, "to the extent the Makah seek a reallocation of the 1987 harvest or challenge the Secretary's inter-tribal allocation decisions, the absent tribes may have an interest in the suit." But it distinguished a separate claim seeking a court order that, in the future, the procedures used to allocate fishing rights be changed.

As another example, consider Ford Motor Co. v. Bisanz Brothers, 249 F.2d 22 (8th Cir. 1957). Property owners sued a railroad to enjoin it from using a spur line that led to a Ford plant, but Ford was not joined as a party to the suit. Were the plaintiffs successful, the railroad would be forbidden to continue picking up cars at the Ford plant, affecting Ford's ability to get its cars to market.. See also Picciotto v. Continental Cas. Co., 512 F.3d 9 (1st Cir. 2008) (adverse ruling in federal-court case could deprive party to state-court case of insurance coverage for possible liability in that case but she was not named a party to the federal case).

In *Camacho*, are comparable arguments applicable? Would real harm come to the Mexican baseball teams due to the outcome of this suit? If the court is correct that it may be called upon to pass on the validity of the alleged contract with the Red Devils, would this court's finding that the contract is invalid really impair the Mexican team's ability to seek legal relief on the ground that the contract is valid? See Taylor v. Sturgell (infra p. 1238), holding that nonparties are bound only in very rare circumstances. On the other hand, what harm comes to the Mexican team if the court rules the contract is valid? As we shall see in Chapter 13, it may be that plaintiffs would then be precluded from re-litigating that decision in later litigation with the Mexican team. So one might say that it's better off not being joined.

When we address intervention, infra p. 296, we will see that intervention can be denied if the court concludes that the current party "adequately represents" the nonparty. There is no such provision in Rule 19, but courts sometimes take that question into account in evaluating whether the nonparty's interests will be prejudiced by litigation in its absence. For example, consider Salt River Project Agricultural Improvement and Power Dist. v. Lee, 672 F.3d 1176 (9th Cir. 2012), an action seeking a declaration that Navajo Nation officials did not have authority to regulate labor relations at plaintiffs' plants in regard to Navajo employees. Defendant officials moved to dismiss because the Navajo Nation, protected by sovereign immunity, was not a party. The court of appeals reversed dismissal because "the Navajo official defendants can be expected to adequately represent the Navajo Nation's interests," and "there is no reason to believe that the Navajo official defendants cannot or will not make any reasonable argument that the tribe would make if it were a party." Id. at 1180.

It is not likely that in *Camacho* the current defendants would similarly represent the Mexican nonparties' interests. But it is worth noting that the Mexican nonparties have another remedy if they are actually interested in this lawsuit. Recall what the Capassos did in Band's Refuse Removal v. Borough of Fair Lawn (supra p. 3) when they wanted to protect their interests. Such a person can often *intervene* in the lawsuit, thereby solving the Rule 19 problem. Indeed, wouldn't there have been a Rule 19 argument in *Band's Refuse*? Should failure to seek intervention support the inference that the nonparty is not really concerned about being joined? For further discussion of intervention, see infra p. 296.

(c) *Inconsistent obligations:* Rule 19 also says that a nonparty is a required party when its absence leaves an existing party with a "substantial" risk of "incurring double, multiple, or otherwise inconsistent obligations." This does not mean every potentially inconsistent outcome compels joinder. For example, suppose plaintiff sues one of two joint tortfeasors and loses. Would that mean that the risk plaintiff would sue the other joint tortfeasor in a separate suit makes the joint tortfeasor a required party? We have already seen that joint tortfeasors are not required parties. "Inconsistent obligations arise only when a party cannot simultaneously comply with the orders of different courts." School Dist. of City of Pontiac v. Sec'y of the U.S. Dep't of Educ., 584 F.3d 253, 282 (6th Cir. 2009); see also Delgado v. Plaza Las Ams., Inc., 339 F.3d 1, 3 (1st Cir. 1998) ("Inconsistent obligations occur when a party is unable to comply with one court's order without breaching another court's order").

Recall Ford v. Bisanz Brothers, cited above, involving the neighbors' suit against the railroad to enjoin use of the railroad spur line. Suppose Ford had a contract requiring the railroad to pick up cars at the Ford plant. Were the court in the neighbors' suit to enjoin use of the spur line, Ford might sue to enforce its contract, requiring use of the spur line. That "whipsaw" situation is what the rule identifies.

Could this problem arise in *Camacho*? One question would be the what relief plaintiffs seek in the current suit. If it is only a money judgment, it is difficult to see how it could produce the difficulty to which this provision is directed. If plaintiffs seek an injunction of some sort requiring the Red Sox to allow Pesqueira to play for the team, it could be that another court could impose liability on the Red Sox for interference with the Red Devils' rights. Would that be an incompatible obligation within the meaning of Rule 19? Shouldn't the Red Sox be allowed to assert an indemnity claim against Pesqueira if there such a suit for interference with contractual rights? Is there a "substantial risk" that the Red Sox will be left holding the bag?

Suits for money can present incompatible obligation problems. For example, consider a life insurance company sued separately by the two grandchildren of the insured, each claiming to be entitled to the entire policy amount. The insurance company may acknowledge that it must pay the proceeds to the proper claimant, but deny that both are entitled to the full amount. But the insurance company runs the risk, if it loses both suits on inconsistent decisions about which claimant is the right one, of having to pay twice. That was what happened in New York Life Ins. Co. v. Dunlevy, 241 U.S. 518 (1916), and Congress promptly passed the federal Interpleader Act to provide a remedy for "stakeholders" in that position. See infra p. 286 for coverage of interpleader.

When this sort of problem does arise, it may often be that the defendant originally sued can also use a counterclaim or a third-party claim to add the nonparty to the case. For discussion, see Impleader (infra p. 278) and Counterclaims and Cross-Claims (infra p. 284). As we will see in Chapter 10, there is broad "supplemental jurisdiction" to add such claims to pending federal lawsuits.

3.   *Joining the nonparties*: The solution to a Rule 19(a) problem is not ordinarily dismissal, but joinder of the required parties. The burden of joining them falls on plaintiff. As in many cases, the obstacle to joining them may be jurisdictional. Plaintiffs in *Camacho*, who are not United States citizens, are foreign nationals, and the Mexican teams are also. So there would not be diversity between them to permit this suit to proceed in federal court. See Chapter 10 for further discussion. It may also be difficult for a U.S. court to exercise personal jurisdiction over these foreign nonparties. If it lacks personal jurisdiction, a U.S. court cannot compel them to appear to defend a suit in this country. See Chapter 9 for further discussion. Does that suggest a reason why they would not intervene in this case?

4.   *To dismiss or not?* Rule 19(b) addresses the court's choice when confronted with nonparties who cannot be joined. In *Camacho*, the judge concludes after considering all four of the criteria listed in the rule that dismissal is warranted "in equity and good conscience." In *Camacho*, what alternative remedy does plaintiff have? Suit in a state court would solve the diversity of citizenship problem, but it is not clear that any American court could exercise personal jurisdiction. Though plaintiffs could sue the Mexican teams in Mexico, it may be that they would not be able to exert personal jurisdiction over the current defendants in a Mexican court.

A court that finds there is no other court for plaintiffs, at least in America, is not precluded from dismissing. Thus, in Republic of Philippines v. Pimentel,

553 U.S. 851 (2008). the Supreme Court held that American proceedings seeking to enforce a human rights judgment against former Philippine President Marcos by seizing assets in an account Marcos opened in the U.S. had to be dismissed because the current government of the Philippines claimed to own the money and could not be added to an American case on grounds of sovereign immunity. "Dismissal under Rule 19(b) will mean, in some instances, that plaintiffs will be left without a forum for definitive resolution of their claims. But that result is contemplated under the doctrine of foreign sovereign immunity." No similar doctrine seems to apply in *Camacho*.

5.   *Recurrent scenarios:* Due to the 1966 amendments to Rule 19, putting a label on an absent party does not necessarily determine whether it is a party to be joined if feasible as a case-by-case analysis is required. But labels are still sometimes found attractive by courts; for example, it is still often said that *joint tortfeasors* and *potential indemnitors* are not required to be joined if feasible. Consider cases involving the following categories of absent parties: *subsidiaries and third-party beneficiaries*, WMX Technologies, Inc. v. Jackson, 168 F.R.D. 64 (M.D.Ala. 1996) (not required parties); *limited partners*, Schmidt v. E.N. Maisel and Associates, 105 F.R.D. 157 (N.D. Ill. 1985) (found to be indispensable parties); Northrop Corp. v. McDonnell Douglas Corp., 705 F.2d 1030 (9th Cir.1983) (not required parties); *joint obligees*, 7 Wright, Miller & Kane, Federal Practice & Procedure: Civil § 1613, ftns. 12, 13 (generally treated as indispensable parties); *joint obligors*, id., ftn. 8 (generally treated as required, but not indispensable, parties). Treatment under Rule 19 will often turn on the particular circumstances. See Spiller v. Tennessee Trailers, Inc., 97 F.R.D. 347 (N.D.Ga. 1982) (since the applicable state law requires privity of contract for a breach of warranty claim, retailer is a necessary party in a suit against the manufacturer, and where, as here, there was an issue as to what role each played in the events precipitating the injury, both were required for complete relief; retailer also found to be indispensable).

E. IMPLEADER (RULE 14)

"Impleader" has its roots in the "vouching to warranty" practice at common law where a person whose title to land was challenged could vouch in the grantor of the land who had warranted the title. The term "implead," however, has taken on a much broader meaning as it is used today in Rule 14. It refers to the right of a defendant to bring in a new party who may be liable for plaintiff's claim against it, under what we now call "third party practice."

CLARK v. ASSOCIATES COMMERCIAL CORP

United States District Court, District of Kansas, 1993
149 F.R.D. 629

BELOT, DISTRICT JUDGE.

[Plaintiff sued Associates Commercial for damages to his property and person (including a broken leg) arising out of Associates' agents'

repossession by force of a tractor that was collateral for a loan that
Associates had made to plaintiff. The complaint alleged causes of action in
tort and contract (by negative implication in the security agreement
prohibiting the secured party from proceeding contrary to plaintiff's rights
under the Uniform Commercial Code). Defendant Associates then filed a
third-party complaint seeking indemnity from its employee (Howard) and
two parties who assisted him in the repossession (Clark, who is no relation
to plaintiff, and Lett). The third-party defendants moved to dismiss the
third-party complaint, and plaintiff moved to strike the third-party
complaint or, in the alternative, for a separate trial of the issues it raised.]

Defendant Associates Commercial Corp. ("Associates") alleges in its
third-party complaint that it hired Bob Howard, who—without the
knowledge of Associates—subcontracted with Clark Investigation &
Recovery ("Clark") to repossess plaintiff's tractor-trailer unit. Associates
further alleges that Randall Lett and an unknown second person were
employees of Clark, and that these employees conducted the actual
repossession of the collateral. Plaintiff alleges that the repossession was
effected through a breach of peace, and that Clark and its employees were
agents of Associates. Associates brings an indemnity claim against third-
party defendants Howard, Clark, and Lett for any amount that Associates
may be found liable to plaintiff.

* * *

Third-party defendants allege that Associates' claim is based upon
"implied indemnity" under the rubric of the "active/passive" dichotomy,
which is no longer recognized in Kansas. Third-party defendants note that
under the Kansas comparative fault statute, each defendant is liable only
in proportion to his relative fault. Thus, because impleader is proper only
if the party has a right to relief under the governing substantive law, third-
party defendants contend that Associates has no valid claim for indemnity
against them.

This argument is meritless. The basis for Associates' indemnity claim
against third-party defendants is an agency theory, whereby Associates
seeks to hold its alleged agents liable for any amounts that Associates is
found liable to plaintiff. Although third-party defendants correctly note
that Kansas no longer recognizes implied indemnity based upon the
"active" wrong of another,[1] no Kansas case has questioned the viability of

---

[1] The court notes, however, that the Kansas comparative fault statute only applies to
negligent tortious conduct, and that joint and several liability remains the law as to intentional
tortfeasors. Moreover, the Kansas Supreme Court has expressly held that an employer who
negligently hires an intentional tortfeasor may not proportionately reduce his liability to a plaintiff
injured by that employee. Regardless of whether Associates becomes liable to plaintiff vicariously
under respondeat superior, or directly under plaintiff's claim of negligent retention, the Kansas
comparative fault statute would not allow Associates to reduce its liability for the intentional torts
of its agents. Thus, not only do third-party defendants fail to recognize that Associates' indemnity
claim is properly based on agency principles, third-party defendants have also proceeded from the

implied indemnity based upon agency principles. Indeed, Kansas continues to recognize the right of an employer to seek indemnity against his employee for liability resulting from the employee's tortious acts. Thus, because Associates has sued each third-party defendant as a person "who is or may be liable to the third-party plaintiff for all or part of the plaintiff's claim against the third-party plaintiff," Fed.R.Civ.P. 14(a), Associates has properly impleaded third-party defendants.

The third-party complaint is also opposed by plaintiff.[3] Plaintiff argues that his claims against Associates are based upon duties imposed under the Uniform Commercial Code and by contract, and thus, that third-party defendants have "no duty" under the contract between plaintiff and Associates. A proper third-party complaint, however, does not depend upon the existence of a duty on the part of the third-party defendant toward the plaintiff. To the contrary, impleader is proper *only* if the third-party defendant "is or may be liable *to the third-party plaintiff* for all or part of the plaintiff's claim against the third-party plaintiff. . . ." Fed.R.Civ.P. 14(a). Although plaintiff correctly quotes the rule that "a defendant has no right under Rule 14(a) to implead a non-party who is only liable to plaintiff," plaintiff fails to appreciate that this very rule defeats his argument.

Moreover, contrary to plaintiff's belief, a third-party defendant need not be "necessarily liable over" to the third-party plaintiff in the event the third-party plaintiff is found liable toward the plaintiff. A third-party defendant must be "liable over" to the defendant only in the sense that the third-party claim is derivative of, and dependent upon, the success of the plaintiff's claim. Although Rule 14 does not allow a defendant to assert an independent claim for relief from a liability that does not arise out of the plaintiff's claim against the defendant, Rule 14(a) expressly allows impleader of a person who "is or *may be* liable to the third-party plaintiff for all or part of the plaintiff's claim against the third-party plaintiff." (emphasis added). Thus, "[t]he third-party claim need not be based on the same theory as the main claim," and "impleader is proper even though the third-party defendant's liability is not automatically established once the third-party plaintiff's liability to the original plaintiff has been determined." 6 C. Wright, A. Miller, & M. Kane, Federal Practice and Procedure § 1446, at 372 & 373 (2d ed. 1990).

Nor does the court find any relevance to plaintiff's observation that it is "inconsistent" for Associates to deny the existence of an agency relationship between it and third-party defendants, while at the same time

---

erroneous legal premise that Associates may not be found jointly and severally liable for plaintiff's injuries.

   [3]   The court will consider plaintiff's substantive objections to Associates' claims against third-party defendants, for Fed.R.Civ.P. 14(a) expressly provides that "*[a]ny party* may move to strike the third-party claim, or for its severance or separate trial." (emphasis added). [This rule language has been revised slightly.—Eds.]

Associates claims indemnity based upon this relationship. In essence, plaintiff argues that Associates is not entitled to plead alternative or inconsistent claims and defenses, contrary to the permissibility of this practice under Fed.R.Civ.P. 8(a) and (e)(2).

The court finds that Associates has stated a valid claim for indemnity against third-party defendants.

Plaintiff also opposes impleader on the ground that the inclusion of Associates' indemnity claims against third-party defendants will unduly complicate the original suit.

Whether to allow a defendant to prosecute a third-party proceeding under Rule 14 rests within the sound discretion of the trial court. In exercising its discretion, the court is mindful that the purpose of Rule 14 is

> to accomplish in one proceeding the adjudication of the rights of all persons concerned in the controversy and to prevent the necessity of trying several related claims in different lawsuits. The rule should be liberally construed to effectuate its intended purposes.

United States v. Acord, 209 F.2d 709, 712 (10th Cir.), cert. denied, 347 U.S. 975 (1954). Thus, the court should generally allow impleader of a proper third-party action unless it will result in some prejudice to the other parties.

The court finds no merit to plaintiff's fear of confusing the issues. Indeed, many of the issues are so closely related that resolution of plaintiff's claims might well collaterally estop Associates from relitigating these issues in a separate proceeding—to the significant prejudice of Associates. For example, the primary basis on which plaintiff seeks to hold Associates liable for the acts of its agents is respondeat superior, which, if meritorious, would then allow Associates to recover against its agents.

The court finds that the practical and equitable considerations overwhelmingly favor trial of all claims herein to a single jury. The motion to strike the third-party complaint or separate trial will therefore be denied.

* * *

[The third-party defendants also moved to dismiss defendant Associates' claims against them for indemnity for any punitive damages awarded to plaintiff against defendant. The court found that, under the applicable state law, punitive damages could be awarded against a principal for acts of its agents.]

Because plaintiff has stated a viable claim for punitive damages against Associates, and because Associates has stated an indemnity claim against third-party defendants for any amounts for which Associates is held vicariously liable to plaintiff, the court rejects the substantive arguments of third-party defendants.

NOTES AND QUESTIONS

1.   Why do you think the plaintiff objected to the third-party complaint? Must he have standing to do so? See footnote 3. Does the plaintiff have different reasons for objecting to the third-party complaint than do the third-party defendants?

2.   Must the third-party defendants be "necessarily liable over" to the defendant to permit impleader under Rule 14? Rule 14 only requires that the third-party defendant "is or may be liable to the third-party plaintiff for all or part of the plaintiff's claim against the third-party plaintiff," and such liability need not be automatically established by a finding that the third-party plaintiff is liable to the plaintiff. Is the question and amount of indemnity from the third-party defendant determined in the same suit? How is that done?

3.   It is inconsistent for the defendant Associates to deny (in reference to the claims of the plaintiff) that the third-party defendants were acting as its agents while asserting (in reference to its third-party complaint claims for indemnity) that there was an agency relationship. Why is this permitted? Recall McCormick v. Kopmann, supra p. 142. Is it relevant that there is efficiency in not having to redetermine in another lawsuit whether there was an agency relationship that would support an indemnity claim against the third-party defendants?

4.   Note that the substantive law of Kansas governs whether the defendant has a right to indemnity. Once having determined that there is a right to indemnity under state law, the court then found that the third-party complaint satisfied the requirements of Rule 14 by impleading persons who may be derivatively liable for the plaintiff's claim against the defendant.

5.   Rule 13(h) provides that "Rules 19 and 20 govern the addition of a person as a party to a counterclaim or a crossclaim." There is no requirement that the claim against such additional parties must be derivative, as opposed to simply arising out of the same transaction. Why is joinder more limited under Rule 14?

6.   In Augenti v. Cappellini v. Holy Spirit Association for the Unification of World Christianity, 30 Fed.R.Serv.2d 382 (M.D.Pa.1980), the plaintiff sued a "deprogrammer" who had been hired by plaintiff's parents to hold him against his will for five weeks and make him give up his association with the Unification Church. He alleged that defendant had violated his constitutional rights. Defendant filed a third-party complaint seeking compensatory and punitive damages against the Unification Church, its President, and its attorney, with the following counts:

     a.   Champerty and maintenance based on a contract between the Church and plaintiff whereby it agreed to pay the costs of bringing this action and plaintiff agreed to reimburse it out of any recovery.

b. Conspiracy between plaintiff and the Church to deprive defendant of his constitutional rights of freedom of speech and association with former members of the Unification Church in violation of a federal civil rights statute.

c. Intentional infliction of emotional distress through harassment of defendant by surveillance of his home, trespass, and instigation of frivolous law suits.

d. Libel and defamation against the attorney who filed the original complaint.

On motion of the third-party defendants, the court struck the third party complaint, reasoning as follows (30 Fed.Rules Serv.2d at 385–86):

This concept of derivative liability is central to the application of Rule 14. The typical fact pattern in which federal courts have permitted third-party practice is where one event gives rise to double liability, defendant to plaintiff and third-party defendant to defendant. Since Rule 14 relies on the discretion of the court in its application, the Rule had been broadly interpreted. However, there is still a requirement of some causal connection between the original action and the action brought in the third-party suit.

The proposed third-party complaint in this action, though related to the original action, does not bear this causal connection to the main action. The original action arose out of the events which occurred in December 1977 and January through February of 1978, when defendant Cappellini and others sought to persuade Frank Augenti to abandon his membership in the Unification Church through the deprogramming process. All of the counts in the original action are concerned with this discrete set of events—the issuance of the original guardianship order and Frank's subsequent deprogramming.

The proposed third-party action arose out of the filing of the main lawsuit and events which occurred afterward—the signing of the contract between Frank Augenti and the Unification Church, and the alleged harassment and alleged injuries to the third-party plaintiff as an individual. If the church were found liable to him on these claims it would not be as a direct result of the determination of the main claim. These third-party claims are independent.

* * *

Allowing the joinder of the third-party claim here would serve to complicate the case. It would broaden the scope of the evidence to be presented from Frank Augenti's personal involvement with the Unification Church and whether any of his Constitutionally protected rights were violated, or whether there was any tortious conduct engaged in by his family and the "de-programmers," to include testimony about the church in general and the methods it uses to protect its members. This expansion of the issues would not further the purposes of Rule 14 to avoid circuitry of action, but would further complicate what has already become a complex lawsuit. Presentation to the jury of so many claims related in such a tenuous way to those initially brought by the original plaintiff may prove to be unduly prejudicial to the original plaintiff.

Is the concept of derivative liability well suited to avoid the kind of complication of the case that the court feared? Couldn't such concerns be solved by an order under Rule 42 that the parts of the case be handled separately?

7.   In Klotz v. Superior Electric Products Corp. v. Butz, 498 F.Supp. 1099 (E.D.Pa.1980), plaintiff sued Superior, alleging that she had contracted trichinosis after eating a pork sausage cooked on a "Super-electric Super Twin-Burger" cooker manufactured and sold by Superior. She alleged that she had followed cooking directions supplied by Superior but that, due to a defect in the cooker, the sausage was not properly cooked. Superior then impleaded Wilkes College, alleging that the plaintiff's trichinosis resulted from her ingesting pork in the college cafeteria on July 8, and not from the July 9 incident involving the cooker. Wilkes College moved to dismiss the third-party complaint against it as improper under Rule 14(a) because the liability asserted against it was not derivative. How should the court rule? Would the complication factors cited in *Augenti* (in note 6 above) be present here?

F.   COUNTERCLAIMS AND CROSS-CLAIMS (RULE 13)

Counterclaims and cross-claims are not primarily devices for bringing in additional parties, but they permit expansion of the issues in the suit and may bring in additional parties as well. They serve the important interest of fairness by allowing a party to make claims against one who has made claims against him and the interest of economy and efficiency in permitting claims between existing parties in the same suit.

Rule 13(a) is a sort of rule-mandated res judicata. It has the effect of barring a party from recovering on a claim which at the time of serving the pleading the pleader has against any opposing party, if it "arises out of the transaction or occurrence that is the subject matter of the opposing party's claim." It has been considered in Chapter 3. See supra pp. 225–229.

Rule 13(b) sets out a liberal permissive counterclaim rule, allowing a party to bring as a counterclaim any claim it has against the opposing party. A permissive counterclaim is, by definition, one that does not arise out of the same transaction or occurrence. It has the potential for permitting a number of different claims that would not constitute a convenient trial package. But it is consistent with Rule 18(a)'s allowance of joinder of claims in pleading without a requirement that they be related.

The solution to badly-matched claims is severance and separate trial. See Rule 42(b).

A cross-claim, authorized under Rule 13(g), allows a claim against a co-party (i.e., co-plaintiffs, co-defendants, or co-third-party defendants). It is limited to claims "arising out of the transaction or occurrence that is the subject matter either of the original action or of a counterclaim therein or relating to any property that is the subject matter of the original action."

Under Rule 13(h), the addition of claims can result in addition of parties if they can be sued as additional parties to the counterclaim or cross-claim "in accordance with the provisions of Rules 19 and 20." This means that so long as a current party to the litigation can assert a counterclaim or cross-claim under Rule 13, it can add parties to that claim provided that its claim against the added parties arises from the same transaction or series thereof within the meaning of Rule 20.

NOTES AND QUESTIONS

1.   Why must cross-claims arise out of the same transaction or occurrence as the original claim, while permissive counterclaims need not?

2.   Why are cross-claims permissive, thus allowing a party to hold them back and sue in another suit? Note, however, that res judicata or collateral estoppel may affect the right of a party to sue later.

"Do it!"

3.   Consider the following situation in terms of the availability of claims between the parties:

A, B, and C were involved in a three-way auto accident. Each of them received serious personal injuries, and all three cars that they were driving were badly damaged. There is reason to believe that the negligence of each of them in driving may have caused or contributed to the accident.

A's car had been repaired the day before the accident by D, an auto dealer. There is reason to believe that D's negligent failure to fix the brakes may have caused or contributed to the accident.

The car B was driving was owned by O. O lent his car to B knowing that B had received several citations for reckless driving. The law of the state makes the owner of a car liable for the conduct of a person to whom he has negligently entrusted it if he knew that the entrustee was a reckless driver. It also treats the borrower of a car as an agent of the owner, allowing the owner to recover from the agent for liability imposed on the owner as a result of the agent's negligence to which the owner did not contribute.

C's car was manufactured by M, an auto manufacturer. There is reason to believe that the car had a design defect in the steering mechanism that caused or contributed to the accident.

Assume that A sues B in federal court. What claims should B assert in reply? In turn, what claims should be made in reply to the claims asserted by

B, and by any other parties brought into the action. You will find it helpful to use a diagram.

4.   For an analysis of the complications that can arise due to the varying treatment of co-party and third-party claims, see Greenbaum, Jacks or Better to Open: Procedural Limitations on Co-Party and Third-Party Claims, 74 Minn.L.Rev. 507 (1990).

G. INTERPLEADER (RULE 22 AND 28 U.S.C.A. § 1335)

Interpleader has ancient origins in common law, but it was equity that developed it into a suitable device for permitting a person faced with conflicting claims to a limited fund or property (referred to as the "stake") to bring all the claimants into a single proceeding. In this manner, the stakeholder could avoid the unfairness of inconsistent judgments or multiple liability that might result if the claimants were to sue individually. Interpleader allowed the stakeholder, fearing separate suits by individual claimants, to institute its own action in which all the claimants would be required to litigate their claims simultaneously.

Classically, the "strict" bill of interpleader was said to be limited by four technical requirements, the meaning and purpose of which were never altogether clear:

> (1) The same thing, debt, or duty must be claimed by both or all the parties against whom the relief is demanded; (2) All their adverse titles or claims must be dependent on or be derived from a common source; (3) The person asking the relief—the plaintiff— must not have or claim any interest in the subject matter; (4) He must have incurred no independent liability to either of the claimants; that is, he must stand perfectly indifferent between them, in the position merely of a stakeholder.

4 J. Pomeroy, Equity Jurisprudence § 1322 (5th ed. 1941).

According to one group of commentators, "[i]f the court demanded literal adherence to these requirements, the range of situations in which equitable interpleader could be used was very limited and applied to only a few of the instances in which plaintiff might be exposed to double vexation. It is not surprising, therefore, that many courts honored these strictures in name only." 7 C. Wright, A. Miller & M. Kane, Federal Practice and Procedure: Civil 2d § 1701 at 526 (3d ed. 2001). In any event, the historical accuracy of these requirements has been questioned. See Hazard & Moskovitz, An Historical and Critical Analysis of Interpleader, 52 Calif.L.Rev. 706 (1964). Early on, equity courts developed a method of circumventing the requirement that the stakeholder must claim no interest in the stake by developing the bill "in the nature of interpleader," which allowed a stakeholder to claim all or part of the stake itself. However, this device could be employed only if some independent basis of equity jurisdiction existed. Today, all four of the classical limitations have, for all practical purposes, been abandoned, either explicitly or implicitly. See C. Wright & M. Kane, Law of Federal Courts § 74 (6th ed. 2002).

The availability of interpleader was restricted by the Supreme Court's decision in New York Life Insurance Co. v. Dunlevy, 241 U.S. 518 (1916), which held that personal jurisdiction could not be obtained unless all the claimants were personally served within the territorial limits of the forum state. This meant that businesses and insurance companies engaged in interstate commerce, which were often confronted with conflicting claims to a fund or property by persons from different states, could not use a single interpleader suit and were often forced to defend multiple suits in different states.

This situation prompted Congress to overrule *Dunlevy* by a federal interpleader statute passed in 1917. It was considerably revised in 1936, essentially into the form now found in 28 U.S.C.A. § 1335 (referred to as "statutory interpleader"). A question still remained, after the passage of the interpleader statutes, as to whether federal courts retained their traditional equity jurisdiction over interpleader actions. This was resolved with the adoption in 1938 of the Federal Rules containing Rule 22 which provided for an interpleader action based on general federal court jurisdiction (federal question or diversity). Called "rule interpleader," Rule 22 also considerably expanded the scope of traditional equitable interpleader.

Thus, today we have two sources of interpleader—*statutory* and *rule*. They have been applied very similarly as to the scope of the interpleader remedy, but, as will be seen, they have quite different provisions as to jurisdiction and venue. They are both available, but because of the differences in jurisdictional and venue requirements a party that can use one in a particular situation may not be able to use the other.

STATE FARM FIRE & CASUALTY CO. V. TASHIRE

Supreme Court of the United States, 1967
386 U.S. 523

JUSTICE FORTAS delivered the opinion of the Court.

Early one September morning in 1964, a Greyhound bus proceeding northward through Shasta County, California, collided with a southbound pickup truck. Two of the passengers aboard the bus were killed. Thirty-three others were injured, as were the bus driver, the driver of the truck and its lone passenger. One of the dead and 10 of the injured passengers were Canadians; the rest of the individuals involved were citizens of five American States. The ensuing litigation led to the present case, which raises important questions concerning administration of the interpleader remedy in the federal courts.

The litigation began when four of the injured passengers filed suit in California state courts, seeking damages in excess of $1,000,000. Named as defendants were Greyhound Lines, Inc., a California corporation; Theron Nauta, the bus driver; Ellis Clark, who drove the truck; and Kenneth Glasgow, the passenger in the truck who was apparently its owner as well. Each of the individual defendants was a citizen and resident of Oregon. Before these cases could come to trial and before other suits were filed in California or elsewhere, petitioner State Farm Fire & Casualty Company, an Illinois corporation, brought this action in the nature of interpleader in the United States District Court for the District of Oregon.

In its complaint State Farm asserted that at the time of the Shasta County collision it had in force an insurance policy with respect to Ellis Clark, driver of the truck, providing for bodily injury liability up to $10,000 per person and $20,000 per occurrence and for legal representation of Clark in actions covered by the policy. It asserted that actions already filed in California and others which it anticipated would be filed far exceeded in aggregate damages sought the amount of its maximum liability under the policy. Accordingly, it paid into court the sum of $20,000 and asked the court (1) to require all claimants to establish their claims against Clark and his insurer in this single proceeding and in no other, and (2) to discharge State Farm from all further obligations under its policy— including its duty to defend Clark in lawsuits arising from the accident. Alternatively, State Farm expressed its conviction that the policy issued to Clark excluded from coverage accidents resulting from his operation of a truck which belonged to another and was being used in the business of another. The complaint, therefore, requested that the court decree that the insurer owed no duty to Clark and was not liable on the policy, and it asked the court to refund the $20,000 deposit.

Joined as defendants were Clark, Glasgow, Nauta, Greyhound Lines, and each of the prospective claimants. Jurisdiction was predicated upon 28 U.S.C. § 1335, the federal interpleader statute,[1] and upon general diversity of citizenship, there being diversity between two or more of the claimants to the fund and between State Farm and all of the named defendants.

---

[1] 28 U.S.C. § 1335(a) provides: "The district courts shall have original jurisdiction of any civil action of interpleader or in the nature of interpleader filed by any person, firm, or corporation, association, or society having in his or its custody or possession money or property of the value of $500 or more, or having issued a . . . policy of insurance . . . of value or amount of $500 or more . . . if

"(1) Two or more adverse claimants, of diverse citizenship as defined in section 1332 of this title, are claiming or may claim to be entitled to such money or property, or to any one or more of the benefits arising by virtue of any . . . policy . . .; and if (2) the plaintiff has . . . paid . . . the amount due under such obligation into the registry of the court, there to abide the judgment of the court. . . ."

An order issued, requiring the defendants to show cause why they should not be restrained from filing or prosecuting "any proceeding in any state or United States Court affecting the property or obligation involved in this interpleader action, and specifically against the plaintiff and the defendant Ellis D. Clark." Personal service was effected on each of the American defendants, and registered mail was employed to reach the 11 Canadian claimants. Defendants Nauta, Greyhound, and several of the injured passengers responded, contending that the policy did cover this accident and advancing various arguments for the position that interpleader was either impermissible or inappropriate in the present circumstances. Greyhound, however, soon switched sides and moved that the court broaden any injunction to include Nauta and Greyhound among those who could not be sued except within the confines of the interpleader proceeding.

When a temporary injunction along the lines sought by State Farm was issued by the United States District Court for the District of Oregon, the present respondents moved to dismiss the action and, in the alternative, for a change of venue—to the Northern District of California, in which district the collision had occurred. After a hearing, the court declined to dissolve the temporary injunction, but continued the motion for a change of venue. The injunction was later broadened to include the protection sought by Greyhound, but modified to permit the filing—although not the prosecution—of suits. The injunction, therefore, provided that all suits against Clark, State Farm, Greyhound, and Nauta be prosecuted in the interpleader proceeding.

On interlocutory appeal, the Court of Appeals for the Ninth Circuit reversed. The court found it unnecessary to reach respondents' contentions relating to service of process and the scope of the injunction, for it concluded that interpleader was not available in the circumstances of this case. It held that in States like Oregon which do not permit "direct action" suits against insurance companies until judgments are obtained against the insured, the insurance companies may not invoke federal interpleader until the claims against the insured, the alleged tortfeasor, have been reduced to judgment. Until that is done, said the court, claimants with unliquidated tort claims are not "claimants" within the meaning of § 1335, nor are they "persons having claims against the plaintiff"* within the meaning of Rule 22 of the Federal Rules of Civil Procedure.[3] In accord with

---

*   This rule language has been revised slightly.—Eds.

[3]   We need not pass upon the Court of Appeals' conclusions with respect to the interpretation of interpleader under Rule 22, which provides that "(1) Persons having claims against the plaintiff may be joined as defendants and required to interplead when their claims are such that the plaintiff is or may be exposed to double or multiple liability. . . ." First, as we indicate today, this action was properly brought under § 1335. Second, State Farm did not purport to invoke Rule 22. Third, State Farm could not have invoked it in light of venue and service of process limitations. Whereas statutory interpleader may be brought in the district where any claimant resides (28 U.S.C. § 1397), Rule interpleader based upon diversity of citizenship may be brought only in the

that view, it directed dissolution of the temporary injunction and dismissal of the action. Because the Court of Appeals' decision on this point conflicts with those of other federal courts, and concerns a matter of significance to the administration of federal interpleader, we granted certiorari. Although we reverse the decision of the Court of Appeals upon the jurisdictional question, we direct a substantial modification of the District Court's injunction for reasons which will appear.

Before considering the issues presented by the petition for certiorari, we find it necessary to dispose of a question neither raised by the parties nor passed upon by the courts below. Since the matter concerns our jurisdiction, we raise it on our own motion. The interpleader statute, 28 U.S.C. § 1335, applies where there are "Two or more adverse claimants, of diverse citizenship. . . ." This provision has been uniformly construed to require only "minimal diversity," that is, diversity of citizenship between two or more claimants, without regard to the circumstance that other rival claimants may be co-citizens. The language of the statute, the legislative purpose broadly to remedy the problems posed by multiple claimants to a single fund, and the consistent judicial interpretation tacitly accepted by Congress, persuade us that the statute requires no more. There remains, however, the question whether such a statutory construction is consistent with Article III of our Constitution, which extends the federal judicial power to "Controversies . . . between citizens of different States . . . and between a State, or the Citizens thereof, and foreign States, Citizens or Subjects." In Strawbridge v. Curtiss, 3 Cranch 267 (1806), this Court held that the diversity of citizenship statute required "complete diversity": where co-citizens appeared on both sides of a dispute, jurisdiction was lost. But Chief Justice Marshall there purported to construe only "The words of the act of congress," not the Constitution itself. And in a variety of contexts this Court and the lower courts have concluded that Article III poses no obstacle to the legislative extension of federal jurisdiction, founded on diversity, so long as any two adverse parties are not co-citizens. Accordingly, we conclude that the present case is properly in the federal courts.

Ct. has jurisdiction

II

We do not agree with the Court of Appeals that, in the absence of a state law or contractual provision for "direct action" suits against the insurance company, the company must wait until persons asserting claims against its insured have reduced those claims to judgment before seeking

---

district where all plaintiffs or all defendants reside (28 U.S.C. § 1391(a)). [After 1993 amendments, this statute provides that venue is permissible where any defendant resides if all defendants reside in the same state, where a substantial part of the events occurred (or property that is the subject of the action is located), or where defendants are subject to personal jurisdiction if there is no other district where the action can be brought.—Eds.] And whereas statutory interpleader enables a plaintiff to employ nationwide service of process (28 U.S.C. § 2361), service of process under Rule 22 is confined to that provided in Rule 4.

to invoke the benefits of federal interpleader. That may have been a tenable position under the 1926 and 1936 interpleader statutes. These statutes did not carry forward the language in the 1917 Act authorizing interpleader where adverse claimants "may claim" benefits as well as where they "are claiming" them. In 1948, however, in the revision of the Judicial Code, the "may claim" language was restored. Until the decision below, every court confronted by the question has concluded that the 1948 revision removed whatever requirement there might previously have been that the insurance company wait until at least two claimants reduced their claims to judgments. The commentators are in accord.

Considerations of judicial administration demonstrate the soundness of this view which, in any event, seems compelled by the language of the present statute, which is remedial and to be liberally construed. Were an insurance company required to await reduction of claims to judgment, the first claimant to obtain such a judgment or to negotiate a settlement might appropriate all or a disproportionate slice of the fund before his fellow claimants were able to establish their claims. The difficulties such a race to judgment pose for the insurer, and the unfairness which may result to some claimants, were among the principal evils the interpleader device was intended to remedy.

III

The fact that State Farm had properly invoked the interpleader jurisdiction under § 1335 did not, however, entitle it to an order both enjoining prosecution of suits against it outside the confines of the interpleader proceeding and also extending such protection to its insured, the alleged tortfeasor. Still less was Greyhound Lines entitled to have that order expanded so as to protect itself and its driver, also alleged to be tortfeasors, from suits brought by its passengers in various state or federal courts. Here, the scope of the litigation, in terms of parties and claims, was vastly more extensive than the confines of the "fund," the deposited proceeds of the insurance policy. In these circumstances, the mere existence of such a fund cannot, by use of interpleader, be employed to accomplish purposes that exceed the needs of orderly contest with respect to the fund.

There are situations, of a type not present here, where the effect of interpleader is to confine the total litigation to a single forum and proceeding. One such case is where a stakeholder, faced with rival claims to the fund itself, acknowledges—or denies—his liability to one or the other of the claimants. In this situation, the fund itself is the target of the claimants. It marks the outer limits of the controversy. It is, therefore, reasonable and sensible that interpleader, in discharge of its office to protect the fund, should also protect the stakeholder from vexatious and multiple litigation. In this context, the suits sought to be enjoined are squarely within the language of 28 U.S.C. § 2361, which provides in part:

Alternative situation [handwritten margin note]

"In any civil action of interpleader or in the nature of interpleader under section 1335 of this title, a district court may issue its process for all claimants and enter its order restraining them from instituting or prosecuting *any proceeding* in any State or United States court *affecting the property, instrument or obligation involved in the interpleader action. . . .*" (Emphasis added.)

But the present case is another matter. Here, an accident has happened. Thirty-five passengers or their representatives have claims which they wish to press against a variety of defendants: the bus company, its driver, the owner of the truck, and the truck driver. The circumstance that one of the prospective defendants happens to have an insurance policy is a fortuitous event which should not of itself shape the nature of the ensuing litigation. For example, a resident of California, injured in California aboard a bus owned by a California corporation should not be forced to sue that corporation anywhere but in California simply because another prospective defendant carried an insurance policy. And an insurance company whose maximum interest in the case cannot exceed $20,000 and who in fact asserts that it has no interest at all, should not be allowed to determine that dozens of tort plaintiffs must be compelled to press their claims—even those claims which are not against the insured and which in no event could be satisfied out of the meager insurance fund— in a single forum of the insurance company's choosing. There is nothing in the statutory scheme, and very little in the judicial and academic commentary upon that scheme, which requires that the tail be allowed to wag the dog in this fashion.

State Farm's interest in this case, which is the fulcrum of the interpleader procedure, is confined to its $20,000 fund. That interest receives full vindication when the court restrains claimants from seeking to enforce against the insurance company any judgment obtained against its insured, except in the interpleader proceeding itself. To the extent that the District Court sought to control claimants' lawsuits against the insured and other alleged tortfeasors, it exceeded the powers granted to it by the statutory scheme.

We recognize, of course, that our view of interpleader means that it cannot be used to solve all the vexing problems of multiparty litigation arising out of a mass tort. But interpleader was never intended to perform such a function, to be an all-purpose "bill of peace." Had it been so intended, careful provision would necessarily have been made to insure that a party with little or no interest in the outcome of a complex controversy should not strip truly interested parties of substantial rights—such as the right to choose the forum in which to establish their claims, subject to generally applicable rules of jurisdiction, venue, service of process, removal, and change of venue. None of the legislative and academic sponsors of a modern federal interpleader device viewed their accomplishment as a "bill of peace," capable of sweeping dozens of lawsuits out of the various state and federal courts in which they were brought and into a single interpleader proceeding. * * *

In light of the evidence that federal interpleader was not intended to serve the function of a "bill of peace" in the context of multiparty litigation arising out of a mass tort, of the anomalous power which such a construction of the statute would give the stakeholder, and of the thrust of the statute and the purpose it was intended to serve, we hold that the interpleader statute did not authorize the injunction entered in the present case. Upon remand, the injunction is to be modified consistently with this opinion.

[Dissenting opinion of JUSTICE DOUGLAS omitted.]

NOTES AND QUESTIONS

1.   The Court of Appeals in *Tashire* ruled that State Farm could not invoke interpleader until the claimants had reduced their claims to judgment (in the absence of a state "direct action" statute that allowed the claimants to sue the insurance company directly). The Supreme Court rejected that position, pointing out that § 1335 allows interpleader by claimants who are claiming or "may claim" to be entitled to money or property. Rule 22(1), referring to situations where a plaintiff is "or may be" exposed to multiple liability, also allows an insurance company to sue in interpleader without there first being a judgment against its insured. Notice that although suit had been filed by the claimants in *Tashire* before State Farm filed its interpleader action, a prior suit (or even a formal demand for payment) is not necessary to allow a stakeholder with a genuine anticipation of double exposure to invoke interpleader.

2.   Why wasn't State Farm allowed to invoke interpleader to prevent prosecution of the suits against its insured (Clark), Greyhound, and Greyhound's driver? Why wasn't the liability insurance policy "fund" which State Farm held as stakeholder sufficient to force all of the suits arising out of the same accident to be tried in the interpleader action?

3.   Could the defendant Greyhound have filed its own interpleader action on the ground that it was exposed to the possibility of multiple and inconsistent suits? Notice that, unlike State Farm, whose liability was limited to the amount of the liability insurance policy, Greyhound's liability was unlimited. For interpleader, there must be an identifiable limited fund ("the stake"). Although it will usually be money or an insurance obligation, it may be any protectable property interest. 7 C. Wright, A. Miller, & M. Kane, *Federal Practice and Procedure* § 1704, at 546 (3d ed. 2001). Interpleader has been allowed as to conflicting claims to an El Greco painting, United States v. Herce, 334 F. Supp. 111 (S.D.N.Y.1971), and rights to use (as opposed to ownership, which was not disputed) an original print of the silent film "Birth

of a Nation." <u>United States v. American Film Institute</u>, 79 F.R.D. 374 (D.D.C.1978).

4.   As a result of the Court's denial in *Tashire* of interpleader protection against the prosecution of separate suits against the defendants, there will be multiple litigation, including (1) this federal interpleader action limited to the conflicting claims to the amount of State Farm's liability policy, (2) the four pending California suits, and (3) whatever suits are filed by or on behalf of the other thirty-one passengers. Multiple litigation has a number of drawbacks. It wastes judicial time and resources, can result in inconsistent judgments that are an embarrassment to a legal system that adheres to the principle of "like treatment for like cases," and creates enormous problems in determining the preclusive effects of the judgments on other similar cases. But the Supreme Court was unwilling to view interpleader as a grand mechanism for unitary disposition of related disputes (as in the "bill of peace," the forerunner of the class action), and ruled that the right to the plaintiffs' choice of forum could not be denied.

5.   Interpleader is not limited to the *Tashire* situation in which the stakeholder sues the claimants in an original interpleader action. Defensive interpleader is available to a stakeholder who is sued by one of the claimants, allowing the stakeholder to interplead the other claimants by way of a third-party claim, cross-claim, or counterclaim. The language of Rule 22(1) expressly authorizes interpleader by cross-claim and counterclaim, and precedents have also extended it to third-party claims and intervention. Although § 1335 does not expressly refer to defensive interpleader, it has been held to permit it by counterclaim. 7 C. Wright, A. Miller, & M. Kane, Federal Practice and Procedure § 1708 (3d ed. 2001). A defendant stakeholder should not be able to claim that absent claimants are indispensable under Rule 19 where it has the power to bring them in through defensive interpleader. See Advisory Committee Notes on the 1966 Amendments to Rule 19.

6.   In contrast to the practice at common law, today a party invoking interpleader is not required to admit liability to any of the claimants. The stakeholder may plead in the alternative that it is not liable, as when an insurance company, exposed to multiple claims on a policy, contends that the terms of the policy have not been satisfied.

7.   An interpleader action has two stages—the first concerns whether the stakeholder has a genuine fear of exposure to multiple liability upon the same obligation, and the second concerns the merits of the claims of the claimants. A court should base its ruling on a request for interpleader solely on a determination of the first stage, which is satisfied by proof of good faith fear of multiple exposure. The merits of the claims should be reserved for the second stage of the proceeding.

8.   As footnote 3 of *Tashire* suggests, the primary differences between statutory and rule interpleader are found in the requirements for diversity, service of process, and venue. Actions brought under rule interpleader are governed by the general statutes and rules governing diversity subject matter

jurisdiction (28 U.S.C.A. § 1332), service of process (Rule 4), and venue (28 U.S.C.A. § 1391). Thus Rule 22(1) actions require complete diversity between the stakeholders, on one side, and the claimants, on the other, as well as $75,000 in controversy. However, statutory interpleader contains special provisions for these matters: diversity is only required as between the claimants, and only $500 is required for the amount in controversy (28 U.S.C.A. § 1335); there is nationwide service of process (28 U.S.C.A. § 2361); and venue lies in the district of the residence of one or more claimants (28 U.S.C.A. § 1397). The following chart shows these differences:

	Diversity	Venue	Service
Rule Interpleader	Between stakeholder & all claimants (complete diversity)	Residence of any defendant (if all defendants reside in the same state), or where a substantial part of events occurred or property located, or where any defendant is subject to personal jurisdiction (if there is no district where the action can otherwise be brought) (§ 1391(a))	As under Rule 4
Statutory Interpleader (28 U.S.C.A. § 1335)	Between two or more claimants (minimal diversity)	Residence of one of more claimants § 1397	Nationwide § 2361

9.   There is also a difference between rule and statutory interpleader as to the authority of the court to enjoin other suits by the claimants. In rule interpleader, the "Anti-Injunction Act," 28 U.S.C.A. § 2283, provides the only exception that could conceivably allow a federal court to enjoin ongoing state proceedings, that is, "where necessary in aid of its jurisdiction," a provision which has received an extremely narrow construction. However, the Act also provides an exception when "expressly authorized by Act of Congress," and statutory interpleader under 28 U.S.C.A. § 2361 expressly allows an order restraining claimants "from instituting or prosecuting any proceeding in any State or United States court affecting the property, instrument or obligation involved in the interpleader action until further order of the court."

H. INTERVENTION (RULE 24)

Intervention, unlike most of the other joinder devices already discussed, does not have a long history in Anglo-American jurisprudence. It arose in statutes after the adoption of code pleading, and is peculiarly the product of the twentieth century.

Intervention is a device for an outsider who has an interest in a lawsuit to voluntarily join it as a party. Sometimes an intervenor has an obvious interest in a suit. The intervenor might, for example, be someone who should have been joined but was not due to insufficient contacts with the forum state to support personal jurisdiction. Indeed, very similar language to that used in Rule 19(a) to describe parties who should be joined if feasible is used in Rule 24(a) to describe intervention of right. If such a person wants voluntarily to enter the suit, Rule 24(a) should allow that. Sometimes, however, a person seeking intervention has a much less obvious interest in the suit, as, for example, someone or some organization that is concerned about governmental action or policy. Rule 24(b) recognizes that intervention may be useful to the court even if a party lacks the compelling interest of an intervenor of right. Permissive intervention, however, is left to the discretion of the court.

NATURAL RESOURCES DEFENSE COUNCIL, INC. V. UNITED STATES NUCLEAR REGULATORY COMMISSION

United States Court of Appeals, Tenth Circuit, 1978
578 F.2d 1341

Before DOYLE and LOGAN, CIRCUIT JUDGES, And STANLEY, SENIOR DISTRICT JUDGE.

WILLIAM E. DOYLE, CIRCUIT JUDGE.

The American Mining Congress and Kerr-McGee Nuclear Corporation seek review of the order of the United States District Court for the District of New Mexico denying their motions to intervene as a matter of right or on a permissive basis, pursuant to Rule 24(a)(2) and (b), Fed.R.Civil Proc.

The underlying action in which the movants requested intervention was instituted by the Natural Resources Defense Council, Inc., and others. In the action, declaratory and injunctive relief is directed to the United States Nuclear Regulatory Commission (NRC) and the New Mexico Environmental Improvement Agency (NMEIA), prohibiting those agencies from issuing licenses for the operation of uranium mills in New Mexico without first preparing environmental impact statements. Kerr-McGee and United Nuclear are potential recipients of the licenses.

Congress, in the Atomic Energy Act of 1954, 42 U.S.C. §§ 2011–2296, has authorized the NRC to issue such licenses. NMEIA is involved because under § 274(b) of the Act, 42 U.S.C. § 2021(b) (1970), the NRC is authorized to enter into agreements with the states allowing the states to issue licenses. Such agreements have been made with about 25 states including New Mexico. Thus, the action below in effect seeks to prevent the use of § 274(b) of the Act so as to avoid the requirement of an impact statement for which provision is made in the National Environmental Policy Act.

42 U.S.C. § 4332(2)(c) (1970) requires that a detailed environmental impact statement must be prepared by all federal agencies "in every recommendation or report on proposals for legislation and other major Federal actions significantly affecting the quality of the human environment." The complaint cites this requirement and alleges that an environmental impact statement would ordinarily be required here as a prerequisite to the issuance of licenses for the operation of uranium mills were it not for the arrangement which gives jurisdiction to the state. It further alleges that such statements are now prepared by the NRC in states that have not entered into agreements with the NRC, but that the NRC does not prepare such statements where there is an agreement with a state such as New Mexico. Plaintiff contends that the granting of licenses by state agencies predicated on delegation of authority from the NRC causes the NRC to consider the aspect of "major federal action" to be thereby eliminated. The New Mexico agency, NMEIA, which grants the license, does not prepare environmental impact statements since it is not a federal agency and is not required either by its agreement with NRC or by state law to prepare such a statement.

The relief sought by the plaintiffs' complaint is, *first,* [a declaration] that NRC's involvement in the licensing procedure in New Mexico is, notwithstanding the delegation to the state, sufficient to constitute major federal action, whereby the impact statement requirement is not eliminated. *Second,* that if an impact statement is not required in connection with the granting of licenses, the New Mexico program is in conflict with § 274(d)(2) of the Atomic Energy Act of 1954, 42 U.S.C. § 2021(d)(2) (1970).

The motion of United Nuclear Corporation to intervene is not opposed by the parties and was granted. On May 3, 1977, the date that the complaint herein was filed, NMEIA granted a license to United Nuclear to operate a uranium mill at Church Rock, New Mexico. The complaint seeks to enjoin the issuance of the license thus granted.

It was after that that Kerr-McGee Nuclear Corporation, Anaconda Company, Gulf Oil Corporation, Phillips Petroleum Company, and the American Mining Congress filed motions to intervene. These motions, insofar as they sought intervention as of right, were denied on the ground that the interests of the parties or movants would be adequately represented by United Nuclear. Permissive intervention was also denied.

* * *

The district court's order denying intervention by the several corporations focused on whether the interest of the party seeking to intervene was adequately represented by a fellow member of the industry. * * * The court decided that the interests of the movants were adequately protected by United Nuclear, which possessed the necessary experience and knowledge in a complex area of business, whereby the representative's capability was competent to meet the demands. The court thought that to allow the intervention would engender delay and produce unwieldy procedure; and that the movants' requirements were met by allowing the filing of *amicus curiae* briefs.

Our conclusion is that the interests of movants in the subject matter [are] sufficient to satisfy the requirements of Rule 24 and that the threat of loss of their interest and inability to participate is of such magnitude as to impair their ability to advance their interest.

I.

The position adopted by the trial court that Kerr-McGee was adequately represented dispensed with the need for the court to consider the question whether Kerr-McGee had an interest in the litigation before the court. Plaintiffs-appellees maintain that the appellants do not have the requisite interest because they are not directly involved; that the controversy centers on the effort of Natural Resources Defense Council, Inc. to prevent the issuance of a license to United Nuclear unless and until an environmental impact statement is issued. The question then is whether the contention made is a correct concept of interest. Strictly to require that the movant in intervention have a *direct* interest in the outcome of the lawsuit strikes us as being too narrow a construction of Rule 24(a)(2). Kerr-McGee argues that the meaning of interest is one which, if they do not prevail in the intervention, threatens them with a disposition of the action which may, as a practical matter, impair or impede their efforts to protect the interest. Thus, we are asked to interpret interest in relationship to the second criterion in Rule 24(a)(2), impairment or impeding ability to protect the interest.

The Supreme Court has said that the interest must be a significantly protectable interest. See Donaldson v. United States, 400 U.S. 517 (1971). The Supreme Court held that a taxpayer did not have a right to intervene in a judicial enforcement proceeding seeking issuance of an Internal Revenue summons ordering production of business records of his employer. The narrowness of the *summons proceeding* was noted, and it was said that an objection of the taxpayer could be raised at the proper time in a subsequent trial.

Cascade Natural Gas Corp. v. El Paso Natural Gas Co., 386 U.S. 129, 135–36 (1967), held that the interest claimed by the applicant in intervention did not have to be a direct interest in the property or transaction at issue provided that it was an interest that would be impaired by the outcome. There Cascade's source of supply would have been a new company created by an antitrust divestiture, a significant change. In view of this consequence of the litigation, it was held that Cascade had a sufficient interest. See also Allard v. Frizzell, 536 F.2d 1332, 1334 n. 1 (10th Cir.1976). In *Allard* it was ruled that the applicant in intervention did not have a sufficient interest. Movant's interest there was general and somewhat abstract.

In our case the matter of immediate interest is, of course, the issuance and delivery of the license sought by United Nuclear. However, the consequence of the litigation could well be the imposition of the requirement that an environmental impact statement be prepared before granting any uranium mill license in New Mexico, or, secondly, it could result in an injunction terminating or suspending the agreement between NRC and NMEIA. Either consequence would be felt by United Nuclear and to some degree, of course, by Kerr-McGee, which is said to be one of the largest holders of uranium properties in New Mexico. It operates a uranium mill in Grants, New Mexico, pursuant to an NMEIA license, which application for renewal is pending. A decision in favor of the plaintiffs, which is not unlikely, could have a profound effect upon Kerr-McGee. Hence, it does have an interest within the meaning of Rule 24(a)(2). This interest of Kerr-McGee is in sharp contrast to the minimal interest which was present in *Allard,* wherein it was an interest of environmental groups in the protection of living birds. This was considered insufficient to justify intervention in a case involving feathers which are part of Indian artifacts. Their interest was said to be limited to a general interest in the public. The interest asserted on behalf of Kerr-McGee and the American Mining Congress is one which is a genuine threat to Kerr-McGee and the members of the American Mining Congress to a substantial degree.

We do not suggest that Kerr-McGee could expect better treatment from state authorities than federal. We do recognize that a change in procedure would produce impairing complications.

II.

The next question is whether, assuming the existence of an interest, the chance of impairment is sufficient to fulfill the requirement of Rule 24(a)(2).

As already noted, the question of impairment is not separate from the question of existence of an interest. The appellants both claim an interest in licenses that are now before NMEIA or will be in the future. If the relief sought by the plaintiffs is granted, there can be little question but that the interests of the American Mining Congress and of Kerr-McGee would be affected. Plaintiffs contend, however, that appellants would not be bound by such a result if they are not participants. Kerr-McGee points out that even though it may not be res judicata, still it would have a stare decisis effect. Moreover, with NRC and NMEIA as parties, the result might be more profound than stare decisis.

It should be pointed out that the Rule refers to impairment "as a practical matter." Thus, the court is not limited to consequences of a strictly legal nature. The court may consider any significant legal effect in the applicant's interest and it is not restricted to a rigid res judicata test. Hence, the stare decisis effect might be sufficient to satisfy the requirement. It is said that where, as here, the case is of first impression, the stare decisis effect would be important.

Finally, the considerations for requiring an environmental impact statement will be relatively the same in respect to the issuance of a uranium mining license in every instance. Hence, to say that it can be repeatedly litigated is not an answer, for the chance of getting a contrary result in a case which is substantially similar on its facts to one previously adjudicated seems remote.

We are of the opinion, therefore, that appellants have satisfied the impairment criterion.

III.

The final question is whether the trial court was correct in its conclusion that United Nuclear would adequately represent Kerr-McGee and the American Mining Congress.

The finding and conclusion was that the representation would be adequate because United Nuclear, a fellow member of the industry, has interests which were the same as those of the appellants and possessed the same level of knowledge and experience with the ability and willingness to pursue the matter and could adequately represent Kerr-McGee and the members of the American Mining Congress.

We have held in accordance with Trbovich v. UMW, 404 U.S. 528, 538 n. 10 (1972), that the burden continues to be on the petitioner or movant in intervention to show that the representation by parties may be inadequate. We have also recognized the holding in *Trbovich* that the burden is minimal; that it is enough to show that the representation "may be" inadequate.

United Nuclear is situated somewhat differently in this case than are the other members of the industry since it has been granted its license. From this it is urged by Kerr-McGee that United Nuclear may be ready to compromise the case by obtaining a mere declaration that while environmental impact statements should be issued, this requirement need be prospective only, whereby it would not affect them. While we see this as a remote possibility, we gravely doubt that United Nuclear would opt for such a result. It is true, however, that United Nuclear has a defense of laches that is not available to Kerr-McGee or the others.

7A C. Wright & A. Miller, Federal Practice & Procedure, § 1909, at 524 (1972), says:

> [I]f [an applicant's] interest is similar to, but not identical with, that of one of the parties, a discriminating judgment is required on the circumstances of the particular case, but he ordinarily should be allowed to intervene unless it is clear that the party will provide adequate representation for the absentee.

While the interest of the two applicants may appear similar, there is no way to say that there is no possibility that they will not be different and the possibility of divergence of interest need not be great in order to satisfy the burden of the applicants.

There are other reasons for allowing intervention. There is some value in having the parties before the court so that they will be bound by the result. American Mining Congress represents a number of companies having a wide variety of interests. This can, therefore, provide a useful supplement to the defense of the case. The same can be said of Kerr-McGee.

The trial court was concerned that the addition of these movants would make the litigation unwieldy. If the intervenors are limited to this group, unwieldiness does not become a problem which the trial court cannot control. It does not appear that there would be a need for additional parties in view of the presence of the American Mining Congress. While we do not express an opinion on the possibilities of further additions, we wish to make clear that the present holdings that the two applicants should be allowed to intervene does not say that others should be added. The two appellants here have satisfied their burden of the three requirements of Rule 24(a)(2). Consequently, they should be and they are hereby allowed to intervene. Accordingly, we need not determine whether the district court erred in denying permissive intervention under Rule 24(b).

The order of the district court is reversed and the cause is remanded with instructions to the trial court to grant the appellants, Kerr-McGee's and American Mining Congress', motions to intervene.

NOTES AND QUESTIONS

1.   We first saw intervention in Band's Refuse Removal, Inc. v. Borough of Fair Lawn, supra p. 3, where the Capassos intervened in the suit. Was intervention there proper under the standards of Rule 24?

2.   Compare Rule 19(a)(1)(B) with Rule 24(a)(2). Does their similarity mean that, whenever an intervenor qualifies under Rule 24(a)(2), all others who have the same characteristics should also be treated as necessary parties under Rule 19(a)? Is one rule narrower in scope than the other? If so, why is it permissible to deny intervention to parties who qualify under Rule 24(a)(2) if they are adequately represented? Note that there is no similar provision in Rule 19, except to the extent that it is somehow implicit in Rule 19(b).

3.   The definition of interest under Rule 24(a) is discussed in some detail below. Assuming the intervenor claims the right kind of interest, intervention of right is proper only if that interest will be impaired should intervention be denied. The court suggests that the stare decisis effect should be sufficient. Consider Olympus Corp. v. United States, 627 F.Supp. 911 (E.D.N.Y.1985), in which the exclusive U.S. distributor of Olympus-brand optical products sued customs officials challenging regulations that allowed importation of "gray market" Olympus products—products imported by persons other than the manufacturer's authorized representative. 47th Street Photo, which imported a substantial quantity of Olympus "gray market" products, and K-Mart Corporation, which purchased other "gray market" goods and said it was a "potential customer" of Olympus "gray market" products, moved to intervene. The court found that 47th Street Photo possessed an adequate interest to intervene as of right, but not K-Mart. Why? How could 47th Street Photo's interest be impaired by the action? The court stated: "Although apprehension concerning the force of *stare decisis* will not support intervention in all cases, its effect under the circumstances presented here, presenting a significant case of apparent first impression, suffices." Who could intervene as of right in a case in which plaintiff seeks to persuade a court in a state that presently treats contributory negligence as a complete defense to switch to a comparative negligence regime?

4.   Once the intervenor can show prospective impairment of the right kind of interest, intervention is to be denied only if the intervenor's interests are adequately represented by the present parties. The intervenor need only show that "representation of his interest 'may be' inadequate; and the burden of making that showing should be treated as minimal." Trbovich v. United Mine Workers, 404 U.S. 528, 538 n. 10 (1972). However, "[w]hen the party seeking intervention has the same ultimate objective as a party to the suit, a presumption arises that its interests are adequately represented, against which the petitioner must demonstrate adversity of interest, collusion, or nonfeasance." International Tank Terminals, Ltd. v. M/V Acadia Forest, 579 F.2d 964, 967 (5th Cir.1978). See also Supreme Beef Processors, Inc. v. U.S. Dept. of Agriculture, 2000 WL 127281 (N.D.Tex) (in suit by beef processor challenging Department of Agriculture regulations governing processing of meat and poultry, intervention by trade association of packers, processors, and distributors denied, finding claim of a broader interest was not sufficient where the same objective and relief were sought). Why weren't Kerr-McGee and the American Mining Congress adequately represented by United Nuclear? Would others interested in the business be deemed adequately represented by Kerr-McGee and the American Mining Congress should they try to intervene?

5.   Consider the application of these intervention criteria in Grutter v. Bollinger, 188 F.3d 394 (6th Cir.1999). Plaintiffs were white applicants rejected for admission by the University of Michigan. They claimed that the university illegally considered race in making admissions decisions, and sought an injunction against future consideration of race. Seventeen African-American and Hispanic individuals who intended to apply to the university and non-profit organizations dedicated to preserving higher educational

opportunities for minority students sought to intervene on the side of the defendant university. The district court denied intervention.

The court of appeals reversed. Noting that the Sixth Circuit takes an expansive view of the interest sufficient to justify intervention of right, the court found that requirement satisfied because "[t]he proposed intervenors have enunciated a specific interest in the subject matter of this case, namely their interest in gaining admission to the University." There was "little room for doubt" that access to the university would be impaired for such applicants if the university were precluded from considering race as a factor in admissions, the court added, citing recent experiences in California and Texas as evidence. The university was not an adequate representative for the intervenors, moreover, because it was subject to internal and external institutional pressures that might prevent it from asserting some defenses of affirmative action, and because it had less to lose than the intervenors did. On this last point, one judge dissented, asserting that the university had "zealously defend[ed] its voluntarily-adopted admissions policies." Is the court's reasoning persuasive?

6. Intervention must be "timely." Rule 24(a) & (b). In United Airlines, Inc. v. McDonald, 432 U.S. 385 (1977), an application for intervention, made only after the intervenor learned that the plaintiffs in this sex discrimination case would not appeal the denial of class certification, was found to have been made "as soon as it became clear" that her interests were no longer protected by the class representatives. Stallworth v. Monsanto Co., 558 F.2d 257 (5th Cir.1977), listed four factors for assessing timeliness: 1) when the intervenor knew or should have known of his interest in the case, 2) whether there was prejudice to existing parties from the delay in seeking intervention, 3) whether there would be prejudice to the intervenor if intervention were denied, and 4) any unusual circumstances.

7. To what extent is an intervenor bound by rulings made by the court before its intervention? See Hall County Historical Society, Inc. v. Georgia Dept. of Transp., 447 F. Supp. 741, 746 n. 1 (N.D.Ga.1978) ("Although an intervenor as of right is entitled to fully litigate the merits by pleading and setting forth additional claims and defenses where they arise from the same transaction(s) as the main claim(s) or are ancillary thereto, it is also well settled that an intervenor in equitable proceedings is bound by all prior orders and decrees as though he had been a party from the inception of the suit.").

8. Under Rule 24(a) intervention is "of right." What rights does that mean the intervenor has? One of the concerns of the district court in denying intervention to Kerr-McGee and the American Mining Congress was that their presence would unduly complicate the case. What could it do to minimize those problems? In Stringfellow v. Concerned Neighbors in Action, 480 U.S. 370 (1987), the neighbors' association was allowed to intervene in an action brought by the United States and the State of California concerning the Stringfellow Acid Pits, an abandoned hazardous waste disposal site. The trial court limited the intervenors in three ways: (1) Intervenors could not assert a claim for relief that was not already raised because that would "expand an already complex

litigation, and could jeopardize the possibility of settlement"; (2) Intervenors could not seek a share of the government's recovery of clean-up costs; (3) Intervenors could not file motions or initiate discovery without first conferring with all the litigants and obtaining permission from at least one of the others. The Supreme Court rejected arguments that these limitations amounted to a complete denial of intervention. Justice Brennan, concurring, noted that "restrictions on participation may also be placed on an intervenor of right and on an original party." For another example, see United States v. Reserve Mining Co., 56 F.R.D. 408 (D.Minn.1972) (requiring intervenors to make uniform presentations and agree on witnesses to be called).

9.   Had there been an applicable fee-shifting statute in the *Natural Resources Defense Council* case, would the intervenors have run the risk of liability for part of plaintiffs' fees if plaintiffs were ultimately successful? In Independent Federation of Flight Attendants v. Zipes, 491 U.S. 754 (1989), a sex discrimination action, other employees were allowed to intervene to challenge a settlement between plaintiffs and the employer. When plaintiffs prevailed against the intervenors, the district court then awarded plaintiffs some $180,000 under the applicable fee-shifting statute for the fees incurred during this litigation against intervenors.

The Supreme Court reversed, interpreting the employment discrimination fee-shifting statute as allowing such an award against intervenors under the same standard as govern an award against an unsuccessful plaintiff (see supra p. 103 n. 2)—where intervenor's assertions were "frivolous, unreasonable, or without foundation." The Court reasoned that "losing intervenors * * * have not been found to have violated anyone's civil rights" and that intervention by "employees innocent of any wrongdoing" would be "particularly welcome" in assessing prospective remedies in employment discrimination cases.

10.   Can a government agency intervene in a private suit involving the interpretation of a statute or regulation if it feels that the suit may create a bad precedent that will affect its enforcement responsibilities? See Blake v. Pallan, 554 F.2d 947 (9th Cir.1977), where a state Commissioner of Corporations was not allowed to intervene in a private securities fraud suit based on federal securities statutes on which the California securities statutes were modeled.

11.   *Intervention for a limited purpose*: The constraints on intervention may be viewed differently when a party seeks to intervene for a limited purpose and not to litigate the validity of the claim asserted by plaintiff. For example, in Sackman v. Liggett Group, 167 F.R.D. 6 (E.D.N.Y.1996), nonparty tobacco companies were allowed to intervene as of right in a smoker's personal injury action against a cigarette manufacturer for the limited purpose of contesting an order permitting plaintiff to discover certain documents that allegedly showed improper conduct by the companies.

THE DEFINITION OF "INTEREST" IN RULE 24(a)(2)

Rule 24(a)(2) applies "when the applicant claims an interest relating to the property or transaction which is the subject of the action." What sort of interest is sufficient to invoke Rule 24(a)(2)? *Natural Resources Defense Council* cites Donaldson v. United States, 400 U.S. 517 (1971), as establishing that the interest must be a "significantly protectable interest." This is in contrast to the requirement at an earlier time that the interest must be a "legal interest," that is, that an intervenor must actually have a legally-protectable interest, such as a property right, in the matter being sued on. But just exactly what the "significantly protectable interest" test requires is a matter of continuing debate because *Donaldson* was one of three cases decided by the Supreme Court between 1967 and 1972 that are not entirely consistent. All three of these cases are cited in the *Natural Resources Defense Council* decision and in many other intervention cases.

The earliest of the three cases was Cascade Natural Gas Corp. v. El Paso Natural Gas Co., 386 U.S. 129 (1967). After El Paso's acquisition of the Pacific Northwest Pipeline Corp. was found to violate the antitrust laws, the court undertook proceedings to consider the remedy of divestiture. Intervention was sought by *California*, the market for most of El Paso's gas, which wanted to assure that Pacific Northwest "would be restored as an effective competitor in California;" *Southern California Edison*, "a large industrial user of natural gas purchasing from El Paso sources and desirous of retaining competition in California;" and *Cascade*, a natural gas utility that had used Pacific Northwest as its sole supplier and would use its successor after the divestiture. The Court found that intervention as of right should have been granted, because the intervenors were so situated as to be adversely affected "by a merger that reduces the competitive factor in natural gas available to Californians." This decision was widely taken to represent a broad interpretation of the "interest" required for Rule 24(a)(2), including non-legally protected interests, such as economic concerns.

In *Donaldson,* the Court implied a narrower concept of "interest." There, in furtherance of an investigation of petitioner's tax returns, the Internal Revenue Service issued summonses to petitioner's putative former employer, Acme, for production of its records of petitioner's employment and compensation during the years under investigation. Petitioner sought to intervene in the enforcement proceeding. In rejecting intervention as of right, the Court reasoned:

> The material sought * * * consists only of Acme's routine business records in which the taxpayer has no proprietary interest of any kind * * *. Donaldson's only interest—and of course it looms large in his eyes—lies in the fact that those records presumably contain details of Acme-to-Donaldson payments possessing significance for federal income tax purposes.

This asserted interest, however, is nothing more than a desire by Donaldson to counter and overcome * * * Acme's willingness, under summons, to comply and to produce records.

* * * This interest cannot be the kind contemplated by Rule 24(a)(2) * * *. What is obviously meant there is a significantly protectable interest. And the taxpayer, to the extent that he has such a protectable interest, as, for example, by way of privilege, or to the extent he may claim abuse of process, may always assert that interest or that claim in due course at its proper place in any subsequent trial.

Thus, while the Court in *Cascade* seemed to focus upon pragmatic or economic factors in defining "interest," in *Donaldson* the Court refused intervention, despite an admittedly strong *practical* interest on the part of the intervenor, because no "significantly protectable interest" was asserted. Is what the Court meant that the intervenor was asserting no *legally-protected* interest in Acme's production of his employment records?

In the third case, Trbovich v. United Mine Workers, 404 U.S. 528 (1972), a union member sought to intervene in an action by the Secretary of Labor to set aside a union election for violating the Labor-Management Reporting and Disclosure Act. Only the Secretary was authorized to file suits under the Act, and union members were prohibited from filing private suits. The Supreme Court upheld the intervention even though he had no right to file suit himself and made no mention of *Donaldson*.

A subsequent Fifth Circuit opinion, New Orleans Public Service, Inc. (*NOPSI*) v. United Gas Pipe Line Co., 732 F.2d 452 (5th Cir.1984), was unwilling to read *Trbovich* as retreating from the requirement of a "significantly protectable interest." It saw the substantive right being litigated in *Trbovich* as the right to have elections conducted in conformity with the Act and concluded that the union member's interest in having elections so conducted "was within the zone of interests protected by the [Act's] substantive provision regulating such elections." Being within the zone of interests intended to be protected by a statute would thus satisfy the "significantly protectable interest" test.

In contrast to *Trbovich*, the interest in *NOPSI* was found insufficient to allow intervention. The City of New Orleans sought to intervene on its own behalf and on behalf of rate-paying customers in a suit brought by the local utility against its natural gas supplier challenging a rate increase as violating their supply contract. Since this was simply a breach of contract suit between two private companies to which the city was not a party, the city had no "significantly protectable interest.": "What is required is that the interest be one which the substantive law recognizes as belonging to or being owned by the applicant. The real party in interest requirement of Rule 17(a) applies to intervenors as well as plaintiffs, as does the rule that a party has no standing to assert a right if it is not his own." The court noted that this was not a case of the city seeking to assert its regulatory rights in a public law suit, and that "the only 'interest' asserted as a basis for intervention is a purely economic interest" that "alone is insufficient, as a legally protectable interest."

The court in *Natural Resources Defense Council* found that the interest of Kerr-McGee was "in sharp contrast to the minimal interest which was present in *Allard*, wherein it was an interest of environmental groups in the protection of living birds." There environmental groups sought to intervene in a suit by sellers of Indian artifacts challenging the constitutionality of a federal act that forbade use of the feathers of protected birds. The interest in *Allard*, the court said, was "general and somewhat abstract" and was "limited to a general interest in the public." Why is this an insufficient interest? Is it that if an interest is too general and shared by too many members of the public, there will be no easy way to limit intervenors (for example, general interests in protecting the environment or aesthetics, or reflecting philosophical, political, or religious views)? Is an individual financial, or "pocket-book" interest, required to assure that an interest is not too general or abstract? Is this consistent with the comment in NOPSI that a "purely economic interest" interest is insufficient?

Sometimes intervenors with strongly-held religious, social, or political views seek to intervene in cases involving issues central to those views. Should those interests suffice? In Planned Parenthood v. Citizens for Community Action, 558 F.2d 861 (8th Cir.1977), a citizens group opposed to abortion sought to intervene in a suit by a family planning clinic challenging an ordinance imposing a moratorium on construction of abortion facilities. The court held that the intervenors had a significantly protectable interest in protecting property values because some lived in the vicinity and a real estate expert opined that presence of an abortion clinic would lower their property values. Should anti-abortion views alone suffice? Contrast Keith v. Daley, 764 F.2d 1265 (7th Cir.1985), upholding denial of intervention by the Illinois Pro-Life Coalition (IPC) in an action seeking to enjoin enforcement of an anti-abortion law:

> In an America whose freedom is secured by its ever vigilant guard on the openness of its marketplace of ideas, IPC is encouraged to thrive, and to speak, lobby, promote, and persuade, so that its principles may become, if it is the will of the majority, the law of the land. Such a priceless right to free expression, however, does not also suggest that IPC has a right to intervene in every lawsuit involving abortion rights, or to forever defend statutes it helped to enact. Rule 24(a) precludes a conception of lawsuits, even public lawsuits, as necessary forums for such public policy debates.

Standing: The question whether intervenors must satisfy standing requirements remains open. In Diamond v. Charles, 476 U.S. 54 (1986), the Court did not decide the question. A doctor who opposed abortion was allowed to intervene on the defense side in an action against Illinois officials challenging the state's abortion law. After the lower courts held the law unconstitutional, the state officials declined to seek Supreme Court review, but the intervenor did. The Court dismissed the appeal: "Diamond's status as an intervenor below, whether permissive or as of right, does not confer standing sufficient to keep the case alive in the absence of the State on this appeal. Although intervenors are considered parties entitled, among other things, to seek review by this Court, an intervenor's right to continue a suit in the absence of the party on whose side intervention was permitted is contingent on a showing by the intervenor that he fulfills the requirements of Article III." The Court reached a similar conclusion in Hollingsworth v. Perry, 570 U.S. 693 (2013). But the question whether they must satisfy standing to intervene in the district court remains open. For lower court treatment of the question, compare Ruiz v. Estelle, 161 F.3d 814 (5th Cir.1998) (intervenors need not possess standing) with Mova Pharmaceutical Corp. v. Shalala, 140 F.3d 1060 (D.C.Cir.1998) (party that seeks to intervene as of right must demonstrate standing).

I. CLASS ACTIONS (RULE 23)

"The class action was an invention of equity . . . mothered by the practical necessity of providing a procedural device so that mere numbers would not disable large groups of individuals, united in interest, from enforcing their equitable rights nor grant them immunity from their equitable wrongs." Montgomery Ward & Co. v. Langer, 168 F.2d 182, 187 (8th Cir.1948). The modern class action is one of the most versatile and powerful joinder devices, offering enormous savings of judicial resources but also providing a significant potential for abuse.

The class action provided in equity was confined to the limited situation when joint rights or rights against a specific property were asserted. An example is the 1921 case Supreme Tribe of Ben-Hur v. Cauble, 255 U.S. 356 (1921). Several members of the fraternal organization were allowed to sue on behalf of all 70,000 members to overturn a reorganization that had unfavorably reclassified their insurance certificates. The class members all had a joint property interest that was threatened by the same conduct of the defendant. However, suits involving such a close identity of interests are not common, and thus class actions at this time were still rare.

The great change came in 1966 when the federal class action rule, Rule 23, was amended. The new Federal Rules in 1938 had divided class actions into three categories based on "jural relationships"—called true, hybrid, and spurious. The distinctions among these categories were difficult to maintain, and students should be happy to know that the 1966 amendments did away with them. The 1966 amendments created three new categories of class actions—referred to as (b)(1), (b)(2), and (b)(3) class actions. The limited situations like *Ben Hur* where there is a close identity of interests and compelling reasons to avoid individual litigation were essentially preserved as *(b)(1)(A)* and *(b)(1)(B)* class actions. These categories involve situations like those calling for compulsory joinder under Rule 19. The two new categories—*(b)(2)* and *(b)(3)*—would bring about great changes in class action practice. For a detailed review of the 1966 revisions, see Rabiej, The Making of Class Action Rule 23—What Were We Thinking?, 24 Miss. Col. L. Rev. 323 (2005).

The *(b)(2) class action* is a suit for injunctive or declaratory relief against a party who had acted or refused to act on grounds generally applicable to the class. The paradigms are the "civil rights" suits of the 1960s and 1970s that brought an end to segregation and enforced the civil rights acts, and the "institutional reform" suits of the 1970s and 1980s that applied constitutional and statutory standards to institutions like police departments, prisons, mental hospitals, and welfare agencies. The principal defendants were often either governmental bodies or companies charged with unfair employment practices, and although there were complaints of abusive class actions, many class actions were successful, and significant reforms were sometimes achieved.

The second new category (the *(b)(3) class action*) was more problematic. It is required that "questions of law or fact common to class members predominate" and that a class action is "superior" to other available methods for the adjudication of the controversy. Unlike the other categories, a (b)(3) class action can be for monetary damages, and so there was now money to be had, providing new entrepreneurial incentives for the plaintiffs' bar.

For the first couple of decades after 1966, most (b)(3) class actions were based on federal statutes such as antitrust, securities fraud, and civil rights. However, by the 1980s, class action suits were being filed for a broad spectrum of product liability, mass tort, commercial, and consumer claims. Class actions for mass torts arising from an accident, product defect, or exposure to a harmful substance became highly controversial. Since mass torts often involve individualized circumstances as to a class member's exposure to an environmental or other condition or use of a product, and as to damages, and class certification is still hard to come by in such cases. See, e.g., Southwestern Ref. Co. v. Bernal, 22 S.W.3d 425 (Tex.2000) (denying certification of a class of persons exposed to toxic substances as a result of an explosion).

1. THE PROBLEM OF REPRESENTATION

The class action is a representative suit by which the class representative or representatives sue on behalf of class members similarly situated:

> The class representatives are self-appointed, having talked with a lawyer and decided that they want to sue on behalf of the class. This may be done for a variety of reasons. The person suing may genuinely feel that the defendant whose conduct harmed him should also have to answer to other persons similarly harmed. Or, on talking with a lawyer, he may have learned that his possible recovery in an individual suit is too small to justify the expense of the litigation, and he can only get a lawyer to take the case if the lawyer can obtain his fees and litigation expenses out of the benefits to a class as a whole. Many class actions are primarily the creation of a lawyer or law firm that recruit the representative plaintiffs and finance the costs of the suit. Indeed, "entrepreneurial litigation," in which the class attorneys are the primary interested parties in the suit, is the subject of much debate in the American class action scene.

* * *

> By allowing individuals to sue not only for themselves, but also on behalf of others similarly situated, the class action "empowers plaintiffs to bring cases that otherwise either would not be possible or would only be possible in a very different form." Business critics see this in consumer suits as enabling "lawyers [to] seek out opportunities to bring these large-scale suits in the expectation that they will receive large fees, whether or not the suit has underlying merit and whether or not the individuals on whose behalf the suit is brought benefit significantly from its resolution." Consumer advocates, on the other hand, see it as providing "a means of bringing a legal action on behalf of a large number of consumers who may be harmed when corporations engage in wrongful behavior" that can "succeed in eliminating inappropriate business practices that would otherwise impose unwarranted costs on individuals."

Sherman, "American Class Actions: Significant Features and Developing Alternatives in Foreign Legal Systems," 215 F.R.D. 130, 139 (2003); Sherman, Consumer Class Actions: Who Are the Real Winners?, 56 Maine L. Rev. 223 (2004).

The class representative(s) and class counsel have the authority to act on behalf of the class and thus have fiduciary responsibilities to the class. If they are not successful and lose the class action suit, the class members will be bound by the judgment. The prerequisites for a class action (which will be taken up in the next section) require that the claims of the class representative(s) must be "typical" of the claims of the class members and that there is "adequacy of representation" by both the class representative(s) and attorney(s).

In a landmark case predating the 1966 amendments to the class action rule, Hansberry v. Lee, the Supreme Court made it clear that there are constitutional due process limitations on the preclusive effect of a class action judgment.

HANSBERRY V. LEE

Supreme Court of the United States, 1940
311 U.S. 32

A non-party is only precluded by res judicata when their interests have been adequately represented, even if the original suit was a class action.

JUSTICE STONE delivered the opinion of the Court.

covenant: WHITES ONLY
It's Settled Res J.

The question is whether the Supreme Court of Illinois, by its adjudication that petitioners in this case are bound by a judgment rendered in an earlier litigation to which they were not parties, has deprived them of the due process of law guaranteed by the Fourteenth Amendment.

[The Hansberrys, who were African American, bought and moved into a home in Chicago in an area covered by a racially restrictive covenant. The area was bounded by 60th and 63rd streets and Cottage Grove and South Park (now Martin Luther King Memorial Drive) and included about 500 homes. In reaction, owners of neighboring homes sued in an Illinois state court to void the sale to the Hansberrys. The Hansberrys defended on the ground that the covenant never became effective because it wasn't signed by 95% of the homeowners in the area, as required by its terms. The trial court found that only 54% of the landowners had signed the agreement.

The trial court nevertheless voided the sale to the Hansberrys and ordered them to move out because it found that they were bound by a decision that the covenant was valid in Burke v. Kleiman, an earlier suit to enforce the covenant in an Illinois state court. That suit was filed at the instance of the Woodlawn Property Owners Association, a neighborhood association, against Kleiman, a white property owner who rented to an African American, and Hall, his African-American tenant. It was brought "on behalf of" all landowners in the area and alleged that the covenant had been signed by the required 95% of the owners. Defendants in the Burke case stipulated that the requisite number of signatures had been obtained and defended on the ground that the covenant should no longer be enforceable due to changed conditions. The court in Burke rejected that defense and held the agreement enforceable.

In Hansberry, the trial court found that it could not reopen the issue because Burke had been a class action that was binding on the Hansberrys' grantor (who, as a property owner, was a member of the class), and Burke had decided that there were enough signatures. The Illinois Supreme

Court, noting that "[i]t cannot be seriously contended that [the *Burke* case] was not properly a representative suit," affirmed. It concluded that the stipulation in *Burke* that 95% had signed, while factually inaccurate, had not been collusive or fraudulent.] — *??? [handwritten]*

W.T.F. ??? [handwritten]

State courts are free to attach such descriptive labels to litigations before them as they may choose and to attribute to them such consequences as they think appropriate under state constitutions and laws, subject only to the requirements of the Constitution of the United States. But when the judgment of a state court, ascribing to the judgment of another court the binding force and effect of res judicata, is challenged for want of due process it becomes the duty of this Court to examine the course of procedure in both litigations to ascertain whether the litigant whose rights have thus been adjudicated has been afforded such notice and opportunity to be heard as are requisite to the due process which the Constitution prescribes.

Res Judicata [handwritten]

It is a principle of general application in Anglo-American jurisprudence that one is not bound by a judgment in personam in a litigation in which he is not designated as a party or to which he has not been made a party by service of process. Pennoyer v. Neff, 95 U.S. 714 (1877). A judgment rendered in such circumstances is not entitled to the full faith and credit which the Constitution and statute of the United States prescribe,* and judicial action enforcing it against the person or property of the absent party is not that due process which the Fifth and Fourteenth Amendments require.

To these general rules there is a recognized exception that, to an extent not precisely defined by judicial opinion, the judgment in a "class" or "representative" suit, to which some members of the class are parties, may bind members of the class or those represented who were not made parties to it.

The class suit was an invention of equity to enable it to proceed to a decree in suits where the number of those interested in the subject of the litigation is so great that their joinder as parties in conformity to the usual rules of procedure is impracticable. Courts are not infrequently called upon to proceed with causes in which the number of those interested in the litigation is so great as to make difficult or impossible the joinder of all because some are not within the jurisdiction or because their whereabouts is unknown or where if all were made parties to the suit its continued abatement by the death of some would prevent or unduly delay a decree. In such cases where the interests of those not joined are of the same class as the interests of those who are, and where it is considered that the latter fairly represent the former in the prosecution of the litigation of the issues in which all have a common interest, the court will proceed to a decree.

---

* See U.S. Const. Art. IV, § 1; 28 U.S.C. § 1738.—Eds.

It is evident that the considerations which may induce a court thus to proceed, despite a technical defect of parties, may differ from those which must be taken into account in determining whether the absent parties are bound by the decree or, if it is adjudged that they are, in ascertaining whether such an adjudication satisfies the requirements of due process and of full faith and credit. Nevertheless there is scope within the framework of the Constitution for holding in appropriate cases that a judgment rendered in a class suit is res judicata as to members of the class who are not formal parties to the suit. Here, as elsewhere, the Fourteenth Amendment does not compel state courts or legislatures to adopt any particular rule for establishing the conclusiveness of judgments in class suits; nor does it compel the adoption of the particular rules thought by this court to be appropriate for the federal courts. With a proper regard for divergent local institutions and interests, this Court is justified in saying that there has been a failure of due process only in those cases where it cannot be said that the procedure adopted, fairly insures the protection of the interests of absent parties who are to be bound by it.

It is familiar doctrine of the federal courts that members of a class not present as parties to the litigation may be bound by the judgment where they are in fact adequately represented by parties who are present, or where they actually participate in the conduct of the litigation in which members of the class are present as parties, or where the interest of the members of the class, some of whom are present as parties, is joint, or where for any other reason the relationship between the parties present and those who are absent is such as legally to entitle the former to stand in judgment for the latter.

In all such cases, so far as it can be said that the members of the class who are present are, by generally recognized rules of law, entitled to stand in judgment for those who are not, we may assume for present purposes that such procedure affords a protection to the parties who are represented though absent, which would satisfy the requirements of due process and full faith and credit. * * * We decide only that the procedure and the course of litigation sustained here by the plea of res judicata do not satisfy these requirements.

The restrictive agreement did not purport to create a joint obligation or liability. If valid and effective its promises were the several obligations of the signers and those claiming under them. The promises ran severally to every other signer. It is plain that in such circumstances all those alleged to be bound by the agreement would not constitute a single class in any litigation brought to enforce it. Those who sought to secure its benefits by enforcing it could not be said to be in the same class with or represent those whose interest was in resisting performance, for the agreement by its terms imposes obligations and confers rights on the owner of each plot of land who signs it. If those who thus seek to secure the benefits of the agreement were rightly regarded by the state Supreme Court as constituting a class, it is evident that those signers or their successors who are interested in challenging the validity of the agreement and resisting its performance are not of the same class in the sense that their interests are identical so that any group who had elected to enforce rights conferred by the agreement could be said to be acting in the interest of any others who were free to deny its obligation.

Because of the dual and potentially conflicting interests of those who are putative parties to the agreement in compelling or resisting its performance, it is impossible to say, solely because they are parties to it, that any two of them are of the same class. Nor without more, and with the due regard for the protection of the rights of absent parties which due process exacts, can some be permitted to stand in judgment for all.

It is one thing to say that some members of a class may represent other members in a litigation where the sole and common interest of the class in the litigation, is either to assert a common right or to challenge an asserted obligation. It is quite another to hold that all those who are free alternatively either to assert rights or to challenge them are of a single class, so that any group merely because it is of the class so constituted, may be deemed adequately to represent any others of the class in litigating their interests in either alternative. Such a selection of representatives for purposes of litigation, whose substantial interests are not necessarily or even probably the same as those whom they are deemed to represent, does not afford that protection to absent parties which due process requires. The doctrine of representation of absent parties in a class suit has not hitherto been thought to go so far. Apart from the opportunities it would afford for the fraudulent and collusive sacrifice of the rights of absent parties, we think that the representation in this case no more satisfies the requirements of due process than a trial by a judicial officer who is in such situation that he may have an interest in the outcome of the litigation in conflict with that of the litigants.

The plaintiffs in the *Burke* case sought to compel performance of the agreement in behalf of themselves and all others similarly situated. They did not designate the defendants in the suit as a class or seek any injunction or other relief against others than the named defendants, and the decree which was entered did not purport to bind others. In seeking to enforce the agreement the plaintiffs in that suit were not representing the petitioners here whose substantial interest is in resisting performance. The defendants in the first suit were not treated by the pleadings or decree as representing others or as foreclosing by their defense the rights of others, and even though nominal defendants, it does not appear that their interest in defeating the contract outweighed their interest in establishing its validity. For a court in this situation to ascribe to either the plaintiffs or defendants the performance of such functions on behalf of petitioners here, is to attribute to them a power that it cannot be said that they had assumed to exercise, and a responsibility which, in view of their dual interests it does not appear that they could rightly discharge.

JUSTICE MCREYNOLDS, JUSTICE ROBERTS and JUSTICE REED concur in the result.

NOTES AND QUESTIONS

1. *Postscript*: Some time after the Supreme Court decided this case, the Hansberrys, reportedly disgusted with racism in this country, moved to Mexico. In 1950 their daughter Lorraine, who had been seven years old when they moved into the house involved in the suit, moved to New York to pursue a career as a writer. In 1958 she published a play entitled "A Raisin in the Sun," in which a central event is the effort of a black family on the South Side of Chicago to move into an all-white area over the objections of the local neighborhood association. The play won the New York Drama Critics Circle Award for 1958–59. Ms. Hansberry died of cancer in 1965, at the age of 34. For more background on the case, see Tidmarsh, The Story of Hansberry: The Foundation for Modern Class Actions, in Civil Procedure Stories 233 (2d ed. 2008); Kamp, The History Behind Hansberry v. Lee, 20 U.C. Davis L. Rev. 481 (1987). In 1948, the Supreme Court held that the Fourteenth Amendment forbade states from enforcing racially restrictive covenants. Shelley v. Kraemer, 334 U.S. 1 (1948).

2. Why should the law ever deputize one person to represent another in litigation? In some instances this is done because a person is incompetent. Cf. Rule 17(c). In general, however, we insist that a person represent her own interest, as Rule 17 emphasizes. The original justification for representative litigation in class actions was, as the Court points out in *Hansberry,* simple necessity. Where those interested in the suit were too numerous to be joined, the court would disregard this "mere technical defect of parties" and proceed with the case. If the requirement that "those interested in the suit" are too numerous to be joined is treated as a "mere technical defect," the way is open to require only, as does the present Rule 23(a)(1), that "the class" is too numerous to be joined—whether or not the potential class members are currently "interested in the suit" or not. What then is the justification for a class action?

3. What is a "class"? The Court says that persons sought to be bound by the agreement would not constitute a single class since some would support enforcement of the covenant and others would oppose it. Should it matter whether the class members conceive themselves to be linked together? Professor Yeazell has traced the origin of the modern class action to medieval group litigation, in which suits by or against groups such as the tenants of a certain village were common. But in medieval cases the group was really that—a functioning social entity—and group litigation merely recognized this social reality. Moreover, there was substantial effort to ensure that the group had actually deputized the person who purported to represent it. See S.

Yeazell, From Medieval Group Litigation to the Modern Class Action (1987). Other countries experimenting with some form of "representative" or "group" actions tend to require a closer tie between the class members, for example, members of a consumer association or an environmental organization. Gidi, Class Actions in Brazil—A Model for Civil Law Countries, 51 Am. J. Comp. L. 311 (2003); Sherman, Group Litigation Under Foreign Legal Systems: Variations and Alternatives to American Class Actions, 52 DePaul L. Rev. 401, 418–424 (2002). The modern class action, by way of contrast, usually agglomerates people who otherwise have no ties to one another. Does this suggest special reasons for worry about the problem of representation?

4.   The Court points out that plaintiffs in *Burke* did not take the precaution of designating the defendants in that case as representatives of a defendant class of homeowners opposed to the enforcement of the covenant. Had they done so, would defendants there have been proper representatives for the Hansberrys? Could the white landlord there have adequately represented the interest of African Americans like the Hansberrys? Would the African-American tenant in that case have been an adequate representative for others, like the Hansberrys, who wanted to buy homes in the area?

Consider how much more difficult it is to identify an adequate representative for a *defendant* class. "[N]amed defendants almost never choose their role as class champion—it is a potentially onerous one thrust upon them by their opponents. * * * But courts must not readily accede to the wishes of named defendants in this area, for to permit them to abdicate so easily would utterly vitiate the effectiveness of the defendant class action as an instrument of correcting widespread illegality." Marcera v. Chinlund, 595 F.2d 1231, 1239 (2d Cir.), vacated on other grounds, 442 U.S. 915 (1979).

5.   Defendants in the *Burke* case stipulated that the 95% signature requirement had been satisfied. Assuming that this was not collusive, but merely an honest mistake, would it show that they were inadequate representatives? Wouldn't a later plaintiff always have some criticism of the unsuccessful prosecution of the earlier case?

6.   The problem of representation results from the courts' insistence that the class action proceed much like an individual lawsuit, with the class representative controlling the case and standing in judgment for the members of the class; hence the focus on the congruence between the class representative's interests and those of the class members. Would it make more sense for the court itself to take control of class actions in order to protect the interests of the class? In some ways, it does. See Rule 23(e) (class action can be settled only with approval of the court). Would it be proper to expand the court's role to make it responsible for the entire development and prosecution of the suit? Cf. Band's Refuse Removal, Inc. v. Borough of Fair Lawn, supra p. 3.

Criticisms of securities fraud class actions led to congressional action in the 1995 Private Securities Litigation Reform Act (PSLRA), 15 U.S.C.A. § 78u–4(a)(3)(B)(i). Recall the discussion of the PSLRA in Chapter 3, supra pp. 160–

177. It directs the initial plaintiff to provide detailed notice about the claims to other investors, inviting them to express an interest in serving as "lead plaintiff." The court will then appoint as lead plaintiff the person "most capable of adequately representing the interests of class members." The court must presume that "the person or group of persons . . . that has the largest financial interest in the relief sought by the class" is best qualified, although the presumption can be rebutted. The lead plaintiff then chooses the class counsel who need not be the attorney(s) who filed the class action. Should this serve as a model for other class actions? What might be the disadvantages in, for example, a consumer or mass tort class action?

Maybe too much hassle to do frequently?

7. Adequacy of representation concerns have generally focused on the adequacy of class counsel and ensuring that the named class representatives will protect the interests of the other members of the class. Rule 23(g), added in 2003, requires the court to appoint class counsel only after scrutinizing her for adequacy, and specifies that class counsel's duty is to "represent the interests of the class." What if those interests diverge from the interests of the class representative? Who should determine what those interests are in cases like *Hansberry*? Sometimes, as in school desegregation litigation, members of the excluded group may favor improvement of their existing facilities over integration into those traditionally used by whites. For discussion of these sorts of problems, see Bell, Serving Two Masters: Integration Ideals and Client Interests in School Desegregation Litigation, 85 Yale L.J. 470 (1976) (describing tension between the goal of integration and parental desires to place more emphasis on educational quality); cf. Rubenstein, Divided We Litigate: Addressing Disputes Among Group Members and Lawyers in Civil Rights Campaigns, 106 Yale L.J. 1623 (1997) (discussing the tension between individualism and group interests).

8. In *Stephenson v. Dow Chemical Co.*, 273 F.3d 249 (2d Cir.2001), aff'd per curiam, 539 U.S. 111 (2003), the Supreme Court affirmed a Second Circuit opinion that allowed two Vietnam War veterans to collaterally attack a class action judgment for inadequate representation. They had been members of a class of service members exposed to Agent Orange in Vietnam. The class action had been settled almost twenty years before, see supra pp. 23–24, but the settlement did not provide for any recovery by persons who, like the plaintiffs, manifested disease after the trust fund had been closed in 1994. Invoking the due process clause, the court found they had not been adequately represented. Does this undermine the finality of class action judgments? This case is considered in more detail, in Chapter 13, infra p. 1271.

2. THE STANDARDS FOR CERTIFICATION

In addition to creating the three categories of class actions set out in subsection (b) (see supra pp. 308–309) the 1966 amendments to Rule 23 established four general prerequisites for class certification—numerosity, commonality, typicality, and adequacy of representation. See Rule 23(a). Every class action must satisfy all four of these prerequisites as well as meeting the criteria for one of the (b)(1), (2), or (3) categories of class action.

A.   Rule 23(b)(2) Class Actions

Skipping

WALTERS V. RENO

United States Court of Appeals, Ninth Circuit, 1998
145 F.3d 1032

Before: GOODWIN, and REINHARDT, Circuit Judges, and KING, SENIOR DISTRICT JUDGE.

REINHARDT, CIRCUIT JUDGE:

* * *

The plaintiffs brought suit against the government on behalf of themselves and similarly situated noncitizens, seeking declaratory and injunctive relief on the ground that the administrative procedures used by the INS to obtain final orders under the document fraud provisions of the Immigration and Naturalization Act of 1990 ("INA" or "the Act") violated their rights to procedural due process. Under § 274C of the Act, 8 U.S.C. § 1324c, the INS may issue an unappealable final order against an alien who has been accused of document fraud if the alien does not request a hearing in writing within 60 days of receiving the notice of intent to fine ("the fine notice") and the notice of rights/waiver ("the rights/waiver notice") forms. Such an order renders the alien deportable and permanently excludable. Deportation is automatic, except in narrowly limited circumstances. If the alien signs a statement waiving his rights with respect to the document fraud charges, including his right to a hearing, the INS will immediately issue an unappealable final order assessing a fine and requiring the alien to cease and desist from his wrongful conduct, but the ultimate result that ordinarily will follow soon thereafter will be the issuance of an order of deportation.

In their complaint, the plaintiffs contend that despite the dramatic immigration consequences for those charged with violating the document fraud provisions of the INA, the forms served on aliens in connection with these charges are dense and written in complex, legal language. The plaintiffs allege that on account of the confusing nature of the forms, aliens in document fraud proceedings are not adequately informed of the steps they must take in order to contest the charges brought against them and thus do not learn how to obtain a hearing on them. Moreover, they allege, they do not learn the true consequences of failing to request that hearing. They also challenge the general procedures by which the forms are presented to them. The plaintiffs moved to certify a class of approximately 4,000 aliens who had been or were subject to final orders, and moved for the entry of a preliminary injunction, summary judgment, a permanent injunction, and an order requiring the INS to reopen each plaintiff's document fraud case and provide hearings if necessary.

In March 1996, Judge Coughenour certified the plaintiffs as a class with the following characteristics:

> All non-citizens who have or will become subject to a final order under § 274C of the Immigration and Naturalization Act because they received notice forms that did not adequately advise them of their rights, of the consequences of waiving their rights or of the consequences of failing to request a hearing.

Under the district court's order, an individual alien can establish his status as a class member by attesting that he did not understand either his rights in the document fraud proceedings or the consequences of waiving his rights. In the same order, Judge Coughenour ruled on summary judgment that the procedures and forms used by the INS in document fraud cases are unconstitutional because they deny aliens their rights to due process of law. The court also granted permanent injunctive relief; the terms of the injunction were to be decided after the parties submitted proposals to the court.

In October 1996, Judge Coughenour entered final judgment in favor of the plaintiffs and granted a permanent injunction requiring the INS to take a variety of actions to remedy the constitutional violations. According to the terms of the injunction, the INS must: (1) revise the two misleading forms (the fine notice and the rights/waiver notice); (2) send notice to possible class members at their last known addresses, and, through a publicity campaign that must include specific attempts to contact all class members inside and outside of the country, publicize the opportunity for class members to reopen their document fraud proceedings; (3) refrain from deporting noncitizens on the basis of § 274C final orders that were entered without a hearing until class members have the opportunity to pursue reopening procedures; (4) reopen § 274C proceedings for each class member who was subject to a § 274C final order, unless the government can show that alien received adequate notice; (5) parole or make other arrangements for class members outside the United States to pursue reopened proceedings; and (6) recharge any alien charged with deficient forms who failed to request a hearing but has not yet been subjected to a final order, unless the government can show that the alien received adequate notice.

* * *

Although there is no question that the United States has extraordinarily broad powers in the area of immigration and border control, it is also well established that aliens facing deportation from this country are entitled to due process rights under the Fifth Amendment. As the Supreme Court has explained on a number of occasions, "once [an] alien gains admission to our country and begins to develop the ties that go with permanent residence his constitutional status changes accordingly." *Landon v. Plasencia,* 459 U.S. 21, 32 (1982). Thus, the government is not free to deport an alien from the United States unless it has first accorded him the most basic procedural protections—notice and a hearing at a meaningful time and in a meaningful manner.[2] The plaintiffs assert that the INS regularly violates these constitutional precepts in the context of document fraud proceedings.

At the heart of this case is the plaintiffs' allegation that the procedures by which INS agents procured waivers of the right to a hearing in document fraud proceedings were constitutionally deficient because the forms used in connection with these proceedings did not adequately inform aliens of their right to a hearing or of the drastic immigration consequences that would ensue if the alien failed to request a hearing. As a result, the aliens' waivers were not made knowingly and voluntarily. These procedures, the plaintiffs contend, have been employed nationwide by the INS in virtually every case in which the government has charged an alien with committing document fraud.

* * *

[A]n alien charged with civil document fraud receives three forms advising him of two hearings. One hearing, he is told—the hearing on the document fraud charges, the consequence for which is stated to be a fine and a cease and desist order—will be held only if the alien submits a written request. The other hearing, the alien is advised—the hearing on the far graver issue whether he will be deported—will be held automatically, without the need for him to do anything. He is also told that at *that* hearing he will be able to respond to the allegations that constitute the basis for the threatened deportation. None of the forms advises the alien that if he fails to request a *separate* hearing on the document fraud charges, the deportation hearing he receives will ordinarily be meaningless, that he will be found deportable and excludable on the ground of document fraud without any further opportunity to challenge that determination, and that his deportation will in most instances be virtually automatic.

Summary Judgment

As a threshold matter, we must determine whether the district court's grant of summary judgment was proper. * * *

The district court concluded that the plaintiffs were entitled to summary judgment because the INS procedures for securing waivers of a hearing on document fraud charges create an unacceptable risk of confusion likely to result in erroneous deportation.

* * *

---

[2] A waiver of either of these basic rights is valid only if the government demonstrates that the alien intentionally relinquished a known right or privilege.

Given the essential facts that determine the outcome in this case—the complexity and ineptness of the forms and the fact that they are designed to provide essential information of constitutional significance to persons of foreign birth—we conclude that the district court properly found that no issues of material fact precluded summary judgment.

Due Process Analysis

According to the government, the district court's legal conclusions regarding the constitutionality of the INS forms are erroneous, and it advances the following arguments in support of this position: (1) the contents of the forms adequately apprise the alien of his rights and the direct consequences of waiving those rights, and due process does not require that forms, such as the waiver of rights form, be in any language other than English; (2) in applying *Mathews v. Eldridge,* 424 U.S. 319 (1976), [supra p. 51 n. 6], the district court erred in calculating the various interests at stake and, as a consequence, misapplied the balancing test; and (3) even if there was a constitutional violation, the plaintiffs failed to demonstrate that any prejudice flowed therefrom.

[The court concludes that the forms "are not only confusing, they are affirmatively misleading."]

The government maintains that the district court erred in evaluating the relevant interests under the calculus established in *Mathews v. Eldridge.* As the *Mathews* balancing test makes clear, whether a particular procedure is sufficient to satisfy due process depends on the circumstances. Thus,

> [i]n evaluating the procedures in any case, the courts must consider the interest at stake for the individual, the risk of an erroneous deprivation of the interest through the procedures used as well as the probable value of additional or different procedural safeguards, and the interest of the government in using the current procedures rather than additional or different procedures.

Id. at 34 (citing *Mathews,* 424 U.S. at 319). We agree with the district court that the relevant factors weigh in favor of altering the document fraud forms.

It is clear that the plaintiffs' interests in this case are significant. *See Plasencia,* 459 U.S. at 34 (noting that the alien's interest in deportation proceedings "is, without question, a weighty one" because "[s]he stands to lose the right 'to stay and live and work in this land of freedom.' ") (quoting *Bridges v. Wixon,* 326 U.S. 135, 154 (1945)). The government's interests in the administration of its immigration laws and in preventing document fraud are likewise considerable. Striking the proper balance between these interests can be achieved by adopting procedures that reduce the risk of erroneous deprivation without imposing an undue burden on the government.

Requiring the government to alter slightly its procedures in document fraud proceedings will achieve the desired effect—additional safeguards—without visiting upon it any inordinate hardship. Specifically, it is possible to reduce the risk of erroneous deprivation (*i.e.,* erroneous deportation) by ensuring that aliens facing charges of document fraud are adequately notified that they *must* request a separate hearing to contest those charges and that their failure to do so will ordinarily foreclose their ability to challenge their status as deportable aliens. Providing constitutionally adequate notice requires only minor changes in the content of the forms themselves and equally slight adaptations in the INS's method of presenting the forms. Requiring the INS to ensure that there are no significant inconsistencies in the written language of forms that affect whether or not an alien will be rendered deportable and permanently excludable, and requiring minor modifications to the written content of the forms will not be unduly burdensome, particularly in light of the benefits of such safeguards.

Prejudice

* * *

When it is necessary to demonstrate prejudice as a result of a constitutional violation, the alien must show that the inadequate procedures occurred "in a manner so as potentially to affect the outcome of the proceedings." *Hartooni v. INS,* 21 F.3d 336, 340 (9th Cir.1994); *see also United States v. Jimenez-Marmolejo,* 104 F.3d 1083, 1086 (9th Cir.1996) (holding that in order to show prejudice, an alien need not prove that he would not have been deported, just that he had "plausible grounds for relief"). Ordinarily, there must be plausible scenarios in which the outcome of the proceedings would have been different, absent the constitutional violation.

Here, the district court determined that at least two class plaintiffs had demonstrated that the lack of adequate notice as to their document fraud proceedings potentially affected the outcome of their document fraud proceedings. In the cases of Ninfa Guerrero de Adames and Antonio Santana-Alvarez, the district court found that each had a viable legal defense to the charges that had been brought against them. With respect to Adames, the district court found that she could have made a persuasive argument that the document fraud charges, as applied to her, violated the prohibition against ex post facto laws. In Santana-Alvarez's case, the district court found that he had a strong legal argument that his conduct did not constitute a violation of the document fraud laws. There is no evidence to suggest that these findings are erroneous. The district court determined that if Adames and Santana-Alvarez had not waived their right to a hearing, they might have been able to defend against the charges successfully. Accordingly, the district court concluded that the lack of notice regarding the right to a hearing potentially affected the outcome of the proceedings.

We agree with the district court that Adames and Santana-Alvarez are not precluded from showing prejudice simply because they admitted, while testifying under grants of immunity, that they had used fraudulent immigration documents. It is sufficient for purposes of showing prejudice that the plaintiffs have demonstrated *plausible* grounds for relief. The potential legal defenses identified by the district court satisfy this standard.

Class Certification

Rule 23(a) provides that a court should certify a class only if the following prerequisites are met: (1) the class is too numerous, making joinder of the parties impracticable; (2) common questions of law or fact exist among the class members; (3) the claims of the class representatives are typical of the claims of the class; and (4) the class representatives will adequately represent the interest of the class. In addition to satisfying the mandatory prerequisites in Rule 23(a), the potential class members must also demonstrate that they meet at least one of the alternative requirements under Rule 23(b). In this case, the government disputes the existence of two of these requirements—commonality and adequacy of representation. Additionally, the government challenges the district court's certification of the class under Rule 23(b)(2).

Commonality

Requiring there to be common questions of law or fact prior to certifying a class serves chiefly two purposes: (1) ensuring that absentee members are fairly and adequately represented; and (2) ensuring practical and efficient case management. In this case, each class member raises the same constitutional question: whether the nationwide procedures used by INS in document fraud proceedings sufficiently apprise aliens of their constitutional right to a hearing, thereby satisfying the notice component of due process.

The government maintains that the commonality requirement is lacking because the actual experiences of the class members are not sufficiently similar. Some individual INS agents and branch offices, for example, have consistently disregarded the Agency's official policy regarding the use of forms in § 274C proceedings and have instituted supplemental explanations of the potential immigration consequences. Therefore, some aliens who were subject to document fraud charges may have received adequate notice in spite of the constitutionally deficient official procedures.

To support its contention that the class members' claims lack commonality, the government points to terms of the injunction that provide for individualized proceedings. Specifically, it relies on the portions of the injunction providing the government with the opportunity to demonstrate that an individual class member "received constitutionally adequate notice despite having received the section 274C notice forms that the Court has found defective." According to the government, these proceedings demonstrate that there is no common factual or legal basis for the class claims; if commonality existed, there would be no need for such individualized procedures.

We think the government misses the point. There is nothing wrong with the district court's presumption that the INS actually employed its constitutionally deficient policies and procedures. The government made no showing in the district court that its procedures were modified by more than just a few agents and branch offices. Thus, it is reasonable to presume that class members involved in document fraud proceedings did not receive due process because of the inadequate forms. Moreover, as the district court observed, it would be "a twisted result" to permit an administrative agency to avoid nationwide litigation that challenges the constitutionality of its general practices simply by pointing to minor variations in procedure among branch offices and individual INS agents, particularly because the variations were designed to avoid the precise constitutional inadequacies identified by the plaintiffs in this action.

The government further argues that commonality is nonexistent on account of factual distinctions in the class members' underlying claims. Differences among the class members with respect to the merits of their actual document fraud cases, however, are simply insufficient to defeat the propriety of class certification. What makes the plaintiffs' claims suitable for a class action is the common allegation that the INS's procedures provide insufficient notice. *See Forbush v. J.C. Penney Co., Inc.,* 994 F.2d 1101, 1106 (5th Cir.1993) (noting that the need for subsequent individual proceedings, even complex ones, "does not supply a basis for concluding that [the named plaintiff] has not met the commonality requirement").

Adequacy of Representation

Requiring the claims of the class representatives to be adequately representative of the class as a whole ensures that the interests of absent class members are adequately protected. *Hansberry v. Lee,* 311 U.S. 32, 42 (1940). Whether the class representatives satisfy the adequacy requirement depends on "the qualifications of counsel for the representatives, an absence of antagonism, a sharing of interests between representatives and absentees, and the unlikelihood that the suit is collusive." Here, the district court specifically found that the attorneys for the class representatives were well qualified and that the class representatives themselves were adequate because they were not antagonistic to the interests of the class and were "interested and involved in obtaining relief."

In challenging the adequacy of the class representatives, the government primarily relies on the fact that some of the named plaintiffs have admitted under grants of immunity that they committed document fraud. According to the government, these admissions preclude the possibility that these representative class members would have prevailed at a hearing on their document fraud charges, and because some of the class representatives cannot demonstrate prejudice—which, as we noted above, the parties assume to be a prerequisite to a finding of a due process violation—the class representatives are hindered in their ability to represent the class before the district court.

We find no merit in the government's position. Once again, the government erroneously emphasizes factual differences in the merits of the underlying document fraud charges. Such differences have no bearing on the class representatives' abilities to pursue the class claims vigorously and represent the interests of the absentee class members. Moreover, we note that the government's argument is particularly weak in light of the fact that the class representatives have been so successful in their efforts to obtain relief for the entire class.

Rule 23(b)(2) Certification

Related to the commonality issue is the government's challenge to the district court's finding that the class was properly certified pursuant to Rule 23(b)(2). Certification under Rule 23(b)(2) is appropriate in cases in which

> the party opposing the class has acted or refused to act on grounds generally applicable to the class, thereby making appropriate final injunctive relief or corresponding declaratory relief with respect to the class as a whole.*

Fed.R.Civ.P. 23(b)(2). Here, the district court found certification proper because the plaintiffs claimed that the INS's practices in document fraud proceedings were violative of due process. The forms and procedures in question were used by the INS in document fraud cases on a nationwide basis. Further, the plaintiffs sought injunctive, not monetary relief.

With respect to certification under Rule 23(b)(2), the government's primary objection appears to be that certifying this class does not further the purposes of Rule 23. Again, the government points to the individual proceedings that will result from the district court's injunction as evidence that judicial efficiency will actually be undermined by the class action. While the government correctly observes that numerous individual administrative proceedings may flow from the district court's decision, it fails to acknowledge that the district court's decision eliminates the need for individual litigation regarding the constitutionality of INS's official forms and procedures. Absent a class action decision, individual aliens

---

*   This rule language has been revised slightly.—Eds.

across the country could file complaints against the INS in federal court, each of them raising precisely the same legal challenge to the constitutionality of the § 274C forms. Contrary to the government's assertion, therefore, class certification in this case is entirely proper in light of the general purposes of Rule 23, avoiding duplicative litigation.

We note that with respect to 23(b)(2) in particular, the government's dogged focus on the factual differences among the class members appears to demonstrate a fundamental misunderstanding of the rule. Although common issues must predominate for class certification under Rule 23(b)(3), no such requirement exists under 23(b)(2). It is sufficient if class members complain of a pattern or practice that is generally applicable to the class as a whole. Even if some class members have not been injured by the challenged practice, a class may nevertheless be appropriate. *See* 7A Charles Alan Wright, Arthur R. Miller & Mary Kay Kane, *Federal Practice & Procedure* § 1775 (2d ed. 1986) ("All the class members need not be aggrieved by or desire to challenge the defendant's conduct in order for some of them to seek relief under Rule 23(b)(2)."); *see also Adamson v. Bowen,* 855 F.2d 668, 676 (10th Cir.1988) (emphasizing that although "the claims of individual class members may differ factually," certification under Rule 23(b)(2) is a proper vehicle for challenging "a common policy").

Moreover, the claims raised by the plaintiffs in this action are precisely the sorts of claims that Rule 23(b)(2) was designed to facilitate. As the Advisory Committee Notes explain, 23(b)(2) was adopted in order to permit the prosecution of civil rights actions.

According to the government, even if we uphold the district court's rulings with respect to the constitutional claims and class certification, we should nonetheless find that the district court erred in granting permanent injunctive relief.

[The court finds that injunctive relief is appropriate as it had determined that the forms were constitutionally defective (satisfying the "likelihood of success" requirement), monetary or other legal remedies were inadequate, and plaintiffs would suffer irreparable injury if the procedures were continued.]

Once a class has been certified and a constitutional violation has been ascertained, the district court retains broad discretion in fashioning a remedy. We review the terms of the district court's injunction for abuse of discretion. Here, the injunction serves a narrow purpose and is carefully tailored to achieve that goal. The order is designed to allow the members of the class to reopen their document fraud and deportation proceedings, thereby remedying the lack of adequate notice.

At the outset of its attack on the terms of the injunction, the government objects to the district court's issuing an injunction that provides classwide relief. Citing *Lewis v. Casey,* 518 U.S. 343 (1996), the government maintains that the systemwide relief mandated by the injunction is unwarranted because the plaintiffs only demonstrated that the constitutional violation prejudiced a few individuals. In *Lewis,* the Supreme Court reversed as overly broad an injunction that essentially called for an overhaul of law libraries in the Arizona prison system pursuant to *Bounds v. Smith,* 430 U.S. 817 (1977). Because there were only two instances in which prisoners were hindered from pursuing their legal claims due to the inadequacy of the prison law libraries, the Supreme Court held that systemwide relief was inappropriate.

In *Lewis,* the constitutional violation was not the violation of the right to adequate law libraries in prisons, but was instead the deprivation of the right of meaningful access to the courts. There was no showing that more than two prisoners suffered deprivation of that constitutional right and thus there was no showing of the need for systemwide relief. By contrast, the constitutional violation in this case is the inadequate notice itself. Thus, once the district court determined that the constitutionally insufficient forms and procedures were employed by the INS on a *systemwide* basis, the court had also determined systemwide injury. Every alien who received the fine notice and the rights/waiver notice forms suffered an injury because he did not receive the notice to which he was constitutionally entitled. Moreover, the lack of notice directly resulted in the failure of the class members to obtain constitutionally required hearings—a further constitutional injury.

* * *

[W]e uphold the district court's grant of summary judgment and, with one minor exception, the terms of its injunction. We remand so that the district court may modify its order granting permanent injunctive relief in accordance with this opinion and may take whatever other action it ma deem appropriate.

NOTES AND QUESTIONS

1.   Walters v. Reno was a (b)(2) class action seeking only injunctive relief. The Advisory Committee notes recognized that cases might be brought for injunctive or declaratory relief in which damages would also be recoverable, stating that (b)(2) "does not extend to cases in which the appropriate final relief relates exclusively or predominantly to money damages." Why is it important to determine whether a claim for damages is inconsistent with a (b)(2) class? Why shouldn't plaintiffs in such cases simply seek certification of a (b)(3) class, which was created for seeking damages? The reason is that there are two additional requirements for a (b)(3) class—that common questions *"predominate"* and that class treatment is *"superior"* to other methods of resolving the dispute (these will be considered in connection with the next case). Note the comment in Walters v. Reno that there is no "predominance" requirement for a (b)(2) class. As courts in recent years have often applied

these requirements to refuse to certify a class under (b)(3), plaintiffs' attorneys have tried to fit their cases under (b)(2). Some courts allowed certification of "hybrid" class actions—a (b)(2) class for injunctive relief, and then a (b)(3) class for damages which might require severing off certain individual issues for individual trials. *Allison* rejected such "hybrid" classes. The Supreme Court's 2011 *Wal-Mart* decision (infra pp. 340–343) followed this reasoning.

2.   A *Rule 23(b)(1) class action* is also mandatory, based on the necessity for a class action to avert unfairness that could result from multiple individual suits. In a (b)(1)(A) class, the unfairness is to the party opposing the class who may be subjected to "inconsistent or varying adjudications" resulting in "incompatible standards" if there were individual suits by class members. This refers to the opposing party's uncertainty as to what standards it must follow in its future conduct, as in the risk of being subjected to incompatible affirmative relief (for example, a defendant corporation being subjected to differing injunctions as to how it must treat various classes of stockholders). But this does not encompass the risk that individual suits by class members might result in different adjudications as to *damages*, see Alexander Grant & Co. v. McAlister, 116 F.R.D. 583 (S.D. Ohio 1987), and so, for example, it would not justify a mandatory class of bus passengers suing the bus company for injuries from the same accident.

3.   A *Rule 23(b)(1)(B) class action*, which is also mandatory without a right to opt out, is based on unfairness to missing class members if there were individual suits by class members. It applies if individual adjudications, "as a practical matter, would be dispositive of the interests of the other members not parties to the individual adjudications or would substantially impair or impede their ability to protect their interests." The paradigm is where individual suits could exhaust a "limited fund" to which all class members have a claim, and thus, as a practical matter, would impair the missing class members' rights. Cf. State Farm Fire & Casualty Co. v. Tashire, supra p.287 (insurance proceeds insufficient to pay all accident victims).

4.   The denial of a right to opt out in 23(b)(1) and (2) class actions where monetary relief is also sought, raises possible constitutional problems. Phillips Petroleum Co. v. Shutts, 472 U.S. 797 (1985), suggested that due process may require that "an absent plaintiff be provided with an opportunity to remove himself from the class by executing and returning an 'opt out' or 'request for exclusion' form to the court," if monetary claims are involved. However, the Supreme Court has not decided the issue. A 2003 amendment to Rule 23 (c)(2)(A) allows a judge to order that notice be given to individual class members in (b)(1) and (b)(2) class actions, which one might expect when the judge feels due process so requires.

5.   The numerosity of the class was not challenged in *Walters*. The test for numerosity is whether "the class is so numerous that joinder of all members is impracticable." Because there is no mystical number at which the numerosity requirement is established, courts have found this element satisfied when the putative class consists of as few as 25 to 40 class members. See Markham v. White, 171 F.R.D. 217, 221 (N.D.Ill.1997) (35–40 class

members); Hendricks-Robinson v. Excel Corp., 164 F.R.D. 667, 671 (C.D.Ill.1996) (38 class members); Riordan v. Smith Barney, 113 F.R.D. 60, 62 (N.D.Ill.1986) (29 class members). However, numerosity was found lacking in State of Utah v. American Pipe & Const. Co., 49 F.R.D. 17 (C.D.Cal.1969), where there were 350 potential class numbers. Courts look to such factors as the relative difficulties of joinder versus class treatment, whether individual joinder might still be accompanied by representation by a single attorney and identical pleadings, and the geographical location of the potential plaintiffs.

B.   Rule 23(b)(3) Class Actions

Rule 23(b)(3) was added in 1966, and "unlike the other categories, a (b)(3) class action is for monetary damages, and so there was now money to be had, providing new entrepreneurial incentives for the plaintiffs' bar." Sherman, Consumer Class Actions: Who Are the Real Winners?, 56 Maine L. Rev. 223, 224 (2004). A high percentage of class actions today are brought under (b)(3) for a broad spectrum of product liability, commercial, environmental, and consumer claims under state laws and such federal causes of action as antitrust, securities fraud, and civil rights. The advisory committee had commented that mass torts are inappropriate for class certification. Advisory Committee Notes to Amendments to Rule 23, 39 F.R.D. 69, 103 (1966).

BUTLER v. SEARS, ROEBUCK AND CO.

United States Court of Appeals, Seventh Circuit. 2012
702 F.3d 359

Before POSNER, RIPPE, HAMILTON, CIRCUIT JUDGES.

POSNER, CIRCUIT JUDGE.

The parties to this class action suit, which is based on the warranty laws of six states, petitioned us to review separate orders by the district court ruling on motions for class certification filed by the plaintiffs. Fed.R.Civ.P. 23(f). The suit is really two class actions because the classes have different members and different claims, and therefore they should have been severed, though both arise from alleged defects in Kenmore-brand Sears washing machines sold in overlapping periods beginning in 2001 and 2004. One class action complains of a defect that causes mold (the "mold claim"), the other of a defect that stops the machine inopportunely (the "control unit claim"). The district court denied certification of the class complaining about the defect that causes mold and granted certification of the class complaining about the defect that causes the sudden stoppage. The denial of certification of the mold class precipitated the petition for review by the plaintiffs who are complaining about the mold, while the grant of certification to the plaintiffs (a different set of named plaintiffs) complaining about the stoppage precipitated Sears's petition for review.

We have accepted the appeals in order to clarify the concept of "predominance" in class action litigation. Rule 23(b)(3) conditions the maintenance of a class action on a finding by the district court "that the questions of fact or law common to class members predominate over any questions affecting only individual members." If there are no common questions or only common questions, the issue of predominance is automatically resolved. Any other case requires "weighing" unweighted factors, which is the kind of subjective determination that usually—including the determination whether to certify a class—is left to the district court, subject to light appellate review.

The mold claim pertains to all Kenmore-brand frontloading "high efficiency" washing machines manufactured by Whirlpool Corporation and sold by Sears since 2001. The claim is that because of the low volume of water used in these machines and the low temperature of the water, compared to the volume and temperature of the water in the traditional top-loading machine, they don't clean themselves adequately and as a result biofilm—a mass of microbes—forms in the machine's drum (where the washing occurs) and creates mold, which emits bad odors. Traditional household cleaners do not eliminate the biofilm, the mold, or the odors. Roughly 200,000 of these Kenmore-brand machines are sold each year and there have been many thousands of complaints of bad odors by the owners. Sears contended that Whirlpool (which remember is the actual manufacturer of the washing machines, not Sears) made a number of design modifications as a result of which different models are differently defective and some perhaps not at all, and therefore common questions of fact concerning the mold problem and its consequences do not predominate over individual questions of fact. The judge accepted this argument; it is the ground on which she denied the motion to certify the mold class.

Although Sears contends that during the period covered by the complaint it sold 27 different Kenmore-brand models, Whirlpool made only five design changes that relate to mold. The basic question in the litigation—were the machines defective in permitting mold to accumulate and generate noxious odors is common to the entire mold class, although the answer may vary with the differences in design. The individual questions are the amount of damages owed particular class members (the owners of the washing machines).

Predominance is a question of efficiency. Is it more efficient, in terms both of economy of judicial resources and of the expense of litigation to the parties, to decide some issues on a class basis or all issues in separate trials? A class action is the more efficient procedure for determining liability and damages in a case such as this, involving a defect that may have imposed costs on tens of thousands of consumers yet not a cost to any one of them large enough to justify the expense of an individual suit. If necessary a determination of liability could be followed by individual hearings to determine the damages sustained by each class member (probably capped at the cost of replacing a defective washing machine—there doesn't seem to be a claim that the odors caused an illness that might support a claim for products liability as distinct from one for breach of warranty). But probably the parties would agree on a schedule of damages based on the cost of fixing or replacing class members' mold-contaminated washing machines. The class action procedure would be efficient not only in cost, but also in efficacy, if we are right that the stakes in an individual case would be too small to justify the expense of suing, in which event denial of class certification would preclude any relief.

Sears argues that most members of the plaintiff class did not experience a mold problem. But if so that is an argument not for refusing to certify the class but for certifying it and then entering a judgment that will largely exonerate Sears—a course it should welcome, as all class members who had not opted out of the class action would be bound by the judgment.

In two states [California and Illinois], or possibly three [Texas] of the six states in which members of the class reside, a defective product can be the subject of a successful suit for breach of warranty even if the defect has not yet caused any harm. If, as appears to be the case, the defect in a Kenmore-brand washing machine can precipitate a mold problem at any time, the defect is an expected harm, just as having symptomless high blood pressure creates harm in the form of an abnormally high risk of stroke. A person who feels fine, despite having high blood pressure, and will continue feeling fine until he has a stroke or heart attack, would expect compensation for an unlawful act that had caused his high blood pressure even though he has yet to suffer the consequences. Every class member who claims an odor problem will have to prove odor in order to obtain damages, but class members who have not yet encountered odor can still obtain damages for breach of warranty, where state law allows such relief—relief for an expected rather than for only a realized harm from a product defect covered by an express or implied warranty.

Sears does not contend that any of Whirlpool's design changes eliminated the odor problem but only that they reduced its incidence or gravity. The number of buyers of each design of the Kenmore-brand machine who encountered mold would have been large even if those who bought later in the product cycle were less likely to encounter the problem. Should it turn out as the litigation progresses that there are large differences in the mold defect among the five differently designed washing machines, the judge may wish to create subclasses; but that possibility is not an obstacle to certification of a single mold class at this juncture.

Sears argues inconsequently that it did not know about the defects in all the different models. But liability for breach of warranty is strict. Sears may be able by means of a suit for contribution or indemnity to shift the cost of any damages it incurs in the present case to Whirlpool, but that is not a defense to liability. Sears also makes arguments that were not considered by the district court, such as that mold problems may reflect how the owner of a washing machine uses it. That would be a defense of mishandling to the charge of breach of warranty. Sears offers no details.

The Sixth Circuit recently upheld the certification of a single mold class in a case, identical to this one (except that it did not involve the other claim in this case, the control unit claim), against Whirlpool. *In re Whirlpool Corp. Front-Loading Washer Products Liability Litigation,* 678 F.3d 409 (6th Cir.2012). For us to uphold the district court's refusal to certify such a class would be to create an intercircuit conflict—and a gratuitous one, because, as should be apparent from the preceding discussion, we agree with the Sixth Circuit's decision.

We turn to Sears's appeal from the certification of a class of buyers of Kenmore-brand washing machines who incurred a harm because of the defective control unit. Each washing machine has a computer device that gives instructions to the machine's moving parts. This "central control unit" consists of circuit boards that are soldered together. In 2004 a company called Bitron that supplied the central control units in the Kenmore-brand washing machines altered its manufacturing process in a way that inadvertently damaged the layer of solder, causing some of the control units mistakenly to "believe" that a serious error had occurred and therefore to order the machine to shut down even though nothing was the matter with it. Sears is alleged to have known about the problem but to have charged each owner of a defective machine hundreds of dollars to repair the central control unit. The defect was corrected in 2005 but Sears continued to ship machines containing the earlier-manufactured, defective control units.

The principal issue is whether the control unit was indeed defective. The only individual issues—issues found in virtually every class action in which damages are sought—concern the amount of harm to particular class members. It is more efficient for the question whether the washing machines were defective—the question common to all class members—to be resolved in a single proceeding than for it to be litigated separately in hundreds of different trials, though, were that approach taken, at some point principles of res judicata or collateral estoppel would resolve the common issue for the remaining cases.

Again the district court will want to consider whether to create different subclasses of the control unit class for the different states. That should depend on whether there are big enough differences among the relevant laws of those states to make it impossible to draft a single, coherent set of jury instructions should the case ever go to trial before a jury.

To summarize, the denial of class certification regarding the mold claim is reversed and the grant of class certification regarding the control unit claim is affirmed.

NOTES AND QUESTIONS

1. On *certiorari*, the Supreme Court vacated the class certification in *Butler* and remanded to the Seventh Circuit for reconsideration in light of a recent Court decision. On remand, the Seventh Circuit, in another opinion by Judge Posner, adhered to its previous decision. 727 F.3d 796 (2013).

2. How did the *Butler* opinion deal with the fact that damages are individualized issues that require individual determinations as to each class member? There is always a question in cases seeking damages as to whether having to try individual damages separately as to each class member obviates the efficiency that can be accorded by a class action. Bifurcation has long been adopted by courts to separate issues that go to liability from individualized issues as to damages. In complex cases, courts have moved beyond liability/damages bifurcation to order separate trials of segmented issues as to both liability and damages (for example, the BP Oil Spill Litigation, which involved multiple defendants and tens of thousands of claimants based on a number of different causes of action in tort, statutes, and maritime law). In class actions there is authority under Rule 23(c)(4) to certify classes "with respect to particular issues," often referred to as "issues classes." The result can be "phased trials" which are an extension of bifurcation by dividing the presentation of a case into separate phases that might be tried at different times with intervals between them so the parties can prepare for the next phase.

Judge Posner said "if necessary a determination of liability could be followed by individual hearings to determine the damages sustained by each class member." Some district court judges have conducted individual or small group trials of class members as to their damages, but increasingly cases have instead allowed classwide evidence as to damages that can be extrapolated to each individual class member. Judge Posner commented that damages could "probably [be] capped at the cost of replacing a defective washing machine— there doesn't seem to be a claim that the odors caused an illness that might support a claim for products liability as distinct from one for breach of warranty)." He also said that "probably the parties would agree on a schedule of damages based on the cost of fixing or replacing class members' mold-contaminated washing machines," which is a classic way to determine damages on a classwide basis.

3. The contours of the predominance requirement have not been exactly established by the courts. "Unfortunately, Rule 23(b)(3) does not specify precisely what the word "predominate" means, and the case law does not provide any sort of checklist test for determining the sufficiency of the common questions necessary to comply with the rule. Given that the "nature of the evidence that will suffice to resolve a question determines whether the question is common or individual," Nolen, "Predominance and Superiority," in

American Bar Association *A Practitioner's Guide to Class Actions* Chapter 3, E, p. 87 (2d ed. 2017).

4.   Other federal circuit courts have not been as accommodating to the "predominance" requirement as was *Butler*. Various circuit courts have taken different approaches to the standard for determining whether the predominance of common questions requirement is satisfied. *See, e.g.,* Sacred Heart Health Systems, Inc. v. Humana Military Healthcare Services, Inc., 601 F.3d 1159 (11th Cir. 2010) ("Whether an issue predominates can only be determined after considering what value the resolution of the class-wide issue will have in each class member's underlying cause of action." Common issues of fact and law predominate if they " 'have a *direct impact* on every class member's effort to establish liability' *that is more substantial than the impact of individualized issues* in resolving the claim or claims of each class member."); CGC Holding Co. LLC v. Broad & Cassel, 773 F.3d 1078 (10th Cir. 2014) (predominance prong asks whether the common, aggregation-enabling issues in the case are more prevalent or important than the non-common, aggregation-defeating, individual issues).

CONSUMER CLASS ACTIONS

Nationwide consumer class actions would seem to be efficient, as the *Butler* case finds, when based on an identical misrepresentation or defect in a product or service. Consumer suits are often based on state consumer protection statutes, a number of which do not require "reliance" as do common law fraud or misrepresentation. Although many states' consumer protection statutes are quite similar, differences may prevent a nationwide class action (although a small selective group of state statutes as subclasses can sometimes succeed). A Ninth Circuit decision, Mazza v. American Honda Motor Co., 666 F.3d 581 (9th Cir. 2012), could further limit the availability of consumer class actions with class members' different states. The court held that a nationwide class of consumers could not be certified under the California Unfair Competition Law, False Advertising Law, and Consumer Legal Remedies Act because it would impair other states' interests. In In re Hyundai and Kia Fuel Economy Litig., 881 F.3d 679 (9th Cir. 2018), the court rejected certification for purposes of settlement.

State-law causes of action for fraud and misrepresentation generally require the plaintiff to prove reliance. Recall Insolia v. Philip Morris, Inc., supra p. 261. Thus even if common misrepresentations were made to the class members, proof of reliance normally requires individualized evidence which could predominate over evidence as to common issues. In federal securities fraud cases, the Supreme Court adopted a "fraud on the market" theory that "where materially misleading statements have been disseminated into an impersonal, well-developed market for securities, the reliance of individual plaintiffs on the integrity of the market may be presumed." Basic Inc. v. Levinson, 485 U.S. 224, 248 (1988). Some courts have been willing to presume reliance in situations other than where there is a regulated market like the stock exchange. See Shores v. Sklar, 647 F.2d 462 (5th Cir.1981) (reliance is presumed where the misrepresentations at issue arise from "material" omissions); cf. Affiliated Ute Citizens v. United States, 406 U.S. 128 (1972) (when an omission is involved, individualized proof of reliance is not required if the omission is material). However, individual proof of reliance is still required in many states in common-law fraud cases, generally preventing common issues from predominating so as to allow class certification.

Because reliance is required for an action in fraud in many states, consumer class actions are often based instead on a contract theory, i.e., that the buyer did not receive the "benefit of the bargain" which he was promised (for example, a product without defects or an insurance policy without unauthorized additional premiums or charges). Another approach is to sue under a state's unfair, deceptive trade practices, or consumer protection statute, which, in many cases, do not require proof of individual reliance on misrepresentations.

Consumer class actions can be "negative value" cases, that is, often alleging that consumers have lost small amounts of money due to the misrepresentations of the seller or the defectiveness of the product are a paradigm for a "negative value" case. No one could justify the costs of litigation to sue individually, or could even find a lawyer to take the case on a contingency, without the prospect of recovering a fee based on the benefit achieved for a class. Consumer suits have been filed against manufacturers and retailers of products and against such service industries as banks, insurers, health care providers, and telephone/communications companies. If based on a claim of misrepresentations, when the same misrepresentations have been made to all class members, as in a printed prospectus or advertisement, evidence of the wrongful conduct can often be presented on a classwide basis, and common questions may predominate. Even when misrepresentations to class members are not uniform, a common policy or course of fraudulent conduct may still satisfy commonality. Recall Walters v. Reno, supra p. 318 As Judge Posner noticed, about the time that *Butler* was decided, the Sixth Circuit upheld the certification of a mold class in a case identical to *Butler*, In re Whirlpool Front-Loaded Washers Product Liability Litigation, 678 F.3d 409 (6th Cir. 2012). Whirlpool argued that commonality could not be met because the washers were built over a period of years on twenty-one different models and consumer laundry habits vary widely by household. The 6th Circuit found that "common questions predominate over individual ones and that the class action mechanism is the superior method to resolve these claims fairly and efficiently. This is especially true since class members are not likely to file individual actions because the cost of litigation would dwarf any potential recovery." *Id.* at 419. The opinion cited Amchem Products, Inc. v. Windsor, 521 U.S, 581, 617(1997), which noted that in drafting Rule 23(b)(3), "the Advisory Committee had dominantly in mind vindication of 'the rights of groups of people who individually would be without effective strength to bring their opponents into court at all');. The 6th Circuit concluded that whether design defects in the [washers] proximately caused mold or mildew to grow and whether Whirlpool adequately warned consumers about the propensity for mold growth are liability issues common to the plaintiff class. These issues are capable of classwide resolution because they are central to the validity of each plaintiff's legal claims and they will generate common answers likely to drive the resolution of the lawsuit."

But see Andrews v. American Tel. & Tel. Co., 95 F.3d 1014, 1023 (11th Cir.1996)(a common policy of failure to monitor fraudulent use of an 800 number found insufficient to establish predominance of common issues because "as a practical matter, the resolution of this overarching common issue breaks down into an unmanageable variety of individual legal and factual issues").

Consumer class actions are often criticized for resulting in only small recoveries for class members and large fees for the attorneys. Defenders of the class action reply that the objective of class actions is not only compensation, but also deterrence and disgorgement of wrongful profits. In most "negative value" cases, where the expected recovery is less than the cost of litigation, wrongdoers might never have to answer for their conduct if a class action were not available. However, such deterrence is obtained at the cost of providing handsome incentives to lawyers to finance and litigate class actions. "For good or for bad, Americans have rejected the kind of broad governmental regulation of business that is often found in European countries. The American preference for market approaches results in an opportunity for litigation fueled by entrepreneurial lawyers to enforce laws, regulations, and standards." Sherman, Consumer Class Actions: Who Are the Real Winners?, 56 Maine L. Rev. 223, 231–32 (2004). A Rand Corporation report on class actions commented:

> The key public policy question is whether the entrepreneurial behavior of private attorneys produces litigation that is socially beneficial. Whereas *public* attorneys general may be reluctant to bring meritorious suits because of financial or political constraints, *private* attorneys general may be too willing to bring nonmeritorious suits if these suits produce generous financial rewards for them.

D. Hensler et al., Class Action Dilemmas: Pursuing Public Goals for Private Gain 72 (Rand Inst. for Civil Justice 2000).

"Coupon settlements," in which class members are awarded coupons that can be reclaimed for services or products of the defendant rather than cash, became a controversial topic in the 1990s. For example, in In re General Motors Corp. Pickup Truck Fuel Tank Prod. Liabil. Litig., 55 F.3d 768 (3d Cir.1995), the class alleged that pickup trucks sold by defendant were defective because they had side-mounted gas tanks that might burst into flame in a crash. The district court approved a settlement giving class members a nontransferable $1,000 discount certificate that could be used within 15 months to buy a new G.M. truck or van, or exchanged for a $500 discount certificate that could be transferred to somebody who wanted to buy such a G.M. product. Class counsel were to be paid $9.5 million by G.M. Objectors challenged the settlement as inadequate for class members and argued that it should not be approved under Rule 23(e). The court of appeals agreed, finding the settlement to be "a sophisticated GM marketing program." There was reason to doubt that many class members would want to use the certificate within the allowed 15-month period. The option of selling a coupon was hamstrung by the delay involved in exchanging the original $1,000 certificate for the $500 transferable one, and there was no indication that there would be a market for the $500 certificate either.

A judge, in approving a class settlement, must scrutinize carefully the fairness of such settlements. Only when the defendant is on the verge of bankruptcy and a coupon is the only reasonable way to get any value for class members may coupon settlements be appropriate. The Class Action Fairness Act of 2005 permits coupon settlements only after a hearing and a court finding that the settlement is "fair, reasonable and adequate for class members." 28 U.S.C.A. § 1712(e). It also provides that "the portion of an attorney's fee award to class counsel that is attributable to the award of coupons shall be based on the value to class members of the coupons that are redeemed." 28 U.S.C.A. § 1712(b).

MASS TORT CLASS ACTIONS

A mass tort involves a large number of individuals asserting claims for injuries arising out of the same use of a product, environmental condition, or conduct caused by the same defendant(s). Examples are mass accidents (like a plane crash or collapse of a building), environmental disasters (like the escape of toxic chemicals into the air or water or failures in connection with a natural disaster), or the malfunction of a defective product (like prescription drugs, autos, or construction materials). With the expansion of Rule 23 (and its counterparts in states), mass tort class actions came to command a great deal of attention in the courts. "As the courts became swamped with individual suits arising out of the same products—asbestos, Agent Orange, Dalkon Shield, PCB's, breast implants—judges turned to class actions as a means of avoiding the delay and expense of trying separate suits. Nevertheless, mass torts often involve individualized circumstances as to a class member's exposure or use of a product, as well as to damages, and class certification is still hard to come by in such cases." Sherman, supra, at 225.

As we have seen, Insolia v. Philip Morris, Inc., supra p. 261 refused to allow three ex-smokers who had contracted tobacco-related diseases from joining in a suit against tobacco companies alleged to have conspired to deceive customers about the addictive and deadly characteristics of cigarettes. The court found the circumstances of each smoker's use of tobacco and injuries too individualized to make a convenient trial package for joinder under Rule 20. It had earlier refused to certify the case as a class action.

Rule 23(b)(3) was added in 1966, and "unlike the other categories, a (b)(3) class action is for monetary damages, and so there was now money to be had, providing new entrepreneurial incentives for the plaintiffs' bar." Sherman, Consumer Class Actions: Who Are the Real Winners?, 56 Maine L. Rev. 223, 224 (2004). A high percentage of class actions today are brought under (b)(3) for a broad spectrum of product liability, commercial, environmental, and consumer claims under state laws and such federal causes of action as antitrust, securities fraud, and civil rights. The advisory committee had commented that mass torts are inappropriate for class certification. 39 F.R.D. 69, 103 (1966), Advisory Committee Notes to Amendments to Rule 23. However, the complexity of modern society is reflected in recent years by an enormous increase in (or awareness of) mass torts.

After many refusals of courts to certify class actions in product liability suits against manufacturers of asbestos, the Fifth Circuit in Jenkins v. Raymark Indus., Inc., 782 F.2d 468 (5th Cir.1986), upheld the class certification for almost a thousand asbestos cases pending in one district court. It agreed with the district judge's conclusion that "[c]onsiderable savings, both for the litigants and for the court, could be gained by resolving [the "state of the art" defense, i.e., whether the manufacturers could have produced a safer product given what was known at the time] and other defense and defense-related questions, including product identification, product defectiveness, gross negligence and punitive damages, in one class trial." Over the following decade, a number of courts, both federal and state, certified mass tort class actions. E.g., Sterling v. Velsicol Chemical Corp., 855 F.2d 1188 (6th Cir.1988) (class action for leakage of toxics from landfill).

Mass torts may vary in their suitability for class action treatment. Those most amenable are mass accident cases, like a train wreck, plane crash, or collapse of a bridge or building, where the focus of a common trial will be on the single event and the conduct of the defendant in bringing it about. Liability and causation issues are generally common, and defensive issues involving the conduct of the plaintiffs are minimal. The more difficult cases are those involving exposure to environmental conditions, medicines, or products. Cases involving exposure of many persons to toxic substances at different times and places could still be suitable for aggregate treatment if the focus of the suit will be on the single course of conduct or condition at a single site without likelihood of individualized defensive or causation issues. Tending towards the side disfavoring aggregation would be mass toxic tort suits in which large numbers of persons claim exposure under very differing conditions to a product or substance which is only harmful under certain circumstances relating to individual characteristics and in which the conduct of each class member may give rise to differing defenses to which the defendant is entitled under substantive law. Where would *Castano* fit on this continuum?

By the mid-1990s, there was a strong movement, particularly in certain federal circuit courts, in reaction against what was considered excessive and inappropriate use of class actions. The Sixth and Seventh Circuits imposed stricter standards on mass tort class actions. In In re American Medical Systems, Inc., 75 F.3d 1069 (6th Cir.1996), the court issued a writ of mandamus overturning certification of a nationwide class of recipients of defendant's allegedly defective penile implants. It found that individualized issues would predominate since class members had used at least ten different models of the prosthesis and their legal claims would "differ depending upon the model and the year it was issued." It faulted the record below as showing "not even the hint of any serious consideration by the judge of commonality" and "no serious consideration" to the typicality requirement in circumstances where "it should have been obvious to the district judge that it needed to 'probe behind the pleadings'" on this subject. The judge also failed to consider how variations in the law of different jurisdictions would affect handling the claims in one class action.

Mass tort class actions were dealt another blow in Matter of Rhone-Poulenc Rorer Inc., 51 F.3d 1293 (7th Cir.), cert. denied, 516 U.S. 867 (1995), in which the court of appeals granted a writ of mandate overturning the trial judge's order for a class action trial of common issues in a suit against manufacturers of blood solids. Plaintiffs were hemophiliacs who had become infected with HIV due to tainted blood solids. Judge Posner, writing for the court, focused particularly on the attempt to represent a nationwide class where different state laws would likely apply depending on the where the class member was exposed to the defective product. He found the trial judge's proposal to meld the law of fifty jurisdictions into an "Esperanto instruction" that would not necessarily be the law of any state inadequate for dealing with the conflict of laws problem.

Castano v. The American Tobacco Co., 84 F.3d 734 (5th Cir. 1996), rejected a class action against tobacco companies for fraudently failing to inform customers that nicotine is addictive and manipulating the nicotine level to sustain their addictive nature. The opinion noted that "in a multi-state class action, variations in state law may swamp any common issues and defeat predominance" and found that the lower court's consideration of state law variations had been inadequate. This has been read as "imposing stringent tests on potential class plaintiffs that district courts must apply: The plaintiff has the burden of satisfying the court that class treatment is appropriate, the trial court must conduct a rigorous de novo review of state law, and conditional certification cannot justify a court's overlooking problems with predominance or superiority. See Spence v. Glock, 227 F.3d 308 (5th Cir.2000) (in nationwide class action against Georgia gun manufacturer for design defect, there was insufficient comparative analysis of the laws of Georgia and other states to support a finding, under the forum state's choice of law rules, that Georgia law would apply); In re Bridgestone/Firestone, Inc., 288 F.3d 1012 (7th Cir.2002) (in product defect class action, the forum state's choice of law rules would call for application of the laws of the fifty states where the injury occurred rather than the principal place of business of the defendants).

EMPLOYMENT DISCRIMINATION CLASS ACTIONS

A long awaited decision by the Supreme Court as to at least some of the class action issues on which lower courts had differed was Wal-Mart Stores, Inc. v. Dukes, 131 S.Ct. 2541 (2011). In a 5 to 4 decision written by Justice Scalia, it resolved some of those issues, but it has also given rise to attempts by plaintiffs and some lower courts to distinguish or limit its rather strong language. *Wal-Mart* was an employment discrimination case, and there also remain questions as to its application to other kinds of class actions.

Discrimination cases brought under various federal civil rights statutes were a paradigm for Rule 23 (b)(2) class actions, which are allowed when only injunctive or declaratory relief is sought. However, Title VII of the Civil Rights Act of 1964, prohibiting employment discrimination based on race, color, religion, sex or national origin, also provided for back pay. Thus an employment discrimination suit could be brought under Title VII for both injunctive relief such as reinstatement or promotion, and also for back pay. Back pay was considered an equitable remedy, rather than damages, and did not entitle the parties to a right to jury trial (which the bill's sponsors wanted to avoid, given the largely white juries that prevailed at that time in the South).

In 1991, Congress amended Title VII so it would allow punitive and compensatory damages for intentional discrimination and a right to jury trial. 42 U.S.C. § 1981a(a)(1) (2000). The purpose was to provide "additional remedies under Federal law * * * needed to deter * * * intentional discrimination in the workplace." However, the Fifth Circuit, in Allison v. Citgo Petroleum Corp., 151 F. 3d 402 (5th Cir. 1998), held that a (b)(2) class could not be certified because the damages now available were not merely "incidental" to the declaratory and injunctive relief sought. "Monetary relief predominates in (b)(2) class actions," the court stated, "unless it is incidental to requested injunctive or declaratory relief," that is, "damages that flow directly from liability to the class as a whole on the claims forming the basis of the injunctive or declaratory relief. Ideally, incidental damages should be only those to which class members automatically would be entitled once liability to the class as a whole is established" and must be "capable of computation by means of objective standards and not dependent in any significant way on the intangible, subjective differences of each class member's circumstances." [Note that sampling to avoid trying damages for each individual case had been rejected by certain lower courts in such situations. See Cimino v. Raymark Industries, Inc., 151 F.3d 297 (5th Cir. 1998).]

The Second Circuit in Robinson v. Metro-North Commuter R.R. Co., 267 F.3d 147 (2d Cir. 2001), rejected *Allison*'s interpretation of the "incidental damages" requirement, saying it should be left to the discretion of the district court, applying an "ad hoc" test to evaluate the significance of the injunctive relief to the plaintiffs in determining whether a reasonable plaintiff would seek it if money damages were not available. In a subsequent opinion in In re Monumental Life Insurance Co., 365 F.3d 408 (5th Cir. 2004), a discrimination suit brought under a post-Civil War civil rights statute (§ 1981), the Fifth Circuit seemed to modify the strictness of *Allison*. The suit alleged that African-Americans had been charged higher premiums over many years and sought injunctive relief requiring the defendant insurance companies to reform existing policies and make "restitution" of the value of overcharges. The Fifth Circuit found that "equitable monetary relief is compatible with a rule 23(b)(2) class," and that "such damages flow from liability in much the same manner that an award of backpay results from a finding of employment discrimination."

Whether a (b)(2) class is permissible when large sums of money are also sought was one of the issues addressed in *Wal-Mart*. In *Wal-Mart* a class of current and former female employees of Wal-Mart (some one and a half million) alleged that the discretion exercised by their local supervisors over pay and promotion violated Title VII by discriminating against women. In addition to injunctive and declaratory relief, they sought an award of back pay which, for the class, would be in the hundreds of million dollars. The Supreme Court reversed the district court and Ninth Circuit Court of Appeals certification of a class action, holding that the Rule 23 requirements were not satisfied.

The district court had certified a (b)(2) class, finding the back pay to be "incidental." Justice Scalia's majority opinion endorsed the Fifth Circuit's *Allison* view that monetary relief is only "incidental" if it flows directly from liability to the class as a whole and would not require additional hearings as to each individual (which were not satisfied in this case). It did not decide "whether there are any forms of 'incidental' monetary relief that are consistent" with its interpretation. However, the majority concluded that, "at a minimum, claims for individualized" or "no[n-]incidental" monetary "relief do not satisfy the Rule." The dissent by Justice Ginsburg agreed that the case should not have been certified under (b)(2)(although not addressing what the standard for "incidental" should be), but maintained that it could meet the requirements for a (b)(3) class.

In addition to its rejection of a (b)(2) class action based on a strict reading of when damages can be considered "incidental," the majority opinion scrutinized the "commonality" requirement under Rule 23(a)(2) (as applied to these facts). Citing its earlier employment discrimination decision (General Telephone Co. of Southwest v. Falcon, 457 U.S. 147 (1982)), the Court said that "commonality requires the plaintiff to demonstrate that the class members have suffered the same injury." Their claims must depend upon a "common contention" that "will resolve an issue that is central to the validity of each one of the claims in one stroke." The proposed class in *Wal-Mart* did not meet this standard because the plaintiffs could not identify any "specific employment practice" that would "tie all their 1.5 million claims together." The plaintiffs relied on "Wal-Mart's policy of allowing discretion by local supervisors over employment matters." The Court found that they had "not identified a common mode of exercising discretion that pervades the entire company." Given Wal-Mart's size and geographical scope (3,400 stores in all 50 states), "it is quite unbelievable that all managers would exercise their discretion in a common way without some common direction."

The majority opinion rejected the plaintiffs' statistical evidence showing region by region lower wages and promotions of women than in the available pool. The opinion found that such statistics did not take into consideration "differences between the various stores as to the available pool or for the claims of managers that they have been applying sex-neutral, performance-based criteria". The opinion concluded that there was "not even a single common question" because" there was no convincing proof of a companywide discriminatory pay and promotion policy."

Justice Ginsburg objected that the requirement of commonality under Rule 23(a)(2) was not that all questions of law or fact were common, but only that there be "one significant issue in common." She saw the majority's emphasis on differences between class members as mimicking the Rule 23(b)(3) "predominance" requirement. Most courts had previously viewed the 23(a)(2) commonality requirement as easy to satisfy. Justice Ginsburg viewed the Court's stringent reading of commonality as setting up a barrier that would preclude further analysis of the different requirements of the three Rule 23(b) types of class actions. Apparently concerned about an expansive application of the majority opinion, she noted that "individual differences should not bar a Rule 23(b)(1) or Rule 23(b)(2) class, so long as the Rule 23(a) threshold is met."

Addressing the sufficiency of the evidence provided by the plaintiffs, Justice Ginsburg noted that, as found by the district court, "women fill 70 percent of the hourly jobs in the retailer's stores but make up only 33 percent of management employees" and "the higher one looks in the organization the lower the percentage of women." Justice Scalia had emphasized that "Wal-Mart's announced policy forbids sex discrimination" and that "pay and promotion decisions at Wal-Mart are generally committed to local managers' broad discretion, which is exercised in a largely subjective manner." The district court had found the systems of compensation and promotion were "sufficiently similar" and "operated uniformly across stores." Justice Ginsburg contended that placing discretion in store managers under these circumstances could demonstrate a companywide policy:

The practice of delegating to supervisors large discretion to make personnel decisions, uncontrolled by formal standards, has long been known to have the potential to produce disparate effects. Managers, like all humankind, may be prey to biases of which they are unaware. The risk of discrimination is heightened when those managers are predominantly of one sex, and are steeped in a corporate culture that perpetuates gender stereotypes.

Finally, the Court unanimously rejected what it called the Ninth Circuit's "novel project" of avoiding individual determinations through the use of statistical sampling, particularly as to damages. Awarding classwide damages on the basis of sampling would " 'abridge, enlarge or modify' " the substantive rights at issue by preventing Wal-Mart from "litigat[ing] its statutory defenses to individual claims." The Court said that the Ninth Circuit's "Trial by Formula" transgressed due process principles that animate Rule 23 and guide courts in its interpretation. The unanimous holding could apply beyond the Rule 23(b)(2) and Title VII contexts—constraining the ability of litigants to use statistical or sampling techniques in large class actions.

NOTICE

For a class to be certified under Rule 23(b)(3), "the court must direct to class members the best notice practicable under the circumstances, including individual notice to all members who can be identified through reasonable effort." Rule 23(c)(1)(A). As beefed up by the 2003 amendments to Rule 23, the rule requires that the notice must "concisely and clearly state in plain, easily understood language" certain specifics about the action, that "a class member may enter an appearance though an attorney" if desired, and that "the court will exclude from the class any member who requests exclusion." Rule 23(c).

Eisen v. Carlisle & Jacquelin, 417 U.S. 156 (1974), addressed the notice requirement. It was a class action brought on behalf of some six million purchasers of odd-lot shares of stock alleging improper charges. The district court found that only 2.25 million of the class members could be identified, but, because of the cost, ordered that individual notice would only be sent to those who had ten or more odd-lot trades and to 5,000 others to be selected at random. Plaintiff was also required to take out advertisements in the Wall Street Journal and New York and California papers.

The Supreme Court rejected this approach, noting that due process required that notice "reasonably calculated, under all the circumstances, to apprise interested parties of the pendency of the action and afford them an opportunity to present their objections." Mullane v. Central Hanover Bank & Trust Co., 339 U.S. 306 (1950). It therefore interpreted Rule 23(c)(2) as requiring individual notice to all the 2.25 million class members who were identifiable through reasonable notice. Furthermore, it ruled that the plaintiff had to bear the cost of the notice, reversing the district court's order that defendants pay 90% of the cost. A judge, it stated, has no authority to conduct a preliminary inquiry into the merits of a suit in order to determine whether it may be maintained as a class action, and therefore "a plaintiff must initially bear the cost of notice to the class" (except in situations where a fiduciary duty pre-existed between plaintiff and defendant, as in a shareholder derivative suit).

By imposing the cost of notice on plaintiffs, *Eisen* made class actions with a large number of class members difficult to finance. Class members could not generally be expected to pay for notice costs, and it is perhaps not surprising that most (b)(3) class actions would have to be financed by the attorneys, thus further encouraging the "entrepreneurial" nature of class action practice.

Another cost factor that plaintiffs must confront in many cases is the expense of identifying class members so that notice can be sent to them. In Oppenheimer Fund, Inc. v. Sanders, 437 U.S. 340 (1978), involving a plaintiff class of securities purchasers, the Court held that defendant could not be required through discovery to compile a list of securities purchasers from its records where the effort would require computer operations costing over $16,000. The Court acknowledged that discovery could be used "to illuminate issues upon which a district court must pass in deciding whether a suit should proceed as a class action under Rule 23, such as numerosity, common questions and adequacy of representation," but concluded that the requested list did not serve this function.

In many consumer and product liability class actions where there are insufficient records of purchase, notice must be made through publication in newspapers, periodicals, radio, television, or the Internet, or through posting in places calculated to be seen by class members. Publication may sometimes be ordered as an extra precaution even when individual notice is given, in recognition of the fact that, in our mobile society, many notices sent to the last-known address will be returned or never reach the addressee. Since a high percentage of class actions are settled, the notice often comes for the first time when the parties have entered a settlement agreement and the court has approved a "settlement class" subject to notice, right to opt out, and opportunity to object by the class members.

The Class Action Fairness Act of 2005 added a requirement that defendants provide state and federal officials with notice of any proposed settlement. See 28 U.S.C.A. § 1715.

OPT-OUT RIGHTS IN 23(b)(3) CLASS ACTIONS

The 1966 amendments abandoned the "opt-in" requirement that was contained in the old rule. In a (b)(3) suit for damages, the notice to the putative class members will tell them that they need not take any action if they want to be a member of the class, and that unless they mail in an "opt-out" form, they will be bound by the results of the litigation. One who "opts out" will be excluded as a member of the class and can pursue the claim on her own if she wishes. However, the percentage of "opt outs" in most class actions is small. This might be explained by the fact that many class members, particularly in consumer and product liability cases, are content to have the case brought on their behalf without any demands on them, or simply by the natural inclination of people toward inaction in such situations. The RAND study of class actions commented:

> Most individuals are too preoccupied with daily life and too uninformed about the law to pay attention to whether they are being overcharged or otherwise inappropriately treated by those with whom they do business. Even if they believe that there is something inappropriate about a transaction, individuals are likely just to "lump it," rather than expend the time and energy necessary to remedy a perceived wrong.

D. Hensler et al., Class Action Dilemmas: Pursuing Public Goals for Private Gain 68 (2000).

On the other hand, the low rate of opt-outs could indicate the disinterest of class members in the suit and put into question the fairness of allowing self-appointed class representatives and attorneys to leverage their case through disinterested absent class members. Business interests have urged a change in the rule to require an affirmative act to "opt in."

Consider the following argument:

> By establishing membership in the class through the inherently passive procedure of opt-out, Rule 23 creates a framework for litigation that undermines the essential premises of the private compensatory model of adjudication. * * *

> At its start, the inherent passivity brought about by the use of opt-out sets the groundwork for an entirely comatose class of plaintiffs, who have never chosen to enforce their private rights and are even unaware that a suit has been brought on their behalf. At its close, even a successful class action may fail to

vindicate class members' private rights by providing meaningful compensation—a result easily predictable at the outset of the suit, because of the inherent impossibility of translating a class-based award into concrete, individualized damage awards to class members. In one sense or another, both of the bookends contribute to the ultimate transformation of the class action from an aggregative private compensatory action into what amounts to a pure bounty hunter action.

Redish, Class Actions and the Democratic Difficulty: Rethinking the Intersection of Private Litigation and Public Goals, 2003 U. Chi. Legal Forum 71, 94.

NOTICE IN (b)(1) AND (b)(2) CLASSES

Rule 23(b)(1) and (b)(2) class actions are mandatory, that is, there is no requirement that the class members receive notice or have a right to opt out. It was assumed that the interests of the class members were so cohesive (as in a (b)(2) suit for injunctive relief that would benefit the whole class) or that the necessity for class treatment was so great (as in a (b)(1) action where individual suits would prejudice the individual class members) that class members should not be allowed to split off and bring suits individually. However, under an amendment to Rule 23(c) in 2003, the judge may order that notice be given to the individual class members, although it is still to be seen if this option is much used. The Advisory Committee Notes state that the judge's discretion to order notice "should be exercised with care." They also comment that notice in (b)(1) and (b)(2) class actions is generally less important because opt-outs are not permitted and the costs may "cripple actions that do not seek damages." Informal methods, such as "[a] simple posting in a place visited by many class members, directing attention to a source of more detailed information, may suffice."

SETTLEMENT CLASSES

In Amchem Products, Inc. v. Windsor, 521 U.S. 591 (1997), the Supreme Court addressed a settlement class action. Before the suit was even filed, twenty asbestos manufacturers had reached an agreement with leading asbestos plaintiffs lawyers for settlement of a class action on behalf of all people in the U.S. who had been exposed occupationally to defendants' asbestos products but had not yet filed suit for personal injuries, and on behalf of the members of the exposed workers' families. The settlement included instances in which no disease had yet manifested itself ("future claims") as well as those in which the class member had suffered a medical consequence but had not yet sued. The Supreme Court found that the attempt to lump all future claimants together in a single class action was inappropriate and overturned the class certification. Among other things, the conflicts of interest between those with presently manifested disease and future claimants could not be ignored. The Court urged that there must be a "structural assurance of fair and adequate representation," seemingly calling for creation of appropriate subclasses, each with its own attorney.

"Limited fund" mass tort class actions: Recall that interpleader is available when there are multiple claimants against a limited fund. In some mass tort cases, it has seemed that the claims made against defendants outstrip their assets and insurance, and efforts have been made to use this predicament as a ground for certification of a "mandatory" (no opt out) class action under Rule 23(b)(1)(B). There have long been questions about whether this practice was consistent with the rule. See Marcus, They Can't Do That, Can They? Tort Reform Via Rule 23, 80 Cornell L. Rev. 858, 877–81 (1995) (arguing that the rule does not work in such situations). In Ortiz v. Fibreboard Corp., 527 U.S. 815 (1999), the Supreme Court overturned a limited fund class certification in an asbestos personal injury case but suggested that there might be situations in which this technique could be used. For an examination of the questions left unanswered by *Ortiz*, see Marcus, Benign Neglect Reconsidered, 148 U.Pa.L.Rev. 2009 (2000).

CHAPTER 5

OBTAINING INFORMATION FOR TRIAL

■ ■ ■

The common law pleading system, with its insistence on formulation of a single issue, left the parties relatively focused on the subjects that would be addressed at trial. But the common law provided no further assistance to the parties in obtaining information to prepare for trial. Instead (except for a "bill of discovery" in equity) the trial was a realm for surprise and dramatic maneuver.

As procedure evolved away from the common law approach to pleadings, it also shifted toward a regime of increased pre-trial disclosure of evidence. Building on the discovery practices at equity, the reformers provided for compelled revelation of information. The Federal Rules of Civil Procedure completed this development; Rule 26(a) now mandates certain disclosures, and Rule 26(b)(1) provides a broad scope of discovery. Rules 27 through 35 provide a number of tools the parties may use to obtain this information. Altogether, these rules prompted a "revolution" in discovery practice. Subrin, Fishing Expeditions Allowed: The Historical Background of the 1938 Federal Discovery Rules, 39 Bos. Col. L. Rev. 691, 718–19 (1998).

The rest of the world, however, approaches these questions differently; almost no other country has discovery near the scale of the U.S. See Subrin, Discovery in Global Perspective: Are We Nuts?, 52 DePaul L. Rev. 299 (2002); Marcus, Extremism in the Pursuit of Truth is Our "Virtue": The American Infatuation With Broad Discovery, in Truth And Efficiency in Civil Litigation (C.H. van Rhee & A. Uzelac, ed., 2012) at 165. Some countries have even enacted "blocking" statutes designed to prevent compliance with American discovery within their borders. Some non-Americans argue that broader discovery should be adopted in the rest of the world, see K. Huang, Introducing Discovery Into Civil Law (2003), but that has not happened to any substantial degree.

Broad discovery can be viewed as an integral feature of American civil litigation: "Broad discovery is thus not a mere procedural rule. Rather, it has become, at least in our era, a procedural institution perhaps of virtually constitutional foundation." Hazard, From Whom No Secrets Are Hid, 76 Tex. L. Rev. 1665, 1694 (1998); see also Oliva & Beety, Discovering Forensic Fraud, 112 Nw.L.Rev. 121 (2017) (urging adoption of broad discovery in criminal cases to combat misuse of "scientific" evidence). Those who propose changing American discovery are even sometimes labeled "unAmerican," while those favoring change sometimes say that American exceptionalism regarding discovery is itself "unAmerican." Marcus, Misgivings About American Exceptionalism: Court Access as a Zero-Sum Game, in Revisiting Procedural Human Rights: The Changing Face of Civil Justice (A. Uzelac & C.H. van Rhee eds., 2017) at 53, 54. Responding to such concerns, in 2011, Congress convened a hearing on "Costs and Burdens of Civil Discovery." Hearing of the Subcommittee on the Constitution of the House Judiciary Committee, Serial No. 112–72 (Dec. 13, 2011). These matters continue to be hotly debated.

A. THE PROMISE AND REALITY OF BROAD DISCOVERY

(not reviewing in class)

Hickman v. Taylor, 329 U.S. 495 (1947):

JUSTICE MURPHY delivered the opinion of the Court.

[This case established what is known as the work product immunity to discovery, and is reproduced at p. 397 infra. It was the Court's first major discovery decision after adoption of the Federal Rules of Civil Procedure, and the Court therefore explained its general attitude toward the purpose of discovery.]

The pre-trial deposition-discovery mechanism established by Rules 26 to 37 is one of the most significant innovations of the Federal Rules of Civil Procedure. Under the prior federal practice, the pre-trial functions of notice giving, issue-formulation and fact-revelation were performed primarily and inadequately by the pleadings. Inquiry into the issues and the facts before the trial was narrowly confined and often cumbersome in method. The new rules, however, restrict the pleadings to the task of general notice-giving and invest the deposition-discovery process with a vital role in the preparation for trial. The various instruments of discovery now serve (1) as a device, along with the pretrial hearing under Rule 16, to narrow and clarify the basic issues between the parties, and (2) as a device for ascertaining the facts, or information as to the existence of whereabouts of facts, relative to those issues. Thus civil trials in the federal courts no longer need be carried on in the dark. The way is now clear, consistent with recognized privileges for the parties to obtain the fullest possible knowledge of the issues and facts before the trial.

* * *

No longer can the time-honored cry of "fishing expedition" serve to preclude a party from inquiring into the facts underlying his opponent's case. Mutual knowledge of all the relevant facts gathered by both parties is essential to proper litigation. To that end, either party may compel the other to disgorge whatever facts he has in his possession. The deposition-discovery procedure simply advances the stage at which the disclosure can be compelled from the time of trial to the period preceding it, thus reducing the possibility of surprise.

NOTES AND QUESTIONS

1.   The optimistic enthusiasm of Hickman v. Taylor somewhat dimmed over time. Beginning in the 1970s, there were repeated expressions of concern about the cost of discovery. Since the 1970s, the trend in rule changes has been to promote specificity and judicial control. See Marcus, Discovery Containment Redux, 39 Bos.Col.L.Rev. 747 (1998). Professor Friedenthal argued that "[i]t is not surprising to find that the battle over specificity has shifted from pleading to discovery. The relationship between the policy of pleading and that of discovery is obvious. The very purpose of permitting pleadings based upon good faith speculation must be to permit plaintiffs to employ the discovery provisions to determine whether a valid case in fact exists." Friedenthal, A Divided Supreme Court Adopts Discovery Amendments to the Federal Rules of Civil Procedure, 69 Calif.L.Rev. 806, 816 (1981). But as we shall see shortly, the amendments adopted in 2015 continued this trend toward discovery constraint.

2.   Recall that Rule 11 requires that a party investigate a claim before presenting it in court, and provides that a lawyer signing a complaint certifies that it has evidentiary support or is likely to after discovery. Should discovery be available to assist a party in gathering this evidentiary support? Rule 27 does allow pre-suit discovery to preserve evidence when the party seeking this discovery shows that it is unable to commence litigation. But courts have resisted permitting such discovery to satisfy Rule 11 obligations or determine whether a prospective plaintiff has a valid claim. See Gordo-Gonzalez v. U.S., 873 F.3d 32, 37 n. 3 (1st Cir. 2017) (Litigants "are not entitled to use discovery to find out whether they have a cause of action.").

Courts have, however, permitted discovery to obtain facts to be used in amending pleadings in suits already on file. See, e.g., Remmes v. Int'l Flavors & Fragrances, Inc., 453 F.Supp.2d 1058 (N.D. Iowa 2006) (plaintiff could use facts learned through discovery to satisfy the particularity requirements of Rule 9(b)); Zavala v. Wal-Mart Stores, Inc., 393 F.Supp.2d 295 (D.N.J. 2005) (permitting plaintiff some discovery prior to filing an amended complaint is justified when the complaint states a claim but lacks sufficient detail). Recall also the suggestion that, if pleading requirements become more demanding, there should also be earlier opportunities for discovery. See supra p. 203 n. 6. Should courts be more receptive to use of discovery to determine whether there is a claim? In some states, pre-suit discovery is more readily available and may provide an important assist for those seeking access to justice. See Hoffman, Access to Information, Access to Justice: The Role of Presuit Investigatory Discovery, 40 U. Mich. J. L. Rev. 217 (2007) (evaluating Texas provision allowing presuit discovery and finding that it may promote access to justice).

3.   Although many lawyers and judges have strong views on the desirability of broad discovery, there has been a limited empirical basis for determining whether there are widespread problems with the operation of

discovery. It seems clear that American litigation costs more than litigation in other countries, and that broad discovery is a significant part of that cost. But there is considerable evidence that, in most cases, discovery is proportional to the stakes involved in the case. Thus, a 2009 study by the Federal Judicial Center about discovery in a randomly-selected set of closed cases revealed that about half the lawyers who handled the cases regarded discovery costs as "just the right amount" in light of the client's stakes in the case, and only about 5% said that the discovery costs were much too much in light of the stakes. Lee & Willging, Federal Judicial Center National Case-based Civil Rules Study 28 (Oct. 2009). Nonetheless, very serious concerns exist about overdiscovery in a significant number of cases. See, e.g., Final Report of the Joint Project of the American College of Trial Lawyers Task Force on Discovery and the Institute for the Advancement of the American Legal System (April 15, 2009) (concluding that "discovery can cost far too much and can become an end in itself"). The push for "proportionality" in discovery has been building for a long time.

Doing some /*not reviewing in*/ *Class*

IN RE CONVERGENT TECHNOLOGIES SECURITIES LITIGATION

United States District Court, Northern District of California, 1985
108 F.R.D. 328

BRAZIL, U.S. MAGISTRATE.

The principal issue in this discovery dispute can be simply framed: when (at which juncture in the pretrial period) should plaintiffs answer "contention" interrogatories served by defendants. The parties do *not* disagree about *whether* the questions should be answered. The sole question is when.

Counsel already have spent upwards of $40,000 of their clients' money on this one discovery dispute.[3] That fact strikes this court as strong evidence that there has been in this case a major breakdown in what is supposed to be the self-executing system of pretrial discovery. The spirit of Rule 26,[4] as amended in 1983, has been violated. So has the spirit of Rule

Q: To Who?

---

[3]   The $40,000 figure does not include money counsel spent drafting, serving and initially objecting to the interrogatories themselves.

[4]   The following provisions were added to Rule 26 in 1983. Subparagraph (b)(1) [now in (b)(1) and (b)(2)(C)] was amended to include this paragraph:

> The frequency or extent of use of the discovery methods set forth in subdivision (a) shall be limited by the court if it determines that: (i) the discovery sought is unreasonably cumulative or duplicative, or is obtainable from some other source that is more convenient, less burdensome, or less expensive; (ii) the party seeking discovery has had ample opportunity by discovery in the action to obtain the information sought; or (iii) the discovery is unduly burdensome or expensive, taking into account the needs of the case, the amount in controversy, limitations on the parties' resources, and the importance of the issues at stake in the litigation. The court may act upon its own initiative after reasonable notice or pursuant to a motion under subdivision (c). Fed.R.Civ.P. 26(b)(1).

1, which declares that the purpose of the Federal Rules of Civil Procedure is "to secure the just, speedy, and inexpensive determination of every action." The discovery system depends absolutely on good faith and common sense from counsel. The courts, sorely pressed by demands to try cases promptly and to rule thoughtfully on potentially case-dispositive motions, simply do not have the resources to police closely the operation of the discovery process. The whole system of civil adjudication would ground to a virtual halt if the courts were forced to intervene in even a modest percentage of discovery transactions. That fact should impose on counsel an acute sense of responsibility about how they handle discovery matters. They should strive to be cooperative, practical and sensible, and should turn to the courts (or take positions that force others to turn to the courts) only in extraordinary situations that implicate truly significant interests.

These are not simply the sentiments of an idealistic and frustrated magistrate. They are the law. They were clearly made so by the 1983 amendments to Rule 26. Those amendments formally interred any argument that discovery should be a free form exercise conducted in a free for all spirit. Discovery is not now and never was free. Discovery is expensive. The drafters of the 1983 amendments to sections (b) and (g) of Rule 26 formally recognized that fact by superimposing the concept of proportionality on all behavior in the discovery arena. It is no longer sufficient, as a precondition for conducting discovery, to show that the information sought "appears reasonably calculated to lead to the discovery of admissible evidence." After satisfying this threshold requirement counsel also must make a common sense determination, taking into account all the circumstances, that the information sought is of sufficient potential significance to justify the burden the discovery probe would

---

In addition, a new subparagraph (g) was added:

> Every request for discovery or response or objection thereto made by a party represented by an attorney shall be signed by at least one attorney of record in his individual name, whose address shall be stated. A party who is not represented by an attorney shall sign the request, response, or objection and state his address. The signature of the attorney or party constitutes a certification that he has read the request, response, or objection, and that to the best of his knowledge, information, and belief formed after a reasonable inquiry it is: (1) consistent with these rules and warranted by existing law or a good faith argument for the extension, modification, or reversal of existing law; (2) not interposed for any improper purpose, such as to harass or to cause unnecessary delay or needless increase in the cost of litigation; and (3) not unreasonable or unduly burdensome or expensive, given the needs of the case, the discovery already had in the case, the amount in controversy, and the importance of the issues at stake in the litigation. If a request, response, or objection is not signed, it shall be stricken unless it is signed promptly after the omission is called to the attention of the party making the request, response, or objection and a party shall not be obligated to take any action with respect to it until it is signed.

> If a certification is made in violation of the rule, the court, upon motion or upon its own initiative, shall impose upon the person who made the certification, the party on whose behalf the request, response, or objection is made, or both, an appropriate sanction, which may include an order to pay the amount of the reasonable expenses incurred because of the violation, including a reasonable attorney's fee.

Fed.R.Civ.P. 26(g) (as amended Apr. 28, 1983, eff. Aug. 1, 1983). [This rule language has been revised.—Eds.]

impose, that the discovery tool selected is the most efficacious of the means that might be used to acquire the desired information (taking into account cost effectiveness and the nature of the information being sought), and that the timing of the probe is sensible, i.e., that there is no other juncture in the pretrial period when there would be a clearly happier balance between the benefit derived from and the burdens imposed by the particular discovery effort.

This articulation of the responsibilities counsel must assume in conducting or responding to discovery may make it appear that the 1983 amendments require counsel to conduct complex analyses each time they take action in the discovery arena. Not so. What the 1983 amendments require is, at heart, very simple: good faith and common sense. Counsel can satisfy these requirements by not using or responding to discovery for some ulterior purpose and by exercising straight forward judgment. The questions are simply stated: 1) what information am I really likely to need and 2) what is the most cost effective way to get it. Tailoring probes and responses to the real issues in the case at hand, rather than relying on stock questions or knee jerk objections and evasive responses, is all that is required.

The problem, one senses, is not that the requirements the law imposes are too subtle. Rather, the problem is more likely to be that counsel are less interested in satisfying the law's requirements than in seeking tactical advantages. At least in cases involving big economic stakes, good faith and common sense hardly seem to be the dominant forces. Instead, it appears that the root evil in complex civil litigation continues to be the pervasiveness of gaming. Civil litigation is too often civil only on the surface. Underneath, it is obsession with pursuit of procedural or psychological edge. In adopting the 1983 amendments, the rulemakers have unequivocally condemned that obsession.

[The court then turned to the question of timing. Defendants had served more than 1,000 questions, many of them seeking to elicit the facts plaintiffs contended supported certain of their allegations about what defendants had done in violation of the securities laws. Noting that contention interrogatories "can be almost mindlessly generated," and that they are unlikely to produce useful information until discovery is completed if they focus on defendants' conduct, the court directed that plaintiffs be excused from responding to most of the interrogatories until they had completed a substantial amount of discovery, particularly document inspection.]

PROPORTIONALITY AND THE 2015 RULE AMENDMENTS

In *Convergent Technologies*, Magistrate Judge Brazil emphasized the importance of then-recent amendments to the discovery rules. To some extent, he was reflecting his heartfelt views. See Brazil, The Adversary

Character of Civil Discovery: A Critique, 31 Vand.L.Rev. 1348 (1978) (written while Brazil was a law professor). But as he said in *Convergent Technologies*, the 1983 amendments to the discovery rules installed a new expectation, which came to be called "proportionality." The Reporter who drafted these rule changes even said that these changes constituted "a 180 degree shift" in the rules' orientation. A. Miller, The August 1983 Amendments to the Federal Rules of Civil Procedure: Promoting Effective Case Management and Lawyer Responsibility 32–33 (1984).

Things did not change so quickly: "In all likelihood, Professor Miller was premature in that announcement. When I prepared the second edition of the *Federal Practice & Procedure* volumes addressing discovery a decade later, I added a new section dealing with proportionality, but had to report that '[t]he [proportionality] amendment itself seems to have created only a ripple in the case law.' But by the time the third edition appeared in 2010, things had changed, and I could report that 'attention to the proportionality provisions has grown since 1994, and endorsement of their use has widened.' " Marcus, "Looking Backward" to 1938, 162 U.Pa.L.Rev. 1691, 1717 (2014).

As amended Dec. 1, 2015, Rule 26(b)(1) says that discovery is available "regarding any nonprivileged matter that is relevant to any party's claim or defense *and proportional to the needs of the case*." The italics identify the words added by amendment. At least some regard this rule change as a watershed. See Steinman, The End of an Era: Federal Civil Procedure After the 2015 Amendments, 66 Emory L.J. 1 (2016); Berman, Reinventing Discovery Under the New Federal Rules, 42 Litigation 22, 22 (Spring 2016) ("It's a whole new ball game."); compare Pulgram, The Discovery Rules Have Changed: But Will We?, 42 Litigation 18 (Spring 2016).

Another change to the rules emphasizes something else Judge Brazil said in *Convergent Technologies*—the importance of cooperation. As amended in 2015, Rule 1 now says that the rules "should be construed, administered, *and employed by the court and the parties* to secure the just, speedy, and inexpensive determination of every action and proceeding." The italics again identify the words added by amendment. The rule does not command cooperation, but the Committee Note does emphasize that "[e]ffective advocacy is consistent with—and indeed depends upon— cooperative and proportional use of procedure." For general discussion, see Marcus, Cooperation and Litigation: Thoughts on the American Experience, 61 Kan.L.Rev. 821 (2013).

It is too early to be certain whether these rule changes will result in changes in lawyer behavior in discovery. It is clear that some hope that they will. Thus, in his 2015 year-end report on the state of the federal judiciary Chief Justice Roberts said that "[t]he amendments may not look like a big deal at first glance, but they are." In his view, that was because the amendments adopted, "as a fundamental principle, that lawyers must size and shape their discovery requests to the requisites of a case." In addition, he stressed that the amended rules "emphasize the crucial role of federal judges in engaging in early and effective case management." At least some judges were listening to the Chief Justice. See, e.g., Waters v. Drake, 222 F.Supp.3d 582, 605 (S.D.Ohio 2016) (quoting Chief Justice Roberts and saying that "[t]he proportionality standard is the instrument by which judges and practitioners are to bring about a change in the culture of discovery").

As we move through the issues raised in this chapter, keep this orientation in mind. Later we will consider how the specific factors that bear on proportionality should be addressed.

NOTES AND QUESTIONS

1. *Importance of proportionality*: Obviously the 2015 rule amendments put proportionality in a central position in determining the scope or amount of discovery that is appropriate in a given case. As *Convergent Technologies* emphasizes, that thrust has been central to the discovery rules since the mid 1980s. To some extent, it may seem odd that there is any need to emphasize this concern. For example, it is difficult to imagine that many lawyers would say they want to engage in "disproportionate" discovery.

But there are surely counterpressures. One is that lawsuits are often important vehicles in the vindication of rights in American society. Such cases cannot be properly valued purely in terms of the amount of money in dispute. One example we encountered in Chapter 2 is the question of what is a "reasonable" attorney fee award in a case that vindicates the plaintiff's constitutional rights. See Venegas v. Mitchell, supra p. 98. The monetary recovery may be limited many such cases, but the amount of attorney work necessary to secure that result could be very substantial. The concept of proportionality therefore should not deprive the lawyer of fair compensation for that work.

Sensitivity to that concern appears in the first factor that Rule 26(b)(1) says should be considered in determining what is proportional—"the importance of the issues at stake in the action." The Committee Note elaborates, invoking the original purpose of this provision in 1983:

> [M]onetary stakes are only one factor, to be balanced against other factors. The 1983 Committee Note recognized "the significance of the substantive issues, as measured in philosophic, social, or institutional terms. Thus the rule recognizes that many cases in public policy spheres, such as employment practices, free speech, and other matters, may have importance far beyond the monetary amount involves."

But there must be a limit to even these considerations. "Thou shalt not ration justice" is a stirring credo, but the willingness of litigants to overuse discovery is a counterweight. Reconsider this concern when we examine who should pay the cost of responding to discovery, infra p. 395 n. 4.

2. *Concern with strategic overuse or misuse of discovery*: American discovery is distinctive in the world. It operates in our adversary system, in which litigants may sometimes exploit every tool available to achieve advantages over their opponents. Aggressive discovery that imposes costs on the opposing party may sometimes be a temptation. Certainly some repeat litigants in U.S. courts object that they must comply with burdensome discovery demands for information that the requesting party seems not to use in the litigation.

At times, there may be "collateral" considerations that explain a party's desire for broad discovery. To take a recent example, consider IMDB.com v. Becerra, 257 F.Supp.3d 1099 (N.D.Cal.2017). IMDB.com provides a resource that some law students have probably used—information about the entertainment industry. At the urging of the Screen Actors Guild, the California Legislature adopted legislation forbidding the posting online of information about the ages of people in that industry, which the Guild claimed fostered age discrimination. IMDB sued the California Attorney General to enjoin enforcement of the statute on First Amendment free speech grounds, and the government asserted in defense that the legislation was justified by the need to combat age discrimination in the entertainment industry.

The government proposed to do discovery in the IMDB case about various matters, including any efforts of IMDB to lobby against the legislation. The judge held the discovery improper, noting that "[i]n a normal civil case, these kinds of irrelevant and burdensome discovery requests are merely annoying. But this is a First Amendment case." Id. at 1102. He elaborated, invoking proportionality:

> The government's theory is that IMDB's responses to these requests may reveal that people in the entertainment industry commit age discrimination. The idea that such information would be unearthed is, to put it charitably, fanciful. Therefore, it does not appear that the requests are "relevant to any party's claim or defense." Moreover, to the extent that this type of information might be revealed, it's difficult to understand how it would help the government defend the statute. Therefore, the burdens these requests impose on IMDB are not "proportional to the needs of the case."

For another example of a suspicious discovery foray, consider Henry v. Morgan's Hotel Group, Inc., 2016 WL 303114 (S.D.N.Y, Jan. 25, 2016). Plaintiff was a waiter who sued a restaurant operator for which he had worked, claiming race and sexual orientation discrimination. Defendant served subpoenas on plaintiff's three previous employers, seeking all materials they had about plaintiff. As the court noted in ruling the discovery disproportionate, if plaintiff again sought employment from these entities his chances of getting hired "might well be adversely affected by the fact that his records had been subpoenaed in this lawsuit." Defendant's speculation about whether plaintiff was truthful with his prior employers "has little, if any, bearing" on whether defendant discriminated against him.

3.   It may be that American lawyers instinctively seek more information than they need. For one thing, "the quality of 'hired gun' is close to the heart and substance of the litigating lawyer's role." Frankel, The Search for Truth: An Umpireal View, 123 U.Pa.L.Rev. 1031 (1975). But pursuit of more discovery may result from "nonconsequentialist reasoning"—"the heuristic that more information must be better, without regard to the cost of the information or the need for it." Wistrich & Rachlinski, How Lawyers' Intuitions Prolong Litigation, 86 S.Cal.L.Rev. 571, 604–06 (2013):

> Litigators thus suffer from a double distortion: they overvalue the additional information and undervalue the costs incurred by the responding party in providing the information. Lawyers also likely do not realize that the additional information might hinder or distort their own judgment.

Adversarial System
the cost to your
opponent is value
to you.

4.   *The English experience with proportionality*: The English legal system employs a "loser pays" approach that can prompt excessive investment in litigation as a way to ensure recovery of costs and attorney fees instead of concentration on the result on the merits. Recall p. 103 n. 1 (describing the English experience with this tendency to over-invest in litigation). In the mid 1990s, the English system of costs recovery was revised to install proportionality as a central concern. See A. Zuckerman, Civil Procedure 1–3 (2003) (describing the new emphasis on proportionality as a "radical departure from past practice"). Yet concern with excessive costs persisted, leading to a 2009 recommendation by Lord Justice Jackson that recovery of even "necessary" costs could be denied if they were disproportionate:

> Disproportionate costs do not become proportionate because they were necessary. If the level of costs incurred is out of proportion to the circumstances of the case, they cannot become proportionate simply because they were "necessary" in order to bring or defend the claim. * * * The fact that it was necessary to incur certain costs in order to prove or disprove a head of claim is obviously relevant, but it is not decisive of the question whether such costs were proportionate.

R. Jackson, Review of Civil Litigation Costs: Final Report 37 (2009).

5.   *A German advantage?*: Professor Langbein has endorsed the German approach, which leaves fact investigation to the judge while otherwise adopting an adversary approach to litigation:

> This all-or-nothing argument [that the investigative judge undermines the adversary system] overlooks the fundamental distinction between fact-gathering and the rest of civil litigation. Outside the realm of fact-gathering, German civil procedure is about as adversarial as our own. Both systems welcome the lawyerly contribution to identifying legal issues and sharpening legal analysis. German civil procedure is materially less adversarial than our own

only in the fact-gathering function, where partisanship has such potential to pollute the sources of truth.

Accordingly, the proper question is not whether to have lawyers, but how to use them; not whether to have an adversarial component to civil procedure, but how to prevent adversarial excesses. If we were to incorporate the essential lesson of the German system in our own procedure, we would still have a strongly adversarial civil procedure. We would not, however, have coached witnesses and litigation-biased experts.

Langbein, The German Advantage in Civil Procedure, 52 U.Chi.L.Rev. 823, 842–43 (1985). Recall Band's Refuse Removal, Inc. v. Borough of Fair Lawn, supra p. 3, as an example of zealous judicial fact-gathering. Should we expect most judges to be equally zealous? If not, would it be better to equip the parties to gather their own evidence?

6. *Employing proportionality*: As the proportionality principle permeates American discovery, it will become increasingly important to address these concerns, and you should keep them in mind as you approach the issues presented in the remainder of this chapter. For an analysis of proportionality from the perspective of economic theory, see Gelbach & Kobayashi, The Law and Economics of Proportionality in Discovery, 50 Ga.L.Rev. 1093 (2016).

B. THE DISCOVERY DEVICES

If he would be a great lawyer, he must first consent to become a great drudge.

—Daniel Webster

Whether or not one must be a drudge to prepare a case properly, it is apparent that one must be discerning in using the tools of modern discovery. To a large extent, the lawyer's choice among the devices in a given case depends upon tactical considerations canvassed at the end of this section. There are also legal limitations on the use of the various discovery devices, most of which are spelled out in the Rules themselves. We will survey some practicalities of the more important discovery devices and raise some questions about the application of those legal limitations.

INITIAL DISCLOSURE

As demonstrated by In re Convergent Technologies, supra p. 352, discovery can use up a great deal of time and money. In order to reduce some of the cost and adversary maneuvering, in the 1980s courts began insisting that parties turn over "core materials" before formal discovery began. See Marcus, Of Babies and Bathwater: The Prospects for Procedural Progress, 59 Brooklyn L. Rev. 761, 805–12 (1993) (describing the evolution of this practice). In 1992, the state courts in Arizona adopted a rule making initial disclosure mandatory. Other states have adopted similar rules.

In the federal courts, initial disclosure was added in Rule 26(a)(1) in 1993. When adopted, it called for disclosure of any information "relevant to disputed facts alleged with particularity in the pleadings" and therefore was extremely controversial because it seemed to compromise the loyalty a lawyer owed to the client by requiring in some instances that information harmful to the client be turned over. For example, Justice Scalia dissented from adoption of this requirement (146 F.R.D. at 511 (1993)):

> The proposed new regime does not fit comfortably within the American judicial system, which relies on adversarial litigation to develop the facts before a neutral decisionmaker. By placing upon lawyers the obligation to disclose information damaging to their clients—on their own initiative, and in a context where the lines between what must be disclosed and what need not be disclosed are not clear but require the exercise of considerable judgment— the new Rule would place intolerable strain upon lawyers' ethical duty to represent their clients and not to assist the opposing side. Requiring a lawyer to make a judgment as to what information is "relevant to disputed facts" plainly requires him to use his professional skills in the service of the adversary.

In 2000, the rule was changed to direct only that a party disclose witnesses and documents it "may use to support its claims or defenses." There is thus no current directive to turn over harmful information unless it is formally requested through discovery. Some lawyers say that initial disclosure under the amended rule provides modest benefits, if any.

One might ask why any requirement was needed at all to prompt parties to reveal the strengths of their cases to their opponents. Indeed, there have long been reports that litigants do so in the absence of a rule requirement during negotiation with the other side. Moreover, Rule 11's safe harbor provisions (see supra p. 158) may also prompt parties to do so in an attempt to persuade the other side to drop a claim or defense. Besides these incentives and the fact that Rule 26(a)(1) now requires it, initial disclosure is enforced by Rule 37(c)(1), which forbids use of materials that should have been disclosed but were not. This means that if a party tries to present evidence that should have been disclosed, the opposing party can argue that this evidence should not be considered. That argument can be made at trial, and also with regard to pretrial motions such as summary judgment motions. So a party has an incentive to disclose materials that it may want to use at trial or to support or oppose a motion for summary judgment. Although Rule 37(c)(1) says that the court may permit the materials to be used even if they were not disclosed, there can be considerable risk for a party that tries to use something it has not disclosed.

Some hoped that disclosure would supplant formal discovery in many cases, but that does not seem to have happened. One reason is that disclosure does not include information harmful to the disclosing party's

Q: I Disc. in relationship to specifically lawyers or to actual defendants as well?

SEC. B   THE DISCOVERY DEVICES   361

position; only discovery exists to elicit that sort of information. Another is that, given the American adversarial litigation background, it would seem against the grain to insist that a party trust its adversary to make full disclosure. For the present and the foreseeable future, then, formal discovery is likely to follow initial disclosure in most cases. But at the same time, parties must be thorough in deciding what to disclose for fear that failure to do so may deprive them of important evidence later in the case.

REQUESTS FOR PRODUCTION   *Rule 34*

Rule 34 permits parties to demand an opportunity to inspect, copy, test or sample documents, electronically stored information or tangible things possessed by other parties. This opportunity can be critical to effective development of a case. Technological advances have greatly increased the amount of information available to most people and organizations. Documents don't forget, as witnesses are wont to do, so that they provide not only evidence but a starting place for examining witnesses in deposition and preparing witnesses for deposition.

The procedure for using this discovery tool is simple. If plaintiff wants to inspect material under defendant's control, plaintiff's lawyer sends a request for production to defendant's lawyer. The request should describe the documents with "reasonable particularity." While parties sometimes specify the precise items they desire (e.g., "the letter to plaintiff dated July 1, 2017"), they often rely on a categorical description (e.g., "all documents or electronically stored information that relate or refer to the meeting between plaintiff and defendant on July 1, 2017"). Often the discovering party does not know much about what information the other parties possess. Because Rule 26(a)(1)(A)(ii) calls for parties to disclose some pertinent information about such materials before formal discovery begins, parties may be able to identify and describe with specificity those they wish to request under Rule 34.

A Rule 34 request calls for the responding party to assemble the requested information in its "possession, custody, or control." The "control" idea has been extended to require efforts to obtain documents from others, where the party responding to discovery is believed to have "influence" over the possessor of the documents. See Tomlinson v. El Paso Corp., 245 F.R.D. 474 (D. Colo. 2007) (employer controlled electronic pension records maintained by company that administered its pension plan because the law required employer to supervise the plan); In re Auction House Antitrust Litig., 196 F.R.D. 444 (S.D.N.Y.2000) (defendant had control of information possessed by former CEO who was required by his termination agreement to provide information to defendant).

It should be apparent that such a request can seek a large amount of information. For example, consider a hypothetical Rule 34 request for "all documents or information regarding the evening of July 1, 2017." Assume the litigation focuses on events on the night of July 1, and that a party to the litigation went out with friends for dinner and a movie that night. That could make the information sought relevant. On its face, that request calls for the responding party to collect all communications, including email, texts, voicemail and credit card billings relating what happened that evening. That could call for a lot of effort. As a result, Rule 34 requests are the most frequent source of proportionality objections. Whatever else might prove to be drudgery, one can be confident that the process of reviewing materials to prepare them for production to the other side is often genuine drudgery.

The responding party can raise those concerns in its formal response to a Rule 34 request. As amended in 2015, Rule 34(b)(2)(B) says that such a response may state objections, but must "state with specificity the grounds for objecting to the request, including the reasons." The response also must state the date on which the information that will be produced is to be provided, and Rule 34(b)(2)(C) requires that the response state whether any responsive materials are actually being withheld on the basis of the objection. Preparing that detail for the Rule 34(b) response could itself be drudgery.

The ideal of the "cooperation" thrust of the 2015 amendments is that the parties work out a reasonable way to handle the challenges of identifying and producing the materials sought. We will return to these topics below. See The Challenges of E-Discovery, infra p. 369. Another rule change in 2015 may facilitate that effort: Rule 26(d)(2) now authorizes "early Rule 34 requests," which can be served before the parties' discovery-planning meeting under Rule 26(f) and provide a concrete focus for devising a discovery plan that is proportional and workable.

Rule 34 also authorizes entry onto property for purposes of testing or measuring. These requests are much less frequent, but they can generate controversy. One recurrent controversy involves requests by disabled plaintiffs for access to defendants' premises to determine whether they comply with legal requirements. In Wiele v. Zenith Arizona, Inc., 278 F.R.D. 477 (D.Az.2012), for example, the court limited a wheelchair-using hotel guest plaintiff to inspection of barriers that actually would affect her disability. See also Hoewischer v. Deerwood Village Mall, LLC, 281 F.R.D. 665 (M.D.Fla.2011) (inspection limited to exclude areas not affecting plaintiff's particular disability); McConnell v. Canadian Pacific Realty Co., 280 F.R.D. 188 (M.D.Pa.2011) (inspection limited to mobility barriers, excluding assessment of ADA compliance unrelated to mobility).

If a party wants to examine materials or premises possessed by a nonparty, a similar procedure is used but a subpoena is required. Rule 45 authorizes a subpoena to command a nonparty to produce designated documents or electronically stored information in its control or permit inspection of premises. The subpoena rule also requires the serving party to "take reasonable steps to avoid imposing undue burden or expense" on a person subject to a subpoena, and it may be that courts will be more solicitous of nonparties' objections to subpoenas than parties' objections to discovery.

INTERROGATORIES *Rule 33*

Rule 33 permits any party to send written questions to another party that must be answered under oath. Since the responding party is usually required to make reasonable efforts to obtain the information sought, this discovery tool may appear extremely valuable because it could allow a party to do much or all of its pretrial preparation fairly inexpensively. The reality, however, has been disappointing. One problem has been that interrogatories are too susceptible to abuse. Questions that are simple to write may be very burdensome to answer. Rule 33(a) now limits the number of interrogatories to 25 per party absent stipulation or court order.

Another problem is that interrogatory answers are almost invariably written by lawyers who wish to avoid disclosing harmful information. As a result, the answers tend to reveal very little even though they are long (for these lawyers have word processors also), and to indulge in generalities where the discovering party wants specifics. Perhaps the most basic difficulty with interrogatories is that they are ill suited to effective exploration of much information that is critical in litigation. Where a narrative answer is sought, for example, an interrogatory often fails to do the job.

Interrogatories can, however, be very useful for identifying witnesses and discovering the location of documents or other tangible evidence, although that task may be eased by Rule 26(a)(1) initial disclosure. They can also be used to obtain precise information (e.g., "State the number of widgets defendant sold in this state during each month in 2017."). Due to the responding party's duty to obtain information to respond, interrogatories can be particularly useful to a party confronted by a large organizational opponent.

One type of question deserves special note—the "contention" interrogatory. Rule 33(a)(2) makes it clear that questions are not improper merely because they seek to elicit an opinion, even where they seek an opinion about the application of law to fact. In practice, contention interrogatories are an effective way of exploring the basis for an adversary's position, but the court may defer the duty to answer until discovery has been completed. Recall In re Convergent Technologies Securities Litigation, supra p. 352. Such questions may provide the predicate for a motion for summary judgment based on non-existence of evidence supporting a critical part of plaintiff's case. Keep these discovery problems in mind when you read Celotex Corp. v. Catrett, infra p. 454.

DEPOSITIONS *Rule 30*

The deposition permits the questioner to compel the witness to answer questions fairly spontaneously and allows the interrogating party to follow up on the answers, particularly unexpected revelations, with further questions. The flexibility and importance of depositions mandate intense preparation on the part of both the interrogating party and the witness. Depositions are the most expensive form of discovery in terms of overall litigation expenditure. But lawyers say that they are worth it. Consider Levin & Powell, Weaving a Nursing Home Deposition Strategy, Trial Magazine, Dec. 2012, at 40, 41:

> Nursing home cases are won in depositions. When conducted properly, depositions in these cases are powerful weapons to illustrate the safety rules, violations of the safety rules, and the resulting harm to your client. You can use depositions to anticipate, undermine, defuse, and reverse common defenses. With skilled deposition techniques, you can bolster your retained experts' opinions through the testimony of the defendant's own employees, while also discrediting and disarming the defense experts. Preparation is essential, and before the deposition you must anticipate the possible defenses and think of ways to defuse them.

Rule 30(b)(1) allows any party to schedule a deposition on "reasonable written notice." Rule 30(a)(2)(A) imposes a numerical limit of ten depositions per side, and Rule 30(d)(1) limits each deposition to "one day of seven hours." The interrogating party can also ask the witness to bring documents along, but that invokes the time limits of Rule 34. See Rule 30(b)(2). If the witness is a party, nothing further need be done to compel the witness to attend, and Rule 37(b) sanctions can be applied when a party witness fails to appear. See Rule 37(d). Otherwise, the party seeking discovery must also serve a subpoena to ensure the attendance of the witness. See Rule 45.

[handwritten margin note: if non-Party →]

Depositions usually do not occur in the courthouse unless the court itself is supervising the deposition in an effort to iron out conflicts between the lawyers (a rare thing). Ordinarily the interrogating lawyer will designate her own office as the place of the deposition. When the attendance of the witness must be compelled by subpoena, the geographical limitations applicable to a subpoena apply. With the deposition of a party, however, there are no explicit geographical limitations, and disputes about the location may arise if the witness is located at some distance from the interrogating lawyer. If the parties cannot resolve these disputes by themselves, they may ask the court to do so. Courts are more likely to require the plaintiff who has sued away from home to travel to the jurisdiction where the suit was filed than to require the distant defendant to come to the jurisdiction where the suit is pending for his deposition. But see Ocasek v. Hegglund, 116 F.R.D. 154 (D.Wyo.1987) (singer Bruce Springsteen not required to appear for deposition in Wyoming even though he is nominal plaintiff in suit filed there).

Before the deposition, the witness will usually consult with her attorney about the deposition process and the subjects that are likely to be covered, a process often called "woodshedding the witness." See Maloney, Preparing the Expert Witness for Deposition, Today's General Counsel, Feb./Mar. 2017, at 48; Berman, Reinventing Witness Preparation, 41 Litigation 20 (Summer 2015); Schaeffer, When Your Client Testifies, Trial Mag., July 2011, at 23. With party witnesses, the woodshedding process can be very protracted. The witness's lawyer tries to alert the witness to the pitfalls she will confront and may school the witness in revealing as little as possible. Whether or not witnesses would testify more accurately and honestly without preparation, woodshedding is ingrained in our current adversary system to the extent that the lawyer who does not prepare a witness may be charged with failing to satisfy his professional obligations.

Occurring as it usually does in a lawyer's office, the deposition itself appears informal in many ways; it looks more like a business meeting than a court hearing. Ordinarily, the interrogating attorney will sit at one side of the table facing the witness, with the court reporter between them. The witness's attorney will sit next to the witness, and lawyers for other parties will sit at other points in the room. The participants may be quite relaxed about matters of personal deportment and dress. But in one regard the deposition is not informal—anything that is transcribed by the reporter ("on the record") may be available for use in the case as though it occurred in open court (to the extent it is admissible). Before the questioning begins, the witness is given the oath, and the interrogating attorney then starts asking questions and continues until she has no further questions to ask.

Although the main actors are the interrogating attorney and the witness, the witness's attorney is not inactive. Instead, she listens to the questions and can object when they are improper. On one level, the pressure to object is moderate since the only objections that are waived are objections on grounds that could be obviated if made at the deposition. Rule 32(d)(3)(B). Thus, where the objection is to the form of the question (that it is leading, or compound, or confusing) the question could be rephrased to avoid the difficulty. Indeed, Rule 30(c)(2) states that if there are objections, "the examination still proceeds; the testimony is taken subject to any objection," so objections seem ineffective even to prevent improper inquires. Why, then, would the lawyer object?

The reality has been that too often objections have been used to continue the woodshedding process mentioned above concerning deposition preparation, and instructions to the witness not to answer "improper" questions were actually used to suggest answers or interfere with the taking of the deposition. In Hall v. Clifton Precision, 150 F.R.D. 525 (E.D.Pa.1993), the court reasoned that "[t]he witness comes to the deposition to testify, not to indulge in a parody of Charlie McCarthy, with lawyers coaching or bending the witness's words to mold a legally convenient record." It therefore ordered that there be no off-the-record consultation between lawyer and witness during the taking of the deposition, including during recesses, except to determine if a privilege applied. Rule 30(c) provides explicit constraints on the behavior of the lawyer for the witness. Rule 30(c)(2) directs that objections "must be stated concisely and in a non-argumentative and nonsuggestive manner." It adds that a lawyer may instruct a witness not to answer only to preserve a privilege, to enforce a limitation on discovery imposed by the judge in this case, or to permit a motion for a protective order. In addition, Rule 30(d)(2) authorizes sanctions on anyone who "impedes, delays, or frustrates the fair examination of the deponent," and for other misconduct in a deposition.

Traditionally, depositions have been recorded by court reporters who used special machines to take notes of the questions and answers. Rule 30(b)(3)(A) now permits a party noticing a deposition to select videotape or audiotape as well as the traditional method. Rule 30(b)(3)(B) allows any other party to designate another method (at its own expense). Lawyers may prefer a videotaped deposition where the witness will not be available to testify at trial because reading aloud from the deposition transcript tends to be extremely boring. Rule 32(c) accordingly expresses a preference for use at trial of a nonstenographic recording if one exists.

For further reading, see S. Israel, Taking and Defending Depositions (2d ed. 2017); P. Miller & P. Scoptur, Advanced Deposition Strategy and Practice (2017); and the Aug., 2017, issue of Trial Magazine ("The Ins and Outs of Depositions").

PHYSICAL OR MENTAL EXAMINATION   *Rule 35*

Physical or mental examinations are the only discovery tools for which a stipulation or advance court approval is necessary. Rule 35(a) provides that, when the mental or physical condition of a party or a person under the legal control of a party is "in controversy," a court may, for good cause, order the person to submit to an examination by a "suitably licensed or certified examiner."

The most common use of Rule 35 examinations involves personal injury plaintiffs who have put their physical condition "in issue." Consider that some examinations may involve discomfort, inconvenience, or even risk for the person examined, and you will understand why parties seeking such examinations must demonstrate that there is good cause for the examination. They must also demonstrate that the mental or physical condition of the party to be examined is "in controversy" in the case. There is no such thing as a subpoena to require a nonparty to submit to such a procedure.

In Schlagenhauf v. Holder, 379 U.S. 104 (1964), which arose out of a rear-end collision when a bus hit a tractor-trailer, the owners of the tractor-trailer contended that the defendant bus driver had impaired vision. After the district court ordered the driver to submit to nine medical examinations by specialists in internal medicine, ophthalmology, neurology, and psychiatry, the Supreme Court held that the order was not supported by a sufficient showing. It said that Rule 35 requires that a request for an examination be based on something more than "mere conclusory allegations of the pleadings," though it distinguished the situation of a personal injury plaintiff. Given the potential intrusiveness of some sorts of examinations, consider how proportionality should be implemented under Rule 35. For example, should every plaintiff claiming emotional distress damages be subject to psychiatric examination? For a general discussion of leave to examine parties, see C. Wright, A. Miller & R. Marcus, Federal Practice & Procedure § 2234.1 (3d ed. 2010).

DISCOVERY SEQUENCE AND TACTICS

Now that you have some familiarity with the operation of the discovery devices, it is worthwhile to introduce some of the tactical considerations that bear on use of these devices.

The starting point is the pleading stage:

> Establish facts through the pleadings. The complaint is often the plaintiff's first discovery device. A carefully drafted complaint can streamline the discovery process by eliminating unnecessary time and expense. In order to do this, numbered individual paragraphs should generally contain only one central thought or factual allegation. Eliminate all unnecessary adjectives and adverbs. It is always tempting to use the complaint as a polemic, but it is almost always inappropriate and strategically wrong.
>
> A nonargumentative and simple paragraph within a complaint may very well elicit an admission in the answer, thereby conclusively establishing the facts alleged in that particular paragraph. An admission of a particular factual allegation in a complaint will not preclude further discovery on that factual issue, but it will establish some central facts early on that could greatly assist subsequent discovery motions or a defense against a motion to dismiss or a motion for summary judgment.

Fox, Planning and Conducting a Discovery Program, 7 Litigation 13, 14 (Summer 1981). Would this lead to good pleading? See Rule 10(b).

Rule 26(f)(3) directs the parties to confer and design a "discovery plan" shortly after the suit is filed, and to submit the plan to the court in time for consideration in connection with the Rule 16(b) scheduling order (which is, among other things, to set a time limit for discovery). Rule 26(d) permits formal discovery only after that conference has occurred, although initial disclosure may occur before, during, or after the conference and "early" Rule 34 requests may be delivered before the conference though responses are not due until 30 days after the conference. Because the discovery plan may control the sequence and content of discovery, lawyers need to give it considerable thought. Different cases call for different tactics. Some will begin with interrogatories to get basic information, although many will opt instead to seek production of documents initially in order to get a full grounding in the documentary side of the case.

In some instances, however, one might want to start with depositions. For example, some say that "[d]epositions get a case moving better than any other discovery device," in part because "there is no time lag between the time questions are asked and answers obtained," and because refusals to answer are rare since questions can be immediately rephrased to follow up. Fox, supra, 7 Litigation at 17. There can be drawbacks to speed, however, since one cannot compel the witness to bring documents without allowing the time for a document production, and there is a significant likelihood under Rule 30(a)(2)(A)(ii) that an early witness will not be subject to recall later in the discovery process when more information is available for questions.

Other sequence issues depend upon the way in which early discovery unfolds. One kind of discovery may be necessary to lay the groundwork for another kind. Thus, interrogatories may be necessary to locate documents and witnesses, requests for documents to obtain the materials needed to prepare for depositions, and depositions to lay the groundwork for a request for a medical examination. Similarly, it may often happen that judges actively managing discovery will entertain requests to expand discovery on the basis of a showing that useful information has been obtained through completed discovery that points up the need for more.

Not only must lawyers grapple with these sorts of tactical issues, they also confront tactical problems with ethical overtones. A common example is the (maladroit) discovery request. Suppose your opponent has made a request for production that arguably covers certain damaging materials from your client's files, but only in a very indirect way. Can you make a good faith argument that the request does not actually ask for the damaging material, knowing all the while that your opponent would certainly want this material if aware of it? Should you be "cooperative" and hand it over anyway? If you can make the argument in good faith, should you? If there is a substantial likelihood that the material will come out later in the case anyway, it might be best to turn it over now rather than highlighting its importance (and providing an occasion for allegations of concealing evidence) when the material surfaces later.

THE CHALLENGES OF E-DISCOVERY

For the American lawyer in the 21st century, the most formidable sort of discovery may involve electronically stored information, often called E-Discovery. As people have come to rely increasingly on electronic means to communicate, store information and generate documents, discovery has increasingly focused on electronically stored information. Lawyers have learned to "follow the e-mail trail." As one lawyer put it, "What I've found is that when you've got the e-mails, people remember lots and lots of things." Geier, A Defense Win in "Enron Country," Nat. L.J., Jan. 23, 2006, at 6. Some even suggest that E-Discovery might be "considered a specialized substantive expertise in the same vein as, for example, patent law." Kwuon & Wan, High Steps for Missteps in EDD, N.J.L.J., Dec. 31, 2007, at E2. In the words of a federal judge speaking at a conference, "E-Discovery is pervasive. It's like understanding civil procedure. You're not going to be a civil litigator without understanding the rules of civil procedure. Similarly, you're no long going to be able to conduct litigation of any complexity without understanding E-Discovery." Dysart, Learn or Lose, ABA Journal, April 2014, at 32. The State Bar of California has issued an opinion that attorney competence must include "a basic understanding of, and facility with, issues related to e-discovery." Formal Opinion 11–0004, State Bar Standing Committee on Professional Responsibility and Conduct. The issues cannot be covered in sufficient detail in this book, but many law schools offer courses in the subject. See S. Scheindlin, D. Capra & The Sedona Conference, Electronic Discovery and Digital Evidence (3d ed. 2015).

A moment's reflection should suggest why this topic is so important. Consider, for example, how much digital information is available about you. Would your litigation adversary find that information potentially useful? Colleges and law schools reportedly use that information in making admissions decisions. See Lee, Law Schools Use Google and Facebook to Screen Applicants, S.F. Daily Jour., Oct. 26, 2011, at 5; Belkin & Porter, Web Profiles Haunt Students, Wall St. J., Oct. 4, 2012, at A3 (regarding use of online information in undergraduate admissions). The police seek this information to build a case. See Ruderman & Edwards, Police Sought Cellphones of Bystanders Who Captured Fatal Times Square Shooting, N.Y. Times, Aug. 15, 2012, at A19: "In the age of the ubiquitous smartphone, it is increasingly common for crimes, shootings involving the police and catastrophes to be captured on video, often prompting investigators to seek the video as evidence to help them piece together what happened." So also with civil cases. See Eder & Valentino-DeVries, A Spy-Gear Arms Race Transforms Modern Divorce, Wall St.J., Oct. 6–7, 2012, at A1 (describing use of electronic surveillance information in divorce cases).

Social media, in particular, have played a growing role. "Every litigator has probably experienced firsthand or at least heard about a situation in which information from a social media site played a significant role in a case." Akin, How to Discover and Use Social Media-Related Evidence, 37 Litigation 32 (Winter 2011); see also Mix, Discovery of Social Media, 2011 Fed.Cts.L.Rev. 5. As the court said in EEOC v. Simply Storage Manag. LLC, 270 F.R.D. 430 (S.D.Ind.2010), "[d]iscovery of [social network sites] requires the application of basic discovery principles in a novel context." In this sexual harassment case, defendant sought discovery of plaintiffs' social media postings, and the court ordered disclosure of anything that would "reveal, refer, or relate to any emotion, feeling or mental state," as well as any picture of a plaintiff posted during the pertinent time period, which "may reveal the claimant's emotional or mental status." Privacy settings were irrelevant to discovery because "a person's expectation and intent that her communications be maintained as private is not a legitimate basis for shielding those communications from discovery." See also Mailhoit v. Home Depot, U.S.A., Inc., 285 F.R.D. 566 (C.D. Cal. 2012) (defendant seeks discovery from plaintiff's postings on Facebook and LinkedIn to test plaintiff's claims that she suffers from post traumatic stress disorder, depression and isolation, and has cut herself off from friends); Offenback v. L.M. Bowman, Inc., 2011 WL 2491371 (M.D. Pa. 2011) (court conducts in camera review of plaintiff's Facebook account and produces a few items to defendant).

These new challenges have produced new litigation costs. In part, that's due to the ever-expanding amount of digital data. "Every day, 23 billion text messages, and 205 billion emails are sent globally." Building a Lean In-House E-Discovery Strategy, Legaltech News, June 2016, at 1-SS. "More data has been created in the last two years than in the entire previous history of the human race and the amount of data is predicted to grow 10-fold by 2020." Gordon v. T.G.R. Logistics, Inc., 321 F.R.D. 401, 403 (D.Wyo.2017). Partly as a consequence, the expenditure on E-Discovery has escalated. "The worldwide e-discovery market surpassed $10 billion during 2015." Silverstein, E-Discovery Market Hits $10B, Legaltech News, Feb 2016, at 17. It is forecast to reach almost $22 billion by 2022. Legaltech News, April 2016, at 23.

But technology may also reduce the cost of some discovery activities. For generations, young lawyers have spent countless hours reviewing material slated for possible production to determine whether it is responsive to a discovery request. Given the volumes of data now potentially available, that sort of review is probably no longer possible in many cases. Instead, "technology assisted review" relies on artificial intelligence principles to develop an algorithm to separate responsive from non-responsive materials. For discussion, see Grossman & Cormack, Technology Assisted Review in E-Discovery Can be More Effective and More Efficient Than Exhaustive Manual Review, 17 Rich.J.L. & Tech. 11

(2011); Coke, Predictive Coding: A Trial Court Judge's Perspective, 26 Regent U.L.Rev. 71 (2013).

The importance of E-Discovery may escalate more due to the increasing use of objects that are part of the "Internet of Things," including a wide variety of items such as GPS devices in autos, fitbits, and many others. According to Post, Discovering the Internet of Things, Legaltech News, Jan. 1, 2015, by late 2014 some 10 billion such devices were in place, and the number would likely rise to 75 billion by 2020, making this development a "defining moment in technology history." Compare Castellanos, When the Cloud Isn't Fast Enough, Wall St.J., Jan. 4, 2018 (predicting that 20.4 billion devices will be in use by 2020). See also Warren, Thanks to the IoT, This Isn't 2006's E-Discovery, Legaltech News, Jan. 18, 2018 (discovery regarding the Internet of Things is "the new pardigm").

Information from such sources is already being used in wage and hour suits to challenge employee claims that they have been working so much that they are due overtime pay. For example, an E-Discovery representative asserted that "we've been able to assess billions of location and time records to understand when and where employees were during their claims of overtime." Collecting Your Company's Digital Breadcrumbs, Metropolitan Corporate Counsel, Dec 2017, at 7. See, e.g., Crabtree v. Angie's List, Inc., 2017 WL 413242 (S.D.Ind., Jan. 31, 2017), a Fair Labor Standards Act suit in which plaintiffs claimed they worked 12-hour days but were paid only for 8 hours a day. Defendant sought discovery of GPS and location service data from plaintiffs' personal cell phones. Defendant said this information would enable it to "construct a detailed and accurate timeline of when Plaintiffs were or were not working. * * * GPS data would identify whether Plaintiffs left for the day, left for lunch or some other unpaid break during that four-hour window when they were still logged on to SalesForce." The court refused discovery on the ground that it would be unduly intrude into plaintiffs' privacy.

[handwritten margin note: Ex: of denial of usage or location data.]

Entering law students should appreciate that the electronic skills they have developed while growing up will therefore be important in handling discovery; indeed, they may possess an advantage over prior generations of lawyers in dealing with such materials. For lawyers and judges, amendments to the Federal Rules in 2006 provided some guidance on problems specific to E-Discovery. Thus, Rule 26(f)(3)(C) calls for consideration of E-Discovery during the design of the discovery plan, and Rule 34(b) provides direction on the form for production of electronically stored information. Rule 26(b)(2)(B) excuses initial production of "inaccessible" electronically stored information to reduce unnecessary costs. As amended in 2015, Rule 37(e) provides some limits on sanctions for loss of digital information. Similar provisions have been adopted by many state courts. See Marcus, E-Discovery Beyond the Federal Rules, 37 U.

Balt. L. Rev. 321 (2008). Altogether, however, much depends on the parties' arrangements rather than precise provisions in the rules; as the first lawyers who have grown up in the Digital Age, you will take an active role in shaping E-Discovery practices.

It is therefore important that you keep in the back of your mind the extent to which American society's shift to relying on electronic communications affects what information is available through discovery and the means of obtaining that information. Only one of the principal cases that follows is an E-Discovery case (McPeek v. Ashcroft, infra p. 387), but each of the situations you will study might have to be handled somewhat differently in the Digital Age.

NOTES AND QUESTIONS

1. *Discovery from nonparties*: As suggested above, discovery from non-parties is more limited than discovery from parties. For example, there is no way to send interrogatories to nonparties, and nonparties are not subject to court-ordered physical examinations under Rule 35. But Rule 45 empowers attorneys to issue subpoenas directing nonparties to provide discovery comparable to what is allowed from parties under Rules 30 (depositions) and 34 (requests for production). Consider the following hypothetical: You wish to obtain information about the eyesight of a nonparty witness to the accident that prompted the lawsuit. How can you do so under the current discovery rules? Cf. Harris v. Athol-Royalston Regional School Dist., 206 F.R.D. 30 (D.Mass.2002) (court orders handwriting exemplars and fingerprints from nonparty personnel of defendant).

Rule 45 also requires that parties avoid unduly burdening nonparties and alert them in the subpoena itself to the right to seek a protective order. Among other things, the court may require the party seeking discovery to reimburse the nonparty for the costs of responding. This cost can be substantial. For example, in United States v. Columbia Broadcasting System, Inc., 666 F.2d 364 (9th Cir.1982), defendant television networks subpoenaed material from five producers of television programming. To comply with the document requests, the producers hired lawyers, had thousands of boxes of documents reviewed and eventually had 17 officers and employees deposed over a period of more than 80 days. They then asked for $2.3 million to compensate them for the cost of responding to this discovery, and the appellate court reversed the trial judge's refusal to award any compensation: "Although party witnesses must generally bear the burden of discovery costs, the rationale for the general rule is inapplicable where the discovery demands are made on nonparties. Nonparty witnesses are powerless to control the scope of litigation and discovery, and should not be forced to subsidize an unreasonable share of the costs of a litigation to which they were not a party." Are nonparties really in a position that is so different from defendants?

Given this difference in treatment between party and nonparty discovery, one solution to discovery problems is to name as parties all those from whom one will seek discovery. Is this solution ethical? Is it consistent with Rule 11? *→ Violates Rule 11(b)*

↳ No. It only to cut $, def. not.

2.   *Discovery from a corporate party:* Discovery from a corporate or other organizational party may be more difficult because both responsibility and knowledge are diffuse. Consider Judge Frank Theis's description of difficulties encountered by plaintiffs in cases involving the Dalkon Shield, a contraceptive product that allegedly caused serious injuries to women who used it: "The project manager for Dalkon Shield explains that a particular question should have gone to the medical department, the medical department representative explains that the question was really [in] the bailiwick of the quality control department. The quality control department representative explains that the project manager was the one with the authority to make a decision on that question. * * * [I]t is not at all unusual for the hard questions posed in Dalkon Shield cases to be unanswerable by anyone from Robins." Lord, The Dalkon Shield Litigation: Revised Annotated Reprimand, 9 Hamline L. Rev. 7, 11 (1986).

One antidote for this merry-go-round problem (called "bandying") is to use interrogatories to identify the persons within the organization who have knowledge about the matter at issue. Initial disclosure pursuant to Rule 26(a)(1)(A) of identities of people with pertinent information may be another. Rule 30(b)(6) provides yet another: It permits a party to notice a deposition of a corporation, partnership, or government agency, whether or not a party, with a description of the matters to be covered, and to require the organization to designate a person able to answer questions on that subject. See In re Vitamins Antitrust Litigation, 216 F.R.D. 168 (D.C.D.C.2003) (defendant and its lawyer would be sanctioned for failure to produce a knowledgeable witness to testify).

3.   *Requests for admissions:* Rule 36 authorizes what appears to be another discovery tool: It permits any party to send requests to any other party asking for an admission of the truth of any matter within the scope of Rule 26(b). The responding party is deemed to have admitted these matters unless he denies them, and denials must "fairly respond to the substance of the matter." Cf. Rule 8(b). Where a matter is admitted, it is deemed conclusively established for the purpose of the litigation at hand, but the admission cannot be used in any other litigation.

Technically requests for admission are not discovery devices but more analogous to pleadings. In reality, however, they can form a part of a discovery package, and parties often serve them coupled with interrogatories asking for specifics about any matters that are denied. Some courts have expressed concern that requests for admissions have been used too often and too early; parties should not be expected to be in a position to make admissions, they reason, until substantial discovery has been completed. Nevertheless, these requests are quite useful to establish the genuineness of documents and to verify basic facts that are within the knowledge of the party.

4. *Admissibility at trial:* Besides assisting parties in locating information, discovery can yield evidence that is admissible at trial. In general, the admissibility of such materials depends on the rules of evidence. Thus, documents obtained through discovery may not be admissible unless "authenticated" (see Fed.R.Evid. 901–02), perhaps by a request for admission of their genuineness. Since virtually all discovery produces evidence that is hearsay, the elaborate rules governing admissibility of hearsay (see Fed.R.Evid. 801–07) play a large role in admission of the fruits of discovery.

Rule 32(a) provides some specifics regarding depositions: Beyond uses allowed by the Federal Rules of Evidence, any deposition may be used for impeachment at trial, the deposition of a party (or a representative designated under Rule 30(b)(6)) may be used by an adverse party for any purpose, and the deposition of a witness may be used for any purpose if the witness is not present at trial and the witness's absence has not been procured by the party offering the deposition.

5. *Discovery disputes:* As should be apparent, discovery matters often cause disputes between the parties, and ultimately the party seeking discovery can ask the court to compel the desired response (see infra pp. 434–441). In part because these disputes often revolve around scheduling details and the like, judges became impatient with parties who squabbled and ran to court to resolve their differences. Consider the following judicial reaction: "If there is a hell to which disputatious, uncivil, vituperative lawyers go, let it be one in which the damned are eternally locked in discovery disputes with other lawyers of equally repugnant attributes." Dahl v. City of Huntington Beach, 84 F.3d 363, 364 (9th Cir.1996). Rule 37 requires that a motion to compel be accompanied by "a certification that the movant has in good faith conferred or attempted to confer with the person or party failing to make disclosure or discovery in an effort to obtain it without court action." Rule 37(a)(1); see also Rule 37(d)(1)(B).

6. *Duty to supplement:* It often happens that a party acquires or remembers additional responsive information after responding to discovery. Rule 26(e) provides that whenever "in some material respect the disclosure or response is incomplete or incorrect" the response must be supplemented. Rule 26(e) does not apply if the additional information has "otherwise been made known to the other parties during the discovery process or in writing." Failure to supplement is subject to sanctions. See Rule 37(c)(1).

Spoliation

7. *Preservation of evidence:* Nobody keeps everything forever, but failure to keep items sought through discovery can lead to sanctions for spoliation. The exact dimensions of the duty to preserve evidence and the exact time when that duty comes into play are sometimes uncertain. But failure to retain information under circumstances indicating a desire to suppress evidence can result in very severe sanctions, including criminal convictions. It may be that negligence is enough fault to justify serious sanctions. In Silvestri v. General Motors Corp., 271 F.3d 583 (4th Cir.2001), a plaintiff who claimed his serious injuries resulted from a malfunction of the air bag in somebody else's car suffered dismissal due to his failure to arrange for G.M. to have a chance to

inspect the car before the owner sold it. Compare Menz v. New Holland North America, Inc., 440 F.3d 1002 (8th Cir. 2006) (reversing dismissal of suit by farmer injured in tractor accident although he repaired the tractor before filing suit, thereby preventing defendant from examining the tractor before it was repaired).

Preservation can be particularly challenging with electronically stored information, because it is often voluminous, may be altered easily (and unintentionally), and can be located in many places. See Katiroll Co. v. Kati Roll and Platters, Inc., 2011 WL 3583408 (D.N.J. 2011) (spoliation claims including alteration of Facebook account). As handheld devices become more popular, and more and more employees work from home or on the road, the range of possible locations of potentially relevant material has grown. As amended in 2015, Rule 37(e) provides that courts may use curative measures to respond to the loss of electronically stored information that should have been preserved if the party did not take "reasonable steps" to preserve in anticipation of litigation.

8.   *Discovery abroad:* Increasingly, litigation in American courts involves litigants or witnesses who are in other countries. American courts can issue "letters rogatory" seeking assistance of foreign courts in obtaining discovery for use in American courts. See 28 U.S.C.A. § 1781. Recall, however, that discovery in other countries is much more limited than American discovery. See supra pp. 349–350. The Hague Convention on Taking Evidence Abroad has since 1972 provided procedures for judicial authorities in signatory countries to obtain discovery in other signatory countries. The Supreme Court has held that district courts may decide on a case-by-case basis whether to employ this Convention. Societe Nationale Industrielle Aerospatiale v. United States District Court, 482 U.S. 522 (1987). But because they view American discovery as unduly intrusive, many countries have adopted "blocking" laws that forbid or limit compliance with discovery efforts within their borders. The U.S. also offers foreign litigants access to American discovery. A statute authorizes district courts to order discovery in this country for use in litigation pending in another country. See 28 U.S.C.A. § 1782; Intel Corp. v. Advanced Micro Devices, Inc., 542 U.S. 241 (2004) (party seeking discovery in U.S. need not show that the information sought would be discoverable in the country in which the proceeding is pending).

An additional potential tension is that many other countries not only eschew discovery but also have very vibrant privacy laws, including the "right to be forgotten" recognized in some countries. These laws forbid "processing" of private information, and regard discovery as forbidden processing. They may regard as "private" anything that identifies a person, including an email on the company system from one employee of a company to another employee of the company. Needless to say, that sort of material is routinely turned over in American discovery. At least one lawyer in France has been prosecuted for cooperating with American discovery; more vigorous enforcement of EU privacy restrictions may occur in the future. When information originally developed by American companies is stored on servers in the EU (perhaps due to "cloud" storage), the EU may regard it as subject to EU privacy restrictions even though it originated in the U.S. There is a potential for serious conflict along the lines that prompted the enactment of "blocking" statutes, mentioned above.

C. MANAGING THE SCOPE AND BURDEN OF DISCOVERY

Doing Some   *(not reviewing in class)*

DAVIS V. ROSS

United States District Court, Southern District of New York, 1985
107 F.R.D. 326

ROBERT L. CARTER, DISTRICT JUDGE.

Plaintiff Gail Davis has instituted this defamation action, seeking one million dollars in compensatory damages and one million dollars in punitive damages, based on an October 11, 1983 letter written and disseminated by defendant Diana Ross. [Davis alleged in her complaint that, from January, 1982, until she voluntarily resigned in November, 1982, she was employed as executive assistant to Ross, a well-known recording artist. The October 11, 1983, letter stated in part:

To Whom it May Concern:

The following [seven] people are no longer in my employment:

Gail Davis

If I let an employee go, it's because either their work or their personal habits are not acceptable to me. I do not recommend these people. In fact, if you hear from these people, and they use my name as a reference I wish to be contacted.

Plaintiff sued, claiming that the letter was false in asserting that Ross fired her, that she was fired because of inadequate work or personal habits, and that her inadequacies warranted Ross' recommendation that she not be hired. The district court granted Ross' motion to dismiss on the ground that, as a matter of law, the text of the letter was not libelous but only expressed Ross' personal dissatisfaction rather than making a representation of fact about Davis's job performance. 602 F.Supp. 504 (S.D.N.Y. 1984). The court of appeals reversed and remanded, reasoning that the letter was susceptible to several interpretations, at least one of which is defamatory. 754 F.2d 80 (2d Cir.1985).] * * * The case is currently before the court on the parties' cross-motions to compel discovery.

Davis seeks discovery of three sets of data. First, she wishes to obtain information concerning Ross' net worth and annual income. Davis argues that this material is discoverable because evidence of a defendant's wealth is relevant in an action for punitive damages. Rupert v. Sellers, 48 A.D.2d 265, 368 N.Y.S.2d 904 (4th Dep't 1975).

The New York courts have recognized, however, that a plaintiff's interest in proving the amount of the defendant's wealth must be balanced against the defendant's right to privacy and general desire not to divulge his or her financial status—especially since plausible claims for punitive damages can easily be made in many actions. Consequently, the rule in New York is that "evidence of defendant's wealth [can] not be brought out upon trial unless and until the jury [brings] in a special verdict that plaintiff is entitled to punitive damages against defendant." [Rupert v. Sellers, 48 A.D.2d] at 272, 368 N.Y.S.2d at 912. Discovery of defendant's net wealth will become necessary only in the event plaintiff obtains such a special verdict.

Davis argues that the rule of Rupert v. Sellers should not govern this case because she entered into a confidentiality order which, she says, should eliminate any concern for privacy on defendant's part. Defendant responds, quite rightly, that the existence of a confidentiality order does not undermine the rationale of Rupert v. Sellers. Ross should not be compelled to disclose private facts to anyone—even to someone who has agreed to keep the information confidential—until it is found that plaintiff is entitled to punitive damages. * * * The motion to compel discovery of Ross' wealth and income is denied.

Plaintiff's second discovery request is for documents reflecting billings by the law firm of Loeb & Loeb and/or John Frankenheimer (a partner in the firm) to Ross and to entities in which she has an interest, and for the records reflecting payment of such bills. Plaintiff argues that this material is discoverable because the defendant has stated that Frankenheimer will be an important witness; therefore, plaintiff asserts, the amount of fees Ross paid Frankenheimer would be relevant to the issue of Frankenheimer's bias and credibility.

Plaintiff is entitled to probe for bias by inquiring into the existence and nature of the relationship between Frankenheimer and Ross. Specifically, plaintiff may discover what, if any, fee arrangements and retainer agreements were entered into between the two. However, the amount of fees earned, without more, is not probative of a witness' bias. Even where a witness' entire livelihood derives from employment by the party for whom he testifies, courts have declined to infer bias from the mere fact of employment. In this case, the court is especially reluctant to pry into the details of the attorney-client relationship or to order burdensome discovery. Consequently, plaintiff's motion to compel discovery of legal fees is denied.

Plaintiff's third request is to discover the names of other employees who have complained about defendant, and the nature of their complaints. Plaintiff's argument for discoverability rests on the Second Circuit's interpretation of the allegedly libelous letter in question. In the letter, Ross stated that Davis no longer worked for her, and then wrote: "If I let an employee go, it is because their work or their personal habits are not acceptable to me. I do not recommend these people." According to the Court of Appeals, the statement, "I do not recommend these people," tends to objectify Ross' evaluation of Davis, and implies that others would also find Davis' work or personal habits unacceptable.

Plaintiff argues that the truth of this statement—that Davis' work or personal habits are objectively unacceptable—will be at issue. Consequently, plaintiff asserts, the material sought is discoverable because "[i]f in fact it was defendant's personality that was a problem and not plaintiff's the jury would be entitled to conclude that there was nothing objectionable about plaintiff's work or personal habits and that defendant is liable for defamation."

The logic of plaintiff's argument is tenuous. Whether Ross is a "good" or "bad" employer, popular or unpopular with employees, is not probative of whether Davis' personal or work habits were objectively satisfactory. Even if other employees have complained about Ross, that would not affect a jury's assessment of Davis' personal or work habits one way or the other. The issue in this case is whether Ross libeled Davis, and the material plaintiff seeks to discover does not bear on that.

Plaintiff also argues that the information is discoverable because it bears on Ross' credibility. The court simply does not see the connection between Ross' reputation as an employer and her capacity for truth-telling. In short, the information sought by plaintiff is irrelevant to any material issue, and is not calculated to lead to any admissible evidence. Consequently, plaintiff's motion is denied.

The court turns now to the motion to compel discovery brought by defendant. Ross seeks discovery of Davis' treatment by a psychiatrist during the period Davis worked for Ross, arguing that the material is relevant and that any physician-patient privilege has been waived.

When the mental or physical condition of the plaintiff is in issue, the physician-patient privilege is waived and cannot be invoked to foreclose discovery of relevant evidence. Defendant argues that plaintiff put her mental condition in issue when she sued to recover for "great mental pain and anguish" (Complaint ¶ 17).

It is generally true that "[w]here compensation is sought for personal injury, the health of the plaintiff before and after the accident may be inquired into. This principle would seem to have equal applicability to an emotional or mental injury when that is what a plaintiff seeks compensation for." Miller v. Colonial Refrigerated Transportation, Inc., 81 F.R.D. 741, 742 (M.D.Pa.1979). See also Mancinelli v. Texas Eastern Transmission Corp., 34 A.D.2d 535, 308 N.Y.S.2d 882 (1st Dep't 1970) (psychiatric treatment held relevant and discoverable when damages sought for mental injury); Awtry v. United States, 27 F.R.D. 399, 402 (S.D.N.Y.1961) (plaintiff's medical and psychiatric history discoverable where plaintiff alleged mental anguish as result of the entry on his medical chart that he was a hypochondriac).

Plaintiff argues, however, that her mental condition is not in issue, notwithstanding her claim for mental pain and anguish, because her action is one for libel per se and in such actions under New York law, general damages are presumed and need not be specifically pleaded or proved. Under plaintiff's view of New York law, it is unnecessary for her to prove either the existence or amount of damages. Consequently, plaintiff argues, information relating to the existence or amount of mental pain and anguish is not relevant and therefore not discoverable.

Defendant contends that New York's rule permitting recovery for presumed damages in libel cases has been overruled by Gertz v. Robert Welch, Inc., 418 U.S. 323 (1974), and that New York courts, in conformance with the Supreme Court's ruling, now require plaintiffs in cases of libel per se to prove they were damaged (in the absence of a showing of actual malice). [The court found that Gertz had been modified by a later Supreme Court decision, and that the New York courts might return to their former rule, as plaintiff urged.] * * *

[E]ven if plaintiff's view of the law prevails and presumed damages are reinstated, that does not mean that information relating to the existence or amount of damages is irrelevant or not discoverable. General damages may be presumed, but defendant must be permitted to rebut the presumption, to try to disprove the existence of damage. Moreover, the amount of damages will always be in issue; plaintiff seeks one million dollars in compensatory damages, and evidence must be introduced to demonstrate that the award should be more than nominal. See Wood v. Lee, 41 A.D.2d 730, 341 N.Y.S.2d 738 (1st Dep't 1973) (it is assumed that defamation causes some damage though it be nominal). Plaintiff may not sue to recover for mental pain and anguish, only to deny the defendant the evidence she needs to argue that there was no damage, or that the amount of compensation sought is excessive.[5]

Accordingly, defendant's motion to compel discovery of plaintiff's treatment by a psychiatrist is granted.

NOTES AND QUESTIONS

1.   The district judge had earlier dismissed plaintiff's suit on the ground that she had failed to state a claim. Here the court denies all plaintiff's discovery requests and grants defendant's discovery request. Could the court's view of the merits have affected its ruling on the discovery issues? Should it?

---

[5]   Defendant also argues that the psychiatric material is relevant to the issue of whether the allegedly libelous statement was true—whether Davis' personal or work habits truly were objectively unacceptable. In light of the court's decision based on the relevance of the material to the issue of damages, it is unnecessary to reach defendant's other argument.

See Rule 26(b)(2)(C). The judge's discovery rulings can be debated; do not assume they all represent "the law."

2.   It should be apparent that the concept of relevance is critical to the scope of discovery. Relevance analysis has developed in evidence law; Fed. R.Evid. 402 declares that all relevant evidence is admissible, but the law has not developed a precise standard for determining what is relevant. Fed. R. Evid. 401 thus states that " '[r]elevant evidence' means evidence having any tendency to make the existence of any fact that is of consequence to the determination of the action more probable or less probable than it would be without the evidence." The Advisory Committee notes explain how the rule should be applied:

> Relevancy is not an inherent characteristic of any item of evidence but exists only as a relation between an item of evidence and a matter properly provable in the case. Does the item of evidence tend to prove the matter sought to be proved? Whether the relationship exists depends upon the principles evolved by experience or science, applied logically to the situation at hand. The rule summarizes this relationship as a "tendency to make the existence" of the fact to be proved "more probable or less probable."

> * * *

> The rule uses the phrase "fact that is of consequence to the determination of the action" to describe the kind of fact of which proof may properly be directed. * * * The fact to be proved may be ultimate, intermediate, or evidentiary; it matters not, so long as it is of consequence to the determination of the action.

How does this relevance reasoning apply to the types of information in dispute in Davis v. Ross? How does the court decide what is a "fact of consequence" in the case?

3.   Why is information about Ross's financial condition relevant? Would it be relevant to determine whether Ross could pay a judgment? Note that Rule 26(a)(1)(A)(iv) now requires disclosure of insurance policies. When discovery of these was first authorized, the Advisory Committee explained this provision as follows:

> Disclosure of insurance coverage will enable counsel for both sides to make the same realistic appraisal of the case, so that settlement and litigation strategy are based on knowledge and not speculation. It will conduce to settlement and avoid protracted litigation in some cases, though in others it may have the opposite effect. The [rule] is limited to insurance coverage, which should be distinguished from any other facts concerning defendant's financial status (1) because insurance is an asset created specifically to satisfy the claim; (2) because the insurance company ordinarily controls the litigation; (3) because information about coverage is available only from defendant or his insurer; and (4) because disclosure does not involve a significant invasion of privacy.

How persuasive is this reasoning? Should it apply more generally to information about the financial condition of a defendant?

4.   With respect to the financial information sought by plaintiff in Davis v. Ross, the court relies on New York rules governing timing of admission of such material into evidence at trials. How can those rules have any bearing on whether discovery should be allowed? Should discovery regarding the extent of plaintiff's damages await a jury determination that defendant is liable for them? Compare Cal. Civ. Code § 3295(c) (precluding discovery by plaintiff regarding defendant's financial condition until plaintiff establishes a "substantial probability" of prevailing on punitive damages).

The court's principal concern seems to be protecting Ross' privacy. Should privacy concerns prompt courts to narrow discovery? A highly-respected former federal judge has noted that "[a] foreigner watching the discovery proceedings in a civil suit would never suspect that this country has a highly-prized tradition of privacy enshrined in the Fourth Amendment." Rifkind, Are We Asking Too Much of Our Courts?, 70 F.R.D. 96, 107 (1976). For an example of discovery intrusiveness, consider Zises v. Department of Social Services, 112 F.R.D. 223 (E.D.N.Y.1986). Plaintiff in a Title VII employment discrimination suit for sexual harassment revealed in her deposition that during the period in question she had kept an extensive "journal," writing 20 to 30 pages daily in a "stream of unconscious becoming conscious." Because plaintiff testified that she wrote about her experiences at work, the court ordered her to turn over the journal to defendant, and plaintiff decided to abandon her suit rather than turn over her journals. See also Simpson v. University of Colorado, 220 F.R.D. 354 (D.Colo.2004) (student suing university for sexual harassment had to turn over diary entries). Is financial information particularly sensitive? See Pasternak v. Dow Kim, 275 F.R.D. 461 (S.D.N.Y.2011) (denying discovery of financial information on ground it is highly sensitive).

[handwritten margin note: Being Forced to turn over diary entries.]

When privacy interests are involved, should the courts routinely issue protective orders to limit the disclosure of discovered material if discovery is ordered? Absent a protective order, is there any limitation on what Ross does with the information she obtains through discovery about Davis' psychiatric treatment? "Generally speaking, when a party obtains documents or information through the discovery process, he can 'use that information in any way which the law permits.' The discovery rules themselves place no limitations on what a party may do with the materials obtained in discovery." In re Halkin, 598 F.2d 176, 188 (D.C.Cir.1979). In Seattle Times Co. v. Rhinehart, 467 U.S. 20 (1984), however, the Supreme Court endorsed broad discretion for imposition of limitations on dissemination of discovered material where supported by "good cause." For an argument that more weight should be given to limiting use of discovered material to preparation for trial, see Marcus, Myth and Reality in Protective Order Litigation, 69 Cornell L.Rev. 1 (1983).

5.   *Privacy and social media*: The pervasive use of social media has opened vast new vistas of discovery, particularly in litigation involving individuals who have participated in social media. Consider how the courts

should weigh privacy interests in this context. In general, there is no immunity to discovery for social networking site. E.g. Gondola v. USMD PPM, LLC, 223 F.Supp.3d 575 (N.D.Tex.2016); Tompkins v. Detroit Metropolitan Airport, 278 F.R.D. 387, 388 (E.D.Mich.2012). But the courts have not entirely disregarded privacy interests in evaluating discovery requests for such material. For example, in Gordon v. T.G.R. Logistics, Inc., 321 F.R.D. 401 (D.Wyo.2017), the court declined to order plaintiff to provide discovery of her entire social media communication history for three years prior to the accident in which she was seriously injured, rejecting defendant's argument that it needed access to challenge plaintiff's claims for emotional distress (id. at 405–06):

> Defendants have been effectively defending such garden variety emotional distress claims for many years and such claims typically make up a small part of the damages in physical injury cases. * * * This Court has not been provided with any authority for the proposition that access to social media prior to the date of the accident would significantly contribute to the evaluation and diagnosis of these conditions.

Nonetheless, the court did order production of social media postings subsequent to the accident relating to significant emotional turmoil, mental disability or ability, or significant events that could reasonably be expected to result in emotional distress, and it cautioned that plaintiff "is to err on the side of disclosure" in deciding what should be produced. Id. at 406 n. 2.

In Gondola v. USMD PPM, LLC, supra, an employment discrimination action, the court rejected defendant's request that plaintiffs produce all information related to their postings on social networking sites: "A party is no more entitled to such unfettered access to an opponent's social networking communications than it is to rummage through the desk drawers and closets of his opponent's home." Instead, it ordered counsel to confer and develop a more limited focus for the Rule 34 request to "include information, messages, and postings on social networking sites relevant to the claims and defenses in this case, such as any mention of Defendant (by name or otherwise) by Plaintiffs, any discussion of the termination of their employment by Defendant, any discussion of Plaintiffs' job searches after leaving Defendant, and any effects that their termination by Defendant had on Plaintiffs."

Had plaintiff and defendant in Davis v. Ross engaged in the level of social media activity that is now common, what access should they have been able to obtain via discovery? Should the court limit what they did with that information?

6.　　Should confidentiality concerns other than privacy justify denial of discovery? Consider Coca-Cola Bottling Co. v. Coca-Cola Co., 107 F.R.D. 288 (D.Del.1985), in which plaintiffs sought to compel defendant to turn over "one of the best-kept trade secrets in the world," the formula for Coca-Cola. Only two people in the company knew the formula, which was kept in a bank vault in Atlanta, Georgia, that could be opened only upon a resolution by the Company's board of directors. Plaintiffs were independent bottlers who produced the drink by mixing syrup they bought from the company with carbonated water. In 1921, they had entered into contracts that specified the price they would have to pay for "Coca-Cola Bottling syrup." When Diet Coke was introduced in 1982, the company claimed that it was not covered by the contracts because Coca-Cola and Diet Coke were different products. Plaintiffs sued to enforce their contractual right to buy diet Coke syrup at the contractual price and sought the formula because it bore on the question whether these were different products. Eventually the discovery dispute expanded to include old Coke ("Coca-Cola Classic"), new Coke and caffeine free Coke.

The court granted plaintiffs' motion:

The issue squarely presented by plaintiffs' motion to compel is whether plaintiffs' need for the secret formula outweighs defendant's need for protection of its trade secrets. In considering this dispute, I am well aware of the fact that disclosure of trade secrets in litigation, even with the use of an appropriate protective order, could "become by indirection the means of ruining an honest and profitable enterprise." Moreover, I am also aware that an order compelling disclosure of the Company's secret formula could be a bludgeon in the hands of plaintiffs to force a favorable settlement. On the other hand, unless defendant is required to respond to plaintiffs' discovery, plaintiffs will be unable to learn whether defendant has done them a wrong. Except for a few privileged matters, nothing is sacred in civil litigation; even the legendary barriers erected by the Coca-Cola Company to keep its formulae from the world must fall if the formulae are needed to allow plaintiffs and the Court to determine the truth in these disputes.

* * *

As in most disputes over the discoverability of trade secrets, the necessity of the discovery for the complete formulae follows logically from the determination that the formulae are relevant. Plaintiffs need the complete formulae in order to address the product identity issue by comparing the ingredients of the various soft drinks involved. Plaintiffs cannot respond to the assertions of defendant's experts that diet Coke and Coca-Cola are two products unless plaintiffs' experts can analyze the complete formulae and explain why the products are the same. * * *

The potential harm that would come from public disclosure of the formulae for old Coke, new Coke, diet Coke, and caffeine free Coke is great, but virtually all of that harm can be eliminated with stringent protective orders and other safeguards. Because plaintiffs are Coca-Cola bottlers, they will have an incentive to keep the formulae secret. The likelihood of harm is less than if defendant's trade secrets were disclosed in litigation to competitors. The potential for harm from protected disclosure of the formulae for old Coke, new

Coke, diet Coke, and caffeine free Coke is outweighed by the plaintiffs' need for the information.

Is this information less confidential than financial information about Diana Ross? Is the need for the information greater? What protective order provision should the court use to protect the company? Couldn't a similar order be fashioned to protect Ross' privacy interest?

7.   Should protective orders also be granted for business information that is not, like the formula for Coca-Cola, a trade secret? There has been much consternation about the possibility that information about allegedly dangerous products has been produced through discovery but has been kept from the general public under protective orders. See, e.g., Cipollone v. Liggett Group, Inc., 785 F.2d 1108 (3d Cir.1986), cert. denied, 484 U.S. 976 (1987) (protective order applied to all discovery in tobacco products liability litigation). Some states have imposed restrictions on protective orders in cases involving "public health hazards." See Florida "Sunshine in Litigation Act," Fla.Stats. § 69.081; Tex.R.Civ.P. 76a. Should discovery be used as a device to provide the public with information? For discussion see Marcus, The Discovery Confidentiality Controversy, 1991 U.Ill.L.Rev. 457; Miller, Confidentiality, Protective Orders, and Public Access to the Courts, 105 Harv.L.Rev. 427 (1991).

8.   Should the court in Davis v. Ross have been solicitous of plaintiff's desire to keep confidential her treatment by a psychiatrist while she was working for Ross? Besides damages, would information about this treatment be relevant to other issues in the case? See the court's footnote 5. Yet this relevant evidence may be unavailable due to the psychotherapist-patient privilege. The court holds that plaintiff has waived this privilege by placing her mental condition at issue in her claim for mental pain and anguish. Is this fair?

9.   Could defendant also require plaintiff to submit to a mental examination regarding her pain and suffering claim? In Vinson v. Superior Court, 740 P.2d 404 (Cal.1987), plaintiff sought damages for mental distress in her sexual harassment employment discrimination suit. The state supreme court refused to overturn an order that she undergo a psychological examination. It noted that "plaintiff haled defendants into court and accused them of causing her various mental and emotional ailments" and that her mental state was therefore in controversy. It added, however, that "[a] simple sexual harassment claim asking for compensation for having to endure an oppressive work environment or for wages lost following an unjust dismissal would not normally create a controversy regarding the plaintiff's mental state." Id. at 409; see also Robinson v. Jacksonville Shipyards, Inc., 118 F.R.D. 525, 531 (N.D.Fla.1988) ("ruling in favor of a mental examination * * * would endorse mental examinations in every Title VII hostile work environment sexual harassment case").

Covering in fac[l]

KOZLOWSKI V. SEARS, ROEBUCK & CO.

United States District Court, District of Massachusetts, 1976
73 F.R.D. 73

- Show us your complaints case

JULIAN, SENIOR DISTRICT JUDGE.

Item in "scope of disc."

Burden shifted to other party to defend withholding

A brief statement of the prior events in this case suffices to explain the present posture of the defendant's motion to remove the default judgment. Plaintiff, a minor, was severely burned on November 11, 1970, in Royal Oak, Michigan, when a pair of pajamas allegedly manufactured and marketed by defendant was "caused to ignite." Plaintiff commenced this product liability action on April 9, 1975, asserting claims sounding in negligence, breach of warranty, and strict liability in tort.

On July 17, 1975, the plaintiff filed a "Request to Produce" pursuant to Rule 34, Federal Rules of Civil Procedure, seeking, among other items, a record of all complaints and communications concerning personal injuries or death allegedly caused by the burning of children's nightwear which had been manufactured or marketed by the defendant, Sears, Roebuck & Co. On August 8, 1975, the defendant filed a motion to quash. The plaintiff opposed the defendant's motion to quash and filed a motion to compel discovery pursuant to Rule 37, Federal Rules of Civil Procedure. On January 22, 1976, United States Magistrate Princi filed a "Memorandum and Order," after a hearing on the motions, overruling the defendant's objections and ordering production within thirty days of all thirty-one items.[2] Because the material was not forthcoming, the plaintiff filed, on April 16, 1976, a motion for entry of judgment by default against the defendant, pursuant to Rule 37, Federal Rules of Civil Procedure. On July 14, 1976, this Court, finding that the defendant's failure to comply with a previous discovery order was "willful and deliberate," entered a judgment by default against the defendant on the issue of liability, but conditioned its removal upon the defendant's "full compliance" with the Court's discovery order on or before September 15, 1976. On September 14, 1976, the defendant filed the instant motion to remove the judgment by default. The Court held a hearing on the motion on October 20, 1976, and took it under advisement. On the basis of that hearing, the Court finds that the defendant has failed substantially to comply fully with the Court's July 14 Order, and thus has not fulfilled the condition for removal of the default judgment.

The Court now denies defendant's motion for reasons hereinafter stated.

In the instant case, information concerning accidents similar to the one alleged in the complaint is clearly relevant to the issues of whether the pajamas allegedly marketed by the defendant were an unreasonably

---

[2] The Magistrate's order modified the plaintiff's request to produce as to twenty-five of the items by imposing a time limit on the materials requested of five years prior and three years subsequent to November 11, 1970.

dangerous product and whether the defendant knew, or in the exercise of due care should have known, of that danger. Furthermore, even though the records of similar suits might be inadmissible in evidence (Narring v. Sears, Roebuck & Co., 59 Mich.App. 717, 229 N.W.2d 901 (1975) (circumstances of prior accident were too dissimilar to accident alleged in complaint)), the records might contain facts which would lead to the discovery of admissible evidence. See Rule 26(b)(1). Accordingly, most courts have held that the existence and nature of other complaints in product liability cases is a proper subject for pretrial discovery.

Nevertheless, information of similar complaints has not been produced by the defendant. The defendant has contended throughout this litigation and reiterated at the October 20 hearing that because of its longstanding practice of indexing claims alphabetically by name of claimant, rather than by type of product, there is no practical way for anyone to determine whether there have been any complaints similar to those alleged in the complaint at bar, "other than [by] going through all of the . . . claims . . . in the Sears Index . . . which is the equivalent of an impossible task." No evidence has been produced tending to establish the truth of this representation.

> *If it were true, would it matter?*

Under Rule 34, Fed.R.Civ.P., the party from whom discovery is sought has the burden of showing some sufficient reason why discovery should not be allowed, once it has been determined that the items sought are properly within the scope of Rule 26(b). Merely because compliance with a "Request for Production" would be costly or time-consuming is not ordinarily sufficient reason to grant a protective order where the requested material is relevant and necessary to the discovery of evidence.

In the instant case, the requested documents are clearly within the scope of Rule 26(b), Fed.R.Civ.P., the plaintiff has a demonstrable need for the documents, the defendant undisputedly has possession of them, and the plaintiff has no other access to them. Thus, the defendant has a duty pursuant to Rule 34, Fed.R.Civ.P., to produce its records of similar suits. The defendant seeks to absolve itself of this responsibility by alleging the herculean effort which would be necessary to locate the documents. The defendant may not excuse itself from compliance with Rule 34, Fed. R.Civ.P., by utilizing a system of record-keeping which conceals rather than discloses relevant records, or makes it unduly difficult to identify or locate them, thus rendering the production of the documents an excessively burdensome and costly expedition. To allow a defendant whose business generates massive records to frustrate discovery by creating an inadequate filing system, and then claiming undue burden, would defeat the purposes of the discovery rules.

* * *

Finally, the defendant makes a confusing offer to finance the transportation to Chicago, Illinois (where the records are kept), by the plaintiff's attorney so that he may either attempt to locate the desired documents among the defendant's massive files, or else verify for himself the impossibility of such a task. The defendant has in essence told the plaintiff that, if he wishes, he may hunt through all its documents and find the information for himself. "This amounts to nothing more than a gigantic 'do it yourself' kit." This Court will not shift the financial burden of discovery onto the discovering party, in this case an indigent plaintiff, where the costliness of the discovery procedure involved is entirely a product of the defendant's self-serving indexing scheme over which the plaintiff has no control.

(covering in full)

McPeek v. Ashcroft

United States District Court, District of Columbia, 2001
202 F.R.D. 31

Facciola, United States Magistrate Judge

Plaintiff, Steven McPeek, began working for the Bureau of Prisons ("BOP") on May 27, 1986. He insists that, upon his promotion to Assistant to the Director in 1990, then-Director of the BOP, J. Michael Quinlan ("Quinlan"), began to sexually harass him and did so for the next two years. Plaintiff then filed an informal complaint against Quinlan, with the Department of Justice ("DOJ") Equal Employment Opportunity Staff. The matter was investigated and culminated in a Settlement Agreement on September 30, 1992. The agreement required that McPeek's complaints about Quinlan be kept confidential by both sides and that McPeek be transferred to the Management and Planning Staff ("MPS"), Justice Management Division ("JMD"), of DOJ. By 1994, plaintiff was working for the Justice Performance Review ("JPR"), under the Office of Policy Development and would ultimately become the Deputy Director of JPR, where he reported to Robert F. Diegelman ("Diegelman"), Director of MPS.

Plaintiff's complaint identifies two forms of retaliation. He first complains that, despite the confidentiality of the settlement agreement, his claims against Quinlan were known by the people with whom he worked and that he suffered humiliation and retaliation at their hands. He then complains that, after hiring counsel in July 1998 to pursue formal legal remedies beginning with EEO counseling, he suffered renewed retaliation efforts.

In responding to plaintiff's discovery, defendants have searched for electronic and paper documents. Since defendants have already searched for electronic records, they do not quarrel with their obligation to do so. During discovery, the producing party has an obligation to search available electronic systems for the information demanded. See Fed.R.Civ.P. 34(a) (document(s) include "data compilations from which information can be obtained"). Plaintiff, however, wants more. He wants to force DOJ to search its backup systems since they might yield, for example, data that was ultimately deleted by the user but was stored on the backup tape and remains there today.

Defendants protest that the remote possibility that such a search will yield relevant evidence cannot possibly justify the costs involved. In support of that claim, defendants submit the declaration of Billy Hoppis, Branch Chief within the JMD office responsible for technology services. Hoppis explains that for the period 1992–1998, the DOJ computer system was known as "Eagle." In 1998, DOJ computers were briefly connected to a system called "JCON1." From 1998 to the present, they have been connected to "JCON2."

There was never a system-wide backup policy for Eagle servers. Each DOJ building had a server and an administrator who had his or her own backup policies. DOJ never intended a system which perfectly preserved all data. The purpose of having a backup system and retaining the tapes was to permit recovery from a disaster, not archival preservation. As a result, there are backup tapes for some periods of time but not others. Additionally, Hoppis explains:

> These backup tapes record only a "snapshot" of the contents of a user's working directory and emails (in the inbox, outbox, and trash) as of the specific date and time the backup was run, and therefore do not necessarily contain all emails sent or from a user, or all documents. In addition, unless a user deletes emails or documents between backups, each backup tape might contain many duplicate emails and documents that were captured on previous backup tapes.

Finally, the backup tapes have to be "restored" or rendered readable by returning the files to a source (i.e., a disk or hard drive) from which they can be read by the application which originally created them. Then, someone would have to review the restored file, whether a word processing document or e-mail, and determine whether it falls within one of plaintiff's document requests. Hoppis estimates that using JCON2, the present operating system, merely restoring the e-mail from a single backup tape would take eight hours at a cost of no less than $93 per hour.

Using traditional search methods to locate paper records in a digital world presents unique problems. In a traditional "paper" case, the producing party searches where she thinks appropriate for the documents requested under Fed.R.Civ.P. 34. She is aided by the fact that files are traditionally organized by subject or chronology ("chron" files), such as all the files of a particular person, independent of subject. Backup tapes are by their nature indiscriminate. They capture all information at a given time and from a given server but do not catalogue it by subject matter.

Unlike a labeled file cabinet or paper files organized under an index, the collection of data by the backup tapes in this case was random. It must be remembered that the DOJ's use of a backup "synch" software system was not for the purpose of creating a perfect mirror image of each user's hard drive. Instead, the system was designed to prevent disaster, i.e., the destruction of all the data being produced on a given day if the network system crashed. Once the day ended and the system had not crashed, the system administrator could breathe a sigh of relief. She may then have maintained that day's backup tapes for some period of time, but then eventually taped over them. This explains why the tapes that remain today, ones which I ordered preserved, are tapes for certain days or periods of time but not for others and therefore not in perfect (or for that matter imperfect) chronological order.

It is therefore impossible to know in advance what is on these backup tapes. There is a theoretical possibility that there may be something on the tapes that is relevant to a claim or defense, for example, a subsequently deleted e-mail that might be evidence of a retaliatory motive. That possibility exists because other information establishes that the persons plaintiff claims retaliated against him used their computers for word processing and e-mail, and the backup tapes may have captured what those persons have since deleted from their computer files.

DOJ has chosen not to search these backup tapes and therefore runs the risk that the trial judge may give the jury an instruction that this failure to search permits the inference that the unfound files would contain information detrimental to DOJ. Conversely, the trial judge may ultimately determine that an instruction should not be given, and therefore DOJ lacks any incentive to conduct a search. Given the potential costs involved, a defendant may be more than willing to decline to search the backup tapes and take the chance that either the court will not give such an instruction at trial, or that if such an instruction is given, defendant will still prevail. In any event, a substantial number of civil cases settle and discovery advances the prospects of settlement. Any potential advancement of settlement would be foregone if the defendant has the option of choosing not to do the search and there is good reason to think that information on the backup tapes might induce one party or the other to settle.

There is certainly no controlling authority for the proposition that restoring all backup tapes is necessary in every case. The Federal Rules of Civil Procedure do not require such a search, and the handful of cases are idiosyncratic and provide little guidance. The one judicial rationale that has emerged is that producing backup tapes is a cost of doing business in the computer age. In re Brand Name Prescription Drugs, 1995 WL 360526 at * 3 (N.D.Ill., June 15, 1995). But, that assumes an alternative. It is impossible to walk ten feet into the office of a private business or government agency without seeing a network computer, which is on a server, which, in turn, is being backed up on tape (or some other media) on a daily, weekly or monthly basis. What alternative is there? Quill pens?

Furthermore, making the producing party pay for all costs of restoration as a cost of its "choice" to use computers creates a disincentive for the requesting party to demand anything less than all of the tapes. American lawyers engaged in discovery have never been accused of asking for too little. To the contrary, like the Rolling Stones, they hope that if they ask for what they want, they will get what they need. They hardly need any more encouragement to demand as much as they can from their opponent.

The converse solution is to make the party seeking the restoration of the backup tapes pay for them, so that the requesting party literally gets what it pays for. Those who favor a "market" economic approach to the law would argue that charging the requesting party would guarantee that the requesting party would only demand what it needs. Under that rationale, shifting the cost of production solves the problem.

But, there are two problems with that analysis. First, a strict cost-based approach ignores the fact that a government agency is not a profit-producing entity and it cannot be said that paying costs in this case would yield the same "profit" that other foregone economic activity would yield. Additionally, the government, which has no fewer rights than anyone else, has to insist that its employees do the restoration lest confidential information be seen by someone not employed by the government who has no right to see it. The reality, therefore, is that a government employee will be diverted from his ordinary duties to search backup tapes. When employees are thus diverted from their ordinary duties, the function of the agency suffers to the detriment of the taxpayers. Moreover, if government agencies are consistently required to pay for the restoration of backup tapes, they may be sorely tempted not to have such systems. There lies disaster; one shudders to think what would happen if the computer system at the Social Security Administration crashed and there was no backup system. While the notion that government agencies and businesses will not have backup systems if they are forced to restore them whenever they are sued may seem fanciful, courts should not lead them into temptation.

Second, if it is reasonably certain that the backup tapes contain information that is relevant to a claim or defense, shifting all costs to the requesting party means that the requesting party will have to pay for the agency to search the backup tapes even though the requesting party would not have to pay for such a search of a "paper" depository.

A fairer approach borrows, by analogy, from the economic principle of "marginal utility." The more likely it is that the backup tape contains information that is relevant to a claim or defense, the fairer it is that the government agency search at its own expense. The less likely it is, the more unjust it would be to make the agency search at its own expense. The difference is "at the margin."

Finally, economic considerations have to be pertinent if the court is to remain faithful to its responsibility to prevent "undue burden or expense". Fed.R.Civ.P. 26(c). If the likelihood of finding something was the only criterion, there is a risk that someone will have to spend hundreds of thousands of dollars to produce a single e-mail. That is an awfully expensive needle to justify searching a haystack. It must be recalled that ordering the producing party to restore backup tapes upon a showing of likelihood that they will contain relevant information in every case gives the plaintiff a gigantic club with which to beat his opponent into settlement. No corporate president in her right mind would fail to settle a lawsuit for $100,000 if the restoration of backup tapes would cost $300,000. While that scenario might warm the cockles of certain lawyers' hearts, no one would accuse it of being just.

Given the complicated questions presented, the clash of policies and the lack of precedential guidance, I have decided to take small steps and perform, as it were, a test run. Accordingly, I will order DOJ to perform a backup restoration of the e-mails attributable to Diegelman's computer during the period of July 1, 1998 to July 1, 1999. I have chosen this period because a letter from plaintiff's counsel to DOJ, complaining of retaliation and threatening to file an administrative claim, is dated July 2, 1998, and it seems to me a convenient and rational starting point to search for evidence of retaliation. I have chosen e-mail because of its universal use and because I am hoping that the restoration will yield both the e-mails Diegelman sent and those he received.

The DOJ will have to carefully document the time and money spent in doing the search. It will then have to search in the restored e-mails for any document responsive to any of plaintiff's requests for production of documents. Upon the completion of this search, the DOJ will then file a comprehensive, sworn certification of the time and money spent and the results of the search. Once it does, I will permit the parties an opportunity to argue why the results and the expense do or do not justify any further search.

NOTES AND QUESTIONS

1. *Changes wrought by rule amendments*: Since these cases were decided, significant rule changes have occurred. In 2006, Rule 26(b)(2)(B) (bearing directly on the problem presented in *McPeek*) was adopted. Then in 2015, proportionality was moved directly into the definition of the scope of discovery. Recall Proportionality and the 2015 Rule Amendments, supra p. 354. Review Rules 26(b)(1) and (b)(2)(B). One important question is whether these amendments made a sea change in the discovery landscape.

In *Kozlowski*, the judge said that "[m]erely because compliance with a 'Request for Production' would be costly or time-consuming is not ordinarily sufficient reason to grant a protective order where the requested material is relevant and necessary to the discovery of evidence." The judge in *McPeek* has a decidedly different attitude about the value of further efforts to locate responsive materials. It should be apparent that the *McPeek* court's attitude is in step with the contemporary rules, and that the judge's attitude in *Kozlowski* seems out of step. Which attitude makes more sense to you? The judge in *McPeek* refers to the risk that discovery could give plaintiff "a gigantic club with which to beat his opponent into settlement." Is it likely that corporate defendants like Sears, Roebuck would succumb to that club?

Focusing on the current Rule 26(b)(1) proportionality factors, is it clear that either of these discovery disputes would be resolved significantly differently if presented now? One possible difference is that the rules now forbid "boilerplate" objections. For example, in Orchestratehr, Inc. v. Trombetta, 178 F.Supp.3d 476 (N.D.Tex.2016), defendants objected that responding would be "unduly burdensome and expensive." The court flatly rejected those objections, invoking the 2015 amendments (id. at 507):

> [G]eneral objections like these are invalid. Objections to discovery must be made with specificity, and the responding party has the obligation to explain and support its objections. Amended Federal Rule of Civil Procedure 34(b)(2) effectively codifies this requirement.

Did the defendants in these two cases do what the current rules require?

2.   *Burden of proof on burden of production*: A concern expressed by some about the 2015 amendments was that the proponent of discovery would have to demonstrate affirmatively that the proposed discovery was not unduly burdensome to the other side, even though it would not often have the information needed to make that showing. The Committee Note accompanying this rule change explains that it "does not change the existing responsibilities of the court and the parties to consider proportionality, and the change does not place on the party seeking discovery the burden of addressing all proportionality considerations." The Note continues:

> The parties may begin discovery without a full appreciation of the factors that bear on proportionality. A party requesting discovery, for example, may have little information about the burden or expense of responding. A party requested to provide discovery may have little information about the importance of the discovery in resolving the issues as understood by the requesting party. Many of these uncertainties should be addressed and reduced in the parties' Rule 26(f) conference and in scheduling and pretrial conferences with the court. * * * A party claiming undue burden or expense ordinarily has far better information—perhaps the only information—with respect to that part of the determination. A party claiming that a request is important to resolve the issues should be able to explain the ways in

which the underlying information bears on an issue as that party understands them.

Did the parties behave in this manner in either *Kozlowski* or *McPeek*?

3. *Application of the proportionality factors*: Consider the proportionality factors specified in Rule 26(b)(1). How should they be applied in these cases.

(a) *Importance of the issues*: The Committee Note acknowledges that cases involving "public policy" issues or "vitally important personal or public values" could call for expansive discovery even if they involved limited monetary stakes. Perhaps the paradigm example would be Brown v. Board of Education, the Supreme Court's 1954 decision declaring racial segregation in public schools unconstitutional. How should the issues in *Kozlowski* and *McPeek* be regarded?

(b) *The amount in controversy*: One might say this factor points in a different direction from the first factor. A litigant who says she is asserting a matter of "principle" might seek to justify extremely burdensome discovery on that ground. On the other hand, when the monetary stakes are enormous—consider some class actions—that might validate discovery that in ordinary cases would seem wasteful. How should *Kozlowski* and *McPeek* be regarded on this score?

(c) *The parties' relative access to information*: This factor was added to the list after public comment raised concerns about the proportionality provision. How should it be applied in *Kozlowski* and *McPeek*?

(d) *The parties' resources*: The Committee Note says that "consideration of the parties' resources does not foreclose discovery requests addressed to an impecunious party, nor justify unlimited discovery requests addressed to a wealthy party." Assuming plaintiffs in *Kozlowski* were of moderate means, how should this consideration be applied? In *McPeek*, had the defendant demanded that plaintiff produce all his email messages and social media posts about his alleged harasser or about retaliation against him, whether or not he had deleted them, how should this factor affect the decision whether to order production? Should it be thought that the government's resources are unlimited?

(e) *The importance of the discovery in resolving the issues*: Should all the discovery sought in *Kozlowski* be regarded as important in resolving the issues presented in that case? Consider whether all communications Sears had received about burning of children's nightwear really would be important to resolving the case before the court. Note the way in which the Magistrate Judge modified the discovery request before ordering Sears to comply.

Compare Fassett v. Sears Holdings Corp., 319 F.R.D. 143 (M.D.Pa.2017), in which plaintiff sued for severe injuries he sustained after being burned when gasoline sprayed on him from the gas cap of his riding lawnmower and ignited. He made a broad discovery request for Sears to produce information about any alternative cap designs considered for such devices. Noting that "discovery is not properly construed as an all-or-nothing game," id. at 153, the court explained how one should approach this issue (id. at 147):

> I hold that in a products liability suit such as this one, faithful adherence to the amended Rule 26(b)(1)'s renewed proportionality mandate is furthered considerably by implementation of a sliding scale analysis: material corresponding to alternative designs or components that exhibit significant similarities to the design or component at issue should be discoverable in the greatest quantities and for the most varied purposes; however, material corresponding to alternative designs or components that share less in common with the contested design or component should be incrementally less discoverable—and for more limited purposes—as those similarities diminish.

(f)   *The burden compared to the benefit*: Consider where Sears would look for responsive material in Fassett v. Sears Holding Corp, the 2017 lawnmower case in note 3(e) above. How much would be in hard copy as opposed to digital form? How should a party with digital information seek material responsive to a discovery request?

In Meredith v. United Collection Bureau, Inc., 319 F.R.D. 240 (N.D.Ohio 2017), plaintiff sued defendant after receiving a number of calls on her cellular phone from automatic telephone dialing systems operated by defendant, which she asserted violated the Telephone Consumer Protection Act. She sued on behalf of a class of others who received similar calls from defendant, and sought discovery about calls made to others. Defendant objected that it would have to conduct a manual review of more than 278,000 calls to respond to this request. Id. at 242. Plaintiff urged that the solution was to query defendant's database for responsive information, but defendant argued that such a request was not authorized because it did not seek electronically stored information as it was stored in the regular course of defendant's business, and because writing a program to perform the query would take a few days and might interfere with its ability to conduct its business during regular business hours. The court rejected defendant's argument, quoting another judge's resolution of a similar issue in a patent infringement dispute between Apple Corp. and Samsung (id. at 243):

> Apple does have financial databases that it could query to generate at least some of the reports sought by Samsung. While this court has held that a party should not be required to create completely new documents, that is not the same as requiring a party to query an existing dynamic database for relevant information. Courts regularly require parties to produce reports from dynamic databases, holding "the technical burden . . . of creating a new dataset for the instant litigation does not excuse compelling production."

In the automatic dialing case, the court found that "[w]hile Defendant has shown that there will be some burden to it in responding to Plaintiff's request, the burden does not outweigh the likely benefit of production." Id. at 244.

How should courts approach this balance in employment discrimination cases? Consider Hollander v. American Cyanamid Co., 895 F.2d 80 (2d Cir.1990), an Age Discrimination in Employment Act suit by a fired manager. The appellate court held that the district judge had improperly refused to require an answer to plaintiff's interrogatory about all other management personnel over 40 whom defendant had fired in the previous five years:

> Because employers rarely leave a paper trail—or "smoking gun"— attesting to discriminatory intent, disparate treatment plaintiffs often must build their cases from pieces of circumstantial evidence which cumulatively undercut the credibility of various explanations offered by the employer. * * * The district court's refusal to compel an answer from American Cyanamid deprived Hollander of evidence potentially helpful to his attempt to assemble such a quantum of circumstantial evidence supporting his argument of pretext.

4. *Who should pay the cost of responding?*: The 2015 amendments also amended Rule 26(c)(1)(B), which now authorizes protective orders including "allocation of expenses" for discovery. The Committee Note cautions: "Recognizing the authority does not imply that cost-shifting should become a common practice. Courts and parties should continue to assume that a responding party ordinarily bears the costs of responding." Consider the incentive structure that results from the presumption that the responding party should bear the cost. See Redish & McNamara, Back to the Future: Cost Allocation and Modern Procedural Theory, 79 Geo. Wash. L. Rev. 773 (2011) (urging that quantum meruit theories should compel the requesting party to reimburse the responding party for the cost of complying with discovery requests).

In some American court systems, responding parties may sometimes be entitled to routine reimbursement. In Toshiba America Electronic Components, Inc. v. Superior Court, 21 Cal.Rptr.3d 532 (Cal.Ct.App.2004), the court held that a California statute required the demanding party to pay the cost of conversion of backup tapes unless the trial court finds that the conversion of the tapes was not necessary, or that the cost was not reasonable. Cal. Civ. Pro. § 2031.280(c) says that "if necessary, the responding party at the reasonable expense of the demanding party shall, through detecting devices, translate any data compilations included in the demand into reasonably usable form." Toshiba said it had over 800 backup tapes, and that the cost of restoring them would be $1.5–1.9 million. The court recognized that the California provision "conflicts with the federal rule, but it appears that the Legislature intended it to be that way." Therefore it was not a matter of discretion for the trial court, and Toshiba had a right to be paid the reasonable cost of restoring the tapes.

5. In *Kozlowski*, the court says that the cost of responding is the result of Sears' "self-serving indexing scheme." Should that concern bear on cost allocation? Would it matter if Sears' system conformed to "industry practice"? Should companies be expected to set up their information systems in a way to assists their litigation adversaries?

6.   In terms of burden, compare Rule 33(d), regarding interrogatories, which provides the responding party with the option of inviting the other side to generate the requested information from the producing party's records. Is that like what the *Kozlowski* court called "a gigantic do-it-yourself kit"? Note that it requires that the producing party affirm that "the burden of deriving or ascertaining the answer is substantially the same for either party."

Rule 34 does not have a "look at my files" option similar to the provisions of Rule 33(d). Ordinarily, the responding party must locate and assemble the items requested at its own expense. That is what Sears was refusing to do, since plaintiff did not want all files on complaints, but only those regarding burning children's pajamas. If the requests are broad, however, culling responsive information from the mass of unrequested documents may impose a burden similar to the Rule 33(d) situation. But Rule 34(b)(2)(E)(i) does give the producing party a choice between organizing the produced documents in accordance with the requests or as they are kept in the usual course of business. There is disagreement on whether the party seeking discovery can insist that the producing party organize the material in accord with the requests. Compare Sherman & Kinnard, Federal Court Discovery in the 80's—Making the Rules Work, 95 F.R.D. 245, 256–57 (1982) (arguing that "[i]n a case like *Kozlowski*, the discovered party should only be allowed to produce its documents as kept in the usual course of business if that method is shown to provide sufficient indexing so that relevant documents can be found") with 8A C. Wright, A. Miller & R. Marcus, Federal Practice & Procedure § 2213 (3d ed. 2010) (arguing that rearrangement of files is not required).

7.   Cases like *McPeek* can raise significant privacy issues as well as cost issues. Consider the range of personal matters that may be discussed in e-mail or otherwise be stored on a computer hard drive. See, e.g., Fraser v. Nationwide Mutual Ins. Co., 352 F.3d 107 (3d Cir.2003) (defendant employer did not violate plaintiff employee's privacy rights by reviewing plaintiff's e-mail because it was stored on defendant's system).

D. EXEMPTIONS FROM DISCOVERY

Even though relevant, "privileged" material is exempt from discovery. Probably the most important privilege from the perspective of lawyers is the attorney-client privilege, discussed in Upjohn Co. v. United States, infra p. 408. It protects confidential communications between lawyer and client in which the client seeks legal advice. The idea is to promote full disclosure by the client to the lawyer. At the time Hickman v. Taylor was decided, the rules contained no further provisions about exemptions from discovery; Rule 26(b)(3) (dealing with "trial preparation materials") and Rules 26(a)(2) and 26(b)(4) (dealing with discovery from experts) were added later.

HICKMAN V. TAYLOR

Supreme Court of the United States, 1947
329 U.S. 495

JUSTICE MURPHY delivered the opinion of the Court.

This case presents an important problem under the Federal Rules of Civil Procedure as to the extent to which a party may inquire into oral and written statements of witnesses, or other information, secured by an adverse party's counsel in the course of preparation for possible litigation after a claim has arisen. Examination into a person's files and records, including those resulting from the professional activities of an attorney, must be judged with care. It is not without reason that various safeguards have been established to preclude unwarranted excursions into the privacy of a man's work. At the same time, public policy supports reasonable and necessary inquiries. Properly to balance these competing interests is a delicate and difficult task.

On February 7, 1943, the tug "J.M. Taylor" sank while engaged in helping to tow a car float of the Baltimore & Ohio Railroad across the Delaware River at Philadelphia. The accident was apparently unusual in nature, the cause of it still being unknown. Five of the nine crew members were drowned. Three days later the tug owners and the underwriters employed a law firm, of which respondent Fortenbaugh is a member, to defend them against potential suits by representatives of the deceased crew members and to sue the railroad for damages to the tug.

A public hearing was held on March 4, 1943, before the United States Steamboat Inspectors, at which the four survivors were examined. This testimony was recorded and made available to all interested parties. Shortly thereafter, Fortenbaugh privately interviewed the survivors and took statements from them with an eye toward the anticipated litigation; the survivors signed these statements on March 29. Fortenbaugh also interviewed other persons believed to have some information relating to the accident and in some cases he made memoranda of what they told him. At the time when Fortenbaugh secured the statements of the survivors, representatives of two of the deceased crew members had been in communication with him. Ultimately claims were presented by representatives of all five of the deceased; four of the claims, however, were settled without litigation. The fifth claimant, petitioner herein, brought suit in a federal court under the Jones Act on November 26, 1943, naming as defendants the two tug owners, individually and as partners, and the railroad.

One year later, petitioner filed 39 interrogatories directed to the tug owners. The 38th interrogatory read: "State whether any statements of the members of the crews of the Tugs 'J.M. Taylor' and 'Philadelphia' or of any other vessel were taken in connection with the towing of the car float and the sinking of the Tug 'John M. Taylor'. Attach hereto exact copies of all such statements if in writing, and if oral, set forth in detail the exact provisions of any such oral statements or reports."

Supplemental interrogatories asked whether any oral or written statements, records, reports or other memoranda had been made concerning any matter relative to the towing operation, the sinking of the tug, the salvaging and repair of the tug, and the death of the deceased. If the answer was in the affirmative, the tug owners were then requested to set forth the nature of all such records, reports, statements or other memoranda.

The tug owners, through Fortenbaugh, answered all of the interrogatories except No. 38 and the supplemental ones just described. While admitting that statements of the survivors had been taken, they declined to summarize or set forth the contents. They did so on the ground that such requests called "for privileged matter obtained in preparation for litigation" and constituted "an attempt to obtain indirectly counsel's private files." It was claimed that answering these requests "would involve practically turning over not only the complete files, but also the telephone records and, almost, the thoughts of counsel."

In connection with the hearing on these objections, Fortenbaugh made a written statement and gave an informal oral deposition explaining the circumstances under which he had taken the statements. But he was not expressly asked in the deposition to produce the statements. The District Court for the Eastern District of Pennsylvania, sitting en banc, held that the requested matters were not privileged. The court then decreed that the tug owners and Fortenbaugh, as counsel and agent for the tug owners forthwith "Answer Plaintiff's 38th interrogatory and supplemental interrogatories; produce all written statements of witnesses obtained by Mr. Fortenbaugh, as counsel and agent for Defendants; state in substance any fact concerning this case which Defendants learned through oral statements made by witnesses to Mr. Fortenbaugh whether or not included in his private memoranda and produce Mr. Fortenbaugh's memoranda containing statements of fact by witnesses or to submit these memoranda to the Court for determination of those portions which should be revealed to Plaintiff." Upon their refusal, the court adjudged them in contempt and ordered them imprisoned until they complied.

The Third Circuit Court of Appeals, also sitting en banc, reversed the judgment of the District Court. It held that the information here sought was part of the "work product of the lawyer" and hence privileged from discovery under the Federal Rules of Civil Procedure. The importance of the problem, which has engendered a great divergence of views among district courts, led us to grant certiorari.

[Before turning to the merits, the Court dealt with what it deemed a "procedural irregularity" regarding the discovery tools employed. Prior court approval was then required for production of documents under Rule

34, so that to the extent plaintiff was trying to obtain documents by using interrogatories, he had employed the wrong device. While "[a] party clearly cannot refuse to answer interrogatories on the ground the information sought is solely within the knowledge of his attorney," the Court saw plaintiff's interrogatories as tantamount to a document production request. Noting that "[t]he deposition-discovery rules create integrated procedural devices," however, the Court declined to decide the case on this ground. Instead, the Court emphasized the need for a liberal interpretation of the discovery rules, see supra p. 350, and turned to "the basic question at stake," which it described as "whether any of those devices may be used to inquire into materials collected by an adverse party's counsel in the course of preparation for possible litigation." It concluded that the materials sought were not covered by the attorney-client privilege because "the protective cloak of this privilege does not extend to information which an attorney secures from a witness while acting for his client in anticipation of litigation. Nor does this privilege concern the memoranda, briefs, communications and other writings prepared by counsel for his own use in prosecuting his client's case."]

* * *

But the impropriety of invoking that privilege does not provide an answer to the problem before us. Petitioner has made more than an ordinary request for relevant, non-privileged facts in the possession of his adversaries or their counsel. He has sought discovery as of right of oral and written statements of witnesses whose identity is well known and whose availability to petitioner appears unimpaired. He has sought production of these matters after making the most searching inquiries of his opponents as to the circumstances surrounding the fatal accident, which inquiries were sworn to have been answered to the best of their information and belief. Interrogatories were directed toward all the events prior to, during and subsequent to the sinking of the tug. Full and honest answers to such broad inquiries would necessarily have included all pertinent information gleaned by Fortenbaugh through his interviews with the witnesses. Petitioner makes no suggestion, and we cannot assume, that the tug owners or Fortenbaugh were incomplete or dishonest in the framing of their answers. In addition, petitioner was free to examine the public testimony of the witnesses taken before the United States Steamboat Inspectors. We are thus dealing with an attempt to secure the production of written statements and mental impressions contained in the files and the mind of the attorney Fortenbaugh without any showing of necessity or any indication or claim that denial of such production would unduly prejudice the preparation of petitioner's case or cause him any hardship or injustice. For aught that appears, the essence of what petitioner seeks either has been revealed to him already through the interrogatories or is readily available to him direct from the witnesses for the asking.

The District Court, after hearing objections to petitioner's request, commanded Fortenbaugh to produce all written statements of witnesses and to state in substance any facts learned through oral statements of witnesses to him. Fortenbaugh was to submit any memoranda he had made of the oral statements so that the court might determine what portions should be revealed to petitioner. All of this was ordered without any showing by petitioner, or any requirement that he make a proper showing, of the necessity for the production of any of this material or any demonstration that denial of production would cause hardship or injustice. The court simply ordered production on the theory that the facts sought were material and were not privileged as constituting attorney-client communications.

In our opinion, neither Rule 26 nor any other rule dealing with discovery contemplates production under such circumstances. That is not because the subject matter is privileged or irrelevant, as those concepts are used in these rules.[9] Here is simply an attempt, without purported necessity or justification, to secure written statements, private memoranda and personal recollections prepared or formed by an adverse party's counsel in the course of his legal duties. As such, it falls outside the arena of discovery and contravenes the public policy underlying the orderly prosecution and defense of legal claims. Not even the most liberal of discovery theories can justify unwarranted inquiries into the files and the mental impressions of an attorney.

Historically, a lawyer is an officer of the court and is bound to work for the advancement of justice while faithfully protecting the rightful interests of his clients. In performing his various duties, however, it is essential that a lawyer work with a certain degree of privacy, free from unnecessary intrusion by opposing parties and their counsel. Proper preparation of a client's case demands that he assemble information, sift what he considers to be the relevant from the irrelevant facts, prepare his legal theories and plan his strategy without undue and needless interference. That is the historical and the necessary way in which lawyers act within the framework of our system of jurisprudence to promote justice and to protect their clients' interests. This work is reflected, of course, in interviews, statements, memoranda, correspondence, briefs, mental impressions,

---

[9]   The English courts have developed the concept of privilege to include all documents prepared by or for counsel with a view to litigation. "All documents which are called into existence for the purpose—but not necessarily the sole purpose—of assisting the deponent or his legal advisers in any actual or anticipated litigation are privileged from production. . . . Thus all proofs, briefs, draft pleadings, etc., are privileged; but not counsel's endorsement on the outside of his brief . . ., nor any deposition or notes of evidence given publicly in open Court. . . . So are all papers prepared by any agent of the party bona fide for the use of his solicitor for the purposes of the action, whether in fact so used or not. . . . Reports by a company's servant, if made in the ordinary course of routine, are not privileged, even though it is desirable that the solicitor should have them and they are subsequently sent to him; but if the solicitor has requested that such documents shall always be prepared for his use and this was one of the reasons why they were prepared, they need not be disclosed." Odgers on Pleading and Practice (12th ed., 1939), p. 264.

personal beliefs, and countless other tangible and intangible ways—aptly though roughly termed by the Circuit Court of Appeals in this case as the "work product of the lawyer." Were such materials open to opposing counsel on mere demand, much of what is now put down in writing would remain unwritten. An attorney's thoughts, heretofore inviolate, would not be his own. Inefficiency, unfairness and sharp practices would inevitably develop in the giving of legal advice and in the preparation of cases for trial. The effect on the legal profession would be demoralizing. And the interests of the clients and the cause of justice would be poorly served.

We do not mean to say that all written materials obtained or prepared by an adversary's counsel with an eye toward litigation are necessarily free from discovery in all cases. Where relevant and non-privileged facts remain hidden in an attorney's file and where production of those facts is essential to the preparation of one's case, discovery may properly be had. Such written statements and documents might, under certain circumstances, be admissible in evidence or give clues as to the existence or location of relevant facts. Or they might be useful for purposes of impeachment or corroboration. And production might be justified where the witnesses are no longer available or can be reached only with difficulty. Were production of written statements and documents to be precluded under such circumstances, the liberal ideals of the deposition-discovery portions of the Federal Rules of Civil Procedure would be stripped of much of their meaning. But the general policy against invading the privacy of an attorney's course of preparation is so well recognized and so essential to an orderly working of our system of legal procedure that a burden rests on the one who would invade that privacy to establish adequate reasons to justify production through a subpoena or court order. That burden, we believe, is necessarily implicit in the rules as now constituted.

Rule 30(b),* as presently written, gives the trial judge the requisite discretion to make a judgment as to whether discovery should be allowed as to written statements secured from witnesses. But in the instant case there was no room for that discretion to operate in favor of the petitioner. No attempt was made to establish any reason why Fortenbaugh should be forced to produce the written statements. There was only a naked, general demand for these materials as of right and a finding by the District Court that no recognizable privilege was involved. That was insufficient to justify discovery under these circumstances and the court should have sustained the refusal of the tug owners and Fortenbaugh to produce.

But as to oral statements made by witnesses to Fortenbaugh, whether presently in the form of his mental impressions or memoranda, we do not believe that any showing of necessity can be made under the circumstances of this case so as to justify production. Under ordinary conditions, forcing

---

*   Under the 1970 amendments, Rule 30(b) was moved to Rule 26, where it appears as Rule 26(c).—Eds.

an attorney to repeat or write out all that witnesses have told him and to deliver the account to his adversary gives rise to grave dangers of inaccuracy and untrustworthiness. No legitimate purpose is served by such production. The practice forces the attorney to testify as to what he remembers or what he saw fit to write down regarding witnesses' remarks. Such testimony could not qualify as evidence; and to use it for impeachment or corroborative purposes would make the attorney much less an officer of the court and much more an ordinary witness. The standards of the profession would thereby suffer.

Denial of production of this nature does not mean that any material, non-privileged facts can be hidden from the petitioner in this case. He need not be unduly hindered in the preparation of his case, in the discovery of facts or in his anticipation of his opponents' position. Searching interrogatories directed to Fortenbaugh and the tug owners, production of written documents and statements upon a proper showing and direct interviews with the witnesses themselves all serve to reveal the facts in Fortenbaugh's possession to the fullest possible extent consistent with public policy. Petitioner's counsel frankly admits that he wants the oral statements only to help prepare himself to examine witnesses and to make sure that he has overlooked nothing. That is insufficient under the circumstances to permit him an exception to the policy underlying the privacy of Fortenbaugh's professional activities. If there should be a rare situation justifying production of these matters, petitioner's case is not of that type.

JUSTICE JACKSON, concurring.

* * *

The primary effect of the practice advocated here would be on the legal profession itself. But it too often is overlooked that the lawyer and the law office are indispensable parts of our administration of justice. Law-abiding people can go nowhere else to learn the ever changing and constantly multiplying rules by which they must behave and to obtain redress for their wrongs. The welfare and tone of the legal profession is therefore of prime consequence to society, which would feel the consequences of such a practice as petitioner urges secondarily but certainly.

Counsel for the petitioner candidly said on argument that he wanted this information to help prepare himself to examine witnesses, to make sure he overlooked nothing. He bases his claim to it in his brief on the view that the Rules were to do away with the old situation where a law suit developed into "a battle of wits between counsel." But a common law trial is and always should be an adversary proceeding. Discovery was hardly intended to enable a learned profession to perform its functions either without wits or on wits borrowed from the adversary.

The real purpose and the probable effect of the practice ordered by the district court would be to put trials on a level even lower than a "battle of wits." I can conceive of no practice more demoralizing to the Bar than to require a lawyer to write out and deliver to his adversary an account of what witnesses have told him. Even if his recollection were perfect, the statement would be his language permeated with his inferences. Every one who has tried it knows that it is almost impossible so fairly to record the expressions and emphasis of a witness that when he testifies in the environment of the court and under the influence of the leading question there will not be departures in some respects. Whenever the testimony of the witness would differ from the "exact" statement the lawyer had delivered, the lawyer's statement would be whipped out to impeach the witness. Counsel producing his adversary's "inexact" statement could lose nothing by saying, "Here is a contradiction, gentlemen of the jury. I do not know whether it is my adversary or his witness who is not telling the truth, but one is not." Of course, if this practice were adopted, that scene would be repeated over and over again. The lawyer who delivers such statements often would find himself branded a deceiver afraid to take the stand to support his own version of the witness's conversation with him, or else he will have to go on the stand to defend his own credibility—perhaps against that of his chief witness, or possibly even his client.

Every lawyer dislikes to take the witness stand and will do so only for grave reasons. This is partly because it is not his role; he is almost invariably a poor witness. But he steps out of professional character to do it. He regrets it; the profession discourages it. But the practice advocated here is one which would force him to be a witness, not as to what he has seen or done but as to other witnesses' stories, and not because he wants to do so but in self-defense.

And what is the lawyer to do who has interviewed one whom he believes to be a biased, lying or hostile witness to get his unfavorable statements and know what to meet? He must record and deliver such statements even though he would not vouch for the credibility of the witness by calling him. Perhaps the other side would not want to call him either, but the attorney is open to the charge of suppressing evidence at the trial if he fails to call such a hostile witness even though he never regarded him as reliable or truthful.

JUSTICE FRANKFURTER joins in this opinion.

NOTES AND QUESTIONS

1.   Rule 26, as written in 1947, exempted only "privileged" information from discovery, but the Court in *Hickman* simultaneously declares that the material sought is not privileged and that it is not discoverable although relevant. Are the Court's reasons persuasive in view of its emphasis on the

broad discovery authorized under the federal rules? Consider Professor Cooper's evaluation:

Clearly no one would argue today that a court should be forced to determine a law suit on the basis of inadequate information in order to preserve for one party the advantages gained by luck, skill, or wealth. Discovery itself rests on the impatient rejection of any assertion of a proprietary privilege to prevail because of unilateral ignorance; if there is some "unfairness" in unbridled discovery, it must be sought in terms of interference with the just disposition of litigation.

In searching for interference with the litigation process, the Court's stern reference to "inefficiency, unfairness and sharp practices," and its clarion cry against demoralizing the legal profession, make heady reading. Unfortunately, they add nothing but an obscuring color of rhetoric to the implicit proposition that the adversary system of litigation cannot function in an atmosphere of complete candor; if no one mourns the sporting theory of justice, still there must be an area of gamesmanship in which fear of the unknown enforces an honesty which mere ethics could not achieve. The fact that litigation has remained adversarial in form and an operational reality must be thought to be responsible for generating pressure toward winning representation, which could lead to dishonest tactics if there were no limits on discovery.

Lacking any basis in controllable or even measurable experience to test such a fear about the effects of discovery, it would be difficult to quarrel with it except by advancing an intuition that no such special protection is really needed. And intuition tugs at least as strongly toward the proposition that discovery can best serve the ultimate truth-finding purposes of the adversary system if its equalizing function is subject to some such limitations. As long as the attorney is charged with the duty of presenting the most favorable case possible for his client, there will be the temptations and impetus of advocacy to strain his ultimate obligation to justice as well as to victory. Perfect knowledge of every item of proof and argument, of the complete trial "strategy" of opposing counsel, would often result— unconsciously in most cases—in a development of position and response calculated to impede rather than advance the search for whatever truth ex post inquiry can obtain.

Cooper, Work Product of the Rulesmakers, 53 Minn.L.Rev. 1269, 1274–75 (1969); compare Wells, The Attorney Work Product Doctrine and Carry-Over Immunity: An Assessment of Their Justifications, 47 U.Pitt.L.Rev. 675, 683 (1986) ("a closer look at the specific rationales [for the work product rule], however, suggests that the work product immunity is largely designed to protect lawyers from themselves and their own unprofessionalism, rather than from their adversaries").

2. If the idea behind work product protection is to preserve some element of surprise for trial, similar concerns have surfaced in connection with certain types of impeachment evidence which might be rendered ineffective if the witness could find out about it before testifying. As one judge put it, "[a] certain amount of surprise is often a catalyst which precipitates the truth. * * * [T]here are facile witnesses whose interest in 'knowing the truth before trial' is prompted primarily by a desire to find the most plausible ways to defeat the truth." Margeson v. Boston & Maine R.R., 16 F.R.D. 200, 201 (D.Mass.1954). Accordingly, some judges have denied access to tools of impeachment such as films showing that the plaintiff is not as badly injured as he claims. Does such a procedure subject parties to unfair risks at trial? See Boldt v. Sanders, 111 N.W.2d 225 (Minn.1961) ("it is implicit in [defendant's] position that witnesses whose testimony is designed to impeach invariably have a monopoly on virtue and that evidence to which the attempted impeachment is directed is, without exception, fraudulent"). See Denham & Bales, The Discoverability of Surveillance Videotapes Under the Federal Rules, 52 Baylor L. Rev. 753 (2000).

3. The simple expedient of taking the deposition of the other side's lawyer might not have occurred to lawyers at the time *Hickman* was decided, but by the 1980s that had changed: "In recent years, the boundaries of discovery have steadily expanded, and it appears that the practice of taking the deposition of opposing counsel has become an increasingly popular vehicle of discovery. To be sure, the Federal Rules of Civil Procedure do not specifically prohibit the taking of opposing counsel's deposition. See Fed. R.Civ.P. 30(a)(1) (a party may take the deposition of 'any person'). We view the increasing practice of taking opposing counsel's deposition as a negative development in the area of litigation, and one that should be employed only in limited circumstances." Shelton v. American Motors Corp., 805 F.2d 1323, 1327 (8th Cir.1986). If the work product doctrine is available to resist improper questions, is the taking of the lawyer's deposition a significant threat to work product concerns? See In re Subpoena Issued to Dennis Friedman, 350 F.3d 65 (2d Cir. 2003) (rejecting rule that would "automatically insulate" lawyers from depositions, and focusing on "whether the proposed deposition would entail an inappropriate burden or hardship").

4. The *Hickman* Court's refusal to call work product a privilege persists among some. See Cohn, The Work-Product Doctrine: Protection, Not Privilege, 71 Geo.L.J. 917 (1983). But the only sense in which it is not a privilege is that it is not absolute, as the attorney-client privilege is supposed to be. The Court may have rejected the privilege designation in *Hickman* due to embarrassment: "the Court was once more trapped by an apparently felt necessity of saving face by refusing to admit that a contingency had arisen which the rules had not foreseen or had dealt with improvidently." Cleary, Hickman v. Jencks: Jurisprudence of the Adversary System, 14 Vand.L.Rev. 865, 866 (1961). Even the Court itself has since referred to it as "the work product privilege." F.T.C. v. Grolier Inc., 462 U.S. 19, 26 (1983).

5.   In 1970, the Court adopted Rule 26(b)(3), which formally incorporated protection for "trial preparation materials" into the rules. In what way is the protection afforded by Rule 26(b)(3) different from that provided in Hickman? See Marcus, The Story of *Hickman*: Preserving Adversarial Incentives While Embracing Broad Discovery, in Civil Procedure Stories (2d ed. 2008) at 323, 347–48 (comparing Rule 26(b)(3) and *Hickman*). For example, consider:

(a)   Would *Hickman* have provided any protection had the statements in that case been taken by an insurance adjuster? How would these be handled under the rule?

(b)   Would Rule 26(b)(3) provide Fortenbaugh any basis for refusing in his deposition to answer questions about what he recalled of his interviews with the witnesses?

6.   Both *Hickman* and Rule 26(b)(3) direct that special protection be afforded the kind of material whose revelation Professor Cooper found most troubling—information about trial strategy. Are there any circumstances under which such materials should be turned over? In Duplan Corp. v. Moulinage et Retorderie de Chavanoz, 509 F.2d 730 (4th Cir.1974), cert. denied, 420 U.S. 997 (1975), the court concluded that "no showing of relevance, substantial need or undue hardship should justify compelled disclosure of an attorney's mental impressions, conclusions, opinion or legal theories." See also Cal.Code Civ.Proc. § 2018.030(a): "A writing that reflects an attorney's impressions, conclusions, opinions, or legal research or theories is not discoverable under any circumstances." In Holmgren v. State Farm Mut. Auto. Ins. Co., 976 F.2d 573 (9th Cir.1992), a bad faith action against an insurer, the court upheld discovery of memoranda prepared by defendant's adjuster even though it was opinion work product. It found that the adjuster's opinions were "directly in issue" and concluded that Rule 26(b)(3) "permits discovery when mental impressions are the pivotal issue in the current litigation and the need for the material is compelling."

7.   Work product protection is available only if material is produced in anticipation of litigation. Why is this consideration important to the policies furthered by the doctrine? How likely must litigation appear? Although four of the five possible claims in *Hickman* were settled, it is doubtful that a court would hold that in such a situation there was not a sufficient likelihood of litigation, but the doctrine does not protect all attorney action, only that directed toward preparation for trial. Thus, in United States v. El Paso Co., 682 F.2d 530 (5th Cir.1982), cert. denied, 466 U.S. 944 (1984), the court, noting that "determining whether a document is prepared in anticipation of litigation is a slippery task," held that El Paso's "tax pool analysis" of its potential exposure for underpayment of taxes was part of its ordinary accounting procedure and therefore not entitled to protection. Ordinarily, the anticipation of litigation test looks to the date a document came into existence, the date of attorney involvement, and the date on which suit was first filed or threatened. Material generated in the ordinary course of business is usually not considered to have been developed in anticipation of litigation. See generally Note, Work

Product Discovery: A Multifactor Approach to the Anticipation of Litigation Requirement in Federal Rule of Civil Procedure 26(b)(3), 66 Iowa L.Rev. 1277 (1981).

8.   If litigation is too remote a prospect to afford protection to some attorney work, does the fact that the litigation for which the work was done has ended mean that the protection should be removed in a second, unrelated litigation? The lower courts have divided on this question, some ruling that the protection only endures in "related" litigation. In Federal Trade Comm'n v. Grolier Inc., 462 U.S. 19 (1983), the Court confronted the question whether work product generated in connection with terminated litigation could be withheld from a request under the Freedom of Information Act because it was still protected by the doctrine. The Court held that the material could be withheld, but did not hold that the same would be true in civil litigation.

Justice Brennan, concurring, urged that the protection should be permanent:

> [D]isclosure of work product connected to prior litigation can cause real harm to the interests of the attorney and his client even after the controversy in the prior litigation is resolved. Many government agencies, for example, deal with hundreds or thousands of essentially similar cases in which they must decide whether and how to conduct enforcement litigation. Few of these cases will be "related" to each other in the sense of involving the same private parties or arising out of the same set of historical facts; yet large classes of them may present recurring, parallel factual settings and identical legal and policy considerations. It would be of substantial benefit to an opposing party (and of corresponding detriment to an agency) if the party could obtain work product generated by the agency in connection with earlier, similar litigation against other persons. * * * Any litigants who face litigation of a commonly recurring type— liability insurers, manufacturers of consumer products or machinery, large-scale employers, securities brokers, regulated industries, civil rights or civil liberties organizations, and so on—have an acute interest in keeping private the manner in which they conduct and settle their recurring legal disputes.

How persuasive are these arguments? Do they provide a basis for a blanket rule that work product protection can endure forever?

9.   The Court in *Hickman* emphasized the duty of the party to provide, in response to discovery, factual information learned by its attorney. Why won't this deter the lawyer from investigating? Can a litigant simply ask its opponent to describe in detail all investigation done by its attorney? See U.S. v. All Assets Held at Bank Julius Baer & Co., 270 F.R.D. 220 (D.D.C.2017) (discovery seeking the identity of every person interviewed by counsel invaded work product, but discovery could seek the identity of all people with knowledge about the issues in the case). To the extent that the witnesses were unearthed by counsel, how meaningful is this distinction?

10. Note the special treatment of witness statements in Rule 26(b)(3)(C). Why should they be treated in a different way? Consider the ultimate fate of the statements in *Hickman* itself:

> After fighting for the right to secure the statements of the accident witnesses from Fortenbaugh's file all the way to the Supreme Court, Freedman [plaintiff's lawyer] objected to the admission of the very same material at Hickman's trial. His objection, moreover, was sustained. Freedman today explains his objection by claiming that the statements must have been all favorable to Fortenbaugh's client, or else he would not have taken them. "When my opponent takes a statement from a witness, I'm going to fight like hell to keep it out."

Coady, Dredging the Depths of Hickman v. Taylor, Harvard Law Record, May 6, 1977, at 7.

11. What showing should be required to justify discovery of work product? Could plaintiff have made a showing in *Hickman*? See Vallabharapurapu v. Burger King Corp., 276 F.R.D. 611 (N.D.Cal.2011) (defendant ordered to produce architectural surveys of over 600 restaurants in class action about disability access; it would take plaintiffs over two years, at a cost of at least $630,000, to compile this information); Coogan v. Cornet Transportation Co., 199 F.R.D. 166 (D.Md.2001) (plaintiffs would be allowed to obtain the statement prepared by one defendant at the scene of the accident because it captured defendant's immediate perceptions of the accident); compare Goodyear Tire & Rubber Co. v. Chiles Power Supply, Inc., 190 F.R.D. 532 (N.D.Ind.1999) (witness statements prepared by defendant's insurer need not be produced; although three years had passed, plaintiff offered no evidence to show that it was prevented from obtaining the information it desired). Would the fact that there was a record of the hearing before the U.S. Steamboat Inspectors affect the decision whether plaintiff in *Hickman* had made the showing?

UPJOHN CO. V. UNITED STATES

Supreme Court of the United States, 1981
449 U.S. 383

JUSTICE REHNQUIST delivered the opinion of the Court.

* * *

I

Petitioner Upjohn Co. manufactures and sells pharmaceuticals here and abroad. In January 1976 independent accountants conducting an audit of one of Upjohn's foreign subsidiaries discovered that the subsidiary made payments to or for the benefit of foreign government officials in order to secure government business. The accountants so informed petitioner Mr. Gerard Thomas, Upjohn's Vice President, Secretary, and General Counsel. Thomas is a member of the Michigan and New York Bars, and has been Upjohn's General Counsel for 20 years. He consulted with outside counsel and R.T. Parfet, Jr., Upjohn's Chairman of the Board. It was decided that the company would conduct an internal investigation of what were termed "questionable payments." As part of this investigation the attorneys prepared a letter containing a questionnaire which was sent to "All Foreign General and Area Managers" over the chairman's signature. The letter began by noting recent disclosures that several American companies made "possibly illegal" payments to foreign government officials and emphasized that the management needed full information concerning any such payments made by Upjohn. The letter indicated that the chairman had asked Thomas, identified as "the company's General Counsel," "to conduct an investigation for the purpose of determining the nature and magnitude of any payments made by the Upjohn Company or any of its subsidiaries to any employee or official of a foreign government." The questionnaire sought detailed information concerning such payments. Managers were instructed to treat the investigation as "highly confidential" and not to discuss it with anyone other than Upjohn employees who might be helpful in providing the requested information. Responses were to be sent directly to Thomas. Thomas and outside counsel also interviewed the recipients of the questionnaire and some 33 other Upjohn officers or employees as part of the investigation.

On March 26, 1976, the company voluntarily submitted a preliminary report to the Securities and Exchange Commission on Form 8-K disclosing certain questionable payments. A copy of the report was simultaneously submitted to the Internal Revenue Service, which immediately began an investigation to determine the tax consequences of the payments. Special agents conducting the investigation were given lists by Upjohn of all those interviewed and all who had responded to the questionnaire. On November 23, 1976, the Service issued a summons pursuant to 26 U.S.C. § 7602 demanding production of:

> "All files relative to the investigation conducted under the supervision of Gerard Thomas to identify payments to employees of foreign governments and any political contributions made by the Upjohn Company or any of its affiliates since January 1, 1971 and to determine whether any funds of the Upjohn Company had been improperly accounted for on the corporate books during the same period."

> "The records should include but not be limited to written questionnaires sent to managers of the Upjohn Company's foreign affiliates, and memorandums or notes of the interviews conducted in the United States and abroad with officers and employees of the Upjohn Company and its subsidiaries."

The company declined to produce the documents specified in the second paragraph on the grounds that they were protected from disclosure by the attorney-client privilege and constituted the work product of attorneys prepared in anticipation of litigation. On August 31, 1977, the United States filed a petition seeking enforcement of the summons under 26 U.S.C. §§ 7402(b) and 7604(a) in the United States District Court for the Western District of Michigan. That court adopted the recommendation of a Magistrate who concluded that the summons should be enforced. Petitioners appealed to the Court of Appeals for the Sixth Circuit which rejected the Magistrate's finding of a waiver of the attorney-client privilege, but agreed that the privilege did not apply "[t]o the extent that the communications were made by officers and agents not responsible for directing Upjohn's actions in response to legal advice . . . for the simple reason that the communications were not the 'client's.' " The court reasoned that accepting petitioners' claim for a broader application of the privilege would encourage upper-echelon management to ignore unpleasant facts and create too broad a "zone of silence." Noting that Upjohn's counsel had interviewed officials such as the Chairman and President, the Court of Appeals remanded to the District Court so that a determination of who was within the "control group" could be made. In a concluding footnote the court stated that the work-product doctrine "is not applicable to administrative summonses issued under 26 U.S.C. § 7602."

II

Federal Rule of Evidence 501 provides that "the privilege of a witness . . . shall be governed by the principles of the common law as they may be interpreted by the courts of the United States in light of reason and experience." The attorney-client privilege is the oldest of the privileges for confidential communications known to the common law. Its purpose is to encourage full and frank communication between attorneys and their clients and thereby promote broader public interests in the observance of law and administration of justice. The privilege recognizes that sound legal advice or advocacy serves public ends and that such advice or advocacy depends upon the lawyer's being fully informed by the client. As we stated last Term in Trammel v. United States, 445 U.S. 40, 51 (1980): "The lawyer-client privilege rests on the need for the advocate and counselor to know all that relates to the client's reasons for seeking representation if the professional mission is to be carried out." And in Fisher v. United States, 425 U.S. 391, 403 (1976), we recognized the purpose of the privilege to be "to encourage clients to make full disclosure to their attorneys." This rationale for the privilege has long been recognized by the Court. Admittedly complications in the application of the privilege arise when the client is a corporation, which in theory is an artificial creature of the law, and not an individual; but this Court has assumed that the privilege applies when the client is a corporation, and the Government does not contest the general proposition.

The Court of Appeals, however, considered the application of the privilege in the corporate context to present a "different problem," since the client was an inanimate entity and "only the senior management, guiding and integrating the several operations, . . . can be said to possess an identity analogous to the corporation as a whole." 600 F.2d at 1226. The first case to articulate the so-called "control group test" adopted by the court below, Philadelphia v. Westinghouse Electric Corp., 210 F.Supp. 483, 485 (E.D.Pa. 1962), reflected a similar conceptual approach:

> "Keeping in mind that the question is, Is it the corporation which is seeking the lawyer's advice when the asserted privileged communication is made? the most satisfactory solution, I think, is that if the employee making the communication, of whatever rank he may be, is in a position to control or even to take a substantial part in a decision about any action which the corporation may take upon the advice of the attorney, . . . then, in effect, *he is (or personifies) the corporation* when he makes his disclosure to the lawyer and the privilege would apply." (Emphasis supplied.)

Such a view, we think, overlooks the fact that the privilege exists to protect not only the giving of professional advice to those who can act on it but also the giving of information to the lawyer to enable him to give sound and informed advice. The first step in the resolution of any legal problem is ascertaining the factual background and sifting through the facts with an eye to the legally relevant. See ABA Code of Professional Responsibility, Ethical Consideration 4–1:

> "A lawyer should be fully informed of all the facts of the matter he is handling in order for his client to obtain the full advantage of our legal system. It is for the lawyer in the exercise of his independent professional judgment to separate the relevant and important from the irrelevant and unimportant. The observance of the ethical obligation of a lawyer to hold inviolate the confidences and secrets of his client not only facilitates the full development of facts essential to proper representation of the client but also encourages laymen to seek early legal assistance."

In the case of the individual client the provider of information and the person who acts on the lawyer's advice are one and the same. In the corporate context, however, it will frequently be employees beyond the control group as defined by the court below—"officers and agents . . . responsible for directing [the company's] actions in response to legal advice"—who will possess the information needed by the corporation's lawyers. Middle-level—and indeed lower-level—employees can, by actions within the scope of their employment, embroil the corporation in serious legal difficulties, and it is only natural that these employees would have the relevant information needed by corporate counsel if he is adequately to advise the client with respect to such actual or potential difficulties. This fact was noted in Diversified Industries, Inc. v. Meredith, 572 F.2d 596 (C.A.8 1977) (en banc):

"In a corporation, it may be necessary to glean information relevant to a legal problem from middle management or non-management personnel as well as from top executives. The attorney dealing with a complex legal problem 'is thus faced with a "Hobson's choice". If he interviews employees not having "the very highest authority," their communications to him will not be privileged. If, on the other hand, he interviews only those employees with the "very highest authority", he may find it extremely difficult, if not impossible, to determine what happened.' "

The control group test adopted by the court below thus frustrates the very purpose of the privilege by discouraging the communication of relevant information by employees of the client to attorneys seeking to render legal advice to the client corporation. The attorney's advice will also frequently be more significant to noncontrol group members than to those who officially sanction the advice, and the control group test makes it more difficult to convey full and frank legal advice to the employees who will put into effect the client corporation's policy.

The narrow scope given the attorney-client privilege by the court below not only makes it difficult for corporate attorneys to formulate sound advice when their client is faced with a specific legal problem but also threatens to limit the valuable efforts of corporate counsel to ensure their client's compliance with the law. In light of the vast and complicated array of regulatory legislation confronting the modern corporation, corporations, unlike most individuals, "constantly go to lawyers to find out how to obey the law," particularly since compliance with the law in this area is hardly an instinctive matter, see, e.g., United States v. United States Gypsum Co., 438 U.S. 422, 440–441 (1978) ("the behavior proscribed by the (Sherman) Act is often difficult to distinguish from the gray zone of socially acceptable and economically justifiable business conduct").[2] The test adopted by the court below is difficult to apply in practice, though no abstractly formulated and unvarying "test" will necessarily enable courts to decide questions such as this with mathematical precision. But if the purpose of the attorney-client privilege is to be served, the attorney and client must be able to predict with some degree of certainty whether particular discussions will be protected. An uncertain privilege, or one which purports to be certain but results in widely varying applications by the courts, is little better than no privilege at all. The very terms of the test adopted by the court below suggest the unpredictability of its application. The test restricts the

---

[2]   The Government argues that the risk of civil or criminal liability suffices to ensure that corporations will seek legal advice in the absence of the protection of the privilege. This response ignores the fact that the depth and quality of any investigations to ensure compliance with the law would suffer, even were they undertaken. The response also proves too much, since it applies to all communications covered by the privilege: an individual trying to comply with the law or faced with a legal problem also has strong incentive to disclose information to his lawyer, yet the common law has recognized the value of the privilege in further facilitating communications.

availability of the privilege to those officers who play a "substantial role" in deciding and directing a corporation's legal response. Disparate decisions in cases applying this test illustrate its unpredictability. Compare, e.g., Hogan v. Zletz, 43 F.R.D. 308, 315–316 (N.D.Okl.1967), aff'd in part sub nom. Natta v. Hogan, 392 F.2d 686 (C.A.10 1968) (control group includes managers and assistant managers of patent division and research and development department), with Congoleum Industries, Inc. v. GAF Corp., 49 F.R.D. 82, 83–85 (E.D.Pa.1969), aff'd, 478 F.2d 1398 (C.A.3 1973) (control group includes only division and corporate vice presidents, and not two directors of research and vice president for production and research).

The communications at issue were made by Upjohn employees[3] to counsel for Upjohn acting as such, at the direction of corporate superiors in order to secure legal advice from counsel. As the Magistrate found, "Mr. Thomas consulted with the Chairman of the Board and outside counsel and thereafter conducted a factual investigation to determine the nature and extent of the questionable payments and to be in a position to give legal advice to the company with respect to the payments." Information, not available from upper-echelon management, was needed to supply a basis for legal advice concerning compliance with securities and tax laws, foreign laws, currency regulations, duties to shareholders, and potential litigation in each of these areas. The communications concerned matters within the scope of the employees' corporate duties, and the employees themselves were sufficiently aware that they were being questioned in order that the corporation could obtain legal advice. The questionnaire identified Thomas as "the company's General Counsel" and referred in its opening sentence to the possible illegality of payments such as the ones on which information was sought. A statement of policy accompanying the questionnaire clearly indicated the legal implications of the investigation. The policy statement was issued "in order that there be no uncertainty in the future as to the policy with respect to the practices which are the subject of this investigation." It began "Upjohn will comply with all laws and regulations," and stated that commissions or payments "will not be used as a subterfuge for bribes or illegal payments" and that all payments must be "proper and legal." Any future agreements with foreign distributors or agents were to be approved "by a company attorney" and any questions concerning the policy were to be referred "to the company's General Counsel." This statement was issued to Upjohn employees worldwide, so that even those interviewees not receiving a questionnaire were aware of the legal implications of the interviews. Pursuant to explicit instructions from the Chairman of the Board, the communications were considered "highly confidential" when made, and have been kept confidential by the company.

---

[3] Seven of the eighty-six employees interviewed by counsel had terminated their employment with Upjohn at the time of the interview. Petitioners argue that the privilege should nonetheless apply to communications by these former employees concerning activities during their period of employment. Neither the District Court nor the Court of Appeals had occasion to address this issue, and we decline to decide it without the benefit of treatment below.

Consistent with the underlying purposes of the attorney-client privilege, these communications must be protected against compelled disclosure.

The Court of Appeals declined to extend the attorney-client privilege beyond the limits of the control group test for fear that doing so would entail severe burdens on discovery and create a broad "zone of silence" over corporate affairs. Application of the attorney-client privilege to communications such as those involved here, however, puts the adversary in no worse position than if the communications had never taken place. The privilege only protects disclosure of communications; it does not protect disclosure of the underlying facts by those who communicated with the attorney:

> "[T]he protection of the privilege extends only to communications and not to facts. A fact is one thing and a communication concerning that fact is an entirely different thing. The client cannot be compelled to answer the question, 'What did you say or write to the attorney?' but may not refuse to disclose any relevant fact within his knowledge merely because he incorporated a statement of such fact into his communication to his attorney." Philadelphia v. Westinghouse Electric Corp., 205 F.Supp. 830, 831 (E.D.Pa.1962).

See also State ex rel. Dudek v. Circuit Court, 34 Wis.2d 559, 580, 150 N.W.2d 387, 399 (1967) ("the courts have noted that a party cannot conceal a fact merely by revealing it to his lawyer"). Here the Government was free to question the employees who communicated with Thomas and outside counsel. Upjohn has provided the IRS with a list of such employees, and the IRS has already interviewed some 25 of them. While it would probably be more convenient for the Government to secure the results of petitioner's internal investigation by simply subpoenaing the questionnaires and notes taken by petitioner's attorneys, such considerations of convenience do not overcome the policies served by the attorney-client privilege. As Justice Jackson noted in his concurring opinion in Hickman v. Taylor, 329 U.S., at 516: "Discovery was hardly intended to enable a learned profession to perform its functions . . . on wits borrowed from the adversary."

* * *

III

Our decision that the communications by Upjohn employees to counsel are covered by the attorney-client privilege disposes of the case so far as the responses to the questionnaires and any notes reflecting responses to interview questions are concerned. The summons reaches further, however, and Thomas has testified that his notes and memoranda of interviews go beyond recording responses to his questions. To the extent that the material subject to the summons is not protected by the attorney-client privilege as disclosing communications between an employee and counsel, we must reach the ruling by the Court of Appeals that the work-product doctrine does not apply to summonses issued under 26 U.S.C. § 7602.[6]

* * *

While conceding the applicability of the work-product doctrine, the Government asserts that it has made a sufficient showing of necessity to overcome its protections. The Magistrate apparently so found. The Government relies on the following language in Hickman:

> "We do not mean to say that all written materials obtained or prepared by an adversary's counsel with an eye toward litigation are necessarily free from discovery in all cases. Where relevant and nonprivileged facts remain hidden in an attorney's file and where production of those facts is essential to the preparation of one's case, discovery may properly be had. . . . And production might be justified where the witnesses are no longer available or can be reached only with difficulty."

The Government stresses that interviewees are scattered across the globe and that Upjohn has forbidden its employees to answer questions it considers irrelevant. The above-quoted language from *Hickman*, however, did not apply to "oral statements made by witnesses . . . whether presently in the form of [the attorney's] mental impressions or memoranda." As to such material the Court did "not believe that any showing of necessity can be made under the circumstances of this case so as to justify production. . . . If there should be a rare situation justifying production of these matters petitioner's case is not of that type." Forcing an attorney to disclose notes and memoranda of witnesses' oral statements is particularly disfavored because it tends to reveal the attorney's mental processes.[8]

Rule 26 accords special protection to work product revealing the attorney's mental processes. The Rule permits disclosure of documents and tangible things constituting attorney work product upon a showing of substantial need and inability to obtain the equivalent without undue hardship. This was the standard applied by the Magistrate. Rule 26 goes on, however, to state that "[i]n ordering discovery of such materials when the required showing has been made, the court shall protect against disclosure of the mental impressions, conclusions, opinions or legal theories of an attorney or other representative of a party concerning the litigation." Although this language does not specifically refer to memoranda based on

---

[6]   The following discussion will also be relevant to counsel's notes and memoranda of interviews with the seven former employees should it be determined that the attorney-client privilege does not apply to them. See n. 3, supra.

[8]   Thomas described his notes of the interviews as containing "what I considered to be the important questions, the substance of the responses to them, my beliefs as to the importance of these, my beliefs as to how they related to the inquiry, my thoughts as to how they related to other questions. In some instances they might even suggest other questions that I would have to ask or things that I needed to find elsewhere."

oral statements of witnesses, the *Hickman* court stressed the danger that compelled disclosure of such memoranda would reveal the attorney's mental processes. It is clear that this is the sort of material the draftsmen of the Rule had in mind as deserving special protection.

Based on the foregoing, some courts have concluded that no showing of necessity can overcome protection of work product which is based on oral statements from witnesses. Those courts declining to adopt an absolute rule have nonetheless recognized that such material is entitled to special protection. We do not decide the issue at this time. It is clear that the Magistrate applied the wrong standard when he concluded that the Government had made a sufficient showing of necessity to overcome the protections of the work-product doctrine. * * * While we are not prepared at this juncture to say that such material is always protected by the workproduct rule, we think a far stronger showing of necessity and unavailability by other means than was made by the Government or applied by the Magistrate in this case would be necessary to compel disclosure.

[Opinion of CHIEF JUSTICE BURGER, concurring in part and concurring in the judgment, omitted.]

NOTES AND QUESTIONS

1.   A person asserting the attorney-client privilege must satisfy a number of requirements to show that it applies. A widely-cited statement of the requirements lists eight: "(1) Where legal advice of any kind is sought (2) from a professional legal adviser in his capacity as such, (3) the communications relating to that purpose, (4) made in confidence (5) by the client, (6) are at his instance permanently protected (7) from disclosure by himself or by the legal adviser, (8) except the protection be waived." 8 Wigmore on Evidence § 2292 (McNaughton ed. 1961). Does the Court in *Upjohn* adhere to this traditional definition? For example, is item no. 5 essential in the Court's view?

2.   Given the truth-seeking purposes for discovery, does the attorney-client privilege further interests that justify denying access to this highly-probative evidence? The Court in *Upjohn* articulates the traditional analysis, commonly referred to as the utilitarian analysis—that the objective is to promote full client disclosure to the attorney. But there has never been empirical evidence that the existence of the privilege promotes disclosure by clients. E.g., Louisell, Confidentiality, Conformity and Confusion: Privileges in Federal Court Today, 31 Tulane L.Rev. 101, 112 (1956) (disclosure promotion theory premised on "sheer speculation"). Although lawyers can emphasize the existence of the privilege to their clients, it is not at all clear that clients place great importance on the existence of the privilege in deciding what to tell their lawyers. Moreover, since the lawyer can also tell the client that full disclosure is essential to valid legal advice, the client considering withholding information from the lawyer confronts a Hobson's choice since the risk of keeping the

lawyer in the dark may seem as great as the risk of disclosure. Since the lawyer can also inform the client that only she (the lawyer) can decide whether the information is harmful, there would seem to be substantial pressures toward full candor with the lawyer. Why, then, have the privilege? The Supreme Court continues to believe in the importance of the privilege. See Swidler & Berlin v. United States, 524 U.S. 399 (1998) (privilege should continue to apply after the client's death because otherwise clients might be reluctant to confide in lawyers).

3.   Does the Court in *Upjohn* actually adopt a utilitarian rationale for the privilege? Why protect what the attorney tells the client? Why not limit the privilege to those client confidences that the client would not reveal to the lawyer absent the privilege? See Wiessenberger, Toward Precision in the Application of the Attorney-Client Privilege for Corporations, 65 Iowa L. Rev. 899, 918–19 (1980) (adoption of a but-for analysis under which privilege attaches only if statement would not have been made absent privilege). How easily could a court fragment a lawyer-client conversation, protecting some parts but not others?

4.   Assuming that the privilege generally promotes full client disclosure, how does it do so with regard to the lower-level corporate employees excluded from coverage by the control group test? The corporation can use the information they reveal to its lawyer as a basis for firing or disciplining them. Moreover, unless there is a personal attorney-client relation between the employee and the lawyer, the corporation can unilaterally decide to turn the employee's revelations over to the authorities. Accordingly, it has long been recognized that the corporate employee may have interests adverse to the employer in an investigation, and that the best solution may be to provide separate representation for the employee. See O'Leary, Criminal Antitrust and the Corporate Executive: The Man in the Middle, 63 A.B.A.J. 1389 (1977). How then can the Court even suggest that the privilege may apply to communications with former employees?

Does *Upjohn* really focus on the motivations of the employees at all? Consider Professor Salzburg's views:

> In their search to expand the privilege beyond the narrow control group formulation, the courts seem to inquire whether, without a guarantee of confidentiality, a lawyer will be reluctant to talk with employees of a corporation who have information—i.e., witness employees. The courts arrive at an affirmative answer. In the process, the courts assume that if lawyers would be reluctant to talk with employees, employees would be equally reluctant to talk with lawyers. * * * [T]he employee who talks without being a client might suffer for his cooperation. Such an employee, who is actually willing to talk without protection of the privilege, is like any witness who is willing to talk. The lawyer's apprehensiveness about possibly finding out information that might turn out to be detrimental to the corporation would be no different when he seeks out an employee than when he seeks out any other witness. The correct question for

courts to ask, therefore, is whether a witness insists upon establishment of an attorney-client relationship and, thus, the protection of a privilege, before speaking with the corporation's attorney. Only where the answer to this question is affirmative is the attorney-client privilege properly applicable.

Saltzburg, Corporate and Related Attorney-Client Privilege Claims: A Suggested Approach, 12 Hofstra L.Rev. 279, 302–03 (1984).

5.   If the Court's real concern is with the lawyer's motivations, is the additional stimulus to investigate provided by the protection necessary? The lawyer has an ethical duty to investigate. Putting that aside, could the lawyer disregard potentially harmful evidence? As one experienced lawyer observed: "Even lawyers in jurisdictions which followed the severely limited 'control group' test had to pretty well ignore it because they could not otherwise serve their clients. It has never made any sense to remain deliberately ignorant of the facts because of a fear of adverse discovery." Panel Discussion, Antitrust Investigations After *Upjohn*, 51 Antitrust L.J. 127, 133 (1982). Moreover, federal-court interpretations of privilege are not binding on the state courts, so that material that is privileged in federal court might be subject to disclosure in state court where the control group test still prevails. See, e.g., Consolidation Coal Co. v. Bucyrus-Erie Co., 432 N.E.2d 250 (Ill.1982) (retaining control group test under Illinois law). Indeed, under Fed.R.Evid. 501, state rules of privilege apply in federal court where the issue involved is governed by state law.

6.   Under *Upjohn* should the witness statements in *Hickman* that were obtained from crew members who were employed by the defendant partnership have been covered by the attorney-client privilege?

7.   Note the Court's handling of the work product issue in *Upjohn*. Does discovery of the materials involved there endanger the policies the Court is seeking to further?

8.   When the attorney-client privilege applies, it can easily be lost. As Davis v. Ross, supra p. 376, suggests, privileged materials may be discovered where the privilege holder has taken a litigation stance that puts them "at issue." This reasoning can be applied to the attorney-client privilege. See, e.g., Pitney-Bowes, Inc. v. Mestre, 86 F.R.D. 444 (S.D.Fla.1980) (By suing for reformation of contract on grounds of mutual mistake, plaintiff waived attorney-client privilege regarding communications concerning the meaning of agreement). Other grounds for waiver abound. Thus, any revelation of privileged material to the opponent or to someone else may result in a waiver, as does the use of privileged material in witness preparation. While supposedly "absolute," then, the protection accorded by the privilege is also very fragile. But see Fed.R.Evid. 502 (protecting against waiver for inadvertent production in discovery of privileged material). Does this fact further undermine the utility of the privilege in promoting full client disclosure? Should the same waiver approach be applied to work product protection? For an argument that courts should find waivers only where warranted by the risk of unfair selective

use of privileged material to distort the truth, see Marcus, The Perils of Privilege: Waiver and the Litigator, 84 Mich.L.Rev. 1605 (1986).

IN RE SHELL OIL REFINERY

United States District Court, Eastern District of Louisiana, 1990
132 F.R.D. 437

MENTZ, DISTRICT JUDGE.

The court addresses here the plaintiffs' request for discovery of the defendant's experts. The defense experts include some who are expected to testify at trial and some who are not expected to testify at trial. The court finds that while discovery of experts expected to testify at trial is premature, the plaintiffs are not entitled to any discovery of experts not expected to testify at trial.

On May 5, 1988, the catalytic cracking unit (CCU) at the Shell Oil Refinery, Norco, Louisiana, exploded. The first of several suits ultimately certified as a class action was filed that day. The day after the explosion, the parties entered an agreement giving the Plaintiff's Legal Committee (PLC) and its experts access to the CCU to inspect, measure, and photograph. Following their agreement, Shell Oil Company (Shell) preserved all materials tagged by the PLC, as well as additional materials Shell wanted preserved.

Later, Shell conducted at its research facility metallurgical and chemical tests on material removed from the explosion site. R.E. Nordstrom and Paul A. Nelson are two Shell employees who were present during the testing. The PLC's experts observed certain of these tests.

From the beginning of this case, both the PLC and Shell retained experts and actively investigated the cause of the explosion. Three months post-explosion, the court ordered: "Any expert who has visited the Norco plant and will be an expert witness at trial shall submit a preliminary report to the court on Friday, September 23, 1988." Shell submitted five reports: two from its in-house employees, R.E. Nordstrom and Paul A. Nelson; one from Failure Analysis Associates; one from Arthur D. Little, Inc.; and one from Hercules, Inc. The PLC submitted three expert reports: one from C H & A Engineering Group; one from Metallurgical & Materials Technologies, Inc.; and one from Perez Architects. The parties did not exchange the preliminary expert reports until later, in April, 1989.

During the course of this litigation, the PLC filed several motions seeking expert discovery, particularly the identity of Shell's experts and the results of the tests conducted by Shell on the CCU material. In each instance, the court ruled against allowing the discovery, unless Shell intended to use the expert or test result at trial.

Before the court is the PLC's Motion for Reconsideration of the Court's August 21, 1989, Ruling. Specifically, the PLC seeks the results of tests conducted by Shell on material from the CCU and leave of court to depose the authors of the preliminary expert reports. Shell states that it has not yet decided which test results and experts it intends to use at trial. Shell also states that it does not intend to call Nordstrom and Nelson at trial or to use either of their preliminary expert reports.

EXPERTS EXPECTED TO BE CALLED AT TRIAL

Although Fed.R.Civ.P. 26(b)(4)(A) allows for interrogatory discovery of experts expected to be called at trial,* the court has discretion in this complex class action to control the sequence of discovery. The Case Management Order (CMO), adopted by the court on August 13, 1990, governs the time frame for discovery of experts. Under the CMO, the parties need not disclose the identity of experts expected to be called at trial until March 1, 1991. The exchange of expert reports is May 1, 1991 and expert depositions start on June 15, 1991. At this time, Shell has no obligation to decide which experts it will call at trial or disclose information about any experts expected to be called at trial. As stated in the Advisory Committee Notes to Rule 26:

> The procedure established in subsection (b)(4)(A) holds the risk [that one side will benefit unduly from the other side's better preparation] to a minimum. Discovery is limited to trial witnesses, and may be obtained only at a time when the parties know who their expert will be. A party must as a practical matter prepare his own case in advance of that time, for he can hardly hope to build his case out of his opponent's expertise.

Those who will testify at trial often cannot be identified until the later stages of litigation. Therefore, the court finds that the PLC's attempt to obtain discovery from experts expected to be called at trial is premature.

EXPERTS NOT EXPECTED TO BE CALLED AT TRIAL

Under Fed.R.Civ.P. 26(b)(4)[(D)], the facts known and opinions held by non-testifying experts who are retained or specially employed in anticipation of litigation or preparation for trial are subject to discovery only in exceptional circumstances. This Rule recognizes that with non-testifying experts, there is no need to obtain discovery for effective cross-examination. See Hoover v. United States Dep't of the Interior, 611 F.2d 1132, 1142 (5th Cir.1980) ("The primary purpose of [Rule 26(b)(4)(A)'s required disclosures about experts expected to be called at trial] is to permit the opposing party to prepare an effective cross-examination.") The Rule is also designed to prevent a party from building his case on the diligent preparation of his adversary. See Pielemeier, Discovery of Non-

---

* After this case was decided, the Federal Rules regarding testifying experts were amended. Rule 26(a)(2) was added, requiring disclosure regarding such testimony, and Rule 26(b)(4)(A) was amended to permit the deposition of each testifying expert. See infra p. 425 n. 3.—Eds.

Testifying "In-House" Experts Under the Federal Rules of Civil Procedure, 58 Ind.L.J. 597, 607–08 (1984).

Shell has stated its intention not to call at trial its in-house experts, Nordstrom and Nelson. No one disputes that Nordstrom and Nelson are experts. Even though Shell submitted the reports of Nordstrom and Nelson as preliminary reports of experts it expected to call at trial, Shell's later decision not to call them at trial is permissible. Prior to the court-imposed deadline for exchange of witness lists, a party is free to make strategic decisions changing an anticipated witness to a non-witness. Thus, Nordstrom and Nelson are properly designated as non-testifying experts.

The PLC maintains that Nordstrom and Nelson should be treated as ordinary witnesses under Fed.R.Civ.P. 26(b)(1) because they are in-house experts who would have performed the tests in question as part of their regular duties regardless of litigation. Alternatively, the PLC maintains that if Nordstrom and Nelson are non-testifying experts retained or specially employed in anticipation of litigation, then under Fed.R.Civ.P. 26(b)(4)[(D)] their facts and opinions are discoverable because of exceptional circumstances requiring great expense to duplicate the tests performed by Shell.

Nordstrom is the Manager of Heat Transfer and Pressure Equipment for Shell. His duties consist of technical input on operations and on design and construction of new facilities. Nelson is a Research Manager whose duties consist of managing 11 research engineers and nine technicians for Shell. Their affidavits show that during the week following the explosion, Shell's legal department and outside counsel requested them to help the investigation team defend the lawsuits filed against Shell. Also, in September, 1988, James Blasek, outside counsel for Shell, requested Nordstrom and Nelson to prepare preliminary reports of their investigation and study of the explosion. Nordstrom and Nelson sent their preliminary reports to only Blasek. Although Nordstrom and Nelson have not been assigned to work exclusively on this litigation, they remain available to assist outside counsel on an as needed basis.

The affidavits show that there can be no serious dispute that Nordstrom and Nelson's investigation and study of the explosion was in anticipation of litigation. Whether they were "retained or specially employed" within the meaning of Fed.R.Civ.P. 26(b)(4)[(D)] is a closer question.

The courts and other legal authority are not in agreement on the question of whether an in-house expert can be "retained or specially employed".

The court finds that the persuasive authority favors application of Rule 26(b)(4)[(D)] to non-testifying in-house experts. To rule otherwise would encourage economic waste by requiring an employer to hire independent experts to obtain the protection of Rule 26(b)(4). Protection of an in-house expert's opinion supports improved public safety and other social benefits of self-analysis. That the work of an in-house expert is used not only to defend a lawsuit but also to improve a company's operations or product design does not remove him from the parameters of Rule 26(b)(4)[(D)].

Not all in-house experts fall within the parameters of the retained or specially employed language of Rule 26(b)(4)[(D)]. The Advisory Committee Notes exclude from the scope of Rule 26(b)(4)([D]) "an expert who is simply a general employee of the party not specially employed on the case." Those in-house experts who are not retained or specially employed should be treated as ordinary witnesses under Rule 26(b)(1), and if their work was in anticipation of litigation or preparation of trial, then discovery must be analyzed under the work product doctrine, Rule 26(b)(3).

Neither the Rule nor the Notes explain when a general employee may become retained or specially employed. Some courts have found that the terms retained or specially employed mean "something more than simply the assignment of a current employee to a particular problem raised by current litigation." See Kansas-Nebraska Natural Gas Co., Inc. [v. Marathon Oil Co.], 109 F.R.D. at 16 [D.Neb.1983]. To the contrary, other authority suggests that "a regular employee may become specially employed when he is designated and assigned by a party to apply his expertise to a particular matter in anticipation of litigation or for trial." Pielemeier, supra, 58 Ind.L.J. at 605.

Whether an in-house expert is retained or specially employed must be decided case-by-case. In this case, the court finds that Nordstrom and Nelson were retained or specially employed by Shell in preparation for trial. Shell's attorneys engaged Nordstrom and Nelson to perform specific tasks to help them defend the lawsuit. At the direction of Shell's legal department and outside counsel, Nordstrom and Nelson investigated and studied the cause of the explosion, and prepared preliminary reports. Copies of the reports were sent only to Shell's outside counsel. Although Nordstrom and Nelson might have studied the cause of the explosion regardless of litigation, their usual duties do not include litigation assistance. That Nordstrom and Nelson were not paid additional compensation or assigned exclusively to the litigation is not conclusive. An in-house expert may be specially employed without additional compensation or an exclusive assignment.

Having found that Nordstrom and Nelson are experts retained or specially employed in preparation for trial, the court must determine whether exceptional circumstances exist to permit discovery. A party seeking to show exceptional circumstances under Rule 26(b)(4)[(D)] carries a heavy burden. The exceptional circumstances requirement has been interpreted by the courts to mean an inability to obtain equivalent information from other sources.

The plaintiffs offered the affidavit of Thomas Shelton, President of Metallurgical and Materials Technology, Inc., to show that this case meets the exceptional circumstances requirement. Mr. Shelton was present at certain of the tests conducted by Shell and estimates that the total cost to duplicate the investigation and testing performed by Shell would be in the range of $230,000 to $315,000. The plaintiffs cited Pearl Brewing Co. v. Jos. Schlitz Brewing Co., 415 F.Supp. 1122 (S.D.Tex.1976), to show that expense can satisfy the exceptional circumstances requirement. In that antitrust case, the plaintiff's experts, who were not expected to be called at trial, created a complicated computer program for a beer marketing distribution model. The plaintiff's expert to be called at trial relied on this model in reaching his conclusions. The court found that the defendant's expert would be unable to understand the model without explanations of the undefined short-hand codes used in the computer program. For defendant's expert to attempt to unravel the short-hand codes alone would be unduly time consuming and expensive. The court granted discovery of the code explanations only. The court noted that the defendant was not trying to find support for his case out of the plaintiff's efforts, but only expediting analysis of the plaintiff's trial expert's conclusions. In other words, the defendant was not going to rely on the plaintiff's distribution model to support its defense, but needed to know the codes in order for its expert to analyze the plaintiff's trial expert's conclusions.

In contrast, the plaintiffs in the case at bar do not seek Shell's test results to understand how Shell's experts will substantiate their conclusions at trial. The plaintiffs want Shell's test results to avoid the expense of conducting their own tests. To allow discovery of Shell's test results under these circumstances would defeat the Rule's intended purposes of protecting trial strategy and preventing one party from having a free ride at the expense of the other party.

The plaintiffs can obtain the substantial equivalent by having their own experts conduct tests. As a result of the parties' consent agreements, the PLC had access to the CCU for a total of fifteen days beginning on May 7 through June 3, 1988. The plaintiffs also have access to the materials tested by Shell. Aside from having to pay for their own testing, the plaintiffs will suffer no loss. During the period set aside for expert discovery, the parties can discover the basis for each other's expert's conclusions, including information received from non-testifying experts. For these reasons, the plaintiffs have failed to show exceptional circumstances.

NOTES AND QUESTIONS

1.   Discovery regarding experts is important because experts are important in litigation. In some cases, such as medical malpractice, the substantive law may require expert testimony. That imperative sometimes leads to pressures on prospective expert witnesses who are called upon to testify against their professional peers. See, e.g., DiPaola, Cohen & Roberts, Silence of the Experts, Trial, Oct. 2004, at 20 (reporting that peer review and ethics panels of medical doctors have increasingly focused on the conduct of doctors who testify for medical malpractice plaintiffs, sometimes urging that the medical licenses of these doctors be suspended or revoked due to their testimony). In Austin v. American Ass'n of Neurological Surgeons, 253 F.3d 967 (7th Cir.2001), a doctor who was suspended from a medical association for six months after giving "irresponsible" testimony against another member sued the association. The court upheld dismissal of the suit because membership in the association was not necessary to practice medicine.

More generally, even though it is not required by law in many kinds of cases, expert testimony is very common. A survey of 529 civil trials before juries in California in the mid 1980s showed that experts testified in 86% of those cases and that an average of 3.8 experts testified per case. Gross, Expert Evidence, 1991 Wis.L.Rev. 1113, 1119; see also Green, Expert Witnesses and Sufficiency of Evidence in Toxic Substances Litigation, 86 Nw.U.L.Rev. 643, 669 (1992) (between 1974 and 1989, number of regularly-testifying experts in Cook County, Ill., increased 1500%, from 188 to 3100).

In *Shell Oil Refinery* the court states that all agree Nordstrom and Nelson are experts. Who else qualifies? In evidentiary terms, the consequence of being designated an expert is that a witness is allowed to express opinions (rather than only describing what she observed) while testifying. Fed.R.Evid. 702 authorizes such opinion testimony by "a witness qualified as an expert by knowledge, skill, experience, training, or education" where "scientific, technical, or other specialized knowledge will assist the trier of fact to understand the evidence or determine a fact at issue." Besides people with advanced training, this could include auto mechanics and others who have specialized knowledge beyond the customary ken.

Concerns have been raised about inappropriate use of unfounded "scientific" theories in litigation. For an attack on this supposed problem, see P. Huber, Galileo's Revenge: Junk Science in the Courtroom (1991). In Daubert v. Merrell Dow Pharmaceuticals, Inc., 509 U.S. 579 (1993), the Court refined the proper approach to such problems, emphasizing that the court must preliminarily find that "in order to qualify as 'scientific knowledge,' an inference or assertion must be derived by the scientific method." Kumho Tire Co. v. Carmichael, 526 U.S. 137 (1999), held that courts should undertake a similar screening effort with regard to engineers and other experts who are not scientists but who testify based on technical or other specialized knowledge. For an examination of the resulting issues, see D. Faigman, D. Kaye, M. Saks, J. Sanders & E. Cheng, Modern Scientific Evidence (2017–18).

2.   Why does Rule 26(b)(4) provide special protections for expert information? "This 'non-testifying expert' privilege is distinct from the work-product doctrine and the attorney-client privilege." Genesco, Inc. v. Visa U.S.A., Inc., 296 F.R.D. 559, 580 (M.D.Tenn.2014). "[T]he expert, unlike an ordinary witness, has no unique knowledge. That is, the other side, at least in theory, can obtain the same information merely by engaging an expert of its own. Hence, it may be argued that a lawyer could want to obtain information from his adversary's expert only to avoid doing any preparation himself, and to save his client considerable expense. Ultimately this could lead to a deterioration in case presentation and lower the standards of the bar generally." Friedenthal, Discovery and Use of an Adverse Party's Expert Information, 14 Stan.L.Rev. 455, 482–83 (1962). Are these concerns applicable in the Shell Oil Refinery case?

3.   Regarding those experts who will testify at trial, from 1970 until 1993 Rule 26(b)(4)(A) provided that the only discovery of right was by interrogatory, and that further discovery could be had only by agreement or court order. Note that in *Shell Oil Refinery* the court replaced this regime with an order calling for identification of experts and exchange of expert reports, followed by depositions. As amended in 1993 and 2010, Rules 26(a)(2) and 26(b)(4) provide by rule for similar handling of experts who will testify at trial.

(a)   *Disclosure of identity of expert witness:* Rule 26(a)(2)(A) requires each party to disclose "any witness it may use at trial to present evidence under Federal Rule of Evidence 702, 703, or 705." This disclosure requirement may apply to witnesses who are also going to provide factual testimony. For example, if Nordstrom and Nelson were at the plant at the time of the explosion of the Catalytic Cracking Unit, they might offer testimony about the circumstances at the time of the explosion. Some of their testimony might draw on their expertise, and therefore fall within Evidence Rule 702. If so, they would have to be disclosed as expert witnesses. Some such witnesses, such as treating doctors in a personal injury case, are in no sense specially retained to prepare evidence for the trial.

(b)   *Reports by specially retained expert witnesses:* Usually these witnesses are hired by the lawyers to assist in preparing the case. Rule 26(a)(2)(B) directs that they prepare rather elaborate reports. Until 2010, the rule was interpreted to require disclosure of all communications between the expert and the hiring lawyer; some said this was important to limit the lawyer's ability to influence the expert's testimony. But the rule was amended in 2010 to limit the disclosure requirement to "facts or data considered by the witness" in order to provide confidentiality for much lawyer-expert communication. See also Rules 26(b)(4)(B) and (C); Sara Lee Corp. v. Kraft Foods, Inc., 273 F.R.D. 416, 419 (N.D.Ill.2011) (explaining that the prior rule "increased discovery costs and impeded effective communication between attorneys and their experts, sometimes even inducing parties to retain two separate sets of experts—one for consultation and another to testify").

(c)   *Disclosures regarding anticipated expert testimony of experts not specially retained:* Rule 26(a)(2)(C) requires the attorneys to provide disclosure regarding the anticipated opinions of expert witnesses who were not specially retained. The goal of this provision is to ensure there is some disclosure regarding these opinions, although the disclosure is not nearly so thorough as the report required of experts who were specially retained.

(d) *Exclusion of evidence when disclosures not made:* Rule 37(c)(1) provides that opinions that should have been disclosed but were not should be excluded at the trial, and courts have often done so. See, e.g., Hoffman v. Caterpillar, Inc., 368 F.3d 709 (7th Cir.2004) (expert opinion excluded because disclosures were not amended to include a videotape viewed by the expert); Macaulay v. Anas, 321 F.3d 45 (1st Cir.2003) (expert precluded from testifying because supplemental report adding a new theory of liability was not submitted until more than a month after the deadline for submitting expert reports).

(e) *Paying the other side's expert:* Usually a party need not pay a deposition witness to testify. But Rule 26(b)(4)(E) directs that the party seeking discovery pay the fee of an expert for responding to discovery. This payment requirement recognizes that expert opinions are different from other evidence. Sometimes courts blanch at the amounts requested. See, e.g., Fisher-Price, Inc. v. Safety 1st, Inc., 217 F.R.D. 329 (D.Del.2003) (expert not entitled to be paid $495 per hour for performing administrative tasks that could easily have been delegated to assistants); Frederick v. Columbia University, 212 F.R.D. 176 (S.D.N.Y.2003) (hourly fee of $975 demanded by plaintiff's expert was unreasonable); Jochims v. Isuzu Motors, Ltd., 141 F.R.D. 493, 497 (S.D.Iowa 1992) ("Continuing escalation of expert witness fees and the all too frequent attitude of experts that their fees should be set at the maximum-the-traffic-will-bear is of great concern."). Compare Scheinholtz v. Bridgestone/Firestone, Inc., 187 F.R.D. 221 (E.D.Pa. 1999) (court sets unusually high rate of $600 per hour for expert's time because defendants had agreed to pay that amount).

4.   Rule 26(b)(4)(D) addresses discovery regarding experts specially retained to prepare for trial but not expected to be called as witnesses, like Nordstrom and Nelson. Why would such people be retained? If you were the lawyer for a party in *Shell Oil Refinery*, would you need an expert like Nordstrom or Nelson to assist you in preparing your case? Assuming the other parties have many other experts to choose among, are there special reasons for limiting discovery regarding the views and knowledge of these expert consultants? As the court explained in Rubel v. Eli Lilly & Co., 160 F.R.D. 458, 460 (S.D.N.Y.1995), "there is an important interest in allowing counsel to obtain the expert advice they need in order properly to evaluate and present their clients' positions without fear that every consultation with an expert may yield grist for the adversary's mill." See also In re Pizza Time Theatre Securities Litigation, 113 F.R.D. 94, 98 (N.D.Cal.1986): "[A] lawyer's decision about which experts to consult, but not to call as a witness, also is a matter that implicates values that the work product doctrine was designed to protect. * * * A lawyer's decisions about which people to use in confidence for which

purposes in preparing a case for trial is as central to lawyering strategy as one can get."

5.   Why doesn't Shell want to call Nordstrom and Nelson as witnesses at trial? Suppose one of the plaintiffs in *Shell Oil Refinery* needs expert medical testimony concerning the extent of injuries and therefore visits and is examined by doctors X, Y and Z on recommendation of her lawyer. If Dr. Z submits a report to the lawyer saying that the plaintiff is not really injured and the lawyer therefore decides to call Dr. X or Dr. Y, should Dr. Z's report be discoverable? In Coates v. AC & S, Inc., 133 F.R.D. 109 (E.D.La.1990), an action against an asbestos producer, after plaintiff died of lung cancer defendant sent tissue samples to several expert consultants. Plaintiff sought copies of the reports made by all the experts even though they would not all testify, and the court granted the motion "in an effort to curtail the 'shopping' of tissue samples," which it viewed as falling within the extraordinary circumstances limitation on discovery regarding nontestifying experts. Contrast Eliasen v. Hamilton, 111 F.R.D. 396, 401 (N.D.Ill.1986): "Even if we assume that plaintiffs chose not to use Gruy because he did not tell them what they wanted to hear, this is not only perfectly permissible, but * * * the very purpose of the rule is to protect plaintiffs from having Gruy's testimony used by their opponent." See also Dominguez v. Syntex Laboratories, Inc., 149 F.R.D. 158, 163 (S.D.Ind.1993) ("Visiting two experts for the purposes of litigation can hardly be considered 'expert shopping.' * * * If an expert botches the evaluation or uses unaccepted methodology, a litigant should not be expected to live with only that evaluation and divulge the results for use by his opponent.").

If expert-shopping is not an exceptional circumstance warranting discovery regarding retained but nontestifying experts, what would suffice? Suppose that only Shell's experts had examined the site in the days after the explosion. The Reporter for the committee that drafted Rule what is now 26(b)(4)(D) offered two illustrations of extraordinary circumstances in a program on those amendments:

> (a)   Circumstances in which an expert employed by the party seeking discovery could not conduct important experiments and tests because an item of equipment, etc., needed for the tests had been destroyed or is otherwise not available. If the party from whom the discovery is sought had been able to have its experts test the item before its destruction or nonavailability, then information obtained from those tests might be discoverable.

> (b)   Circumstances in which it might be impossible for a party to obtain its own expert. Such circumstances would occur when the number of experts in a field is small and their time is already fully retained by others.

Sacks, Seminar on Discovery, Atlanta, Ga., Sept. 26–27, 1970, quoted in Ager v. Jane C. Stormont Hospital & Training School, 622 F.2d 496, 503–04 n. 8 (10th Cir.1980). As a possible example of situation (a) above, consider Layman

v. Jr. Players Golf Academy, Inc., 314 F.R.D. 379 (D.S.C.2016), a suit against the Academy by the family of a former student who claimed she was bullied there. Plaintiffs employed a bullying expert. The expert report plaintiffs served included the expert's notes on his interview with the student. Then plaintiffs decided not to call the expert as a witness, and defendant noticed the expert's deposition because the student, during her deposition, offered a different version of pertinent events from the version in the expert's notes. The court ruled that these disparities provided exceptional circumstances that justified permitting a deposition of the nontestifying expert about what the student told him.

In Commissioner of the Dep't of Planning & Nat. Res. v. Century Aluminum Co., 279 F.R.D. 317 (D.V.I.2012), environmental authorities sued two companies that operated an oil refinery for alleged contamination of adjacent waters. After suit was filed, defendants' lawyers hired marine biology consultants to examine the area, but the consultants were not listed as trial witnesses. Plaintiff sought production of their scientific data and recorded observations, arguing that exceptional circumstances were present because the constantly changing marine environment made all such data crucial. The court rejected the argument (id. at 319):

> We acknowledge that the precise conditions extant at the time the defendants' consultants performed their dives are not capable of duplication. Nevertheless, we disagree that this is an exceptional circumstance requiring production of those test results and observations under Rule 26(b)(4)(D). The data and observations at issue, while unique, do not relate to a moment in time critical to the litigation. Unlike oil spills caused by a tanker ship running aground or an explosion on an offshore drilling platform, the alleged environmental damage in this case is not traceable to a single event. * * * There has been no indication that any environmental damage has significantly abated or disappeared due to the passage of time.

In *Shell Oil Refinery*, the court treated the roughly $300,000 cost of duplicating the analysis performed by defendant as insufficient to constitute extraordinary circumstances. Compare Bank Brussels Lambert v. Chase Manhattan Bank, 175 F.R.D. 34 (S.D.N.Y.1997), in which plaintiff retained Arthur Andersen & Co. to analyze the financial condition of a failing company, and Andersen based its advice on 10,000 hours spent by its personnel reviewing the company's financial records before those files were put into storage when the company failed. Noting that it was likely that documents were rearranged and that some were lost over the two years before defendant was sued, the court held that extraordinary circumstances had been established for access to Andersen's work.

6.   Should regular employees like Nordstrom and Nelson be covered by Rule 26(b)(4)(D)? "[R]ule 26(b)(4)[(D)] permits a party to engage in discovery with respect to information consultative experts acquired prior to being retained by an opposing party." Rocky Mountain Natural Gas Co. v. Cooper Industries, Inc., 166 F.R.D. 481, 482 (D.Colo.1996). After the court in *Shell Oil*

made the ruling above, plaintiffs noticed the depositions of ten Shell employees, including Nordstrom and Nelson, explaining that they wanted to examine these witnesses about pre-explosion conditions at the refinery. Shell moved to quash the deposition notices, and the court denied the motion, amending its earlier ruling to say that it "applies only to facts known and opinions held by Nordstrom and Nelson subsequent to being specially employed in preparation for litigation." In re Shell Oil Refinery, 134 F.R.D. 148, 151 (E.D.La.1990). Shell argued that "as a practical matter pre- and post-retention knowledge cannot be segregated for the purposes of discovery," id. at 150, but the court was not moved by that difficulty.

Arguably, permitting an employer to use the "non-testifying expert" privilege to shelter its employees from discovery might present risks of abuse. Consider Ely v. Cabot Oil & Gas Corp., 2015 WL 6447557 (M.D.Pa., Oct. 26, 2015), involving water contamination. Late in the litigation, defendant added an affirmative defense that plaintiffs had failed to mitigate their damages because they did not use a type of water treatment system used by the company that provided defendant's water treatment system. Before it asserted that affirmative defense, defendant had identified an employee of this company as an expert witness, but it then de-designated him. Plaintiffs sought to take his deposition anyway, and the court found that he was in a position similar to that of a regular employee of a party, and authorized a limited deposition, explaining its decision as follows:

> [A] leading treatise has indicated "that the number of situations in which the protective provisions of the Rule would come into effect is small." Tellabs Operations, Inc. v. Fujitsu, Ltd., 283 F.R.D. 374, 376 (N.D.Ill.2012) (citing to 8A Wright, Miller & Marcus, Federal Practice & Procedure, § 2023 at 126 (2010)). In that treatise, the authors observe that "[t]here is a legitimate concern that a party may try to immunize its employees who are actors or viewers against proper discovery by designating them experts retained for work on the case," and thus they warn that "courts should be exceedingly skeptical when employees who have otherwise discoverable information are designated 'experts,' and efforts must be made to preserve the opportunity to discover that information."

7.   One partial exception to the ban on discovery of litigation-preparation work by non-testifying experts is Rule 35(b)(1), involving court-ordered examinations of parties. The rule says that the party subject to the examination has a right to receive a copy of the report. In Downs v. River City Group, LLC, 288 F.R.D. 507 (D.Nev.2013), defendant, responding to plaintiff's claim that she had suffered severe emotional distress, obtained a court order that plaintiff submit to examinations by a psychologist and a psychiatrist. Defendant then listed the psychiatrist, but not the psychologist, as an expert witness. Plaintiff, who had obtained a copy of the psychologist's report pursuant to Rule 35(b)(1), designated the psychologist as a witness she would call at trial. Defendant moved to strike this designation on the basis that no

exceptional circumstances were shown. Concluding that plaintiff could obtain similar expertise from a witness of her own, the court granted the motion.

8.   In *Shell Oil*, trial witnesses had not yet been designated. What if a party designates an expert and then retracts the designation? In Durflinger v. Artiles, 727 F.2d 888 (10th Cir.1984), where plaintiff decided not to call a certain doctor after listing him as a trial witness, the court upheld an order preventing defendant from calling the doctor at trial on the ground that defendant had "circumvented the discovery process and subverted the principle of fairness that underlies Rule 26(b)(4)([D])." Should the court instead have allowed defendant to call the doctor as a witness but forbidden reference to the fact the doctor was originally retained by plaintiff? The court found this protection sufficient in Granger v. Wisner, 656 P.2d 1238 (Az.1982), although it recognized the perils:

> Jurors unfamiliar with the role of counsel in adversary proceedings might well assume that plaintiff's counsel had suppressed evidence which he had an obligation to offer. Such a reaction could destroy counsel's credibility in the eyes of the jury. * * *
>
> If the plaintiff sought to attack the expert's qualifications or credentials, he might well have some concern that the defendant would attempt to rehabilitate the witness by showing that plaintiff's counsel had thought well enough of the witness to consult him on this very case. Arguably, that consultation might be an admission that plaintiff believed the witness to be qualified.

656 P.2d at 1242–43. See also Agron v. Columbia University, 176 F.R.D. 445 (S.D.N.Y.1997) (psychiatric expert previously retained by plaintiff could testify for defendant at trial providing that there was no mention that the witness had been retained originally by plaintiff); compare Healy v. Counts, 100 F.R.D. 493, 496 (D.Colo.1984) ("I do not agree that such a restriction on defense counsel could adequately protect the plaintiffs here."). For discussion, see Easton, "Red Rover, Red Rover, Send That Expert Right Over": Clearing the Way for Parties to Introduce the Testimony of Their Opponents' Expert Witnesses, 55 S.M.U.L.Rev. 427 (2002) (arguing for broadening the opportunity to call the opponent's expert).

9.   Sometimes, however, there are experts with no affiliation at all to a party. Consider, for example, the possibility that Professor A is a leading expert on catalytic cracking units like the one that exploded and had authored a leading article on defects leading to explosions. Could a party happy with Professor A's views in the article subpoena her to testify at trial? Could a party expecting her article to be used in evidence against it subpoena her research data in an effort to discredit her conclusions? Remember that Rule 26(b)(4) only limits discovery of material prepared in anticipation of litigation. See Wright v. Jeep Corp., 547 F.Supp. 871, 874 (E.D.Mich.1982) (professor who wrote report on Jeep turnovers ordered to submit to deposition); Application of American Tobacco Co., 880 F.2d 1520 (2d Cir.1989) (medical researcher who had published studies on synergistic effect of exposure to asbestos and smoking

required to supply tobacco companies with research data); see generally Marcus, Discovery Along the Litigation/Science Interface, 57 Brooklyn L.Rev. 381 (1991). But see Rule 45 (providing that a subpoena seeking disclosure of "an unretained expert's opinion or information that does not describe specific occurrences in dispute and results from the expert's study that was not requested by a party" may be quashed or modified unless the party serving the subpoena shows substantial need for the information and assures that the recipient of the subpoena will be reasonably compensated).

10. If an expert testifies but does a poor job, can she be held liable for that? In Marrogi v. Howard, 282 F.3d 854 (5th Cir.2002), plaintiff's expert was tripped up by mistakes in his deposition during a suit against plaintiff's former employer, and the employer was able to obtain summary judgment. Plaintiff then sued the expert for malpractice. The district court dismissed the case based on the normal rule that witnesses are immune from suit for their testimony in litigation, but the court of appeals reversed based on an exception to the immunity rule for retained experts providing litigation services.

E. INVESTIGATION—FACT GATHERING WITHOUT JUDICIAL ASSISTANCE

Corley v. Rosewood Care Center, Inc., 142 F.3d 1041 (7th Cir.1998):

Before CUMMINGS, RIPPLE, and ROVNER, CIRCUIT JUDGES.

ILANA DIAMOND ROVNER, CIRCUIT JUDGE.

[In this RICO action based on defendants' alleged bait and switch tactics in connection with nursing home services, plaintiff had been conducting interviews with non-party witnesses under oath and with a court reporter present. The witnesses evidently participated voluntarily in this activity. When defendant found out, it persuaded the district court to grant a protective order requiring plaintiff to give notice of these sessions as though they were depositions. The appellate court held that this order was wrong.]

The district court viewed Corley's investigative technique as tantamount to a deposition under the Federal Rules. * * * But we see nothing in the Federal Rules that would support such a restriction on counsel's private inquiry into the facts underlying his client's claim. * * * [A]lthough court reporters were present and witnesses presumably were questioned under oath, the interviews in fact were not depositions precisely because Corley had not complied with the requirements of Rule 30(b). The statements thus could not be used as depositions under Rule 32.

But the fact that the statements could not be used as depositions does not mean, as the district judge apparently assumed, that Corley was not entitled to take them. The Supreme Court has long recognized that as part of his investigation and trial preparation, counsel may choose to take sworn statements from individuals having knowledge of the claims or defenses at issue. See Hickman v. Taylor. [The court also noted that Rule 26(b)(3)(C) explicitly contemplates that witness statements may include a "stenographic, mechanical, electrical, or other recording."] This portion of Rule 26 therefore assumes that the taking of a witness statement is entirely proper, even where the statement is recorded and transcribed by a court reporter, and the rule proceeds to address the circumstances under which the statement may be discoverable. In light of that, there would seem to be no basis for restricting Corley's chosen investigative method of taking sworn statements from potential non-party witnesses. The Federal Rules of Civil Procedure do not prohibit that technique; the rules instead are concerned only with whether the statements are discoverable and with the uses to which they may be put at trial.

NOTES AND QUESTIONS

1.   Although we have concentrated thus far in this chapter on the use of the power of the court to extract information, it is important to realize that a great deal of extremely useful information is available for the asking. Moreover, Rule 11 requires prefiling investigation by an attorney before taking a position in litigation. Consider Ingebretsen, Crafting a Discovery Plan, 33 Litigation 27, 29 (Summer 2007):

> Informal interviews of third-party witnesses are an underutilized and effective discovery technique. They cost significantly less than depositions, allow you to get information without the distracting presence of opposing counsel, and can engender a level of trust and cooperation between the third party and your client. Third-party witnesses, even if they do not have a dog in the fight, often develop a sense of righteous indignation when they learn the position your opponent has taken or is expected to take. They may become sympathetic to your client's plight and invested in seeing that the truth, as they know it, comes out.

See also In re Testosterone Replacement Therapy Liabil. Lit., 167 F.Supp.3d 936, 937 (N.D.Ill.2016) ("In a typical case, there are no restrictions on a party's contacts with a fact witness.").

2.   Given the utility of informal interviews with willing witnesses, why would a lawyer ever choose to take the deposition of such a person? Cf. Rule 27 (authorizing a pre-litigation deposition to preserve testimony of a witness who may become unavailable). Consider the views of the court in International Business Machines Corporation v. Edelstein, 526 F.2d 37 (2d Cir.1975): "In contrast to the pretrial interview with prospective witnesses, a deposition serves an entirely different purpose, which is to perpetuate testimony, to have it available for use or confrontation at the trial, or to have the witness committed to a specific representation for such facts as he might present. A desire to depose formally would arise normally after preliminary interviews might have caused counsel to decide to take a deposition." The court also noted

that "[i]t is the common experience of counsel at the trial bar that a potential witness, upon reflection, will often change, modify or expand upon his original statement and that a second or third interview will be productive of greater accuracy."

3.   The attorney's freedom to interview witnesses stops, however, with the opposing party because rules of professional responsibility forbid a lawyer to talk to an opposing party who is represented by counsel unless the party's lawyer consents. With corporate or other organizational parties, this rule becomes difficult to apply. In Niesig v. Team I, 558 N.E.2d 1030 (N.Y.1990), the court held that counsel may not interview corporate employees whose acts or omissions in the matter under inquiry are binding on the corporation, or whose acts are imputed to the corporation for purposes of its liability. See also Cagguila v. Wyeth Laboratories, Inc., 127 F.R.D. 653, 654 (E.D.Pa.1989) ("In such an uncertain area of ethical conduct, we believe that a prudent attorney would have given notice to opposing counsel of the intent to take such a statement.").

In Mompoint v. Lotus Devel. Corp., 110 F.R.D. 414 (D.Mass.1986), the court refused to go this far. Plaintiff claimed that he had been fired because he was black and a Haitian. Defendant claimed it fired him because it had received complaints from female employees that plaintiff had pressured them for sexual favors. Defendant moved for a protective order against interviews with these women by plaintiff's counsel. The court found that the complaints related to matters within the scope of their employment, but that there was no good cause to forbid interviews, citing Professor Leubsdorf's arguments: "The public interest in obtaining testimony should not be frustrated by the massive embargo that a warned employer could impose." Leubsdorf, Communicating with Another Lawyer's Client: The Lawyer's Veto and the Client's Interests, 127 U.Pa.L.Rev. 683, 708 (1979). The court did, however, order that plaintiff himself should not be present during any of these interviews.

4.   Should there be any other court-ordered limitations on evidence gathering outside the discovery process? Compare Nemir v. Mitsubishi Motors Corp., 381 F.3d 540 (6th Cir.2004) (overturning district court order forbidding plaintiff's lawyer from contacting defendant's consumers because there was no showing of pertinent harm to defendant); Todd v. Montoya, 791 F.Supp.2d 1060 (D.N.M.2011) (refusing to disqualify plaintiff's attorney for having his investigator obtain a statement from 18-year-old defendant) with Cordy v. Sherwin-Williams Co., 156 F.R.D. 575 (D.N.J.1994) (disqualifying defense counsel for contacting an expert who had a written agreement with plaintiff's counsel to work for plaintiff on the case). See also Martinez v. Carson, 697 F.3d 1252 (10th Cir. 2012) (witness interviews that "proceeded essentially like depositions" violated district court's discovery stay).

5.   On analogy to decisions suppressing evidence in criminal cases, civil litigants sometimes try to suppress evidence that is illegally seized. Thus, in State of Iowa v. Union Asphalt & Roadoils, Inc., 281 F.Supp. 391 (S.D.Iowa 1968), affirmed sub nom. Standard Oil Co. v. State of Iowa, 408 F.2d 1171 (8th Cir.1969), the state's attorney general had sent his assistants and police

officers into the offices of certain defendants just before he filed suit, and these agents carted away "substantially all of the business records contained in the offices." Noting the quasi-criminal nature of antitrust suits, and the use of official powers to effect seizure, the court ordered the return of all the material but refused to forbid the state from using discovery to obtain that material again. Compare Suburban Sew 'N Sweep, Inc. v. Swiss-Bernina, Inc., 91 F.R.D. 254 (N.D.Ill.1981), in which plaintiff embarked on a pretrial campaign of searching through the trash dumpster outside defendant's offices and found a number of items that would be privileged under the attorney-client privilege. The court refused to order these materials returned despite their privileged character, reasoning that defendant had not made sufficient efforts to maintain the confidentiality of the material. See also Sackler v. Sackler, 203 N.E.2d 481 (N.Y.1964) ("Any court is taking extreme measures when it refuses convincing evidence because of the way it was procured. Proof of guilt collected in raids by private detectives has been, pursuant to rules not heretofore questioned, the basis for thousands of divorce decrees in our State."); Epstein v. Epstein, 843 F.3d 1147 (7th Cir. 2016) (wife placed device on husband's computer that forwarded his email to her, providing the basis for her adultery divorce suit in state court, prompting husband to sue wife and her lawyer in federal court for violation of the federal Wiretapping Act).

F. ENFORCING THE DISCOVERY RULES—SANCTIONS

CINE FORTY-SECOND STREET THEATRE CORP. V. ALLIED ARTISTS PICTURES CORP.

United States Court of Appeals, Second Circuit, 1979
602 F.2d 1062

BEFORE KAUFMAN, CHIEF JUDGE, and OAKES and MESKILL, CIRCUIT JUDGES.

IRVING R. KAUFMAN, CHIEF JUDGE.

Appellee Cine Forty-Second Street Theatre Corp. ("Cine"), has operated a movie theater in New York City's Times Square area since July 1974. It alleges that those owning neighboring theaters on West Forty-Second Street (the "exhibitors") attempted through abuse of City agency processes to prevent the opening of its theater. When this tactic was unsuccessful, Cine contends, the exhibitors entered into a conspiracy with certain motion picture distributors to cut off its access to first-run, quality films. Bringing suit on August 1, 1975, Cine claimed $3,000,000 in treble damages under the antitrust laws, and sought an injunction against the defendants' alleged anticompetitive practices.

On November 6, 1975, the eleven defendants served plaintiff with a set of consolidated interrogatories. Cine thereupon secured its adversaries' consent to defer discovery on the crucial issue of damages until it could retain an expert to review the rival exhibitors' box office receipts. Not until four months after the deadline upon which the parties had agreed, however, did Cine file its first set of answers to the remaining interrogatories. Moreover, even casual scrutiny reveals the patent inadequacy of these responses. Many were bare, ambiguous cross-references to general answers elsewhere in the responses. Highly specific questions concerning the design of Cine's theater were answered with architectural drawings that did not even purport to show the dimensions requested.

Although Cine now complains bitterly that these interrogatories amounted to pure harassment, it never moved to strike them as irrelevant or as harassing. Rather, it filed supplemental answers, which were similarly deficient, and then failed to obey two subsequent orders from Magistrate Gershon compelling discovery. At a hearing in October of 1977, the magistrate found Cine's disobedience to have been willful, and assessed $500 in costs against it. Soon afterwards, she further warned plaintiff that any further noncompliance would result in dismissal.

By the summer of 1977, as this conflict was coming to a head, Cine had still not retained the expert it claimed was necessary to respond to the damages interrogatories. Magistrate Gershon quite reasonably and leniently ordered Cine merely to produce a plan to answer, but this yielded no result. The magistrate then directed Cine to answer the damages interrogatories, admonishing its counsel that future nonfeasance would be viewed in light of past derelictions. Cine did file two sets of answers, one over two months late and both seriously deficient.

The responses omitted, inter alia, any information concerning significant time periods for which Cine claimed injury. Moreover, they failed to provide any indication as to the method of calculating a major portion of the alleged damages. Thereupon, at an unrecorded hearing held on September 7, 1978, Magistrate Gershon once again held off the imposition of final sanctions in these already over-protracted discovery proceedings and ordered the defects cured, on pain of dismissal of the complaint. Cine stood mute, neither appealing from, objecting to, nor complying with the order. On September 20, the defendants moved before the magistrate for dismissal of the complaint, citing plaintiff's failure to obey the order requiring responses on damages.

At a formal hearing on October 19, 1978, Cine's attorney argued that several months earlier he and defense counsel had reached an "understanding," pursuant to which a deposition of Cine's principal officer, Clark, would replace the answers at issue. Cine has never introduced any written evidence or corroborative testimony demonstrating the existence of such an understanding. In any case, the magistrate's subsequent oral order compelling answers to the interrogatories would have superseded it.

Accordingly, Magistrate Gershon found that Cine had no basis for assuming that the answers were not due on the dates set in her orders. After noting plaintiff's history of disobedience in the face of her own repeated warnings, the magistrate concluded that Cine's present non-compliance was willful.[5] "[T]he plaintiff," she stated, "has decided when it will be cooperative and when it will not be cooperative, and that it does not have any right to do." She thereupon recommended to the district court that Cine be precluded from introducing evidence with respect to damages. This sanction was, of course, tantamount to a dismissal of Cine's damage claim, but left standing its claim for injunctive relief.

Judge Goettel, the district judge to whom Magistrate Gershon's order was submitted for approval, reacted to Cine's behavior as did Magistrate Gershon. He wrote, "[i]f there were ever a case in which drastic sanctions were justified, this is it." But Judge Goettel could not fully accept the magistrate's finding of willfulness. "[T]he actions of plaintiff's counsel," he concluded, were either willful or a total dereliction of professional responsibility. No other conclusion is possible. However, in the absence of a written direction, it is virtually impossible to establish that the attorney's action was in fact willful, rather than grossly negligent.

The district judge thus apparently believed it possible that Cine's counsel, confused as to the precise terms of Magistrate Gershon's oral orders, could have thought in good faith that the answers were not due. Action taken upon that baseless belief, however, was, at the very least, grossly negligent. The district court "regretfully" concluded that under Flaks v. Koegel, 504 F.2d 702 (2d Cir.1974), it lacked the power, absent a finding of willfulness, to impose the extreme sanction recommended by the magistrate. Instead, the court merely assessed costs in the amount of $1,000.[6] But, recognizing that he might have "misperceive[d] the controlling law of this circuit," Judge Goettel certified this interlocutory appeal on his own motion under 28 U.S.C. § 1292(b).

On reargument, Judge Goettel expressed some doubt regarding the correctness of his prior decision. In light of plaintiff's subsequent response to the damages interrogatories, however, the court adhered to its earlier view.

The question before us is whether a grossly negligent failure to obey an order compelling discovery may justify the severest disciplinary measures available under Fed.R.Civ.P. 37. This rule provides a spectrum of sanctions. The mildest is an order to reimburse the opposing party for

---

[5]   In light of our holding, it is not necessary for us to consider Cine's contention that a written order is, as a matter of law, a necessary prerequisite to a finding of "willfulness" under Rule 37. We note, en passant, however, that in Independent Investors Protective League v. Touche Ross & Co., 25 F.R.Serv.2d 222, 224, and Henry v. Sneiders, 490 F.2d 315, 318 (9th Cir.), cert. denied, 419 U.S. 832 (1974), preclusion was upheld on the basis of orders announced in open court.

[6]   Defendants estimate that their actual costs in seeking to compel discovery total at least $50,000.

expenses caused by the failure to cooperate. More stringent are orders striking out portions of the pleadings, prohibiting the introduction of evidence on particular points and deeming disputed issues determined adversely to the position of the disobedient party. Harshest of all are orders of dismissal and default judgment.

These sanctions serve a threefold purpose. Preclusionary orders ensure that a party will not be able to profit from its own failure to comply. Rule 37 strictures are also specific deterrents and, like civil contempt, they seek to secure compliance with the particular order at hand. Finally, although the most drastic sanctions may not be imposed as "mere penalties," Hammond Packing Co. v. Arkansas, 212 U.S. 322 (1909); see Hovey v. Elliott, 167 U.S. 409 (1897), courts are free to consider the general deterrent effect their orders may have on the instant case and on other litigation, provided that the party on whom they are imposed is, in some sense, at fault. National Hockey League v. Metropolitan Hockey Club, Inc., 427 U.S. 639 (1976) (per curiam); Societe Internationale Pour Participations Industrielles et Commerciales v. Rogers, 357 U.S. 197 (1958).

Where the party makes good faith efforts to comply, and is thwarted by circumstances beyond his control, for example a foreign criminal statute prohibiting disclosure of the documents at issue, an order dismissing the complaint would deprive the party of a property interest without due process of law. See Societe Internationale, supra, 357 U.S. at 212, 78 S.Ct. 1087. It would, after all, be unfair and irrational to prevent a party from being heard solely because of a nonculpable failure to meet the terms of a discovery order. Indeed, such measures would be gratuitous, for if the party is unable to obey there can be no effective deterrence, general or specific. Accordingly, "Rule 37 should not be construed to authorize dismissal of [a] complaint because of petitioner's noncompliance with a pretrial production order when it has been established that failure to comply has been due to inability, and not to willfulness, bad faith, or any fault of petitioner." Societe Internationale, supra, 357 U.S. at 212.

The lower court did not determine whether willfulness caused plaintiff's failure to respond. It was possible, Judge Goettel apparently believed, that Cine's counsel simply did not understand the exact requirements of the magistrate's unwritten order compelling discovery. If so, Cine's failure to answer the damages interrogatories might not rise to the level of "willfulness" or "bad faith" for both of these conditions imply a deliberate disregard of the lawful orders of the court. The question, then, is whether gross negligence amounting to a "total dereliction of professional responsibility," but not a conscious disregard of court orders, is properly embraced within the "fault" component of Societe Internationale's triple criterion. Fault, of course, is a broad and amorphous concept, and the Courts of Appeals have had considerable difficulty construing it in this context. Indeed, one court defined "fault" by the apparent oxymoron "intentional negligence." Thus, commentators have opined that an element of willfulness or conscious disregard of the court's orders is a prerequisite to the harsher categories of Rule 37 sanctions. But the appellate cases commonly cited for this proposition hold only that dismissal is an abuse of discretion where failure to comply was not the result of the fault of any party.

Unless we are to assume that the Court chose its words carelessly, we must accord the term "fault" a meaning of its own within the Societe Internationale triad. And plainly, if "fault" has any meaning not subsumed by "willfulness" and "bad faith," it must at least cover gross negligence of the type present in this case. * * *

In the final analysis, however, this question cannot turn solely upon a definition of terms. We believe that our view advances the basic purposes of Rule 37, while respecting the demands of due process. The principal objective of the general deterrent policy of National Hockey is strict adherence to the "responsibilities counsel owe to the Court and to their opponents," 427 U.S. at 640. Negligent, no less than intentional, wrongs are fit subjects for general deterrence. And gross professional incompetence no less than deliberate tactical intransigence may be responsible for the interminable delays and costs that plague modern complex lawsuits. An undertaking on the scale of the large contemporary suit brooks none of the dilation, posturing, and harassment once expected in litigation. The parties, and particularly their lawyers, must rise to the freedom granted by the Rules and cooperate in good faith both in question and response.

Considerations of fair play may dictate that courts eschew the harshest sanctions provided by Rule 37 where failure to comply is due to a mere oversight of counsel amounting to no more than simple negligence. But where gross professional negligence has been found—that is, where counsel clearly should have understood his duty to the court—the full range of sanctions may be marshalled. Indeed, in this day of burgeoning, costly and protracted litigation courts should not shrink from imposing harsh sanctions where, as in this case, they are clearly warranted.

A litigant chooses counsel at his peril, Link v. Wabash Railroad Co., 370 U.S. 626 (1962), and here, as in countless other contexts, counsel's disregard of his professional responsibilities can lead to extinction of his client's claim.[10] See, e.g., Anderson v. Air West, Inc., 542 F.2d 522 (9th Cir.1976) (dismissal for failure to proceed with due diligence); RePass v. Vreeland, 357 F.2d 801 (3d Cir.1966) (negligent failure to file suit within

---

[10] The acts and omissions of counsel are normally wholly attributable to the client. This case does not present the extraordinary circumstance of complete disappearance or mental illness of counsel that justified relief in Vindigni v. Meyer, 441 F.2d 376 (2d Cir.1971) and United States v. Cirami, 563 F.2d 26 (2d Cir.1977). Indeed, by Magistrate Gershon's finding and counsel's own admission, Clark, Cine's principal officer, was aware of every aspect of discovery and intimately involved with the progress of the case.

statute of limitations); Universal Film Exchanges, Inc. v. Lust, 479 F.2d 573 (4th Cir.1973) (party not relieved under Fed.R.Civ.P. 60(b) from summary judgment where counsel's failure to proffer defenses was grossly, rather than excusably, negligent).

Plaintiff urges that because it has at last filed answers to the damage interrogatories, it should be permitted to prove its losses at trial. But it forgets that sanctions must be weighed in light of the full record in the case. Furthermore, "[i]f parties are allowed to flout their obligations, choosing to wait to make a response until a trial court has lost patience with them, the effect will be to embroil trial judges in day-to-day supervision of discovery, a result directly contrary to the overall scheme of the federal discovery rules." Moreover, as we have indicated, compulsion of performance in the particular case at hand is not the sole function of Rule 37 sanctions. Under the deterrence principle of National Hockey, plaintiff's hopelessly belated compliance should not be accorded great weight. Any other conclusion would encourage dilatory tactics, and compliance with discovery orders would come only when the backs of counsel and the litigants were against the wall.

In light of the fact that plaintiff, through its undeniable fault, has frozen this litigation in the discovery phase for nearly four years, we see no reason to burden the court below with extensive proceedings on remand. Judge Goettel's opinion makes it abundantly clear that but for his misinterpretation of the governing law in this circuit, he would have wholeheartedly adopted Magistrate Gershon's original recommendation. Accordingly, the judge's order declining to adopt the magistrate's recommendation that proof of damages be precluded is reversed.

[Concurring opinion of JUDGE OAKES omitted.]

NOTES AND QUESTIONS

1.   How would similar damages issues be handled now? See Rules 26(a)(1)(A)(iii); 37(c)(1). How easily could plaintiff comply with such a disclosure requirement?

2.   Should discovery sanctions be employed aggressively? Judicial enthusiasm for imposing serious sanctions has seemed to wax and wane. Until the 1980s, judges were supposedly averse to using sanctions, but by the dawn of the 21st century some thought they were too prone to be aggressive. Certainly dramatic sanctions are used on occasion. See F.D.I.C. v. Hurwitz, 384 F.Supp.2d 1039 (S.D. Tex. 2005) (imposing sanctions totalling over $72 million on plaintiff for various types of misconduct, including during discovery). The frequency of dismissal or entry of default for violating discovery orders has increased. See 8B C. Wright, A. Miller & R. Marcus, Fed. Prac. & Pro. § 2289 (3d ed. 2010).

3.   Imposing fines or costs on a party is different from deciding the merits of the case against it due to discovery violations. The need to base

judgments on the merits of the case has constitutional stature. In Hovey v. Elliott, 167 U.S. 409 (1897), the Court held that due process precludes a court from entering judgment against a party as punishment for disobeying an order because a litigant has a right to have the case decided on the merits. In Hammond Packing Co. v. Arkansas, 212 U.S. 322 (1909), however, the Court upheld default as a sanction against a party that failed to produce documents. It distinguished Hovey on the ground that this disobedience went to the merits because it supported a presumption that the party withheld evidence that would show that its position in the litigation was groundless. Will all willful refusals to comply with discovery support such a presumption? In what ways was such a merits inference justified in *Cine Forty-Second Street*?

4.   A related due process requirement discussed by the court in *Cine Forty-Second Street* is the insistence that fault be found before extreme discovery sanctions are used. This requirement flows from Societe Internationale v. Rogers, 357 U.S. 197 (1958), in which the district court dismissed plaintiff's suit when plaintiff failed to produce documents on the ground that Swiss law forbade disclosure of the documents. The Supreme Court reversed, finding that dismissal was not justified because the district court had concluded that plaintiff had tried to comply in good faith with the production order. Citing "serious constitutional questions," the Court said that Rule 37 "should not be construed to authorize dismissal of [a] complaint because of [a plaintiff's] noncompliance with a pretrial production order when it has been established that failure to comply has been due to inability, and not to willfulness, bad faith, or any fault of [plaintiff]." How does this standard apply in Cine Forty-Second Street?

5.   Under *Cine Forty-Second Street*, what degree of fault is required for "ultimate" sanctions? Would ordinary negligence be sufficient? Why is that not "fault"? See Note, Defining a Feasible Culpability Threshold for the Imposition of Severe Discovery Sanctions, 65 Minn.L.Rev. 137, 148 (1980) (ordinary negligence threshold "may be the inevitable outgrowth of the * * * Cine position"). Courts of appeals have developed various multifactor tests to guide this decision. See Universal Health Group v. Allstate Ins. Co., 703 F.3d 953, 956 (6th Cir. 2013), calling for consideration of the following factors:

> (1)   whether the party's failure is due to willfulness, bad faith, or fault; (2) whether the adversary was prejudiced by the dismissed party's conduct; (3) whether the dismissed party was warned that failure to cooperate could lead to dismissal; and (4) whether less drastic sanctions were imposed or considered before dismissal was considered.

But the ultimate sanction decision is left to the district judge; even if the disobedience that draws the "ultimate" sanction seems minor, it may be viewed in the context of the party's overall record of recalcitrance. E360 Insight, Inc. v. Spamhaus Project, 658 F.3d 637 (7th Cir. 2011).

6.   Where the necessary quantum of fault is found, should the court automatically use the most stringent sanctions? Why does Rule 37(b)(2)

provide such a variety of sanctions? Compare Heartland Bank v. Heartland Home Finance, Inc., 335 F.3d 810 (8th Cir.2003) (district court's exclusion of plaintiff's nine witnesses for misleading defendant was unduly severe; the court should have considered the possibility of lesser sanctions) with Angulo-Alvarez v. Aponte de la Torre, 170 F.3d 246 (1st Cir.1999) (district court did not abuse its discretion in dismissing without first considering less severe sanctions). Is a requirement that lesser sanctions be considered dictated by the due process requirement that sanctions be based on legitimate presumptions about the merits of the case? In *Cine Forty-Second Street*, for example, did plaintiff's failure to respond to discovery support any presumption about its belief in its case on liability, as opposed to damages? If not, would dismissal of plaintiff's entire case have been an abuse of discretion?

Would a requirement that lesser sanctions be considered be consistent with the Supreme Court's pronouncement that "the most severe in the spectrum of sanctions provided by statute or rule must be available to the district court in appropriate cases, not merely to penalize those whose conduct may be deemed to warrant such a sanction, but to deter those who might be tempted to such conduct in the absence of such a deterrent." National Hockey League v. Metropolitan Hockey Club, Inc., 427 U.S. 639 (1976).

7.   Lest it be thought that lower courts invariably impose maximum sanctions, consider Coca-Cola Bottling Co. v. Coca-Cola Co., 110 F.R.D. 363 (D.Del.1986), in which defendant refused to comply with the court's order that it produce the secret formula for Coca-Cola (see supra p. 382 n. 6). Even though the decision to disobey the order was clearly the willful decision of the client, the court denied plaintiffs' motion for entry of default. It emphasized that the sanction must be "just" and relate to the issue to which the discovery in question was directed and that defendant had not otherwise been dilatory in discovery. It therefore crafted an elaborate order concerning assumptions of fact and limitations on defendant's evidence to assure that "plaintiffs are entitled to the advantage of every possible inference that fairly could be drawn from the formulae evidence sought." See 110 F.R.D. at 374–77. Should courts be required to fashion such elaborate orders to avoid ultimate sanctions against those who disobey their discovery orders?

CHAPTER 6

ADJUDICATION BEFORE TRIAL: SUMMARY JUDGMENT

■ ■ ■

The procedural device of summary judgment provides an opportunity for either party to win a case prior to trial by demonstrating, in the words of Rule 56(a) of the Federal Rules of Civil Procedure, "that there is no genuine issue as to any material fact and that the moving party is entitled to a judgment as a matter of law." The procedure is often employed "to identify claimants who lack evidence sufficient to reach the jury and who will therefore probably suffer a directed verdict or its equivalent at trial." Louis, Federal Summary Judgment Doctrine: A Critical Analysis, 83 Yale L.J. 745 (1974). As one court put it, summary judgment "is the put up or shut up moment in a lawsuit, when a party must show what evidence it has that would convince a trier of fact to accept its version of the events." Hammel v. Eau Galle Cheese Factory, 407 F.3d 852, 859 (7th Cir. 2005). For a discussion of the history and policies of summary judgment, see Miller, The Pretrial Rush to Judgment: Are the "Litigation Explosion," "Liability Crisis," and Efficiency Cliches Eroding Our Day in Court and Jury Trial Commitments?, 78 N.Y.U. L. Rev. 982 (2003).

What function does summary judgment serve that is not served by the motion to dismiss? One commentator states that "the motion for summary judgment has become the first real opportunity [in the course of a litigation] for identifying factually deficient claims or defenses." Louis, 83 Yale L.J. at 746. Why isn't this function already performed by the motion to dismiss?

It has been argued that summary judgment assumes special importance in a "notice pleading" system, such as the one adopted by the Federal Rules of Civil Procedure. See, e.g., E. Brunet, J. Parry & M. Redish, Summary Judgment: Federal Law and Practice 6–8 (2017); Marcus, The Revival of Fact Pleading Under the Federal Rules of Civil Procedure, 86 Colum.L.Rev. 433, 484–94 (1986). Why do you think this is so?

Might it be deemed improper to grant summary judgment prior to the conduct of discovery? See Fed. R. Civ. P. 56 (d). If so, does the device really avoid the problems for defendants generally associated with notice pleading? For a discussion of the timing of a summary judgment motion, see Brunet, The Timing of Summary Judgment, 198 F.R.D. 679 (2001).

Summary judgment can play an important role in modern civil procedure. To understand the nature of that role, it is first necessary to comprehend the nature and requirements of the device itself. To that end, this Chapter is divided into two sections. The first describes the concept of "burden shifting", which essentially constitutes the mechanics of the summary judgment device. The second section considers the standard of proof employed in deciding whether a summary judgment motion is to be granted.

A. THE NATURE OF THE SUMMARY JUDGMENT DEVICE: THE CONCEPT OF BURDEN SHIFTING

AN INTRODUCTION TO THE CONCEPT OF BURDEN OF PROOF

In a certain sense, a summary judgment motion seeks to establish that the party against whom the motion is made lacks sufficient evidence to meet his "burden of proof." But that term is ambiguous; as Professor Fleming James has written, "[t]he term 'burden of proof' is used in our law to refer to two separate and quite different concepts. * * * The two distinct concepts may be referred to as (1) the risk of non-persuasion, or the burden of persuasion or simply persuasion burden; (2) the duty of producing evidence, the burden of going forward with the evidence, or simply the production burden or the burden of evidence." James, Burdens of Proof, 47 Va.L.Rev. 51 (1961). Fundamentally, the burden of persuasion concerns which party must convince the trier of fact at trial of the accuracy of its factual assertions, while the burden of production concerns whether a party has sufficient evidence to go to trial in the first place. The summary judgment device is concerned exclusively with the latter burden.

Professor James describes the burden of persuasion in this manner:

Wherever in human affairs a question of the existence or nonexistence of a fact is to be decided by somebody, there is the possibility that the decider, or trier of the fact, may at the end of his deliberations be in doubt on the question submitted to him. On all the material before him, he may, for example, regard the existence or non-existence of the fact as equally likely—a matter in equipoise. * * * Where the parties to a civil action are in dispute over a material issue of fact, then that party who will lose if the trier's mind is in equipoise may be said to bear the risk that the trier will not be affirmatively persuaded or the risk of non-persuasion upon that issue.

* * *

Where an issue of fact is tried to a jury, it is the members of the jury whose minds may be in doubt or equipoise and the judge is not directly concerned in solving the problem. Under our system, however, the court does not leave this problem entirely to the jury, but attempts to formulate guides or tests for them in its charge. * * *

The usual formulation of the test in civil cases is that there must be a *preponderance of evidence* in favor of the party having the persuasion burden (the proponent) before he is entitled to a verdict. * * * The general statement is usually explained as referring not to the number of witnesses or quantity of evidence but to the convincing force of the evidence. [47 Va.L.Rev. at 52–53.]

Note that while the notion of burden of proof in civil cases depending on the preponderance of the evidence is now well established, apparently it was not used until the nineteenth century. See Leubsdorf, The Surprising History of the Preponderance Standard of Civil Proof, 67 Fla.L.Rev. 1569 (2015).

While the concept of burden of persuasion is designed to guide the fact finder (often the jury), the burden of production concept serves as a means of controlling the jury: unless the party upon whom that burden has been placed presents sufficient evidence to support a verdict in his favor, the judge will take the case out of the hands of the jury by granting a directed verdict, because a jury verdict in that party's favor would be irrational. In Professor James' words, "[t]he concept of the production burden is addressed to the court's function, not the jury's. It is simply a device whereby the court determines whether, if the trial were stopped at any given point, it would send the case to the jury. If not, the court decides the case and the jury has no role to play. If the case is sent to the jury, the production burden drops out of the case and has no role to play. The jury will be concerned only with the persuasion burden." 47 Va. L. Rev. at 57.

To be able to get his case to a jury, then, the party with the burden of production must present evidence sufficient to meet that burden—i.e. enough evidence that a reasonable finder of fact *could* find for him. It is, of course, no small task to determine in a particular case what evidence is sufficient to meet that standard. To a certain extent, that issue is examined in Section B of this chapter, and it is also discussed in Chapter 8, concerning the motions for directed verdict and judgment notwithstanding the verdict.

One further idea should be mentioned: the concept of burden shifting. Once the court has placed the burden of persuasion on a party (usually the plaintiff, except as to proof of affirmative defenses), the burden generally remains on that party throughout the litigation. In contrast, the burden of production may shift from party to party. A party with a burden of production may conceivably do more than simply *meet* his burden (i.e. present enough evidence that a reasonable finder of fact *could* find for him).

He may *shift* his burden, by presenting enough evidence that a reasonable finder of fact *must* find for him. At that point, the burden of production has shifted to the opposing party, who then must respond with evidence of his own, sufficient to *allow* a reasonable finder of fact to find for him. If he fails, the case will not go to the jury. If he succeeds in *meeting* his newly-imposed burden, the case will go to the jury. If, however, he responds with enough evidence of his own that, on the basis of that evidence, a reasonable finder of fact *must* find for him, he has effectively *shifted* the burden of production back onto the party who had it initially. In this manner, the burden of production can be shifted from one party to the other. If at some point the party with the burden of production *meets* but *does not shift* the burden, this means that the court has concluded that a fact finder could reasonably find for either party.

To understand exactly how the burden of production functions in the use of the summary judgment device, it is first necessary to understand the relationship between the motions for summary judgment and judgment as a matter of law.

SUMMARY JUDGMENT AND JUDGMENT AS A MATTER OF LAW CONTRASTED

Like a motion for summary judgment, a motion for judgment as a matter of law (previously referred to as "directed verdict" and "judgment n.o.v.") seeks to establish that the non-movant has failed to meet his burden of production. It has been suggested that because summary judgment comes at a relatively early stage in the litigation, courts should be more reluctant to grant summary judgment than to direct a verdict. However, the Supreme Court has held that the standard of proof to be applied is identical in both motions. Reeves v. Sanderson Plumbing Products, Inc., 530 U.S. 133 (2000); Anderson v. Liberty Lobby, Inc., 477 U.S. 242 (1986) (discussed infra p. 483). Compare Miller, The Pretrial Rush to Judgment: Are the "Litigation Explosion," "Liability Crisis," and Efficiency Cliches Eroding Our Day in Court and Jury Trial Commitments?, 78 N.Y.U. L. Rev. 982, 1061 (2003) (referring to "the radical difference in the timing and context of the two motions"). See also Clark, A Different Tack: The Case for a Least Restrictive Means Requirement for Summary Judgment, 40 Dayton L. Rev. 333, 360–61 (2016) (arguing that a judge deciding a case on a motion for judgment as a matter of law is more likely to reach the correct result than on a motion for summary judgment).

At trial, the party who does not have the burden of production may, at the close of his opponent's case, move for judgment as a matter of law without presenting any evidence of his own. At that point, the court will inquire whether the evidence presented by the non-movant meets his burden of production—whether a finder of fact could reasonably find for that party on the basis of the evidence presented. It is unclear, however, whether a party seeking summary judgment may, in the pre-trial stage, simply demand that the opposing party present his evidence to establish that the opponent has met its burden of production. This is so, even though the party moving for summary judgment would not have the burden of production at trial, and at that time could move for judgment as a matter of law—presenting the exact same issue raised on the summary judgment motion—without presenting any of its own evidence.

The following cases and commentary consider the showing that the party moving for summary judgment must make to invoke the court's review of the other side's ability to satisfy its burden of production before trial. One should be careful, however, to distinguish between the two concepts, and focus on the ways in which the moving party's initial showing compares to the burden of production.

Case about Summary judgement

(10/31/18)

ADICKES V. S.H. KRESS & CO.
Supreme Court of the United States, 1970
398 U.S. 144

White woman w/ Black students denied service and arrested

JUSTICE HARLAN delivered the opinion of the Court.

[Petitioner Sandra Adickes, a white New York schoolteacher, taught at a Mississippi "Freedom School" during the summer of 1964. One day, she went into the lunchroom of Kress's store in Hattiesburg, Miss., accompanied by six African American students at the school. The store refused to serve her, and she was arrested for vagrancy by two police officers shortly after she left the store. She sued Kress in federal court in New York under 42 U.S.C.A. § 1983, alleging that there was a conspiracy between Kress and the police to arrest her because she was in the company of African Americans.

After some discovery, Kress moved for summary judgment. It relied on the deposition of its employee Mr. Powell, the manager of the lunchroom, who stated that, due to the "explosive" situation in the store he used a prearranged signal to Ms. Baggett, one of the waitresses, that petitioner not be served. He stated further that he had no communication with the police about petitioner. In addition, Kress submitted the affidavits of the two arresting officers and the chief of police, all asserting that there had been no request from Powell that petitioner be arrested. Kress also pointed out that in her deposition petitioner admitted she had no knowledge of any communications between any Kress employee and the police. Petitioner relied in response on an unsworn statement from a Kress employee that one of the arresting officers had been in the store on the day she was arrested, and the hearsay statement of one of the six students, described in plaintiff's deposition, about seeing an officer in the store.

The district court granted summary judgment, ruling that petitioner had "failed to allege any facts from which a conspiracy might be inferred." The court of appeals affirmed. On appeal, the Supreme Court recognized that under section 1983 petitioner had to prove "state action" by showing "that Kress' employee, in the course of employment, and a Hattiesburg policeman somehow reached an understanding * * * to cause her subsequent arrest because she was a white person in the company of Negroes." It nevertheless reversed.]

In granting respondent's motion, the District Court simply stated that there was "no evidence in the complaint or in the affidavits and other papers from which a 'reasonably-minded person' might draw an inference of conspiracy." Our own scrutiny of the factual allegations of petitioner's complaint, as well as the material found in the affidavits and depositions presented by Kress to the District Court, however, convinces us that summary judgment was improper here, for we think respondent failed to carry its burden of showing the absence of any genuine issue of fact.

* * *

We think that on the basis of this record, it was error to grant summary judgment. As the moving party, respondent had the burden of showing the absence of a genuine issue as to any material fact, and for these purposes the material it lodged must be viewed in the light most favorable to the opposing party. Respondent here did not carry its burden because of its failure to foreclose the possibility that there was a policeman in the Kress store while petitioner was awaiting service, and that this policeman reached an understanding with some Kress employee that petitioner not be served.

It is true that Mr. Powell, the store manager, claimed in his deposition that he had not seen or communicated with a policeman prior to his tacit signal to Miss Baggett, the supervisor of the food counter. But respondent did not submit any affidavits from Miss Baggett, or from Miss Freeman, the waitress who actually refused petitioner service, either of whom might well have seen and communicated with a policeman in the store. Further, we find it particularly noteworthy that the two officers involved in the arrest each failed in his affidavit to foreclose the possibility (1) that he was in the store while petitioner was there; and (2) that, upon seeing petitioner with Negroes, he communicated his disapproval to a Kress employee, thereby influencing the decision not to serve petitioner.*

Given these unexplained gaps in the materials submitted by respondent, we conclude that respondent failed to fulfill its initial burden

_____

*   The affidavits of the officers each stated: "This arrest was made on the public streets of Hattiesburg, Mississippi, and was an officers' discretion arrest. I had not consulted with Mr. G.T. Powell, Manager of S.H. Kress and Company in Hattiesburg, and did not know his name until this date. No one at the Kress store asked that the arrest be made and I did not consult with anyone prior to the arrest."—Eds.

of demonstrating what is a critical element in this aspect of the case—that there was no policeman in the store. If a policeman were present, we think it would be open to a jury, in light of the sequence that followed, to infer from the circumstances that the policeman and a Kress employee had a "meeting of the minds" and thus reached an understanding that petitioner should be refused service. * * * [W]e think respondent's failure to show there was no policeman in the store requires reversal.

Pointing to Rule 56(e), as amended in 1963, respondent argues that it was incumbent on petitioner to come forward with an affidavit properly asserting the presence of the policeman in the store, if she were to rely on that fact to avoid summary judgment. Respondent notes in this regard that none of the materials upon which petitioner relied met the requirements of Rule 56(e).**

This argument does not withstand scrutiny, however, for both the commentary on and background of the 1963 amendment conclusively show that it was not intended to modify the burden of the moving party under Rule 56(c) to show initially the absence of a genuine issue concerning any material fact. The Advisory Committee note on the amendment states that the changes were not designed to "affect the ordinary standards applicable to the summary judgment." And, in a comment directed specifically to a contention like respondent's, the Committee stated that "[w]here the evidentiary matter in support of the motion does not establish the absence of a genuine issue, summary judgment must be denied *even if no opposing evidentiary matter is presented.*" Because respondent did not meet its initial burden of establishing the absence of a policeman in the store, petitioner here was not required to come forward with suitable opposing affidavits.

If respondent had met its initial burden by, for example, submitting affidavits from the policemen denying their presence in the store at the time in question, Rule 56(e) would then have required petitioner to have done more than simply rely on the contrary allegation in her complaint. To have avoided conceding this fact for purposes of summary judgment, petitioner would have had to come forward with either (1) the affidavit of someone who saw the policeman in the store or (2) an affidavit under Rule 56(f) [now Rule 56(d)—Eds.] explaining why at that time it was impractical to do so.

[Justice Marshall took no part in the decision. Justice Black, in a separate opinion, concurred in the judgment, reasoning that "[t]he

---

** The version of Rule 56(e) referred to in text was changed to the current version in 2010.—Eds. Prior to its amendment the relevant portion of Rule 56(e) read as follows: "When a motion for summary judgment is made and supported as provided in this rule, an adverse party may not rest upon the mere allegations or denials of the adverse party's pleading, but the adverse party's response, by affidavits or as otherwise provided in this rule, must set forth specific facts showing that there is a genuine issue for trial. If the adverse party does not so respond, summary judgement, if appropriate, shall be entered against the adverse party."

existence or nonexistence of a conspiracy is essentially a factual issue that the jury, not the trial judge, should decide. * * * The advantages of trial before a live jury with live witnesses, and all the possibilities of considering the human factors, should not be eliminated by substituting trial by affidavit and the sterile bareness of summary judgment." Justice Douglas dissented in part on other grounds, and Justice Brennan concurred in part and dissented in part, also on other grounds.]

THE MOVANT'S BURDEN IN SUMMARY JUDGMENT

At trial, assuming that the plaintiff has the burden of production, once the plaintiff has presented its case to the jury the defendant may move for judgment as a matter of law (formerly known as directed verdict) pursuant to Rule 50, asserting that the plaintiff has failed to produce sufficient evidence to justify a rational finder of fact's judgment in plaintiff's favor. For example, if in *Adickes* at trial the plaintiff had presented her evidence to support her allegation of conspiracy, the defendant could have moved for judgment as a matter of law on the grounds that plaintiff had failed to meet her burden of production. Yet because *Adickes* involved defendant's summary judgment motion prior to trial, rather than a motion for judgment as a matter of law at trial, the Supreme Court held that the motion must be denied because in support of its motion the defendant had failed to foreclose the possibility that the policemen had been in the store at the time plaintiff had been ordered to leave. Thus, the Court appeared to indicate that a movant's burden in making a summary judgment motion may be much heavier than the burden on a movant at trial who does not have the burden of production.

Does it make sense to place a significant burden of production on a movant for summary judgment, when that party would have absolutely no burden of production at trial, other than the burden simply to move for judgment as a matter of law by pointing to the inadequacies in her opponent's case? Isn't the point of summary judgment to determine whether a trial would be unnecessary? Why, then, shouldn't we want to know, at the summary judgment stage, whether the party who has the burden of production at trial (as the plaintiff in *Adickes* would on the issue of conspiracy) will have sufficient evidence at that point to satisfy that burden? After all, we will find that out at trial on the defendant's motion for judgment as a matter of law anyway once the plaintiff has had an opportunity to present its evidence; why not find it out at the summary judgment stage, to avoid having a trial in the first place?

Professor Martin Louis criticized the Court's approach to the movant's burden in *Adickes,* arguing that "[i]mposing such a requirement on the movant makes it extremely difficult for him to compel the opposing party to preview his proof, even though the latter will bear the production burden at trial and even though it appears doubtful that he could discharge it. Thus the opposing party could sometimes defeat a motion for summary judgment simply by withholding proof, the inadequacy of which, if disclosed, would probably lead to his defeat." Louis, Federal Summary Judgment Doctrine: A Critical Analysis, 83 Yale L.J. 745, 752 (1974). Moreover, he noted that use of the approach employed in *Adickes* is inconsistent with the relaxed pleading requirement of the Federal Rules: "[A] conclusory, factually deficient pleading will usually survive a motion to dismiss. If the party moving for summary judgment must discharge a rigorous proof burden regardless of whether he would bear the burden of proof at trial, he could almost never compel the pleader to demonstrate that he can prove the essential elements which he was in the past required to allege in detail. As a result the movant could rarely intercept a factually deficient claim or defense. Given the severe congestion of most court dockets, such an interpretation of the Federal Rules of Civil Procedure is most unfortunate." Id. at 752. He therefore concluded that the burden imposed on a movant for summary judgment who does not have the burden of production at trial should be reduced.

Professor Louis was unwilling, however, to completely remove the burden on a summary judgment movant who would not have the burden of production at trial. Instead, he believed that "a movant who would not have the trial proof burden clearly must support his motion with some affidavits or other materials showing or at least suggesting the nonexistence of an essential element of the opposing party's case. A more lenient requirement would permit him to harass the opposing party too easily." He believed that "if [the moving party] fails to discharge the burden, his motion fails, even though the opposing party makes no response. * * * [I]f he discharges this burden, he should be deemed to have established the nonexistence of the essential element in question unless the opposing party responds adequately." Id. at 750.

According to Professor Louis, "[t]here are essentially two methods by which the moving party can discharge his burden. First, through discovery he can obtain a preview of his opponent's evidence on an essential element and contend, in support of his motion, that the evidence is insufficient to discharge the opponent's production burden. If his contention is correct he discharges his own burden and shifts to the opposing party the onus of producing additional evidence or excusing his failure to do so under Rule 56(f) [now Rule 56(d)—Eds.] Second, by previewing his own proof, he can attempt to show the nonexistence of an essential element asserted by the opposing party. He can, of course, combine these two approaches." Id. at 750. If a movant who would not have the production burden at trial chooses Professor Louis's second method, Louis would require that she present only evidence sufficient to *meet* a burden of production—i.e., enough evidence so that a reasonable factfinder *could* find for her. In this important sense, Louis's approach imposes a more lenient burden on the movant than that imposed under the approach invoked in *Adickes,* which effectively required the movant to *shift* a burden onto the nonmovant (i.e., present enough evidence that a reasonable finder of fact *must* find for him), even when the movant would have had no production burden at trial.

Several years later, Professor David Currie concurred in Professor Louis's criticism of *Adickes,* but argued that Louis had not gone far enough: "The purpose of rule 56 requires that summary judgment be granted if and only if the evidence before the court would justify a directed verdict if presented at trial. Consequently [Rule 56] should be amended to make clear that a motion for summary judgment, without more, puts an opposing party with the burden of proof [at trial] to the task of producing evidence sufficient to sustain a favorable verdict." Currie, Thoughts on Directed Verdicts and Summary Judgment, 45 U. Chi. L. Rev. 72, 79 (1977). Thus, Currie would have imposed no more burden on a movant for summary judgment than he would have at trial; if the movant would have no burden of production at trial, Currie would impose no additional burden on that movant at the summary judgment stage.

Currie dismissed Louis's concern that the absence of any burden of production on the movant for summary judgment might unduly burden or harass the plaintiff: "This fear seems unfounded, for discovery can require far more burdensome disclosure, and the evidence must in any event be prepared for trial." Id. at 78. Of course, the motion for summary judgment might require the plaintiff to prepare his evidence at an earlier point than he would be required to, were he to be preparing for trial. But should that burden *necessarily* be deemed "undue"? Consider Rule 56(d); does that provision provide sufficient case-by-case protection to a nonmovant who has not been given sufficient time to prepare his evidence? See Jacked Up, LLC v. Sara Lee Corp., 854 F.3d 797 (5th Cir. 2017) (requests for additional time to respond should be "liberally granted," but the party seeking more time must set forth a plausible basis for believing that further facts will emerge and explain how those would impact the motion). Consider also Rule 11, which is today a far more substantial barrier to the making of harassing motions for summary judgment than it was at the time that either Louis or Currie wrote.

Professor Melissa Nelken has argued that "[i]f defendants seek to avoid the delay and expense of trial, at a minimum [on a summary judgment motion] they should shoulder the expense of doing sufficient discovery to show that the plaintiff does not have a case." Nelken, One Step Forward, Two Steps Back: Summary Judgment After *Celotex,* 40 Hastings L.J. 53, 66 (1988). See also Nissan Fire & Marine Ins. Co. v. Fritz Companies, 210 F.3d 1099, 1105 (9th Cir. 2000) ("In a typical case, in order to carry its initial burden of production by pointing to the absence of evidence to support the nonmoving party's claim or defense, the moving party will have made reasonable efforts, using the normal tools of discovery, to discover whether the nonmoving party has enough evidence to carry its burden of persuasion at trial."). On the other hand, it has been argued that "[i]mposition of the burden upon the movant as suggested by Professor Nelken * * * appears to amount to little more than extracting a toll for the making of a summary judgment motion." E. Brunet & M. Redish, Summary Judgment: Federal Law and Practice 108 (3d ed. 2006). But see Friedenthal, Cases on Summary Judgment: Has There Been a Material Change in Standards?, 63 Notre Dame L. Rev. 770, 776 (1988):

> [T]here are many cases, undoubtedly the vast majority, in which the litigants are fully aware that the party with the burden of production (at trial) is able to call witnesses on its behalf who will carry its burden of producing evidence. Any "automatic" rule requiring all such parties to make a showing would be extremely wasteful. If one could, merely by filing an unsupported motion, force an opponent to make a substantial showing, there would be a strong incentive to make such a filing, if for no other reason than to harass the other party and raise its costs of litigation.

Which of the three approaches comports most closely with the approach employed in *Adickes*? How persuasive is Professor Currie's criticism of *Adickes*?

Recall that Professor Louis suggests that one way in which a moving party can satisfy his burden in moving for summary judgment is to present a preview of his own proof. What tactical considerations would affect a party's willingness to make such a presentation? Would his opponent be able through discovery to require him to do so?

The other avenue identified by Professor Louis is that the moving party can use discovery to obtain a preview of his opponent's evidence. Will he encounter work product obstacles at that point? Cf. Rule 26(b)(3) (regarding opinion work product). Does your answer to that question depend on who has the burden of pleading and proof with regard to the issue involved? What happens if the party to whom the discovery is directed says "I have not completed my investigation and discovery yet and therefore cannot respond"? Cf. Rule 56(d).

There are, then, three basic approaches to the question of what burden a movant for summary judgment should bear. Under the approach employed in *Adickes*, in order to require a nonmovant to respond, a movant must establish the truth of her position, whether or not she would have the burden of production at trial. This approach is often associated with Professor J. William Moore. 6 J. W. Moore, Federal Practice and Procedure ¶ 56.15[3] (2nd ed.). Under Professor Louis's approach, the movant would have only to meet a burden of production, or to demonstrate—through discovery—the absence of proof of an essential element of the nonmovant's case. Professor Currie, in contrast, would treat summary judgment in the same manner as a motion for judgment as a matter of law at trial pursuant to Rule 50, imposing no burden of production on a movant who would not bear the burden of production at trial, in order to require the nonmovant to come forward with her supporting evidence. Note, however, that under all three approaches, a movant for summary judgment who would bear the burden of production at trial must *shift* the burden before the nonmovant will be required to respond.

Consider whether in the following case the Supreme Court adhered to the approach it had chosen in *Adickes*. If your answer is no, consider whether it replaced it with Louis's approach, Currie's approach, or something in between.

CELOTEX CORP. V. CATRETT
Supreme Court of the United States, 1986
477 U.S. 317

• Asbestos Case
• Summary jud.
req.

JUSTICE REHNQUIST delivered the opinion of the Court.

The United States District Court for the District of Columbia granted the motion of petitioner Celotex Corporation for summary judgment against respondent Catrett because the latter was unable to produce evidence in support of her allegation in her wrongful death complaint that the decedent had been exposed to petitioner's asbestos products. A divided panel of the Court of Appeals for the District of Columbia Circuit reversed, however, holding that petitioner's failure to support its motion with evidence tending to negate such exposure precluded the entry of summary judgment in its favor. * * *

Respondent commenced this lawsuit in September 1980, alleging that the death in 1979 of her husband, Louis H. Catrett, resulted from his exposure to products containing asbestos manufactured or distributed by 15 named corporations. Respondent's complaint sounded in negligence, breach of warranty, and strict liability. Two of the defendants filed motions challenging the District Court's in personam jurisdiction, and the remaining 13, including petitioner, filed motions for summary judgment. Petitioner's motion, which was first filed in September 1981, argued that summary judgment was proper because respondent had "failed to produce evidence that any [Celotex] product . . . was the proximate cause of the injuries alleged within the jurisdictional limits of [the District] Court." In particular, petitioner noted that respondent had failed to identify, in answering interrogatories specifically requesting such information, any witnesses who could testify about the decedent's exposure to petitioner's asbestos products. In response to petitioner's summary judgment motion, respondent then produced three documents which she claimed "demonstrate that there is a genuine material factual dispute" as to whether the decedent had ever been exposed to petitioner's asbestos products. The three documents included a transcript of a deposition of the decedent, a letter from an official of one of the decedent's former employers whom petitioner planned to call as a trial witness, and a letter from an insurance company to respondent's attorney, all tending to establish that the decedent had been exposed to petitioner's asbestos products in Chicago during 1970–1971. Petitioner, in turn, argued that the three documents were inadmissible hearsay and thus could not be considered in opposition to the summary judgment motion.

In July 1982, almost two years after the commencement of the lawsuit, the District Court granted all of the motions filed by the various defendants. The court explained that it was granting petitioner's summary judgment motion because "there [was] no showing that the plaintiff was exposed to the defendant Celotex's product in the District of Columbia [or elsewhere] within the statutory period." Respondent appealed only the grant of summary judgment in favor of petitioner, and a divided panel of the District of Columbia Circuit reversed. The majority of the Court of Appeals held that petitioner's summary judgment motion was rendered "fatally defective" by the fact that petitioner "made no effort to adduce any evidence, in the form of affidavits or otherwise, to support its motion." According to the majority, Rule 56(e) of the Federal Rules of Civil Procedure, and this Court's decision in Adickes v. S.H. Kress & Co., 398 U.S. 144, 159 (1970), establish that "the party opposing the motion for summary judgment bears the burden of responding *only after* the moving party has met its burden of coming forward with proof of the absence of any genuine issues of material fact." The majority therefore declined to consider petitioner's argument that none of the evidence produced by respondent in opposition to the motion for summary judgment would have been admissible at trial. The dissenting judge argued that "[t]he majority errs in supposing that a party seeking summary judgment must always make an affirmative evidentiary showing, even in cases where there is not a triable, factual dispute." Id. at 167, 756 F.2d, at 188 (Bork, J., dissenting).

We think that the position taken by the majority of the Court of Appeals is inconsistent with the standard for summary judgment set forth in Rule 56(c)* of the Federal Rules of Civil Procedure. Under Rule 56(c), summary judgment is proper "if the pleadings, depositions, answers to interrogatories, and admissions on file, together with the affidavits, if any, show that there is no genuine issue as to any material fact and that the moving party is entitled to a judgment as a matter of law." In our view, the plain language of Rule 56(c) mandates the entry of summary judgment, after adequate time for discovery and upon motion, against a party who fails to make a showing sufficient to establish the existence of an element essential to that party's case, and on which that party will bear the burden of proof at trial. In such a situation, there can be "no genuine issue as to any material fact," since a complete failure of proof concerning an essential element of the nonmoving party's case necessarily renders all other facts immaterial. The moving party is "entitled to judgment as a matter of law" because the nonmoving party has failed to make a sufficient showing on an

---

*   Note that the relevant portion of the rule is now included in Rule 56(a).—Eds.

essential element of her case with respect to which she has the burden of proof. "[T]h[e] standard [for granting summary judgment] mirrors the standard for a directed verdict under Federal Rule of Civil Procedure 50(a)." Anderson v. Liberty Lobby, Inc., 477 U.S. 242, 250 (1986).

Of course, a party seeking summary judgment always bears the initial responsibility of informing the district court of the basis for its motion, and identifying those portions of "the pleadings, depositions, answers to interrogatories, and admissions on file, together with the affidavits, if any," which it believes demonstrate the absence of a genuine issue of material fact. But unlike the Court of Appeals, we find no express or implied requirement in Rule 56 that the moving party support its motion with affidavits or other similar materials *negating* the opponent's claim. On the contrary, Rule 56(c), which refers to "the affidavits, *if any*" (emphasis added), suggests the absence of such a requirement.* And if there were any doubt about the meaning of Rule 56(c) in this regard, such doubt is clearly removed by Rules 56(a) and (b), which provide that claimants and defendants, respectively, may move for summary judgment *"with or without supporting affidavits"* (emphasis added). The import of these subsections is that, regardless of whether the moving party accompanies its summary judgment motion with affidavits, the motion may, and should, be granted so long as whatever is before the district court demonstrates that the standard for the entry of summary judgment, as set forth in Rule 56(c), is satisfied. One of the principal purposes of the summary judgment rule is to isolate and dispose of factually unsupported claims or defenses, and we think it should be interpreted in a way that allows it to accomplish this purpose.[5]

Respondent argues, however, that Rule 56(e), by its terms, places on the nonmoving party the burden of coming forward with rebuttal affidavits, or other specified kinds of materials, only in response to a motion for summary judgment "made and supported as provided in this rule." According to respondent's argument, since petitioner did not "support" its motion with affidavits, summary judgment was improper in this case. But as we have already explained, a motion for summary judgment may be made pursuant to Rule 56 "with or without supporting affidavits." In cases like the instant one, where the nonmoving party will bear the burden of proof at trial on a dispositive issue, a summary judgment motion may properly be made in reliance solely on the "pleadings, depositions, answers to interrogatories, and admissions on file." Such a motion, whether or not accompanied by affidavits, will be "made and supported as provided in this rule," and Rule 56(e) therefore requires the nonmoving party to go beyond the pleadings and by her own affidavits, or by the "depositions, answers to

---

    *   This rule language has been slightly revised.—Eds.

    5   See Louis, Federal Summary Judgment Doctrine: A Critical Analysis, 83 Yale L.J. 745, 752 (1974); Currie, Thoughts on Directed Verdicts and Summary Judgment, 45 U.Chi.L.Rev. 72, 79 (1977).

interrogatories, and admissions on file," designate "specific facts showing that there is a genuine issue for trial."

We do not mean that the nonmoving party must produce evidence in a form that would be admissible at trial in order to avoid summary judgment. Obviously, Rule 56 does not require the nonmoving party to depose her own witnesses. Rule 56(e) permits a proper summary judgment motion to be opposed by any of the kinds of evidentiary materials listed in Rule 56(c), except the mere pleadings themselves, and it is from this list that one would normally expect the nonmoving party to make the showing to which we have referred.

The Court of Appeals in this case felt itself constrained, however, by language in our decision in Adickes v. S.H. Kress & Co., 398 U.S. 144 (1970). There we held that summary judgment had been improperly entered in favor of the defendant restaurant in an action brought under 42 U.S.C. § 1983. In the course of its opinion, the *Adickes* Court said that "both the commentary on and the background of the 1963 Amendment conclusively show that it was not intended to modify the burden of the moving party . . . to show initially the absence of a genuine issue concerning any material fact." We think that this statement is accurate in a literal sense, since we fully agree with the *Adickes* Court that the 1963 Amendment to Rule 56(e) was not designed to modify the burden of making the showing generally required by Rule 56(c). It also appears to us that, on the basis of the showing before the Court in *Adickes,* the motion for summary judgment in that case should have been denied. But we do not think the *Adickes* language quoted above should be construed to mean that the burden is on the party moving for summary judgment to produce evidence showing the absence of a genuine issue of material fact, even with respect to an issue on which the nonmoving party bears the burden of proof. Instead, as we have explained, the burden on the moving party may be discharged by "showing"—that is, pointing out to the District Court—that there is an absence of evidence to support the nonmoving party's case.

The last two sentences of Rule 56(e) were added, as this Court indicated in *Adickes,* to disapprove a line of cases allowing a party opposing summary judgment to resist a properly made motion by reference only to its pleadings. While the *Adickes* Court was undoubtedly correct in concluding that these two sentences were not intended to *reduce* the burden of the moving party, it is also obvious that they were not adopted to *add to* that burden. Yet that is exactly the result which the reasoning of the Court of Appeals would produce; in effect, an amendment to Rule 56(e) designed to *facilitate* the granting of motions for summary judgment would be interpreted to make it *more difficult* to grant such motions. Nothing in the two sentences themselves requires this result, for the reasons we have previously indicated, and we now put to rest any inference that they do so.

Our conclusion is bolstered by the fact that district courts are widely acknowledged to possess the power to enter summary judgments *sua sponte,* so long as the losing party was on notice that she had to come forward with all of her evidence. * * * It would surely defy common sense to hold that the District Court could have entered summary judgment *sua sponte* in favor of petitioner in the instant case, but that petitioner's filing of a motion requesting such a disposition precluded the District Court from ordering it.

Respondent commenced this action in September 1980, and petitioner's motion was filed in September 1981. The parties had conducted discovery, and no serious claim can be made that respondent was in any sense "railroaded" by a premature motion for summary judgment. Any potential problem with such premature motions can be adequately dealt with under Rule 56(f)[now 56(d)—Eds.], which allows a summary judgment motion to be denied, or the hearing on the motion to be continued, if the nonmoving party has not had an opportunity to make full discovery.

In this Court, respondent's brief and oral argument have been devoted as much to the proposition that an adequate showing of exposure to petitioner's asbestos products was made as to the proposition that no such showing should have been required. But the Court of Appeals declined to address either the adequacy of the showing made by respondent in opposition to petitioner's motion for summary judgment, or the question whether such a showing, if reduced to admissible evidence, would be sufficient to carry respondent's burden of proof at trial. We think the Court of Appeals with its superior knowledge of local law is better suited than we are to make these determinations in the first instance.

* * * Summary judgment procedure is properly regarded not as a disfavored procedural shortcut, but rather as an integral part of the Federal Rules as a whole, which are designed "to secure the just, speedy and inexpensive determination of every action." Fed.Rule Civ.Proc. 1; see Schwarzer, Summary Judgment Under the Federal Rules: Defining Genuine Issues of Material Fact, 99 F.R.D. 465, 467 (1984). Before the shift to "notice pleading" accomplished by the Federal Rules, motions to dismiss a complaint or to strike a defense were the principal tools by which factually insufficient claims or defenses could be isolated and prevented from going to trial with the attendant unwarranted consumption of public and private resources. But with the advent of "notice pleading," the motion to dismiss seldom fulfills this function any more, and its place has been taken by the motion for summary judgment. Rule 56 must be construed with due regard not only for the rights of persons asserting claims and defenses that are adequately based in fact to have those claims and defenses tried to a jury, but also for the rights of persons opposing such claims and defenses to demonstrate in the manner provided by the Rule, prior to trial, that the claims and defenses have no factual basis.

The judgment of the Court of Appeals is accordingly reversed, and the case is remanded for further proceedings consistent with this opinion.

JUSTICE WHITE, concurring in the Court's opinion and judgment.

I agree that the Court of Appeals was wrong in holding that the moving defendant must always support his motion with evidence or affidavits showing the absence of a genuine dispute about a material fact. I also agree that the movant may rely on depositions, answers to interrogatories and the like to demonstrate that the plaintiff has no evidence to prove his case and hence that there can be no factual dispute. But the movant must discharge the burden the rules place upon him: It is not enough to move for summary judgment without supporting the motion in any way or with a conclusory assertion that the plaintiff has no evidence to prove his case.

A plaintiff need not initiate any discovery or reveal his witnesses or evidence unless required to do so under the discovery rules or by court order. Of course, he must respond if required to do so; but he need not also depose his witnesses or obtain their affidavits to defeat a summary judgment motion asserting only that he has failed to produce any support for his case. It is the defendant's task to negate, if he can, the claimed basis for the suit.

Petitioner Celotex does not dispute that if respondent has named a witness to support her claim, summary judgment should not be granted without Celotex somehow showing that the named witness' possible testimony raises no genuine issue of material fact. It asserts, however, that respondent has failed on request to produce any basis for her case. Respondent, on the other hand, does not contend that she was not obligated to reveal her witnesses and evidence but insists that she has revealed enough to defeat the motion for summary judgment. Because the Court of Appeals found it unnecessary to address this aspect of the case, I agree that the case should be remanded for further proceedings.

JUSTICE BRENNAN, with whom THE CHIEF JUSTICE and JUSTICE BLACKMUN join, dissenting.

This case requires the Court to determine whether Celotex satisfied its initial burden of production in moving for summary judgment on the ground that the plaintiff lacked evidence to establish an essential element of her case at trial. I do not disagree with the Court's legal analysis. The Court clearly rejects the ruling of the Court of Appeals that the defendant must provide affirmative evidence disproving the plaintiff's case. Beyond this, however, the Court has not clearly explained what is required of a moving party seeking summary judgment on the ground that the nonmoving party cannot prove its case.[1] This lack of clarity is unfortunate:

---

[1] It is also unclear what the Court of Appeals is supposed to do in this case on remand. Justice White—who has provided the Court's fifth vote—plainly believes that the Court of Appeals should reevaluate whether the defendant met its initial burden of production. However, the

district courts must routinely decide summary judgment motions, and the Court's opinion will very likely create confusion. For this reason, even if I agreed with the Court's result, I would have written separately to explain more clearly the law in this area. However, because I believe that Celotex did not meet its burden of production under Federal Rule of Civil Procedure 56, I respectfully dissent from the Court's judgment.

Summary judgment is appropriate where the Court is satisfied "that there is no genuine issue as to any material fact and that the moving party is entitled to a judgment as a matter of law." Fed.Rule Civ.Proc. 56(c).* The burden of establishing the nonexistence of a "genuine issue" is on the party moving for summary judgment. * * * This burden has two distinct components: an initial burden of production, which shifts to the nonmoving party if satisfied by the moving party; and an ultimate burden of persuasion, which always remains on the moving party. * * * The court need not decide whether the moving party has satisfied its ultimate burden of persuasion[2] unless and until the Court finds that the moving party has discharged its initial burden of production. * * *

The burden of production imposed by Rule 56 requires the moving party to make a prima facie showing that it is entitled to summary judgment. * * * The manner in which this showing can be made depends upon which party will bear the burden of persuasion on the challenged claim at trial. If the moving party will bear the burden of persuasion at trial, that party must support its motion with credible evidence—using any of the materials specified in Rule 56(c)—that would entitle it to a directed verdict if not controverted at trial. Such an affirmative showing shifts the burden of production to the party opposing the motion and requires that party either to produce evidentiary materials that demonstrate the existence of a "genuine issue" for trial or to submit an affidavit requesting additional time for discovery. * * *

---

decision to reverse rather than to vacate the judgment below implies that the Court of Appeals should assume that Celotex has met its initial burden of production and ask only whether the plaintiff responded adequately, and, if so, whether the defendant has met its ultimate burden of persuasion that no genuine issue exists for trial. Absent some clearer expression from the Court to the contrary, Justice White's understanding would seem to be controlling.

* The relevant provision is now Rule 56(a).—Eds.

[2] The burden of persuasion imposed on a moving party by Rule 56 is a stringent one. Summary judgment should not be granted unless it is clear that a trial is unnecessary, Anderson v. Liberty Lobby, Inc., 477 U.S. 242, 250 (1986), and any doubt as to the existence of a genuine issue for trial should be resolved against the moving party, Adickes v. S.H. Kress & Co., 398 U.S. 144, 158–159 (1970). In determining whether a moving party has met its burden of persuasion, the court is obliged to take account of the entire setting of the case and must consider all papers of record as well as any materials prepared for the motion. As explained by the Court of Appeals for the Third Circuit in In re Japanese Electronic Products Antitrust Litigation, 723 F.2d 238 (1983), rev'd on other grounds sub nom. Matsushita Electric Industrial Co. v. Zenith Radio Corp., 475 U.S. 574 (1986), "[i]f . . . there is any evidence in the record from any source from which a reasonable inference in the [nonmoving party's] favor may be drawn, the moving party simply cannot obtain a summary judgment. . . ." 723 F.2d, at 258.

If the burden of persuasion at trial would be on the nonmoving party, the party moving for summary judgment may satisfy Rule 56's burden of production in either of two ways. First, the moving party may submit affirmative evidence that negates an essential element of the nonmoving party's claim. Second, the moving party may demonstrate to the Court that the nonmoving party's evidence is insufficient to establish an essential element of the nonmoving party's claim. See 10A C. Wright, A. Miller & M. Kay Kane § 2727, pp. 130–131; Louis, Federal Summary Judgment Doctrine: A Critical Analysis, 83 Yale L.J. 745, 750 (1974) (hereinafter Louis). If the nonmoving party cannot muster sufficient evidence to make out its claim, a trial would be useless and the moving party is entitled to summary judgment as a matter of law. Anderson v. Liberty Lobby, Inc., 477 U.S. 242, 250 (1986).

Where the moving party adopts this second option and seeks summary judgment on the ground that the nonmoving party—who will bear the burden of persuasion at trial—has no evidence, the mechanics of discharging Rule 56's burden of production are somewhat trickier. Plainly, a conclusory assertion that the nonmoving party has no evidence is insufficient. * * * Such a "burden" of production is no burden at all and would simply permit summary judgment procedure to be converted into a tool for harassment. * * * Rather, as the Court confirms, a party who moves for summary judgment on the ground that the nonmoving party has no evidence must affirmatively show the absence of evidence in the record. This may require the moving party to depose the nonmoving party's witnesses or to establish the inadequacy of documentary evidence. If there is literally no evidence in the record, the moving party may demonstrate this by reviewing for the court the admissions, interrogatories and other exchanges between the parties that are in the record. Either way, however, the moving party must affirmatively demonstrate that there is no evidence in the record to support a judgment for the nonmoving party.

If the moving party has not fully discharged this initial burden of production, its motion for summary judgment must be denied, and the Court need not consider whether the moving party has met its ultimate burden of persuasion. Accordingly, the nonmoving party may defeat a motion for summary judgment that asserts that the nonmoving party has no evidence by calling the Court's attention to supporting evidence already in the record that was overlooked or ignored by the moving party. In that event, the moving party must respond by making an attempt to demonstrate the inadequacy of this evidence, for it is only by attacking all the record evidence allegedly supporting the nonmoving party that a party seeking summary judgment satisfies Rule 56's burden of production.[3]

---

[3]   Once the moving party has attacked whatever record evidence—if any—the nonmoving party purports to rely upon, the burden of production shifts to the nonmoving party, who must either (1) rehabilitate the evidence attacked in the moving party's papers, (2) produce additional

Thus, if the record disclosed that the moving party had overlooked a witness who would provide relevant testimony for the nonmoving party at trial, the Court could not find that the moving party had discharged its initial burden of production unless the moving party sought to demonstrate the inadequacy of this witness' testimony. Absent such a demonstration, summary judgment would have to be denied on the ground that the moving party had failed to meet its burden of production under Rule 56.

The result in Adickes v. S.H. Kress & Co., supra, is fully consistent with these principles. In that case, petitioner was refused service in respondent's lunchroom and then was arrested for vagrancy by a local policeman as she left. Petitioner brought an action under 42 U.S.C. § 1983 claiming that the refusal of service and subsequent arrest were the product of a conspiracy between respondent and the police; as proof of this conspiracy, petitioner's complaint alleged that the arresting officer was in respondent's store at the time service was refused. Respondent subsequently moved for summary judgment on the ground that there was no actual evidence in the record from which a jury could draw an inference of conspiracy. In response, petitioner pointed to a statement from her own deposition and an unsworn statement by a Kress employee, both already in the record and both ignored by respondent, that the policeman who arrested petitioner was in the store at the time she was refused service. We agreed that "[i]f a policeman were present, . . . it would be open to a jury, in light of the sequence that followed, to infer from the circumstances that the policeman and Kress employee had a 'meeting of the minds' and thus reached an understanding that petitioner should be refused service." Consequently, we held that it was error to grant summary judgment "on the basis of this record" because respondent had "failed to fulfill its initial burden" of demonstrating that there was no evidence that there was a policeman in the store.

The opinion of the Court in *Adickes* has sometimes been read to hold that summary judgment was inappropriate because the respondent had not submitted affirmative evidence to negate the possibility that there was a policeman in the store. The Court of Appeals apparently read *Adickes* this way and therefore required Celotex to submit evidence establishing that plaintiff's decedent had not been exposed to Celotex asbestos. I agree with the Court that this reading of *Adickes* was erroneous and that Celotex could seek summary judgment on the ground that plaintiff could not prove exposure to Celotex asbestos at trial. However, Celotex was still required to satisfy its initial burden of production.

---

evidence showing the existence of a genuine issue for trial as provided in Rule 56(e), or (3) submit an affidavit explaining why further discovery is necessary as provided in Rule 56(f). Summary judgment should be granted if the nonmoving party fails to respond in one or more of these ways, or if, after the nonmoving party responds, the court determines that the moving party has met its ultimate burden of persuading the court that there is no genuine issue of material fact for trial.

I do not read the Court's opinion to say anything inconsistent with or different than the preceding discussion. My disagreement with the Court concerns the application of these principles to the facts of this case.

Defendant Celotex sought summary judgment on the ground that plaintiff had "failed to produce" any evidence that her decedent had ever been exposed to Celotex asbestos. Celotex supported this motion with a 2-page "Statement of Material Facts as to Which There is No Genuine Issue" and a 3-page "Memorandum of Points and Authorities" which asserted that the plaintiff had failed to identify any evidence in responding to two sets of interrogatories propounded by Celotex and that therefore the record was "totally devoid" of evidence to support plaintiff's claim.

Approximately three months earlier, Celotex had filed an essentially identical motion. Plaintiff responded to this earlier motion by producing three pieces of evidence which she claimed "[a]t the very least . . . demonstrate that there is a genuine factual dispute for trial": (1) a letter from an insurance representative of another defendant describing asbestos products to which plaintiff's decedent had been exposed, (2) a letter from T.R. Hoff, a former supervisor of decedent, describing asbestos products to which decedent had been exposed; and (3) a copy of decedent's deposition from earlier workmen's compensation proceedings. Plaintiff also apparently indicated at that time that she intended to call Mr. Hoff as a witness at trial.

Celotex subsequently withdrew its first motion for summary judgment. However, as a result of this motion, when Celotex filed its second summary judgment motion, the record did contain evidence—including at least one witness—supporting plaintiff's claim. Indeed, counsel for Celotex admitted to this Court at oral argument that Celotex was aware of this evidence and of plaintiff's intention to call Mr. Hoff as a witness at trial when the second summary judgment motion was filed. Moreover, plaintiff's response to Celotex' second motion pointed to this evidence—noting that it had already been provided to counsel for Celotex in connection with the first motion—and argued that Celotex had failed to "meet its burden of proving that there is no genuine factual dispute for trial."

On these facts, there is simply no question that Celotex failed to discharge its initial burden of production. Having chosen to base its motion on the argument that there was no evidence in the record to support plaintiff's claim, Celotex was not free to ignore supporting evidence that the record clearly contained. Rather, Celotex was required, as an initial matter, to attack the adequacy of this evidence. Celotex' failure to fulfill this simple requirement constituted a failure to discharge its initial burden of production under Rule 56, and thereby rendered summary judgment improper.

This case is indistinguishable from *Adickes*. Here, as there, the defendant moved for summary judgment on the ground that the record contained no evidence to support an essential element of the plaintiff's claim. Here, as there, the plaintiff responded by drawing the court's attention to evidence that was already in the record and that had been ignored by the moving party. Consequently, here, as there, summary judgment should be denied on the ground that the moving party failed to satisfy its initial burden of production.

[The dissenting opinion of JUSTICE STEVENS is omitted.]

NOTES AND QUESTIONS

1.   Does the decision in *Celotex* represent a major alteration in the *Adickes* approach? Do either the majority or dissent in *Celotex* believe that it does? Consider Nissan Fire & Marine Ins. Co. v. Fritz Companies, 210 F.3d 1099, 1103–04 (9th Cir.2000):

> We believe that the perceived tension between *Adickes* and *Celotex* may be explained by the fact that the cases focused on different questions. The central question in *Adickes* was whether the moving party had carried its initial burden of production by producing affirmative evidence negating an essential element of the nonmoving party's claim. The central question in *Celotex* was whether the moving party had carried its initial burden of production by showing that the nonmoving party did not have enough evidence to carry its ultimate burden of persuasion at trial. In other words, *Adickes* and *Celotex* dealt with two different methods by which a moving party can carry its initial burden of production.

But see Edwards v. Princess Cruise Lines, Ltd., 471 F. Supp.2d 1027, 1029 (N.D.Cal. 2007): "To the extent that plaintiff relies on *Adickes v. S.H. Kress* for the proposition that a movant must 'disprove' an essential element of the non-movant's case, that case has been superseded in pertinent part by *Celotex*. . . ."

Relying in large part on *Adickes,* the lower court in *Celotex* had stated (756 F.2d at 184–85):

> It is firmly established that the party opposing the motion for summary judgment bears the burden of responding *only after* the moving party has met its burden of coming forward with proof of the absence of any genuine issues of material fact.

> At trial, of course, Mrs. Catrett would have the burden of proving by admissible evidence that her husband's exposure to Celotex's products had proximately caused his death. If Mrs. Catrett failed to satisfy her burden, then her case would be vulnerable to a motion for a directed verdict. However, * * * the party moving for summary judgment carries the burden of proving the absence of a material issue of fact "even on issues where the other party would have the burden of proof at trial."

> In this case Celotex proffered nothing. It advanced only the naked allegation that the *plaintiff* had not come forward in discovery

with evidence to support her allegations of decedent's exposure to the defendant's product. Under settled rules, that barebones approach will not do. Mrs. Catrett was simply not required, given this state of the record, to offer any evidence in response.

Is this an accurate characterization of the standard of *Adickes?* Why did the Supreme Court reverse? On remand from the Supreme Court, the same panel of the court of appeals held that plaintiff's reliance on the letter from the official of Louis Catrett's former employer, coupled with plaintiff's indication that this official would be a witness at trial, sufficed to show a genuine issue as to whether Catrett was exposed to Celotex products. 826 F.2d 33 (D.C.Cir.1987). Again dissenting, Judge Bork argued that the letter was not admissible and that plaintiff had made no showing that the official had personal knowledge of such exposure.

2.   To which scholarly approach is the standard adopted by Justice Rehnquist in *Celotex* closer, Professor Currie's or Professor Louis'? Is it identical to either one? Consider the relevance of Rule 56(c)(1) in answering this question.

The majority of post-*Celotex* lower courts have read that decision not to impose a significant triggering burden on a movant who lacks the burden of production at trial. Indeed, many lower court decisions following *Celotex* have either reduced the burden dramatically or ignored it completely. See, e.g., Chao v. Hall Holding Co., Inc., 285 F.3d 415 (6th Cir. 2002), cert. denied, 537 U.S. 1168 (2003); Adler v. Wal-Mart Stores, Inc. 144 F.3d 664 (10th Cir. 1998); Elkins v. Richardson-Merrell, Inc., 8 F.3d 1068 (6th Cir.1993); Whetstine v. Gates Rubber Co., 895 F.2d 388 (7th Cir.1990); Kauffman v. Puerto Rico Telephone Co., 841 F.2d 1169 (1st Cir.1988). But see Clark v. Coats & Clark, Inc., 929 F.2d 604 (11th Cir.1991). In that case, the district court had granted defendant's summary judgment motion on the ground that plaintiffs would not be able to prove their case. The appellate court reversed on the ground that defendant had not satisfied its initial burden to justify summary judgment. It concluded "emphatically" that "*Celotex* did not overrule *Adickes*," and was an "exception" for an "uncommon situation"—"where neither party could prove either the affirmative or the negative of an essential element of the claim." This decision has been criticized as "contrary to the letter and spirit of *Celotex*" because it overlooked the Supreme Court's statement that summary judgment is "an integral part of the Federal Rules as a whole" and recalls the "wariness (if not downright hostility) toward summary judgment common prior to [*Celotex*]." Schwarzer & Hirsch, Summary Judgment After *Eastman Kodak*, 45 Hast. L.J. 1, 12–13 (1993). See also Russ v. International Paper Co., 943 F.2d 589, 591 (5th Cir.1991): "[T]he district court * * * cite[s] language from * * * *Celotex* and other cases suggesting that summary judgment is appropriate anytime a party fails to establish the existence of an element essential to his case and on which he will bear the burden of proof at trial. * * * This is incorrect. * * * *Celotex* makes clear that before the non-moving party is required to produce evidence in opposition to the motion, the moving party must first satisfy its obligation of demonstrating that there are no factual issues warranting trial." Is this an accurate reading of *Celotex*? To a similar effect see Hunter v. Caliber Sys., 220 F.3d 702, 725–26 (6th Cir. 2000).

3.   Recall the initial disclosure provisions of Rule 26(a)(1). Once the disclosure exchange is completed, would defendant be in a position to move for summary judgment on the ground that plaintiff has disclosed no evidence to support his or her claims? Could plaintiff then oppose the motion with material not previously disclosed? See Rule 37(c)(1).

4.   In his dissent, Justice Brennan contends that the only difference between his opinion and that of the majority is in the application of an accepted general standard to the facts. Do you agree that the two opinions adopt the same general approach to the movant's burden?

In footnote 2 of his dissent, Justice Brennan refers to "[t]he burden of persuasion imposed on a moving party by Rule 56." Does the summary judgment procedure actually have anything to do with the "burden of persuasion," as that term is traditionally defined? See the discussion of Professor James' work, supra pp. 444–445. What do you suppose Justice Brennan means by his use of the term? In footnote 1, he refers to a movant's "ultimate burden of persuasion that no genuine issue exists for trial." Does this statement provide a clue as to his meaning?

5.   Does Justice Brennan adopt Professor Louis's approach to the ways in which the moving party may generate the material needed to make the showing required to support summary judgment? Does he give proper weight to the difficulties the moving party may confront in fashioning discovery to obtain this information?

6.   Given possible uncertainty about whether the moving party has satisfied its initial burden, how does the responding party decide what needs to be submitted in opposition to a motion for summary judgment? Should the court first appraise the movant's showing and then advise the other side on whether it need bother to submit responsive materials? Although no courts require that the judge make that sort of initial appraisal, some do require that pro se litigants be advised (either by the judge or the moving party) of the general requirements that Rule 56 imposes on a party responding to a motion for summary judgment. See, e.g., Irby v. New York City Transit Auth., 262 F.3d 412 (2d Cir. 2001) ("the moving party should routinely provide a pro se party with notice of the requirements of Rule 56"); Stratton v. Buck, 697 F.3d 1104 (9th Cir.2012) (requiring similar notice when judge converts motion to dismiss into summary-judgment motion pursuant to Rule 12(d)). How well does such a burden fit within the adversary system? See Rand v. Rowland, 154 F.3d 952, 968 (9th Cir. 1998) (dissenting opinion) ("We are not supposed to be advocates for a class of litigants, and it is hard to help pro ses very much without being unfair to their adversaries.").

7.   Does the Court in *Celotex* relieve plaintiff of the obligation of coming forward with admissible evidence? See Rule 56(c)(4), which provides that affidavits or declarations used to support or oppose a summary judgment motion must "set out facts that would be admissible in evidence. . . ."

8.   The Court in *Celotex* points out that plaintiff was not "railroaded" by a premature motion for summary judgment, suggesting that such problems can be dealt with under what is now Rule 56(d). Does that provision protect plaintiffs adequately against premature motions? See Coleman, The *Celotex* Initial Burden Standard and an Opportunity to "Revivify" Rule 56, 32 So. Ill. L.J. 295 (2008) (reporting that pre-discovery motions for summary judgment do not occur). Should the court permit discovery on issues not raised by the summary judgment motion? With regard to discovery directed toward the issue raised by the summary judgment motion, must plaintiff make a showing that the discovery is likely to produce material that will defeat the motion? Consider the Second Circuit's test for the sufficiency of an affidavit under what was then Rule 56(f) but is currently dealt with in Rule 56(d): "The affidavit must include the nature of the uncompleted discovery; how the facts sought are reasonably expected to create a genuine issue of material fact; what efforts the affiant has made to obtain these facts; and why these efforts were unsuccessful." See Paddington Partners v. Bouchard, 34 F.3d 1132, 1138 (2d Cir.1994).

9.   It has been said that *Celotex* "worked a systemic sea change" in promoting summary judgment. Shadur, Trials or Tribulations (Rule 56 Style), 29 Litigation 5 (Winter 2003); see also Gonzalez, Depositions in the Age of Summary Judgment, Trial, Aug. 2004, at 20 ("The most dramatic change in employment discrimination litigation over the past two decades is the federal judiciary's increased use of summary judgment.") If so, is that necessarily a bad result? For a criticism of the trend towards the greater availability of summary judgment thought to be manifested in decisions such as *Celotex*, see generally Stempel, A Distorted Mirror: The Supreme Court's Shimmering View of Summary Judgment, Directed Verdict, and the Adjudication Process, 49 Ohio St. L.J. 95 (1988). See also Issacharoff & Loewenstein, Second Thoughts About Summary Judgments, 100 Yale L.J. 73 (1990) (arguing that expanded use of summary judgment after *Celotex* alters the balance of power in pretrial by raising costs and risks to plaintiffs and has a further adverse effect on settlement when a summary judgment motion has been denied). Should *Celotex* be viewed instead as a positive development? See Redish, Summary Judgment and the Vanishing Trial: Implications of the Litigation Matrix, 57 Stan. L. Rev. 1329 (2005) (praising *Celotex*'s removal of "external barriers" to a trial court's reaching the merits of a summary judgment motion). See also Steinman, The Irrepressible Myth of *Celotex*: Reconsidering Summary Judgment Burdens Twenty Years After the Trilogy, 63 Wash. & Lee L. Rev. 81, 87 (2006) (reporting that *Celotex* and other Supreme Court summary judgment decisions are very heavily cited); Brunet, The Efficiency of Summary Judgment, 43 Loy. U. Chi. L.J. 689 (2012) (emphasizing "numerous positive features associated with the summary judgment procedure").

More recently, doubt has been raised about *Celotex*'s input on the rate of summary judgment awards in federal court. According to Professor Linda Mullenix, for example, neither *Celotex* nor the other 1986 summary judgment decisions of the Supreme Court had a significant impact on the extent to which summary judgment has been awarded. In support, she relies on empirical studies conducted by the Federal Judicial Center. Mullenix, The 25th

Anniversary of the Summary Judgment Trilogy: Much Ado About Very Little, 43 Loy. U. Chi. L. J. 561 (2012). Does the fact that empirical studies fail to demonstrate an increase in the rate of summary judgment awards necessarily mean that *Celotex* has had no meaningful impact? On the issue, See Thomas, Keynote: Before and After the Summary Judgment Trilogy, 43 Loy. U. Chi. L. J. 499 (2012) (arguing that "the trend. . .toward decision making by judges and lawyers and away from juries is remarkable and unmistakable").

Some states have also changed their practices. California decisions, for example, instructed that summary judgment in California courts should generally conform to *Celotex*. See, e.g., Aguilar v. Atlantic Richfield Co., 24 P.3d 493 (Cal. S.Ct. 2001). The California Legislature, however, responded by amending the state's summary judgment statute to require 75 days notice of a summary judgment motion, and to extend the time further if the party seeking summary judgment has unreasonably failed to allow discovery. See Cal. Code Civ. Proc. § 437c(a). But not all states have accepted the decision. See, e.g., Orvis v. Johnson, 177 P.3d 600, 604 (Utah 2008): "While [*Celotex*] has been the law in the federal courts for over two decades now, it is not Utah law."

10. One area in which the award of summary judgment has increased is employment discrimination. See, e.g., Schneider, The Changing Shape of Federal Pre-Trail Practice: The Disparate Impact on Civil Rights and Employment Discrimination Cases, 158 U. Pa. L. Rev. 517 (2010) (criticizing alleged overuse of summary judgment in civil rights cases). Some have therefore suggested that a much stricter standard be employed for the award of summary judgment in employment discrimination cases. However, in Torgerson v. City of Rochester, 643 F.3d 1031 (8th Cir. 2011), the Eighth Circuit rejected recognition of such an exception. Relying heavily on *Celotex*, the court noted that summary judgment is "designed for every action." Id. at 1031. The court concluded that "[t] here is no 'discrimination case exception' to the application of summary judgment, which is a useful pretrial tool to determine whether any case, including one alleging discrimination, merits a trail." Id.

11. Note that Justice Rehnquist relies in part on a trial court's ability to award summary judgment *sua sponte*. This means that the court may award summary judgment, even though neither party has formally moved for it. However, it is generally error for the district court to award summary judgment *sua sponte* without providing notice to the party against whom the award has been made. Bendet v. Sandoz Pharmaceuticals Corp., 308 F.3d 907, 911–12 (8th Cir. 2002). But see Geraghty and Miller, Inc. v. Conoco, Inc., 234 F.3d 917 (5th Cir. 2000) (district court's award of *sua sponte* summary judgment without notice was harmless error because the court had accepted and considered the losing party's brief and gave it an opportunity to be heard on all issues). According to one court, while granting summary judgment *sua sponte* "is permissible * * * it is a hazardous procedure which warrants special caution." Osler Institute, Inc. v. Forde, 333 F.3d 832, 836 (7th Cir. 2003), cert. denied, 540 U.S. 1177 (2004).

B. MEETING THE BURDEN OF PRODUCTION: DETERMINING THE APPROPRIATE STANDARD

In the previous section, we examined exactly what a party who moves for summary judgment must produce in order to trigger the need for a response from the non-movant. Once the response is triggered, it is necessary to determine what evidence the non-movant must produce in order to avoid summary judgment.

If the non-movant would have the burden of production at trial, it must respond with sufficient evidence that a reasonable finder of fact *could* find in its favor—i.e., it must meet its burden of production. If the non-movant would not have the burden of production at trial, however, everyone agrees that the only way that a movant may obtain summary judgment is by *shifting* the burden of production—i.e., by providing sufficient evidence that, absent a response from the non-movant, a reasonable fact finder would have to find for the movant because it would be unreasonable to do otherwise.

In this section, we consider what constitutes evidence sufficient to meet a party's burden of production—in other words, when has a party presented enough evidence that a reasonable jury could find for him?

ARNSTEIN V. PORTER
United States Court of Appeals, Second Circuit, 1946
154 F.2d 464

Before L. HAND, CLARK, and FRANK, CIRCUIT JUDGES.

FRANK, CIRCUIT JUDGE.

[Plaintiff Arnstein sued noted song writer Cole Porter for copyright infringement, alleging that numerous well-known songs by the defendant were actually taken from a number of songs copyrighted by plaintiff. Plaintiff claimed that defendant "had stooges right along to follow me, watch me, and live in the same apartment with me", and that plaintiff's room had been ransacked on several occasions. Asked in his deposition how he knew that defendant had anything to do with any of these breakins, plaintiff responded, "I don't know that he had to do with it, but I only know that he could have." Defendant in his deposition denied that he had ever seen or heard any of plaintiff's compositions or had had any acquaintance with persons who might have stolen any of them. The trial court granted defendant's summary judgment motion, and plaintiff, appearing *pro se*, appealed. The Court of Appeals reversed.]

The principal question on this appeal is whether the lower court, under Rule 56, properly deprived plaintiff of a trial of his copyright infringement action. * * * [I]t is important to avoid confusing two separate elements essential to a plaintiff's case in such a suit: (a) that defendant copied from plaintiff's copyrighted work and (b) that the copying (assuming it to be proved) went so far as to constitute improper appropriation.

As to the first—copying—the evidence may consist (a) of defendant's admission that he copied or (b) circumstantial evidence—usually evidence of access—from which the trier of the facts may reasonably infer copying.

* * *

After listening * * * to the compositions as played in the phonograph recordings submitted by defendant, we find similarities [between plaintiff's and defendant's compositions]; but we hold that unquestionably, standing alone, they do not compel the conclusion, or permit the inference, that defendant copied. The similarities, however, are sufficient so that, if there is enough evidence of access to permit the case to go to the jury, the jury may properly infer that the similarities did not result from coincidence.

Summary judgment was, then, proper if indubitably defendant did not have access to plaintiff's compositions. Plainly that presents an issue of fact. On that issue, the district judge, who heard no oral testimony, had before him the depositions of plaintiff and defendant. The judge characterized plaintiff's story as "fantastic"; and, in the light of the references in his opinion to defendant's deposition, the judge obviously accepted defendant's denial of access and copying. Although part of plaintiff's testimony on deposition (as to "stooges" and the like) does seem "fantastic," yet plaintiff's credibility, even as to those improbabilities, should be left to the jury. If evidence is "of a kind that greatly taxes the credulity of the judge, he can say so, or, if he totally disbelieves it, he may announce that fact, leaving the jury free to believe it or not." If, said Winslow, J., "evidence is to be always disbelieved because the story told seems remarkable or impossible, then a party whose rights depend on the proof of some facts out of the usual course of events will always be denied justice simply because his story is improbable." [Marston v. Dresen, 85 Wis. 530, 535, 55 N.W. 896, 899 (1893).] We should not overlook the shrewd proverbial admonition that sometimes truth is stranger than fiction.

But even if we were to disregard the improbable aspect of plaintiff's story, there remain parts by no means "fantastic." On the record now before us, more than a million copies of one of his compositions were sold; copies of others were sold in smaller quantities or distributed to radio stations or band leaders or publishers, or the pieces were publicly performed. If, after hearing both parties testify, the jury disbelieves defendant's denials, it can, from such facts, reasonably infer access. It follows that, as credibility is unavoidably involved, a genuine issue of material fact presents itself. With credibility a vital factor, plaintiff is entitled to a trial where the jury can observe the witnesses while testifying. Plaintiff must not be deprived of the invaluable privilege of cross-examining the defendant—the "crucial test of credibility"—in the presence of the jury. Plaintiff, or a lawyer on his behalf, on such examination may elicit damaging admissions from defendant; more important, plaintiff may persuade the jury, observing defendant's manner when testifying, that the defendant is unworthy of belief.

CLARK, J.,* dissenting.

Under the procedure employed, the parties were entitled to require discovery of the case relied on by the other. This they did by each taking the deposition of the other, resulting in a categorical denial by defendant of having ever seen or heard plaintiff's compositions and no showing by plaintiff of any evidence of access worthy of submission to any trier of fact. * * * My brothers, in a trusting belief in the virtues of cross-examination, rely upon a trial to develop more. But cross-examination can hardly construct a whole case without some factual basis on which to start. * * *

Since the legal issue seems thus clear to me, I am loath to believe that my colleagues will uphold a final judgment of plagiarism on a record such as this. The present holding is therefore one of those procedural mountains which develop where it is thought that justice must be temporarily sacrificed, lest a mistaken precedent be set at large. The conclusion that the precedent would be mistaken appears to rest on two premises: a belief in the efficacy of the jury to settle issues of plagiarism, and a dislike of the rule established by the supreme court as to summary judgments. Now, as to the first, I am not one to condemn jury trials (cf. Frank, Law and the Modern Mind) since I think it has a place among other quite finite methods of fact-finding. * * * [But] surely we cannot now say that a verdict should not be directed. * * *

The second premise—dislike of the summary-judgment rule—I find difficult to appraise or understand. [Judge Clark found the majority's opinion to suggest a special limitation on summary judgment in copyright cases.] * * * [S]ince, however, the clear-cut provisions of f.r. 56 conspicuously do not contain either a restriction on the kinds of actions to which it is applicable (unlike most state summary procedures), or any presumption against its use, it is necessary to refashion the rule. * * * that is a novel method of amending rules of procedure. It subverts the plans and hopes of the profession for careful, informed study leading to the adoption and to the amendment of simple rules which shall be uniform throughout the country. * * *

In fact, however, cases, texts, and articles without dissent accept and approve the summary judgment as an integral and useful part of the procedural system envisaged by the rules. * * * It is, indeed, more necessary in the system of simple pleading now enforced in the federal

---

* Judge Clark served as reporter of the committee that drafted the Federal Rules of Civil Procedure, and he was reporter to the Advisory Committee on the Civil Rules when this case was decided. He had early favored summary judgment over pleadings motions as a way to decide the merits of cases. See Smith, Judge Charles E. Clark and the Federal Rules of Civil Procedure, 85 Yale L.J. 914, 918–19.—Eds.

courts; for under older procedures, useless and unnecessary trials could be avoided, in theory at least, by the then existing demurrer and motion practice. But that stresses pleading forms, rather than the merits, while summary judgment and its popular correlative, pre-trial procedure, f.r.16, go directly to the merits. One unfortunate consequence of eliminating summary procedure is that it affords support for the plea of return to the old demurrer, which, however clumsily, did get rid of some of the cases which did not deserve a protracted and expensive trial. Of course it is error to deny trial when there is a genuine dispute of facts; but it is just as much error—perhaps more in cases of hardship, or where impetus is given to strike suits—to deny or postpone judgment where the ultimate legal result is clearly indicated.

DYER v. MACDOUGALL

United States Court of Appeals, Second Circuit, 1952
201 F.2d 265

Before SWAN, CHIEF JUDGE, and L. HAND and FRANK, CIRCUIT JUDGES.

L. HAND, CIRCUIT JUDGE.

This case comes up on appeal by the plaintiff from a judgment summarily dismissing the third and fourth counts of a complaint for libel and slander. * * * We may start with the amended complaint, which was filed on November 24, 1950. It was in four counts, of which the first alleged that the defendant, Albert E. MacDougall, had said of the plaintiff at a directors' meeting of the "Queensboro Corporation": "You are stabbing me in the back." The second count alleged that MacDougall had written a letter to one Dorothy Russell Hope, the plaintiff's wife's sister, containing the words: "He"—the plaintiff—"has made false statements to my clients in Philadelphia," and "He has presented bills for work he has not done." The third count alleged that MacDougall had said to a lawyer, named Almirall, that a letter sent out by the plaintiff to the shareholders of the "Queensboro Corporation" was "a blackmailing letter." The fourth count alleged that MacDougall's wife, as MacDougall's agent, had said to Mrs. Hope that the plaintiff had "written and sent out a blackmailing letter."

On December 26, 1950, the defendants, before answer, moved for judgment summarily dismissing the second, third and fourth counts, supporting their motion by affidavits of MacDougall, MacDougall's wife, and Almirall, and by a deposition of Mrs. Hope, which the plaintiff himself had already taken. Each of the defendants unequivocally denied the utterance of the slanders attributed to him or her; and Almirall and Mrs. Hope denied that he or she had heard the slanders uttered. On his part the plaintiff replied with several affidavits of his own, the contents of all of which would, however, be inadmissible as evidence at a trial upon the issue of utterance. On January 24, 1951, the defendants filed an unverified answer denying the defamatory utterances, and on the same day they brought on their motion for hearing before Judge Kennedy. He offered the plaintiff an opportunity to take depositions of Mr. and Mrs. MacDougall and of Almirall, and a second deposition of Mrs. Hope; and by consent the case was then adjourned to allow the plaintiff to take the depositions. However, towards the end of October 1951, he told the court that he did not wish to do so, and on December 28, 1951 * * * the judge decided the defendants' motion by summarily dismissing the third and fourth counts on the ground that upon the trial the plaintiff would have no evidence to offer in support of the slanders except the testimony of witnesses, all of whom would deny their utterance.

* * *

The question is whether, in view of the defendants' affidavits and Mrs. Hope's deposition, there was any "genuine issue" under Rule 56(c)* as to the utterance of the slanders. The defendants had the burden of proving that there was no such issue; on the other hand, at a trial the plaintiff would have the burden of proving the utterances; and therefore, if the defendants on the motion succeeded in proving that the plaintiff would not have enough evidence to go to the jury on the issue, the judgment was right. As the plaintiff has refused to avail himself of the privilege under Rule 56(f)** of examining by deposition the witnesses whom the defendants proposed to call at the trial, we must assume that what they said in their affidavits they would have repeated in their depositions; and that what they would have said in their depositions, they would say at a trial, with one possible exception, the consideration of which we will postpone for the time being. With that reserved we will therefore first discuss the judgment on the assumption that the record before us contains all the testimony that would appear at a trial in support of the slanders. * * *

[If] the cause went to trial, the plaintiff would have no witnesses by whom he could prove the slanders alleged in the third and fourth counts, except the two defendants, Almirall and Mrs. Hope; and they would all deny that the slanders had been uttered. On such a showing how could he escape a directed verdict? It is true that the carriage, behavior, bearing, manner and appearance of a witness—in short, his "demeanor"—is a part of the evidence. The words used are by no means all that we rely on in making up our minds about the truth of a question that arises in our ordinary affairs, and it is abundantly settled that a jury is as little confined to them as we are. They may, and indeed they should, take into consideration the whole nexus of sense impressions which they get from a witness. This we have again and again declared, and have rested our affirmance of findings of fact of a judge, or of a jury, on the hypothesis that this part of the evidence may have turned the scale.[7] Moreover, such

---

*   The relevant provision today is Rule 56(a).—Eds.

**   The relevant provision today is Rule 56(d).—Eds.

[7]   Arnstein v. Porter, 2 Cir., 154 F.2d 464.

evidence may satisfy the tribunal, not only that the witness' testimony is not true, but that the truth is the opposite of his story; for the denial of one, who has a motive to deny, may be uttered with such hesitation, discomfort, arrogance or defiance, as to give assurance that he is fabricating, and that, if he is, there is no alternative but to assume the truth of what he denies.

Nevertheless, although it is therefore true that in strict theory a party having the affirmative might succeed in convincing a jury of the truth of his allegations in spite of the fact that all the witnesses denied them, we think it plain that a verdict would nevertheless have to be directed against him. This is owing to the fact that otherwise in such cases there could not be an effective appeal from the judge's disposition of a motion for a directed verdict. He, who has seen and heard the "demeanor" evidence, may have been right or wrong in thinking that it gave rational support to a verdict; yet, since that evidence has disappeared, it will be impossible for an appellate court to say which he was. Thus, he would become the final arbiter in all cases where the evidence of witnesses present in court might be determinative. We need not say that in setting aside a verdict the judge has not a broader discretion than in directing one; for we have before us only the equivalent of a direction. It may be argued that such a ruling may deprive a party of a possibly rational verdict, and indeed that is theoretically true, although the occasions must be to the last degree rare in which the chance so denied is more than fanciful. Nevertheless we do not hesitate to set against the chance so lost, the protection of a review of the judge's decision.

There remains the second point which we reserved for separate discussion: i.e. whether by an examination in open court the plaintiff might extract from the four witnesses admissions which he would not have got on the depositions that he refused. Although this is also at best a tenuous possibility, we need not say that there could never be situations in which it might justify denying summary judgment. It might appear for example that upon a deposition a witness had been recalcitrant, or crafty, or defiant, or evasive, so that the immediate presence of a judge in a courtroom was likely to make him tell more. That would be another matter; and it might be enough. But the plaintiff is in no position to invoke such a possibility for he has refused to try out these witnesses upon deposition, where he might discover whether there was any basis for supposing that awe of a judge was necessary to make them more amenable. A priori we will not assume that that is true. The course of procedural reform has all indeed been towards bringing witnesses before the tribunal when it is possible; but that is not so much because more testimony can be got out of them as because only so can the "demeanor" evidence be brought before the tribunal.

Judgment affirmed.

[Concurring opinion of JUDGE FRANK omitted.]

NOTES AND QUESTIONS

1. The Cole Porter songs involved in *Arnstein* included "Begin the Bequine," "Night and Day," "You'd Be So Nice to Come Home To," "My Heart Belongs to Daddy," and "Don't Fence Me In." On remand, Arnstein lost at trial. According to Arnstein's biographer, "[t]he outcome was never much in doubt." Gary A. Rosen, Unfair to Genius: The Strange and Litigious Career of Ira B. Arnstein 235 (2012). After the jury's verdict in his favor, Porter moved for an award of attorneys' fees. The judge awarded the "relatively nominal sum of $2,500... [B]ut since Arnstein couldn't pay it anyway, the paltry amount scarcely mattered." The jury's verdict was summarily affirmed on appeal. Id. at 236. For a discussion of the entire case, see id. at 215–36.

2. For a thorough discussion of both *Arnstein* and the Clark-Frank debate, see Wald, Summary Judgment at Sixty, 76 Tex. L. Rev. 1897, 1898–1904 (1998). According to Judge Wald, "the disagreement between Judges Frank and Clark offers a penetrating preview of the extreme version of the pro- and anti-summary judgment positions that we see among current judges." Id. at 1903.

3. How persuasive is the court's reasoning in *Dyer*? In a separate concurring opinion, Judge Frank criticized the logic of Judge Hand's opinion:

> Judge Hand's opinion states that, if defendant and the other witnesses testified, the trial court, evaluating their credibility in the light of their demeanor as witnesses, could rationally find not only that defendant's denial was false, but that the opposite was true, i.e., that defendant had made the slanderous statement. Yet Judge Hand holds that a trial judge in a jury trial of such a case would be obliged not to let the jury reach a verdict for plaintiff on that rational basis. As I understand Judge Hand, he says that the result of holding otherwise would be that the trial judge's disposition of a motion for a directed verdict (or a verdict n.o.v.) could not be effectively reviewed on appeal. On that ground alone—i.e., the supposed obstacle, in a jury trial of such a case, to review of a directed verdict—Judge Hand's opinion affirms the summary judgment for defendant here.

>   * * *

> Judge Hand argues from the alleged unreviewability of a directed verdict in a case like this, if demeanor were a factor. But this argument cuts too far. For, if Judge Hand is correct, the same difficulty will attend the review of any directed verdict in any case where any important evidence consists of oral testimony. In any such case, one could say, as Judge Hand says here: If the jury (should the case go to the jury) could rely on "demeanor evidence," then necessarily the trial judge could do likewise, on a motion for a directed verdict; and if he could, no directed verdict would be reviewable when important testimony in oral. But this is exactly not the rule in the federal courts: The well-settled rule is that, in passing on a motion for a directed verdict the trial judge always must utterly

disregard his own views of witnesses' credibility, and therefore of their demeanor; that he believes or disbelieves some of the testimony is irrelevant.

4.   Demeanor evidence may usually be relied upon by the jury to disbelieve witnesses with impeccable credentials; as is often said, a scoundrel's testimony could be believed over the testimony of 40 bishops. Does the law give too much weight to demeanor evidence? In general, the mannerisms that people tend to associate with lying are characteristics of people who are simply nervous. Many witnesses are nervous about testifying, and it may be that some liars are not nervous about lying. This should make us a bit uneasy about the heavy emphasis placed on demeanor evidence. Moreover, some psychological research indicates that people are not effective at detecting lies from observing the speaker. See, e.g., Bond, Kahler & Paolicelli, The Miscommunication of Deception: An Adaptive Perspective, 21 J. Exper. Social Psych. 331 (1985) (subjects of experiment were not much better than chance in detecting liars, presumably because they placed reliance on factors such as gestures that do not invariably indicate lying); Zuckerman, Koestner & Driver, Beliefs About Cues Associated with Deception, 6 J. Nonverbal Behavior 105 (Winter 1981) (subjects who answered questionnaire revealed about 10% accuracy in identifying those cues actually associated with lying). One very early study even concluded that people make *more* accurate decisions on the basis of written materials than observation of witnesses. Marston, Studies in Testimony, 15 J.Amer.Inst.Crim.Law & Criminology 5, 22–26 (1924). These studies do not provide conclusive evidence that the law's reliance on demeanor evidence is misplaced since they do not recreate the trial atmosphere accurately enough for such a conclusion, but they do provide a basis for caution in assuming that demeanor evidence is critical to accurate results. Compare United States v. Thoms, 684 F. 3d 893, 903 (9th Cir. 2012) (We * * * do not think we overvalue the importance of live testimony.").

5.   While Judge Frank, the author of *Arnstein*, rejected Judge Hand's reasoning in *Dyer*, he ultimately concurred in the court's judgment. Can *Arnstein* and *Dyer* be reconciled? Judge Frank believed that the facts in *Dyer* were "most unusual: The plaintiff asserts that in his absence he was slandered by defendant in the presence of but two other persons. As this fact is denied by all three, only plaintiff's own suit serves to publicize the alleged slander. In these peculiar circumstances, the plaintiff should not have the chance at a trial to discharge his burden of proof by nothing except the trial court's disbelief in the oral testimony of witnesses all of whom will deny that the alleged slanderous statement was made." Is this suggested distinction between *Dyer* and *Arnstein* persuasive? See Springer v. Durflinger, 518 F.3d 479 (7th Cir. 2008) ("When challenges to a witness's credibility are all a plaintiff relies on, and he has shown no independent facts—no proof—to support his claims, summary judgment in favor of the defendant is proper").

6.   If the decisions are, in fact, irreconcilable, which position do you find more compelling? Does your answer depend on how important we deem the litigants' access to a jury? As Judge Clark noted in his *Arnstein* dissent, Judge

Frank was one of the harshest critics of the use of the jury. See, e.g., J. Frank, Law and the Modern Mind 191–93 (Anchor ed. 1963):

> Proclaiming that we have a government of laws, we have, in jury cases, created a government of often ignorant and prejudiced men. * * * [A]re jurors good fact-finders? * * * Is it likely that twelve men, summoned from all sorts of occupations, unaccustomed to the machinery of the law, unacquainted with their own mental workings and not known to one another, can, in the scant time allowed them for deliberation, do as good a job in weighing conflicting testimony as an experienced judge? Can they as well see through the story of the glib liar, or of the unconsciously biased but conscientious witness, or as ably allow for the stage fright which often makes the honest but cautious man speak falteringly on the witness stand? It is hard to conceive that any astute person can take seriously the stereotyped praise of the jury. * * *

Is Judge Frank's position on summary judgment in *Arnstein* inconsistent with his views on the value of the jury? See R. Glennon, The Iconoclast as Reformer 156–57 (1985) (describing Frank's view that summary judgment should be curtailed *because* juries act unpredictably, and perhaps irrationally).

7.   Whatever the wisdom of overriding a jury decision, appellate courts have not been reluctant to reverse district court decisions granting summary judgment, and the fact that the district judge has seen things one way ordinarily has no influence on the appellate court. In *Arnstein,* for example, the appellate judges substituted their reaction to the recordings of the songs involved for the district judge's. Was this proper? For a later example, consider Twentieth Century-Fox Film Corp. v. MCA, Inc., 715 F.2d 1327 (9th Cir.1983), in which the producer of the film "Star Wars" sued the maker of the television show "Battlestar: Galactica" for copyright infringement. The district court granted summary judgment, finding that defendant's television show was so dissimilar from plaintiff's movie that there was no genuine dispute about whether they were substantially similar. The appellate panel disagreed: "After viewing the Star Wars and Battlestar motion pictures, we conclude that the films do in fact raise genuine issues of material fact as to whether only the Star Wars idea or the expression of that idea was copied." Does this kind of second guessing on appeal provide an important protection for the right to jury trial?

8.   In his opinion for the court in Doehler Metal Furniture Co. v. United States, 149 F.2d 130, 135 (2d Cir.1945), Judge Frank developed the so-called "slightest doubt" test for summary judgment: "We take this occasion to suggest that trial judges should exercise great care in granting motions for summary judgment. A litigant has a right to a trial where there is the slightest doubt as to the facts." To what extent does Judge Frank's opinion in *Arnstein* reflect this approach? The "slightest doubt" test for summary judgment is criticized in E. Brunet & M. Redish, Summary Judgment: Federal Law and Practice 127 (3d ed. 2006): "[Judge Frank's] language [in *Doehler*] is remarkable both for its negative attitude toward the use of summary judgment and for its complete failure to provide a clear legal source for the 'slightest doubt' standard. * * *

Judge Frank's *Doehler* opinion casts a negative light upon the summary judgment mechanism and, if widely accepted, would deter most judges from seriously thinking about granting a Rule 56 motion." More recent decisions have generally rejected the approach of *Arnstein*. As the Second Circuit stated in Beal v. Lindsay, 468 F.2d 287, 291 (2d Cir.1972), "The rule of Arnstein v. Porter * * * that summary judgment may not be rendered when there is the 'slightest doubt' as to the facts no longer is good law." See also Heyman v. Commerce & Industry Insurance Co., 524 F.2d 1317, 1319 (2d Cir.1975).

Judge Jack Weinstein has argued that "the 'slightest doubt' test, if it is taken seriously, means that summary judgment is almost never to be used—a pity in this critical time of overstrained legal resources." Chubbs v. City of New York, 324 F.Supp. 1183, 1189 (E.D.N.Y.1971). Thus, although several decisions continue to speak in terms of the "slightest doubt" test, the majority of cases today demand a stronger evidentiary showing by a nonmovant who will bear the burden of production at trial.

9.   A strong argument could be fashioned that the Supreme Court effectively put an end to the "slightest doubt" test in Matsushita Electric Industrial Co. v. Zenith Radio Corp., 475 U.S. 574 (1986). The case involved a factually complex antitrust suit, brought by American television manufacturers, alleging a conspiracy by 21 firms—either Japanese manufacturers or American firms controlled by Japanese parent companies— "to raise, fix and maintain artificially *high* prices for television receivers sold by [defendants] in Japan and, at the same time, to fix and maintain *low* prices for television receivers exported to and sold in the United States." These "low prices" were allegedly set at levels that produced substantial losses for defendants. This conduct was claimed to violate, *inter alia,* section 1 of the Sherman Act, which prohibits combinations or conspiracies in restraint of trade.

After several years of discovery, defendants moved for summary judgment, and the district court granted the motion, finding no genuine issue of material fact as to the existence of the conspiracy. The Third Circuit Court of Appeals reversed, but the Supreme Court agreed with the district court that summary judgment was proper. The Court reasoned that, when the moving party has carried its burden, the opposing party must "do more than simply show that there is some metaphysical doubt as to the material facts." If the factual material renders plaintiff's claim "implausible—if the claim is one that simply makes no economic sense—respondents must come forward with more persuasive evidence to support their claim than would otherwise be necessary." In the case before it, the Court found that the alleged conspiracy "is economically irrational and practically infeasible" because predatory pricing schemes are "rarely tried, and even more rarely successful." Accordingly, the plaintiffs had to come forward with evidence showing that the inference of conspiracy "is reasonable in light of the competing inferences of independent action." In particular, the absence of a persuasive motive for defendants to conspire as plaintiffs alleged demonstrated that summary judgment was appropriate:

Lack of motive bears on the range of permissible conclusions that might be drawn from ambiguous evidence: if petitioners had no rational economic motive to conspire, and if their conduct is consistent with other, equally plausible explanations, the conduct does not give rise to an inference of conspiracy. * * * In sum, in light of the absence of any rational motive to conspire, neither petitioners' pricing practices, nor their conduct in the Japanese market, nor their agreements respecting prices and distribution in the American market, suffice to create a "genuine issue for trial."

The Court indicated that "[t]o support a motion for summary judgment in a plaintiff seeking damages for violation of § 1 [of the Sherman Act] must present evidence that 'tends to exclude the possibility' that the alleged conspirators acted independently." 475 U.S. at 588.

Four justices dissented. Is the Court's reasoning a proper approach to summary judgment? Compare Bell Atlantic Corp. v. Twombly, supra p. 184, discussing pleading of antitrust conspiracy claims. The Supreme Court has continued to assert that raising a mere "metaphysical doubt" as to the facts is insufficient to avoid summary judgment. See Scott v. Harris, 550 U.S. 372, 127 S.Ct. 1769 (2007).

10. Post-*Matsushita* lower court decisions have sought to clarify that decision's "tends to exclude" standard. In Publication Paper Antitrust Litigation, 690 F.3d 51 (2d Cir. 2012), the Second Circuit noted that "where a plaintiff's theory of recovery is implausible, it takes 'strong direct or circumstantial evidence' to satisfy *Matsushita's* 'tend to exclude' standard. . . . By contrast, broader inferences are permitted, and the 'tends to exclude' standard is more easily satisfied, when the conspiracy is economically sensible for the alleged conspirators to undertake and 'the challenged activities could not reasonably be perceived as procompetitive.' " Id. at 63 (quoting In re Flat Glass Antitrust Litigation, 385 F. 3d 5, 358 (3d Cir. 2004). See also Apex Oil Co. v. DiMauro, 822 F. 2d 246 (2d Cir. 1984).

11. Summary judgment problems become more difficult when issues of motive and intent are presented. See, for example, Poller v. Columbia Broadcasting System, Inc., 368 U.S. 464 (1962) (whether motivation for purchase of a television station was anticompetitive). In cases where the critical issue is defendant's state of mind or intent when he engaged in conduct he admittedly undertook, should it ever be possible to grant summary judgment in favor of defendant based on his affidavit or deposition testimony averring that he did not entertain the forbidden state of mind? Recall Adickes v. S.H. Kress & Co., supra p. 447. The general rule, not surprisingly, is that it should not because here, at least, the jury should be allowed to view the defendant's demeanor when he testifies. The *Poller* decision has on occasion been construed to hold that summary judgment is generally inappropriate in so-called "complex cases." See, e.g., Timberlane Lumber Co. v. Bank of America, 549 F.2d 597, 602 (9th Cir.1976). Consider the impact of *Matsushita* on a doctrine calling for special reluctance to employ summary judgment in

complex cases. To the extent *Poller* was properly read to establish such a doctrine, does it survive *Matsushita*?

More recent lower court decisions generally reject the slightest doubt test. See, e.g., Shah v. Racetrac Petroleum Co., 338 F.3d 557, 566 (6th Cir. 2003) (noting that "the 'mere possibility' of a factual dispute does not suffice to create a triable case"); Harriscom Svenska, AB v. Harris Corp., 3 F.3d 576, 580 (2d Cir. 1993) (nonmovant "must demonstrate more than 'some metaphysical doubt' as to the material facts").

12.   The general rule that summary judgment is inappropriate in cases raising issues of state of mind could affect the substantive law. For example, public officials charged with violation of citizens' constitutional rights may raise an affirmative defense of qualified, or "good faith" immunity. Traditionally, this was said to depend on whether the official knew or should have known that the action would violate a plaintiff's constitutional rights, and immunity would be unavailable if the official acted with the malicious intention of depriving plaintiff of his rights. In Harlow v. Fitzgerald, 457 U.S. 800 (1982), the Court reasoned that this approach was unsatisfactory because, under Rule 56, "an official's good faith has been considered to be a question of fact that some courts have regarded as inherently requiring resolution by a jury." To remedy this problem and facilitate summary judgment, the Court held that the immunity defense should be judged under an objective standard, looking to whether a reasonable official in defendant's position would have realized at the time of the action in question that it was forbidden. Moreover, this determination should, the Court held, be made on the basis of the state of the law, and without discovery. The Court concluded that "[b]y defining the limits of qualified immunity essentially in objective terms, we provide no license to lawless conduct." Do you agree? Does this approach provide a useful solution to the impediment to summary judgment ordinarily presented in a case where the defendant's state of mind has traditionally been said to be relevant? For another discussion of *Harlow,* see p. 1099 n. 4.

Post-*Harlow* decisions have reaffirmed the Supreme Court's desire to employ summary judgment as a means of reducing the costs of civil rights litigation. For example, in Anderson v. Creighton, 483 U.S. 635 (1987), the Court once again asserted summary judgment's significance in the disposition of civil rights claims on the basis of the qualified immunity defense. Justice Scalia, writing for the Court, mandated a fact-specific examination into the objective reasonableness test set forth initially in *Harlow*, rejecting the application of the "clearly established law" test at an abstract generalized level. Under *Anderson*, the constitutional rights alleged to have been violated must be " 'clearly established' in a more particularized, and hence more relevant, sense." 483 U.S. at 640. As in *Harlow*, the *Anderson* Court recognized the need "to protect public officials from the 'broad-ranging discovery' that can be 'peculiarly disruptive of effective government.' " Id. at 646 n. 6 (quoting *Harlow*). On the general subject, see McKenzie, The Doctrine of Qualified Immunity in Section 1983 Actions: Resolution of the Immunity Issue on Summary Judgment, 25 Suffolk L.Rev. 673 (1991). In a more recent decision, however, the Court made clear that even where claims of officer immunity are raised by the defendant in a civil rights action, summary judgment is not always appropriate. In Tolan v. Cotton, 134 S.Ct. 1861 (2014), the Court reversed the Fifth Circuit's affirmance of an award of summary judgment in an officer immunity case. The Court found that in holding that a police officer's actions did not violate clearly established law and were therefore shielded by officer immunity, the lower court had improperly failed to view the evidence at summary judgment in the light most favorable to the plaintiff as the nonmovant.

13. The above discussion deals with cases in which the party moving for summary judgment does not have the burden of production at trial. What standard should apply where the party seeking summary judgment does have the burden? Recall that it is possible for a party with the burden of production to shift that burden by producing such compelling evidence that no reasonable finder of fact could decide against him. That same idea applies to the movant who has the burden of proof; his showing to obtain summary judgment must shift the burden of production to the opposing party, and unless that party produces evidence permitting a decision in his favor, summary judgment should be entered.

14. If plaintiff will have to prove his case by more than a preponderance of evidence (the usual standard in civil cases), should that affect the summary judgment decision? Note the treatment of the problem in Anderson v. Liberty Lobby, Inc., 477 U.S. 242 (1986), discussed in the material on summary judgment in defamation cases that follows.

15. *"Sham" affidavits*: The court may not weigh evidence in deciding a summary judgment motion, but sometimes courts will disregard affidavits that appear to create an issue. "If a party who has been examined at length on deposition could raise an issue of fact simply by submitting an affidavit contradicting his own prior testimony, this would greatly diminish the utility of summary judgment as a procedure for screening out sham issues of fact." Perma Research & Devel. Co. v. Singer Co., 410 F.2d 572, 578 (2d Cir. 1969); see also Burns v. Board of County Commissioners, 330 F.3d 1275 (10th Cir. 2003) (court disregards plaintiff's "corrections" to deposition answers on the ground that trying to vary deposition testimony using a "correction sheet" should not be different from using an affidavit). But if there is a viable explanation for the change, the affidavit may be credited. Cf. McCormick v. City of Fort Lauderdale, 333 F.3d 1234 (11th Cir. 2003) (court credits plaintiff's affidavit contradicting his own sworn initial statement to police because plaintiff offered a plausible explanation for the differences). How different is this practice from weighing evidence? See also Rule 56(h).

16. *Summary judgment and videotape evidence*: To what extent is it appropriate for the court, in deciding whether summary judgment should be granted, to make its own judgment on the probative impact of video evidence of the relevant events? In Scott v. Harris, 550 U.S. 372 (2007), the Supreme Court held that a summary judgment motion should be granted, on the basis of its own perception of a videotape of the relevant events. The plaintiff had

sued the defendant, a county deputy, for violation of his Fourth Amendment rights. Plaintiff alleged that the defendants used undue force by terminating a high-speech car chase by ramming the rear of plaintiff's vehicle, causing it to leave the road and crash, thereby rendering him a quadriplegic. The defendant had moved for summary judgment on the grounds that he had acted reasonably under the circumstances and was therefore protected by qualified officer immunity. In support, he relied on a videotape of the chase, made from his police car. Plaintiff claimed in opposition that he had not posed a hazard because he was always in control of his vehicle. Although the lower courts had held that the issue of the videotape's import was one for the jury, the Supreme Court reversed. Justice Scalia, writing for the Court, noted that the videotape "resembles a Hollywood-style car chase of the most frightening sort," and posed a substantial and immediate risk of serious physical injury to others, rendering the defendant's decision to ram the plaintiff's vehicle a reasonable act. The Court held that where the record blatantly contradicts plaintiff's version of events so that no reasonable person could believe it, summary judgment is appropriate.

According to one group of commentators, "the Court in *Scott* was wrong to privilege its own view." Kahan, Hoffman & Braman, Whose Eyes Are You Going to Believe? Scott v. Harris and the Perils of Cognitive Illiberalism, 122 Harv. L. Rev. 837 (2009). *Scott,* they assert, "is the only case in which the Supreme Court has invoked brute sense impressions to justify its decision." The authors showed the videotape to a diverse sample of 1,350 Americans. While overall a majority agreed with the Court's resolution of the key issues, within the sample were found sharp differences of opinion along cultural, ideological and other lines.

Does the fact that not all members of the sample agreed with the Court's perception necessarily mean that the Court's decision to award summary judgment was wrong? Isn't it at least possible, if not likely, that in any case in which a court grants summary judgment, there would be potential jurors who would have disagreed and found for the nonmovant? Doesn't a court grant summary judgment for the very purpose of preventing such jurors from getting the opportunity to find for the nonmovant on irrational grounds? Why, then, should it be at all relevant that there are, in fact, people who would have found for the nonmovant?

17.   It has been suggested that summary judgment is a threat to the constitutionally embodied value of jury trial, and as a result, a violation of the Seventh Amendment right to a jury trial in civil cases. See, e.g., S. Thomas, The Missing American Jury (2016); Thomas, The Unconstitutionality of Summary Judgment: A Status Report, 93 Iowa L. Rev. 1613 (2008) (discussing how the federal courts have dealt with the issue); Thomas, Why Summary Judgment is Unconstitutional, 93 Va. L. Rev. 139 (2007) (arguing that the summary judgment is unconstitutional and that Supreme Court has never resolved the issue); Miller, The Pretrial Rush to Judgment: Are the "Litigation Explosion," "Liability Crisis," and Efficiency Cliches Eroding Our Day in Court and Jury Trial Commitments?, 78 N.Y.U. L. Rev. 982, 1093 (2003) (noting that

"hyperactive use of pretrial motions threatens long-standing constitutional values"); Mollica, Federal Summary Judgment at High Tide, 84 Marq. L. Rev. 141, 181–205 (2000) (current applications of summary judgment "press against tolerable constitutional limits"). But see Brunet, Summary Judgment is Constitutional, 93 Iowa L. Rev. 1625 (2008). Others have questioned the extent to which the device actually produces litigation efficiency. See Rave, Note, Questioning the Efficiency of Summary Judgment, 81 N.Y.U. L. Rev. 875, 876 (2006), arguing that "[w]hile it seems intuitive that avoiding costly trials would save money, that savings is only realized when summary judgment is granted. Modern summary judgment, however, is a frequently used motion that is costly to oppose and, if not granted often enough, may be a net drain on society." How persuasive is this criticism? If one assumes its validity, to what conclusion does it lead—the need to deter summary judgment motions, or the need to grant more of them? Could the answer be to do both?

SUMMARY JUDGMENT IN DEFAMATION CASES

In New York Times Co. v. Sullivan, 376 U.S. 254 (1964), the Supreme Court held that the First Amendment right of free expression prohibits the imposition of damages for defamation of a public official, unless the defamation was published with "actual malice"—defined as knowledge of falsity or reckless disregard of truth or falsity. The Court has since extended this modified constitutional protection to defamation of public figures, as well as public officials.

Constitutional protection in these cases will turn on whether the defamatory statement was made with "actual malice." Because of the importance of the constitutional right involved, the Court held that the plaintiff must prove the presence of actual malice by "clear and convincing evidence," a standard of proof more strict than the traditional "preponderance of the evidence" standard normally employed in civil cases.

The possible use of summary judgment in these cases raises the question whether the presence of the higher burden of proof on the plaintiff should dictate a more lenient standard for the granting of such a motion made by the defendant. The Court considered this issue in Anderson v. Liberty Lobby, Inc., 477 U.S. 242 (1986). Justice White, speaking for six Justices, initially concluded that the inquiry on a summary judgment motion "mirrors the standard for a directed verdict * * * which is that the trial judge must direct a verdict if, under the governing law, there can be but one reasonable conclusion as to the verdict." The Court then concluded that on either motion, the ruling "necessarily implicates the substantive evidentiary standard of proof that would apply at the trial on the merits." Therefore "where the First Amendment mandates a 'clear and convincing' standard, the trial judge in disposing of a directed verdict motion should consider whether a reasonable factfinder could conclude, for example, that the plaintiff had shown actual malice with convincing clarity."

The Court emphasized that its holding "does not denigrate the role of the jury. It by no means authorizes trial on affidavits. Credibility determinations, the weighing of the evidence, and the drawing of legitimate inferences from the facts are jury functions, not those of a judge, whether he is ruling on a motion for summary judgment or for a directed verdict."

Finding "the Court's analysis * * * deeply flawed," Justice Brennan dissented. He contended that "the Court's opinion is * * * full of language which could surely be understood as an invitation—if not an instruction—to trial courts to assess and weigh evidence much as a juror would," and expressed the fear "that this new rule * * * will transform what is meant to provide an expedited 'summary' procedure into a full blown paper trial on the merits."

Justice Rehnquist, joined by Chief Justice Burger, also dissented, finding the Court's holding to be "a procedural requirement engrafted onto Rule 56," contrary to the Court's previous statements that no special procedural protections are to be granted to defendants in defamation actions "in addition to the constitutional protections embodied in the substantive laws." Calder v. Jones, 465 U.S. 783, 790–91 (1984) (reproduced infra p. 756 on a different point).

Do you agree with Justice Rehnquist that the Court's approach extends special procedural protection to defamation defendants? Should the invocation of plaintiff's trial standard of proof be extended to other types of cases?

CHAPTER 7

JUDICIAL SUPERVISION OF PRETRIAL AND PROMOTION OF SETTLEMENT

■ ■ ■

We are now ready to turn to the formal pretrial procedures that seek to prepare a case for trial and, if possible, to accomplish its early settlement. Beginning in the 1970's, this phase of litigation came under increasing judicial supervision as federal courts in particular have embraced the "managerial judge" model.[1] The two basic principles of effective case management are said to be that judges must show commitment, leadership, and supervision from the earliest stages and that they must establish clear timetables for different phases of a case's progress.[2]

The primary tool for judicial supervision is Rule 16, although judges have also invoked inherent powers for their pretrial-management rulings. Rule 16, as adopted in 1938, conceived of the pretrial conference as the means of preparing a case for trial. It was to take place just before trial and served to finalize such matters as contested issues, lists of witnesses and documents, and stipulations. "But federal courts came to appreciate more fully the value of earlier pretrial planning, and Rule 16 was amended in 1983 to provide for two types of pretrial conferences—'scheduling and planning' and 'final.' * * * The rule states the purpose of the 'scheduling and planning' conference in clear case-management terms: expediting disposition, 'establishing early and continuing control so that the case will not be protracted because of lack of management,' 'discouraging wasteful pretrial activities,' 'improving the quality of the trial through more thorough preparation,' and facilitating settlement."[3] We will consider this expanded role of the pretrial conference in the first section of this chapter.

Promotion of settlement is also an increasingly significant aspect of judicial supervision of pretrial. At the end of Chapter 2 (supra pp. 106–122), we briefly considered available alternatives to trial, including both

---

[1] See Marcus, Reining in the American Litigator: The New Role of American Judges, 27 Hast.Int'l & Compar.L.Rev. 3 (2003); Peckham, A Judicial Response to the Cost of Litigation: Case Management, Two-Stage Discovery Planning and Alternative Dispute Resolution, 37 Rutgers L. Rev. 253 (1985) (offering empirical evidence that managerial judging "substantially reduced" delay in federal district courts). This development has also been criticized. Resnik, Managerial Judges, 96 Harv.L.Rev. 374 (1982).

[2] Solomon & Somerlot, American Bar Association, Caseflow Management in the Trial Court: Now and for the Future 1, 12–13, 24–28 (1987).

[3] Sherman, A Process Model and Agenda for Civil Justice Reforms in the States, 46 Stan.L.Rev. 1553, 1564 (1994).

processes that are outside the court system and those that have been made an integral part of pretrial procedures. As we observed there, settlement conferences with a judge have been a traditional vehicle for judicial promotion of settlement. However, the explosion of new settlement devices that has accompanied the ADR movement has led many courts to adopt other means of promoting settlement. In the second section of this chapter, we will consider some of the principal settlement devices that use intervention by third parties, and, in the third section, we will examine incentives to settle through shifting of attorney's fees and sanctions.

A. PRETRIAL CONFERENCE

Central to the relaxed standards of pleading adopted in the Federal Rules of Civil Procedure in 1938 was the premise that it is unreasonable to expect the parties to have full knowledge of all relevant facts at the pleading stage. Therefore it was understood that pleadings would be acceptable even if framed in general terms. It was during the discovery process, following the pleading stage, that the parties would be expected to obtain the bulk of the relevant factual information necessary for trial.

While the system adopted in the Federal Rules generally reduced the level of knowledge and information required at the pleading stage, it simultaneously attempted to increase dramatically the level of information possessed by the parties at trial. This seeming paradox was rationalized by a single overriding normative principle: The adjudicatory process should be viewed as a search for the truth, rather than purely as a game of competitive skill in mastering the technicalities of pleading or in orchestrating surprises at trial.

The one procedural device essential to achievement of these goals was the pretrial conference, provided for in Rule 16, a practice that found its origins in a procedure employed by the Circuit Court of Wayne County, Michigan in the 1930's.[4] At the pretrial conference, the parties were expected—*after* completion of discovery—to provide the type of factual detail no longer required in their pleadings. Also at the pretrial conference, the parties were to provide to the opposition information concerning how they intended to prove their cases at trial.

Rule 16 provides that the court may order the attorneys and any unrepresented parties to appear for one or more pretrial conferences for such purposes as:

(1) expediting disposition of the action;

(2) establishing early and continuing control so that the case will not be protracted because of lack of management;

---

[4] See Sunderland, The Theory and Practice of Pre-Trial Procedure, 36 Mich.L.Rev. 215 (1937).

(3)   discouraging wasteful pretrial activities;

(4)   improving the quality of trial through more thorough preparation; and

(5)   facilitating settlement.

After the conference, the court should issue an order "reciting the action taken," and this order "controls the course of the action unless the court modifies it." Rule 16(e) provides that a court may hold a "final pretrial conference to formulate a trial plan, including a plan to facilitate the admission of evidence." This conference must be held as close to the start of the trial as is reasonable and be attended by at least one attorney who will conduct the trial for each party and by any unrepresented party.

The pretrial conference authorized by Rule 16 was designed to familiarize the litigants and the court with issues actually involved in a lawsuit so that the parties could accurately appraise their cases and substantially reduce the danger of surprise at trial. See generally 6A C. Wright, A. Miller & M. Kane, Federal Practice and Procedure §§ 1522–26 (3d ed. 2010). According to Judge Charles Clark, Reporter for the original Advisory Committee that wrote the Federal Rules, "simplification of the issues" was "perhaps the over-all purpose of the entire rule. * * * The judge finds out what the case is all about, how much is admitted on each side, and how much not, and then he goes on to the question of manner of proof. This is pre-trial at its most effective level."[5]

A study conducted in the 1960's evaluated New Jersey's state pretrial conference device in the context of personal injury actions. The study concluded that the pretrial conference served a number of important and beneficial functions, including increasing the chance the case will be well presented, eliminating inefficiencies at trial, and improving the settlement process.[6]

In light of these beneficial functions, one might wonder why the rule does not mandate the use of the pretrial conference in every case, rather than leaving the matter to the trial court's discretion. The answer is that "there always has been some question whether the time and effort consumed by the pretrial conference might not offset the benefits it supposedly yields and a concern that the time of judges and lawyers can be better spent in other pursuits."[7] In simple suits where trial would require a relatively brief period of time, a pretrial conference could consume more time than it saved. It was therefore thought wise to allow the judge to make the determination concerning the appropriateness of the conference on a case-by-case basis. However, certain of the busier districts, such as the

---

[5]   Clark, Objectives of Pre-Trial Procedure, 17 Ohio St.L.J. 163, 167 (1956).

[6]   M. Rosenberg, The Pretrial Conference and Effective Justice (1964).

[7]   6A C. Wright, A. Miller & M. Kane, Federal Practice & Procedure § 1522.

District of Columbia and the Southern District of New York, adopted a local rule requiring a pretrial conference in all cases.

Rule 16 still provides that the holding of a pretrial conference lies in the court's discretion, but there are now mandatory aspects of the rule concerning scheduling. Rule 26(f) directs the parties to meet and confer regarding a number of topics "at least 21 days before a scheduling conference is held or a scheduling order is due under Rule 16(b)." This meeting is to yield a report to be submitted to the court within ten days of the meeting detailing a discovery plan for the case and possibly including other topics. Rule 16(b) requires the court to issue a "scheduling order" after consulting with the parties at a "scheduling conference or by telephone, mail, or other means," or after receiving the parties' report under Rule 26(f). The scheduling order shall be issued within 90 days after service of the complaint on any defendant or 60 days after any defendant has appeared. The order must limit the time to join other parties, amend the pleadings, complete discovery, and file motions, and can address such other matters as modifying the extent of discovery or protection of privileged material.

While the original Rule 16 contemplated the holding of only one conference, presumably at the close of discovery, in the more protracted and complex cases one conference proved to be inadequate to ensure efficient judicial management. Therefore Rule 16 now authorizes the holding of more than one conference, and provides for the holding of a "Final Pretrial Conference," to "be held as close to the time of trial as reasonable under the circumstances," for the purpose of "formulat[ing] a plan for trial, including a program for facilitating the admission of evidence."

The original Rule 16 made no express provision for sanctions for an attorney's failure to appear at or cooperate in a pretrial conference, but the Supreme Court recognized the trial judge's inherent authority to impose sanctions in such situations.[8] The rule now expressly provides for the imposition of sanctions in Rule 16(f).[9]

NOTES AND QUESTIONS

1.   In Chapter 1 we noted the growing involvement of federal judges in controlling cases assigned to them and explored some aspects of judges' authority under Rule 16. Note the way in which the rule's requirement that the judge impose scheduling deadlines in every case tends to prompt judges to take control of cases from an early date. The managerial judging approach has attracted attention overseas; in the mid-1990s it was proposed as a new model for handling civil litigation in England. For discussion, see Marcus, "Deja Vu All Over Again?" An American Reaction to the Woolf Report, in Reform of Civil

---

[8]   See, e.g. Link v. Wabash R. Co., 370 U.S. 626 (1962).

[9]   See Kothe v. Smith, supra p. 19.

Procedure (A. Zuckerman & R. Cranston, eds., 1995), at 219; N. Andrews, English Civil Procedure 337 (2003) (case management is a "cornerstone" of English procedure under the new procedure code).

2.   As we saw in Band's Refuse Removal, Inc. v. Borough of Fair Lawn, supra p. 3, discovery may be used to probe an opponent's expected evidence for trial. Even if the parties don't focus their discovery on trial evidence, Rule 26(a)(3) requires disclosure at least 30 days before trial of the identities of likely witnesses and documents or other exhibits that the parties expect to offer at trial. It further provides that if the parties don't serve objections within 14 days after service of these disclosures most objections otherwise allowed by the Federal Rules of Evidence are waived.

As a part of case management under Rule 16, some courts require considerably more. Before the final pretrial conference, courts may require that the parties submit a statement that lists all undisputed facts and factual issues, identifies and briefs all disputed points of law, lists all witnesses likely to be called together with a brief statement describing the substance of their testimony, lists all exhibits to be offered in evidence, and proposes voir dire questions, jury instructions and verdict forms. Some courts require that such specifics be provided in a joint pretrial statement. Preparing such statements involves a great deal of effort for the lawyers. Is that effort wasted if the case settles on the courthouse steps? Would a lawyer be able to prepare properly for trial without making such an effort?

3.   There have been cases where the appellate courts have found that district courts have gone too far in imposing pretrial requirements. For example, in McCargo v. Hedrick, 545 F.2d 393 (4th Cir.1976), the trial court's local rule on joint pretrial statements filled eleven single-spaced pages. After completing the 120-day discovery period allowed in this case, counsel for both sides began a 16-month effort to submit a pretrial statement that satisfied the rule, only to have each version rejected by the court. At the end of this time, the district court dismissed the case for failure to comply with the local rule. Noting that "[t]he facts of this case illustrate the burden put upon litigants and their counsel by a pretrial procedure that appears to have become an end in itself," the appellate court held that the local rule exceeded the district court's authority under Rule 16 as then written. It concluded (id. at 401):

> Ours is an adversary system of justice. Local Rule 2.08 is inquisitorial in tone and purpose. In our system lawyers worry about the whereabouts of witnesses. The court does not. Lawyers worry about proof. The court does not—except in the rare case of collusion. Lawyers get the case ready for trial. The court does not. Local Rule 2.08 subordinates the role of the lawyer to that of the administering magistrate, reducing counsel to the role of clerical assistants who are to anticipate imaginatively what other matters ought to be embraced within an endless pretrial order.

4.   If a final pretrial order is entered, it governs the action and may be changed only to prevent "manifest injustice." What does this mean? One form

of injustice can be surprise to the opponent, the matter that worried the appellate court in Band's Refuse Removal, Inc. v. Borough of Fair Lawn, supra p. 3. Recall the way in which Rule 15(b) treats that concern to allow amendment of the pleadings to conform to the evidence if the other party would not be prejudiced. See supra p. 235. Does Rule 16 impose on the party seeking to change the final pretrial order a higher burden than one seeking to amend at trial under Rule 15(b)? See Wallin v. Fuller, 476 F.2d 1204, 1209 (5th Cir.1973) ("It is unlikely that the pretrial order under Rule 16 was intended to make the pleadings, and therefore Rule 15, obsolete").

But will a relaxed attitude undermine the purposes of the pretrial conference? "Unless pretrial orders are honored and enforced, the objectives of the pretrial conference to simplify issues and avoid unnecessary proof by obtaining admissions of fact will be jeopardized if not entirely nullified. * * * Disregard of these principles would bring back the days of trial by ambush and discourage timely preparation by the parties for trial." United States v. First National Bank of Circle, 652 F.2d 882, 886 (9th Cir.1981). Reacting to concerns about reliance and the importance that pretrial orders be enforced, courts have therefore forbidden the calling of witnesses not listed and excluded evidence not identified in the orders.

5.   The use of sanctions under Rule 16 raises difficult issues concerning the court's power to require participation in a settlement conference, explored in the following case.

G. HEILEMAN BREWING CO. v. JOSEPH OAT CORP.

United States Court of Appeal, Seventh Circuit, 1989
871 F.2d 648

Before BAUER, CHIEF JUDGE, CUMMINGS, WOOD, JR., CUDAHY, POSNER, COFFEY, FLAUM, EASTERBROOK, RIPPLE, MANION and KANNE, CIRCUIT JUDGES.

KANNE, CIRCUIT JUDGE.

May a federal district court order litigants—even those represented by counsel—to appear before it in person at a pretrial conference for the purpose of discussing the posture and settlement of the litigants' case? After reviewing the Federal Rules of Civil Procedure and federal district courts' inherent authority to manage and control the litigation before them, we answer this question in the affirmative and conclude that a district court may sanction a litigant for failing to comply with such an order.

I. Background

A federal magistrate ordered Joseph Oat Corporation to send a "corporate representative with authority to settle" to a pretrial conference to discuss disputed factual and legal issues and the possibility of settlement. Although counsel for Oat Corporation appeared, accompanied by another attorney who was authorized to speak on behalf of the principals of the corporation, no principal or corporate representative personally attended the conference. The court determined that the failure of Oat Corporation to send a principal of the corporation to the pretrial conference violated its order. Consequently, the district court imposed a sanction of $5,860.01 upon Oat Corporation pursuant to Federal Rule of Civil Procedure 16(f). This amount represented the costs and attorneys' fees of the opposing parties attending the conference.

II. The Appeal

Oat Corporation appeals, claiming that the district court did not have the authority to order litigants represented by counsel to appear at the pretrial settlement conference. Specifically, Oat Corporation contends that, by negative implication, the language of Rule 16(a)(5) prohibits a district court from directing represented litigants to attend pretrial conferences. That is, because Rule 16 expressly refers to "attorneys for the parties and any unrepresented parties" in introductory paragraph (a), a district court may not go beyond that language to devise procedures which direct the pretrial appearance of parties represented by counsel. Consequently, Oat Corporation concludes that the court lacked the authority to order the pretrial attendance of its corporate representatives and, even if the court possessed such authority, the court abused its discretion to exercise that power in this case. Finally, Oat Corporation argues that the court abused its discretion to enter sanctions.

A. Authority to Order Attendance

First, we must address Oat Corporation's contention that a federal district court lacks the authority to order litigants who are represented by counsel to appear at a pretrial conference. Our analysis requires us to review the Federal Rules of Civil Procedure and district courts' inherent authority to manage the progress of litigation.

Rule 16 addresses the use of pretrial conferences to formulate and narrow issues for trial as well as to discuss means for dispensing with the need for costly and unnecessary litigation. As we stated in Link v. Wabash R.R., 291 F.2d 542, 547 (7th Cir.1961), aff'd, 370 U.S. 626 (1962):

> Pre-trial procedure has become an integrated part of the judicial process on the trial level. Courts must be free to use it and to control and enforce its operation. Otherwise, the orderly administration of justice will be removed from control of the trial court and placed in the hands of counsel. We do not believe such a course is within the contemplation of the law.

The pretrial settlement of litigation has been advocated and used as a means to alleviate overcrowded dockets, and courts have practiced numerous and varied types of pretrial settlement techniques for many years. Since 1983, Rule 16 has expressly provided that settlement of a case is one of several subjects which should be pursued and discussed vigorously during pretrial conferences.

The language of Rule 16 does not give any direction to the district court upon the issue of a court's authority to order litigants who are represented by counsel to appear for pretrial proceedings. Instead, Rule 16 merely refers to the participation of trial advocates—attorneys of record and pro se litigants. However, the Federal Rules of Civil Procedure do not completely describe and limit the power of the federal courts. HMG Property Investors, Inc. v. Parque Indus. Rio Canas, Inc., 847 F.2d 908, 915 (1st Cir.1988).

The concept that district courts exercise procedural authority outside the explicit language of the rules of civil procedure is not frequently documented, but valid nevertheless. The Supreme Court has acknowledged that the provisions of the Federal Rules of Civil Procedure are not intended to be the exclusive authority for actions to be taken by district courts. Link v. Wabash R.R., 370 U.S. 626 (1962).* * *

In this case, we are required to determine whether a court's power to order the pretrial appearance of litigants who are represented by counsel is inconsistent with, or in derogation of, Rule 16. We must remember that Rule 1 states, with unmistakable clarity, that the Federal Rules of Civil Procedure "shall be construed to secure the just, speedy, and inexpensive determination of every action." This language explicitly indicates that the federal rules are to be liberally construed. There is no place in the federal civil procedural system for the proposition that rules having the force of statute, though in derogation of the common law, are to be strictly construed.

"[The] spirit, intent, and purpose [of Rule 16] is . . . broadly remedial, allowing courts to actively manage the preparation of cases for trial." In re Baker, 744 F.2d 1438, 1440 (10th Cir.1984) (en banc), cert. denied, 471 U.S. 1014 (1985). Rule 16 is not designed as a device to restrict or limit the authority of the district judge in the conduct of pretrial conferences. As the Tenth Circuit Court of Appeals sitting en banc stated in Baker, "the spirit and purpose of the amendments to Rule 16 always have been within the inherent power of the courts to manage their affairs as an independent constitutional branch of government."

We agree with this interpretation of Rule 16. The wording of the rule and the accompanying commentary make plain that the entire thrust of the amendment to Rule 16 was to urge judges to make wider use of their powers and to manage actively their dockets from an early stage. We therefore conclude that our interpretation of Rule 16 to allow district courts to order represented parties to appear at pretrial settlement conferences merely represents another application of a district judge's inherent authority to preserve the efficiency, and more importantly the integrity, of the judicial process.* * *

B. Exercise of Authority to Order Attendance

Having determined that the district court possessed the power and authority to order the represented litigants to appear at the pretrial settlement conference, we now must examine whether the court abused its discretion to issue such an order.

At the outset, it is important to note that a district court cannot coerce settlement. Kothe v. Smith, 771 F.2d 667, 669 (2d Cir.1985).[8] In this case, considerable concern has been generated because the court ordered "corporate representatives with authority to settle" to attend the conference. In our view, "authority to settle," when used in the context of this case, means that the "corporate representative" attending the pretrial conference was required to hold a position within the corporate entity allowing him to speak definitively and to commit the corporation to a particular position in the litigation. We do not view "authority to settle" as a requirement that corporate representatives must come to court willing to settle on someone else's terms, but only that they come to court in order to consider the possibility of settlement.

As Chief Judge Crabb set forth in her decision which we now review:

> There is no indication ... that the magistrate's order contemplated requiring Joseph Oat ... to agree to any particular form of settlement or even to agree to settlement at all. The only requirement imposed by the magistrate was that the representative [of Oat Corporation] be present with full authority to settle, should terms for settlement be proposed that were acceptable to [Oat Corporation].

If this case represented a situation where Oat Corporation had sent a corporate representative and was sanctioned because that person refused to make an offer to pay money—that is, refused to submit to settlement coercion—we would be faced with a decidedly different issue—a situation we would not countenance.

The Advisory Committee Notes to Rule 16 state that "[a]lthough it is not the purpose of Rule 16(c)[9] to impose settlement negotiations on unwilling litigants, it is believed that providing a neutral forum for discussing [settlement] might foster it." These Notes clearly draw a distinction between being required to attend a settlement conference and being required to participate in settlement negotiations. Thus, under the scheme of pretrial settlement conferences, the corporate representative remains free, on behalf of the corporate entity, to propose terms of

---

[8]   Likewise, a court cannot compel parties to stipulate to facts. J.F. Constr. Co., v. Anderson Safeway Guard Rail Corp., 542 F.2d 1318 (7th Cir.1976) (per curiam). Nor can a court compel litigants to participate in a nonbinding summary jury trial. Strandell [v. Jackson County], 838 F.2d [884] at 887 [(7th Cir.1987)]. In the same vein, a court cannot force a party to engage in discovery. Identiseal Corp. v. Positive Identification Sys., Inc., 560 F.2d 298 (7th Cir.1977).

settlement independently—but he may be required to state those terms in a pretrial conference before a judge or magistrate.

As an alternative position, Oat Corporation argues that the court abused its discretion to order corporate representatives of the litigants to attend the pretrial settlement conference. Oat Corporation determined that because its business was a "going concern":

> It would be unreasonable for the magistrate to require the president of that corporation to leave his business [in Camden, New Jersey] to travel to Madison, Wisconsin, to participate in a settlement conference. The expense and burden on the part of Joseph Oat to comply with this order was clearly unreasonable. Consequently, Oat Corporation believes that the district court abused its authority.

We recognize, as did the district court, that circumstances could arise in which requiring a corporate representative (or any litigant) to appear at a pretrial settlement conference would be so onerous, so clearly unproductive, or so expensive in relation to the size, value, and complexity of the case that it might be an abuse of discretion. Moreover, "[b]ecause inherent powers are shielded from direct democratic controls, they must be exercised with restraint and discretion." However, the facts and circumstances of this case clearly support the court's actions to require the corporate representatives of the litigants to attend the pretrial conference personally.

This litigation involved a claim for $4 million—a claim which turned upon the resolution of complex factual and legal issues. The litigants expected the trial to last from one to three months and all parties stood to incur substantial legal fees and trial expenses. This trial also would have preempted a large segment of judicial time—not an insignificant factor. Thus, because the stakes were high, we do not believe that the burden of requiring a corporate representative to attend a pretrial settlement conference was out of proportion to the benefits to be gained, not only by the litigants but also by the court.

Additionally, the corporation did send an attorney, Mr. Fitzpatrick, from Philadelphia, Pennsylvania to Madison, Wisconsin to "speak for" the principals of the corporation. It is difficult to see how the expenses involved in sending Mr. Fitzpatrick from Philadelphia to Madison would have greatly exceeded the expenses involved in sending a corporate representative from Camden to Madison. Consequently, we do not think the expenses and distance to be traveled are unreasonable in this case.

Furthermore, no objection to the magistrate's order was made prior to the date the pretrial conference resumed. Oat Corporation contacted the magistrate's office concerning the order's requirements and was advised of the requirements now at issue. However, Oat Corporation never objected to its terms, either when it was issued or when Oat Corporation sought clarification. Consequently, Oat Corporation was left with only one course of action: it had to comply fully with the letter and intent of the order and argue about its reasonableness later.

We thus conclude that the court did not abuse its authority and discretion to order a representative of the Oat Corporation to appear for the pretrial settlement conference on December 19.

C. Sanctions

Finally, we must determine whether the court abused its discretion by sanctioning Oat Corporation for failing to comply with the order to appear at the pretrial settlement conference. Oat Corporation argues that the instructions directing the appearance of corporate representatives were unclear and ambiguous. Consequently, it concludes that the sanctions were improper.

Absent an abuse of discretion, we may not disturb a district court's imposition of sanctions for failure of a party to comply with a pretrial order. The issue on review is not whether we would have imposed these costs upon Oat Corporation, but whether the district court abused its discretion in doing so.

Oat Corporation contends that the presence of Mr. Fitzpatrick, as an attorney authorized to speak on behalf of the principals of Oat Corporation, satisfied the requirement that its "corporate representative" attend the December 19 settlement conference. Oat Corporation argues that nothing in either the November 19, 1984 order or the December 14, 1984 order would lead a reasonable person to conclude that a representative or principal from the Joseph Oat Corporation was required to attend the conference personally—in effect arguing that sanctions cannot be imposed because the order failed to require a particular person to attend the conference.

We believe that Oat Corporation was well aware of what the court expected. While the November order may have been somewhat ambiguous, any ambiguity was eliminated by the magistrate's remarks from the bench on December 14, the written order of December 18, and the direction obtained by counsel from the magistrate's clerk.

* * *

III. Conclusion

We hold that Rule 16 does not limit, but rather is enhanced by, the inherent authority of federal courts to order litigants represented by counsel to attend pretrial conferences for the purpose of discussing settlement. Oat Corporation violated the district court's order requiring it to have a corporate representative attend the pretrial settlement conference on December 19, 1984. Under these circumstances, the district court did not abuse its discretion by imposing sanctions for Oat Corporation's failure to comply with the pretrial order.

POSNER, CIRCUIT JUDGE, dissenting.

Rule 16(a) of the Federal Rules of Civil Procedure authorizes a district court to "direct the attorneys for the parties and any *unrepresented* parties to appear before it for a [pretrial] conference."* The word I have italicized could be thought to carry the negative implication that no represented party may be directed to appear—that was the panel's conclusion—but I hesitate to so conclude in a case that can be decided on a narrower ground.

The main purpose of the pretrial conference is to get ready for trial. For that purpose, only the attorneys need be present, unless a party is acting as his own attorney. The only possible reason for wanting a represented party to be present is to enable the judge or magistrate to explore settlement with the principals rather than with just their agents. Some district judges and magistrates distrust the willingness or ability of attorneys to convey to their clients adequate information bearing on the desirability and terms of settling a case in lieu of pressing forward to trial. The distrust is warranted in some cases, I am sure; but warranted or not, it is what lies behind the concern that the panel opinion had stripped the district courts of a valuable settlement tool—and this at a time of heavy, and growing, federal judicial caseloads. The concern may well be exaggerated, however. The panel opinion may have had little practical significance; it is the rare attorney who will invite a district judge's displeasure by defying a request to produce the client for a pretrial conference.

The question of the district court's power to summon a represented party to a settlement conference is a difficult one. On the one hand, nothing in Rule 16 or in any other rule or statute confers such a power, and there are obvious dangers in too broad an interpretation of the federal courts' inherent power to regulate their procedure. One danger is that it encourages judicial high-handedness ("power corrupts"); several years ago one of the district judges in this circuit ordered Acting Secretary of Labor Brock to appear before him for settlement discussions on the very day Brock was scheduled to appear before the Senate for his confirmation hearing. The broader concern illustrated by the Brock episode is that in their zeal to settle cases judges may ignore the value of other people's time. One reason people hire lawyers is to economize on their own investment of time in resolving disputes. It is pertinent to note in this connection that Oat is a defendant in this case; it didn't want its executives' time occupied with this litigation.

On the other hand, die Not bricht Eisen ["necessity breaks iron"]. Attorneys often are imperfect agents of their clients, and the workload of

---

*   This rule language has been revised slightly.—Eds.

our district courts is so heavy that we should hesitate to deprive them of a potentially useful tool for effecting settlement, even if there is some difficulty in finding a legal basis for the tool. Although few attorneys will defy a district court's request to produce the client, those few cases may be the very ones where the client's presence would be most conducive to settlement. If I am right that Rule 16(a) empowers a district court to summon unrepresented parties to a pretrial conference only because their presence may be necessary to get ready for trial, we need not infer that the draftsmen meant to forbid the summoning of represented parties for purposes of exploring settlement. The draftsmen may have been unaware that district courts were asserting a power to command the presence of a represented party to explore settlement. We should hesitate to infer inadvertent prohibitions.

The narrowly "legal" considerations bearing on the question whether district courts have the power asserted by the magistrate in this case are sufficiently equivocal to authorize—indeed compel—us to consider the practical consequences for settlement before deciding what the answer should be. Unfortunately we have insufficient information about those consequences to be able to give a confident answer, but fortunately we need not answer the question in this case—so clear is it that the magistrate abused his discretion, which is to say, acted unreasonably, in demanding that Oat Corporation send an executive having "full settlement authority" to the pretrial conference. This demand, which is different from a demand that a party who has not closed the door to settlement send an executive to discuss possible terms, would be defensible only if litigants had a duty to bargain in good faith over settlement before resorting to trial, and neither Rule 16 nor any other rule, statute, or doctrine imposes such a duty on federal litigants. There is no federal judicial power to coerce settlement. Oat had made clear that it was not prepared to settle the case on any terms that required it to pay money. That was its prerogative, which once exercised made the magistrate's continued insistence on Oat's sending an executive to Madison arbitrary, unreasonable, willful, and indeed petulant. This is apart from the fact that since no one officer of Oat may have had authority to settle the case, compliance with the demand might have required Oat to ship its entire board of directors to Madison. Ultimately Oat did make a money settlement, but there is no indication that it would have settled sooner if only it had complied with the magistrate's demand for the dispatch of an executive possessing "full settlement authority." * * *

COFFEY, CIRCUIT JUDGE, with whom EASTERBROOK, RIPPLE and MANION, CIRCUIT JUDGES, join, dissenting.

* * * Unlike the majority, I am convinced that Rule 16 does not authorize a trial judge to require a represented party litigant to attend a pretrial conference together with his or her attorney because the rule

mandates in clear and unambiguous terms that only an unrepresented party litigant and attorneys may be ordered to appear.

[The opinion goes on to reject "inherent authority" to compel the presence of represented parties.]

EASTERBROOK, CIRCUIT JUDGE, with whom POSNER, COFFEY, and MANION, CIRCUIT JUDGES, join, dissenting.

Our case has three logically separate issues. First, whether a district court may demand the attendance of someone other than the party's counsel of record. Second, whether the court may insist that this additional person be an employee rather than an agent selected for the occasion. Third, whether the court may insist that the representative have "full settlement authority"—meaning the authority to agree to pay cash in settlement (maybe authority without cap, although that was not clear). Even if one resolves the first issue as the majority does, it does not follow that district courts have the second or third powers, or that their exercise here was prudent.

The proposition that a magistrate may require a firm to send an employee rather than a representative is puzzling. Corporate "employees" are simply agents of the firm. Corporations choose their agents and decide what powers to give them. Which agents have which powers is a matter of internal corporate affairs. Joseph Oat Corp. sent to the conference not only its counsel of record but also John Fitzpatrick, who had authority to speak for Oat. Now Mr. Fitzpatrick is an attorney, which raised the magistrate's hackles, but why should this count against him? Because Fitzpatrick is a part-time rather than a full-time agent of the corporation? Why can't the corporation make its own decision about how much of the agent's time to hire? Is Oat being held in contempt because it is too small to have a cadre of legal employees—because its general counsel practices with a law firm rather than being "in house"?

At all events, the use of outside attorneys as negotiators is common. * * *

As for the third subject, whether the representative must have "settlement authority": the magistrate's only reason for ordering a corporate representative to come was to facilitate settlement then and there. As I understand Magistrate Groh's opinion, and Judge Crabb's, the directive was to send a person with "full settlement authority". Fitzpatrick was deemed inadequate only because he was under instructions not to pay money. E.g.: "While Mr. Fitzpatrick claimed authority to speak for Oat, he stated that he had no authority to make a [monetary] offer. *Thus*, no representative of Oat or National having authority to settle the case was present at the conference as the order directed" (magistrate's opinion, emphasis added). On learning that Fitzpatrick did not command Oat's treasury, the magistrate ejected him from the conference and never listened to what he had to say on Oat's behalf, never learned whether Fitzpatrick might be receptive to others' proposals. (We know that Oat ultimately did settle the case for money, after it took part in and "prevailed" at a summary jury trial—participation and payment each demonstrating Oat's willingness to consider settlement.) The magistrate's approach implies that if the Chairman and CEO of Oat had arrived with instructions from the Board to settle the case without paying cash, and to negotiate and bring back for the Board's consideration any financial proposals, Oat still would have been in contempt.

Both magistrate and judge demanded the presence not of a "corporate representative" in the sense of a full-time employee but of a representative with "full authority to settle". Most corporations reserve power to agree (as opposed to power to discuss) to senior managers or to their boards of directors—the difference depending on the amounts involved. Heileman wanted $4 million, a sum within the province of the board rather than a single executive even for firms much larger than Oat. Fitzpatrick came with power to discuss and recommend; he could settle the case on terms other than cash; he lacked only power to sign a check. The magistrate's order therefore must have required either (a) changing the allocation of responsibility within the corporation, or (b) sending a quorum of Oat's Board.

Magistrate Groh exercised a power unknown even in labor law, where there is a duty to bargain in good faith. 29 U.S.C. § 158(d). Labor and management commonly negotiate through persons with the authority to discuss but not agree. The negotiators report back to management and the union, each of which reserves power to reject or approve the position of its agent. We know from Fed.R.Civ.P. 16—and especially from the Advisory Committee's comment to Rule 16(c) that the Rule's "reference to 'authority' is not intended to insist upon the ability to settle the litigation"—that the parties cannot be compelled to negotiate "in good faith". A defendant convinced it did no wrong may insist on total vindication. Rule 68, which requires a party who turns down a settlement proposal to bear costs only if that party does worse at trial, implies the same thing. Yet if parties are not obliged to negotiate in good faith, on what ground can they be obliged to come with authority to settle on the spot—an authority agents need not carry even when the law requires negotiation? The order we affirm today compels persons who have committed no wrong, who pass every requirement of Rules 11 and 68, who want only the opportunity to receive a decision on the merits, to come to court with open checkbooks on pain of being held in contempt.

Settling litigation is valuable, and courts should promote it. Is settlement of litigation more valuable than settlement of labor disputes, so that courts may do what the NLRB may not? The statutory framework— bona fide negotiations required in labor law but not in litigation—suggests the opposite. Does the desirability of settlement imply that rules of state law allocating authority within a corporation must yield? We have held in other cases that settlements must be negotiated within the framework of existing rules; the desire to get a case over and done with does not justify modifying generally applicable norms.

[Dissenting opinions of JUDGES RIPPLE and MANION omitted.]

NOTES AND QUESTIONS

1.   The majority opinion in *Heileman* conceded that circumstances could arise in which requiring a corporate representative to appear "would be so onerous, so clearly unproductive, or so expensive in relation to the size, value, and complexity of the case that it might be an abuse of discretion." However, it found no such situation here, where the claim was sizable ($4 million) and turned on complex factual and legal issues, where the trial was expected to be lengthy (one to three months), and where the corporation had sent an attorney from Philadelphia to speak for the principals, whose expenses would not have exceeded sending a corporate representative from Camden. Would any or a number of these facts, if changed, have made the attendance order impermissible?

2.   Judge Posner, dissenting, expressed the concern "that in their zeal to settle cases judges may ignore the value of other people's time." Surely there are circumstances when an attorney can adequately represent a party and when requiring a non-attorney representative is unnecessarily wasteful. How does the majority opinion deal with this point? Do the efficiency and proportionality considerations identified by the majority provide appropriate guidance for case-by-case determinations?

3.   Judge Easterbrook, also dissenting, argued that many firms send their lawyer to negotiate in collective bargaining or merger talks, and that a lawyer is no less suited to negotiating in a settlement conference. However, ADR places great importance on having in attendance the person who will make the ultimate decision to settle so that she could hear, see, and participate in the proceedings, in short so that she can be affected by the discussion and interaction with the other side and the judge. Would an appropriate test be that if a lawyer is the sole representative she should be essentially the *alter ego* of the corporate decision-maker, with similar knowledge, reactions, interests, and settlement authority?

4.   Professor Riskin examined the advantages and disadvantages of client attendance at settlement conferences and ADR proceedings that offers useful guidance for courts. Riskin, The Represented Client in a Settlement Conference: The Lessons of *G. Heileman Brewing Co. v. Joseph Oat Corp.,* 69 Wash.U.L.Rev. 1059, 1099–1102 (1991). Advantages include giving the client a chance to tell his story in his own words, learning about the strengths and weaknesses of both sides, permitting him to act on new information, allowing cooperation and momentum to build in the offer process, clearing up miscommunications about facts and interests between lawyers and clients, and

providing information to spot opportunities for problem-solving situations. Medina v. Pile Trucking Inc., 2012 WL 4742424,*4 (C.D. Cal.) sanctioned defendants for failing to appear at a settlement conference, noting that their presence was required "precisely because they are the integral participants in this lawsuit. For one thing, they are the ones who retain actual personal knowledge of the events at issue."

Disadvantages include the risk that the client may give away valuable information that could leave him vulnerable to exploitation or weaken his case, that exposure to the other side's behavior will anger or harden some clients, or that direct communication will cause a flare-up and loss of objectivity. Riskin concluded that client attendance is likely to be useful in an ADR process that has such features as "participatory lawyer-client relationships, problem-solving negotiation, and judicial interventions emphasizing facilitation rather than pressure."

5.   Should there be an exception to the client attendance requirement when a named party has no real interest in the case? "Under standard insurance policy provisions, the insurance company has sole authority over the defense of cases, including whether to settle or go to trial. The insurance company representative, therefore, is the crucial person on the defense side for settlement negotiations. The insured defendant may have some interest in the case since its conduct is in question, but determination of that issue may have no monetary consequence to it." Sherman, Court-Mandated Alternative Dispute Resolution: What Form of Participation Should Be Required?, 46 S.M.U.L.Rev. 2079, 2105 (1993) (arguing that settlement conference orders should not require an insured defendant to attend "when it has no realistic exposure over policy limits and when its consent to settle is not required"). Might not the parties still benefit from confronting the person on the other side of an accident, hopefully bringing some emotional closure that would make even the plaintiff more willing to settle?

Can both an insured defendant and the insurer's representative be ordered to attend a settlement conference? In In re Novak, 932 F.2d 1397 (11th Cir.1991), the district court in a medical malpractice action directed the defendant's lawyer to find out who at the defendant's insurer had "full settlement authority" after the lawyer stated in a pretrial conference that he would have to check with the insurer before increasing defendant's settlement offer. On being told that the person with such authority was Novak, the judge ordered him to appear for a settlement conference and fined him when he did not. The appellate court agreed with *Heileman* that there is inherent power to require a party to send a person with full settlement authority to a pretrial conference, but held that there is no similar authority to require a nonparty insurer to attend.

In Kamaunu v. Kaaea, 57 P.3d 428, 430 n. 3 (Haw. 2002), the plaintiff sought sanctions against the defendant, alleging failure of the insurer's representative to have adequate settlement authority and to make a genuine offer at a court-ordered settlement conference. The Hawaii Supreme Court noted that in cases of no-fault insurance, "the authority to settle a case generally lies with the defendant's insurer, especially where the settlement value does not exceed the insured's policy limits." It was thus unwilling to find that the defendant's presence at the settlement conference could make up for the insurer's representative not having adequate settlement authority "unless the defendant, in fact, had authority to settle the case."

6.   "Courts routinely include in ADR orders a requirement that the parties and counsel come to the proceeding with settlement authority. This is based on the frequent experience that a settlement is less likely to be achieved if persons not in attendance must still approve the settlement agreed upon. Coming without full settlement authority has also been seen as an illegitimate tactic used by parties, particularly insurance companies, to allow the negotiator to claim inability to bargain outside of a prescribed range and to allow absent officials to disavow agreements made by their negotiating representative as outside their authority." Sherman, Court-Mandated Alternative Dispute Resolution: What Form of Participation Should Be Required? 46 S.M.U.L.Rev. 2079, 2103 (1993).

7.   How broad must the settlement authority be? The S.D. California local rule quoted in note 5 above requires "full and unlimited authority." A court order in that district added: "Full settlement authority means that the individuals at the settlement conference must be authorized to explore settlement options fully and to agree at that time to any settlement terms acceptable to the parties." Santangelo v. California Business Bureau, Inc., 2010 WL 4941878, *1, fn 1 (S.D.Cal.). It has been said that the person who attends must have "unfettered discretion and authority" to change the settlement position of a party. Pitman v. Brinker Int'l, Inc., 216 F.R.D. 481, 485–86 (D. Ariz. 2003).

8.   Lockhart v. Patel, 115 F.R.D. 44, 45 (E.D.Ky.1987), provides an example of an insurance company's noncompliance with such an order. After a nonbinding summary jury trial awarded the plaintiff $200,000 for a lost eye in a medical malpractice case, the plaintiff agreed to settle for $175,000, but the attorney for the doctor's insurer told the judge he was only authorized to offer $125,000 and not to negotiate any further. The judge then called a settlement conference, directing the defense attorney to bring the home-office representative of the insurance company who had issued these instructions and a representative with equal authority. He said: "Tell them not to send some flunky who has no authority to negotiate. I want someone who can enter into a settlement in this range without having to call anyone else." The defense attorney brought an adjuster from the local office who advised the court that her instructions from the home office were to reiterate the previous offer "and not to bother to call them back if it were not accepted." The judge then made findings that the insurer "had deliberately refused to obey the order of the court," striking the pleadings of the defendant, declaring him in default, and ordering a show cause hearing why the insurer should not be punished for criminal contempt. Later that day, the insurer settled for $175,000. At the contempt hearing, the judge accepted the assurances of the insurer that "it had all been a misunderstanding" and permitted it to purge itself with a letter of apology from its Chief Executive Officer.

Consider the following comment on *Lockhart* [from Sherman, supra note 6, at 2107–08]:

> *Lockhart* is an appropriate fact situation for sanctions. Defendant's refusal to send a representative with any settlement authority at all, other than to reiterate the previous offer, insured that the conference would be a futile proceeding. Requiring settlement authority does not coerce a party into settling for any specific amount, and litigant autonomy cannot justify ignoring a requirement directed at avoiding wasteful negotiation tactics.
>
> The hard cases arise when the representative's settlement authority is more ambiguous than in *Lockhart*. Assume that an insurance company sends a representative with authority to settle only up to $10,000, on the basis that it has thoroughly reviewed the case and is convinced that there is no liability at all and, that, in any event, the reasonable damages are much smaller than that amount. Surely the company should not be required to give its representative authority to settle at a higher amount when it has concluded that there is no justification for doing so. But the key inquiry is what the representative's instructions are. If he is sent without authority to consider any settlement above $10,000, this is essentially a "no authority" case as in *Lockhart*. A court should be entitled to require that the representative at least be open to hearing the arguments of the other side with the possibility of settling at any amount found to be persuasive, even though the representative understands that the company has evaluated the case as not worth more than $10,000. If his authority and instructions are so limited that he is deaf to any persuasion, then he is not the proper representative with adequate authority that the court has ordered.

9. It is clear that parties may not be sanctioned for sending a representative who lacks authority simply because they refuse to make an offer or counter offer. *Kamauno*, quoted in note 5 above, determined that the trial court's imposition of sanctions on defendant was based on "failure to make a monetary settlement offer and his firm intention to go to trial." It found that the fact that defendant made only a "walk-away" offer (a dismissal with each side bearing its own costs and no recovery for the plaintiff) was not grounds for sanctions. It quoted *Heileman* for the proposition that sanctions would not be appropriate "[i]f this case represented a situation where [defendant] had sent a corporate representative and was sanctioned because that person refused to make an offer to pay money—that is, refused to submit to settlement coercion—we would be faced with a decidedly different issue—a situation we would not countenance." However, an absolute limitation on authority to settle for no more than a certain sum does not comply with the authority requirement. Nick v. Morgan's Foods, Inc., 270 F.3d 590, 595–97 (8th Cir. 2001)(also holding that a client can be sanctioned for the conduct of his attorney).

10. Sending a person with settlement authority becomes more complicated when such authority resides in a body such as a city council or corporate board. See Nueces County v. De Pena, 953 S.W.2d 835 (Tex.App.1997) (in suit against county, county judge could not be required to attend mediation since settlement authority lay in commissioners' court). Perhaps all that can be expected is that the representative be part of that body and that any settlement reached be subject to being confirmed by the body. Compare In re United States, 149 F.3d 332 (5th Cir.1998) (district court did not abuse its discretion in ordering the government to send a person with full settlement authority to mediation, at least where the government agreed to the mediation). The problems of requiring an insurer's representative or governmental official to attend a mediation with adequate settlement authority were arguably eased by 1993 amendments permitting availability by telephone.

11. In 1993, Rule 16(c) was amended, and it now provides that "[i]f appropriate, the court may require that a party or its representative be present or reasonably available by other means to consider possible settlement." The 1993 Advisory Committee Note also mentions that this might include "a representative from an insurance company." Citing *Heileman*, the Note states that the telephone provision "is not intended to limit the reasonable exercise of the court's inherent powers." Are the two really compatible? The Fifth Circuit, in In re Stone, 986 F.2d 898 (5th Cir.1993), recommended a "practical approach" to settlement authority requirements imposed on governmental officials, such as allowing the official with ultimate authority to be fully prepared and available by telephone at the time of the conference. But see Raad v. Wal-Mart Stores, Inc., 1998 WL 272879 (D.Neb. 1998) (upholding sanctions for nonattendance at mediation of corporate representative who only made himself available by telephone).

Whether a high-ranking official who possesses settlement authority must always attend in person, or can be in touch long-distance, depends on the facts of the individual case. U.S. v. U.S. Dist. Court for Northern Mariana Islands, 694 F.3d 1051 (9th Cir. 2012) was a multi-million dollar suit against the U.S. for return of allegedly erroneous tax payments. Because of the size of the claim, the lowest-ranking official authorized to settle the case was the officer in charge of the Tax Division of the Department of Justice, the Assistant Attorney General of the Tax Division. The judge ordered her to attend the initial settlement conference (to be held in Idaho). The Ninth Circuit granted a writ of mandamus overturning that order, finding that the judge had abused his discretion. It said the federal government is "not like any other litigant." The Tax Division had 549 pending civil cases that involved more than $2 million, and "the government has good reasons for not delegating greater authority to settle to more officials" in the interests of "centralized decision making." "Another important factor" was that this was the first settlement conference in the case; "the court did not have a basis to conclude that the direct involvement of the critical decision maker for the federal government was needed to achieve a settlement." The court expressed agreement with the Fifth Circuit's "practical approach" in *In re Stone*, which would "consider whether a representative may be effectively available as needed during a settlement conference without physical attendance." However, it added: "If it turns out that the district court's 'reasonable efforts' to conduct settlement efforts are 'thwarted because the government official with settlement authority will not communicate with the government counsel or the court in a timely manner,' then we also agree with the Fifth Circuit that 'the court, as a last resort, can require the appropriate officials with full settlement authority to attend.'"

12. Rule 16(f) sanctions have been assessed for failure to comply with orders relating to the timing of settlement offers. The flood of asbestos cases lead federal district courts to adopt local rules requiring parties to settle, if they are going to settle, by a certain date before the commencement of the trial. The purpose was to force parties to give earlier attention to settlement and to avoid last minute settlements just before or during the trial that are disruptive of a court's trial schedule and of the ability of parties in other cases to rely on trial dates. In Newton v. A.C. & S., 918 F.2d 1121 (3d Cir.1990), the district court set a deadline for settling asbestos cases of two weeks prior to the trial date, with sanctions to be imposed for later settlement. In these cases consolidated for appeal, the plaintiffs settled with some defendants before trial, but after the settlement deadline, settled with others on the day trial was to begin, and settled with one defendant after several days of trial.

The appellate court approved the district court's use of deadlines as consistent with Rule 16 "to maximize the efficiency of the court system by insisting that attorneys and clients cooperate with the court and abandon practices which unreasonably interfere with the expeditious management of cases." It also approved the use of sanctions, but not as they were imposed in these cases. The district court levied fines only on the settling defendants. The appellate court said that, in the absence of a finding of fault, "disparate treatment of plaintiffs and defendants may not be countenanced." (Note the similarity to the one-sided imposition of sanctions for failing to settle in Kothe v. Smith, supra p. 19.) The court of appeals criticized the district judge's apparent belief that since the defendants "controlled the purse strings essential to a settlement," imposing fines against them alone "would be an effective measure to compel a relaxation of the purse strings and induce settlement." Can a court ever take into account the fact that defendant corporations or insurance companies are often repeat players and that fines could discourage them from delaying inevitable settlements?

13. In White v. Raymark Industries, Inc., 783 F.2d 1175 (4th Cir.1986), the district court assessed jurors' costs in the amount of $2,000 against a defendant pursuant to a local rule imposing costs on parties for settling cases without giving the clerk's office one day's notice. The Fourth Circuit upheld the assessment based on inherent judicial authority. It noted that "despite plaintiff's vigorous attempts to reach a settlement" in the week before the trial, the defendant's counsel was prohibited from agreeing on a settlement figure without permission of an official of the insurance carrier who could not be reached.

In contrast, in State of Wisconsin v. American Family Mut. Ins. Co., 451 N.W.2d 429 (Wis. 1990), the Wisconsin Supreme Court found no inherent authority for a trial court to impose a sanction on a party for disrupting its calendar by a last-minute settlement. Under the court's practice, in order to obtain a "stipulated" trial date, the parties had to agree that if the case were settled after a certain date, a penalty (in this case $20,000, the difference between the parties' offers) would be paid into the court's general fund. Had they chosen not to stipulate, the parties would have been given a "stacked" trial date which would normally involve having their case set with four other cases and running a risk of being unable to go to trial on that date. The Supreme Court found that the penalty was inconsistent with state statutes and precedents and actually restricted a party's ability to control prosecution of the case.

14. A settlement conference with the judge who will try the case raises a concern that the parties will either not be entirely candid or will feel pressured to agree to a certain settlement so as not to displease the judge. For this reason, some district courts provide that a magistrate judge or a different district judge will conduct pretrial settlement conferences. Mediation before a neutral mediator unconnected with the court is another alternative. (See discussion of mediation, infra p. 509).

In Horrocks v. Daggett County, 460 F.Supp.2d 1274 (D.Utah 2006), the trial judge, in a case for overtime wages under the Fair Labor Standards Act, asked the parties at a settlement conference whether it would be useful if he gave a specific dollar amount of what he believed would be a fair resolution of the case. When both sides agreed, he said he thought a fair resolution would be a payment of $4,000 to plaintiff (she had sought $11,000), along with half of her attorneys' fees. The parties did not reach a settlement, and the County moved to disqualify the judge. 28 U.S.C. § 455(a) states that "[a]ny justice, judge, or magistrate of the United States shall disqualify himself in any proceeding in which his impartiality might reasonably be questioned." Where a judge is to serve as the trier of fact, cases have held that he should not recommend a settlement figure before trial. First Wisconsin National Bank of Rice Lake v. Klapmeier, 526 F.2d 77 (8th Cir. 1975); United States v. Pfizer, Inc., 560 F.2d 319 (8th Cir. 1977). The judge in Horrocks found that this admonition did not apply to him because the case would be tried by a jury and there would be no suggestion of bias where the jury would be the trier of fact. He also found inapplicable a local rule that a judge holding a settlement conference shall not communicate with the trial judge as to what was said in discussions during the conference. He found this would only apply where a case has been referred to another judge for a settlement conference, while here the judge who held the conference would also try the case. Citing Heileman, the judge concluded that the Rule 16 authority "to order represented parties to appear at pretrial settlement conferences merely represents another application of a district judge's inherent authority to preserve the efficiency, and more importantly the integrity, of the judicial process."

15. A danger in having a judge or magistrate preside at a settlement conference is that "reality testing" with a party may be seen as coercive. In Gevas v. Ghosh, 566 F.3d 717, 718–20 (7th Cir. 2009), a party sought to void a settlement agreement he had entered into after the conference on the ground that the magistrate had attempted to coerce him into settling by telling him at the outset of the conference that his case was meritless. The appellate court said that coercion occurs when a judge threatens to penalize a party that refuses to settle, but that a judge "is not prohibited from expressing a negative opinion of a party's claim during discussion as a means to foster an agreement." It found no threat by the judge to penalize the party for not settling.

16. It must be remembered that use of a settlement conference is still a matter for the discretion of the judge, see Kelley v. Board of Educ. of City of Chicago, 2012 WL 1108135 (N.D. Ill.) (declining to order an immediate settlement conference at the point when the parties were skirmishing over a motion to compel responses to written discovery).

B. SETTLEMENT DEVICES USING INTERVENTION BY THIRD PARTIES

Although Rule 16, when adopted in 1938, contemplated that the pretrial conference would be the primary tool for judicial preparation of a case for trial, four decades later the courts were most concerned with the "litigation explosion" and how to settle cases short of trial. In 1983, the rule was amended to add "facilitating settlement" to the subjects to be discussed at a pretrial conference. Then in 1993, it was amended again to expressly allow consideration of "settlement and the use of special procedures to assist in resolving the dispute when authorized by statute or local rule." By this time the "ADR movement" was in full flower.

The ADR movement began with an expansion of mediation. Once primarily used in family law cases, it became a popular process in the 1960's and 1970's for a broader range of disputes. "Neighborhood justice" centers sprang up to encourage members of communities to work out their differences rather than relying on the establishment courts and police. Churches and mediation centers became a source of essentially free mediation services. Concurrently the business community, concerned with the spiraling costs of litigation, embraced "settlement promotion" through both mediation and new techniques for resolving disputes. Lawyers increasingly took training in mediation and other ADR processes and soon dominated the field of third-party neutrals who assist in settlement.

Finally, ADR became "court-annexed."[10] Courts adopted rules making mediation and other ADR devices an integral part of litigation. In an attempt to achieve earlier settlements and reduce costs, court rules and individual judges encouraged (and increasingly required) parties to go

---

[10] See Sherman, The Impact on Litigation Strategy of Integrating Alternative Dispute Resolution into the Pretrial Process, 168 F.R.D. 75 (1996).

through an ADR process before they would be allowed to proceed towards trial. Different courts began to experiment with different types of processes. The Civil Justice Reform Act of 1990[11] adopted a decentralized model. It authorized courts by local rule to adopt one or more forms of ADR—which by this time included mediation, neutral evaluation, non-binding arbitration, summary jury trials, and mini-trials. This encouraged further experimentation, and reports back to Congress were required.

Reconciling the methodology, values, and objectives of ADR and trials within an integrated litigation process is no easy task. The procedural differences between a binding adjudicatory process (such as a trial) and a nonbinding facilitative process (like mediation) are considerable. These include such basic process features as the form of presentation, the kind of evidence and argumentation permitted, the role of the decision maker or audience, and the legal effect of the outcome. Of course, integrating ADR into the litigation process does not result in a single, amalgamated proceeding, and most ADR processes do not mimic a trial. Attorneys must therefore anticipate having to participate in two very different procedures. It is difficult to engraft an ADR proceeding onto the usual pretrial process without affecting the way attorneys investigate and prepare their cases for both the ADR and the trial proceedings. Furthermore, the act of going through an ADR process, in which evidence and arguments are presented in a rather different manner than in a trial, can not help but affect the conduct of a subsequent trial.

A great deal of experimentation with different kinds of ADR processes has now taken place in both federal and state courts.[12] These processes have in common the use of third-party neutrals to assist the parties in achieving settlement. They differ as to such features as the degree of procedural formality, the level of intrusiveness of the neutral, the time at which the process is invoked, and the manner of selecting the neutral. All of these processes are non-binding, and, unless the parties agree to a particular settlement, they will be entitled to go forward with a trial.

The principal ADR processes that have emerged can be roughly placed on a continuum from the least formal, with the neutral playing primarily the role of facilitating discussion and consideration of settlement options (such as mediation), to the most formal with the neutral playing a "reality testing," "evaluative," or "fact-finding" role (such as court-annexed arbitration, mini-trial, and summary jury trial).[13] We will take them up in the order of least formal to most formal.

---

[11] 28 U.S.C. § 471 et seq.

[12] See Stienstra, ADR in the Federal District Courts: An Initial Report (Federal Judicial Center, Nov. 16, 2011).

[13] See further discussion of the various ADR categories in Rau, Sherman & Peppet, Processes of Dispute Resolution: The Role of Lawyers 545–78 (4th ed. 2006).

1. MEDIATION

Mediation is a broad term used to describe the process by which a third party facilitates communication between parties to a dispute, and aids them in finding a solution. The "classical" format for mediation involves a mediator sitting at a table with the parties in an informal atmosphere. The mediator usually makes introductory remarks; then the parties or their counsel present their version of the dispute. This is followed by a dialogue guided by the mediator, which includes gathering information, identifying problems, generating options, and bargaining—the aim of which is to resolve the dispute and write a settlement agreement. At some stage, the mediator may also decide to move the parties into separate rooms with the mediator shuttling back and forth between them, conveying information, arguments and offers from the other side.

Participation in court-annexed mediation may not be entirely voluntary. Statutes and court rules now often require parties to participate in mediation as part of the pre-trial process (see further discussion, infra pp. 519–520). But although participation may be required, agreeing to settle is not, and settlement will only be achieved if the parties come to an agreement as a result of the mediation.[14] "Mediation has emerged as the primary ADR process in the federal district courts," and over half of the 94 federal court districts offer or require mediation.[15]

Mediators may be selected in a variety of ways. Many court-annexed mediation programs allow the parties to select their own mediators, or, if they cannot agree, provide for selection by the court from a roster of qualified mediators. Some simply provide that the court will select the mediator. Because mediation has been an essentially private form of dispute resolution, governmental regulation is minimal. Unlike other professions—ranging from attorneys and psychologists to therapists and cosmetologists—mediators have not been subjected to governmental supervision over such matters as licensing, training, professional standards, and discipline. A number of professional mediation organizations certify mediators as having satisfied certain requirements as to training and experience, but there is no formal licensing of mediators.[16] Court-annexed mediation programs typically require completion of a basic 40-hour training course in mediation, with advanced training required for certain kinds of cases like family law. A few state-court mediation programs have certification requirements for mediators, with their state

---

[14] There are mediation-arbitration ("med-arb") hybrids that begin with mediation, but if the parties cannot reach a settlement, the mediator may decide the case as an arbitrator if agreed in advance by the parties.

[15] Plapinger & Stienstra, ADR and Settlement in the Federal District Courts: A Sourcebook for Judges and Lawyers, Alternative Dispute Resolution: The Litigator's Handbook, eds. Atlas, Huber & Trachte-Huber, 399 (ABA Section of Litigation 2000).

[16] See ABA Section of Dispute Resolution, Task Force on Credentialing, Final Report, Aug. 2012.

Supreme Court or affiliate entities serving as the credentialing body (e.g., Florida, Virginia, Georgia, and Tennessee).

As courts began to annex mediation as an integral part of the trial process, lawyers have become the largest profession performing as mediators. Most are part-time, doing mediation as an adjunct to their law practice, although some confine their practice exclusively to mediation. In certain kinds of cases, non-lawyers also often serve as mediators (for example, psychologists in family disputes, social workers in juvenile or community matters, criminologists in victim-offender confrontations, engineers or architects in construction disputes, or labor specialists in labor/employment relations). Some courts have staff mediators to conduct mediations (for example, in California in family law cases[17]). Prior experience in litigation is often desired in a mediator, particularly by parties' attorneys, and many full-time mediators are former litigators or judges. Typically mediators make known their fee schedules in advance, whether they are appointed by the court or selected by the parties. Mediator fees may be assessed by the court as costs, and are often split between the parties.

2. EARLY NEUTRAL EVALUATION (ENE)

The Early Neutral Evaluation (ENE) program, now used in a number of federal district courts, was first created by the U.S. District Court for the N.D. California.[18] Under it, a neutral—usually a respected lawyer with expertise in the subject matter of the case—meets with the parties and their lawyers for a couple of hours not long after the filing of the case and gives them a frank assessment of their cases. "Typically, one of the clients begins a narrative presentation of the case, without being led by the lawyer. After both sides have presented, the evaluator asks questions. The evaluator tries to help the parties to identify common ground, and to convert this to stipulations or informal agreements. The effort during the process is to isolate the areas of disagreement most central to the case."[19]

After the discussion, the evaluator leaves the room and writes her evaluation of the value of the case and two or three key analytical points. If the plaintiff wins, the evaluator ascribes a range of damages. Before giving the parties the evaluation, the evaluator asks if they wish to discuss settlement before they see it. Some 25% of cases have settled at this point. If they opt not to discuss settlement, the evaluator explains the evaluation. She then "outlines a case development plan, identifying key areas of

---

[17] California requires conciliation where child custody is in issue. West's Ann. Cal.Civ.Code § 4607.

[18] See W. Brazil, Early Neutral Evaluation (ABA 2012); Brazil, Kahn, Newman & Gold, Early Neutral Evaluation: An Experimental Effort to Expedite Dispute Resolution, 69 Judicature 279 (1986).

[19] Lawyers Get Tips on Using Early Neutral Evaluation, 4 ADR Rep. 124, at 124–25 (April 12, 1990).

disagreement and suggesting ways to posture the case and to conduct discovery as efficiently as possible. The evaluator is required to do case planning. The parties are required to listen, but not to agree. They may decide to come back for a follow-up settlement conference."

ENE provides a fairly pristine form of "evaluative" ADR. Although the outside attorney may facilitate discussion, her principal role is to hear each side's case and give them an objective assessment. Unlike mediation, both the presentation and the evaluation tend to be couched in terms of the legal issues. ENE serves as an early planning, as well as a settlement, device. It is hoped that by receiving an early assessment from an impartial outsider, the attorneys will be able either to settle then or to structure their cases so that settlement or a smoother trial is possible in the future.

3. COURT-ANNEXED ARBITRATION

Based on an experiment in the Pennsylvania courts in the 1950s, court-annexed (sometimes called non-binding) arbitration has become the second most used ADR process. The experiment was based on the premise that parties are more likely to settle if they are given an opportunity to present their cases in an abbreviated form to three neutral attorneys who would render a non-binding judgment. This would provide an opportunity to "reality test" by comparing the presentation of their case with that of their opponent and to see how neutrals who were familiar with the law would assess the cases.

A study of one of the programs in Pittsburgh found a high settlement rate and general satisfaction with the program by litigants and attorneys. "The private, informal arbitration procedure, conducted by three ordinary attorneys in business suits, sitting without a jury around a table in a small hearing room" clearly did not fit the trial paradigm of "a black-robed judge, conducting a public trial before a jury, in a formal courtroom environment."[20] Nevertheless, only a small percentage of litigants interviewed said they would have preferred to have a judge or jury hear their case. The reason, the study concluded, was that the litigants were satisfied with a speedy, inexpensive procedure that provides a full hearing before an impartial third party:

> They wanted an opportunity to have their case heard and decided by an impartial third party. When this requirement was met, they reported that the arbitration process had been "fair." When asked why they had come to this conclusion, they were unlikely to offer elaborate rationales. "They heard us both out, listened the same

---

[20] Adler, Hensler & Nelson, Simple Justice: How Litigants Fare in the Pittsburgh Arbitral Program 87–94 (1983).

to both sides," or "We got an equal chance to tell our stories," were typical responses.[21]

The Civil Justice Reform Act of 1990[22] required each district court to study and develop a civil justice "expense and delay reduction" plan, including consideration of ADR programs. A number of federal district courts provided for court-annexed arbitration, either mandatory or voluntary. However, a Rand study of the effectiveness of the CJRA found no major effect of court-annexed arbitration on the time to disposition, lawyer work hours, or lawyer satisfaction.[23] In 1997, Congress reauthorized the twenty district court arbitration programs that had been adopted in pilot districts.[24] Although court-annexed arbitration continues to be one of several ADR alternatives in federal courts, the Rand study noted "a marked shift in half of the pilot districts toward other structured and administratively supported ADR programs—especially mandatory or voluntary mediation and early neutral evaluation."[25] Court-annexed arbitration thus had fallen out of favor with some courts and attorneys, and when the Alternative Dispute Resolution Act of 1998 required every district to authorize at least one type of ADR by local rule, it required consent by the parties for court-annexed arbitration (which was also limited to non-Constitutional right cases involving less than $15,000).[26]

In the typical federal court-annexed arbitration program, a roster of lawyers who are willing to serve as arbitrators is maintained by the court. A list of lawyers who have been randomly selected is submitted to counsel, who are instructed to strike one name and return the list to the court. The three attorneys whose names remain are then asked to serve as the arbitration panel. At the hearing, counsel make a summarized presentation of their cases without live witnesses. The arbitrators confer and render a non-binding decision. The parties and their counsel may be given an opportunity to discuss the case informally with the arbitrators. Parties can demand a trial de novo within 30 days after entry of judgment if they post an amount equal to the arbitrators' fees (which was typically set at $75 per day of hearing for each arbitrator, a recognition that the lawyers were essentially serving pro bono). This amount is returned if the

---

[21] Id. at 9.

[22] 28 U.S.C.A. §§ 471–82.

[23] See J. Kakalik et al., Just, Speedy, and Inexpensive? An Evaluation of Judicial Case Management Under the Civil Justice Reform Act (Rand, Inst. of Civ. Just., 1996). However, there have been criticisms of the methodology and limited samples used in the Rand study. See Statement of Concerns Regarding the Rand ADR Study (CPR Inst. for Disp. Res., March 14, 1997).

[24] 111 Stat. 1173 (1997). However, the next year a bill requiring all federal district courts to use mandatory court-annexed arbitration in cases involving less than a certain dollar amount failed, and instead, the Alternative Dispute Resolution Act of 1998, 112 Stat. 2993 (1998), gave federal district courts power to refer cases to mediation and early neutral evaluation, but to court-annexed arbitration only if the parties consent.

[25] Kakalik, supra note 23, at 17.

[26] 28 U.S.C. §§ 654–58.

party obtains a judgment more favorable than the arbitration award; otherwise, it is forfeited to the government. Upon the filing of a de novo demand, the judgment entered on the arbitrators' award is vacated, and the award sealed pending the final outcome of the case.[27]

Court-annexed arbitration is generally expected to take place early in the litigation, without an opportunity for full discovery. It is viewed as a quick and inexpensive alternative to litigation; Judge Harry Edwards has referred to it as a "poor man's mini-trial."[28] Parties are encouraged to decide what discovery is crucial to the hearing and conduct that discovery in advance of arbitration. One of the principal advantages of court-annexed arbitration as a settlement device is that it functions without a judge and thus frees up judicial time. It is also considerably less expensive than a trial. The form of presentation is through summarization of evidence in a relatively short proceeding, usually less than half a day.

4. SUMMARY JURY TRIAL

A summary jury trial is a shortened trial, usually lasting less than a day, in which the lawyers summarize their cases before a jury empanelled under usual procedures. A judge or magistrate presides. Some brief testimony may be heard from key witnesses, such as the parties, but most of the testimony will be summarized by the attorneys based on depositions, other discovery, and affidavits. The jury verdict is only advisory and non-binding on the parties—although the jurors are not usually told this.

The summary jury trial was developed in 1980 by Judge Thomas Lambros, of the U.S. District Court for the Northern District of Ohio, for two personal injury suits that he believed should have settled: "The reason that they didn't was that counsel and their clients felt that they could obtain a better resolution from a jury than their pretrial settlement negotiations. It occurred to me that if only the parties could gaze into a crystal ball and be able to predict, with a reasonable amount of certainty, what a jury could do in their respective cases, the parties and counsel would be more willing to reach a settlement rather than going through the expense and aggravation of a full jury trial." [29]

Discovery should be completed before a summary jury trial. The parties have to submit lists of the witnesses whose testimony will be summarized and must "present all procedural and evidentiary questions which foreseeably will arise during the course of the summary jury trial," on which the judge will rule, minimizing the need for objections.

As described by Judge Lambros, the proceedings are not open to the public and, unless ordered by the Court, are not recorded. Counsel may, if

---

[27] Meierhoefer & Seron, Court-Annexed Arbitration in the Western District of Texas 3 (1989).

[28] Edwards, Alternative Dispute Resolution: Panacea or Anathema?, 99 Harv.L.Rev. 668, 673 (1986).

[29] Lambros, The Summary Jury Trial, 103 F.R.D. 461, 463 (1984).

so desired, arrange for a court reporter to be in attendance. All evidence is presented through the attorneys, and opening and closing arguments are amalgamated with a narrative overview of the trial proofs. In non-complex cases, as little as one hour of time may be allotted to each side to present their case to the jury, with a further opportunity for short rebuttal.

No testimony is taken by sworn witnesses. Counsel simply summarize the anticipated testimony of trial witnesses and are free to present exhibits to the jury. Counsel are limited to presenting representations of evidence that would be admissible at trial. Representations of facts must be supportable by reference to discovery materials such as depositions, stipulations, documents, and formal admissions, or by a professional representation that counsel has spoken with the witness and is repeating that which the witness stated. Statements, reports, and depositions may be read from, but not at undue length.

Following counsels' presentation, the jury is given an abbreviated charge and then retires to deliberate. The jury may return a consensus verdict or separate, individual verdicts that list each juror's opinion of liability and damages. While consensus verdicts are encouraged, separate, individual verdicts do afford counsel substantial insight into the individual juror's perceptions and may suggest an equitable basis for settlement.

Summarization Techniques

Summarization of evidence by lawyers, rather than live testimony, is central to the time savings offered by the summary jury trial. This has been criticized by Professor Brunet, as an inferior form of presenting information because it "can be only an imperfect perception."[30] "Moreover, attorney witness summations cannot resolve factual questions of veracity and credibility. Any lawyer who has ever tried a case knows that the trier of fact has expertise in discerning witness credibility and veracity. A full trial achieves careful consideration of issues of witness believability. These advantages of trial are absent from summary jury trial. Attorney witness summaries simply are incomparable to actual consideration of witness demeanor. As Judge Posner has stated, 'We do not need a jury of laymen to decide which of two lawyers is more credible.' Posner, The Summary Jury Trial and Other Methods of Alternative Dispute Resolution: Some Cautionary Observations, 53 U.Chi.L.Rev. 366, 374 (1986)."

On the other hand, a summary jury trial is not intended as a substitute for a trial, but as a device to provide "reality testing" conducive to a settlement short of trial. But see Marcus, Completing Equity's Conquest? Reflections on the Future of Trial Under the Federal Rules of Civil Procedure, 50 U.Pitt.L.Rev. 725 (1988) (suggesting that, for some purposes,

---

[30] Brunet, Questioning the Quality of Alternative Dispute Resolution, 62 Tulane L.Rev. 1, 40 (1987).

summary jury trial is analogous to trial). The issue is whether it can provide a sufficiently reliable overview to give some confidence that it will result in a fair settlement. Consider Sherman, Reshaping the Lawyer's Skills for Court-Supervised ADR, 51 Tex.Bar.J. 47, 47–49 (1988):

> The art of summarization is the centerpiece of court-supervised ADR proceedings. It is already familiar to attorneys who, in letters, memoranda, and briefs, are constantly called on to boil down information, synthesize it, and present it in a shortened form. Perhaps the closest analogues to this skill in litigation are found in closing argument to the jury, appellate argument, presentations to administrative agencies, and "written narrative statements.
>
> A genuine concern is that there is no opportunity for cross-examination which may be necessary to assess credibility when there is disputed testimony. Cross-examination, however, may take place on deposition. It is up to counsel to convey through his summarization the effect of the cross-examination and any discrepancies and flaws in the witness' total testimony. The ADR decision-maker, however, will not have the opportunity to observe the witness and assess his credibility, and, in certain cases, that can be a significant loss. For this reason, allowing brief appearances of witnesses or showing portions of a videotaped deposition seems desirable, and courts should be open to allowing such developments. A check on counsels' inventiveness in a summary jury trial in describing the expected testimony is that they must have a basis for the assertions they make about the evidence.

Is there any check on a counsel's misstating what he has been told in private by a potential witness? Indeed, is there any check on a counsel's misstating or embellishing his summary of the deposition or other discovery? The primary check is the ability of the opposing counsel to set the record straight in her own presentation. Objections are possible, though not encouraged. Perhaps most importantly, it should be kept in mind that the summary jury verdict is advisory only, and a verdict that the other party will not accept because she feels she has been overreached in the summary jury trial is worth very little.

Limited Benefits?

Although a summary jury trial provides perhaps the best estimate of how a jury would decide a case, questions have been raised as to whether it really results in a savings of effort. Most cases settle anyway. Moreover, using this method seems not to result in significant savings of attorney time (since full pretrial preparation is necessary) or judge time (since the judge must rule on a variety of trial-related matters and must preside at the summary jury trial). For a skeptical examination of the claims of cost and time savings in a summary jury trial, see Posner, The Summary Jury Trial and Other Methods of Alternative Dispute Resolution: Some Cautionary Observations, 53 U.Chi.L.Rev. 366 (1986). Perhaps because so many resources go into a summary jury trial—which will be wasted if one of the parties will not accept the verdict—it has slipped far behind mediation, settlement conference, ENE, and court-annexed arbitration as most-used ADR processes. Although many federal courts authorize its use, only a small number of cases are referred to a summary jury trial.[31] Nevertheless experimentation with summary jury trials can help to develop lawyer's skills in presenting their cases in much shortened form for settlement purpose, obviating the need for a full blown trial.

Confidentiality

Since summary jury trials are non-binding, it is important that what is said in them and the jury's decision will be inadmissible in any later proceedings. As a form of compromise negotiations, the summary jury trial enjoys the protections of Fed.R.Evid. 408: Evidence of "furnishing or offering or promising to furnish—or accepting or offering or promising to accept—a valuable consideration in compromising or attempting to compromise the claim" which was disputed as to either validity or amount, is not admissible to prove liability for or invalidity of the claim or its amount. Evidence of conduct or statements made in compromise negotiations is likewise not admissible. However, Rule 408 only goes to admissibility, and not discovery, and if the parties are to be assured that discovery may not be used in the future, by their opponent or third parties, as to what was said or decided in the summary jury trial, a privilege under common law or statute is necessary.

Note that the summary jury trial is closed to the public. Yet Judge Lambros says it is essential that the event take place in a courtroom, presided over by a judge or magistrate, using jurors summoned by public authorities. In Cincinnati Gas & Elec. Co. v. General Elec. Co., 117 F.R.D. 597 (S.D.Ohio 1987), affirmed, 854 F.2d 900 (6th Cir.1988). the court denied newspapers access to a summary jury trial. The newspapers argued that trials are public events, but the judge rejected the analogy "because the purpose of the summary jury trial is settlement by means of giving the parties insights into the strengths and weaknesses of their case" and "as a matter of necessity, not all of the evidence that would be presented at trial will be covered by the summary proceeding."

The underlying litigation in *Cincinnati Gas* concerned the safety of a nuclear reactor. Plaintiff alleged that due to poor design the reactor was unable to withstand the pressures generated by the nuclear steam supply

---

[31] See Stienstra, supra note 12.

system and therefore was unable to contain radioactive steam. After the secret summary jury trial, the case was settled for an amount reportedly exceeding $75 million. Should the press and residents of the area where the reactor is located have been given access to the evidence summarized during the summary jury trial? Federal Reserve Bank v. Carey-Canada, Inc., 123 F.R.D. 603, 607 (D.Minn.1988), did require the parties in an asbestos liability case to participate in a summary jury trial without their consent and followed *Cincinnati Gas* in closing it to the public.

5. MINI-TRIAL

The term "mini-trial" was attached by a *New York Times* story to a formal settlement device created in 1977 in connection with a corporate dispute. It is not strictly speaking a trial at all, but a process that combines elements of adjudication with other processes such as negotiation and mediation. It refers to a proceeding, usually presided over by a neutral advisor, in which each side presents its case in shortened form to the persons who have ultimate settlement authority (often the corporate Chief Executive Officers, or persons with settlement authority over the particular dispute) as a prelude to settlement negotiations between them. The term is sometimes incorrectly used to refer to any form of shortened or summarized trial (rather than using the more specific titles, such as "summary jury trial" or "court-annexed arbitration").

The "mini-trial" was created for disputes involving corporate parties and has been primarily conducted by private organizations like the CPR Institute for Dispute Resolution, an association of corporations that promotes resolution of disputes without trials.[32] However, some courts have found it to be a useful settlement device, and it has been "court-annexed" in some cases by orders that the parties conduct a mini-trial.

A principal reason for creation of the mini-trial was to "return the dispute to the businessmen."[33] Often litigated matters result from business arrangements that have failed in some way, and the corporate managers shy away from them. Whether or not the corporate manager who oversees the litigation was personally responsible for the matter that is in litigation, he is unlikely to advance his career through association with that unhappy episode. Hence the tendency to leave the matter to the lawyers; if the case turns out unsuccessfully, the result can be blamed on them. Throughout the litigation the lawyers are likely to have to combat this tendency in order to prompt the client to take some responsibility for the conduct of the case. By shifting the responsibility for the outcome back to the client, advocates of the mini-trial argue, it can perform an important function. The process also directly involves the decision-makers who have settlement authority

---

[32] See Fine, The CPR Legal Program Mini-Trial Workbook (Center for Public Resources, now CPR Institute for Dispute Resolution, 1985).

[33] Olson, An Alternative for Large Case Dispute Resolution, 6 Litigation 22 (1980).

in the settlement process. The decision-makers may, for the first time, hear the weak points in their case when there is a summarized presentation of the evidence.

When mini-trial treatment is proposed, the parties may be expected to work out an agreement providing for specific procedures. For example, a Handbook prepared for the Center for Public Resources[34] lays out ground rules on presentations and includes a schedule calling for trial within six weeks, with only two weeks for discovery. The mini-trial itself is projected to last 2½ days: plaintiff's case-in-chief on the first afternoon, defendant's rebuttal and plaintiff's response on the following morning, defendant's case-in-chief on the second afternoon, and plaintiff's rebuttal and defendant's response on the second morning. Question and answer sessions for the neutral advisor are interspersed throughout, and the third afternoon is reserved for negotiations without the advisor. If a settlement is not reached, the advisor may be summoned back to participate in negotiations.

Advantages of the mini-trial include the flexibility for parties to select their own timetable, location, rules and procedures, and neutral advisor; the benefit of directing presentations to the decision-making officials; and the salutary role of a respected neutral advisor in being able to go beyond the power of a judge to ask questions and provide reality-testing. Minitrials still tend to be conducted by private organizations, like the CPR Institute for Dispute Resolution, and not pursuant to court order, although a number of local rules list the mini-trial among the authorized court-annexed ADR processes

C. OBLIGATION TO PARTICIPATE IN ADR SETTLEMENT PROCESSES

As ADR settlement procedures, particularly mediation, have increasingly provided an alternative to settlement conferences conducted by the judge, the question of mandatory participation and costs has arisen. *Heileman* found that Rule 16 provides authority for federal judges to require parties to attend pretrial settlement conferences with settlement authority. But the ADR devices we have just discussed are a little different from a judicial settlement conference. They involve a third-party neutral and contemplate some form of presentation of arguments, and perhaps evidence, which might go beyond what is expected in just a pretrial conference with a judge. Rule 16 was amended in 1993 to include in the list of proper subjects for discussion at a pretrial conference "settlement and the use of special procedures to assist in resolving the dispute when authorized by statute or local rule." The limitation "when authorized by state or local rule" might be read as an indication that "special procedures"

---

[34] E. Green, The CPR Legal Program Mini-Trial Handbooks in Corporate Dispute Management 111–14 (1981).

require more than just discussion in a settlement conference and therefore should be specifically authorized by statute or rule.

Court orders to participate in mediation, the least structured of the ADR processes, have been upheld against a variety of challenges. See Montgomery v. Louis Trauth Dairy, Inc., 164 F.R.D. 469 (S.D. Ohio 1996)(finding authority in Rule 16). These include claims of unconstitutionality (for example, that it forces parties to participate in an expensive process that detracts from their absolute right to a trial by jury) and lack of authority (that the judge or district court has not authorized the process). In In re Atlantic Pipe Corporation, 304 F.3d 135 (1st Cir. 2002), the First Circuit found that a local rule that only provided for mediation by a judicial officer did not authorize mediation before a private mediator. It also found that neither the ADR Act of 1998 (which authorized district courts to adopt ADR procedures) nor amended Rule 16 (that allowed use of special procedures to aid settlement) provided authority because both said the processes must be authorized by local court rule. However, it found inherent power in the district judge (reminiscent of the majority's position in *Heileman* to "order non-consensual mediation in those cases in which that step seems reasonably likely to serve the interests of justice":

Requiring the parties to pay for an ADR professional(s), even when referral is made by the court without the consent of the parties, was once controversial but has gradually become an accepted practice. In a summary jury trial, of course, the cost of the judge and jurors is borne by the court (as is the cost of the judge in a settlement conference). But other ADR devices—and particularly mediation—require a trained professional. Thirty years ago, mediators and court-annexed arbitrators often volunteered their services for little or no pay. In the formative years, ADR neutrals were generally satisfied with the honor of being listed on a federal district court panel and the opportunity to gain experience, but the picture is quite different today. Most district courts now authorize payments of ADR neutrals and place responsibility for neutrals' fees on the parties.

The justification for making mandatory a highly unstructured process like mediation rests in part on the fact that so little is required of the parties. They are not required to present evidence, make arguments, or engage in offers and counteroffers, but only to listen and attempt in good faith to settle.[35] But as the ADR processes move along a continuum toward more structured processes, there is more procedural formality which calls

---

[35] Court orders often provide that the parties will attend the mediation and "participate in good faith." The vagueness of that standard, its possible intrusion on the right of parties not to settle, and difficulty in applying sanctions to enforce it have been considerably discussed. Compare Sherman, Court-Mandated Alternative Dispute Resolution: What Form of Participation Should be Required?, 46 S.M.U.L.Rev. 2079, 2089–94 (1993) (proposing a "minimal meaningful participation" standard rather than "good faith") and Kovach, Lawyer Ethics in Mediation: Time for a Requirement of Good Faith, 4 Dispute Res. 9 (1997) (arguing that a good faith standard is necessary to accomplish the objectives of mediation).

on the parties to make presentations of evidence and arguments. The most structured process is the summary jury trial, which looks very much like a regular trial except that most of the evidence is presented in summarized form and rules of evidence are not generally enforced. Then the question arises as to whether a party can be required to put on a trial run of its case in a non-binding proceeding, when it would prefer to hold its ammunition for the real trial.

The Seventh Circuit in Strandell v. Jackson County, 838 F.2d 884 (7th Cir. 1987), held that a district judge does not possess inherent power to compel participation in a summary jury trial. The plaintiff's attorney objected that he would have to disclose work-product statements he had obtained from twenty-one witnesses which had been denied to defendants for failure to establish substantial need and undue hardship (see Rule 26(b)(3)). The court said mandatory participation in a summary jury trial would "affect seriously the well-established rules concerning discovery and work-product privilege."

The Sixth Circuit followed *Strandell* in In re NLO, Inc., 5 F.3d 154 (6th Cir. 1993), but other courts did not. See Federal Reserve Bank of Minneapolis v. Carey-Canada, Inc., 123 F.R.D. 603, 605 (D.Minn. 1988)(rejecting the Strandell concerns over adding cost without benefit and premature disclosure of one's case); In re Atlantic Pipe Corp., 304 F.3d 135 (1st Cir. 2002)(stating that compulsory ADR, in this case mediation, "could yield significant benefits even if one or more parties object").

D. INCENTIVES TO SETTLE THROUGH SHIFTING OF ATTORNEY'S FEES AND COSTS

MAREK V. CHESNY

Supreme Court of the United States, 1985
473 U.S. 1

CHIEF JUSTICE BURGER delivered the opinion of the Court.

We granted certiorari to decide whether attorney's fees incurred by a plaintiff subsequent to an offer of settlement under Federal Rule of Civil Procedure 68 must be paid by the defendant under 42 U.S.C. § 1988, when the plaintiff recovers a judgment less than the offer.

I

Petitioners, three police officers, in answering a call on a domestic disturbance, shot and killed respondent's adult son. Respondent, in his own behalf and as administrator of his son's estate, filed suit against the officers in the United States District Court under 42 U.S.C. § 1983 and state tort law.

Prior to trial, petitioners made a timely offer of settlement "for a sum, including costs now accrued and attorney's fees, of ONE HUNDRED THOUSAND ($100,000) DOLLARS." Respondent did not accept the offer. The case went to trial and respondent was awarded $5,000 on the state-law "wrongful death" claim, $52,000 for the § 1983 violation, and $3,000 in punitive damages.

Respondent filed a request for $171,692.47 in costs, including attorney's fees. This amount included costs incurred after the settlement offer. Petitioners opposed the claim for post-offer costs, relying on Federal Rule of Civil Procedure 68, which shifts to the plaintiff all "costs" incurred subsequent to an offer of judgment not exceeded by the ultimate recovery at trial. Petitioners argued that attorney's fees are part of the "costs" covered by Rule 68. The District Court agreed with petitioners and declined to award respondent "costs, including attorney's fees, incurred after the offer of judgment." The parties subsequently agreed that $32,000 fairly represented the allowable costs, including attorney's fees, accrued prior to petitioner's offer of settlement.[1] Respondent appealed the denial of post-offer costs.

The Court of Appeals reversed. The court rejected what it termed the "rather mechanical linking up of Rule 68 and section 1988." It stated that the District Court's reading of Rule 68 and § 1988, while "in a sense logical," would put civil rights plaintiffs and counsel in a "predicament" that "cuts against the grain of section 1988." Plaintiffs' attorneys, the court reasoned, would be forced to "think very hard" before rejecting even an inadequate offer, and would be deterred from bringing good faith actions because of the prospect of losing the right to attorney's fees if a settlement offer more favorable than the ultimate recovery were rejected. The court concluded that "[t]he legislators who enacted section 1988 would not have wanted its effectiveness blunted because of a little known rule of court."

We granted certiorari. We reverse.

II

Rule 68 provides that if a timely pretrial offer of settlement is not accepted and "the judgment finally obtained by the offeree is not more favorable than the offer, the offeree must pay *the costs incurred after the making of the offer*." Fed.Rule Civ.Proc. 68 (emphasis added)[This rule language has been revised slightly. Eds.] The plain purpose of Rule 68 is to encourage settlement and avoid litigation. Delta Air Lines, Inc. v. August, 450 U.S. 346 (1981). The Rule prompts both parties to a suit to evaluate the risks and costs of litigation, and to balance them against the likelihood of success upon trial on the merits. This case requires us to decide whether the offer in this case was a proper one under Rule 68, and whether the term

---

[1]   The District Court refused to shift to respondent any costs accrued by petitioners. Petitioners do not contest that ruling.

"costs" as used in Rule 68 includes attorney's fees awardable under 42 U.S.C. § 1988.

A

The first question we address is whether petitioners' offer was valid under Rule 68. Respondent contends that the offer was invalid because it lumped petitioners' proposal for damages with their proposal for costs. Respondent argues that Rule 68 requires that an offer must separately recite the amount that the defendant is offering in settlement of the substantive claim and the amount he is offering to cover accrued costs. Only if the offer is bifurcated, he contends, so that it is clear how much the defendant is offering for the substantive claim, can a plaintiff possibly assess whether it would be wise to accept the offer. * * *

If defendants are not allowed to make lump sum offers that would, if accepted, represent their total liability, they would understandably be reluctant to make settlement offers. As the Court of Appeals observed, "many a defendant would be unwilling to make a binding settlement offer on terms that left it exposed to liability for attorney's fees in whatever amount the court might fix on motion of the plaintiff."

Contrary to respondent's suggestion, reading the Rule in this way does not frustrate plaintiffs' efforts to determine whether defendants' offers are adequate. At the time an offer is made, the plaintiff knows the amount in damages caused by the challenged conduct. The plaintiff also knows, or can ascertain, the costs then accrued. A reasonable determination whether to accept the offer can be made by simply adding these two figures and comparing the sum to the amount offered. Respondent is troubled that a plaintiff will not know whether the offer on the substantive claim would be exceeded at trial, but this is so whenever an offer of settlement is made. In any event, requiring itemization of damages separate from costs would not in any way help plaintiffs know in advance whether the judgment at trial will exceed a defendant's offer.

* * *

B

The second question we address is whether the term "costs" in Rule 68 includes attorney's fees awardable under 42 U.S.C. § 1988. By the time the Federal Rules of Civil Procedure were adopted in 1938, federal statutes had authorized and defined awards of costs to prevailing parties for more than 85 years. See generally Alyeska Pipeline Service Co. v. Wilderness Society, 421 U.S. 240 (1975). Unlike in England, such "costs" generally had not included attorney's fees; under the "American Rule," each party had been required to bear its own attorney's fees. The "American Rule" as applied in federal courts, however, had become subject to certain exceptions by the late 1930's. Some of these exceptions had evolved as a product of the "inherent power in the courts to allow attorney's fees in particular situations." But most of the exceptions were found in federal statutes that directed courts to award attorney's fees as part of costs in particular cases.

Section 407 of the Communications Act of 1934, for example, provided in relevant part that, "[i]f the petitioner shall finally prevail, he shall be allowed a reasonable attorney's fee, to be taxed and collected as a part of the costs of the suit." 47 U.S.C. § 407. There was identical language in Section 3(p) of the Railway Labor Act, 45 U.S.C. § 153(p) (1934 ed.). Section 40 of the Copyright Act of 1909, 17 U.S.C. § 40 (1934 ed.), allowed a court to "award to the prevailing party a reasonable attorney's fee as part of the costs." And other statutes contained similar provisions that included attorney's fees as part of awardable "costs." See, e.g., the Clayton Act, 15 U.S.C. § 15 (1934 ed.); the Securities Act of 1933, 15 U.S.C. § 77k(e) (1934 ed.); the Securities Exchange Act of 1934, 15 U.S.C. §§ 78i(e), 78r(a) (1934 ed.).

The authors of Federal Rule of Civil Procedure 68 were fully aware of these exceptions to the American Rule. The Advisory Committee's Note to Rule 54(d) contains an extensive list of the federal statutes which allowed for costs in particular cases; of the 25 "statutes as to costs" set forth in the final paragraph of the Note, no fewer than 11 allowed for attorney's fees as part of costs. Against this background of varying definitions of "costs," the drafters of Rule 68 did not define the term; nor is there any explanation whatever as to its intended meaning in the history of the Rule.

In this setting, given the importance of "costs" to the Rule, it is very unlikely that this omission was mere oversight; on the contrary, the most reasonable inference is that the term "costs" in Rule 68 was intended to refer to all costs properly awardable under the relevant substantive statute or other authority. In other words, all costs properly awardable in an action are to be considered within the scope of Rule 68 "costs." Thus, absent Congressional expressions to the contrary, where the underlying statute defines "costs" to include attorney's fees, we are satisfied such fees are to be included as costs for purposes of Rule 68.

Here, respondents sued under 42 U.S.C. § 1983. Pursuant to the Civil Rights Attorney's Fees Awards Act of 1976, 42 U.S.C. § 1988, a prevailing party in a § 1983 action may be awarded attorney's fees "as part of the costs." Since Congress expressly included attorney's fees as "costs" available to a plaintiff in a § 1983 suit, such fees are subject to the cost-shifting provision of Rule 68. This "plain meaning" interpretation of the interplay between Rule 68 and § 1988 is the only construction that gives meaning to each word in both Rule 68 and § 1988.[2]

---

[2] Respondents suggest that Roadway Express, Inc. v. Piper, 447 U.S. 752 (1980), requires a different result. *Roadway Express,* however, is not relevant to our decision today. In *Roadway,* attorney's fees were sought as part of costs under 28 U.S.C. § 1927, which allows the imposition of costs as a penalty on attorneys for vexatiously multiplying litigation. We held in *Roadway Express* that § 1927 came with its own statutory definition of costs, and that this definition did not include

Unlike the Court of Appeals, we do not believe that this "plain meaning" construction of the statute and the Rule will frustrate Congress' objective in § 1988 of ensuring that civil rights plaintiffs obtain "effective access to the judicial process." Merely subjecting civil rights plaintiffs to the settlement provision of Rule 68 does not curtail their access to the courts, or significantly deter them from bringing suit. Application of Rule 68 will serve as a disincentive for the plaintiff's attorney to continue litigation after the defendant makes a settlement offer. There is no evidence, however, that Congress, in considering § 1988, had any thought that civil rights claims were to be on any different footing from other civil claims insofar as settlement is concerned. Indeed, Congress made clear its concern that civil rights plaintiffs not be penalized for "helping to lessen docket congestion" by settling their cases out of court. See H.R.Rep.No. 94–1588, p. 7 (1976).

Moreover, Rule 68's policy of encouraging settlements is neutral, favoring neither plaintiffs nor defendants; it expresses a clear policy of favoring settlement of all lawsuits. Civil rights plaintiffs—along with other plaintiffs—who reject an offer more favorable than what is thereafter recovered at trial will not recover attorney's fees for services performed after the offer is rejected. But, since the Rule is neutral, many civil rights plaintiffs will benefit from the offers of settlement encouraged by Rule 68. Some plaintiffs will receive compensation in settlement where, on trial, they might not have recovered, or would have recovered less than what was offered. And, even for those who would prevail at trial, settlement will provide them with compensation at an earlier date without the burdens, stress, and time of litigation. In short, settlements rather than litigation will serve the interests of plaintiffs as well as defendants.

To be sure, application of Rule 68 will require plaintiffs to "think very hard" about whether continued litigation is worthwhile; that is precisely what Rule 68 contemplates. This effect of Rule 68, however, is in no sense inconsistent with the congressional policies underlying § 1983 and § 1988. Section 1988 authorizes courts to award only "reasonable" attorney's fees to prevailing parties. In Hensley v. Eckerhart, 461 U.S. 424 (1983), we held that "the most critical factor" in determining a reasonable fee "is the degree of success obtained." We specifically noted that prevailing at trial "may say little about whether the expenditure of counsel's time was reasonable in relation to the success achieved." In a case where a rejected settlement offer exceeds the ultimate recovery, the plaintiff—although technically the prevailing party—has not received any monetary benefits from the post-offer services of his attorney. This case presents a good example: the $139,692 in post-offer legal services resulted in a recovery $8,000 less than petitioner's settlement offer. Given Congress' focus on the success achieved,

---

attorney's fees. The critical distinction here is that Rule 68 does not come with a definition of costs; rather, it incorporates the definition of costs that otherwise applies to the case.

we are not persuaded that shifting the post-offer costs to respondent in these circumstances would in any sense thwart its intent under § 1988.

Rather than "cutting against the grain" of § 1988, as the Court of Appeals held, we are convinced that applying Rule 68 in the context of a § 1983 action is consistent with the policies and objectives of § 1988. Section 1988 encourages plaintiffs to bring meritorious civil rights suits; Rule 68 simply encourages settlements. There is nothing incompatible in these two objectives.

[Concurring opinions of JUSTICES POWELL and REHNQUIST omitted.]

JUSTICE BRENNAN, with whom JUSTICE MARSHALL and JUSTICE BLACKMUN join, dissenting.

The question presented by this case is whether the term "costs" as it is used in Rule 68 of the Federal Rules of Civil Procedure and elsewhere throughout the Rules refers simply to those taxable costs defined in 28 U.S.C. § 1920 and traditionally understood as "costs"—court's fees, printing expenses, and the like—or instead includes attorney's fees when an underlying fees-award statute happens to refer to fees "as part of" the awardable costs. Relying on what it recurrently emphasizes is the "plain language" of one such statute, 42 U.S.C. § 1988,[3] the Court today holds that a prevailing civil-rights litigant entitled to fees under that statute is per se barred by Rule 68 from recovering any fees for work performed after rejecting a settlement offer where he ultimately recovers less than the proffered amount in settlement.

I dissent. The Court's reasoning is wholly inconsistent with the history and structure of the Federal Rules, and its application to the over 100 attorney's fees statutes enacted by Congress will produce absurd variations in Rule 68's operation based on nothing more than picayune differences in statutory phraseology. Neither Congress nor the drafters of the Rules could possibly have intended such inexplicable variations in settlement incentives. Moreover, the Court's interpretation will "seriously undermine the purposes behind the attorney's fees provisions" of the civil-rights laws, Delta Air Lines, Inc. v. August, 450 U.S. 346 (1981) (REHNQUIST, J., dissenting)—provisions imposed by Congress pursuant to § 5 of the Fourteenth Amendment. * * *

The Court's "plain language" analysis goes as follows: Section 1988 provides that a "prevailing party" may recover "a reasonable attorney's fee as part of the costs." Rule 68 in turn provides that, where an offeree obtains a judgment for less than the amount of a previous settlement offer, "the offeree must pay the costs incurred after the making of the offer." Because

---

[3]   Civil Rights Attorney's Fees Awards Act of 1976, 42 U.S.C. § 1988. That section provides in relevant part that "[i]n any action or proceeding to enforce a provision of sections 1981, 1982, 1983, 1985, and 1986 of this title, title IX of Public Law 92–318, or title VI of the Civil Rights Act of 1964, the court, in its discretion, may allow the prevailing party, other than the United States, a reasonable attorney's fee as part of the costs."

"attorney's fees" are "costs," the Court concludes, the "plain meaning" of Rule 68 per se prohibits a prevailing civil-rights plaintiff from recovering fees incurred after he rejected the proposed out-of-court settlement.

The Court's "plain language" approach is, as Judge Posner's opinion for the court below noted, "in a sense logical." However, while the starting point in interpreting statutes and rules is always the plain words themselves, "[t]he particular inquiry is not what is the abstract force of the words or what they may comprehend, but in what sense were they intended to be understood or what understanding they convey when used in the particular act." [2A C. Sands, Sutherland on Statutory Construction § 46.07, p. 110.] We previously have been confronted with "superficially appealing argument[s]" strikingly similar to those adopted by the Court today, and we have found that they "cannot survive careful consideration." Roadway Express, Inc. v. Piper, 447 U.S. 752 (1980). So here.

In *Roadway Express*, the petitioner argued that under 28 U.S.C. § 1927,[6] "costs" should be interpreted to include attorney's fees when the underlying fees-award statute provided for fees "as part of the costs." We rejected that argument, concluding that "costs" as it was used in § 1927 had a well-settled meaning limited to the traditional taxable items of costs set forth in 28 U.S.C. § 1920. * * *

The Court today restricts its discussion of *Roadway* to a single footnote, urging that that case "is not relevant to our decision" because "section 1927 came with its own statutory definition of costs" whereas "Rule 68 does not come with a definition of costs." But this purported "distinction" merely begs the question. As in *Roadway,* the question we face is whether a cost-shifting provision "come[s] with a definition of costs"—that set forth in § 1920 in an effort "to standardize the treatment of costs in federal courts"—or instead may vary wildly in meaning depending on the phraseology of the underlying fees-award statute. The parties' arguments in this case and in *Roadway* are virtually interchangeable, and our analysis is not much advanced simply by the conclusory statement that the cases are different.

For a number of reasons, "costs" as that term is used in the Federal Rules should be interpreted uniformly in accordance with the definition of costs set forth in § 1920:

First. The limited history of the costs provisions in the Federal Rules suggests that the drafters intended "costs" to mean only taxable costs traditionally allowed under the common law or pursuant to the statutory predecessor of § 1920. Nowhere was it suggested that the meaning of taxable "costs" might vary from case to case depending on the language of

---

[6]   That section provided that any attorney "who so multiplies the proceedings in any case as to increase costs unreasonably and vexatiously may be required by the court to satisfy personally such excess costs." The section was amended after *Roadway Express* to require the payment of "excess costs, expenses, and attorneys' fees reasonably incurred because of such conduct."

the substantive statute involved—a practice that would have cut against the drafters' intent to create uniform procedures applicable to "every action" in federal court. Fed.Rule Civ.Proc. 1.

Second. The Rules provide that "costs" may automatically be taxed by the clerk of the court on one day's notice, Fed. Rule Civ. Proc. 54(d)— strongly suggesting that "costs" were intended to refer only to those routine, readily determinable charges that could appropriately be left to a clerk, and as to which a single day's notice of settlement would be appropriate. Attorney's fees, which are awardable only by the court and which frequently entail lengthy disputes and hearings, obviously do not fall within that category.

Third. When particular provisions of the Federal Rules are intended to encompass attorney's fees, they do so explicitly. Eleven different provisions of the Rules authorize a court to award attorney's fees as "expenses" in particular circumstances, demonstrating that the drafters knew the difference, and intended a difference, between "costs," "expenses," and "attorney's fees."

Fourth. With the exception of one recent Court of Appeals opinion and two recent District Court opinions, the Court can point to no authority suggesting that courts or attorneys have ever viewed the cost-shifting provisions of Rule 68 as including attorney's fees. Yet Rule 68 has been in effect for 47 years, and potentially could have been applied to numerous fee statutes during this time. "The fact that the defense bar did not develop a practice of seeking" to shift or reduce fees under Rule 68 "is persuasive evidence that trial lawyers have interpreted the Rule in accordance with" the definition of costs in § 1920. Delta Air Lines, Inc. v. August, 450 U.S., at 360.

Fifth. We previously have held that words and phrases in the Federal Rules must be given a consistent usage and be read *in pari materia,* reasoning that to do otherwise would "attribute a schizophrenic intent to the drafters." Applying the Court's "plain language" approach consistently throughout the Rules, however, would produce absurd results that would turn statutes like § 1988 on their heads. * * * For example, Rule 54(d) provides that "costs shall be allowed as of course to the prevailing party unless the court otherwise directs."* Similarly, the plain language of Rule 68 provides that a plaintiff covered by the Rule "must pay the costs incurred after the making of the offer"—language requiring the plaintiff to bear both his post-offer costs and the defendant's post-offer costs. If "costs" as used in these provisions were interpreted to include attorney's fees by virtue of the wording of § 1988, losing civil-rights plaintiffs would be required by the "plain language" of Rule 54(d) to pay the defendant's attorney's fees, and prevailing plaintiffs falling within Rule 68 would be required to bear the defendant's post-offer attorney's fees.

* * * If the word "costs" does subsume attorney's fees, this "would alter fundamentally the nature of" civil-rights attorney's fee legislation. Roadway Express, Inc. v. Piper, 447 U.S., at 762. To avoid this extreme result while still interpreting Rule 68 to include fees in some circumstances, however, the Court would have to "select on an ad hoc basis those features of § 1988 . . . that should be read into" Rule 68—a process of construction that would constitute nothing short of "standardless judicial lawmaking."[16]

Sixth. As with all of the Federal Rules, the drafters intended Rule 68 to have a uniform, consistent application in all proceedings in federal court. In accordance with this intent, Rule 68 should be interpreted to provide uniform, consistent incentives "to encourage the settlement of litigation." Delta Air Lines, Inc. v. August, supra, 450 U.S., at 352. Yet today's decision will lead to dramatically different settlement incentives depending on minor variations in the phraseology of the underlying fees-award statutes—distinctions that would appear to be nothing short of irrational and for which the Court has no plausible explanation.

Congress has enacted well over 100 attorney's fees statutes, many of which would appear to be affected by today's decision. As the Appendix to this dissent [listing these statutes] illustrates, Congress has employed a variety of slightly different wordings in these statutes. It sometimes has referred to the awarding of "attorney's fees as part of the costs," to "costs including attorney's fees," and to "attorney's fees and other litigation costs." Under the "plain language" approach of today's decision, Rule 68 will operate to include the potential loss of otherwise-recoverable attorney's fees as an incentive to settlement in litigation under these statutes. But Congress frequently has referred in other statutes to the awarding of "costs and a reasonable attorney's fee," of "costs together with a reasonable attorney's fee," or simply of "attorney's fees" without reference to costs. Under the Court's "plain language" analysis, Rule 68 obviously will not include the potential loss of otherwise-recoverable attorney's fees as a settlement incentive in litigation under these statutes because they do not refer to fees "as" costs.

The result is to sanction a senseless patchwork of fee-shifting that flies in the face of the fundamental purpose of the Federal Rules—the provision of uniform and consistent procedure in federal courts. Such a construction will "introduce into [Rule 68] distinctions unrelated to its goal . . . and [will]

---

[16] It also might be argued that a defendant may not recover post-offer attorney's fees under the "plain language" of Rule 68 because he is not the "prevailing party" within the meaning of § 1988. We have made clear, however, that a party may "prevail" under § 1988 on some elements of the litigation but not on others. Thus while the plaintiff would prevail for purposes of preoffer fees, the defendant could be viewed as the prevailing party for purposes of the postoffer fees. Shifting fees to the defendant in such circumstances would plainly violate § 1988 for the reasons set forth above in text, and the substantive standards of § 1988 must therefore override the otherwise "plain language" approach taken by the Court.

result in virtually random application of the Rule." Roadway Express, Inc. v. Piper, supra, 447 U.S., at 761–762. * * *

Although the Court's opinion fails to discuss any of the problems reviewed above, it does devote some space to arguing that its interpretation of Rule 68 "is in no sense inconsistent with the Congressional policies underlying § 1983 and § 1988." The Court goes so far as to assert that its interpretation fits in smoothly with § 1988 as interpreted by Hensley v. Eckerhart, 461 U.S. 424 (1983).

The Court is wrong. Congress has instructed that attorney's fee entitlement under § 1988 be governed by a reasonableness standard. Until today the Court always has recognized that this standard precludes reliance on any mechanical "bright-line" rules automatically denying a portion of fees, acknowledging that such "mathematical approach[es]" provide "little aid in determining what is a reasonable fee in light of all the relevant factors." Although the starting point is always "the number of hours reasonably expended on the litigation," this "does not end the inquiry": a number of considerations set forth in the legislative history of § 1988 "may lead the district court to adjust the fee upward or downward." We also have emphasized that the district court "necessarily has discretion in making this equitable judgment" because of its "superior understanding of the litigation." Section 1988's reasonableness standard is, in sum, "acutely sensitive to the merits of an action and to antidiscrimination policy." Roadway Express, Inc. v. Piper, 447 U.S., at 762.

Rule 68, on the other hand, is not "sensitive" at all to the merits of an action and to antidiscrimination policy. It is a mechanical *per se* provision automatically shifting "costs" incurred after an offer is rejected, and it deprives a district court of all discretion with respect to the matter by using "the strongest verb of its type known to the English language—'must.'" Delta Air Lines, Inc. v. August, 450 U.S., at 369. The potential for conflict between § 1988 and Rule 68 could not be more apparent.[40]

Of course, a civil-rights plaintiff who unreasonably fails to accept a settlement offer, and who thereafter recovers less than the proffered amount in settlement, is barred under § 1988 itself from recovering fees for unproductive work performed in the wake of the rejection. This is because "the extent of a plaintiff's success is a crucial factor in determining the proper amount of an award of attorney's fees," hours that are "excessive, redundant, or otherwise unnecessary" must be excluded from that calculus. To this extent, the results might sometimes be the same under either § 1988's reasonableness inquiry or the Court's wooden application of Rule 68. Had the Court allowed the Seventh Circuit's remand in the instant case

---

[40] It might be argued that Rule 68's offer-of-judgment provisions merely serve to define one aspect of "reasonableness" within the meaning of Hensley v. Eckerhart, supra. This argument is foreclosed by Congress' rejection of *per se* "mathematical approach[es]" that would "end the inquiry" without allowing consideration of "all the relevant factors."

to stand, for example, the District Court after conducting the appropriate inquiry might well have determined that much or even all of the respondent's post offer fees were not properly awardable.

But the results under § 1988 and Rule 68 will not always be congruent, because § 1988 mandates the careful consideration of a broad range of other factors and accords appropriate leeway to the district court's informed discretion. Contrary to the Court's protestations, it is not at all clear that "[t]his case presents a good example" of the smooth interplay of § 1988 and Rule 68, because there has never been an evidentiary consideration of the reasonableness or unreasonableness of the respondent's fee request. It is clear, however, that under the Court's interpretation of Rule 68 a plaintiff who ultimately recovers only slightly less than the proffered amount in settlement will *per se* be barred from recovering trial fees even if he otherwise "has obtained excellent results" in litigation that will have far-reaching benefit to the public interest. Today's decision necessarily will require the disallowance of some fees that otherwise would have passed muster under § 1988's reasonableness standard,[41] and there is nothing in § 1988's legislative history even vaguely suggesting that Congress intended such a result.

* * *

Other difficulties will follow from the Court's decision. For example, if a plaintiff recovers less money than was offered before trial but obtains potentially far-reaching injunctive or declaratory relief, it is altogether unclear how the Court intends judges to go about quantifying the "value" of the plaintiff's success.[48] * * * These are difficult policy questions, and I do not mean to suggest that stronger settlement incentives would necessarily conflict with the effective enforcement of the civil-rights laws. But contrary to the Court's 4-paragraph discussion, the policy considerations do not all point in one direction, and the question of whether and to what extent attorney's fees should be included within Rule 68 has provoked sharp debate in Congress, on the Advisory Committee on the Federal Rules, and among commentators. The Court has offered up some

---

[41] Indeed, the "plain language" of § 1988 authorizes the inclusion as "costs" only of those attorney's fees that have been determined to be "reasonable," so the cost-shifting provisions of Rule 68 necessarily will come into play only with respect to reasonable attorney's fees.

[48] For example, a plaintiff who is unable to prove actual damages at trial and recovers only nominal damages of $1, but who nevertheless demonstrates the unconstitutionality of the challenged practice and obtains an injunction, is surely a "prevailing party" within the meaning of § 1988. If the plaintiff had earlier rejected an offer of $500 to "get rid" of the controversy, the damages portion of his suit will fall within Rule 68 as interpreted by today's decision. Yet we previously have emphasized that "a plaintiff who failed to recover damages but obtained injunctive relief, or vice versa, may recover a fee award based on all hours reasonably expended if the relief obtained justified that expenditure of attorney time." Hensley v. Eckerhart, supra, 461 U.S., at 435–436, n. 11. Although courts must therefore evaluate the "value" of nonpecuniary relief before deciding whether the "judgment" was "more favorable than the offer" within the meaning of Rule 68, the uncertainty in making such assessments surely will add pressures on a plaintiff to settle his suit even if by doing so he abandons an opportunity to obtain potentially far-reaching nonmonetary relief—a discouraging incentive entirely at odds with Congress' intent.

interesting arguments based on an economic analysis of settlement incentives and aggregate results. But I believe Judge Posner had the better of this argument in concluding that the incentives created by interpreting Rule 68 in its current form to include attorney's fees would "cu[t] against the grain of section 1988," and that in any event a modification of Rule 68 to encompass fees is for Congress, not the courts.

NOTES AND QUESTIONS

1. In *Marek* the Court assumes that the goal of Rule 68 is to promote settlement. Bone, "To Encourage Settlement": Rule 68, Offers of Judgment, and the History of the Federal Rules of Civil Procedure, 102 Nwn. U. L. Rev. 1561 (2008), argues that the conventional view of Rule 68 is wrong. The state rules on which Rule 68 was based "were designed to prevent plaintiffs from imposing costs unfairly when the defendant offered what the plaintiff was entitled to receive from trial, and to enable defendants to avoid paying those costs when the plaintiff persisted with the suit. The text of Rule 68 makes much more sense when it is viewed in these fairness terms. The current interpretation of Rule 68 as a settlement promotion tool became entrenched in the 1970s and 1980s when concerns about litigation costs, case backlogs, and litigation delays produced an intense interest in settling cases." Id. at 1562.

Would a rule promoting settlement be desirable? Other researchers found that, by requiring that defendants consent to entry of judgment, current Rule 68 actually deters defendants from making qualifying offers. See Lewis & Eaton, Rule 68 Offers of Judgment: The Practices and Opinions of Experienced Civil Rights and Employment Discrimination Attorneys, 241 F.R.D. 332 (2007). They proposed that a new rule be adopted to promote settlement offers by both plaintiffs and defendants. See Lewis & Eaton, The Contours of a New FRCP, Rule 68.1: A Proposed Two-Way Offer of Settlement Provision for Federal Fee-Shifting Cases, 252 F.R.D. 551 (2009).

2. *Marek* should be read against the backdrop of the American rule that the prevailing party is not entitled to recover attorney's fees from the loser, as we have seen in Chapter 2, supra pp. 102–103 n. 1. That rule is reflected in Rule 54(d), which provides that only costs as described in 28 U.S.C.A. § 1920 (which does not include attorney's fees) are ordinarily recoverable by the prevailing party.

3. What is the effect of the American rule on settlement of cases? Does it cause parties who are confident of success nevertheless to settle for a reduced amount to avoid incurring further litigation costs? If so, is that a good thing? In England, where bilateral fee shifting is routine, it is not designed to offer full indemnity. Instead, "policymakers were concerned that giving full control over the accumulation of costs to the successful party would produce unfair and excessive fees. Requiring the loser to pay the full amount of fees might encourage the winner to prolong the litigation; on the other hand, requiring the winner to absorb a portion of the fees might encourage settlement or, at least, serve as a brake against dilatory tactics, harassment, or other abusive

litigation practices." Tomkins & Willging, Taxation of Attorneys' Fees: Practices in English, Alaskan and Federal Courts 7–8 (1986).

4.   Fee-shifting statutes like 42 U.S.C.A. § 1988 alter the American rule by providing that the prevailing party can recover attorneys' fees. Section 1988 has been interpreted to direct a pro-plaintiff attitude toward fee-shifting, making recovery of fees by plaintiffs routine, but allowing defendants to recover fees only if plaintiff sues without valid grounds or frivolously. Other fee-shifting statutes have been read to be bilateral and permit winning plaintiffs and defendants equal opportunities to recover fees. See Fogerty v. Fantasy, Inc., 510 U.S. 51 (1994) (refusing to find a pro-plaintiff bias in the fee-shifting provisions of the Copyright Act, 17 U.S.C.A. § 505).

5.   What happens when there is a verdict for the defendant? In Delta Air Lines, Inc. v. August, 450 U.S. 346 (1981), the Court held that "the plain language of Rule 68 confines its effects to * * * [cases] in which the plaintiff has obtained a judgment" which is not more favorable than the offer of judgment. Thus, Rule 68 is not applicable if the judgment is for the defendant. "There is irony in this interpretation of Rule 68: a plaintiff who suffers a defendant's judgment at trial might end up better off under the attorney's fee shifting provision than if there had been a plaintiff's verdict that was less favorable than the offer that the plaintiff turned down. The virtue of this literal interpretation of the rule, however, is to prevent defendants from making token, rather than serious, offers for small amounts (say $1) in order to invoke cost shifting in every case that results in a defendant's verdict. For this reason, proposals to change Rule 68 generally have chosen to leave the Delta interpretation intact." Sherman, From "Loser Pays" to Modified Offer of Judgment Rules, 76 Tex. L. Rev. 1863, 1881 (1998). Note that a plaintiff who obtains a verdict on liability, but receives no damages, may still have to pay Rule 68 costs. See Tunison v. Continental Airlines Corp., 162 F.3d 1187 (D.C.Cir.1998) (although no damages were awarded, plaintiff was required to pay defendant's post-offer costs because plaintiff refused a Rule 68 offer and obtained a verdict).

6.   In Marek, Justice Brennan relied heavily on Roadway Express, Inc. v. Piper, 447 U.S. 752 (1980), which held that the word "costs" in 28 U.S.C.A. § 1927 (which authorized imposition of "costs" on attorneys whose tactics unduly prolong or complicate litigation) did not include attorney's fees. The majority says that this case is distinguishable because § 1927 "came with its own statutory definition of costs." But in Roadway Express, Justice Powell, writing for the Court, said that "[s]ection 1927 * * * does not define the critical word. Only if 'costs' includes attorneys fees can § 1927 support the sanction in this case." Since costs were not understood to include fees in 1813, when the original version of § 1927 was enacted, the Court held that attorney fees were not included in the term.

7.   Inconsistent interpretations of other statutes as to whether the word "costs" was intended to include attorney fees raise doubts as to the certainty of the Marek majority based on textual language. For example, Rule 41(d) provides that if a plaintiff who previously dismissed an action files an action

based on the same claim against the same defendant, "the court may order the plaintiff to pay all or part of the costs of that previous action." The circuit and district courts have reached varying conclusions as to whether the word "costs" includes attorney's fees. Compare Meredith v. Stovall, 216 F.3d 1087 (10th Cir. 2000) (finding no abuse of discretion in district court's award of attorney's fees pursuant to Rule 41(d)), and Evans v. Safeway Stores, Inc., 623 F.2d 121, 122 (8th Cir.1980) (affirming a Rule 41(d) award of attorney's fees without substantive discussion), with Esposito v. Piatrowski, 223 F.3d 497, 501 (7th Cir.2000) (holding that a party may recover reasonable attorney's fees as part of its "costs" under Rule 41(d) only where the underlying statute defines costs to include attorney's fees), and Rogers v. Wal-Mart Stores, Inc., 230 F.3d 868, 875 (6th Cir.2000) (vacating Rule 41(d) award of attorney's fees, because they are not expressly provided for by the rule).

8. In TM, LLC v. Anderson, 2012 WL 4483180 (E.D.N.C.), the defendant sought to recover his attorney fees of $61,000 because the plaintiff had previously dismissed the case without prejudice. The court stated that "plaintiff's dismissal of one suit in search of a more favorable ruling in another court is precisely the type of forum shopping conduct that Rule 41(d) was enacted to address." However, it noted that the plain language of the rule provided only for an award of "costs" and that "the law generally recognizes a difference between the terms 'costs' and 'attorney's fees.'" It declined to extend *Marek to* Rule 41(d). "To award attorney's fees under Rule 41(d), only when a party would be entitled to recover them as costs in the cause of action underlying the first dismissed suit, serves the remedial purpose of the Rule without offense to the long standing principle that, absent Congressional intent, attorney's fees are not recoverable costs." Since attorney's fees are not recoverable under the state Uniform Fraudulent Transfer Act on which the claim was based, the defendant could not recover its attorney's fees.

9. Should Rule 68 be interpreted to allow losing defendants in civil rights cases to recover their own attorney's fees if they made Rule 68 offers more favorable than the judgment won by the plaintiff? How would you argue against that result? See Crossman v. Marcoccio, 806 F.2d 329 (1st Cir.1986), cert. denied, 481 U.S. 1029 (1987) (defendant's fees not shifted because they were not "properly awardable").

10. *Marek* was viewed by the plaintiff's bar, and particularly the pro bono and civil rights bar, as a backdoor way to deny prevailing plaintiffs their attorney's fees. Consider this strategic use of Rule 68 by defendants: "A defendant can put the plaintiff's recovery of his attorney's fees in jeopardy by making a lump sum offer and specifying that this sum is intended to include costs. The dilemma of a plaintiff's lawyer in such a situation can be intense: Any statutory attorney's fees the plaintiff might recover can be a negotiable item on the table, and his client, who has no liability for those statutory fee amounts if not awarded, has discretion to accept or reject the settlement offer." Sherman, supra note 5, 76 Tex. L. Rev. at 1878–79. Evans v. Jeff D., 475 U.S. 717 (1986), intensified this dilemma. There the defendant offered to settle only if the plaintiff's lawyer waived his statutory fees altogether, but offered terms

very favorable to the client. The Supreme Court held that a settlement offer may link the relief on the merits to a waiver of statutory attorneys' fees, confirming "the possibility of a tradeoff between merits relief and attorney's fees." Do these decisions improperly discourage access to the courts?

11. Rule 68 applies only if the judgment eventually obtained by plaintiff is "not more favorable" than the offer. If plaintiff seeks money, as in *Marek,* the comparison is relatively simple. But real difficulties can emerge in cases seeking equitable relief. Consider Reiter v. MTA New York City Transit Auth., 457 F.3d 224 (2d Cir. 2006), in which plaintiff made a Title VII claim after he was demoted from his position as Deputy Vice President of Engineering Services. In that position, he was one of thirteen senior executives who reported directly to the Senior Vice-President and had eight senior executives reporting to him. He got a corner office with a front view of Manhattan. After his demotion, he was assigned to one of the smallest of defendant's departments, had no staff, and nobody reported to him. He claimed that his demotion was retaliation for complaints about bias, and sought monetary relief and restoration to his former job. Before trial, defendants made a Rule 68 offer of $20,001 plus attorney's fees accrued to date, but no restoration of defendant's job. Plaintiff did not accept the offer, and at trial won a verdict of $140,000 and restoration to his former job. The district court granted defendants' motion for a new trial, however, unless plaintiff accepted a remittitur of the monetary award to only $10,000. Plaintiff accepted the remittitur, and the district court then denied attorney's fees for the work done after rejection of the Rule 68 offer on the ground that the equitable relief restoring plaintiff to his former job had "no significant value."

The court of appeals reversed, finding the conclusion that restoration to the former job had no significant value to be clearly erroneous. In its view, defendant bore the burden of showing that the offer was more favorable than the ultimate judgment, and failed because restoring plaintiff to his former position was "of considerable importance under Title VII's remedial framework." Finding that the lower court's assumption was that the restoration to his former job was worth less than the $10,001 difference between the offer and the monetary relief rewarded, the court explained:

> We have no difficulty concluding that any senior executive worthy of the title * * * would, at a moment's notice, exchange a job with no staff, no budget, no direct reports, and a work force of ten for a job with 900 employees and eight senior direct reports in a department with a billion-dollar budget. Further, we have no difficulty opining that any such rational executive would more likely than not jump at the chance if it were priced at just $10,000—an amount totaling less than 10% of a single year's salary. In sum, while monetizing equitable relief will, in many instances, pose vexing problems * * * we have little difficulty concluding that Reiter ultimately recovered more than the Offer and that, consequently, it did not cut off his entitlement to post-Offer attorneys' fees.

Compare Leach v. Northern Telecom, Inc., 141 F.R.D. 420, 428 (E.D.N.C. 1991) ("If the monetary relief awarded falls short of that offered, but equitable relief is also awarded, the trial judge can then determine whether the relief awarded, as a package, is more or less favorable than that offered."). See also Note, Federal Rule 68 Offers of Judgment and Equitable Relief: Where Angels Fear To Tread, 70 Tex. L. Rev. 465 (1991).

12. The Civil Rights Act of 1991, Pub.L.No. 102–166, 105 Stat. 1071, "respond[ed] to a number of recent decisions of the United States Supreme Court that had sharply cut back on the scope and effectiveness of . . . important [civil rights laws that ban discrimination in employment]." H.R.Rep.No. 102–40(II), at 2. *Marek* was one of those cases. Therefore, a Title VII employment discrimination case, Gudenkauf v. Stauffer Communications, Inc., 158 F.3d 1074 (10th Cir. 1998), held that the plaintiff's failure to do better than a Rule 68 offer of $7,500 would not prevent her from recovering her attorney's fees and costs as prevailing party. While 42 U.S.C. § 2000e–2(k) of Title VII was not changed from stating that fees are to be awarded "as part of" the costs, the 1991 amendment to § (g)(2)(B) provides that a court may award attorney's fees "and" costs. The court found this was intended to overrule *Marek* as the legislative history of the 1991 Act specifically disapproved of the Marek decision and proposed to amend subsection (k) to avoid its application." *Marek*, the House report said, "is particularly problematic in the context of Title VII, because it may impede private actions, which Congress has relied upon for enforcement of the statute's guarantees and advancement of the public's interest." But see Bell v. Board of County Com'rs of Jefferson County, 2005 WL 361510 (D.Kan.), reading *Gudenkauf* as affirming the attorney fee award in reliance on § (g)(2)(B), which authorizes attorney's fees in a Title VII mixed motive case even though the plaintiff is not entitled to damages, while this is not a mixed motive case and thus plaintiff's request for attorney fees must be denied under 42 U.S.C. § 1988).

13. Employment cases brought under the Fair Labor Standards Act (FLSA) and Age Discrimination in Employment Act (ADEA) have also been held not to be governed by *Marek* as to recovery of attorney's fees and costs despite a plaintiff's failure to do better than a Rule 68 offer. Dalal v. Alliant Techsystems, Inc., 182 F.3d 757 (10th Cir. 1999) (ADEA); Mogilevsky v. Bally Total Fitness Corp., 311 F.Supp.2d 212 (D. Mass. 2004) (FLSA). However, although Rule 68 may not completely bar recovery for attorney's fees, the refusal of the offer can still be a factor in a court's determination of the amount of attorneys fees due. *Dalal* held that, while Rule 68 did not bar an award of post-offer attorney's fees under the ADEA, "the reasonableness calculation must take the fact of the Rule 68 offer into account." The Tenth Circuit held that the district court did not abuse its discretion in "award[ing] only half of the fees generated after the Rule 68 offer to reflect plaintiff's limited success." See also Anderson v. Unum Life Ins. Co. of America, 2007 WL 604728 (M.D.Ala. 2007)(in a suit under the Employee Retirement Income Security Act (ERISA), which provides for recovery of attorney's fees "in addition" to costs, Rule 68 did not bar recovery of attorney's fees, but since the offer to settle was substantial and the difference between the offer and ultimate award was

minimal, the judge could consider the refusal of the offer as a factor in awarding less than the full attorneys fees).

14. In Johnson v. Midwest ATM, Inc., 2012 WL 3113861 (D. Minn.), plaintiff who was charged a $2.50 user fee after withdrawing money from an ATM, sued under the Electronic Funds Transfer Act (EFTA), alleging that no notice was posted on the exterior of the ATM. Unlike the statute in *Marek*, the court said, the EFTA mandates cost, "together with a reasonable attorney's fee." "Because the EFTA separates costs and fees, the Rule 68 limitation on costs does not apply to attorney's fees." See also Zortman v. J.C. Christensen & Assoc., Inc., 2012 WL 1563918 (D.Minn.) (finding identical language in the Fair Debt Collection Practices Act prevented the *Marek* ruling against recovery of attorney's fees from applying).

15. Courts have refused to extend *Marek* to settlement offers made outside of the context of Rule 68. Martino v. Massachusetts Bay Transportation Authority, 230 F.Supp.2d 195 (D.Mass. 2002) (failure of jury verdict of $50,000 to do better than $75,000 offer made orally in mediation would not prevent plaintiff from recovering attorney's fees and costs).

16. Rule 68 only allows defendants to make offers to plaintiffs. Should plaintiffs get an equivalent opportunity to apply settlement pressure to defendants by making offers of judgment to them? Compare Cal. Code Civ. Proc. § 998 (allowing any party to make such an offer to any other party). Throughout the first half of the 1980s, there were proposals to change Rule 68, generally designed to make it bilateral (i.e., to allow plaintiffs to make such offers as well), to provide explicitly for fee shifting in some situations, and to limit shifting to cases in which a party unreasonably rejected a Rule 68 offer. For an examination of the reform movement, see Simon, The Riddle of Rule 68, 54 Geo.Wash.L.Rev. 1 (1985). Further proposals for reform have been made. See Schwarzer, Fee-Shifting Offers of Judgment—An Approach to Reducing the Cost of Litigation, 76 Judicature 147 (1992); Rowe & Vidmar, Empirical Research on Offers of Settlement: A Preliminary Report, 51 Law & Contemp. Probs 13 (1988).

17. The House of Representatives passed a modified offer of judgment rule in 1995 (dubbed "loser pays") that, as part of the GOP "Contract with America," allowed either party to make an offer and, if refused and the ultimate judgment were not more favorable than the offer, the offeree would have to pay the offeror's costs, including attorney's fees. This led the American Bar Association to convene a task force to study the issue in light of expressed concerns that the bill would disproportionately impact plaintiffs who would be deterred from seeking access to the courts by the risk of having to pay the defendants' attorney's fees. The task force concluded that allowing attorney's fees to be shifted under an offer of judgment rule could promote settlement, but that safeguards were needed to mitigate the disproportionate adverse effect upon plaintiffs. It proposed a rule that included a fee shifting formula that gave an offeree a margin of error of 25% before cost shifting was triggered by not doing as well as the ultimate judgment obtained; limiting liability for the offeror's attorney's fees to an amount equal to the offeree's attorney's fees;

and giving the court discretion to reduce or eliminate cost shifting to avoid undue hardship. See Sherman, supra note 5, 76 Tex.L.Rev. at 1185–1891. Neither the House bill nor the ABA proposal became law. "Loser pays" proposals continue to be proposed by business interests. See "Greater Justice, Lower Cost: How a 'Loser Pays' Rule Would Improve the American Legal System," Manhattan Institute for Policy Research Civil Justice Report (December 2008), http://www.manhattan-institute.org/html/cjr_11.htm (proposal endorsed by former NYC Mayor Rudy Giuliani).

18. An expanded "offer of judgment" rule has been part of the "tort reform" proposals urged by business interests in many states. The most sweeping was passed and signed into law in Texas, effective on January 1, 2004. It allows claimants or defendants to make offers and provides for the shifting of litigation expenses, including attorney's fees, fees of two testifying expert witnesses, and post-rejection litigation costs when the judgment is less favorable to the offeree by at least 20%. The Texas Supreme Court adopted rules implementing the procedure. 3 McDonald & Carlson, Texas Civil Practice, §§ 17.32–17.36 (2004). The approach in *Marek* is followed: "A party against whom litigation costs are awarded may not recover attorney fees and costs under another law incurred after the date the party rejected the settlement offer made the basis of the award." Tex.R.Civ.P. 167.4(f). In 2011, Texas adopted a further "loser pays" rule. HB274 allows winning parties to recover litigation costs in breach of contract suits or if a judge grants a motion to dismiss.

19. Mediation and offer of judgment rules are both procedural devices that seek to promote settlement. They have generally functioned independently, and they have differing sanction regimes to enforce compliance with their requirements. Mediation rules may impose sanctions, often including cost-shifting, for failure of a party to comply with the requirements of an order for court-ordered mediation. An offer of judgment could be made in conjunction with mediation, thus providing an additional incentive to settle. The procedural rules of at least two states—Minnesota and Michigan—call for interaction between the two regimes. Consider Sherman & Fairman, Interplay Between Mediation and Offer of Judgment Rule Sanctions, 26 Ohio St. J. on Dis. Resol. 327, 356 (2011):

"Federal Rule 68 and state offer of judgment rules modeled after it are destined to remain underutilized tools for settlement unless changes are made. The experience of states like Minnesota and Michigan provide considerable guidance. The scope of Federal Rule 68 must be broadened to allow plaintiffs to make offers and to allow the shifting of attorney's fees under certain circumstances. The potential use of Federal Rule 68 should be discussed during pretrial conferences, and Federal Rule 16 can be easily amended to make this explicit. Similarly, mediators should be instructed to consider the impact of Federal Rule 68 in their facilitation of court-connected mediation. While attaching cost-shifting directly to orders to mediate is unwise, adoption of a case evaluation process with cost-shifting provides the promise of additional incentives to settle. If implemented, the changes suggested here would allow offer of judgment rules and mediation practice to work in tandem to encourage settlement."

CHAPTER 8

TRIAL

■ ■ ■

Cases that cannot be decided on the basis of pretrial submissions must go to trial unless settled. A thousand years ago, a trial had few of the aspects of modern trials. Indeed, the orientation of trial methods was antirational because people believed that they were not competent to decide questions of guilt or innocence. Thus, at least in criminal matters, trial might be by ordeal on the theory that the outcome would be determined by God. The Norman Conquest introduced trial by jury to England, but that method of trial also differed greatly from the current jury trial. The original version depended on a jury composed of people who already had information about the matter in dispute. Rather than receiving information about the dispute, the jurors were expected to investigate as necessary to acquire any further information they needed to resolve the controversy. See Marcus, The Tudor Treason Trials: Some Reflections on the Emergence of Forensic Themes, 1984 U.Ill.L.Rev. 675, 681–82. Gradually this model evolved into our current jury trial.

We have already discussed the pretrial conference, an event of increasing importance in organizing trials, in Chapter 7 (supra pp. 486–490). In this chapter we examine the current handling of trials by first canvassing the phases of a jury trial. We then turn to the rules governing whether the right to jury trial exists under the Seventh Amendment, and the interaction of that right with the various devices by which the judge can control the jury's verdict.

A. THE PHASES OF A TRIAL

Modern jury trials are, in a sense, largely theatrical events. Mastering the techniques of this type of theater is the work of a lifetime. In law school, it is the work of courses on trial practice. Moreover, the legal rules that apply to in-court activities are assigned principally to the course on evidence, and beyond the scope of this book. This section briefly canvasses the phases of a trial to acquaint you with them in a general way. We will examine some of these topics more carefully later in the chapter.

1. JURY SELECTION

In jury trials, the first thing that must be done is to select a jury. This process involves questioning jurors about their possible biases or acquaintance with the parties or issues involved in the suit. Unlike the early English jury, the contemporary American jury should consist of persons entirely ignorant of the dispute. Juror selection can be extremely important, as the composition of the jury is thought by many to have a substantial effect on the outcome of the suit. For an examination of the process, see Jury Selection, infra p. 610.

2. OPENING STATEMENTS

Because the jurors know nothing about the case, the lawyers get a chance to tell them something about it before the presentation of evidence begins. The presentation of the evidence is sometimes disjointed and difficult to follow because witnesses may be called in the order that is convenient for them, and they can only testify about events they know personally. Thus the jury might not appreciate the relation between a witness's story and the overall case unless it had been given some sort of roadmap to the whole case. The function of the opening statement is to provide that roadmap, but what the lawyers tell the jury is not itself evidence.

3. PRESENTATION OF EVIDENCE

Needless to say, the presentation of evidence is the heart of a trial, and provides the focus of most of the forensic talents of the lawyers.

(a) *Sequence:* Because the jury is thought to be most attentive at the beginning of the trial, the question of sequence of presentation becomes important. The usual formulation is that the party with the burden of proof on an issue goes first (with the "case-in-chief"). When that is completed, the other side gets to present opposing evidence, to which the party with the burden of proof may respond with rebuttal evidence, which the other side may then rebut, until there is no further evidence to be presented. Customarily, this means that the plaintiff goes first with its case-in-chief on the claims against defendant. The defendant then responds with opposing evidence and, if there is a counterclaim, its case-in-chief on the counterclaim. Each successive round after that should be limited to material responsive to that presented by the opponent in its preceding opportunity to offer evidence.

(b) *Manner of presentation:* Our system relies on the witnesses—not the lawyers—to tell the jury what they know. Among other things, a "foundation" can be provided for documentary or other tangible evidence by testimony from a witness identifying an object. For an example, see Guenther v. Armstrong Rubber Co., infra p. 645, in which the dispute concerns testimony about whether a certain tire was the tire that exploded and injured the plaintiff.

There are several reasons for this method. For one thing, witnesses don't know what is relevant, and they need some direction from the lawyers. Moreover, some of the information that witnesses possess may be inadmissible. Using a question-and-answer format permits the opposing party to object to the question before the witness answers, thus keeping the information from the jury if the objection is sustained. Because the lawyer may exert too much influence over the witness, we generally insist that lawyers questioning witnesses who are not antagonistic to the lawyer's position use "non-leading" questions. See Fed.R.Evid. 611(c). A leading question is a question that suggests the answer the lawyer desires. Ordinarily these rules are relaxed to speed the testimony.

(c) *Exclusion of evidence:* The law of evidence allows litigants to prevent their opponents from presenting certain things to the jury. In general, the Federal Rules of Evidence incline toward allowing the jury to hear all relevant evidence unless its probative value is substantially outweighed by other factors. Detailed study of these rules must await a course on evidence, but general reference to some of them should be helpful by way of orientation.

Relevance and countervailing prejudice: We have already seen that Fed.R.Evid. 401 makes relevant any evidence that has *some* tendency to make a fact of consequence more or less likely. See supra p. 380 n. 2. More refined analysis permits some evaluation of the probative value of relevant pieces of evidence. Under Fed.R.Evid. 403, relevant evidence may be excluded "if its probative value is substantially outweighed by the danger of unfair prejudice, confusion of the issues, or misleading the jury, or by considerations of undue delay, waste of time, or needless presentation of cumulative evidence." While courts are not quick to use this power, it permits particularized recalibration of the wide-open relevance standards of Rule 401. In some cases, it is used simply to speed up the trial by curtailing unnecessary proof.

More significantly, Rule 403 gives courts a tool to prevent the jury from learning about something that is relevant for one reason but which invites the jury to decide the case on a ground not authorized by law. The usual reason a party offers evidence is to prejudice the position of its opponent, so that is hardly a reason to exclude the evidence. When the main impact of the evidence is to invite a decision on a ground not authorized by law, however, the risk of distorting the outcome justifies exclusion of the evidence. For example, in a personal injury case a verdict for plaintiff was overturned. The appellate court noted that the case for liability was thin, but did not fault the trial court for allowing plaintiff to put on evidence regarding damages, including psychiatric testimony that persons with depression as severe as plaintiff's may commit suicide when confronted with other adversity. But the court found "much too inflammatory" plaintiff's further effort "to forge a direct link between a substantial award to him in this case and his continued life. The jury was clearly told that the plaintiff would commit suicide if their verdict was not a generous award to him." Gibson v. Caterpillar Tractor Co., 20 Fed. R. Evid. Serv. 144 (4th

Cir.1986). Was this relevant? Was the appellate court right in forbidding it?

More specifically, Rule 404 forbids "character" evidence offered to prove that on a certain occasion a person acted in conformity with his or her character. This provision reflects the belief that liability, civil or criminal, should depend on what a person did on a certain occasion, not an assessment of whether he is a "good" or "bad" person. This rule becomes particularly important in criminal cases, where the defendant's past convictions are usually excluded in order to avoid the risk that the jury would convict in order to get this "bad person" off the streets. But when a party testifies, evidence relevant to his character for truthfulness may be explored, and prior convictions (or other misconduct) are more readily admitted. See Fed.R.Evid. 608; 609.

Competence: Only persons who can perceive events and relate what they saw under oath are permitted to testify. Fed.R.Evid. 601; 603. Beyond that, Rule 602 permits a witness to testify only about matters within his personal knowledge.

Hearsay: Probably the best known evidence rule, the rule against hearsay is an important way of ensuring that the witness has personal knowledge, rather than simply repeating what somebody else said. It forbids a witness from proving something by means of an out-of-court assertion that it is true. See Fed.R.Evid. 801(c). In difficult cases, the application of this concept is extremely challenging. But even hearsay evidence is often admissible under one or more exceptions to the ban on hearsay. See Fed. R. Evid. 801(d); 803; 804.

Privileges: In Chapter 5 we examined some issues of privilege. In addition to the attorney-client privilege, the common law has recognized privileges for communications between a doctor and patient, priest and parishioner, husband and wife, and some others in confidential relationships. Unlike other rules of evidence, the ban on evidence of such communications is unrelated to its probative value. Instead, courts are forbidden to intrude into these relationships for policy reasons deemed to outweigh the value of such evidence to accurate decisions at trial.

Need to Object: The above rules are not self-executing, and a judge will rarely prevent a party from introducing improper evidence unless the other side objects. In the tumult of trial, lawyers often overlook grounds for objection, and even where they recognize that the evidence being offered is improper, lawyers may choose not to object for strategic reasons. As you should appreciate, effective use of the rules of evidence takes years to master.

When a party objects, the court must rule on the objection. If the objection is sustained, the witness is told not to answer the question. If the objection is overruled, the evidence is admitted. The objecting party may then argue on appeal or in support of a motion for a new trial that the objection should have been sustained. To succeed on that argument, however, the objecting party must be reasonably specific about the grounds for objection. See Fed. R. Evid. 103. For example, Perry Mason's perennial objection—"irrelevant, incompetent and immaterial"—covers almost the entire gamut of evidence law and would likely be held to be too general to require a judge to survey all possible grounds for objection and determine whether any is applicable (a point seemingly always missed by Mason's perennial opponent, Hamilton Burger).

(d) *Motion for judgment as a matter of law:* At any time before the case is submitted to the jury after the non-movant has been fully heard, any party may move for judgment as a matter of law, formerly called a directed verdict. To prevail on such a motion, the party must show that the opposing party has failed to satisfy its burden of production, and that judgment should therefore be entered in the moving party's favor. The defendant may make this motion at the close of the plaintiff's case-in-chief without prejudice to the right to offer evidence if the motion is denied. If the motion is granted, the court need not submit the matter to the jury. See Fed.R.Civ.P. 50(a).

4. ARGUMENT

Once all the evidence is in and the parties have rested their cases, the lawyers are allowed to argue the case to the jury. Ordinarily the plaintiff gets to argue first, then the defendant responds, and the plaintiff gets the closing chance to address the jury.

The argument allows the lawyers to weave together all the evidence in the manner most favorable to their clients and to urge the jury to accept their view of the facts. They may also relate the evidence to the legal issues the judge will cover in the instructions. In doing so, they are accorded wide latitude in suggesting inferences that can be drawn from the evidence. There are, however, some limits beyond which they should not go. First, they are limited to "fair comment" on the evidence. Broad though this is, it excludes open invitations to decide the case on an improper ground. At some point, for instance, the lawyer for a local plaintiff will be reprimanded for suggesting to the jury that it decide for the plaintiff because the defendant is from another state. Second, the lawyer may not in argument try to offer new evidence to the jury; counsel must argue on the basis of the evidence actually received, rather than presenting additional information. Third, counsel are not to insinuate their personal beliefs into the case. Thus, defendant's lawyer may not assure the jury that "I wouldn't be here before you today if I didn't know in my heart that defendant has not wronged plaintiff."

5. INSTRUCTIONS

After the lawyers finish their closing arguments, the judge instructs the jury on the legal rules that govern the case. This activity gives the judge the "last word," and is the means by which the judge sets the scene for the jury to apply the law to the facts it finds. The respective roles of judge and jury are outlined in the following introductory instruction designed for the commencement of trial:

> After the evidence has been heard and arguments and instructions are finished, you will meet to make your decision. You will determine the facts from all the testimony that you hear and the other evidence that is presented. You are the sole and exclusive judges of the facts. I must stress that you are required to accept the rules of law that I give you, whether or not you agree with them.
>
> The law permits me to comment on the evidence in the case during the trial or while instructing the jury. Such comments are only expressions of my opinion as to the facts. You may disregard these comments entirely, because you are to determine for yourself the weight of the evidence and the credibility of each of the witnesses.

3 K. O'Malley, J. Grenig & W. Lee, Federal Jury Practice and Instructions § 101.10 (5th ed. 2000); see Thornburg, The Power and the Process: Instructions and the Civil Jury, 66 Fordham L. Rev. 1837 (1998).

Once the evidence is in, the judge is to be more specific about the way the jury should approach the evidence. As noted above, in federal court the judge may "comment" on the evidence by expressing an opinion about which party's evidence seemed forceful, truthful, etc. This practice rejects the view of some states that such comments invade the province of the jury. See Evans v. Wright, 505 F.2d 287, 289 (4th Cir.1974) ("a United States district judge is not a bump on a log"). But the jury remains the prime arbiter of factual issues, as revealed in the following instruction on the jury's role in evaluating the evidence. Keep these rules in mind as you examine the standards for taking the case from the jury:

> As the sole judges of the facts, you must determine which of the witnesses you believe, what portion of their testimony you accept and what weight you attach to it. At times during the trial I sustained objections to questions asked without permitting the witness to answer or, where an answer has been made, instructed that it be stricken from the record and that you disregard it and dismiss it from your minds. You may not draw any inference from an unanswered question nor may you consider testimony which has been stricken in reaching your decision. The law requires that your decision be made solely upon the competent evidence before

you. Such items as I exclude from your consideration were excluded because they are not legally admissible.

The law does not, however, require you to accept all of the evidence I admitted, even though it be competent. In determining what evidence you will accept you might make your own evaluation of the testimony given by each of the witnesses, and determine the degree of weight you choose to give to his testimony. The testimony of a witness may fail to conform to the facts as they occurred because he is intentionally telling a falsehood, because he did not accurately see or hear that about which he testifies, because his recollection of the event is faulty, or because he has not expressed himself clearly in giving his testimony. There is no magical formula by which one may evaluate testimony. You bring with you to this courtroom all of the experience and background of your lives. In your everyday affairs you determine for yourselves the reliability or unreliability of statements made to you by others. The same tests that you use in your everyday dealings are the tests which you apply in your deliberations. The interest or lack of interest of any witness in the outcome of this case, the bias or prejudice of a witness, if there be any, the age, the appearance, the manner in which the witness gives his testimony on the stand, the opportunity that the witness had to observe the facts concerning which he testifies, the probability or improbability of the witness' testimony when viewed in the light of all of the other evidence in the case, are all items to be taken into your consideration in determining the weight, if any, you will assign to that witness' testimony. If such considerations make it appear that there is a discrepancy in the evidence, you will have to consider whether the apparent discrepancy may not be reconciled by fitting the two stories together. If, however, that is not possible, you will then have to determine which of the conflicting versions you will accept.

2 E. Devitt & C. Blackmar, Federal Jury Practice and Instructions § 72.01 (3d ed. 1977).

In addition, the judge instructs the jury on the substantive rules that apply to the case. For example, the following is an instruction on the burden of persuasion. Recall the introduction to this subject in Chapter 6, supra p. 444:

Plaintiff _____ has the burden in a civil action, such as this, to prove every essential element of [*plaintiff's*] claim by a preponderance of the evidence. If plaintiff _____ should fail to establish any essential element of [*plaintiff's*] claim by a preponderance of the evidence, you should find for the defendant as to that claim.

"Establish by a preponderance of the evidence" means to prove that something is more likely so than not so. In other words, a preponderance of the evidence in the case means such evidence as, when considered and compared with the evidence opposed to it, has more convincing force, and produces in your minds belief that what is sought to be proved is more likely true than not true. This standard does not require proof to an absolute certainty, since proof to an absolute certainty is seldom possible in any case.

In determining whether any fact in issue has been proved by a preponderance of the evidence in the case, the jury may, unless otherwise instructed, consider the testimony of all witnesses, regardless of who may have called them, and all exhibits received in evidence, regardless of who may have produced them.

3 K. O'Malley, J. Grenig & W. Lee, supra, § 104.01. Further instructions would spell out the elements of plaintiff's case, and of any affirmative defenses, on which defendant would of course have the burden.

6. JURY DELIBERATION AND VERDICT

The judge's instructions will conclude with directions to the jury to retire to a jury room and deliberate. Ordinarily the first order of business for the jury is to select a foreperson who will chair the further deliberations. Then the jury is to deliberate. The following instruction summarizes the way in which the jurors are supposed to approach the deliberation process:

It is your duty, as jurors, to consult with one another and to deliberate with a view to reaching an agreement, if you can do so without disregard of individual judgment. You must each decide the case for yourself, but only after an impartial consideration of the evidence in the case with your fellow jurors. In the course of your deliberations, do not hesitate to reexamine your own views, and change your opinion, if convinced it is erroneous. But do not surrender your honest conviction as to the weight or effect of evidence, solely because of the opinion of your fellow jurors, or for the mere purpose of returning a verdict.

Remember at all times that you are not partisans. You are judges—judges of the facts. Your sole interest is to seek the truth from the evidence in the case.

3 K. O'Malley, J. Grenig & W. Lee, supra, § 106.01. Keep these guidelines in mind as you examine the materials on juror impeachment of the verdict, infra p. 695.

Once the jury reaches a verdict, it reports its decision on the verdict form it was given during the instructions. We will consider verdict forms in connection with Whitlock v. Jackson, infra p. 683. The judge then calls the parties into the courtroom, where the jury has reassembled, and asks the jurors if the verdict is their verdict. The loser may then have the jury "polled," which means that the judge will ask each juror individually if the verdict was his or her verdict. Unless there is dissent, the verdict will be accepted, and judgment entered thereon. When further consideration of the verdict may be necessary (as in a complicated plaintiff's verdict or where special verdicts are used), the judge may defer entering judgment until a later time.

7.   POST-TRIAL MOTIONS AND JUDGMENT

We will consider the standards governing post-trial motions in some detail. See infra pp. 613–703. There are two types of motions. First, there is the renewed motion for a judgment as a matter of law, formerly called judgment N.O.V. (notwithstanding the verdict), by which the dissatisfied litigant asks the court to enter judgment in its favor even though the jury decided the case the other way. As a prerequisite to such relief, in federal court the moving party must have made a motion for judgment as a matter of law before the jury deliberations. Fed. R. Civ. P. 50(b). Second, there is the motion for a new trial, in which the loser asks the court to set aside the verdict and order a retrial. See Fed.R.Civ.P. 59. The new trial motion may result in an order known as remittitur or additur, in which the judge orders that a new trial occur unless the other side agrees to a change in the amount of damages. If the verdict-winner accepts, judgment is entered in the amount selected by the judge.

B.   SEVENTH AMENDMENT RIGHT TO JURY TRIAL

The Seventh Amendment to the United States Constitution provides:

> In suits at common law, where the value in controversy shall exceed twenty dollars, the right of trial by jury shall be preserved, and no fact tried by a jury, shall be otherwise re-examined in any Court of the United States, than according to the rules of the common law.

The Amendment contains two parts: one describing the circumstances under which a litigant has a right to a jury trial, and the other indicating what controls the court may impose upon a jury in a case in which the right is guaranteed. Thus, the second portion of the Amendment comes into play only after it has initially been determined that a right to a jury trial exists in the first place. Section C of this chapter, dealing with judicial control of the verdict, will examine the scope of the Amendment's second part. This section, on the other hand, focuses exclusively on the initial question of when a right to jury trial itself is guaranteed.

According to one commentator, the Seventh Amendment was added to the Bill of Rights in order to serve as a check on unrepresentative, unaccountable federal judges: "In 1789 there was a shared perception that guaranteeing the right to civil jury trials was important. Without an impartial jury, the individual citizen had no ability to check the power of the sovereign in a civil courtroom. Legislators and presidents are elected. Federal judges serve for life." Klein, The Myth of How to Interpret the Seventh Amendment Right to a Civil Jury Trial, 53 Ohio St. L.J. 1005, 1032 (1992). The same commentator asserts: "The Anti-Federalists distrusted the Federalists' assurance that civil juries were inviolate. The amendment the Anti-Federalists demanded reflected their belief that absent explicit language to the contrary, juries could slowly disappear from the civil courtroom, leaving judges as courtroom kings. The principle captured in the amendment is that this specter of unchecked authority was unacceptable." Id. at 1034. For analysis of the history of the Seventh Amendment's adoption, see Henderson, The Background of the Seventh Amendment, 80 Harv. L. Rev. 289 (1966); Wolfram, The Constitutional History of the Seventh Amendment, 57 Minn.L.Rev. 639 (1973).

By its terms, the Amendment appears to dictate a form of historical inquiry: Use of the word "preserved" has caused the Seventh Amendment to hold a unique position in the realm of constitutional interpretation. For many years following the Amendment's adoption, it was thought that its interpretation was to be governed by an exclusively historical test. See Dimick v. Schiedt, 293 U.S. 474, 476 (1935), infra p. 669: "In order to ascertain the scope and meaning of the Seventh Amendment, resort must be had to the appropriate rules of the common law established at the time of the adoption of that constitutional provision in 1791." It is generally thought that the historical test was intended to look to the 1791 common law practice of England, rather than that of the states. See Wolfram, The Constitutional History of the Seventh Amendment, 57 Minn.L.Rev. 639, 640 (1973). Use of a strict historical test presents obvious problems. It is often difficult to determine what issues were, under the common law of England in 1791, "legal," for which a jury trial could be had, and which were "equitable," for which there was no right to jury trial.

Application of the historical test is further complicated by the merger of law and equity in the federal system. Attempting to determine what the English practice was in 1791 is sufficiently difficult without the additional burden of translating that practice into terms of merged procedures. See generally Redish, Seventh Amendment Right to Jury Trial: A Study in the Irrationality of Rational Decision Making, 70 Nw.U.L.Rev. 486 (1975). The cases in this section concern the Supreme Court's attempt to interpret the historically-oriented Seventh Amendment in light of modern procedural developments.

Before we turn to these problems, however, it is instructive, if only as background, to consider the question whether, wholly apart from its constitutional status, the continued widespread use of the civil jury makes practical sense. In this regard, it is interesting to note that England, the source of our concept of civil jury trial, has largely abandoned the concept.

The arguments against the civil jury can be grouped into three basic categories: delay caused by use of juries; juror incompetence; and juror prejudice. In the words of one commentator, "As a scientific method of settling disputes the general verdict rates a little higher than the ordeal, compurgation or trial by battle." L. Green, Judge and Jury 353 (1930). See also J. Frank, Courts on Trial 179 (1949).

Particular attention has been paid by both courts and commentators to problems that may arise from the use of juries in cases that are highly complex, either legally or factually. The issue is examined in detail infra at p. 603.

Not all commentators on the civil jury are critical, however. Professor Harry Kalven, for example, asserted that "there is much evidence that most people, once actually serving in a trial, become highly serious and responsible toward their task and toward the joint effort to deliberate through to a verdict." Kalven, The Dignity of the Civil Jury, 50 Va.L.Rev. 1055, 1062 (1964).

The English legal historian William Holdsworth listed what he saw as the basic advantages of the civil jury: (1) the jury can bring "average common sense" to bear upon the facts; (2) the findings of the jury do not result in the creation of binding precedent, thus permitting the jury to decide "hard cases" without making bad law; (3) a jury helps to preserve the dignity of the bench by relieving the judge of the responsibility of decision; (4) the jury members themselves are educated by their exposure to and participation in the administration of justice; and (5) the jury makes the law intelligible by constantly bringing the rules of the law to the touchstone of common sense. 1 W. Holdsworth, A History of English Law 348–50 (6th ed. 1938). According to a jury critic, "the argument for the jury system most frequently advanced * * * [is] that legal rules often work injustice, and that juries, through their general verdicts, wisely nullify those rules." J. Frank, supra at 127. Judge Frank rejected this defense, however, because "[i]t asserts that, desirably, each jury is a twelve-man ephemeral legislature, not elected by the voters, but empowered to destroy what the elected legislators have enacted or authorized." Id. at 129–30.

For additional defenses of the civil jury, see Note, Developments in the Law: The Civil Jury, 110 Harv. L. Rev. 1408 (1997). There it is argued that "the very fact that the civil jury is a democratic institution composed of laypersons fosters a sense of inclusion and participation that reflects and generates popular endorsement of the judicial system. The citizen jury confers legitimacy on judicial actions by identifying the actions of government with those of the people, both actually and vicariously." Id. at 1433. But see Lilly, The Decline of the American Jury, 72 U.Colo.L.Rev. 53 (2001): "[S]ubtle, long-term trends in the nature of litigation and the selection of juries pose serious questions about the potential of American juries to adequately perform their traditional roles."

BEACON THEATRES, INC. V. WESTOVER
Supreme Court of the United States, 1959
359 U.S. 500

JUSTICE BLACK delivered the opinion of the Court.

Petitioner, Beacon Theatres, Inc., sought by mandamus to require a district judge in the Southern District of California to vacate certain orders alleged to deprive it of a jury trial of issues arising in a suit brought against it by Fox West Coast Theatres, Inc. The Court of Appeals for the Ninth Circuit refused the writ, holding that the trial judge had acted within his proper discretion in denying petitioner's request for a jury. We granted certiorari, because "Maintenance of the jury as a fact-finding body is of such importance and occupies so firm a place in our history and jurisprudence that any seeming curtailment of the right to a jury trial should be scrutinized with the utmost care." Dimick v. Schiedt, 293 U.S. 474, 486.

Fox had asked for declaratory relief against Beacon alleging a controversy arising under the Sherman Antitrust Act, 15 U.S.C. §§ 1, 2, and under the Clayton Act, 15 U.S.C. § 15, which authorizes suits for treble damages against Sherman Act violators. According to the complaint Fox operates a movie theatre in San Bernardino, California, and has long been exhibiting films under contracts with movie distributors. These contracts grant it the exclusive right to show "first run" pictures in the "San Bernardino competitive area" and provide for "clearance"—a period of time during which no other theatre can exhibit the same pictures. After building a drive-in theatre about 11 miles from San Bernardino, Beacon notified Fox that it considered contracts barring simultaneous exhibitions of first-run films in the two theatres to be overt acts in violation of the antitrust laws. Fox's complaint alleged that this notification, together with threats of treble damage suits against Fox and its distributors, gave rise to "duress and coercion" which deprived Fox of a valuable property right, the right to negotiate for exclusive first-run contracts. Unless Beacon was restrained, the complaint continued, irreparable harm would result. Accordingly, while its pleading was styled a "Complaint for Declaratory Relief," Fox prayed both for a declaration that a grant of clearance between the Fox and Beacon theatres is reasonable and not in violation of the antitrust laws, and for an injunction, pending final resolution of the litigation, to prevent Beacon from instituting any action under the antitrust laws against Fox and its distributors arising out of the controversy alleged in the complaint. Beacon filed an answer, a counterclaim against Fox, and a cross-claim against an exhibitor who had intervened. These denied the threats and asserted that there was no substantial competition between the two theatres, that the clearances granted were therefore unreasonable, and that a conspiracy existed between Fox and its distributors to manipulate contracts and clearances so as to restrain trade and monopolize first-run pictures in violation of the antitrust laws. Treble damages were asked.

Beacon demanded a jury trial of the factual issues in the case as provided by Federal Rule of Civil Procedure 38(b). The District Court, however, viewed the issues raised by the "Complaint for Declaratory Relief," including the question of competition between the two theatres, as essentially equitable. Acting under the purported authority of Rules 42(b) and 57, it directed that these issues be tried to the court before jury determination of the validity of the charges of antitrust violations made in the counterclaim and cross-claim. A common issue of the "Complaint for Declaratory Relief," the counterclaim, and the cross-claim was the reasonableness of the clearances granted to Fox, which depended, in part, on the existence of competition between the two theatres. Thus the effect of the action of the District Court could be, as the Court of Appeals believed, "to limit the petitioner's opportunity fully to try to a jury every issue which has a bearing upon its treble damage suit," for determination of the issue of clearances by the judge might "operate either by way of res judicata or collateral estoppel so as to conclude both parties with respect thereto at the subsequent trial of the treble damage claim."

* * *

[I]f Beacon would have been entitled to a jury trial in a treble damage suit against Fox it cannot be deprived of that right merely because Fox took advantage of the availability of declaratory relief to sue Beacon first. Since the right to trial by jury applies to treble damage suits under the antitrust laws, and is, in fact, an essential part of the congressional plan for making competition rather than monopoly the rule of trade, the Sherman and Clayton Act issues on which Fox sought a declaration were essentially jury questions.

Nevertheless the Court of Appeals refused to upset the order of the district judge. It held that the question of whether a right to jury trial existed was to be judged by Fox's complaint read as a whole. In addition to seeking a declaratory judgment, the court said, Fox's complaint can be read as making out a valid plea for injunctive relief, thus stating a claim traditionally cognizable in equity. A party who is entitled to maintain a suit in equity for an injunction, said the court, may have all the issues in his suit determined by the judge without a jury regardless of whether legal rights are involved. The court then rejected the argument that equitable relief, traditionally available only when legal remedies are inadequate, was rendered unnecessary in this case by the filing of the counterclaim and cross-claim which presented all the issues necessary to a determination of the right to injunctive relief. Relying on American Life Ins. Co. v. Stewart, 300 U.S. 203, 215, decided before the enactment of the Federal Rules of Civil Procedure, it invoked the principle that a court sitting in equity could retain jurisdiction even though later a legal remedy became available. In such instances the equity court had discretion to enjoin the later lawsuit in order to allow the whole dispute to be determined in one case in one court. Reasoning by analogy, the Court of Appeals held it was not an abuse of discretion for the district judge, acting under Federal Rule of Civil Procedure 42(b), to try the equitable cause first even though this might, through collateral estoppel, prevent a full jury trial of the counterclaim and cross-claim which were as effectively stopped as by an equity injunction.

Beacon takes issue with the holding of the Court of Appeals that the complaint stated a claim upon which equitable relief could be granted. As initially filed the complaint alleged that threats of lawsuits by petitioner against Fox and its distributors were causing irreparable harm to Fox's business relationships. The prayer for relief, however, made no mention of the threats but asked only that pending litigation of the claim for declaratory judgment, Beacon be enjoined from beginning any lawsuits under the antitrust laws against Fox and its distributors arising out of the controversy alleged in the complaint. Evidently of the opinion that this prayer did not state a good claim for equitable relief, the Court of Appeals construed it to include a request for an injunction against threats of lawsuits. This liberal construction of a pleading is in line with Rule 8 of the Federal Rules of Civil Procedure. See Conley v. Gibson, 355 U.S. 41, 47–48. Assuming that the pleadings can be construed to support such a request and assuming additionally that the complaint can be read as alleging the kind of harassment by a multiplicity of lawsuits which would *traditionally* have justified equity to take jurisdiction and settle the case in one suit, we are nevertheless of the opinion that, under the Declaratory Judgment Act and the Federal Rules of Civil Procedure, neither claim can justify denying Beacon a trial by jury of all the issues in the antitrust controversy.

The basis of injunctive relief in the federal courts has always been irreparable harm and inadequacy of legal remedies. At least as much is required to justify a trial court in using its discretion under the Federal Rules to allow claims of equitable origins to be tried ahead of legal ones, since this has the same effect as an equitable injunction of the legal claims. And it is immaterial, in judging if that discretion is properly employed, that before the Federal Rules and the Declaratory Judgment Act were passed, courts of equity, exercising a jurisdiction separate from courts of law, were, in some cases, allowed to enjoin subsequent legal actions between the same parties involving the same controversy. This was because the subsequent legal action, though providing an opportunity to try the case to a jury, might not protect the right of the equity plaintiff to a fair and orderly adjudication of the controversy. Under such circumstances the legal remedy could quite naturally be deemed inadequate. Inadequacy of remedy and irreparable harm are practical terms, however. As such their existence today must be determined, not by precedents decided under discarded procedures, but in the light of the remedies now made available by the Declaratory Judgment Act and the Federal Rules.

Viewed in this manner, the use of discretion by the trial court under Rule 42(b) to deprive Beacon of a full jury trial on its counterclaim and cross-claim, as well as on Fox's plea for declaratory relief, cannot be justified. Under the Federal Rules the same court may try both legal and equitable causes in the same action. Thus any defenses, equitable or legal, Fox may have to charges of antitrust violations can be raised either in its suit for declaratory relief or in answer to Beacon's counterclaim. On proper showing, harassment by threats of other suits, or other suits actually brought, involving the issues being tried in this case, could be temporarily enjoined pending the outcome of this litigation. Whatever permanent injunctive relief Fox might be entitled to on the basis of the decision in this case could, of course, be given by the court after the jury renders its verdict. In this way the issues between these parties could be settled in one suit giving Beacon a full jury trial of every antitrust issue. By contrast, the holding of the court below while granting Fox no additional protection unless the avoidance of jury trial be considered as such, would compel Beacon to split his antitrust case, trying part to a judge and part to a jury. Such a result, which involves the postponement and subordination of Fox's own legal claim for declaratory relief as well as of the counterclaim which Beacon was compelled by the Federal Rules to bring, is not permissible.

* * * Since in the federal courts equity has always acted only when legal remedies were inadequate, the expansion of adequate legal remedies provided by the Declaratory Judgment Act and the Federal Rules necessarily affects the scope of equity. Thus, the justification for equity's deciding legal issues once it obtains jurisdiction, and refusing to dismiss a case, merely because subsequently a legal remedy becomes available, must be re-evaluated in the light of the liberal joinder provisions of the Federal Rules which allow legal and equitable causes to be brought and resolved in one civil action. Similarly the need for, and therefore, the availability of such equitable remedies as Bills of Peace, Quia Timet and Injunction must be reconsidered in view of the existence of the Declaratory Judgment Act as well as the liberal joinder provision of the Rules. This is not only in accord with the spirit of the Rules and the Act but is required by the provision in the Rules that "[t]he right of trial by jury as declared by the Seventh Amendment to the Constitution or as given by a statute of the United States shall be preserved . . . inviolate."

If there should be cases where the availability of declaratory judgment or joinder in one suit of legal and equitable causes would not in all respects protect the plaintiff seeking equitable relief from irreparable harm while affording a jury trial in the legal cause, the trial court will necessarily have to use its discretion in deciding whether the legal or equitable cause should be tried first. Since the right to jury trial is a constitutional one, however, while no similar requirement protects trials by the court, that discretion is very narrowly limited and must, wherever possible, be exercised to preserve jury trial. As this Court said in Scott v. Neely, 140 U.S. 106, 109–110: "In the Federal courts this [jury] right cannot be dispensed with, except by the assent of the parties entitled to it; nor can it be impaired by any blending with a claim, properly cognizable at law, of a demand for equitable relief in aid of the legal action, or during its pendency." This long-standing principle of equity dictates that only under the most imperative circumstances, circumstances which in view of the flexible procedures of the Federal Rules we cannot now anticipate, can the right to a jury trial of legal issues be lost through prior determination of equitable claims. As we have shown, this is far from being such a case.

* * *

The judgment of the Court of Appeals is reversed.

JUSTICE FRANKFURTER took no part in the consideration or decision of this case.

JUSTICE STEWART, with whom JUSTICE HARLAN and JUSTICE WHITTAKER concur, dissenting.

There can be no doubt that a litigant is entitled to a writ of mandamus to protect a clear constitutional or statutory right to a jury trial. But there was no denial of such a right here. The district judge simply exercised his inherent discretion, now explicitly confirmed by the Federal Rules of Civil Procedure, to schedule the trial of an equitable claim in advance of an action at law. Even an abuse of such discretion could not, I think, be attacked by the extraordinary writ of mandamus. In any event no abuse of discretion is apparent in this case.

The complaint filed by Fox stated a claim traditionally cognizable in equity. That claim, in brief, was that Beacon had wrongfully interfered with the right of Fox to compete freely with Beacon and other distributors for the licensing of films for first-run exhibition in the San Bernardino area. The complaint alleged that the plaintiff was without an adequate remedy at law and would be irreparably harmed unless the defendant were restrained from continuing to interfere—by coercion and threats of litigation—with the plaintiff's lawful business relationships.

The Court of Appeals found that the complaint, although inartistically drawn, contained allegations entitling the petitioner to equitable relief. That finding is accepted in the prevailing opinion today. If the complaint had been answered simply by a general denial, therefore, the issues would under traditional principles have been triable as a proceeding in equity. Instead of just putting in issue the allegations of the complaint, however, Beacon filed pleadings which affirmatively alleged the existence of a broad conspiracy among the plaintiff and other theatre owners to monopolize the first-run exhibition of films in the San Bernardino area, to refrain from competing among themselves, and to discriminate against Beacon in granting film licenses. Based upon these allegations, Beacon asked damages in the amount of $300,000. Clearly these conspiracy allegations stated a cause of action triable as of right by a jury. What was demanded by Beacon, however, was a jury trial not only of this cause of action, but also of the issues presented by the original complaint.

Upon motion of Fox the trial judge ordered the original action for declaratory and equitable relief to be tried separately to the court and in advance of the trial of the defendant's counterclaim and cross-claim for damages. The court's order, which carefully preserved the right to trial by jury upon the conspiracy and damage issues raised by the counterclaim and cross-claim, was in conformity with the specific provisions of the Federal Rules of Civil Procedure. Yet it is decided today that the Court of Appeals must compel the district judge to rescind it.

Assuming the existence of a factual issue common both to the plaintiff's original action and the defendant's counterclaim for damages, I cannot agree that the District Court must be compelled to try the counterclaim first. It is, of course, a matter of no great moment in what order the issues between the parties in the present litigation are tried. What is disturbing is the process by which the Court arrives at its decision—a process which appears to disregard the historic relationship between equity and law.

I

The Court suggests that "the expansion of adequate legal remedies provided by the Declaratory Judgment Act . . . necessarily affects the scope of equity." Does the Court mean to say that the mere availability of an action for a declaratory judgment operates to furnish "an adequate remedy at law" so as to deprive a court of equity of the power to act? That novel line of reasoning is at least implied in the Court's opinion. But the Declaratory Judgment Act did not "expand" the substantive law. That Act merely provided a new statutory remedy, neither legal nor equitable, but available in the areas of both equity and law. When declaratory relief is sought, the right to trial by jury depends upon the basic context in which the issues are presented. If the basic issues in an action for declaratory relief are of a kind traditionally cognizable in equity, e.g., a suit for cancellation of a written instrument, the declaratory judgment is not a "remedy at law." If, on the other hand, the issues arise in a context traditionally cognizable at common law, the right to a jury trial of course remains unimpaired, even though the only relief demanded is a declaratory judgment.

Thus, if in this case the complaint had asked merely for a judgment declaring that the plaintiff's specified manner of business dealings with distributors and other exhibitors did not render it liable to Beacon under the antitrust laws, this would have been simply a "juxtaposition of parties" case in which Beacon could have demanded a jury trial. But the complaint in the present case, as the Court recognizes, presented issues of exclusively equitable cognizance, going well beyond a mere defense to any subsequent action at law. Fox sought from the court protection against Beacon's allegedly unlawful interference with its business relationships—protection which this Court seems to recognize might not have been afforded by a declaratory judgment, unsupplemented by equitable relief. The availability of a declaratory judgment did not, therefore, operate to confer upon Beacon the right to trial by jury with respect to the issues raised by the complaint.

II

The Court's opinion does not, of course, hold or even suggest that a court of equity may never determine "legal rights". For indeed it is precisely such rights which the Chancellor, when his jurisdiction has been properly invoked, has often been called upon to decide. Issues of fact are rarely either "legal" or "equitable." All depends upon the context in which they arise. * * *

Though apparently not disputing these principles, the Court holds, quite apart from its reliance upon the Declaratory Judgment Act, that Beacon by filing its counterclaim and cross-claim acquired a right to trial by jury of issues which otherwise would have been properly triable to the court. Support for this position is found in the principle that, "in the federal courts equity has always acted only when legal remedies were inadequate. . . ." Yet that principle is not employed in its traditional sense as a limitation upon the exercise of power by a court of equity. This is apparent in the Court's recognition that the allegations of the complaint entitled Fox to equitable relief—relief to which Fox would not have been entitled if it had had an adequate remedy at law. Instead, the principle is employed today to mean that because it is possible under the counterclaim to have a jury trial of the factual issue of substantial competition, that issue must be tried by a jury, even though the issue was primarily presented in the original claim for equitable relief. This is a marked departure from long-settled principles.

It has been an established rule "that equitable jurisdiction existing at the filing of a bill is not destroyed because an adequate legal remedy may have become available thereafter." American Life Ins. Co. v. Stewart, 300 U.S. 203, 215. It has also been long settled that the District Court in its discretion may order the trial of a suit in equity in advance of an action at law between the same parties, even if there is a factual issue common to both. In the words of Mr. Justice Cardozo, writing for a unanimous Court in American Life Ins. Co. v. Stewart, supra:

"A court has control over its own docket. . . . In the exercise of a sound discretion it may hold one lawsuit in abeyance to abide the outcome of another, especially where the parties and the issues are the same. . . . If request had been made by the respondents to suspend the suits in equity till the other causes were disposed of, the District Court could have considered whether justice would not be done by pursuing such a course, the remedy in equity being exceptional and the outcome of necessity. . . . There would be many circumstances to be weighed, as, for instance, the condition of the court calendar, whether the insurer had been precipitate or its adversaries dilatory, as well as other factors. In the end, benefit and hardship would have to be set off, the one against the other, and a balance ascertained." 300 U.S. 203, 215–216.[9]

III

The Court today sweeps away these basic principles as "precedents decided under discarded procedures." It suggests that the Federal Rules of Civil Procedure have somehow worked an "expansion of adequate legal remedies" so as to oust the District Courts of equitable jurisdiction, as well as to deprive them of their traditional power to control their own dockets. But obviously the Federal Rules could not and did not "expand" the substantive law one whit.

Like the Declaratory Judgment Act, the Federal Rules preserve inviolate the right to trial by jury in actions historically cognizable at common law, as under the Constitution they must. They do not create a right of trial by jury where that right "does not exist under the Constitution or statutes of the United States." Rule 39(a). Since Beacon's counterclaim was compulsory under the Rules, see Rule 13(a), it is apparent that by filing it Beacon could not be held to have waived its jury rights.[12] But neither can the counterclaim be held to have transformed Fox's original complaint into an action at law.

The Rules make possible the trial of legal and equitable claims in the same proceeding, but they expressly affirm the power of a trial judge to determine the order in which claims shall be heard. Rule 42(b). Certainly the Federal Rules were not intended to undermine the basic structure of equity jurisprudence, developed over the centuries and explicitly recognized in the United States Constitution.

Dairy Queen, Inc. v. Wood, 369 U.S. 469 (1962):

JUSTICE BLACK delivered the opinion of the Court.

The United States District Court for the Eastern District of Pennsylvania granted a motion to strike petitioner's demand for a trial by jury in an action now pending before it on the alternative grounds that either the action was "purely equitable" or, if not purely equitable,

---

[9]   It is arguable that if a case factually similar to American Life Ins. Co. v. Stewart were to arise under the Declaratory Judgment Act, the defendant would be entitled to a jury trial.

[12]   This is not, of course, to suggest that the filing of a permissive "legal" counterclaim to an "equitable" complaint would amount to a waiver of jury rights on the issues raised by the counterclaim.

whatever legal issues that were raised were "incidental" to equitable issues, and, in either case, no right to trial by jury existed.

* * *

At the outset, we may dispose of one of the grounds upon which the trial court acted * * *—that based upon the view that the right to trial by jury may be lost as to legal issues where those issues are characterized as "incidental" to equitable issues—for our previous decisions make it plain that no such rule may be applied in the federal courts. In Scott v. Neely, decided in 1891, this Court held that a court of equity could not even take jurisdiction of a suit "in which a claim properly cognizable only at law is united in the same pleadings with a claim for equitable relief." [140 U.S. 106, 117 (1891).] That holding, which was based upon both the historical separation between law and equity and the duty of the Court to insure "that the right to a trial by a jury in the legal action may be preserved intact," created considerable inconvenience in that it necessitated two separate trials in the same case whenever that case contained both legal and equitable claims. Consequently, when the procedure in the federal courts was modernized by the adoption of the Federal Rules of Civil Procedure in 1938, it was deemed advisable to abandon that part of the holding of Scott v. Neely which rested upon the separation of law and equity and to permit the joinder of legal and equitable claims in a single action. [The Court quoted Rule 18.]

The Federal Rules did not, however, purport to change the basic holding of Scott v. Neely that the right to trial by jury of legal claims must be preserved. Quite the contrary, Rule 38(a) expressly reaffirms that constitutional principle. * * * Nonetheless, after the adoption of the Federal Rules, attempts were made indirectly to undercut that right by having federal courts in which cases involving both legal and equitable claims were filed decide the equitable claim first. The result of this procedure in those cases in which it was followed was that any issue common to both the legal and equitable claims was finally determined by the court and the party seeking trial by jury on the legal claim was deprived of that right as to these common issues. This procedure finally came before us in Beacon Theatres, Inc. v. Westover[, 359 U.S. 500 (1959)], a case which, like this one, arose from the denial of a petition for mandamus to compel a district judge to vacate his order striking a demand for trial by jury.

Our decision reversing that case not only emphasizes the responsibility of the Federal Courts of Appeals to grant mandamus where necessary to protect the constitutional right to trial by jury but also limits the issues open for determination here by defining the protection to which that right is entitled in cases involving both legal and equitable claims. The holding in *Beacon Theaters* was that where both legal and equitable issues are presented in a single case, "only under the most imperative circumstances, circumstances which in view of the flexible procedures of the Federal Rules we cannot now anticipate, can the right to a jury trial of legal issues be lost through prior determination of equitable claims." That holding, of course, applies whether the trial judge chooses to characterize the legal issues presented as "incidental" to the equitable issues or not. Consequently, in a case such as this where there cannot even be a contention of such "imperative circumstances," *Beacon Theaters* requires that any legal issues for which a trial by jury is timely and properly demanded be submitted to a jury. There being no question of the timeliness or correctness of the demand involved here, the sole question which we must decide is whether the action now pending before the District Court contains legal issues.

* * *

The District Court proceeding arises out of a controversy between petitioner and the respondent owners of the trademark "DAIRY QUEEN" with regard to a written licensing contract * * * under which petitioners agreed to pay some $150,000 for the exclusive right to use that trademark in certain portions of Pennsylvania. * * * In August 1960, the respondents wrote petitioner a letter in which they claimed that petitioner had committed "a material breach of that contract" by defaulting on the contract's payment provisions and notified petitioner of the termination of the contract and the cancellation of petitioner's right to use the trademark unless this claimed default was remedied immediately. When petitioner continued to deal with the trademark despite the notice of termination, the respondents brought an action based upon their view that a material breach of contract had occurred.

* * * [The complaint prayed for] (1) temporary and permanent injunctions to restrain petitioner from any future use of or dealing in the franchise and the trademark; (2) an accounting to determine the exact amount of money owing by petitioner and a judgment for that amount; and (3) an injunction pending accounting to prevent petitioner from collecting any money from "Dairy Queen" stores in the territory.

* * *

Petitioner's contention * * * is that insofar as the complaint requests a money judgment it presents a claim which is unquestionably legal. We agree with that contention. The most natural construction of the respondents' claim for a money judgment would seem to be that it is a claim that they are entitled to recover whatever was owed them under the contract as of the date of its purported termination plus damages for infringement of their trademark since that date. Alternatively, the complaint could be construed to set forth a full claim based upon both of these theories—that is, a claim that the respondents were entitled to recover both the debt due under the contract and damages for trademark infringement for the entire period of the alleged breach including that before the termination of the contract. Or it might possibly be construed to set forth a claim for recovery based completely on either one of these two theories—that is, a claim based solely upon the contract for the entire period both before and after the attempted termination on the theory that the termination, having been ignored, was of no consequence, or a claim based solely upon the charge of infringement on the theory that the contract, having been breached, could not be used as a defense to an infringement action even for the period prior to its termination. We find it unnecessary to resolve this ambiguity in the respondents' complaint because we think it plain that their claim for a money judgment is a claim wholly legal in its nature however the complaint is construed. As an action on a debt allegedly due under a contract, it would be difficult to conceive of an action of a more traditional legal character. And as an action for damages based upon a change of trademark infringement it would be no less subject to cognizance by a court of law.

The respondents' contention that this money claim is "purely equitable" is based primarily upon the fact that their complaint is cast in terms of an "accounting," rather than in terms of an action for "debt" or "damages." But the constitutional right to trial by jury cannot be made to depend upon the choice of words used in the pleadings. The necessary prerequisite to the right to maintain a suit for an equitable accounting, like all other equitable remedies, is, as we pointed out in *Beacon Theatres,* the absence of an adequate remedy at law. Consequently, in order to maintain such a suit on a cause of action cognizable at law, as this one is, the plaintiff must be able to show that "accounts between the parties" are of such a "complicated nature" that only a court of equity can satisfactorily unravel them. In view of the powers given to District Courts by Federal Rule of Civil Procedure 53(b) to appoint masters to assist the jury in those exceptional cases where the legal issues are too complicated for the jury adequately to handle alone, the burden of such a showing is considerably increased and it will indeed be a rare case in which it can be met. Be that as it may, this is certainly not such a case. A jury, under proper instructions from the court, could readily determine the recovery, if any, to be had here, whether the theory finally settled upon is that of breach of contract, that of trademark infringement, or any combination of the two. The legal remedy cannot be characterized as inadequate merely because the measure of damages may necessitate a look into petitioner's business records.

Nor is the legal claim here rendered "purely equitable" by the nature of the defenses interposed by petitioner. Petitioner's primary defense to the charge of breach of contract—that is, that the contract was modified by a subsequent oral agreement—presents a purely legal question having nothing whatever to do either with novation, as the district judge suggested, or reformation, as suggested by the respondents here. Such a defense goes to the question of just what, under the law, the contract between the respondents and petitioner is and, in an action to collect a debt for breach of a contract between these parties, petitioner has a right to have the jury determine not only whether the contract has been breached and the extent of the damages if any but also just what the contract is.

* * *

We conclude therefore that the district judge erred in refusing to grant petitioner's demand for a trial by jury on the factual issues related to the question of whether there has been a breach of contract. Since these issues are common with those upon which respondents' claim to equitable relief is based, the legal claims involved in the action must be determined prior to any final court determination of respondents' equitable claims. * * *

[Justice Stewart concurred in the result. Justices Frankfurter and White took no part in the consideration or decision of the case. Justice Harlan, joined by Justice Douglas, concurred separately: " * * * [W]hat is involved in this case is nothing more than a joinder in one complaint for prayers for both legal and equitable relief. In such circumstances, under principles long since established, the petitioner cannot be deprived of his constitutional right to a jury trial on the 'legal' claim contained in the complaint."]

NOTES AND QUESTIONS

1.   Prior to *Beacon Theatres,* the Supreme Court had explicitly stated that the existence of the Seventh Amendment right to jury trial was to be determined by a historical analysis of common law practice prior to 1791, the year of the Amendment's adoption. See, e.g., Dimick v. Schiedt, 293 U.S. 474, 476 (1935), infra p. 669. Since historically there existed a right to jury trial in suits at law but not in equity, it was generally assumed that the Amendment's applicability was to be determined by an analysis of whether the case historically would have been deemed "legal" or "equitable". Do the decisions in *Beacon Theatres* and *Dairy Queen* reject this historical mode of inquiry? If not, do they modify it at all? See Redish, Seventh Amendment Right to Jury Trial: A Study in the Irrationality of Rational Decision Making, 70 Nw.U.L.Rev. 486, 496 (1975): "[T]he Court in *Beacon Theatres* appears to find that the Seventh Amendment's purpose was not to freeze the jury trial picture as it existed in 1791, but rather to dictate that in 'legal,' but not 'equitable,' cases there was to be a right to jury trial. Since equity acts only when the remedy at law is inadequate, the Court concluded that today the legal remedy in *Beacon Theatres* is not inadequate and, therefore, despite historical practice, the case is no longer equitable."

It should be noted that any attempt strictly to reproduce today the historical divisions between law and equity as of 1791 is no simple task, in part because "[b]efore the adoption of the [state and federal] constitutions the line between law and equity * * * was not a fixed and static one. There was a continual process of borrowing by one jurisdiction from the other; there were less frequent instances of a sloughing off of older functions * * *." F. James,

Civil Procedure 340–41 (1965). See also Shapiro & Coquillette, The Fetish of Jury Trial in Civil Cases: A Comment on Rachal v. Hill, 85 Harv.L.Rev. 442, 449 (1971). On the pre-constitutional practice, see generally Wolfram, The Constitutional History of the Seventh Amendment, 57 Minn.L.Rev. 639 (1973).

2. One commentator has suggested that the decision in *Beacon Theatres* "fits well with the conception of the Constitution as a durable document providing continuingly useful standards for an evolving society." McCoid, Procedural Reform and the Right to Jury Trial: A Study of Beacon Theatres, Inc. v. Westover, 116 U.Pa.L.Rev. 1, 11 (1967).

3. Should either or both parties have a constitutional right to jury trial, where plaintiff sues for breach of contract and seeks both damages (legal relief) and specific performance (equitable relief)? How would a strict historical test (i.e. examination of the English practice in 1791, when law courts and equity courts were separate) apply? How would the approach taken in *Beacon Theatres* apply? Professors Wright and Kane have contended that use of a purely historical test in such cases "must fail," because it attempts "to classify a hybrid form of lawsuit that could never have existed in the ancient days." C. Wright & M. Kane, Law of Federal Courts 655 (7th ed. 2011). Does this fact make it impossible to determine how the issue would have been resolved historically? They add that "[i]f the problem cannot be solved by history, resort must be had to policy, and the relevant policy, expressed in the Seventh Amendment, is favorable to jury trial." Id. Does the Seventh Amendment indicate a "policy" in favor of jury trial, even in a case where historically no such right existed?

4. Note that the suit in *Beacon Theatres* sought treble damages for violation of the federal antitrust laws. Obviously the federal antitrust statutes did not exist at common law prior to 1791. How, under a historical test, can the Court assume that there exists a right to jury trial in a suit under these laws? We will consider this problem in Curtis v. Loether, infra pp. 574–576.

5. Fox's original complaint in *Beacon Theatres* sought a declaratory judgment. Does the Court hold that declaratory judgment is a legal remedy? If so, why wasn't there a right to jury trial on Fox's suit, even absent the counterclaim? Note that if a declaratory judgment is not obeyed, the prevailing party can obtain an injunction. See 28 U.S.C.A. § 2201. Why wouldn't that remedy be adequate in any suit in which the plaintiff ultimately desired an injunction to compel compliance with the decision on the merits? See G. Hazard, J. Leubsdorf & D. Bassett, Civil Procedure § 12.11 (6th ed. 2011) (raising the possibility that *Beacon* could be construed to support the questionable conclusion that all claims are legal).

6. A considerably narrower interpretation of the Seventh Amendment than that adopted in *Beacon Theatres* and *Dairy Queen* is advocated in Schwartz, "Everything Depends on How You Draw the Lines": An Alternative Interpretation of the Seventh Amendment, 6 Seton Hall Const. L.J. 599 (1996). Schwartz argues that "the Seventh Amendment is not a guarantee of civil jury trial at all. Rather, it is an authorization to Congress to pass laws requiring

jury trials in cases in which the legislature sees fit and an assurance that such laws will not violate the Constitution. When the Seventh Amendment dictated that the right to civil jury trial was preserved, it meant that it was not abolished." She relies on the fact that when the Constitution was going through the ratification process the Anti-Federalists argued that the document's silence as to the availability of civil jury rendered the use of juries impermissible. The amendment, she contends, was adopted in response to this concern. In support of this conclusion, Schwartz emphasizes Hamilton's response that the Constitution intended instead to leave the decision concerning the use of civil juries to Congress. Does this point support or undermine her position?

For the most part, the other of the first eight amendments included in the Bill of Rights were inserted not to emphasize congressional power to protect the rights in question but rather to insulate those rights from congressional interference. Should the Seventh Amendment, in contrast, be construed solely as the guarantee of congressional authority? Schwartz argues in support of such a distinction on the grounds that only the Seventh Amendment includes the word, "preserved." To what extent does use of this word support her position?

THE "CLEAN-UP" DOCTRINE

Note that the Court in *Dairy Queen,* in response to the argument "that the right to trial by jury may be lost as to legal issues where those issues are characterized as 'incidental' to equitable issues," stated that "our previous decisions make it plain that no such rule may be applied in the federal courts." This response has been criticized as historically inaccurate. F. James, Civil Procedure 374 n. 14 (1965). In fact, the practice rejected by the Court, generally referred to as the "clean-up" doctrine, had a long history. See generally Levin, Equitable Clean-Up and the Jury: A Suggested Orientation, 100 U.Pa.L.Rev. 320 (1951). Why do you suppose equity courts had traditionally assumed authority to resolve "legal" matters that were deemed "incidental" to the primary equitable issues? See Levin, 100 U.Pa.L.Rev. at 320: "Sound considerations of policy lay behind * * * [the] 'clean-up rule,' considerations which loom large and real against the background of two entirely independent systems of trial courts." In light of this pragmatic rationale for the "clean-up" doctrine, might the Court in *Dairy Queen,* applying the approach taken in *Beacon Theatres,* have been able to reject its use in a system in which law and equity have been merged?

Four years after *Dairy Queen,* the Supreme Court itself relied on a form of the "clean-up" doctrine in Katchen v. Landy, 382 U.S. 323 (1966). A trustee in bankruptcy sought to recoup money which the bankrupt had paid to a claimant in the bankruptcy proceeding on the ground that it constituted a voidable preference. The claimant sought a jury trial, arguing that if he had chosen not to file a claim with the bankruptcy court, the trustee would have been forced to sue him, in which case petitioner could have obtained a jury trial.

Though the Court acknowledged that the claimant might be entitled to a jury trial in a plenary action on the preference, it rejected his claim to a right to a jury trial in the course of the bankruptcy proceeding. Acceptance of the jury trial argument, Justice White reasoned, would require that in every similar case "the proceedings on allowance of claims must be suspended and a plenary suit initiated, with all the delay and expense that course would entail." The Court rejected the jury trial right, because "incidental" legal questions could be handled by the bankruptcy court, acting as a court of equity. Is it possible to justify use of the "clean-up" rule in *Katchen* while rejecting its use in *Dairy Queen?*

The Court in *Katchen* distinguished *Beacon Theatres* and *Dairy Queen* on the ground that neither case had "involved a specific statutory scheme contemplating the prompt trial of a disputed claim without the intervention of a jury." Does this statement imply that the Court in *Katchen* was balancing the constitutional right to jury trial against the need for governmental convenience? See Comment, The Seventh Amendment and Civil Rights Statutes: History Adrift in a Maelstrom, 68 Nw.U.L.Rev. 503 (1973). If so, do you think this is a proper mode of constitutional analysis? Should a "statutory scheme" take precedence over a constitutional right? On the issue of the right to jury trial in bankruptcy cases, see infra pp. 601–602.

ROSS V. BERNHARD

Supreme Court of the United States, 1970
396 U.S. 531

JUSTICE WHITE delivered the opinion of the Court.

* * * Whether the [Seventh] Amendment guarantees the right to a jury trial in stockholders' derivative actions is the issue now before us.

Petitioners brought this derivative suit in federal court against the directors of their closed end investment company, the Lehman Corporation and the corporation's brokers, Lehman Brothers. They contended that Lehman Brothers controlled the corporation through an illegally large representation on the corporation's board of directors, in violation of the Investment Company Act of 1940, 15 U.S.C.A. §§ 80a–1 to 52, and used this control to extract excessive brokerage fees from the corporation. The directors of the corporation were accused of converting corporate assets and of "gross abuse of trust, gross misconduct, willful misfeasance, bad faith, [and] gross negligence." Both the individual defendants and Lehman Brothers were accused of breaches of fiduciary duty. * * * Petitioners requested that the defendants "account for and pay to the Corporation for their profits and gains and its losses." Petitioners also demanded a jury trial on the corporation's claims.

On motion to strike petitioners' jury trial demand, the District Court held that a shareholder's right to a jury on his corporation's cause of action was to be judged as if the corporation were itself the plaintiff. Only the shareholder's initial claim to speak for the corporation had to be tried to the judge. * * * The Court of Appeals reversed, holding that a derivative action was entirely equitable in nature, and no jury was available to try any part of it. * * *

We reverse the holding of the Court of Appeals that in no event does the right to a jury trial preserved by the Seventh Amendment extend to derivative actions brought by the stockholders of a corporation. We hold that the right to jury trial attaches to those issues in derivative actions as to which the corporation, if it had been suing in its own right, would have been entitled to a jury.

The Seventh Amendment preserves to litigants the right to jury trial in suits at common law—

> "not merely suits, which the common law recognized among its old and settled proceedings, but suits in which legal rights were to be ascertained and determined, in contradistinction to those where equitable rights alone were recognized, and equitable remedies were administered. . . . In a just sense, the amendment then may well be construed to embrace all suits, which are not of equity and admiralty jurisdiction, whatever may be the peculiar form which they may assume to settle legal rights." Parsons v. Bedford, Breedlove & Robeson, 3 Pet. 433, 447 (1830).

However difficult it may have been to define with precision the line between actions at law dealing with legal rights and suits in equity dealing with equitable matters, some proceedings were unmistakably actions at law triable to a jury. The Seventh Amendment, for example, entitled the parties to a jury trial in actions for damages to a person or property, for libel and slander, for recovery of land, and for conversion of personal property. Just as clearly, a corporation, although an artificial being, was commonly entitled to sue and be sued in the usual forms of action, at least in its own State. Whether the corporation was viewed as an entity separate from its stockholders or as a device permitting its stockholders to carry on their business and to sue and be sued, a corporation's suit to enforce a legal right was an action at common law carrying the right to jury trial at the time the Seventh Amendment was adopted.

The common law refused, however, to permit stockholders to call corporate managers to account in actions at law. The possibilities for abuse, thus presented, were not ignored by corporate officers and directors. Early in the 19th century, equity provided relief both in this country and in

England. Without detailing these developments, it suffices to say that the remedy in this country * * * provided redress not only against faithless officers and directors but also against third parties who had damaged or threatened the corporate properties and whom the corporation through its managers refused to pursue. The remedy made available in equity was the derivative suit, viewed in this country as a suit to enforce a corporate cause of action against officers, directors, and third parties. As elaborated in the cases, one precondition for the suit was a valid claim on which the corporation could have sued; another was that the corporation itself had refused to proceed after suitable demand, unless excused by extraordinary conditions. Thus the dual nature of the stockholder's action: first, the plaintiff's right to sue on behalf of the corporation and, second, the merits of the corporation's claim itself.

Derivative suits posed no Seventh Amendment problems where the action against the directors and third parties would have been by a bill in equity had the corporation brought the suit. Our concern is with cases based upon a legal claim of the corporation against directors or third parties. Does the trial of such claims at the suit of a stockholder and without a jury violate the Seventh Amendment?

* * *

What can be gleaned from this Court's opinions is not inconsistent with the general understanding, reflected by the state court decisions and secondary sources, that equity could properly resolve corporate claims of any kind without a jury when properly pleaded in derivative suits complying with the equity rules.

Such was the prevailing opinion when the Federal Rules of Civil Procedure were adopted in 1938. It continued until 1963 when the Court of Appeals for the Ninth Circuit, relying on the Federal Rules as construed and applied in Beacon Theatres, Inc. v. Westover, and Dairy Queen, Inc. v. Wood, required the legal issues in a derivative suit to be tried to a jury. * * *

Under [*Beacon Theatres* and *Dairy Queen*], where equitable and legal claims are joined in the same action, there is a right to jury trial on the legal claims which must not be infringed either by trying the legal issues as incidental to the equitable ones or by a court trial of a common issue existing between the claims. The Seventh Amendment question depends on the nature of the issue to be tried rather than the character of the overall action.[10] The principle of these cases bears heavily on derivative actions.

We have noted that the derivative suit has dual aspects: first, the stockholder's right to sue on behalf of the corporation, historically an

---

[10] As our cases indicate, the "legal" nature of an issue is determined by considering, first, the pre-merger custom with reference to such questions; second, the remedy sought; and, third, the practical abilities and limitations of juries. Of these factors, the first, requiring extensive and possibly abstruse historical inquiry, is obviously the most difficult to apply. See James, Right to a Jury Trial in Civil Actions, 72 Yale L.J. 655 (1963).

equitable matter; second, the claim of the corporation against directors or third parties on which, if the corporation had sued and the claim presented legal issues, the company could demand a jury trial. * * * [L]egal claims are not magically converted into equitable issues by their presentation to a court of equity in a derivative suit. The claim pressed by the stockholder against directors or third parties "is not his own but the corporation's." Koster v. Lumbermens Mut. Cas. Co., 330 U.S. 518, 522 (1947). The corporation is a necessary party to the action; without it the case cannot proceed. Although named a defendant, it is the real party in interest, the stockholder being at best the nominal plaintiff. The proceeds of the action belong to the corporation and it is bound by the result of the suit. The heart of the action is the corporate claim. If it presents a legal issue, one entitling the corporation to a jury trial under the Seventh Amendment, the right to a jury is not forfeited merely because the stockholder's right to sue must first be adjudicated as an equitable issue triable to the court. *Beacon* and *Dairy Queen* require no less.

If under older procedures, now discarded, a court of equity could properly try the legal claims of the corporation presented in a derivative suit, it was because irreparable injury was threatened and no remedy at law existed as long as the stockholder was without standing to sue and the corporation itself refused to pursue its own remedies. Indeed, from 1789 until 1938, the judicial code expressly forbade courts of equity from entertaining any suit for which there was an adequate remedy at law. * * * If, before 1938, the law had borrowed from equity, as it borrowed other things, the idea that stockholders could litigate for their recalcitrant corporation, the corporate claim, if legal, would undoubtedly have been tried to a jury.

Of course, this did not occur, but the Federal Rules had a similar impact. Actions are no longer brought as actions at law or suits in equity. Under the Rules there is only one action, a "civil action" in which all claims may be joined and all remedies are available. Purely procedural impediments to the presentation of any issue by any party, based on the difference between law and equity, were destroyed. In a civil action presenting a stockholder's derivative claim, the court after passing upon the plaintiff's right to sue on behalf of the corporation is now able to try the corporate claim for damages with the aid of a jury. Separable claims may be tried separately, Fed.Rule Civ.Proc. 42(b), or legal and equitable issues may be handled in the same trial. The historical rule preventing a court of law from entertaining a shareholder's suit on behalf of the corporation is obsolete; it is no longer tenable for a district court, administering both law and equity in the same action, to deny legal remedies to a corporation, merely because the corporation's spokesmen are its shareholders rather than its directors. Under the rules, law and equity are procedurally combined; nothing turns now upon the form of the action or the procedural devices by which the parties happen to come before the court. The "expansion of adequate legal remedies provided by . . . the Federal Rules necessarily affects the scope of equity." Beacon Theatres, Inc. v. Westover.

Thus, for example, before-merger class actions were largely a device of equity, and there was no right to a jury even on issues that might, under other circumstances, have been tried to a jury. Although at least one post-merger court held that the device was not available to try legal issues, it now seems settled in the lower federal courts that class action plaintiffs may obtain a jury trial on any legal issues they present.

Derivative suits have been described as one kind of "true" class action. We are inclined to agree with the description, at least to the extent it recognizes that the derivative suit and the class action were both ways of allowing parties to be heard in equity who could not speak at law.[15] After adoption of the rules there is no longer any procedural obstacle to the assertion of legal rights before juries, however the party may have acquired standing to assert those rights. Given the availability in a derivative action of both legal and equitable remedies, we think the Seventh Amendment preserves to the parties in a stockholder's suit the same right to a jury trial that historically belonged to the corporation and to those against whom the corporation pressed its legal claims.

In the instant case we have no doubt that the corporation's claim is, at least in part, a legal one. The relief sought is money damages. There are allegations in the complaint of a breach of fiduciary duty, but there are also allegations of ordinary breach of contract and gross negligence. The corporation, had it sued on its own behalf, would have been entitled to a jury's determination, at a minimum, of its damages against its broker under the brokerage contract and of its rights against its own directors because of their negligence. Under these circumstances it is unnecessary to decide whether the corporation's other claims are also properly triable to a jury. Dairy Queen, Inc. v. Wood.

JUSTICE STEWART, with whom THE CHIEF JUSTICE and JUSTICE HARLAN join, dissenting.

In holding as it does that the plaintiff in a shareholder's derivative suit is constitutionally entitled to a jury trial, the Court today seems to rely upon some sort of ill-defined combination of the Seventh Amendment and the Federal Rules of Civil Procedure. Somehow the Amendment and the Rules magically interact to do what each separately was expressly intended

---

[15] Other equitable devices are used under the rules without depriving the parties employing them of the right to a jury trial on legal issues. For example, although the right to intervene may in some cases be limited, when intervention is permitted generally, the intervenor has a right to a jury trial on any legal issues he presents. A similar development seems to be taking place in the lower courts in interpleader actions. Before merger interpleader actions lay only in equity, and there was no right to a jury even on issues that might, under other circumstances, have been tried to a jury. This view continued for some time after merger.

not to do, namely, to enlarge the right to a jury trial in civil actions brought in the courts of the United States.

The Seventh Amendment, by its terms, does not extend, but merely preserves the right to a jury trial "[i]n Suits at common law." All agree that this means the reach of the Amendment is limited to those actions that were tried to the jury in 1791 when the Amendment was adopted.[1] Suits in equity, which were historically tried to the court, were therefore unaffected by it. Similarly, Rule 38 of the Federal Rules has no bearing on the right to a jury trial in suits in equity, for it simply preserves inviolate "[t]he right of trial by jury as declared by the Seventh Amendment." Thus this Rule, like the Amendment itself, neither restricts nor enlarges the right to jury trial. Indeed nothing in the Federal Rules can rightly be construed to enlarge the right of jury trial, for in the legislation authorizing the Rules, Congress expressly provided that they "shall neither abridge, enlarge, nor modify the substantive rights of any litigant." See 28 U.S.C. § 2072. I take this plain, simple, and straightforward language to mean that after the promulgation of the Federal Rules, as before, the constitutional right to a jury trial attaches only to suits at common law. So, apparently, has every federal court that has discussed the issue. Since, as the Court concedes, a shareholder's derivative suit could be brought only in equity, it would seem to me to follow by the most elementary logic that in such suits there is no constitutional right to a trial by jury. Today the Court tosses aside history, logic and over 100 years of firm precedent to hold that the plaintiff in a shareholder's derivative suit does indeed have a constitutional right to a trial by jury. This holding has a questionable basis in policy[5] and no basis whatever in the Constitution.

The Court begins by assuming the "dual nature" of the shareholder's action. While the plaintiff's right to get into court at all is conceded to be equitable, once he is there the Court says his claim is to be viewed as though it were the claim of the corporation itself. If the corporation would have been entitled to a jury trial on such a claim, then, it is said, so would the shareholder. This conceptualization is without any historical basis. For the fact is that a shareholder's suit was not originally viewed in this country, or in England, as a suit to enforce a corporate cause of action. Rather, the shareholder's suit was initially permitted only against the managers of the corporation—not third parties—and it was conceived of as an equitable action to enforce the right of a beneficiary against his trustee. The shareholder was not, therefore, in court to enforce indirectly the

---

[1]   Where a new cause of action is created by Congress, and nothing is said about how it is to be tried, the jury trial issue is determined by fitting the cause into its nearest historical analogy. See James, Right to a Jury Trial in Civil Actions, 72 Yale L.J. 655.

[5]   See, e.g., Frank, Courts on Trial 110–11 (1949). Certainly there is no consensus among commentators on the desirability of jury trials in civil actions generally. Particularly where the issues in the case are complex as they are likely to be in a derivative suit much can be said for allowing the court discretion to try the case itself. See discussion in 5 J. Moore, Federal Practice ¶ 38.02[1].

corporate right of action, but to enforce directly his own equitable right of action against an unfaithful fiduciary. Later the rights of the shareholder were enlarged to encompass suits against third parties harming the corporation, but "the postulated 'corporate cause of action' has never been thought to describe an actual historical class of suit which was recognized by courts of law." [Note, The Right to a Jury Trial in a Stockholder's Derivative Action, 74 Yale L.J. 725, 730 (1965)]. Indeed the commentators, including those cited by the Court as postulating the analytic duality of the shareholder's derivative suit, recognize that historically the suit has in practice always been treated as a single cause tried exclusively in equity. They agree that there is therefore no constitutional right to a jury trial even where there might have been one had the corporation itself brought the suit.

This has been not simply the "general" or "prevailing" view in the federal courts as the Court says, but the unanimous view with the single exception of the Ninth Circuit's 1963 decision in DePinto v. Provident Security Life Ins. Co., 323 F.2d 826, a decision that has since been followed by no court until the present case. The Court would have us discount all those decisions rendered before 1938, when the Federal Rules of Civil Procedure were adopted, because it says that before the promulgation of the Rules, "[p]urely procedural impediments" somehow blocked the exercise of a constitutional right. In itself this would seem a rather shaky premise upon which to build an argument. But the Court's position is still further weakened by the fact that any "[p]urely procedural impediments" to a jury trial in a derivative suit were eliminated, not in 1938, but at least as early as 1912. For Rule 23 of the Equity Rules of that year provided that if a "matter ordinarily determinable at law" arose in an equity suit it should "be determined in that suit according to the principles applicable, without sending the case or question to the law side of the court." These applicable principles included the right of jury trial. Consequently, when the Court said in United Copper Co. v. Amalgamated Copper Co., 244 U.S. 261, 264, that "it is clear" that the remedy of a stockholder seeking to enforce the rights of a corporation—whatever their nature—is not in law but in equity, it was not because there were "procedural impediments" to a jury trial on any "legal issues." Rather, it was because the suit itself was conceived of as a wholly equitable cause of action.

* * *

These pre-1938 cases, then, firmly establish the unitary, equitable basis of shareholders' derivative suits and in no way support the Court's holding here. But, the Court says, whatever the situation may have been before 1938, the Federal Rules of Civil Procedure of that year, at least as construed in our decisions more than 20 years later in Beacon Theatres, Inc. v. Westover, and Dairy Queen, Inc. v. Wood, in any event require the conclusion reached today. I can find nothing in either of these cases that leads to that conclusion.

* * *

It is true that in *Beacon Theatres* it was stated that the 1938 Rules did diminish the scope of federal equity jurisdiction in certain particulars. But the Court's effort to force the facts of this case into the mold of *Beacon Theatres* and *Dairy Queen* simply does not succeed. Those cases involved a combination of historically separable suits, one in law and one in equity. Their facts fit the pattern of cases where, before the Rules, the equity court would have disposed of the equitable claim and would then have either retained jurisdiction over the suit, despite the availability of adequate legal remedies, or enjoined a subsequent legal action between the same parties involving the same controversy.

But the present case is not one involving traditionally equitable claims by one party, and traditionally legal claims by the other. Nor is it a suit in which the plaintiff is asserting a combination of legal and equitable claims. For, as we have seen, a derivative suit has always been conceived of as a single, unitary, equitable cause of action. It is for this reason, and not because of "procedural impediments," that the courts of equity did not transfer derivative suits to the law side. In short, the cause of action is wholly a creature of equity. And whatever else can be said of *Beacon Theatres* and *Dairy Queen,* they did not cast aside altogether the historic division between equity and law.

If history is to be so cavalierly dismissed, the derivative suit can, of course, be artificially broken down into separable elements. But so then can any traditionally equitable cause of action, and the logic of the Court's position would lead to the virtual elimination of all equity jurisdiction. An equitable suit for an injunction, for instance, often involves issues of fact which, if damages had been sought, would have been triable to a jury. Does this mean that in a suit asking only for injunctive relief these factual issues must be tried to the jury, with the judge left to decide only whether, given the jury's findings, an injunction is the appropriate remedy? Certainly the Federal Rules make it possible to try a suit for an injunction in that way, but even more certainly they were not intended to have any such effect. Yet the Court's approach, it seems, would require that if any "legal issue" procedurally could be tried to a jury, it constitutionally must be tried to a jury.

The fact is, of course, that there are, for the most part, no such things as inherently "legal issues" or inherently "equitable issues." There are only factual issues, and, "like chameleons [they] take their color from surrounding circumstances."[12] Thus the Court's "nature of the issue" approach is hardly meaningful.

* * *

The Court's decision today can perhaps be explained as a reflection of an unarticulated but apparently overpowering bias in favor of jury trials in civil actions. It certainly cannot be explained in terms of either the Federal Rules or the Constitution.

NOTES AND QUESTIONS

1.   There is no doubt that historically, the *Ross* case would have been deemed purely equitable. Does the majority legitimately reach the conclusion that the right to jury trial applies? Does the approach to the law-equity distinction adopted in *Beacon Theatres* [supra p. 550] support the Court's conclusion?

2.   One commentator has suggested that while in part *Ross* relied on historical analysis, "[a]t another point in its opinion * * * the Court gave reason to speculate that the historical test might be subject to substantial modification in future cases." Wolfram, The Constitutional History of the Seventh Amendment, 57 Minn.L.Rev. 639, 643 (1973). Professor Wolfram was referring to footnote 10 of the Court's opinion, where it noted that "the practical abilities and limitations of juries" was a factor relevant to the determination of the constitutional right to jury trial. With the exception of the case of an accounting, it had never been thought that the presence of the constitutional right was to be determined by an assessment of a jury's capabilities.

Professor Wolfram applauded this development: "If precedent is not an insurmountable obstacle, then one may hope that the time is near when the dead hand of the historical test will be lifted from the seventh amendment." 57 Minn.L.Rev. at 747. Do you agree with Professor Wolfram's sentiments? Does the language of the Seventh Amendment allow the court to ignore "the dead hand of the historical test"? Should that matter?

3.   *Ross* shows that sometimes procedural innovation can give rise to a right to jury trial in a case where it would not have been available at common law. Procedural innovation can work the other way as well. Thus, in Parklane Hosiery Co. v. Shore, 439 U.S. 322 (1979), the Court abandoned the common law rule that collateral estoppel could only be asserted by one who was a party to the prior litigation whose results were urged as binding in the present suit. The Court therefore held that plaintiffs in a securities fraud action could rely on the findings of an earlier suit brought by the SEC against defendants. This issue is covered in Chapter 13. See infra p. 1257.

---

[12] James, supra n. 1, at 692. As Professor Moore has put it, "Whether issues are legal or equitable may, of course, depend upon the manner in which they are presented. . . . " 5 J. Moore, Federal Practice ¶ 38.04[1], n. 40. And he, along with virtually every other commentator, concludes that if the issues are presented in a shareholder's derivative suit they are equitable and the plaintiff has no constitutional right to have them tried by a jury. 5 J. Moore, Federal Practice ¶ 38.38[4].

Defendants in *Parklane* also argued that abandoning the requirement of mutuality for collateral estoppel deprived them of their right to a jury trial in the private securities fraud action since the earlier SEC suit had been tried to a judge. Pointing out that *Beacon Theatres* assumed that the judge's findings from a prior equitable action would bind the later litigation of the same issues between the same parties, the Court saw no reason for a different result where the party relying on estoppel had not been involved in the earlier proceeding.

"A litigant who has lost because of adverse factual findings in an equity action is equally deprived of a jury trial whether he is estopped from relitigating the factual issues against the same party or a new party. In either case, the party against whom estoppel is asserted has litigated questions of fact, and has had the facts determined against him in an earlier proceeding. In either case there is no further factfinding function for the jury to perform, since the common factual issues have been resolved in the previous action".

Only Justice Rehnquist dissented, reasoning that "the development of nonmutual estoppel is a substantial departure from the common law and its use in this case completely deprives petitioners of their right to have a jury determine contested issues of fact. I am simply unwilling to accept the Court's presumption that the complete extinguishment of petitioners' right to trial by jury can be justified as a mere change in 'procedural incident or detail.' " Justice Rehnquist based his conclusion on the great importance the framers of the Seventh Amendment placed on the jury trial.

Does *Parklane* signal a shift in attitude toward the right to jury trial? May other procedures be developed that deny a jury where it would have been available at common law?

4.   In Lytle v. Household Manufacturing, Inc., 494 U.S. 545 (1990), the Supreme Court refused to extend the reach of *Parklane*. The Court held that the Seventh Amendment precludes according collateral estoppel effect to a district court's determinations of issues that are common to both equitable and legal claims where the court resolved the equitable claims first solely because it had erroneously dismissed the legal claims. The plaintiff had sued under both Title VII of the Civil Rights Act of 1964 and 42 U.S.C.A. § 1981, alleging that the defendant had terminated his employment because of his race and had retaliated against him for filing a charge with the Equal Employment Opportunity Commission. The district court dismissed the § 1981 claim, to which the jury trial right applied, and conducted a bench trial on the Title VII claims, which it deemed equitable. While the court of appeals reversed the district court's dismissal of the § 1981 claim, it nevertheless held that that court's findings on the Title VII issue were collateral estoppel on the § 1981 claim.

In reversing, Justice Marshall, speaking for the Court, distinguished *Parklane* (494 U.S. at 550–52):

Only the District Court's erroneous dismissal of the § 1981 claims enabled that court to resolve issues common to both claims, issues that otherwise would have been resolved by a jury. But for that erroneous ruling, this case would be indistinguishable from *Beacon Theatres* and *Dairy Queen*. It would be anomalous to hold that a district court may not deprive a litigant of his right to a jury trial by resolving an equitable claim before a jury hears a legal claim raising common issues, but that a court may accomplish the same result by erroneously dismissing the legal claim. Such a holding would be particularly unfair here because [plaintiff] was required to join his legal and equitable claims to avoid the bar of res judicata.

CURTIS V. LOETHER
Supreme Court of the United States, 1974
415 U.S. 189

JUSTICE MARSHALL delivered the opinion of the Court.

Section 812 of the Civil Rights Act of 1968 authorizes private plaintiffs to bring civil actions to redress violations of Title VIII, the fair housing provisions of the Act, and provides that "[t]he court may grant as relief, as it deems appropriate, any permanent or temporary injunction, temporary restraining order, or other order, and may award to the plaintiff actual damages and not more than $1,000 punitive damages. . . ." The question presented in this case is whether the Civil Rights Act or the Seventh Amendment requires a jury trial upon demand by one of the parties in an action for damages and injunctive relief under this section.

Petitioner, a Negro woman, brought this action under § 812, claiming that respondents, who are white, had refused to rent an apartment to her because of her race, in violation of § 804(a) of the Act. In her complaint she sought only injunctive relief and punitive damages; a claim for compensatory damages was later added. * * * Respondents made a timely demand for jury trial in their answer. The District Court, however, held that jury trial was neither authorized by Title VIII nor required by the Seventh Amendment, and denied the jury request. * * *

The Court of Appeals reversed on the jury trial issue.

* * *

The legislative history on the jury trial question is sparse, and what little is available is ambiguous. There seems to be some indication that supporters of Title VIII were concerned that the possibility of racial prejudice on juries might reduce the effectiveness of civil rights damages actions. * * * We see no point to giving extended consideration to these arguments, however, for we think it is clear that the Seventh Amendment entitles either party to demand a jury trial in an action for damages in the federal courts under § 812.

* * * Although the thrust of the Amendment was to preserve right to jury trial as it existed in 1791, it has long been settled that the right

extends beyond the common-law forms of action recognized at that time. Mr. Justice Story established the basic principle in 1830:

"The phrase 'common law,' found in this clause, is used in contradistinction to equity, and admiralty, and maritime jurisprudence.... By *common law*, [the Framers of the Amendment] meant . . . not merely suits, which the *common* law recognized among its old and settled proceedings, but suits in which *legal* rights were to be ascertained and determined, in contradistinction to those where equitable rights alone were recognized, and equitable remedies were administered.... In a just sense, the amendment then may well be construed to embrace all suits which are not of equity and admiralty jurisdiction, whatever might be the peculiar form which they may assume to settle legal rights." Parsons v. Bedford, 3 Pet. 433, 446–447 (1830) (emphasis in original).

Petitioner nevertheless argues that the Amendment is inapplicable to new causes of action created by congressional enactment. As the Court of Appeals observed, however, we have considered the applicability of the constitutional right to jury trial in actions enforcing statutory rights "as a matter too obvious to be doubted." * * * Whatever doubt may have existed should now be dispelled. The Seventh Amendment does apply to actions enforcing statutory rights, and requires a jury trial upon demand, if the statute creates legal rights and remedies, enforceable in an action for damages in the ordinary courts of law.

We think it is clear that a damages action under § 812 is an action to enforce "legal rights" within the meaning of our Seventh Amendment decisions. A damages action under the statute sounds basically in tort— the statute merely defines a new legal duty, and authorizes the courts to compensate a plaintiff for the injury caused by the defendant's wrongful breach. * * * [T]his cause of action is analogous to a number of tort actions recognized at common law. More important, the relief sought here—actual and punitive damages—is the traditional form of relief offered in the courts of law.

NLRB v. Jones & Laughlin Steel Corp., 301 U.S. 1 (1937), relied on by petitioner, lends no support to her statutory-rights argument. The Court there upheld the award of back pay without jury trial in an NLRB unfair labor practice proceeding, rejecting a Seventh Amendment claim on the ground that the case involved a "statutory proceeding" and "not a suit at common law or in the nature of such a suit." *Jones & Laughlin* merely stands for the proposition that the Seventh Amendment is generally inapplicable in administrative proceedings, where jury trials would be incompatible with the whole concept of administrative adjudication and would substantially interfere with the NLRB's role in the statutory scheme. Katchen v. Landy [supra p. 563, also relied upon by petitioner, is to like effect. * * * These cases uphold congressional power to entrust enforcement of statutory rights to an administrative process or specialized court of equity free from the strictures of the Seventh Amendment. But when Congress provides for enforcement of statutory rights in an ordinary civil action in the district courts, where there is obviously no functional justification for denying the jury trial right, a jury trial must be available if the action involves rights and remedies of the sort typically enforced in an action at law.

* * *

We need not, and do not, go so far as to say that any award of monetary relief must necessarily be "legal" relief. A comparison of Title VIII with Title VII of the Civil Rights Act of 1964, where the courts of appeals have held that jury trial is not required in an action for reinstatement and back pay, is instructive, although we of course express no view on the jury trial issue in that context. In Title VII cases the courts of appeals have characterized back pay as an integral part of an equitable remedy, a form of restitution. But the statutory language on which this characterization is based—

> "[T]he court may enjoin the respondent from engaging in such unlawful employment practice, and order such affirmative action as may be appropriate, which may include, but is not limited to, reinstatement or hiring of employees, with or without back pay . . . or any other equitable relief as the court deems appropriate," 42 U.S.C. § 2000e–5(g).

contrasts sharply with § 812's simple authorization of an action for actual and punitive damages. In Title VII cases, also, the courts have relied on the fact that the decision whether to award back pay is committed to the discretion of the trial judge. There is no comparable discretion here: if a plaintiff proves unlawful discrimination and actual damages, he is entitled to judgment for that amount. Nor is there any sense in which the award here can be viewed as requiring the defendant to disgorge funds wrongfully withheld from the plaintiff. Whatever may be the merit of the "equitable" characterization in Title VII cases, there is surely no basis for characterizing the award of compensatory and punitive damages here as equitable relief.

We are not oblivious to the force of petitioner's policy arguments. Jury trials may delay to some extent the disposition of Title VIII damages actions. * * * We recognize, too, the possibility that jury prejudice may deprive a victim of discrimination of the verdict to which he or she is entitled. * * * More fundamentally, however, these considerations are insufficient to overcome the clear command of the Seventh Amendment.

NOTES AND QUESTIONS

1. After *Curtis,* what is left of the balancing approach to Seventh Amendment analysis arguably implied in footnote 10 of *Ross* and in Katchen v. Landy?

2. Does the Court in *Curtis* satisfactorily distinguish cases arising under Title VII of the 1964 Civil Rights Act from Title VIII cases under the Civil Rights Act of 1968? If a complaining party alleges that he was not hired because of his race, is it proper to characterize his damage claim as "backpay"? In section 102 of the Civil Rights Act of 1991, Pub. L. No. 102–166, 105 Stat. 1071 (1991), Congress provided a statutory right to jury trial in Title VII actions when a complaining party seeks compensatory or punitive damages. However, Congress excluded backpay from the definition of "compensatory damages."

3. In Pernell v. Southall Realty, 416 U.S. 363 (1974), the Supreme Court held that the Seventh Amendment guaranteed a right to jury trial in a landlord's suit to recover possession of real property from his tenant under § 16–1501 of the District of Columbia Code, stating:

> This Court has long assumed that actions to recover land, like actions for damages to a person or property, are actions at law triable to a jury. * * *
>
> Respondent suggests, however, that these precedents should be limited to actions to recover property where title is in issue and that actions brought under § 16–1501 should be distinguished * * *. The distinction between title to and possession of property, of course, was well recognized at common law. But however relevant it was for certain purposes, it had no bearing on the right to a jury trial.
>
> * * *
>
> In particular, ejectment became the principal means employed by landlords to evict tenants for overstaying the terms of their leases, nonpayment of rent, or other breach of lease covenants. * * *
>
> Notwithstanding this history, the Court of Appeals reasoned that an action under § 16–1501 was not the "equivalent" of an action of ejectment. * * * Since, in its opinion, neither § 16–1501 nor its equivalent existed at common law, the Court of Appeals held that the Seventh Amendment did not guarantee the right to jury trial.
>
> In our view, this analysis is fundamentally at odds with the test we have formulated for resolving Seventh Amendment questions.

The Court then quoted Parsons v. Bedford, which was relied on in *Curtis:* "whether or not a close equivalent to § 16–1501 existed in England in 1791 is irrelevant for Seventh Amendment purposes, for that Amendment requires trial by jury in actions unheard of at common law, provided that the action involves rights and remedies of the sort traditionally enforced in an action at law, rather than in an action in equity or admiralty."

4.   Note that in Curtis v. Loether the proponents of jury trial are the defendants, while the party opposing it is the plaintiff. Consider how this alignment may reflect the arguments that might have moved Congress to desire that Title VIII claims not give rise to a jury trial. The actual outcome, however, may not have been as anticipated; one commentator reported that before Curtis v. Loether was decided, the usual plaintiff judgments ranged from $1,500 to $2,500, while after the decision they increased to a usual range on $10,000 to $50,000. See Susz, Federal Fair Housing, 89 Case & Comment 30, 30–31 (May–June 1984).

5.   Note that Congress may choose to provide a *statutory* right to jury trial, when the Seventh Amendment does not itself dictate such a right. It is generally thought that there is no constitutional right to a non-jury trial. See 9 Wright & Miller, Federal Practice and Procedure § 2302.

Tull v. United States, 481 U.S. 412 (1987):

JUSTICE BRENNAN delivered the opinion of the Court.

[The government charged petitioner with dumping fill in wetlands in violation of the Clean Water Act, 33 U.S.C. §§ 1311; 1344; 1362. The Act authorizes both an injunction and a civil penalty of up to $10,000 per day during the period of the violation. The government sought both. Petitioner demanded a jury trial, but the trial court refused the demand. After a 15-day bench trial it found violations of the Act and fined petitioner $75,000, with further fines to follow unless petitioner undertook extremely expensive restoration efforts. The Supreme Court first held that petitioner had a right to jury trial on the question of violation of the Act.]

The petitioner analogizes this Government suit * * * to an action in debt within the jurisdiction of English courts of law. Prior to the enactment of the Seventh Amendment, English courts had held that a civil penalty suit was a particular species of an action in debt that was within the jurisdiction of the courts of law.

* * *

The Government argues, however, that—rather than an action in debt—the closer historical analogue is an action to abate a public nuisance.

* * *

Whether, as the Government argues, a public nuisance action is a better analogy than an action in debt is debatable. But we need not decide the question. As Pernell v. Southhall Realty [supra p. 577 n. 3] cautioned, the fact that the subject matter of a modern statutory action and an 18th-century English action are close equivalents "is irrelevant for Seventh Amendment purposes," because "that Amendment requires trial by jury in actions unheard of at common law." It suffices that we conclude that both the public nuisance action and the action in debt are appropriate analogies to the instant statutory action. * * *

We need not rest our conclusion on what has been called an "abstruse historical" search for the nearest 18th-century analogue. Ross v. Bernhard, [396 U.S. at 548] n. 10. We reiterate our previously expressed view that characterizing the relief sought is "[m]ore important" than finding a precisely analogous common law cause of action in determining whether the Seventh Amendment guarantees a jury trial. Curtis v. Loether, [supra p. 574.]

A civil penalty was a type of remedy at common law that could only be enforced in courts of law. Remedies intended to punish culpable individuals, as opposed to those intended simply to extract compensation or restore the status quo, were issued by courts of law, not courts of equity. [This] action * * * is of this character. [The Act] does not direct that the "civil penalty" imposed be calculated solely on the basis of equitable determinations, such as the profits gained from violations of the statute, but simply imposes a maximum penalty of $10,000 per day of violation. * * * [The Act's] authorization of punishment to further retribution and deterrence clearly evidences that this subsection reflects more than a concern to provide equitable relief. * * * Because the nature of the relief authorized by [the Act] was traditionally available only in a court of law, the petitioner in this present action is entitled to a jury trial on demand.

The punitive nature of the relief sought in the present case is made apparent by a comparison with the relief sought in an action to abate a public nuisance. A public nuisance action was a classic example of the kind of suit that relied on the injunctive relief provided by courts of equity.

[The Court went on, however, to hold that there was no right to jury determination of the amount of civil penalties.]

The Seventh Amendment is silent on the question whether a jury must determine the remedy in a trial in which it must determine liability.[9] The answer must depend on whether the jury must shoulder this responsibility to preserve the "substance of the common-law right of trial by jury." Is a jury role necessary for that purpose? We do not think so. * * * The assessment of civil penalties * * * cannot be said to involve "the substance

---

[9]   Nothing in the Amendment's language suggests that the right to a jury trial extends to the remedy phase of a civil trial. * * * We have been presented with no evidence that the Framers meant to extend the right to a jury to the remedy phase of a civil trial.

of a common-law right to a trial by jury," nor a "fundamental element of a jury trial."

Congress' assignment of the determination of the amount of civil penalties to trial judges therefore does not infringe on the constitutional right to a jury trial.

JUSTICE SCALIA, joined by JUSTICE STEVENS, concurring in part and dissenting in part.

[Justice Scalia agreed that petitioner was entitled to a jury trial on the question of violation, but disagreed with the majority about the assessment of the civil penalty.]

[I]n my view the right to trial by jury on whether a civil penalty of unspecified amount is assessable also involves a right to trial by jury on what the amount should be. * * *

While purporting to base its determination (quite correctly) upon historical practice, the Court creates a form of civil adjudication I have never encountered. I can recall no precedent for judgment of civil liability by jury but assessment of amount by the court. Even punitive damages are assessed by the jury when liability is determined in that fashion. * * * Since, as the Court correctly reasons, the proper analogue to a civil-fine action is the common-law action for debt, the government need only prove liability by a preponderance of the evidence; but must, as in any action for debt, accept the amount of award determined not by its own officials but by twelve private citizens. If that tends to discourage the government from proceeding in this fashion, I doubt that the Founding Fathers would be upset.

NOTES AND QUESTIONS

1.   Does the Court in *Tull* abandon or rely on the historical test in reaching its decision? Does it purport to do both? *Can* it logically do both?

2.   *The law-fact distinction*: As *Tull* illustrates, even where the Seventh Amendment dictates a jury trial right, it does so only to issues of fact, not to issues of law. Distinguishing between the two has not always been an easy task. The Supreme Court devoted attention to this question in Markman v. Westview Instruments, Inc., 517 U.S. 370 (1996), the Court held that construction of a patent, including terms of art, is exclusively within the province of the court, rather than the jury. In reaching this conclusion, the Court initially looked to historical practice. However, where such practice, either directly or by analogy, does not provide an answer, the Court will "consider both the relative interpretive skills of judges and juries and the statutory policies that ought to be furthered by the allocation." Such "functional considerations" may indicate that "as a matter of the sound administration of justice, one judicial actor is better positioned than another to decide the issue in question." Id. at 388, quoting Miller v. Fenton, 474 U.S.

104, 114 (1985). *Markman* is defended in Kirgis, The Right to a Jury Decision On Questions of Fact Under the Seventh Amendment, 64 Ohio St. L. J. 1125 (2003). On the general issue of the law-fact distinction, see Sward, The Seventh Amendment and the Alchemy of Fact and Law, 33 Seton Hall L. Rev. 573 (2003). On the general issue of the role of the Seventh Amendment in patent cases, see Herlihy, Appellate Review of Patent Claim Construction: Should the Federal Circuit be its own Lexicographer in Matters Related to the Seventh Amendment?, 15 Mich. Telecomm. & Tech. L. Rev. 469 (2009).

3.   In Feltner v. Columbia Pictures Television, Inc., 523 U.S. 340 (1998), the Court held that the Seventh Amendment right to jury trial applied to the determination of the amount of damages in a suit under section 504(c) of the Copyright Act, 17 U.S.C. § 504(c). That provision permits a copyright owner "to recover, instead of actual damages and profits, an award of statutory damages . . ., in a sum of not less than $500 or more than $20,000 as the court considers just." Although the Court held that Congress had not created a statutory right to jury trial in section 504(c), it nevertheless found that a jury trial right was provided by the Seventh Amendment.

The Court initially concluded that although the statutory right had not itself existed at common law, historical analogues did in fact exist, and those analogues demonstrated that historically such a right was one at law. The Court further pointed to the "general rule" that monetary relief is legal, and noted that "an award of statutory damages may serve purposes traditionally associated with legal relief, such as compensation and punishment." Because suits under the statute are suits at law, the Court held that the Seventh Amendment dictated a right to jury trial.

The Court further held that the jury trial right dictated that the jury find damages, as well as liability, because "there is overwhelming evidence that the consistent practice at common law was for juries to award damages." The fact that the damages were discretionary did not affect the constitutional requirement that the jury decide damages, because "there is historical evidence that cases involving discretionary monetary relief were tried before juries."

The Court rejected Columbia's reliance on *Tull*: "In *Tull* . . . we were presented with no evidence that juries historically had determined the amount of civil penalties to be paid to the Government. Moreover, the awarding of civil penalties to the Government could be viewed as analogous to sentencing in a criminal proceeding. . . . Here, of course, there is no similar analogy, and there is clear and direct historical evidence that juries, both as a general matter and in copyright cases, set the amount of damages awarded to a successful plaintiff." How persuasive is the Court's asserted distinction of *Tull*? Might the Court's analogy of civil penalties to criminal sentencing prove too much? If a civil penalty is analogous to criminal sentencing, why do the traditional procedural protections of the criminal law (for example, requirement of proof beyond a reasonable doubt and the right to confront accusers) not also apply to civil penalty actions?

4.   *Punitive damages and the law-fact distinction*: Should the question as to whether or not a punitive damage award should be deemed excessive be considered an issue of fact or of law? In BMW of North America, Inc. v. Gore, 517 U.S. 559 (1996), the Supreme Court held that a punitive damage award may be unconstitutionally excessive. In Cooper Industries, Inc. v. Leatherman Tool Group, Inc., 532 U.S. 424 (2001), the Court held that "[b]ecause the jury's award of punitive damages does not constitute a finding of 'fact,' appellate review of the District Court's determination that an award is consistent with due process does not implicate the Seventh Amendment. . . ." Id. at 437. Why should the award of punitive damages be deemed a question of law? Is it that it is unlike the measure of actual damages, in that actual damage awards present a question of historical predictive fact, while punitive damages are comparable to civil fines? If, as the Court concludes, the award of punitive damages is not a finding of fact, why is it decided by the jury in the first place?

5.   One method of tort reform attempted by numerous state legislatures in recent years has been the imposition of statutory caps on the amount of damages to be awarded in a variety of common law tort actions. Do such caps violate the Seventh Amendment in federal court diversity suits? One commentator believes that they do. See Murphy, Determining Compensation: The Tension Between Legislative Power and Jury Authority, 74 Tex. L. Rev. 345 (1995). Professor Murphy notes that "[b]efore adoption of the Seventh Amendment, English juries had long assessed compensatory damages because of their factfinding role." Should statutory caps be viewed as an invasion of the jury's traditional role? Consider the following response: Statutory caps on damages are properly viewed not as a legislative interference with jury factfinding, but rather as a legislative alteration in the governing substantive law.

TEAMSTERS LOCAL NO. 391 V. TERRY

Supreme Court of the United States, 1990
494 U.S. 558

JUSTICE MARSHALL delivered the opinion of the Court except as to Part III-A.

This case presents the question whether an employee who seeks relief in the form of backpay for a union's alleged breach of its duty of fair representation has a right to trial by jury. We hold that the Seventh Amendment entitles such a plaintiff to a jury trial.

I

McLean Trucking Company and the Chauffeurs, Teamsters, and Helpers Local Union No. 391 were parties to a collective-bargaining agreement that governed the terms and conditions of employment at McLean's terminals. The 27 respondents were employed by McLean as truckdrivers in bargaining units covered by the agreement, and all were members of the Union.

[Respondents objected to various employment practices used by McLean that impaired their seniority rights, alleging breaches of the collective bargaining agreement. They filed a grievance with the union, and the grievance committee ordered McLean to alter its practices. When their seniority rights were again impaired, respondents filed subsequent grievances. This time the union declined to refer them to the grievance committee on the ground that the relevant issues had been determined in the prior proceeding.]

In July 1983, respondents filed an action in District Court, alleging that McLean had breached the collective-bargaining agreement in violation of § 301 of the Labor Management Relations Act, 1947, and that the Union had violated its duty of fair representation. Respondents requested a permanent injunction requiring the defendants to cease their illegal acts and to reinstate them to their proper seniority status; in addition, they sought, *inter alia,* compensatory damages for lost wages and health benefits. In 1986 McLean filed for bankruptcy; subsequently, the action against it was voluntarily dismissed, along with all claims for injunctive relief.

Respondents had requested a jury trial in their pleadings. The Union moved to strike the jury demand on the ground that no right to a jury trial exists in a duty of fair representation suit. The District Court denied the motion to strike. After an interlocutory appeal, the Fourth Circuit affirmed the trial court, holding that the Seventh Amendment entitled respondents to a jury trial of their claim for monetary relief. We granted the petition for certiorari to resolve a circuit conflict on this issue, and now affirm the judgment of the Fourth Circuit.

II

The duty of fair representation is inferred from unions' exclusive authority under the National Labor Relations Act, to represent all employees in a bargaining unit. The duty requires a union "to serve the interests of all members without hostility or discrimination toward any, to exercise its discretion with complete good faith and honesty, and to avoid arbitrary conduct." A union must discharge its duty both in bargaining with the employer and in its enforcement of the resulting collective bargaining agreement. Thus, the Union here was required to pursue respondents' grievances in a manner consistent with the principles of fair representation.

Because most collective-bargaining agreements accord finality to grievance or arbitration procedures established by the collective-bargaining agreement, an employee normally cannot bring a § 301 action against an employer unless he can show that the union breached its duty of fair representation in its handling of his grievance. Whether the employee sues both the labor union and the employer or only one of those entities, he must prove the same two facts to recover money damages: that the employer's action violated the terms of the collective-bargaining agreement and that the union breached its duty of fair representation.

III

We turn now to the constitutional issue presented in this case—whether respondents are entitled to a jury trial. * * *

To determine whether a particular action will resolve legal rights, we examine both the nature of the issues involved and the remedy sought. "First, we compare the statutory action to 18th-century actions brought in the courts of England prior to the merger of the courts of law and equity. Second, we examine the remedy sought and determine whether it is legal or equitable in nature." Tull [v. United States.] The second inquiry is the more important in our analysis.[4]

A

An action for breach of a union's duty of fair representation was unknown in 18th-century England; in fact, collective-bargaining was unlawful. We must therefore look for an analogous cause of action that existed in the 18th century to determine whether the nature of this duty of fair representation suit is legal or equitable.

The Union contends that this duty of fair representation action resembles a suit brought to vacate an arbitration award because respondents seek to set aside the result of the grievance process. In the 18th Century, an action to set aside an arbitration award was considered equitable. * * *

The arbitration analogy is inapposite, however, to the Seventh Amendment question posed in this case. No grievance committee has considered respondents' claim that the Union violated its duty of fair representation; the grievance process was concerned only with the employer's alleged breach of the collective-bargaining agreement. Thus, respondents' claim against the Union cannot be characterized as an action to vacate an arbitration award because " '[t]he arbitration proceeding did not, and indeed, could not, resolve the employee's claim against the union. . . . Because no arbitrator has decided the primary issue presented by this claim, no arbitration award need be undone, even if the employee ultimately prevails.' " DelCostello [v. Teamsters, 462 U.S. 151, 167 (1983)].

---

[4] Justice Stevens' analysis emphasizes a third consideration, namely whether "the issues [presented by the claim] are typical grist for the jury's judgment." This Court, however, has never relied on this consideration "as an independent basis for extending the right to a jury trial under the Seventh Amendment." Tull v. United States [supra p. 615]. We recently noted that this consideration is relevant only to the determination "whether Congress has permissibly entrusted the resolution of certain disputes to an administrative agency or specialized court of equity, and whether jury trials would impair the functioning of the legislative scheme." Granfinanciera, S.A. v. Nordberg [infra p. 638. n. 6]. No one disputes that an action for breach of the duty of fair representation may properly be brought in an Article III court; thus, the factor does not affect our analysis.

The Union next argues that respondents' duty of fair representation action is comparable to an action by a trust beneficiary against a trustee for breach of fiduciary duty. Such actions were within the exclusive jurisdiction of courts of equity. This analogy is far more persuasive than the arbitration analogy. Just as a trustee must act in the best interests of the beneficiaries, a union, as the exclusive representative of the workers, must exercise its power to act on behalf of the employees in good faith. Moreover, just as a beneficiary does not directly control the actions of a trustee, an individual employee lacks direct control over a union's actions taken on his behalf.

The trust analogy extends to a union's handling of grievances. In most cases, a trustee has the exclusive authority to sue third parties who injure the beneficiaries' interest in the trust, including any legal claim the trustee holds in trust for the beneficiaries. The trustee then has the sole responsibility for determining whether to settle, arbitrate, or otherwise dispose of the claim. Similarly, the union typically has broad discretion in its decision whether and how to pursue an employee's grievance against an employer. Just as a trust beneficiary can sue to enforce a contract entered into on his behalf by the trustee only if the trustee "improperly refuses or neglects to bring an action against the third person," Restatement (Second) of Trusts, § 282(2), so an employee can sue his employer for a breach of the collective-bargaining agreement only if he shows that the union breached its duty of fair representation in its handling of the grievance.

Respondents contend that their duty of fair representation suit is less like a trust action than an attorney malpractice action which was historically an action at law. * * * We find that, in the context of the Seventh Amendment inquiry, the attorney malpractice analogy does not capture the relationship between the union and the represented employees as fully as the trust analogy does.

The attorney malpractice analogy is inadequate in several respects. Although an attorney malpractice suit is in some ways similar to a suit alleging a union's breach of its fiduciary duty, the two actions are fundamentally different. The nature of an action is in large part controlled by the nature of the underlying relationship between the parties. Unlike employees represented by a union, a client controls the significant decisions concerning his representation. Moreover, a client can fire his attorney if he is dissatisfied with his attorney's performance. This option is not available to an individual employee who is unhappy with a union's representation, unless a majority of the members of the bargaining unit share his dissatisfaction. Thus, we find the malpractice analogy less convincing than the trust analogy.

Nevertheless, the trust analogy does not persuade us to characterize respondents' claim as wholly equitable. The Union's argument mischaracterizes the nature of our comparison of the action before us to

18th-century forms of action. As we observed in Ross v. Bernhard, [supra p. 564], "The Seventh Amendment question depends on the nature of the *issue* to be tried rather than the character of the overall action." * * * [T]o recover from the Union here, respondents must prove both that McLean violated § 301 by breaching the collective-bargaining agreement and that the Union breached its duty of fair representation.[6] When viewed in isolation, the duty of fair representation issue is analogous to a claim against a trustee for breach of fiduciary duty. The § 301 issue, however, is comparable to a breach of contract claim—a legal issue.

Respondents' action against the Union thus encompasses both equitable and legal issues. The first part of our Seventh Amendment inquiry, then, leaves us in equipoise as to whether respondents are entitled to a jury trial.

B

Our determination under the first part of the Seventh Amendment analysis is only preliminary. In this case, the only remedy sought is a request for compensatory damages representing backpay and benefits. Generally, an action for money damages was "the traditional form of relief offered in the courts of law." Curtis v. Loether, 415 U.S. 189, 196 (1974). This Court has not, however, held that "any award of monetary relief must *necessarily* be 'legal' relief." *Ibid.* (emphasis added). Nonetheless, because we conclude that the remedy respondents seek has none of the attributes that must be present before we will find an exception to the general rule and characterize damages as equitable, we find that the remedy sought by respondents is legal.

First, we have characterized damages as equitable where they are restitutionary, such as in "action[s] for disgorgement of improper profits," *Tull,* 481 U.S., at 424. The backpay sought by respondents is not money wrongfully held by the Union, but wages and benefits they would have received from McLean had the Union processed the employees' grievances properly. Such relief is not restitutionary.

Second, a monetary award "incidental to or intertwined with injunctive relief" may be equitable. *Tull,* supra, 481 U.S., at 424. Because

---

[6]   The dissent characterizes this opinion as "pars[ing] legal elements out of equitable claims". The question whether the Seventh Amendment analysis requires an examination of the nature of each element of a typical claim is not presented by this case. The claim we confront here is not typical; instead, it is a claim consisting of discrete issues that would normally be brought as two claims, one against the employer and one against the union. Had the employer remained a defendant in this action, the dissent would surely agree that the 301 claim against the employer was a separate claim. The Seventh Amendment analysis should not turn on the ability of the plaintiff to maintain his suit against both defendants, when the issues in the suit remain the same even when he can sue only the union. Consideration of the nature of the two issues in this hybrid action is therefore warranted.

respondents seek only money damages, this characteristic is clearly absent from the case.[8]

The Union argues that the backpay relief sought here must nonetheless be considered equitable because this Court has labeled backpay awarded under Title VII, 42 U.S.C. § 2000e et seq. (1982 ed.), as equitable. It contends that the Title VII analogy is compelling in the context of the duty of fair representation because its backpay provision was based on the NLRA provision governing backpay awards for unfair labor practices. We are not convinced.

The Court has never held that a plaintiff seeking backpay under Title VII has a right to a jury trial. Assuming, without deciding, that such a Title VII plaintiff has no right to a jury trial, the Union's argument does not persuade us that respondents are not entitled to a jury trial here. Congress specifically characterized backpay under Title VII as a form of "equitable relief." 42 U.S.C. § 2000e–5(g) (1982 ed.) ("[T]he court may . . . order such affirmative action as may be appropriate, which may include, but is not limited to, reinstatement or hiring of employees, with or without back pay . . ., or any other equitable relief as the court deems appropriate"). See also Curtis v. Loether [supra p. 574] (distinguishing backpay under Title VII from damages under Title VIII, the fair housing provision of the Civil Rights Act, which the Court characterized as "legal" for Seventh Amendment purposes). Congress made no similar pronouncement regarding the duty of fair representation. Furthermore, the Court has noted that backpay sought from an employer under Title VII would generally be restitutionary in nature, in contrast to the damages sought here from the Union. Thus, the remedy sought in this duty of fair representation case is clearly different from backpay sought for violations of Title VII.

Moreover, the fact that Title VII's backpay provision may have been modeled on a provision in the NLRA concerning remedies for unfair labor practices does not require that the backpay remedy available here be considered equitable. The Union apparently reasons that if Title VII is comparable to one labor law remedy it is comparable to all remedies available in the NLRA context. Although both the duty of fair

---

[8]   Both the Union and the dissent argue that the backpay award sought here is equitable because it is closely analogous to damages awarded to beneficiaries for a trustee's breach of trust. Such damages were available only in courts of equity because those courts had exclusive jurisdiction over actions involving a trustee's breach of his fiduciary duties.

The Union's argument, however, conflates the two parts of our Seventh Amendment inquiry. Under the dissent's approach, if the action at issue were analogous to an 18th-century action within the exclusive jurisdiction of the courts of equity, we would necessarily conclude that the remedy sought was also equitable because it would have been unavailable in a court of law. This view would, in effect, make the first part of our inquiry dispositive. We have clearly held, however, that the second part of the inquiry the nature of the relief is more important to the Seventh Amendment determination. The second part of the analysis, therefore, should not replicate the "abstruse historical" inquiry of the first part, Ross, but requires consideration of the general types of relief provided by courts of law and equity.

representation and the unfair labor practice provisions of the NLRA are components of national labor policy, their purposes are not identical. Unlike the unfair labor practice provisions of the NLRA, which are concerned primarily with the public interest in effecting federal labor policy, the duty of fair representation targets " 'the wrong done the individual employee.' " Electrical Workers v. Foust, 442 U.S. 42, 49, n. 12 (1979) (quoting Vaca v. Sipes, 386 U.S., at 182, n. 8 (emphasis deleted). Thus, the remedies appropriate for unfair labor practices may differ from the remedies for a breach of the duty of fair representation, given the need to vindicate different goals. Certainly, the connection between backpay under Title VII and damages under the unfair labor practice provision of the NLRA does not require us to find a parallel connection between Title VII backpay and money damages for breach of the duty of fair representation.

We hold, then, that the remedy of backpay sought in this duty of fair representation action is legal in nature. Considering both parts of the Seventh Amendment inquiry, we find that respondents are entitled to a jury trial on all issues presented in their suit.

IV

On balance, our analysis of the nature of respondents' duty of fair representation action and the remedy they seek convinces us that this action is a legal one. Although the search for an adequate 18th-century analog revealed that the claim includes both legal and equitable issues, the money damages respondents seek are the type of relief traditionally awarded by courts of law. Thus, the Seventh Amendment entitles respondents to a jury trial, and we therefore affirm the judgment of the Court of Appeals.

JUSTICE BRENNAN, concurring in part and concurring in the judgment.

I agree with the Court that respondents seek a remedy that is legal in nature and that the Seventh Amendment entitles respondents to a jury trial on their duty of fair representation claims. I therefore join Parts I, II, III-B, and IV of the Court's opinion. I do not join that part of the opinion which reprises the particular historical analysis this Court has employed to determine whether a claim is a "Suit at common law" under the Seventh Amendment, because I believe the historical test can and should be simplified.

The current test, first expounded in *Curtis v. Loether,* requires a court to compare the right at issue to 18th-century English forms of action to determine whether the historically analogous right was vindicated in an action at law or in equity, and to examine whether the remedy sought is legal or equitable in nature. However, this Court, in expounding the test, has repeatedly discounted the significance of the analogous form of action for deciding where the Seventh Amendment applies. I think it is time we dispense with it altogether.[1] I would decide Seventh Amendment questions on the basis of the relief sought. If the relief is legal in nature, i.e., if it is the kind of relief that historically was available from courts of law, I would hold that the parties have a constitutional right to a trial by jury—unless Congress has permissibly delegated the particular dispute to a non-Article III decisionmaker and jury trials would frustrate Congress' purposes in enacting a particular statutory scheme.[2]

I believe that our insistence that the jury trial right hinges in part on a comparison of the substantive right at issue to forms of action used in English courts 200 years ago needlessly convolutes our Seventh Amendment jurisprudence. For the past decade and a half, this Court has explained that the two parts of the historical test are not equal in weight, that the nature of the remedy is more important than the nature of the right. Since the existence of a right to jury trial therefore turns on the nature of the remedy, absent congressional delegation to a specialized decisionmaker,[3] there remains little purpose to our rattling through dusty attics of ancient writs. The time has come to borrow William of Occam's razor and sever this portion of our analysis.

We have long acknowledged that, of the factors relevant to the jury trial right, comparison of the claim to ancient forms of action, "requiring extensive and possibly abstruse historical inquiry, is obviously the most difficult to apply." Ross v. Bernhard, 396 U.S. 531, 538, n. 10 (1970). Requiring judges, with neither the training nor time necessary for reputable historical scholarship, to root through the tangle of primary and secondary sources to determine which of a hundred or so writs is analogous to the right at issue has embroiled courts in recondite controversies better left to legal historians. For example, in *Granfinanciera, S.A.,* [infra, p. 601 n. 6], * * * both Justice White, in dissent, and I, writing for the Court, struggled with the question whether an equity court would have heard the suit that was comparable to the modern statutory action at issue. * * *

---

[1]   I therefore also do not join Part III of Justice Marshall's opinion because it considers which 18th-century actions are comparable to the modern-day statutory claim brought here.

[2]   As the majority notes, ante at n. 4, where Congress has delegated a particular claim to an administrative agency or specialized court of equity, a court must consider whether the delegation is a permissible one and "whether jury trials would impair the functioning of the legislative scheme." Granfinanciera, S.A. v. Nordberg, 492 U.S. 33, 42 (1989). These questions are not implicated in this case, as it is undisputed that an action for breach of the duty of fair representation may be brought in an Article III court.

[3]   Even where Congress has assigned resolution of a dispute to a specialized forum, the right to a jury trial does not turn on whether the analogous 18th-century action was legal or equitable. As we explained in *Granfinanciera, S.A., supra,* at n. 4, a court first looks to the analogous historical form of action and the nature of the relief sought, allotting greater weight to the nature of the relief. If this inquiry leads the court to conclude that the party is entitled to a jury trial, the court must consider whether the party is asserting a public right or private right distinction contingent on the government's role in creating the right, and whether jury trials would impair the functioning of the legislative scheme. The result of the search for a historical analog is subordinate to the nature of the relief sought and irrelevant to the subsequent inquiry.

To be sure, it is neither unusual nor embarrassing for members of a court to disagree and disagree vehemently. But it better behooves judges to disagree within the province of judicial expertise. Furthermore, inquiries into the appropriate historical analogs for the rights at issue are not necessarily susceptible of sound resolution under the best of circumstances. * * *

In addition, modern statutory rights did not exist in the 18th-century and even the most exacting historical research may not elicit a clear historical analog. The right at issue here, for example, is a creature of modern labor law quite foreign to Georgian England. * * * I have grappled with this kind of inquiry for three decades on this Court and have come to the realization that engaging in such inquiries is impracticable and unilluminating.

To rest the historical test required by the Seventh Amendment solely on the nature of the relief sought would not, of course, offer the federal courts a rule that is in all cases self-executing. Courts will still be required to ask which remedies were traditionally available at law and which only in equity. But this inquiry involves fewer variables and simpler choices, on the whole, and is far more manageable than the scholasticist debates in which we have been engaged. Moreover, the rule I propose would remain true to the Seventh Amendment, as it is undisputed that, historically, "[j]urisdictional lines [between law and equity] were primarily a matter of remedy." McCoid, Procedural Reform and the Right to Jury Trial: A Study of Beacon Theatres, Inc. v. Westover, 116 U.Pa.L.Rev. 1 (1967). See also Redish, Seventh Amendment Right to Jury Trial: A Study in the Irrationality of Rational Decision Making, 70 Nw.U.L.Rev. 486, 490 (1975) ("In the majority of cases at common law, the equitable or legal nature of a suit was determined not by the substantive nature of the cause of action but by the remedy sought").[7]

---

[7] There are, to be sure, some who advocate abolishing the historical test altogether. See, e.g., Wolfram, The Constitutional History of the Seventh Amendment, 57 Minn.L.Rev. 639, 742 47 (1973). Contrary to the intimations in Justice Kennedy's dissent, I am not among them. I believe that it is imperative to retain a historical test, for determining when parties have a right to jury trial, for precisely the same reasons Justice Kennedy, does. It is mandated by the language of the Seventh Amendment and it is a bulwark against those who would restrict a right our forefathers held indispensible. Like Justice Kennedy, I have no doubt that courts can and do look to legal history for the answers to constitutional questions, and therefore the Seventh Amendment test I propose today obligates courts to do exactly that.

Where Justice Kennedy and I differ is in our evaluations of which historical test provides the more reliable results. That three learned Justices of the Supreme Court cannot arrive at the same conclusion in this very case, on what is essentially a question of fact, does not speak well for the judicial solvency of the current test. My concern is not merely the competence of courts to delve into this peculiarly recalcitrant aspect of legal history and certainly not, as Justice Kennedy summarizes it, the "competence of the Court to understand legal history" in general. My concern is that all too often the first prong of the current test requires courts to measure modern statutory actions against 18th-century English actions so remote in form and concept that there is no firm basis for comparison. In such cases, the result is less the discovery of a historical analog than the manufacture of a historical fiction. By contrast, the nature of relief available today corresponds

This is not to say that the resulting division between claims entitled to jury trials and claims not so entitled would exactly mirror the division between law and equity in England in 1791. But it is too late in the day for this Court to profess that the Seventh Amendment preserves the right to jury trial only in cases that would have been heard in the British law courts of the 18th century. * * *

Indeed, given this Court's repeated insistence that the nature of the remedy is always to be given more weight than the nature of the historically analogous right, it is unlikely that the simplified Seventh Amendment analysis I propose will result in different decisions than the analysis in current use. In the unusual circumstance that the nature of the remedy could be characterized equally as legal or equitable, I submit that the comparison of a contemporary statutory action unheard of in the 18th century to some ill-fitting ancient writ is too shaky a basis for the resolution of an issue as significant as the availability of a trial by jury. If, in the rare case, a tie-breaker is needed, let us break the tie in favor of jury trial.

What Blackstone described as "the glory of the English law" and "the most transcendent privilege which any subject can enjoy," 3 W. Blackstone, Commentaries, was crucial in the eyes of those who founded this country. The encroachment on civil jury trial by colonial administrators was a "deeply divisive issue in the years just preceding the outbreak of hostilities between the colonies and England," and all thirteen States reinstituted the right after hostilities ensued. Wolfram, The Constitutional History of the Seventh Amendment, 57 Minn.L.Rev. 639, 654–655 (1973). "In fact, '[t]he right to trial by jury was probably the only one universally secured by the first American constitutions.'" Id., at 655 (quoting L. Levy, Freedom of Speech and Press in Early American History—Legacy of Suppression 281 (1963 reprint)). Fear of a federal government that had not guaranteed jury trial in civil cases, voiced first at the Philadelphia Convention in 1787 and regularly during the ratification debates, was the concern that precipitated the maelstrom over the need for a bill of rights in the United States Constitution.

* * *

We can guard this right and save our courts from needless and intractable excursions into increasingly unfamiliar territory simply by retiring that prong of our Seventh Amendment test which we have already cast into a certain doubt. If we are not prepared to accord the nature of the historical analog sufficient weight for this factor to affect the outcome of our inquiry, except in the rarest of hypothetical cases, what reason do we have for insisting that federal judges proceed with this arduous inquiry? It

---

more directly to the nature of relief available in Georgian England. Thus the historical test I propose, focusing on the nature of the relief sought, is not only more manageable than the current test, it is more reliably grounded in history.

is time we read the writing on the wall, especially as we ourselves put it there.

JUSTICE STEVENS, concurring in part and concurring in the judgment.

Because I believe the Court has made this case unnecessarily difficult by exaggerating the importance of finding a precise common-law analogue to the duty of fair representation, I do not join Part III-A of its opinion. Ironically, by stressing the importance of identifying an exact analogue the Court has diminished the utility of looking for any analogue.

As I have suggested in the past, I believe the duty of fair representation action resembles a common law action against an attorney for malpractice more closely than it does any other form of action. Of course, this action is not an exact counterpart to a malpractice suit. Indeed, by definition, no recently recognized form of action—whether the product of express congressional enactment or of judicial interpretation—can have a precise analogue in 17th or 18th century English law. Were it otherwise the form of action would not in fact be "recently recognized."

But the Court surely overstates this action's similarity to an action against a trustee. Collective bargaining involves no settlor, no trust corpus, and no trust instrument executed to convey property to beneficiaries chosen at the settlor's pleasure. Nor are these distinctions reified matters of pure form. The law of trusts originated to expand the varieties of land ownership in feudal England, and evolved to protect the paternalistic beneficence of the wealthy, often between generations and always over time. Beneficiaries are protected from their own judgment. The attorney-client relationship, by contrast, advances the client's interests in dealings with adverse parties. Clients are saved from their lack of skill, but their judgment is honored. Union members, as a group, accordingly have the power to hire, fire, and direct the actions of their representatives—prerogatives anathema to the paternalistic forms of the equitable trust.[2]

Equitable reasoning calibrated by the sophisticated judgment of the jurist, the accountant, and the chancellor is thus appropriately invoked when the impact of a trustee's conduct on the future interests of contingent remaindermen must be reviewed. However, the common sense understanding of the jury, selected to represent the community, is appropriately invoked when disputes in the factory, the warehouse, and the garage must be resolved. In most duty of fair representation cases, the issues, which require an understanding of the realities of employment relationships, are typical grist for the jury's judgment. Indeed, the law

---

[2]   Indeed, to make sense of the trust analogy, the majority must apparently be willing to assume that the union members, considered collectively, are both beneficiary and settlor, and that the settlor retains considerable power over the corpus, including the power to revoke the trust. That is an odd sort of trust.

defining the union's duty of fair representation has developed in cases tried to juries. * * *

As the Court correctly observed in Curtis v. Loether, "in an ordinary civil action in the district courts, where there is obviously no functional justification for denying the jury trial right, a jury trial must be available if the action involves rights and remedies of the sort typically enforced in an action at law." * * * Duty of fair representation suits are for the most part ordinary civil actions involving the stuff of contract and malpractice disputes. There is accordingly no ground for excluding these actions from the jury right.

In my view, the evolution of this doctrine through suits tried to juries, the useful analogy to common-law malpractice cases, and the well-recognized duty to scrutinize any proposed curtailment of the right to a jury trial "with the utmost care," provide a plainly sufficient basis for the Court's holding today. I therefore join its judgment and all of its opinion except for Part III-A.

JUSTICE KENNEDY, with whom JUSTICE O'CONNOR and JUSTICE SCALIA join, dissenting.

This case asks whether the Seventh Amendment guarantees the respondent union members a jury trial in a duty of fair representation action against their labor union. The Court is quite correct, in my view, in its formulation of the initial premises that must govern the case. Under Curtis v. Loether, the right to a jury trial in a statutory action depends on the presence of "legal rights and remedies." To determine whether rights and remedies in a duty of fair representation action are legal in character, we must compare the action to the 18th-century cases permitted in the law courts of England, and we must examine the nature of the relief sought. I agree also with those Members of the Court who find that the duty of fair representation action resembles an equitable trust action more than a suit for malpractice.

I disagree with the analytic innovation of the Court that identification of the trust action as a model for modern duty of fair representation actions is insufficient to decide the case. The Seventh Amendment requires us to determine whether the duty of fair representation action "is more similar to cases that were tried in courts of law than to suits tried in courts of equity." Tull v. United States, 481 U.S. 412, 417 (1987). Having made this decision in favor of an equitable action, our inquiry should end. Because the Court disagrees with this proposition, I dissent.

I

Both the union and the respondents identify historical actions to which they find the duty of fair representation action most analogous. * * *

Justice Marshall, speaking for four Members of the Court, states an important and correct reason for finding the trust model better than the malpractice analogy. He observes that the client of an attorney, unlike a union member or beneficiary, controls the significant decisions concerning his litigation and can fire the attorney if not satisfied. Put another way, although a lawyer acts as an agent of his client, unions and trustees do not serve as agents of their members and beneficiaries in the conventional sense of being subject to their direction and control in pursuing claims. An individual union member cannot require his union to pursue a claim and cannot choose a different representative. A trustee, likewise, may exercise proper discretion in deciding whether to press claims held in trust, and in general does not act as an agent of his beneficiaries. * * *

Further considerations fortify the conclusion that the trust analogy is the controlling one here. A union's duty of fair representation accords with a trustee's duty of impartiality. The duty of fair representation requires a union "to make an honest effort to serve the interests of all of [its] members, without hostility to any." Ford Motor Co. v. Huffman, 345 U.S. 330, 337 (1953). This standard may require a union to act for the benefit of employees who, as in this case, have antithetical interests. Trust law, in a similar manner, long has required trustees to serve the interests of all beneficiaries with impartiality.

A lawyer's duty of loyalty is cast in different terms. Although the union is charged with the responsibility of reconciling the positions of its members, the lawyer's duty of loyalty long has precluded the representation of conflicting interests. A lawyer, at least absent knowing waiver by the parties, could not represent both the respondents and the senior laid-off workers as the union has done in this case.

The relief available in a duty of fair representation action also makes the trust action the better model. To remedy a breach of the duty of fair representation, a court must issue an award "fashioned to make the injured employee whole." Electrical Workers v. Foust, 442 U.S. 42, 49 (1979). The court may order an injunction compelling the union, if it is still able, to pursue the employee's claim, and may require monetary compensation, but it cannot award exemplary or punitive damages. This relief parallels the remedies prevailing in the courts of equity in actions against trustees for failing to pursue claims.

These remedies differ somewhat from those available in attorney malpractice actions. Because legal malpractice was a common law claim, clients sued their attorneys for breach of professional obligations in the law courts. No one maintains that clients could obtain from these courts the injunctive relief offered in duty of fair representation actions. The evidence suggests that compensatory damages in malpractice cases resembled the monetary relief now awarded in duty of fair representation actions. Yet, as a historical matter, juries did have the authority to award exemplary damages in at least some tort actions. * * *

For all these reasons, the suit here resembles a trust action, not a legal malpractice action. By this I do not imply that a union acts as a trustee in all instances or that trust law, as a general matter, should inform any particular aspects of federal labor law. Obvious differences between a union and a trustee will exist in other contexts. I would conclude only that, under the analysis directed by our precedents, the respondents may not insist on a jury trial. When all rights and remedies are considered, their action resembles a suit heard by the courts of equity more than a case heard by the courts of law. From this alone it follows that the respondents have no jury trial right on their duty of fair representation claims against the union.

II

The Court relies on two lines of precedents to overcome the conclusion that the trust action should serve as the controlling model. The first consists of cases in which the Court has considered simplifications in litigation resulting from modern procedural reforms in the federal courts. Justice Marshall asserts that these cases show that the Court must look at the character of individual issues rather than claims as a whole. The second line addresses the significance of the remedy in determining the equitable or legal nature of an action for the purpose of choosing the most appropriate analogy. Under these cases, the Court decides that the respondents have a right to a jury because they seek money damages. These authorities do not support the Court's holding.

A

In three cases we have found a right to trial by jury where there are legal claims that, for procedural reasons, a plaintiff could have or must have raised in the courts of equity before the systems merged. * * * [Justice Kennedy here discusses *Beacon Theatres, Dairy Queen,* and *Ross.*]

These three cases responded to the difficulties created by a merged court system. They stand for the proposition that, because distinct courts of equity no longer exist, the possibility or necessity of using former equitable procedures to press a legal claim no longer will determine the right to a jury. Justice Marshall reads these cases to require a jury trial whenever a cause of action contains legal issues and would require a jury trial in this case because the respondents must prove a breach of the collective-bargaining agreement as one element of their claim.

I disagree. The respondents, as shown above, are asserting an equitable claim. Having reached this conclusion, the *Beacon, Dairy Queen,* and *Ross* cases are inapplicable. Although we have divided self-standing legal claims from equitable declaratory, accounting, and derivative procedures, we have never parsed legal elements out of equitable claims absent specific procedural justifications. Actions which, beyond all question, are equitable in nature may involve some predicate inquiry that would be submitted to a jury in other contexts. For example, just as the plaintiff in a duty of fair representation action against his union must show breach of the collective-bargaining agreement as an initial matter, in an action against a trustee for failing to pursue a claim the beneficiary must show that the claim had some merit. But the question of the claim's validity, even if the claim raises contract issues, would not bring the jury right into play in a suit against a trustee.

Our own writing confirms the consistency of this view with respect to the action before us. We have not deemed the elements of a duty of fair representation action to be independent of each other. Proving breach of the collective-bargaining agreement is but a preliminary and indispensable step to obtaining relief in a duty of fair representation action. * * * The absence of distinct equitable courts provides no procedural reason for wresting one of these elements from the other.

B

The Court also rules that, despite the appropriateness of the trust analogy as a whole, the respondents have a right to a jury trial because they seek money damages. The nature of the remedy remains a factor of considerable importance in determining whether a statutory action had a legal or equitable analog in 1791, but we have not adopted a rule that a statutory action permitting damages is by definition more analogous to a legal action than to any equitable suit. In each case, we look to the remedy to determine whether, taken with other factors, it places an action within the definition of "suits at common law."

In *Curtis,* for example, we ruled that the availability of actual and punitive damages made a statutory anti-discrimination action resemble a legal tort action more than any equitable action. We made explicit that we did not "go so far as to say that any award of monetary relief must necessarily be 'legal' relief." Although monetary damages might cause some statutory actions to resemble tort suits, the presence of monetary damages in this duty of fair representation action does not make it more analogous to a legal action than to an equitable action. Indeed, as shown above, the injunctive and monetary remedies available make the duty of fair representation suit less analogous to a malpractice action than to a suit against a trustee.

* * *

* * * The courts of equity could and did award the kind of damages sought by the respondents here. The respondents' mere request for backpay in no way entitles them to a jury under the Seventh Amendment.

III

The Court must adhere to the historical test in determining the right to a jury because the language of the Constitution requires it. The Seventh Amendment "preserves" the right to jury trial in civil cases. We cannot preserve a right existing in 1791 unless we look to history to identify it. Our precedents are in full agreement with this reasoning and insist on adherence to the historical test. No alternatives short of rewriting the Constitution exist. * * * If we abandon the plain language of the Constitution to expand the jury right, we may expect Courts with opposing views to curtail it in the future.

It is true that a historical inquiry into the distinction between law and equity may require us to enter into a domain becoming less familiar with time. Two centuries have passed since the Seventh Amendment's ratification and the incompleteness of our historical records makes it difficult to know the nature of certain actions in 1791. The historical test, nonetheless, has received more criticism than it deserves. Although our application of the analysis in some cases may seem biased in favor of jury trials, the test has not become a nullity. We do not require juries in all statutory actions. * * *

I would hesitate to abandon or curtail the historical test out of concern for the competence of the Court to understand legal history. We do look to history for the answers to constitutional questions. Although opinions will differ on what this history shows, the approach has no less validity in the Seventh Amendment context than elsewhere.

If Congress has not provided for a jury trial, we are confined to the Seventh Amendment to determine whether one is required. Our own views respecting the wisdom of using a jury should be put aside. Like Justice Brennan, I admire the jury process. Other judges have taken the opposite view. See, e.g., J. Frank, Law and the Modern Mind 170–185 (1931). But the judgment of our own times is not always preferable to the lessons of history. Our whole constitutional experience teaches that history must inform the judicial inquiry. Our obligation to the Constitution and its Bill of Rights, no less than the compact we have with the generation that wrote them for us, do not permit us to disregard provisions that some may think to be mere matters of historical form.

* * *

NOTES AND QUESTIONS

1.   Which historical analogy considered by the Court do you find to be closer to the cause of action provided in section 301? Should it matter, for purposes of determining the Seventh Amendment right?

2.   Note that the Court in *Terry* indicates that in the two-part historical test outlined in *Tull,* "[t]he second inquiry is the more important in our

analysis." Do you understand why? Under this weighted approach, what function does the first element of the test actually serve? Does it serve *any* real function?

3.   In applying the second part of the *Tull* test, the Court distinguished the award of backpay under Title VII of the 1964 Civil Rights Act. How persuasive is the asserted basis of distinction?

4.   *Terry* was deemed controlling in Wooddell v. International Brotherhood of Electrical Workers, Local 71, 502 U.S. 93 (1991). Plaintiff alleged that the Local had violated his rights under Title I of the Labor Management Reporting and Disclosure Act of 1959, by discriminating against him in job referrals in the operation of a hiring hall provided for in the Local's collective-bargaining contracts with electrical contractors. He sought injunctive relief, lost wages and benefits, additional compensatory damages, punitive damages, and attorney's fees. Plaintiff argued "that, although he seeks injunctive relief as well as damages, the injunctive relief is incidental to the damages, and not vice versa, and that his claim for lost wages cannot be treated as restitutionary incident to an order reinstating him to a job from which he has been terminated, as the damages sought are for pay for jobs to which the union failed to refer him." 502 U.S. at 97–98. The Court agreed, holding that the jury trial right applied under *Terry.*

THE RIGHT TO JURY TRIAL IN STATUTORILY-CREATED ADMINISTRATIVE PROCEEDINGS

In NLRB v. Jones & Laughlin Steel Corp., 301 U.S. 1 (1937), discussed in Curtis v. Loether, supra p. 574, the Supreme Court denied a right to jury trial in an administrative proceeding for a back-pay order, despite the argument that an award of back pay was analogous to an award of damages at common law. The Court reasoned that the Seventh Amendment "has no application to cases where recovery of money damages is an incident to equitable relief even though damages might have been recovered in an action at law." The Court, in other words, relied on a form of the "clean-up" doctrine.

The Court also rejected the jury trial right because "[t]he instant case is not a suit at common law or in the nature of such a suit. The proceeding is one unknown at the common law. It is a statutory proceeding. Reinstatement of the employee and payment for time lost are requirements imposed for violation of the statute and are remedies appropriate to its enforcement."

In Atlas Roofing Co., Inc. v. Occupational Safety and Health Review Commission, 430 U.S. 442 (1977), the Supreme Court held that the Seventh Amendment does not preclude Congress from assigning to an administrative agency the task of adjudicating violations of the Occupational Safety and Health Act of 1970. The Act "created a new statutory duty to avoid maintaining unsafe or unhealthy working conditions," and authorized the Commission to impose civil penalties on any employer maintaining any unsafe working condition. Justice White, speaking for the Court, acknowledged the rule of Parsons v. Bedford, that the right to jury trial in a suit brought pursuant to a new statute is determined by analogy to common law practice. It had been argued "that a suit in federal court by the Government for civil penalties for violation of a statute is a suit for a money judgment which is classically a suit at common law, and that the defendant therefore has a Seventh Amendment right to a jury determination of all issues of fact in such a case." But the Court rejected this argument:

> At least in cases in which "public rights" are being litigated—e.g., cases in which the Government sues in its sovereign capacity to enforce public rights created by statutes within the power of Congress to enact—the Seventh Amendment does not prohibit Congress from assigning the factfinding function and initial adjudication to an administrative forum with which the jury would be incompatible.

* * *

> Congress is not required by the Seventh Amendment to choke the already crowded federal courts with new types of litigation or prevented from committing some new types of litigation to administrative agencies with special competence in the relevant field. This is the case even if the Seventh Amendment would have required a jury where the adjudication of those rights is assigned to a federal court of law instead of an administrative agency.

In response to the argument "that the right to jury trial was never intended to depend on the identity of the forum to which Congress has chosen to submit a dispute; otherwise, * * * Congress could utterly destroy the right to a jury trial by always providing for administrative rather than judicial resolution of the vast range of cases that now arise in the courts," Justice White reasoned:

> Our prior cases support administrative factfinding in only those situations involving "public rights" * * *. Wholly private tort, contract, and property cases as well as a vast range of other cases, are not at all implicated.

> More to the point, it is apparent from the history of jury trial in civil matters that factfinding * * * was never the exclusive province of the jury under the English or American legal systems at the time of the adoption of the Seventh Amendment; and the question whether a fact would be found by a jury turned to a considerable degree on the nature of the forum in which a litigant found himself. Critical factfinding was performed without juries

in suits in equity, and there were no juries in admiralty; nor were there juries in the military justice system.

* * *

The point is that the Seventh Amendment was never intended to establish the jury as the exclusive mechanism for factfinding in civil cases. It took the existing legal order as it found it * * *. We cannot conclude that the Amendment rendered Congress powerless—when it concluded that remedies available in courts of law were inadequate to cope with a problem within Congress' power to regulate—to create new public rights and remedies by statute and commit their enforcement, if it chose, to a tribunal other than a court of law—such as an administrative agency—in which facts are not found by juries.

NOTES AND QUESTIONS

1. Did the Court in *Curtis* adequately distinguish *Jones & Laughlin?*

2. Re-examine Justice Story's reasoning in Parsons v. Bedford, quoted in Ross v. Bernhard, supra p. 564. which the Court in Curtis v. Loether cites as establishing the "basic principle" that guides decisions in the area. Are NLRB v. Jones & Laughlin Steel Corp. or Atlas Roofing Co. v. OSHA consistent with *Parsons?* If not, is *Parsons'* continuing vitality undermined by these decisions?

3. Why is the fact that a so-called "public right," rather than a "private right", is involved so essential to the denial of the jury trial right in *Atlas Roofing?* Is there anything in the text of the Seventh Amendment to indicate the dichotomy's importance? Note that at common law, there is no evidence to indicate that the law-equity dichotomy, on which the jury trial right is largely determined, in any way turned on a distinction between "public" and "private" rights. Given the Court's emphasis on the "public"/"private" right distinction, is there any way logically to limit the distinction's effect to *administrative* proceedings? If a "public" right were adjudicated in a federal court, rather than before an administrative tribunal, should the Court's logic apply to deny a jury trial right? If not, should the distinction make any difference in an administrative proceeding, either?

4. Note that in *Atlas Roofing,* Justice White states that use of a jury would be "incompatible" with an administrative proceeding. Does this amount to a balancing of the Seventh Amendment right against competing governmental interests? If so, is such a practice consistent with the Court's attitude towards balancing expressed in *Curtis?*

5. To support its conclusion concerning the absence of a right to jury trial, the Court in *Atlas Roofing* relied on Supreme Court precedents dating from the year 1856. According to one commentator, the fact that "[t]here is no attempt in *Atlas Roofing* to follow the classic doctrine that the scope of the seventh amendment is determined by reference to the common law of 1791" is

"unusual". Kirst, Administrative Penalties and the Civil Jury: The Supreme
Court's Assault on the Seventh Amendment, 126 U.Pa.L.Rev. 1281, 1282–83
(1978). Professor Kirst believes that "*Atlas* demonstrates how easily a modern
court can misinterpret the seventh amendment if the analysis begins in the
middle of the historical development." Id. at 1283.

    6.   In Granfinanciera, S.A. v. Nordberg, 492 U.S. 33 (1989), the Supreme
Court held that the Seventh Amendment was violated by the denial of a jury
trial for the defendant in a suit by the trustee in bankruptcy to recover an
allegedly fraudulent monetary transfer from the bankrupt shortly before filing
for bankruptcy (called a "fraudulent conveyance"). Though bankruptcy courts
are not exactly like administrative agencies, their judges—like those in charge
of agencies—lack the salary and tenure protections of Article III of the
Constitution, which are given to judges of the United States district courts and
courts of appeals. Since the 1984 amendments to the Bankruptcy Reform Act
of 1978, Pub. L. 95–598, 92 Stat. 2549, bankruptcy judges have been considered
adjuncts to the district courts, enabling them to adjudicate private rights
involving the bankrupt. Using the historical inquiry of Tull v. United States
(supra p. 578), Justice Brennan, writing for the Court, concluded that "actions
to recover preferential or fraudulent transfers were often brought at law in late
18th-century England," and that "[t]hese actions, like all suits at law, were
conducted before juries."

    Justice Brennan acknowledged that "[i]n *Atlas Roofing*, we noted that
'when Congress creates new statutory 'public rights,' it may assign their
adjudication to an administrative agency with which a jury trial would be
incompatible, without violating the Seventh Amendment's injunction. . . .' "
However, he noted that Congress "lacks the power to strip parties contesting
matters of private right of their constitutional right to a trial by jury." Applying
the controlling standard that a "public right" is "a seemingly 'private' right
[created by Congress] that is so closely integrated into a public regulatory
scheme as to be a matter appropriate for agency resolution with limited
involvement by the Article III judiciary," Brennan concluded that "a
bankruptcy trustee's right to recover a fraudulent conveyance . . . seems to us
more accurately characterized as a private rather than a public right. . . ." He
therefore held that the jury trial right applied.

    In dissent, Justice White argued that Katchen v. Landy (supra p. 563)
"dispositively settles the question before us today: like the petitioner in
Katchen, petitioners in this case have no Seventh Amendment right to jury
trial when respondent trustee seeks to avoid the fraudulent transfer they
received." Justice Brennan, however, found *Katchen* distinguishable. He
reasoned that under *Katchen* "a creditor's right to a jury trial on a bankruptcy
trustee's preference claim depends on whether the creditor has submitted a
claim against the estate. . . ." Do you agree with Justice Brennan's distinction?

    In finding that a Seventh Amendment right existed, the majority in
Granfinanciera conceded that it "owe[s] some deference to Congress' judgment"
on constitutional issues, but denies the existence of evidence demonstrating
that Congress had exercised any such judgment in the present case. It also

denied that the provision of a jury trial right would dismantle Congress's statutory scheme. Should the case have been decided differently if either or both of these questions had been resolved differently?

In Langenkamp v. Culp, 498 U.S. 42 (1990) (per curiam), the Supreme Court considered "the question whether creditors who submit a claim against a bankruptcy estate and are then sued by the trustee in bankruptcy to recover allegedly preferential monetary transfers are entitled to jury trial under the Seventh Amendment." Id. at 42–43 . The Court answered that question in the negative. In so doing, the Court distinguished *Granfinanciera* (498 U.S. at 4):

> In *Granfinanciera* we recognized that by filing a claim against a bankruptcy estate the creditor triggers the process of "allowance and disallowance of claims," thereby subjecting himself to the bankruptcy court's equitable power. If the creditor is met, in turn, with a preference action from the trustee, that action becomes part of the claims-allowance process which is triable only in equity. In other words, the creditor's claim and the ensuing preference action by the trustee become integral to the restructuring of the debtor-creditor relationship through the bankruptcy court's *equity jurisdiction*. As such, there is no Seventh Amendment right to a jury trial. If a party does *not* submit a claim against the bankruptcy estate, however, the trustee can recover allegedly preferential transfers only by filing what amounts to a legal action to recover a monetary transfer. In those circumstances the preference defendant is entitled to a jury trial.

7. The *Granfinanciera* Court left unresolved "whether the Seventh Amendment or Article III allows jury trials * * * to be held before non-Article III bankruptcy judges * * * ." In 1994, Congress enacted the Bankruptcy Reform Act of 1994, which included the following provision:

> If the right to a jury trial applies in a proceeding that may be heard under this section by a bankruptcy judge, the bankruptcy judge may conduct the jury trial if specially designated to exercise such jurisdiction by the district court and with the express consent of all the parties.

§ 112, Bankruptcy Reform Act of 1994, 103 P.L. 394; 108 Stat. 4106. On the issue of jury trials in bankruptcy proceedings, see generally Symposium, Jury Trials in Bankruptcy Courts, 65 Am. Bank. L.J. 1 (1991).

8. For a critical view of the Supreme Court's modern doctrine concerning the role of the Seventh Amendment in administrative proceedings, see Redish & LaFave, Seventh Amendment Right to Jury Trial in Non-Article III Proceedings: A Study in Dysfunctional Constitutional Theory, 4 Wm. & Mary Bill of Rts. L.J. 407 (1995). There it is argued: "[T]he Court's exclusion of the jury trial right from most cases of congressional transfer of adjudication to a non-Article III forum can be rationalized only by means of a principle of functionalism. Under this principle, the Court allows the Congress to conclude that the needs of a particular legislative scheme require adjudication without

jury trial. The Court does this, despite its assumption that absent such congressional action, the Seventh Amendment would dictate existence of the jury trial right. Judicial revocation of an otherwise applicable constitutional right solely because of a congressional judgment of incompatibility of that right with a legislative scheme effectively inverts ... fundamental precepts of American constitutional theory." See also Klein, The Validity of the Public Rights Doctrine in Light of the Historical Rationale of the Seventh Amendment, 21 Hastings Const. L.Q. 1013 (1994), where it is argued that the analysis dictating the absence of the Seventh Amendment right to non-Article III proceedings "rests on the faulty premise that the Seventh Amendment only applies to Article III courts." Professor Klein asserts that "the Seventh Amendment applies to the dispute resolution of all claims sounding in common law. . . ."

9. For a detailed examination of the public right-private right distinction, see M. Redish, Federal Jurisdiction: Tensions in the Allocation of Judicial Power 53–82 (2d ed. 1990).

COMPLEX CASES AND THE RIGHT TO JURY TRIAL

It has been argued that because jurors are generally incapable of comprehending all of the issues and evidence in so-called complex litigation, a "complexity" exception to the Seventh Amendment right to jury trial should be recognized in those cases. Is recognition of such an exception consistent with the Supreme Court's traditional approach to Seventh Amendment interpretation? Of what relevance is footnote 10 of *Ross* (supra p. 564)? Alternatively, it has been argued that use of a jury trial in complex cases violates the Fifth Amendment right to due process.

In In re Japanese Electronic Products Antitrust Litigation, 631 F.2d 1069 (3d Cir.1980), the Third Circuit rejected a generalized, historically-based exception to the jury trial right on the basis of complexity. However, the court found that "the principles that define the procedural requirement of due process would seem to impose some limitations on the range of cases that may be submitted to a jury." The court explained its reasoning in the following manner:

> The primary value promoted by due process in factfinding procedures is "to minimize the risk of erroneous decisions." A jury that cannot understand the evidence and the legal rules to be applied provides no reliable safeguard against erroneous decisions. Moreover, in the context of a completely adversary proceeding, like a civil trial, due process requires that "the decisionmaker's conclusion . . . rest solely on the legal rules and evidence adduced at the hearing." Unless the jury can understand the legal rules and evidence, we cannot realistically expect that the jury will rest its decision on them.

* * *

If a particular lawsuit is so complex that a jury cannot satisfy this requirement of due process but is nonetheless an action at law, we face a conflict between the requirements of the fifth and seventh amendments. In this situation, we must balance the constitutionally protected interests, as they are implicated in this particular context, and reach the most reasonable accommodation between the two constitutional provisions.

* * *

We believe that when a jury is unable to perform its decisionmaking task with a reasonable understanding of the evidence and legal rules, it undermines the ability of a district court to render basic justice.

The loss of the right to jury trial in a suit found too complex for a jury does not implicate the same fundamental concerns. The absence of a jury trial requirement in equitable and maritime actions indicates that federal courts can provide fair trials and can grant principles of basic justice without the aid of a jury.

* * *

We do not believe that a due process limitation allows the district courts a substantial amount of discretion to deny jury trials. Because preservation of the right to jury trial remains a constitutionally protected interest, denials of jury trial on grounds of complexity should be confined to suits in which due process clearly requires a nonjury trial. This implies a high standard. It is not enough that trial to the court would be preferable. The complexity of a suit must be so great that it renders the suit beyond the ability of a jury to decide by rational means with a reasonable understanding of the evidence and applicable legal rules.

Judge Gibbons dissented from this due process analysis:

> [T]he majority has substituted for an express guarantee in the Bill of Rights a rule of district court discretion that in practice will be virtually unreviewable, and therefore largely unfettered.

* * *

The majority opinion attempts to objectify the factors that bear upon complexity, but in the end the factors which are identified will permit the exercise of trial court discretion. I fear that the exercise of that discretion will sometimes be influenced by unarticulated sympathies for or hostilities toward the underlying policies sought to be advanced in the lawsuit.

* * *

Part of my difficulty with the majority's position probably results from a perception of the nature of the judicial process and the role of juries in that process. It is often said that the judicial process involves the search for objective truth whether the trial is to the court or to a jury. * * * In the process of gaining public acceptance for the imposition of sanctions, the role of the jury is highly significant. * * * Any erosion of citizen participation in the sanctioning system is in the long run likely * * * to result in a reduction in the moral authority that supports the process.

In In re U.S. Financial Securities Litigation, 609 F.2d 411 (9th Cir.1979), cert. denied, 446 U.S. 929 (1980), the court rejected any exception to the Seventh Amendment for complex cases. In so doing, it rejected reliance for such an exception on both footnote 10 of *Ross* and on the Due Process Clause:

No Supreme Court decision prior to *Ross* even utilized a test even partially dependent upon an inquiry into the abilities of jurors.

* * *

While the Supreme Court has never specifically repudiated the third factor in the *Ross* footnote, it has never met with general acceptance by the courts. In the *Ross* decision itself, the Court did not consider the practical abilities and limitations of juries.

* * *

The appellees argued [in this case] that their rights to due process under the Fifth Amendment would be violated if this case was tried to a jury. * * *

We assume, without deciding, that there is such a right to a "competent" fact-finder. However, we do not agree with the two assumptions upon which the argument is based, that is, the complexity and the inability of a jury to serve as fact-finder.

* * *

Many cases appear overwhelmingly complicated in their early stages. Nevertheless, by the time such cases go to trial, what had initially appeared as an impossible array of facts and issues has been synthesized into a coherent theory by the efforts of counsel. * * *

Also, the trial judge has the power and the authority to control, manage and direct the course of complex cases. * * *

* * *

Not only do we refuse to read a complexity exception into the Seventh Amendment, but we also express grave reservations about whether a meaningful test could be developed were we to find such an exception.

Which position do you find more persuasive? See Lempert, Civil Juries and Complex Cases: Let's Not Rush to Judgment, 80 Mich.L.Rev. 68, 87–88 (1981): "[R]elying on the fifth amendment is discomfitting. Contrary to the usual canons of statutory construction, this approach prefers general language to specific language. * * * To rest the denial of the right to jury trial on due process grounds, one must see due process * * * as requiring the denial of one of the specific procedural guarantees of the Bill of Rights."

Certain scholars have argued in support of an historically-based exception to the jury trial right, even in cases seeking otherwise purely legal relief, on complexity grounds. For example, English legal scholar Lord Patrick Devlin, in an article derived from a study commissioned by a Washington, D.C. law firm that represented an amicus curiae opponent to jury trial in In re Japanese Antitrust Litigation, supra, expressed the view "that the practical abilities and limitations of juries would have been a factor very much in the mind of a Chancellor in 1791" in deciding whether to assert equitable jurisdiction, and that "if in any particular case he had thought the 'practical abilities' not up to the complexities of the case, he would have had the power to stop the suit at common law. And further, such a use of the power would not have been considered at all outrageous, but on the contrary as in tune with the accepted relationship between equity and the common law." Devlin, Jury Trial of Complex Cases: English Practices at the Time of the Seventh Amendment, 80 Colum.L.Rev. 43, 107 (1980).

Taking the opposite side of the historical debate, in an article commissioned by the lawyers for the plaintiffs in In re Japanese Antitrust Litigation, Professor (now Judge) Morris Arnold concluded:

A diligent search of the available sources has not revealed any evidence of an eighteenth-century American or English belief that complexity was a ground for the exercise of equitable jurisdiction. In the nineteenth century, statements to that effect can be discovered but their lineage is in no sense ancient or otherwise distinguished. On the contrary, there is ample evidence that the jury was revered in most of the American colonies, so much so that jury trial found a regular place in Chancery, a practice that would have raised eyebrows in England. * * * There thus seems to be no good historical foundation for the argument that plaintiffs may be denied the right to a jury trial because their cases are complex.

Arnold, A Historical Inquiry Into the Right to Trial by Jury in Complex Civil Litigation, 128 U.Pa.L.Rev. 829, 848 (1980).

A response to Arnold's article argued "that Professor Arnold's conclusions rest upon an incomplete examination of the historical evidence." Campbell & Le Poidevin, Complex Cases and Jury Trials: A Reply to Professor Arnold, 128 U.Pa.L.Rev. 965 (1980). They criticized Arnold for focusing on the history of *American* "special affection" for the jury trial, when it is well established that it is *English* common law practice that determines the Seventh Amendment right. They agree with Lord Devlin's historical conclusions about the nature of English practice.

A number of years prior to this debate, Professor Fleming James stated what had been the generally accepted view of historical practice: "At no time in history was the line dividing equity from law altogether—or even largely—the product of a rational choice between issues which were better suited to court or to jury trial. * * * Rather, the choice between law and equity frequently was made upon consideration of other factors." F. James, Civil Procedure 344 (1965). Is this position reconcilable with that of Lord Devlin?

One non-historian legal scholar, commenting on this debate, concluded that "[a]s I read the evidence, it appears that the historical test gives little comfort to those who wish to read a complexity exception into the seventh amendment. There are a few early cases in which judges, choosing not to empanel juries, disparage the ability of jurors to deal with the litigation in question, but these cases appear to invoke disputes not remediable at law in the first instance. Even if one could discover a case where jury trial was denied although the action was unquestionably legal, it would not establish a *pattern* of denying jury trials in complex cases. The case would be more properly read as an aberrational decision that cannot be the measure of the right the framers of the seventh amendment intended to preserve." Lempert, Civil Juries and Complex Cases: Let's Not Rush to Judgment, 80 Mich.L.Rev. 68, 74 (1981). Professor Lempert further commented that "[w]hat is most notable about the attempts to find an eighteenth-century complexity exception to the right to jury trial is not the evidence presented, but that which is not given. * * * Had there been a complexity exception, we would expect to see a number of cases that make use of it, but we are not even presented with cases where counsel argued fruitlessly for one." Id. at 75.

One commentator has suggested that in most cases "[b]y implementing procedural devices already in place, courts can satisfy the requirements of both the Fifth Amendment and the Seventh Amendment, without unnecessarily balancing one against the other. Thus, jurors can decide complex cases without violating due process and retain their important role as a check on the government." Note, Taking the "Complexity" Out of Complex Litigation: Preserving the Constitutional Right to a Civil Jury Trial, 28 Val. U.L. Rev. 337, 359 (1993). The commentator places reliance on the use of masters, magistrates and court-appointed experts, as well as resort to special verdicts and the assumption by the trial judge of "an active role in determining how the trial will be structured." The same commentator suggests that "as a last resort, where a judge determines that a case is simply too complex for a traditional jury * * * a specially qualified jury must be implemented." Id. at 341. See also Lansing & Miley, The Right to a Jury Trial in Complex Commercial Litigation: A Comparative Law Perspective, 14 Loy. L.A. Int'l & Comp. L.J. 121 (1991); Bownes, Should Trial By Jury Be Eliminated in Complex Cases?, 1 Risk: Issues Health & Safety 75 (1990).

Another commentator has argued that "[s]pecial juries, chosen for their particular knowledge or experience, could help eliminate [the] current problems of jury confusion and lead to better decisions." Sutton, A More Rational Approach to Complex Civil Litigation in the Federal Courts: The Special Jury, 1990 U. Chi. Legal F. 575. See also Drazan, The Case for Special Juries in Toxic Tort Litigation, 72 Judicature 292 (1989). Should such a practice be found to violate the Seventh Amendment? Cf. Schwarzer, Reforming Jury Trials, 132 F.R.D. 575, 580 (1991):

The process of calling prospective jurors is designed to produce a representative cross-section of the population for jury service. There is no right, however, to have a representative cross-section on any particular jury; indeed, there would be no way to achieve this result. Nor is there a right to a randomly selected jury. Thus, there is no reason why, from among a venire randomly called for service in a case, one should not select those who by education and experience seem to be best qualified to decide the particular case.

Professor Steven Friedland has suggested that problems of juror competence may be reduced by encouraging a more active role for the jurors in the trial process. In performing such a role, jurors would "ask questions, take notes, or otherwise play a more active role in the system generally. . . ." Friedland, The Competency and Responsibility of Jurors in Deciding Cases, 85 Nw.U.L.Rev. 190, 218 (1990). See also Schwarzer, Reforming Jury Trials, 132 F.R.D. 575 (1991); Heuer & Penrod, Some Suggestions for the Critical Appraisal of a More-Active Jury, 85 Nw.U.L.Rev. 226 (1990); Lilly, The Decline of the American Jury, 72 U.Colo.L.Rev. 53 (2001).

THE SEVENTH AMENDMENT AND JURY SIZE

To what extent does the constitutional right to jury trial guarantee a jury consisting of twelve members, as used at common law? In Williams v. Florida, 399 U.S. 78 (1970), the Supreme Court held that a state could, consistently with the Sixth Amendment's right to jury trial in criminal cases as applied to the states through the Fourteenth Amendment's due process clause, employ a jury of six, or perhaps even fewer members.

In Colgrove v. Battin, 413 U.S. 149 (1973), the Court upheld the constitutionality of a district court's local rule providing for a six-member jury in all civil cases:

> We can only conclude * * * that by referring to the "common law," the Framers of the Seventh Amendment were concerned with preserving the *right* of trial by jury in civil cases where it existed at common law, rather than the various incidents of trial by jury. In short, what was said in *Williams* with respect to the criminal jury is equally applicable here: constitutional history reveals no intention on the part of the Framers "to equate the constitutional and common-law characteristics of the jury."

> * * *

> In *Williams,* we rejected the notion that "the reliability of the jury as a factfinder . . . [is] a function of its size," * * * and nothing has been suggested to lead us to alter that conclusion.

> * * *

> Thus, while we express no view as to whether any number less than six would suffice, we conclude that a jury of six satisfies the Seventh Amendment's guarantee of trial by jury in civil cases.

A number of federal districts have provided by local rule for six-member juries. Cf. Rule 48. Acceptance of six-member juries has, how-ever, been the subject of criticism:

> If the jury size is reduced from twelve to six, [lawyers'] perception of the approximate balance between jury and bench trial will be disturbed. Henceforth, the "gamble" with a jury will be significantly greater than the "gamble" with a judge and, as a result, more lawyers might waive their right to a jury, perhaps a consequence not unexpected by those who initiated the reform.

> In addition to the tendency to be less representative and to produce more varied damage verdicts, the six-member jury is likely to yield fewer examples of that treasured, paradoxical phenomenon—the hung jury. Hung juries almost always arise from situations in which there were originally several dissenters. Even if only one holds out, his having once been the member of a group is essential in sustaining him against the majority's efforts to make the verdict unanimous. Fewer hung juries can be expected in six-member juries for two reasons: first, * * * there will be fewer holders of minority positions on the jury; second, if a dissenter appears, he is more likely to be the only one on the jury. Lacking any associate to support his position, he is more likely to abandon it.

> * * *

From the foregoing discussion, it would appear that the Court's holding in *Williams* rests on a poor foundation. In several important respects, the six-member jury performs differently than the twelve-member jury. The Court probably suspected that some differences in composition and performance would exist between the types of juries but thought them negligibly small. It would seem that the Court has underestimated their magnitude.

* * *

[T]he change in verdicts that might be expected from the deduction of the twelve-member jury to six members is by no means negligible.

Zeisel, . . . and Then There Were None: The Diminution of the Federal Jury, 38 U.Chi.L.Rev. 710 (1971); see also ABA Comm. On Federal Civil Procedure, The Importance of the Twelve-Member Jury in the Federal Courts, 205 F.R.D. 249 (2002) (arguing against shrinkage of the jury). Would the Court's logic in *Williams* and *Colgrove* also justify replacement of the traditional juror unanimity requirement with a majority-rule principle?

JURY SELECTION

Assuming there is a right to jury trial, one must select a jury. In general, litigants are entitled to fair and impartial jurors representing a cross-section of the community. Thiel v. Southern Pac. Co., 328 U.S. 217 (1946). To implement this, the Juror Selection and Service Act of 1968, 28 U.S.C.A. §§ 1861 et seq., directs that the clerk of the court use a selection method that ensures that potential jurors are "selected at random from a fair cross section of the community." Ordinarily voter registration lists are employed for this purpose, although some have urged that they be supplemented because voter registration patterns vary significantly among different groups. See Kairys, Kadane & Lehockzy, Jury Representativeness: A Mandate for Multiple Source Lists, 65 Calif.L.Rev. 776 (1977).

The resulting group of potential jurors, often called the array, is summoned to the courthouse and directed to a jury assembly room, where the clerk determines whether the prospective jurors satisfy the statutory qualifications, such as the ability to understand the English language. See 28 U.S.C.A. § 1865(b). Qualifying persons are then given some instruction on the duties of jurors, assigned in groups of approximately fifty (called jury panels) and directed to report to specific courtrooms. Using a random process, the courtroom deputy clerk then selects enough prospective jurors from the panel to fill the seats in the jury box. Up to this point, except for challenges to the array on the ground that the selection method was not calculated to yield a fair cross section of the community, neither judges nor lawyers are involved in the jury selection process.

Once prospective jurors are seated in the jury box, the judge and lawyers address the question whether any of them should be excused "for cause." In general, the reasons for excusing jurors for cause relate to their ability to be fair and impartial. Thus, if a juror is acquainted with one of the parties or witnesses or lawyers that may be grounds for excusing the juror if it could affect his attitude toward the case. Similarly, a juror whose personal experiences might result in partiality may be excused. For example, a juror who has lost a limb in an accident may be inappropriate for a personal injury suit involving loss of a limb. Finally, some jurors may have such extensive personal commitments that these would distract them from jury service. For example, a juror who is raising three small children might on that ground be excused, but judges are increasingly strict in their willingness to allow such excuses. Lawyers, it should be noted, are not generally exempt from the civic duty to serve on juries. Any potential jurors who are excused are replaced with others from the panel selected at random by the courtroom deputy, and these are also screened to determine if they should be excused for cause.

Even if there is no ground for excusing jurors for cause, the jury selection process is not over because the parties retain what are called peremptory challenges. In federal court each side has three of these. See 28 U.S.C.A. § 1870. Traditionally it has been said that a party may excuse any juror using such a challenge for any reason whatsoever. The ability of parties to use peremptory challenges in a discriminatory manner has been severely limited. See Edmonson v. Leesville Concrete Co., 500 U.S. 614 (1991) (race-based peremptory challenges in civil litigation between private parties violate the equal protection clause of the Constitution); J.E.B. v. Alabama *ex rel.* T.B., 511 U.S. 127 (1994) (exclusion of all men from jury in paternity case unconstitutional because it discriminates on grounds of gender). Some suggest that untrammeled use of peremptory challenges is a thing of the past.

Decisions about excusing prospective jurors for cause or peremptorily must be based on information about them. To develop such information, jurors are questioned at the beginning of the trial in a process known as voir dire. Although voir dire is done by lawyers in many state courts, in federal court it is usually done by judges. See Fed.R.Civ.P. 47(a). Many lawyers feel that judicial control unduly limits their ability to get a "feel" for the jury, but judges justify the practice as a way to expedite voir dire and prevent lawyers from converting it into an indoctrination session. Judges will nevertheless entertain suggestions about areas for inquiry, and sometimes they are reversed for refusing such requests.

What happens if a juror fails to respond accurately in voir dire? In McDonough Power Equip., Inc. v. Greenwood, 464 U.S. 548 (1984), after the jury returned a verdict for plaintiff in a personal injury suit it was discovered that one juror had not revealed, during voir dire questioning about injuries to members of jurors' families, that his son had once been injured. The Supreme Court reversed a decision granting a new trial on this ground. It reasoned that the juror had acted in good faith, and that insisting on more than good faith asks for "something closer to perfection than our judicial system can be expected to give" because a litigant "is entitled to a fair trial, but not a perfect one."

The limitations on voir dire inquiry, and the possibility of inaccurate responses, have increasingly prompted lawyers to supplement voir dire with independent research. Indeed, judges may often refuse to allow inquiry during voir dire into areas that might be pertinent to the decision whether to exercise a peremptory challenge because they have no bearing on whether a juror should be excused for cause. But the judge will usually inquire into background information about jurors such as their addresses, types of employment and educational backgrounds. Lawyers nowadays find that Facebook, Snapchat, Pinterest, Twitter and LinkedIn enable them to "learn about jurors' lives, professions, political ideologies, interests, and potential biases that may not be apparent during voir dire." Vaughn, Screening the Jury Pool, Trial Mag., Sept. 2016, at 40. In addition, jury questionnaires may increasingly ask jurors to disclose details about their lives, though those sorts of inquiries are more common in criminal than civil cases. See Cliffford, TV Habits? Medical History? Tests for Jury Duty Get Personal, N.Y. Times, Aug. 21, 2015. These methods have supplemented or replaced the surveys lawyers have used in the past to provide demographic correlates that lawyers can use to predict how given potential jurors would react. Regarding those techniques, see Saks, The Limits of Scientific Jury Selection: Ethical and Empirical, 17 Jurimetrics 3, 7–8 (1976) (explaining that such data provide probabilities about juror attitudes, "not how any particular 54-year-old male Republican entrepreneur will vote").

NOTES AND QUESTIONS

1. As in so many other areas, the jury selection process relies in large part on the adversary initiative of the litigants rather than the court. Would complete control by the judge be more likely to assure impartial juries? Are the parties likely to try to get impartial jurors? Would plaintiff want to excuse a juror with a pro-plaintiff bias?

2. Assuming peremptory challenges may be used on any basis a party deems important, should voir dire be directed at the areas parties feel are significant to the exercise of the peremptory challenges? If judges imposed no limits on the subject matter of questions during voir dire, would there nevertheless be practical impediments to questioning about subjects jurors might be embarrassed to discuss?

3. Will judges' unwillingness to allow litigants a free hand in voir dire encourage them to rely more heavily on other juror investigation? Contacting

prospective jurors outside of court may be unethical under rules against attempts to influence jurors improperly. Survey research avoids ethical problems. However, it is expensive because large numbers of people must be questioned about a variety of pertinent matters to determine the correlation between background characteristics and attitudes toward the issues involved in the case. Will limitations on voir dire magnify the advantages that wealthy litigants have over litigants who cannot afford such research? If so, what effect, if any, should that fact have?

C. JUDICIAL CONTROL OF THE VERDICT

1. JUDGMENT AS A MATTER OF LAW (FORMERLY DIRECTED VERDICT AND J.N.O.V.)

Instructions to the jury are, of course, one form of judicial control, but judgment as a matter of law is a much more drastic form. Judgment as a matter of law is provided for in Rule 50(a) of the Federal Rules of Civil Procedure. The practice "enables the court to determine whether there is any question of fact to be submitted to the jury and whether any finding other than the one requested would be erroneous as a matter of law." 9A C. Wright & A. Miller, Federal Practice and Procedure § 2521. Motions for judgment as a matter of law may be made by either party at the close of her opponent's evidence. For the motion to be granted the court must find that there is insufficient evidence to go to the jury or that the evidence is so compelling that only one result could follow. In this way the motion for judgment as a matter of law acts effectively like a delayed summary judgment motion, in that it determines that there are no genuine issues of fact for the jury. Thus, while courts might be somewhat more hesitant to grant summary judgment than judgment as a matter of law because of the relative point in the litigation at which the two motions are made, essentially the same analysis concerning the meeting and shifting of the burden of production discussed in conjunction with summary judgment (see supra pp. 444–446) applies to the motion for judgment as a matter of law. The party with the burden of production at trial must present enough evidence so that a reasonable jury could find for him. His opponent's motion for judgment as a matter of law asks the court to make this determination before sending the case to the jury. However, a party with the burden of production may present evidence so persuasive that a reasonable jury would have to find for him. In such an event, that party, too, can obtain a judgment as a matter of law.

Prior to its amendment in 1991, Rule 50 provided for two different motions to control the jury's verdict, directed verdict and judgment notwithstanding the verdict (generally described as "judgment n.o.v."). Under the prior Rule 50(a), a party could move for directed verdict before the case was submitted to the jury; under prior Rule 50(b), a party against whom a jury verdict was rendered could seek judgment n.o.v. Other than this difference in timing, the two motions were identical. In combining the two motions into a motion for judgment as a matter of law, the Advisory Committee expressed the view that the "directed verdict" terminology was both misleading and anachronistic. It believed that use of the phrase, "judgment as a matter of law", underscores the connection between the two rules and reveals the common identity of the motions for directed verdict and judgment n.o.v. The change, then, was, for all practical purposes, one in name only. In many state judicial systems, the traditional nomenclature is still used.

In analyzing the scope of the motion for judgment as a matter of law, two distinct issues must be considered: (1) whether the motion is consistent with constitutional dictates concerning the role of the jury, and (2) the method for determining whether there exists sufficient evidence for a "reasonable" jury to find for a particular party. The first case in this section, Galloway v. United States, presents both issues, while the final two cases raise different aspects of the second issue.

The courts have developed acronyms for the motion available under amended Rule 50. See, e.g., Weese v. Schukman, 98 F.3d 542, 545 (10th Cir.1996) (JML); McKeel v. City of Pine Bluff, 73 F.3d 207, 212 (8th Cir.1996) (JAML); Jennings v. Jones, 587 F.3d 430 (1st Cir. 2009) (JMOL).

GALLOWAY V. UNITED STATES
Supreme Court of the United States, 1943
319 U.S. 372

JUSTICE RUTLEDGE delivered the opinion of the Court.

Petitioner seeks benefits for total and permanent disability by reason of insanity he claims existed May 31, 1919. On that day his policy of yearly renewable term insurance lapsed for nonpayment of premium.[1]

The suit was filed June 15, 1938. At the close of all the evidence the District Court granted the Government's motion for a directed verdict. Judgment was entered accordingly. The Circuit Court of Appeals affirmed. Both courts held the evidence legally insufficient to sustain a verdict for petitioner. He says this was erroneous and, in effect, deprived him of trial by jury, contrary to the Seventh Amendment.

---

[1] The contract was issued pursuant to the War Risk Insurance Act and insured against death or total permanent disability. Pursuant to statutory authority, T.D. 20 W.R., promulgated March 9, 1918, provided:

"Any impairment of mind or body which renders it impossible for the disabled person to follow continuously any substantially gainful occupation shall be deemed . . . to be total disability.

"Total disability shall be deemed to be permanent whenever it is founded upon conditions which render it reasonably certain that it will continue throughout the life of the person suffering from it. . . ."

The constitutional argument, as petitioner has made it, does not challenge generally the power of federal courts to withhold or withdraw from the jury cases in which the claimant puts forward insufficient evidence to support a verdict. The contention is merely that his case as made was substantial, the courts' decisions to the contrary were wrong, and therefore their effect has been to deprive him of a jury trial. * * * Upon the record and the issues as the parties have made them, the only question is whether the evidence was sufficient to sustain a verdict for petitioner. On that basis, we think the judgments must be affirmed.

I.

Certain facts are undisputed. Petitioner worked as a longshoreman in Philadelphia and elsewhere prior to enlistment in the Army November 1, 1917. He became a cook in a machine gun battalion. His unit arrived in France in April, 1918. He served actively until September 24. From then to the following January he was in a hospital with influenza. He then returned to active duty. He came back to the United States, and received honorable discharge April 29, 1919. He enlisted in the Navy January 15, 1920, and was discharged for bad conduct in July. The following December he again enlisted in the Army and served until May, 1922, when he deserted. Thereafter he was carried on the Army records as a deserter.

In 1930 began a series of medical examinations by Veterans' Bureau physicians. On May 19 that year his condition was diagnosed as "Moron, low grade; observation, dementia praecox, simple type." In November, 1931, further examination gave the diagnosis, "Psychosis with other diseases or conditions (organic disease of the central nervous system—type undetermined)." In July, 1934, still another examination was made, with diagnosis: "Psychosis manic and depressive insanity incompetent; hypertension, moderate; otitis media, chronic, left; varicose veins left, mild; abscessed teeth roots; myocarditis, mild."

Petitioner's wife, the nominal party in this suit, was appointed guardian of his person and estate in February, 1932. Claim for insurance benefits was made in June, 1934, and was finally denied by the Board of Veterans' Appeals in January, 1936. This suit followed two and a half years later.

Petitioner concededly is now totally and permanently disabled by reason of insanity and has been for some time prior to institution of this suit. It is conceded also that he was sound in mind and body until he arrived in France in April, 1918.

The theory of his case is that the strain of active service abroad brought on an immediate change, which was the beginning of a mental breakdown that has grown worse continuously through all the later years. Essential in this is the view it had become a total and permanent disability not later than May 31, 1919 [when the policy lapsed].

The evidence to support this theory falls naturally into three periods, namely, that prior to 1923; the interval from then to 1930; and that following 1930. It consists in proof of incidents occurring in France to show the beginnings of change; testimony of changed appearance and behavior in the years immediately following petitioner's return to the United States as compared with those prior to his departure; the medical evidence of insanity accumulated in the years following 1930; and finally the evidence of a physician, given largely as medical opinion, which seeks to tie all the other evidence together as foundation for the conclusion, expressed as of 1941, that petitioner's disability was total and permanent as of a time not later than May of 1919.

Documentary exhibits included military, naval and Veterans' Bureau records. Testimony was given by deposition or at the trial chiefly by five witnesses. One, O'Neill, was a fellow worker and friend from boyhood; two, Wells and Tanikawa, served with petitioner overseas; Lt. Col. Albert K. Mathews, who was an Army chaplain, observed him or another person of the same name at an Army hospital in California during early 1920; and Dr. Wilder, a physician, examined him shortly before the trial and supplied the only expert testimony in his behalf. The petitioner also put into evidence the depositions of Commander Platt and Lt. Col. James E. Matthews, his superior officers in the Navy and the Army, respectively, during 1920–22.

[Petitioner's fellow soldiers testified about various incidents in France demonstrating bizarre behavior on petitioner's part (including screaming a false alarm of a German attack while on guard duty on the Marne), and his friend testified about the dramatic change in petitioner's behavior after he returned from France.]

Lt. Col. (Chaplain) Mathews said he observed a Private Joseph Galloway, who was a prisoner for desertion and a patient in the mental ward at Fort MacArthur Station Hospital, California, during a six weeks period early in 1920. The chaplain's testimony gives strong evidence the man he observed was insane. However, there is a fatal weakness in this evidence. In his direct testimony, which was taken by deposition, the chaplain said he was certain that the soldier was petitioner. When confronted with the undisputed fact that petitioner was on active duty in the Navy during the first half of 1920, the witness at first stated that he might have been mistaken as to the time of his observation. Subsequently he reasserted the accuracy of his original statement as to the time of observation, but admitted that he might have been mistaken in believing that the patient-prisoner was petitioner. In this connection he volunteered the statement, "Might I add, sir, that I could not now identify that soldier if I were to meet him face to face, and that is because of the long lapse of time." The patient whom the witness saw was confined to his bed. The record is barren of other evidence, whether by the hospital's or the Army's records or otherwise, to show that petitioner was either patient or prisoner at Fort MacArthur in 1920 or at any other time.

Commander Platt testified that petitioner caused considerable trouble by disobedience and leaving ship without permission during his naval service in the first half of 1920. After "repeated warnings and punishments, leading to court martials," he was sentenced to a bad conduct discharge.

* * *

Dr. Wilder was the key witness. He disclaimed specializing in mental disease, but qualified as having given it "special attention." He first saw petitioner shortly before the trial, examined him "several times." He concluded petitioner's ailment "is a schizophrenic branch or form of praecox." Dr. Wilder heard the testimony and read the depositions of the other witnesses, and examined the documentary evidence. Basing his judgment upon this material, with inferences drawn from it, he concluded petitioner was born with "an inherent instability," though he remained normal until he went to France; began there "to be subjected to the strain of military life, then he began to go to pieces." In May, 1919, petitioner "was still suffering from the acuteness of the breakdown. . . . He is going down hill still, but the thing began with the breakdown. . . ." Petitioner was "definitely insane, yes, sir," in 1920 and "has been insane at all times, at least since July, 1918, the time of this episode on the Marne"; that is, "to the point that he was unable to adapt himself. I don't mean he has not had moments when he could not perform some routine tasks," but "from an occupational standpoint . . . he has been insane." He could follow "a mere matter of routine," but would have no incentive, would not keep a steady job, come to work on time, or do anything he didn't want to do. * * *

However, the witness knew "nothing whatever except his getting married" about petitioner's activities between 1925 and 1930, and what he knew of them between 1922 and 1925 was based entirely on O'Neill's testimony and a paper not of record here. Dr. Wilder at first regarded knowledge concerning what petitioner was doing between 1925 and 1930 as not essential. "We have a continuing disease, quite obviously beginning during his military service, and quite obviously continuing in 1930, and the *minor incidents* don't seem to me—" (Emphasis added.) Counsel for the government interrupted to inquire, "Well, if he was continuously employed for eight hours a day from 1925 to 1930 would that have any bearing?" The witness replied, "It would have a great deal." Upon further questioning, however, he reverted to his first position, stating it would not be necessary or helpful for him to know what petitioner was doing from 1925 to 1930: "I testified from the information I had."

This, we think, is the crux of the case and distinguishes it from the cases on which petitioner has relied.[8] His burden was to prove total and permanent disability as of a date not later than May 31, 1919. He has undertaken to do this by showing incipience of mental disability shortly before that time and its continuance and progression throughout the succeeding years. He has clearly established incidence of total and permanent disability as of some period prior to 1938, when he began this suit.[9] For our purposes this may be taken as medically established by the Veterans' Bureau examination and diagnosis of July, 1934.

But if the record is taken to show that some form of mental disability existed in 1930, which later became total and permanent, petitioner's problem remains to demonstrate by more than speculative inference that this condition itself began on or before May 31, 1919 and continuously existed or progressed through the intervening years to 1930.

To show origin before the crucial date, he gives evidence of two abnormal incidents occurring while he was in France, one creating the disturbance before he came near the fighting front, the other yelling that the Germans were coming when he was on guard duty at the Marne. There is no other evidence of abnormal behavior during his entire service of more than a year abroad.

That he was court martialed for these sporadic acts and bound and gagged for one does not prove he was insane or had then a general breakdown in "an already fragile mental constitution," which the vicissitudes of a longshoreman's life had not been able to crack.

To these two incidents petitioner adds the testimony of O'Neill that he looked and acted like a wreck, compared with his former self, when he returned from France about a month before the crucial date, and O'Neill's vague recollections that this condition continued through the next two, three, four or five years.

O'Neill's testimony apparently takes no account of petitioner's having spent 101 days in a hospital in France with influenza just before he came home. But, given the utmost credence, as is required, it does no more than show that petitioner was subject to alternating periods of gaiety and depression for some indefinite period after his return, extending perhaps as late as 1922. But because of its vagueness as to time, dates, frequency

---

[8] None of them exhibits a period of comparable length as to which evidence is wholly lacking and under circumstances which preclude inference the omission was unintentional.

[9] He has not established a fixed date at which contemporaneous medical examination, both physical and mental, establishes totality and permanence prior to Dr. Wilder's examinations in 1941. Dr. Wilder testified that on the evidence concerning petitioner's behavior at the time of his discharge in 1919, and without reference to the testimony as to later conduct, including O'Neill's, he would reserve his opinion on whether petitioner was then "crazy"—"I wouldn't have enough—."

of opportunity for observation, and specific incident, O'Neill's testimony concerning the period from 1922 to 1925 is hardly more than speculative.

We have then the two incidents in France followed by O'Neill's testimony of petitioner's changed condition in 1919 and its continuance to 1922.[11] * * * Then follows a chasm of eight years. The only evidence we have concerning this period is the fact that petitioner married his present guardian at some time within it, an act from which in the legal sense no inference of insanity can be drawn.

This period was eight years of continuous insanity, according to the inference petitioner would be allowed to have drawn. If so, he should have no need of inference. Insanity so long and continuously sustained does not hide itself from the eyes and ears of witnesses. The assiduity which produced the evidence of two "crazy" incidents during a year and a half in France should produce one during eight years or, for that matter, five years in the United States.

Inference is capable of bridging many gaps. But not, in these circumstances, one so wide and deep as this. Knowledge of petitioner's activities and behavior from 1922 or 1925 to 1930 was peculiarly within his ken and that of his wife, who has litigated this cause in his and presumably, though indirectly, in her own behalf. His was the burden to show continuous disability. What he did in this time, or did not do, was vital to his case. Apart from the mere fact of his marriage, the record is blank for five years and almost blank for eight. For all that appears, he may have worked full time and continuously for five and perhaps for eight, with only a possible single interruption.

No favorable inference can be drawn from the omission. It was not one of oversight or inability to secure proof. That is shown by the thoroughness with which the record was prepared for all other periods, before and after this one, and by the fact petitioner's wife, though she married him during the period and was available, did not testify. The only reasonable conclusion is that petitioner, or those who acted for him, deliberately chose, for reasons no doubt considered sufficient (and which we do not criticize, since such matters including tactical ones, are for the judgment of counsel) to present no evidence or perhaps to withhold evidence readily available concerning this long interval, and to trust to the genius of expert medical inference and judicial laxity to bridge this canyon.

---

[11] Chaplain Mathews' testimony would be highly probative of insanity existing early in 1920, if petitioner were sufficiently identified as its subject. However, the bare inference of identity which might otherwise be drawn from the mere identity of names cannot be made reasonably in view of its overwhelming contradiction by other evidence presented by petitioner and the failure to produce records from Fort MacArthur Hospital or the Army or from persons who knew the fact that petitioner had been there at any time. The omission eloquently testifies in a manner which no inference could overcome that petitioner never was there. The chaplain's testimony therefore should have been stricken, had the case gone to the jury, and petitioner can derive no aid from it here.

In the circumstances exhibited, the former is not equal to the feat, and the latter will not permit it. No case has been cited and none has been found in which inference, however expert, has been permitted to make so broad a leap and take the place of evidence which, according to all reason, must have been at hand. To allow this would permit the substitution of inference, tenuous at best, not merely for evidence absent because impossible or difficult to secure, but for evidence disclosed to be available and not produced. This would substitute speculation for proof. Furthermore, the inference would be more plausible perhaps if the evidence of insanity as of May, 1919, were stronger than it is, such for instance as Chaplain Mathews' testimony would have furnished if it could be taken as applying to petitioner. But, on this record, the evidence of insanity as of that time is thin at best, if it can be regarded as at all more than speculative.

Beyond this, there is nothing to show totality or permanence. These come only by what the Circuit Court of Appeals rightly characterized as "long-range retroactive diagnosis." That might suffice, notwithstanding this crucial inference was a matter of opinion, if there were factual evidence over which the medical eye could travel and find continuity through the intervening years. But eight years are too many to permit it to skip, when the bridgeheads (if the figure may be changed) at each end are no stronger than they are here, and when the seer first denies, then admits, then denies again, that what took place in this time would make "a great deal" of difference in what he saw. Expert medical inference rightly can do much. But we think the feat attempted here too large for its accomplishment.

* * *

III.

What has been said disposes of the case as the parties have made it. For that reason perhaps nothing more need be said. But objection has been advanced that, in some manner not wholly clear, the directed verdict practice offends the Seventh Amendment.

It may be noted, first, that the Amendment has no application of its own force to this case. The suit is one to enforce a monetary claim against the United States. It hardly can be maintained that under the common law in 1791 jury trial was a matter of right for persons asserting claims against the sovereign.[17] Whatever force the Amendment has therefore is derived because Congress in the legislation cited has made it applicable. Even so, the objection made on the score of its requirements is untenable.

If the intention is to claim generally that the Amendment deprives the federal courts of power to direct a verdict for insufficiency of evidence, the

---

[17] Neither the Amendment's terms nor its history suggest it was intended to extend to such claims. The Court of Claims has functioned for almost a century without affording jury trial in cases of this sort and without offending the requirements of the Amendment. McElrath v. United States, 102 U.S. 426; see Richardson, History, Jurisdiction and Practice of the Court of Claims (2d ed. 1885).

short answer is the contention has been foreclosed by repeated decisions made here consistently for nearly a century. More recently the practice has been approved explicitly in the promulgation of the Federal Rules of Civil Procedure. Cf. Rule 50. The objection therefore comes too late.

Furthermore, the argument from history is not convincing. It is not that "the rules of the common law" in 1791 deprived trial courts of power to withdraw cases from the jury, because not made out, or appellate courts of power to review such determinations. The jury was not absolute master of fact in 1791. Then as now courts excluded evidence for irrelevancy and relevant proof for other reasons. The argument concedes they weighed the evidence, not only piecemeal but in toto for submission to the jury, by at least two procedures, the demurrer to the evidence and the motion for a new trial. The objection is not therefore to the basic thing, which is the power of the court to withhold cases from the jury or set aside the verdict for insufficiency of the evidence. It is rather to incidental or collateral effects, namely, that the directed verdict as now administered differs from both those procedures because, on the one hand, allegedly higher standards of proof are required and, on the other, different consequences follow as to further maintenance of the litigation. Apart from the standards of proof, the argument appears to urge that in 1791, a litigant could challenge his opponent's evidence, either by the demurrer, which when determined ended the litigation, or by motion for a new trial which if successful, gave the adversary another chance to prove his case; and therefore the Amendment excluded any challenge to which one or the other of these consequences does not attach.

The Amendment did not bind the federal courts to the exact procedural incidents or details of jury trial according to the common law in 1791, any more than it tied them to the common-law system of pleading or the specific rules of evidence then prevailing. Nor were "the rules of the common law" then prevalent, including those relating to the procedure by which the judge regulated the jury's role on questions of fact, crystalized in a fixed and immutable system. On the contrary, they were constantly changing and developing during the late eighteenth and early nineteenth centuries. In 1791 this process already had resulted in widely divergent common-law rules on procedural matters among the states, and between them and England. And none of the contemporaneous rules regarding judicial control of the evidence going to juries or its sufficiency to support a verdict had reached any precise, much less final, form. In addition, the passage of time has obscured much of the procedure which then may have had more or less definite form, even for historical purposes.

This difficulty, no doubt, accounts for the amorphous character of the objection now advanced, which insists, not that any single one of the features criticized, but that the cumulative total or the alternative effect of all, was embodied in the Amendment. The more logical conclusion, we

think, and the one which both history and the previous decisions here
support, is that the Amendment was designed to preserve the basic
institution of jury trial in only its most fundamental elements, not the great
mass of procedural forms and details, varying even then so widely among
common-law jurisdictions.

Apart from the uncertainty and the variety of conclusions which
follows from an effort at purely historical accuracy, the consequences
flowing from the view asserted are sufficient to refute it. It may be doubted
that the Amendment requires challenge to an opponent's case to be made
without reference to the merits of one's own and at the price of all
opportunity to have it considered. On the other hand, there is equal room
for disbelieving it compels endless repetition of litigation and unlimited
chance, by education gained at the opposing party's expense, for perfecting
a case at other trials. The essential inconsistency of these alternatives
would seem sufficient to refute that either or both, to the exclusion of all
others, received constitutional sanctity by the Amendment's force. The first
alternative, drawn from the demurrer to the evidence, attributes to the
Amendment the effect of forcing one admission because another and an
entirely different one is made,[28] and thereby compels conclusion of the
litigation once and for all. The true effect of imposing such a risk would not
be to guarantee the plaintiff a jury trial. It would be rather to deprive the
defendant (or the plaintiff if he were the challenger) of that right; or, if not
that, then of the right to challenge the legal sufficiency of the opposing case.
The Amendment was not framed or adopted to deprive either party of
either right. It is impartial in its guaranty of both. To posit assertion of one
upon sacrifice of the other would dilute and distort the full protection
intended. The admitted validity of the practice on the motion for a new trial
goes far to demonstrate this.[29] It negatives any idea that the challenge
must be made at such a risk as the demurrer imposed. As for the other
alternative, it is not urged that the Amendment guarantees another trial
whenever challenge to the sufficiency of evidence is sustained. That

---

[28] By conceding the full scope of an opponent's evidence and asserting its insufficiency in law,
which is one thing, the challenger must be taken, perforce the Amendment, also to admit he has
no case, if the other's evidence is found legally sufficient, which is quite another thing. In effect,
one must stake his case, not upon its own merit on the facts, but on the chance he may be right in
regarding his opponent's as wanting in probative content. If he takes the gamble and loses, he pays
with his own case, regardless of its merit and without opportunity for the jury to consider it. To
force this choice and yet deny that afforded by the directed verdict would be to embed in the
Constitution the hypertechnicality of common-law pleading and procedure in their heyday.

[29] Under that practice the moving party receives the benefit of jury evaluation of his own
case and of challenge to his opponent's for insufficiency. If he loses on the challenge, the litigation
is ended. But this is not because, in making it, he is forced to admit his own is insufficient. It is
rather for the reasons that the court finds the opposite party's evidence is legally sufficient and
the jury has found it outweighs his own. There is thus no forced surrender of one right from
assertion of another.

On the other hand, if the challenger wins, there is another trial. But this is because he has
sought it, not because the Amendment guarantees it.

argument, in turn, is precluded by the practice on demurrer to the evidence.

Each of the classical modes of challenge, therefore, disproves the notion that the characteristic feature of the other, for effect upon continuing the litigation, became a part of the Seventh Amendment's guaranty to the exclusion of all others. That guaranty did not incorporate conflicting constitutional policies, that challenge to an opposing case must be made with the effect of terminating the litigation finally and, at the same time, with the opposite effect of requiring another trial. Alternatives so contradictory give room, not for the inference that one or the other is required, but rather for the view that neither is essential.

Finally, the objection appears to be directed generally at the standards of proof judges have required for submission of evidence to the jury. But standards, contrary to the objection's assumption, cannot be framed wholesale for the great variety of situations in respect to which the question arises. Nor is the matter greatly aided by substituting one general formula for another. It hardly affords help to insist upon "substantial evidence" rather than "some evidence" or "any evidence," or vice versa. The matter is essentially one to be worked out in particular situations and for particular types of cases. Whatever may be the general formulation, the essential requirement is that mere speculation be not allowed to do duty for probative facts, after making due allowance for all reasonably possible inferences favoring the party whose case is attacked. The mere difference in labels used to describe this standard, whether it is applied under the demurrer to the evidence or on motion for a directed verdict, cannot amount to a departure from "the rules of the common law" which the Amendment requires to be followed. If there is abuse in this respect, the obvious remedy is by correction on appellate review.

Judged by this requirement, or by any standard other than sheer speculation, we are unable to conclude that one whose burden, by the nature of his claim, is to show continuing and total disability for nearly twenty years supplies the essential proof of continuity when he wholly omits to show his whereabouts, activities or condition for five years, although the record discloses evidence must have been available, and, further, throws no light upon three additional years, except for one vaguely described and dated visit to his former home. Nothing in the Seventh Amendment requires it should be allowed to join forces with the jury system to bring about such a result. That guaranty requires that the jury be allowed to make reasonable inferences from facts proven in evidence having a reasonable tendency to sustain them. It permits expert opinion to have the force of fact when based on facts which sustain it. But it does not require that experts or the jury be permitted to make inferences from the withholding of crucial facts, favorable in their effects to the party who has the evidence of them in his peculiar knowledge and possession, but elects to keep it so. The words "total and permanent" are the statute's, not our own. They mean something more than incipient or occasional disability. We hardly need add that we give full credence to all of the testimony. But that cannot cure its inherent vagueness or supply essential elements omitted or withheld.

JUSTICE BLACK, with whom JUSTICE DOUGLAS and JUSTICE MURPHY concur, dissenting.

The Seventh Amendment to the Constitution provides:

> "In suits at common law, where the value in controversy shall exceed twenty dollars, the right of trial by jury shall be preserved, and no fact tried by a jury shall be otherwise re-examined in any Court of the United States, than according to the rules of the common law."

The Court here re-examines testimony offered in a common law suit, weighs conflicting evidence, and holds that the litigant may never take this case to a jury. The founders of our government thought that trial of fact by juries rather than by judges was an essential bulwark of civil liberty. For this reason, among others, they adopted Article III, § 2 of the Constitution, and the Sixth and Seventh Amendments. Today's decision marks a continuation of the gradual process of judicial erosion which in one hundred fifty years has slowly worn away a major portion of the essential guarantee of the Seventh Amendment.

The principal method by which judges prevented cases from going to the jury in the Seventeenth and Eighteenth Centuries was by the demurrer to the evidence, under which the defendant at the end of the trial admitted all facts shown by the plaintiff as well as all inferences which might be drawn from the facts, and asked for a ruling of the Court on the "law of the case." This practice fell into disuse in England in 1793, Gibson v. Hunter, 2 H.Bl. 187, and in the United States federal courts in 1826, Fowle v. Alexandria, 11 Wheat. 320, 6 L.Ed. 484. The power of federal judges to comment to the jury on the evidence gave them additional influence. The right of involuntary non-suit of a plaintiff, which might have been used to expand judicial power at jury expense was at first denied federal courts.

As Hamilton had declared in The Federalist, the basic judicial control of the jury function was in the court's power to order a new trial. In 1830, this Court said: "The only modes known to the common law to re-examine such facts, are the granting of a new trial by the court where the issue was tried, or to which the record was properly returnable; or the award of a venire facias de novo, by an appellate court, for some error of law which intervened in the proceedings." Parsons v. Bedford, 3 Pet. at page 448. That retrial by a new jury rather than factual reevaluation by a court is a constitutional right of genuine value was restated as recently as Slocum v. New York Life Insurance Co., 228 U.S. 364.

A long step toward the determination of fact by judges instead of by juries was the invention of the directed verdict. In 1850, what seems to have been the first directed verdict case considered by this Court, Parks v. Ross, 11 How. 362, 374, was presented for decision. The Court held that the directed verdict serves the same purpose as the demurrer to the evidence, and that since there was "no evidence whatever" on the critical issue in the case, the directed verdict was approved. The decision was an innovation, a departure from the traditional rule restated only fifteen years before in Greenleaf v. Birth, 1835, 9 Pet. 292, 299, in which this Court had said: "Where there is no evidence tending to prove a particular fact, the courts are bound so to instruct the jury, when requested; but they cannot legally give any instruction which shall take from the jury the right of weighing the evidence and determining what effect it shall have."

This new device contained potentialities for judicial control of the jury which had not existed in the demurrer to the evidence. In the first place, demurring to the evidence was risky business, for in so doing the party not only admitted the truth of all the testimony against him but also all reasonable inferences which might be drawn from it; and upon joinder in demurrer the case was withdrawn from the jury while the court proceeded to give final judgment either for or against the demurrant. Imposition of this risk was no mere technicality; for by making withdrawal of a case from the jury dangerous to the moving litigant's cause, the early law went far to assure that facts would never be examined except by a jury. Under the directed verdict practice the moving party takes no such chance, for if his motion is denied, instead of suffering a directed verdict against him, his case merely continues into the hands of the jury. The litigant not only takes no risk by a motion for a directed verdict, but in making such a motion gives himself two opportunities to avoid the jury's decision; for under the federal variant of judgment notwithstanding the verdict, the judge may reserve opinion on the motion for a directed verdict and then give judgment for the moving party after the jury was formally found against him. In the second place, under the directed verdict practice the courts soon abandoned the "admission of all facts and reasonable inferences" standard referred to, and created the so-called "substantial evidence" rule which permitted directed verdicts even though there was far more evidence in the case than a plaintiff would have needed to withstand a demurrer.

The substantial evidence rule did not spring into existence immediately upon the adoption of the directed verdict device. For a few more years federal judges held to the traditional rule that juries might pass finally on facts if there was "any evidence" to support a party's contention. The rule that a case must go to the jury unless there was "no evidence" was completely repudiated in Schuylkill and Dauphin Improvement Co. v. Munson, 1871, 14 Wall. 442, 447, 448, upon which the Court today relies in part. There the Court declared that "some" evidence was not enough— there must be evidence sufficiently persuasive to the judge so that he thinks "a jury can properly proceed." The traditional rule was given an ugly name, "the scintilla rule", to hasten its demise. For a time traces of the old formula remained, but the new spirit prevailed. The same transition from jury supremacy to jury subordination through judicial decisions took place in State courts.

* * *

Today the Court comes dangerously close to weighing the credibility of a witness and rejecting his testimony because the majority do not believe it.

The story thus briefly told depicts the constriction of a constitutional civil right and should not be continued.

* * *

The call for the true application of the Seventh Amendment is not to words, but to the spirit of honest desire to see that constitutional right preserved. Either the judge or the jury must decide facts and, to the extent that we take this responsibility, we lessen the jury function. Our duty to preserve this one of the Bill of Rights may be peculiarly difficult, for here it is our own power which we must restrain. * * * As for myself, I believe that a verdict should be directed, if at all, only when, without weighing the credibility of the witnesses, there is in the evidence no room whatever for honest difference of opinion over the factual issue in controversy. I shall continue to believe that in all other cases a judge should, in obedience to the command of the Seventh Amendment, not interfere with the jury's function. Since this is a matter of high constitutional importance, appellate courts should be alert to insure the preservation of this constitutional right even though each case necessarily turns on its peculiar circumstances.

* * *

This case graphically illustrates the injustice resulting from permitting judges to direct verdicts instead of requiring them to await a jury decision and then, if necessary, allow a new trial. The chief reason given for approving a directed verdict against this petitioner is that no evidence except expert medical testimony was offered for a five to eight year period. Perhaps, now that the petitioner knows he has insufficient evidence to satisfy a jury, he would be able to fill this time gap to meet any judge's demand. If a court would point out on a motion for new trial that the evidence as to this particular period was too weak, the petitioner would be given an opportunity to buttress the physician's evidence. If, as the Court believes, insufficient evidence has been offered to sustain a jury verdict for the petitioner, we should at least authorize a new trial. * * *

I believe that there is a reasonable difference of opinion as to whether the petitioner was totally and permanently disabled by reason of insanity on May 31, 1919, and that his case therefore should have been allowed to go to the jury. The testimony of fellow soldiers, friends, supervisors, and of a medical expert whose integrity and ability is not challenged cannot be rejected by any process available to me as a judge.

NOTES AND QUESTIONS

1.   Note that the Seventh Amendment contains two distinct clauses. The first concerns whether a constitutional right to jury trial exists at all. We have already considered the interpretation of that clause extensively in Section B of this chapter. The other clause, relevant only after one has initially concluded that the jury trial right applies, concerns the scope of the limitations that can be placed on performance of the jury's function. *Galloway*'s constitutional discussion primarily constitutes an interpretation of this latter clause to determine whether the directed verdict properly empowers the court to take the task of fact finding away from the jury in certain instances.

2.   The Court's discussion of the constitutionality of the directed verdict is largely dictum, in light of its holding that the Seventh Amendment was inapplicable in *Galloway*. On what basis did the Court reach this conclusion? Cf. Osborn v. Haley, 549 U.S. 225, 252 (2007) (Seventh Amendment right "does not apply to proceedings against the sovereign."). Is its reasoning persuasive? In answering, examine the language of the Seventh Amendment, and consider the approach to Seventh Amendment application adopted by Justice Story in Parsons v. Bedford, 28 U.S. (3 Pet.) 433, 447, used by the Court to the present day. See, e.g., Curtis v. Loether, supra p. 574. If one were to assume that by its nature the right asserted in *Galloway* was "legal", should the Seventh Amendment apply, even though in 1791, at the time of the amendment's ratification, there were no suits against the sovereign? Consider the following argument: Because it is established that Congress need not allow private individuals to sue the government, it can take the lesser step of allowing such suits only on the condition that the individual waive his Seventh Amendment right to jury trial.

3.   Justice Rutledge acknowledges that the directed verdict, at least in its modern form, did not exist at common law. Yet the second clause of the Seventh Amendment provides that jury fact finding may be reviewed only in accordance with procedures in existence at common law—i.e., at the time of the amendment's ratification in 1791. How, then, does Justice Rutledge reach the conclusion that the directed verdict is constitutional? What common law practices does he rely on to justify the directed verdict? In what ways did those practices differ from the modern directed verdict? Do you agree with Justice Rutledge that those differences are insufficient to distinguish those practices from the directed verdict?

4.   What is the basis of Justice Black's dissent on the constitutional issue? Who do you think gets the better of the argument? Do you agree with Professor Cooper that the majority's response to Justice Black is "unduly facile"? Cooper, Directions for Directed Verdicts: A Compass for Federal Courts, 55 Minn.L.Rev. 903, 917 (1971). For a comprehensive examination of the history of the directed verdict and its predecessor, see id. at 909–27. See

also Blume, Origin and Development of the Directed Verdict, 48 Mich.L.Rev. 555 (1950). For a critique of Justice Black's assumptions about early jury practices, see Woolhandler & Collins, The Article III Jury, 87 Va. L. Rev. 587 (2001) (arguing that Justice Black's view was incorrect because "pre-modern federal control of juries by the elaboration of law, the direction of verdicts, and the liberal use of commentary on the evidence along with new trials likely exceeded the overall level of modern judicial controls").

5. Assuming directed verdict is constitutional, was it properly invoked on the evidence presented in *Galloway?* To what extent is the decision to award directed verdict simply an illustration of the commonplace inference that when a party fails to produce evidence within its control the evidence would probably hurt the party's case. Even if this were true, would it justify a directed verdict, or simply influence the fact finder's decision? Would the jury have had to speculate in order to find for Galloway? If so, would that speculation have been anything more than the type of inferential process we normally expect juries to undertake? Is the majority or Justice Black more persuasive on this issue?

Justice Black argues that the majority improperly adopts a "substantial evidence" standard—unless the party with the burden of production produces "substantial evidence" to support its claim, directed verdict will be granted. Black says directed verdict should be granted only when the party opposing the motion has absolutely no supporting evidence—what he claims has been pejoratively labeled the "scintilla rule," since that was always the standard employed historically. How does Justice Rutledge respond to this contention? Consider how these differing standards may be applied in the next case.

6. Note that the attack on the directed verdict might also have been made against summary judgment. The English developed summary procedures in the 19th century in suits against debtors who failed to offer evidence to support their defenses. When the District of Columbia adopted a similar rule, the Supreme Court held that it did not violate the right of a debtor to trial by jury where the debtor failed to submit an affidavit showing that there was a real issue for trial:

> If it were true that the rule deprived the plaintiff in error of the right to trial by jury, we should pronounce it void without reference to cases. But it does not do so. It prescribes the means of making an issue. The purpose of the rule is to preserve the court from frivolous defenses and to defeat attempts to use formal pleading as means to delay the recovery of just demands.

Fidelity & Deposit Co. v. United States, 187 U.S. 315, 320, 23 S.Ct. 120, 122, 47 L.Ed. 194 (1902).

More recently, Professor Thomas has mounted a Seventh Amendment challenge to summary judgment, arguing that summary judgment differs fundamentally from common law procedures establishing judicial checks on the jury's factfinding province. See generally S. Thomas, The Missing American Jury: Restoring the Fundamental Constitutional Role of the Criminal, Civil, and Grand Juries (2016). See also Thomas, Why Summary

Judgment is Unconstitutional, 93 Va.L.Rev. 139 (2007). See also the responses by Professors Brunet and Nelson to Thomas's theory, Brunet, Summary Judgment is Constitutional, 93 Iowa L. Rev. 1625 (2008); Nelson, Summary Judgment and the Progressive Constitution, 93 Iowa L. Rev. 1653 (2008), as well as her reply, Thomas, Why Summary Judgment Is Still Unconstitutional: A Reply to Professors Brunet and Nelson, 93 Iowa L. Rev. 1667 (2008). See also Thomas, The Unconstitutionality of Summary Judgment: A Status Report, 93 Iowa L. Rev. 1613 (2008).

Relying in large part on its decision in *Fidelity & Deposit Co.*, the Supreme Court has held that the directive of the Private Securities Litigation Reform Act requiring the trial court to draw factual inferences concerning scienter in securities fraud cases did not unconstitutionally usurp the jury's function. It reasoned that the purpose of both challenged procedures "simply 'prescribe[ ] the means of making an issue,'" and "when '[t]he issue [was] made as prescribed, the right of trial by jury accrues.'" Tellabs, Inc. v. Makor Issues & Rights, Ltd., 551 U.S. 308 (2007), quoting *Fidelity & Deposit Co.*, 187 U.S. at 320. This case is reproduced in the pleading chapter, supra p. 161.

For a discussion of Seventh Amendment challenges to the rule 12(b)(6) motion to dismiss under the standards imposed by *Twombly* and *Iqbal* [supra pp. 184–198], see Thomas, Why the Motion to Dismiss is Now Unconstitutional, 92 Minn.L.Rev. 1851 (2008). See also Klein, Is Ashcroft v. Iqbal the Death (Finally) of the "Historical Test" for Interpreting the Seventh Amendment?, 88 Neb. L. Rev. 467 (2010).

THE CONSTITUTIONALITY OF JUDGMENT AS A MATTER OF LAW AFTER VERDICT

Recall that prior to its amendment in 1991, Rule 50(a) provided for two distinct procedures, directed verdict (sought before the case is sent to the jury) and judgment n.o.v., or judgment notwithstanding the verdict (sought after the jury's verdict). Though the 1991 amendment replaced both procedures with the motion for judgment as a matter of law (see supra p. 613), the constitutional issues raised by the former judgment n.o.v. practice remain unchanged.

As was true of directed verdict, the motion for judgment n.o.v. faced a serious constitutional challenge under the Seventh Amendment. In fact, in Slocum v. New York Life Insurance Co., 228 U.S. 364 (1913), the Supreme Court, in an opinion by Justice Van Devanter, held judgment n.o.v. to be unconstitutional, because it did not exist at common law. While at common law a court could order a new trial because of plaintiff's failure to present sufficient evidence, this was fundamentally different, the Supreme Court reasoned, from the court's entry of a judgment in defendant's favor. The Court also acknowledged the common law practice of demurrer to the evidence (discussed in *Galloway*), and, despite the controversy surrounding the issue in *Galloway* some thirty years later, assumed the validity of the directed verdict practice. However, the Court saw qualitative differences between these practices and the judgment n.o.v.:

> At the trial the defendant requested that a verdict in its favor be directed, and had the court indicated its purpose to do that, it would have been open to the plaintiff, under the then prevailing practice, to take a voluntary nonsuit, which would have enabled her to make a fuller and better presentation of her case, if the facts permitted, at another trial in a new suit.

If, on the other hand, the jury's verdict were rejected by the court and a judgment for the other party entered, the opportunity for a voluntary nonsuit would no longer be available. Today, a party could not take a voluntary nonsuit this late in the proceeding, without the court's permission. Fed.R.Civ.P. 41(a). In light of this fact, would the approach to Seventh Amendment interpretation adopted in *Galloway* lead to a finding that judgment n.o.v. is constitutional today?

Slocum has never been formally overruled. However, in Baltimore & Carolina Line, Inc. v. Redman, 295 U.S. 654 (1935), the Court, once again in an opinion by Justice Van Devanter, effectively sapped the strength from *Slocum*. The Court found the case to present "[a] very different situation" from *Slocum,* because in *Redman* "[t]he trial court expressly reserved its ruling on the defendant's motions to dismiss and for a directed verdict * * *." This practice, the Court concluded, was valid at common law. Thus, when the trial judge invalidated the jury's verdict, he was not granting a motion for judgment n.o.v.; he was merely making a ruling on the directed verdict motion which he had reserved prior to trial.

In 2006, Rule 50 was amended to remove the former requirement that the moving party must file the motion for judgment as a matter of law "at the close of all the evidence," in order to preserve the right to move again after verdict, although a pre-verdict motion is still required. Instead, the rule now allows the motion to be made at any time before the case is submitted to the jury and after the opposing party has been fully heard on the issue. The accompanying Committee Note indicates that the continued requirement of a motion prior to submission to the jury satisfies the Seventh Amendment.

Why might a judge who has denied a motion for judgment as a matter of law under Rule 50(a) be willing to grant that motion when renewed by the moving party following the jury's verdict?

While a Rule 50(a) motion is deemed to serve as a prerequisite for filing a post-verdict Rule 50(b) motion, on occasion courts have softened that requirement under the circumstances of a given case. See, e.g., E.E.O.C. v. Western Trading Co., 291 F.R.D. 615 (D. Colo. 2013) (court allows Rule 50(b) motion despite absence of pre-verdict Rule 50(a) motion because plaintiffs had argued during the jury charge conference that there was insufficient evidence to warrant a mitigation of damages instruction). In light of *Redman,* supra, is such a practice constitutional?

LAVENDER V. KURN

Supreme Court of the United States, 1946
327 U.S. 645

JUSTICE MURPHY delivered the opinion of the Court.

The Federal Employers' Liability Act permits recovery for personal injuries to an employee of a railroad engaged in interstate commerce if such injuries result "in whole or in part from the negligence of any of the officers, agents, or employees of such carrier, or by reason of any defect or insufficiency, due to its negligence, in its cars, engines, appliances, machinery, track, roadbed, works, boats, wharves, or other equipment." 45 U.S.C. § 51, 45 U.S.C.A. § 51.

Petitioner, the administrator of the estate of L. E. Haney, brought this suit under the Act against the respondent trustees of the St. Louis-San Francisco Railway Company (Frisco) and the respondent Illinois Central Railroad Company. It was charged that Haney, while employed as a switchtender by the respondents in the switchyard of the Grand Central Station in Memphis, Tennessee, was killed as a result of respondents' negligence. Following a trial in the Circuit Court of the City of St. Louis, Missouri, the jury returned a verdict in favor of petitioner and awarded damages in the amount of $30,000. Judgment was entered accordingly. On appeal, however, the Supreme Court of Missouri reversed the judgment, holding that there was no substantial evidence of negligence to support the submission of the case to the jury. We granted certiorari to review the propriety of the Supreme Court's action under the circumstances of this case.

It was admitted that Haney was employed by the Illinois Central, or a subsidiary corporation thereof, as a switchtender in the railroad yards near the Grand Central Station, which was owned by the Illinois Central. His duties included the throwing of switches for the Illinois Central as well as for the Frisco and other railroads using that station. * * *

The Illinois Central tracks run north and south directly past and into the Grand Central Station. About 2700 feet south of the station the Frisco tracks cross at right angles to the Illinois Central tracks. A westbound Frisco train wishing to use the station must stop some 250 feet or more west of this crossing and back into the station over a switch line curving east and north. The events in issue center about the switch several feet north of the main Frisco tracks at the point where the switch line branches off. This switch controls the tracks at this point.

It was very dark on the evening of December 21, 1939. At about 7:30 p.m. a westbound interstate Frisco passenger train stopped on the Frisco main line, its rear some 20 or 30 feet west of the switch. Haney, in the performance of his duties, threw or opened the switch to permit the train to back into the station. The respondents claimed that Haney was then required to cross to the south side of the track before the train passed the switch; and the conductor of the train testified that he saw Haney so cross. But there was also evidence that Haney's duties required him to wait at the switch north of the track until the train had cleared, close the switch, return to his shanty near the crossing and change the signals from red to green to permit trains on the Illinois Central tracks to use the crossing. The Frisco train cleared the switch, backing at the rate of 8 or 10 miles per hour. But the switch remained open and the signals still were red. Upon investigation Haney was found north of the track near the switch lying face down on the ground, unconscious. An ambulance was called, but he was dead upon arrival at the hospital.

Haney had been struck in the back of the head, causing a fractured skull from which he died. There were no known eye-witnesses to the fatal blow. Although it is not clear there is evidence that his body was extended north and south, the head to the south. Apparently he had fallen forward to the south; his face was bruised on the left side from hitting the ground and there were marks indicating that his toes had dragged a few inches southward as he fell. His head was about 5½ feet north of the Frisco tracks. Estimates ranged from 2 feet to 14 feet as to how far west of the switch he lay.

The injury to Haney's head was evidenced by a gash about two inches long from which blood flowed. The back of Haney's white cap had a corresponding black mark about an inch and a half long and an inch wide, running at an angle downward to the right of the center of the back of the head. A spot of blood was later found at a point 3 or 4 feet north of the tracks. The conclusion following an autopsy was that Haney's skull was fractured by "some fast moving small round object." One of the examining doctors testified that such an object might have been attached to a train backing at the rate of 8 or 10 miles per hour. But he also admitted that the fracture might have resulted from a blow from a pipe or club or some similar round object in the hands of an individual.

Petitioner's theory is that Haney was struck by the curled end or tip of a mail hook hanging down loosely on the outside of the mail car of the backing train. This curled end was 73 inches above the top of the rail, which was 7 inches high. The overhang of the mail car in relation to the rails was about 2 to 2½ feet. The evidence indicated that when the mail car swayed or moved around a curve the mail hook might pivot, its curled end swinging out as much as 12 to 14 inches. The curled end could thus be swung out to a point 3 to 3½ feet from the rail and about 73 inches above the top of the rail. Both east and west of the switch, however, was an uneven mound of cinders and dirt rising at its highest points 18 to 24 inches above the top of the rails. Witnesses differed as to how close the mound approached the rails, the estimates varying from 3 to 15 feet. But taking the figures most favorable to the petitioner, the mound extended to a point 6 to 12 inches north of the overhanging side of the mail car. If the mail hook end swung out 12 to 14 inches it would be 49 to 55 inches above the highest parts of the mound. Haney was 67½ inches tall. If he had been standing on the mound about a foot from the side of the mail car he could have been hit by the end of the mail hook, the exact point of contact depending upon the height of the mound at the particular point. His wound was about 4 inches below the top of his head, or 63½ inches above the point where he stood on the mound—well within the possible range of the mail hook end.

Respondents' theory is that Haney was murdered. They point to the estimates that the mound was 10 to 15 feet north of the rail, making it impossible for the mail hook end to reach a point of contact with Haney's head. Photographs were placed in the record to support the claim that the ground was level north of the rail for at least 10 feet. Moreover, it appears that the area immediately surrounding the switch was quite dark. Witnesses stated that it was so dark that it was impossible to see a 3-inch pipe 25 feet away. It also appears that many hoboes and tramps frequented the area at night in order to get rides on freight trains. Haney carried a pistol to protect himself. This pistol was found loose under his body by those who came to his rescue. It was testified, however, that the pistol had apparently slipped out of his pocket or scabbard as he fell. Haney's clothes were not disarranged and there was no evidence of a struggle or fight. No rods, pipes or weapons of any kind, except Haney's own pistol, were found near the scene. Moreover, his gold watch and diamond ring were still on him after he was struck. Six days later his unsoiled billfold was found on a high board fence about a block from the place where Haney was struck and near the point where he had been placed in an ambulance. It contained his social security card and other effects, but no money. His wife testified that he "never carried much money, not very much more than $10." Such were the facts in relation to respondents' theory of murder.

Finally, one of the Frisco foremen testified that he arrived at the scene shortly after Haney was found injured. He later examined the fireman's side of the train very carefully and found nothing sticking out or in disorder. In explaining why he examined this side of the train so carefully he stated that while he was at the scene of the accident "someone said they thought that train No. 106 backing in to Grand Central Station is what struck this man" and that Haney "was supposed to have been struck by something protruding on the side of the train." The foreman testified that these statements were made by an unknown Illinois Central switchman standing near the fallen body of Haney. The foreman admitted that the switchman "didn't see the accident." This testimony was admitted by the trial court over the strenuous objections of respondents' counsel that it was mere hearsay falling outside the res gestae rule.

The jury was instructed that Frisco's trustees were liable if it was found that they negligently permitted a rod or other object to extend out from the side of the train as it backed past Haney and that Haney was killed as the direct result of such negligence, if any. The jury was further told that Illinois Central was liable if it was found that the company negligently maintained an unsafe and dangerous place for Haney to work, in that the ground was high and uneven and the light insufficient and inadequate, and that Haney was injured and killed as a direct result of the said place being unsafe and dangerous. This latter instruction as to Illinois Central did not require the jury to find that Haney was killed by something protruding from the train.

The [Missouri] Supreme Court, in upsetting the jury's verdict against both the Frisco trustees and the Illinois Central, admitted that "It could be inferred from the facts that Haney could have been struck by the mail hook knob *if* he were standing on the south side of the mound and the mail hook extended out as far as 12 or 14 inches." But it held that "all reasonable minds would agree that it would be mere speculation and conjecture to say that Haney was struck by the mail hook" and that "plaintiff failed to make a submissible case on that question." It also ruled that there "was no substantial evidence that the uneven ground and insufficient light were cause or contributing causes of the death of Haney." Finally, the Supreme Court held that the testimony of the foreman as to the statement made to him by the unknown switchman was inadmissible under the *res gestae* rule since the switchman spoke from what he had heard rather than from his own knowledge.

We hold, however, that there was sufficient evidence of negligence on the part of both the Frisco trustee and the Illinois Central to justify the submission of the case to the jury and to require appellate courts to abide by the verdict rendered by the jury.

The evidence we have already detailed demonstrates that there was evidence from which it might be inferred that the end of the mail hook struck Haney in the back of the head, an inference that the [State] Supreme Court admitted could be drawn. That inference is not rendered unreasonable by the fact that Haney apparently fell forward toward the main Frisco track so that his head was 5½ feet north of the rail. He may well have been struck and then wandered in a daze to the point where he fell forward. The testimony as to blood marks some distance away from his head lends credence to that possibility, indicating that he did not fall immediately upon being hit. When that is added to the evidence most favorable to the petitioner as to the height and swing-out of the hook, the height and location of the mound and the nature of Haney's duties, the inference that Haney was killed by the hook cannot be said to be unsupported by probative facts or to be so unreasonable as to warrant taking the case from the jury.

It is true that there is evidence tending to show that it was physically and mathematically impossible for the hook to strike Haney. And there are facts from which it might reasonably be inferred that Haney was murdered. But such evidence has become irrelevant upon appeal, there being a reasonable basis in the record for inferring that the hook struck Haney. The jury having made that inference, the respondents were not free to relitigate the factual dispute in a reviewing court. Under these circumstances it would be an undue invasion of the jury's historic function for an appellate court to weigh the conflicting evidence, judge the credibility of witnesses and arrive at a conclusion opposite from the one reached by the jury.

It is no answer to say that the jury's verdict involved speculation and conjecture. Whenever facts are in dispute or the evidence is such that fair-minded men may draw different inferences, a measure of speculation and conjecture is required on the part of those whose duty it is to settle the dispute by choosing what seems to them to be the most reasonable inference. Only when there is a complete absence of probative facts to support the conclusion reached does a reversible error appear. But where, as here, there is an evidentiary basis for the jury's verdict, the jury is free to discard or disbelieve whatever facts are inconsistent with its conclusion. And the appellate court's function is exhausted when that evidentiary basis becomes apparent, it being immaterial that the court might draw a contrary inference or feel that another conclusion is more reasonable.

We are unable, therefore, to sanction a reversal of the jury's verdict against Frisco's trustees. Nor can we approve any disturbance in the verdict as to Illinois Central. The evidence was uncontradicted that it was very dark at the place where Haney was working and the surrounding ground was high and uneven. The evidence also showed that this area was entirely within the domination and control of Illinois Central despite the fact that the area was technically located in a public street of the City of Memphis. It was not unreasonable to conclude that these conditions constituted an unsafe and dangerous working place and that such conditions contributed in part to Haney's death, assuming that it resulted primarily from the mail hook striking his head.

* * *

The judgment of the Supreme Court of Missouri is reversed and the case is remanded for whatever further proceedings may be necessary not inconsistent with this opinion.

THE CHIEF JUSTICE and JUSTICE FRANKFURTER concur in the result.

JUSTICE REED dissents.

JUSTICE JACKSON took no part in the consideration or decision of this case.

NOTES AND QUESTIONS

1.   In ruling on a motion for judgment as a matter of law under rule 50, the court "must take the evidence and all reasonable inferences therefrom in the light most flattering to the nonmovant." Trainor v. HEI Hospitality, LLC, 699 F.3d 19 (1st Cir. 2012). In ruling on the motion, the court "may not consider the credibility of witnesses, resolve conflicts in testimony, or evaluate the weight of the evidence." Wagenmann v. Adams, 829 F. 2d 196, 200 (1st Cir. 1987). In the words of one court, "[a] district court should grant judgment as a matter of law when the plaintiff presents no legally sufficient evidentiary basis for a reasonable jury to find for him on a material element of his cause of action." Collins v. Marriott International, 749 F.3d 951, 957 (11th Cir. 2014). "[T]he court should review all of the evidence in the record," but in doing so "the court must draw all reasonable inferences in favor of the nonmoving party, and it may not make credibility determinations or weigh the evidence." Reeves v. Sanderson Plumbing Products, Inc., 530 U.S. 133, 150 (2000).

2.   If you were a member of the jury in *Lavender,* how would you have decided how the decedent had been killed? Could your decision be anything more than speculation? Do you agree with the comment that "a study of the evidence in [*Lavender*] would lead me at least to the conclusion that there was no more reason for attributing the accident to the railroad's negligence, than to the deceased man's negligence, or the vicious act of a third person, or a combination of circumstances involving no fault on anyone's part"? Jaffe, Res Ipsa Loquitur Vindicated, 1 Buffalo L.Rev. 1, 14 (1951). If so, does it follow that the Court's decision to allow the case to go to the jury was wrong?

Consider the argument in James, Sufficiency of the Evidence and Jury-Control Devices Available Before Verdict, 47 Va.L.Rev. 218, 221–22 (1961):

> Where from the proven facts the nonexistence of the fact to be inferred appears to be just as probable as its existence (or more probable than its existence), then the conclusion that it exists is a matter of speculation, surmise, and conjecture, and a jury will not be allowed to draw it. This test suggests mathematical precision, but the suggestion is spurious. For one thing, we lack the quantitative data about most matters which would be needed to make meaningful statements in terms of probabilities. * * *

> Another flaw in the test as usually formulated lies in the possibility that courts may not mean it to be taken literally anyhow. * * *

> It appears then that the test, formulated in terms which suggest objective, scientific precision, is in fact one which gives the courts little guidance and great latitude. * * * Instead, courts are constantly asserting or assuming broad generalizations about human behavior and all sorts of other matters which either rest on their own very fallible notions about such things * * * or spring from considerations of policy and expediency.

How does the decision in *Lavender* respond to this kind of argument? Could the Court's opinion fairly be characterized as saying that it is incorrect to take cases away from the jury when the jury's conclusion would be no more than speculation, because the *only* occasions when a court *should* send a case to a jury are those in which an element of speculation is required? Does the fact the jury has such difficulty choosing between plaintiff's version and defendant's version mean that plaintiff has offered substantial evidence?

On this question, consider the following argument:

> The plaintiff [in *Lavender*] had presented sufficient evidence that a reasonable finder of fact could, not unreasonably, infer that the facts happened as alleged. True, the defendant had also presented sufficient evidence to support a contrary inference. But if we could be sure in every case what events had taken place, either way, there would never be a need for a jury. Cases are sent to a jury only when reasonable people can differ over the outcome. This means that a finding either way would not be deemed unreasonable—simply another way of saying that we cannot be certain of the events.

Redish, Summary Judgment and the Vanishing Trial: Implications of the Litigation Matrix, 57 Stan. L. Rev. 1329, 1353 (2005).

3.   *Lavender* was a suit under the Federal Employers' Liability Act, a law enacted by Congress to provide special protection to railroad workers against railroad negligence. As Professor Cooper states, "it is no secret that FELA cases involve special reasons for allowing juries a wide discretion in fact inference and in law application * * *. The consequence of a mistaken denial of recovery for the injured plaintiff is disaster; the consequence of a verdict imposing liability after dispensing with any real requirement of negligence is that one more easily anticipated cost is added to the many costs of railroading. Although it may sometimes seem that railroads are less than ideally situated for absorbing or redistributing extra costs, there can be no question that they are far better situated than their injured workmen. That the seventh amendment is appropriately applied to preserve this area for jury justice does not mean that it is appropriately applied to require allowing an equivalent scope of jury freedom in areas where it may be more capricious or arbitrary." 55 Minn.L.Rev. at 926–27. See also Jaffe, supra, 1 Buffalo L.Rev. at 14–15: "We must not go too fast in drawing conclusions from Lavender v. Kurn. The FELA serves as a glorified workmen's compensation, and the Supreme Court has gone very far in dispensing with meaningful notions of both negligence and actual causation." Jaffe adds, however, "that there are similar trends in the automobile and railroad crossing cases." Id. at 15. Is there anything in the *Lavender* opinion to indicate that it was intended to be limited to FELA cases? For a discussion of the reasons for *not* limiting *Lavender* to FELA cases, see C. Wright & M. Kane, Law of Federal Courts 685 (7th ed. 2011).

A number of courts to have specifically considered the question have confined *Lavender* to cases arising under pro-plaintiff congressional statutes, such as the FELA and the Jones Act (authorizing negligence suits by seamen). See, e.g., Boeing Co. v. Shipman, 411 F.2d 365, 370–73 (5th Cir.1969):

> FELA cases * * * are statutory negligence actions. * * * [I]t is clear that the congressional intent in enacting the FELA was to secure jury determinations in a larger proportion of cases than would be true of ordinary common law actions.

> * * *

> As a corollary to the unique statutory context of FELA actions, it is apparent that in the general run of cases federal courts have rejected the legendary "scintilla" test. * * * [T]he FELA test should not be employed as a vehicle to re-establish the "scintilla" rule which has been so firmly rejected by the federal judiciary.

> Although the Supreme Court has not answered the question of law, no Circuit Court of the United States * * * has held that the FELA test of sufficiency of evidence is applicable in non-FELA cases. * * *

The court then articulated what it considered the applicable standard in non-FELA cases (id. at 374–75):

> On motions for directed verdict and for judgment notwithstanding the verdict the Court should consider all of the evidence—not just that evidence which supports the non-mover's case—but in the light and with all reasonable inferences most favorable to the party opposed to the motion. If the facts and inferences point so strongly and overwhelmingly in favor of one party that the Court believes that reasonable men could not arrive at a contrary verdict, granting of the motions is proper. * * * A mere scintilla of evidence is insufficient to present a question for the jury. The motions for directed verdict and judgment n.o.v. should not be decided by which side has the better of the case, nor should they be granted only when there is a complete absence of probative facts to support a jury verdict. There must be a conflict in substantial evidence to create a jury question. However, it is the function of the jury as the traditional finder of the facts, and not the Court, to weigh conflicting evidence and inferences, and determine the credibility of witnesses.

See also Farpella-Crosby v. Horizon Health Care, 97 F.3d 803, 805 (5th Cir. 1996) (applying *Boeing* standard). Does it make sense to decide a directed verdict motion without looking at the evidence presented by the movant, as well as by the nonmovant?

In Boeing Co. v. Shipman, supra, Judge Rives dissented on the rejection of *Lavender*. Though he expressed no doubt "that the so-called 'scintilla' test has been firmly rejected by the Supreme Court and other federal courts in all jury cases including FELA cases," he also noted that the use of the term "substantial evidence" is "misleading," if not "erroneous," because "[t]he word 'substantial,' used in its legal sense, can equally well connote either a *qualitative* or a *quantitative* meaning." He further noted "that, notwithstanding all the variations which the Supreme Court has played on its sufficiency theme, I have been unable to find a single instance in which the Supreme Court has used 'substantial' in any of its articulations of the constitutional standard." 411 F.2d at 393–94. Certain courts have applied the *Lavender* standard to non-FELA cases as well. See, e.g., Howard v. McCrory Corp., 601 F.2d 133 (4th Cir.1979); Wratchford v. S. J. Groves & Sons Co., 405 F.2d 1061 (4th Cir.1969); Lones v. Detroit, Toledo and Ironton R. Co., 398 F.2d 914 (6th Cir.1968), cert. denied, 393 U.S. 1063, 89 S.Ct. 714, 21 L.Ed.2d 705 (1969).

4.   Compare *Lavender* to the Supreme Court's decision in an earlier FELA case, Pennsylvania R. Co. v. Chamberlain, 288 U.S. 333 (1933). This was an action to recover for the death of a brakeman, alleged to have been caused by the railroad's negligence. The brakeman was riding on a string of two cars while assisting in the breaking and making up of trains in the yard. Immediately behind him was a string of nine cars. Both strings were descending from a hump in the track through the force of gravity. His body was found next to the track some distance past the hump, and plaintiff's theory was that the railroad employees piloting the nine-car string allowed it to hit his string, causing him to be thrown off the cars and killed. However, the three employees riding the nine-car string testified that their string never collided with his string, and their testimony was corroborated by other employees in a position to see.

The only witness to testify for plaintiff was one Bainbridge, who said he was standing close to the hump. He saw the deceased riding at the rear of his string as it went by him and then saw the nine-car string pass by at a somewhat greater speed. Bainbridge looked away, heard a "loud crash" (which he said was not an unusual event in the yard and did not cause him to turn around at once), and when he turned around again, saw the two strings together, still moving, and the deceased no longer in sight. Later he heard shouts and went to the spot where the deceased's body was found.

The Supreme Court affirmed a directed verdict in favor of the defendant. It conceded that "where there is a direct conflict of testimony upon a matter of fact, the question must be left to the jury to determine, without regard to the number of witnesses upon either side." However, it found that "here there really is no conflict in the testimony as to the facts" because the defendant's witnesses all flatly testified that there was no collision between the two strings and "Bainbridge did not say there was such a collision." It concluded that the case "belong[s] to that class of cases where proven facts give equal support to each of two inconsistent inferences; in which event, neither of them being established, judgment, as a matter of law, must go against the party upon whom rests the necessity of sustaining one of those inferences as against the other, before he is entitled to recover." A verdict in plaintiff's favor, said the Court, "would have rested upon mere speculation and conjecture." Is it possible to reconcile this holding with that of *Lavender*? If not, which of the two makes more sense as a measure of the sufficiency of the evidence?

The *Chamberlain* decision also went on to characterize Bainbridge's testimony:

> Not only is Bainbridge's testimony considered as a whole suspicious, insubstantial and insufficient, but his statement that when he turned shortly after hearing the crash the two strings were moving together is simply incredible, if he meant thereby to be understood as saying that he saw the two in contact. * * * [H]e was paying slight and only occasional attention to what was going on. The cars were eight or nine hundred feet from where he stood and moving almost directly away from him, his angle of vision being only 3E 33O from a straight line. At that sharp angle and from that distance, near dusk of a misty evening (as the proof shows), the practical impossibility of the witness being able to see whether the front of the nine-car string was in contact with the back of the two-car string is apparent. And, certainly, in the light of these conditions, no verdict based upon a statement so unbelievable reasonably could be sustained as against the positive testimony to the contrary of unimpeached witnesses, all in a position to see, as this witness was not, the precise relations of the cars to one another. The fact that these witnesses were employees of the petitioner, under the circumstances here disclosed, does not impair this conclusion.

What contrary arguments could be made on plaintiff's behalf concerning the nature and strength of Bainbridge's testimony? Is this argument by the Court concerning the incredibility of Bainbridge's testimony and his inability to have had sense perception a different rationale from its earlier argument that the evidence was insufficient because it gave equal support to two inconsistent inferences?

5.   Also compare to *Lavender* another FELA case, Brady v. Southern Ry. Co., 320 U.S. 476 (1943), where the Court, in affirming a state court holding that the plaintiff's case should not have been submitted to a jury, stated: "The weight of the evidence under the Employers' Liability Act must be more than a scintilla before the case may be properly left to the discretion of the trier of fact * * *. When the evidence is such that without weighing the credibility of the witnesses there can be but one reasonable conclusion as to the verdict, the court should determine the proceedings by non-suit, directed verdict or otherwise in accordance with the applicable practice without submission to the jury * * *." *Lavender* was decided three years later. Are the two decisions inconsistent? Some decisions have read *Brady* to disapprove *Lavender*'s invocation of the scintilla rule, even in FELA cases. See, e.g., Aparicio v. Norfolk & Western Railway Co., 84 F.3d 803, 810 (6th Cir. 1996). However, while the standard under the FELA now appears to demand more than a scintilla, it nevertheless continues to be less demanding than the traditional burden. Mullahon v. Union Pacific R.R., 64 F.3d 1358, 1363 (9th Cir. 1995) (referring to standard in FELA cases as "less stringent."). For a discussion of

these decisions, see Dorsaneo, Judges, Juries and Reviewing Courts, 53 S.M.U.L.Rev. 1497 (2000); Ayres, Judicial Nullification of the Right to Trial by Jury by "Evolving" Standards of Appellate Review, 60 Baylor L. Rev. 337, 445–49 (2008).

6.   *The "substantial evidence" and "scintilla" rules:* Recall the discussion in Justice Black's dissent in *Galloway* concerning these alternative approaches to the measure of the sufficiency of the evidence. Would it be accurate to characterize *Lavender* as an illustration of the "scintilla" rule and *Chamberlain* as an illustration of the "substantial evidence" rule? According to Professor James, "[i]t is a judicial legend that there once was a 'scintilla rule' under which a verdict could be directed only where there was literally no evidence for proponent, but if there ever was such a notion all that remains of it today is its universal repudiation." 47 Va.L.Rev. at 218–19. Today, it seems reasonably clear that the general trend in the courts has been toward the use of the substantial evidence test and increased court control. As one modern court of appeals has phrased the standard, "[j]udgment as a matter of law is proper when the record contains no proof beyond speculation to support the verdict." Larson v. Miller, 76 F.3d 1446, 1452 (8th Cir. 1996) (en banc). See also Sassaman v. Heart City Toyota, 879 F.Supp. 901, 907 (N.D.Ind.1994) ("a mere scintilla of evidence is not sufficient to support the jury's verdict."). Thus, to the extent *Lavender* does represent adoption of the "scintilla" rule, it appears to have been limited to its specific context.

7.   *Judgment as a matter of law in employment discrimination suits:* In addition to FELA suits, courts have developed judgment as a matter of law standards that are specific to a number of federal statutes creating substantive causes of action for discrimination in employment. Included are suits under the Age Discrimination in Employment Act (ADEA), 29 U.S.C. §§ 621–634, which prohibits age discrimination against workers, and suits for racial or gender-based discrimination pursuant to Title VII of the Civil Rights Act of 1964, 42 U.S.C. § 2000e et seq.

One who sues for violation of these statutory protections bears an initial burden to establish a prima facie case of discrimination. Meeting this burden is "not onerous." Sanchez v. Puerto Rico Oil Co., 37 F.3d 712, 719 (1st Cir. 1994). "All that is needed is the production of admissible evidence which, if uncontradicted, would justify a legal conclusion of discrimination." Id. "Once the plaintiff establishes the prima facie requirements, a rebuttable presumption that the employer engaged in intentional age based discrimination attaches. * * * The burden then shifts to the employer to articulate a legitimate, nondiscriminatory reason for the decision. If the employer meets its burden, the presumption of discrimination vanishes." Brennan v. GTE Government Systems Corp., 150 F.3d 21, 25 (1st Cir. 1998). At that point, the court, in ruling on a motion for judgment as a matter of law, asks "whether the evidence as a whole would permit a reasonable factfinder to conclude that the proffered reason was pretextual and the true reason was an age-based animus." Id. This "three-step" burden-shifting framework was originally set out by the Supreme Court in McDonnell Douglas Corp. v. Green,

411 U.S. 792 (1973), and Texas Department of Community Affairs v. Burdine, 450 U.S. 248 (1981).

In St. Mary's Honor Center v. Hicks, 509 U.S. 502 (1993), the Supreme Court discussed how to assess a motion for judgment as a matter of law in light of this burden-shifting framework. The Court stated: "The fact finder's disbelief of the reasons put forward by the defendant (particularly if disbelief is accompanied by a suspicion of mendacity) may, together with the elements of the prima facie case, suffice to show intentional discrimination. Thus, rejection of the defendant's proffered reasons will permit the trier of fact to infer the ultimate fact of intentional discrimination." 509 U.S. at 511.

In Reeves v. Sanderson Plumbing Products, Inc., 530 U.S. 133 (2000), the Supreme Court reaffirmed *Hicks*, holding that "a plaintiff's prima facie case, combined with sufficient evidence to find that the employer's asserted justification is false, may permit the trier of fact to conclude that the employer unlawfully discriminated." Id. at 148. The Court added, however, that "[t]his is not to say that such a showing by the plaintiff will *always* be adequate to sustain a jury's finding of liability. Certainly there will be instances where, although the plaintiff has established a prima facie case and set forth sufficient evidence to reject the defendant's explanation, no rational factfinder could conclude that the action was discriminatory. For instance, an employer would be entitled to judgment as a matter of law if the record conclusively revealed some other, nondiscriminatory reason for the employer's decision, or if the plaintiff created only a weak issue of fact as to whether the employer's reason was untrue and there was abundant and uncontroverted independent evidence that no discrimination had occurred." Id. Contrast the standards for judgment as a matter of law in Title VII cases with the pleading requirements imposed in suits brought pursuant to the same statute, discussed in Swierkiewicz v. Sorema N.A., 534 U.S. 506 (2002), supra p. 177.

JUDGMENT AS A MATTER OF LAW AND LAW APPLICATION

Note that in *Lavender* plaintiff also sought to recover on the theory that the Illinois Central Railroad negligently maintained an unsafe place for Haney to work. Besides raising questions of historical fact, this claim called for the application of a reasonableness standard to the historical facts as found. Particularly in negligence actions, the jury has an important function to play in this law application process even where there is no dispute as to the historical facts. See generally Weiner, The Civil Jury and the Law-Fact Distinction, 54 Calif.L.Rev. 1867 (1966).

For example, in Sioux City & P. Railroad Co. v. Stout, 84 U.S. (17 Wall.) 657 (1873), plaintiff, a small child, was injured by an unlocked railroad turntable on which he was playing. Because there was no dispute about the location of the turntable, the absence of a lock, and other circumstances, the railroad contended that the question whether it had been guilty of negligence was a question of law for the judge. The Supreme Court disagreed:

It is true, in many cases, that where the facts are undisputed the effect of them is for the judgment of the court, and not for the decision of the jury. This is true in that class of cases where the existence of such facts comes in question rather than where deductions or inferences are to be made from the facts. If a deed be given in evidence, a contract proven, or its breach testified to, the existence of such deed, contract, or breach, there being nothing in derogation of the evidence, is no doubt to be ruled as a question of law. In some cases, too, the necessary inference from the proof is so certain that it may be ruled as a question of law. If a sane man voluntarily throws himself in contact with a passing engine, there being nothing to counteract the effect of this action, it may be ruled as a matter of law that the injury to him resulted from his own fault, and that no action can be sustained by him or his representatives. * * * But these are extreme cases. The range between them is almost infinite in variety and extent. It is in relation to these intermediate cases that the opposite rule prevails. Upon the facts proven in such cases, it is a matter of judgment and discretion, of sound inference, what is the deduction to be drawn from the undisputed facts. Certain facts we may suppose to be clearly established from which one sensible, impartial man would infer that proper care had not been used, and that negligence existed; another man equally sensible and equally impartial would infer that proper care had been used, and that there was no negligence. It is this class of cases and those akin to it that the law commits to the decisions of a jury. * * * It is assumed that twelve men know more of the common affairs of life than does one man, that they can draw wiser and safer conclusions from admitted facts thus occurring than can a single judge.

BURDEN SHIFTING AND SUBSTANTIVE POLICY

While the issues of directed verdict standards and burden shifting are essentially procedural issues, as the discussion of FELA cases (supra p. 637 n. 3) demonstrates, substantive policy considerations have influenced these issues. The classic illustration is Summers v. Tice, 199 P.2d 1 (Cal.1948). Plaintiff was injured when two hunters negligently shot in his direction. It was impossible to determine which of the two shots caused the injury. The defendants nevertheless were held liable as joint tortfeasors. In order to avoid liability, then, one of the defendants would have to demonstrate that his shot did not cause plaintiff's injury, thereby imposing full damages on the other defendant. What are the likely reasons for such a rule? To what dangers, if any, might it give rise?

Summers, in modified form, was relied on by the California Supreme Court in Sindell v. Abbott Laboratories, 607 P.2d 924 (Cal.1980), cert.

denied sub nom. Upjohn Co. v. Sindell, 449 U.S. 912 (1980). The plaintiff, the daughter of a woman who had taken the drug DES as a miscarriage preventative during pregnancy, sued many years later claiming she developed cancer as a result of her mother's ingestion of the drug. She sued eleven named drug companies, as well as other unnamed manufacturers of DES, claiming all had acted negligently in the sale and handling of the drug. However, she was unable to establish which of the companies—named or unnamed—manufactured the specific drug ingested by her mother. The state supreme court refused to dismiss the complaint:

> The most persuasive reason for finding plaintiff states a cause of action is that advanced in *Summers*: as between an innocent plaintiff and negligent defendants, the latter should bear the cost of the injury. Here, as in *Summers,* plaintiff is not at fault in failing to provide evidence of causation, and although the absence of such evidence is not attributable to the defendants either, their conduct in marketing a drug the effects of which are delayed for many years played a significant role in creating the unavailability of proof.

> From a broader policy standpoint, defendants are better able to bear the cost of injury resulting from the manufacture of a defective product. * * *

> Where, as here, all defendants produced a drug from an identical formula and the manufacturer of the DES which caused plaintiff's injuries cannot be identified through no fault of plaintiff, a modification of the rule of *Summers* is warranted. * * *

> [W]e hold it to be reasonable in the present context to measure the likelihood that any of the defendants supplied the product which allegedly injured plaintiff by the percentage which the DES sold by each of them for the purpose of preventing miscarriage bears to the entire production of the drug sold by all for that purpose. * * *

> Each defendant will be held liable for the proportion of the judgment represented by its share of the market unless it demonstrates that it could not have made the product which caused plaintiff's injuries. * * *

> Under this approach, each manufacturer's liability would approximate its responsibility for the injuries caused by its own products.

Is this a perversion of purely procedural factfinding devices in individual cases, or does it represent a legitimate blending of substantive social policy with a procedural mechanism? Cf. Goldman v. Johns-Manville Sales Corp., 514 N.E.2d 691 (Ohio 1987) (market share liability theory rejected where it could not be shown that all products to which injured party was exposed were completely fungible). For a thorough discussion of the market share theory, see Kurczi v. Eli Lilly and Co., 113 F.3d 1426 (6th Cir. 1997).

GUENTHER V. ARMSTRONG RUBBER CO.

United States Court of Appeals, Third Circuit, 1969
406 F.2d 1315

Before MCLAUGHLIN, STALEY and VAN DUSEN, CIRCUIT JUDGES.

GERALD MCLAUGHLIN, CIRCUIT JUDGE.

This is an ordinary products liability negligence claim. It is in the Federal courts solely by reason of diversity of citizenship between the parties. It has one rather unusual situation which was the sole reason for the direction of verdict below in favor of the defendant and is the only question on appeal.

The facts are simple. Plaintiff-appellant is a mechanic who on May 21, 1965 was employed by Sears Roebuck & Company at its place of business in the Pittsburgh, Pennsylvania area. His main work was installing automobile tires and batteries. On the particular day he was in the process of putting four summer tires on an automobile. He first removed the four tires which were on the car. Without any complications he then put on three of the new ones. As he was adjusting the fourth tire, it exploded and threw him about six feet away. He was unconscious for a few seconds. He was later taken to the Pittsburgh Hospital where he was given emergency treatment. Robert W. Small, the Sears Service Center Manager at the time, was a witness on behalf of the plaintiff. He said he was in the Service building when the explosion occurred and that he rushed from his office to the tire center. Mr. Guenther was on the floor about four feet from the tire machine. There was a tire on the machine. After Mr. Guenther was removed to the ambulance, Mr. Small had the tire taken to his office where he checked out its serial numbers.

In November 1966, Messrs. Drozness, plaintiff's expert, and Dunlop, the defense expert, examined the tire in Mr. Small's office. That tire was in the court at the trial. It was admitted on behalf of the defendant regarding that tire "This is our tire, our experts have told you that." Mr. Drozness was called as an expert on behalf of the plaintiff. The defense asked for an offer of proof. Plaintiff's attorney stated that Mr. Drozness "has already been identified by Mr. Small as having examined the tire involved in the accident. I am going to put him on to testify that it had a broken bead, that he went over the history of the mounting procedure used by Mr. Guenther and as a basis of that, he concludes that this is a manufacturer's defect." In response to the court's query, plaintiff's attorney continued to outline his theory of the defendant's liability, stating as to the jury, "If they accept Small's testimony and they accept the tire as given by Mr. Drozness which has a broken bead in it and if they are on the basis of a hypothetical inquiry wherein I intend to tell him, repeat how the Plaintiff put it on the machine and everything and that it had no apparent defects." The attorney went on to say he expected to develop that in the expert's opinion the tire had not been damaged by handling and that the broken bead was a manufacturer's defect. The defense attorney objected to the testimonial offer and was sustained by the judge.

Plaintiff, as a witness, carefully outlined the steps he had taken in mounting the fourth tire. He said that after he had the tire in position and he started to put air into it "Well, it started to come up, the bead, and when it hit the rim it just let loose and exploded." The tire which Mr. Small had testified was on the machine and which he had brought to his office was a "white wall". Mr. Guenther testified that the tire he was mounting and which exploded was a "black wall". He said it was a fifteen inch and that the white wall in court was a thirteen inch. He was asked "How do you remember that the one you were mounting was black?" He answered "I just remember it was." He said he remembered it was fifteen inch because the automobile was a Chrysler "55 or 56" which takes "15 inch".

With respect to the identification of the white wall tire in court, the defense attorney, addressing the court with reference to the proposed evidence of Mr. Drozness, said "He is going to say he examined a tire, how is he going to identify it?" Plaintiff's counsel answered, "Small has already said the tire Drozness examined is the tire in Court." The judge commented "That may be sufficient identity if Drozness examined the tire Small produced." Defense counsel said, "Judge, it seems to me that they are going to rely on Small to establish the identity." The judge asked "Well, with that offer, do you object to his testimony?" Counsel replied "I certainly do your Honor." The judge sustained the motion for a directed verdict in favor of the defendant.

Later, in denying the motion for a new trial, the judge specifically found as to the tire produced by Sears Roebuck manager Small which was marked as a trial exhibit, that, "This tire was admittedly manufactured by Defendant. It is this tire which Plaintiff's expert examined and would testify was defective." The court concluded that "To allow this is to fly directly in the face of Plaintiff's clear and unequivocal denial that this was the tire that injured him. We believe that Plaintiff is bound by this testimony." The judge therefore upheld his trial conclusion of a directed verdict in favor of the defendant. The lower court decision centered entirely upon the testimony of the plaintiff that it was a "black wall" tire which exploded, threw him six feet and rendered him unconscious.

* * *

The foundation of plaintiff's cause is that he was injured by a bursting tire which he had been adjusting on the tire machine in front of him and which was still on the machine after it had exploded. There is a disagreement between plaintiff and his witness Small as to whether that particular tire was a "black wall" or a "white wall". On such detail we do not think it is the function of the court to conclude plaintiff's cause of action by directing a verdict against him. In this instance no reason appears why a jury should not be able to readily resolve the problem in dispute at this time in this appeal.

It is also urged for appellant that his claim should have been allowed to go to the jury * * * founded on evidence that the defendant made from 75 to 80 per cent of the tires the particular Sears Roebuck store had for sale. It is true that the trial court in holding that plaintiff's evidence of identification failed, relied on Kamosky v. Owens-Illinois Glass Co., 89 F.Supp. 561 (M.D.Pa.1950), affd. p.c. 185 F.2d 674 (3 Cir.1950). It is also true that in *Kamosky* there was only a 10 to 15 per cent likelihood of liability of the alleged offending article. Even so as we see it there was no justification for allowing plaintiff's case on that so-called probability hypothesis to go to the jury. The latter's verdict would at best be a guess. It could not be reasonably supported.

The judgment of the District Court will be reversed and the case remanded for a new trial on the merits.

NOTES AND QUESTIONS

1.   The facts of *Guenther* present a problem of proof similar to that found in what has been referred to by academics as the "blue bus" hypothetical:

> While driving late at night on a dark, two-laned road, a person confronts an oncoming bus speeding down the centerline of the road in the opposite direction. In the glare of the headlights, the person sees that the vehicle is a bus, but cannot otherwise identify it. He swerves to avoid a collision, and his car hits a tree. The bus speeds past without stopping. The injured person later sues the Blue Bus Company. He proves, in addition to the facts stated above, that the Blue Bus Company owns and operates 80% of the buses that run on the road where the accident occurred. Can he win?

Nesson, The Evidence or the Event? On Judicial Proof and the Acceptability of Verdicts, 98 Harv.L.Rev. 1357, 1378 (1985). For a case strikingly similar to this example, see Smith v. Rapid Transit, Inc., 58 N.E.2d 754 (Mass.1945).

In commenting on this hypothetical, Professor Nesson writes: "one can conclude from the evidence that the plaintiff was probably injured by a blue bus, and yet not be entirely satisfied with the conclusion that a blue bus injured the plaintiff. The evidence seems not to be about the specific event in question, but rather about a class of events (all cases involving unidentified busses). It suggests only that the defendant causes a majority but not all of a class of events. It offers no basis for a leap to a conclusion about any specific event. Although the information about the class suggests it is more probable than not that the defendant caused any given accident, a finding for any one plaintiff would logically extend to every plaintiff in the class." Nesson, Agent Orange Meets the Blue Bus: Factfinding at the Frontier of Knowledge, 66 B.U.L.Rev. 521, 522 (1986).

2.   In the *Kamosky* case, mentioned in the *Guenther* opinion, the plaintiff attempted to establish that a bottle involved in an accident was one of defendant's by producing evidence that (1) defendant had manufactured the overwhelming portion of the new bottles used by the bottler from whom ultimately the bottle in question had been obtained, and (2) between 10% and 15% of the bottles used by the bottler during the relevant time period were in fact new bottles. On this evidence, the court directed a verdict for the defendant, and a motion to set aside the directed verdict was denied: "Such was clearly not substantial evidence from which the jury, without guessing, might find that Owens did manufacture, produce, handle, or process the bottle which exploded." Do you agree with the trial court in *Guenther* that the two cases are indistinguishable?

3.   Would the *Guenther* court have reached the same conclusion on plaintiff's "probability" argument had 99.9% of the tires in the store in question been manufactured by the defendant? *Should* it reach the same conclusion in such a case? Cf. Nesson, 66 B.U.L.Rev. at 522, n. 3: "At some point, high probability alone is sufficient to produce an acceptable verdict. In the blue bus hypothetical * * * evidence indicating a 55% likelihood that the plaintiff should recover presents a problem, whereas evidence indicating a 95% likelihood might not. Reaching a conclusion involves putting doubt aside. The difficulty of doing so will vary with the intensity of the doubt, the degree to which we are concerned about making a mistake, and the rationalizations we have to help us conclude."

For a comparison with *Guenther*, consider Kramer v. Weedhopper of Utah, Inc., 490 N.E.2d 104 (Ill.App.1986). The case was a products liability suit, turning largely on the question of who had distributed an allegedly defective bolt used on an airplane that had crashed. Defendant Lawrence had distributed 90% of the bolts used by the airplane manufacturer, while Hughes Aviation supplied the remainder. No other evidence existed to demonstrate who had distributed the bolt. Lawrence was granted summary judgment, but the appellate court reversed:

> The parties here do not seriously dispute that the elements of a product liability action may be proved inferentially or by direct or circumstantial evidence. The dispute centers, instead, on whether the fact that Lawrence supplied 90% of the bolts * * * is sufficient circumstantial evidence to avoid entry of summary judgment. Circumstantial evidence consists of facts or circumstances which give rise to a reasonable inference of the truth of an underlying fact. * * * Such evidence must have reasonable probative force; the jury will not be allowed to engage in conjecture, surmise or speculation. * * *

> The focus must then be on what quantum of evidence is sufficient for an inference to be reasonable. This measure has eluded specific

standardization and enumeration. * * * Generally, the test of reasonableness resolves into a question of probability: is the inferred occurrence more probable than not, or is it merely possible.

* * * Evidence showing that defendant was the exclusive distributor of a product would strongly support plaintiff's case when defendant's identification can be proved only circumstantially; but when two suppliers of an allegedly dangerous product exist, under circumstances which show that a defendant supplied 90% of the parts used, this evidence is sufficient to withstand a motion for summary judgment.

* * * Defendant was allegedly the most probable cause of plaintiff's injury. The defects in plaintiff's proof are such that affect the weight which should be accorded the evidence, not whether the evidence initially poses a genuine material triable question of fact.

One judge dissented, arguing: "Liability is not based on a balancing of probabilities, but on a finding of fact." He relied in part on *Guenther* for his decision that plaintiff's evidence was insufficient to go to the jury.

4.   Should probability evidence be limited to issues of identification? Consider the following case: Plaintiff is cut on his arm by flying glass, caused by defendant's negligence. A scar forms at the location of the injury, and, a number of years later, a skin cancer develops on the exact location of the scar. Expert witnesses testify that there is no medical basis on which to believe that such an injury is likely to give rise to skin cancer. Should the court grant a directed verdict on the causation issue? Cf. Kramer Service, Inc. v. Wilkins, 186 So. 625 (Miss.1939), in which the court precluded recovery for such a cancer by a plaintiff whose expert witness testified the trauma could cause skin cancer, but only in one of a hundred cases. The court reasoned that "[p]ossibilities will not sustain a verdict."

5.   One group of commentators has argued that "jurors should be allowed to use [social science] research to help them decide the dispute at hand, but this general research should be communicated via judicial instruction that reflects the reliable general causation principles revealed by the research. The jurors would then be in a position to apply the general social framework to the specific evidence produced at trial, if they believed such application was warranted." Monahan, Walker & Mitchell, Contextual Evidence of Gender Discrimination: The Ascendance of "Social Frameworks," 94 Va. L. Rev. 1715, 1726 (2008). See also Walker & Monahan, Social Frameworks: A New Use of Social Science in Law, 73 Va. L. Rev. 559 (1987). This method would be employed instead of utilizing expert witnesses for the parties to introduce social science research to the jury. Do you foresee risks with their approach? Do its benefits outweigh those risks? These commentators themselves have acknowledged that "experience has shown that jury instructions are rarely seen as a feasible method of communicating contextual information to juries, and that courts will typically allow general information from social science

research to be conveyed to the jury by expert witnesses." 94 Va. L. Rev. at 1748. Are there significant risks with use of their method, as well?

6.   To what extent does the question of whether there exists sufficient evidence for a case to go to the jury lend itself to the application of mathematical-statistical probability theory? See generally Cullison, Probability Analysis of Judicial Fact-Finding: A Preliminary Outline of The Subjective Approach, 1 Tol.L.Rev. 538 (1969).

Professor Nesson has argued: " '[P]robability' as we use the term in law, particularly in the civil standard of proof, is not a hard-edged mathematical concept. It is, rather, a concept that incorporates less rigid ideas of justice and reflects the judicial function of resolving disputes in the real world, where values shift and knowledge is uncertain. An outcome is 'probable' if it best accomplishes a just and acceptable resolution of the dispute. Probability, as a legal concept in the law of proof, suggests wisdom, probity, and approbation— not favorable betting odds." Nesson, Agent Orange Meets the Blue Bus: Factfinding at the Frontier of Knowledge, 66 B.U.L.Rev. 521 (1986). See also Tribe, Trial by Mathematics: Precision and Ritual in the Legal Process, 84 Harv.L.Rev. 1329 (1971).

To illustrate his point, Nesson cites a portion of the "Agent Orange" litigation, in which former servicemen sued the government for damages they claimed to have incurred as a result of their use of the defoliant, Agent Orange, in Vietnam. In re "Agent Orange" Prod. Liab. Litig., 611 F.Supp. 1223 (E.D.N.Y.1985), affirmed on other grounds, 818 F.2d 187 (2d Cir.1987), cert. denied, 487 U.S. 1234 (1988). Though the plaintiffs involved in the class action recovered a large amount as part of a settlement, the court granted summary judgment against those plaintiffs who had opted out of the class, because "[i]n Judge Weinstein's view, the epidemiological studies on Agent Orange so clearly failed to prove any causative link between exposure to Agent Orange and cancers, birth defects, and other illnesses, that * * * [none] of the * * * opt-out plaintiffs presented a factual dispute." 66 B.U.L.Rev. at 525. Nesson is critical of the court's approach:

> [Judge Weinstein's] view reflects an erroneous and hard-edged statistical concept of probability, which obscures the differences between law and science. Although he has settled the Agent Orange cases, his approach, if it becomes dogma, will gravely incapacitate the dispute-resolving powers of courts in toxic tort cases. It leaves entirely to defendants the range between what jurors and members of the public can rationally believe, and what statisticians can prove.

While there were no studies linking the chemical in Agent Orange to cancer in humans (though there were such studies as to animals), Nesson notes that "[t]he etiology of cancer is not yet known; scientists cannot explain at a cellular level the mechanism of causation." 66 B.U.L.Rev. at 526. He draws a distinction between "scientific proof" and "legal proof" (66 B.U.L.Rev. at 529– 30):

An imaginative scientist exploring the hypothesis that a given toxic agent causes cancer is very likely to suspend scientific judgment on the ultimate question of causation until more testing or study can be done to eliminate alternative hypotheses. A doctor or lawyer or judge, on the other hand, often does not have the luxury of postponing a decision. Often he makes a judgment once he reaches a reasonable working conclusion. Likewise, we ask juries to come to conclusions without insisting on waiting for scientific demonstration. The legal standard of proof would seem to require only a rational basis for the expert's opinion—a standard far short of scientific demonstration.

In response, Professor Ronald Allen writes:

If the issue was whether any rational jury could find for the plaintiff, then Weinstein did his job—no rational jury could so find based upon the evidence before the court. If, by contrast, the issue was whether *any* jury could find for the plaintiff, then obviously Weinstein did not do his job. The only way to find out if a jury would return a plaintiff's verdict is to let it hear the case. * * *

Now [under Nesson's view] we see that "what actually happened" does not matter. Rather, whatever a jury decided will be promulgated as "what actually happened" no matter how irrational or lawless it might be. I do not believe the rest of us are that gullible. We know that there is the risk that any small group of people making a decision might act in an irrational fashion. There is also a risk that such a group might reach a result for the wrong reason. In either case, such decisions should not be allowed precisely because they diverge from reality as we are able to reconstruct it. It is a tenet of our civilization that legal rights and obligations should, in general, rest on as accurate a reconstruction of reality as is feasible in the context of any particular dispute.

Allen, Rationality, Mythology, and the "Acceptability of Verdicts" Thesis, 66 B.U.L.Rev. 541, 561–62 (1986).

Might the court in the *Agent Orange* case have appropriately utilized the burden-shifting approach employed by the California Supreme Court in Summers v. Tice and the DES litigation [supra p. 643]? Were the causation problems in *Summers* comparable to those in *Agent Orange*?

7.   In cases like *Agent Orange,* could the causation problem be solved by using a different procedural device? Professor David Rosenberg has argued that the class action offers a solution because it permits the judicial system to aggregate exposed individuals into a group and impose on the defendant who is responsible for their exposure liability equal to the population-wide increase in the incidence of disease due to the exposure. This money could then create a fund that could be used to compensate those suffering from the disease even though there is no way to be certain which of them would not have gotten the disease in the absence of exposure. See Rosenberg, The Causal Connection in Mass Exposure Cases: A "Public Law" Vision of the Tort System, 97 Harv.

L.Rev. 851 (1984). Would this be fair to defendants? Should courts countenance a device that transfers money from defendants to people they have not injured? Is it even fair to all of the plaintiffs? See Redish & Berlow, The Class Action as Political Theory, 85 Wash. U. L. Rev. 753, 786 (2007) (criticizing Rosenberg's approach because it ignores "the individual plaintiff's ability to control the protection of his individually held legal rights.").

8. While the court in *Guenther* rejected plaintiff's "probability" argument as a basis for denying a directed verdict motion, it ultimately reversed the granting of the directed verdict, because a jury could reasonably believe plaintiff's witness, rather than plaintiff's own recollection, on the nature of the exploding tire. Would the jury have been "guessing" any less in making this judgment than in deciding, on the basis of the applicable statistics, whether the tire had actually been manufactured by the defendant? Is the jury "guessing" any less when it decides the cause of the switchman's death in *Lavender?* Do you think the Supreme Court that decided *Lavender* would have affirmed a grant of directed verdict in *Guenther?* See Figueroa v. Mazza, 825 F.3d 89, 106 (2d Cir. 2016) ("A party that admits on the witness stand a fact damaging to his case is ordinarily free to contradict that fact through the testimony of other witnesses and argue that their testimony should be believed over his own.").

2. MOTION FOR NEW TRIAL

AHERN V. SCHOLZ

United States Court of Appeals First Circuit, 1996
85 F.3d 774

Before TORRUELLA, CHIEF JUDGE, BOWNES, SENIOR CIRCUIT JUDGE, and STAHL, CIRCUIT JUDGE.

TORRUELLA, CHIEF JUDGE.

The parties in this breach of contract case, a successful musician and his former manager, dispute whether royalties from record albums have been accounted for and paid to each other. The appeal is from a final judgment by the district court after a jury trial, disposing of all claims in respect to all parties.

In this case, the parties dispute many of the facts and the inferences to be drawn from them. Thus we start with a sketch of the basic facts, and address the individual issues in more detail below. Appellant and cross-appellee Donald Thomas Scholz ("Scholz") is a musician, composer, and record producer who was, and is, a member of the musical group BOSTON ("BOSTON"). In late 1975, Scholz entered into three agreements with appellee and cross-appellant Paul F. Ahern ("Ahern"), who was engaged in the business of promoting and managing music groups, and his then partner, Charles McKenzie ("McKenzie") (collectively, the "1975 Agreements"). First, Scholz made a recording agreement (the "Recording

Agreement") with Ahern and McKenzie d/b/a P.C. Productions, to which Bradley Delp, the lead singer of BOSTON, was also a party. Second was a management agreement (the "Management Agreement"), also between Scholz and P.C. Productions, under which Ahern and McKenzie were appointed Scholz' exclusive personal managers worldwide. The third agreement was a songwriter agreement made between Scholz and Ahern, under which Scholz was obligated to furnish Ahern his exclusive songwriting services for a period of five years.

In early 1976, CBS Records ("CBS") and Ahern Associates, a business name of Ahern and McKenzie, entered into a recording agreement for the exclusive recording services of BOSTON. The group's first album (the "first album") was released in 1976, and sold approximately 11 million copies—one of the highest-selling debut albums ever. Its second album (the "second album") was released in August 1978, and sold approximately 6 million copies.

In 1978, Scholz and the other members of BOSTON entered into a modification agreement with Ahern and P.C. Productions, dated April 24, 1978. Among other things, the First Modification Agreement modified the 1975 Agreements and changed the financial relationship between Scholz and his managers. Ahern and McKenzie dissolved their partnership. A few years later, in May of 1981, Ahern and Scholz, individually and under various business names, entered into a further modification agreement (the "Further Modification Agreement" or "FMA"), which is at the heart of this dispute. Ahern ceased to be Scholz' manager.

In 1982, with the third album not yet released, CBS cut off the payment of royalties generated from the first and second albums. In 1983, CBS brought suit against Scholz, Ahern, and the members of BOSTON for failure to timely deliver record albums. Scholz' counsel in that action was Donald S. Engel ("Engel"); Ahern had his own counsel. While that litigation was pending, the third album was released by MCA Records ("MCA") in 1986 and sold well over 4 million copies. At the close of trial—seven years after the CBS litigation began—the jury found that Scholz was not in breach of contract. Scholz incurred legal fees of about $3.4 million dollars.

In February 1991, Ahern commenced this action against Scholz for breach of the FMA claiming a failure to pay royalties due under the third album. Scholz asserted various affirmative defenses and counterclaims against Ahern, including breach of the FMA. During trial, Engel, Scholz' lead trial counsel, was twice called as a witness. At the close of the evidence, the court granted Scholz' directed verdict dismissing Ahern's Count III for fraud and IV for breach of implied covenant of good faith and fair dealing. The court also granted Ahern's motion for directed verdict dismissing Scholz' First, Second, and Third Counterclaims and his Third, Fourth, and Fifth affirmative defenses. Only the parties' respective breach of contract claims went to the jury. The jury found that Scholz breached section 5.2.1 of the FMA to pay Ahern royalties from the third album, and found that Ahern had not breached the FMA to account for and pay Scholz royalties due from the first and second albums. It awarded Ahern $547,007 in damages.

The trial court sitting without a jury also found Scholz had breached the FMA, and heard Ahern's Count II for declaratory relief and Count V for violation of Mass. Gen. L. ch. 93A and Scholz' Fifth Counterclaim for recision of contract for failure to obtain a license. The court denied the declaratory relief Ahern sought in Count I, and awarded him costs, interest and attorney's fees pursuant to Count V for violation of Mass. Gen. L. ch. 93A §§ 2 & 11. The court denied the relief sought by Scholz in his Fifth Counterclaim and held that he waived his Counts VI and VII at oral argument. After a hearing on Ahern's bill of costs and application for reasonable attorney's fees and interest, the court awarded Ahern $265,000 in attorney's fees and $135,000 in costs.

The district court denied, without a hearing, Scholz' motion for a new trial, motion to amend the court's memorandum and order and judgment entered thereon, motion to admit new evidence, and motion to amend the court's memorandum and order and the judgment entered thereon regarding Scholz' Sixth Counterclaim. This appeal followed.

Appellant first argues that the district court erred in denying his motion for a new trial, made pursuant to Fed.R.Civ.P. 59(a). We therefore review the record below to determine whether the evidence required that the district court grant the motion for a new trial. In reviewing the record of the 16-day trial, we note that both parties presented extensive evidence. The jury heard testimony regarding a history that spans two decades, involves at least seven contracts, includes detailed numerical accounting, and references more than half a dozen other legal battles. The parties called a total of fifteen witnesses, seven of whom, including Ahern, Scholz, and Engel, Scholz' counsel, testified twice. In short, the jury faced a complex and sometimes conflicting set of facts in making its decision as to whether either, neither, or both parties breached the 1981 Further Modification Agreement. Ultimately, we find that the jury's verdict was not against the clear weight of the evidence, and the district court did not abuse its discretion in so finding.

A. STANDARD OF REVIEW

"A verdict may be set aside and new trial ordered 'when the verdict is against the clear weight of the evidence, or is based upon evidence which is false, or will result in a clear miscarriage of justice.'" Phav v. Trueblood, Inc., 915 F.2d 764, 766 (1st Cir.1990) (quoting Torres-Troche v. Municipality of Yauco, 873 F.2d 499 (1st Cir.1989)); see Fed.R.Civ.P. 59(a) * * *. In reaching its decision, "the district court has broad legal authority to determine whether or not a jury's verdict is against the 'clear weight of the evidence.'" de Perez [v. Hospital del Maestro], 910 F.2d at 1006.

Nonetheless, "the trial judge's discretion, although great, must be exercised with due regard to the rights of both parties to have questions which are fairly open resolved finally by the jury at a single trial." Coffran v. Hitchcock Clinic, Inc., 683 F.2d 5, 6 (1st Cir.), cert. denied, 459 U.S. 1087 (1982); Thus, the district court judge "cannot displace a jury's verdict merely because he disagrees with it or would have found otherwise in a bench trial." "The mere fact that a contrary verdict may have been equally—or even more easily—supportable furnishes no cognizable ground for granting a new trial." Freeman v. Package Mach. Co., 865 F.2d 1331, 1333–34 (1st Cir.1988).

Our review is circumscribed: we will disturb the district court's ruling on appellant's motion for a new trial only where there has been a clear abuse of discretion. In order to determine whether such an abuse occurred here, we must review the record below. We do this not in the role of "a thirteenth juror," assessing the credibility of witnesses and weighing testimony, but rather to isolate the factual basis for the trial court's ruling and provide the foundation for our action today. "So long as a reasonable basis exists for the jury's verdict, we will not disturb the district court's ruling on appeal."

With our standard of review established, we turn to Scholz' argument and the record below. We address each of the two breach of contract claims the jury decided in turn.

B. Did Ahern Breach the FMA?

Scholz argues that Ahern breached his obligations under the 1981 FMA to both account for and pay to Scholz, every six months, his share of the royalties from the compositions on the first and second albums: indeed, Ahern admitted at trial that he had failed to make some payments he owed Scholz under the FMA. The jury and the trial court disagreed with Scholz, however, and found that Ahern's breach of the FMA was not material. The question facing us, then, is whether the district court abused its discretion in finding that the jury's decision was not against the weight of the evidence. After careful review of the record, we find no abuse of discretion in the lower court's decision not to disturb the jury's finding.

Scholz argues at some length on appeal that Ahern's breach was by definition material, both for his failure to account and his failure to pay. As for the first contention, we note that while Scholz' reading of the FMA as requiring that Ahern render Scholz direct accountings every six months is a convincing one, it is not the only plausible one. Indeed, Ahern contends that the FMA only required him to send irrevocable letters of direction to various entities involved directing them to send Scholz his share of the royalties when collected. In the end, it would not be against the clear weight of the evidence to find that letters of directions would satisfy Ahern's accounting obligations under the FMA, and that such letters were sent. Therefore, Ahern's failure to account every six months was not a material breach.

As for the second contention, Scholz supports his position that Ahern's failure to pay constitutes a separate, material breach by drawing on both New York and Massachusetts case law. He points to the Second Circuit's refusal to overturn summary judgment in ARP Films, Inc. v. Marvel Entertainment Group, Inc., 952 F.2d 643, 649 (2d Cir.1991). In that case, where plaintiffs failed to account and pay royalties in excess of $400,000, the court stated that the district court correctly concluded that the breach by plaintiffs in failing to make the payments and provide the reports required * * * was material as a matter of law, thus authorizing Marvel to terminate the contract. [The parties' agreement] explicitly singled out plaintiffs' obligation to provide "prompt accounting" for distributions as a term and condition of the agreement, the substantial breach of which authorized Marvel to terminate the license provided by the agreement. In addition, failure to tender payment is generally deemed a material breach of contract. Finally, as the district court found, and the subsequent accounting confirmed, the amounts withheld from Marvel by plaintiffs were very substantial. * * * Scholz argues that Ahern's breach, spanning thirteen years, is more egregious than these cases of a six-month failure to pay concession and rental fees, four-month failure to pay license and lease fees, and seven-month failure to pay (and five-month failure to account). Therefore, Scholz concludes, Ahern's failure to pay Scholz at least $459,000 is clearly a substantial breach.

We are not convinced. We remind appellant that under our standard of review, we do not sit as a juror, evaluating credibility and weighing evidence, as he seems to ask us to do. Rather, we simply weigh whether the district court committed a clear abuse of its discretion in determining that the jury verdict was not against the clear weight of the evidence. Our review of the record reveals that Ahern's counsel presented testimony questioning, to varying degrees, nine of the thirteen items of the estimate Scholz' accounting expert made of how much Ahern owed Scholz. Phillip Ames ("Ames"), a certified public accountant who served as business manager for both Ahern and BOSTON from 1976 through sometime in 1981 or 1982, made several estimates of how much Ahern owed Scholz, which he labeled "ball park figures." While we note that Ames' final estimate was $277,000, for a total of $459,000 with interest, we cannot assume that the jury accepted this figure as gospel. Given that Ahern sought over a million dollars in principal and interest from Scholz, the jury may reasonably have found that the Ames figure was not a substantial breach in the particular context of this case. It may have determined that the amount of money Ahern owed, taken in the perspective of the contract, Ahern's obligations, and the total amounts of money concerned, was not so significant a breach as to violate "an essential and inducing feature of the contract." Finally, addressing the case law Scholz relies on for support, we note that here, unlike in those cases, the amount of money owed was in question.

Ultimately, examining the record in full, the evidence clearly provides the jury and trial court with a basis for finding that Ahern did not substantially breach the FMA. As this Circuit stated on another occasion,

> We can understand how a jury might have decided for [defendant] on the basis of this evidence. But the jury did not do this; it decided for [plaintiff]. We do not see how one could say that the jury clearly made a mistake. We do not see how one could say that the evidence overwhelmingly favored the [defendant]. Rather, the evidence simply was mixed and contradictory. de Perez, 910 F.2d at 1008.

Therefore we cannot say that the district court committed a clear breach of its discretion on this point.

* * *

[The court ultimately reversed on other grounds and remanded for retrial].

NOTES AND QUESTIONS

1.   How does the standard for granting the motion for new trial differ from that employed when judgment as a matter of law is sought after a verdict has been returned? See Rule 59(a)(1). At a minimum, it is said that the court may weigh the evidence in ruling on a motion for new trial. But how can this be consistent with the right to jury trial? Keep in mind the historical directive embodied in the Seventh Amendment's second clause. See *Galloway*, supra p. 614.

The famous English judge, Lord Mansfield, said that "[t]rials by jury, in civil causes, could not subsist now without a power, *somewhere*, to grant new trials. * * * It is an absolute necessity to justice, that there should, upon many occasions, be opportunities of reconsidering the cause by a new trial." Bright v. Eynon, 97 Eng.Rep. 365 (K.B. 1757). As an American judge put it, "the exercise of this power is not in derogation of the right of trial by jury but is one of the historic safeguards of that right." Aetna Casualty & Surety Co. v. Yeatts, 122 F.2d 350, 353 (4th Cir.1941).

2.   It is often said that there is effectively no appellate review of a trial judge's *grant* of a motion for a new trial. Why? Keep in mind that as a general rule, appeal may be taken only from final judgments. On the other hand, it has been suggested that, at least as a theoretical matter, appellate review of a *grant* of a new trial is more appropriate than review of a *denial*, because "[t]o allow appellate review of the judge's refusal to [grant a motion for new trial] would mean that the verdict could be set aside solely by judges who were not present at the trial even though the trial judge, by denying the motion for new

trial, has found that the verdict is not contrary to the clear weight of the evidence." C. Wright & M. Kane, Law of Federal Courts 681 (7th ed. 2011).

The court in *Ahern* states that an appellate court will reverse a denial of a new trial motion because the verdict was against the weight of the evidence only if the district judge committed abuse of discretion. But consider the approach of the court in Lind v. Schenley Industries, Inc., 278 F.2d 79, 88 (3d Cir.), cert. denied, 364 U.S. 835 (1960):

> It is frequently stated that a motion for a new trial [on the ground that the verdict is against the weight of the evidence] ordinarily is nonreviewable because within the discretion of the trial court. * * * But this discretion must still be exercised in accordance with ascertainable legal standards and if an appellate court is shown special or unusual circumstances which clearly indicate an abuse of discretion in that the trial court failed to apply correctly the proper standards, reversal is possible. * * * Concededly appellate courts rarely find that the trial court abused its discretion.

Plaintiff in *Lind* was a former employee of defendant who claimed that his superior, Kaufman, had orally promised him a special commission that would have been more than five times his salary and would have made him the highest paid employee in the company. He sued for the commission. Defendant denied that the promise had been made, but the jury found in plaintiff's favor. The trial judge granted defendant a judgment n.o.v. and, in the alternative, a new trial should the judgment n.o.v. be overturned. The appellate court reversed the judgment n.o.v. and held that the new trial was improper:

> Where a trial is long and complicated and deals with a subject matter not lying within the ordinary knowledge of jurors a verdict should be scrutinized more closely by the trial judge than is necessary where the litigation deals with material which is familiar and simple, the evidence relating to ordinary commercial practices. An example of subject matter unfamiliar to a layman would be a case requiring a jury to pass upon the nature of an alleged newly discovered organic compound in an infringement action. A prime example of subject matter lying well within the comprehension of jurors is presented by the circumstances at bar.

> The subject matter of the litigation before us is simple and easily comprehended by an intelligent layman. The jury's main function was to determine the veracity of the witnesses: i.e., what testimony should be believed. If Lind's testimony and that of Mrs. Kennan, Kaufman's secretary [who claimed she witnessed the promise], was deemed credible, Lind presented a convincing, indeed an overwhelming case. We must conclude that the jury did believe this testimony and that the court below substituted its judgment for that of the jury on this issue and thereby abused legal discretion.

Is this approach sensible?

3.   *Ahern* is relied upon in Jennings v. Jones, 587 F.3d 430 (1st Cir. 2009). There the court held in a civil rights suit alleging excessive force by a police officer that the district court had not abused its discretion in granting the defendant's motion for a new trial. In its holding, the court emphasized the significant differences between the questions the district court asks itself on a motion for judgment as a matter of law under Rule 50 on the one hand and on a motion for new trial under Rule 59, on the other. However, the court emphasized that "trial judges do not sit as thirteenth jurors empowered to reject any verdict with which they disagree." The court also emphasized the "circumscribed" nature of appellate review in this context: "we may reverse only when there is an abuse of discretion."

4.   Should the court, ruling on a motion for new trial, concern itself with distortion in the outcome due to poor lawyering? Consider Vance v. Texas A & M University System, 117 F.R.D. 93 (S.D.Tex.1987), in which the judge granted a mistrial on the ground plaintiff's lawyer was "completely unorganized and ineffective." The judge reasoned that "[a] trial judge is not a mere observer of the proceedings, nor an umpire. He or she has the affirmative duty to ensure that litigants have a full and complete opportunity to present their case to the trier of fact for determination." Recall Band's Refuse Removal, Inc. v. Borough of Fair Lawn, supra p. 3. Is this attitude consistent with the proper role of the judge outlined there?

5.   The above discussion relates to new trials granted because the judge concludes that the verdict is against the clear weight of the evidence. Verdict losers may also argue that they deserve a new trial because of errors in the handling of the trial. See, e.g., People v. Hutchinson, infra p. . How should the court address such arguments? See Rule 61. Should the judge's uneasiness with the result bear on his assessment of the importance of the errors?

THE INTERSECTION BETWEEN JUDGMENT AS A MATTER OF LAW AND MOTION FOR NEW TRIAL

Rules 50(b), (c), and (e) establish a framework for the intersection between the motions for judgment as a matter of law and new trial. Rule 50(b) provides that a party who lost at trial may renew its motion for judgment as a matter of law, and "may include an alternative or joint request for a new trial under Rule 59." Rule 50(c)(1) provides that "[i]f the court grants a renewed motion for judgment as a matter of law, it must also conditionally rule on any motion for a new trial by determining whether a new trial should be granted if the judgment is later vacated or reversed." In so doing, "the court must state the grounds for conditionally granting or denying the motion for new trial." According to Rule 50(c)(2), when a conditional new trial motion is granted by the trial court and the judgment granting judgment as a matter of law has been reversed on appeal, "the new trial must proceed unless the appellate court orders otherwise." But if the motion for new trial has been conditionally denied by the trial court, the party making that conditional motion (i.e., the party who lost at trial but won on its post-trial motion for judgment as a matter of law) may on appeal assert the conditional denial of its new trial motion as error. "[I]f the judgment is reversed, the case must proceed as the appellate court orders."

Under Rule 50(e), if the trial court denies the motion for judgment as a matter of law, "the prevailing party [i.e., the party who won both at trial and on the loser's motion for judgment as a matter of law after trial] may, as appellee, assert grounds entitling it to a new trial should the appellate court conclude that the trial court erred in denying the motion. If the appellate court reverses the judgment, it may order a new trial, direct the trial court to determine whether a new trial should be granted, or direct the entry of judgment."

Consider initially the alternative new trial motion procedure provided for in Rule 50(b). Can you imagine circumstances under which the trial court would deny the motion for judgment as a matter of law, but nevertheless grant the alternative motion for new trial? The most obvious possibility is that while the court does not believe that the nonmovant's evidence is so deficient that it was unreasonable for the jury to find for that party, the court is nevertheless firmly convinced that a verdict on behalf of the non-movant is against the clear weight of the evidence. In other words, because the standard for granting a new trial on the grounds that the verdict is against the clear weight of the evidence is less deferential to the jury than is the standard employed on a motion for judgment as a matter of law, it is conceivable that the court would conclude that the non-movant's evidence failed to satisfy the former standard, even though it did satisfy the latter standard. Also, a trial court may choose to grant the alternative motion for new trial under Rule 50(b), despite denying the motion for judgment as a matter of law, because it believes it committed an error at trial—for example, in improperly refusing to admit some of the non-movant's evidence.

Rule 50(c)(1) concerns the situation in which the trial court has granted the renewed motion for judgment as a matter of law under Rule 50(b). The provision requires the trial court also to rule, hypothetically, on the motion for new trial. At the trial level, the ruling on the alternative new trial motion is hypothetical, because the court's granting of the motion for judgment as a matter of law has the effect of mooting, at least for immediate purposes, the merits of the new trial motion: Having had judgment entered in his favor as a matter of law, the movant naturally is no longer interested in having its new trial motion granted. The rule requires the hypothetical ruling, however, to take of the possibility that the trial court's grant of the motion for judgment as a matter of law will ultimately be reversed on appeal. Rule 50(c)(1) provides that in such an event, if the trial court has conditionally granted the new motion, the new trial proceeds unless otherwise ordered by the appellate court. If, on the other hand, the trial court denied the alternative new trial motion, the appellee on appeal may assert that ruling as error.

Rule 50(e) concerns the situation in which the trial court has denied the motion for judgment as a matter of law. The provision allows the appellee—i.e., the party who both won at trial and defeated the motion for judgment as a matter of law in the trial court—to argue that in the event the trial court's denial of judgment as a matter of law is reversed he should nevertheless be granted a new trial. Can you understand why, purely as a strategic matter, appellees might be reluctant to make such an argument to the appellate court?

One issue that has arisen concerns the ability of the appellate court to enter judgment on behalf of the party who made a motion for judgment as a matter of law when the appellate court has reversed the trial court's denial of that motion. If the appellee has argued that it should be granted a new trial in the event that the appellate court reverses the denial of the judgment as a matter of law, and the appellate court nevertheless enters judgment for the appellant, it would necessarily mean that the appellate court had rejected the appellee's request for a new trial. The question is whether Rule 50(e) authorizes the appellate court to reject the request for a new trial itself, or instead requires it to remand to the trial court to rule on such a request.

In Neely v. Martin K. Eby Construction Co., Inc., 386 U.S. 317 (1967), the Supreme Court held that the appellate court, where it reverses a denial of a motion for judgment as a matter of law, may simply direct entry of judgment for the appellant, even when the appellee has asked for a new trial in the event the denial of judgment as a matter of law is reversed.

Justice White, writing for the majority, conceded that often the request for a new trial should be ruled upon by the trial court, rather than by the appellate court, "because of the trial judge's firsthand knowledge of witnesses, testimony, and issues—because of his 'feel' for the overall case." He added that "obviously judgment for defendant-appellant should not be ordered where the plaintiff-appellee urges grounds for a nonsuit or new trial which should more appropriately be addressed to the trial court." However, he further noted that "these considerations do not justify an ironclad rule that the court of appeals should never order dismissal or judgment for defendant where plaintiff's verdict has been set aside on appeal. Such a rule would not serve the purpose of Rule 50 to speed litigation and to avoid unnecessary retrials."

Justice White noted one example where entry of judgment for the appellant would be appropriate: "situations where the defendant's grounds for setting aside the jury's verdict raise questions of subject matter jurisdiction or dispositive issues of law which, if resolved in defendant's favor, must necessarily terminate the litigation." Further, he pointed to situations in which the asserted basis for new trial by appellee would concern pure issues of law, for which no deference to the trial court would be required.

Justice Black dissented. He did so in part on the grounds that in such a situation the appellate court "is entirely powerless to order the trial court to dismiss the case, thus depriving the verdict winner of any opportunity to present a motion for new trial to the trial judge who is thoroughly familiar with the case."

Consider the language of Rule 50(e). Does it authorize the appellate court to enter judgment on behalf of appellant where the appellee has argued that it should be granted a new trial in the event that the trial court's denial of judgment as a matter of law is reversed?

Less than a year after deciding *Neely,* the Supreme Court in Iacurci v. Lummus Co., 387 U.S. 86 (1967), emphasized the need to remand to the trial court where it has greater expertise. The jury there returned a verdict for plaintiff and answered yes to one of five parts of an interrogatory to the jury about ways in which defendant might have been negligent, failing to answer the other four parts. The appellate court, inferring from the jury's silence on the other four parts of the interrogatory to the jury that it found no negligence as to those matters, directed entry of judgment for defendant upon finding that the evidence was insufficient to justify a verdict for plaintiff on the ground selected by the jury. The Supreme Court vacated and remanded with directions that the new trial issue be sent back to the district judge: "Under these circumstances, we think the Court of Appeals erred in directing entry of judgment for respondent; the case should have been remanded to the Trial Judge, who was in the best position to pass upon the question of a new trial in light of the evidence, his charge to the jury, and the jury's verdict and interrogatory answers." How often will that not be true?

Professor Louis concluded that "[a]fter *Iacurci,* the courts of appeals should ordinarily reject only those requests for a new trial, the grant of which by the trial court would constitute an abuse of discretion." Louis, Post-Verdict Rulings on the Sufficiency of the Evidence: Neely v. Martin K. Eby Construction Co. Revisited, 1975 Wis.L.Rev. 503, 516. Would that approach have justified the action by the court of appeals in *Neely*? Should it be an abuse of discretion to grant plaintiff a new trial where plaintiff has failed to satisfy the burden of production in the first trial?

In Weisgram v. Marley Co., 528 U.S. 440 (2000), the Supreme Court held that what is now Rule 50(e) [previously Rule 50(d)] authorizes an appellate court to direct the entry of judgment as a matter of law when it determines that evidence was erroneously admitted at trial and that the remaining, properly admitted evidence is insufficient to constitute a submissible case. The Court rejected plaintiff's argument that under such circumstances the appellate court may not order entry of judgment for the verdict loser, instead having to remand the case to the case to the trial court for a new trial determination. It found unpersuasive plaintiff's argument "that allowing courts of appeals to direct the entry of judgment for defendants will punish plaintiffs who could have shored up their cases by other means had they known their expert testimony would be found inadmissable," because it viewed both parties on notice as to the possibility that judgment would be entered contrary to the jury verdict due to exclusion of evidence. The Court found *Neely*'s reasoning applicable to the situation in *Weisgram*.

A number of commentators had criticized the decision in *Neely*. See, e.g., Note, Post-Verdict Motions Under Rule 50: Protecting the Verdict Winner, 53 Minn.L.Rev. 358 (1968); Note, Civil Procedure—Federal Rule 50(d)—Disposition of Cases by the Court of Appeals After Granting Judgment Notwithstanding the Verdict, 47 N.C.L.Rev. 162 (1968). Professor Louis, however, defended it. Though he asserts that "courts of appeals should ordinarily not make such discretionary determinations," he finds that this does not "establish or even suggest that they cannot screen out cases beyond the scope of legitimate discretion. Admittedly the courts have sometimes attempted to overreach this function, and may seek to do so in the future. But the Supreme Court has thwarted such efforts in the past and presumably would continue to do so." Louis, supra, 1975 Wis.L.Rev. at 520.

In Unitherm Food Systems, Inc. v. Swift-Eckrich, Inc., 546 U.S. 394 (2006), the Supreme Court held that in a case in which the defendant had made a preverdict motion for judgment as a matter of law under Rule 50(a)(2) but had failed to renew its preverdict motion as specified in Rule 50(b), the court of appeals had no authority to review the trial court's denial of the defendant's original motion. "A postverdict motion is necessary," the Court reasoned, "because '[d]etermination of whether a new trial should be granted or a judgment entered under Rule 50(b) calls for the judgment in the first instance of the judge who saw and heard the witnesses and has the feel of the case which no appellate printed transcript can impart.'" 546 U.S. at 401.

In a footnote, the Court noted that neither *Neely* nor *Weisgram* "undermine[s] our judgment about the benefit of postverdict input from the district court. In those cases this Court determined that an appellate court may, in certain circumstances, direct the entry of judgment when it reverses the district court's denial of a Rule 50(b) motion. But in such circumstances the district court will have an opportunity to consider the propriety of entering judgment or ordering a new trial by virtue of the postverdict motion. 546 U.S. at 401, n. 3. For a discussion of *Unitherm* and its implications, see Childress, Revolving Trapdoors: Preserving Sufficiency Review of the Civil Jury After *Unitherm* and Amended Rule 50, 26 Review of Litig. 239 (2007).

Post-*Unitherm* cases in the lower courts show that the decision has been confined to challenges to the sufficiency of the evidence. See, e.g., Linden v. CNH America, LLC, 673 F.3d 829 (8th Cir. 2012) ("The *Unitherm* opinion includes language that, when read out of context, indicates that an appeal may never be taken unless a postverdict motion is filed. * * * However, in addressing whether this language extends to all post-trial appeals, appeals courts have uniformly limited it to sufficiency of the evidence challenge where parties fail to file a postverdict motion under Rule 50(b) after the *denial* of a Rule 50(a) preverdict motion. Reading *Unitherm* more broadly would dramatically alter the well-accepted rule that an objection at trial generally preserves an issue for review on appeal."). See also Belk Inc. v. Meyer Corp.), 679 F. 3d 146 (4th Cir. 2012).

RELIEF FROM JUDGMENT UNDER RULE 60(b)

A motion for new trial under Rule 59 must be made "no later than 28 days after the entry of judgment." Rule 59(b). However, Rule 60(b) provides a mechanism by which a party may obtain relief from a judgment at a later time. Note that it only applies to *final* judgment; the court usually may reconsider any earlier decision before final judgment.

What are the competing policy considerations that might influence a court's predisposition towards motions under Rule 60(b)? See Comment, Rule 60(b): Survey and Proposal for General Reform, 60 Calif.L.Rev. 531, 533 (1972): "Rule 60(b) is an attempt to reconcile the values of finality and doing individual justice. * * * Besides helping to keep societal peace and protecting an individual litigant from harassment, finality lends stability and predictability to judicial activity—qualities essential to any institution charged with settling disputes authoritatively. On the other hand, the rigidity of absolute finality could be intolerable."

While motions under Rule 60(b) must be made "within a reasonable time" and when made on grounds of mistake, inadvertence, surprise, excusable neglect, newly discovered evidence, or misrepresentation, "no more than one year after entry of the judgment," it also provides that the Rule does not limit a court's power "to entertain an independent action." Generally an independent action is allowed where a party has been denied an opportunity to present his claims fairly. But this second action is limited by the doctrine of res judicata, which is said to preclude relitigation in an independent action not only of issues actually litigated but also of issues open to litigation in the prior action. See Comment, supra, 60 Calif.L.Rev. at 542–43. How often will this option be available?

Because finality furthers highly important values, relief under Rule 60(b) is extremely difficult to obtain. Nevertheless, it is useful to consider some of the rule's provisions:

Mistake: Rule 60(b)(1) allows a party to ask that judgment be set aside on grounds of "mistake, inadvertence, surprise, or excusable neglect."

Except for default cases, where such relief may often be obtained on the ground that defendant failed through mistake to file an answer (recall Shepard Claims Serv. v. William Darrah & Assoc., supra p. 208), it is difficult to justify such relief on the ground that a party simply made a mistake, and bad lawyering ordinarily will not provide a basis for granting relief on this ground.

Newly discovered evidence: Rule 60(b)(2) authorizes setting aside a judgment where the loser presents newly discovered evidence. The standard for allowing relief under this provision is the same as the approach under Rule 59 to a motion for a new trial on grounds of newly discovered evidence. See 11 C. Wright & A. Miller, Federal Practice & Procedure § 2859. What factors should the court consider in evaluating such a motion? Consider that the rule indicates that the proffered material be evidence, be newly discovered, and not have been discoverable in time with due diligence.

Fraud: Rule 60(b)(3) provides that fraud or other misconduct of a party is a ground for setting aside a final judgment or order. The rule abandons the former idea that relief should only be accorded for "extrinsic" fraud, but concern about making relief readily available persists. Consider how often the loser may claim that the winner's witnesses lied during the trial. Should this be a ground for a second trial? If so, what is the purpose of a trial in which the jury is supposed to determine the truth?

The Supreme Court early announced that "the mischief of retrying every case in which the judgment or decree [was] rendered on false testimony * * * would be greater, by reason of the endless nature of the strife, than any compensation arising from doing justice in individual cases." United States v. Throckmorton, 98 U.S. (8 Otto) 61, 68–69 (1878). Since then, courts have relaxed their attitude, but the difficulties confronting the moving party are reflected in the following observations by Justice Brennan, at the time a member of the New Jersey Supreme Court:

> Perjured testimony that warrants disturbance of a final judgment must be shown by clear, convincing and satisfactory evidence to have been, not false merely, but to have been willfully and purposely falsely given, and to have been material to the issue tried and not merely cumulative but probably to have controlled the result. Further, a party seeking to be relieved from the judgment must show that the fact of the falsity of the testimony could not have been discovered by reasonable diligence in time to offset it at the trial * * *.

Shammas v. Shammas, 88 A.2d 204, 209 (N.J.1952).

Particular difficulty arises if the alleged perjury came not from a party but from some other witness. In Harre v. A.H. Robins Co., 750 F.2d 1501 (11th Cir.1985), one of defendant's experts claimed that he had performed tests on the Dalkon Shield contraceptive device, which was produced by defendant, and determined that it did not cause infections in women, but later testimony by the same witness in another case showed that he had not done any such experiments. Stressing the fact that the same lawyer represented defendant in both cases, the appellate court directed a new trial. It reasoned that the issue on which the witness testified—defect of the product—was the "ultimate issue in the case" and that the lawyers knew or should have known of the falsity of the testimony. The witness himself was later indicted for obstructing justice but was acquitted. See Harre v. A.H. Robins Co., 866 F.2d 1303 (11th Cir.1989). On the other hand, in Metlyn Realty Corp. v. Esmark, Inc., 763 F.2d 826 (7th Cir.1985), the trial court approved the settlement of a class action after a hearing in which an expert gave his opinion on the value of corporate shares in issue. After the court approved the settlement, objectors moved to set aside the resulting judgment on the ground that the witness had lied about his experience. The appellate court upheld denial of the Rule 60 motion, noting that "[e]xpert witnesses such as Levy are free agents. Parties and counsel have an obligation not to deceive the court about the witness and to correct statements they know to be false, but they are not responsible for the details of the witness's testimony."

In Pumphrey v. K.W. Thompson Tool Co., 62 F.3d 1128 (9th Cir. 1995), the court upheld relief under Rule 60(b) to set aside a judgment for fraud on the court. Defendant in that product liability action had not revealed that, in addition to the test film it showed at trial in which the product did not malfunction, there was another test film showing the very malfunction in question. Indeed, "[t]he trial video was made because the test shown on the original video did not turn out as planned." Id. at 1131. Because defendant's general counsel was involved in this chicanery, and defendant also answered interrogatories falsely, there was fraud on the court. See also Lonsdorf v. Seefeldt, 47 F.3d 893 (7th Cir.1995) (relief justified because document used at trial had been altered).

Other reasons: Rule 60(b)(6) provides that a party may be relieved from a final judgment for "any other reason that justifies relief." Do you think it is wise to include such an open-ended authorization? See United States v. Buck, 281 F.3d 1336, 1340 (10th Cir. 2002) ("If there is ever to be closure to litigation, such motions should be granted only for compelling reasons."). The provision was added as part of the 1946 amendment, in part in response to an article, Moore & Rogers, Federal Relief From Civil Judgments, 55 Yale L.J. 623, 688 (1946), which argued:

> [I]t is productive of harsh and inequitable results to enumerate exclusive situations when relief can be afforded by motion; and when this is done, courts will invent some means of escape as by the doctrine of inherent power, or the doctrine that the term of the court gives power.

Note that the one-year time limit in Rule 60(b) applies only to reasons (1), (2), and (3), i.e., mistake, etc., newly discovered evidence, and fraud, etc. Can it be avoided by simply filing under reason (6)? The answer is, not if the real reason is one of the other specified reasons, which is likely in most cases. As stated in Stradley v. Cortez, 518 F.2d 488, 493–94 (3d Cir.1975): "[P]laintiff can use Rule 60(b)(6) as a means of avoiding the time bars * * * only upon a showing that (1) the reason for the relief sought under 60(b)(6) is not embraced within the various provisions of 60(b)(1–5) and (2) exceptional circumstances exist which warrant the granting of relief." See also United States v. Buck, 281 F.3d 1336 (10th Cir. 2002).

Courts have been especially cautious in invoking Rule 60(b)(6). See, e.g., Ford Motor Co. v. Mustangs Unlimited, Inc., 487 F.3d 465, 468 (6th Cir. 2007) (recognizing uniquely limited availability of Rule 60(b)(6) motions). They have emphasized that "a motion under Rule 60(b) is not a second opportunity for the losing party to make its strongest case, to rehash arguments or to dress up arguments that previously failed." Kustom Signals, Inc. v. Applied Concepts, Inc., 247 F.Supp.2d 1233, 1235 (D. Kan. 2003).

For a hard-nosed application of the requirements of Rule 60(b), consider Brandon v. Chicago Board of Education, 143 F.3d 293 (7th Cir.1998). Plaintiff filed an ADA action in August, 1995, and the clerk's office somehow entered the wrong name and address for his lawyer while docketing the case. Accordingly, from that point forward all communications from the court were sent to a lawyer with a name similar to plaintiff's lawyer and an office near the office of plaintiff's lawyer. This lawyer sent the notices back to the clerk, explaining that this was not his case, but the clerk's office still did not catch the error. As a result, plaintiff's actual lawyer never received two status hearing notices and the court dismissed for nonprosecution when counsel did not appear. The dismissal was also misdirected by the clerk's office. In late 1996, counsel for plaintiff visited the clerk's office and discovered that "his case had been quite active without him." He promptly filed a Rule 60(b) motion, but it was by then one year and three days after the date the case had been dismissed. Plaintiff argued that this should not matter because he could rely on the fallback provisions of Rule 60(b)(6), but the court of appeals ruled that Rule 60(b)(1) was the pertinent provision because it applies to errors by the court as well as those of the parties. Accordingly, Rule 60(b)(6) could not apply. Probably the lawyer should have wondered about the case much sooner, but this case nevertheless emphasizes the limitations on relief under Rule 60(b).

On the general issue, see Kane, Relief From Federal Judgments: A Morass Unrelieved by a Rule, 30 Hastings L.J. 41 (1978); Wham, Federal District Court Rule 60(b): A Humane Rule Gone Wrong, 49 A.B.A.J. 566 (1963).

The Supreme Court has recognized that Rule 60(b) may play an important role in allowing modifications of decrees in institutional reform litigation. See Rufo v. Inmates of Suffolk County Jail, 502 U.S. 367, 380 (1992): "The upsurge in institutional reform litigation since Brown v. Board of Education * * * has made the ability of a district court to modify a decree in response to changed circumstances all the more important. Because such decrees often remain in place for extended periods of time, the likelihood of significant changes occurring during the life of the decree is increased." The Court noted that "[t]he experience of the district and circuit courts in implementing and modifying such decrees has demonstrated that a flexible approach is often essential to achieving the goals of reform litigation." Id. The Court therefore held that modification, under Rule 60(b)(5), of consent decrees in institutional reform litigation is not to be measured by the "grievous wrong" standard that had previously been employed in other contexts.

In United States v. Beggerly, 524 U.S. 38 (1998), the Court addressed the requirements for an independent action to set aside a judgment. In 1979, the government had sought to quiet its title to an island in the Gulf of Mexico from some 200 people who claimed ownership interests in the island. The government's position was that no such interests could exist because the United States never patented the property. During discovery, defendants sought proof of their title, but the government reported that a search of official records included nothing showing that the island had ever been granted to private land-owners. The claimants settled with the government, and judgment was entered in accordance with the settlement.

Some years later, a specialist hired by claimants found materials in the National Archives that they argued showed that the island was granted to a private party before it became part of the United States. That would mean that the title did not pass to the United States in the Louisiana Purchase, and might mean that claimants' title to the land was superior to the government's. They filed a suit asking the court to set aside the earlier judgment and award much more than the settlement amount. Although the district court dismissed for lack of jurisdiction, the Court of Appeals reversed on the ground that the suit satisfied the requirements for an "independent action" identified in Rule 60(b).

The Supreme Court reversed. The Court agreed that the district court could entertain the suit without an independent basis for jurisdiction, for ancillary jurisdiction would justify entertaining the suit to set aside the judgment entered by the federal court. But this suit did not satisfy the requirements for a meritorious independent action. All claimants alleged was that the government had failed to provide relevant information in the earlier case, and that would at best come under Rule 60(b)(3), which is subject to a one-year limitation. Independent actions should be reserved for those cases of "injustices which * * * are deemed sufficiently gross to demand a departure" from res judicata. Although fraud would suffice, the Court held that claimants' allegations in this case "do not approach this demanding standard."

3.   REMITTITUR AND ADDITUR

DIMICK V. SCHIEDT

Supreme Court of the United States, 1935
293 U.S. 474

JUSTICE SUTHERLAND delivered the opinion of the Court.

This is an action brought by respondent (plaintiff) against petitioner (defendant) in the federal District Court for the District of Massachusetts to recover damages for a personal injury resulting from the alleged negligent operation of an automobile on a public highway in Massachusetts. The jury returned a verdict in favor of respondent for the sum of $500. Respondent moved for a new trial on the grounds that the verdict was contrary to the weight of the evidence, that it was a compromise verdict, and that the damages allowed were inadequate. The trial court ordered a new trial upon the last-named ground, unless petitioner would consent to an increase of the damages to the sum of $1,500. Respondent's consent was neither required nor given. Petitioner, however, consented to the increase, and, in accordance with the order of the court, a denial of the motion for new trial automatically followed. Respondent appealed to the Circuit Court of Appeals, where the judgment was reversed; the court holding that the conditional order violated the Seventh Amendment of the Federal Constitution in respect of the right of trial by jury. That court recognized the doctrine, frequently stated by this court, that in the case of an excessive verdict it is within the power of the trial court to grant defendant's motion for a new trial unless plaintiff remit the amount deemed to be excessive, but held that the trial court was without power to condition the allowance of plaintiff's motion for a new trial upon the refusal of defendant to consent to an increase in the amount of damages.

* * *

Section 269 of the Judicial Code, as amended, U.S.C. title 28, § 391 (28 U.S.C.A. § 391), confers upon all federal courts power to grant new trials "in cases where there has been a trial by jury, for reasons for which new trials have usually been granted in the courts of law. . . ."

In order to ascertain the scope and meaning of the Seventh Amendment, resort must be had to the appropriate rules of the common law established at the time of the adoption of that constitutional provision in 1791. A careful examination of the English reports prior to that time fails to disclose any authoritative decision sustaining the power of an

English court to increase, either absolutely or conditionally, the amount fixed by the verdict of a jury in an action at law, with certain exceptions.

* * *

From the foregoing, and from many other English authorities which we have examined but deem it unnecessary to cite, we conclude that, while there was some practice to the contrary in respect of *decreasing* damages, the established practice and the rule of the common law, as it existed in England at the time of the adoption of the Constitution, forbade the court to *increase* the amount of damages awarded by a jury in actions such as that here under consideration.

We could well rest this opinion upon that conclusion, were it not for the contention that our federal courts from a very early day have upheld the authority of a trial court to deny a motion for new trial because damages were found to be excessive, if plaintiff would consent to remit the excessive amount, and that this holding requires us to recognize a similar rule in respect of increasing damages found to be grossly inadequate. There is a decision by Mr. Justice Story, sitting on circuit, authorizing such a remittitur, as early as 1822. Blunt v. Little, Fed.Cas.No. 1,578, 3 Mason, 102. There, the jury returned a verdict for $2,000 damages, suffered as a result of a malicious arrest. Defendant moved for a new trial on the ground that the damages were excessive. The court asserted its power to grant a new trial upon that ground, but directed that the cause should be submitted to another jury unless plaintiff was willing to remit $500 of the damages. This view of the matter was accepted by this court in Northern Pacific R. Co. v. Herbert, 116 U.S. 642, 646, 647, and has been many times reiterated.

Since the decision of Mr. Justice Story in 1822, this court has never expressed doubt in respect of the rule, and it has been uniformly applied by the lower federal courts. It is, however, remarkable that in none of these cases was there any real attempt to ascertain the common-law rule on the subject. Mr. Justice Story, in the *Blunt* Case, cited two English cases antedating the Constitution in support simply of his conclusion that the court had power to grant a new trial for excessive damages, and thereupon announced without more that, unless the plaintiff should be willing to remit $500 of his damages, the cause would be submitted to another jury. For the latter conclusion, no authority whatever was cited. The plaintiff remitted the amount, and the motion was overruled.

* * *

In the last analysis, the sole support for the decisions of this court and that of Mr. Justice Story, so far as they are pertinent to cases like that now in hand, must rest upon the practice of some of the English judges—a practice which has been condemned as opposed to the principles of the common law by every *reasoned* English decision, both before and after the adoption of the Federal Constitution, which we have been able to find.

In the light reflected by the foregoing review of the English decisions and commentators, it therefore may be that, if the question of remittitur were now before us for the first time, it would be decided otherwise. But, first announced by Mr. Justice Story in 1822, the doctrine has been accepted as the law for more than a hundred years and uniformly applied in the federal courts during that time. And, as it finds some support in the practice of the English courts prior to the adoption of the Constitution, we may assume that in a case involving a remittitur, which this case does not, the doctrine would not be reconsidered or disturbed at this late day.

Nevertheless, this court in a very special sense is charged with the duty of construing and upholding the Constitution; and, in the discharge of that important duty, it ever must be alert to see that a doubtful precedent be not extended by mere analogy to a different case if the result will be to weaken or subvert what it conceives to be a principle of the fundamental law of the land.

That rule applies with peculiar force to the present case * * *. That is to say, the power to conditionally increase the verdict of a jury does not follow as a necessary corollary from the power to conditionally decrease it. As the court below correctly pointed out, in the case of a conditional remittitur, "a jury has already awarded a sum in excess of that fixed by the court as a basis for a remittitur, which, at least, finds some support in the early English practice; while in the second case no jury has ever passed on the increased amount, and the practice has no precedent according to the rules of the common law."

* * *

The controlling distinction between the power of the court and that of the jury is that the former has the power to determine the law and the latter to determine the facts. In dealing with questions like the one now under consideration, that distinction must be borne steadily in mind. Where the verdict returned by a jury is palpably and grossly inadequate or excessive, it should not be permitted to stand; but, in that event, both parties remain entitled, as they were entitled in the first instance, to have a jury properly determine the question of liability and the extent of the injury by an assessment of damages. Both are questions of fact. Where the verdict is excessive, the practice of substituting a remission of the excess for a new trial is not without plausible support in the view that what remains is included in the verdict along with the unlawful excess—in the sense that it has been found by the jury—and that the remittitur has the effect of merely lopping off an excrescence. But, where the verdict is too small, an increase by the court is a bald addition of something which in no sense can be said to be included in the verdict. When, therefore, the trial court here found that the damages awarded by the jury were so inadequate as to entitle plaintiff to a new trial, how can it be held, with any semblance of reason, that that court, with the consent of the defendant only, may, by assessing an additional amount of damages, bring the constitutional right of the plaintiff to a jury trial to an end in respect of a matter of fact which no jury has ever passed upon either explicitly or by implication? To so hold is obviously to compel the plaintiff to forego his constitutional right to the verdict of a jury and accept "an assessment partly made by a jury which has acted improperly, and partly by a tribunal which has no power to assess." [Lionel Barber & Co. v. Deutsche Bank, [1919] A.C. 304, 335.]

It is said that the common law is susceptible of growth and adaptation to new circumstances and situations, and that the courts have power to declare and effectuate what is the present rule in respect of a given subject without regard to the old rule; and some attempt is made to apply that principle here. The common law is not immutable, but flexible, and upon its own principles adapts itself to varying conditions. But here we are dealing with a constitutional provision which has in effect adopted the rules of the common law in respect of trial by jury as these rules existed in 1791. To effectuate any change in these rules is not to deal with the common law, *qua* common law, but to alter the Constitution. * * *

It is worthy of note that, while for more than a century the federal courts have followed the approved practice of conditioning the allowance of a new trial on the consent of plaintiff to remit excessive damages, no federal court, so far as we can discover, has ever undertaken similarly to increase the damages, although there are numerous cases where motions for new trial have been made and granted on the ground that the verdict was inadequate. This, it is true, is but negative evidence; but it is negative evidence of more than ordinary value. For, when we consider that during the great length of time mentioned the federal courts were constantly applying the rule in respect of the remission of excessive damages, the circumstance that the practice here in question in respect of inadequate damages was never followed or, apparently, its approval even suggested, seems highly significant as indicating a lack of judicial belief in the existence of the power.

JUSTICE STONE [joined by CHIEF JUSTICE HUGHES and JUSTICES BRANDEIS and CARDOZO], dissenting:

I think the judgment should be reversed.

What the trial court has done is to deny a motion for a new trial, for what seemed to it a good reason: That the defendant had given his binding consent to an increased recovery, which the court thought to be adequate, and thus to remove any substantial ground for awarding a new trial. In denying the motion, the trial judge relied on two rules of the common law which have received complete acceptance for centuries. One is that the court has power to act upon a motion to set aside the verdict of a jury because inadequate or excessive, and in its discretion to grant or deny a new trial. The other, which is implicit in the first, is that it has power to determine, as a matter of law, the upper and lower limits within which recovery by a plaintiff will be permitted and the authority to set aside a verdict which is not within those limits.

As a corollary to these rules is the further one of the common law, long accepted in the federal courts, that the exercise of judicial discretion in denying a motion for a new trial, on the ground that the verdict is too small or too large, is not subject to review on writ of error or appeal. This is but a special application of the more general rule that an appellate court will not re-examine the facts which induced the trial court to grant or deny a new trial.

If the effect of what is now decided is to liberalize the traditional common-law practice so that the denial of a motion for a new trial, made on the ground that the verdict is excessive or inadequate, is subject to some sort of appellate review, the change need not be regarded as unwelcome, even though no statute has authorized it. But the question remains whether, in exercising this power of review, the trial judge should be reversed.

The decision of the Court is rested on the ground that the Constitution prohibits the trial judge from adopting the practice. Accordingly, I address myself to the question of power without stopping to comment on the generally recognized advantages of the practice as a means of securing substantial justice and bringing the litigation to a more speedy and economical conclusion than would be possible by a new trial to a jury, or the extent to which that or analogous practice has been adopted and found useful in the courts of the several states. The question is a narrow one: Whether there is anything in the Seventh Amendment or in the rules of the common law, as it had developed before the adoption of the amendment, which would require a federal appellate court to set aside the denial of the motion merely because the particular reasons which moved the trial judge to deny it are not shown to have similarly moved any English judge before 1791.

There is nothing in its history or language to suggest that the amendment had any purpose but to preserve the essentials of the jury trial as it was known to the common law before the adoption of the Constitution. For that reason this Court has often refused to construe it as intended to perpetuate in changeless form the *minutiae* of trial practice as it existed in the English courts in 1791. From the beginning, its language has been regarded as but subservient to the single purpose of the amendment, to preserve the essentials of the jury trial in actions at law, serving to distinguish them from suits in equity and admiralty, and to safeguard the jury's function from any encroachment which the common law did not permit.

Thus interpreted, the Seventh Amendment guarantees that suitors in actions at law shall have the benefits of trial of issues of fact by a jury, but it does not prescribe any particular procedure by which these benefits shall be obtained, or forbid any which does not curtail the function of the jury to decide questions of fact as it did before the adoption of the amendment. It does not restrict the court's control of the jury's verdict, as it had previously been exercised, and it does not confine the trial judge, in determining what issues are for the jury and what for the court, to the particular forms of trial practice in vogue in 1791.

Thus this Court has held that a federal court, without the consent of the parties, may constitutionally appoint auditors to hear testimony, examine books and accounts, and frame and report upon issues of fact, as an aid to the jury in arriving at its verdict, Ex parte Peterson, 253 U.S. 300; it may require both a general and a special verdict and set aside the general verdict for the plaintiff and direct a verdict for the defendant on the basis of the facts specially found, Walker v. New Mexico & Southern Pacific R. Co., 165 U.S. 593; and it may accept so much of the verdict as declares that the plaintiff is entitled to recover, and set aside so much of it as fixes the amount of the damages, and order a new trial of that issue alone, Gasoline Products Co., Inc. v. Champlin Refining Co., 283 U.S. 494. Yet none of these procedures was known to the common law. In fact, the very practice, so firmly imbedded in federal procedure, of making a motion for a new trial directly to the trial judge, instead of to the court *en banc,* was never adopted by the common law. But this Court has found in the Seventh Amendment no bar to the adoption by the federal courts of these novel methods of dealing with the verdict of a jury, for they left unimpaired the function of the jury to decide issues of fact, which it had exercised before the adoption of the amendment.

If we apply that test to the present case, it is evident that the jury's function has not been curtailed. After the issues of fact had been submitted to the jury and its verdict taken, the trial judge was authorized to entertain a motion to set aside the verdict and, as an incident, to determine the legal limits of a proper verdict. A denial of the motion out of hand, however inadequate the verdict, was not an encroachment upon the province of the jury as the common law defined it. It would seem not to be any the more so here because the exercise of the judge's discretion was affected by his knowledge of the fact that a proper recovery had been assured to the plaintiff by the consent of the defendant. Thus the plaintiff has suffered no infringement of a right by the denial of his motion. The defendant has suffered none because he has consented to the increased recovery, of which he does not complain.

It is upon these grounds, as well as the further one that the denial of a new trial may not be reviewed upon appeal, that this Court has upheld the practice of the remittitur.

The defendant, who has formally consented to pay the increased amount, cannot complain. The plaintiff has suffered no denial of a right because the court, staying its hand, has left the verdict undisturbed, as it lawfully might have done if the defendant had refused to pay more than the verdict. The fact that in one case the recovery is less than the amount of the verdict, and that in the other it is greater, would seem to be without significance. For in neither does the jury return a verdict for the amount actually recovered, and in both the amount of recovery was fixed, not by the verdict, but by the consent of the party resisting the motion for a new trial.

The question with which we are now concerned—what considerations shall govern an appellate review of this discretionary action of the trial court—is one unknown to the common law, which provided for no such review. We are afforded but a meager and fragmentary guide if our review is to be controlled by the Seventh Amendment, read as though it had incorporated by reference the particular details of English trial practice exhibited by the law books in 1791. * * *

If our only guide is to be this scant record of the practice of controlling the jury's verdict, however fragmentary the state of its development at this period, and if we must deny any possibility of change, development, or improvement, then it must be admitted that search of the legal scrap heap of a century and a half ago may commit us to the incongruous position in which we are left by the present decision: A federal trial court may deny a motion for a new trial where the plaintiff consents to decrease the judgment to a proper amount, but it is powerless to deny the motion if its judgment is influenced by the defendant's consent to a comparable increase in the recovery.

But I cannot agree that we are circumscribed by so narrow and rigid a conception of the common law. * * * When the Constitution was adopted, the common law was something more than a miscellaneous collection of precedents. It was a system, then a growth of some five centuries, to guide judicial decision. One of its principles, certainly as important as any other, and that which assured the possibility of the continuing vitality and usefulness of the system, was its capacity for growth and development, and its adaptability to every new situation to which it might be needful to apply it. "This flexibility and capacity for growth and adaptation is," as the Court declared in Hurtado v. California, 110 U.S. 516, 530, "the peculiar boast and excellence of the common law."

* * * If this Court could thus, in conformity to common law, substitute a new rule for an old one because it was more consonant with modern conditions, it would seem that no violence would be done to the common law by extending the principle of the remittitur to the case where the verdict is inadequate, although the common law had made no rule on the subject in 1791; and that we could not rightly refuse to apply to either the

principle of general application, that it is competent to exercise a discretionary power to grant or withhold relief in any way which is not unjust.

* * *

To me it seems an indefensible anachronism for the law to reject the like principle of decision, in reviewing on appeal denials of motions for new trials, where the plaintiff has consented to decrease the judgment or the defendant has consented to increase it by the proper amount, or to apply it in the one case and reject it in the other. It is difficult to see upon what principle the denial of a motion for a new trial, which for centuries has been regarded as so much a matter of discretion that it is not disturbed when its only support may be a bad or inadequate reason, may nevertheless be set aside on appeal when it is supported by a good one: That the defendant has bound himself to pay an increased amount of damages which the court judicially knows is within the limits of a proper verdict.

NOTES AND QUESTIONS

1. "Remittitur is the procedure by which a trial judge gives a plaintiff who has received an excessively favorable jury verdict the option of accepting a specified reduction in the jury verdict or submitting to a new trial. Since its approval by a federal court in 1822, remittitur has been accepted and employed by the courts of the United States. Despite this century and a half of use, the procedures and standards utilized by the federal courts have been, and still are, far from uniform." Note, Remittitur Practice in the Federal Courts, 76 Colum.L.Rev. 299 (1976). Note, however, the possible limits of the remittitur concept. For example, in Tronzo v. Biomet, Inc., 236 F.3d 1342 (Fed. Cir. 2001), the court rejected plaintiff's argument that it was unconstitutional legal error for the district court to fail to award him a new trial after he had rejected a reduction in his award and instead directly implement the reduction. The Federal Circuit held that the judicially imposed reduction in damages did not constitute a remittitur: "[I]n the present case, the district court did not reweigh any evidence, nor did it exercise its discretion in computing the damages award. Instead, the court awarded the maximum damages possible given the lack of competent evidence in the record. * * * Thus, representing this issue to the jury would have been pointless because, as a matter of law, the compensatory damages award could not exceed [the amount] already awarded." How persuasive is the court's distinction between cases in which the district court reduces damages as excessive (remittitur) and those in which the district court reduces damages due to "the lack of competent evidence in the record" supporting the award? If there exists competent evidence supporting the jury's award, should the court be granting remittitur in the first place?

Contrast the situation in Tronzo with that in Ross v. Kansas City Power & Light Co., 293 F.3d 1041 (8th Cir. 2002), where the court held a plaintiff was not entitled to remittitur's option of a new trial when the district court reduced the award of punitive damages because it was deemed to be unconstitutionally excessive. "[T]he court's mandatory [and constitutionally dictated] review of a punitive damages award," the court concluded, "does not implicate the Seventh Amendment. The plaintiff's consent to a constitutional reduction of a punitive damages award is 'irrelevant' because the court must decide the issue as a matter of law." See also Cooper Industries, Inc. v. Leatherman Tool Group, Inc., 532 U.S. 424, 437 (2001) ("Because the jury's award of punitive damages does not constitute a finding of 'fact,' appellate review of the district court's determination that an award is consistent with due process does not implicate. . . . Seventh Amendment concerns. . . .") What, according to the Court in Dimick, are the bases for distinguishing between additur and remittitur for purposes of the Seventh Amendment? Are they persuasive?

2.   On what grounds does Justice Stone dissent? Compare his analysis to that of Justice Rutledge, speaking for the Court, in *Galloway,* supra p. 614. Note that *Galloway* was decided a number of years after *Dimick.* Though *Galloway* itself concerned the constitutionality of only the directed verdict, might the opinion's reasoning be relied upon to uphold the modern use of additur? It should be noted, however, that the Supreme Court has never taken this step. Thus, *Dimick* remains controlling in the federal courts. However, many state courts, not bound by the Seventh Amendment, have upheld the constitutionality of additur under state constitutional jury trial provisions. See, e.g., Fisch v. Manger, 130 A.2d 815 (N.J.1957). Sometimes they use it aggressively. See Cunningham, Judge Tacks $5.3 Million Onto Jury's Award, S.F. Recorder, July 18, 2002 at 1 (judge increased award of $713,000 for pain and suffering by $5.3 million).

3.   One scholar has argued that, despite the reasoning in *Dimick*, remittitur is unconstitutional. Thomas, Re-Examining the Constitutionality of Remittitur Under the Seventh Amendment, 64 Ohio St. L. J. 731 (2003). According to Professor Thomas, "[t]he study of the English cases at the time of the Seventh Amendment's adoption shows that remittitur as presently practiced by the federal courts did not exist at common law in 1791." Id. at 793. Even if one were to accept an "evolving" view of the Seventh Amendment right, she argues, remittitur should be deemed unconstitutional because "[w]hen faced with the possibility of a new trial or alternatively, a remittitur, the plaintiff has no real choice to take a new trial . . . because even if the second trial results in a verdict that is greater or the same as the previous jury's verdict, the same judge will oversee the case, and that judge has already determined the maximum amount that a reasonable jury could award under the facts." Id. at 734.

4.   Although *Dimick* remains good law [See, e.g., ClearOne Communications, Inc. v. Biamp Systems, 653 F.3d 1163 (10th Cir. 2011); Azimi v. Jordan's Meats, Inc., 456 F.3d 228 (1st Cir. 2006)], the additur practice has nevertheless been utilized sporadically in the federal courts. See Liriano v. Hobart Corp., 170 F.3d 264 (2d Cir.1999) (upholding district court's "adjustment" of a jury verdict to include a hospital bill); E.E.O.C. v. Massey Yardley Chrysler Plymouth, Inc., 117 F.3d 1244 (11th Cir. 1997). In Hattaway v. McMillian, 903 F.2d 1440 (11th Cir.1990), the federal trial court had ordered

an additur pursuant to a Florida statute. While the appellate court expressly acknowledged "that the order of an additur by a federal court violates the seventh amendment right to a jury trial in civil cases," citing *Dimick*, it found the additur order to be non-appealable. In so holding it relied, by analogy, on a long line of decisions, reaffirmed in Donovan v. Penn Shipping Co., 429 U.S. 648 (1977) (per curiam), which "forbid the plaintiff from accepting a remittitur—even under protest—and then appealing the order granting the remittitur." 903 F.2d at 1451. Though the court acknowledged "that there are no federal cases applying these principles [of non-appealability] to an additur order," and that on the merits "the district court erred in ordering the defendant to choose between accepting either the additur or a new trial," it nevertheless left "untouched the district court's judgment on this issue." Id. See also Millennium Partners, L.P. v. Colmar Storage, LLC, 494 F.3d 1293, 1303 (11th Cir. 2007) (exception to *Dimick* has been recognized where jury has found underlying liability and there is no genuine issue as to the correct amount of damages); Sulzer Carbomedics, Inc. v. Oregon Cardio-Devices, Inc., 257 F.3d 449 (5th Cir. 2001).

Does the *Donovan* rule make any sense in its original context of remittitur? If a party agrees to a remittitur only under protest, can that party rationally be deemed to have voluntarily waived any objection? What alternative does a plaintiff who finds a remittitur unacceptable have? If the plaintiff refuses to agree to the remittitur, the trial judge will order a new trial—a non-appealable interlocutory order. As a practical matter, then, under the *Donovan* rule, how often is a plaintiff likely to be able to obtain appellate review of a trial court's conditional order of remittitur? If the answer is almost never, is that necessarily a bad result? (It should be noted, however, that when the trial court *denies* a defendant's motion for new trial, that decision will be subject to appellate review as part of the normal process of appeal from the final judgment in favor of the plaintiff). See also Anderson v. Roberson, 249 F.3d 539, 542 (6th Cir. 2001) ("a district court order giving the plaintiff a choice between remittitur or a new trial is not a final, appealable order.")

Does any basis exist on which to distinguish the appealability of an additur order from a remittitur order? Note that in the case of a remittitur, the party seeking appellate review—the plaintiff—was victorious at trial and continues to retain an award of damages while in the case of additur the party seeking appellate review is the defendant, who lost at trial as well as on the additur motion. Is that a proper basis of distinction, for purposes of appealability? How relevant is the fact that any appeal from a remittitur can challenge only the propriety of remittitur in that particular case, while an appeal from an additur challenges what is unambiguously an unconstitutional order by the trial court?

Note that where a trial court has, purportedly through the use of remittitur, denied an entire award of punitive damages, an appeals court may view the trial court's decision as a judgment as a matter of law, and therefore appealable. See Hill v. Marshall, 962 F.2d 1209 (6th Cir.1992).

5.   On occasion, the federal courts allow a trial court to increase the amount of an award, distinguishing the increase from the unconstitutional practice of additur. For example, in Gibeau v. Nellis, 18 F.3d 107 (2d Cir.1994), the court held that nominal damages had to be awarded in a civil rights case pursuant to § 1983 where liability had been found by the jury, even though the jury awarded no damages. The court reached this conclusion, despite its recognition that, under *Dimick*, "a federal court's increase of a jury award would constitute impermissible additur where it would violate the Seventh Amendment right to a jury trial." Id. at 110. The court found *Dimick* inapplicable, because its decision that nominal damages had to be awarded was compelled by substantive law. For a contrary decision, holding that *Dimick* precludes reversal of a jury's failure to award nominal damages in a civil rights case, see Walker v. Anderson Electrical Connectors, 944 F.2d 841 (11th Cir.1991). For another example of an appellate court's authorization of a trial court's increase in a jury's award despite the unconstitutionality of the additur practice, see Roman v. Western Mfg., Inc., 691 F.3d 686 (5th Cir. 2012) (trial court's increase in damages for medical expenses from jury's award of $15,000 to an amount in excess of $168,000 did not violate Seventh Amendment's reexamination clause because the damages were uncontested, the correct figure was divined as a matter of law and plaintiff was not made to choose between increase in damage award and new trial).

6.   In his dissent in *Dimick*, Justice Stone argues that the power to determine the upper and lower limits of acceptable verdicts is implicit in the power to set aside the verdict of a jury and grant a retrial. Is this "greater includes the lesser" argument persuasive? Would it justify a judge's decision to instruct the jury on the upper and lower limits of acceptable recoveries during a second trial? If so, should the judge so instruct the jury in the first trial?

7.   Is there some reason why the jury's mistake about the amount of damages should be peculiarly vulnerable to meddling after-the-fact by the judge? Should judges be allowed to change verdicts to reflect other disagreements with the jury's decision? Consider Akermanis v. Sea-Land Serv., Inc., 688 F.2d 898 (2d Cir.1982), where the jury determined that plaintiff's contributory negligence was a four percent cause of the accident for which it found plaintiff had suffered damages totalling $528,000. On defendant's motion for a new trial, the judge found no fault with the jury's measurement of damages, but concluded that the four percent figure for plaintiff's responsibility was "clear and serious error." Finding that 25 percent would be more appropriate, the trial judge granted defendant's motion conditioned on reduction in the verdict to reflect the increase of plaintiff's responsibility to 25 percent. Plaintiff accepted.

The court of appeals held that this procedure was invalid under Dimick v. Schiedt:

> [W]e note a fundamental difference between the use of remittitur to decrease a determination of damages and its use here to increase a contributory negligence percentage. Though both have the same ultimate consequence of reducing the amount of the judgment that

the plaintiff is invited to accept as the price of avoiding a new trial, the means by which the reduction is accomplished differ in a way that is critical to determining the lawfulness of the technique. A conditional reduction of a damage calculation leaves in the judgment a portion of what the jury awarded, a circumstance that the Supreme Court considered crucial to its willingness to permit remittitur while rejecting additur in *Dimick*. In this case, however, the conditional adjustment of the contributory negligence percentage inserts into the judgment something beyond what the jury found: a conclusion that the plaintiff's negligence was responsible for a greater share of the accident than the jury had thought. In *Dimick,* the four dissenters thought it was needlessly artificial to deny a trial judge the authority to condition a new trial order on payment of an additur while permitting him to use the device of remittitur. In either circumstance, they argued, the judge is simply conditioning the new trial order on the minimum adjustment necessary to render the verdict within the bounds of reasonableness. But their view did not prevail. We are therefore bound to apply the rationale of the *Dimick* majority, which, as we understand it, precludes any adjustment that extends a jury's finding, even if that extension results in a reduced monetary judgment.

Does this case correctly read *Dimick?* Would the *Dimick* dissenters have approved what the judge did in this case?

8.   *Determining when remittitur is appropriate*: As is the case in ruling on a motion for a judgment as a matter of law, a trial court is not permitted to usurp the jury's factfinding function merely because the court would have awarded less had it been the factfinder. Rather, according to one court, "[r]emittitur is appropriate only when the error in the verdict results from a specific misconception on the part of the jury and can be mechanically corrected without resolving a disputed issue of fact." Control Terminals, Inc. v. Airline Management Group, Inc., 931 F.2d 62 (10th Cir.1991). Another phrasing of the test is whether the amount of damages found by the jury is so excessive and exorbitant as to show passion and prejudice on the part of the jury. See, e.g., Gorsalitz v. Olin Mathieson Chemical Corp., 429 F.2d 1033 (5th Cir.1970). It has been suggested that the use of remittitur has increased in recent years. See Comment, Appellate Control of Excessive Jury Verdicts Since Gasperini v. Center for Humanities: From Nisi Prius Courts to "Gasperini Hearings," 66 U.Cin. L. Rev. 1323 (1998) (referring to "[t]he current unbridled use of remittitur by federal trial and appellate courts)." For a critical view of this development, see Dooley, Our Jury, Our Selves: The Power, Perception and Politics of the Civil Jury, 80 Cornell L. Rev. 325 (1995); Comment, Gasperini v. Center for Humanities: Clarifying Federal Appellate Review or Judicial License in Tort Reform?, 32 New England L. Rev. 853 (1998).

A number of federal courts have sought to determine whether a jury award is excessive through resort to so-called "comparability" analysis, i.e., reviewing damage awards by comparison to amounts awarded in other similar cases. See, e.g., Mathie v. Fries, 121 F.3d 808, 813–14 (2d Cir.1997) ("the determination of whether a damage award exceeds a reasonable range 'should not be made in a vacuum,' but should include consideration of the amounts awarded in other, comparable cases."); Hetzel v. County of Prince William, 89 F.3d 169, 173 (4th Cir. 1996) (instructing district court, upon remand, to examine awards in cases "which are comparable to what would be an appropriate award"). Cf. Gasperini v. Center for Humanities, Inc., 518 U.S. 415 (1996), infra p. 1014. According to one commentator, use of comparability analysis "has become a widespread practice among federal courts." Elsevier, Out-of-Line: Federal Courts Using Comparability to Review Damage Awards, 33 Georgia L. Rev. 243 (1998).

The same commentator refers to the use of comparability analysis as "a highly suspect, if not unconstitutional, practice." Id. at 244. He suggests that "in practice a comparability analysis can be easily manipulated, thereby allowing a court to justify its assertion that a damage award is excessive." Id. at 257. Pursuant to the analysis used by the Court in Dimick v. Schiedt, how would a court properly go about deciding whether a particular version of remittitur practice violated the Seventh Amendment?

9.   *Deciding the size of the remittitur*: Once a court decides that a remittitur is appropriate because the jury's award of damages is excessive, it must decide the amount of damages to be reduced. There are three basic methods for determining this amount: by reducing the award to (1) the minimum amount the jury might have awarded, (2) the amount the court itself believes should have been awarded, and (3) the maximum amount that a reasonable jury could have awarded. It has been argued that "[i]t is questionable whether an actual measuring rod can be constructed" and that "it may be that judicial corrections of jury awards in this area can only reflect the personal predictions of particular judges or groups of judges." Comment, Remittitur Review: Constitutionality and Efficiency in Liquidated and Unliquidated Damage Cases, 43 U.Chi.L.Rev. 376, 394 (1976). See also Carlin, Remittiturs and Additurs, 49 W.Va.L.Q. 1 (1942).

A leading treatise asserts that the "maximum recovery" rule is the only standard that "has any reasonable claim of being consistent with the Seventh Amendment." 11 C. Wright, A. Miller & M. Kane, Federal Practice & Procedure § 2815. Do you agree? It has been argued that "[t]he maximum recovery rule would * * * be the most effective [standard] in reducing caseloads." Note, Remittitur Practice in the Federal Courts, 76 Colum.L.Rev. 299, 309 (1976). Why? See id. The same commentator contends, however, that the "maximum recovery" rule is "the most inequitable in terms of fairness to the defendant." Id. Why? See Note, Constitutional Law—Right to Jury Trial—Judicial Use of Additurs in Correcting Insufficient Damage Verdicts, 21 Va.L.Rev. 666, 672 (1935). In defense of the "maximum recovery" rule, the court in Earl v. Bouchard Transportation Co., Inc., 917 F.2d 1320 (2d Cir.1990), argued that "[t]o obtain a 'fair' judgment on damages in a case such as this, the law has traditionally deferred to the decision of a jury of laymen drawn from the community at large, and not to the 'seasoned judgment' of the trial judge." Id. at 1329.

The intermediate standard was forcefully advocated by Professor J.W. Moore, who reasoned that the standard "gives the defendant the benefit of the full supervisory power of the trial court, and yet the plaintiff still has his option to refuse to remit. And it moderately serves the function of remittitur aimed at avoiding the judicial waste of a new trial, for the plaintiff still has a strong incentive to remit." 6A Moore's Federal Practice ¶ 59.08[7] (2d ed. 1989). Professor Moore attacked the maximum recovery standard, because if "the trial court fixes the residue at the lowest amount that it would permit a verdict to stand, this constitutes a considerable intrusion upon the jury's function and the plaintiff's incentive in remitting is reduced to a minimum." Id.

Why might a court employ the "minimum recovery" standard? See Meissner v. Papas, 35 F.Supp. 676, 677 (E.D.Wis.1940) ("in order to protect the party obliged to pay against a judge's assessment of damages, the court determines from the evidence the lowest amount that an impartial jury properly instructed would reasonably award"). Might a defendant properly support use of such a rule by arguing "that but for the procedure of remittitur he would be entitled to a new trial"? Note, Remittitur Practice in the Federal Courts, 76 Colum.L.Rev. 299, 309 (1976).

10. Recall the discussion of pain and suffering awards in note 5 after Carey v. Piphus, supra p. 69. Is this sort of compensation inherently resistant to judicial scrutiny because it depends so largely on the jury's determination of a proper amount of compensation? Does the prospect of judicial revision of pain and suffering awards remove some concerns about the untrammeled nature of jury discretion in the area?

Empirical research indicates that post-trial revisions of the amount awarded significantly reduce the amount collected in cases where plaintiffs win verdicts. See generally M. Shanley & M. Peterson, Post-Trial Adjustments to Jury Awards (1987). Examining all plaintiff verdicts, this study of state courts in California and Illinois found that the amount actually paid plaintiff was lower than the amount awarded plaintiff in 25% of cases involving plaintiff verdicts. Most such reductions were the result of settlements, but nearly a quarter were by court action, which tended to occur more often in cases with high verdicts. As to those, the authors report that "[v]erdicts reduced by the courts involved the largest verdicts and quite substantial reductions in jury awards. The average verdict in such trials is nearly $780,000, but the average payment by defendants is less than half that amount." Id. at 45. Does this evidence on judges' actual reductions indicate that efforts to devise caps for such awards are unnecessary?

11. *Partial new trial*: Another new trial possibility is that the trial court may conclude that a new trial is appropriate only as to certain issues, such as the amount of damages. In Gasoline Products Co. v. Champlin Refining Co., 283 U.S. 494 (1931), the Court stated that a partial new trial "may not properly be resorted to unless it clearly appears that the issue to be retried is so distinct

and separable from the others that a trial of it alone may be had without injustice." What sort of injustice might be relevant? In *Dimick*, would a retrial limited to the amount of damages be proper?

4.   THE NATURE OF THE VERDICT

WHITLOCK V. JACKSON

United States District Court, Southern District of Indiana, 1991
754 F.Supp. 1394

McKINNEY, DISTRICT JUDGE.

This action was brought by Eileen Whitlock, as administratrix of the estate of her brother, Richard Gaisor. The suit alleged that on August 20, 1986, the defendants arrested Gaisor and inflicted serious injuries that caused his death. The suit alleged numerous violations of both state and federal laws, and sought compensatory and punitive damages. Following a trial, the jury returned a verdict in favor of the plaintiff and against the defendants for the sum of $29,700.

The plaintiff now argues that inconsistencies in the jury's answers to special interrogatories require an additur or, in the alternative, a new trial. The plaintiff's motion raises two broad issues. First, did the plaintiff's failure to object to the alleged inconsistencies constitute a waiver, thus preventing review? Second, if no waiver occurred, are there in fact inconsistencies in the interrogatories that require a new trial?

A. WAIVER

The defendants assert that the plaintiff's failure to object to the allegedly inconsistent answers to interrogatories prior to the jury's discharge constitutes waiver of the issue. In support of this argument, the defendants cite Strauss v. Stratojac Corp., 810 F.2d 679 (7th Cir.1987), wherein the Seventh Circuit held that the failure to raise a timely objection did indeed constitute a waiver pursuant to Rule 49(b).[2] Citation to *Strauss*, however, presupposes either that the special interrogatories in the case at bar were submitted under Rule 49(b), or that the waiver doctrine is equally applicable under both Rule 49(a) and (b).[*]

Rule 49(a) governs "special verdicts," and states in relevant part that district courts may require a jury to return "a special written finding upon each issue of fact . . . or it may use such other method of submitting the issues and requiring the written findings thereon as it deems most appropriate." Rule 49(b) governs "general verdicts accompanied by answers

---

[2]   In addition, the court in *Strauss* qualified its holding somewhat, stating, "We realize that, at some future date, we might encounter a case where the inconsistency in the special interrogatories is so obvious that it would be proper to hold that the trial judge had an independent responsibility to act despite trial counsel's silence."

[*]   The rule language has been slightly revised.—Eds.

to interrogatories," and provides in part that a district court "may submit to the jury, together with the appropriate forms for a general verdict, written interrogatories upon one or more issues of fact. . . ."

In the case at bar the Court did not clearly indicate whether it was proceeding under Rule 49(a) or (b). The "verdict form" submitted to the jury in this cause contained numerous specialized questions, requiring either a "yes" or "no" answer or an amount of damages. However, no actual verdict was given to the jury, and the "final verdict" in this case was completed by the Court.

In Bonin v. Tour West, Inc., 896 F.2d 1260, 1262 (10th Cir.1990), the district court used a verdict form that mirrors the form used in the case at bar. The verdict form in *Bonin* required the jury to answer "yes" or "no" to questions regarding negligence, proportion fault among the parties, and then assess damages. The defendant in *Bonin* argued that the plaintiffs waived their right to contest any inconsistencies in the jury's answers because no objection was made prior to the discharge of the jury. In reviewing the verdict form, the court of appeals stated, "The court, here, did not submit a general verdict coupled with written interrogatories under Rule 49(b) to the jury. Rather, the court gave the jury a special verdict in the form described in Rule 49(a)."

Similarly, the procedure employed by this Court closely parallels the procedure employed under Rule 49(a). This is especially true in that no "general verdict" was given to the jury, and that Rule 49(a) provides the more flexible approach whereby a district court may require "special written finding(s) upon each issue of fact" or it may use "such other method . . . as it deems most appropriate."

While the need to distinguish between Rule 49(a) and (b) may appear inconsequential, it is in fact critical. As the court went on to say in *Bonin*: Unlike Rule 49(b), Rule 49(a) does not contain a specific direction to send the jury back for further deliberations in the event of an inconsistency in the jury's answers. Therefore, Rule 49(a) does not require a party to object to the inconsistencies in order to preserve his right to challenge the inconsistencies in a subsequent motion or on appeal. Id. (citation omitted).

Thus, the defendants' reflexive citation to *Strauss* and the Rule 49(b) standard is incorrect if the *Bonin* analysis is applied in the Seventh Circuit. Unfortunately, this issue has not been clearly resolved. In Bates v. Jean, 745 F.2d 1146, 1150 (7th Cir.1984), the Seventh Circuit ruled that a pro se plaintiff who failed to object to inconsistent verdicts under Rule 49(a) was not precluded from arguing inconsistency on appeal. However, the plaintiff's pro se status was the motivation for the appellate court's ruling, not the application of Rule 49(a).

In fact, the *Bates* court noted that the circuit courts of appeal are split on their interpretation of the waiver doctrine under Rule 49(a), and expressly refused to decide the issue. * * *

The split among the circuits is apparent. * * *

Absent a clear directive on the waiver issue from the Seventh Circuit, this Court is instructed to give "respectful consideration" to the decisions of other circuits. Given the split in the circuits, this consideration requires choosing one alternative over another. For several reasons, this Court is compelled to reject waiver under Rule 49(a).

First, the greater weight of authority supports rejecting the waiver approach. The majority of the circuits so hold, and it is respectfully submitted that those circuits holding otherwise have done so on insufficient authority. * * * The second reason compelling this Court to reject waiver as a bar involves the Seventh Amendment. It has been said that the Seventh Amendment creates a "delicate balance" between judge and jury which must be maintained, as explained in Mercer v. Long Mfg. N.C., Inc., 671 F.2d 946, 948 n. 1 (5th Cir.1982). The *Mercer* court stated:

> The legal error resulting from the entry of a judgment based on inconsistent special interrogatories is one which undermines the validity and integrity of the judgment and may, in fact, run afoul of the Seventh Amendment by allowing the District Court to usurp the jury's function. The Seventh Amendment creates a delicate balance.

Finally, the language of Rule 49(a) and (b) differs in a pivotal way, thus supporting waiver only under Rule 49(b) practice. Rule 49(b) states in relevant part, "When the answers are inconsistent with each other and one or more is likewise inconsistent with the general verdict, judgment shall not be entered, but the court shall return the jury for further consideration of its answers and verdict or shall order a new trial."* Rule 49(a) is devoid of any direction that the jury shall be returned "for further consideration." Given that Rule 49(a) does not provide for this procedure, it is difficult to understand how the failure to object waives any rights under the Rule.

In commenting on practice under Rule 49(a), one scholar has flatly stated, "It would appear that a party does not waive his right to object to inconsistencies in the special interrogatories on appeal if he does not object at trial." 5A J. Moore & J. Lucas, Moore's Federal Practice § 49.03[4] (2d ed. 1990). For all the foregoing reasons, this Court agrees. Accordingly, the plaintiff has not waived the right to challenge alleged inconsistencies in the special interrogatories.

---

*   This rule language has been revised slightly.—Eds.

B. ALLEGED INCONSISTENCIES

Having found no waiver occurred, the Court must address the plaintiff's claim of inconsistencies in the special interrogatories.

This cause was put to the jury against three defendants: Indiana State Police Sgt. Donald Jackson, and Marion County Sheriff Deputies Glenn Thompson and Terrence Cress. Recovery was sought against defendant Jackson on the basis of the Fourth Amendment (unreasonable excessive force in a seizure), the Fifth and Fourteenth Amendments (denial of medical treatment in violation of due process), wrongful death, and assault and battery. Recovery was sought against defendants Cress and Thompson under the Fifth and Fourteenth Amendments (excessive force in violation of due process), wrongful death, and assault and battery.

The jury declined to hold the defendants liable for any constitutional violations, nor did the jury find the defendants' acts to have proximately caused the death of Gaisor, who died from a ruptured aneurism. Instead, the jury found the defendants liable for battery only, and awarded compensatory damages of $3,700 against Jackson, $1,500 against Cress, and $2,000 against Thompson. Additionally, the jury awarded punitive damages of $10,000 against Jackson, $4,000 against Cress, and $8,500 against Thompson. Judgment was entered accordingly.

The plaintiff's motion argues an inconsistency exists in that the jury awarded punitive damages, but failed to find a violation of constitutional proportions. The plaintiff argues that the "verdict form is inconsistent in that it must have simultaneously found that the actions of the defendants violated the constitutional rights of the plaintiff."

The starting point for resolving this issue is that in considering a motion for a new trial the Court is required to harmonize the answers on a special verdict if possible under a fair reading of them. In addition, the Court must search for a reasonable way to read the verdicts as expressing a coherent view of the case, and if there is any way to view a case that makes the jury's answers to the special interrogatories consistent, they must be resolved that way even if strained.

In the case at bar, the plaintiff essentially argues that it was inconsistent for the jury to have found that the defendants battered the plaintiff, and that the defendants should be liable for punitive damages, but not find the defendants liable for torts of a constitutional magnitude. The Court disagrees, as demonstrated by reviewing the jury's findings as to each defendant.

As for defendant Jackson, the jury found his conduct constituted battery, but declined to find unreasonable excessive force in a seizure (Fourth Amendment), or a denial of medical treatment violative of due process (Fifth and Fourteenth Amendments). The defendant correctly points out that the evidence supports a finding that Jackson struck Gaisor after Gaisor was handcuffed and in police custody. Thus, it was not inconsistent for the jury to find that the seizure was lawfully conducted, but that thereafter Jackson battered Gaisor.

This analysis relies on the premise that the Fourth Amendment protects against unreasonable force during an arrest, but that after the arrest has been effected the Fourth Amendment drops out and Fifth Amendment substantive due process protections are triggered. * * *

Thus, no legal reason prevented the jury from denying relief on Fourth Amendment grounds if it found that Gaisor was battered after his seizure was effected. Given that the jury's conclusions can be so reconciled, the Court will not inquire further. If the plaintiff had sought recovery from Jackson on the basis of Fifth Amendment substantive due process for use of unreasonably excessive force, an instruction reflecting this fact should have been submitted, and an objection should have been made if the Court failed to offer the tendered instruction.

It was not inconsistent for the jury to find a state law battery violation, and to additionally find that the defendants did not violate the Constitution by using unreasonably excessive force. A plaintiff's constitutional protection "is not co-extensive with that afforded the common law tort action for battery." Santiago v. Yarde, 487 F.Supp. 52, 54 (S.D.N.Y. 1980). The often-stated rule applicable here is that not every wrong rises to the level of a constitutional violation for the purposes of 42 U.S.C. § 1983.

The imposition of punitive damages in this case presents a much closer question, but does not alter the result. The punitive damages instruction given to the jury allowed for the imposition of punitive damages for various alternative reasons, including "malice." The instructions and special interrogatories allowed the jury to find the defendants intentionally touched Gaisor in a rude manner, and that this was done with malice, yet determine that this touching did not involve unreasonably reckless and excessive force. Such a determination is not necessarily inconsistent given the conflicting nature of the testimony. The number of times the defendants struck Gaisor was in dispute, as was the amount of force used. Given that this Court must make every effort to view the jury's answers to the special interrogatories as consistent, the jury could properly have believed the defendants' version that only minimal force was used, and that reckless and excessive force was not involved.

The answers to interrogatories imply that the jury found the force used on Gaisor constituted battery and involved malice. This is not the same as finding the force was constitutionally excessive. The fact that the jury found the defendants' acts were not the proximate cause of Gaisor's death speaks loudly on this point. Accordingly, the jury could have found that Thompson and Cress each struck a blow to Gaisor, and did so maliciously, yet concluded that such conduct did not involve reckless and excessive force. In other words, evidence of a single blow of modest force delivered with malicious intent might not carry the day on a claim that the defendants' conduct on the whole involved reckless and excessive force.

Furthermore, the jury was instructed that it could award punitive damages "to deter others from like offenses." Therefore, the award of punitive damages in this case could have been rooted in a desire to deter other police officers from engaging in similar batteries. Arguably this "deterrent" aspect of punitive damages involves a reason for awarding punitive damages, which comes into play only after the jury has found malice or the like. Nevertheless, the jury was entitled to award punitive damages as a deterrent to others without finding the defendants' conduct constitutionally prohibited.

Thus, it is speculation to graft upon the jury's imposition of punitive damages the additional conclusion that Gaisor's constitutional rights were violated. To so hold, in view of the plaintiff's argument, would have required instructing the jury that if it found that Gaisor was battered, and if it found that punitive damages were appropriate, it also must find Fifth and Fourteenth Amendment violations. The plaintiff has not presented this Court with any supporting authority for such an instruction.

Lost in the plaintiff's argument for a new trial is an understanding of the message contained in the jury's verdict. The plaintiff's complaint sought recovery on the basis of alleged constitutional violations, wrongful death, and state tort claims. The jury returned a verdict in the plaintiff's favor on the battery claim only, plus a modest award of punitive damages. The evidence showed that on the night of Gaisor's arrest, he had been drinking, he disobeyed a police directive to discard a whiskey bottle, and was combative with police, both at the time of his arrest and later at the hospital.

Accordingly, in awarding approximately $30,000 in damages, including an award of punitive damages, the jury stated that Gaisor had been wronged, and that the defendants acted improperly. However, the jury verdict is just as significant for what it did not say. It did not say that Gaisor's constitutional rights were violated, or that the defendants were responsible for Gaisor's death. The answers to interrogatories reflect this fact and are not inconsistent.

C. CONCLUSION

In conclusion, the Court finds that the plaintiff did not waive the right to object to any alleged inconsistencies in the special interrogatories. However, the Court has reviewed the jury's responses to these interrogatories and for the reasons discussed herein finds that they may be viewed as consistent. Accordingly, the plaintiff's motion for additur or for a new trial is DENIED.

NOTES AND QUESTIONS

1.   The practice set out in Rule 49(a) is known as the "special verdict." It was developed as an alternative to the general verdict, under which the jury provides nothing more than its ultimate verdict. Under the procedure set out in Rule 49(a), the judge propounds a series of written questions to the jury about the facts of the case and enters a verdict based on her assessment of those answers. In the words of one court: "If the jury announces only its ultimate conclusions, it returns an ordinary general verdict; if it makes factual findings in addition to the ultimate legal conclusions, it returns a general verdict with interrogatories [provided for in Rule 49(b)]. If it returns only factual findings, leaving the court to determine the ultimate legal result, it returns a special verdict [pursuant to Rule 49(a)]." Zhang v. American Gem Seafoods, Inc., 339 F.3d 1020, 1031 (9th Cir. 2003).

What is the rationale for Rule 49(a)? Is it a good idea? See Brodin, Accuracy, Efficiency, and Accountability in the Litigation Process—The Case for the Fact Verdict, 59 U. Cin. L. Rev. 15, 22 (1990), suggesting that routine use of the special verdict "has the significant potential for enhancing the reliability and efficiency of our judicial dispute resolution process." See also Sutton, A More Rational Approach to Complex Civil Litigation in the Federal Courts: The Special Jury, 1990 U. Chi. Legal F. 575; Faulkner, Using the Special Verdict to Manage Complex Cases and Avoid Compromise Verdicts, 21 Ariz. St.L.J. 297 (1989).

Note that use of "Rule 49(a) is permissive, not obligatory." Santos v. Posadas De Puerto Rico Associates, Inc., 452 F.3d 59, 65 (1st Cir. 2006). "Consequently, a district court's decision not to adopt a special verdict form proposed by a party is subject to review only for abuse of discretion." Id.

2.   Does Rule 49(a) reflect a fundamental mistrust of the jury system? If so, in what way does it control the jury more than the general verdict procedure does? Justices Black and Douglas, strong supporters of the civil jury, characterized the special verdict as "but another means utilized by courts to weaken the constitutional power of juries and to vest judges with more power to decide cases according to their own judgments." Minority Statement of Justices Black and Douglas, Opposing the 1963 Amendments to the Federal Rules of Civil Procedure, 374 U.S. 861, 865 (1963). The jurist traditionally associated with support of the special verdict procedure is Judge Jerome Frank, long a critic of the jury system. Consider his views in Courts on Trial: Myth and Reality in American Justice 141 (1949):

> A special verdict would seem to do away with some of the most objectionable features of trial by jury. The division of functions between jury and judge is apparently assured, the one attending to the facts alone, the other to the legal rules alone. The jury seems, by this device, to be shorn of its power to ignore the rules or to make rules to suit itself. * * * The finding of facts, says Sunderland, "is much better done by means of the special verdict. Every advantage which the jury is popularly supposed to have over the [judge] as a

trier of facts is retained, with the very great additional advantage that the analysis and separation of the facts in the case which the court and the attorney must necessarily effect in employing the special verdict, materially reduce the chance of error. It is easy to make mistakes in dealing at large with aggregates of facts. The special verdict compels detailed consideration. But above all it enables the public, the parties and the court to see what the jury has really done. * * * The morale of the jury also is aided by throwing off the cloak of secrecy, for only through publicity is there developed the proper feeling of responsibility in public servants. So far, then, as the facts go, they can be much more effectively, conveniently, and usefully tried by abandoning the general verdict. * * * The special verdict is devised for the express purpose of escaping the sham of false appearances."

For an argument that special verdicts simplify issues so much that when the judge moves to apply the law to the jury's factfinding, the judge may reach legal conclusions which the jury would have rejected, see Iuliano, Jury Voting Paradoxes, 113 Mich. L. Rev. 405 (2014).

3. Do you see any disadvantages of the special verdict? Consider the argument in C. Wright & M. Kane, Law of Federal Courts 674 (7th ed. 2011):

The use of special verdicts is intended to emphasize the facts, prevent the jury from acting on bias, and make the law more scientific. Little is gained, however, by making the law more scientific if, in the process, it becomes harder to achieve substantial justice. Some of the most famous students of the judicial process have argued that one of the purposes of the jury system is to permit the jury to temper strict rules of law by the demands and necessities of substantial justice, thereby adding a much needed element of flexibility. Those who share this conception of the role of the jury rightly fear that it will be limited or defeated by the special verdict practice * * *.

Consider also the response to this type of argument by Judge Frank:

The general-verdict jury trial, in practice, negates that which the dogma of precise legal predictability maintains to be the nature of law. A better instrument could scarcely be imagined for achieving uncertainty, capriciousness, lack of uniformity, disregard of former decisions—utter unpredictability.

* * *

[T]o preserve the self-delusion of legal fixity, certainty and impartiality, in many cases we hand over the determination of legal rights and liabilities to the whims of twelve men casually gathered together.

The demand for an impossible legal stability, resulting from an infantile longing to find a father-substitute in the law, thus actually leads, in the use of the jury, to a capriciousness that is unnecessary and socially harmful.

J. Frank, Law and the Modern Mind 186–92 (1930).

Should the jury be thought to possess authority to "nullify" unjust legal rules by means of the general verdict? Consider the following argument: "Many may applaud when a jury, under the protection and guise of its general verdict, effectively repeals the law of contributory negligence and replaces it with a crude form of case-by-case, comparative negligence. Perhaps many of those same individuals, however, would be outraged by a jury's blatant disregard of a judge's instructions in a civil rights action because the jurors do not agree with the application of section 1983 to a suit by a black against a local police officer. Yet if we accept the jury's power to disregard the law and do what it deems to be 'justice' in the former, does it not become intellectually awkward to deny it in the latter? Even if the answer is no, it must be realized that if we are to allow the former it is, as a practical matter, virtually impossible to prevent the latter." Redish, Seventh Amendment Right to Jury Trial: A Study in the Irrationality of Rational Decision Making, 70 Nw.U.L.Rev. 486, 508 (1975).

4.   Whatever their impact on jury nullification, special verdicts may be especially appropriate in complex cases: "Special verdicts reduce jury confusion in factually and legally complex cases by identifying and organizing the issues in the case and by simplifying the instructions given to the jury." Note, Resolving Inconsistencies in Federal Special Verdicts, 53 Ford.L.Rev. 1089, 1090–91 (1985). Several federal courts have agreed. In SCM Corp. v. Xerox Corp., 463 F.Supp. 983 (D.Conn.1978), affirmed and remanded, 645 F.2d 1195 (2d Cir.1981), cert. denied, 455 U.S. 1016 (1982), an antitrust suit involving 215 days of evidence presentation, the trial judge stated that "the sheer volume and complexity of the evidence necessitated focusing the jury's attention on specific issues to be sure that orderly decision-making occurred." Id. at 988.

5.   Other than possible interferences with the jury's "law-making" function, does the special verdict have any disadvantages? Is there any value to cloaking jury decision-making in secrecy? Are there any risks to finding out more about the jury's reasoning process? Consider Sunderland, Verdicts, General and Special, 29 Yale L.J. 253, 262 (1920):

The real objection to the special verdict is that it is an honest portrayal of the truth, and the truth is too awkward a thing to fit the technical demands of the record. The record must be absolutely flawless, but such a result is possible only by concealing, not by excluding mistakes. This is the great technical merit of the general verdict. It covers up all the shortcomings which frail human nature is unable to eliminate from the trial of a case. In the abysmal abstraction of the general verdict concrete details are swallowed up, and the eye of the law, searching anxiously for the realization of logical perfection, is satisfied. In short, the general verdict is valued for what it does, not for what it is. It serves as the great procedural opiate, which draws the curtain upon human errors and soothes us with the assurance that we have attained the unattainable.

6.   What is the difference between Rules 49(a) and 49(b)? See Lavoie v. Pacific Press & Shear Co., 975 F.2d 48, 53 (2d Cir.1992): "The distinction between the two provisions is that under Rule 49(a) the jury answers primarily factual questions for the benefit of the trial court which then applies the law to those answers. Under Rule 49(b), the jury after being fully instructed answers the interrogatories, renders a general verdict and the trial court enters judgment on the jury's verdict." Why might a judge prefer to use Rule 49(b), instead of Rule 49(a)?

Rule 49(b) has been the subject of heavy criticism. Judge John R. Brown has argued that "Rule 49(b) offers, so far as I can see, nothing but trouble because it seeks to mold a general verdict and special answers with the high likelihood of conflict which extinguishes both. Rule 49(a), on the other hand, if used with skill and resourcefulness, melds the general *charge* (not verdict) with the special answers to specific controlling issues of fact or legal fact." Brown, Federal Special Verdicts: The Doubt Eliminator, 44 F.R.D. 338, 339–40 (1967).

Lawyers may regard the decision whether to favor use of Rule 49(b) special interrogatories tactically, depending on their confidence that they will win:

> In planning, recognize that the possibility of an inconsistency is highest when the jury is given special interrogatories, somewhat lower when there are multiple defendants and claims, and nonexistent when the jury returns a single, general verdict. Some cagey trial lawyers (whose identities will be protected here) will take this into account when deciding whether to seek special interrogatories or a single, general verdict. If you are confident of a win, a general verdict eliminates arguments about any inconsistency. If you sense a disaster, numerous special interrogatories afford more potential for inconsistency. You might want to think about this and plan ahead.

Douglas, What to Do When the Jury Gets it Wrong, 33 Litigation 20 (Fall 2006). Does this provide an explanation why some judges would resist using special interrogatories?

7.   What if the inconsistency is not between jury answers to interrogatories and the jury verdict, but rather between the jury's verdict and unsolicited written statements included by the jury along with its answers? See Riddle v. Tex-Fin, Inc., 719 F. Supp. 2d 742, 750 (S.D. Tex. 2010) (recognizing that courts are permitted "to consider unsolicited jury answers or statements if they cast doubt on the unqualified nature of the verdict.")

8.   *Whitlock* deals with the issue of whether a plaintiff's failure to object to allegedly inconsistent jury answers to interrogatories constitutes waiver of that objection. The court in *Whitlock* sides with those courts that have found

the waiver principle, which is expressly incorporated into Rule 49(b), inapplicable to cases employing Rule 49(a). As to the role of waiver under Rule 49(b), see, e.g., Diamond Shamrock Corp. v. Zinke & Trumbo, Ltd., 791 F.2d 1416 (10th Cir.1986). What are the competing considerations? Is there some basis for finding waiver under Rule 49(b) when the party fails to object to the inconsistencies prior to dismissal of the jury that is inapplicable to the situation under Rule 49(a)? Does the text of the rule resolve the waiver issue under Rule 49(a)?

9. A different waiver issue may also arise concerning the relationship between Rules 49(a) and 49(b). Note that Rule 49(a)(3) explicitly provides that "[a] party waives the right to jury trial on any issue of fact raised by the pleadings or evidence but not submitted to the jury unless, before the jury retires, the party demands its submission to the jury." Rule 49(b) does not contain a similar waiver provision. See Bradway v. Gonzales, 26 F.3d 313 (2d Cir.1994).

10. When, as in *Whitlock*, the answers are alleged to be inconsistent, "jury verdicts must be interpreted so as to avoid inconsistency wherever possible * * *." Freeman v. Chicago Park District, 189 F.3d 613, 615 (7th Cir. 1999). Courts believe that they "should do what we can to save the verdict against the spectre of inconsistency." American Casualty Co. v. B. Cianciolo, Inc., 987 F.2d 1302 (7th Cir. 1993).

11. The use of special verdicts or interrogatories poses problems as to how narrow or broad the questions should be. In Texas, where the jury is not allowed to render a general verdict but must answer questions that the judge will then convert into a verdict, an ordinary case once generated dozens of issues, with a separate question as to each claim or defense. In negligence cases, for example, the jury was required to answer as to each act of negligence alleged (e.g., speeding, failure to apply brakes, failure to keep a proper lookout, etc.), forcing them to agree on the specific act of negligence. All answers had to be consistent, and it is not surprising that the practice was favored by the defense bar. For an argument against requiring unanimity on such specifics by a present Supreme Court Justice, see Ginsburg, Special Findings and Jury Unanimity in Federal Courts, 65 Colum. L. Rev.256 (1965). However, "broad-form" submission of questions is now required in Texas (which is consistent with the usual practice in federal courts under Rule 49). See Lemos v. Montez, 680 S.W.2d 798, 801 (Tex.1984); Tex.R.Civ.P. 277. Use of questions has the advantage over a general verdict of guiding the jury's deliberations and obtaining precise answers that may be necessary pursuant to the substantive law, as in the case of comparative negligence or responsibility. Thus, the Texas Pattern Jury Charge book has suggested the following questions for a basic automobile negligence case [1 Tex. Pattern Jury Charges §§ 4.1, 4.3, 8.2 (2003)]:

> Did the negligence, if any, of those named below proximately cause the [occurrence] [injury] [occurrence or injury] in question?

a.   Don Davis [defendant]   _____

b.   Paul Payne [plaintiff]   _____

c.   Sam Settlor [if plaintiff has previously settled with another person claimed to be responsible]   _____

d.   Responsible Ray [a responsible third party]   _____

e.   Connie Contributor [a contribution defendant]   _____

What percent of the negligence that caused the [*occurrence*] [*injury*] [*occurrence or injury*] do you find to be attributable to each of those listed below and found by you, in your answer to Question _____ [*4.1 or other applicable liability question*], to have been negligent?

a.   Don Davis   _____%

b.   Paul Payne   _____%

c.   Sam Settlor   _____%

d.   Responsible Ray   _____%

       Total   _____100%

What sum of money, if paid now in cash, would fairly and reasonably compensate Paul Payne for his injuries, if any, that resulted from the occurrence in question?

Consider the elements of damages listed below and none other. Consider each element separately. Do not award any sum of money on any element if you have otherwise, under some other element, awarded a sum of money for the same loss. That is, do not compensate twice for the same loss, if any. Do not include interest or any amount of damages you find.

a.   Physical pain and mental anguish.

b.   Loss of earning capacity.

c.   Disfigurement.

d.   Physical impairment.

e.   Medical care expenses.

Do not reduce the amounts, if any, in your answers because of the negligence, if any, of *Paul Payne*.

Answer in dollars and cents for damages, if any, that—

       were sustained in the past;   Answer: _____

       in reasonable probability will be sustained in the future.   Answer: _____

5. JUROR IMPEACHMENT OF THE VERDICT

Sopp v. Smith, 377 P.2d 649 (Cal.1963):

SCHAUER, J.

[Plaintiff in a negligence action arising out of an automobile accident sought a new trial on the basis of a juror's affidavit that after all the evidence had been presented, he took a drive to the scene of the accident and tested the claims of some of the witnesses. The trial court denied the motion on the grounds that the affidavit was inadmissible. The California Supreme Court affirmed on the basis of the rule in Kollert v. Cundiff, 329 P.2d 897 Cal. (1958): "It is the general rule in California that affidavits of jurors may not be used to impeach a verdict."]

The *Kollert* case also points out that California recognizes two exceptions to the rule, one created by statute (resort to chance, Code Civ.Proc. § 657, subd. 2), and the other by judicial decision (bias or disqualification of a juror concealed by false answers on *voir dire*), * * * and further emphasizes that "The problem involves the balancing of two conflicting policies. It is, of course, necessary to prevent instability of verdicts, fraud, and harassment of jurors, and, on the other hand, it is desirable to give the losing party relief from wrongful conduct by the jury. * * *" Having thus expressly recognized and considered the conflicting policies, we rejected plaintiffs' plea to create a further exception.

PETERS, J.

I dissent.

The majority, following the rule of stare decisis, adhere to a court created doctrine first announced by Judge Mansfield in Vaise v. Delaval, 1 Term R. 11, 99 Eng.Rep. 944 (K.B.1785). That rule is that affidavits of jurors may not be used to impeach their verdict. The only reason given by the majority, other than stare decisis, is public policy, at best a vague and uncertain guide * * *.

Dean Wigmore has demonstrated to a certainty that before 1785 the rule was well settled that jurors could, as to overt acts showing misconduct, impeach their own verdict. The Dean has also pointed out that the only reason given by Judge Mansfield for adopting the new rule was his belief that under no circumstances should a witness be heard to allege his own turpitude. That doctrine, involving the admissibility of voluntary confessions, has long been overruled in practically all American jurisdictions, including California.

* * *

Wigmore demonstrates to a certainty that there is no reason in law or logic for continuing the rule * * *.

Iowa has taken the lead in liberalizing the Mansfield rule. At least 12 jurisdictions, by judicial decision, have modified the strict Mansfield rule. * * *

The Iowa rule is based upon the distinction between extrinsic or overt acts which may be corroborated or disproved, such as access to improper matter or an illegal method of reaching a verdict, and intrinsic matters which "inhere in the verdict itself" and hence are known only to the individual juror, such as misunderstanding or prejudice. Because matters which "inhere" in the verdict, including the thought processes and motives of the juror in reaching his decision, are not readily capable of being either corroborated or disproved they should be excluded.

* * *

I would hold that as to overt acts of misconduct a juror, on motion for a new trial, may testify to such misconduct, and that the trial court erred in excluding such testimony from its consideration.

PEOPLE V. HUTCHINSON
Supreme Court of California, 1969
455 P.2d 132

TRAYNOR, CHIEF JUSTICE.

[Convicted of possession of marijuana for sale, defendant argued on appeal that there was insufficient evidence to support his conviction and that the trial court committed prejudicial error in refusing to consider a juror's affidavit he offered in support of his motion for a new trial.]

* * *

In support of his motion for a new trial defendant submitted an affidavit of a juror alleging misconduct on the part of the bailiff.[1] The trial

---

[1] "I hereby certify and declare that I was a juror on the above-entitled case and that the following is my recollection of the activities of the bailiff in regard to this case. The Judge stated from the Bench that we would go to dinner at 6:00 p.m., if we had not reached a verdict. At 6:00 p.m. we were not taken to dinner.

"It was not until about 6:30 when the bailiff came in, and at our request. At this time inquiry of him was made as to when we would get to dinner. At this point he replied words to the effect: 'If you go out to eat, you will be locked up overnight.' At some time during the deliberations in the late afternoon, after 6:30, the bailiff came in and said words to this effect: 'If you knew what was going on out there, you would be shivering in your boots.' At one time when he entered, around 7:00, he seemed quite angry and put out. He said words, 'This is it.' We replied, 'Give us a few more minutes and we can come to a verdict.' He gave us about five or ten minutes and said if we had not reached a verdict that was it. I feel that we were definitely rushed by the bailiff. When the bailiff came in the last time, I felt we just had to make up our minds and that was it when he came in. He had come in three times and each time he seemed and spoke in a more angry manner. It was my opinion that the entire jury was uncertain as to how to proceed. As a result of his actions, everyone said, 'Hurry up.' It is my opinion that I hurried my verdict and agreed to the compromise verdict in order to prevent the jury from being locked up overnight.

"There were about four of us who felt from the beginning of deliberations that he was not guilty. I was the last holdout on the jury. The verdict for the lesser included was my verdict and court refused to consider the affidavit on the ground that: "They [the jury] can't impeach their own verdict."

The rule that jurors cannot impeach their verdicts, although almost universally assailed by the commentators as without foundation in logic or policy, has been a common law rule in this state since our first volume of reports. The rule first sprang full blown and unprecedented from the opinion of Lord Mansfield in Vaise v. Delaval (1785) 1 T.R. 11, 99 Eng.Rep. 944, and was based on an extension of the principle *nemo turpitudinem suam allegans audietur*—no man shall be heard to allege his own turpitude.[2] With several exceptions, the rule was adopted by the courts in American jurisdictions, including California, even though the principle on which it was originally based was largely repudiated as applied to other areas of the law of evidence. (See 8 Wigmore, Evidence (McNaughton rev. 1961) § 2352, p. 696.)

* * * The rule owes its continuing vitality, not to statute, but to the force of stare decisis (see Sopp v. Smith (1963) 377 P.2d 649 (dissenting opinion, Peters, J.)); and to a variety of legal arguments and public policies that, like the discredited policy against self-stultifying testimony, cannot withstand careful analysis.

In Kollert v. Cundiff, 329 P.2d 897, 900, we stated the rationale presently underlying the rule: "The problem involves the balancing of two conflicting policies. It is, of course, necessary to prevent instability of verdicts, fraud, and harassment of jurors, and, on the other hand, it is desirable to give the losing party relief from wrongful conduct by the jury. The court in McDonald v. Pless, 238 U.S. 264, 267–269, after discussing these policies and stating that the wrong to the individual was the lesser of two evils, concluded that as a general rule the affidavits [of jurors] should be excluded but that there might be instances where the rule could not be applied without 'violating the plainest principles of justice.' " Upon further deliberation we have concluded that there is no substantial conflict of policies and that the wrong to the individual cannot be considered the lesser of two evils.

In the Evidence Code the Legislature has determined that certain facts may be proved to impeach a verdict. "Upon an inquiry as to the validity of a verdict, any otherwise admissible evidence may be received as to statements made, or conduct, conditions, or events occurring, either within or without the jury room, of such a character as is likely to have influenced the verdict improperly. No evidence is admissible to show the effect of such statement, conduct, condition, or event upon a juror either in influencing him to assent to or dissent from the verdict or concerning the mental

---

was the verdict of the entire jury. I heard no vulgarity. I would not desire to sit on another jury if it was handled in the same way that this jury was handled by the bailiff."

[2]   The 12 jurors in Vaise v. Delaval had reached their verdict by lot, conduct that Lord Mansfield classed as a very high misdemeanor.

processes by which it was determined." (Evid.Code, § 1150, subd. (a).) This distinction between proof of overt acts, objectively ascertainable, and proof of the subjective reasoning processes of the individual juror, which can be neither corroborated nor disproved, has been advocated by commentators, adopted by the Uniform Rules of Evidence (rules 41 and 44) and the Model Code of Evidence (rule 301), and has been the basic limitation on proof set by the leading decisions allowing jurors to impeach their verdicts.

Although section 1150 does not alter the rule against impeachment of a verdict by the jurors, its limitation of impeachment evidence to proof of overt conduct, conditions, events, and statements, as suggested by the commentators, vitiates the major policy arguments supporting the common law rule. (See Sopp v. Smith, supra, 377 P.2d 649 (dissenting opinion, Peters, J.).) This limitation prevents one juror from upsetting a verdict of the whole jury by impugning his own or his fellow jurors' mental processes or reasons for assent or dissent. The only improper influences that may be proved under section 1150 to impeach a verdict, therefore, are those open to sight, hearing, and the other senses and thus subject to corroboration. "[T]hese facts can be easily proved or disproved. There is invariably little disagreement as to their occurrence." (Report of the New Jersey Supreme Court Committee on Evidence 80 (1963).) Experience in other jurisdictions that recognize the competency of a juror to impeach his verdict indicates that the admission of jurors' affidavits within the limits set by section 1150 will not result in the widespread upsetting of verdicts. Experience in this state with the present exceptions "indicates that the fears of jury tampering are unrealistic" (6 Cal. Law Revision Com. Reports (1964) 611), and there is no reason to believe that permitting proof of other overt misconduct is more likely to encourage post verdict tampering with the jury than do the present exceptions.

Admission of jurors' affidavits within the limits set by section 1150 protects the stability of verdicts, and allows proof by the best evidence of misconduct on the part of either jurors or third parties that should be exposed, misconduct upon which no verdict should be based. The content and conduct of deliberations may already be exposed by jurors at the trial of one who attempted corruptly to influence the verdict, or, in the case of the present two exceptions to the rule, at motion for new trial. Admission of this best evidence of misconduct or improper influence at a motion for new trial, therefore, would not present a breach in the post verdict privacy of jury deliberations. It would merely insure that evidence of misconduct will be available to the courts, freeing them to determine the substantive questions of whether the particular misconduct is a recognized ground for new trial and whether it has prejudiced the losing party. Admission of jurors' affidavits should also have a further prophylactic effect of stripping from all prejudicial misconduct whatever veil of post verdict secrecy is now reserved for the proper deliberations of the jury. "[T]o hear such proof would have a tendency to diminish such practices and to purify the jury room, by rendering such improprieties capable and probable of exposure, and consequently deterring jurors from resorting to them." (Wright v. Illinois, etc., Tel. Co., 20 Iowa 195, 211.)

We therefore hold that jurors are competent witnesses to prove objective facts to impeach a verdict under section 1150 of the Evidence Code. To the extent that Sopp v. Smith; Kollert v. Cundiff and similar cases are contrary to our conclusion herein, they are overruled.

The bailiff's remarks and the tone of their delivery constitute statements and conduct that are "likely to have influenced the verdict improperly." The affidavit of the juror is therefore admissible to prove the statements and conduct of the bailiff. Since the trial court refused to consider this competent evidence, defendant is entitled to a redetermination of his motion for new trial.

The order granting probation and the order denying the motion for new trial are vacated with directions to the trial court to hear and determine the motion for new trial in accordance with this opinion and to take such further proceedings as are appropriate.

MCCOMB, PETERS, TOBRINER, MOSK, BURKE and SULLIVAN, JJ., concur.

NOTES AND QUESTIONS

1.   The rationale for the traditional rule established by Lord Mansfield in Vaise v. Delaval was described by the Supreme Court in McDonald v. Pless, 238 U.S. 264, 267–68 (1915):

> [L]et it once be established that verdicts solemnly made and publicly returned into court can be attacked and set aside on the testimony of those who took part in their publication and all verdicts could be, and many would be, followed by an inquiry in the hope of discovering something which might invalidate the finding. Jurors would be harassed and beset by the defeated party in an effort to secure from them evidence of facts which might establish misconduct sufficient to set aside a verdict. If evidence thus secured could be thus used, the result would be to make what was intended to be a private deliberation, the constant subject of public investigation—to the destruction of all frankness and freedom of discussion and conference.

See also Lewis, Toward a Limited Right of Access to Jury Deliberation, 58 Fed. Comm. L.J. 195, 205 (2006) ("the courts have long recognized a free-standing commitment to jury secrecy during the deliberative process."); Sanderford, The Sixth Amendment, Rule 606(b), and the Intrusion Into Jury Deliberations of Religious Principles of Decision, 74 Tenn. L. Rev. 167, 178 (2007) (goal is to avoid race between parties to secure evidence from jurors establishing misconduct). But do these arguments justify the *total* ban of juror impeachment established by the *Delaval* rule? What if, during the course of deliberations, one juror pulls out a gun and orders every other juror to vote for the plaintiff? Could one of the jurors impeach the verdict on the basis of this evidence under the *Delaval* rule? Note that the *Delaval* rule "addresses itself to the question of whether a juror shall be allowed to testify to misconduct committed by his own jury panel. The * * * rule distinguishes sharply between the testimony of a juror and that of an outsider. Although a juror would be forbidden to file an affidavit or testify about an irregularity in the jury room, 'some person having seen the transaction through a window, or by some such other means' would be allowed to testify in court or file an affidavit concerning it." Carlson & Sumberg, Attacking Jury Verdicts: Paradigms for Rule Revision, 1977 Ariz.St.L.J. 247, 249 [quoting *Delaval*]. Does this distinction make sense?

2.   Should the judge feel some responsibility to ensure that the jury has not misbehaved in reaching its verdict? Consider Peterson v. Wilson, 141 F.3d 573 (5th Cir.1998), in which the trial judge met with the jurors without notice to counsel after the jury returned a plaintiff's verdict, and discussed the verdict with the jurors. Later, she sua sponte granted a motion for a new trial, explaining that "comments the jurors made to the court after returning the verdict [demonstrated] that the jury completely disregarded the Court's instructions." The court of appeals held that this violated Federal Rule of Evidence 606(b) (note 5 infra), for "—with the possible exception of an instance in which the court's professional curiosity has been piqued but on which no subsequent action is taken by the court—such a meeting is highly irregular if not absolutely impermissible, and, more importantly, that impeachment of the jury verdict on the basis of information obtained in such a discussion constitutes abuse of discretion per se."

3.   In Ballard v. Uribe, 715 P.2d 624 (Cal.1986), Justice Mosk (who had concurred in Justice Traynor's opinion in *Hutchinson*) wrote in a separate concurring opinion:

> I must express my apprehension at an incipient trend, that of losing parties attempting to impeach jury verdicts. * * * Giving such appeals and petitions any credence prevents the finality of judgments, places additional burdens on the judicial process, and contributes to disenchantment with the tort system.

>   Most juror affidavits * * * delve into the subjective concerns of the jurors during their deliberations. When deference is given to such affidavits, encouragement is given to opposing counsel in future cases to engage in postverdict competition to obtain juror affidavits revealing discussions that took place behind the closed doors of the deliberation room. Generally the party with the most resources will win that contest. If affidavits purportedly relating jury discussions are permissible, in the interest of accuracy we may as well install recording devices in jury rooms.

See also In re Hamilton, 84 Cal.Rptr.2d 403 (Cal.1999) (Chin, J., concurring) ("fishing expeditions by litigants who lost at trial must not transform the quest for misconduct claims into the witch hunts of the next millennium.").

4.   The so-called "Iowa rule", discussed in Justice Peters' dissent in *Sopp*, was developed as an attempt to bridge the interests served by the *Delaval* rule on the one hand and the competing interest in a fair and accurate verdict, on the other. Does it successfully achieve this goal? Could a juror impeach his verdict in the circumstances described in note 1 under the Iowa rule? See Carlson & Sumberg, supra, 1977 Ariz.St.L.J. at 257:

> A key to understanding the Iowa rule lies in appreciating which matters do, and which matters do not, "inhere in the verdict." Although there is some disagreement over the precise meaning of the phrase, matters that inhere in the verdict usually are deemed to be those which are personal to the juror, such as his mental operations, emotions, and personal reactions to the arguments of counsel.

5.   Federal Rule of Evidence 606(b) provides:

Rule 606. Juror's Competency as a Witness

* * *

(b) During an Inquiry Into the Validity of a Verdict or Indictment.

> **(1) Prohibited Testimony or Other Evidence**. During an inquiry into the validity of a verdict or indictment, a juror may not testify about any statement made or incident that occurred during the jury's deliberations; the effect of anything on that juror's or another juror's vote; or any juror's mental processes concerning the verdict or indictment. The court may not receive a juror's affidavit or evidence of a juror's statement on these matters.

> **(2)**   Exceptions. A juror may testify about whether:

>> **(A)** extraneous prejudicial information was improperly brought to the jury's attention;

>> **(B)** an outside influence was improperly brought to bear on any juror; or

>> **(C)** a mistake was made in entering the verdict on the verdict form.

6.   Consider how the three rules (Rule 606(b), the Iowa rule, and the Delaval rule) would apply to the following hypotheticals:

(a)   The quotient verdict: The jurors reached a verdict by writing down the amount each thought plaintiff should recover (even if zero) and dividing the total amount by the number of jurors. Cf. Scogin v. Century Fitness, Inc., 780 F.2d 1316 (8th Cir.1985) (evidence of quotient verdict "does not concern extraneous prejudicial information or outside influence being brought to bear upon any juror").

(b)   The notes the jury made while calculating damages indicate that it was confused and as a result awarded the wrong amount. See Ohanian v. Avis Rent A Car System, Inc., 779 F.2d 101 (2d Cir.1985) ("To use jurors' notes to impeach a verdict would, as the Supreme Court in McDonald v. Pless feared, 'make what was intended to be a private deliberation, the constant subject of public investigation—to the destruction of all frankness and freedom of discussion and conference.' ").

(c)   A juror attempts to impeach his verdict by stating that for many hours he had been the last holdout in favor of the ultimate losing party, when his boss, who was also a member of the jury, said to him: "Remember, you have a job, Sam." At that point he switched his vote.

(d)   A juror testifies that during a break in deliberation, the bailiff called him aside and, in discussing an especially recalcitrant juror, pulled his gun out, took out a bullet, and said he could "put her out of her misery." The juror did not tell the recalcitrant juror, but testifies that "it really shook me up." See Sea Hawk Seafoods, Inc. v. Alyeska Pipeline Service Co., 206 F.3d 900 (9th Cir. 2000).

7.   In the 1970s commentators noted that "[s]ome courts are developing new exceptions to the no-impeachment rule for civil cases, and recently enacted codes of evidence are broadly replacing the rule in both civil and criminal litigation in other jurisdictions. However, the most dramatic developments have been in the constitutional area. They point to the probable demise of the [Delaval] rule, at least where activities in the jury room deprive an accused of his constitutional rights in a criminal prosecution." Carlson & Sumberg, supra, 1977 Ariz.St.L.J. at 267.

In Tanner v. United States, 483 U.S. 107 (1987), the Court rejected such arguments by a convicted criminal defendant who relied on a juror affidavit that several jurors were drunk or stoned or both. The juror asserted that he "felt like * * * the jury was one big party." He detailed a rather troubling picture: Four of the jurors customarily drank one to three pitchers of beer at lunch, the foreperson, an alcoholic, usually had a carafe of wine at lunch, four jurors regularly smoked marijuana during the trial, one juror sold a quarter pound of marijuana to another juror in the courthouse during the trial, and one juror took cocaine five times during the trial while another used that drug two or three times. Despite arguments by the dissent that this evidence indicated a violation of due process, the majority held that, like matters of alleged mental or physical incompetence, the evidence related to something "internal" to the verdict and that it was therefore inadmissible. In Warger v. Shavers, 135 S.Ct. 521 (2014), the Court held that a disappointed plaintiff could not rely on a juror affidavit to attempt to prove that another juror had lied in responding to voire dire. The Court concluded that such materials constituted an inquiry into the validity of a verdict for purposes of Rule 606(b).

In Robles v. Exxon Corp., 862 F.2d 1201 (5th Cir.), cert. denied, 490 U.S. 1051 (1989), the court held that a judge's receiving testimony from the jurors after they have returned their verdict, for the purposes of ascertaining that the jury misunderstood its instructions, is absolutely prohibited by Rule 606(b).

8.   It may strike you as unlikely that many jurors would do as the juror did in Sopp v. Smith—make a special trip to visit the site of the accident in suit. But consider how easily an online "visit" might occur today using GoogleEarth or a similar method. See Davenport, Here's Looking at You, Trial Magazine, March 2012, at 18 (quoting a lawyer who says that "jurors have always violated court orders not to do their own research, and technology has only made it easier"); Mastro, Preventing the "Google Mistrial": The Challenge Posed by Jurors Who Use the Internet and Social Media, 37 Litigation 23 (Winter 2011); MacPherson & Bonora, The Wired Juror Unplugged, Trial Magazine, Nov. 2010, at 40. For an example, see Russo v. Takata Corp., 774 N.W.2d 441 (S.D.2009) (juror in wrongful death action learned through online research about defendant that it had been sued by others making similar claims). In California, the Legislature responded by providing in Cal. Code Civ. Proc. § 1209(a) that the following is contempt of court: "Willful disobedience by a juror of a court admonishment related to the prohibition on any form of communication or research about a case, including all forms of electronic or wireless communication or research."

9.   What if a juror admits during deliberations that she lied during voir dire? Can the judge consider that on a challenge to the verdict? In Warger v. Shauers, 135 S.Ct. 521 (2014), the Court held that Rule 606(b) forbids consideration of a juror affidavit reporting that during deliberations another juror revealed personal information inconsistent with her answers during voir dire. "As enacted, Rule 606(b) prohibited the use of *any* evidence of juror deliberations, subject only to the express exceptions for extraneous information and outside influences." Neither of those exceptions applied.

CHAPTER 9

CHOOSING THE FORUM— GEOGRAPHICAL LOCATION

∎ ∎ ∎

Until this point, we have given little attention to the location of the court in which the case is to proceed. In a country the size of the United States, that factor can of course be quite important, as can the question whether the case is in federal or state court. The plaintiff's preferences with regard to location and court system may result from a variety of strategic factors, but they are subject to a number of legal limitations. We turn to those limitations now. In this chapter we consider the geographical location of the court. In the next chapter we address the choice between state and federal court.

In early English procedure, the method for obtaining jurisdiction was often rather primitive, if direct—under the writ of *capias ad respondendum*, the sheriff simply arrested the defendant and, unless bond was posted, put him in jail, there to await trial. Gradually that method was abandoned and, "in the case of a suit against a man, jurisdiction is regarded as established by service [of process], without the need of keeping him in prison to await judgment. It is enough that the personal service shows that he could have been seized and imprisoned." Tyler v. Judges of the Court of Registration, 55 N.E. 812, 814 (Mass.1900) (Holmes, C.J.). Nevertheless, jurisdiction has continued to plague lawyers, judges and law students. As introduced below, the original American formulation relied on the states' power over the person or property of the defendant, but by the mid 20th century more expansive jurisdictional grounds were accepted. Beginning in the 1980s, the Supreme Court cut back on those more expansive jurisdictional theories.

A. THE TRADITIONAL FORMULATION: THE "POWER" THEORY OF JURISDICTION

Q. Vid.

PENNOYER V. NEFF

Supreme Court of the United States, 1877
95 U.S. (5 OTTO) 714

JUSTICE FIELD delivered the opinion of the Court.

[In November, 1865, J.H. Mitchell sued Neff in the Circuit Court of Multnomah County, Oregon, claiming that Neff owed him $253.14 for legal work performed in 1862 and 1863. Shortly after filing the suit, Mitchell submitted his affidavit asserting that Neff was a California resident, but that Mitchell did not know his address. Mitchell also averred that Neff owned property in Oregon, although the record does not reveal what that property was. On the basis of the affidavit, the Oregon court directed that Neff be served by publication. When the defendant's place of residence was known, the Code of Oregon provided that he either be personally served outside the state or that the summons and complaint be mailed to him. But since Neff's address was unknown, the only notice of the suit required was publication once a week for six weeks in the Pacific Christian Advocate, a paper of general circulation in Multnomah County. When Neff failed to answer, Mitchell obtained a default judgment in early 1866. A month later, Neff acquired title to a tract of land in Oregon. Mitchell then executed against this land and bought it at the sheriff's sale for $341.60, presumably the amount of the judgment plus interest and costs. Three days later, on August 10, 1866, he transferred title to Pennoyer.

In September, 1874, Neff sued Pennoyer in federal court in Oregon to recover title to the land, which he alleged was worth $15,000. He contended that the judgment in Mitchell's suit was invalid because the Oregon court had not, despite substituted service under the Oregon procedure, had jurisdiction.]

The Code of Oregon provides for such service [by publication] when an action is brought against a non-resident and absent defendant, who has property within the state. It also provides, where the action is for the recovery of money or damages, for the attachment of the property of the non-resident. And it also declares that no natural person is subject to the jurisdiction of a court of the State, "unless he appear in the court, or be found within the State, or be a resident thereof, or have property therein; and, in the last case, only to the extent of such property at the time the jurisdiction attached." Construing this latter provision to mean, that, in an action for money or damages where a defendant does not appear in the court, and is not found within the State, and is not a resident thereof, but has property therein, the jurisdiction of the court extends only over such property, the declaration expresses a principle of general, if not universal, law. The authority of every tribunal is necessarily restricted by the territorial limits of the State in which it is established. Any attempt to exercise authority beyond those limits would be deemed in every other forum, as has been said by this Court, an illegitimate assumption of power, and be resisted as mere abuse. In this case against the plaintiff, the property here in controversy sold under the judgment rendered was not attached, nor in any way brought under the jurisdiction of the court. Its first connection with the case was caused by a levy of the execution. It was not, therefore, disposed of pursuant to any adjudication, but only in enforcement of a personal judgment, having no relation to the property, rendered against a non-resident without service of process upon him in the action, or his appearance therein.

[The lower court had ruled for Neff on the ground that the affidavit used to prove service by publication was defective because it came from the editor, and the statute called for the affidavit of "the printer, or his foreman, or his principal clerk." The Supreme Court found the affidavit of the editor sufficient under the Oregon statute.]

If, therefore, we were confined to the rulings of the court below upon the defects in the affidavits mentioned, we should be unable to uphold its decision. But it was also contended in that court, and is insisted upon here, that the judgment in the State court against the plaintiff was void for want of personal service of process on him, or of his appearance in the action in which it was rendered, and that the premises in controversy could not be subjected to the payment of the demand of a resident creditor except by a proceeding in rem; that is, by a direct proceeding against the property for that purpose. If these positions are sound, the ruling of the Circuit Court as to the invalidity of that judgment must be sustained, notwithstanding our dissent from the reasons upon which it was made. And that they are sound would seem to follow from two well-established principles of public law respecting the jurisdiction of an independent State over persons and property. The several States of the Union are not, it is true, in every respect independent, many of the rights and powers which originally belonged to them being now vested in the government created by the Constitution. But, except as restrained and limited by that instrument, they possess and exercise the authority of independent States, and the principles of public law to which we have referred are applicable to them. One of these principles is, that every State possesses exclusive jurisdiction and sovereignty over persons and property within its territory. As a consequence, every State has the power to determine for itself the civil status and capacities of its inhabitants; to prescribe the subjects upon which they may contract, the forms and solemnities with which their contracts shall be executed, the rights and obligations arising from them, and the mode in which their validity shall be determined and their obligations enforced; and also to regulate the manner and conditions upon which property situated within such territory, both personal and real, may be acquired, enjoyed, and transferred. The other principle of public law referred to follows from the one mentioned; that is, that no State can exercise direct jurisdiction and authority over persons or property without its territory. Story, Confl. Laws, c. 2; Wheat. Int. Law, pt. 2, c. 2. The several States are of equal dignity and authority, and the independence of one implies the exclusion of power from all others. And so it is laid down by jurists, as an elementary principle, that the laws of one State have no operation outside of its territory, except so far as is allowed by comity; and that no tribunal established by it can extend its process beyond that territory so as to subject either persons or property to its decisions. "Any exertion of authority of this sort beyond this limit," says Story, "is a mere nullity, and incapable of binding such persons or property in any other tribunals." Story, Confl. Laws, sect. 539.

But as contracts made in one State may be enforceable only in another State, and property may be held by non-residents, the exercise of the jurisdiction which every State is admitted to possess over persons and property within its own territory will often affect persons and property without it. To any influence exerted in this way by a State affecting persons resident or property situated elsewhere, no objection can be justly taken; whilst any direct exertion of authority upon them, in an attempt to give ex-territorial operation to its laws, or to enforce an ex-territorial jurisdiction by its tribunals, would be deemed an encroachment upon the independence of the State in which the persons are domiciled or the property is situated, and be resisted as usurpation.

Thus the State, through its tribunals, may compel persons domiciled within its limits to execute, in pursuance of their contracts respecting property elsewhere situated, instruments in such form and with such solemnities as to transfer the title, so far as such formalities can be complied with; and the exercise of this jurisdiction in no manner interferes with the supreme control over the property by the State within which it is situated.

So the State, through its tribunals, may subject property situated within its limits owned by non-residents to the payment of the demand of its own citizens against them; and the exercise of this jurisdiction in no respect infringes upon the sovereignty of the State where the owners are domiciled. Every State owes protection to its own citizens; and, when non-residents deal with them, it is a legitimate and just exercise of authority to hold and appropriate any property owned by such non-residents to satisfy the claims of its citizens. It is in virtue of the State's jurisdiction over the property of the non-resident situated within its limits that its tribunals can inquire into that non-resident's obligations to its own citizens, and the inquiry can then be carried only to the extent necessary to control the disposition of the property. If the non-resident have no property in the State, there is nothing upon which the tribunals can adjudicate.

* * *

If, without personal service, judgments *in personam*, obtained ex parte against non-residents and absent parties, upon mere publication of process, which, in the great majority of cases, would never be seen by the parties interested, could be upheld and enforced, they would be the constant instruments of fraud and oppression. Judgments for all sorts of claims upon contracts and for torts, real or pretended, would be thus obtained, under which property would be seized, when the evidence of the transactions upon which they were founded, if they ever had any existence, had perished.

Substituted service by publication, or in any other authorized form, may be sufficient to inform parties of the object of proceedings taken where property is once brought under the control of the court by seizure or some equivalent act. The law assumes that property is always in the possession of its owner, in person or by agent; and it proceeds upon the theory that its seizure will inform him, not only that it is taken into the custody of the court, but that he must look to any proceedings authorized by law upon such seizure for its condemnation and sale. Such service may also be sufficient in cases where the object of the action is to reach and dispose of property in the State, or of some interest therein, by enforcing a contract or a lien respecting the same, or to partition it among different owners, or, when the public is a party, to condemn and appropriate it for a public purpose. In other words, such service may answer in all actions which are substantially proceedings *in rem*. But where the entire object of the action is to determine the personal rights and obligations of the defendants, that is, where the suit is merely in personam, constructive service in this form upon a non-resident is ineffectual for any purpose. Process from the tribunals of one State cannot run into another State, and summon parties there domiciled to leave its territory and respond to proceedings against them. Publication of process or notice within the State where the tribunal sits cannot create any greater obligation upon the non-resident to appear. Process sent to him out of the State, and process published within it, are equally unavailing in proceedings to establish his personal liability.

The want of authority of the tribunals of a State to adjudicate upon the obligations of non-residents, where they have no property within its limits, is not denied by the court below; but the position is assumed, that, where they have property within the State, it is immaterial whether the property is in the first instance brought under the control of the court by attachment or some other equivalent act, and afterwards applied by its judgment to the satisfaction of demands against its owner; or such demands be first established in a personal action, and the property of the non-resident be afterwards seized and sold on execution. But the answer to this position has already been given in the statement, that the jurisdiction of the court to inquire into and determine his obligations at all is only incidental to its jurisdiction over the property. Its jurisdiction in that respect cannot be made to depend upon facts to be ascertained after it has tried the cause and rendered the judgment. If the judgment be previously void, it will not become valid by the subsequent discovery of property of the defendant, or by his subsequent acquisition of it. The judgment, if void when rendered, will always remain void: it cannot occupy the doubtful position of being valid if property be found, and void if there be none. Even if the position assumed were confined to cases where the non-resident defendant possessed property in the State at the commencement of the action, it would still make the validity of the proceedings and judgment depend upon the question whether, before the levy of the execution, the defendant had or had not disposed of the property. If before the levy the property should be sold, then, according to this position, the judgment would not be binding. This doctrine would introduce a new element of uncertainty in judicial proceedings. The contrary is the law: the validity of every judgment depends upon the jurisdiction of the court before it is rendered, not upon what may occur subsequently. * * *

The force and effect of judgments rendered against non-residents without personal service of process upon them, or their voluntary appearance, have been the subject of frequent consideration in the courts of the United States and of the several States, as attempts have been made to enforce such judgments in States other than those in which they were rendered, under the provision of the Constitution requiring that "full faith and credit shall be given in each State to the public acts, records, and judicial proceedings of every other State;" and the act of Congress providing for the mode of authenticating such acts, records, and proceedings, and declaring that, when thus authenticated, "they shall have such faith and credit given to them in every court within the United States as they have by law or usage in the courts of the State from which they are or shall be taken." In the earlier cases, it was supposed that the act gave to all judgments the same effect in other States which they had by law in the State where rendered. But this view was afterwards qualified so as to make the act applicable only when the court rendering the judgment had jurisdiction of the parties and of the subject matter, and not to preclude an inquiry into the jurisdiction of the court in which the judgment was rendered, or the right of the State itself to exercise authority over the person or the subject-matter.

* * *

Since the adoption of the Fourteenth Amendment to the Federal Constitution, the validity of such judgments may be directly questioned, and their enforcement in the State resisted on the ground that proceedings in a court of justice to determine the personal rights and obligations of parties over whom that court has no jurisdiction do not constitute due process of law. Whatever difficulty may be experienced in giving to those terms a definition which will embrace every permissible exertion of power affecting private rights, and exclude such as is forbidden, there can be no doubt of their meaning when applied to judicial proceedings. They then mean a course of legal proceedings according to those rules and principles which have been established in our systems of jurisprudence for the protection and enforcement of private rights. To give such proceedings any validity, there must be a tribunal competent by its constitution—that is, by the law of its creation—to pass upon the subject-matter of the suit; and, if that involves merely a determination of the personal liability of the defendant, he must be brought within its jurisdiction by service of process within the State, or his voluntary appearance.

Except in cases affecting the personal status of the plaintiff, and cases in which that mode of service may be considered to have been assented to in advance, as hereinafter mentioned, the substituted service of process by publication, allowed by the law of Oregon and by similar laws in other States, where actions are brought against non-residents, is effectual only where, in connection with process against the person for commencing the action, property in the State is brought under the control of the court, and subjected to its disposition by process adapted to that purpose, or where the judgment is sought as a means of reaching such property or affecting some interest therein; in other words, where the action is in the nature of a proceeding in rem. * * *

It is true that, in a strict sense, a proceeding in rem is one taken directly against property, and has for its object the disposition of the property, without reference to the title of individual claimants; but, in a larger and more general sense, the terms are applied to actions between parties, where the direct object is to reach and dispose of property owned by them, or of some interest therein. Such are cases commenced by attachment against the property of debtors, or instituted to partition real estate, foreclose a mortgage, or enforce a lien. So far as they affect property in the State, they are substantially proceedings in rem in the broader sense which we have mentioned.

* * *

To prevent any misapplication of the views expressed in this opinion, it is proper to observe that we do not mean to assert, by anything we have said, that a State may not authorize proceedings to determine the status of one of its citizens towards a non-resident, which would be binding within the State, though made without service of process or personal notice to the non-resident. The jurisdiction which every State possesses to determine the civil status and capacities of all its inhabitants involves authority to prescribe the conditions on which proceedings affecting them may be commenced and carried on within its territory. The State, for example, has absolute right to prescribe the conditions upon which the marriage relation between its own citizens shall be created, and the causes for which it may be dissolved. One of the parties guilty of acts for which, by the law of the State, a dissolution may be granted, may have removed to a State where no dissolution is permitted. The complaining party would, therefore, fail if a divorce were sought in the State of the defendant; and if application could not be made to the tribunals of the complainant's domicile in such case, and proceedings be there instituted without personal service of process or personal notice to the offending party, the injured citizen would be without redress.

Neither do we mean to assert that a State may not require a non-resident entering into a partnership or association within its limits, or making contracts enforceable there, to appoint an agent or representative in the State to receive service of process and notice in legal proceedings instituted with respect to such partnership, association, or contracts, or to designate a place where such service may be made and notice given, and provide, upon their failure, to make such appointment or to designate such place that service may be made upon a public officer designated for that purpose, or in some other prescribed way, and that judgments rendered upon such service may not be binding upon the non-residents both within and without the state. * * * Nor do we doubt that a State, on creating corporations or other institutions for pecuniary or charitable purposes, may provide a mode in which their conduct may be investigated, their obligations enforced, or their charters revoked, which shall require other than personal service upon their officers or members. Parties becoming members of such corporations or institutions would hold their interest subject to the conditions prescribed by law.

In the present case, there is no feature of this kind, and, consequently, no consideration of what would be the effect of such legislation in enforcing the contract of a non-resident can arise. The question here respects only the validity of a money judgment rendered in one State, in an action upon a simple contract against the resident of another, without service of process upon him, or his appearance therein.

[Dissenting opinion of Justice Hunt omitted.]

NOTES AND QUESTIONS

1.   As befits an epic case, Pennoyer v. Neff involves some interesting characters, as Professor Perdue has chronicled. See Perdue, Sin, Scandal, and Substantive Due Process: Personal Jurisdiction and *Pennoyer* Reconsidered, 62 Wash.L.Rev. 479 (1987). Marcus Neff was an illiterate settler who came to Oregon from Iowa by wagon train in 1848 and experienced difficulties qualifying for land for settlers under the Oregon Donation Act. In 1862 he consulted Mitchell for legal services, the nature of which is not clear. Mitchell did not sue for payment until three years later, by which time Neff had moved to California. Mitchell himself was born John Hipple and, while a teacher in Pennsylvania, had been forced to marry a 15 year old student he had seduced. In 1860 he changed his name and headed west, leaving his wife behind but taking along his current paramour and $4,000 of client money from his legal practice. He abandoned the paramour in California and moved to Oregon, where he established a successful law practice and married again without divorcing his first wife. In 1872 Mitchell was elected to the U.S. Senate, and after losing his seat in 1879 he was elected again in 1885 despite scandal due to the publication of love letters from a recent adulterous relationship. Sylvester Pennoyer was also a successful politician. Elected Governor of Oregon in 1887, and still smarting from his loss to Neff, he used his inaugural address to decry the Supreme Court's decision against him as an example of federal judicial usurpation of state power.

2. *Terminology*: Justice Field distinguishes *in personam* and *in rem* jurisdiction. In theory, a judgment is *in personam* when it makes the defendant personally liable. As we have seen in Chapter 2, such a judgment might declare that the defendant is liable to pay money to the plaintiff (damages), or it might order defendant to begin or cease certain activity (injunction). In either instance, the judgment is "personal" to the defendant. Jurisdiction *in rem*, in contrast, focuses on property (the *res*) and permits the court to dispose of the property in accordance with the outcome of the litigation. In practice, this distinction often blurs. The most common form of *in personam* judgment, for money damages, may ordinarily be enforced (as was done in this case) against property of the defendant, so that *in personam* judgments often have an impact on property. A judgment *in rem*, meanwhile, is effective only to the extent that it extinguishes the claimed rights of persons in the property involved, so that it has a personal impact on them despite the description. Whatever the shortcomings of the dichotomy, it is central to the jurisdictional approach of *Pennoyer*.

(a) Jurisdiction *in personam*: A court can enter a valid judgment *in personam* only, the Court held, when jurisdiction has been obtained by personal service of process in the state, although it does not matter that the defendant was present in the state only briefly. The *reductio ad absurdum* on this score to date is Grace v. MacArthur, 170 F.Supp. 442 (E.D.Ark.1959), in which defendant, a passenger on a nonstop commercial airline flight from Memphis, Tennessee, to Dallas, Texas, was served while the plane was over Pine Bluff, Arkansas. The court held that this service was sufficient to subject him to Arkansas jurisdiction, although it recognized "that a time may come, and may not be far distant, when commercial aircraft will fly at altitudes so high that it would be unrealistic to consider them as being within the territorial limits of the United States or of any particular State while flying at such altitudes."

This sort of jurisdiction is popularly known as *"transient" jurisdiction*, because it permits a state to exercise jurisdiction over a defendant served in the state even if he was only present in the state for a short period. Against the background of *capias ad respondendum*, it may seem eminently reasonable to conclude that service alone is sufficient to support jurisdiction. Nevertheless, most other countries do not authorize transient jurisdiction. *Pennoyer*'s casual acceptance of the sufficiency of transient jurisdiction was forcefully challenged in Ehrenzweig, The Transient Rule of Personal Jurisdiction: The "Power" Myth and Forum Conveniens, 65 Yale L.J. 289 (1956). Professor Ehrenzweig argued that, before *Pennoyer*, personal service had been neither essential nor sufficient to support jurisdiction, which he contended depended on issues of convenience and submission by defendant to the power of the court. *Pennoyer*'s prohibition on process beyond the state, however, undermined this flexible structure and paved the way for cases like Grace v. MacArthur, which involved no elements of either convenience or submission by the defendant to jurisdiction of the court. Is there any persuasive justification for treating personal service, without more, as sufficient for jurisdiction? We return to the current validity of transient jurisdiction in Section F of this chapter, infra p. 812.

(b) Jurisdiction *in rem*: Personal service in the jurisdiction is not necessary, however, for the state to exercise its power over property in the state. The presence of property in a state under traditional practice could conceivably give rise to two distinct forms of jurisdiction: *in rem* and *quasi in rem*. In the case of *in rem* jurisdiction, the physical presence of the property within the state vests the state with jurisdiction to adjudicate the rights of any individual—whether in the state or not—in that property. Though this form of jurisdiction conceivably allows the state to adjudicate the rights of individuals located anywhere in the world, it does so only for rights in that particular property.

In rem jurisdiction, standing alone, conferred no authority to assess damages against an individual or in any way control the individual's personal rights apart from his interest in the property. *In rem* jurisdiction appeared in two forms: "pure" *in rem* and actions "in the nature of rem" (sometimes also inexactly referred to as *quasi in rem*). In "pure" *in rem* actions, the state sought to bind the rights of the entire world in a piece of property within the state's borders. For example, consider an action to quiet title; unless the action could bind the entire world, its goal of preserving the uninhibited alienability of property would be undermined. In an action in the nature of rem, while the state sought to bind merely rights in a particular piece of property, it did so only as to specifically named individuals. Thus, a suit to specifically enforce a contract for the sale of land could be viewed either as an *in personam* action (i.e., to determine and control the defendant's personal rights in the property), or as an action in the nature of rem (i.e., to adjudicate rights in property located within the state). Usually, the plaintiff would characterize the action in one form or the other, depending upon which form of jurisdiction provided the state with authority to adjudicate: If the property was located in the state but the defendant was not subject to service, the state could properly characterize the case as in the nature of rem; if, on the other hand, the property was beyond the state's borders but the defendant was subject to service of process, the state would likely deem the case to be *in personam*.

Although as already noted actions in the nature of rem were also sometimes referred to as *quasi in rem*, it is important not to confuse that form of jurisdiction with the more common category of cases described as quasi in rem. In these cases, the action is purely *in personam*; the substance of the case has nothing to do with defendant's property. However, for whatever reason, the state lacks authority to assert *in personam* jurisdiction over the defendant. In such a case, the plaintiff was allowed to assert jurisdiction over the defendant's property within the state by attachment, garnishment, or other process available at the beginning of a suit to allow seizure of property to secure any judgment plaintiff ultimately obtains on the in personam claim. For example, *A* from Illinois sues *B* from New York in Illinois state court for damages of $500,000 for breach of a personal services contract. *B* is not subject to *in personam* jurisdiction in Illinois, but does own a piece of property in that state worth $250,000. Though the property is irrelevant to the substance of the case, *A* is able to sue *B* in Illinois for $250,000—the value of the property—by attaching it at the time suit is filed. If successful, *A* is still able to sue *B* in some other jurisdiction for the remaining amount. *B*, in turn, is traditionally allowed to make a *"limited appearance"* in Illinois: i.e., to appear to defend the suit up to the value of the property, without implicitly consenting to full in personam jurisdiction. Which of these forms of jurisdiction was employed in *Pennoyer*?

Quasi in rem jurisdiction generated its own *reductio ad absurdum*: In Seider v. Roth, 216 N.E.2d 312 (N.Y.1966), the court held that the obligation of an insurer to defend and indemnify the nonresident defendant in an auto accident case is property of the insured that is present in New York if the insurance company does business there, and that the presence of such "property" justifies the exercise of jurisdiction in a suit against the defendant no matter where the accident occurred or where the defendant lives. The Supreme Court rejected this jurisdictional argument in Rush v. Savchuk, infra p. 806 n. 1.

3.   What is the source of the rules on which the Court relies in *Pennoyer*? As Justice Field foresees, the Due Process Clause of the 14th Amendment would thereafter support attacks on jurisdiction as a violation of due process, and in fact due process is the rubric under which the Court has since handled jurisdiction issues. But that amendment did not become effective until 1868, after Mitchell's judgment was entered. Instead, the Court in *Pennoyer* relied on principles of "public law" derived from the international sphere. How relevant are these concepts about the relations of independent nations to the relations of the states of the United States? To the degree they are relevant, what do they have to do with due process, which normally protects the individual against overreaching by the government? For an argument that the due process inquiry should be limited to unfair inconvenience to defendant, see Redish, Due Process, Federalism, and Personal Jurisdiction: A Theoretical Evaluation, 75 Nw.U.L.Rev. 1112 (1981); see also Sachs, *Pennoyer* Was Right: Jurisdiction and General Law, 95 Tex. L. Rev. 1249 (2017) (arguing that courts should abandon the view that Due Process places any limitation on state courts' exercise of personal jurisdiction).

4.   If the proper focus is on the relative rights of states as sovereigns, are limitations on jurisdiction designed to protect defendants or states? If it is the latter, why should these limitations evaporate once the defendant appears in the lawsuit (or flies over the state in an airplane)?

5.   Whatever their source, how well do the postulates upon which the *Pennoyer* Court relies work as a description of the American judicial system? Justice Field asserts confidently that every state has "exclusive jurisdiction" of persons and property within it and, as a corollary, that no state may exercise "direct" jurisdiction over persons or property outside it. But consider:

(a)   If Mitchell had managed to serve Neff in Oregon, couldn't he insist that California give the resulting judgment full faith and credit? If so, he could enforce it against Neff's property in California. Could California, by asserting its "exclusive" jurisdiction over property in California, refuse to enforce the judgment? See U.S. Const., Art. IV § 1.

(b)   If Neff were served with process while temporarily in Oregon, would he be subject to Oregon's "exclusive" jurisdiction? In Milliken v. Meyer, 311 U.S. 457 (1940), the Court held that a state may exercise jurisdiction over one of its citizens even while the citizen is out of the state.

(c)   If Mitchell had attached Neff's Oregon property before judgment was entered by the Oregon court, it appears that Justice Field would have been satisfied. But a piece of property worth $15,000 was a very significant interest in 1866. How realistic is it to say that Oregon is only exercising "indirect" jurisdiction over Neff when it takes that property away from him? For a careful dissection of Pennoyer's premises, see Hazard, A General Theory of State-Court Jurisdiction, 1965 Sup.Ct.Rev. 241, 265–68.

6.   Justice Field himself carefully carves out two exceptions. First, he emphasizes that a state retains the right to determine the status of its citizens, a doctrine that normally is important in family law litigation. One theoretical explanation for this exception is that marital status is somehow a res, so that the jurisdiction is in rem. True, a divorce decree is not *in personam* in that it neither orders the defendant to pay money nor directs him to do or cease doing anything. But it is hard to imagine a judicial action that has a more personal effect on the defendant. Nevertheless, the courts have pursued the in rem reasoning to create the "divisible divorce"—the divorce plaintiff's state has jurisdiction to decree the divorce (in rem) but not to decide questions of alimony or child support obligations involving an absent defendant (in personam). See, e.g., Estin v. Estin, 334 U.S. 541 (1948); Wasserman, Divorce and Domicile: Time to Sever the Knot, 39 Will. & Mary L. Rev. 1 (1997) (tracing the difficulties caused by tying jurisdiction to domicile and proposing solving these problems by statutory action).

The other exception is consent. We treat issues raised by private consent to jurisdiction infra at p. 835. The consent envisioned by the *Pennoyer* Court turned on a state's right to refuse outsiders access to the state, a refusal it could withdraw in return for their submission to its jurisdiction. Because this idea illustrates the way the Court and the states tried to cope with the difficulties caused by the *Pennoyer* construct, we treat it in some detail.

FRAUDULENT INDUCEMENT INTO THE FORUM

It should be apparent that *Pennoyer*'s general requirement of service within the forum was often an obstacle to the exercise of jurisdiction. But the parallel idea that service within the forum was always sufficient for jurisdiction led to troubling results when plaintiff enticed defendant into the state to effect service. In reaction, the courts developed the doctrine of fraudulent inducement, which would invalidate service where plaintiff has lured defendant into the jurisdiction with falsehoods. See, e.g., Wyman v. Newhouse, 93 F.2d 313 (2d Cir.1937) (in suit growing out of adulterous affair between plaintiff and defendant, plaintiff's repeated pleas that defendant come to visit her one last time invalidated service on defendant as he alighted from airplane). This doctrine limits the ability of a plaintiff to invoke the power of a distant state through subterfuge.

The fraudulent inducement doctrine is most difficult to apply to situations where defendant has come into the jurisdiction to negotiate a resolution of an admitted dispute, for in such cases there is no doubt that a dispute exists between the parties and that it may result in litigation. Courts nevertheless have applied the doctrine. For example, in E/M Lubricants, Inc. v. Microfral, S.A.R.L., 91 F.R.D. 235 (N.D.Ill.1981), plaintiff licensed defendant, a French corporation, to use and market plaintiff's patented processes for the treatment of metals. When a dispute arose about defendant's obligation to make certain minimum royalty payments, there was much correspondence attempting to resolve the dispute. Eventually defendant's president suggested that since he was planning a visit to the United States on other business he could meet with plaintiff's president to discuss the dispute, and plaintiff's president agreed to meet in Chicago. On the night before the scheduled meeting, however, defendant's president was served with summons and complaint at his hotel. Defendant moved to dismiss, to which plaintiff responded that the meeting had been defendant's idea and that, in any event, it had not decided to sue until after the meeting was arranged, so there had been no fraud.

The court granted the motion to dismiss. It held the fact that defendant had proposed the meeting irrelevant because its president came to Illinois only to discuss settlement. Compare Schwarz v. Artcraft Silk Hosiery Mills, 110 F.2d 465 (2d Cir.1940) (service in New York at outset of negotiations valid because defendant had come to New York to visit his summer home on Long Island). Accepting plaintiff's claim that it had not decided to sue until the meeting was arranged, the court decided that plaintiff's failure to advise defendant of its change of heart then was deceitful because the earlier discussions gave rise to a duty to speak. The court in *Microfral* found this result compelled by policy as well:

> First and most significantly, it is in the interest of justice to promote the speedy and amicable resolution of disputes as an alternative to legal battle. Conduct such as that engaged in by plaintiff in this case does not further that interest. Out-of-state persons in the shoes of [defendant] will simply forgo the opportunity to negotiate a settlement rather than risk subjecting themselves to service in an unfavorable jurisdiction. It is significant that the interest in informal dispute resolution is compromised whether the plaintiff induces reliance through misrepresentation of his intention from the outset or, as in the instant case, through failure to disclose a subsequent change of heart.

Second, there are enforcement problems if plaintiffs are permitted to escape the reach of the fraudulent enticement doctrine merely by asserting that they did not form the intent to sue until after they had agreed to negotiate. It is extremely easy for a plaintiff to make such an assertion and extremely difficult to disprove it.

But see Sawyer v. LaFlamme, 185 A.2d 466 (Vt.1962), where the court upheld service in the office of plaintiff's lawyer after negotiations had broken down, reasoning that the negotiations were in good faith and there had accordingly been no fraud. If plaintiff in *Microfral* had waited until after negotiations were completed (unsuccessfully) would that have made a difference?

Harris v. Balk, 198 U.S. 215 (1905):

JUSTICE PECKHAM delivered the opinion of the Court:

[While Harris, a resident of North Carolina, was in Maryland on a business trip in 1896, he was served with a writ of garnishment issued by a Maryland court at the request of one Epstein, a Maryland resident. Epstein had a claim for over $300 against another North Carolinian named Balk, and the writ garnished a $180 debt that Harris owed Balk. Harris did not contest the Maryland proceedings and paid the $180 to an attorney for Epstein. Upon his return to North Carolina, barely a week after being garnished in Maryland, Harris was sued by Balk in North Carolina on the $180 debt. Harris defended on the ground that his obligation was extinguished by payment to Epstein. Balk argued, however, that Maryland never obtained jurisdiction because Harris was not a resident of Maryland and Balk had no property there, the situs of the debt being North Carolina, where the loan was made. The North Carolina courts refused to accord the Maryland judgment full faith and credit and granted Balk judgment against Harris for $180. The Supreme Court held that North Carolina had to recognize the Maryland judgment.]

Attachment is the creature of the local law; that is, unless there is a law of the state providing for and permitting the attachment, it cannot be levied there. If there be a law of the state providing for the attachment of the debt, then, if the garnishee be found in that state, and process be personally served upon him therein, we think the court thereby acquires jurisdiction over him, and can garnish the debt due from him to the debtor of the plaintiff, and condemn it, provided the garnishee could himself be sued by his creditor in that state. We do not see how the question of jurisdiction vel non can properly be made to depend upon the so-called original situs of the debt, or upon the character of the stay of the garnishee, whether temporary or permanent, in the state where the attachment is issued. Power over the person of the garnishee confers jurisdiction on the courts of the state where the writ issues. If, while temporarily there, his creditor might sue him there and recover the debt, then he is liable to process of garnishment, no matter where the situs of the debt was originally. We do not see the materiality of the expression "situs of the debt," when used in connection with attachment proceedings. If by situs is meant the place of the creation of the debt, that fact is immaterial. If it be meant that the obligation to pay the debt can only be enforced at the situs thus fixed, we think it plainly untrue. The obligation of the debtor to pay his debt clings to and accompanies him wherever he goes. He is as much bound to pay his debt in a foreign state when therein sued upon his obligation by his creditor, as he was in the state where the debt was contracted. We speak of ordinary debts, such as the one in this case. It would be no defense to such suit for the debtor to plead that he was only in the foreign state casually or temporarily. His obligation to pay would be the same whether he was there in that way or with an intention to remain. It is nothing but the obligation to pay which is garnished or attached. This obligation can be enforced by the courts of the foreign state after personal service of process therein, just as well as by the courts of the domicil of the debtor. If the debtor leaves the foreign state without appearing, a judgment by default may be entered, upon which execution may issue, or the judgment may be sued upon in any other state where the debtor might be found. In such a case the situs is unimportant. It is not a question of possession in the foreign state, for possession cannot be taken of a debt or of the obligation to pay it, as tangible property might be taken possession of. Notice to the debtor (garnishee) and the commencement of the suit, and notice not to pay to his creditor, is all that can be given, whether the garnishee be a mere casual and temporary comer, or a resident of the state where the attachment is laid. His obligation to pay his creditor is thereby arrested, and a lien created upon the debt itself. We can see no reason why the attachment could not be thus laid, provided the creditor of the garnishee could himself sue in that state, and its laws permitted the attachment.

There can be no doubt that Balk, as a citizen of the state of North Carolina, had the right to sue Harris in Maryland to recover the debt which Harris owed him. Being a citizen of North Carolina, he was entitled to all the privileges and immunities of citizens of the several states, one of which is the right to institute actions in the courts of another state.

* * *

It seems to us, therefore, that the judgment against Harris in Maryland, condemning the $180 which he owed to Balk, was a valid judgment, because the court had jurisdiction over the garnishee by personal service of process within the state of Maryland.

It ought to be and it is the object of courts to prevent the payment of any debt twice over. Thus, if Harris, owing a debt to Balk, paid it under a valid judgment against him, to Epstein, he certainly ought not to be compelled to pay it a second time, but should have the right to plead his payment under the Maryland judgment. It is objected, however, that the payment by Harris to Epstein was not under legal compulsion. Harris in truth owed the debt to Balk, which was attached by Epstein. He had, therefore, as we have seen, no defense to set up against the attachment of the debt. Jurisdiction over him personally had been obtained by the Maryland court. As he was absolutely without defense, there was no reason why he should not consent to a judgment impounding the debt, which judgment the plaintiff was legally entitled to, and which he could not prevent. There was no merely voluntary payment within the meaning of that phrase as applicable here.

But most rights may be lost by negligence, and if the garnishee were guilty of negligence in the attachment proceeding, to the damage of Balk, he ought not to be permitted to set up the judgment as a defense. Thus it is recognized as the duty of the garnishee to give notice to his own creditor, if he would protect himself, so that the creditor may have the opportunity to defend himself against the claim of the person suing out the attachment. * * * While the want of notification by the garnishee to his own creditor may have no effect upon the validity of the judgment against the garnishee (the proper publication being made by the plaintiff), we think it has and ought to have an effect upon the right of the garnishee to avail himself of the prior judgment and his payment thereunder. This notification by the garnishee is for the purpose of making sure that his creditor shall have an opportunity to defend the claim made against him in the attachment suit. Fair dealing requires this at the hands of the garnishee. In this case, while neither the defendant nor the garnishee appeared, the court, while condemning the credits attached, could not, by the terms of the Maryland statute, issue the writ of execution unless the plaintiff gave bond or sufficient security before the court awarding the execution, to make restitution of the money paid if the defendant should, at any time within a year and a day, appear in the action and show that the plaintiff's claim, or some part thereof, was not due to the plaintiff. The defendant in error, Balk, had notice of this attachment, certainly within a few days after the issuing thereof and the entry of judgment thereon, because he sued the plaintiff in error to recover his debt within a few days after his [Harris'] return to North Carolina, in which suit the judgment in Maryland was set up by Harris as a plea in bar to Balk's claim. Balk, therefore, had an opportunity for a year and a day after the entry of the judgment to litigate the question of his liability in the Maryland court, and to show that he did not owe the debt, or some part of it, as was claimed by Epstein. He, however, took no proceedings to that end, so far as the record shows, and the reason may be supposed to be that he could not successfully defend the claim, because he admitted in this case that he did, at the time of the attachment proceeding, owe Epstein some $344.

NOTES AND QUESTIONS

1.   If the reasoning of this case seems convoluted, keep in mind that when Epstein filed his suit such stratagems were necessary to solve the jurisdictional problems caused by *Pennoyer*. Would the *Pennoyer* Court have looked favorably on this exercise of jurisdiction?

2.   From the perspective of Balk, and consistent with *Pennoyer*'s outlook, Maryland's jurisdiction is quasi-in-rem. What is it from the perspective of Harris? Suppose that Maryland garnishment procedures resembled *capias ad respondendum* (supra p. 705) and required the sheriff to imprison the garnishee until he paid the money into court. If Maryland lacks jurisdiction, what does Harris do to extricate himself and avoid double liability?

3.   Aside from providing a pretext to get around *Pennoyer*, in rem jurisdiction serves other functions. As we have seen in Chapter 2, prejudgment attachment can secure the plaintiff's right ultimately to recover and post-judgment garnishment can provide a means for enforcing judgments once entered. Beyond that, jurisdiction in rem can often serve very important interests of the state. The Court recognized these interests in Arndt v. Griggs, 134 U.S. 316 (1890):

> If a state has no power to bring a non-resident into its courts for any purposes by publication, it is impotent to perfect the titles of real estate within its limits held by its own citizens; and a cloud cast upon such title by a claim by a non-resident will remain for all time a cloud, unless such non-resident shall voluntarily come into its courts for the purpose of having it adjudicated. But no such imperfections attend the sovereignty of the state. * * * The well-being of every community requires that the title to real estate therein shall be secure, and that there be convenient and certain methods of determining any unsettled questions respecting it. The duty of accomplishing this is local in its nature.

Do any of these justifications for exercise of in rem jurisdiction apply in Harris v. Balk?

4.   The Court reasons that the debt can be attached in Maryland while Harris is there because Balk could then sue him there to collect on the debt. Does Balk's ability to sue Harris in Maryland if he serves him there have anything to do with the situs of the debt? Is there any reason to say that intangible property has a situs for purposes of exercise of quasi-in-rem jurisdiction?

5.   Was notice to Balk critical to the Maryland court's jurisdiction? If so, shouldn't it be Epstein's responsibility to provide notice?

6.   What if Balk denies that he owes money to Epstein? Can he contest the Maryland proceedings without consenting to jurisdiction there over

Start ⟶

Epstein's entire claim? See supra p. 715 for a discussion of limited appearances.

7.   Note that the Court cautions that "[w]e speak of ordinary debts, such as the one in this case." Under substantive law, such as that relating to negotiable instruments, enforcement of an obligation often entails possession of a document evidencing the obligation. Where that is true, the debt would not follow the debtor, and possession of the document would be a prerequisite to exercise of jurisdiction over the obligation.

―――――――

Q. Vid.

Hess v. Pawloski, 274 U.S. 352 (1927):

JUSTICE BUTLER delivered the Opinion of the Court.

[Plaintiff sued defendant, a Pennsylvania resident, in Massachusetts for personal injuries sustained in an auto accident in Massachusetts. Defendant objected to jurisdiction, but his objection was rejected and judgment was entered against him. Jurisdiction was based on a Massachusetts statute providing that the acceptance by a nonresident of the "privilege" of operating a motor vehicle in that state "shall be deemed equivalent to an appointment by such nonresident of the registrar or his successor in office, to be his true and lawful attorney upon whom may be served all lawful processes in any action or proceeding against him, growing out of any accident or collision in which said nonresident may be involved while operating a motor vehicle [in Massachusetts]." Service on the registrar would then be effective to subject defendant to Massachusetts jurisdiction provided plaintiff also "forthwith" sent notice of the service and a copy of the process to defendant by registered mail and obtained a signed return receipt. After plaintiff obtained jurisdiction in this manner, defendant sought Supreme Court review on the ground that he was not subject to Massachusetts jurisdiction, The Supreme Court upheld jurisdiction.]

Collateral Challenge

The process of a court of one State cannot run into another and summon a party there domiciled to respond to proceedings against him. Notice sent outside the state to a nonresident is unavailing to give jurisdiction in an action against him personally for money recovery. Pennoyer v. Neff, 95 U.S. 714. There must be actual service within the State of notice upon him or upon some one authorized to accept service for him. A personal judgment rendered against a nonresident, who has neither been served with process nor appeared in the suit, is without validity. The mere transaction of business in a State by nonresident natural persons does not imply consent to be bound by the process of its courts. Flexner v. Farson, 248 U.S. 289. The power of a State to exclude foreign corporations, although not absolute, but qualified, is the ground on which such an implication is supported as to them. Pennsylvania Fire Insurance Co. v. Gold Issue Mining Co., 243 U.S. 93, 96. But a State may not withhold from nonresident individuals the right of doing business therein. The privileges and immunities clause of the Constitution, § 2, Art. IV, safeguards to the citizens of one State the right "to pass through, or to reside in any other state for purposes of trade, agriculture, professional pursuits, or otherwise." And it prohibits state legislation discriminating against citizens of other states.

Motor vehicles are dangerous machines; and, even when skillfully and carefully operated, their use is attended by serious dangers to persons and property. In the public interest the State may make and enforce regulations reasonably calculated to promote care on the part of all, residents and nonresidents alike, who use its highways. The measure in question operates to require a nonresident to answer for his conduct in the State where arise causes of action alleged against him, as well as to provide for a claimant a convenient method by which he may sue to enforce his rights. Under the statute the implied consent is limited to proceedings growing out of accidents or collisions on a highway in which the nonresident may be involved. It is required that he shall actually receive and receipt for notice of the service and a copy of the process. And it contemplates such continuances as may be found necessary to give reasonable time and opportunity for defense. It makes no hostile discrimination against non-residents, but tends to put them on the same footing as residents. Literal and precise equality in respect of this matter is not attainable; it is not required. The State's power to regulate the use of its highways extends to their use by nonresidents as well as by residents. And, in advance of the operation of a motor vehicle on its highway by a nonresident, the State may require him to appoint one of its officials as his agent on whom process may be served in proceedings growing out of such use. Kane v. New Jersey, 242 U.S. 160, 167. That case recognized power of the State to exclude a nonresident until the formal appointment is made. And, having the power so to exclude, the State may declare that the use of the highway by the nonresident is the equivalent of the appointment of the registrar as agent on whom process may be served. The difference between the formal and implied appointment is not substantial, so far as concerns the application of the due process clause of the Fourteenth Amendment.

NOTES AND QUESTIONS

1. Is the Court's emphasis on the automobile's dangerousness a nonsequitur in light of its emphasis on defendant's implied consent as the basis for finding jurisdiction? Cf. Henry L. Doherty & Co. v. Goodman, 294 U.S. 623 (1935), where the Supreme Court, relying in part on *Hess*, upheld Iowa's authority to assert jurisdiction over a nonresident individual by means of service of process on the individual's agent within the state. Defendant, though never personally within the state, had established an office in the state for dealing in securities. The Court noted that "Iowa treats the business of dealing in corporate securities as exceptional and subjects it to special regulation."

Should that factor be relevant in determining the applicability of *Hess*'s implied consent analysis?

2. Kane v. New Jersey, 242 U.S. 160 (1916), upheld a state requirement that nonresidents who used its highways register, pay a fee, and appoint an agent for service of process. As in *Hess*, the Court emphasized the dangerousness of the car in concluding that the requirement was a reasonable regulation of the use of the highways. To what extent is that sort of state interest in regulating the activity involved essential to its right to condition permission to engage in the activity on consent to jurisdiction? Could Massachusetts exclude people on bicycles or on foot? Cf. Edwards v. California, 314 U.S. 160 (1941) (state statute excluding indigents violates commerce clause).

3. Did Justice Field have implied consent in mind in *Pennoyer*? Consider the analysis of Justice Frankfurter in Olberding v. Illinois Central Ry. Co., 346 U.S. 338 (1953), rejecting a similar argument that defendant had waived his right to object on venue grounds (statutory limitations on the location of suit, see infra p. 842) by driving his truck in the state:

> The defendant may protest to high heaven his unwillingness to be sued and it avails him not. The liability rests on the inroad which the automobile has made on the decision of Pennoyer v. Neff, 95 U.S. 714, as it has on so many aspects of our social scene. The potentialities of damage by a motorist, in a population as mobile as ours, are such that those whom he injures must have opportunities of redress against him provided only that he is afforded an opportunity to defend himself. We have held that this is a fair rule of law as between a resident injured party (for whose protection these statutes are primarily intended) and a non-resident motorist, and that the requirements of due process are therefore met. Hess v. Pawloski, 274 U.S. 352. But to conclude from this holding that the motorist, who never consented to anything and whose consent is altogether immaterial, has actually agreed to be sued and has thus waived his federal venue rights is surely to move in the world of Alice in Wonderland.

4. The Massachusetts statute limited the implied consent to claims arising out of driving in the state. Was that limitation constitutionally required? In Pennsylvania Fire Ins. Co. v. Gold Issue Mining & Milling Co., 243 U.S. 93 (1917), the Court held that a state could constitutionally require that foreign corporations wishing to be authorized to do business consent to suit in all actions, of whatever nature, not just those arising out of the business done in the state. See Note, Registration Statutes, Personal Jurisdiction, and the Problem of Predictability, 103 Colum.L.Rev. 1163 (2003) (arguing that due process precludes general jurisdiction based on corporate registration statutes); King v. American Family Mut. Ins. Co., 632 F.3d 579 (9th Cir. 2011) (holding that partially-completed corporation registration in Montana did not subject insurer that was "99.9% Montana free" to Montana jurisdiction).

5. The consent theory can founder where the state does not have the power to exclude the defendant. Why? In Flexner v. Farson, 248 U.S. 289 (1919), the court refused to allow the consent theory to be applied to a partnership because, under the privileges and immunities clause of the Constitution, the individual partners had the right (not shared by corporations) to engage in business in the state. The Court watered down this holding in Henry L. Doherty & Co. v. Goodman, 294 U.S. 623 (1935), described in note 1 above.

JURISDICTION OVER CORPORATE DEFENDANTS

Corporations presented special difficulties for the *Pennoyer* analysis. Like the automobile, they came to have greater and greater importance in society in the decades after *Pennoyer* was decided. Because they were fictional entities, however, it was difficult to say that they could be found in any particular place for purposes of service. Initially, it was assumed that a corporation could be sued in the state in which it was incorporated, but as corporations began to grow and engage in interstate activities that hardly seemed sufficient. Two types of solutions were found. First, states enacted comprehensive requirements that all corporations engaging in business within their borders register and appoint agents for service of process. Failing that, many of these statutes provided that corporations which engaged in business but did not register would be deemed impliedly to have consented to service on a state official. This was permissible because corporations, unlike individuals, have been held to have no rights under the privileges and immunities clause.

Second, there developed a doctrine of corporate "presence"—a corporation was present wherever it engaged in a sufficient amount of activities, and it could therefore be served like a natural person who was present. Unhappily, this approach used the same label and looked to the same facts as the implied consent theory—"doing business." It is important to note that under the "presence" analysis, whether plaintiff's claim was related to defendant's activities within the state was logically irrelevant. This fact derived from the analogy of the corporate "presence" doctrine to an individual's physical presence within a state as a basis for in personam jurisdiction: Under the "transient" principle, an individual physically present within a state could be subjected to jurisdiction for any suit; similarly, if a corporation were deemed "present," no relationship between the suit and the corporation's in-state activity need be established. Thus, the analysis of "doing business" turned exclusively on an examination of purely quantitative factors, primarily the total amount and continuity of the corporation's business activities in the state. "Continuous and substantial" commercial activity was necessary to constitute presence. See, e.g., the opinion of Judge Cardozo in Tauza v. Susquehanna Coal Company, 115 N.E. 915 (N.Y.1917).

Given these difficulties in adapting *Pennoyer* to suits against corporations, it is not surprising that the Court broke away from *Pennoyer* in a suit against a corporation.

B. THE SHIFT TO MINIMUM CONTACTS

INTERNATIONAL SHOE CO. v. WASHINGTON

Supreme Court of the United States, 1945
326 U.S. 310

CHIEF JUSTICE STONE delivered the opinion of the Court.

The questions for decision are (1) whether, within the limitations of the due process clause of the Fourteenth Amendment, appellant, a Delaware corporation, has by its activities in the State of Washington rendered itself amenable to proceedings in the courts of that state to recover unpaid contributions to the state unemployment compensation fund exacted by state statutes, Washington Unemployment Compensation Act, Washington Revised Statutes, § 9998–103a through § 9998–123a, 1941 Supp., and (2) whether the state can exact those contributions consistently with the due process clause of the Fourteenth Amendment.

The statutes in question set up a comprehensive scheme of unemployment compensation, the costs of which are defrayed by contributions required to be made by employers to a state unemployment compensation fund. The contributions are a specified percentage of the wages payable annually by each employer for his employees' services in the state. The assessment and collection of the contributions and the fund are administered by respondents. Section 14(c) of the Act (Wash.Rev.Stat. 1941 Supp., § 9998–114c) authorizes respondent Commissioner to issue an order and notice of assessment of delinquent contributions upon prescribed personal service of the notice upon the employer if found within the state, or, if not so found, by mailing the notice to the employer by registered mail at his last known address. That section also authorizes the Commissioner to collect the assessment by distraint if it is not paid within ten days after service of the notice. By §§ 14e and 6b the order of assessment may be administratively reviewed by an appeal tribunal within the office of unemployment upon petition of the employer, and this determination is by § 6(i) made subject to judicial review on questions of law by the state Superior Court, with further right of appeal in the state Supreme Court as in other civil cases.

In this case notice of assessment for the years in question was personally served upon a sales solicitor employed by appellant in the State of Washington, and a copy of the notice was mailed by registered mail to appellant at its address in St. Louis, Missouri. Appellant appeared specially before the office of unemployment and moved to set aside the order and notice of assessment on the ground that the service upon appellant's salesman was not proper service upon appellant; that appellant was not a corporation of the State of Washington and was not doing business within the state; that it had no agent within the state upon whom service could be made; and that appellant is not an employer and does not furnish employment within the meaning of the statute.

The motion was heard on evidence and a stipulation of facts by the appeal tribunal which denied the motion and ruled that respondent Commissioner was entitled to recover the unpaid contributions. That action was affirmed by the Commissioner; both the Superior Court and the Supreme Court affirmed. Appellant in each of these courts assailed the statute as applied, as a violation of the due process clause of the Fourteenth Amendment, and as imposing a constitutionally prohibited burden on interstate commerce. The cause comes here on appeal, appellant assigning as error that the challenged statutes as applied infringe the due process clause of the Fourteenth Amendment and the commerce clause.

The facts as found by the appeal tribunal and accepted by the state Superior Court and Supreme Court, are not in dispute. Appellant is a Delaware corporation, having its principal place of business in St. Louis, Missouri, and is engaged in the manufacture and sale of shoes and other footwear. It maintains places of business in several states, other than Washington, at which its manufacturing is carried on and from which its merchandise is distributed interstate through several sales units or branches located outside the State of Washington.

Appellant has no office in Washington and makes no contracts either for sale or purchase of merchandise there. It maintains no stock of merchandise in that state and makes there no deliveries of goods in intrastate commerce. During the years from 1937 to 1940, now in question, appellant employed eleven to thirteen salesmen under direct supervision and control of sales managers located in St. Louis. These salesmen resided in Washington; their principal activities were confined to that state; and they were compensated by commissions based upon the amount of their sales. The commissions for each year totaled more than $31,000. Appellant supplies its salesmen with a line of samples, each consisting of one shoe of a pair, which they display to prospective purchasers. On occasion they rent permanent sample rooms, for exhibiting samples, in business buildings, or rent rooms in hotels or business buildings temporarily for that purpose. The cost of such rentals is reimbursed by appellant.

The authority of the salesmen is limited to exhibiting their samples and soliciting orders from prospective buyers, at prices and on terms fixed by appellant. The salesmen transmit the orders to appellant's office in St. Louis for acceptance or rejection, and when accepted the merchandise for filling the orders is shipped f.o.b. from points outside Washington to the purchasers within the state. All the merchandise shipped into Washington is invoiced at the place of shipment from which collections are made. No salesman has authority to enter into contracts or to make collections.

The Supreme Court of Washington was of opinion that the regular and systematic solicitation of orders in the state by appellant's salesmen, resulting in a continuous flow of appellant's product into the state, was sufficient to constitute doing business in the state so as to make appellant amenable to suit in its courts. But it was also of opinion that there were sufficient additional activities shown to bring the case within the rule frequently stated, that solicitation within a state by the agents of a foreign corporation plus some additional activities there are sufficient to render the corporation amenable to suit brought in the courts of the state to enforce an obligation arising out of its activities there. The court found such additional activities in the salesmen's display of samples sometimes in permanent display rooms, and the salesmen's residence within the state, continued over a period of years, all resulting in a substantial volume of merchandise regularly shipped by appellant to purchasers within the state.

* * *

Appellant also insists that its activities within the state were not sufficient to manifest its "presence" there and that in its absence the state courts were without jurisdiction, that consequently it was a denial of due process for the state to subject appellant to suit. It refers to those cases in which it was said that the mere solicitation of orders for the purchase of goods within a state, to be accepted without the state and filled by shipment of the purchased goods interstate, does not render the corporation seller amenable to suit within the state. And appellant further argues that since it was not present within the state, it is a denial of due process to subject it to taxation or other money exaction. It thus denies the power of the state to lay the tax or to subject appellant to a suit for its collection.

Historically the jurisdiction of courts to render judgment in personam is grounded on their de facto power over the defendant's person. Hence his presence within the territorial jurisdiction of court was prerequisite to its rendition of a judgment personally binding him. Pennoyer v. Neff, 95 U.S. 714, 733. But now that the capias ad respondendum has given way to personal service of summons or other form of notice, due process requires only that in order to subject a defendant to a judgment in personam, if he be not present within the territory of the forum, he have certain minimum contacts with it such that the maintenance of the suit does not offend "traditional notions of fair play and substantial justice." Milliken v. Meyer, 311 U.S. 457, 463.

Since the corporate personality is a fiction, although a fiction intended to be acted upon as though it were a fact, it is clear that unlike an individual its "presence" without, as well as within, the state of its origin can be manifested only by activities carried on in its behalf by those who are authorized to act for it. To say that the corporation is so far "present" there as to satisfy due process requirements, for purposes of taxation or the maintenance of suits against it in the courts of the state, is to beg the question to be decided. For the terms "present" or "presence" are used merely to symbolize those activities of the corporation's agent within the state which courts will deem to be sufficient to satisfy the demands of due process. Those demands may be met by such contacts of the corporation with the state of the forum as make it reasonable, in the context of our federal system of government, to require the corporation to defend the particular suit which is brought there. An "estimate of the inconveniences" which would result to the corporation from a trial away from its "home" or principal place of business is relevant in this connection.

"Presence" in the state in this sense has never been doubted when the activities of the corporation there have not only been continuous and systematic, but also give rise to the liabilities sued on, even though no consent to be sued or authorization to an agent to accept service of process has been given. Conversely it has been generally recognized that the casual presence of the corporate agent or even his conduct of single or isolated items of activities in a state in the corporation's behalf are not enough to subject it to suit on causes of action unconnected with the activities there. To require the corporation in such circumstances to defend the suit away from its home or other jurisdiction where it carries on more substantial activities has been thought to lay too great and unreasonable a burden on the corporation to comport with due process.

While it has been held in cases on which appellant relies that continuous activity of some sort within a state is not enough to support the demand that the corporation be amenable to suits unrelated to that activity, there have been instances in which the continuous corporate operations within a state were thought so substantial and of such a nature as to justify suit against it on causes of action arising from dealings entirely distinct from those activities.

Finally, although the commission of some single or occasional acts of the corporate agent in a state sufficient to impose an obligation or liability on the corporation has not been thought to confer upon the state authority to enforce it, Rosenberg Bros. & Co. v. Curtis Brown Co., 260 U.S. 516, other such acts, because of their nature and quality and the circumstances of their commission, may be deemed sufficient to render the corporation liable to suit. Cf. Kane v. New Jersey, 242 U.S. 160; Hess v. Pawloski, [274 U.S. 352]. True, some of the decisions holding the corporation amenable to suit have been supported by resort to the legal fiction that it has given its consent to service and suit, consent being implied from its presence in the state through the acts of its authorized agents. But more realistically it may be said that those authorized acts were of such a nature as to justify the fiction.

It is evident that the criteria by which we mark the boundary line between those activities which justify the subjection of a corporation to suit, and those which do not, cannot be simply mechanical or quantitative. The test is not merely, as has sometimes been suggested, whether the activity, which the corporation has seen fit to procure through its agents in another state, is a little more or a little less. Whether due process is satisfied must depend rather upon the quality and nature of the activity in relation to the fair and orderly administration of the laws which it was the purpose of the due process clause to insure. That clause does not contemplate that a state may make binding a judgment in personam against an individual or corporate defendant with which the state has no contacts, ties, or relations. Cf. Pennoyer v. Neff, supra.

But to the extent that a corporation exercises the privilege of conducting activities within a state, it enjoys the benefits and protection of the laws of that state. The exercise of that privilege may give rise to obligations; and, so far as those obligations arise out of or are connected with the activities within the state, a procedure which requires the corporation to respond to a suit brought to enforce them can, in most instances, hardly be said to be undue.

Applying these standards, the activities carried on in behalf of appellant in the State of Washington were neither irregular nor casual. They were systematic and continuous throughout the years in question. They resulted in a large volume of interstate business, in the course of which appellant received the benefits and protection of the laws of the state, including the right to resort to the courts for the enforcement of its rights. The obligation which is here sued upon arose out of those very activities. It is evident that these operations establish sufficient contacts or ties with the state of the forum to make it reasonable and just according to our traditional conception of fair play and substantial justice to permit the state to enforce the obligations which appellant has incurred there. Hence we cannot say that the maintenance of the present suit in the State of Washington involves an unreasonable or undue procedure.

JUSTICE BLACK delivered the following opinion.

* * *

[I]t is unthinkable that the vague due process clause was ever intended to prohibit a State from regulating or taxing a business carried on within its boundaries simply because this is done by agents of a corporation organized and having its headquarters elsewhere. To read this into the due process clause would in fact result in depriving a State's citizens of due process by taking from the State the power to protect them in their business dealings within its boundaries with representatives of a foreign corporation. Nothing could be more irrational or more designed to defeat the function of our federative system of government. Certainly a State, at the very least, has power to tax and sue those dealing with its citizens within its boundaries, as we have held before. Were the Court to follow this principle, it would provide a workable standard for cases where, as here, no other questions are involved. The Court has not chosen to do so, but instead has engaged in an unnecessary discussion in the course of which it has announced vague Constitutional criteria applied for the first time to the issue before us. It has thus introduced uncertain elements confusing the simple pattern and tending to curtail the exercise of State powers to an extent not justified by the Constitution.

* * *

I think it a judicial deprivation to condition its exercise upon this Court's notion of "fair play," however appealing that term may be. Nor can I stretch the meaning of due process so far as to authorize this Court to deprive a State of the right to afford judicial protection to its citizens on the ground that it would be more "convenient" for the corporation to be sued somewhere else.

There is a strong emotional appeal in the words "fair play", "justice", and "reasonableness." But they were not chosen by those who wrote the original Constitution or the Fourteenth Amendment as a measuring rod for this Court to use in invalidating State or Federal laws passed by elected legislative representatives. * * * For application of this natural law concept, whether under the terms "reasonableness", "justice", or "fair play", makes judges the supreme arbiters of the country's laws and practices.

NOTES AND QUESTIONS

1.   Chief Justice Stone goes to some lengths to expose the difficulties created by previous theories for jurisdiction over foreign corporations. While one could argue that the new minimum contacts formulation announced in *International Shoe* applies only to corporate defendants, in fact it was held to apply generally to all defendants.

2.   What factors are relevant to a minimum contacts determination whether to exercise jurisdiction over defendant? Obviously plaintiff will have information bearing on some of those factors when the lawsuit is filed, but on others plaintiff will need to do discovery. In Insurance Corp. of Ireland, Ltd. v. Compagnie des Bauxites de Guinee, 456 U.S. 694 (1982), infra p. 830, the Court upheld the power of a court to compel defendant to respond to discovery regarding its contacts with the forum.

3.   The Court's decision does not seem keyed to the precise facts of the case before it, and it provides little insight into proper disposition of jurisdictional challenges in other types of cases. Consider the following alternative scenarios:

(a)   A Washington resident buys a pair of International Shoe shoes at a shoe store in Seattle and is injured in Seattle due to an alleged defect in the shoes. Can he sue International Shoe in Washington to recover for his injuries?

(b) An Oregon resident visiting in Washington buys a pair of International Shoe shoes at a shoe store in Seattle, takes them home to Oregon, and is injured there due to an alleged defect in the shoes. Can she sue International Shoe in Oregon to recover for her injuries? Can she sue in Washington?

(c) A Washington resident visiting in St. Louis buys a pair of International Shoe shoes there, takes them home to Washington and is injured there due to an alleged defect in the shoes. Can he sue International Shoe in Washington to recover for his injuries?

(d) An Oregon shoe retailer meets with International Shoe sales representatives in Seattle and places an order for 100 pairs of International Shoe shoes. International Shoe accepts the order and ships the shoes to Oregon. The retailer sells some, and customers who discover defects in the shoes return them. Can the Oregon retailer sue International Shoe in Oregon to get back the money she paid for the shoes and to recover damages for injury to her business reputation?

(e) Assume the Oregon retailer in the previous example had not paid for the shoes when she received the complaints and that she then refused to pay. Can International Shoe sue her in St. Louis for payment? In Rosenberg Bros. & Co. v. Curtis Brown Co., 260 U.S. 516 (1923), cited in *International Shoe*, an Oklahoma retailer of clothing which regularly purchased a large part of its merchandise from New York, was sued in New York when it failed to pay for some of the merchandise. The Court held that New York could not exercise jurisdiction. It reasoned that "[t]he only business alleged to have been transacted by the company in New York, either then or theretofore, related to such purchases of goods by officers of a foreign corporation. Visits on such business, even if occurring at regular intervals, would not warrant the inference that the corporation was present within the jurisdiction of the State."

(f) If one of the customers of the Oregon retailer in (d) above was injured in Oregon due to the alleged defects in the shoes, could he sue in Oregon to recover for his injuries? If so, would that affect the right of the Oregon resident in (b) above, who bought her shoes in Seattle, to sue in Oregon for injuries received there due to alleged defects in International Shoe shoes?

4.   As should be apparent, much development of the minimum contacts standard would be necessary to make it workable. Justice Black castigated the majority for creating a "natural law" standard infinitely manipulable by judges. His concern, obviously, was that judges would invalidate exercises of state power, as had occurred during the 1920s and 1930s with regard to a great deal of New Deal and similar regulatory legislation. Was his concern realistic? Consider that the jurisdiction decision is usually made by an elected state court judge confronted with a local plaintiff (and constituent), often injured, suing a distant defendant, often a large corporation. In what direction is judicial power likely to be abused?

McGee v. International Life Ins. Co., 355 U.S. 220 (1957):

Opinion of the Court by JUSTICE BLACK, announced by JUSTICE DOUGLAS.

Petitioner, Lulu B. McGee, recovered a judgment in a California state court against respondent, International Life Insurance Company, on a contract of insurance. Respondent was not served with process in California but by registered mail at its principal place of business in Texas. The California court based its jurisdiction on a state statute which subjects foreign corporations to suit in California on insurance contracts with residents of that State even though such corporations cannot be served with process within its borders. [Cal. Ins. Code, §§ 1610–1620.] [Petitioner sought to enforce her default judgment in Texas, but the Texas courts refused to accord it full faith and credit. The Supreme Court reversed.]

The material facts are relatively simple. In 1944, Lowell Franklin, a resident of California, purchased a life insurance policy from the Empire Mutual Insurance Company, an Arizona corporation. In 1948 the respondent agreed with Empire Mutual to assume its insurance obligations. Respondent then mailed a reinsurance certificate to Franklin in California offering to insure him in accordance with the terms of the policy he held with Empire Mutual. He accepted this offer and from that time until his death in 1950 paid premiums by mail from his California home to respondent's Texas office. Petitioner, Franklin's mother, was the beneficiary under the policy. She sent proofs of his death to the respondent but it refused to pay claiming that he had committed suicide. It appears that neither Empire Mutual nor respondent has ever had any office or agent in California. And so far as the record before us shows, respondent has never solicited or done any insurance business in California apart from the policy involved here.

Since Pennoyer v. Neff, 95 U.S. 714, this Court has held that the Due Process Clause of the Fourteenth Amendment places some limit on the power of state courts to enter binding judgments against persons not served with process within their boundaries. But just where this line of limitation falls has been the subject of prolific controversy, particularly with respect to foreign corporations. In a continuing process of evolution this Court accepted and then abandoned "consent," "doing business," and "presence" as the standard for measuring the extent of state judicial power over such corporations. More recently in International Shoe Co. v. State of Washington, 326 U.S. 310, the Court decided that "due process requires only that in order to subject a defendant to a judgment in personam, if he be not present within the territory of the forum, he have certain minimum contacts with it such that the maintenance of the suit does not offend 'traditional notions of fair play and substantial justice.'"

Looking back over this long history of litigation a trend is clearly discernible toward expanding the permissible scope of state jurisdiction over foreign corporations and other nonresidents. In part this is attributable to the fundamental transformation of our national economy over the years. Today many commercial transactions touch two or more States and may involve parties separated by the full continent. With this increasing nationalization of commerce has come a great increase in the amount of business conducted by mail across state lines. At the same time modern transportation and communication have made it much less burdensome for a party sued to defend himself in a State where he engages in economic activity.

Turning to this case we think it apparent that the Due Process Clause did not preclude the California court from entering a judgment binding on respondent. It is sufficient for purposes of due process that the suit was based on a contract which had substantial connection with that State. The contract was delivered in California, the premiums were mailed from there and the insured was a resident of that State when he died. It cannot be denied that California has a manifest interest in providing effective means of redress for its residents when their insurers refuse to pay claims. These residents would be at a severe disadvantage if they were forced to follow the insurance company to a distant State in order to hold it legally accountable. When claims were small or moderate individual claimants frequently could not afford the cost of bringing an action in a foreign forum—thus in effect making the company judgment proof. Often the crucial witnesses—as here on the company's defense of suicide—will be found in the insured's locality. Of course there may be inconvenience to the insurer if it is held amenable to suit in California where it had this contract but certainly nothing which amounts to a denial of due process. There is no contention that respondent did not have adequate notice of the suit or sufficient time to prepare its defenses and appear.

NOTES AND QUESTIONS

1.   In terms of general attitude toward the extent of jurisdiction, *McGee* represented the apogee of liberality by the Supreme Court. In support of this expansive view, Justice Black cites the "fundamental transformation of our national economy" that has occurred since *Pennoyer*. Certainly state lines seem insignificant in terms of the geographic organization of significant parts of our country. One need only consider metropolitan areas that include parts of several states, such as New York and Philadelphia, to recognize that for many purposes our society is not organized along state lines. Should state lines simply be irrelevant, with the burden on the defendant the only significant factor? Would that place due process limitations on the power of a large state to require its own citizens to defend in a distant court of that state?

2.   The Court's opinion suggests that the focus should be on balancing the inconvenience to the plaintiff of suing elsewhere and the inconvenience to the defendant of defending in the forum. How often will such a balance turn out to favor dismissal where the plaintiff is local?

3.   Later in the same term in which it decided *McGee*, the Court sounded a note of caution on overbroad extensions of state court jurisdiction in Hanson v. Denckla, 357 U.S. 235 (1958). This extraordinarily complicated case revolved around the validity of a trust set up in Delaware by Dora Donner, a woman from Pennsylvania who later moved to Florida and died there. The Florida courts held that the trust was invalid. To reach that result, the Florida courts had to find jurisdiction over the Delaware trustee, which was an indispensable party under Florida law.

The Supreme Court reversed on the ground that Florida's exercise of jurisdiction over the trustee was unconstitutional. Chief Justice Warren, writing for the Court, recognized the progressive relaxation of limitations on jurisdiction, but cautioned that "it is a mistake to assume that this trend heralds the eventual demise of all restrictions on the personal jurisdiction of state courts. Those restrictions are more than a guarantee of immunity from inconvenient or distant litigation. They are a consequence of territorial limitations on the power of the respective States. However minimal the burden of defending in a foreign tribunal, a defendant may not be called upon to do so unless he has the 'minimal contacts' with that state that are a prerequisite to its exercise of power over him." It stressed that defendant's contacts with the forum state could not be established by the *unilateral action* of another person, adding that "it is essential in each case that there be some act by which the defendant purposefully avails itself of the privilege of conducting activities within the forum State, thus invoking the benefits and protections of its laws."

This *purposeful availment* requirement seems to be derived from some of the reasoning in *International Shoe*: "[T]o the extent that a corporation exercises the privilege of conducting activities within a state, it enjoys the benefits and protection of the laws of that state. The exercise of that privilege may give rise to obligations, and, so far as those obligations arise out of or are connected with the activities within the state, a procedure which requires the corporation to respond to a suit brought to enforce them can, in most instances, hardly be said to be undue." See supra p. 730.

Nevertheless, the facts in *Hanson* seemed a great deal like *McGee*. For nearly 20 years many believed that *Hanson* was an aberration, but when the Court again addressed the subject, it showed that it was serious about the analytical framework of *Hanson*. Before we examine those developments in Section D of this chapter, however, we shall turn to the states' response to the relaxation of the due process formula.

4.   How should *McGee*'s approach be applied in Gray v. American Radiator & Standard Sanitary Corp., 176 N.E.2d 761 (Ill.1961)? Plaintiff in that case was injured in Illinois due to the explosion of a water heater manufactured by defendant American Radiator at its plant in Pennsylvania. She also sued Titan Valve Manufacturing Co., an Ohio company that manufactured safety valves and supplied them to American Radiator, claiming that the valve in the water heater that exploded was manufactured by Titan. Titan objected to jurisdiction on the ground that it did no business in Illinois and had no agent in the state. It argued that its sales of valves to American

Radiator outside Illinois was not a proper basis for jurisdiction. The court disagreed:

> In the case at bar defendant does not claim that the present use of its product in Illinois is an isolated instance. While the record does not disclose the volume of Titan's business or the territory in which appliances incorporating its valves are marketed, it is a reasonable inference that its commercial transactions, like those of other manufacturers, result in substantial use and consumption in this State. To the extent that its business may be directly affected by transactions occurring here it enjoys benefits from the laws of this State, and it has undoubtedly benefited, to a degree, from the protection which our law has given to the marketing of hot water heaters containing its valves. Where the alleged liability arises, as in this case, from the manufacture of products presumably sold in contemplation of use here, it should not matter that the purchase was made from an independent middleman or that someone other than the defendant shipped the product into this State.

> With the increasing specialization of commercial activity and the growing interdependence of business enterprises it is seldom that a manufacturer deals directly with consumers in other States. The fact that the benefit he derives from its laws is an indirect one, however, does not make it any the less essential to the conduct of his business; and it is not unreasonable, where a cause of action arises from alleged defects in his product, to say that the use of such products in the ordinary course of commerce is sufficient contact with this State to justify a requirement that he defend here.

> As a general proposition, if a corporation elects to sell its products for ultimate use in another State, it is not unjust to hold it answerable there for any damage caused by defects in those products. Advanced means of distribution and other commercial activity have made possible these modern methods of doing business, and have largely effaced the economic significance of State lines. By the same token, today's facilities for transportation and communication have removed much of the difficulty and inconvenience formerly encountered in defending lawsuits brought in other States.

This justification for exercising jurisdiction has come to be known as the *stream of commerce* theory, positing that if a commercial actor puts its products into the stream of commerce with the expectation that they will be marketed in the forum it may be sued in the forum for injuries allegedly resulting there. Is this analysis consistent with *McGee*? Does it comport with the "purposeful availment" analysis of Hanson v. Denckla, supra note 3? We will return to these questions in connection with World-Wide Volkswagen Corp. v. Woodson, infra p. 744, and J. McIntyre Machinery, Ltd. v. Nicastro, infra p. 772.

C. THE STATES' RESPONSE—
LONG-ARM STATUTES

As we have seen, the states responded to *Pennoyer* by creatively fitting their jurisdictional statutes within its framework, particularly by expanding the concept of consent. The relaxation of *Pennoyer* that culminated in *International Shoe* similarly had an effect on state law regarding exercise of jurisdiction. There is no constitutional requirement that a state actually exercise its jurisdiction to the maximum extent permitted by due process, although some legislatures decided to do so. Consider California's straightforward approach: "A court of this state may exercise jurisdiction on any basis not inconsistent with the Constitution of this state or of the United States." Cal.Code Civ.Proc. § 410.10.

Most states, however, were initially more circumspect, enacting statutes that described with some particularity the kinds of cases in which their courts were to exercise jurisdiction. The first comprehensive effort in this regard was the Illinois long-arm statute of 1955 (originally codified as Ill.Rev.Stats. ch. 110, § 17), which provided as follows:

(1) Any person, whether or not a citizen or resident of this State, who in person or through an agent does any of the acts hereinafter enumerated, thereby submits said person, and, if an individual, his personal representative, to the jurisdiction of the courts of this State as to any cause of action arising from the doing of any of said acts:

(a) The transaction of any business within this State;

(b) The commission of a tortious act within this State;

(c) The ownership, use, or possession of any real estate in this State;

(d) Contracting to insure any person, property or risk located within this State at the time of contracting.

The Illinois statute served as a model for the statutes in other states. In Gray v. American Radiator & Standard Sanitary Corp., 176 N.E.2d 761 (Ill.1961) (also discussed supra p. 735 n. 4), the Illinois Supreme Court adopted an expansive interpretation of the provision for jurisdiction on claims arising out of "[t]he commission of a tortious act within this State." Plaintiff there had been injured in Illinois when a water heater exploded. Plaintiff sued not only American Radiator, a Pennsylvania company that manufactured the water heater, but also Titan Valve Manufacturing Co., an Ohio company that supplied American Radiator with valves, including the one in the water heater that exploded. Titan argued that if it had committed a "tortious act," it must have done so in Ohio. Since it had never done any business in Illinois, and sent the valves it sold to American Radiator, it contended that it could not be sued in Illinois.

The court rejected Titan's argument:

> The wrong in the case at bar did not originate in the conduct of a servant physically present here, but arose instead from acts performed at the place of manufacture. Only the consequences occurred in Illinois. It is well established, however, that in law the place of a wrong is where the last event takes place which is necessary to render the actor liable. Restatement, Conflict of Laws, sec. 377. A second indication that the place of injury is the determining factor is found in rules governing the time within which an action must be brought. In applying statutes of limitation our court has computed the period from the time when the injury is done. We think it is clear that the alleged negligence in manufacturing the valve cannot be separated from the resulting injury; and that for present purposes, like those of liability and limitations, the tort was committed in Illinois.
>
> Titan seeks to avoid this result by arguing that instead of using the word "tort," the legislature employed the term "tortious act"; and that the latter refers only to the act or conduct, separate and apart from any consequences thereof. We cannot accept the argument. To be tortious an act must cause injury. The concept of injury is an inseparable part of the phrase. In determining legislative intention courts will read words in their ordinary and popularly understood sense. We think the intent should be determined less from technicalities of definition than from considerations of general purpose and effect. To adopt the criteria urged by defendant would tend to promote litigation over extraneous issues concerning the elements of a tort and the territorial incidence of each, whereas the test should be concerned more with those substantial elements of convenience and justice presumably contemplated by the legislature. As we observed in Nelson v. Miller, 143 N.E.2d 673, the statute contemplates the exertion of jurisdiction over nonresident defendants to the extent permitted by the due-process clause.

Titan's argument seemed to have some force; the New York statute modeled on the Illinois provision was interpreted as Titan had argued. In Feathers v. McLucas, 209 N.E.2d 68 (N.Y.1965), the New York court explicitly disagreed with the Illinois court's approach in *Gray*:

> The language of paragraph 2 [of the New York long-arm statute]— conferring personal jurisdiction over a nondomiciliary "if, in person or through an agent, he . . . commits a tortious act within the state"—is too plain and precise to permit it to be read * * * as if it were synonymous with "commits a tortious act without the state which causes injury within the state." The mere occurrence of the injury in this State certainly cannot serve to transmute an

out-of-state tortious act into one committed here within the sense of the statutory wording.

But it may often be difficult to discern why the legislature would want to close the courthouse door on local plaintiffs seeking compensation from distant defendants. In New York, the New York Legislature responded to the more restrictive interpretation of the New York court by amending its statute to cover tortious acts outside New York causing injury within, so long as defendant "expects or should reasonably expect the act to have consequences in the state and derives substantial revenue from interstate or international commerce."

NOTES AND QUESTIONS

1.   The Illinois court said that it was interpreting the term "tortious act" in its "ordinary and popularly understood sense." Is this persuasive? It also invoked "considerations of general purpose and effect." Would it be reasonable to expect that the Illinois legislature would endorse the interpretation given the statute by the court?

Ultimately the Illinois legislature amended its long-arm statute, and it now appears as § 2–209 of the Illinois Code of Civil Procedure. Subsection (a) repeats the original provisions (quoted supra p. 737) and adds the following additional acts, where the cause of action arises from them (the original (a) through (d) having been renumbered (1) through (4)), among others the following:

(7)   The making or performance of any contract or promise substantially connected with this State;

(10) The acquisition or ownership, possession or control of any asset or thing of value present within this State when ownership, possession or control was acquired;

(11) The breach of any fiduciary duty within this State;

(12) The performance of duties as a director or officer of a corporation organized under the laws of this State or having its principal place of business within this State.

Subsection (b) authorizes jurisdiction "in any action arising within or without this State against any person who:

(1)   Is a natural person present within this State when served;

(2)   Is a natural person domiciled or resident within this State when the cause of action arose, the action was commenced, or process was served;

(3)   Is a corporation organized under the laws of this State; or

(4)   Is a natural person or corporation doing business within this State."

"well, Now
you're on
notice"

Finally, subsection (c) states that "[a] court may also exercise jurisdiction on any other basis now or hereafter permitted by the Illinois Constitution and the Constitution of the United States."

Do these amendments indicate that the court in *Gray* was correct in its interpretation of the original Act? Should the original provisions of the Act continue to be interpreted the same way, given the passage of these amendments?

2.   The *Gray* analysis seemed to permit suit in Illinois on any tort that allegedly had an injurious effect there. But in Green v. Advance Ross Elec. Corp., 427 N.E.2d 1203 (Ill.1981), the court retreated from that view. Plaintiff there, a Delaware corporation headquartered in Illinois, sued a former employee in Illinois for alleged breaches of fiduciary duty that occurred outside Illinois, arguing that the tort had an impact inside Illinois because it harmed the company's financial condition. The Illinois Supreme Court found this effect "too remote," reasoning that plaintiff's interpretation "would be tantamount to permitting a corporation operating nationwide to sue employees, suppliers, customers and perhaps others, at the company's State of incorporation or at its headquarters no matter how far away they lived and worked or their contact with the corporation was." Recall this case when you read Burger King Corp. v. Rudzewicz, infra p. 762.

3.   Other problems can arise from the use of the phrase "tortious act." Until the trial is completed, how can the court know whether defendant has committed a tort? Whatever Titan did in Ohio or Illinois has not been proved to be a tort. Must there be two trials? If plaintiff loses at trial, does that mean there was no jurisdiction to begin with? The problem was early disposed of in Illinois when the statute was interpreted to apply whenever the act as alleged would be tortious. Nelson v. Miller, 143 N.E.2d 673 (Ill.1957); see Currie, The Growth of the Long Arm: Eight Years of Extended Jurisdiction in Illinois, 1963 U.Ill.L.F. 533, 539. Still, the use of substantive law terms in a long-arm statute invites further difficulties.

4.   As a fallback for its statutory interpretation, the court in *Gray* asserts that its long-arm statute extends to the maximum extent permitted by due process. Many state courts have thus interpreted their statutes (see World-Wide Volkswagen v. Woodson, infra p. 744—the Oklahoma statute "has been interpreted as conferring jurisdiction to the limits permitted by the United States Constitution"). This alternative route should be kept in mind. But if the legislature wanted to take the California route it could have done so explicitly; shouldn't the courts exercise some caution? Consider the Illinois Supreme Court's later views on the subject before the legislature adopted the changes described in note 1: "We do not, however, regard this observation as the equivalent of declaring that the construction and application of section 17(1)(b) depend entirely on decisions determining in what circumstances due process requirements would permit long-arm jurisdiction. * * * A statute worded in the way ours is should have a fixed meaning without regard to changing concepts of due process." Green v. Advance Ross Elec. Corp., 427 N.E.2d 1203 (Ill.1981).

5.   Notwithstanding expansive interpretations of long-arm statutes, it is important to keep in mind that they must be satisfied in order for a court to exercise jurisdiction, whether or not the exercise of jurisdiction would be constitutional. As with the due process analysis of prejudgment seizure (see supra pp. 29–64), the starting point for issues of personal jurisdiction is statutory authorization for the assertion of jurisdiction; only when that is satisfied does the question of due process limitations arise. There is no constitutional requirement that a state extend its jurisdiction to the due process limit. See Friedman v. Bloomberg, L.P. 884 F.3d 83, 91 (2d Cir. 2018) ("A plaintiff has no right of access to the courts when, as here, a state's long-arm statute does not provide for jurisdiction over certain out-of-state defendants.").

PERSONAL JURISDICTION IN FEDERAL COURT

At this point, students often suggest that the easy solution to these jurisdictional problems is to sue in federal court. We will deal in the next chapter with subject matter jurisdiction, which governs access to federal court. The personal jurisdiction issue bears separate treatment here, however, because in most cases those jurisdictional problems are identical in state and federal court.

The congruence of personal jurisdiction issues between state and federal courts is hardly obvious, however, and those who assume that there simply is no personal jurisdiction problem in federal court have sensible grounds for their reaction. *Pennoyer*, after all, emphasized the sovereign power of any state over all found within it, so it would seem that the United States could, without encountering any problems of personal jurisdiction, exercise jurisdiction through its courts over anyone served in the country, just as Oregon could have properly exercised jurisdiction over anyone served in that state. Indeed, less than a year after the decision in *Pennoyer*, the Supreme Court suggested that Congress could have created a single federal trial court with nationwide personal jurisdiction. United States v. Union Pacific R. Co., 98 U.S. 569 (1878). Although Congress did not do so, there is certainly room to debate the need for the state-by-state organization that Congress did adopt for the U.S. district courts. Moreover, it has broken almost half the states into more than one district, with California, New York and Texas divided into four districts each. Certainly one could reasonably surmise that these federal courts would not be subject to the same personal jurisdiction limitations as the courts of the states in which they sit, particularly since the 14th Amendment, with its due process clause, applies only to the states and not to the federal government (although the 5th Amendment due process clause does apply to the federal government).

But the reality is different, and raises some extremely slippery issues. Rule 4(k)(1)(A) authorizes exercise of personal jurisdiction by a federal court only to the extent a state court of the state in which it sits, under the state's long-arm statute, could exercise jurisdiction. This normally will invoke an *International Shoe* analysis of minimum contacts with the state even when the plaintiff asserts a federal claim in federal court. Accordingly, with some exceptions noted below, the problems of statutory interpretation and due process are the same whether the case is in federal or state court. Some cavil about this situation, see Berger, Acquiring In Personam Jurisdiction in Federal Question Cases: Procedural Frustration Under Federal Rule of Civil Procedure 4, 1982 Utah L.Rev. 285, but for our purposes it is a working assumption.

One important exception is that Congress has, in some instances, authorized nationwide service of process in specific statutes. See Rule 4(k)(1)(C). Many of these provisions are designed to facilitate the assertion of the claims created by the statutory scheme. See, e.g., 15 U.S.C. § 25 (antitrust claims); 15 U.S.C. §§ 77v(a); 78aa (securities claims). In other situations, nationwide service is designed to provide a forum in federal court that can bind all interested parties where jurisdictional problems might make that impossible in state court. See, e.g., 28 U.S.C. §§ 1335 (interpleader); 28 U.S.C. §§ 1695 (derivative actions); 1697 (multiparty, multiforum litigation); cf. Bankruptcy Rule 7004(d) (authorizing nationwide service in connection with bankruptcy proceedings).

Are there no constitutional protections against unfair inconvenience where nationwide service is permitted? Some have argued that the due process clause of the 5th Amendment, which does bind the United States, should be read to impose similar limitations on nationwide service. Compare Republic of Panama v. BCCI Holdings, 119 F.3d 935 (11th Cir.1997) (5th Amendment does limit federal court assertion of jurisdiction in extraordinarily inconvenient district) with F.T.C. v. Jim Walter Corp., 651 F.2d 251 (5th Cir.1981) (rejecting 5th Amendment limitation on federal court jurisdiction). See generally Fullerton, Constitutional Limits on Nationwide Personal Jurisdiction in the Federal Courts, 79 Nw.U.L.Rev. 1 (1984).

Another exception is Rule 4(k)(1)(B), which authorizes service within 100 miles of the federal courthouse, even though outside the state, where a third party complaint is asserted under Rule 14, or where additional parties are necessary for full adjudication under Rule 19. This is known as *"bulge jurisdiction."* In Coleman v. American Export Isbrandtsen Lines, Inc., 405 F.2d 250 (2d Cir.1968), the court explained that the provision of bulge jurisdiction was designed "to allow complicated controversies to be ended by a single lawsuit if all the necessary third parties could be found within 100 miles of the courthouse."

The special jurisdictional features of a federal court are also invoked by Rule 4(k)(2), with respect to claims based on federal law when "the defendant is not subject to jurisdiction in any state's courts of general jurisdiction." One situation in which this provision would apply is where the forum state's long-arm statute does not authorize exercise of jurisdiction although that would be constitutional, and there are not sufficient contacts with any other state to permit it to exercise jurisdiction. Another is where the defendant's contacts with any particular state are insufficient to support jurisdiction, but its contacts with the country as a whole are sufficient. But how does a plaintiff show that jurisdiction is not possible in any other state? In ISI International, Inc. v. Borden Ladner Gervais LLP, 256 F.3d 548 (7th Cir.2001), the court decided that "[a] defendant who wants to preclude use of Rule 4(k)(2) has only to name some other state in which the suit could proceed. Naming a more appropriate state would amount to a consent to personal jurisdiction there. * * * If, however, the defendant contends that he cannot be sued in the forum state and refuses to identify any other where suit is possible, then the federal court is entitled to use Rule 4(k)(2)." Id. at 552; see also Merial, Ltd. v. Cipla, Ltd., 681 F.3d 1283, 1294–95 (Fed.Cir.2012) (holding that defendant's consent to suit in another forum when it moves to dismiss is not sufficient; the question is whether plaintiff had a unilateral right to sue there).

Pendent personal jurisdiction: The existence of some federal authorizations for nationwide personal jurisdiction explains the emergence of the doctrine of "pendent personal jurisdiction." "Pendent personal jurisdiction is typically found where one or more federal claims for which there is nationwide personal jurisdiction are combined in the same suit with one or more state or federal claims for which there is not nationwide personal jurisdiction." Action Embroidery Corp. v. Atlantic Embroidery, Inc., 368 F.3d 1174, 1180–81 (9th Cir.2004). "Pendent personal jurisdiction * * * exists when a court possesses personal jurisdiction over a defendant for one claim, lacks an independent basis for personal jurisdiction over the defendant for another claim that arises out of the same nucleus of operative fact, and then, because it possesses personal jurisdiction over the first claim, asserts personal jurisdiction over the second claim." United States v. Botefuhr, 309 F.3d 1263, 1272 (10th Cir.2002).

D. REFINING THE MINIMUM CONTACTS ANALYSIS

Since *International Shoe*, courts have sometimes said that issues of personal jurisdiction depended on "gestalt factors," Ticketmaster-New York, Inc. v. Alioto, 26 F.3d 201, 209 (1st Cir.1994), and that resolving these questions was "more an art than a science." Donatelli v. National Hockey League, 893 F.2d 459, 468 n. 7 (1st Cir.1990). After nearly twenty years of silence, the Supreme Court began deciding personal jurisdiction cases again in 1977. As it decided more cases, it refined the minimum contacts standard, although in some ways these refinements resembled what Professor Hazard called "arbitrary particularization." Hazard, A

General Theory of State-Court Jurisdiction, 1965 Sup.Ct.Rev. 241, 283. As you examine these cases, you will note that the Supreme Court's attitude toward personal jurisdiction has become more cautious since McGee v. International Life Ins. Co. (supra p. 733).

WORLD-WIDE VOLKSWAGEN CORP. V. WOODSON

Supreme Court of the United States, 1980
444 U.S. 286

JUSTICE WHITE delivered the opinion of the Court.

The issue before us is whether, consistently with the Due Process Clause of the Fourteenth Amendment, an Oklahoma court may exercise in personam jurisdiction over a nonresident automobile retailer and its wholesale distributor in a products-liability action, when the defendants' only connection with Oklahoma is the fact that an automobile sold in New York to New York residents became involved in an accident in Oklahoma.

I

Respondents Harry and Kay Robinson purchased a new Audi automobile from petitioner Seaway Volkswagen, Inc. (Seaway), in Massena, N.Y., in 1976. The following year the Robinson family, who resided in New York, left that State for a new home in Arizona. As they passed through the State of Oklahoma, another car struck their Audi in the rear, causing a fire which severely burned Kay Robinson and her two children.[1]

The Robinsons subsequently brought a products-liability action in the District Court for Creek County, Okla., claiming that their injuries resulted from defective design and placement of the Audi's gas tank and fuel system. They joined as defendants the automobile's manufacturer, Audi NSU Auto Union Aktiengesellschaft (Audi); its importer, Volkswagen of America, Inc. (Volkswagen); its regional distributor, petitioner World-Wide Volkswagen Corp. (World-Wide); and its retail dealer, petitioner Seaway. Seaway and World-Wide entered special appearances,[3] claiming that Oklahoma's exercise of jurisdiction over them would offend the limitations on the State's jurisdiction imposed by the Due Process Clause of the Fourteenth Amendment.

The facts presented to the District Court showed that World-Wide is incorporated and has its business office in New York. It distributes vehicles, parts, and accessories, under contract with Volkswagen, to retail dealers in New York, New Jersey, and Connecticut. Seaway, one of these

---

[1]   The driver of the other automobile does not figure in the present litigation.

[3]   Volkswagen also entered a special appearance in the District Court, but unlike World-Wide and Seaway did not seek review in the Supreme Court of Oklahoma and is not a petitioner here. Both Volkswagen and Audi remain as defendants in the litigation pending before the District Court in Oklahoma.

retail dealers, is incorporated and has its place of business in New York. Insofar as the record reveals, Seaway and World-Wide are fully independent corporations whose relations with each other and with Volkswagen and Audi are contractual only. Respondents adduced no evidence that either World-Wide or Seaway does any business in Oklahoma, ships or sells any products to or in that State, has an agent to receive process there, or purchases advertisements in any media calculated to reach Oklahoma. In fact, as respondents' counsel conceded at oral argument, there was no showing that any automobile sold by World-Wide or Seaway has ever entered Oklahoma with the single exception of the vehicle involved in the present case. Despite the apparent paucity of contacts between petitioners and Oklahoma, the District Court rejected their constitutional claim and reaffirmed that ruling in denying petitioners' motion for reconsideration. Petitioners then sought a writ of prohibition in the Supreme Court of Oklahoma to restrain the District Judge, respondent Charles S. Woodson, from exercising in personam jurisdiction over them. They renewed their contention that, because they had no "minimal contacts" with the State of Oklahoma, the actions of the District Judge were in violation of their rights under the Due Process Clause.

The Supreme Court of Oklahoma denied the writ, holding that personal jurisdiction over petitioners was authorized by Oklahoma's "long-arm" statute, Okla.Stat., Tit. 12, § 1701.03(a)(4) (1971).[7] Although the court noted that the proper approach was to test jurisdiction against both statutory and constitutional standards, its analysis did not distinguish these questions, probably because § 1701.03(a)(4) has been interpreted as conferring jurisdiction to the limits permitted by the United States Constitution. The court's rationale was contained in the following paragraph:

> "In the case before us, the product being sold and distributed by the petitioners is by its very design and purpose so mobile that petitioners can foresee its possible use in Oklahoma. This is especially true of the distributor, who has the exclusive right to distribute such automobile in New York, New Jersey and Connecticut. The evidence presented below demonstrated that goods sold and distributed by the petitioners were used in the State of Oklahoma, and under the facts we believe it reasonable to infer, given the retail value of the automobile, that the

---

[7]   This subsection provides:

   "A court may exercise personal jurisdiction over a person, who acts directly or by an agent, as to a cause of action or claim for relief arising from the person's . . . causing tortious injury in this state by an act or omission outside this state if he regularly does or solicits business or engages in any other persistent course of conduct, or derives substantial revenue from goods used or consumed or services rendered, in this state. . . ."

The State Supreme Court rejected jurisdiction based on § 1701.03(a)(3), which authorizes jurisdiction over any person "causing tortious injury in this state by an act or omission in this state." Something in addition to the infliction of tortious injury was required.

petitioners derive substantial income from automobiles which
from time to time are used in the State of Oklahoma. This being
the case, we hold that under the facts presented, the trial court
was justified in concluding that the petitioners derive substantial
revenue from goods used or consumed in this State."

We granted certiorari to consider an important constitutional question
with respect to state-court jurisdiction and to resolve a conflict between the
Supreme Court of Oklahoma and the highest courts of at least four other
States. We reverse.

II

The Due Process Clause of the Fourteenth Amendment limits the
power of a state court to render a valid personal judgment against a
nonresident defendant. Kulko v. California Superior Court, 436 U.S. 84, 91
(1978). A judgment rendered in violation of due process is void in the
rendering State and is not entitled to full faith and credit elsewhere.
Pennoyer v. Neff, 95 U.S. 714, 732–733 (1877). Due process requires that
the defendant be given adequate notice of the suit, Mullane v. Central
Hanover Trust Co., 339 U.S. 306, 313–314 (1950), and be subject to the
personal jurisdiction of the court, International Shoe Co. v. Washington,
326 U.S. 310 (1945). In the present case, it is not contended that notice was
inadequate; the only question is whether these particular petitioners were
subject to the jurisdiction of the Oklahoma courts.

As has long been settled, and as we reaffirm today, a state court may
exercise personal jurisdiction over a nonresident defendant only so long as
there exist "minimum contacts" between the defendant and the forum
State. International Shoe Co. v. Washington, supra, at 316. The concept of
minimum contacts, in turn, can be seen to perform two related, but
distinguishable, functions. It protects the defendant against the burdens of
litigating in a distant or inconvenient forum. And it acts to ensure that the
States, through their courts, do not reach out beyond the limits imposed on
them by their status as coequal sovereigns in a federal system.

The protection against inconvenient litigation is typically described in
terms of "reasonableness" or "fairness." We have said that the defendant's
contacts with the forum State must be such that maintenance of the suit
"does not offend 'traditional notions of fair play and substantial justice.' "
International Shoe Co. v. Washington, at 316. The relationship between
the defendant and the forum must be such that it is "reasonable . . . to
require the corporation to defend the particular suit which is brought
there." 326 U.S., at 317. Implicit in this emphasis on reasonableness is the
understanding that the burden on the defendant, while always a primary
concern, will in an appropriate case be considered in light of other relevant
factors, including the forum State's interest in adjudicating the dispute,
see McGee v. International Life Ins. Co., 355 U.S. 220, 223 (1957); the
plaintiff's interest in obtaining convenient and effective relief, see Kulko v.

California Superior Court, 436 U.S., at 92, at least when that interest is not adequately protected by the plaintiff's power to choose the forum, cf. Shaffer v. Heitner, 433 U.S. 186, 211, n. 37 (1977); the interstate judicial system's interest in obtaining the most efficient resolution of controversies; and the shared interest of the several States in furthering fundamental substantive social policies, see Kulko v. California Superior Court, supra, 436 U.S., at 93, 98.

The limits imposed on state jurisdiction by the Due Process Clause, in its role as a guarantor against inconvenient litigation, have been substantially relaxed over the years. As we noted in McGee v. International Life Ins. Co., 355 U.S., at 222–223, this trend is largely attributable to a fundamental transformation in the American economy. * * *

The historical developments noted in *McGee*, of course, have only accelerated in the generation since that case was decided.

Nevertheless, we have never accepted the proposition that state lines are irrelevant for jurisdictional purposes, nor could we, and remain faithful to the principles of interstate federalism embodied in the Constitution. The economic interdependence of the States was foreseen and desired by the Framers. In the Commerce Clause, they provided that the Nation was to be a common market, a "free trade unit" in which the States are debarred from acting as separable economic entities. But the Framers also intended that the States retain many essential attributes of sovereignty, including, in particular, the sovereign power to try causes in their courts. The sovereignty of each State, in turn, implied a limitation on the sovereignty of all of its sister States—a limitation express or implicit in both the original scheme of the Constitution and the Fourteenth Amendment.

Hence, even while abandoning the shibboleth that "[t]he authority of every tribunal is necessarily restricted by the territorial limits of the State in which it is established," Pennoyer v. Neff, 95 U.S., at 720, we emphasized that the reasonableness of asserting jurisdiction over the defendant must be assessed "in the context of our federal system of government," International Shoe Co. v. Washington, 326 U.S., at 317, and stressed that the Due Process Clause ensures not only fairness, but also the "orderly administration of the laws," id., at 319. As we noted in Hanson v. Denckla, 357 U.S. 235, 250–251 (1958):

> "As technological progress has increased the flow of commerce between the States, the need for jurisdiction over nonresidents has undergone a similar increase. At the same time, progress in communications and transportation has made the defense of a suit in a foreign tribunal less burdensome. In response to these changes, the requirements for personal jurisdiction over nonresidents have evolved from the rigid rule of Pennoyer v. Neff, 95 U.S. 714, to the flexible standard of International Shoe Co. v. Washington, 326 U.S. 310. But it is a mistake to assume that this

trend heralds the eventual demise of all restrictions on the personal jurisdiction of state courts. Those restrictions are more than a guarantee of immunity from inconvenient or distant litigation. They are a consequence of territorial limitations on the power of the respective States."

Thus, the Due Process Clause "does not contemplate that a state may make binding a judgment *in personam* against an individual or corporate defendant with which the state has no contacts, ties, or relations." International Shoe Co. v. Washington, 326 U.S., at 319. Even if the defendant would suffer minimal or no inconvenience from being forced to litigate before the tribunals of another State; even if the forum State has a strong interest in applying its law to the controversy; even if the forum State is the most convenient location for litigation, the Due Process Clause, acting as an instrument of interstate federalism, may sometimes act to divest the State of its power to render a valid judgment. Hanson v. Denckla, 357 U.S., at 251, 254.

III

Applying these principles to the case at hand, we find in the record before us a total absence of those affiliating circumstances that are a necessary predicate to any exercise of state-court jurisdiction. Petitioners carry on no activity whatsoever in Oklahoma. They close no sales and perform no services there. They avail themselves of none of the privileges and benefits of Oklahoma law. They solicit no business there either through salespersons or through advertising reasonably calculated to reach the State. Nor does the record show that they regularly sell cars at wholesale or retail to Oklahoma customers or residents or that they indirectly, through others, serve or seek to serve the Oklahoma market. In short, respondents seek to base jurisdiction on one, isolated occurrence and whatever inferences can be drawn therefrom: the fortuitous circumstance that a single Audi automobile, sold in New York to New York residents, happened to suffer an accident while passing through Oklahoma.

It is argued, however, that because an automobile is mobile by its very design and purpose it was "foreseeable" that the Robinsons' Audi would cause injury in Oklahoma. Yet "foreseeability" alone has never been a sufficient benchmark for personal jurisdiction under the Due Process Clause. In Hanson v. Denckla [supra p. 735 n. 3], it was no doubt foreseeable that the settlor of a Delaware trust would subsequently move to Florida and seek to exercise a power of appointment there; yet we held that Florida courts could not constitutionally exercise jurisdiction over a Delaware trustee that had no other contacts with the forum State. In Kulko v. California Superior Court, 436 U.S. 84 (1978), it was surely "foreseeable" that a divorced wife would move to California from New York, the domicile of the marriage, and that a minor daughter would live with the mother. Yet we held that California could not exercise jurisdiction in a child-support action over the former husband who had remained in New York.

If foreseeability were the criterion, a local California tire retailer could be forced to defend in Pennsylvania when a blowout occurs there, see Erlanger Mills, Inc. v. Cohoes Fibre Mills, Inc., 239 F.2d 502, 507 (C.A.4 1956); a Wisconsin seller of a defective automobile jack could be haled before a distant court for damage caused in New Jersey, Reilly v. Phil Tolkan Pontiac, Inc., 372 F.Supp. 1205 (N.J.1974); or a Florida soft-drink concessionaire could be summoned to Alaska to account for injuries happening there, see Uppgren v. Executive Aviation Services, Inc., 304 F.Supp. 165, 170–171 (Minn.1969). Every seller of chattels would in effect appoint the chattel his agent for service of process. His amenability to suit would travel with the chattel.[11] * * *

This is not to say, of course, that foreseeability is wholly irrelevant. But the foreseeability that is critical to due process analysis is not the mere likelihood that a product will find its way into the forum State. Rather, it is that the defendant's conduct and connection with the forum State are such that he should reasonably anticipate being haled into court there. The Due Process Clause, by ensuring the "orderly administration of the laws," International Shoe Co. v. Washington, 326 U.S., at 319, gives a degree of predictability to the legal system that allows potential defendants to structure their primary conduct with some minimum assurance as to where that conduct will and will not render them liable to suit. When a corporation "purposefully avails itself of the privilege of conducting activities within the forum State," Hanson v. Denckla, 357 U.S., at 253, it has clear notice that it is subject to suit there, and can act to alleviate the risk of burdensome litigation by procuring insurance, passing the expected costs on to customers, or, if the risks are too great, severing its connection with the State. Hence if the sale of a product of a manufacturer or distributor such as Audi or Volkswagen is not simply an isolated occurrence, but arises from the efforts of the manufacturer or distributor to serve directly or indirectly, the market for its product in other States, it is not unreasonable to subject it to suit in one of those States if its allegedly defective merchandise has there been the source of injury to its owner or to others. The forum State does not exceed its powers under the Due Process Clause if it asserts personal jurisdiction over a corporation that delivers its products into the stream of commerce with the expectation that they will

---

[11] Respondents' counsel, at oral argument, sought to limit the reach of the foreseeability standard by suggesting that there is something unique about automobiles. It is true that automobiles are uniquely mobile, that they did play a crucial role in the expansion of personal jurisdiction through the fiction of implied consent, e.g., Hess v. Pawloski, 274 U.S. 352 (1927), and that some of the cases have treated the automobile as a "dangerous instrumentality." But today, under the regime of International Shoe, we see no difference for jurisdictional purposes between an automobile and any other chattel. The "dangerous instrumentality" concept apparently was never used to support personal jurisdiction; and to the extent that it has relevance today it bears not on jurisdiction but on the possible desirability of imposing substantive principles of tort law such as strict liability.

be purchased by consumers in the forum State. Cf. Gray v. American Radiator & Standard Sanitary Corp., 176 N.E.2d 761 (Ill.1961).

But there is no such or similar basis for Oklahoma jurisdiction over World-Wide or Seaway in this case. Seaway's sales are made in Massena, N.Y. World-Wide's market, although substantially larger, is limited to dealers in New York, New Jersey, and Connecticut. There is no evidence of record that any automobiles distributed by World-Wide are sold to retail customers outside this tri-state area. It is foreseeable that the purchasers of automobiles sold by World-Wide and Seaway may take them to Oklahoma. But the mere "unilateral activity of those who claim some relationship with a nonresident defendant cannot satisfy the requirement of contact with the forum State." Hanson v. Denckla, at 253.

In a variant on the previous argument, it is contended that jurisdiction can be supported by the fact that petitioners earn substantial revenue from goods used in Oklahoma. The Oklahoma Supreme Court so found, drawing the inference that because one automobile sold by petitioners had been used in Oklahoma, others might have been used there also. While this inference seems less than compelling on the facts of the instant case, we need not question the court's factual findings in order to reject its reasoning.

This argument seems to make the point that the purchase of automobiles in New York, from which the petitioners earn substantial revenue, would not occur but for the fact that the automobiles are capable of use in distant States like Oklahoma. Respondents observe that the very purpose of an automobile is to travel, and that travel of automobiles sold by petitioners is facilitated by an extensive chain of Volkswagen service centers throughout the country, including some in Oklahoma. However, financial benefits accruing to the defendant from a collateral relation to the forum State will not support jurisdiction if they do not stem from a constitutionally cognizable contact with that State. In our view, whatever marginal revenues petitioners may receive by virtue of the fact that their products are capable of use in Oklahoma is far too attenuated a contact to justify that State's exercise of in personam jurisdiction over them.

Because we find that petitioners have no "contacts, ties, or relations" with the State of Oklahoma, International Shoe Co. v. Washington, supra, 326 U.S., at 319, 66 S.Ct., at 159, the judgment of the Supreme Court of Oklahoma is reversed.

JUSTICE MARSHALL, with whom JUSTICE BLACKMUN joins, dissenting.

* * *

I sympathize with the majority's concern that the persons ought to be able to structure their conduct so as not to be subject to suit in distant forums. But that may not always be possible. Some activities by their very nature may foreclose the option of conducting them in such a way as to avoid subjecting oneself to jurisdiction in multiple forums. This is by no means to say that all sellers of automobiles should be subject to suit everywhere; but a distributor of automobiles to a multi-state market and a local automobile dealer who makes himself part of a nationwide network of dealerships can fairly expect that the cars they sell may cause injury in distant States and that they may be called on to defend a resulting lawsuit there.

* * * I believe such contacts are to be found here and that, considering all of the interests and policies at stake, requiring petitioners to defend this action in Oklahoma is not beyond the bounds of the Constitution. Accordingly, I dissent.

[Dissenting opinion of JUSTICE BLACKMUN omitted.]

JUSTICE BRENNAN, dissenting.

* * *

The Court accepts that a State may exercise jurisdiction over a distributor which "serves" that State "indirectly" by "deliver[ing] its products into the stream of commerce with the expectation that they will be purchased by consumers in the forum State." It is difficult to see why the Constitution should distinguish between a case involving goods which reach a distant State through a chain of distribution and a case involving goods which reach the same State because a consumer, using them as the dealer knew the customer would, took them there. In each case the seller purposefully injects the goods into the stream of commerce and those goods predictably are used in the forum State.[12]

* * *

It may be that affirmance of the judgment * * * would approach the outer limits of International Shoe's jurisdictional principle. But that principle, with its almost exclusive focus on the rights of defendants, may be outdated. * * *

The model of society on which the International Shoe Court based its opinion is no longer accurate. Business people, no matter how local their businesses, cannot assume that goods remain in the business' locality. Customers and goods can be anywhere else in the country usually in a matter of hours and always in a matter of a very few days.

* * *

I would * * * strip the defendant of an unjustified veto power over certain very appropriate fora—a power the defendant justifiably enjoyed long ago when communication and travel over long distances were slow and

---

[12] The manufacturer in the case cited by the court, Gray v. American Radiator & Standard Sanitary Corp. [supra p. 735 n. 4], had no more control over which States its goods would reach than did the petitioners in this case.

unpredictable and when notions of state sovereignty were impractical and exaggerated. But I repeat that is not today's world.

NOTES AND QUESTIONS

1.   You may have wondered why plaintiffs would sue the objecting defendants as well as Audi and Volkswagen of America, and why these defendants would pursue the jurisdiction question to the Supreme Court. The curious explanation is that the Robinsons' lawyer wanted to keep the case in state court because juries in the county where the accident happened were known to be friendly to plaintiffs. Because the Robinsons were still technically New Yorkers for purposes of diversity of citizenship (see infra pp. 865–877), it was necessary to sue a New York defendant such as Seaway or World-Wide Volkswagen to prevent removal on grounds of diversity. Audi and Volkswagen of America underwrote the cost of appealing to the Supreme Court so that they could get the case removed to federal court. After removal, the federal jury returned a defense verdict. For a history of the case, see Adams, World-Wide Volkswagen v. Woodson—The Rest of the Story, 72 Neb.L.Rev. 1122 (1993).

2.   *Role of interstate sovereignty in personal jurisdiction decisions:* In *World-Wide Volkswagen*, the Court places great stress on the sovereignty issue in personal jurisdiction. Two years later, however, it watered down this idea in Insurance Corp. of Ireland, Ltd. v. Compagnie des Bauxites de Guinee, 456 U.S. 694 (1982), in upholding a finding of jurisdiction entered as a discovery sanction because defendant had consented to disposition of the jurisdictional issue by the American court (see infra p. 830 for discussion of this aspect of the case):

> The restriction on state sovereign power described in World-Wide Volkswagen Corp., however, must be seen as ultimately a function of the individual liberty interest preserved by the Due Process Clause. That Clause is the only source of the personal jurisdiction requirement and the Clause itself makes no mention of federalism concerns. Furthermore, if the federalism concept operated as an independent restriction on the sovereign power of the court, it would not be possible to waive the personal jurisdiction requirement.

But more recently the Court has again invoked sovereignty as a reason for holding that a state court lacked jurisdiction. In Bristol Myers Squibb Co v. Superior Court, 137 S.Ct. 1773 (2017), the Court rejected jurisdiction, citing *World-Wide Volkswagen* and noting that "at times, this federalism interest may be decisive." We will see interstate sovereignty issues again in J. McIntyre Machinery, Ltd. v. Nicastro, infra p. 772.

Should interstate sovereignty play a significant role in determining the due process limits of personal jurisdiction? Consider the following critique:

> In virtually every other context, due process—in both its substantive and procedural manifestations—has been construed as a protection of private parties from some form of injustice. In the personal jurisdiction context, however, the Court has infused vague concepts

of interstate sovereignty into the due process clause. These limitations on state authority are imposed in the name of the clause, regardless of whether private parties—the ultimate beneficiaries of these protections—are in danger of suffering real injustice. Although the Court has assumed since the time of *Pennoyer* that the due process clause embodies such notions of federalism, it has relied on neither the language, history, nor policy of the due process clause to justify its construction. Indeed, such notions of federalism as limitations on the reach of personal jurisdiction are found nowhere in the body of the Constitution, much less in the terms of the due process clause.

Redish, Due Process, Federalism, and Personal Jurisdiction: A Theoretical Evaluation, 75 Nw.U.L.Rev. 1112, 1113–14 (1981). In keeping with ordinary due process analysis, personal jurisdiction would focus on three factors, "the degree of inconvenience that a defendant would suffer in being forced to litigate in a distant forum, the degree of inconvenience a plaintiff would suffer in being forced to proceed in a different forum, and the state's interest in having its own law resolve the controversy." Id. at 1115. What effect would this approach have on the analysis in *World-Wide Volkswagen*? "The proposed test for personal jurisdiction would eliminate two factors of central importance to the 'minimum contacts' test—concern for prelitigation contacts between the defendant and the forum and for the defendant's awareness of possible suit in that forum—except to the extent such factors relate to the actual burdens of litigation." Id.

3.   The Court couches its general approach in terms of foreseeability. Is this analysis circular? Consider Redish, Due Process, Federalism, and Personal Jurisdiction: A Theoretical Evaluation, 75 Nw.U.L.Rev. 1112 (1981): "If the law were to tell potential litigants that they may be sued in any convenient forum, regardless of their previous contact with the forum, the litigants' reasonable expectations would have to change." Or is circularity in the eyes of the beholder? Consider West American Insurance Company v. Westin, Inc., 337 N.W.2d 676 (Minn.1983), in which the court held that *World-Wide Volkswagen* required reconsideration of two of its earlier decisions upholding jurisdiction over Wisconsin drinking establishments that served Minnesota 18-year-olds in suits by persons injured by those patrons after they returned to Minnesota: "It might be argued that [the earlier decisions] provided this foreseeability. This line of reasoning fails because it is essentially circular. The ultimate question in this case is whether [the earlier decisions] are still good law. To answer this query by arguing that after *World-Wide*, these cases make jurisdiction by Minnesota courts 'reasonably foreseeable' is to say that [the earlier decisions] are valid because [they] are valid." But if all the Wisconsin tavern owners were in fact aware of the earlier decisions, why wouldn't that fact satisfy *World-Wide*?

4.   *World-Wide* was the first products liability personal jurisdiction decision by the Supreme Court. In that setting, the Court tells us that a manufacturer or distributor should foresee being sued in areas it "seeks to serve." How broad is this approach? World-Wide was the distributor for the

states of New York, New Jersey and Connecticut. If it supplied a retailer in Camden, New Jersey, just across the Delaware River from Philadelphia, Pa., and the retailer advertised in the Philadelphia media, would it be found to have sought to serve Pennsylvania? Would that extend also to Delaware if the Philadelphia media reached there?

5.   In *World-Wide Volkswagen*, the Court says that due process permits jurisdiction over "a corporation that delivers its products into the stream of commerce with the expectation that they will be purchased by consumers in the forum State. Cf. Gray v. American Radiator & Standard Sanitary Corp." Recall that in Gray v. American Radiator (supra p. 735 n. 4), the Illinois court upheld jurisdiction in Illinois over an Ohio company that supplied valves to a Pennsylvania company that manufactured water heaters using those valves when one of the water heaters exploded in Illinois, causing the plaintiff's injuries. The reasoning that jurisdiction is proper in such situations is often called the stream of commerce theory. Does the Court endorse that theory in *World-Wide Volkswagen*? We will return to this issue in J. McIntyre Machinery, Ltd. v. Nicastro, infra p. 772.

GENERAL AND SPECIFIC JURISDICTION

Audi did not challenge Oklahoma jurisdiction, and Volkswagen of America did not pursue its initial objection to jurisdiction. They did "seek to serve" Oklahoma, regularly distributing a substantial number of cars in that state. But the Robinsons' purchase of a car in New York is difficult to relate to that distribution in Oklahoma. Focusing on these defendants introduces the distinction between "general jurisdiction" and "specific jurisdiction."

Under the *Pennoyer* world view, jurisdiction depended little on the nature of the claim asserted; service in the forum or seizure of property in the forum were the focus. For corporate defendants, "presence" in the forum came to be the key concern. *International Shoe* replaced that standard with the more nuanced "minimum contacts" approach, which emphasizes the specifics of the underlying claim in making the jurisdictional determination. For example, when the Court upheld jurisdiction in McGee v. International Life Ins. Co., supra p. 733, it surely did not mean that the defendant company could be sued in California by every insured; the Court was upholding jurisdiction only for the suit on the policy issued to a Californian. But as *International Shoe* itself recognized (supra p. 726), "continuous corporate operations within a state [may be] so substantial and of such a nature as to justify suit against in on causes of action arising from dealings entirely distinct form those activities."

In Jurisdiction to Adjudicate: A Suggested Analysis, 79 Harv. L. Rev. 1121 (1966), Professors Arthur von Mehren and Donald Trautman introduced the notion that jurisdiction could be classified as either general or specific. The Supreme Court has since accepted this dichotomy. In

Bristol-Myers Squibb Co. v. Superior Court, 137 S.Ct. 1773 (2017), the Court explained:

> Since our seminal decision in *International Shoe*, our decisions have recognized two types of personal jurisdiction: "general" (sometimes called "all-purpose") jurisdiction and "specific" (sometimes called "case linked") jurisdiction. "For an individual the paradigm forum for the exercise of general jurisdiction is the individual's domicile; for a corporation, it is an equivalent place, one in which the corporation is fairly regarded as at home." A court with general jurisdiction may hear *any* claim against that defendant, even if all the incidents underlying the claim occurred in a different State. But "only a limited set of affiliations with a forum will render a defendant amenable to" general jurisdiction in that State.
>
> Specific jurisdiction is very different. In order for a state court to exercise specific jurisdiction, "the *suit*" must "aris[e] out of or relat[e] to the defendant's contacts with the *forum*." In other words, there must be "an affiliation between the forum and the underlying controversy, principally, [an] activity or an occurrence that takes place in the forum state and is therefore subject to the State's regulation." For this reason, "specific jurisdiction is confined to adjudication of issues deriving from, or connected with, the very controversy that establishes jurisdiction."

We will examine the test for general jurisdiction in section G of this chapter, infra p. 817. For the present, it is enough to understand that the Court has curtailed broad use of this ground for jurisdiction, and that the current standard would mean that neither Audi nor Volkswagen of America would be subject to general jurisdiction in Oklahoma. Could specific jurisdiction be upheld even though it's difficult to see why the Robinsons' claim arose out of these defendants' efforts to serve the Oklahoma market?

The Supreme Court's 2017 decision in Bristol-Myers Squibb Co. v. Superior Court, supra, provides a comparison. Plaintiffs in that case sued in state court in San Francisco, claiming injury due to taking Plavix, a prescription blood thinner made by defendant. Although some of the plaintiffs were Californians, the great majority were not. The Court held that specific jurisdiction could not be exercised over the nonresidents' claims:

> The State Supreme Court found that specific jurisdiction was present without identifying any adequate link between the State and the nonresidents' claims. As noted, the nonresidents were not prescribed Plavix in California, did not purchase Plavix in California, did not ingest Plavix in California, and were not injured by Plavix in California. The mere fact that *other* plaintiffs

were prescribed, obtained, and ingested Plavix in California—and allegedly sustained the same injuries as did the non-residents—does not allow the State to assert specific jurisdiction over the nonresidents' claims. * * * Nor is it sufficient—or even relevant—that [defendant] conducted research in California on matters unrelated to Plavix. What is needed—and what is missing here—is a connection between the forum and the specific claims at issue.

Would this analysis support jurisdiction in Oklahoma over the Robinsons' claims against Audi and Volkswagen of America? Consider the views of Justice Ginsburg, dissenting in J. McIntyre Machinery, Ltd. v. Nicastro, 131 S.Ct. 2780, 2802 (2011) [infra p. 772]: "[N]otably, the foreign manufacturer of the Audi in *World-Wide Volkswagen* did not object to the jurisdiction of the Oklahoma courts and the U.S. importer abandoned its initially stated objection. * * * [T]he Court's opinion indicates that an objection to jurisdiction by the manufacturer or national distributor would have been unavailing." Keep the requirements for specific jurisdiction in mind as you examine the following cases.

Q. Vid.

———————

Calder v. Jones, 465 U.S. 783 (1984):   (11/12/18)

JUSTICE REHNQUIST delivered the opinion of the Court.

[In its October 9, 1979, issue, the National Enquirer (published by a Florida corporation that had its principal place of business in that state) printed a story about Shirley Jones, an entertainer living and working in California. The story made a number of uncomplimentary assertions about Jones, including a report that she drank so heavily as to prevent her from fulfilling her professional obligations. Jones sued the Enquirer for libel in California state court. Perhaps because some 12% of its nationwide circulation of 5 million was sold in California, nearly twice the distribution of any other state, the paper answered without raising any objection to jurisdiction.

Jones also sued Calder, the paper's editor, and South, the reporter whose byline appeared on the story. Both were Florida residents, and they objected to California jurisdiction. South frequently traveled to California on business but claimed he did his research on this story by telephone from Florida to California, although the trial court found that he made one visit to the state in connection with the story. Calder, who "oversees just about every function of the Enquirer," reviewed and approved the subject for the story and edited the article in final form. He also refused Jones' demand for a retraction. But he had visited California only twice—once on pleasure and once to testify at the trial of the unrelated libel suit against the Enquirer brought by entertainer Carol Burnett.

The Supreme Court unanimously upheld jurisdiction, but declined to premise it on South's numerous telephone calls to California and visit to that state.]

The Due Process Clause of the Fourteenth Amendment to the United States Constitution permits personal jurisdiction over a defendant in any State with which the defendant has "certain minimum contacts . . . such that the maintenance of the suit does not offend 'traditional notions of fair play and substantial justice.' " International Shoe Co. v. Washington, 326 U.S. 310, 316 (1945). In judging minimum contacts, a court properly focuses on "the relationship among the defendant, the forum, and the litigation." Shaffer v. Heitner, 433 U.S. 186, 204 (1977). The plaintiff's lack of "contacts" will not defeat otherwise proper jurisdiction, see Keeton v. Hustler Magazine, Inc., 465 U.S. 770, 779–81 (1984), but they may be so manifold as to permit jurisdiction when it would not exist in their absence. Here, the plaintiff is the focus of the activities of the defendants out of which the suit arises.

The allegedly libelous story concerned the California activities of a California resident. It impugned the professionalism of an entertainer whose television career was centered in California. The article was drawn from California sources, and the brunt of the harm, in terms both of respondent's emotional distress and the injury to her professional reputation, was suffered in California. In sum, California is the focal point both of the story and of the harm suffered. Jurisdiction over petitioners is therefore proper in California based on the "effects" of their Florida conduct in California. World-Wide Volkswagen Corp. v. Woodson, 444 U.S. 286, 297–298 (1980).

Petitioners argue that they are not responsible for the circulation of the article in California. A reporter and an editor, they claim, have no direct economic stake in their employer's sales in a distant State. Nor are ordinary employees able to control their employer's marketing activity. The mere fact that they can "foresee" that the article will be circulated and have an effect in California is not sufficient for an assertion of jurisdiction. World-Wide Volkswagen Corp. v. Woodson, 444 U.S., at 295. They do not "in effect appoint the [article their] agent for service of process." World-Wide Volkswagen Corp. v. Woodson, 444 U.S., at 296. Petitioners liken themselves to a welder employed in Florida who works on a boiler which subsequently explodes in California. Cases which hold that jurisdiction will be proper over the manufacturer, Gray v. American Radiator & Standard Sanitary Corp., 176 N.E.2d 761 (Ill.1961), should not be applied to the welder who has no control over and derives no direct benefit from his employer's sales in that distant State.

Petitioners' analogy does not wash. Whatever the status of their hypothetical welder, petitioners are not charged with mere untargeted negligence. Rather, their intentional, and allegedly tortious, actions were expressly aimed at California. Petitioner South wrote and petitioner Calder edited an article that they knew would have a potentially devastating impact upon respondent. And they knew that the brunt of that injury would be felt by respondent in the State in which she lives and works and in which the National Enquirer has its largest circulation. Under the circumstances, petitioners must "reasonably anticipate being haled into court there" to answer for the truth of the statements made in their article. World-Wide Volkswagen Corp. v. Woodson, 444 U.S., at 297; Shaffer v. Heitner, 433 U.S. 186, 216 (1977). An individual injured in California need not go to Florida to seek redress from persons who, though remaining in Florida, knowingly cause the injury in California. Petitioners are correct that their contacts with California are not to be judged according to their employer's activities there. On the other hand, their status as employees does not somehow insulate them from jurisdiction. Each defendant's contacts with the forum State must be assessed individually. In this case, petitioners are primary participants in an alleged wrongdoing intentionally directed at a California resident, and jurisdiction over them is proper on that basis.

NOTES AND QUESTIONS

1.   In Walden v. Fiore, 134 S.Ct. 1115 (2014), the Court unanimously held that *Calder*'s targeting test did not support jurisdiction. Plaintiffs there were professional gamblers traveling from Puerto Rico to Nevada, their part-time home, when a police officer deputized as an agent of the Drug Enforcement Administration seized some $97,000 in cash from their carry-on luggage while they were changing planes at Atlanta airport. As plaintiffs told defendant at the airport, the money was their "bank" and winnings from gambling in Puerto Rico, and they were bound to Las Vegas for more gambling. Plaintiffs claimed that defendant had no probable cause for the seizure and that he later made false statements in an affidavit submitted to the U.S. Attorney in Georgia in connection with possible forfeiture proceedings. Plaintiffs sued in Nevada, arguing that jurisdiction was proper because defendant targeted them by depriving them of the money they needed to pursue their profession in Nevada.

The Court rejected plaintiffs' argument and distinguished *Calder* (id. at 1123–24):

> The crux of *Calder* was that the reputation-based "effects" of the alleged libel connected the defendants to California, not just to the plaintiff. * * * [T]he reputational injury caused by the defendants' story would not have occurred but for the fact that the defendants wrote an article for publication in California that was read by a large number of California citizens. * * * In this way, the "effects" caused by the defendant's article—*i.e.*, the injury to the plaintiff's reputation in the estimation of the California public—connected the defendants' conduct to *California*, not just to a plaintiff who lived there.

The St. in which the injury occurs is the state in which the tort occurs.

(Note Case)

SEC. D   REFINING THE MINIMUM CONTACTS ANALYSIS   759

Compare Indianapolis Colts v. Metropolitan Baltimore Football Club Limited Partnership, 34 F.3d 410 (7th Cir.1994). After the owner of the Baltimore Colts National Football League moved the team to Indianapolis, fans in Baltimore obtained a franchise in the Canadian Football League and prepared to launch a new football team to be called the "Baltimore CFL Colts." The Indianapolis Colts sued in Indiana, claiming trademark infringement, and the court upheld jurisdiction:

> The Indiana Colts use the trademarks they seek to defend in this suit mainly in Indiana. If the trademarks are impaired, as the suit alleges, the injury will be felt mainly in Indiana. By choosing a name that might be found to be confusingly similar to that of the Indianapolis Colts, the defendants assumed the risk of injuring valuable property located in Indiana. Since there can be no tort without an injury, the state in which the injury occurs is the state in which the tort occurs, and someone who commits a tort in Indiana should, one might suppose, be amenable to suit there. This conclusion is supported by the Supreme Court's decision in Calder v. Jones.

The court noted as well that defendants intended to broadcast games involving the new Baltimore team nationwide via cable TV.

(11/12/18)

2.   Keeton v. Hustler Magazine, Inc., 465 U.S. 770 (1984), a companion case to *Calder*, was also a libel suit against a nationally distributed publication. Plaintiff, a New York resident, had first sued defendant, an Ohio corporation, in Ohio. When this suit was dismissed on statute of limitations grounds (considered "procedural" and therefore not on the merits for res judicata purposes), the only state in which the limitations period had not yet run was New Hampshire. Even though she had no prior contacts with New Hampshire, plaintiff filed a second libel suit there. Defendant regularly sold 10,000 to 15,000 copies of its magazine, a very small proportion of the total distribution, in New Hampshire. Under the "single publication rule" (that all damages sustained in all jurisdictions are recoverable in one action), plaintiff sought in the second suit to recover for injuries suffered from the nationwide circulation of the defamation. Reasoning that "the New Hampshire tail is too small to wag so large an out-of-state dog," the lower courts dismissed the case for lack of personal jurisdiction.

The Supreme Court reversed. It found that "regular monthly sales of thousands of magazines cannot by any stretch of the imagination be characterized as random, isolated or fortuitous." Despite the single publication rule, New Hampshire's unusually long statute of limitations, and plaintiff's lack of contacts with the forum, jurisdiction was therefore proper in New Hampshire. The Court reasoned that New Hampshire had a sufficient interest in redressing injuries that occurred within the state because its residents were allegedly misled about plaintiff, and that her reputation was harmed by these misrepresentations even though she was otherwise unknown in New Hampshire. Plaintiff's lack of contacts, although not irrelevant to the issue of state interest, did not foreclose jurisdiction. The Court refused to consider choice of law issues because "any potential unfairness of applying New

Hampshire's statute of limitations to all aspects of this nationwide suit has nothing to do with jurisdiction of the Court to adjudicate the claims," and choice of law concerns "should not distort the jurisdictional inquiry."

3. In Gordy v. Daily News, L.P., 95 F.3d 829 (9th Cir.1996), Berry Gordy, former president of Motown Records, filed suit in California claiming a story in the New York Daily News defamed him. The story was not about California activities of Gordy and did not mention California. More than 99% of the circulation of the paper was distributed within 300 miles of New York City. But the News did deliver 13 copies of its daily edition and 18 copies of its Sunday edition to California recipients. The court upheld jurisdiction: "It is reasonable to expect the bulk of the harm from defamation of an individual to be felt at his domicile. Targeting also occurs because the Daily News regularly distributes from 13 to 18 copies of its publication in California, and the defamatory column contained in those copies causes harm in California." Contrast Fielding v. Hubert Burda Media, Inc., 415 F.3d 419 (5th Cir. 2005), in which plaintiff, originally a Texan but living in Europe, sued for libel due to defendant's publication of a story asserting that her husband had committed adultery while they were living in Berlin. Plaintiff sued in Texas, pointing that about 60 issues of the offending magazine were distributed there and alleging that the story harmed her reputation among her family and friends in Texas. The court held there was no jurisdiction, distinguishing Gordy, because "the articles concerned the German activities of individuals in Germany," and "Germany is the focal point both of the story and the harm suffered."

4. Does the effects analysis give plaintiff too much control over jurisdiction? Consider Burt v. Board of Regents, 757 F.2d 242 (10th Cir.1985). Plaintiff doctor had done his medical residency at the University of Nebraska and then moved to Colorado. He asked Dr. Connolly, the head of the University's Department of Orthopedic Surgery, to provide a reference, and Dr. Connolly said uncomplimentary things about plaintiff. Plaintiff sued Connolly in Colorado, and a divided court of appeals upheld jurisdiction:

> Nor are we persuaded by Dr. Connolly's claim that it violates due process to hale him into court in Colorado because the letter was, in effect, solicited by Dr. Burt, who gave Dr. Connolly's name to the hospitals. Dr. Burt solicited a letter of reference; he did not solicit a malicious falsehood. Taking Dr. Burt's allegations as true, as we must on a motion to dismiss, we hold that no due process notions of fairness are violated by requiring one who intentionally libels another to answer for the truth of his statements in any state where the libel causes harm to the victim. To the extent that Dr. Connolly's statements damage Dr. Burt's reputation and his ability to practice his profession, the damage occurred in Colorado.

Judge Seth dissented:

> In the case before us, the letter was, of course, sent to Colorado but the "focal" point of the story was Nebraska. The letter was about what had taken place in Nebraska, not Colorado. The story was certainly

Interview ≠ Publishing

not drawn from Colorado sources. The action was initiated by plaintiff. We thus have but half a *Calder*.

The Supreme Court granted certiorari in *Burt*, but later dismissed the case as moot. See also Brainerd v. Governors of the University of Alberta, 873 F.2d 1257 (9th Cir.1989) (suit allowed in Arizona for allegedly defamatory statement by vice president of Canadian university about a former faculty member in response to inquiry by the faculty member's present employer, the University of Arizona).

5.   In *Calder*, the Court uses a number of phrases to explain why jurisdiction over Calder and South is different from jurisdiction over the welder who negligently produces a boiler. It says, for example, that they were "primary participants" who are "not charged with mere untargeted negligence." How many other employees of a defendant charged with an intentional tort would be similarly covered by the Court's reasoning? Does it cover non-employees? Suppose that South gathered information for his story from other Floridians who knew Jones. Could they be sued in California when their stories were printed in the Enquirer? In Madara v. Hall, 916 F.2d 1510 (11th Cir.1990), a rock star gave a telephonic interview from New York, his home, to a magazine published in California that was distributed nationwide. When he was sued in Florida for comments made in the interview about a Florida resident, the court held that jurisdiction was not proper: "Simply giving an interview to a reporter is not enough to cause Hall to anticipate being haled into court in Florida. Hall was not the magazine's publisher and did not control its circulation and distribution. * * * Hall's mere awareness, if he indeed was aware, that a small number of copies of the magazine might find their way to Florida is not enough to justify the exercise of personal jurisdiction."

6.   In *Calder*, all the indicators mentioned by the Court point toward jurisdiction in California. Thus, we are told that the article "concerned the California activities of a California resident," and that "the brunt of the harm" was California. How many of these factors need to coalesce to justify jurisdiction on the Court's effects test? Consider:

   (a)   Suppose Jones lived in Arizona when she was not making TV programs. Would jurisdiction then be permissible in both Arizona and California? Would it be permissible in either?

   (b)   Suppose Jones sometimes acted in plays in New York. New York has the second largest circulation of the National Enquirer. Would jurisdiction be permissible there?

7.   How should this jurisdictional theory apply to terrorists that target the U.S.? In Mwani v. bin Laden, 417 F.3d 1 (D.C Cir. 2005), Kenyans injured by the terrorist bombing of the U.S. embassy in Nairobi in 1998 sued Osama bin Laden and al Queda in D.C. district court for orchestrating the bombing. The court found that jurisdiction was proper because bin Laden and al Queda "purposefully directed" their activities at residents of the United States (id. at 13):

In this case, there is no doubt that the defendants "engaged in unabashedly malignant actions directed at [and] felt in this forum." The plaintiffs' allegations were that bin Laden and al Queda orchestrated the bombing of the American embassy in Nairobi, not only to kill both American and Kenyan employees inside the building, but to cause pain and sow terror in the embassy's home country, the United States. Nor were the plaintiffs' allegations and evidence of contacts with the United States limited to the Nairobi bombing. The plaintiffs described an ongoing conspiracy to attack the United States, with overt acts occurring within this country's borders. Putting to one side the acts that took place after the embassy bombing (including the attacks on the World Trade Center and the Pentagon on September 11, 2001), the plaintiffs pointed to the 1993 World Trade Center bombing, as well as to the plot to bomb the United Nations, Federal Plaza, and the Lincoln and Holland Tunnels in New York.

Does the decision mean that anyone injured by an act of terrorism that "targets" America anywhere in the world can sue in U.S. courts? In Piper Aircraft Corp. v. Reyno (infra p. 849) we will see that the Supreme Court sometimes disapproves of suits brought against American companies by foreigners for injuries they suffered in their home countries. Should jurisdiction be extended nonetheless to include the *Mwani* case?

BURGER KING CORP. v. RUDZEWICZ
Supreme Court of the United States, 1985
471 U.S. 462

JUSTICE BRENNAN delivered the opinion of the Court.

The State of Florida's long-arm statute extends jurisdiction to "[a]ny person, whether or not a citizen or resident of this state," who, inter alia, "[b]reach[es] a contract in this state by failing to perform acts required by the contract to be performed in this state," so long as the cause of action arises from the alleged contractual breach. Fla.Stat. § 48.193(1)(g) (Supp. 1984). The United States District Court for the Southern District of Florida, sitting in diversity, relied on this provision in exercising personal jurisdiction over a Michigan resident who allegedly had breached a franchise agreement with a Florida corporation by failing to make required payments in Florida. The question presented is whether this exercise of long-arm jurisdiction offended "traditional conception[s] of fair play and substantial justice" embodied in the Due Process Clause of the Fourteenth Amendment.

I

[Burger King, a Florida corporation headquartered in Florida, operates 3,000 restaurants, 80% through a franchise operation called the "Burger King System" that prescribes uniform standards for format and building design as well as food preparation. Franchisees are therefore required to attend training seminars at Burger King University in Miami and at Whopper College Regional Training Centers around the country. They are subject to "exacting regulation of virtually every conceivable aspect of their operations by Burger King." Ultimate authority rests with Burger King headquarters in Miami, but day-to-day monitoring is conducted through a network of district offices.]

The instant litigation grows out of Burger King's termination of one of its franchisees, and is aptly described by the franchisee as "a divorce proceeding among commercial partners." The appellee John Rudzewicz, a Michigan citizen and resident, is the senior partner in a Detroit accounting firm. In 1978, he was approached by Brian MacShara, the son of a business acquaintance, who suggested that they jointly apply to Burger King for a franchise in the Detroit area. MacShara proposed to serve as the manager of the restaurant if Rudzewicz would put up the investment capital; in exchange, the two would evenly share the profits. Believing that MacShara's idea offered attractive investment and tax-deferral opportunities, Rudzewicz agreed to the venture.

Rudzewicz and MacShara jointly applied for a franchise to Burger King's Birmingham, Michigan district office in the autumn of 1978. Their application was forwarded to Burger King's Miami headquarters, which entered into a preliminary agreement with them in February 1979. During the ensuing four months it was agreed that Rudzewicz and MacShara would assume operation of an existing facility in Drayton Plains, Michigan. MacShara attended the prescribed management courses in Miami during this period, and the franchisees purchased $165,000 worth of restaurant equipment from Burger King's Davmor Industries division in Miami. Even before the final agreements were signed, however, the parties began to disagree over site-development fees, building design, computation of monthly rent, and whether the franchisees would be able to assign their liabilities to a corporation they had formed. During these disputes Rudzewicz and MacShara negotiated both with the Birmingham district office and with the Miami headquarters.[7] With some misgivings, Rudzewicz and MacShara finally obtained limited concessions from the Miami headquarters, signed the final agreements, and commenced operations in June 1979. By signing the final agreements, Rudzewicz obligated himself personally to payments exceeding $1 million over the 20-year franchise relationship.

The Drayton Plains facility apparently enjoyed steady business during the summer of 1979, but patronage declined after a recession began later that year. Rudzewicz and MacShara soon fell far behind in their monthly

---

[7]   Although Rudzewicz and MacShara dealt with the Birmingham district office on a regular basis, they communicated directly with the Miami headquarters in forming the contracts; moreover, they learned that the district office had "very little" decisionmaking authority and accordingly turned directly to headquarters in seeking to resolve their disputes.

payments to Miami. Headquarters sent notices of default, and an extended period of negotiations began among the franchisees, the Birmingham district office, and the Miami headquarters. After several Burger King officials in Miami had engaged in prolonged but ultimately unsuccessful negotiations with the franchisees by mail and by telephone, headquarters terminated the franchise and ordered Rudzewicz and MacShara to vacate the premises. They refused and continued to occupy and operate the facility as a Burger King restaurant.

[Burger King sued Rudzewicz and McShara in Florida for breach of contract, and for tortiously infringing its trademarks and service marks by continuing to operate the Drayton Plains facility. Defendants filed a counterclaim accusing Burger King of violation of Michigan's Franchise Investment Law. After a 3-day bench trial, the district court entered judgement in Burger King's favor for $228,875 in contract damages and ordered defendants to cease operating the restaurant and turn the keys over to Burger King, meanwhile rejecting their counterclaim. McShara did not appeal, and Rudzewicz settled the trademark infringement aspects of the judgment. Accordingly, the Court noted that it did not need to address the extent to which the tortious act provisions of Florida's long-arm statute could apply to out-of-state trademark infringement under Calder v. Jones, supra p. 756.]

II

A

[Justice Brennan summarized the Court's prior rulings on the due process limits on the jurisdiction as designed to give defendants "fair warning that a particular activity may subject them to the jurisdiction of a foreign sovereign" and thereby "give a degree of predictability to the legal system that allows potential defendants to structure their primary conduct with some minimum assurance as to where that conduct will and will not render them liable to suit." The purposeful availment requirement mainly serves that purpose; when a commercial actor has purposefully directed his activities at forum residents "he must present a compelling case that the existence of some other considerations would render jurisdiction unreasonable."]

B

(1)

Applying these principles to the case at hand, we believe there is substantial record evidence supporting the District Court's conclusion that the assertion of personal jurisdiction over Rudzewicz in Florida for the alleged breach of his franchise agreement did not offend due process. At the outset, we note a continued division among lower courts respecting whether and to what extent a contract can constitute a "contact" for purposes of due process analysis. If the question is whether an individual's contract with an out-of-state party alone can automatically establish sufficient minimum contacts in the other party's home forum, we believe the answer clearly is that it cannot. The Court long ago rejected the notion that personal jurisdiction might turn on "mechanical" tests, or on "conceptualistic . . . theories of the place of contracting or of performance." Instead, we have emphasized the need for a "highly realistic" approach that recognizes that a "contract" is "ordinarily but an intermediate step serving to tie up prior business negotiations with future consequences which themselves are the real object of the business transaction." It is these factors—prior negotiations and contemplated future consequences, along with the terms of the contract and the parties' actual course of dealing— that must be evaluated in determining whether the defendant purposefully established minimum contacts within the forum.

In this case, no physical ties to Florida can be attributed to Rudzewicz other than MacShara's brief training course in Miami. Rudzewicz did not maintain offices in Florida and, for all that appears from the record, has never even visited there. Yet this franchise dispute grew directly out of "a contract which had a *substantial* connection with that State." McGee v. International Life Insurance Co., 355 U.S., at 223 (emphasis added). Eschewing the option of operating an independent local enterprise, Rudzewicz deliberately "reach[ed] out beyond" Michigan and negotiated with a Florida corporation for the purchase of a long-term franchise and the manifold benefits that would derive from affiliation with a nationwide organization. Travelers Health Assn. v. Virginia, 339 U.S. [643], at 647 [(1950)]. Upon approval, he entered into a carefully structured 20-year relationship that envisioned continuing and wide-reaching contacts with Burger King in Florida. In light of Rudzewicz's voluntary acceptance of the long-term and exacting regulation of his business from Burger King's Miami headquarters, the "quality and nature" of his relationship to the company in Florida can in no sense be viewed as "random," "fortuitous," or "attenuated." Rudzewicz's refusal to make the contractually required payments in Miami, and his continued use of Burger King's trademarks and confidential business information after his termination, caused foreseeable injuries to the corporation in Florida. For these reasons it was, at the very least, presumptively reasonable for Rudzewicz to be called to account there for such injuries.

The Court of Appeals concluded, however, that in light of the supervision emanating from Burger King's district office in Birmingham, Rudzewicz reasonably believed that "the Michigan office was for all intents and purposes the embodiment of Burger King" and that he therefore had no "reason to anticipate a Burger King suit outside of Michigan." This reasoning overlooks substantial record evidence indicating that Rudzewicz most certainly knew that he was affiliating himself with an enterprise based primarily in Florida. The contract documents themselves emphasize that Burger King's operations are conducted and supervised from the

Miami headquarters, that all relevant notices and payments must be sent there, and that the agreements were made in and enforced from Miami. Moreover, the parties' actual course of dealing repeatedly confirmed that decisionmaking authority was vested in the Miami headquarters and that the district office served largely as an intermediate link between the headquarters and the franchisees. When problems arose over building design, site-development fees, rent computation, and the defaulted payments, Rudzewicz and MacShara learned that the Michigan office was powerless to resolve their disputes and could only channel their communications to Miami. Throughout these disputes, the Miami headquarters and the Michigan franchisees carried on a continuous course of direct communications by mail and by telephone, and it was the Miami headquarters that made the key negotiating decisions out of which the instant litigation arose. See n. 7, supra.

Moreover, we believe the Court of Appeals gave insufficient weight to provisions in the various franchise documents providing that all disputes would be governed by Florida law. The franchise agreement, for example, stated:

> "This Agreement shall become valid when executed and accepted by BKC at Miami, Florida; it shall be deemed made and entered into in the State of Florida and shall be governed and construed under and in accordance with the laws of the State of Florida. The choice of law designation does not require that all suits concerning this Agreement be filed in Florida."

The Court of Appeals reasoned that choice-of-law provisions are irrelevant to the question of personal jurisdiction, relying on Hanson v. Denckla for the proposition that "the center of gravity for choice-of-law purposes does not necessarily confer the sovereign prerogative to assert jurisdiction." This reasoning misperceives the import of the quoted proposition. The Court in *Hanson* and subsequent cases has emphasized that choice-of-law analysis—which focuses on all elements of a transaction, and not simply on the defendant's conduct—is distinct from minimum-contacts jurisdictional analysis—which focuses at the threshold solely on the defendant's purposeful connection to the forum. Nothing in our cases, however, suggests that a choice-of-law provision should be ignored in considering whether a defendant has "purposefully invoked the benefits and protections of a State's laws" for jurisdictional purposes. Although such a provision standing alone would be insufficient to confer jurisdiction, we believe that, when combined with the 20-year interdependent relationship Rudzewicz established with Burger King's Miami headquarters, it reinforced his deliberate affiliation with the forum State and the reasonable foreseeability of possible litigation there. As Judge Johnson argued in his dissent below, Rudzewicz "purposefully availed himself of the benefits and protections of Florida's laws" by entering into contracts expressly providing that those laws would govern franchise disputes.

(2)

[The Court held that defendant did not make a "compelling case" that other factors made Florida's exercise of jurisdiction unreasonable. The state had a legitimate interest in holding defendant answerable on a claim related to the contacts he had established with Florida. Although defendant emphasized that Michigan's Franchise Investment Law was designed to protect franchisees like him, that law did not purport to give Michigan exclusive authority to resolve franchise disputes affecting its residents. Indeed, "minimum-contacts analysis presupposes that two or more States may be interested in the outcome of a dispute." Although defendant argued that there was a "disparity of bargaining power" between him and Burger King, he was an experienced accountant and the district court found that he was an experienced businessman and that he did not act under economic duress.]

III

Notwithstanding these considerations, the Court of Appeals apparently believed that it was necessary to reject jurisdiction in this case as a prophylactic measure, reasoning that an affirmance of the District Court's judgment would result in the exercise of jurisdiction over "out-of-state consumers to collect payments due on modest personal purchases" and would "sow the seeds of default judgments against franchisees owing smaller debts." We share the Court of Appeals' broader concerns and therefore reject any talismanic jurisdictional formulas; "the facts of each case must [always] be weighed" in determining whether personal jurisdiction would comport with "fair play and substantial justice." The "quality and nature" of an interstate transaction may sometimes be so "random," "fortuitous," or "attenuated" that it cannot fairly be said that the potential defendant "should reasonably anticipate being haled into court" in another jurisdiction. We also have emphasized that jurisdiction may not be grounded on a contract whose terms have been obtained through "fraud, undue influence, or overweening bargaining power" and whose application would render litigation "so gravely difficult and inconvenient that [a party] will for all practical purposes be deprived of his day in court." The Bremen v. Zapata Off-Shore Co., 407 U.S., at 12, 18. Cf. Fuentes v. Shevin, 407 U.S. 67, 94–96 (1972); National Equipment Rental, Ltd. v. Szukhent, 375 U.S. 311, 329 (1964) (Black, J., dissenting) (jurisdictional rules may not be employed against small consumers so as to "crippl[e] their defense"). Just as the Due Process Clause allows flexibility in ensuring that commercial actors are not effectively "judgment proof" for the consequences of obligations they voluntarily assume in other States, so too does it prevent rules that would unfairly enable them to obtain default judgments against unwitting customers.

For the reasons set forth above, however, these dangers are not present in the instant case. Because Rudzewicz established a substantial and continuing relationship with Burger King's Miami headquarters, received fair notice from the contract documents and the course of dealing that he might be subject to suit in Florida, and has failed to demonstrate how jurisdiction in that forum would otherwise be fundamentally unfair, we conclude that the District Court's exercise of jurisdiction pursuant to Florida Stat. § 48.193(1)(g) (Supp.1984) did not offend due process. The judgment of the Court of Appeals is accordingly reversed, and the case is remanded for further proceedings consistent with this opinion.

It is so ordered.

JUSTICE POWELL took no part in the consideration or decision of this case.

JUSTICE STEVENS, with whom JUSTICE WHITE joins, dissenting.

In my opinion there is a significant element of unfairness in requiring a franchisee to defend a case of this kind in the forum chosen by the franchisor. It is undisputed that respondent maintained no place of business in Florida, that he had no employees in that State, and that he was not licensed to do business there. Respondent did not prepare his french fries, shakes, and hamburgers in Michigan, and then deliver them into the stream of commerce "with the expectation that they [would] be purchased by consumers in" Florida. To the contrary, respondent did business only in Michigan, his business, property, and payroll taxes were payable in that state, and he sold all of his products there.

Throughout the business relationship, respondent's principal contacts with petitioner were with its Michigan office. Notwithstanding its disclaimer, the Court seems ultimately to rely on nothing more than standard boilerplate language contained in various documents to establish that respondent " 'purposefully availed himself of the benefits and protections of Florida's laws.' " Such superficial analysis creates a potential for unfairness not only in negotiations between franchisors and their franchisees but, more significantly, in the resolution of the disputes that inevitably arise from time to time in such relationships. Judge Vance's opinion for the Court of Appeals for the Eleventh Circuit adequately explains why I would affirm the judgment of that court. I particularly find the following more persuasive than what this Court has written today:

> "Nothing in the course of negotiations gave Rudzewicz reason to anticipate a Burger King suit outside of Michigan. The only face-to-face or even oral contact Rudzewicz had with Burger King throughout months of protracted negotiations was with representatives of the Michigan office. Burger King had the Michigan office interview Rudzewicz and MacShara, appraise their application, discuss price terms, recommend the site which

the defendants finally agreed to, and attend the final closing ceremony. There is no evidence that Rudzewicz ever negotiated with anyone in Miami or even sent mail there during negotiations. He maintained no staff in the state of Florida, and as far as the record reveals, he has never even visited the state.

"The contracts contemplated the startup of a local Michigan restaurant whose profits would derive solely from food sales made to customers in Drayton Plains. The sale, which involved the use of an intangible trademark in Michigan and occupancy of a Burger King facility there, required no performance in the state of Florida. Under the contract, the local Michigan district office was responsible for providing all of the services due Rudzewicz, including advertising and management consultation. Supervision, moreover, emanated from that office alone. To Rudzewicz, the Michigan office was for all intents and purposes the embodiment of Burger King. He had reason to believe that his working relationship with Burger King began and ended in Michigan, not at the distant and anonymous Florida headquarters. . . .

"Given that the office in Rudzewicz' home state conducted all of the negotiations and wholly supervised the contract, we believe that he had reason to assume that the state of the supervisory office would be the same state in which Burger King would file suit. Rudzewicz lacked fair notice that the distant corporate headquarters which insulated itself from direct dealings with him would later seek to assert jurisdiction over him in the courts of its own home state. . . .

"Just as Rudzewicz lacked notice of the possibility of suit in Florida, he was financially unprepared to meet its added costs. The franchise relationship in particular is fraught with potential for financial surprise. The device of the franchise gives local retailers the access to national trademark recognition which enable them to compete with better-financed, more efficient chain stores. This national affiliation, however, does not alter the fact that the typical franchise store is a local concern serving at best a neighborhood or community. Neither the revenues of a local business nor the geographical range of its market prepares the average franchise owner for the cost of distant litigation. . . ."

NOTES AND QUESTIONS

1.   Isn't a fast food outlet much more local than a three-state distributor of cars like World-Wide Volkswagen? Indeed, isn't it more local than an auto retailer like Seaway? Yet the Court here upholds jurisdiction in part because defendants "reached out" beyond Michigan for "the manifold benefits that would derive from affiliation with a nationwide organization." But in *World-*

Wide Volkswagen the Court had rejected the argument that a local retailer relied upon the existence of a nationwide net of service facilities as justifying jurisdiction in Oklahoma. Are the two cases consistent?

2.   When did Rudzewicz "reach out" to Florida? When he filed the initial application at the Birmingham, Michigan, district office of Burger King? When he negotiated by letter with headquarters in Florida? When he signed the franchise agreement? When he and MacShara began operating the outlet?

3.   With respect to reasonableness, the Court says that if defendant "purposefully has directed his activities at forum residents" jurisdiction is appropriate unless it presents "a compelling case that some other considerations would render jurisdiction unreasonable." "Although there is a 'strong presumption of reasonableness' if purposeful availment exists, courts must still consider reasonableness as a separate factor." Budget Blinds, Inc. v. White, 536 F.3d 244, 265 (3d Cir. 2008).

In Asahi Metal Indus. Co. v. Superior Court, 480 U.S. 102 (1987), the Court sharply disagreed about whether the purposeful availment requirement was satisfied, but unanimously agreed that the exercise of jurisdiction could not be sustained because it was not reasonable. The underlying litigation was filed in a California state court after a California motorcycle rider was seriously injured when the tire on his Honda motorcycle burst on the freeway. He sued Honda, which manufactured the motorcycle, and the maker of the inner tube in the tire. The maker of the inner tube, a Taiwanese company, asserted a cross-complaint (like a third-party complaint under Rule 14) against Asahi, a Japanese company that made a valve, claiming that it was defective and caused the accident. The plaintiff (who never sued Asahi) settled all his claims, so the only feature of the litigation that remained by the time the case got to the Supreme Court was an indemnity claim by a Taiwanese company against a Japanese company. The Court stressed the "unique burdens placed upon one who must defend oneself in a foreign legal system," and found no justification for imposing them on Asahi. Although California might have some slight interest in enforcing its safety standards against the component manufacturer, similar pressures would be placed on it by its customers, who were subject to California jurisdiction. See also Benton v. Cameco Corp., 375 F.3d 1070 (10th Cir. 2004) (holding Colorado jurisdiction unreasonable in a suit against a Canadian defendant, partly because the showing of purposeful availment was very weak); contrast Airstech Chem Intern., Ltd. v. Acrylic Fabricators, Inc., 138 F.3d 624 (6th Cir. 1998) ("we think that a Canadian defendant such as AFL bears a significantly lighter burden than does a Japanese defendant—or, for that matter, most other foreign defendants.")

Could the ease of satisfying the reasonableness prong produce undue strictness in interpreting the purposeful availment prong? Consider Freer, Personal Jurisdiction in the Twenty-First Century: The Ironic Legacy of Justice Brennan, 63 S. Car. L. Rev. 551, 563–64 (2012):

> In *Burger King*, Brennan created a presumption that jurisdiction will be proper when the defendant has relevant contacts with the forum.

He placed an inordinately high burden on the defendant to overcome that burden. As a result, a defendant will find it virtually impossible to escape jurisdiction by appealing to fairness factors. Accordingly, the only realistic option for a court wishing to reject personal jurisdiction is to find that the defendant has not forged relevant contacts with forum.

4.   In *Burger King*, the Court finds that the choice-of-law provision in the franchise agreement constituted some purposeful availment by defendants of Florida law. How realistic is that analysis? The franchise agreement could have provided for appointment of a Florida agent for service of process, National Equipment Rental, Inc. v. Szukhent, infra p. 835, and might validly have required that disputes be adjudicated in a certain jurisdiction to the exclusion of all others. See Carnival Cruise Lines, Inc. v. Shute, infra p. 836. Since the agreement in this case did not include any such provisions, does the provision regarding choice of law really notify defendant that he may be sued in Florida?

5.   The Court also treats as significant the fact that defendant entered into "a carefully structured 20-year relationship that envisioned continuing and wide-reaching contacts with Burger King." To get an idea how pervasive that influence might be, consider the following description of the level of control McDonalds exerts over its franchisees:

> In 1958 [McDonalds] put together an operations and training manual for the company that was seventy-five pages long, specifying how almost everything should be done. Hamburgers were always to be placed on the grill in six neat rows; french fries had to be exactly 0.28 inches thick. The McDonalds operations manual today has ten times the number of pages and weighs about four pounds. Known within the company as "the Bible," it contains precise instructions on how various appliances should be used, how each item on the menu should look, and how employees should greet customers. Operators who disobey these rules can lose their franchises. Cooking instructions are not only printed in the manual, they are often designed into the machines. A McDonalds kitchen is full of buzzers and flashing lights that tell employees what to do.

Schlosser, Fast Food Nation 69 (2002). How often will a contractual relationship be so intimate?

6.   For some time before *Burger King* was decided, commentators hoped for clear rules for the handling of jurisdictional issues in breach of contract cases. In Professor Louis' view, "Burger King is not the definitive contract case we had hoped for, and it sheds only a little more light on the basic problem than its predecessors." Louis, Jurisdiction Over Those Who Breach Their Contracts: The Lessons of Burger King, 72 N.C.L.Rev. 55 (1993). He found that tort and contract cases are actually not approached differently; "jurisdiction over the person in both tort and contract cases is readily established when the claim arises out of the personal activities of the defendant within the forum

state or out of the regular shipment of defendant's goods into, or the plaintiff's goods out of, the forum state. Jurisdiction is much more difficult to establish if the defendant has not personally entered the state, the defendant's contacts with the state are few or irregular, and the defendant is a purchaser, particularly a consumer-purchaser." Id. at 63.

J. McINTYRE MACHINERY, LTD. v. NICASTRO

Supreme Court of the United States, 2011
564 U.S. 873

Q. Vid

Plurality

JUSTICE KENNEDY announced the judgment of the Court and delivered an opinion, in which THE CHIEF JUSTICE, JUSTICE SCALIA, and JUSTICE THOMAS join.

Whether a person or entity is subject to the jurisdiction of a state court despite not having been present in the State either at the time of suit or at the time of the alleged injury, and despite not having consented to the exercise of jurisdiction, is a question that arises with great frequency in the routine course of litigation. The rules and standards for determining when a State does or does not have jurisdiction over an absent party have been unclear because of decades-old questions left open in Asahi Metal Industry Co. v. Superior Court, 480 U.S. 102 (1987).

Here, the Supreme Court of New Jersey, relying in part on *Asahi*, held that New Jersey's courts can exercise jurisdiction over a foreign manufacturer of a product so long as the manufacturer "knows or reasonably should know that its products are distributed through a nationwide distribution system that might lead to those products being sold in any of the fifty states." Nicastro v. McIntyre Machinery America, Ltd., 987 A.2d 575, 591, 592 (2010). Applying that test, the court concluded that a British manufacturer of scrap metal machines was subject to jurisdiction in New Jersey, even though at no time had it advertised in, sent goods to, or in any relevant sense targeted the State.

That decision cannot be sustained. Although the New Jersey Supreme Court issued an extensive opinion with careful attention to this Court's cases and to its own precedent, the "stream of commerce" metaphor carried the decision far afield. Due process protects the defendant's right not to be coerced except by lawful judicial power. As a general rule, the exercise of judicial power is not lawful unless the defendant "purposefully avails itself of the privilege of conducting activities within the forum State, thus invoking the benefits and protections of its laws." Hanson v. Denckla, 357 U.S. 235 (1958). There may be exceptions, say, for instance, in cases involving an intentional tort. But the general rule is applicable in this products-liability case, and the so-called "stream-of-commerce" doctrine cannot displace it.

I

This case arises from a products-liability suit filed in New Jersey state court. Robert Nicastro seriously injured his hand while using a metal-shearing machine manufactured by J. McIntyre Machinery, Ltd. (J. McIntyre). The accident occurred in New Jersey, but the machine was manufactured in England, where J. McIntyre is incorporated and operates. The question here is whether the New Jersey courts have jurisdiction over J. McIntyre, notwithstanding the fact that the company at no time either marketed goods in the State or shipped them there. Nicastro was a plaintiff in the New Jersey trial court and is the respondent here; J. McIntyre was a defendant and is now the petitioner.

At oral argument in this Court, Nicastro's counsel stressed three primary facts in defense of New Jersey's assertion of jurisdiction over J. McIntyre.

First, an independent company agreed to sell J. McIntyre's machines in the United States. J. McIntyre itself did not sell its machines to buyers in this country beyond the U.S. distributor, and there is no allegation that the distributor was under J. McIntyre's control.

Second, J. McIntyre officials attended annual conventions for the scrap recycling industry to advertise J. McIntyre's machines alongside the distributor. The conventions took place in various States, but never in New Jersey.

Third, no more than four machines (the record suggests only one), including the machine that caused the injuries that are the basis for this suit, ended up in New Jersey.

In addition to these facts emphasized by petitioner, the New Jersey Supreme Court noted that J. McIntyre held both United States and European patents on its recycling technology. It also noted that the U.S. distributor "structured [its] advertising and sales efforts in accordance with" J. McIntyre's "direction and guidance whenever possible," and that "at least some of the machines were sold on consignment to" the distributor.

In light of these facts, the New Jersey Supreme Court concluded that New Jersey courts could exercise jurisdiction over petitioner without contravention of the Due Process Clause. Jurisdiction was proper, in that court's view, because the injury occurred in New Jersey; because petitioner knew or reasonably should have known "that its products are distributed through a nationwide distribution system that might lead to those products being sold in any of the fifty states"; and because petitioner failed to "take some reasonable step to prevent the distribution of its products in this State."

Both the New Jersey Supreme Court's holding and its account of what it called "[t]he stream-of-commerce doctrine of jurisdiction," were incorrect, however. This Court's Asahi decision may be responsible in part for that court's error regarding the stream of commerce, and this case presents an opportunity to provide greater clarity. *101, Basically trying to*

II   *overturn it.*

The Due Process Clause protects an individual's right to be deprived of life, liberty, or property only by the exercise of lawful power. This is no less true with respect to the power of a sovereign to resolve disputes through judicial process than with respect to the power of a sovereign to prescribe rules of conduct for those within its sphere. As a general rule, neither statute nor judicial decree may bind strangers to the State.

A court may subject a defendant to judgment only when the defendant has sufficient contacts with the sovereign "such that the maintenance of the suit does not offend 'traditional notions of fair play and substantial justice.'" International Shoe Co. v. Washington, 326 U.S. 310, 316 (1945). Freeform notions of fundamental fairness divorced from traditional practice cannot transform a judgment rendered in the absence of authority into law. As a general rule, the sovereign's exercise of power requires some act by which the defendant "purposefully avails itself of the privilege of conducting activities within the forum State, thus invoking the benefits and protections of its laws," Hanson, 357 U.S., at 253, though in some cases, as with an intentional tort, the defendant might well fall within the State's authority by reason of his attempt to obstruct its laws. In products-liability cases like this one, it is the defendant's purposeful availment that makes jurisdiction consistent with "traditional notions of fair play and substantial justice."

A person may submit to a State's authority in a number of ways. There is, of course, explicit consent. E.g., Insurance Corp. of Ireland v. Compagnie des Bauxites de Guinee, 456 U.S. 694, 703 (1982) [infra p. 830]. Presence within a State at the time suit commences through service of process is another example. See Burnham [v. Superior Court, 495 U.S. 604 (1990), infra p. 813]. Citizenship or domicile—or, by analogy, incorporation or principal place of business for corporations—also indicates general submission to a State's powers. Goodyear Dunlop Tires Operations, S.A. v. Brown, [131 S.Ct. 2846 (2011), infra p. 817, a companion case]. Each of these examples reveals circumstances, or a course of conduct, from which it is proper to infer an intention to benefit from and thus an intention to submit to the laws of the forum State. Cf. Burger King Corp. v. Rudzewicz, 471 U.S. 462, 476 (1985) [supra p. 762]. These examples support exercise of the general jurisdiction of the State's courts and allow the State to resolve both matters that originate within the State and those based on activities and events elsewhere. By contrast, those who live or operate primarily outside a State have a due process right not to be subjected to judgment in its courts as a general matter.

There is also a more limited form of submission to a State's authority for disputes that "arise out of or are connected with the activities within the state." International Shoe Co., supra, at 319. Where a defendant "purposefully avails itself of the privilege of conducting activities within the forum State, thus invoking the benefits and protections of its laws," Hanson, supra, at 253, it submits to the judicial power of an otherwise foreign sovereign to the extent that power is exercised in connection with the defendant's activities touching on the State. In other words, submission through contact with and activity directed at a sovereign may justify specific jurisdiction "in a suit arising out of or related to the defendant's contacts with the forum."

The imprecision arising from Asahi, for the most part, results from its statement of the relation between jurisdiction and the "stream of commerce." The stream of commerce, like other metaphors, has its deficiencies as well as its utility. It refers to the movement of goods from manufacturers through distributors to consumers, yet beyond that descriptive purpose its meaning is far from exact. This Court has stated that a defendant's placing goods into the stream of commerce "with the expectation that they will be purchased by consumers within the forum State" may indicate purposeful availment. World-Wide Volkswagen Corp. v. Woodson, 444 U.S. 286, 298 (1980) [supra p. 744] (finding that expectation lacking). But that statement does not amend the general rule of personal jurisdiction. It merely observes that a defendant may in an appropriate case be subject to jurisdiction without entering the forum— itself an unexceptional proposition—as where manufacturers or distributors "seek to serve" a given State's market. The principal inquiry in cases of this sort is whether the defendant's activities manifest an intention to submit to the power of a sovereign. In other words, the defendant must "purposefully avai[l] itself of the privilege of conducting activities within the forum State, thus invoking the benefits and protections of its laws." Hanson, supra, at 735; Insurance Corp., supra, at 704–705 ("[A]ctions of the defendant may amount to a legal submission to the jurisdiction of the court"). Sometimes a defendant does so by sending its goods rather than its agents. The defendant's transmission of goods permits the exercise of jurisdiction only where the defendant can be said to have targeted the forum; as a general rule, it is not enough that the defendant might have predicted that its goods will reach the forum State.

In Asahi, an opinion by Justice Brennan for four Justices outlined a different approach. It discarded the central concept of sovereign authority in favor of considerations of fairness and foreseeability. As that concurrence contended, "jurisdiction premised on the placement of a product into the stream of commerce [without more] is consistent with the Due Process Clause," for "[a]s long as a participant in this process is aware that the final product is being marketed in the forum State, the possibility of a lawsuit there cannot come as a surprise." It was the premise of the concurring opinion that the defendant's ability to anticipate suit renders the assertion of jurisdiction fair. In this way, the opinion made foreseeability the touchstone of jurisdiction.

The standard set forth in Justice Brennan's concurrence was rejected in an opinion written by Justice O'Connor; but the relevant part of that opinion, too, commanded the assent of only four Justices, not a majority of the Court. That opinion stated: "The 'substantial connection' between the defendant and the forum State necessary for a finding of minimum contacts must come about by an action of the defendant purposefully directed toward the forum State. The placement of a product into the stream of commerce, without more, is not an act of the defendant purposefully directed toward the forum State."

Since *Asahi* was decided, the courts have sought to reconcile the competing opinions. But Justice Brennan's concurrence, advocating a rule based on general notions of fairness and foreseeability, is inconsistent with the premises of lawful judicial power. This Court's precedents make clear that it is the defendant's actions, not his expectations, that empower a State's courts to subject him to judgment.

* * *

Two principles are implicit in the foregoing. First, personal jurisdiction requires a forum-by-forum, or sovereign-by-sovereign, analysis. The question is whether a defendant has followed a course of conduct directed at the society or economy existing within the jurisdiction of a given sovereign, so that the sovereign has the power to subject the defendant to judgment concerning that conduct. Personal jurisdiction, of course, restricts "judicial power not as a matter of sovereignty, but as a matter of individual liberty," for due process protects the individual's right to be subject only to lawful power. But whether a judicial judgment is lawful depends on whether the sovereign has authority to render it.

The second principle is a corollary of the first. Because the United States is a distinct sovereign, a defendant may in principle be subject to the jurisdiction of the courts of the United States but not of any particular State. * * * For jurisdiction, a litigant may have the requisite relationship with the United States Government but not with the government of any individual State. That would be an exceptional case, however. If the defendant is a domestic domiciliary, the courts of its home State are available and can exercise general jurisdiction. * * * Furthermore, foreign corporations will often target or concentrate on particular States, subjecting them to specific jurisdiction in those forums.

It must be remembered, however, that although this case and Asahi both involve foreign manufacturers, the undesirable consequences of Justice Brennan's approach are no less significant for domestic producers. The owner of a small Florida farm might sell crops to a large nearby distributor, for example, who might then distribute them to grocers across the country. If foreseeability were the controlling criterion, the farmer could be sued in Alaska or any number of other States' courts without ever leaving town. * * *

The conclusion that the authority to subject a defendant to judgment depends on purposeful availment, consistent with Justice O'Connor's opinion in *Asahi*, does not by itself resolve many difficult questions of jurisdiction that will arise in particular cases. The defendant's conduct and the economic realities of the market the defendant seeks to serve will differ across cases, and judicial exposition will, in common-law fashion, clarify the contours of that principle.

III

In this case, petitioner directed marketing and sales efforts at the United States. It may be that, assuming it were otherwise empowered to legislate on the subject, the Congress could authorize the exercise of jurisdiction in appropriate courts. That circumstance is not presented in this case, however. * * * Here the question concerns the authority of a New Jersey state court to exercise jurisdiction, so it is petitioner's purposeful contacts with New Jersey, not with the United States, that alone are relevant.

Respondent has not established that J. McIntyre engaged in conduct purposefully directed at New Jersey. Recall that respondent's claim of jurisdiction centers on three facts: The distributor agreed to sell J. McIntyre's machines in the United States; J. McIntyre officials attended trade shows in several States but not in New Jersey; and up to four machines ended up in New Jersey. The British manufacturer had no office in New Jersey; it neither paid taxes nor owned property there; and it neither advertised in, nor sent any employees to, the State. Indeed, after discovery the trial court found that the "defendant does not have a single contact with New Jersey short of the machine in question ending up in this state." These facts may reveal an intent to serve the U.S. market, but they do not show that J. McIntyre purposefully availed itself of the New Jersey market.

* * *

Due process protects petitioner's right to be subject only to lawful authority. At no time did petitioner engage in any activities in New Jersey that reveal an intent to invoke or benefit from the protection of its laws. New Jersey is without power to adjudge the rights and liabilities of J. McIntyre, and its exercise of jurisdiction would violate due process. The contrary judgment of the New Jersey Supreme Court is Reversed.

JUSTICE BREYER, with whom JUSTICE ALITO joins, concurring in the judgment.

The Supreme Court of New Jersey adopted a broad understanding of the scope of personal jurisdiction based on its view that "[t]he increasingly fast-paced globalization of the world economy has removed national borders as barriers to trade." I do not doubt that there have been many recent changes in commerce and communication, many of which are not anticipated by our precedents. But this case does not present any of those issues. So I think it unwise to announce a rule of broad applicability without full consideration of the modern-day consequences.

In my view, the outcome of this case is determined by our precedents. Based on the facts found by the New Jersey courts, respondent Robert Nicastro failed to meet his burden to demonstrate that it was constitutionally proper to exercise jurisdiction. [Justice Breyer stressed that the New Jersey court relied on three facts: (1) the American distributor once sold a machine to a New Jersey customer; (2) the British manufacturer wanted to sell to anyone in America willing to buy its machines; and (3) the British manufacturer sent representatives to trade shows in the U.S.]

None of our precedents finds that a single isolated sale, even if accompanied by the kind of sales effort indicated here, is sufficient. [In World-Wide Volkswagen Corp. v. Woodson, 444 U.S. 286 (1980), the Court held that a single sale to a customer who takes a product to the forum state was not sufficient to support jurisdiction. In Justice Breyer's view, the various opinions in Asahi Metal Indus. Co. v. Superior Court, 480 U.S. 102 (1987), had "strongly suggested that a single sale of a product in a State does not constitute an adequate basis for asserting jurisdiction over an out-of-state defendant, even if that defendant places his goods in the stream of commerce fully aware (and hoping) that such a sale will take place."]

Here, the relevant facts found by the New Jersey Supreme Court show no "regular . . . flow" or "regular course" of sales in New Jersey; and there is no "something more," such as special state-related design, advertising, advice, marketing, or anything else. Mr. Nicastro, who here bears the burden of proving jurisdiction, has shown no specific effort by the British Manufacturer to sell in New Jersey. He has introduced no list of potential New Jersey customers who might, for example, have regularly attended trade shows. [That he might have made additional showings, such as the size and scope of New Jersey's scrap-metal business mentioned in Justice Ginsburg's dissent, is not relevant; plaintiff bears the burden of establishing jurisdiction, and the Court should take the facts precisely as the New Jersey courts stated them.]

I would not go further. Because the incident at issue in this case does not implicate modern concerns, and because the factual record leaves many open questions, this is an unsuitable vehicle for making broad pronouncements that refashion basic jurisdictional rules.

The plurality seems to state strict rules that limit jurisdiction where a defendant does not "inten[d] to submit to the power of a sovereign" and cannot "be said to have targeted the forum." But what do those standards mean when a company targets the world by selling products from its Web site? And does it matter if, instead of shipping the products directly, a company consigns the products through an intermediary (say, Amazon.com) who then receives and fulfills the orders? And what if the company markets its products through popup advertisements that it knows will be viewed in a forum? Those issues have serious commercial consequences but are totally absent in this case.

Internet Sales?!

Pop Up adds?

But though I do not agree with the plurality's seemingly strict no-jurisdiction rule, I am not persuaded by the absolute approach adopted by the New Jersey Supreme Court and urged by respondent and his amici. Under that view, a producer is subject to jurisdiction for a products-liability action so long as it "knows or reasonably should know that its products are distributed through a nationwide distribution system that might lead to those products being sold in any of the fifty states." In the context of this case, I cannot agree.

[The absolute rule in favor of jurisdiction would undermine the purposeful availment requirement, which rests upon "a particular notion of defendant-focused fairness."] A rule like the New Jersey Supreme Court's would permit every State to assert jurisdiction in a products-liability suit against any domestic manufacturer who sells its products (made anywhere in the United States) to a national distributor, no matter how large or small the manufacturer, no matter how distant the forum, and no matter how few the number of items that end up in the particular forum at issue. What might appear fair in the case of a large manufacturer which specifically seeks, or expects, an equal-sized distributor to sell its product in a distant State might seem unfair in the case of a small manufacturer (say, an Appalachian potter) who sells his product (cups and saucers) exclusively to a large distributor, who resells a single item (a coffee mug) to a buyer from a distant State (Hawaii). I know too little about the range of these or in-between possibilities to abandon in favor of the more absolute rule what has previously been this Court's less absolute approach.

* * * [M]anufacturers come in many shapes and sizes. It may be fundamentally unfair to require a small Egyptian shirt maker, a Brazilian manufacturing cooperative, or a Kenyan coffee farmer, selling its products through international distributors, to respond to products-liability tort suits in virtually every State in the United States, even those in respect to which the foreign firm has no connection at all but the sale of a single (allegedly defective) good. And a rule like the New Jersey Supreme Court suggests would require every product manufacturer, large or small, selling to American distributors to understand not only the tort law of every State,

but also the wide variance in the way courts within different States apply that law.

I would adhere strictly to our precedents and the limited facts found by the New Jersey Supreme Court. And on those grounds, I do not think we can find jurisdiction in this case. Accordingly, though I agree with the plurality as to the outcome of this case, I concur only in the judgment of that opinion and not its reasoning.

JUSTICE GINSBURG, with whom JUSTICE SOTOMAYOR and JUSTICE KAGAN join, dissenting.

A foreign industrialist seeks to develop a market in the United States for machines it manufactures. It hopes to derive substantial revenue from sales it makes to United States purchasers. Where in the United States buyers reside does not matter to this manufacturer. Its goal is simply to sell as much as it can, wherever it can. It excludes no region or State from the market it wishes to reach. But, all things considered, it prefers to avoid products liability litigation in the United States. To that end, it engages a U.S. distributor to ship its machines stateside. Has it succeeded in escaping personal jurisdiction in a State where one of its products is sold and causes injury or even death to a local user?

* * * Inconceivable as it may have seemed yesterday, the splintered majority today "turn[s] the clock back to the days before modern long-arm statutes when a manufacturer, to avoid being haled into court where a user is injured, need only Pilate-like wash its hands of a product by having independent distributors market it." Weintraub, A Map Out of the Personal Jurisdiction Labyrinth, 28 U.C. Davis L.Rev. 531, 555 (1995).

I

On October 11, 2001, a three-ton metal shearing machine severed four fingers on Robert Nicastro's right hand. Alleging that the machine was a dangerous product defectively made, Nicastro sought compensation from the machine's manufacturer, J. McIntyre Machinery Ltd. (McIntyre UK).

[Justice Ginsburg amplified the factual picture presented by Justices Kennedy and Breyer: McIntyre UK's Web site says that it manufactures "a complete range of equipment for metal recycling." The specific machine involved in this case sold in the U.S. for $24,900. McIntyre's Web site says that the machine has "massive cutting capacity" and is "use[d] throughout the world." New Jersey is "a hotbed of scrap-metal businesses" that, in 2008, processed more scrap metal than any other state. From 1995 to 2001, McIntyre distributed its products in the U.S. through an Ohio-based company named McIntyre Machinery America, its exclusive distributor, but the two companies had no commonality of ownership.

McIntyre America distributed several other McIntyre products in the U.S. in addition to the model that caused plaintiff's injury. McIntyre products had been installed in several states, including Illinois, Iowa, Virginia and Washington. McIntyre America filed for bankruptcy in 2001, and McIntyre UK then authorized a Texas-based company to serve as its exclusive U.S. distributor. McIntyre UK had been named a defendant in lawsuits in Illinois, Kentucky, Massachusetts, and West Virginia. It had products liability insurance coverage. It had never instructed McIntyre U.S. to avoid certain states or regions of this country.

From 1990 to 2005, McIntyre UK representatives attended every convention of the Institute of Scrap Metal Industries. For members, a 10' by 10' booth at the convention costs $3,000. In 1994 or 1995, Frank Curcio, owner of plaintiff's employer (Curcio Scrap Metal), attended the convention in Las Vegas and learned of McIntyre's products; that is evidently how plaintiff's employer happened to acquire the machine involved in the accident.]

In sum, McIntyre UK's regular attendance and exhibitions at ISRI conventions was surely a purposeful step to reach customers for its products "anywhere in the United States." At least as purposeful was McIntyre UK's engagement of McIntyre America as the conduit for sales of McIntyre UK's machines to buyers "throughout the United States." Given McIntyre UK's endeavors to reach and profit from the United States market as a whole, Nicastro's suit, I would hold, has been brought in a forum entirely appropriate for the adjudication of his claim. He alleges that McIntyre UK's shear machine was defectively designed or manufactured and, as a result, caused injury to him at his workplace. The machine arrived in Nicastro's New Jersey workplace not randomly or fortuitously, but as a result of the U.S. connections and distribution system that McIntyre UK deliberately arranged. On what sensible view of the allocation of adjudicatory authority could the place of Nicastro's injury within the United States be deemed off limits for his products liability claim against a foreign manufacturer who targeted the United States (including all the States that constitute the Nation) as the territory it sought to develop?

II

[Justice Ginsburg emphasized that "the constitutional limits on a state's adjudicatory authority derive from considerations of due process, not state sovereignty," and that the Court had similarly discarded reliance on legal fictions such as "presence" and "implied consent." Accordingly, "the plurality's notion that consent is the animating concept draws no support from controlling decisions of this Court." Further, "[t]he plurality's notion that jurisdiction over foreign corporations depends upon the defendant's 'submission' seems scarcely different from the long-discarded fiction of implied consent. It bears emphasis, therefore, that a majority of this Court's members do not share the plurality's view."]

III

This case is illustrative of marketing arrangements for sales in the United States common in today's commercial world. A foreign-country manufacturer engages a U.S. company to promote and distribute the manufacturer's products, not in any particular State, but anywhere and everywhere in the United States the distributor can attract purchasers. The product proves defective and injures a user in the State where the user lives or works. * * *

The modern approach to jurisdiction over corporations and other legal entities, ushered in by *International Shoe*, gave prime place to reason and fairness. Is it not fair and reasonable, given the mode of trading of which this case is an example, to require the international seller to defend at the place its products cause injury? Do not litigational convenience and choice-of-law considerations point in that direction? On what measure of reason and fairness can it be considered undue to require McIntyre UK to defend in New Jersey as an incident of its efforts to develop a market for its industrial machines anywhere and everywhere in the United States? Is not the burden on McIntyre UK to defend in New Jersey fair, i.e., a reasonable cost of transacting business internationally, in comparison to the burden on Nicastro to go to Nottingham, England to gain recompense for an injury he sustained using McIntyre's product at his workplace in Saddle Brook, New Jersey?

McIntyre UK dealt with the United States as a single market. Like most foreign manufacturers, it was concerned not with the prospect of suit in State X as opposed to State Y, but rather with its subjection to suit anywhere in the United States. * * * If McIntyre UK is answerable in the United States at all, is it not "perfectly appropriate to permit the exercise of that jurisdiction . . . at the place of injury"? See Degnan & Kane, The Exercise of Jurisdiction Over and Enforcement of Judgments Against Alien Defendants, 39 Hastings L.J. 799, 813–815 (1988) (noting that "[i]n the international order," the State that counts is the United States, not its component States, and that the fair place of suit within the United States is essentially a question of venue).

In sum, McIntyre UK, by engaging McIntyre America to promote and sell its machines in the United States, "purposefully availed itself" of the United States market nationwide, not a market in a single State or a discrete collection of States. McIntyre UK thereby availed itself of the market of all States in which its products were sold by its exclusive distributor. "Th[e] 'purposeful availment' requirement," this Court has explained, simply "ensures that a defendant will not be haled into a jurisdiction solely as a result of 'random,' 'fortuitous,' or 'attenuated' contacts." Burger King, 471 U.S., at 475. * * * How could McIntyre UK not have intended, by its actions targeting a national market, to sell products in the fourth largest destination for imports among all States of the United States and the largest scrap metal market?

Courts, both state and federal, confronting facts similar to those here, have rightly rejected the conclusion that a manufacturer selling its products across the USA may evade jurisdiction in any and all States, including the State where its defective product is distributed and causes injury. * * *

IV

[Justice Ginsburg distinguished this case from prior cases the Court had decided, urging that none of the Court's prior cases required the conclusion that jurisdiction was absent in the "now-prevalent pattern presented here—a foreign-country manufacturer enlisting a U.S. distributor to develop a market in the United States for the manufacturer's products."]

In World-Wide Volkswagen v. Woodson, supra p. 744, the objecting defendants were a New York dealer and a three-state distributor with activities limited to New York, Connecticut, and New Jersey. Neither the national distributor nor the German manufacturer objected to jurisdiction in the Oklahoma courts, and "the Court's opinion indicates that an objection by the manufacturer or national distributor would have been unavailing."

In Asahi Metal Indus. Co. v. Superior Court, 480 U.S. 102 (1987), all that remained by the time the case got to the Supreme Court was a dispute between a foreign plaintiff from Taiwan and a foreign defendant from Japan about indemnification for amounts paid in settlement of a claim by an American injured in California while using a Japanese-manufactured motorcycle. The Court was unanimous on the bottom-line judgment that, in these circumstances, the exercise of jurisdiction was not reasonable, and the duelling opinions of Justices O'Connor and Brennan about the purposeful availment analysis were not necessary. The objecting defendant there did not seek out U.S. customers, and engaged no distributor to market its products in this country. "To hold that Asahi controls this case would be dead wrong." Justice Ginsburg elaborated on this point in a footnote:

> "The plurality notes the low volume of sales in New Jersey. A $24,900 shearing machine, however, is unlikely to sell in bulk worldwide, much less in any given State. By dollar value, the price of a single machine represents a significant sale. Had a manufacturer sold in New Jersey $24,900 worth of flannel shirts, see Nelson v. Park Industries, Inc., 717 F.2d 1120 (CA 7 1983), cigarette lighters, see Oswalt v. Scripto, Inc., 616 F.2d 191 (CA5 1983), or wire-rope splices, see Hedrick v. Daiko Shoji Co., 715

F.2d 1355 (CA9 1983), the Court would presumably find the defendant amenable to suit in that State."

Justice Ginsburg also argued that the decision against jurisdiction "puts United States plaintiffs at a disadvantage in comparison to similarly situated complainants elsewhere in the world." Under the European Union Regulation on Jurisdiction and the Recognition and Enforcement of Judgments, jurisdiction in tort cases is authorized "in the courts for the place where the harmful event occurred." She attached an Appendix describing 12 American cases "upholding exercise of personal jurisdiction over an alien or out-of-state corporation that, through a distributor, targeted a national market."

She argued further that, in the international sphere, courts have been able to pay proper attention to a defendant "who is a natural or legal person whose economic activities are largely home-based, i.e. entities without designs to gain substantial revenue from sales in distant markets," an approach that "would, to a considerable extent, answer the concerns expressed by Justice Breyer."]

For the reasons stated, I would hold McIntyre UK answerable in New Jersey for the harm Nicastro suffered at his workplace in that State using McIntyre UK's shearing machine. While I dissent from the Court's judgment, I take heart that the plurality opinion does not speak for the Court, for that opinion would take a giant step away from the "notions of fair play and substantial justice" underlying International Shoe.

NOTES AND QUESTIONS

1.   Justice Kennedy says that *Nicastro* offered the Court an opportunity to "provide greater clarity." Did the Court do that? The decision in *Nicastro* has been criticized by commentators. See, e.g., Borchers, J. McIntyre Machinery, Goodyear, and the Incoherence of the Minimum Contacts Test, 44 Creighton L. Rev. 1245, 1245 (2011) (McIntyre "is a disaster"); Carrington, Business Interest and the Long Arm in 2011, 63 S. Car. L. Rev. 637, 637 (2012) ("the Supreme Court has been captured by the Chamber of Commerce"); Peterson, The Timing of Minimum Contacts After Goodyear and McIntyre, 80 Geo. Wash. L. Rev. 202, 241–42 (2011) (the decision "may serve to increase the confusion of the lower courts"). So if you find it difficult to unravel or troubling in its implications, you are not alone.

2.   Would Justice Kennedy's opinion significantly change due process limits on jurisdiction if it were adopted by the full Court? Consider the terms he uses:

(a)   *Submission*: Justice Kennedy argues that the purposeful availment requirement ensures that the defendant has "submitted" to the authority of the state in which the suit is filed. Consider his treatment of the Court's earlier cases. Is it helpful to describe them as involving "submission," or is that merely a label attached to activities found to satisfy the purposeful availment requirement? Compare a case in which a defendant enters an appearance in the proceeding. Can that more easily be regarded as "submission" to the authority of the court? Reconsider this question when you read Insurance Corporation of Ireland, Ltd. v. Compagnie des Bauxites de Guinee, infra p. 830.

(b)   *Sovereignty*: Justice Kennedy emphasizes limits on sovereignty. Is the due process clause really a protector of those interests? See Brilmayer & Smith, The (Theoretical) Future of Personal Jurisdiction: Issues Left Open by Goodyear Dunlop Tires v. Brown and J. McIntyre Machinery v. Nicastro, 63 S. Car. L. Rev. 617, 618 (2012) ("The strongest message from * * * *McIntyre* is a reaffirmation that state sovereignty is central to the Court's philosophy of what it means to have a federal system."). More often, the Supreme Court has emphasized that the states' sovereignty is relevant in considering the authority of the federal government to override the states' latitude to regulate or control certain matters. See Vail, Six Questions in Light of J. McIntyre Machinery, Ltd. v. Nicastro, 63 So. Car. L. Rev. 571, 518–20 (2012) (exploring the sovereignty question). Does *Nicastro* really involve any issue of New Jersey's invasion of the sovereignty of another state?

(c)   *Targeting*: Justice Kennedy also says that it is important to determine whether defendant "targeted" the forum state. Recall that in Calder v. Jones, supra p. 756, the Court contrasted the actions of the objecting defendants to those of a welder whose "untargeted negligence" produced a boiler that exploded in the forum, injuring the plaintiff. Is the "targeted conduct" idea articulated in *Calder* what Justice Kennedy is invoking? Would that mean that plaintiff would have to show that at the time it distributed its products defendant could foretell that the main impact of any resulting harm would be in New Jersey? Recall *Calder*'s companion case, Keeton v. Hustler Magazine, supra p. 759 n. 2, in which the Court upheld jurisdiction in New Hampshire even though very few issues of the magazine were distributed in that state because routine distribution there sufficed to support jurisdiction over the magazine. Justice Kennedy does mention "exceptions * * * in cases involving an intentional tort." For claims like the one in *Nicastro*, it may be that, by "targeting" every state, defendant in effect targeted none.

3.   Justice Kennedy seems to say that he agrees with Justice O'Connor's opinion in Asahi v. Superior Court, 480 U.S. 102 (1987). In that case, a Californian was injured in California when the tire on his motorcycle blew out on a freeway. He sued Honda, which made the motorcycle, and Cheng Shin Rubber Industry Co., a Taiwanese company that manufactured the tube in the tire that blew out. Cheng Shin in turn filed an indemnity claim against Asahi Metal Industry Co. of Japan, which had for several years supplied Cheng Shin with between 100,000 and 500,000 valves per year to incorporate in its tires. Cheng Shin also bought valves from other suppliers, but claimed that the valve on the offending tire was from Asahi, and was defective. Asahi claimed that the valve on that tire was not one of its products. Its sales to Cheng Shin accounted for approximately 1% of its income. Its president submitted an affidavit after it was sued asserting that he never imagined that selling valves to Cheng Shin could lead to his being sued in California.

Justice Brennan concluded that purposeful availment was satisfied under the stream-of-commerce theory. Justice O'Connor disagreed, insisting on what some called "stream-of-commerce plus"—that defendant must do more:

> The placement of a product into the stream of commerce, without more, is not an act of the defendant purposefully directed toward the forum State. Additional conduct of the defendant may indicate an intent or purpose to serve the market in the forum State, for example, designing the product for the market in the forum State, advertising in the forum State, establishing channels for providing regular advice to customers in the forum State, or marketing the product through a distributor who has agreed to serve as the sales agent in the forum State. But a defendant's awareness that the stream of commerce may or will sweep the product into the forum State does not convert the mere act of placing the product into the stream into an act purposefully directed toward the forum State.
>
> Assuming, arguendo, that respondents have established Asahi's awareness that some of the valves sold to Cheng Shin would be incorporated into tire tubes sold in California, respondents have not demonstrated any action by Asahi to purposefully avail itself of the California market. Asahi does not do business in California. It has no office, agents, employees, or property in California. It does not advertise or otherwise solicit business in California. It did not create, control, or employ the distribution system that brought its valves to California. Cf. Hicks v. Kawasaki Heavy Industries, 453 F.Supp. 130 (MD Pa. 1978). There is no evidence that Asahi designed its product in anticipation of sales in California. Cf. Rockwell International Corp. v. Construzioni Aeronautiche Giovanni Agusta, 553 F.Supp. 328 (ED Pa. 1982).

Does Justice Kennedy's opinion in *Nicastro* adopt the same standard? Is there a stronger argument for denying jurisdiction on the facts of *Asahi* than in *Nicastro*? YES

Could Justice O'Connor's standard be satisfied by the facts in *Nicastro*? In *Asahi*, Justice O'Connor cited lower court decisions upholding jurisdiction to illustrate the kind of "plus" she had in mind. In Hicks v. Kawasaki Heavy Industries, 452 F.Supp. 130 (M.D. Pa. 1978), the lower court upheld jurisdiction over a Japanese motorcycle manufacturer that sold its products only to a U.S. distributor over which the manufacturer did not have "corporate control." The district judge felt that it was "doing business by means of indirect shipments into the state." In Rockwell Int'l Corp. v. Construzioni Aeronautiche Giovanni Agusta, 553 F.Supp. 328 (E.D. Pa. 1982), defendant was a French corporation that manufactured ball-bearing assemblies for a particular helicopter and sold the assemblies to its Italian subsidiary, which in turn sold them to an Italian helicopter manufacturer that sold the helicopters to a U.S. distributor in Delaware to sell to purchasers in the U.S. The court held that jurisdiction was proper because defendant had designed its bearing assemblies for use in this make of helicopter and was aware that the product "was targeted for the executive corporate transport market in the United States and Europe." Would Justice Kennedy uphold jurisdiction in these cases?

4.   To a certain extent, *Nicastro* repeats the division in *Asahi*, this time in the contrasting views of Justice Kennedy and Justice Ginsburg. Which approach to purposeful availment should the Court adopt?

Regarding Justice Kennedy's view, consider Lesnick v. Hollingsworth & Vose Co., 35 F.3d 939 (4th Cir.1994), in which the court held jurisdiction improper under *Asahi*. Plaintiff's late husband had smoked cigarettes manufactured by Lorillard, Inc. He died of mesothelioma, a form of cancer caused by exposure to asbestos fibers. In the 1950s Lorillard, a New York company with plants in New Jersey and Kentucky, entered into an arrangement with defendant, a Massachusetts company, to develop a "Micronite Filter" for cigarettes using asbestos fibers. They jointly owned the resulting patent, and defendant sold some 10 billion asbestos-containing filters to Lorillard during the 1950s knowing that they would be incorporated into cigarettes and sold throughout the country. The court concluded that this collaborative arrangement between defendant and Lorillard was not in any way directed toward Maryland, where plaintiff's husband lived and bought the cigarettes that plaintiff claimed caused his mesothelioma. Accordingly, jurisdiction was improper (id. at 945):

> To permit a state to assert jurisdiction over any person in the country whose product is sold in the state simply because a person must expect that to happen destroys the notion of individual sovereignties inherent in our system of federalism. Such a rule would subject defendants to judgment in locations based on the activity of third persons and not the deliberate conduct of the defendant, making it impossible for defendants to plan and structure their business contacts and risks.

Would Justice Kennedy preclude jurisdiction anywhere outside Massachusetts in *Lesnick*? Is the broad stream-of-commerce standard adopted by Justice Ginsburg a better choice? How suitable would it be for the Egyptian shirt maker, the Brazilian manufacturing cooperative, or the Kenyan coffee farmer mentioned by Justice Breyer? And how should this standard be applied to a maker of components rather than the end product? In *Asahi*, for example, Asahi made valves that it sold to Cheng Shin, which in turn made inner tubes it sold to Honda, which put them on motorcycles it sold around the world. Could Asahi have done anything to prevent its products from arriving in California? Suppose it refused to fill Cheng Shin's order without a guarantee that none of its products would be sold in California? Would Cheng Shin want to buy from Asahi and try to honor that promise? Could it do so if it wanted to, given that the ultimate distribution was by Honda, not Cheng Shin?

5.   What is the precedential value of *Nicastro*? The Supreme Court has said that, when one of its decisions is not supported by a majority opinion, "the holding of the Court may be viewed as that position taken by those Members who concurred in the judgments on the narrowest grounds." Marks v. United

States, 430 U.S. 188, 193 (1977); compare Williams, Questioning *Marks*: Plurality Decisions and Precedential Constraint, 69 Stan. L. Rev. 795 (2017) (urging that lower courts use a "shared agreement" approach to discern which reasons led a majority of the Court to support the bottom line decision in a case). That would seem to make Justice Breyer's concurrence dispositive. Does it provide much guidance on how courts should resolve jurisdiction challenges? Justice Breyer says that "[n]one of our precedents finds that a single isolated sale, even if accompanied by the kind of sales effort indicated here, is sufficient." He seems to think that a "regular flow" or "regular course" should be required. Is that consistent with McGee v. International Life Ins. Co., supra p. 733? What should lower courts (and lawyers) do? "Lower courts are already split as to whether Breyer's opinion means that the Court has rejected the Brennan stream of commerce position, or whether the *Nicastro* opinion is so narrow as to have little application beyond factual situations nearly identical to it. Some have even dropped rather unsubtle hints of displeasure at the Court's inability to reach a decision, stating, for example, that '*McIntyre* has little or no precedential value.'" Effron, Letting the Perfect Become the Enemy of the Good: The Relatedness Problem in Personal Jurisdiction, 16 Lewis & Clark L. Rev. 867, 887 (2012).

6.   Is there any state in the U.S. in which Nicastro could sue McIntyre under the Court's decision?

Justice Kennedy suggests that the constraints he sees on the jurisdiction of a state court would not necessarily be a constitutional bar to federal court jurisdiction because McIntyre U.K. clearly did seek to serve the U.S., and it is all one sovereignty. Consider the following possible amendment to Rule 4(k)(2) (removed language overstricken; new language underlined):

> (2)   ~~Federal~~ **Claims Outside State-Court Jurisdiction.** ~~For a claim that arises under federal law,~~ <u>s</u>Serving a summons or filing a waiver of service establishes personal jurisdiction over a defendant if:
>
>> (A)   the defendant is not subject to jurisdiction in any state's courts of general jurisdiction; and
>>
>> (B)   exercising jurisdiction is consistent with the United States Constitution and laws.

Would such an amendment, if effective, be desirable? For an agrument in favor of amending the rule, see Borchers, Extending Federal Rule of Civil Procedure 4(k)(2): A Way to (Partially) Clean Up the Personal Jurisdiction Mess, 67 Amer. U. L. Rev. 413 (2017).

7.   Both *Asahi* and *Nicastro* were products liability suits. Would refusal to uphold jurisdiction in such cases frustrate the goals of tort law? Long ago, privity requirements prevented suits by injured consumers against product manufacturers, but tort law changed. Ever since MacPherson v. Buick Motor Co., 111 N.E. 1050 (N.Y. 1916) and Henningsen v. Bloomfield Motors, Inc., 161 A.2d 69 (N.J. 1960) abandoned the privity requirement for negligence and products liability suits, consumers have had a substantive method for seeking

recovery from manufacturers of defective products. Did *Asahi* (and now *Nicastro*) impose an inappropriate jurisdictional hurdle in their way? See Wiseman, Reconstructing the Citadel: The Advent of Jurisdictional Privity, 54 Ohio St. L. Rev. 403, 443 (1993) ("The synergy developed between the law of products liability, as codified in the Restatement [of Torts], and personal jurisdiction * * * has now been not so neatly undone by a plurality of the Supreme Court in *Asahi*.").

8.   How should *Nicastro* be applied in cases where the out-of-state defendant advertises in the state inviting residents to sample its wares elsewhere? Usually such cases involve a plaintiff injured at defendant's distant establishment. In Shute v. Carnival Cruise Lines, 897 F.2d 377, 380–87 (9th Cir.1990), rev'd on other grounds, 499 U.S. 585 (1991), plaintiffs from the state of Washington booked a Carnival cruise that began in Los Angeles through a travel agent near their home. (The Supreme Court's approach to this case is considered below. See Forum Selection Clauses, infra p. 836.) After being injured during the cruise, plaintiffs sued in their home state. Carnival Lines was not registered to do business in Washington, and owned no property and maintained no office there. Its ships had never called at Washington ports. It did, however, advertise its cruises in local Washington newspapers and provide brochures to local travel agents for distribution to potential customers. It also periodically held seminars for travel agents in the state to inform them about its cruises and encourage them to sell tickets. It paid travel agents a 10% commission for selling tickets. Slightly over 1% of its cruise business was derived from residents of Washington.

The Ninth Circuit upheld jurisdiction, using a three-part analysis. First, it concluded that defendant's act of soliciting business in Washington should be considered purposeful availment to the extent it resulted in transaction of business with residents. Second, the court held that the claim arose out of the defendant's solicitation of business in Washington even though the claim was for negligence on the ship in international waters off Mexico. The court used a "but for" analysis, concluding that the plaintiffs would not have bought a ticket on defendant's cruise but for its solicitation activities directed at Washington travel agents. Finally, drawing on the "presumption of reasonableness" it found in Burger King Corp. v. Rudzewicz, supra p. 762, the court held that defendant had not presented a compelling case that the exercise of jurisdiction would be unreasonable.

Contrast Nowak v. Tak How Investments, Ltd., 94 F.3d 708 (1st Cir.1996), a suit filed in Massachusetts to recover for the drowning of a Massachusetts resident at the Hong Kong Holiday Inn, which was operated by defendant. Defendant had no other business activities besides operation of that hotel, but it had advertised the hotel in some publications that circulated in Massachusetts. The court did not treat this advertising activity as sufficient, and rejected the Ninth Circuit's "but for" causation standard, favoring a proximate causation standard:

> First, proximate or legal cause clearly distinguishes between foreseeable and unforeseeable risks of harm. Foreseeability is a

critical component of the due process inquiry, particularly in evaluating purposeful availment, and we think it also informs the relatedness prong. * * * Adherence to a proximate cause standard is likely to enable defendants better to anticipate which conduct might subject them to a state's jurisdiction than a more tenuous link in the chain of causation. * * *

A "but for" requirement, on the other hand, has in itself no limiting principle; it literally embraces every event that hindsight can logically identify in the causative chain. True, as the Ninth Circuit has noted, courts can use the reasonableness prong to keep Pandora's jar from opening too wide. But to say that the harm that might be done by one factor can be prevented by another is not, after all, an affirmative justification for the former.

Under this standard, the court concluded that jurisdiction was proper because this guest was in Hong Kong due to special rates that were offered to her husband's employer to persuade the employer to have employees stay at this hotel. The court added that "we intend to emphasize the importance of proximate causation, but to allow a slight loosening of that standard when circumstances dictate." It also noted that "it will not always be easy to apply this flexible approach to the particular circumstances, but that is a function of the complexity of this area of the law." Which approach is most in keeping with *Nicastro*?

9. How should jurisdiction be handled under *Nicastro* in a case like *Calder v. Jones* (supra p. 756)? Note Justice Kennedy's reference to "exceptions * * * in cases involving an intentional tort."

10. Justice Breyer cautions that the case before the Court does not involve "modern-day consequences" and "modern concerns," which seem to include the challenge of fashioning jurisdictional rules that will work fairly regarding Internet-based transactions. In Walden v. Fiore, 134 S.Ct. 1115 (2014), the Court held that a police officer who took custody of plaintiffs' "gambling stake" while they were changing planes in Atlanta airport on their way home to Nevada could not be sued in Nevada on the ground that the had "targeted" Nevada residents. The Court declined to use that case to address "modern-day" issues (id. at 1125 n. 9):

> Respondents warn that if we decide petitioner lacks minimum contacts in this case, it will bring about unfairness in cases where intentional torts are committed via the Internet or other electronic means (e.g., fraudulent access of financial accounts or "phishing" schemed). * * * [T]his case does not present the very different questions whether and how a defendant's virtual "presence" and conduct translate into "contacts" with a particular State. To the contrary, there is no question where the conduct giving rise to this litigation took place. Petitioner seized physical cash from respondents in the Atlanta airport, and he later drafted and

forwarded an affidavit in Georgia. We leave questions about virtual contacts for another day.   # Kick That Can Down The Road

We turn to that challenge now. As indicated in the following case, lower courts have found *Walden* to be instructive in addressing jurisdiction with regard to Internet-based activities.

RILLEY V. MONEYMUTUAL LLC   The intrawebs !!!

Supreme Court of Minnesota, 2016
884 N.W.2d 321

ANDERSON, JUSTICE.

This case raises the question of what contacts a defendant must have with Minnesota before our courts can exercise specific personal jurisdiction over that defendant. Appellant MoneyMutual, LLC, claims that the district court erred when it concluded that it could exercise specific personal jurisdiction over MoneyMutual based on MoneyMutual's email correspondence with Minnesota residents and advertising in Minnesota. * * *

MoneyMutual operates a website that allows individuals to apply for short-term loans, commonly known as "payday loans." After an individual submits a loan application through MoneyMutual's website, MoneyMutual "matches" the applicant with a payday lender in its network. For each matched applicant, MoneyMutual receives a "lead" fee from the lender. Respondents are four Minnesota residents who used MoneyMutual's website to obtain payday loans.

Respondents filed a class-action complaint, alleging that MoneyMutual matched respondents with payday lenders that were unlicensed in Minnesota. The complaint also alleged that the terms of the payday loans respondents received were illegal under Minnesota's payday-lending statutes because, among other claims, the annual percentage rates (APRs) advertised by MoneyMutual—which ranged "between 261% and 1304% for a 14 day loan"—exceeded the maximum allowable APRs under Minnesota law. Respondents also claimed that MoneyMutual's website and advertising contained misrepresentations that violated Minnesota's consumer protection statutes.

[MoneyMutual moved to dismiss for lack of personal jurisdiction. The state Supreme Court affirmed denial of this motion.]

The "minimum contacts" necessary to support specific personal jurisdiction over the defendant must focus on "the relationship among the defendant, the forum, and the litigation," and the "defendant's suit-related conduct must create a substantial connection with the forum state," *Walden v. Fiore*, 134 S.Ct. 1115, 1121 (2014), such that the litigation results from alleged harms that "arise out of or relate to" the defendant's contacts with the forum. This minimum-contacts inquiry must "look[ ] to the defendant's contacts with the forum State itself" and not the defendant's " 'random, fortuitous, or attenuated' contacts" with "persons affiliated with the State" or "persons who reside there." *Walden*, 134 S.Ct. at 1122–23. But in some cases, "a defendant's contacts with the forum State may be intertwined with his transactions or interactions with the plaintiff or other parties."

* * *

A

Respondents assert that MoneyMutual made contact with more than 1,000 Minnesotans via email. Specifically, respondents identify three types of emails that MoneyMutual sent to known Minnesota residents. First, after an applicant completed the online application process on MoneyMutual's website, MoneyMutual sent the applicant an email "matching" the applicant with a payday lender in MoneyMutual's network. Second, MoneyMutual sent emails to encourage applicants to complete an unfinished loan application. Finally, MoneyMutual sent emails soliciting prior loan applicants to apply for additional loans.

MoneyMutual argues that these email contacts are irrelevant to the minimum contacts analysis. To support this argument, MoneyMutual and its amici rely heavily on the United States Supreme Court's decision in *Walden* to argue that its interactions with known Minnesota residents are per se insufficient to establish minimum contacts with a Minnesota forum. But * * * *Walden* does not disturb numerous, long-established precedents allowing courts to exercise personal jurisdiction over defendants based in part on commercial contacts with businesses or residents that are located inside the forum.

* * * Here, MoneyMutual's commercial solicitations of over 1,000 loan applicants with known Minnesota addresses were not "random, fortuitous, or attenuated" contacts with forum residents, but rather constitute "intertwined" contacts with both Minnesota residents and the state of Minnesota.

* * *

The United States Supreme Court also has recognized that "a substantial amount of business is transacted solely by mail and wire communications across state lines." *Burger King*, 471 U.S. at 476. And the Court has "consistently rejected the notion that an absence of physical contacts can defeat personal jurisdiction" when "a commercial actor's efforts are 'purposefully directed' toward residents of another State." Id. In this case, Minnesota residents provided MoneyMutual with their personal information and, in return, MoneyMutual matched those residents with potential lenders. * * * Nonetheless, MoneyMutual argues that these contacts should be disregarded because they occurred via email. * * * [T]he proliferation of email has created additional questions regarding the role that electronic long-distance communications should play in establishing personal jurisdiction.

The primary problem with relying on emails to establish personal jurisdiction is that, unlike a letter, the sender of an email may not know the geographic destination of the message. This reality is particularly troublesome because the personal-jurisdiction inquiry must focus on the defendant's contacts with the forum and not merely "random, fortuitous, or attenuated" connections with residents of a forum. If the sender of an email does not know the physical location of the recipient, the fact that the recipient happens to be located in a particular state is the definition of a "random, fortuitous, or attenuated" connection.

As a result of these challenges, three approaches to email-based contacts have developed in federal courts. First, for the above reasons, some courts reject any consideration of email-based contacts. Under a second approach, courts hold that email communications alone are insufficient but that emails are "secondary" contacts that can be added to other types of contacts to support personal jurisdiction. Finally, under a third approach, courts suggest that email-based contacts may establish personal jurisdiction, provided that the context of the email, or other relevant evidence, indicates that the sender knew or had reason to know that the recipient was located, and would receive the email within, a certain forum—or more generally, the plaintiff makes a prima facie showing that the sender "purposefully directed" the email at the forum.

Having considered the body of persuasive authority on this point, we conclude that the third approach, which considers emails just like any other contact with the forum, is the appropriate rule of law. In the modern digital era, with ubiquitous e-commerce and electronic communication, it would be arbitrary to exclude emails from consideration in a minimum contacts analysis, or to limit email to an exclusively supplemental role.

The most reasonable approach is to simply apply the traditional minimum contacts analysis by considering the quantity, nature, and quality of the email contacts, and whether those contacts establish a "substantial connection" between the defendant, the forum, and the litigation, such that the defendant "purposefully availed" himself of the forum and "reasonably anticipate[d] being haled into court" there. The unique characteristics of email as a form of communication necessarily require a district court to consider whether the defendant was aware of the plaintiff's location or at least had reason to believe that the email would be received in a particular jurisdiction.

Here, MoneyMutual's solicitation of and transactions with over 1,000 Minnesotan loan applicants via email demonstrates a "purposeful direction" of litigation-related conduct at Minnesota. Significantly, when MoneyMutual sent emails matching applicants to lenders in its network, those applicants had already completed an online application that showed they were Minnesota residents. Thus, MoneyMutual clearly knew or should have known that emails to these applicants likely would be opened in Minnesota.[12] Similarly, when MoneyMutual sent follow-up emails encouraging prior applicants to seek additional loans, MoneyMutual had sufficient information to know that the applicants were Minnesota residents and that the emails likely were to be opened in Minnesota.

Despite the electronic, email-based nature of these relationships, these contacts demonstrate "purposeful direction" toward Minnesota and a "purposeful availment" of the benefits of doing business in a Minnesota forum—namely, a profitable pool of low-income Minnesota residents that MoneyMutual could match with its payday-lending network to generate lead fees. In other words, MoneyMutual availed itself of a Minnesota forum because it profited by selling lead information to payday lenders about Minnesota residents. These facts, demonstrating a "purposeful availment" of the Minnesota forum, should have caused MoneyMutual to reasonably anticipate being haled into court in Minnesota. Thus, MoneyMutual's emails to respondents are contacts with Minnesota that support the exercise of personal jurisdiction.

B

[Plaintiffs also relied on MoneyMutual's television advertisements that plaintiffs said they saw in Minnesota. The court rejected relying on "purely national advertising as a contact supporting personal jurisdiction because such activity is not purposefully directed at the forum state."]

Most significantly, relying on purely national marketing activity to support minimum contacts appears to be in tension with the United States Supreme Court's holding in J. McIntyre Mach., Ltd. v. Nicastro, 564 U.S. 873, 886 (2011) [supra p. 772] (holding that national "marketing and sales efforts" did not support personal jurisdiction; although it "may reveal an intent to serve the U.S. market," "it is petitioner's purposeful contacts with New Jersey, not with the United States, that alone are relevant"). *Nicastro* may be distinguishable here because the "marketing efforts" in that case consisted solely of attending several national trade shows outside of New Jersey, rather than advertising content that actually appeared in the forum state. Ultimately, however, *Nicastro* provides a guiding principle that efforts to target the national market of the United States do not equate

---

[12] It is no excuse that MoneyMutual's website and email-solicitation systems are automated and depend solely on unilateral activity by users, because MoneyMutual or others under its direction programmed these systems. See uBID, Inc. v. GoDaddy Grp., Inc., 623 F.3d 421, 428 (7th Cir.2010) ("No more persuasive is GoDaddy's argument that its sales to Illinois residents are automated transactions unilaterally initiated by those residents. GoDaddy tells us that its customers enter into most transactions without any human action on GoDaddy's end. But of course the customers . . . are not simply typing their credit card numbers into a web form and hoping they get something in return. GoDaddy itself set the system up this way. It cannot now point to its hundreds of thousands of customers in Illinois and tell us, 'It was all their idea.' ").

to contacts with a particular state simply because that state is a part of the national market.

C

Finally, respondents argue that MoneyMutual targeted the Minnesota market and established contacts with Minnesota through its Google AdWords advertising campaign. * * * According to respondents, Google's "Ad Settings" page indicated that MoneyMutual's ads matched the exact search that the user had entered—in other words, MoneyMutual paid to display those ads to customers who specifically searched for "payday loans Minnesota" or "payday loans Minneapolis." Respondents argue that these advertising purchases show an intent on MoneyMutual's part to target the Minnesota market.

[MoneyMutual argued that its Google AdWords outreach did not target only Minnesota but included other states as well.] This argument fails because it is not necessary to rule out the targeting of other forums, in addition to Minnesota, in order to establish Minnesota's personal jurisdiction over a particular defendant. Hypothetically, if MoneyMutual paid for AdWords directed at other states, such as "payday loan New York," it would not diminish the conclusion that MoneyMutual targeted Minnesota with its AdWords campaign. Rather, it would tend to establish contacts with both Minnesota and New York. * * *

[MoneyMutual argued that its Google AdWords campaign was irrelevant because no claimant alleged having performed a Google search that brought up such an ad.] Although at this early stage of the litigation there is no evidence that the Google Ads actually caused any of the claims, the Google Ads are sufficiently related to the claims of respondents to survive a motion to dismiss. Respondents allege that MoneyMutual's website and advertising violated consumer protection statutes on false advertising and deceptive trade practices and that MoneyMutual conspired with, aided, and abetted, unlicensed payday lenders that extended loans under terms that violated Minnesota law. MoneyMutual's Google Ads, which were targeted at searches including "Minnesota" and "Minneapolis," solicited viewers to apply for these allegedly illegal payday loans by stating, for example: "Apply Online Now www.moneymutual.com Fast Payday Loan—Apply Online! Safe & Bad Credit OK Up to $1,000."

* * * As a result, MoneyMutual's use of Google AdWords advertising that was specifically designed to target Minnesota residents is a relevant contact with the Minnesota forum for the purpose of the minimum contacts analysis.

NOTES AND QUESTIONS

1.   In many ways, this is an easy case. Probably most law students are familiar with similar marketing efforts for various products and services. In

that sense, one might say that MoneyMutual's marketing simply reflects changes in technology, and the fact that new technology is used should not affect jurisdictional analysis. Indeed, the Court recognized in its 1957 decision in McGee v. International Life Ins. Co., supra p. 733, that improved means of communication might affect jurisdictional analysis. Surely it would be easy to conclude that defendant "sought to serve" Minnesota, the phrase used in World-Wide Volkswagen v. Woodson, supra p. 744. But what if Seaway, the New York retailer in that case had set up a web site with a "service questions answered" function that permitted customers to log in and ask its mechanics questions about car performance issues. Would that be "seeking to serve" any place a customer could log on with a question? Consider the court's treatment of defendant's television ads. Should a website that simply invited customers to request goods or services online suffice to support jurisdiction for a claim that the goods or services were defective wherever the purchaser was located? Would it matter of the goods or services were delivered online? Consider Remick v. Manfredy, 238 F.3d 248, 259 n. 3 (3d Cir. 2001): "[M]ere posting of information or advertisements on an Internet website does not confer nationwide personal jurisdiction."

2. Should Internet-based activities be handled under special jurisdictional rules? One view is that "the Internet is no different from the myriad of ways that people from one place injure people in other places. * * * Since the replacement of strict territorialism [in the wake of *International Shoe*, supra p. 726], such interstate activity no longer confounds the courts. There is a rich and complex body of law to test the legitimacy of sovereign claims to regulate and redress interstate claims." Stein, The Unexceptional Problem of Jurisdiction in Cyberspace, 32 Int'l Lawyer 1167, 1180 (1998).

Others are less sanguine about adapting current jurisdictional principles to Internet situations. Consider that "the ease and relative inexpensiveness involved in placing a Web page on the Internet mean that such activity cannot legitimately be viewed as true purposeful availment of those forums [the Internet reaches]. The defendant has not made the type of temporal or financial commitment required in the use of a preexisting communications technology." Redish, Of New Wine in Old Bottles: Personal Jurisdiction, the Internet, and the Nature of Constitutional Evolution, 38 Jurimetrics 575, 590 (1998). As a consequence, the purposeful availment standard may be unsuited to determining jurisdictional issues related to Internet activities (id. at 580):

> [B]ecause of the dramatic and unique ease with which those out-of-staters may make use of the Internet to inflict such harm, it will often be impossible realistically to characterize their activities as the purposeful availment of the jurisdiction's benefits and privileges, i.e., the conscious decision affirmatively to connect oneself with the forum state for the purpose of acquiring benefits and privileges from that state. Use of this standard will therefore effectively prevent individual states from protecting their citizens against Internet harm. At least in the context of the Internet, then, the purposeful availment test fails the traditional utilitarian calculus of procedural

due process, which seeks to draw an appropriate balance between the competing interests of state and litigant.

One reaction is that courts will need to devise tests that protect against jurisdictional overreaching. See Citron, Minimum Contacts in a Borderless World: Voice Over Internet Protocol and the Coming Implosion of Personal Jurisdiction Theory, 39 U.C. Davis L. Rev. 1481 (2006) (arguing that use of VoIP technology means that callers don't know where their calls are going, which "will force the Supreme Court to reconstruct its theory of personal jurisdiction for VoIP-related contacts from the ground up"). But perhaps technology can provide a solution as well as create the problem. For example, "geolocation" technology now enables marketers to determine where they are directing messages. Could that not also be used to limit the impact of Internet-based activities? See Wandell, Geolocation and Jurisdiction: From Purposeful Availment to Avoidance and Targeting on the Internet, 16 J. Tech. Law & Policy 275 (2011) (arguing that failure to use geolocation technology to prevent access from certain states should suffice to establish purposeful availment with respect to those states). Should it matter that, for ordinary people, geolocation technology may be a significant cost? For further discussion of these issues, see Symposium, Personal Jurisdiction in the Internet Age, 98 Nw.U.L.Rev. 409 (2004).

3.   *The* Zippo *test*: One early effort to devise special rules for Internet-based activity was in Zippo Mfg. Co. v. Zippo Dot Com, Inc., 952 F.Supp. 1119 (W.D.Pa.1997), using a "sliding scale" to determine whether a website was "passive" or "interactive" or was an "E-commerce site" to determine whether it provided a basis for jurisdiction. A "passive" site does nothing more than post information. Should that protect against a finding of jurisdiction? Consider the imaginary site www.BombTheBridge.org, which displays a highly detailed set of drawings of San Francisco's Golden Gate Bridge, detailed instructions on how to build a bomb that would bring down the bridge, and instructions on where to place such a bomb to destroy the bridge. Could it be said that this "passive" site targets San Francisco? Compare an "E-commerce" site operated by a small inn in Vermont that permits people to book rooms at the inn online. Should that interactivity make the inn subject to suit wherever a prospective patron could book a room? For discussion, see Trammell & Bambauer, Personal Jurisdiction and the "Interwebs," 100 Cornell L. Rev. 1129, 1149–52 (2015) (describing the *Zippo* test as "both wrong and useless").

4.   Would an expansive attitude toward jurisdiction for online activities sweep too broadly? In Burdick v. Superior Court, 183 Cal.Rptr.3d 1 (Cal.Ct.App.2015), defendant, an Illinois resident, posted on his Facebook page a video that plaintiff, a Californian, claimed was defamatory in his suit in a California state court. The court upheld dismissal for lack of personal jurisdiction. It read the Supreme Court's analysis in Walden v. Fiore, supra p. 758 n. 1 and p. 790 n. 10, to require that the defendant himself establish contacts with the forum state, not merely with the plaintiff. Although it could infer that defendant knew that plaintiff resided in California, the court found that jurisdiction was proper only if "the nonresident defendant expressly aimed

or intentionally targeted his or her intentional conduct at the forum state." It added that "merely posting on the Internet negative comments about the plaintiff and knowing the plaintiff is in the forum state are insufficient to create minimum contacts."

As might be expected, defamation suits based on online access have often presented jurisdictional issues. Here are some examples:

Blumenthal v. Drudge, 992 F.Supp. 44 (D.D.C.1998): The court held that a White House staffer could sue Matt Drudge, an Internet columnist, in D.C. Drudge solicited contributions of information from people in D.C., focused much of his column on activities in the capitol, and visited the District to promote his column.

Young v. New Haven Advocate, 315 F.3d 256 (4th Cir.2002): A Connecticut newspaper published an article about the transfer of Connecticut inmates to a prison in Virginia that was posted in its Web site and could be read on a computer in Virginia. Plaintiff, the warden of the Virginia prison, sued there claiming that the article was libelous, but except for Internet access no copies of the newspaper were distributed in Virginia. The court held there was no jurisdiction.

Griffis v. Luban, 646 N.W.2d 527 (Minn.2002), cert. denied, 538 U.S. 906 (2003): Plaintiff sued defendant in Alabama for posting uncomplimentary assertions about plaintiff on an Internet newsgroup site for those interested in archeology. The Minnesota court held that plaintiff's Alabama default judgment was not entitled to full faith and credit because jurisdiction was not warranted under Calder v. Jones, supra p. 756. The postings were about archaeology and directed, not to Alabama, but to an Internet community likely spread across the country and the world. For further discussion, see Note, A Culture Without Consequences? Redefining Purposeful Availment for Wrongful Online Conduct, 63 Hast. L.J. 1135 (2012) (urging courts to focus on "defendant's specific knowledge and intent").

5. *Copyright or trademark infringement*: In Brayton Purcell, LLP v. Recordon & Recordon, 575 F.3d 981 (9th Cir. 2009), a law firm sued another law firm for copyright violation based on defendant's using text from plaintiff's website on its web site. Under the Ninth Circuit view, venue in copyright cases depends on whether the defendant would be subject to personal jurisdiction in the district in which suit is filed, so the question was whether defendant, a San Diego firm (in the S.D. Cal.) could be sued in the N.D. Cal., where the plaintiff firm was located. Defendants Kathy and Stephen Recordon argued that they never had any clients in the N.D. Cal., and that they therefore could not be sued there.

The defendant law firm had hired a web-design company to add an elder law section to its website, and the plaintiff claimed the web-design company had copied portions of plaintiff's web site verbatim and included them on defendant's web page. Plaintiff marketed itself as a statewide leader on providing elder law representation throughout California, including San Diego. The majority of the appellate court held that this showing sufficed under its "express aiming" standard of purposeful availment, citing an affidavit submitted by plaintiff that elder law is a new area of practice with few entrants, so that potential clients who read both websites might be confused about which firm was the true author of the material. One judge dissented:

> [T]he majority opinion would permit a defendant who resides in Ohio, Florida, or Maine, thousands of miles from the Ninth Circuit, to be sued in the Northern District of California based on nothing more than his knowledge that the plaintiff whose intellectual property rights he allegedly infringed resides in San Francisco. Under the majority's opinion, every website operator faces the potential that he will be hailed into far-away courts based upon allegations of intellectual property infringement, if he happens to know where the alleged owner of the property rights resides.

In Carefirst of Maryland v. Carefirst Pregnancy Centers, Inc., 334 F.3d 390 (4th Cir.2003), a Maryland plaintiff sued a defendant that used the same name in Illinois. Defendant's website sought donations for its Chicago-area activities, but it had only received $1,500 (0.0174%) of its contributions from Maryland residents. The court used the *Zippo* analysis (supra note 3), but held that jurisdiction was improper. Even though defendant's site was "semi-interactive," it did not satisfy this test. In reaching this conclusion, the court recognized that Maryland was the focal point of plaintiff's injuries. But the overall content of defendant's site was "strongly local" in character, directed to the Chicago area. Accordingly, "when [defendant] set up its generally accessible, semi-interactive Internet website, it did not thereby direct electronic activity into Maryland with the manifest intent of engaging in business or other interactions within that state in particular." Id. at 401. The fact that defendant relied on a Maryland company as a web server and to facilitate its acquisition of domain names was de minimis, particularly since the servers themselves were actually located in Massachusetts.

Contrast Dudnikov v. Chalk & Vermilion Fine Arts, Inc., 514 F.3d 1063 (10th Cir.2008), in which Colorado users of eBay sued a British copyright holder for sending eBay a Notice of Copyright Infringement (NOCI) regarding plaintiffs' offer to sell online a fabric containing a design based a famous design by Erte, a 20th century Russian-born French artist. Defendants held the copyright to this Erte design and sent an NOCI to eBay in California, which caused eBay automatically to terminate the auction of the challenged item and notify plaintiffs of the NOCI. Plaintiffs then wrote to defendants by e-mail, explaining that they made their living on eBay and asking that the NOCI be withdrawn in return for plaintiffs' promise not to offer the challenged fabric. Plaintiffs also filed an action in federal court in Colorado seeking a declaratory judgment that their fabric did not infringe defendants' copyrights. Defendant successfully moved to dismiss for lack of jurisdiction, arguing that all they had done was to send a NOCI to eBay in California. The appellate court reversed under *Calder* (id. at 1075):

> [W]hile, as defendants emphasize, the NOCI formally traveled only to California, it can be fairly characterized as an intended means to

the further intended end of cancelling plaintiff's auction in Colorado. In this way, it is something like a bank shot in basketball. A player who shoots the ball off the backboard intends to hit the backboard, but he does so in the service of his further intention of putting the ball into the basket. Here, defendants intended to send the NOCI to eBay in California, but they did so with the ultimate purpose of cancelling plaintiff's auction in Colorado.

In Marvix Photo, Inc. v. Brand Technologies, Inc., 647 F.3d 1218 (9th Cir. 2011), plaintiff, a Florida corporation, took "candid photographs" of the celebrity Fergie in the Bahamas and copyrighted them. Defendant, an Ohio corporation, posted the photos on its website www.celebrity-gossip.net, a remarkably popular website (ranked 3,622 of 180 million websites worldwide). Plaintiff sued in Los Angeles. The district court granted defendant's motion to dismiss, rejecting plaintiff's argument that defendant's activities were inherently directed toward California because it is "the epicenter of celebrities and the entertainment industry." The court of appeals reversed, citing Keeton v. Hustler Magazine (supra p. 759 n. 2) and relying on repeated accessing of defendant's site from California, which showed that defendant wanted "a substantial California viewer base." Like the defendant in *Keeton*, which sent several thousand copies of its magazine each month into New Hampshire, this defendant's penetration into the California market was not "random, isolated, or fortuitous." Casenote, 125 Harv. L. Rev. 634 (2011), argues that this decision was wrong because *Keeton* "was premised on the assumption that thousands of copies of a physical good cannot simply arrive in a locale by chance and thus must have been purposefully directed there." Moreover, "[g]iven the scope of internet viewership, it is hard to imagine any popular website whose viewership does not far exceed the distribution in *Keeton*."

6. *Doing business over the Internet*: In *MoneyMutual*, the jurisdiction decision seemed easy because defendant was engaged in a fairly extensive online commercial activity involving many Minnesota customers. But what does it mean to say that defendant transacts business over the Internet? In some instances, it may be easy to reach this conclusion. For example, some businesses such as Amazon.com operate only on the Internet. Should it be sufficient if defendant made one sale on eBay? In Boschetto v. Hansing, 539 F.3d 1011 (9th Cir.2008), plaintiff filed suit at home in San Francisco when the 1964 Ford Galaxie he purchased for over $34,000 through an eBay auction turned out not to match the description defendants had given. Defendants resided in Wisconsin, and had arranged the sale from there. Regarding the sale as a "one-shot affair" as to which defendants had no control over where the buyer would come from, the court held that it did not support jurisdiction. Contrast Dedvukaj v. Maloney, 447 F.Supp.2d 813, 823 (E.D. Mich. 2006) ("Defendants' use of eBay is regular and systemic"). Should regularly using Craigslist be treated similarly?

E. PRESENCE OF DEFENDANT'S PROPERTY

SHAFFER V. HEITNER

Supreme Court of the United States, 1977
433 U.S. 186

JUSTICE MARSHALL delivered the opinion of the Court.

The controversy in this case concerns the constitutionality of a Delaware statute that allows a court of that State to take jurisdiction of a lawsuit by sequestering any property of the defendant that happens to be located in Delaware. Appellants contend that the sequestration statute as applied in this case violates the Due Process Clause of the Fourteenth Amendment both because it permits the state courts to exercise jurisdiction despite the absence of sufficient contacts among the defendants, the litigation, and the State of Delaware and because it authorizes the deprivation of defendants' property without providing adequate procedural safeguards. We find it necessary to consider only the first of these contentions.

[Heitner, a nonresident of Delaware, owned one share of stock in Greyhound Corp., which was incorporated under Delaware law but had its principal place of business in Phoenix, AZ. He filed a shareholder's derivative suit in state court in Delaware, naming as defendants Greyhound and one of its subsidiaries, and 28 present or former officers or directors of the company or its subsidiary, none of whom resided in Delaware. Heitner alleged that the individual defendants caused Greyhound and the subsidiary to take improper actions in Oregon that caused the corporations to become liable in a private antitrust suit.

Simultaneously with filing the derivative action, Heitner obtained a sequestration order from the Delaware court for seizure of stock and stock options issued by Greyhound to the individual defendants. Under Delaware law, all the stock was considered to be in Delaware even though it appeared that none of the share certificates were in that state, because Delaware law makes the state the situs of ownership of all stock in Delaware corporations. The result of the sequestration order was that none of the individual defendants could transfer ownership of their shares. 21 of the 28 individual defendants owned stock or stock options in the company.

The 21 defendants who owned stock or stock options made due process challenges to the freezing of their stock without prior notice or hearing, relying on Fuentes v. Shevin, supra p. 31, and Mitchell v. W.T. Grant Co., supra p. 45. Noting that under Delaware law sequestration "is a process used to compel the personal appearance of a nonresident defendant to answer and defend a suit," and that it would be lifted as soon as the defendant entered an appearance, the Delaware court rejected this due process challenge. The Supreme Court did not reach this challenge.

The defendants also made due process personal-jurisdiction objections. The Delaware courts rejected those arguments on the ground that the proceeding was based on *quasi in rem* jurisdiction. Addressing this contention, the Supreme Court concluded that the time had come to consider whether the *International Shoe* standard should apply to actions *in rem* as well as to actions *in personam*.]

III

The case for applying to jurisdiction in rem the same test of "fair play and substantial justice" as governs assertions of jurisdiction in personam is simple and straightforward. It is premised on recognition that "[t]he phrase, 'judicial jurisdiction over a thing', is a customary elliptical way of referring to jurisdiction over the interests of persons in a thing." This recognition leads to the conclusion that in order to justify an exercise of jurisdiction in rem, the basis for jurisdiction must be sufficient to justify exercising "jurisdiction over the interests of persons in a thing."[23] The standard for determining whether an exercise of jurisdiction over the interests of persons is consistent with the Due Process Clause is the minimum-contacts standard elucidated in International Shoe.

This argument, of course, does not ignore the fact that the presence of property in a State may bear on the existence of jurisdiction by providing contacts among the forum State, the defendant, and the litigation. For example, when claims to the property itself are the source of the underlying controversy between the plaintiff and the defendant,[24] it would be unusual for the State where the property is located not to have jurisdiction. In such cases, the defendant's claim to property located in the State would normally indicate that he expected to benefit from the State's protection of his interest. The State's strong interests in assuring the marketability of property within its borders and in providing a procedure for peaceful resolution of disputes about the possession of that property would also support jurisdiction, as would the likelihood that important records and witnesses will be found in the State.[28] The presence of property may also favor jurisdiction in cases such as suits for injury suffered on the land of an absentee owner, where the defendant's ownership of the property is

---

[23] It is true that the potential liability of a defendant in an *in rem* action is limited by the value of the property, but that limitation does not affect the argument. The fairness of subjecting a defendant to state-court jurisdiction does not depend on the size of the claim being litigated.

[24] This category included true *in rem* actions and the first type of *quasi in rem* proceedings. See n. 17, supra. [Footnote 17 says as follows: "A judgment *in rem* affects the interests of all persons in designated property. A judgment *quasi in rem* affects the interests of particular persons in designated property. The latter is of two types. In one the plaintiff is seeking to secure a pre-existing claim in the subject property and to extinguish or establish the nonexistence of similar interests in particular persons. In the other the plaintiff seeks to apply what he concedes to be the property of the defendant to a claim against him. Restatement, Judgments, 5–9." Hanson v. Denckla, 357 U.S. 235, 246 n. 12 (1957).]

[28] We do not suggest that these illustrations include all the factors that may affect the decision, nor that the factors we have mentioned are necessarily decisive.

conceded but the cause of action is otherwise related to rights and duties growing out of that ownership.[29]

It appears, therefore, that jurisdiction over many types of actions which now are or might be brought in rem would not be affected by a holding that any assertion of state-court jurisdiction must satisfy the *International Shoe* standard.[30] For the type of quasi in rem action typified by Harris v. Balk [supra p. 718] and the present case, however, accepting the proposed analysis would result in significant change. These are cases where the property which now serves as the basis for state-court jurisdiction is completely unrelated to the plaintiff's cause of action. Thus, although the presence of the defendant's property in a State might suggest the existence of other ties among the defendant, the State, and the litigation, the presence of the property alone would not support the State's jurisdiction. If those other ties did not exist, cases over which the State is now thought to have jurisdiction could not be brought in that forum.

Since acceptance of the *International Shoe* test would most affect this class of cases, we examine the arguments against adopting that standard as they relate to this category of litigation. Before doing so, however, we note that this type of case also presents the clearest illustration of the argument in favor of assessing assertions of jurisdiction by a single standard. For in cases such as *Harris* and this one, the only role played by the property is to provide the basis for bringing the defendant into court. Indeed, the express purpose of the Delaware sequestration procedure is to compel the defendant to enter a personal appearance.[33] In such cases, if a direct assertion of personal jurisdiction over the defendant would violate the Constitution, it would seem that an indirect assertion of that jurisdiction should be equally impermissible.

The primary rationale for treating the presence of property as a sufficient basis for jurisdiction to adjudicate claims over which the State would not have jurisdiction if *International Shoe* applied is that a wrongdoer "should not be able to avoid payment of his obligations by the expedient of removing his assets to a place where he is not subject to an in personam suit." This justification, however, does not explain why jurisdiction should be recognized without regard to whether the property is present in the State because of an effort to avoid the owner's obligations. Nor does it support jurisdiction to adjudicate the underlying claim. At most, it suggests that a State in which property is located should have

---

[29] Cf. Dubin v. City of Philadelphia, 34 Pa.D. & C. 61 (1939). If such an action were brought under the *in rem* jurisdiction rather than under a long-arm statute, it would be a *quasi in rem* action of the second type. See n. [24], supra.

[30] We do not suggest that jurisdictional doctrines other than those discussed in text, such as the particularized rules governing adjudications of status, are inconsistent with the standard of fairness.

[33] This purpose is emphasized by Delaware's refusal to allow any defense on the merits unless a defendant enters a general appearance, thus submitting to full *in personam* liability.

jurisdiction to attach that property, by use of proper procedures, as security for a judgment being sought in a forum where the litigation can be maintained consistently with *International Shoe*. Moreover, we know of nothing to justify the assumption that a debtor can avoid paying his obligations by removing his property to a State in which his creditor cannot obtain personal jurisdiction over him. The Full Faith and Credit Clause, after all, makes the valid in personam judgment of one State enforceable in all other States.[36]

It might also be suggested that allowing in rem jurisdiction avoids the uncertainty inherent in the International Shoe standard and assures a plaintiff of a forum.[37] We believe, however, that the fairness standard of International Shoe can be easily applied in the vast majority of cases. Moreover, when the existence of jurisdiction in a particular forum under International Shoe is unclear, the cost of simplifying the litigation by avoiding the jurisdictional question may be the sacrifice of "fair play and substantial justice." That cost is too high.

We are left, then, to consider the significance of the long history of jurisdiction based solely on the presence of property in a State. Although the theory that territorial power is both essential to and sufficient for jurisdiction has been undermined, we have never held that the presence of property in a State does not automatically confer jurisdiction over the owner's interest in that property. This history must be considered as supporting the proposition that jurisdiction based solely on the presence of property satisfies the demands of due process, cf. Ownbey v. Morgan, 256 U.S. 94, 111 (1921), but it is not decisive. "[T]raditional notions of fair play and substantial justice" can be as readily offended by the perpetuation of ancient forms that are no longer justified as by the adoption of new procedures that are inconsistent with the basic values of our constitutional heritage. Cf. Sniadach v. Family Finance Corp., 395 U.S., at 340. The fiction that an assertion of jurisdiction over property is anything but an assertion of jurisdiction over the owner of the property supports an ancient form without substantial modern justification. Its continued acceptance would serve only to allow state-court jurisdiction that is fundamentally unfair to the defendant.

We therefore conclude that all assertions of state-court jurisdiction must be evaluated according to the standards set forth in *International Shoe* and its progeny.

---

[36] Once it has been determined by a court of competent jurisdiction that the defendant is a debtor of the plaintiff, there would seem to be no unfairness in allowing an action to realize on that debt in a State where the defendant has property, whether or not that State would have jurisdiction to determine the existence of the debt as an original matter.

[37] This case does not raise, and we therefore do not consider, the question whether the presence of a defendant's property in a State is a sufficient basis for jurisdiction when no other forum is available to the plaintiff.

IV

[Heitner contended that the individual defendants' positions as directors or officers of a Delaware corporation supplied the needed contacts with the state, emphasizing the state's interest in supervising the management of a Delaware corporation. Although the Court recognized that, under customary choice of law principles, "the law of the State of incorporation is held to govern the liability," this interest did not support personal jurisdiction in Delaware because the Delaware Legislature had not asserted that supposed state interest in jurisdiction in the state's courts. Moreover, "sequestration can be used in any suit against a nonresident," which demonstrated that *in rem* jurisdiction was not focused on that state interest.]

Appellants have simply had nothing to do with the State of Delaware. Moreover, appellants had no reason to expect to be haled before a Delaware court. Delaware, unlike some States, has not enacted a statute that treats acceptance of a directorship as consent to jurisdiction in the State.

[Justice Rehnquist took no part in the consideration or decision of this case.

Justice Powell concurred in the Court's opinion but said he would reserve judgment on "whether the ownership of some forms of property whose situs is indisputably and permanently located within a State may, without more" be subjected to the state's jurisdiction to the value of the property. "In the case of real property, in particular, preservation of the common-law concept of *quasi in rem* jurisdiction arguably would avoid the uncertainty of the general *International Shoe* standard."

Justice Stevens concurred in the judgment, emphasizing the "fair notice" idea he saw as critical to personal jurisdiction decisions. "If I visit another State, or acquire real estate or open a bank account in it, I knowingly assume some risk that the State will exercise its power over my property or my person while there. My contact with the State, though minimal, gives rise to predictable risks." He agreed with Justice Powell that *quasi in rem* jurisdiction should continue to be available with regard to ownership of real property.

Justice Brennan concurred with the decision that *International Shoe* should apply to assertions of *in rem* jurisdiction, but dissented from the Court's decision that this standard could not be satisfied in the case before the Court. He emphasized the state interest adjudicating a shareholder derivative action involving officers or directors of a corporation chartered by the state, and the fact that by accepting positions with such a corporation these individual defendants associated themselves with the state of Delaware.]

NOTES AND QUESTIONS

1.   The Court elaborated on *Shaffer* three years later in Rush v. Savchuk, 444 U.S. 320 (1980). Plaintiff there had been a passenger in a single-car accident in Indiana, where he then lived, and sued the driver, who was also from Indiana. By the time suit was filed, plaintiff had moved to Minnesota, and plaintiff sued there. One reason why plaintiff sued in Minnesota was that under Indiana law plaintiff's claim was barred by the guest statute and the statute of limitations. It appeared, however, that Minnesota might apply its own law, which had a longer limitations period and no guest statute.

Plaintiff did not serve defendant in Minnesota. Instead, he used a Minnesota procedure that permitted him to garnish State Farm Insurance Co., which had issued defendant an auto liability policy, because Minnesota law treated that obligation of the insurer as property of the insured that was present in the state and subject to garnishment. Without questioning Minnesota's assertion that there was property present, the Court held the exercise of jurisdiction invalid:

> The Minnesota Supreme Court was of the view that the insurance policy was so important to the litigation that it provided contacts sufficient to satisfy due process. The insurance policy is not the subject matter of the case, however, nor is it related to the operative facts of the negligence action. The contractual arrangements between the defendant and the insurer pertain only to the conduct, not the substance of the litigation, and accordingly do not affect the court's jurisdiction unless they demonstrate ties between the defendant and the forum.

> In fact, the fictitious presence of the insurer's obligation in Minnesota does not, without more, provide a basis for concluding that there is any contact in the *International Shoe* sense between Minnesota and the insured. To say that "a debt follows the debtor" is simply to say that intangible property has no actual situs, and a debt may be sued on wherever there is jurisdiction over the debtor. State Farm is "found," in the sense of doing business, in all 50 States and the District of Columbia. Under appellee's theory, the "debt" owed to Rush would be "present" in each of those jurisdictions simultaneously. It is apparent that such a "contact" can have no jurisdictional significance.

2.   Consider the broad possible impact of Delaware's sequestration statute. About 60% of publicly traded corporations in this country were incorporated in Delaware, and about 90% of IPOs (initial public offerings) of new corporations are for corporations organized under Delaware law. Should Delaware be able to freeze all the shares of all those companies as a means of coercing submission to its courts' jurisdiction for any claim against one of the owners of those shares? Note that the state does not even offer nonresident owners the option of a limited appearance (see footnote 33); only a general appearance will end the sequestration of the shares.

3.   Do the objecting defendants actually have property in Delaware? Obviously Delaware says they do, but all the other 49 states say that a share of corporate stock is physically embodied in the share certificate and therefore not in Delaware unless the certificate is present there. Given this disparity in determination of location of property, does the Court have to treat Delaware's deviant rule as significant for jurisdictional purposes?

The Supreme Court has never addressed constitutional limitations on a state's right to claim that there is property within its limits in a case involving personal jurisdiction issues, but it confronted similar issues in Western Union Tel. Co. v. Pennsylvania, 368 U.S. 71 (1961), when Pennsylvania claimed that all undelivered wire orders to send money that originated in Pennsylvania should escheat to the state. While disavowing any claim to the money, Western Union challenged Pennsylvania's right to claim the funds on the ground that other states (such as the state to which the money was to be sent) could claim that the money was located there and make similar escheat claims. The Supreme Court did not dispute the power of a state to claim abandoned property, but held that Pennsylvania had denied Western Union due process because it could not guarantee that no other state would make a conflicting and duplicative claim. Is the Constitution a basis for challenging a state's claim that property is present only when there is a similar risk of double exposure? Couldn't the dual location of stock lead to similar duplicative liability? Compare Blackstone v. Miller, 188 U.S. 189 (1903), upholding multiple death taxation of intangible personal property. On multiple taxation of such property, see generally 2 R. Rotunda & J. Nowak, Constitutional Law: Substance and Procedure §§ 13.2; 13.3 (4th ed. 2007).

4.   The Court says that "all assertions of state-court jurisdiction must be evaluated according to the standards set forth in *International Shoe* and its progeny." Does that mean that the presence of the defendant's property has no relevancy at all? Consider a farm in Delaware inherited by a Californian from her grandmother. Would those facts support a finding of purposeful availment if the granddaughter was two years old at the time of the inheritance and had never set foot in Delaware? Would there be a ground for finding that the granddaughter had "submitted" to the jurisdiction under the approach endorsed by Justice Kennedy in *Nicastro*, supra p. 772? If not, would that mean that Delaware could not use judicial process of eminent domain to obtain title to the land to build a road across it? Similarly, if somebody were injured on the farm allegedly due to failure to maintain it in a safe condition, could attachment of the farm provide a basis for jurisdiction in a suit against the granddaughter as an absentee (and inattentive) landlady?

5.   Recall that in *Nicastro*, supra p. 772, it appeared possible that plaintiff would not be able to sue McIntyre U.K. in any American forum because it had not targeted any particular American state. Assume that McIntyre UK nonetheless has a bank or securities account in New York with a balance of $1 million, and that New York would allow attachment jurisdiction based on seizure of the account. Would it be constitutional for New York to

entertain Nicastro's suit even though (as the Court held) he could not sue in New Jersey? See the Court's footnote 37.

6.   The Court refers to the tripartite division of the Restatement of Judgments among true *in rem*, *quasi in rem* type I and *quasi in rem* type II. Does this division really have a bearing on the jurisdictional determination?

(a)   How many actions are genuine *in rem* actions? The Restatement Second of Judgments, § 6, Comment b, identifies four: admiralty libels in rem, proceedings leading to the forfeiture of a thing to the government, title clearance or registration proceedings, and proceedings to settle an estate. Is jurisdiction of the state where the property is located guaranteed in these cases?

(b)   *Quasi in rem* type I: Is jurisdiction always permissible in cases falling into this category? If so, would it be permissible in a specific performance action against a nonresident purchaser? Does it matter what type of property is involved? What if plaintiff claims that defendant fraudulently obtained $100,000 of plaintiff's money in State A and deposited it in an account in State B? Can plaintiff support jurisdiction in State B on the basis of presence of the bank account? Would that depend on whether plaintiff could establish a right to that $100,000, as opposed to an award of that amount in damages?

(c)   *Quasi in rem* type II: At first blush it would seem that in these cases the presence of property is irrelevant to the jurisdictional determination. But the Court tells us in footnote 29 that some cases that would be denominated type II still involve a pertinent connection between the property and the claim that might make the presence of the property relevant. Thus, it cites Dubin v. Philadelphia, a case in which the court held a nonresident owner of property subject to jurisdiction in a suit by a person injured on the property, relying on an analogy to Hess v. Pawloski (supra p. 772): "It is just as important that nonresident owners of Philadelphia real estate should keep their property in such shape as not to injure our citizens as it is that nonresident owners of cars should drive about our streets with equal care. It is only a short step beyond this to assert that defendants in both classes of cases should be answerable in this forum." Does this mean that the presence of property is relevant for jurisdictional purposes where, on analogy to *Hess*, it would justify an inference of consent to jurisdiction?

7.   Taking its cue from the Court, the Delaware legislature quickly passed a statute making acceptance of the position as director of a Delaware corporation consent to suit there on claims of malfeasance in that position. In Armstrong v. Pomerance, 423 A.2d 174 (Del. 1980), the court rejected a challenge to this statute by directors of a corporation who had never conducted any business in Delaware because defendants were on notice of their exposure to suit. In terms of Justice Stevens' concern that defendant have "fair notice" about susceptibility to suit, why does that matter? Compare Winship, Jurisdiction Over Corporate Officers and the Incoherence of Implied Consent, 2013 U.Ill.L.Rev. 1171 (criticizing Delaware's reliance on "consent" by corporate officers as a basis for jurisdiction). Greyhound responded to this

statute by switching its state of incorporation to Arizona. Perdue, The Story of Shaffer v. Heitner: Allocating Jurisdictional Authority Among the States, in Civil Procedure Stories (2d ed. 2008), at 135, 153. Beginning in 2004, an amendment to the Delaware statute broadened the implied consent to officers of the corporation. See Tit. 10, Del. Code § 3114.

8. After *Shaffer*, one might have expected quasi-in-rem jurisdiction to disappear, but it did not. A survey published in 1990 showed that New York and some other states have continued to use the doctrine where due process would allow assertion of jurisdiction, but "gaps" in their long-arm statutes precluded that. Mushlin, The New Quasi-in-rem Jurisdiction: New York's Revival of a Doctrine Whose Time Has Passed, 55 Brooklyn L. Rev. 1059 (1990). Professor Mushlin argues that this is undesirable because it deprives defendants of the use of their property pending resolution of the litigation, and because it improperly overrides the choice of the legislature in adopting a narrow long-arm statute. See also Note, *Shaffer*, *Burnham*, and New York's Continuing Use of QIR-2 Jurisdiction: A Resurrection of the Power Theory, 45 Emory L.J. 239 (1996).

9. The Anticybersquatting Consumer Protection Act, enacted in 1999, provides remedies against those who improperly obtain rights to Internet domain names based on other parties' trademarks. In cases in which personal jurisdiction over the registrant of the domain name is not possible, the Act permits "an in rem civil action against a domain name in the judicial district in which the domain name registrar, domain name registry, or other domain name authority that registered or assigned the domain name is located." 15 U.S.C. § 1125(d)(2)(A). In Porsche Cars North America, Inc. v. Porsche.Net, 302 F.3d 248 (4th Cir.2002), the court held that domain names are property subject to seizure under the Act, and that this seizure would be permissible whether or not the purported owner of the domain name was subject to personal jurisdiction. See also Office Depot, Inc. v. Zuccarini, 596 F.3d 696 (9th Cir. 2010), holding that a domain name could be seized at the location of the domain name registry in Mountain View, Cal., to execute on a judgment entered by a court with in personam jurisdiction. "[U]nder California law * * * domain names are located where the registry is located for the purpose of asserting quasi in rem jurisdiction." Id. at 703. For discussion, see Allen, In Rem Jurisdiction from *Pennoyer* to *Shaffer* to the Anticybersquatting Consumer Protection Act, 11 Geo. Mason L. Rev. 243 (2002).

10. Should *Shaffer* have overturned such a time-honored procedure as attachment jurisdiction on due process grounds? Keep in mind Justice Marshall's treatment of the evolving nature of "traditional notions of fair play and substantial justice" as you examine the continued validity of service of process within the state to establish jurisdiction, infra p. 812.

CHOICE OF LAW

Law school courses in Conflicts of Law examine in detail the many doctrines that bear on selection of the law to decide cases. With 50 separate jurisdictions, the United States presents a fertile field for conflicts of law.

Except for limitations imposed by jurisdiction and venue, a plaintiff can forum shop for favorable law. Thus, efforts to defeat personal jurisdiction may, as in Rush v. Savchuk (supra p. 806 n. 1), seem to be animated by concerns about choice of law. But the Supreme Court has repeatedly separated issues of choice of law from those of personal jurisdiction. This Note provides only an overview of the choice of law problem.

Choice of Law Principles: Because the handling of choice of law problems has evolved to different points in different states, it is necessary to canvass the history of these different approaches. Early in the 20th century, the prevailing choice of law analysis relied on vested rights concepts resulting in fairly rigid rules that determined which law should be applied to decide a case. Thus, in a suit growing out of an accident, the rules called for application of the law of the place of the accident. Similar rules governed selection of the law in actions for breach of contract (e.g. law of the state where the contract was executed or breached).

These rigid rules offered the advantage of ease of application, but they also had serious disadvantages when they led to results that seemed to make no sense. Taking Rush v. Savchuk (supra p. 806 n. 1) as an example, it seems difficult to justify the availability of the guest statute defense as depending on whether the accident (involving two Indianans) happened in Indiana or just across the state line in Illinois, assuming Illinois had abandoned the guest statute. Similarly, it would seem odd to apply the guest statute to an accident just inside Indiana involving two Illinois residents. Some refinement of the analysis looking to a determination whether Indiana had an interest in application of its guest statute seemed in order.

One of the leading proponents of change was Professor Brainerd Currie, who developed an elaborate method of determining governmental interests designed, at a minimum, to identify cases in which only one state had a real interest in applying its law. To take the Rush v. Savchuk example, so long as both parties involved in the accident are Indianans, it may well be that Illinois has no interest in applying its more liberal rule to permit the passenger to recover from his host even though the accident occurred in Illinois. Similarly, were the accident in Indiana, involving two Illinoisians, it would seem that Indiana has no interest in applying its guest statute to deny the Illinois passenger recovery, while Illinois' abandonment of the guest statute seems to show that it desires to allow recovery.

Currie's methods were often not easy to apply, but they furthered a revolution in conflicts jurisprudence that at least one commentator has described as "without parallel in the history of the common law." Hill, The Judicial Function in Choice of Law, 85 Colum. L. Rev. 1585, 1588 (1985). The dust has yet to settle, however, and the question whether "interest analysis" is a legitimate choice of law tool remains highly controversial.

Obviously this book cannot resolve these ongoing disputes. Instead, it can give some of the flavor of the policy-oriented approach that is evolving around the Restatement (Second) of Conflict of Laws (1971). This Restatement, adopted after 17 years of drafting, calls for application of the law of the state that, with respect to a given issue, is most significantly related to the occurrence and the parties. In section 6 it enumerates a list of factors that should be considered in identifying the state that is most significantly related:

(a)   the needs of the interstate and international systems,

(b)   the relevant policies of the forum,

(c)   the relevant policies of other interested states and the relative interests of those states in the determination of the particular issue,

(d)   the protection of justified expectations,

(e)   the basic policies underlying the particular field of law,

(f)   certainty, predictability and uniformity of result, and

(g)   ease in the determination and application of the law to be applied.

Later sections prescribe specific factors to consider in certain types of cases. See, e.g., §§ 145 (torts); 188 (contracts). Suffice it to say the wife these principles afford state courts substantial latitude in selecting the law to be applied.

Two further points should be made. First, after all the analysis is done, the reality is that courts have a strong tendency to apply their own law, and usually do so. Second, these rules are said to apply only to matters of "substance," leaving matters of "procedure" to local law in the court in which the case is pending. We shall attempt to distinguish between these two concepts in detail in Chapter 11, dealing with the Erie problem, and note here that similar issues can arise in connection with selection of the law of different states. Thus, in Keeton v. Hustler Magazine, Inc. (supra p. 759 n. 2), the dismissal of the first suit brought by plaintiff in Ohio on statute of limitations grounds was not considered res judicata because it was made on a "procedural" ground.

Constitutional limitations: States are not totally free to apply their own law, however. Instead, due process requires that "for a State's substantive law to be selected in a constitutionally permissible manner, that State must have a significant contact or significant aggregation of contacts, creating state interests, such that choice of its law is neither arbitrary nor fundamentally unfair." Allstate Ins. Co. v. Hague, 449 U.S. 302 (1981).

As applied by the courts, this standard is less demanding than the normal minimum contacts standard for personal jurisdiction. In *Allstate*, for instance, plaintiff's husband, a Wisconsin resident, had been killed in a collision in Wisconsin involving two other Wisconsin residents, neither of whom had insurance. But decedent had policies of insurance, issued in Wisconsin on each of the family's three cars (registered in Wisconsin), and each policy had $15,000 coverage for injuries caused by an uninsured motorist. The issue was whether plaintiff should be permitted to "stack" those three policies, thereby obtaining a total recovery of $45,000. Under the law of Wisconsin, stacking was not allowed. Plaintiff had, however, moved to Minnesota after her husband died, and she sued the insurance company there. The Minnesota Supreme Court, concluding that allowing stacking is the "better rule," permitted the higher recovery, and the Supreme Court rejected the insurance company's due process arguments. In an opinion joined by three other justices, Justice Brennan identified three connections between Minnesota and the claim that together permitted application of Minnesota law: (1) The husband worked in Minnesota, commuting there every work day (although he was not on his way to work when he was killed), (2) Allstate was doing business at all times in Minnesota, so that it was familiar with Minnesota's laws (although this fact hardly put it on notice that Minnesota law would be applied to this case), and (3) Plaintiff became a Minnesota resident before the suit was filed (although this was clearly her unilateral activity).

It is unlikely that these factors would have provided a basis for jurisdiction over either of the Wisconsin drivers involved in the accident, so that State courts appear to have more freedom in choice of law than in extensions of personal jurisdiction. For a criticism of *Hague*, see Brilmayer, Legitimate Interests in Multistate Problems: As Between State and Federal Law, 79 Mich.L.Rev. 1315 (1981). For our purposes, it seems likely that a state which has a constitutional basis for exercising jurisdiction would generally be able constitutionally to apply its own law as well if its choice of law analysis points in that direction (as it usually does). In Phillips Petroleum Co. v. Shutts, 472 U.S. 797 (1985), however, the court held that although a state could entertain personal jurisdiction over a nationwide class action on grounds of consent, it could not constitutionally apply its law over defendant's objections to decide the rights of class members who had no contact with the forum.

F. PERSONAL SERVICE WITHIN THE JURISDICTION

In Shaffer v. Heitner, supra p. 801, the Court concluded as follows: "We therefore conclude that all assertions of state-court jurisdiction must be evaluated according to the standards set forth in *International Shoe*." That might lead to the conclusion that another "traditional" basis for personal jurisdiction—service within the state—would no longer suffice to support jurisdiction. In Burnham v. Superior Court, 495 U.S. 604 (1991), *Q. Vid* the Court held that personal service in the forum still sufficed, except that it might not if the defendant's presence in the state were unintentional or unknowing.

Burnham was a marital dispute. Husband and wife were married in West Virginia but soon moved to New Jersey, where they lived for a decade. Then they separated, allegedly with the understanding that the wife would move to California and take their two children with her. According to the wife, the couple agreed that they would file for divorce on grounds of "irreconcilable differences." When the husband filed for divorce in New Jersey a couple of months later, however, he said it was for "desertion." He did not obtain summons in the case or try to serve his wife. When the husband refused to adhere to the agreement about the grounds for divorce, the wife brought suit against him in a California state court for divorce and child and spousal support. Under the "divisible divorce" concept (see supra p. 716 n. 6), the support aspects of the suit could proceed only if there were *in personam* jurisdiction.

Soon after the wife filed the California suit, the husband visited southern California on business, and he then went north to the Bay Area to visit his children and took the older one to the Exploratorium, a museum in San Francisco. When he returned the child to his wife's house, he was served with a summons for the California case. He moved to quash service on the grounds there was no basis for personal jurisdiction, but the California courts denied his motion.

The Supreme Court's decision in Kulko v. Superior Court, 436 U.S. 84 (1978), also involving a divorcing couple, seemed very comparable. Arguably, except for the personal service aspect of *Burnham*, it was a stronger case for jurisdiction in California. The couple there were New Yorkers, but they were married in California in 1959 when the husband was shipping out for military duty in Korea. When he finished his military service, he returned to New York and two children were born there to the couple. In 1972 they separated and agreed that the children would live with the husband during the school year and with the wife during the summers. On that basis, the wife obtained a divorce in Haiti.

The 1972 arrangement in *Kulko* did not last long. In 1973, the couple's daughter decided she wanted to remain with her mother in California and in 1976 their son told his father he also wanted to remain with his mother. As soon as the son arrived in California, the former wife sued there to increase support obligations. The Supreme Court held that California did not have jurisdiction, reasoning: "A father who agrees, in the interests of family harmony and his children's preferences, to allow them to spend more time in California than was required under a separation agreement can hardly be said to have 'purposefully availed himself' of the 'benefits and

Personal
Service Law
basically does
this...

protections' of California's laws." It also said that it did not want to "discourage parents from entering into reasonable visitation agreements." Absent service in the forum, then, there was no jurisdiction over the nonresident spouse.

In *Burnham*, however, the Court was unanimous that jurisdiction was established by personal service on the husband while he was in California. But there was a stark division about the reasons why service was sufficient. Speaking for four Justices, Justice Scalia announced the judgment of the Court, emphasizing the "pedigree" of personal service in the forum, "[a]mong the most firmly established principles of personal jurisdiction in American tradition" at the time the 14th Amendment (containing the due process clause) was adopted in 1868. For him, that pedigree sufficed to establish its constitutionality. He therefore did not conduct any "independent inquiry into the desirability or fairness" of making personal service decisive, recognizing that this attitude was a different "basic approach" to traditional practices from the one adopted to *in rem* jurisdiction in Shaffer v. Heitner, supra p. 801.

Speaking for four other Justices, Justice Brennan concurred in the judgment, but not entirely on the basis of "tradition." Instead, he argued that the historical background mattered because it "provides a defendant voluntarily present in a particular state *today* 'clear notice that [he] is subject to suit' in the forum." (Justice Scalia labeled this argument as "tradition masquerading as 'fairness.'") Justice Brennan also argued that, by visiting a California, the defendant enjoyed the benefits of the state's protections, and he worried that unless transient jurisdiction were upheld "an asymmetry would arise: a transient would have the full benefit of the power the forum State's courts as a plaintiff while retaining immunity from their authority as a defendant."

Justice Stevens, meanwhile, also concurred in the judgment but did not join the opinions of either Justices Scalia or Brennan. In his view, the combined effect of historical evidence, fairness, and common sense meant that "this is indeed a very easy case." Recall that in Shaffer v. Heitner, supra p. 801, he concurred, saying "If I visit another state, * * * I knowingly assume some risk that the state will exercise its power * * * over my person." In a footnote in *Burnham*, he observed wryly: "Perhaps the adage about hard cases making bad law should be revised to cover easy cases."

So personal service remains sufficient all by itself except in the most unusual situations. Justice Brennan's opinion (joined by three others) noted that "there may be cases in which a defendant's involuntary or unknowing presence in a State does not support the exercise of personal jurisdiction over him." And though he generally joined Justice Scalia's opinion, Justice White concurred in a brief opinion saying that he was speaking of "the case where presence in the forum state is intentional, which would almost always be the fact."

NOTES AND QUESTIONS

1.   If personal service should continue to suffice to establish jurisdiction, what is the best reason for that result? Consider the disagreement between Justices Scalia and Brennan concerning the proper due process test. Is Justice Scalia's emphasis on the "pedigree" of transient jurisdiction the proper test? A similar showing could be made concerning the pedigree of quasi-in-rem jurisdiction. Consider Pyrolusite Manganese Co. v. Ward, 73 Ga. 491, 492 (1884): "No one ever dreamed that the attachment laws of the several States authorizing attachments against non-resident defendants, were violative of the Constitution of the United States. Argument is unnecessary." Contrast the approach to pedigree in Shaffer v. Heitner (supra p. 801) and recall Fuentes v. Shevin (supra p. 31), which invalidated attachment statutes on procedural due process grounds.

Justice Scalia justifies the "pedigree" approach by focusing on the word "traditional" in the International Shoe formula. Is this justified? Consider the following criticism:

> By focusing solely on the word, "traditional," Justice Scalia has ignored the words that follow. The Court did not say that due process dictates merely adherence to traditional judicial practices of asserting jurisdiction. Rather, it expressly referred to "traditional notions of fair play and substantial justice." Far from locking in a mindless equation of traditional jurisdictional practice with due process, then, the International Shoe Court was attempting to introduce into jurisdictional analysis the traditional due process concern with fundamental procedural fairness. Justice Scalia's construction is therefore one hundred eighty degrees away from an accurate perception of the International Shoe Court's intent.

Redish, Tradition, Fairness, and Personal Jurisdiction: Due Process and Constitutional Theory After Burnham v. Superior Court, 22 Rutgers L.J. 675, 682 (1991).

2.   If one evaluates transient jurisdiction under contemporary standards of fairness, should it be upheld? Are Justice Brennan's reasons for sustaining jurisdiction based on personal service sufficient to uphold it where jurisdiction could not be upheld without such service?

(a)   Justice Brennan concluded that by visiting California defendant availed himself of the protections of California law. Unless that has some bearing on the claims asserted in the case, should this contact matter? If this contact does suffice, why does personal service in the state matter?

(b)   Justice Brennan argued that a century of judicial practice upholding jurisdiction based on personal service should create reasonable expectations supporting jurisdiction on these grounds. Is this really, as Justice Scalia says, "tradition masquerading as 'fairness.'"? Should the same arguments be available to uphold attachment jurisdiction?

(c) Justice Brennan said that transient jurisdiction overcomes an asymmetry that would otherwise exist since the transient could sue the forum resident in its courts while the resident could not sue the transient. But isn't that asymmetry a consequence of limitations on state court jurisdiction? Since the transient need not personally enter the state to sue the resident there, how does the transient jurisdiction doctrine solve the asymmetry? Cf. Adam v. Saenger (infra pp. 835–836) (by filing suit in California plaintiff consented to jurisdiction on defendant's cross-complaint against him).

3.   As you reflect on contemporary reactions to transient jurisdiction, consider also the following observations:

> If the rule becomes a recognized part of domestic relations law, will it deter a parent from visiting children, particularly in a case like Burnham in which a parent's trip to California was primarily for business purposes? Will parents seek to avoid Burnham by flying children to visit them rather than travelling to the state of residence of the former spouse? Will this added cost decrease the frequency of visits or adversely affect the children? Will a parent enter into a previsit contract with the other parent agreeing not to serve process during the visit? Will such terms be included as a matter of course in initial divorce-custody decrees?

Zeppos, People's Court, 44 Vand.L.Rev. 847, 856–57 (1991). Should these issues bear on the constitutional question presented in *Burnham*?

4.   *Immunity from service*: Rather outdated procedures accorded immunity from service to persons who were in the jurisdiction only to participate in a trial. When *capias ad respondendum* was used, the desire for such immunity was understandable in that the witness might be seized by the sheriff before testifying. More recently, immunity has been justified on the ground that witnesses would otherwise be deterred from coming into the jurisdiction to testify. But how often will the possibility of service actually deter them? Consider Mr. Calder, of Calder v. Jones, supra p. 756. Would he have refused to come to California to testify in Carol Burnett's suit against the National Enquirer for fear that Shirley Jones would serve him with the summons and complaint in her suit? In Kadic v. Karadzic, 70 F.3d 232 (2d Cir.1995), cert. denied, 518 U.S. 1005 (1996), plaintiffs suing Rodovan Karadzic for violations of international law in Bosnia served process on him at the U.N. in New York. The Second Circuit rejected Karadzic's argument that the U.N. headquarters agreement exempted him from service: "Fed.R.Civ.P. 4(e)(2) specifically authorizes personal service of a summons and complaint upon an individual physically present within a judicial district of the United States, and such personal service comports with the requirements of due process for the assertion of personal jurisdiction. See Burnham v. Superior Court."

5.   How should *Burnham* be applied if defendant is a corporation or other similar entity? Recall that serving corporate defendants presented difficult problems under the *Pennoyer* regime. See Jurisdiction over Corporate

Defendants, supra p. 725. Ordinarily even high corporate officers are not found to be authorized to accept service on behalf of the corporation; service on a corporate president taking a vacation cruise in Alaska can provide jurisdiction over the president personally, but not over the corporation. Compare First American Corp. v. Price Waterhouse LLP, 154 F.3d 16 (2d Cir.1998), in which a British accounting partnership (not a corporation) assigned one of its partners to work on an extended basis in New York, where he was served with a subpoena by litigants trying to obtain documents from the partnership. Service on a partner sufficed under New York law as service on the partnership. Citing *Burnham*, the court concluded that the assertion of personal jurisdiction over the British partnership satisfied due process. It noted that the rule authorizing service on a partnership by serving a partner was "a venerable one," and that the partnership should have known it was risking being subject to New York jurisdiction by sending its partner to work in New York.

G. THE GENERAL JURISDICTION ALTERNATIVE

GOODYEAR DUNLOP TIRES OPERATIONS, S.A. v. BROWN

Supreme Court of the United States, 2011
564 U.S. 915

JUSTICE GINSBURG delivered the opinion of the Court.

This case concerns the jurisdiction of state courts over corporations organized and operating abroad. We address, in particular, this question: Are foreign subsidiaries of a United States parent corporation amenable to suit in state court on claims unrelated to any activity of the subsidiaries in the forum State?

A bus accident outside Paris that took the lives of two 13-year-old boys from North Carolina gave rise to the litigation we here consider. Attributing the accident to a defective tire manufactured in Turkey at the plant of a foreign subsidiary of The Goodyear Tire and Rubber Company (Goodyear USA), the boys' parents commenced an action for damages in a North Carolina state court; they named as defendants Goodyear USA, an Ohio corporation, and three of its subsidiaries, organized and operating, respectively, in Turkey, France, and Luxembourg. Goodyear USA, which had plants in North Carolina and regularly engaged in commercial activity there, did not contest the North Carolina court's jurisdiction over it; Goodyear USA's foreign subsidiaries, however, maintained that North Carolina lacked adjudicatory authority over them.

A state court's assertion of jurisdiction exposes defendants to the State's coercive power, and is therefore subject to review for compatibility with the Fourteenth Amendment's Due Process Clause. International Shoe Co. v. Washington, 326 U.S. 310, 316 (1945). Opinions in the wake of the pathmarking International Shoe decision have differentiated between general or all-purpose jurisdiction, and specific or case-linked jurisdiction.

A court may assert general jurisdiction over foreign (sister-state or foreign-country) corporations to hear any and all claims against them when their affiliations with the State are so "continuous and systematic" as to render them essentially at home in the forum State. Specific jurisdiction, on the other hand, depends on an "affiliatio[n] between the forum and the underlying controversy," principally, activity or an occurrence that takes place in the forum State and is therefore subject to the State's regulation. von Mehren & Trautman, Jurisdiction to Adjudicate: A Suggested Analysis, 79 Harv. L.Rev. 1121, 1136 (1966) (hereinafter von Mehren & Trautman); see Brilmayer et al., A General Look at General Jurisdiction, 66 Texas L.Rev. 721, 782 (1988) (hereinafter Brilmayer). In contrast to general, all-purpose jurisdiction, specific jurisdiction is confined to adjudication of "issues deriving from, or connected with, the very controversy that establishes jurisdiction." von Mehren & Trautman 1136.

Because the episode-in-suit, the bus accident, occurred in France, and the tire alleged to have caused the accident was manufactured and sold abroad, North Carolina courts lacked specific jurisdiction to adjudicate the controversy. The North Carolina Court of Appeals so acknowledged. Brown v. Meter, 681 S.E.2d 382, 388 (2009). Were the foreign subsidiaries nonetheless amenable to general jurisdiction in North Carolina courts? Confusing or blending general and specific jurisdictional inquiries, the North Carolina courts answered yes. Some of the tires made abroad by Goodyear's foreign subsidiaries, the North Carolina Court of Appeals stressed, had reached North Carolina through "the stream of commerce"; that connection, the Court of Appeals believed, gave North Carolina courts the handle needed for the exercise of general jurisdiction over the foreign corporations.

A connection so limited between the forum and the foreign corporation, we hold, is an inadequate basis for the exercise of general jurisdiction. Such a connection does not establish the "continuous and systematic" affiliation necessary to empower North Carolina courts to entertain claims unrelated to the foreign corporation's contacts with the State.

I

On April 18, 2004, a bus destined for Charles de Gaulle Airport overturned on a road outside Paris, France. Passengers on the bus were young soccer players from North Carolina beginning their journey home. Two 13-year-olds, Julian Brown and Matthew Helms, sustained fatal injuries. The boys' parents, respondents in this Court, filed a suit for wrongful-death damages in the Superior Court of Onslow County, North Carolina, in their capacity as administrators of the boys' estates. Attributing the accident to a tire that failed when its plies separated, the parents alleged negligence in the "design, construction, testing, and inspection" of the tire.

Goodyear Luxembourg Tires, SA (Goodyear Luxembourg), Goodyear Lastikleri T.A.S. (Goodyear Turkey), and Goodyear Dunlop Tires France, SA (Goodyear France), petitioners here, were named as defendants. Incorporated in Luxembourg, Turkey, and France, respectively, petitioners are indirect subsidiaries of Goodyear USA, an Ohio corporation also named as a defendant in the suit. Petitioners manufacture tires primarily for sale in European and Asian markets. Their tires differ in size and construction from tires ordinarily sold in the United States. They are designed to carry significantly heavier loads, and to serve under road conditions and speed limits in the manufacturers' primary markets.[1]

In contrast to the parent company, Goodyear USA, which does not contest the North Carolina courts' personal jurisdiction over it, petitioners are not registered to do business in North Carolina. They have no place of business, employees, or bank accounts in North Carolina. They do not design, manufacture, or advertise their products in North Carolina. And they do not solicit business in North Carolina or themselves sell or ship tires to North Carolina customers. Even so, a small percentage of petitioners' tires (tens of thousands out of tens of millions manufactured between 2004 and 2007) were distributed within North Carolina by other Goodyear USA affiliates. These tires were typically custom ordered to equip specialized vehicles such as cement mixers, waste haulers, and boat and horse trailers. Petitioners state, and respondents do not here deny, that the type of tire involved in the accident, a Goodyear Regional RHS tire manufactured by Goodyear Turkey, was never distributed in North Carolina.

Petitioners moved to dismiss the claims against them for want of personal jurisdiction. The trial court denied the motion, and the North Carolina Court of Appeals affirmed. Acknowledging that the claims neither "related to, nor . . . ar[o]se from, [petitioners'] contacts with North Carolina," the Court of Appeals confined its analysis to "general rather than specific jurisdiction," which the court recognized required a "higher threshold" showing: A defendant must have "continuous and systematic contacts" with the forum. That threshold was crossed, the court determined, when petitioners placed their tires "in the stream of interstate commerce without any limitation on the extent to which those tires could be sold in North Carolina."

Nothing in the record, the court observed, indicated that petitioners "took any affirmative action to cause tires which they had manufactured to

---

[1]   Respondents portray Goodyear USA's structure as a reprehensible effort to "outsource" all manufacturing, and correspondingly, tort litigation, to foreign jurisdictions. Yet Turkey, where the tire alleged to have caused the accident-n-suit was made, is hardly a strange location for a facility that primarily supplies markets in Europe and Asia.

be shipped into North Carolina." The court found, however, that tires made by petitioners reached North Carolina as a consequence of a "highly-organized distribution process" involving other Goodyear USA subsidiaries. Petitioners, the court noted, made "no attempt to keep these tires from reaching the North Carolina market." Indeed, the very tire involved in the accident, the court observed, conformed to tire standards established by the U.S. Department of Transportation and bore markings required for sale in the United States.[2] As further support, the court invoked North Carolina's "interest in providing a forum in which its citizens are able to seek redress for [their] injuries," and noted the hardship North Carolina plaintiffs would experience "[were they] required to litigate their claims in France," a country to which they have no ties. The North Carolina Supreme Court denied discretionary review.

We granted certiorari to decide whether the general jurisdiction the North Carolina courts asserted over petitioners is consistent with the Due Process Clause of the Fourteenth Amendment.

II

A

The Due Process Clause of the Fourteenth Amendment sets the outer boundaries of a state tribunal's authority to proceed against a defendant. The canonical opinion in this area remains *International Shoe*, in which we held that a State may authorize its courts to exercise personal jurisdiction over an out-of-state defendant if the defendant has "certain minimum contacts with [the State] such that the maintenance of the suit does not offend 'traditional notions of fair play and substantial justice.'"

Endeavoring to give specific content to the "fair play and substantial justice" concept, the Court in *International Shoe* classified cases involving out-of-state corporate defendants. First, as in *International Shoe* itself, jurisdiction unquestionably could be asserted where the corporation's in-state activity is "continuous and systematic" and *that activity gave rise to the episode-in-suit*. Further, the Court observed, the commission of certain "single or occasional acts" in a State may be sufficient to render a corporation answerable in that State with respect to those acts, though not with respect to matters unrelated to the forum connections. The heading courts today use to encompass these two *International Shoe* categories is "specific jurisdiction." Adjudicatory authority is "specific" when the suit "aris[es] out of or relate[s] to the defendant's contacts with the forum."

International Shoe distinguished from cases that fit within the "specific jurisdiction" categories, "instances in which the continuous

---

[2] Such markings do not necessarily show that any of the tires were destined for sale in the United States. To facilitate trade, the Solicitor General explained, the United States encourages other countries to "treat compliance with [Department of Transportation] standards, including use of DOT markings, as evidence that the products are safely manufactured."

corporate operations within a state [are] so substantial and of such a nature as to justify suit against it on causes of action arising from dealings entirely distinct from those activities." Adjudicatory authority so grounded is today called "general jurisdiction." For an individual, the paradigm forum for the exercise of general jurisdiction is the individual's domicile; for a corporation, it is an equivalent place, one in which the corporation is fairly regarded as at home. See Brilmayer 728 (identifying domicile, place of incorporation, and principal place of business as "paradig[m]" bases for the exercise of general jurisdiction).

Since *International Shoe*, this Court's decisions have elaborated primarily on circumstances that warrant the exercise of specific jurisdiction, particularly in cases involving "single or occasional acts" occurring or having their impact within the forum State. As a rule in these cases, this Court has inquired whether there was "some act by which the defendant purposefully avail[ed] itself of the privilege of conducting activities within the forum State, thus invoking the benefits and protections of its laws." Hanson v. Denckla, 357 U.S. 235, 253 (1958). [Justice Ginsburg cited World-Wide Volkswagen Corp. v. Woodson, 444 U.S. 286 (1980), Burger King Corp. v. Rudzewicz, 471 U.S. 462 (1985), and Asahi Metal Industry Co. v. Superior Court, 480 U.S. 102 (1987).] See also Twitchell, The Myth of General Jurisdiction, 101 Harv.L.Rev. 610, 628 (1988) (in the wake of International Shoe, "specific jurisdiction has become the centerpiece of modern jurisdiction theory, while general jurisdiction plays a reduced role").

In only two decisions postdating *International Shoe*, discussed infra, has this Court considered whether an out-of-state corporate defendant's in-state contacts were sufficiently "continuous and systematic" to justify the exercise of general jurisdiction over claims unrelated to those contacts: Perkins v. Benguet Consol. Mining Co., 342 U.S. 437 (1952) (general jurisdiction appropriately exercised over Philippine corporation sued in Ohio, where the company's affairs were overseen during World War II); and Helicopteros [Nacionales de Colombia v. Hall], 466 U.S. 408 [(1984)] (helicopter owned by Colombian corporation crashed in Peru; survivors of U.S. citizens who died in the crash, the Court held, could not maintain wrongful-death actions against the Colombian corporation in Texas, for the corporation's helicopter purchases and purchase-linked activity in Texas were insufficient to subject it to Texas court's general jurisdiction).

B

To justify the exercise of general jurisdiction over petitioners, the North Carolina courts relied on the petitioners' placement of their tires in the "stream of commerce." The stream-of-commerce metaphor has been invoked frequently in lower court decisions permitting "jurisdiction in products liability cases in which the product has traveled through an extensive chain of distribution before reaching the ultimate consumer."

Typically, in such cases, a nonresident defendant, acting outside the forum, places in the stream of commerce a product that ultimately causes harm inside the forum.

Many States have enacted long-arm statutes authorizing courts to exercise specific jurisdiction over manufacturers when the events in suit, or some of them, occurred within the forum state. * * *

The North Carolina court's stream-of-commerce analysis elided the essential difference between case-specific and all-purpose (general) jurisdiction. Flow of a manufacturer's products into the forum, we have explained, may bolster an affiliation germane to specific jurisdiction. But ties serving to bolster the exercise of specific jurisdiction do not warrant a determination that, based on those ties, the forum has general jurisdiction over a defendant.

A corporation's "continuous activity of some sorts within a state," *International Shoe* instructed, "is not enough to support the demand that the corporation be amenable to suits unrelated to that activity." Our 1952 decision in Perkins v. Benguet Consol. Mining Co. remains "[t]he textbook case of general jurisdiction appropriately exercised over a foreign corporation that has not consented to suit in the forum."

Sued in Ohio, the defendant in *Perkins* was a Philippine mining corporation that had ceased activities in the Philippines during World War II. To the extent that the company was conducting any business during and immediately after the Japanese occupation of the Philippines, it was doing so in Ohio: the corporation's president maintained his office there, kept the company files in that office, and supervised from the Ohio office "the necessarily limited wartime activities of the company." Although the claim-in-suit did not arise in Ohio, this Court ruled that it would not violate due process for Ohio to adjudicate the controversy. See Keeton v. Hustler Magazine, Inc., 465 U.S. 770, 779–780, n. 11 (1984) (Ohio's exercise of general jurisdiction was permissible in *Perkins* because "Ohio was the corporation's principal, if temporary, place of business").

We next addressed the exercise of general jurisdiction over an out-of-state corporation over three decades later, in Helicopteros. In that case, survivors of United States citizens who died in a helicopter crash in Peru instituted wrongful-death actions in a Texas state court against the owner and operator of the helicopter, a Colombian corporation. The Colombian corporation had no place of business in Texas and was not licensed to do business there. "Basically, [the company's] contacts with Texas consisted of sending its chief executive officer to Houston for a contract-negotiation session; accepting into its New York bank account checks drawn on a Houston bank; purchasing helicopters, equipment, and training services from [a Texas enterprise] for substantial sums; and sending personnel to [Texas] for training." These links to Texas, we determined, did not "constitute the kind of continuous and systematic general business contacts

. . . found to exist in Perkins," and were insufficient to support the exercise of jurisdiction over a claim that neither "ar[o]se out of . . . no[r] related to" the defendant's activities in Texas.

Helicopteros concluded that "mere purchases [made in the forum State], even if occurring at regular intervals, are not enough to warrant a State's assertion of [general] jurisdiction over a nonresident corporation in a cause of action not related to those purchase transactions." We see no reason to differentiate from the ties to Texas held insufficient in *Helicopteros*, the sales of petitioners' tires sporadically made in North Carolina through intermediaries. Under the sprawling view of general jurisdiction urged by respondents and embraced by the North Carolina Court of Appeals, any substantial manufacturer or seller of goods would be amenable to suit, on any claim for relief, wherever its products are distributed.

Measured against *Helicopteros* and *Perkins*, North Carolina is not a forum in which it would be permissible to subject petitioners to general jurisdiction. Unlike the defendant in *Perkins*, whose sole wartime business activity was conducted in Ohio, petitioners are in no sense at home in North Carolina. Their attenuated connections to the State fall far short of the "the continuous and systematic general business contacts" necessary to empower North Carolina to entertain suit against them on claims unrelated to anything that connects them to the State.[5]

C

[Plaintiffs asserted also that, under a "single enterprise" theory, jurisdiction over the offshore Goodyear entities should be based on the North Carolina contacts of Goodyear USA. But they had not previously urged disregard of the subsidiaries' discrete status, and accordingly forfeited this contention. Moreover, distribution of some of the foreign subsidiaries' tires in North Carolina would not support jurisdiction in this case; "even regularly occurring sales of a product in a State do not justify the exercise of jurisdiction over a claim unrelated to those sales."]

For the reasons stated, the judgment of the North Carolina Court of Appeals is Reversed.

NOTES AND QUESTIONS

1.   In Daimler AG v. Bauman, 134 S.Ct. 746 (2014), the Court applied the *Goodyear* analysis to reject jurisdiction in California with regard to "a claim

---

[5]   As earlier noted, the North Carolina Court of Appeals invoked the States' "well-recognized interest in providing a forum in which its citizens are able to seek redress for injuries that they have sustained." But "[g]eneral jurisdiction to adjudicate has in [United States] practice never been based on the plaintiff's relationship to the forum. There is nothing in [our] law comparable to . . . article 14 of the Civil Code of France (1804) under which the French nationality of the plaintiff is a sufficient ground for jurisdiction." von Mehren & Trautman 1137. When a defendant's act outside the forum causes injury in the forum, by contrast, a plaintiff's residence in the forum may strengthen the case for exercise of specific jurisdiction.

brought by foreign plaintiffs against a foreign defendant based on events occurring entirely outside the United States." Plaintiffs there sought to sue the German car manufacturer of Mercedes Benz cars on claims that its Argentinean subsidiary had, between 1976 and 1983, collaborated with state security forces in Argentina, leading to the torture and murder of workers at the subsidiary's Argentinean plants. Among other claims, plaintiffs sued under the Alien Tort Claims Act, 28 U.S.C. § 1350, and the federal Torture Victim Protection Act. Although the German parent did not itself have a significant presence in California, its American subsidiary (responsible for distributing its cars in this country) was headquartered in New Jersey and had a substantial presence in California. The Ninth Circuit found that the American subsidiary's contacts could be imputed to the German parent on an agency theory, and that the American subsidiary was subject to general jurisdiction in California.

Accepting that the American subsidiary was "at home" in California, and that its contacts could be imputed to the German parent corporation, the Supreme Court held that the German parent was not subject to general jurisdiction under *Goodyear*. Justice Ginsburg rejected the idea that "continuous and systematic" forum contacts could suffice for general jurisdiction, although she acknowledged that in an "exceptional case" a corporation's operations in a state that was not its principal place of business or state of incorporation might suffice to support "all purpose jurisdiction." The Court found the assertion of jurisdiction "exorbitant" (id. at 761):

> If Daimler's California activities sufficed to allow adjudication of this Argentina-rooted case in California, the same global reach would presumably be available in every other State in which [Mercedes Benz] sales are sizable.

In BNSF Ry. Co. v. Tyrell, 137 S.Ct. 1549 (2017), the Court drove home this point in a case involving a domestic defendant. Defendant railroad had over 2,000 miles of track and more than 2,000 employees in Montana, where two injured employees sued it. But neither of the plaintiffs resided in that state or was injured in that state. The Montana state court held that jurisdiction was proper because the railroad was "found within Montana" within the meaning of the state's long-arm statute, but the Supreme Court, again speaking through Justice Ginsburg, held that the magnitude of the defendant's activities in the state is not the measure of general jurisdiction; "a corporation that operates in many places can scarcely be deemed at home in all of them." At the same time, she added, "the business BNSF does in Montana is sufficient to subject the railroad to specific personal jurisdiction in that State on clams related to the business it does in Montana." Id. at 1559.

2.   *Desirability of the "essentially at home" rule for general jurisdiction*: *Goodyear* was the beginning of "a radical departure from decades of case law holding that general jurisdiction was appropriate where a company was doing business in the forum—in the sense of having continuous and systematic general business contacts with the forum." Monestier, Where is Home Depot "At Home"?: *Daimler v. Bauman* and the End of Doing Business Jurisdiction, 66 Hast. L.J. 233, 236 (2014). In a way, the expansive view originated with the

idea of "corporate presence" that guided courts in the early 20th century on when a corporation could be sued in a given state. See Jurisdiction over Corporate Defendants, supra p. 725. Before *Goodyear*, many lower courts had found "doing business" jurisdiction in states that would not be regarded as the "home base" of the defendant corporation. See, e.g., Bryant v. Finnish National Airlines, 208 N.E.2d 439 (N.Y.1965). In that case, a New Yorker injured at Orly Airport in Paris due to the alleged negligence of defendant was allowed to sue in New York although defendant flew no planes to or from the United States. Jurisdiction was based on the fact that it had a one-and-a-half room New York office staffed by three full-time and four part-time employees, who made bookings for air transport services defendant offered in Europe.

Is this recent change desirable? In *Daimler*, the Court said that its new approach will "afford plaintiffs recourse to at least one clear and certain forum in which a corporate defendant may be sued on any and all claims." 134 S.Ct. at 760. The problem presented by alien corporations (see note 7 below) challenges this assumption. Is specific jurisdiction is sufficiently flexible to provide access to court for plaintiffs who deserve it? For example, suppose a North Carolina citizen were injured in North Carolina due to an alleged defect in one of the thousands of Goodyear tires manufactured by the foreign subsidiaries that were distributed in North Carolina. Could that plaintiff sue in North Carolina? Recall J. McIntyre Machinery, Ltd. v. Nicastro, supra p. 772.

Justice Sotomayor dissented vigorously in *Daimler*, supra note 1, arguing that the new standard wrongly broke away from *International Shoe* by introducing a comparative analysis—no matter what the volume or duration of a corporation's activities in the forum state, they would not suffice to support general jurisdiction if its activities elsewhere were more significant. "We used the phrase 'at home' [in *Goodyear*] to signify that in order for an out-of-state defendant to be subject to general jurisdiction, its continuous and substantial contacts with a forum State must be akin to those of a local enterprise that actually is 'at home' in the State." 134 S.Ct. at 769 (Sotomayor, dissenting). As she emphasized, Daimler's sales in California were 2.4% of its worldwide sales of $192 billion, some $4.6 billion, the product of a longstanding presence in the state. Under the *International Shoe* standard, she concluded, that level of activity should suffice without regard to the level of its activities elsewhere.

Justice Sotomayor urged that the majority's rule would deny justice to American plaintiffs (id. at 773):

> Under the majority's rule, for example, a parent whose child is maimed due to the negligence of a foreign hotel owned by a multinational conglomerate will be unable to hold the hotel to account in a single U.S. court, even if the hotel company has a massive presence in multiple States. Similarly, a U.S. business that enters into a contract in a foreign country to sell its products to a multinational company may be unable to seek relief in any U.S. court if the multinational company breaches the contract, even if the company has considerable operations in numerous U.S. forums.

She argued that the reasonableness standard should be employed to limit overly aggressive assertions of general jurisdiction instead of the "essentially at home" standard adopted by the majority.

In *BNSF Ry. Co.*, supra note 1, Justice Sotomayor again dissented, arguing that the decision against jurisdiction in that case in effect renounced the suggestion in *Daimler* that an "exceptional case" might warrant broader application of the general jurisdiction concept, limiting that possibility to "the exact facts of Perkins v. Benguet Consol. Mining Co.," in which corporate headquarters were temporarily located in the forum state.

In Bristol-Myers Squibb Co. v. Superior Court, 137 S.Ct. 1773 (2017), plaintiffs from outside California sued in San Francisco claiming injury due to use of defendant's product Plavix. Defendant was a Delaware corporation with headquarters in New York. Over 50% of its work force was employed in New York or New Jersey, which was the state in which Plavix was developed. But it did have five research facilities in California, employing about 160 people, and employed some 250 sales representatives in the state. Between 2006 and 2012, it took in more than $900 million from sales of Plavix in California, and the non-California plaintiffs were joined in the San Francisco suits by Californians who also claimed injury from Plavix. The California courts used a "sliding scale" approach to justify jurisdiction over the non-Californians' claims based on defendant's employment of hundreds of Californians and receipt of hundreds of millions of dollars for California sales of the product in suit, but the Supreme Court rejected this approach as "a loose and spurious form of general jurisdiction." Id. at 1781.

(The full case is in the Supp. Packet)

Justice Sotomayor again dissented, citing *Daimler*'s narrow view of general jurisdiction: "Today the Court takes its first step toward a similar contraction of specific jurisdiction by holding that a corporation that engages in a nationwide course of conduct cannot be held accountable in a state court by a group of injured people unless all of those people were injured in the forum state." Id. at 1784 (Sotomayor, J., dissenting) She emphasized that the holding might make it impossible for those injured by nationwide distribution of a harmful product to sue together in one consolidated case, particularly if the two or more defendants headquartered in different states were involved in creating and distributing the harmful product but not subject to general jurisdiction in the same state.

3.   *Scope of specific jurisdiction:* Recall the claim against Audi, the German auto manufacturer sued in Oklahoma in World-Wide Volkswagen Corp. v. Woodson, supra p. 744. Would the Robinsons have to rely on general jurisdiction to sue Audi in Oklahoma? See General and Specific Jurisdiction, supra p. 754. Professor Brilmayer has argued that the critical question for specific jurisdiction problems is whether the contacts have substantive relevance to plaintiff's claim whether or not there is a jurisdictional problem in the case:

A contact is related to the controversy if it is the geographical qualification of a fact relevant to the merits. A forum occurrence which would ordinarily be alleged as part of a comparable domestic complaint is a related contact. In contrast, an occurrence in the forum State of no relevance to a totally domestic cause of action is an unrelated contact, a purely jurisdictional allegation with no substantive purpose. If a fact is irrelevant in a purely domestic dispute, it does not suddenly become related to the controversy simply because there are multistate elements.

Brilmayer, How Contacts Count: Due Process Limitations on State Court Jurisdiction, 1980 Sup.Ct.Rev. 77, 82. It this a desirable standard?

Professor Twitchell criticized this approach as underinclusive. In World-Wide Volkswagen v. Woodson (supra p. 744), for example, it would seem that Audi's sales of cars in Oklahoma lacked that sort of relationship to the claim by the Robinsons, who bought their car in New York. She feels that specific jurisdiction should reach such a case:

> [T]he fact that this accident occurred within the forum, coupled with similarity between the manufacturer's conduct in the forum and the conduct underlying the plaintiff's cause of action, * * * makes exercising jurisdiction over this claim particularly reasonable. Having sold and serviced identical cars in the state, the manufacturer will have foreseen such suits and insured against them. Furthermore, the forum has a very strong interest in regulating the manufacturer's conduct in this suit, not just because this particular automobile malfunctioned there, but because state residents are buying many similar cars and operating them on the forum's highways. The fact that the car was not actually sold within the state is, in this context, fortuitous. A court need not decide whether it is fair to hold the manufacturer subject to jurisdiction on all causes of action in the forum in order to decide that it is fair in this particular case. Specific jurisdiction, in which the nature of the cause of action is taken into account when considering fairness, not general jurisdiction, is the key to proper jurisdictional analysis under these circumstances.

Twitchell, The Myth of General Jurisdiction, 101 Harv.L.Rev. 610, 661–62 (1988). Did the Court implicitly endorse this analysis in *World-Wide Volkswagen*?

In response, Professor Brilmayer argued that substantive relevance is a critical element of a sensible test. See Brilmayer, Related Contacts and Personal Jurisdiction, 101 Harv.L.Rev. 1444 (1988). With regard to defective products cases, she raises the "tricky problem of what constitutes adequate similarity. Must it be the identical product that is distributed? A similar make or model? * * * Would assertion of specific jurisdiction require that a similar product sent into the forum state have an identical defect?" With regard to defendant's ability to foresee suit of the character of the suit brought, she adds that "[i]f one assumes that awareness of potential liability to suit on some cause of action in the forum entails awareness of potential liability on other causes of action that did not arise in the forum, then one risks turning specific jurisdiction into general jurisdiction. Under this view, the defendant should be equally unsurprised by any cause of action brought against him or her in the forum: the very definition of general jurisdiction." Id. at 1460–61.

In Bristol-Myers Squibb Co. v. Superior Court, 137 S.Ct. 1773 (2017), supra note 2, the Court seemed to adopt a middle ground. The Court held that specific jurisdiction was not available because the non-California plaintiffs "did not allege that they obtained [the drug] through California physicians or from any other California source; nor did they claim that they were injured by [the drug] or were treated for their injuries in California." In addition, there was no indication that this drug was manufactured, labeled, or processed in the state. Were one or more of those things true, the Court implied, specific jurisdiction could be satisfied even though general jurisdiction would not be available because defendant was "at home" only in New York (the headquarters state) or Delaware (where it was incorporated). As with the claims against Audi and Volkswagen of America in World-Wide Volkswagen v. Woodson (supra p. 744), it seemed that such a local "nexus" would suffice to support specific jurisdiction.

4.   *Definition of "at home":* Will it always be easy to determine where a corporation is "at home"? For purposes of determining citizenship of a corporate party to determine whether there is diversity of citizenship (a topic addressed in Chapter 10), 28 U.S.C. § 1332(c)(1) directs attention to the "principal place of business." But lower courts diverged on application of that term, some emphasizing the place where the corporation has the most employees or most business activity, and others emphasizing the "nerve center," the place where corporate decisions are made. In Hertz Corp. v. Friend, 559 U.S. 77 (2010), the Supreme Court read that statute to adopt the "nerve center" test for that statute. Similarly, the venue statute, 28 U.S.C. § 1391(c)(2), provides that a corporation may be sued in its state of incorporation and where it maintains its "principal place of business." For an argument in favor of this approach for general jurisdiction, see Stein, The Meaning of "Essentially at Home" in Goodyear Dunlop, 63 S. Car. L. Rev. 527 (2012).

Should the same test apply to general jurisdiction? At least in some situations, that might be contested. For example, consider companies (such as Boeing Corporation) that move their headquarters from the original state to another state while maintaining a major presence in their original state. Should they be regarded as "essentially at home" in their original headquarters state even though headquarters have moved?

5.   *General jurisdiction over natural persons:* Contrast the situation with a natural person. The pre-*International Shoe* ruling in Milliken v. Meyer, 311 U.S. 457 (1940), holds that a natural person can be sued in his home state even without personal service within the state. But a natural person is also subject to general jurisdiction whenever he is served within a state. See Burnham v. Superior Court, supra p. 813. There is essentially no similar way to serve a corporation "present" in the forum state.

6.   *Corporate registration statutes:* A possible analogy to service within the state might result from corporate registration statutes. Adopted in the late 19th and early 20th century, these statutes required out-of-state corporations to register to do business in a state in which they were not incorporated, and ordinarily one aspect of registering was to appoint an agent for service of process in the state. In Pennsylvania Fire Ins. Co. v. Gold Issue Mining & Milling Co., 243 U.S. 93 (1917), the Court held that a state could constitutionally require that foreign corporations wishing to be authorized to do business in a state consent to suit there on any claim, of whatever nature, not just those arising out of the business done in the state. Should that remain true?

One question is whether a state registration statute really was intended to reach beyond forum-related claims. In Brown v. Lockheed Martin Corp., 814 F.3d 619 (2d Cir. 2016), the court held that the Connecticut statute "nowhere expressly provides that foreign corporations that register to transact business in the state shall be subject to the 'general jurisdiction' of the Connecticut courts." Id. at 634. The court therefore declined to exercise such jurisdiction based on registration. It added that "the more demanding 'essentially at home' test enunciated in *Goodyear* and *Daimler* suggests that federal due process rights likely constrain an interpretation that transforms a run-of-the-mill registration and appointment statute into corporate 'consent'—perhaps unwitting—to the exercise of general jurisdiction by state courts." See generally Comment, Pennoyer's Ghost: Consent, Registration, Statutes, and General Jurisdiction After *Daimler AG v. Bauman*, 90 N.Y.U. L. Rev. 1609 (2015).

7.   *The problem of alien corporations*: At least with American corporations, there must be some American state where the company is "at home." But that is not true of corporations with headquarters abroad. Consider, for example, the problem confronted by plaintiff in J. McIntyre Machinery, Ltd. v. Nicastro, supra p. 772. Would there be any state in which he could sue the UK maker of the machine that caused his injury in New Jersey? In that case, the plurality opinion suggested that suit could be maintained in a federal court on the basis of "national contacts," premised in that case on the company's targeting of the U.S. market even if it did not particularly target any specific state, such as New Jersey. For an argument that, with alien defendants, national contacts should suffice in both state courts and federal courts, at least for specific jurisdiction, see Dodge & Dodson, Personal Jurisdiction and Aliens, 116 Mich. L. Rev. 1205 (2018).

Alien corporations may become a more common feature of American litigation due to corporate changes undertaken for tax reasons. In the 21th century, American corporations have sometimes entered into what are called "corporate inversions," by which they acquire foreign companies but rearrange matters so that the foreign company becomes the parent company and the American company becomes, in essence, an alien corporation. These corporate changes are designed to produce tax advantages. See Congressional Budget Office, An Analysis of Corporate Inversions, Sept. 18, 2017. If that means that

such companies can also avoid being subject to the jurisdiction of American courts in a significant number of cases because they are not longer subject to general jurisdiction that renders them subject to suit for injuries incurred outside the U.S., there may be an added dividend beyond tax advantages.

8.   *"General" subject matter jurisdiction:* The term "general jurisdiction" is used to describe a very different concept in connection with subject matter jurisdiction, where we will find that some courts (like the federal courts) are allowed only to hear claims of certain types or involving certain minimum or maximum amounts, while others are courts of "general jurisdiction" and may hear claims of all types. Be careful not to confuse the two ideas.

H. LITIGATING JURISDICTION

Insurance Corporation of Ireland, Ltd. v. Compagnie des Bauxites de Guinee, 456 U.S. 694 (1982):

JUSTICE WHITE delivered the opinion of the Court.

[Compagnie des Bauxites de Guinee, a Delaware corporation owned jointly by a Pennsylvania company and the Republic of Guinee, operated bauxite mines in that country. In connection with those operations, it obtained $20 million worth of business interruption insurance, $10 million from an American insurance company and the additional $10 million ("excess" coverage) from 21 foreign insurers on the London insurance market. As a result of mechanical problems at the mine, it lost over $10 million due to a stoppage of work. When the insurers denied that this loss was covered, Compagnie des Bauxites sued in U.S. District Court in Pennsylvania. The American insurer did not challenge jurisdiction, but the foreign insurers raised lack of jurisdiction as a defense in their answers and moved for summary judgment on that ground. Plaintiffs served discovery asking for copies of all business interruption insurance policies that the foreign insurers had issued covering risks in Pennsylvania or delivered in Pennsylvania. After protracted discovery wrangles, including defendants' offer to make 4 million files available in London, the district court ordered the foreign defendants to produce the requested information in Pennsylvania. When they refused, the district court found it had jurisdiction as a sanction under Rule 37(b)(2)(A). On appeal, defendants argued that the trial court could not bootstrap itself into jurisdiction through use of sanctions if it had no jurisdiction. The Supreme Court affirmed.]

The personal jurisdiction requirement recognizes and protects an individual liberty interest. It represents a restriction on judicial power not as a matter of sovereignty, but as a matter of individual liberty. Thus, the test for personal jurisdiction requires that "the maintenance of the suit . . . not offend 'traditional notions of fair play and substantial justice.'"

International Shoe Co. v. Washington, 326 U.S. 310, 316 (1945), quoting Milliken v. Meyer, 311 U.S. 457, 463 (1940).

Because the requirement of personal jurisdiction represents first of all an individual right, it can, like other such rights, be waived. In McDonald v. Mabee, [243 U.S. 90 (1917)], the Court indicated that regardless of the power of the State to serve process, an individual may submit to the jurisdiction of the court by appearance. A variety of legal arrangements [has] been taken to represent express or implied consent to the personal jurisdiction of the court. In National Equipment Rental, Ltd. v. Szukhent, 375 U.S. 311, 316 (1964), we stated that "parties to a contract may agree in advance to submit to the jurisdiction of a given court," and in Petrowski v. Hawkeye-Security Insurance Co., 350 U.S. 495 (1956), the Court upheld the personal jurisdiction of a District Court on the basis of a stipulation entered into by the defendant. In addition, lower federal courts have found such consent implicit in agreements to arbitrate. Furthermore, the Court has upheld state procedures which find constructive consent to the personal jurisdiction of the state court in the voluntary use of certain state procedures. See Adam v. Saenger, 303 U.S. 59, 67–68 (1938). Finally, unlike subject-matter jurisdiction, which even an appellate court may review sua sponte, under Rule 12(h), Federal Rules of Civil Procedure, "[a] defense of lack of jurisdiction over the person . . . is waived" if not timely raised in the answer or a responsive pleading.

In sum, the requirement of personal jurisdiction may be intentionally waived, or for various reasons a defendant may be estopped from raising the issue. These characteristics portray it for what it is—a legal right protecting the individual. The plaintiff's demonstration of certain historical facts may make clear to the court that it has personal jurisdiction over the defendant as a matter of law—i.e., certain factual showings will have legal consequences—but this is not the only way in which the personal jurisdiction of the court may arise. The actions of the defendant may amount to a legal submission to the jurisdiction of the court, whether voluntary or not.

The expression of legal rights is often subject to certain procedural rules: The failure to follow those rules may well result in a curtailment of the rights. Thus, the failure to enter a timely objection to personal jurisdiction constitutes, under Rule 12(h)(1), a waiver of the objection. A sanction under Rule 37(b)(2)(A) consisting of a finding of personal jurisdiction has precisely the same effect. As a general proposition, the Rule 37 sanction applied to a finding of personal jurisdiction creates no more of a due process problem than the Rule 12 waiver.

[The Court noted that discovery sanctions do not violate due process where they are based upon a presumption of fact that the evidence not produced would support the adversary's position. Instead, due process would be offended only if the sanction were imposed solely to punish a party for disobeying the court's order. See supra p. 439 n. 3.]

Petitioners argue that a sanction consisting of a finding of personal jurisdiction differs from all other instances in which a sanction is imposed * * * because a party need not obey the orders of a court until it is established that the court has personal jurisdiction over that party. If there is no obligation to obey a judicial order, a sanction cannot be applied for the failure to comply. Until the court has established personal jurisdiction, moreover, any assertion of judicial power over the party violates due process.

This argument again assumes that there is something unique about the requirement of personal jurisdiction, which prevents it from being established or waived like other rights. A defendant is always free to ignore the judicial proceedings, risk a default judgment, and then challenge that judgment on jurisdictional grounds in a collateral proceeding. By submitting to the jurisdiction of the court for the limited purpose of challenging jurisdiction, the defendant agrees to abide by that court's determination on the issue of jurisdiction: That decision will be res judicata on that issue in any further proceedings.

NOTES AND QUESTIONS

1.   The Court says that what the foreign insurers did was "a legal submission to the jurisdiction of the court." In *Nicastro*, supra p. 772, Justice Kennedy said that the foreign manufacturer did not "submit" to the jurisdiction of the courts of New Jersey. Are the two cases using the word "submit" in the same sense? When did the objecting defendants in *Bauxites* submit to the court's jurisdiction to decide the personal jurisdiction issue? Cf. Fed.R.Civ.P. 12(h). From that moment on, could they ever have withdrawn that consent?

Contrast Mobile Anesthesiologists Chicago, LLC v. Anesthesia Assoc. of Houston Metroplex, P.A., 623 F.3d 440 (7th Cir. 2010), in which a Chicago anesthesiology business sued a one-doctor Houston-based anesthesiology business as a cybersquatter for using a similar name on his website. Plaintiff had recently opened a Houston office, and its lawyer sent defendant a cease-and-desist letter. That was the first defendant had ever heard of plaintiff. Plaintiff promptly sued defendant in Chicago, scheduling a hearing just three weeks later on its preliminary-injunction request. Three days before that hearing, defendant's Texas lawyer filed a motion to continue the preliminary-injunction hearing to obtain time to prepare for it, and then promptly moved to dismiss for lack of personal jurisdiction. The district court granted the motion to dismiss and plaintiff appealed, arguing that the motion to postpone the preliminary-injunction hearing constituted submission to the jurisdiction of the Chicago court. The appellate court disagreed (id. at 443):

These preliminary actions do not come close to what is required for waiver or forfeiture. To waive or forfeit a personal jurisdiction defense, a defendant must give a plaintiff a reasonable expectation that it will defend the suit on the merits or must cause the court to go to some effort that would be wasted if personal jurisdiction is later found lacking. Faced with an impending preliminary injunction hearing and unable to produce its key witness, [defendant] had the right to ask for more time to learn who was suing it and why without losing its right to object to personal jurisdiction.

See also Hedeen, International, LLC v. Zing Toys, Inc., 811 F.3d 904 (7th Cir. 2016) (failure to respond within 21 days of service of the complaint may be a default, but it does not waive a personal jurisdiction objection).

2.   As *Bauxites* suggests, defendants who wish to challenge personal jurisdiction may have to make some hard choices about how best to protect their rights. Since a judgment entered by a court without jurisdiction is not entitled to full faith and credit, defendant may chose to disregard the litigation, permit its default to be entered, and defend against enforcement of the judgment on the ground it is invalid for lack of jurisdiction. *Pennoyer* shows that the validity of the judgment can be litigated later even in the state that entered the judgment. The problem with this approach is that the defendant may be uncertain about how the jurisdictional question will be resolved, given the elasticity of the minimum contacts calculus. If defendant defaults but is wrong about the first court's jurisdiction, it is too late to defend on the merits when that court's default judgment is enforced elsewhere. Thus, a defendant with a valid defense on the merits takes a risk in permitting its default to be entered.

3.   The alternative, obviously, is to litigate jurisdiction as a defense in the distant court where the first action is filed. Should that obviously be the first choice of most defendants, as it was the choice made by defendants in *Bauxites*? If the distant court rejects the jurisdiction argument, defendant has no remedy except appeal. Baldwin v. Iowa State Traveling Men's Ass'n, 283 U.S. 522 (1931), held that a defendant who has litigated jurisdiction and lost is estopped later to claim that the judgment is not entitled to full faith and credit due to lack of jurisdiction. Cf. Durfee v. Duke, 375 U.S. 106 (1963) (estoppel to relitigate subject matter jurisdiction). But it may not be possible to appeal until after trial. As explained in Chapter 12, in many court systems (including the federal courts) there is no right to appeal pretrial rulings like denial of a motion to dismiss for lack of personal jurisdiction until final judgment is entered. Compare Cal.Code Civ.Proc. § 418.10(c) (requiring that defendant seek immediate review by petitioning an appellate court for a writ of mandate or waive objections to jurisdiction).

Accordingly, the defendant usually will have to put on a defense at trial before getting a chance to persuade an appellate court that defending in this jurisdiction is unfairly burdensome. Of course, defendant can take some solace in the hope that the defense will be successful, thereby ending its worries about the case, while the opportunity to overturn an unsuccessful result on the merits with the jurisdictional argument still exists if the trial turns out unfavorably. It may be, however, that the defendant has no right to such an option. In Western Life Indem. Co. v. Rupp, 235 U.S. 261 (1914), the Court upheld the constitutionality of a state court rule requiring defendant whose objection to jurisdiction was rejected to waive the jurisdiction objection as a precondition to the right to defend on the merits.

4.   As *Bauxites* also makes clear, a defendant must take care to avoid losing its objections to jurisdiction unintentionally. Fed.R.Civ.P. 12(h) requires only that the jurisdiction issue be raised at the first opportunity, whether that be a Rule 12 motion or the answer. State court rules may require a *special appearance* to avoid submitting to the jurisdiction of the court by entering a general appearance. See Tex. R. Civ. P. 120a (special appearance required to object to jurisdiction; any other appearance results in consent to jurisdiction).

Even the right to make a special appearance may be a matter of legislative grace, not constitutional right. In York v. Texas, 137 U.S. 15 (1890), the Court upheld a Texas rule (abandoned in 1962) that even an objection to jurisdiction was a general appearance. Reasoning that the entry of a judgment which is void for lack of jurisdiction deprives defendant of nothing, the Court found no violation of due process in denying defendant the opportunity to contest jurisdiction: "It certainly is more convenient that a defendant be permitted to object to the service, and raise the question of jurisdiction, in the first instance, in the court in which the suit is pending. But mere convenience is not substance of right." This attitude reflects an age in which questions of jurisdiction were thought, under the influence of *Pennoyer*, to be clear cut. How realistic is it today to say that a defendant who loses the right to defend on the merits by guessing wrong about jurisdiction loses nothing? Isn't the right to defend on the merits entitled to some recognition?

5.   Once a proper objection to jurisdiction has been made, there may be factual matters that are uncertain, and discovery in aid of jurisdiction may be available to develop information for use on the jurisdictional challenge, as in *Bauxites*. Was it a mistake for defendants to move to dismiss in *Bauxites*? Should their lawyer have alerted them to the possibility of discovery before they filed their motion?

Should burdensome jurisdictional discovery be a frequent thing? For discussion, see 8 C. Wright, A. Miller & R. Marcus, Federal Practice & Procedure § 2008.3 (3d ed. 2010) (examining discovery regarding various jurisdictional issues). Should discovery similar to the discovery involved in *Bauxites* often be necessary? Recall that general jurisdiction is only allowed at the "home base" of the defendant. Would much discovery be required to ascertain where that is? In Daimler AG v. Bauman, 134 S.Ct. 746 (2014), Justice Sotomayor dissented from the Court's general jurisdiction standard, arguing that the Court had "radically expanded the scope of jurisdictional discovery. Id. at 770. But Justice Ginsburg, writing for the Court, reasoned that "it is hard to see why much in the way of discovery would be needed to determine where a corporation is at home." Id. at 762 n. 20. Would more discovery be needed to evaluate specific jurisdiction?

6.   Finally, a very practical note: It should be clear that jurisdictional issues may often turn on factual material; very often that information is supplied by affidavits prepared by the lawyer for the defendant or its employees to sign. Lawyers should be extremely careful in the preparation of these affidavits. Often they will necessarily describe events that lie at the heart of the substantive dispute between the parties. Whatever the disposition of the jurisdiction issue, the affidavits remain. They are signed under oath by persons who may be critical witnesses at trial. Because they are prepared early in the litigation, at a time when attention is centered on the jurisdictional problem, they may be inexact or incomplete about matters that later prove to be critical to the merits. Accordingly, mark well the adage that early affidavits usually come back to haunt a litigant. Where possible, obtain affidavits from persons who won't be witnesses on the merits. Always draft the affidavits with extreme care.

CONSENT TO SUIT IN FORUM

Entering a general appearance constitutes consent to proceeding in the jurisdiction selected by plaintiff. Defendant may consent to jurisdiction in advance of suit. For example, in National Equipment Rental, Ltd. v. Szukhent, 375 U.S. 311 (1964), two Michigan farmers signed National Equipment's form lease for farm equipment. The form provided that they appointed one Florence Weinberg of Long Island City, New York, their agent "for the purpose of accepting service of any process within the State of New York." They were not acquainted with Weinberg, who was the wife of an officer of National Equipment. When problems developed with the equipment, the farmers stopped paying and National Equipment sued them in New York, serving Ms. Weinberg. The farmers claimed that the agency was not valid, particularly in light of Ms. Weinberg's conflict of interest. In a 5–4 decision, the Court disagreed: "Under well-settled general principles of the law of agency Florence Weinberg's prompt acceptance and transmittal to the respondents of the summons and complaint was itself sufficient to validate the agency, even though there was no explicit previous promise on her part to do so." In dissent, Justice Black decried the invitation to insert such a clause in all form contracts. Should the Court have looked to equality of bargaining power between the parties? Cf. D.H. Overmyer Co. v. Frick Co., 405 U.S. 174 (1972) (consent to entry of judgment without prior notice and hearing valid only if bargained for among parties of equal bargaining power). Should the Court have treated the absence of such a provision in the form franchise agreement as significant in its treatment of the choice of law clause in Burger King Corp. v. Rudzewicz, supra p. 762?

By filing a lawsuit, a plaintiff is deemed to have consented to jurisdiction of the court he has selected with respect to defendant's claims against him. Thus, in Adam v. Saenger, 303 U.S. 59 (1938), the Court held that California's provision that the plaintiff's attorney is his agent for service of process on a cross-complaint sufficed to establish California jurisdiction entitling a default judgment entered on the cross-complaint to full faith and credit in plaintiff's home state of Texas. How broad is this consent? Cf. Fed.R.Civ.P. 13(b). Should it apply to claims asserted against the plaintiff by additional parties brought into the action by the defendant? See Nobel Floral, Inc. v. Pasero, 130 Cal.Rptr.2d 881 (Cal.Ct.App.2003) (nonresident who filed suit in California thereby consented to jurisdiction in a later separate suit in California arising from the same transaction).

In Phillips Petroleum Co. v. Shutts, 472 U.S. 797 (1985), the Court held that a similar consent principle permits nationwide class actions, even though the individual class members do not take action to participate in the suit. It stressed that "States place fewer burdens upon absent class plaintiffs than they do upon absent defendants in nonclass suits" because class members "may sit back and allow the litigation to run its course, content in knowing that there are safeguards provided for his protection." It also noted that counterclaims against unnamed class members are extremely rare.

FORUM SELECTION CLAUSES

Another aspect of consent involves the advance choice of the forum for any possible disputes, commonly called a forum selection clause. In The M/S Bremen v. Zapata Off-Shore Co., 407 U.S. 1 (1972), an American company had entered into such a contract with a German company to tow an oil drilling rig from Louisiana to Italy, designating London as the chosen forum. Notwithstanding, the American company filed an action in a U.S. District Court. Recognizing "present-day commercial realities and expanding international trade," the Supreme Court held that the clause should be enforced and the American suit should be dismissed. So a forum selection clause can trump otherwise valid jurisdiction.

In Carnival Cruise Lines, Inc. v. Shute, 499 U.S. 585 (1991), the Court applied the same reasoning to a forum selection clause that was on the back of a cruise line passenger ticket. Although the passengers came from the state of Washington and the cruise in question originated in Los Angeles, the clause said that any suit had to be filed in Florida. The Court found the clause reasonable because Carnival Cruise Lines had its headquarters in Florida and many of its cruises originated there, and because a cruise line would have a "special interest in limiting the fora in which it could potentially be liable to suit." It also observed that "it stands to reason that passengers who purchase tickets containing a forum clause like that at issue in this case benefit in the form of reduced fares reflecting the savings that the cruise line enjoys." Because the clause was not fundamentally unfair, the Court held that the plaintiffs' suit in Washington had to be dismissed. For an example outside the admiralty area, see Caspi v. The Microsoft Network, 732 A.2d 528 (N.J. Super. Ct.1999) (holding that a forum selection clause in the on-line subscription contract for the Microsoft Network is binding).

Is use of forum selection clauses in consumer contracts fair? For criticism, see Purcell, Geography as a Litigation Weapon: Consumers, Forum-Selection Clauses, and the Rehnquist Court, 40 U.C.L.A.L. Rev. 423 (1992).

I. THE REQUIREMENT OF NOTICE

Recall that in *Pennoyer* it was unclear whether the Due Process clause (which had not even gone into effect at the pertinent time) would require notice to the defendant, and that in Harris v. Balk, supra p. 718, the Court seemed to say that the garnishee, not the plaintiff, had the obligation to give notice to be protected by the binding effect of the judgment.

In Mullane v. Central Hanover Bank & Trust Co., 339 U.S. 306 (1950), the Court directly addressed due process notice requirements. In that case, a bank sought an "accounting," a decision that its handling as trustee of combined trust funds containing bequests being administered for a large number of beneficiaries was proper. The effect of the decree would be to extinguish any right of any beneficiary to sue the bank for mishandling the accounts. The only notice given of the proceeding was publication in a newspaper four times of a brief and cryptic advertisement that did not even identify the beneficiaries. This notice effort could be contrasted with the bank's regular correspondence with many of the beneficiaries to remit income and conduct like business. The Court held that this published notice did not satisfy due process.

The Court began by recognizing that "[p]ersonal service of written notice within the jurisdiction is the classic form of notice always adequate in any type of proceeding," but also that alternative means could be used in situations in which that form is impracticable. The fundamental rule is a realistic one that takes account of the demands of the given situation:

> An elementary and fundamental requirement of due process in any proceeding which is to be accorded finality is notice reasonably calculated, under all the circumstances, to apprise interested parties of the pendency of the action and afford them an opportunity to present their objections. The notice must be of such nature as reasonably to convey the required information, and it must afford a reasonable time for those interested to make their appearance. But if with due regard for the practicalities and peculiarities of the case these conditions are reasonably met the constitutional requirements are satisfied. "The criterion is not the possibility of conceivable injury, but the just and reasonable character of the requirements, having reference to the subject with which the statute deals."

The Court added that "[t]he means employed must be such as one desirous of actually informing the absentee might reasonably adopt to accomplish it." Measured by these standards, the newspaper publication by the bank was inadequate. "Chance alone brings to the attention of even a local resident an advertisement in small type inserted in the back pages of a newspaper, and if he makes his home outside the area of the newspaper's normal circulation the odds that the information will never reach him are large indeed." (Recall that the only notice in *Pennoyer* was publication in a local newspaper.)

The *Mullane* Court recognized that notice in some instances might be "reinforced by steps likely to attract the parties' attention to the proceeding." For example, seizure of tangible property would be likely to come to the owner's attention. Cf. Fuentes v. Shevin, supra p. 31. And it may often be permissible to use constructive means of notice with regard to persons missing or unknown. But the bank had names and addresses for many of the beneficiaries, and as to them "we find no tenable ground for dispensing with a serious effort to inform them personally of the accounting, at least by ordinary mail to the record addresses." Notice to some might often be a reasonable substitute for notice to all:

> The individual interest does not stand alone but is identical with that of a class. The rights of each in the integrity of the fund and the fidelity of the trustee are shared by many other beneficiaries. Therefore notice reasonably certain to reach most of those interested in objecting is likely to safeguard the interests of all, since any objections sustained would inure to the benefit of all. We think that under such circumstances reasonable risks that notice might not actually reach every beneficiary are justifiable.

For a thorough history of *Mullane*, see Leubsdorf, Due Process, Common Trust Funds, and the Class Action Wars, 66 Hast. L.J. 1693 (2015).

NOTES AND QUESTIONS

1.   Although *Mullane* suggested that seizure of property might be sufficient to give notice in *in rem* proceedings, in Walker v. City of Hutchinson, 352 U.S. 112 (1956), the Court held that mailed notice to the owner is required in state condemnation proceedings. Recall that in *Pennoyer* seizure of Neff's property in Oregon to enforce Mitchell's judgment in 1866 did not seem to have brought the case to Neff's attention; Neff did not sue to get title back until 1874.

2.   If the defendant's name and address are known, what means of notice are sufficient? The Court in *Mullane* notes that personal service is the "classic form" of notice, and that first class mail is usually sufficient, but it also acknowledges that posting on property may be sufficient. In Greene v. Lindsey, 456 U.S. 444 (1982), tenants at a public housing project challenged the state processes for serving notice of eviction proceedings. The procedure authorized

posting on the door of the apartment, but plaintiffs offered testimony that notices were often torn off doors, and the trial court so found. On this basis the Court, while recognizing that posting may often be sufficient, found the procedure a denial of due process in plaintiffs' case, and that only mailed notice would suffice. Justice O'Connor retorted in dissent:

> The Court * * * holds that notice via the mails is so far superior to posted notice that the difference is of constitutional dimension. How the Court reaches this judgment remains a mystery, especially since the Court is unable, on the present record, to evaluate the risks that notice mailed to public housing projects might fail due to loss, misdelivery, lengthy delay, or theft. Furthermore, the advantages of the mails over posting, if any, are far from obvious. It is no secret, after all, that unattended mailboxes are subject to plundering by thieves. Moreover, unlike the use of the mails, posting notice at least gives assurance that the notice has gotten as far as the tenant's door.

3.   Due process does not guarantee that notice will be received. In Dusenbery v. United States, 534 U.S. 161 (2002), plaintiff claimed that he was denied due process when certified mail notifying him of a forfeiture proceeding was not actually delivered although correctly addressed to him in the prison where he was incarcerated. The Court rejected his argument because due process "requires only that the Government's effort be 'reasonably calculated' to apprise a party of the pendency of the action." But if the plaintiff learns that a reasonable effort to give notice failed, it may be required to do more. Thus, in Jones v. Flowers, 547 U.S. 220 (2006), when the certified mail notice to Jones of foreclosure for failure to pay taxes was returned by the post office, there was a violation of due process because the state went forward with foreclosure anyway. "Deciding to take no further action is not what someone 'desirous of actually informing' Jones would do; such a person would take further reasonable steps if any were available." At least, the notice could be sent again by regular mail, which does not require a signature at the receiving end.

4.   The Court acknowledges in *Mullane* that notice is not required for those who are too difficult to identify or locate. How much effort is required to identify such persons? In Mennonite Board of Missions v. Adams, 462 U.S. 791 (1983), the Court held that a mortgagee is entitled to notice of proceedings to sell the mortgaged property for nonpayment of taxes. It had no difficulty deciding that the mortgagee was reasonably identifiable:

> In this case, the mortgage on file with the county recorder identified the mortgagee only as "MENNONITE BOARD OF MISSIONS a corporation, of Wayne County, in the State of Ohio." We assume that the mortgagee's address could have been ascertained by reasonably diligent efforts. Simply mailing a letter to "Mennonite Board of Missions, Wayne County, Ohio," quite likely would have provided actual notice, given "the well-known skill of postal officials and employees in making proper delivery of letters defectively addressed." We do not suggest, however, that a government body is required to undertake extraordinary efforts to discover the identity

and whereabouts of a mortgagee whose identity is not in the public record.

How much guidance does this give others trying to decide whether they have made sufficient efforts to locate parties with an interest? Should they ask the court to approve their efforts? In certain kinds of proceedings, such as actions to quiet title and to close an estate, judicial approval is sometimes necessary to establish that sufficient efforts have been made to identify and notify those who are interested.

5.   The *Mullane* Court's recognition that, because the beneficiaries constituted "a class," notice was only required to those who could be identified provided a foundation for Rule 23's notice provisions regarding class actions. See Rule 23(c)(2). In Eisen v. Carlisle & Jacquelin, 417 U.S. 156 (1974), the trial judge certified a class action on behalf of six million persons who traded in odd lots of shares on the New York Stock Exchange (blocks of less than 100 or not in multiples of 100 shares). It directed notice of the action (including the right to opt out) be sent to all individuals who had ten or more such trades during the four years in question and to 5,000 others, selected at random, as well as requiring advertisements in a number of papers. Citing *Mullane*, the Supreme Court held that this did not comply with Fed.R.Civ.P. 23(c)(2), which requires "individual notice to all members who can be identified through reasonable effort." About 2.25 million class members could be identified. Was this notice constitutionally required? Would it be necessary if there were no right to opt out?

MANNER OF SERVING PROCESS

The ordinary way to give the defendant notice of the action is through service of the summons and complaint. On one level, of course, that represents the exercise of the court's power over the individual. When *capias ad respondendum* was the method for exercise of that power, service had to be by the sheriff, in person, and notice was not a problem. Given *Pennoyer*'s emphasis on power, notice remained a secondary consideration. Service of process today is still an exercise of the court's power through the summons, which directs the defendant to file an answer. The primary purpose of service provisions, however, is to guarantee that the defendant gets notice of the suit.

As *Mullane* suggests, the variety of methods available for service of process has increased since the day when only the sheriff could do so. Although state procedures may differ, see Hanna v. Plumer, infra p. 988, Fed.R.Civ.P. 4 touches on most of the likely methods. It allows service to be made in most civil cases by any person not a party who is over the age of 18. Rule 4(c)(2). If the defendant is an individual located in a federal judicial district, Rule 4(e)(1) states that service may be accomplished by any means authorized by the law of the state in which the court in which the suit is pending sits, or by the law of the state in which the person is served. Rule 4(e)(2) also authorizes service by personal delivery, or by leaving the summons and complaint at the defendant's "usual place of abode" with a person of "suitable age and discretion who resides there." Rule 4(f) provides directions for service of individuals in foreign countries, and there are further specifics regarding service on corporations (Rule 4(h)), the United States (Rule 4(i)), foreign governments (Rule 4(j)), and infants and incompetent persons (Rule 4(g)).

Rule 4(d) offers an alternative route: the plaintiff may ask the defendant to waive formal service. Waiving service does not waive any objection to jurisdiction or venue. See Rule 4(d)(5). Rule 4(d)(1) imposes a "duty to avoid unnecessary expenses of serving the summons" on a party who receives notice and a request to waive service in the prescribed way by first class mail. It also rewards the defendant who waives service by according a longer time to answer than defendant would have if formally served. A defendant who fails to waive service in response to a request made pursuant to Rule 4(d) shall be assessed costs, which Rule 4(d)(2) says include the costs subsequently incurred in effecting service in a more traditional way along with a reasonable attorneys' fee incurred for the motion to recover the costs. Some states go even further. See, e.g., Cal.Code Civ.Proc. § 415.40 (summons may be served on person outside state by first-class mail, and service is effective without action of defendant on tenth day after mailing).

Should service by e-mail suffice? The easy answer is that Rule 4 does not presently authorize service of process by e-mail. (Rule 5(b)(2)(E) authorizes use of e-mail to serve later filings in some circumstances.) In Rio Properties, Inc. v. Rio International Interlink, Inc., 284 F.3d 1007 (9th Cir.2002), the court upheld a court order authorizing service of process by e-mail under Rule 4(f)(3) on a company with offices in Costa Rica, but the circumstances were quite unusual. Plaintiff asserted a claim that defendant's gambling Web site infringed the trademark of plaintiff's Las Vegas casino. Plaintiff made a variety of efforts to serve defendant by more conventional means but failed. Indeed, defendant had publicly indicated that it generally preferred communication through its e-mail address to any other means. Under these circumstances, the appellate court ruled, the district judge acted properly in authorizing service by e-mail. See also Lexmark Int'l, Inc. v. INK Technologies Printer Supplies, LLC, 295 F.R.D. 259 (S.D.Ohio 2013) (authorizing service by email). For a case authorizing service via Twitter, see St. Francis Assisi v. Kuwait Fin. House, 2016 WL 5725002 (N.D. Cal., Sept. 30, 2016).

For service on a person in another country, the Hague Convention may limit the manner of service permitted. But in Water Splash, Inc. v. Menon, 137 S.Ct. 1504 (2017), the Court held that, because the Convention uses the verb "send" in connection with service of process, service by mail on a defendant residing in Canada was not forbidden by the Convention. Compare Elboied v. Baylock, 299 F.R.D. 105 (E.D.Pa.2014) (holding that the Hague Convention does not allow service by email on a person living in Switzerland).

The person who serves the summons and complaint then makes out a proof of service (Rule 4(*l*)) attesting that service has been accomplished and how it was done. This document is filed, which may be important because Rule 4(m) provides that the action is subject to dismissal unless service is accomplished within 120 days of filing of the action.

As Rule 12(b)(5) indicates, a defendant who does not waive service can contest the sufficiency of service, and such a contest can raise a variety of factual issues. Where, for example, is defendant's "usual place of abode"? Was it sufficient to leave the summons and complaint with the secretary of the president of the defendant corporation? The variety of factual disputes that can arise is beyond the scope of this book, but it is worth noting that courts in general are not receptive to arguments about the manner of service made by defendants who clearly have received notice of the action (although they may be receptive to defendant's objections to the jurisdiction of the court). Where default is involved, however, they are more likely to entertain arguments about whether the manner of service actually gave defendant notice of the suit.

J. VENUE

Venue, meaning place of trial, places a further geographical limitation on plaintiff's options in selecting a forum. Although "[t]erritorial jurisdiction and venue were largely indistinguishable concepts for more than the first half of the existence of the federal courts," Clermont, Restating Territorial Jurisdiction and Venue for State and Federal Courts, 66 Cornell L.Rev. 411, 430 (1981), due to relaxation of restrictions on jurisdiction federal venue requirements now place an additional hurdle in the plaintiff's way. Indeed, some have gone so far as to suggest that "[j]urisdiction must become venue." Ehrenzweig, From State Jurisdiction to Interstate Venue, 50 Ore.L.Rev. 103, 113 (1971).

Before federal venue requirements were adopted, all states had venue provisions of their own, usually limiting the counties in which suit could be brought. Although there are some variations, these statutes tend to look to one or more of the following factors: (1) the location of property involved in the action, (2) the place where the cause of action arose, (3) the location of some particular event or fact, (4) defendant's residence, (5) plaintiff's residence, (6) defendant's place of business, and (7) plaintiff's place of business. See generally Stevens, Venue Statutes: Diagnosis and Proposed Cure, 49 Mich.L.Rev. 307 (1951).

Read 28 U.S.C. §§ 1390 and 1391 and consider the factors employed there. The Supreme Court has explained that "[i]n most instances, the purpose of statutorily specified venue is to protect the defendant against the risk that a plaintiff will select an unfair or inconvenient place of trial." Leroy v. Great Western United Corp., 443 U.S. 173, 183–84 (1979). Before 1966, venue in federal court generally turned on residence of defendants, but this produced "venue gaps" when there was no state in which all defendants resided. In 1966 Congress sought to solve this problem by authorizing venue in the district "where the claim arose." This provision was changed, in turn, in 1990, and the venue statute was further revised in 2011.

BATES v. C & S ADJUSTERS, INC.

United States Court of Appeals, Second Circuit, 1992
980 F.2d 865

Before: OAKES, NEWMAN, and PIERCE, CIRCUIT JUDGES.

JON O. NEWMAN, CIRCUIT JUDGE:

This appeal concerns venue in an action brought under the Fair Debt Collection Practices Act, 15 U.S.C. §§ 1692–1692o (1988). Specifically, the issue is whether venue exists in a district in which the debtor resides and to which a bill collector's demand for payment was forwarded. The issue arises on an appeal by Phillip E. Bates from the May 21, 1992, judgment of the District Court for the Western District of New York, dismissing his complaint because of improper venue. We conclude that venue was proper under 28 U.S.C. § 1391(b)(2) and therefore reverse and remand.

Bates commenced this action in the Western District of New York upon receipt of a collection notice from C & S Adjusters, Inc. ("C & S"). Bates alleged violations of the Fair Debt Collection Practices Act, and demanded statutory damages, costs, and attorney's fees. The facts relevant to venue are not in dispute. Bates incurred the debt in question while he was a resident of the Western District of Pennsylvania. The creditor, a corporation with its principal place of business in that District, referred the account to C & S, a local collection agency which transacts no regular business in New York. Bates had meanwhile moved to the Western District of New York. When C & S mailed a collection notice to Bates at his Pennsylvania address, the Postal Service forwarded the notice to Bates' new address in New York.

In its answer, C & S asserted two affirmative defenses and also counterclaimed for costs, alleging that the action was instituted in bad faith and for purposes of harassment. C & S subsequently filed a motion to dismiss for improper venue, which the District Court granted.

1.   VENUE AND THE 1990 AMENDMENTS TO 28 U.S.C. § 1391(b)

Bates concedes that the only plausible venue provision for this action is 28 U.S.C. § 1391(b)(2), which allows an action to be brought in "a judicial district in which a substantial part of the events or omissions giving rise to the claim occurred." Prior to 1990, section 1391 allowed for venue in "the judicial district . . . in which the claim arose." 28 U.S.C. § 1391(b) (1988). This case represents our first opportunity to consider the significance of the 1990 amendments.

Prior to 1966, venue was proper in federal question cases, absent a special venue statute, only in the defendant's state of citizenship. If a plaintiff sought to sue multiple defendants who were citizens of different states, there might be no district where the entire action could be brought. Congress closed this "venue gap" by adding a provision allowing suit in the district "in which the claim arose." This phrase gave rise to a variety of conflicting interpretations. Some courts thought it meant that there could be only one such district; others believed there could be several. Different tests developed, with courts looking for "substantial contacts," the "weight of contacts," the place of injury or performance, or even to the boundaries of personal jurisdiction under state law.

The Supreme Court gave detailed attention to section 1391(b) in Leroy v. Great Western United Corp., 443 U.S. 173 (1979). The specific holding of *Leroy* was that Great Western, a Texas corporation, which had attempted to take over an Idaho corporation, could not bring suit in Texas against Idaho officials who sought to enforce a state anti-takeover law. Although the effect of the Idaho officials' action might be felt in Texas, the Court rejected this factor as a basis for venue, since it would allow the Idaho officials to be sued anywhere a shareholder of the target corporation could allege that he wanted to accept Great Western's tender offer. The Court made several further observations: (1) the purpose of the 1966 statute was to close venue gaps and should not be read more broadly than necessary to close those gaps; (2) the general purpose of the venue statute was to protect defendants against an unfair or inconvenient trial location; (3) location of evidence and witnesses was a relevant factor; (4) familiarity of the Idaho federal judges with the Idaho anti-takeover statute was a relevant factor; (5) plaintiff's convenience was not a relevant factor; and (6) in only rare cases should there be more than one district in which a claim can be said to arise.

Subsequent to *Leroy* and prior to the 1990 amendment to section 1391(b), most courts have applied at least a form of the "weight of contacts" test. Courts continued to have difficulty in determining whether more than one district could be proper.

Against this background, we understand Congress' 1990 amendment to be at most a marginal expansion of the venue provision. The House Report indicates that the new language was first proposed by the American Law Institute in a 1969 Study, and observes:

The great advantage of referring to the place where things happened . . . is that it avoids the litigation breeding phrase "in which the claim arose." It also avoids the problem created by the frequent cases in which substantial parts of the underlying events have occurred in several districts.

H.R.Rep. No. 734, 101st Cong., 2d Sess. 23, reprinted in 1990 U.S.C.C.A.N. 6860, 6869. Thus it seems clear that *Leroy*'s strong admonition against recognizing multiple venues has been disapproved. Many of the factors in *Leroy*—for instance, the convenience of defendants and the location of evidence and witnesses—are most useful in distinguishing between two or more plausible venues. Since the new statute does not, as a general matter, require the District Court to determine the best venue, these factors will be of less significance. Apart from this point, however, *Leroy* and other precedents remain important sources of guidance.

2.   FAIR DEBT COLLECTION PRACTICES ACT

Under the version of the venue statute in force from 1966 to 1990, at least three District Courts held that venue was proper under the Fair Debt Collection Practices Act in the plaintiff's home district if a collection agency had mailed a collection notice to an address in that district or placed a phone call to a number in that district. None of these cases involved the unusual fact, present in this case, that the defendant did not deliberately direct a communication to the plaintiff's district.

We conclude, however, that this difference is inconsequential, at least under the current venue statute. The statutory standard for venue focuses not on whether a defendant has made a deliberate contact—a factor relevant in the analysis of personal jurisdiction[1]—but on the location where events occurred. Under the new version of section 1391(b)(2), we must determine only whether a "substantial part of the events . . . giving rise to the claim" occurred in the Western District of New York.

In adopting this statute, Congress was concerned about the harmful effect of abusive debt practices on consumers. See 15 U.S.C. § 1692(a) ("Abusive debt collection practices contribute to the number of personal bankruptcies, to marital instability, to the loss of jobs, and to invasions of individual privacy."). This harm does not occur until receipt of the collection notice. Indeed, if the notice were lost in the mail, it is unlikely that a violation of the Act would have occurred.[2] Moreover, a debt collection agency sends its dunning letters so that they will be received. Forwarding such letters to the district to which a debtor has moved is an important

---

[1]   C & S has waived whatever claim it might have had that the District Court lacked personal jurisdiction over it. Waiver resulted from C & S's failure to allege lack of personal jurisdiction in its answer or motion to dismiss. See Fed. R. Civ. P. 12(b)(2), (h).

[2]   Although we need not decide the issue today, we note that at least one court has indicated that a plaintiff's cause of action might not accrue until receipt of the collection notice for purposes of the Act's one-year statute of limitations. 15 U.S.C. § 1692k(d) (1988). See Seabrook v. Onondaga Bureau of Medical Economists, Inc., 705 F.Supp. 82, 83 (N.D.N.Y.1989) ("more likely" that statute would start to run only "on the date the debtor received the communication"). But see Mattson v. U.S. West Communications, Inc., 967 F.2d 259, 261 (8th Cir. 1992) (statute starts to run on date of mailing); Drumright v. Collection Recovery, Inc., 500 F.Supp. 1 (M.D.Tenn.1980) (statute starts to rule on date of mailing for some violations).

step in the collection process. If the bill collector prefers not to be challenged for its collection practices outside the district of a debtor's original residence, the envelope can be marked "do not forward." We conclude that receipt of a collection notice is a substantial part of the events giving rise to a claim under the Fair Debt Collection Practices Act.

The relevant factors identified in *Leroy* add support to our conclusion. Although "bona fide error" can be a defense to liability under the Act, 15 U.S.C. § 1692k(c), the alleged violations of the Act turn largely not on the collection agency's intent, but on the content of the collection notice. The most relevant evidence—the collection notice—is located in the Western District of New York. Because the collection agency appears not to have marked the notice with instructions not to forward, and has not objected to the assertion of personal jurisdiction, trial in the Western District of New York would not be unfair.

NOTES AND QUESTIONS

1. Defendant C & S is a corporation. Why isn't its venue objection overcome by 28 U.S.C. § 1391(c)(2)? Note that under this provision venue has become jurisdiction rather than the other way around, as Professor Ehrenzweig urged (see supra p. 842). Should venue provide greater limits on suits against non-corporate defendants than personal jurisdiction requirements?

As interpreted by the Second Circuit, how does the venue requirement of § 1391(b)(2) compare to personal jurisdiction analysis? Could it be said that defendant C & S purposefully availed with respect to New York in a way that would support jurisdiction in New York? Would it be important that under some views (see the court's footnote 2) the claim was not actionable until receipt of the letter?

2. Before the 2011 amendment, § 1391 made no special provision for determining residence for entities other than corporations. See Denver and Rio Grande Western R.R. Co. v. Brotherhood of Railroad Trainmen, 387 U.S. 556 (1967) (holding that Congress left it to the courts to determine the residency of a labor union). § 1391(c)(2) now provides statutory guidance regarding venue for any "entity with the capacity to sue or be sued in its common name under the applicable law." What does that mean? See Rule 17(b)(3) (providing direction to determine which state's law should be used to determine whether a partnership or unincorporated association may sue or be sued in its common name).

The amended statute does continue to treat corporations somewhat differently in § 1391(d), which carries forward provisions for states with multiple districts and directs the court to determine whether the contacts with its district would be sufficient to subject the corporate defendant to personal jurisdiction if the district were a separate state. If not, the court is to determine which district in the state has "the most significant contacts." How readily can this be done? Consider, for example, the distinction between the Southern

District of New York (Manhattan) and the Eastern District of New York (Brooklyn).

3.   For a "natural person" (a human being), § 1391(c)(1) provides that the court should look to the person's domicile as the residence for venue purposes. This provision resolved a split among the lower courts, some of which suggested the possibility that the state in which a person had a summer home could also be the residence for venue purposes. See H. Rep. No. 112–10 pp. 20–21 (2011) (explaining the use of "domicile"). We will see that the same concept governs diversity of citizenship subject-matter jurisdiction. See infra pp. 875–877. The treatment for venue purposes should be essentially the same. § 1391(c)(1) includes "an alien lawfully admitted for permanent residence in the United States." Thus, such a person may object to venue in any district not her residence. Contrast § 1391(c)(3) for "a defendant not resident in the United States." The diversity-jurisdiction statute also has applications specific to such people.

4.   Is the court's application of § 1391(b)(2) in *Bates* persuasive? Consider the explanation of this provision offered by another court: "[T]he current statutory language still favors the defendant in a venue dispute by requiring that the events or omissions supporting a claim be 'substantial.' Events or omissions that might only have some tangential connection with the dispute in litigation are not enough. * * * The test for determining venue is not the defendant's 'contacts' with a particular district, but rather the location of those 'events or omissions giving rise to the claim,' theoretically a more easily demonstrable circumstance than where a 'claim arose.' " Cottman Transmission Systems, Inc. v. Martino, 36 F.3d 291 (3d Cir.1994). Compare the Supreme Court's decision in *Leroy*, discussed in the court's opinion. In that case, Idaho officials acting pursuant to an Idaho anti-takeover law directed a cease and desist order to a company headquartered in Texas to prevent it from undertaking an impending tender offer for shares of a company with substantial Idaho operations. The company sued in Texas, asserting that the Idaho officials lacked authority to prevent the tender offer. Would the result be the same under the new statute?

5.   For a contrast to *Bates*, consider Database America, Inc. v. Bellsouth Advertising & Publishing Corp., 825 F.Supp. 1216 (D.N.J.1993). Plaintiff, a New Jersey company, was in the business of marketing information drawn from a number of sources including the telephone yellow pages. Defendant, which compiles and publishes yellow pages for nine southeastern states, sent a letter to plaintiff asserting that plaintiff was violating defendant's copyright and instructing plaintiff to stop doing so. Plaintiff responded with a suit in New Jersey seeking a declaratory judgment that it had not infringed or that the copyright was not valid. The court concluded that venue was not proper under § 1392(b)(2):

> [I]t is difficult to accept the assertion that merely sending a cease and desist letter into a forum, in a declaratory judgment action for non-infringement and/or copyright invalidity, constitutes "substantial" activity as the term is used in Section 1391(b)(2). While such a letter

> may provoke an alleged infringer to file such a lawsuit, the letter
> itself has nothing to do with whether the copyright is valid or whether
> infringement has occurred. In other words, * * * the cease and desist
> letter does not constitute a "substantial" activity "giving rise to the
> claim[s]."

Id. at 1225. The court emphasized that the only elements of copyright
infringement are ownership of a valid copyright and copying of parts of an
original copyrighted work, and concluded that all such activities by defendant
had occurred in Georgia, where it was headquartered. But usually in an action
for declaratory relief the plaintiff must demonstrate that there is a genuine
controversy between the parties; wouldn't the cease and desist letter matter
for that? Does the nature of the claim asserted in *Bates* lead to a different
result? See also Gulf Ins. Co. v. Glasbrenner, 417 F.3d 353 (2d Cir. 2005) ("for
venue to be proper, *significant* events or omissions *material* to the plaintiff's
claim must have occurred in the district in question, even if other material
events occurred elsewhere").

    6.   In other instances, the new statute may create difficulties similar to
those we have already encountered in jurisdiction cases. "The ALI's test for
transactional venue is more liberal than the 'in which the claim arose' test, but
hardly comes warranted as less likely to be 'litigation breeding.' " Oakley,
Recent Statutory Changes in the Law of Federal Jurisdiction and Venue: The
Judicial Improvements Acts of 1988 and 1990, 24 U.C.Davis L.Rev. 735, 775
(1991). Consider:

    Where does an "omission" occur? In Burger King Corp. v. Rudzewicz
(supra p. 762), would it be fair to say that defendant's failure to make payments
that the contract said should be made in Florida was an omission in Florida?
Compare Cottman Transmission Systems, Inc. v. Martino, 36 F.3d 291 (3d Cir.
1994), in which plaintiff franchisor claimed that defendant franchisee had
violated his contract by continuing to operate transmission repair facilities in
Michigan, thereby violating plaintiff's trademark rights. The court held that
defendant's alleged failure to pay license fees in Pennsylvania, where plaintiff
was headquartered, and his failure to return advertising items to
Pennsylvania, did not support venue in Pennsylvania. "The omissions that
Cottman cites—Martino's failure to return various materials and failure to
remit payments—actually occurred in Michigan, not in Pennsylvania. Even
though the result was Cottman's non-receipt of those items in Pennsylvania,
the omissions bringing about this result actually occurred in Michigan." Id. at
295.

    Where does an "event" occur? In Calder v. Jones (supra p. 756), did the
events occur in Florida, where the allegedly defamatory story was written and
published, or in California, where the defamation was circulated? When the
action upon which the claim is based has been done on the Internet, where
should venue treat it as having occurred?

    What events or omissions "give rise to" a claim so as to matter for venue
purposes? Should inquiry be limited to those that form a basis for liability

under the applicable substantive law? Should events not essential to liability be disregarded? Should only matters that are properly included in the complaint be considered?

What is a "substantial part" of these events or omissions? In proposing this standard, the American Law Institute admitted that "[i]t is true that there may be controversy over what constitutes 'a substantial part,'" but concluded that this prospect did not matter because "this is most likely to occur when a plaintiff is taking a deliberate chance in an effort to gain a desired forum." In Keeton v. Hustler Magazine (supra p. 759 n. 2), plaintiff sued in New Hampshire although only a small portion of defendant's sales containing the allegedly defamatory article occurred there. Was that a substantial part? If not, were the sales of National Enquirers in California a substantial part in Calder v. Jones (supra p. 756)?

7.   What is the focus of the § 1391(b)(3), sometimes called the fallback option? In Atlantic Marine Constr. Co. v. U.S. District Court, 571 U.S. 49 (2013), the Court explained that it "reflect[s] Congress' intent that venue should always lie in *some* federal court whenever federal courts have personal jurisdiction over the defendant. [It] ensures that so long as a federal court has personal jurisdiction over a defendant, venue will always lie somewhere."

8.   Besides the general venue statute, Congress has provided special venue provisions in a number of areas. See generally 15 C. Wright, A. Miller & E. Cooper, Federal Practice & Procedure §§ 3816–25. Sometimes those provisions may constrict available venues. For example, in TC Heartland LLC v. Kraft Foods Group Brands LLC, 137 S.Ct. 1514 (2017), the Court held that 28 U.S.C. § 1400(b), the special venue statute for patent cases, was narrower than § 1391(c), because it said that venue is allowed only where a domestic corporation "resides," which means its state of incorporation.

9.   Note that if personal jurisdiction can be obtained but the federal venue limitations preclude suit in a federal court, it may still be possible to sue in state court if the venue rules are different there.

10.   *Local actions*: Until 2011, there were different venue rules for "local actions" involving real property and "transitory actions." Those distinctions have been abolished. See § 1391(a)(2).

K. DISCRETIONARY DECLINE OF JURISDICTION

PIPER AIRCRAFT CO. v. REYNO
Supreme Court of the United States, 1981
454 U.S. 235

JUSTICE MARSHALL delivered the opinion of the Court.

These cases arise out of an air crash that took place in Scotland. Respondent, acting as representative of the estates of several Scottish citizens killed in the accident, brought wrongful-death actions against petitioners that were ultimately transferred to the United States District

Court for the Middle District of Pennsylvania. Petitioners moved to dismiss on the ground of forum non conveniens. After noting that an alternative forum existed in Scotland, the District Court granted their motions. The United States Court of Appeals for the Third Circuit reversed. The Court of Appeals based its decision, at least in part, on the ground that dismissal is automatically barred where the law of the alternative forum is less favorable to the plaintiff than the law of the forum chosen by the plaintiff. Because we conclude that the possibility of an unfavorable change in law should not, by itself, bar dismissal, and because we conclude that the District Court did not otherwise abuse its discretion, we reverse.

I

A

In July 1976, a small commercial aircraft crashed in the Scottish highlands during the course of a charter flight from Blackpool to Perth. The pilot and five passengers were killed instantly. The decedents were all Scottish subjects and residents, as are their heirs and next of kin. There were no eyewitnesses to the accident. At the time of the crash the plane was subject to Scottish air traffic control.

The aircraft, a twin-engine Piper Aztec, was manufactured in Pennsylvania by petitioner Piper Aircraft Co. (Piper). The propellers were manufactured in Ohio by petitioner Hartzell Propeller, Inc. (Hartzell). At the time of the crash the aircraft was registered in Great Britain and was owned and maintained by Air Navigation and Trading Co., Ltd. (Air Navigation). It was operated by McDonald Aviation, Ltd. (McDonald), a Scottish air taxi service. Both Air Navigation and McDonald were organized in the United Kingdom. The wreckage of the plane is now in a hangar in Farnsborough, England.

The British Department of Trade investigated the accident shortly after it occurred. A preliminary report found that the plane crashed after developing a spin, and suggested that mechanical failure in the plane or the propeller was responsible. At Hartzell's request, this report was reviewed by a three-member Review Board, which held a 9-day adversary hearing attended by all interested parties. The Review Board found no evidence of defective equipment and indicated that pilot error may have contributed to the accident. The pilot, who had obtained his commercial pilot's license only three months earlier, was flying over high ground at an altitude considerably lower than the minimum height required by his company's operations manual.

In July 1977, a California probate court appointed respondent Gaynell Reyno administratrix of the estates of the five passengers. Reyno is not related to and does not know any of the decedents or their survivors; she was a legal secretary to the attorney who filed this lawsuit. Several days after her appointment, Reyno commenced separate wrongful-death actions against Piper and Hartzell in the Superior Court of California, claiming negligence and strict liability. Air Navigation, McDonald, and the estate of the pilot are not parties to this litigation. The survivors of the five passengers whose estates are represented by Reyno filed a separate action in the United Kingdom against Air Navigation, McDonald, and the pilot's estate. Reyno candidly admits that the action against Piper and Hartzell was filed in the United States because its laws regarding liability, capacity to sue, and damages are more favorable to her position than are those of Scotland. Scottish law does not recognize strict liability in tort. Moreover, it permits wrongful-death actions only when brought by a decedent's relatives. The relatives may sue only for "loss of support and society."

On petitioners' motion, the suit was removed to the United States District Court for the Central District of California. Piper then moved for transfer to the United States District Court for the Middle District of Pennsylvania, pursuant to 28 U.S.C. § 1404(a). Hartzell moved to dismiss for lack of personal jurisdiction, or in the alternative, to transfer.[5] In December 1977, the District Court quashed service on Hartzell and transferred the case to the Middle District of Pennsylvania. Respondent then properly served process on Hartzell.

B

In May 1978, after the suit had been transferred, both Hartzell and Piper moved to dismiss the action on the ground of forum non conveniens. The District Court granted these motions in October 1979. It relied on the balancing test set forth by this Court in Gulf Oil Corp. v. Gilbert, 330 U.S. 501 (1947), and its companion case, Koster v. Lumbermens Mut. Cas. Co., 330 U.S. 518 (1947). In those decisions, the Court stated that a plaintiff's choice of forum should rarely be disturbed. However, when an alternative forum has jurisdiction to hear the case, and when trial in the chosen forum would "establish . . . oppressiveness and vexation to a defendant . . . out of all proportion to plaintiff's convenience," or when the "chosen forum [is] inappropriate because of considerations affecting the court's own administrative and legal problems," the court may, in the exercise of its sound discretion, dismiss the case. Koster, supra, at 524. To guide trial court discretion, the Court provided a list of "private interest factors" affecting the convenience of the litigants, and a list of "public interest factors" affecting the convenience of the forum. Gilbert, supra, 330 U.S. at 508–509.[6]

---

[5]   The District Court concluded that it could not assert personal jurisdiction over Hartzell consistent with due process. However, it decided not to dismiss Hartzell because the corporation would be amenable to process in Pennsylvania.

[6]   The factors pertaining to the private interests of the litigants included the "relative ease of access to sources of proof; availability of compulsory process for attendance of unwilling, and the cost of obtaining attendance of willing, witnesses; possibility of view of premises, if view would be appropriate to the action; and all other practical problems that make trial of a case easy, expeditious and inexpensive." *Gilbert*, 330 U.S., at 508. The public factors bearing on the question

[The district court granted the motion. With regard to private interests, it acknowledged that evidence about the design and manufacture of the plane was in the United States, but otherwise found the connections with Scotland "compelling." Moreover, it found plaintiffs choice of forum unimportant since all the real parties in interest were foreign. Concerning public interests, it determined that Pennsylvania law would apply to the claim against Piper and Scottish law to the claim against Hartzell.[8] This disparity, it concluded, would confuse the jury and, to the extent Scottish law had to be applied, the court as well.]

C

On appeal, the United States Court of Appeals for the Third Circuit reversed and remanded for trial. The decision to reverse appears to be based on two alternative grounds. First, the Court held that the District Court abused its discretion in conducting the Gilbert analysis. Second, the Court held that dismissal is never appropriate where the law of the alternative forum is less favorable to the plaintiff. [The appellate court bolstered this point by deciding that American law would apply to the claims against both defendants.[10]]

II

The Court of Appeals erred in holding that plaintiffs may defeat a motion to dismiss on the ground of forum non conveniens merely by showing that the substantive law that would be applied in the alternative forum is less favorable to the plaintiffs than that of the present forum. The possibility of a change in substantive law should ordinarily not be given conclusive or even substantial weight in the forum non conveniens inquiry.

---

included the administrative difficulties flowing from court congestion; the "local interest in having localized controversies decided at home"; the interest in having the trial of a diversity case in a forum that is at home with the law that must govern the action; the avoidance of unnecessary problems in conflict of laws, or in the application of foreign law; and the unfairness of burdening citizens of an unrelated forum with jury duty.

[8]   Under Klaxon v. Stentor Electric Mfg. Co., 313 U.S. 487 (1941), a court ordinarily must apply the choice-of-law rules of the State in which it sits. However, where a case is transferred pursuant to 28 U.S.C. § 1404(a), it must apply the choice-of-law rules of the State from which the case was transferred. Van Dusen v. Barrack, 376 U.S. 612 (1964). Relying on these two cases, the District Court concluded that California choice-of-law rules would apply to Piper, and Pennsylvania choice-of-law rules would apply to Hartzell. It further concluded that California applied a "governmental interests" analysis in resolving choice-of-law problems, and that Pennsylvania employed a "significant contacts" analysis. The court used the "governmental interests" analysis to determine that Pennsylvania rules would apply to Piper, and the "significant contacts" analysis to determine that Scottish liability rules would apply to Hartzell. [This is the Court's footnote—Eds.]

[10]   The Court of Appeals agreed with the District Court that California choice-of-law rules applied to Piper, and that Pennsylvania choice-of-law rules applied to Hartzell, see no. 8, supra. It did not agree, however that California used a "governmental interests" analysis and that Pennsylvania used a "significant contacts" analysis. Rather, it believed that both jurisdictions employed the "false conflicts" test. Applying this test, it concluded that Ohio and Pennsylvania had greater policy interests in the dispute than Scotland, and that American law would apply to both Piper and Hartzell. [This is the Court's footnote—Eds.]

We expressly rejected the position adopted by the Court of Appeals in our decision in Canada Malting Co. v. Paterson Steamships, 285 U.S. 413 (1932). That case arose out of a collision between two vessels in American waters. The Canadian owners of cargo lost in the accident sued the Canadian owners of one of the vessels in Federal District Court. The cargo owners chose an American court in large part because the relevant American liability rules were more favorable than the Canadian rules. The District Court dismissed on grounds of forum non conveniens. The plaintiffs argued that dismissal was inappropriate because Canadian laws were less favorable to them. This Court nonetheless affirmed:

> "We have no occasion to enquire by what law the rights of the parties are governed, as we are of the opinion that, under any view of that question, it lay within the discretion of the District Court to decline to assume jurisdiction over the controversy. . . . '[T]he court will not take cognizance of the case if justice would be as well done by remitting the parties to their home forum.' "

The Court further stated that "[t]here was no basis for the contention that the District Court abused its discretion."

* * *

In fact, if conclusive or substantial weight were given to the possibility of a change in law, the forum non conveniens doctrine would become virtually useless. Jurisdiction and venue requirements are often easily satisfied. As a result, many plaintiffs are able to choose from among several forums. Ordinarily, these plaintiffs will select that forum whose choice-of-law rules are most advantageous. Thus, if the possibility of an unfavorable change in substantive law is given substantial weight in the forum non conveniens inquiry, dismissal would rarely be proper.

* * *

At least where the foreign plaintiff named an American manufacturer as defendant,[17] a court could not dismiss the case on grounds of forum non conveniens where dismissal might lead to an unfavorable change in law. The American courts, which are already extremely attractive to foreign plaintiffs, would become even more attractive. The flow of litigation into the United States would increase and further congest already crowded courts.

The Court of Appeals based its decision, at least in part, on an analogy between dismissals on grounds of forum non conveniens and transfers between federal courts pursuant to § 1404(a). In Van Dusen v. Barrack,

---

[17] In fact, the defendants might not even have to be American. A foreign plaintiff seeking damages for an accident that occurred abroad might be able to obtain service of process on a foreign defendant who does business in the United States. Under the Court of Appeals' holding, dismissal would be barred if the law of the alternative forum were less favorable to the plaintiff—even though none of the parties are American, and even though there is absolutely no nexus between the subject matter of the litigation and the United States.

376 U.S. 612 (1964), this Court ruled that a § 1404(a) transfer should not result in a change in the applicable law. Relying on dictum in an earlier Third Circuit opinion interpreting Van Dusen, the court below held that principle is also applicable to a dismissal on forum non conveniens grounds. However, § 1404(a) transfers are different than dismissals on the ground of forum non conveniens.

Congress enacted § 1404(a) to permit change of venue between federal courts. Although the statute was drafted in accordance with the doctrine of forum non conveniens, it was intended to be a revision rather than a codification of the common law. Norwood v. Kirkpatrick, 349 U.S. 29 (1955). District courts were given more discretion to transfer under § 1404(a) than they had to dismiss on grounds of forum non conveniens. The reasoning employed in Van Dusen v. Barrack is simply inapplicable to dismissals on grounds of forum non conveniens. That case did not discuss the common-law doctrine. Rather, it focused on "the construction and application" of § 1404(a). Emphasizing the remedial purpose of the statute, *Barrack* concluded that Congress could not have intended a transfer to be accompanied by a change in law. The statute was designed as a "federal housekeeping measure," allowing easy change of venue within a unified federal system. The Court feared that if a change in venue were accompanied by a change in law, forum-shopping parties would take unfair advantage of the relaxed standards for transfer. The rule was necessary to ensure the just and efficient operation of the statute.

We do not hold that the possibility of an unfavorable change in law should never be a relevant consideration in a forum non conveniens inquiry. Of course, if the remedy provided by the alternative forum is so clearly inadequate or unsatisfactory that it is no remedy at all, the unfavorable change in law may be given substantial weight; the district court may conclude that dismissal would not be in the interests of justice.[22] In these cases, however, the remedies that would be provided by the Scottish courts do not fall within this category. Although the relatives of the decedents may not be able to rely on a strict liability theory, and although their potential damages award may be smaller, there is no danger that they will be deprived of any remedy or treated unfairly.

---

[22] At the outset of any forum non conveniens inquiry, the court must determine whether there exists an alternative forum. Ordinarily, this requirement will be satisfied when the defendant is "amenable to process" in the other jurisdiction. *Gilbert*, 330 U.S., at 506–507. In rare circumstances, however, where the remedy offered by the other forum is clearly unsatisfactory, the other forum may not be an adequate alternative, and the initial requirement may not be satisfied. Thus, for example, dismissal would not be appropriate where the alternative forum does not permit litigation of the subject matter of the dispute. Cf. Phoenix Canada Oil Co., Ltd. v. Texaco, Inc, 78 F.R.D. 445 (Del.1978) (court refuses to dismiss, where alternative forum is Ecuador, it is unclear whether Ecuadorean tribunal will hear the case, and there is no generally codified Ecuadorean legal remedy for the unjust enrichment and tort claims asserted).

III

The Court of Appeals also erred in rejecting the District Court's Gilbert analysis. The Court of Appeals stated that more weight should have been given to the plaintiff's choice of forum, and criticized the District Court's analysis of the private and public interests. However, the District Court's decision regarding the deference due plaintiff's choice of forum was appropriate. Furthermore, we do not believe that the District Court abused its discretion in weighing the private and public interests.

A

The District Court acknowledged that there is ordinarily a strong presumption in favor of the plaintiff's choice of forum, which may be overcome only when the private and public interest factors clearly point towards trial in the alternative forum. It held, however, that the presumption applies with less force when the plaintiff or real parties in interest are foreign.

The District Court's distinction between resident or citizen plaintiffs and foreign plaintiffs is fully justified. In Koster, the Court indicated that a plaintiff's choice of forum is entitled to greater deference when the plaintiff has chosen the home forum. 330 U.S., at 524.[23] When the home forum has been chosen, it is reasonable to assume that this choice is convenient. When the plaintiff is foreign, however, this assumption is much less reasonable. Because the central purpose of any forum non conveniens inquiry is to ensure that the trial is convenient, a foreign plaintiff's choice deserves less deference.[24]

B

The forum non conveniens determination is committed to the sound discretion of the trial court. It may be reversed only when there has been a clear abuse of discretion; where the court has considered all relevant public and private interest factors, and where its balancing of these factors is reasonable, its decision deserves substantial deference.

(1)

In analyzing the private interest factors, the District Court stated that the connections with Scotland are "overwhelming." This characterization

---

[23] Citizens or residents deserve somewhat more deference than foreign plaintiffs, but dismissal should not be automatically barred when a plaintiff has filed suit in his home forum. As always, if the balance of conveniences suggests that trial in the chosen forum would be unnecessarily burdensome for the defendant or the court, dismissal is proper.

[24] Respondent argues that since plaintiffs will ordinarily file suit in the jurisdiction that offers the most favorable law, establishing a strong presumption in favor of both home and foreign plaintiffs will ensure that defendants will always be held to the highest possible standard of accountability for their purported wrongdoing. However, the deference accorded to a plaintiff's choice of forum has never been intended to guarantee that the plaintiff will be able to select the law that will govern the case.

may be somewhat exaggerated. Particularly with respect to the question of relative ease of access to sources of proof, the private interests point in both directions. As respondent emphasizes, records concerning the design, manufacture, and testing of the propeller and plane are located in the United States. She would have greater access to sources of proof relevant to her strict liability and negligence theories if trial were held here.[25] However, the District Court did not act unreasonably in concluding that fewer evidentiary problems would be posed if the trial were held in Scotland. A large proportion of the relevant evidence is located in Great Britain.

The Court of Appeals found that the problems of proof could not be given any weight because Piper and Hartzell failed to describe with specificity the evidence they would not be able to obtain if trial were held in the United States. It suggested that defendants seeking forum non conveniens dismissal must submit affidavits identifying the witnesses they would call and the testimony these witnesses would provide if the trial were held in the alternative forum. Such detail is not necessary. Piper and Hartzell have moved for dismissal precisely because many crucial witnesses are located beyond the reach of compulsory process, and thus are difficult to identify or interview. Requiring extensive investigation would defeat the purpose of their motion. Of course, defendants must provide enough information to enable the District Court to balance the parties' interests. Our examination of the record convinces us that sufficient information was provided here. Both Piper and Hartzell submitted affidavits describing the evidentiary problems they would face if the trial were held in the United States.[27]

The District Court correctly concluded that the problems posed by the inability to implead potential third-party defendants clearly supported holding the trial in Scotland. Joinder of the pilot's estate, Air Navigation, and McDonald is crucial to the presentation of petitioners' defense. If Piper and Hartzell can show that the accident was caused not by a design defect, but rather by the negligence of the pilot, the plane's owners, or the charter company, they will be relieved of all liability. It is true, of course, that if Hartzell and Piper were found liable after a trial in the United States, they could institute an action for indemnity or contribution against these parties in Scotland. It would be far more convenient, however, to resolve all claims in one trial. The Court of Appeals rejected this argument. Forcing petitioners to rely on actions for indemnity or contributions would be

---

[25] In the future, where similar problems are presented, district courts might dismiss subject to the condition that defendant corporations agree to provide records relevant to the plaintiff's claims.

[27] The affidavit provided to the District Court by Piper states that it would call the following witnesses: the relatives of the decedents; the owners and employees of McDonald; the persons responsible for the training and licensing of the pilot; the persons responsible for servicing and maintaining the aircraft; and two or three of its own employees involved in the design and manufacture of the aircraft.

"burdensome" but not "unfair." Finding that trial in the plaintiff's chosen forum would be burdensome, however, is sufficient to support dismissal on grounds of forum non conveniens.

(2)

The District Court's review of the factors relating to the public interest was also reasonable. On the basis of its choice-of-law analysis, it concluded that if the case were tried in the Middle District of Pennsylvania, Pennsylvania law would apply to Piper and Scottish law to Hartzell. It stated that a trial involving two sets of laws would be confusing to the jury. It also noted its own lack of familiarity with Scottish law. Consideration of these problems was clearly appropriate under Gilbert; in that case we explicitly held that the need to apply foreign law pointed towards dismissal. The Court of Appeals found that the District Court's choice-of law analysis was incorrect, and that American law would apply to both Hartzell and Piper. Thus, lack of familiarity with foreign law would not be a problem. Even if the Court of Appeals' conclusion is correct, however, all other public interest factors favored trial in Scotland.

Scotland has a very strong interest in this litigation. The accident occurred in its airspace. All of the decedents were Scottish. Apart from Piper and Hartzell, all potential plaintiffs and defendants are either Scottish or English. As we stated in *Gilbert*, there is "a local interest in having localized controversies decided at home." Respondent argues that American citizens have an interest in ensuring that American manufacturers are deterred from producing defective products, and that additional deterrence might be obtained if Piper and Hartzell were tried in the United States, where they could be sued on the basis of both negligence and strict liability. However, the incremental deterrence that would be gained if this trial were held in an American court is likely to be insignificant. The American interest in this accident is simply not sufficient to justify the enormous commitment of judicial time and resources that would inevitably be required if the case were to be tried here.

[Opinions of Justice Stevens, dissenting (joined by Justice Brennan), and Justice White, concurring in part and dissenting in part, omitted. Neither Justice Powell nor Justice O'Connor took part in the decision.]

NOTES AND QUESTIONS

1.   *Transfer*: Plaintiff originally sued in state court in California, but since defendants removed to federal court it was possible to transfer to Pennsylvania, where Piper's plant is located. Under 28 U.S.C.A. § 1404(a), unless all parties consent, transfer is permitted only to a district where the action might have been brought, which has been interpreted to mean a district in which plaintiff could satisfy both personal jurisdiction and venue requirements as to all defendants. Hoffman v. Blaski, 363 U.S. 335 (1960). Why was Pennsylvania such a jurisdiction?

§ 1404(a) directs the court to transfer "[f]or the convenience of parties and witnesses, in the interest of justice." In general, it is said that the showing for a transfer need not be so compelling as that required for a forum non conveniens dismissal. How should the California court have evaluated these factors in connection with Piper's transfer motion? What information would it need to make its decision?

Hartzell moved to dismiss in the California federal court on the ground that it was not subject to personal jurisdiction there. Recall J. McIntyre Machinery, Ltd. v. Nicastro, supra p. 772. Assuming that there was no valid basis for jurisdiction over Hartzell in California, the California federal court nevertheless could transfer because 28 U.S.C.A. § 1406(a) permits transfer where suit is filed in a district that is not a proper venue. In Goldlawr, Inc. v. Heiman, 369 U.S. 463 (1962), the Court held that this allowed transfer even if jurisdiction were improper in the original district because that would "remov[e] whatever obstacles may impede an expeditious and orderly adjudication of cases and controversies on their merits." Should a court without jurisdiction do so? In Nichols v. G.D. Searle & Co., 991 F.2d 1195 (4th Cir.1993), the court upheld the district court's refusal to transfer, reasoning that "a district court acts within its discretion when it finds that the interest of justice is not served by allowing a plaintiff whose attorney committed an obvious error in filing the plaintiffs action in the wrong court, and thereby imposed substantial unnecessary costs on both the defendant and the legal system, simply to transfer his/her action to the proper court, with no cost to him/herself or his/her attorney." Id. at 1201.

Given the ultimate disposition in *Reyno*, it would seem that the California federal court might better have dismissed the entire action on forum non conveniens grounds. Where the showing of inconvenience is sufficient to justify dismissal, is transfer nevertheless preferable? The consensus has been that, in federal court, the court should transfer rather than dismiss no matter how forceful the showing, an attitude that compounds choice of law problems (see note 2 below).

Yet another transfer provision is 28 U.S.C. § 1407, which authorizes the Judicial Panel on Multidistrict Litigation to transfer all cases raising common questions of fact or law to a single district for all pretrial purposes. This transfer provision has assumed great importance for "mass torts." See Dodge, Facilitative Judging: Organizational Design in Mass-Multidistrict Litigation, 64 Emory L.J. 329, 331 (2014) (citing 2014 study saying that, if one excludes prisoner and social security cases, over 45% of pending federal civil cases were subject to a multidistrict transfer order).

2.   *Choice of law*: Choice of law complications arise after transfer. The problem is whether the defendant should get "a change of law as a bonus for a change of venue" if transfer is granted. See Wells v. Simonds Abrasive Co., 345 U.S. 514, 522 (1953) (Jackson, J., dissenting). In Van Dusen v. Barrack, 376 U.S. 612 (1964), the Court interpreted § 1404(a) as preserving the plaintiff's choice of law resulting from the freedom to select the initial forum under broad venue provisions, so that the transferee court applies the law that would have

been applied in the transferor court. In some ways this seems illogical. Consider Marcus, Conflicts Among Circuits and Transfers Within the Federal Judicial System, 93 Yale L.J. 677, 698 (1984):

> The transfer section is intended, on a case-by-case basis, to accomplish the original objective of venue provisions and limit a plaintiff's ability to impose undue geographical burdens on a defendant. Once plaintiff's original choice of forum has been overridden by a transfer, the reason for giving plaintiff a broad choice of venues in the first place ceases to apply. Indeed, any connection between the convenience of the forum and the choice of law would point to preferring the law of the transferee. Ironically, however, even though his choice of location has been taken away from him, plaintiff's incidental choice of law is still protected under a theory of acquired rights.

This outcome, however, merely recognizes that, within constitutional limits on choice of law, states may select the law to apply. There is no federal principle that overrides that choice, and § 1404(a) was not intended to be one. Indeed, in Ferens v. John Deere Co., 494 U.S. 516 (1990), the Court held that transferor law applies even if the *plaintiff* makes the § 1404(a) motion. The Court reasoned that otherwise plaintiffs would not make such motions, and that defendants who chose not to make them would thereby inflict on plaintiffs (and the court) the inconvenience of trial in a distant forum. Justice Scalia dissented, arguing that it was "unlikely that Congress meant to provide the plaintiff with a vehicle by which to appropriate the law of a distant and inconvenient forum in which he does not intend to litigate, and to carry that prize back to the State in which he wishes to try the case." But where, as with Hartzell, the original forum lacked jurisdiction or venue, the law of the transferee will apply after the transfer. Ellis v. Great Southwestern Corp., 646 F.2d 1099 (5th Cir.1981).

The requirement that plaintiff find a place where jurisdiction can be satisfied in order to "appropriate" favorable law may not impose strict limits on forum shopping by plaintiffs. Is that a bad thing? In re Coudert Bros. LLP, 673 F.3d 180 (2d Cir. 2012), reasons that "interstate forum shopping has come to be perceived less as a necessary evil of federalism and more as a right to be enjoyed by plaintiffs and protected for their benefit." "Van Dusen, in other words, is far less concerned about the fact that plaintiffs may engage in interstate forum shopping, on the basis of competing choice of law doctrines than it is with making sure that *only* plaintiffs engage in forum shopping. * * * Any remaining doubt about the Supreme Court's tolerance for inter-state forum shopping by plaintiffs was put to rest by *Ferens*. * * * While recognizing its rule would allow plaintiffs to separate their shopping for favorable choice of law rules from their ultimate choice of forum, the Court [in *Ferens*] believed a plaintiff's right to shop for favorable choice of law rules is so important that it should not be compromised 'by being put to a choice between a choice of law versus a forum.'" Id. at 189.

3.   *Effect of narrowing grounds for general jurisdiction*: Recall that the Supreme Court has narrowed the grounds for general jurisdiction. See Goodyear Dunlop Tires Operations, S.A. v. Brown, supra p. 817, limiting general jurisdiction to the place where the defendant is "essentially at home." See Daimler, AG v. Bauman, supra p. 823 n. 1 (directing dismissal for lack of jurisdiction in suit by Argentinean plaintiffs against German company for atrocities committed in Argentina). Compare the Court's footnote 17 (referring to a foreign plaintiff "able to obtain service of process on a foreign defendant who does business in the United States"). For an argument that the narrowing of general jurisdiction makes the use of forum non conveniens "dangerously redundant," see Gardner, Retiring Forum Non Conveniens, 92 N.Y.U. L. Rev. 390 (2017). The occasions in which non-American defendants will be subject to general jurisdiction in the U.S. have probably diminished, but for American companies, like Piper, the possibility still exists in their home state or state of incorporation.

4.   *Effect of a forum selection clause*: As explained in Forum Selection Clauses, supra p. 836, parties may select a forum for resolving contract disputes in their contract. In Atlantic Marine Constr. Co. v. U.S. District Court, 571 U.S. 49 (2013), the Court held that "a proper application of § 1404(a) requires that a forum-selection clause be 'given controlling weight in all but the most exceptional case.'" The court "should not consider arguments about the parties' private interests. When parties agree to a forum-selection clause, they waive the right to challenge the preselected forum as inconvenient." The court may rely on the public-interest factors, but "those factors will rarely defeat a transfer motion." In addition, the Court held that Van Dusen v. Barrack, 376 U.S. 612 (1964) (directing that the choice-of-law rules of the transferor court should apply after transfer) does not apply when transfer is pursuant to a forum selection clause.

5.   Should guarding plaintiffs' efforts to forum shop for favorable law stop at the water's edge? In *Reyno*, the district court in Pennsylvania concluded that Pennsylvania law would apply to the claim against Piper, and the Court of Appeals concluded that Ohio law would apply to the claim against Hartzell. The Supreme Court does not reject these conclusions. Does the fact that American law would be applied indicate that there is an American interest in having this case decided under American law? Under Klaxon Co. v. Stentor Electric Mfg. Co., 313 U.S. 487 (1941), a district court sitting in a diversity case must apply the choice of law rules of the state in which it sits. Does forum non conveniens threaten to undermine this system? Consider Stein, Forum Non Conveniens and the Redundancy of Court-Access Doctrine, 133 U.Pa.L.Rev. 781, 827–28 (1985): "[T]he district court in *Reyno* would not have been permitted to disregard Pennsylvania's interest analysis for choice-of-law purposes simply because it believed that Scottish interests in the controversy were paramount. Nonetheless, the very same result—application of Scottish law in a Scottish court—was achieved for the very same reason—paramount Scottish interests."

Balanced against an American interest in applying American law is the spectre of a flood of essentially foreign cases clogging American courts. How realistic is this concern? Consider the views of an English judge in Smith Kline & French Laboratories Ltd. v. Bloch, [1983] 1 W.L.R. 730 (C.A. 1982):

> As a moth is drawn to the light, so is a litigant drawn to the United States. If he can only get his case into their courts, he stands to win a fortune. At no cost to himself, and at no risk of having to pay anything to the other side. The lawyers there will conduct the case "on spec" as we say, or on a "contingency fee" as they say. * * * There is also in the United States a right to trial by jury. These are prone to award fabulous damages. They are notoriously sympathetic and know that the lawyers will take their 40 per cent. All this means that the defendant can be readily forced into a settlement. The plaintiff holds all the cards.

Is it better that plaintiff or defendant hold all the cards? A study of the fate of suits dismissed by American courts on forum non conveniens grounds showed that not one resulted in a plaintiff victory in a foreign court, although some were settled. See Clermont, The Story of Piper: Forum Matters, in Civil Procedure Stories (2d ed. 2008), at 199, 222–23. Does this finding show that dismissal should be harder to obtain? If the English judge quoted above was right that in America the plaintiff "holds all the cards," isn't a lower success rate elsewhere what one would expect? Does that mean forum non conveniens dismissal should never be granted?

6. *Deferring to plaintiff's choice of forum*: While upholding dismissal, in *Reyno* the Court reiterates the ordinary refrain that the plaintiff's choice of forum is not to be disturbed except upon a compelling showing. Similar language can be found in transfer cases under § 1404(a). Why should plaintiff be accorded this solicitude in close cases (i.e., where the choice of forum seems highly questionable)?

In *Reyno*, the Court avoids this roadblock by saying that the plaintiff's choice is not important when she is foreign. Does this mean a non-American, or a person not suing in her home state? In any event, why should it matter? Had one of the victims of the crash had a daughter living in Los Angeles who filed a wrongful death action there, would the fact that she had sued at home invoke the presumption in her favor? If the presumption depends on the presence of witnesses and evidence in the forum, then what does the fact that it is plaintiff's home add to the weight of those factors?

In Iragorri v. United Technologies Corp., 274 F.3d 65 (2d Cir.2001), the court explored the weight the court should give to plaintiff's interest in suing in the forum. Plaintiffs were U.S. domiciliaries, but nationals of Colombia, suing for an injury that was inflicted in Colombia. They sued in Connecticut, although they lived in Florida, because two of the defendants had headquarters there. The district court dismissed on forum non conveniens grounds, but the appellate court vacated for further consideration. It found the Supreme Court's observations about suit in this country by foreigners to be "part of a broader principle under which the degree of deference to be given to a plaintiff's choice of forum moves on a sliding scale. * * * The more it appears that a domestic or foreign plaintiff's choice of forum has been dictated by reasons that the law recognizes as valid, the greater the deference that will be given to the plaintiff's forum choice." This, in turn, should look to whether there is a "bona fide connection" between the suit and the U.S. The fact that plaintiffs here were not living in Connecticut should not be controlling since they had to sue where they could get personal jurisdiction. Compare Iragorri v. International Elevator, Inc., 203 F.3d 8 (1st Cir.2000) (upholding dismissal of the same plaintiffs' claim against a different defendant arising out of the same incident in Colombia).

7.   *Conditional dismissals*: The court may, while dismissing, require defendant to make certain concessions to plaintiff in connection with litigation elsewhere. Courts often require stipulations waiving statutes of limitation or consenting to jurisdiction before agreeing to dismiss on forum non conveniens grounds. There are limits on the power to insist on such conditions. In In re Union Carbide Corp. Gas Plant Disaster at Bhopal, India, 809 F.2d 195 (2d Cir.), cert. denied, 484 U.S. 871 (1987), the district judge required Union Carbide to agree to discovery in India according to the Federal Rules of Civil Procedure, which are much broader than Indian practice, as a condition for dismissing. Is it appropriate for an American court thus to supplant Indian procedure? The appellate court revoked the condition because "[b]asic justice requires that both sides be treated equally."

8.   *Inadequate alternative forum*: The Court says that, even where dismissal otherwise is appropriate, it may be denied if the foreign remedy is "no remedy at all." What does this mean? In footnote 22, it favorably cites a case that refused to dismiss unjust enrichment tort claims because the law of Ecuador, the alternative forum, did not recognize such claims. But why isn't Scotland's decision not to allow strict liability claims similarly a bar to dismissal? See Aguinda v. Texaco, Inc., 303 F.3d 470 (2d Cir.2002), upholding dismissal of suit for environmental harm by citizens of Ecuador despite plaintiffs' contentions that there were no parallel claims under local law and that the courts in Ecuador were not independent. In order to justify dismissal, Texaco had to persuade the American court that the courts of Ecuador provided an adequate alternative forum. Plaintiffs did indeed pursue their claims in Ecuador and eventually obtained a multi-billion dollar judgment against Chevron (which acquired Texaco after the forum non dismissal). Chevron has argued that the American courts should not enforce this judgment because the Ecuadorian courts acted improperly in entering it. See In re Chevron Corp., 650 F.3d 276, 282 n. 7 (3d Cir.2011) (describing Chevron's campaign of U.S. discovery to attack the validity of the Ecuadorian judgment as "unique in the annals of American judicial history").

More generally, globalization seems to have brought more litigation to American courts, and forum non conveniens is frequently invoked against such suits. It is not clear that these rulings are all consistent with each other, although each case is, of course, dependent on its own facts. In Carijano v.

Occidental Petroleum Co., 626 F.3d 1137 (9th Cir. 2010), indigenous people from Peru accused an American oil company of causing severe environmental damage and sought to sue under the California Unfair Competition Law. The appellate court reversed dismissal, characterizing forum non dismissal as a "drastic exercise" of the court's inherent power and an "exceptional tool." It credited plaintiffs' assertion that courts in Peru were biased against indigenous people, and criticized the district judge for failing to consider whether Peruvian law offers any remedy comparable to California's Unfair Competition Law, a provision that is quite remarkable in this country. See also Halo Creative & Design Ltd. v. Comptoir des Indes, Inc., 816 F.3d 1366 (Fed. Cir. 2016) (error to dismiss copyright claim brought by Hong Kong plaintiff against Canadian defendant because defendant did not demonstrate that a Canadian court would afford a remedy for copyright infringement occurring in the U.S.).

Contrast Tazoe v. Airbus S.A.S., 631 F.3d 1321 (11th Cir. 2011), upholding dismissal of a suit arising from "the worst accident in Brazilian aviation history," a crash killing 187 people when a commercial airliner overran a rain-soaked runway at a Sao Paolo airport. All killed in the crash were Brazilian except for one American, but the defendants came from many places, many with American contacts. Stressing that it reviewed only for an abuse of discretion, the appellate court noted that other American federal courts had found the courts of Brazil to be an adequate alternative forum, that Brazil allowed similar causes of action, and that much evidence (including the flight recorder) were in Brazil.

CHAPTER 10

SUBJECT MATTER JURISDICTION— CHOOSING BETWEEN STATE AND FEDERAL COURT

■ ■ ■

Putting aside questions of geographical location, plaintiffs must also select a court with authority to decide the case, or with what is often termed subject matter jurisdiction. Court systems may allocate decisional authority or jurisdiction to a range of different courts. Thus, many states have simplified small claims courts with jurisdiction over claims up to a certain dollar limit; other states assign certain types of claims (such as divorce or probate matters) to specialized courts. Most states have one court of "general" subject matter jurisdiction as well that has broad authority to decide most claims, including those that rest on both state and federal law theories of liability.

Choosing a court with proper subject matter jurisdiction raises issues conceptually separate from the problems of personal jurisdiction we considered in the previous chapter. Hence, one may say generally that a plaintiff must select a court that has personal jurisdiction over the defendant and subject matter jurisdiction over the claim. The two concepts, though separate, often overlap in confusing ways. For example, the existence of subject matter jurisdiction over claims against a defendant corporation may depend on the corporation's state of citizenship. The same contacts that support a finding of citizenship for purposes of subject matter jurisdiction may also give rise to a finding that the corporation has subjected itself to the state's "general" personal jurisdiction. You should distinguish between a court's subject matter jurisdiction and its ability to assert "general" personal jurisdiction over a particular defendant.

The various allocations of subject matter jurisdiction in state court systems are beyond the scope of this book. Instead, we will focus on the limited subject matter jurisdiction of the federal courts. For most purposes, the rules governing federal jurisdiction are the same whether the plaintiff has initially sued in federal court, or the defendant has "removed" the case to federal court from state court.

A. DIVERSITY OF CITIZENSHIP

Article III of the Constitution authorizes the federal courts to hear controversies between citizens of different states as well as disputes

865 *Start*
865-891

involving foreign nationals. In the Judiciary Act of 1789, Congress vested federal courts with jurisdiction of such cases in the predecessor to 28 U.S.C. § 1332. In Strawbridge v. Curtiss, 7 U.S. (3 Cranch) 267 (1806), the Court held that the statute required "complete diversity," that no defendant could be a citizen of the same state as any plaintiff. Read Article III §§ 1 and 2 of the Constitution, section 1332 and Rule 8(a)(1).

Q. V. d

MAS V. PERRY

United States Court of Appeals, Fifth Circuit, 1974
489 F.2d 1396

Before WISDOM, AINSWORTH and CLARK, CIRCUIT JUDGES.

AINSWORTH, CIRCUIT JUDGE.

This case presents questions pertaining to federal diversity jurisdiction under 28 U.S.C. § 1332, which, pursuant to article III, section 2 of the Constitution, provides for original jurisdiction in federal district courts of all civil actions that are between, inter alia, citizens of different States or citizens of a State and citizens of foreign states and in which the amount in controversy is more than $10,000.

Appellees Jean Paul Mas, a citizen of France, and Judy Mas were married at her home in Jackson, Mississippi. Prior to their marriage, Mr. and Mrs. Mas were graduate assistants, pursuing coursework as well as performing teaching duties, for approximately nine months and one year, respectively, at Louisiana State University in Baton Rouge, Louisiana. Shortly after their marriage, they returned to Baton Rouge to resume their duties as graduate assistants at LSU. They remained in Baton Rouge for approximately two more years, after which they moved to Park Ridge, Illinois. At the time of the trial in this case, it was their intention to return to Baton Rouge while Mr. Mas finished his studies for the degree of Doctor of Philosophy. Mr. and Mrs. Mas were undecided as to where they would reside after that.

Upon their return to Baton Rouge after their marriage, appellees rented an apartment from appellant Oliver H. Perry, a citizen of Louisiana. This appeal arises from a final judgment entered on a jury verdict awarding $5,000 to Mr. Mas and $15,000 to Mrs. Mas for damages incurred by them as a result of the discovery that their bedroom and bathroom contained "two-way" mirrors and that they had been watched through them by the appellant during three of the first four months of their marriage.

At the close of the appellees' case at trial, appellant made an oral motion to dismiss for lack of jurisdiction. The motion was denied by the district court. Before this Court, appellant challenges the final judgment below solely on jurisdictional grounds, contending that appellees failed to prove diversity of citizenship among the parties and that the requisite jurisdictional amount is lacking with respect to Mr. Mas. Finding no merit to these contentions, we affirm. Under section 1332(a)(2), the federal judicial power extends to the claim of Mr. Mas, a citizen of France, against the appellant, a citizen of Louisiana. Since we conclude that Mrs. Mas is a citizen of Mississippi for diversity purposes, the district court also properly had jurisdiction under section 1332(a)(1) of her claim.

It has long been the general rule that complete diversity of parties is required in order that diversity jurisdiction obtain; that is, no party on one side may be a citizen of the same State as any party on the other side. Strawbridge v. Curtiss, 7 U.S. (3 Cranch) 267 (1806). This determination of one's State citizenship for diversity purposes is controlled by federal law, not by the law of any State. As is the case in other areas of federal jurisdiction, the diverse citizenship among adverse parties must be present at the time the complaint is filed. Jurisdiction is unaffected by subsequent changes in the citizenship of the parties. The burden of pleading the diverse citizenship is upon the party invoking federal jurisdiction, and if the diversity jurisdiction is properly challenged, that party also bears the burden of proof.

To be a citizen of a State within the meaning of section 1332, a natural person must be both a citizen of the United States, and a domiciliary of that State. For diversity purposes, citizenship means domicile; mere residence in the State is not sufficient.

A person's domicile is the place of "his true, fixed, and permanent home and principal establishment, and to which he has the intention of returning whenever he is absent therefrom. . ." A change of domicile may be effected only by a combination of two elements: (a) taking up residence in a different domicile with (b) the intention to remain there.

It is clear that at the time of her marriage, Mrs. Mas was a domiciliary of the State of Mississippi. While it is generally the case that the domicile of the wife—and, consequently, her State citizenship for purposes of diversity jurisdiction—is deemed to be that of her husband, we find no precedent for extending this concept to the situation here, in which the husband is a citizen of a foreign state but resides in the United States. Indeed, such a fiction would work absurd results on the facts before us. If Mr. Mas were considered a domiciliary of France—as he would be since he had lived in Louisiana as a student-teaching assistant prior to filing this suit—then Mrs. Mas would also be deemed a domiciliary, and thus, fictionally at least, a citizen of France. She would not be a citizen of any State and could not sue in a federal court on that basis; nor could she invoke alienage jurisdiction to bring her claim in federal court, since she is not an alien. On the other hand, if Mrs. Mas's domicile were Louisiana, she would become a Louisiana citizen for diversity purposes and could not bring suit with her husband against appellant, also a Louisiana citizen, on the basis of diversity jurisdiction. These are curious results under a rule arising from the theoretical identity of person and interest of the married couple.

An American woman is not deemed to have lost her United States citizenship solely by reason of her marriage to an alien. 8 U.S.C. § 1489. Similarly, we conclude that for diversity purposes a woman does not have her domicile or State citizenship changed solely by reason of her marriage to an alien.

Mrs. Mas's Mississippi domicile was disturbed neither by her year in Louisiana prior to her marriage nor as a result of the time she and her husband spent at LSU. Though she testified that after her marriage she had no intention of returning to her parents' home in Mississippi, Mrs. Mas did not effect a change of domicile since she and Mr. Mas were in Louisiana only as students and lacked the requisite intention to remain there. Until she acquires a new domicile, she remains a domiciliary, and thus a citizen, of Mississippi.[2]

Appellant also contends that Mr. Mas's claim should have been dismissed for failure to establish the requisite jurisdictional amount for diversity cases of more than $10,000. In their complaint Mr. and Mrs. Mas alleged that they had each been damaged in the amount of $100,000. As we have noted, Mr. Mas ultimately recovered $5,000.

It is well settled that the amount in controversy is determined by the amount claimed by the plaintiff in good faith. Federal jurisdiction is not lost because a judgment of less than the jurisdictional amount is awarded. That Mr. Mas recovered only $5,000 is, therefore, not compelling. As the Supreme Court stated in St. Paul Mercury Indemnity Co. v. Red Cab Co., 303 U.S. 283, 288–290:

The sum claimed by the plaintiff controls if the claim is apparently made in good faith.

It must appear to a legal certainty that the claim is really for less than the jurisdictional amount to justify dismissal. The inability of the plaintiff to recover an amount adequate to give the court jurisdiction does not show his bad faith or oust the jurisdiction. . .

. . . His good faith in choosing the federal forum is open to challenge not only by resort to the face of his complaint, but by the facts disclosed at trial, and if from either source it is clear that his claim never could have amounted to the sum necessary to give jurisdiction there is no injustice in dismissing the suit.

Having heard the evidence presented at the trial, the district court concluded that the appellees properly met the requirements of section 1332 with respect to jurisdictional amount. Upon examination of the record in

---

[2] The original complaint in this case was filed within several days of Mr. and Mrs. Mas's realization that they had been watched through the mirrors, quite some time before they moved to Park Ridge, Illinois. Because the district court's jurisdiction is not affected by actions of the parties subsequent to the commencement of the suit, the testimony concerning Mr. and Mrs. Mas's moves after that time is not determinative of the issue of diverse citizenship, though it is of interest insofar as it supports their lack of intent to remain permanently in Louisiana.

this case, we are also satisfied that the requisite amount was in controversy.

Thus the power of the federal district court to entertain the claims of appellees in this case stands on two separate legs of diversity jurisdiction: a claim by an alien against a State citizen; and an action between citizens of different States. We also note, however, the propriety of having the federal district court entertain a spouse's action against a defendant, where the district court already has jurisdiction over a claim, arising from the same transaction, by the other spouse against the same defendant. In the case before us, such a result is particularly desirable. The claims of Mr. and Mrs. Mas arise from the same operative facts, and there was almost complete interdependence between their claims with respect to the proof required and the issues raised at trial. Thus, since the district court had jurisdiction of Mr. Mas's action, sound judicial administration militates strongly in favor of federal jurisdiction of Mrs. Mas's claim.

NOTES AND QUESTIONS

1.   Consider the complete diversity rule in light of the rationale for federal jurisdiction over cases involving citizens of different states and citizens or subject of foreign states ("foreign nationals").[1] Although the historical record is rather thin on the question, Article III apparently provides for diversity and foreign national jurisdiction to afford a safety valve against state court prejudice against outsiders. If that is true, the risk of local prejudice against husband Mas might justify federal jurisdiction, without regard to the citizenship of his wife. Judged from the vantage point of local prejudice, the complete diversity requirement is hard to justify: "[W]ho can say whether a Vermont jury, concentrating attention on the one Vermont defendant, would shut its eyes to the merits of the complainants' case, or, realizing that its fellow citizen was only one of a crowd, would deal fairly and squarely with all? A theory so little founded on realities could hardly be expected to furnish a satisfactory answer to a new and difficult question." Friendly, The Historic Basis of Diversity Jurisdiction, 41 Harv.L.Rev. 483, 509 (1928). Cf. Jones, Finishing a Friendly Argument: The Jury and the Historical Origins of Diversity Jurisdiction, 82 N.Y.U.L. Rev. 997 (2007) (arguing that diversity jurisdiction was meant to transfer decisions from state to federal juries and describing the way federal officials controlled juror selection). For criticism of the policy underlying the complete diversity requirement, see Redish, Reassessing the Allocation of Judicial Business Between State and Federal Courts: Federal Jurisdiction and "the Martian Chronicles", 78 Va. L. Rev. 1769, 1803–06 (1992). A similar rule of complete diversity often applies to suits

---

[1]   Article III of the Constitution extends jurisdiction to certain controversies involving "citizens or subjects of foreign states." The Judiciary Act of 1789 referred instead to "aliens" in conferring jurisdiction on the federal courts and it became common to refer to alienage jurisdiction. See An Act to Establish the Judicial Courts of the United States, ch. 23, 1 Stat. 73, §§ 11, 12, 13 (1789). Current law follows the language of Article III in extending jurisdiction to certain claims involving "citizens or subjects of a foreign state." 28 U.S.C. § 1332(a)(2)–(3). For simplicity, the casebook will describe such persons as foreign nationals.

involving foreign nationals; diversity does not exist if there are foreign nationals on both sides of the case, even if they are citizens or subjects of different countries. See Ruhrgas AG v. Marathon Oil Co., 526 U.S. 574 (1999) (joinder of foreign national plaintiff and defendant defeats complete diversity).

2.   Whatever the wisdom of the complete diversity rule, the Court made clear in State Farm Fire & Cas. Co. v. Tashire, supra p. 287, that it is not constitutionally required. The Court upheld the requirement of "minimal diversity" in the federal interpleader statute: "Article III poses no obstacle to the legislative extension of federal jurisdiction, founded on diversity, so long as any two adverse parties are not co-citizens." Congress has adopted two important statutes in reliance on the minimal diversity holding of *Tashire*. The Multiparty, Multiforum Trial Jurisdiction Act of 2002 (MMTJA) seeks to sweep into federal court all claims arising from any single disaster at a discrete location (such as a fire or plane crash or terrorist attack) that results in the death of more than 75 individuals. Pub. L. No. 107–273, 116 Stat. 1758. More significantly, in terms of impact on federal dockets, the Class Action Fairness Act of 2005 (CAFA), Pub. L. No. 109–2, 119 Stat. 4, empowers the district courts to hear many state law class actions in which the aggregate value of the claims exceeds $5 million and diversity of citizenship exists between any member of the class and any defendant. See 28 U.S.C. § 1332(d). For evaluations of the jurisdictional ramifications, see Marcus, Assessing CAFA's Stated Jurisdictional Policy, 156 U. Pa. L. Rev. 1765 (2008); Pfander, Protective Jurisdiction, Aggregate Litigation, and the Limits of Article III, 95 Cal. L. Rev. 1423 (2007).

3.   As Mas v. Perry demonstrates, the definition of citizenship for diversity jurisdiction incorporates the concept of domicile, which is slightly different from residence. In a highly mobile society like ours, does this difference matter? The idea, as indicated in Mas v. Perry, is that a person must be present in a new state with the intention to remain indefinitely before her domicile changes. Consider how this intention element would influence the domicile determination in the following situations:

(a)   A domiciliary of New York was convicted of a crime and incarcerated in Indiana. Prisoner intended to return to New York after period of incarceration ended. Held: prisoner had no intention to make the state of incarceration a permanent home, so the old domicile of New York remains unchanged. See Denlinger v. Brennan, 87 F.3d 214 (7th Cir. 1996).

(b)   A domiciliary of Missouri moved to Ohio to take a year-long course of studies as a prelude to conducting a national job search and taking the best job offered. Held: temporary residence to pursue studies did not effect a change in domicile. See Holmes v. Sopuch, 639 F.2d 431 (8th Cir. 1981).

(c)   A woman living in Illinois suffered a stroke and was taken by relatives and guardians to live in Ohio, where she was placed in assisted care facility and declared incompetent. Held: recognizing an exception to the requirement of a voluntary intent to change domiciles, court concludes that a guardian can change an incompetent person's domicile on her behalf. See Dakuras v. Edwards, 312 F.3d 256 (7th Cir. 2002).

(d)   What should be the citizenship of a homeless person? In O'Neal v. Atwal, 425 F.Supp.2d 944 (W.D. Wis. 2006), plaintiff was homeless but listed an address in Alabama in his complaint. Plaintiff had been in homeless shelters in Wisconsin, and in jail in Minnesota. In order to determine whether there was diversity of citizenship, the judge required plaintiff to answer such questions as where he had lived, whether and where he had ever had employment, whether and where he had ever registered to vote. See id. at 947. Does a person make the sort of conscious decision to become homeless and to move from state to state that the law should regard as expressing an intent to change one's domicile?

4.   How should the domicile test apply to the wife in Mas v. Perry? At least three different possible domiciles present themselves.

(a)   France. Some old cases would more or less automatically assign women the citizenship or domicile of their husbands. If that approach were applied to Ms. Mas, she could be considered to share the domicile of her husband, France. But the premise seems flawed; in an era of bicoastal marriages, spouses do not always share their partners' domicile and the modern cases so reflect. If Ms. Mas were considered a domiciliary of France, she would fall into the stateless-person exception to diversity jurisdiction. See Newman-Green, Inc. v. Alfonzo-Larrain, 490 U.S. 826, 828 (1989) ("The [exception applies when an individual], although a United States citizen, has no domicile in any State. He is therefore 'stateless' for purposes of § 1332(a)(2)."). Lacking state citizenship, the stateless person cannot sue or be sued in federal court on the basis of diversity.

(b)   Mississippi. As the court explains, Ms. Mas was a domiciliary of Mississippi before she married her husband. Should she be considered a Mississippi citizen even though she has no intention to return? In general, the law treats a person's old domicile as presumptively continuing until such time as the person makes a change. Thus, for example, the student in Holmes v. Sopuch, supra note 3(b), was viewed as a Missouri domiciliary, even though he was living in Ohio and had no specific intention to return to Missouri.

(c)   Louisiana. Ms. Mas made her home in Louisiana while she and her husband completed their studies. She thus has the requisite presence in the state. Did she also have the requisite intent to make a change in her domicile? Students who move to a new state solely to study do not typically do so with the intent necessary to change their domicile. But when a student gets married and leaves home with no intention of returning, there may be a stronger argument for viewing her as a domiciliary of the state where she lives and studies. The court appears to admit as much at the end of its opinion, but viewed the clear existence of jurisdiction over the husband's claim as an argument in favor of hearing the wife's claim as well. Is it appropriate for the court to expand its jurisdiction to encompass related claims and parties that do not themselves satisfy the elements of federal jurisdiction? We will return to this question later in the chapter in considering supplemental jurisdiction, 28 U.S.C. § 1367.

5.   Since Mas v. Perry was decided, 28 U.S.C. § 1332(a) has been twice amended to address the assertion of jurisdiction over claims involving foreign nationals admitted to the United States as lawful permanent residents (LPRs). In the first amendment, section 1332(a) deemed "an alien admitted to the United States for permanent residence" to be a citizen of the foreign national's state of domicile. The apparent goal of the provision was to prevent the assertion of jurisdiction in a dispute between a citizen of one state and an LPR living in the same state. See Foy v. Schantz, Schatzman & Aaronson, P.A., 108 F.3d 1347 (11th Cir. 1997) (holding that the reference to permanent resident aliens encompasses only "those aliens who have been accorded permanent resident status by" the federal government and have received green cards). Despite Congress's apparent desire to curtail jurisdiction, some courts read the statute as expanding federal subject matter jurisdiction by opening the courts to an action between two LPRs who happen to be residents (and deemed citizens) of different states or between an LPR and any foreign national who lacks a green card. See C. Wright & M. Kane, Law of Federal Courts 156 (7th ed. 2011) (concluding that the power of Congress to open courts to suit between resident foreign nationals domiciled in different states is "extremely doubtful"; Article III makes no provision for jurisdiction over disputes between foreign nationals).

A further amendment, effective in 2012, produced the current version of section 1332(a)(2). How did Congress address the potential for jurisdictional expansion caused by the deeming provision? Was its fix successful?

6.   *Dual nationals*: How do courts determine the citizenship of a person who holds dual citizenship? In Aly v. Hanzada for Import & Export Ltd, 864 F.3d 844 (8th Cir. 2017), the plaintiff was a citizen of both the United States and Egypt. He brought suit against Hanzada (an Egyptian firm) for breach of a contract relating to the importation of meat products. Aly made his home in Ohio. The Eighth Circuit held that Aly was a citizen of Ohio for diversity purposes: "An individual who resides in more than one State is regarded, for purposes of federal subject-matter (diversity) jurisdiction, as a citizen of but one State." Id. at 848 (quoting Wachovia Bank v. Schmidt, 546 U.S. 303, 318 (2006)). This made Aly a citizen of Ohio, and only Ohio, for purposes of § 1332(a) because an individual is a "citizen" of only one place. The Eighth Circuit also invoked the Seventh Circuit's widely adopted *Sadat* rule: "only the American nationality of the dual citizen should be recognized under 28 U.S.C. § 1332(a)." See Aly, 864 F.3d at 848 (citing Sadat v. Mertes, 615 F.2d 1176, 1187 (7th Cir. 1980)). *See also* Molinos Valle Del Cibao, C. por A. v. Lama, 633 F.3d 1330, 1341 (11th Cir. 2011) (same).

7.   It should be apparent that diversity jurisdiction is often manipulable. 28 U.S.C. § 1359 seeks to control such manipulation: "A district court shall not have jurisdiction of a civil action in which any party, by assignment or otherwise, has been improperly or collusively made or joined to invoke the jurisdiction of such court." In Kramer v. Caribbean Mills, Inc., 394 U.S. 823

(1969), a Panamanian corporation assigned its claim against a Haitian corporation to a Texas lawyer in return for one dollar and a promise that the Texan would remit 95% of any amounts he recovered. The assignment was admittedly intended to create diversity, but it was evidently valid as a matter of Texas law. The Court nevertheless held that this strategy would not create diversity for jurisdictional purposes: "If federal jurisdiction could be created by assignments of this kind, which are easy to arrange and involve few disadvantages for the assignor, then a vast quantity of ordinary contract and tort litigation could be channeled into the federal courts at the will of one of the parties." At the same time, the Court was careful to note that "where the transfer of a claim is absolute, with the transferor retaining no interest in the subject matter, then the transfer is not 'improperly or collusively made,' regardless of the transferor's motive." In contrast to this prohibition of assignments to create diversity, federal law does not in general prohibit the joinder of parties or claims to *defeat* diversity. What accounts for this difference in treatment?

Before 1988, there was much opportunity to create or defeat diversity when a claim was made on behalf of an estate by selecting an executor or administrator of the desired citizenship. Cf. Piper Aircraft Co. v. Reyno, supra p. 849. In 1988, Congress amended 28 U.S.C. § 1332(c) to provide that for purposes of diversity the representative of an estate would be deemed a citizen of the same state as the decedent. For discussion, see Nicolas, Fighting the Probate Mafia: A Dissection of the Probate Exception to Federal Court Jurisdiction, 74 S.Cal.L.Rev. 1479 (2001).

8.   Problems have also arisen in determining whether there is diversity when plaintiff names fictitious "John Doe" defendants. In general, it is said that for a plaintiff to sue Doe defendants in federal court on grounds of diversity she must plead that they are of diverse citizenship. See C. Wright & M. Kane, Law of Federal Courts 189–90 (7th ed. 2011). For purposes of removal on grounds of diversity of a case originally filed in state court, 28 U.S.C. § 1441(a) provides that defendants sued under fictitious names shall be disregarded.

9.   What happens if, after litigation proceeds in federal court for some time, the district court dismisses for want of subject matter jurisdiction? While such a disposition does not preclude further litigation in a competent court, the relevant statute of limitations may bar the filing of a new lawsuit. To deal with this problem of timeliness, many states have adopted "saving statutes," which give the plaintiff a grace period (ranging from 30 days to a full year) to re-file in state court following the dismissal. See generally W. Ferguson, The Statute of Limitations Savings Statutes (1978) (listing some thirty states with such statutes). For example, Illinois permits re-filing following a voluntary dismissal, a dismissal for lack of jurisdiction, and certain other kinds of dismissal. See 735 Ill.Comp.Stat. 5/13–217 (West 2008).

In a state that lacks a saving statute, defendants may be tempted to lull plaintiffs into thinking that jurisdiction is proper until it is too late to re-file suit in state court. Federal courts have dealt with such behavior by imposing sanctions on counsel for concealing, or failing to exercise proper diligence in discovering, the absence of diversity. See, e.g., Belleville Catering Co. v. Champaign Market Place, LLC, 350 F.3d 691 (7th Cir. 2003) (dismissing action for lack of complete diversity and directing counsel for both parties to relitigate the matter in state court without charging their clients any further fees). In a case where one party misleads the court, would it be lawful for the district court to impose a finding of jurisdiction by estoppel? Unlike personal jurisdiction, subject matter jurisdiction cannot be based on consent or action of the parties or on theories of estoppel. See 13 C. Wright, A. Miller, E. Cooper & R. Freer, Federal Practice and Procedure § 3522 (3d ed. 2008). But cf. Note, Second Bites at the Jurisdictional Apple: A Proposal for Preventing False Assertions of Diversity of Citizenship, 41 Hast.L.J. 1417 (1990) (urging estoppel against belated challenges to existence of diversity). Is it wise to have rules of subject matter jurisdiction that invite chicanery? Is it possible to suppress the efforts of litigants to gain strategic advantage through forum selection?

10. Even where diversity is present, federal courts have traditionally refused to entertain certain kinds of cases. One such category of excluded cases involves domestic relations issues. In Ankenbrandt v. Richards, 504 U.S. 689 (1992), plaintiff sued her former husband, on behalf of their children, for damages for abuse of the children while they were visiting their father. The district court dismissed, but the Supreme Court reversed. While concluding that "[t]he domestic relations exception * * * divests the federal courts of power to issue divorce, alimony, and child custody decrees," the Court found this exception inapplicable to plaintiffs' suit for tort damages. Compare Matusow v. Trans-County Title Agency, LLC, 545 F.3d 241 (3d Cir. 2008) (action to quiet title to real property that was the subject of an agreement entered as part of a divorce proceeding would not interfere with state court authority over the divorce and property settlement and did not fall within the domestic relations exception). For a summary of the domestic relations exception and an argument for its narrow application, see Pfander & Damrau, A Non-Contentious Account of Article III's Domestic Relations Exception, 92 Notre Dame L. Rev. 117 (2016).

A second category of cases in which federal courts refuse jurisdiction despite diversity are those that involve the probate of an estate. In Marshall v. Marshall, 547 U.S. 293 (2006), the Court narrowly defined the probate exception as reserving to state courts

> the probate of a will and the administration of a decedent's estate; it also precludes federal courts from endeavoring to dispose of property that is in the custody of a state probate court. But it does not bar federal courts from adjudicating matters outside those confines and otherwise within federal jurisdiction.

Accordingly, the Court found that the probate exception did not prevent a federal bankruptcy court from hearing a claim by widow Anna Nicole Smith for tortious interference with her receipt of a gift from her aged husband despite the pendency of related proceedings in a Texas probate court. In a subsequent decision in the same long-running case, the Court ruled that Congress had violated Article III of the Constitution in authorizing a non-Article III federal bankruptcy court to hear the tortious interference claim. See Stern v. Marshall, 131 S.Ct. 2594 (2011). Those interested in the background to the legal dispute may consult In re Marshall, 600 F.3d 1037 (9th Cir. 2010). For an overview of the history of the probate exception and an argument that it derives from the inability of the federal courts to hear uncontested matters of state law, see Pfander & Downey, In Search of the Probate Exception, 67 Vand. L. Rev. 1533 (2014).

11. Plaintiffs can cure jurisdictional problems created by the lack of complete diversity by dismissing as to the non-diverse defendant unless that defendant is indispensable under Rule 19(b). In Newman-Green, Inc. v. Alfonzo-Larrain, 490 U.S. 826 (1989), the Court held that Rule 21 permits this solution even if the case is on appeal when the lack-of-diversity problem appears. Compare Grupo Dataflux v. Atlas Global Group, L.P., 541 U.S. 567 (2004), holding that the withdrawal of two non-diverse partners from plaintiff partnership due to commercial developments before trial could not cure the lack of diversity at the beginning of the lawsuit. Four justices dissented, arguing that jurisdiction should be found because there had been minimal diversity throughout, and complete diversity by the time of trial.

CORPORATE AND ASSOCIATION CITIZENSHIP

As for corporate parties, section 1332(c) provides that a corporation is a citizen of every State and foreign state in which it is incorporated and "the State or foreign state where it has its principal place of business." Although a corporation ordinarily has but one state of incorporation, some corporations choose to incorporate in more than one state (and would thus become citizens of all such states for diversity purposes). In addition, corporations have but one "principal" place of business. In Hertz Corp. v. Friend, 559 U.S. 77 (2010), the Supreme Court defined the corporation's principal place of business (some fifty years after the language was added to the judicial code). The dispute involved the rental car company, Hertz, which had its corporate headquarters in New Jersey and did business in all fifty states. The lower court had ruled that Hertz was to be regarded as having its principal place of business in California, the state in which it conducted more business operations and from which it derived more rental revenues than any other state. But the Supreme Court reversed, declaring that the corporation's principal place of business is "the place where the corporation's high level officers direct, control, and coordinate the corporation's activities," *i.e.,* its "nerve center." Id. at 92–93. In explaining the virtues of a simple jurisdictional test, the Court observed that "[c]omplex tests produce appeals and reversals, encourage gamesmanship, and, again, diminish the likelihood that results and settlements will reflect a claim's legal and factual merits." Id. at 94. The Court hypothesized a situation in which a corporation's visible business activities take place in New Jersey, while its top officers direct those activities from across the

Hudson river in New York. In such a situation, the Court explained that the principal place of business would be New York. Id. at 96.

Has the *Hertz* Court's goal of simplicity and administrability been achieved? Consider Harrison v. Granite Bay Care, Inc., 811 F.3d 36 (1st Cir. 2016). The corporate defendant did business in Maine, alone, but its corporate operations were directed by its owners and directors from New Hampshire, where they lived. Despite the fact that the corporation maintained an administrative office in Maine, the court ruled that the nerve center of the firm was in New Hampshire. Contrasting the old locus of operations test, the court observed that the *Hertz* nerve center test simplified an analysis that would have otherwise been "extraordinarily close." Id. at 41 n. 5. Can the concept of a corporate nerve center remain straightforward in a world of telecommuting and virtual conferences? Amazon, the on-line retail giant, announced its intention to create a second headquarters (HQ2) to supplement its longtime center in Seattle, Washington. See Amazon is Planning a Second Headquarters with 50,000 Jobs, N.Y. Times, Sept. 7, 2017. Amazon CEO Jeff Bezos was quoted as saying HQ2 would be a "full equal to our Seattle headquarters" and executives could base their teams in either place. Would the nerve center test as applied to an Amazon with two equal HQs ascribe the firm's citizenship to the place where Bezos happens to work?

However simple the nerve center proves to be in practice, one can fairly ask if the Court has achieved comparable simplicity in the development of the citizenship rules that govern other associations, business and otherwise. Unlike corporations, unincorporated associations are not treated as separate entities for diversity purposes, and in determining diversity one must treat the association as a citizen of every state in which its members are citizens. See United Steelworkers of America v. R.H. Bouligny, Inc., 382 U.S. 145 (1965). In Carden v. Arkoma Associates, 494 U.S. 185 (1990), the Court refused to liken a limited partnership to a corporation and therefore chose to consider the citizenship of all the partners, full and limited. Even though the limited partners had little or no right to influence the operation of the enterprise, and were therefore in a position similar to the shareholders of a corporation, the Court held that their citizenship should be counted for purposes of determining the existence of diversity. See Carden, 494 U.S. at 195–96. See also Underwriters at Lloyd's of London v. Osting-Schwinn, 613 F.3d 1079 (11th Cir. 2010) (holding that, as an unincorporated association of "names," the insurance syndicate Lloyds of London must allege the citizenship of each "name" or principal when invoking the diversity jurisdiction of the federal courts).

Lower courts have generally followed *Carden* in evaluating the citizenship of limited liability companies, or LLCs. See Johnson v. Smithkline Beecham Corp., 724 F.3d 337 (3d Cir. 2013); Harvey v. Grey

Wolf Drilling Co., 542 F.3d 1077 (5th Cir. 2008) (collecting cases). LLCs have grown in number and complexity in the past twenty years, combining some of the advantages of partnerships with the limited liability that has long been the hallmark of incorporated firms. To get some idea of the growth, consider a report on the jurisdictional treatment of LLCs and other unincorporated associations: in 1993, roughly 275,000 limited partnerships and only 17,335 LLCs filed federal tax returns; by 2008, over 534,000 limited partnerships and over 1,898,000 LLCs filed federal tax returns. See ABA Section on Litigation, Report to the House of Delegates at 4 (August 2015) (available https://www.americanbar.org). The combination of unincorporated status and widely dispersed ownership means that disputes involving LLCs often fail to satisfy the complete diversity rule. The ABA recommended new legislation that would assign all unincorporated associations the citizenship of their principal place business and their state of organization. Id. at 6.

In Navarro Savings Ass'n v. Lee, 446 U.S. 458 (1980), the Court held that for a Massachusetts business trust only the citizenship of the trustees need be considered in determining diversity because they possess "certain customary powers to hold, manage, and dispose of assets for the benefit of others." See also Supreme Tribe of Ben-Hur v. Cauble, 255 U.S. 356 (1921) (in class action only the citizenship of the class representatives need be considered in determining diversity).

In Americold Realty Trust v. Conagra Foods, Inc., 136 S.Ct. 1012 (2016), the Court held unanimously that a Maryland real estate trust did not have the citizenship for diversity purposes of only its Maryland principal place of business. The Court admitted that the question of citizenship "can become metaphysical when applied to legal entities." Id. at 1014. Plaintiff argued that the Maryland setup was sufficiently similar to a corporation to make the trust a separate entity for purposes of citizenship. The Court rejected this argument: "So long as an entity is unincorporated, we apply our 'oft-repeated rule' that it possesses the citizenship of all its members." Id. at 1016. That included every "shareholder" in a Maryland trust because "[t]hese shareholders appear to be in the same position as the shareholders of a joint-stock company or the partners of a limited partnership." Id. at 1016. Navarro Savings Ass'n v. Lee, supra, was distinguishable because it "confirmed a separate rule that when a trustee files a lawsuit in *her* name, her jurisdictional citizenship is the State to which she belongs."

AMOUNT IN CONTROVERSY

To qualify for federal jurisdiction on grounds of diversity, plaintiff must establish not only complete diversity but also that more than $75,000 is in controversy. From the outset, there has been such a monetary minimum for federal diversity jurisdiction. In 1789, it was set at $500. It was increased to $2,000 in 1887, $3,000 in 1911, to $10,000 in 1958, to

$50,000 in 1988, and to $75,000 in 1996. There have been suggestions to "index" the figure so it could fluctuate in accordance with the Consumer Price Index or some similar measure of inflation. The idea behind this minimum is to exclude inconsequential cases from the federal courts while keeping the federal court doors open to all and not just the well-to-do.

In Mas v. Perry, defendant argued that plaintiff husband, who had recovered only $5,000, had not satisfied the then-applicable $10,000 jurisdictional minimum requirement. Rejecting this argument, the court quoted the governing standard from St. Paul Mercury Indem. Co. v. Red Cab Co., 303 U.S. 283 (1938). See p. 868 supra. Reread that standard and consider the difficulties that arise in applying it, discussed below.

NOTES AND QUESTIONS

1.   In Mas v. Perry, both husband and wife claimed $100,000 in damages and yet the jury awarded them only $5,000 and $15,000 respectively. Why does the court focus on the amount claimed in good faith rather than on the actual amount recovered? Would the suit have satisfied the jurisdictional minimum requirements if defendant had spied on them only once? If so, would jurisdiction be proper if they had merely been brushing their teeth on that occasion?

2.   Suppose that in a case like Mas v. Perry, defendant had failed to return plaintiffs' security deposit and other property valued at $5000. Could they have satisfied today's $75,000 jurisdictional requirement in a suit for the return of their deposit and property by adding a claim for punitive damages? In such a situation the court would be faced with two somewhat separate questions. First, as a matter of applicable substantive law, is this sort of recovery permitted? Second, if so, is this claim made in good faith? The questions tend to blend in practice. Much may depend on whether the plaintiff has alleged facts that will give rise to punitive damages of that amount. Recent Supreme Court decisions, invoking the Due Process Clause as a limit on punitive damages, suggest a third layer of inquiry. In State Farm Mut. Auto Ins. Co. v. Campbell, 538 U.S. 408, 424–25 (2003), the Supreme Court suggested that punitive damages that exceed compensatory damages by a ratio greater than four to one or perhaps nine to one (a "single digit" ratio) might violate due process. Some lower courts have relied on the single digit ratio in evaluating whether the combination of punitive and compensatory damages will meet the jurisdictional threshold. In LM Ins. Co. v. Spaulding Enterprises, Inc., 533 F.3d 542, 552 (7th Cir. 2008), the court determined that compensatory damages of $20,000 were at issue. After concluding that punitive damages were available as a matter of law, the court reasoned that it would take a $55,000 punitive award to meet the jurisdictional minimum. Such a punitive award would represent 2.75 times the amount of compensatory damages, well within the single digit ratio discussed in State Farm. The court accordingly upheld jurisdiction. By contrast, the ratio in the hypothetical suit for the return of the security deposit and property would approach 14 to 1 ($70,000 to $5000).

Does the use of a ratio to evaluate the allowable amount of punitive damages satisfy the legal certainty standard in *Red Cab*?

3.   Much of the difficulty in assessing the jurisdictional value of personal injury claims stems from the lack of a precise way to value emotional distress damages. In general, the courts have been relatively lenient in permitting such damages to satisfy the threshold, provided that the plaintiff himself or herself has suffered relatively significant personal injuries. See Stewart v. Tupperware Corp., 356 F.3d 335, 337–38 (1st Cir. 2004) (injuries in automobile accident included hospital bills and impairment of function; emotional injuries were potentially significant enough to meet the minimum). Where the plaintiff suffers no personal injury herself, however, courts may be less willing to presume large, attendant emotional distress. See Rosario Ortega v. Star-Kist Foods, Inc., 370 F.3d 124, 128 (1st Cir. 2004) (mother's distress at child's injury was not sufficiently serious to satisfy the amount in controversy, where out-of-pocket losses to mother were relatively modest), reversed on other grounds, 545 U.S. 546 (2005).

4.   How carefully should the court scrutinize the claim in considering a challenge to the jurisdictional amount? In general, "[i]n contrast to a motion to dismiss for failure to state a claim, in deciding a motion to dismiss for lack of subject matter jurisdiction, the court accepts as true only uncontroverted allegations of the complaint. * * * [D]isputed facts outside the pleadings are subject to the fact-finding of the court." Engage Learning, Inc. v. Salazar, 660 F.3d 1346, 1355 (Fed. Cir. 2011). Consider Scherer v. Equitable Life Assur. Society, 347 F.3d 394 (2d Cir.2003), in which defendant argued that the amount in controversy requirement was not satisfied because almost all of plaintiff's claims were barred by res judicata, leaving claims insufficient to support jurisdiction. The court stressed that jurisdiction had to be determined based on the allegations of the complaint, and rejected defendant's arguments (id. at 397–98):

> [A]ffirmative "defenses asserted on the merits" may not be used to whittle down the amount in controversy. Were such defenses to affect the jurisdictional amount, we have said, "doubt and uncertainty would surround the jurisdictional base of most diversity litigation from complaint to final judgment[, and i]ssues going to a federal court's power to decide would be hopelessly confused with the merits themselves." Even where the complaint itself "discloses the existence of a valid defense," we have declined to consider it in determining whether the jurisdictional test is met.
>
> The rule that affirmative defenses may not be used in determining the jurisdictional amount does not appear to depend on whether a colorable argument against the defense has been advanced. * * *

This may seem paradoxical: if it can be said "to a legal certainty" that the defense in question is a winning defense, ought it not be considered for amount-in-controversy purposes? One plausible answer is that because affirmative defenses can be waived the court cannot *at the time of filing* be certain that any given affirmative defense will be applied to the case. Can you distinguish the punitive damage example, where due process operates as a defense to an excessive award?

Compare the situation in Freeland v. Liberty Mut. Fire Ins. Co., 632 F.3d 250 (6th Cir. 2011), where the appellate court dismissed on its own motion because a declaratory judgment action against an insurance company was for exactly $75,000, and therefore fell one penny short of the jurisdictional minimum. Plaintiff insureds filed a declaratory judgment action against their insurer claiming that the $25,000 per accident limit for uninsured motorist coverage was inapplicable because the insurer had failed to make required disclosures, and that the $100,000 policy limit for other accidents applied. The insurer had already offered plaintiffs the $25,000 before they sued. Under these circumstances, only $75,000 was actually in controversy (id. at 253): In order for the district court to have original jurisdiction, "the matter *in controversy*" must "exceed[ ] the sum or value of $75,000." The words "in controversy" have to mean something. Congress could have written § 1332 to require only that "the matter exceed the sum or value of $75,000," in which case jurisdiction might be appropriate here. But there is simply no controversy over the first $25,000 of coverage. If the [plaintiffs] lose, they will keep that amount of coverage. Indeed, as the [plaintiffs] acknowledged in their complaint in state court, [the insurer] had already offered [them] this amount. The dispute—the controversy—is only over the next $75,000. The court distinguished a situation in which a defendant has made a settlement offer of a certain amount: "If plaintiff sues defendant for $100,000, defendant cannot defeat federal jurisdiction simply by offering to settle the case for $40,000." But in this case the insurer's "acknowledgement that there is no dispute over the first $25,000 of coverage" was different.

Also consider Esquilin-Mendoza v. Don King Productions, Inc., 638 F.3d 1 (1st Cir. 2011), where the court explored what it described as a "confusing" "contested territory" in St Paul Mercury Indem. Co. v. Red Cab Co., 303 U.S. 283 (1938). On the one hand, the Supreme Court said that "[t]he sum claimed by the plaintiff controls if the claim is apparently made in good faith." On the other hand, the case also says dismissal is required when it appears "to a legal certainty that the claim is really for less than the jurisdictional amount." The complaint sought $1 million associated with the wrongful seizure and detention of plaintiff's SUV to satisfy a default judgment in a prior action. But the complaint admitted that liability had correctly attached in the prior action; the party seizing the SUV had only mistakenly described the plaintiff's marital status. The court observed: "Therefore, notwithstanding her presumable good faith in making the claim, we find it clear to a legal certainty that the plaintiff Delia Esquilin has no legal entitlement to damages for emotional injury resulting from a judgment against her and the consequent seizure of her car. * * * [N]otwithstanding its insignificant mistake as to her marital status, [defendant] was entitled to judgment against Delia, the owner of Delia's Tacos, and to seize her car in its execution." Id. at 5. How different is this from deciding the merits to determine whether there is jurisdiction?

5.   In Pershing, LLC v. Kiebach, 819 F.3d 179 (5th Cir. 2016), the court applied the amount in controversy requirement to an action to confirm an arbitration award. Claimants sought to recover some $80 million in losses they suffered in R. Allen Stanford's Ponzi scheme from an outfit they claimed had failed to disclose adverse financial information. An arbitration panel set up under the aegis of the Financial Industry Regulatory Authority, Inc. (FINRA— a private self-regulatory body and successor to the National Association of Securities Dealers) rejected their main claims, but did award them about $10,000 in compensation for certain arbitration-related expenses. The defendant then filed a motion to confirm the arbitration award, which the claimants moved to dismiss for lack of subject matter jurisdiction, citing the $75,000 jurisdictional minimum. Meanwhile, the claimants filed an action to vacate the arbitrators' award in state court. The district court upheld its jurisdiction and certified the question under 28 U.S.C. § 1292(b). The Fifth Circuit affirmed. It found a division in the circuits between the "demand approach" (focusing on the amount sought in the arbitration proceeding) and the "award approach" (focusing on the award actually made by the arbitration panel). It opted for the demand approach because that (1) recognizes the true scope of the controversy; (2) avoids the application of different standards to a petition to compel arbitration (where the demand approach surely must be applied) and one to confirm the award; and (3) allows the district court to exercise jurisdiction coextensive with its diversity jurisdiction in the absence of an agreement to arbitrate. A concurring judge worried that the majority's ruling was too broad.

6.   Actions for nonmonetary relief pose great problems. In general, the amount in controversy is to be determined by reference to the value of the relief sought. But courts are split on whether the relief should be valued from the plaintiff's perspective (value to plaintiff) or the defendant's (cost to defendant). For example, in Glenwood Light & Water Co. v. Mutual Light, Heat & Power Co., 239 U.S. 121(1915), plaintiff sued to restrain defendant from erecting poles and wires in a way that would injure plaintiff's poles and wires. The trial court dismissed because the cost to defendant of changing its method would be less than the jurisdictional amount, but the Supreme Court reversed, holding that plaintiff's right to conduct its business free of wrongful interference had a value far in excess of the jurisdictional amount. Compare C. Wright & M. Kane, Law of Federal Courts 204–07 (7th ed. 2011) (supporting jurisdiction if amount exceeds jurisdictional minimum from viewpoint of either plaintiff or defendant); Macken ex rel. Macken v. Jensen, 333 F.3d 797 (7th Cir. 2003) (following the plaintiff-or-defendant view in valuing the object in controversy) with CE Design Ltd v. American Economy Ins. Co., 755 F.3d 39 (1st Cir. 2014) (holding that the amount in controversy in a suit seeking declaratory relief was the monetary value to the plaintiff of the relief being sought); Cohen v. Office Depot, Inc., 204 F.3d 1069 (11th Cir. 2000) (same). In Note, Diversity Jurisdiction and Injunctive Relief: Using a "Moving-Party Approach" to Value the Amount in Controversy, 95 Minn.L.Rev. 1930 (2011), the author explores the various approaches the courts have used in dealing with this problem, and

endorses an approach that focuses on the value from the perspective of the party invoking federal-court jurisdiction.

7.   The joinder rules lead to counter-intuitive results regarding aggregation of claims to satisfy the jurisdictional minimum. Rule 18 allows plaintiff to combine into one suit all the claims it has against a particular defendant, no matter how unrelated. A long line of cases holds that the aggregate total of all the claims, however unrelated, comprises the jurisdictional amount. By contrast, where several plaintiffs join under Rule 20 in asserting claims against a defendant that all derive from the same transaction or occurrence, they cannot aggregate their related claims to satisfy the jurisdictional minimum. See Clark v. Paul Gray, Inc., 306 U.S. 583 (1939). Similarly, in class actions the Supreme Court held that the claims of class members may not be aggregated to meet the jurisdictional minimum. See Snyder v. Harris, 394 U.S. 332 (1969). The Class Action Fairness Act of 2005, however, added § 1332(d), which authorizes jurisdiction over certain class actions in which an aggregate of at least $5 million is sought by the class. Moreover, as noted infra p. 918, the Supreme Court has interpreted 28 U.S.C. § 1367 to extend supplemental jurisdiction to the related but below-threshold claims of diverse citizen plaintiffs joined under Rules 20 or 23, provided at least one plaintiff submits claims that satisfy the threshold.

8.   Related problems arise with respect to a counterclaim by defendant. If it is permissive, it cannot be added to the amount of the claim to satisfy the amount in controversy requirement where the plaintiff's claim is less than the jurisdictional amount. Even if it is compulsory, taking account of the value of the counterclaim would run afoul of the notion that jurisdiction must be determined from the face of the plaintiff's complaint. Cf. Louisville & Nashville R.R. v. Mottley, infra p. 883, but see Spectacor Management Group v. Brown, 131 F.3d 120 (3d Cir.1997) (holding that a compulsory counterclaim is included in "the substance of the controversy"). In removal situations, a stronger argument can be made for considering the counterclaim if it is compulsory under state law and the defendant would, in effect, be marooned in state court because plaintiff sued there first and has a claim insufficient to satisfy the jurisdictional minimum. In evaluating the problem of the marooned defendant, keep in mind that the defendant in the state court action could often file a stand-alone action in federal court, asserting as a plaintiff the same claim that would appear in state court as a compulsory counterclaim. In the event of such overlapping litigation, the first judgment would often preclude further litigation in the other forum. These complexities help to explain why it is difficult to generalize confidently about the treatment of counterclaims. See generally 14A C. Wright, A. Miller & E. Cooper, Federal Practice & Procedure § 3706 (4th ed. 2008).

B. FEDERAL QUESTION

Article III, § 2 of the Constitution extends the judicial power to "all Cases, in Law and Equity, arising under this Constitution, the Laws of the United States, and Treaties made, or which shall be made, under their

Authority." But aside from a brief period at the dawn of the nineteenth century, Congress did not vest the lower federal courts with general jurisdiction over cases raising federal questions until 1875, when it passed the predecessor to 28 U.S.C. § 1331: "The district courts shall have original jurisdiction of all civil actions arising under the Constitution, laws, or treaties of the United States."

In interpreting this language, the Supreme Court has performed a sorting function. Parties can bring disputes within federal jurisdiction to the district courts, either as an original matter or by removal. The remaining disputes must be handled in the first instance by the state courts (subject to the possibility of review in the Supreme Court on issues of federal law). As you consider the cases below, give some thought to the values that should inform this sorting process. One starting point has been to view the federal district courts as the forum of choice for disputes that implicate the interpretation of federal law. Disputes controlled by state law, by contrast, remain in state court unless the elements of diversity jurisdiction are satisfied. Jurisdictional policy often emphasizes the need for relatively clear rules that will enable the parties and the courts to resolve jurisdictional issues correctly at the outset of the litigation. Rules that look to subsequent events, or that require the exercise of judicial discretion, can undermine the goal of jurisdictional clarity.

1. THE WELL-PLEADED COMPLAINT RULE

LOUISVILLE & NASHVILLE R.R. v. MOTTLEY

Supreme Court of the United States, 1908
211 U.S. 149

Q. v: d

JUSTICE MOODY delivered the opinion of the Court.

The appellees (husband and wife), being residents and citizens of Kentucky, brought this suit in equity in the circuit court of the United States for the western district of Kentucky against the appellant, a railroad company and a citizen of the same state. The object of the suit was to compel the specific performance of the following contract:

Louisville, Ky., Oct. 2d, 1871.

The Louisville & Nashville Railroad Company, in consideration that E. L. Mottley and wife, Annie E. Mottley, have this day released company from all damages or claims for damages for injuries received by them on the 7th of September, 1871, in consequence of a collision of trains on the railroad of said company at Randolph's Station, Jefferson County, Kentucky, hereby agrees to issue free passes on said railroad and branches now existing or to exist, to said E. L. & Annie E. Mottley for the remainder of the present year, and thereafter to renew said passes annually during the lives of said Mottley and wife or either of them.

The bill alleged that in September, 1871, plaintiffs, while passengers upon the defendant railroad, were injured by the defendant's negligence, and released their respective claims for damages in consideration of the agreement for transportation during their lives, expressed in the contract. It is alleged that the contract was performed by the defendant up to January 1, 1907, when the defendant declined to renew the passes. The bill then alleges that the refusal to comply with the contract was based solely upon that part of the act of Congress of June 29, 1906, which forbids the giving of free passes or free transportation. The bill further alleges: First, that the act of Congress referred to does not prohibit the giving of passes under the circumstances of this case; and, second, that, if the law is to be construed as prohibiting such passes, it is in conflict with the 5th Amendment of the Constitution, because it deprives the plaintiffs of their property without due process of law. The defendant demurred to the bill. The judge of the circuit court overruled the demurrer, entered a decree for the relief prayed for, and the defendant appealed directly to this court.

Two questions of law were raised by the demurrer to the bill, were brought here by appeal, and have been argued before us. They are, first, whether that part of the act of Congress of June 29, 1906, which forbids the giving of free passes or the collection of any different compensation for transportation of passengers than that specified in the tariff filed, makes it unlawful to perform a contract for transportation of persons who, in good faith, before the passage of the act, had accepted such contract in satisfaction of a valid cause of action against the railroad; and, second, whether the statute, if it should be construed to render such a contract unlawful, is in violation of the 5th Amendment of the Constitution of the United States. We do not deem it necessary, however, to consider either of these questions, because, in our opinion, the court below was without jurisdiction of the cause. Neither party has questioned that jurisdiction, but it is the duty of this court to see to it that the jurisdiction of the circuit court, which is defined and limited by statute, is not exceeded. This duty we have frequently performed of our own motion.

There was no diversity of citizenship, and it is not and cannot be suggested that there was any ground of jurisdiction, except that the case was a "suit . . . arising under the Constitution or laws of the United States." [The Court here cited the predecessor to 28 U.S.C. § 1331.] It is the settled interpretation of these words, as used in this statute, conferring jurisdiction, that a suit arises under the Constitution and laws of the United States only when the plaintiff's statement of his own cause of action shows that it is based upon those laws or that Constitution. It is not enough that the plaintiff alleges some anticipated defense to his cause of action, and asserts that the defense is invalidated by some provision of the

Constitution of the United States. Although such allegations show that very likely, in the course of the litigation, a question under the Constitution would arise, they do not show that the suit, that is, the plaintiff's original cause of action, arises under the Constitution. * * * [I]n Boston & M. Consol. Copper & S. Min. Co. v. Montana Ore Purchasing Co. 188 U.S. 632, the plaintiff brought suit in the circuit court of the United States for the conversion of copper ore and for an injunction against its continuance. The plaintiff then alleged, for the purpose of showing jurisdiction, in substance, that the defendant would set up in defense certain laws of the United States. The cause was held to be beyond the jurisdiction of the circuit court, the court saying, by Mr. Justice Peckham:

> "It would be wholly unnecessary and improper, in order to prove complainant's cause of action, to go into any matters of defense which the defendants might possibly set up, and then attempt to reply to such defense, and thus, if possible, to show that a Federal question might or probably would arise in the course of the trial of the case. To allege such defense and then make an answer to it before the defendant has the opportunity to itself plead or prove its own defense is inconsistent with any known rule of pleading, so far as we are aware, and is improper.

> "The rule is a reasonable and just one that the complainant in the first instance shall be confined to a statement of its cause of action, leaving to the defendant to set up in his answer what his defense is, and, if anything more than a denial of complainant's cause of action, imposing upon the defendant the burden of proving such defense."

* * *

The application of this rule to the case at bar is decisive against the jurisdiction of the circuit court.

NOTES AND QUESTIONS

1. Note that the Court raised subject matter jurisdiction on its own motion. Unlike personal jurisdiction, subject matter jurisdiction is never waived during the course of the case; the parties cannot by agreement confer this type of jurisdiction on a court that does not have it. See Fed.R.Civ.P. 12(h)(3). Is there a reason why the two types of jurisdiction should be treated so differently?

Different treatment is not required in all cases, however. In Ruhrgas AG v. Marathon Oil Co., 526 U.S. 574 (1999), the district court dismissed a removed action for lack of personal jurisdiction even though there were also objections to the court's subject-matter jurisdiction. Citing an earlier Supreme Court decision that said subject-matter jurisdiction must be established before a decision on the merits, the court of appeals reversed on the ground that personal jurisdiction may never be resolved before subject-matter jurisdiction. Holding that "there is no unyielding jurisdictional hierarchy," the Supreme Court reversed unanimously. Although subject-matter jurisdictional limitations are not waivable and personal jurisdiction limitations may easily be waived, "[t]hese distinctions do not mean that subject-matter jurisdiction is ever and always the more 'fundamental.'" Accordingly, although usually subject-matter jurisdiction question would come first, a district court has discretion to turn to personal jurisdiction if the subject-matter jurisdiction question presents particularly thorny problems. See also Sinochem Int'l Co. v. Malaysia Int'l Shipping Co., 549 U.S. 422 (2007) (upholding dismissal on grounds of forum non conveniens even where doubts persist as to personal or subject matter jurisdiction). See generally Idleman, The Emergence of Jurisdictional Resequencing in the Federal Courts, 87 Cornell L.Rev. 1 (2001) (criticizing this approach); Dodson, Hybridizing Jurisdiction, 99 Calif. L. Rev. 1439 (2011).

2.   It is generally said that the court's jurisdiction must be determined from the plaintiff's complaint, so the Court's adoption of the *well-pleaded complaint rule* to determine whether there is federal question jurisdiction seems natural. Yet even the Supreme Court has seemed ambivalent about the rule:

> It is possible to conceive of a rational jurisdictional system in which the answer as well as the complaint would be consulted before a determination was made whether the case "arose under" federal law, or in which original and removal jurisdiction were not co-extensive. Indeed, until the 1887 amendments to the 1875 Act [granting federal question jurisdiction to the federal courts], the well-pleaded complaint rule was not applied in full force to cases removed from state court; the defendant's petition for removal could furnish the necessary guarantee that the case necessarily presented a substantial question of federal law. Commentators have repeatedly proposed that some mechanism be established to permit removal of cases in which a federal defense may be dispositive. But those proposals have not been adopted.

Franchise Tax Board v. Construction Laborers Vacation Trust, 463 U.S. 1, 10 n. 9 (1983). For an attack on the rule, see Doernberg, There's No Reason For It; It's Just Our Policy: Why the Well-Pleaded Complaint Rule Sabotages the Purpose of Federal Question Jurisdiction, 38 Hast.L.J. 597 (1987). Nonetheless, the Court generally adheres to the view that "Congress has not authorized removal based on a defense, or anticipated defense federal in character." Rivet v. Regions Bank, 522 U.S. 470 (1998).

Are there justifications for the rule that outweigh its drawbacks? Consider:

(a)   The rule requires that the court determine whether the complaint is "well pleaded," so it should disregard superfluous references to federal law that the plaintiff has inserted in an effort to obtain federal jurisdiction. In 1908, it was still thought that distinctions between "ultimate facts" and "mere evidence" could be drawn in a meaningful way, but the adoption of Rule 8(a)(2) shows that the federal system has moved away from that idea. Moreover, as we have seen in Chapter III, distinguishing between matters that are part of plaintiff's pleading burden and those which are affirmative defenses is often difficult. Putting aside these difficulties of application, the rule invites circumvention by the adept; "[i]t is too late in the day to deny that inventive pleading plays some part in conferring jurisdiction upon the federal courts." American Invs-Co Countryside, Inc. v. Riverdale Bank, 596 F.2d 211, 216 (7th Cir.1979).

(b) Assuming that distinctions between proper and improper pleading, and between defenses and claims, can be made, do those distinctions provide a sensible guiding line for federal jurisdiction? Is there less federal interest in a federal defense than a federal issue properly included in plaintiff's complaint? Consider a libel action against a newspaper which claims that the First Amendment protects its right to publish. Although the freedom of speech issue is a defense, it is surely one in which there is a great federal interest. Indeed, the Supremacy Clause, U.S. Const. art. VI, commands state judges to give effect to valid First Amendment defenses. Was Congress anxious to assure access to a federal judge for litigants raising such issues when it created federal question jurisdiction? In evaluating this question, consider that Congress expressly permits defendants in a narrow range of cases to remove an action to federal court on the basis of a federal question defense. See 28 U.S.C. § 1442 (federal officer and agency defendants); § 1442a (members of the armed forces); § 1443 (defendants who cannot enforce their civil rights in state court). One prominent critic of proposals to expand removal jurisdiction to include federal defenses has argued that defendants could too easily formulate colorable federal defenses to shift litigation over state law matters into federal court. See R. Posner, The Federal Courts: Challenge and Reform 302–03 (2d ed. 1996). But is that any less true as to federal issues raised in the complaint? For criticism of the well-pleaded complaint rule, see Redish, Reassessing the Allocation of Judicial Business Between State and Federal Courts: Federal Jurisdiction and "the Martian Chronicles", 78 Va. L. Rev. 1769, 1794–97 (1992).

(c) Like a federal-law defense, a federal-law counterclaim would seem to fail the well-pleaded complaint test. Cf. Holmes Group, Inc. v. Vornado Air Circulation Systems, Inc., 535 U.S. 826 (2002) (noting, in the specialized context of patent litigation, that reliance on counterclaim to establish "arising under" jurisdiction would undermine plaintiff's role as master of the complaint; would radically expand the universe of potentially removable claims; and would undermine the "clarity and ease of administration" of the well-pleaded-complaint doctrine). Consider also Vaden v. Discovery Bank, 556 U.S. 49 (2009). The bank sued Vaden in Maryland state court on "a garden-variety, state-law-based contract claim" for over $10,000 allegedly due on a credit card. Vaden responded with a class action counterclaim, claiming that the bank's finance charges, interest, and late fees violated Maryland's usury laws. The credit card agreement had an arbitration clause, but neither the bank nor

Vaden invoked it while the case was pending in state court. Contending that the Federal Deposit Insurance Act preempted the state-law usury claims, the bank filed a new action in federal court, seeking arbitration under the Federal Arbitration Act. The FAA itself did not create federal jurisdiction, and the Court therefore looked to the underlying dispute in deciding whether jurisdiction existed. Applying the well-pleaded complaint rule, the majority held that the federal court lacked jurisdiction:

> Nor can federal jurisdiction rest upon an actual or anticipated counterclaim. We so ruled, emphatically, in *Holmes Group* [supra]. Without dissent, the Court held in *Holmes Group* that a federal counterclaim, even when compulsory, does not establish "arising under" jurisdiction. Adhering assiduously to the well-pleaded complaint rule, the Court observed that it would undermine the clarity and simplicity of that rule if federal courts were required to consider the contents not only of the complaint but also of responsive pleadings in determining whether a case arises under federal law.

Vaden, 556 U.S. at 60–61. Note, however, that the "America Invents Act," signed in September 2011, included statutory amendments (called the "Holmes Group fix" because they were designed to undo the effects of the specific ruling in that case) that authorize the exercise of removal jurisdiction over patent-law counterclaims. See 28 U.S.C. § 1454. That specific measure leaves in place the general well-pleaded complaint rule and the rule's implication that federal-law counterclaims do not confer jurisdiction under section 1331.

(d) At the time of the *Mottley* decision, litigants in state court had an absolute right to appeal to the Supreme Court when the state courts finally rejected controlling claims or defenses based on federal law. By insisting on the well-pleaded complaint rule, the Court did not lock the parties into state court, but simply required them to litigate there first, subject to its own review of any final decision that presented a dispositive federal issue. Today, by contrast, state court litigants have no right to appellate review of their federal claims and defenses; the Court exercises discretion over what cases to review and takes only some ten to twenty cases each year from the state courts. Does this change in the prospects for federal review of state court decisions help to explain some of the criticism of the well-pleaded complaint rule? Chapter 12 explores the Supreme Court's appellate jurisdiction, infra at p. 1057.

3.   Having lost their federal court judgment on jurisdictional grounds in 1908, the Mottleys promptly sued in a Kentucky state court, raising the same arguments. The state court ordered the railroad to resume issuing free passes to them. The railroad appealed and the Supreme Court again took away the Mottleys' victory, reaching the merits and rejecting both their statutory construction and constitutional arguments. Louisville & Nashville R.R. v. Mottley, 219 U.S. 467 (1911). How could the Court have had authority under Article III to hear the appeal in light of its decision in 1908 that the case did not arise under federal law?

The Court derives its appellate jurisdiction not from 28 U.S.C. § 1331, but from a separate set of statutory provisions. See 28 U.S.C. §§ 1253–59. Its power to review a state court decision depends not on the presence of a well-pleaded federal question on the face of the state court complaint, but on the existence of a dispositive federal question in a final state court judgment. See 28 U.S.C. § 1257. (State court *judgments* may turn on federal law, as in the second *Mottley* decision, even where the *complaint* was based entirely on state law and the federal issues were introduced into the case by way of defense or counterclaim.) In this respect, the constitutional provision for the exercise of arising-under jurisdiction in Article III can be viewed as extending more broadly than the statutory provision for original federal-question jurisdiction in the federal district courts. Thus, there is no question that a newspaper with the First Amendment defense in a libel suit may seek Supreme Court review if that defense is rejected. See, e.g., New York Times Co. v. Sullivan, 376 U.S. 254 (1964).

4. The constitutional grant of arising-under jurisdiction has been interpreted more broadly than § 1331 in yet another respect. In Osborn v. Bank of the United States, 22 U.S. (9 Wheat.) 738 (1824), the Court broadly defined the power of Congress to assign original jurisdiction to the lower federal courts. The statute at issue in *Osborn* had, as the Court read it, granted federal courts jurisdiction over any action to which the Bank of the United States was a party. Many of those actions would have turned entirely on state law. But Chief Justice Marshall, writing for the Court, found this acceptable under Article III; as a federal creation, the Bank's capacity to sue would depend on federal law. At the time Marshall wrote, the states hotly contested the constitutionality of the Bank. See McCulloch v. Maryland, 17 U.S. (4 Wheat.) 316 (1819). But once the question of the Bank's legality was resolved, it would not likely arise again by way of defense to claims brought by the Bank. This fact did not trouble Marshall: "The question [of the Bank's capacity to sue] forms an original ingredient in every cause. Whether it be in fact relied on or not, in the defense, it is still a part of the cause, and may be relied upon." While Marshall's account suggests a willingness to uphold federal jurisdiction based on challenges to the Bank's capacity to sue that were in fact never raised, scholars argue that Marshall did not mean to go quite that far. See Bellia, The Origins of Article III "Arising Under" Jurisdiction, 57 Duke L.J. 263 (2007).

In American National Red Cross v. S.G., 505 U.S. 247 (1992), the Court held that the federal statute chartering the Red Cross conferred original federal court jurisdiction because it authorized the organization "to sue or be sued in courts of law and equity, State or Federal, within the jurisdiction of the United States." Regarding the constitutionality of this interpretation, the Court said: "As long ago as *Osborn,* the Court held that Article Ill's 'arising under' jurisdiction is broad enough to authorize Congress to confer federal court jurisdiction over actions involving federally chartered corporations." While the constitutional principle in *Osborn* and *American Red Cross* has not been questioned in later cases involving the sue-and-be-sued provisions of corporate charters, the Court has looked closely at the charter's language to ensure that Congress meant to confer jurisdiction rather than capacity. See

Lightfoot v. Cendant Mortgage Corp., 137 S.Ct. 553 (2017) (concluding that charter provision, authorizing Fannie Mae "to sue and to be sued, and to complain and to defend, in any court of competent jurisdiction, State or Federal," conferred capacity to sue rather than federal subject matter jurisdiction).

Does the *Osborn* view overextend federal judicial power? Some have argued that it would permit Congress to assign all land disputes in the western states to the federal courts, even though their outcome would be controlled by state law, because they depend ultimately upon original federal land grants. Similarly, the dissent in *Osborn* claimed that the theory of the case would permit Congress to allow all naturalized citizens to sue or be sued in federal court on ordinary contract and tort claims. In both of the hypothesized statutes, state law would control the dispute's resolution. What federal interest would Congress advance through such jurisdictional grants? Does the absence of any such interest minimize the possibility that Congress will confer expansive grants of federal-question jurisdiction? Whether or not Congress would choose to exercise it, the power obviously extends more broadly than § 1331.

5.   The application of the well-pleaded complaint rule was blurred further by the adoption of the Declaratory Judgment Act, 28 U.S.C. §§ 2201– 02. In allowing suit for a declaration of the rights of the parties in a "case of actual controversy," the Act contemplates that litigants in the position of the Mottleys will include reference to the federal defense in an action to declare that the defense is not valid. In other words, in a real sense the complaint's reference to the federal issue would be "well pleaded." However, in Skelly Oil Co. v. Phillips Petroleum Co., 339 U.S. 667 (1950), the Court ruled that the references to federal defenses in a Declaratory Judgment Act proceeding otherwise governed by state law would not confer federal jurisdiction. Noting that to rule otherwise would "turn into the federal courts a vast current of litigation indubitably arising under State law," the Court emphasized that the Act did not broaden federal jurisdiction: "To sanction suits for declaratory relief as within the jurisdiction of the District Courts merely because, as in this case, artful pleading anticipates a defense based on federal law would contravene the whole trend of jurisdictional legislation by Congress, disregard the effective functioning of the federal judicial system and distort the limited procedural purpose of the Declaratory Judgment Act." Accordingly, there is federal question jurisdiction only when the coercive action would itself be within federal jurisdiction. For a criticism of this decision, see M. Redish, Federal Jurisdiction: Tensions in the Allocation of Judicial Power 108–10 (2d ed. 1990).

Is the result in *Skelly Oil* compelled by *Mottley?* Whatever the risk of error in the plaintiff's anticipation of federal defenses in the *Mottley* situation, the declaratory judgment plaintiff *must* show an actual dispute between the parties about federal law. In Franchise Tax Board v. Construction Laborers Vacation Trust, 463 U.S. 1 (1983), the state taxing authority sought a declaratory judgment in state court that, despite the federal Employment Retirement Income Security Act (ERISA), it could collect unpaid state income taxes by levying on taxpayers' funds held in trust pursuant to ERISA by defendants. As the Board alleged in its complaint, defendants took the position that ERISA precluded such action, and it seemed clear that this was the only disputed legal issue in the case. But when defendants removed the case to federal court, the Supreme Court somewhat reluctantly held that *Skelly Oil* should be extended to apply to actions brought under state declaratory judgment acts as well: "The issue is an important one, which affects thousands of federally regulated trusts and all non-federal tax collection systems, and it must eventually receive a definitive, uniform resolution. Nevertheless, for reasons involving perhaps more history than logic, we hold that the lower federal courts had no jurisdiction to decide the question in the case before us."

6.   Should preemption be a ground for exercising federal jurisdiction? Ordinarily preemption is said to be a defense to a state law cause of action and therefore, under *Mottley,* it provides no basis for federal jurisdiction under § 1331, even where the preemption issue is raised in a declaratory judgment action, as the Court held in *Franchise Tax Board.* But there are exceptions. In a puzzling but well established line of cases, the Court has permitted a party to invoke federal question jurisdiction in seeking injunctive and declaratory relief against state laws on grounds of preemption. See, e.g., Sprint Communications, Inc. v. Jacobs, 571 U.S. 69 (2013) (citing Verizon Maryland, Inc. v. Public Servs. Comm'n, 535 U.S. 635, 642 (2002), for the proposition that right to seek injunctive relief against preempted state law does not violate the well-pleaded complaint rule); Shaw v. Delta Air Lines, Inc., 463 U.S. 85, 96 n.14 (1983) (same). One can best perhaps rationalize the cases as recognizing that federal law creates an implied right of action to enforce the federal interest in the displacement (under the Supremacy Clause) of preempted state law, although that's a conclusion the Court has rejected in other settings. We consider the jurisdictional significance of the implied right of action below at pp. 899–900.

A second line of cases gives rise to what has been termed the complete preemption doctrine:

> One corollary of the well-pleaded complaint rule developed in the case law, however, is that Congress may so completely pre-empt a particular area, that any civil complaint raising this select group of claims is necessarily federal in character. For 20 years, this Court has singled out claims pre-empted by § 301 of the Labor Management Relations Act (LMRA), 29 U.S.C. § 185, for such special treatment. Avco Corp. v. Machinists, 390 U.S. 557 (1968).

> The necessary ground of decision [in *Avco]* was that the preemptive force of § 301 is so powerful as to displace entirely any state cause of action "for violation of contracts between an employer and a labor organization." Any such suit is purely a creature of federal law, notwithstanding the fact that state law would provide a cause of action in the absence of § 301.

Metropolitan Life Ins. Co. v. Taylor, 481 U.S. 58, 64 (1987) (quoting *Franchise Tax Board*). In *Metropolitan Life* the Court held that plaintiff's state law claim regarding benefits under employee benefit plan had been "displaced" by the Employee Retirement Security Act (ERISA), 29 U.S.C. §§ 1001 et seq., because the legislative history said that they should be handled "in similar fashion to those brought under section 301 of the Labor-Management Relations Act," which the Court took to be a "specific reference to the *Avco* rule."

In attempting to rationalize the complete preemption doctrine, the Court has emphasized two factors: that the statute at issue must completely preempt state law causes of action and that it must create a federal cause of action that Congress regarded as the exclusive basis for seeking to remedy the conduct at issue in the complaint. See Beneficial Nat. Bank v. Anderson, 539 U.S. 1 (2003) (National Bank Act completely preempts state-law usury claim against a national bank). Compare Caterpillar Inc. v. Williams, 482 U.S. 386 (1987), in which the Court found that LMRA § 301 did not displace claims by employees for violation of contractual undertakings independent of the collective bargaining agreement.

7.   Except in cases where federal law displaces state claims, plaintiff is ordinarily free to rely solely on state law grounds and thereby defeat federal jurisdiction. But in a footnote in Federated Department Stores, Inc. v. Moitie, 452 U.S. 394 (1981), the Court suggested that "artful pleading" could not be used to avoid federal jurisdiction. In Rivet v. Regions Bank, 522 U.S. 470 (1998), however, the Court ruled that unless there is a completely preemptive federal statute (see note 6 above), the well-pleaded complaint rule precludes consideration of claims the plaintiff has declined to raise. For discussion, see Miller, Artful Pleading: A Doctrine in Search of Definition, 76 Tex. L. Rev. 1781 (1998); Seinfeld, The Puzzle of Complete Preemption, 155 U. Pa. L. Rev. 557 (2007). *Moitie* is discussed in connection with a different issue, infra p. 1185.

2.   STATE LAW CLAIMS WITH FEDERAL INGREDIENTS

GUNN V. MINTON

Supreme Court of the United States, 2013
568 U.S. 251

CHIEF JUSTICE ROBERTS delivered the opinion for a unanimous Court.

Federal courts have exclusive jurisdiction over cases "arising under any Act of Congress relating to patents." 28 U.S.C. § 1338(a). The question presented is whether a state law claim alleging legal malpractice in the handling of a patent case must be brought in federal court.

I

In the early 1990s, respondent Vernon Minton developed a computer program and telecommunications network designed to facilitate securities trading. In March 1995, he leased the system—known as the Texas Computer Exchange Network, or TEXCEN—to R.M. Stark & Co., a securities brokerage. A little over a year later, he applied for a patent for an interactive securities trading system that was based substantially on TEXCEN. The U.S. Patent and Trademark Office issued the patent in January 2000.

Patent in hand, Minton filed a patent infringement suit in Federal District Court against the National Association of Securities Dealers, Inc. (NASD) and the NASDAQ Stock Market, Inc. He was represented by Jerry Gunn and the other petitioners. NASD and NASDAQ moved for summary judgment on the ground that Minton's patent was invalid under the "on sale" bar, 35 U.S.C. § 102(b). That provision specifies that an inventor is not entitled to a patent if "the invention was . . . on sale in [the United States], more than one year prior to the date of the application," and Minton had leased TEXCEN to Stark more than one year prior to filing his patent application. Rejecting Minton's argument that there were differences between TEXCEN and the patented system that precluded application of the on-sale bar, the District Court granted the summary judgment motion and declared Minton's patent invalid. * * *

Minton then filed a motion for reconsideration in the District Court, arguing for the first time that the lease agreement with Stark was part of ongoing testing of TEXCEN and therefore fell within the "experimental use" exception to the on-sale bar. * * * The District Court denied the motion. * * *

Minton appealed to the U.S. Court of Appeals for the Federal Circuit. That court affirmed, concluding that the District Court had appropriately held Minton's experimental-use argument waived. * * *

Minton, convinced that his attorneys' failure to raise the experimental-use argument earlier had cost him the lawsuit and led to invalidation of his patent, brought this malpractice action in Texas state court. His former lawyers defended on the ground that the lease to Stark was not, in fact, for an experimental use, and that therefore Minton's patent infringement claims would have failed even if the experimental-use argument had been timely raised. The trial court agreed, holding that Minton had put forward "less than a scintilla of proof" that the lease had been for an experimental purpose. It accordingly granted summary judgment to Gunn and the other lawyer defendants.

On appeal, Minton raised a new argument: Because his legal malpractice claim was based on an alleged error in a patent case, it "aris[es] under" federal patent law for purposes of 28 U.S.C. § 1338(a). And because, under § 1338(a), "[n]o State court shall have jurisdiction over any claim for relief arising under any Act of Congress relating to patents," the Texas court—where Minton had originally brought his malpractice claim—lacked subject matter jurisdiction to decide the case. Accordingly, Minton argued, the trial court's order should be vacated and the case dismissed, leaving Minton free to start over in the Federal District Court.

A divided panel of the Court of Appeals of Texas rejected Minton's argument. Applying the test we articulated in Grable & Sons Metal Products, Inc. v. Darue Engineering & Mfg., 545 U.S. 308, 314 (2005), it held that the federal interests implicated by Minton's state law claim were not sufficiently substantial to trigger § 1338 "arising under" jurisdiction. It also held that finding exclusive federal jurisdiction over state legal malpractice actions would, contrary to *Grable*'s commands, disturb the balance of federal and state judicial responsibilities. Proceeding to the merits of Minton's malpractice claim, the Court of Appeals affirmed the trial court's determination that Minton had failed to establish experimental use and that arguments on that ground therefore would not have saved his infringement suit.

The Supreme Court of Texas reversed, relying heavily on a pair of cases from the U.S. Court of Appeals for the Federal Circuit. * * * The Court concluded that Minton's claim involved "a substantial federal issue" within the meaning of *Grable* "because the success of Minton's malpractice claim is reliant upon the viability of the experimental use exception as a defense to the on-sale bar." Adjudication of Minton's claim in federal court was consistent with the appropriate balance between federal and state judicial responsibilities, it held, because "the federal government and patent litigants have an interest in the uniform application of patent law by courts well-versed in that subject matter." * * *

II

"Federal courts are courts of limited jurisdiction," possessing "only that power authorized by Constitution and statute." Kokkonen v. Guardian Life Ins. Co. of America, 511 U.S. 375, 377 (1994). There is no dispute that the Constitution permits Congress to extend federal court jurisdiction to a case such as this one, see Osborn v. Bank of United States, 9 Wheat. 738, 823–824 (1824); the question is whether Congress has done so, see Powell v. McCormack, 395 U.S. 486 (1969).

As relevant here, Congress has authorized the federal district courts to exercise original jurisdiction in "all civil actions arising under the Constitution, laws, or treaties of the United States," 28 U.S.C. § 1331, and, more particularly, over "any civil action arising under any Act of Congress relating to patents," § 1338(a). Adhering to the demands of "[l]inguistic consistency," we have interpreted the phrase "arising under" in both sections identically, applying our § 1331 and § 1338(a) precedents interchangeably. See Christianson v. Colt Industries Operating Corp., 486 U.S. 800, 808–809 (1988). For cases falling within the patent-specific arising under jurisdiction of § 1338(a), however, Congress has not only provided for federal jurisdiction but also eliminated state jurisdiction, decreeing that "[n]o State court shall have jurisdiction over any claim for relief arising under any Act of Congress relating to patents." § 1338(a) (2006 ed., Supp. V). To determine whether jurisdiction was proper in the

Texas courts, therefore, we must determine whether it would have been proper in a federal district court—whether, that is, the case "aris[es] under any Act of Congress relating to patents."

For statutory purposes, a case can "aris[e] under" federal law in two ways. Most directly, a case arises under federal law when federal law creates the cause of action asserted. * * *

But even where a claim finds its origins in state rather than federal law—as Minton's legal malpractice claim indisputably does—we have identified a "special and small category" of cases in which arising under jurisdiction still lies. Empire Healthchoice Assurance, Inc. v. McVeigh, 547 U.S. 677, 699 (2006). In outlining the contours of this slim category, we do not paint on a blank canvas. Unfortunately, the canvas looks like one that Jackson Pollock got to first. * * *

In an effort to bring some order to this unruly doctrine several Terms ago, we condensed our prior cases into the following inquiry: Does the "state-law claim necessarily raise a stated federal issue, actually disputed and substantial, which a federal forum may entertain without disturbing any congressionally approved balance of federal and state judicial responsibilities"? *Grable*, 545 U.S., at 314. That is, federal jurisdiction over a state law claim will lie if a federal issue is: (1) necessarily raised, (2) actually disputed, (3) substantial, and (4) capable of resolution in federal court without disrupting the federal-state balance approved by Congress. Where all four of these requirements are met, we held, jurisdiction is proper because there is a "serious federal interest in claiming the advantages thought to be inherent in a federal forum," which can be vindicated without disrupting Congress's intended division of labor between state and federal courts. Id., at 313–314.

III

Applying *Grable*'s inquiry here, it is clear that Minton's legal malpractice claim does not arise under federal patent law. Indeed, for the reasons we discuss, we are comfortable concluding that state legal malpractice claims based on underlying patent matters will rarely, if ever, arise under federal patent law for purposes of § 1338(a). Although such cases may necessarily raise disputed questions of patent law, those cases are by their nature unlikely to have the sort of significance for the federal system necessary to establish jurisdiction.

A

To begin, we acknowledge that resolution of a federal patent question is "necessary" to Minton's case. * * * To prevail on his legal malpractice claim * * * Minton must show that he would have prevailed in his federal patent infringement case if only petitioners had timely made an experimental-use argument on his behalf. That will necessarily require application of patent law to the facts of Minton's case.

B

The federal issue is also "actually disputed" here—indeed, on the merits, it is the central point of dispute. * * *

C

Minton's argument founders on *Grable*'s next requirement, however, for the federal issue in this case is not substantial in the relevant sense. In reaching the opposite conclusion, the Supreme Court of Texas focused on the importance of the issue to the plaintiff's case and to the parties before it. * * * As our past cases show, however, it is not enough that the federal issue be significant to the particular parties in the immediate suit; that will always be true when the state claim "necessarily raise[s]" a disputed federal issue, as *Grable* separately requires. The substantiality inquiry under *Grable* looks instead to the importance of the issue to the federal system as a whole.

[margin note: Prof. says this is the key line.]

In *Grable* itself, for example, the Internal Revenue Service had seized property from the plaintiff and sold it to satisfy the plaintiff's federal tax delinquency. * * * In holding that the case arose under federal law, we primarily focused not on the interests of the litigants themselves, but rather on the broader significance of the notice question for the Federal Government. We emphasized the Government's "strong interest" in being able to recover delinquent taxes through seizure and sale of property, which in turn "require[d] clear terms of notice to allow buyers . . . to satisfy themselves that the Service has touched the bases necessary for good title." The Government's "direct interest in the availability of a federal forum to vindicate its own administrative action" made the question "an important issue of federal law that sensibly belong[ed] in a federal court."

A second illustration of the sort of substantiality we require comes from Smith v. Kansas City Title & Trust Co., 255 U.S. 180 (1921), which *Grable* described as "[t]he classic example" of a state claim arising under federal law. * * * We held that the case arose under federal law, because the "decision depends upon the determination" of "the constitutional validity of an act of Congress which is directly drawn in question." Again, the relevant point was not the importance of the question to the parties alone but rather the importance more generally of a determination that the Government "securities were issued under an unconstitutional law, and hence of no validity."

Here, the federal issue carries no such significance. Because of the backward-looking nature of a legal malpractice claim, the question is posed in a merely hypothetical sense: If Minton's lawyers had raised a timely experimental-use argument, would the result in the patent infringement proceeding have been different? No matter how the state courts resolve that hypothetical "case within a case," it will not change the real-world result of the prior federal patent litigation. Minton's patent will remain invalid.

Nor will allowing state courts to resolve these cases undermine "the development of a uniform body of [patent] law." Bonito Boats, Inc. v. Thunder Craft Boats, Inc., 489 U.S. 141, 162 (1989). Congress ensured such uniformity by vesting exclusive jurisdiction over actual patent cases in the federal district courts and exclusive appellate jurisdiction in the Federal Circuit. See 28 U.S.C. §§ 1338(a), 1295(a)(1). In resolving the nonhypothetical patent questions those cases present, the federal courts are of course not bound by state court case-within-a-case patent rulings. See Tafflin v. Levitt, 493 U.S. 455, 465 (1990). In any event, the state court case-within-a-case inquiry asks what would have happened in the prior federal proceeding if a particular argument had been made. In answering that question, state courts can be expected to hew closely to the pertinent federal precedents. It is those precedents, after all, that would have applied had the argument been made.

As for more novel questions of patent law that may arise for the first time in a state court "case within a case," they will at some point be decided by a federal court in the context of an actual patent case, with review in the Federal Circuit. If the question arises frequently, it will soon be resolved within the federal system, laying to rest any contrary state court precedent; if it does not arise frequently, it is unlikely to implicate substantial federal interests. The present case is "poles apart from Grable," in which a state court's resolution of the federal question "would be controlling in numerous other cases." Empire Healthchoice Assurance, Inc., 547 U.S., at 700.

Minton also suggests that state courts' answers to hypothetical patent questions can sometimes have real-world effect on other patents through issue preclusion. * * * It is unclear whether this is true. * * * But even assuming that a state court's case-within-a-case adjudication may be preclusive under some circumstances, the result would be limited to the parties and patents that had been before the state court. Such "fact-bound and situation-specific" effects are not sufficient to establish federal arising under jurisdiction. Empire Healthchoice Assurance, Inc., at 701.

Nor can we accept the suggestion that the federal courts' greater familiarity with patent law means that legal malpractice cases like this one belong in federal court. It is true that a similar interest was among those we considered in Grable, 545 U.S., at 314. But the possibility that a state court will incorrectly resolve a state claim is not, by itself, enough to trigger the federal courts' exclusive patent jurisdiction, even if the potential error finds its root in a misunderstanding of patent law.

There is no doubt that resolution of a patent issue in the context of a state legal malpractice action can be vitally important to the particular parties in that case. But something more, demonstrating that the question is significant to the federal system as a whole, is needed. That is missing here.

D

It follows from the foregoing that *Grable*'s fourth requirement is also not met. That requirement is concerned with the appropriate "balance of federal and state judicial responsibilities." Ibid. We have already explained the absence of a substantial federal issue within the meaning of *Grable*. The States, on the other hand, have "a special responsibility for maintaining standards among members of the licensed professions." Ohralik v. Ohio State Bar Assn., 436 U.S. 447 (1978). * * * We have no reason to suppose that Congress—in establishing exclusive federal jurisdiction over patent cases—meant to bar from state courts state legal malpractice claims simply because they require resolution of a hypothetical patent issue. * * *

The judgment of the Supreme Court of Texas is reversed, and the case is remanded for further proceedings not inconsistent with this opinion.

NOTES AND QUESTIONS

1.   As we have seen, the analysis of federal question jurisdiction begins with a consideration of the body of law that provides for or creates the claims asserted in the complaint. Federal question jurisdiction has been generally upheld where federal law creates the right to sue. Conversely, when state law creates the right of action, courts usually treat the claim as arising under state law and as a matter for state court adjudication (at least in the absence of diversity of citizenship). Justice Holmes argued that the jurisdictional inquiry should end there: he took the view that claims arise under the body of law, state or federal, that creates the right of action. See American Well Works Co. v. Layne & Bowler Co., 241 U.S. 257 (1916). But the Court has not adopted the Holmes view; it has on occasion refused federal jurisdiction over claims created by a federal statute and has, more frequently, allowed jurisdiction over state-created claims with embedded federal ingredients (thereby creating the Jackson Pollock canvas to which the Chief Justice referred in Gunn v. Minton). A quick summary follows of the decisions on which the *Gunn* Court relied.

2.   In Smith v. Kansas City Title & Trust Co., 255 U.S. 180 (1921), a shareholder of the defendant corporation brought suit in federal court to enjoin the company from investing in bonds issued under the authority of the Federal Farm Loan Act. The complaint alleged that Missouri law imposed a fiduciary duty on the corporation, limiting its investments to bonds that had been duly issued and validly authorized. The complaint further alleged that the Congress could not, consistent with the Constitution, adopt the Federal Farm Loan Act or authorize the issuance of the bonds in question. Thus, a state created cause of action for breach of fiduciary duty raised a federal question concerning the power of Congress to adopt the challenged legislation. The Court upheld the jurisdiction, reasoning that the "right to relief depends on the construction or application of the Constitution or laws of the United States" and "rests upon a

reasonable foundation." Justice Holmes dissented from the assertion of jurisdiction on the ground that state law created the cause of action.

3.   In Moore v. Chesapeake & Ohio Ry., 291 U.S. 205 (1934), by contrast, the Court refused to allow jurisdiction over the claim of an injured railroad worker. There, the plaintiff brought suit under a Kentucky statute that allowed recovery of damages for personal injuries and declared that doctrines of contributory negligence and assumption of the risk were inapplicable when the employer/defendant had violated a federal safety standard. Moore alleged that his injuries resulted from the defendant's failure to comply with the Federal Safety Appliance Act, which regulated the safety of coupling devices on railroad cars. The Court found that the state-created claim did not arise under federal law, despite the reference to federal law. As the Court explained, the federal statute "touched the duty of the [employer] at a single point and, save as provided in the statute, the right of the plaintiff to recover was left to be determined by the law of the state." One text proposed to reconcile the cases by noting that the federal elements in *Moore* would have entered the case as affirmative defenses in violation of the well-pleaded complaint rule. See R. Fallon, D. Meltzer & D. Shapiro, Hart & Wechsler's Federal Courts and the Federal System 135 n. 2 (6th ed. Supp. 2008).

4.   Many years after *Smith* and *Moore,* the Court decided Merrell Dow Pharmaceuticals, Inc. v. Thompson, 478 U.S. 804 (1986).

(a)   *The regulatory backdrop*: Merrell Dow marketed the drug Bendectin in the United States, Canada, and Europe to treat nausea and morning sickness in pregnant women. Some women who took the drug gave birth to children with birth defects. State and federal law could in theory provide at least three different kinds of remedies for such personal injuries. The children (or their guardians) might bring suit under state law, seeking damages for negligence or failure to warn. Alternatively, the children might ask the federal regulatory agency, here the Food and Drug Administration, to pursue some sort of enforcement action against the company on their behalf. Finally, the children might bring suit under federal law, provided that the Act of Congress creates both a federal right to properly labeled drugs and a federal right of action that empowers individuals to bring suit for damages for any personal injuries suffered as a result of mislabeling or misbranding. In deciding what course of action to pursue, the lawyer for the plaintiffs would necessarily consult the federal statute, here the Federal Food Drug and Cosmetic Act (FDCA), 52 Stat. 1040, as amended, and the cases that define the availability of federal rights of action.

Although the FDCA empowers the *FDA* to regulate drug safety and labeling, it does not create an express federal right of action enabling *individuals* to sue for personal injuries caused by violations of the Act. But Congress's failure to provide explicitly for personal injury litigation does not necessarily foreclose it. Congress may have assumed the existence of *state* law tort remedies and provided supplementary federal regulations. Alternatively Congress may have put in place a regulatory scheme that assumes or "implies" the existence of a *federal* right of action for damages. To some extent, the plaintiff (as master of the complaint) can structure the litigation as she sees fit, bringing suit on the basis of state common law or on the basis of a federal implied right of action or both. Both strategies have risks: the court might decline to recognize an implied federal right of action, a prospect increasingly likely given the Supreme Court's oft-stated reluctance to embrace a right of action that Congress has not seen fit to furnish itself. Moreover, the court might find that federal law preempts the state common law claims, depending on whether Congress expected the federal administrative enforcement option to exclude state remedies.

Lawyers evaluating the choices available in the *Merrell Dow* litigation would understand that the federal courts generally treat the assertion of an implied federal right of action as conferring subject matter jurisdiction on the district courts under 28 U.S.C. § 1331. The fact that the court may reject the purported federal claim on the merits does not preclude subject matter jurisdiction from attaching. In Bell v. Hood, 327 U.S. 678 (1946), the Court rejected an attempt to link the jurisdictional inquiry to a determination whether the complaint states a claim for relief. To decide if there is federal question jurisdiction, the court "must look to the way the complaint is drawn to see if it is drawn so as to claim a right to recover under the Constitution and laws of the United States. * * * [I]t is well settled that the failure to state a proper cause of action calls for a judgment on the merits and not a dismissal for want of jurisdiction." In Bell v. Hood, the Court went on, however, to distinguish cases "where the alleged claim under the Constitution or federal statutes clearly appears to be immaterial and made solely for the purpose of obtaining jurisdiction, or where the claim is wholly insubstantial and frivolous." In such cases, dismissal for lack of jurisdiction is proper. The Court's distinction apparently seeks to ensure that the lower courts have jurisdiction to make binding determinations of doubtful causes of action. Of course, if the Supreme Court were definitively to reject the claim that a particular statute gives rise to an implied right of action, the allegation of such an action would lack the colorable foundation needed to confer jurisdiction. By contrast, if the Court were to recognize a particular implied right of action, there would be no question that § 1331 would provide federal jurisdiction over that claim.

(b) *The Ohio litigation*: The Thompsons and McTavishes, from Canada and Scotland respectively, filed their personal injury claims in Ohio state court. They did not allege the existence of an implied federal right of action, but sought recovery on state common law theories of liability. Plaintiffs sought to avoid removal of their action because federal courts had previously dismissed lawsuits by overseas victims on forum non conveniens grounds; plaintiffs did so by withholding any federal claims and by suing the defendant in its Ohio state of incorporation (which under 28 U.S.C. § 1441(b) would preclude removal on the basis of diversity of citizenship). As a strategic matter, the plaintiffs apparently believed that the state court would allow the claims to proceed to trial (declining to apply the federal doctrine of forum non conveniens).

The defendant, Merrell Dow, removed anyway. Count IV of the six-count complaint alleged that Merrell Dow had been negligent in failing to warn about the dangers of Bendectin. In support of this negligence claim, plaintiffs alleged that the drug had been misbranded in violation of the FDCA. Relying on *Smith v. Kansas City Title & Trust,* the district court found that Count IV presented a state-created negligence cause of action with a federal statutory ingredient. After confirming its jurisdiction, the district court dismissed for forum non conveniens. The Sixth Circuit reversed, viewing the federal issues as too insubstantial to warrant federal jurisdiction.

(c)   *The majority opinion*: The Supreme Court affirmed in an opinion by Justice Stevens for himself and four others. The Court first noted the importance of making "sensitive judgments about congressional intent, judicial power, and the federal system." In assessing congressional intent, the Court continued:

> In this case, both parties agree with the Court of Appeals' conclusion that there is no federal cause of action for FDCA violations. For purposes of our decision, we assume that this is a correct interpretation of the FDCA. Thus, as the case comes to us, it is appropriate to assume that, under the settled framework for evaluating whether a federal cause of action lies, some combination of the following factors is present: (1) the plaintiffs are not part of the class for whose special benefit the statute was passed; (2) the indicia of legislative intent reveal no congressional purpose to provide a private cause of action; (3) a federal cause of action would not further the underlying purposes of the legislative scheme; and (4) the respondents' cause of action is a subject traditionally relegated to state law. In short, Congress did not intend a private federal remedy for violations of the statute that it enacted.

The Court pointed out that it had concluded in prior cases that implying a private federal remedy would "flout congressional intent" in situations that did not satisfy its four-part test. To permit a federal court to entertain a state-law claim based on a federal statute that would not support a direct federal claim, it concluded, would similarly "flout" congressional intent. Having thus emphasized the negative implications that flowed from Congress's failure to create an express right of action, the Court considered three more arguments advanced in support of jurisdiction.

> First, petitioner contends that the case represents a straightforward application of the statement in *Franchise Tax Board* [supra p. 890 n. 5] that federal-question jurisdiction is appropriate when "it appears that some substantial, disputed question of federal law is a necessary element of one of the well-pleaded state claims." *Franchise Tax Board,* however, did not purport to disturb the long-settled understanding that the mere presence of a federal issue in a state cause of action does not automatically confer federal-question jurisdiction. * * *

Far from creating some kind of automatic test, *Franchise Tax Board* thus candidly recognized the need for careful judgments about the exercise of federal judicial power in an area of uncertain jurisdiction. Given the significance of the assumed congressional determination to preclude federal private remedies, the presence of the federal issue as an element of the state tort is not the kind of adjudication for which jurisdiction would serve congressional purposes and the federal system. This conclusion is fully consistent with the very sentence relied on so heavily by petitioner. We simply conclude that the congressional determination that there should be no federal remedy for the violation of this federal statute is tantamount to a congressional conclusion that the presence of a claimed violation of the statute as an element of a state cause of action is insufficiently "substantial" to confer federal-question jurisdiction.

In accompanying footnote 12, Justice Stevens added the following comment:

Several commentators have suggested that our § 1331 decisions can best be understood as an evaluation of the nature of the federal interest at stake. See, e.g., Shapiro, Jurisdiction and Discretion, 60 N.Y.U.L. Rev. 543, 568 (1985). * * *

Focusing on the nature of the federal interest, moreover, suggests that the widely perceived "irreconcilable" conflict between the finding of federal jurisdiction in Smith v. Kansas City Title & Trust Co., 255 U.S. 180 (1921), and the finding of no jurisdiction in Moore v. Chesapeake & Ohio R. Co., 291 U.S. 205 (1934), see, e.g., M. Redish, Federal Jurisdiction: Tensions in the Allocation of Judicial Power 67 (1980), is far from clear. For the difference in results can be seen as manifestations of the differences in the nature of the federal issues at stake. In *Smith,* as the Court emphasized, the issue was the constitutionality of an important federal statute. In *Moore,* in contrast, the Court emphasized that the violation of the federal standard as an element of state tort recovery did not fundamentally change the state tort nature of the action.

Returning to its consideration of petitioner's arguments, the Court rejected the contention that the assertion of federal jurisdiction was necessary to help ensure uniform interpretation of federal law:

In addition to the significance of the congressional decision to preclude a federal remedy, we do not agree with petitioner's characterization of the federal interest and its implications for federal-question jurisdiction. To the extent that petitioner is arguing that state use and interpretation of the FDCA pose a threat to the order and stability of the FDCA regime, petitioner should be arguing, not that federal courts should be able to review and enforce state FDCA-based causes of action as an aspect of federal-question jurisdiction, but that the FDCA preempts state-court jurisdiction over the issue in dispute. Petitioner's concern about the uniformity of interpretation, moreover, is considerably mitigated by the fact that, even if there is no original district court jurisdiction for these kinds of action, this Court retains power to review the decision of a federal issue in a state cause of action.

Finally, the Court evaluated the argument that "special circumstances" justified federal-question jurisdiction.

> Petitioner emphasizes that it is unclear whether the FDCA applies to sales in Canada and Scotland; there is, therefore, a special reason for having a federal court answer the novel federal question relating to the extraterritorial meaning of the Act. We reject this argument. * * * The novelty of an FDCA issue is not sufficient to give it status as a federal cause of action; nor should it be sufficient to give a state-based FDCA claim status as a jurisdiction-triggering federal question.

(d)   *The dissent*: Speaking for four members of the Court, Justice Brennan wrote a strong dissent. He began with the assumption that *Smith* remained good law and argued that any substantial federal ingredient in a state-created cause of action should suffice to confer federal question jurisdiction. Justice Brennan also responded to the claims in Justice Stevens' footnote 12.

> In one sense, the Court is correct in asserting that we can reconcile *Smith* and *Moore* on the ground that the "nature" of the federal interest was more significant in *Smith* than in *Moore*. Indeed, as the Court appears to believe, we could reconcile many of the seemingly inconsistent results that have been reached under § 1331 with such a test. But this is so only because a test based upon an ad hoc evaluation of the importance of the federal issue is infinitely malleable: at what point does a federal interest become strong enough to create jurisdiction? * * * However, the inevitable—and undesirable—result of a test such as that suggested in the Court's footnote 12 is that federal jurisdiction turns in every case on an appraisal of the federal issue, its importance and its relation to state law issues. Yet it is precisely because the Court believes that federal jurisdiction would be "ill-served" by such a case-by-case appraisal that it rejects petitioners' claim that the difficulty and importance of the statutory issue presented by their claim suffices to confer jurisdiction under § 1331. The Court cannot have it both ways.

4.   In the wake of *Merrell Dow,* lower courts struggled to apply the Court's analysis to other situations in which state-created claims included federal ingredients. For a summary, see Note, Mr. *Smith* Goes to Federal Court: Federal Question Jurisdiction Post *Merrell Dow,* 115 Harv.L.Rev. 2272 (2002) (reporting that the lower courts have "split nearly evenly" on whether *Smith* jurisdiction is allowed only in situations in which there is an implied private federal cause of action). For a critique of the *Merrell Dow* approach, see

M. Redish, Federal Jurisdiction: Tensions in the Allocation of Judicial Power 104 (2d ed. 1990) ("a congressional decision not to provide a federal remedy does not necessarily imply congressional disapproval of the provision of a federal forum for adjudication of a state cause of action turning on the interpretation of that federal statute").

5.   In Grable & Sons Metal Products, Inc. v. Darue Engineering & Manufacturing, 545 U.S. 308 (2005), the Court granted review to address the uncertainty after *Merrell Dow*. The case began when the Internal Revenue Service seized Michigan real property belonging to Grable & Sons to satisfy Grable's federal tax delinquency. The Tax Code required the IRS to give notice of the seizure, and there is no dispute that Grable received actual notice by certified mail before the IRS sold the property to respondent Darue Engineering & Manufacturing. Grable did not exercise its statutory right to redeem the property, and after the redemption period had passed, the Government gave Darue a quitclaim deed. Five years later, Grable brought a quiet title action in state court, claiming that Darue's record title was invalid because the IRS had failed to comply with a federal statute requiring it to notify Grable of its seizure of the property by personal service on "the owner of the property [or] left at his usual place of abode or business." Darue removed the action on the theory that the state-created quiet title action included an issue of federal law (does the IRS's failure to comply with the statutory rules of service invalidate the delinquency sale) and thus arose under federal law.

In an opinion by Justice Souter, the Court upheld federal jurisdiction. He described the prevailing doctrine as follows:

> It has in fact become a constant refrain in such cases that federal jurisdiction demands not only a contested federal issue, but a substantial one, indicating a serious federal interest in claiming the advantages thought to be inherent in a federal forum.

> But even when the state action discloses a contested and substantial federal question, the exercise of federal jurisdiction is subject to a possible veto. For the federal issue will ultimately qualify for a federal forum only if federal jurisdiction is consistent with congressional judgment about the sound division of labor between state and federal courts governing the application of § 1331. . . . Because arising-under jurisdiction to hear a state-law claim always raises the possibility of upsetting the state-federal line drawn (or at least assumed) by Congress, the presence of a disputed federal issue and the ostensible importance of a federal forum are never necessarily dispositive; there must always be an assessment of any disruptive portent in exercising federal jurisdiction.

> These considerations have kept us from stating a "single, precise, all-embracing" test for jurisdiction over federal issues

embedded in state-law claims between nondiverse parties. We have not kept them out simply because they appeared in state raiment, as Justice Holmes would have done, but neither have we treated "federal issue" as a password opening federal courts to any state action embracing a point of federal law. Instead, the question is, does a state-law claim necessarily raise a stated federal issue, actually disputed and substantial, which a federal forum may entertain without disturbing any congressionally approved balance of federal and state judicial responsibilities.

Applying this test, the Court found that jurisdiction was proper. The meaning of the federal tax provision was said to an important issue of federal law (a conclusion the federal government supported as an amicus, arguing in favor of jurisdiction). Moreover, the Court found that it would be the "rare" state title case that would present a contested issue of federal law, meaning that the assertion of federal jurisdiction would "portend only a microscopic effect on the federal-state division of labor." Finally, the Court found nothing in *Merrell Dow* to the contrary. While the cases were similar in that Congress had failed to provide a private federal cause of action to enforce both the FDA labeling requirement and the right to quiet title in IRS tax sales, the Court found the legislative omission more meaningful in *Merrell Dow* than in *Grable & Sons*:

> ... Expressing concern over the "increased volume of federal litigation," and noting the importance of adhering to "legislative intent," *Merrell Dow* thought it improbable that the Congress, having made no provision for a federal cause of action, would have meant to welcome any state-law tort case implicating federal law "solely because the violation of the federal statute is said to [create] a rebuttable presumption [of negligence] ... under state law." ... *Merrell Dow's* analysis thus fits within the framework of examining the importance of having a federal forum for the issue, and the consistency of such a forum with Congress's intended division of labor between state and federal courts.

> As already indicated, however, a comparable analysis yields a different jurisdictional conclusion in this case. Although Congress also indicated ambivalence in this case by providing no private right of action to Grable, it is the rare state quiet title action that involves contested issues of federal law. Consequently, jurisdiction over actions like Grable's would not materially affect, or threaten to affect, the normal currents of litigation. Given the absence of threatening structural consequences and the clear interest the Government, its buyers, and its delinquents have in the availability of a federal forum, there is no good reason to shirk from federal jurisdiction over the dispositive and contested federal issue at the heart of the state-law title claim.

6.   Justice Souter's approach bears some resemblance to that sketched in Shapiro, Jurisdiction and Discretion, 60 N.Y.U.L. Rev. 543 (1985), which argued that courts evaluating federal ingredient claims should consider the nature of the federal interest and the impact on the federal docket. A similar suggestion appeared in *Merrell Dow's* footnote 12. Will such a case-by-case discretionary analysis lead to an acceptable level of clarity in the articulation of jurisdictional rules? Is discretion more defensible at the Supreme Court than it would be in the jurisdictional decisions of the lower federal courts? Was Justice Thomas right, concurring in *Grable & Sons*, to urge the Court to consider the Holmes test as an alternative? For a criticism of the Holmes test, arguing that it does not explain the cases or provide the clarity often claimed for it, see Mulligan, A Unified Theory of 28 U.S.C. Section 1331 Jurisdiction, 61 Vand. L. Rev. 1667 (2008). For his part, Justice Souter summarized the majority's approach with the pithy recognition that, after *Merrell Dow*, "Justice Holmes was still dissenting." Grable & Sons, 545 U.S. at 318.

7.   In Smith v. Kansas City Title, note 2 supra, the Court upheld jurisdiction and then ruled on the merits, rejecting the challenge to the constitutionality of the issuance of federal bonds. In a replay of the *Smith* case, raising the same constitutional challenge to federal bonds, the federal issue might be seen as lacking the substantiality and actually-disputed quality needed to confer jurisdiction. *Grable & Sons* might thus usher in a world in which jurisdiction expands initially to allow the federal courts to resolve the disputed issue of federal law and then contracts after the issue has been settled. Does this accordion-like quality argue against the *Grable & Sons* approach (on the ground that it produces inconsistent results) or in favor of it (on the basis that it opens the federal courts only so long as necessary to address a disputed federal issue and then lets predominantly state law issues return to state court). With its focus on actual disputes over substantial issues of federal law, does *Grable & Sons* cast doubt on the Court's approach to jurisdiction over declaratory judgment proceedings? On the well-pleaded complaint rule?

How insubstantial must a federal question be before a federal court can dismiss it out of hand for want of subject matter jurisdiction under Bell v. Hood, 327 U.S. 678 (1946). In Shapiro v. McManus, 136 S.Ct. 450 (2015), the issue arose in connection with a federal law that requires a three-judge federal court to hear federal constitutional challenges to state apportionment of congressional districts. In *Shapiro*, a single district judge dismissed without first triggering the three-judge court procedure, having concluded that the plaintiff failed to state a claim for relief. Speaking through Justice Scalia, the Court unanimously held this was improper, quoting *Bell v. Hood* (id. at 455–56):

We have long distinguished between failing to raise a substantial federal question for jurisdictional purposes * * * and failing to state a claim for relief on the merits; only "wholly insubstantial and frivolous" claims implicate the former. Absent such frivolity, "the failure to state a proper cause of action calls for a judgment on the merits and not for a dismissal for want of jurisdiction."

Because the plaintiff's claim was not frivolous, the district court lacked authority to dismiss it for want of jurisdiction and was required to trigger a three-judge court for any ruling on the merits.

8. In City of Chicago v. International College of Surgeons, 522 U.S. 156 (1997), the Court held that a federal law element of a state law claim sufficed to create jurisdiction under § 1331. The International College of Surgeons (ICS) sought review in state court of the decision of the Chicago Landmarks Commission to designate two buildings the College owned as landmarks; such designation meant that the College could not develop the property in the way it wanted. Among the grounds for overturning the Commission's decision were federal constitutional contentions based on the takings clause, due process clause and equal protection clause of the Fifth and Fourteenth amendments. These federal constitutional claims were raised by a cause of action created by state law, namely, the Illinois Administrative Procedure Act. What role should 42 U.S.C. § 1983 play in the analysis of such an invocation of federal jurisdiction after *Grable & Sons?* Section 1983 authorizes a federal law claim to remedy constitutional violations under color of state law and the federal and state courts routinely assert concurrent jurisdiction over such claims.

9. Does the Supreme Court in *Gunn v. Minton* apply the *Grable & Sons* test or modify it?

(a) Would the federal issue in *Grable & Sons* qualify as significant or substantial within the meaning of *Gunn?* Would any state court resolution of the legality of the IRS delinquency sale bind a future federal court in a later proceeding between different parties that presented the same issue?

(b) How much emphasis does the *Gunn* Court place on the docket impact of shifting lawyer malpractice claims to federal court? Do you agree with its assessment of the likely docket impact?

(c) How attentive is the *Gunn* Court to congressional signals? Does the grant of exclusive federal jurisdiction over patent claims (something missing in *Grable & Sons* and *Merrell Dow*) deserve greater attention than it receives in the Court's opinion? Does the exclusively federal quality of patent litigation support an argument for federalizing the standards that govern the duties of the federal patent bar.

10. Note that the *Gunn* Court says both that § 1331 and § 1338(a) are to be interpreted "identically" and that "state legal malpractice claims based on underlying patent matters will rarely, if ever, arise under federal patent law for purposes of § 1338(a)." Could one fashion an argument that the conferral of exclusive patent jurisdiction gave rise to a national patent bar with distinctive norms of professional responsibility? Why do you think Congress conferred exclusive jurisdiction over patent cases on the federal courts? Should those reasons give rise to a presumption of federal jurisdiction for cases in which a patent issue is embedded in a state cause of action? In other words, *should* the

Court interpret § 1338(a) (and other grants of exclusive jurisdiction) identically to § 1331?

As noted above, see p. 888, in 2011, Congress adopted the America Invents Act, Pub. L. No 112–29, 125 Stat. 284. The Act expanded the exclusive jurisdiction of the district courts by foreclosing State courts from hearing "any claim for relief arising under any Act of Congress relating to patents" and other forms of intellectual property. See 28 U.S.C. § 1338(a). In addition, the Act rejected the well-pleaded complaint rule by expressly authorizing removal of civil actions in which "any party asserts a claim for relief" under the patent laws. See 28 U.S.C. § 1454(a). The provision overruled the Court's decision in Holmes Group, Inc. v. Vornado Air Circulation Systems, Inc., 535 U.S. 826 (2002), which had applied the well-pleaded complaint rule in refusing to allow the assertion of federal question removal jurisdiction over defendant's compulsory counterclaim under the patent laws. Did this congressional signal deserve consideration in the *Gunn* Court's decision to treat arising-under jurisdiction identically in patent cases?

In Merrill, Lynch, Pierce, Fenner & Smith, Inc. v. Manning, 136 S.Ct. 1562 (2016), the Court applied the *Gunn* ingredient test to a dispute that implicated the federal securities laws. Manning sued in state court on a state law cause of action. Merrill, Lynch removed, arguing that the claim fell within the Exchange Act's provision for exclusive federal jurisdiction over suits "brought to enforce" certain elements of that Act. The Court concluded that the general "arising-under" test of federal question jurisdiction, imported from section 1331 doctrine, was to govern suits that implicate the Exchange Act as well. That meant that suits brought formally on the basis of state law were subject to removal only if they meet the *Gunn* test for jurisdiction over state-created causes of action with federal ingredients. *Merrill, Lynch* continues the Court's recent practice (as reflected in *Gunn*) of refusing to articulate a separate body of jurisdictional law for specialized bodies of federal law, even where Congress has conferred exclusive jurisdiction over suits that implicate that law. The Court explained that it has done so both to simplify and clarify its jurisdictional law and to preserve room for the state courts to hear matters adjacent to federal regulatory schemes. Id. at 1574–75.

11. A different jurisdictional problem arises when Congress provides a separate grant of jurisdiction over claims that rest entirely or predominantly on state law. Such specialized jurisdictional statutes do not call for an interpretation of the general federal-question provision in § 1331, but invite consideration of whether Congress has exceeded the bounds of Article III. See Osborn v. Bank of the United States, supra, p. 889. In general, Congress cannot simply transfer state law claims to federal court (in the absence of diversity) and state law claims cannot be said to arise under a federal statute that does nothing more than provide the federal courts with jurisdiction. (Consider why this conclusion follows from the notion that Article III of the Constitution imposes limits on the scope of federal jurisdiction.) Given trends in federal regulation, Congress rarely assigns state law claims to federal court without providing some federal rules for decision of the case. When it does, the Court

will often work around the problem, either by narrowing the scope of federal jurisdiction or by reading some federal substance into what might otherwise operate as a jurisdictional provision. See Mesa v. California, 489 U.S. 121 (1989) (federal officers may not remove action from state to federal court unless they tender a defense governed by federal law); Textile Workers Union v. Lincoln Mills, 353 U.S. 448 (1957) (law to be applied in suits to enforce collective bargaining agreements between unions and employers was federal common law, "which the courts must fashion from the policy of our national labor laws").

C. THE PENUMBRA OF FEDERAL JUDICIAL POWER—SUPPLEMENTAL JURISDICTION

Having found a basis for the exercise of federal jurisdiction, courts (and parties) must consider the extent of that jurisdiction. Regarding the constitutional scope of federal-question jurisdiction, the Supreme Court early took a broad view. In Osborn v. Bank of the United States, 22 U.S. 738 (1824), the Court held that Congress could grant the federal courts jurisdiction over "a whole case," so long as a federal issue was an "ingredient in the original cause" asserted. Even though it early interpreted the diversity-jurisdiction statute to require complete diversity (Strawbridge v. Curtiss, supra p. 866), the Court held that the Constitution required only minimal diversity. See State Farm Fire & Cas. Co. v. Tashire, supra p. 287. These decisions provided the foundation for the judicial expansion of federal jurisdiction through the recognition of pendent claim, pendent party, and ancillary forms of jurisdiction. This section will sketch the developments that led to the adoption of the supplemental jurisdiction statute, 28 U.S.C. § 1367, and the interpretive issues that have arisen since its adoption.

1. CODIFYING SUPPLEMENTAL JURISDICTION

Q. v. b

UNITED MINE WORKERS V. GIBBS
Supreme Court of the United States, 1966
383 U.S. 715

JUSTICE BRENNAN delivered the opinion of the Court.

[In 1960, a coal mine in Tennessee closed its doors and laid off 100 workers, all members of the local affiliate of the United Mine Workers. Later that year, the mine proposed to re-open, but employing members of the rival Southern Labor Union. Paul Gibbs was the supervisor of the new venture and had contracted to haul the coal to markets. When the UMW's local union members learned of the plan to re-open, they conducted a violent assault on the operation. Later, UMW officials instituted a nonviolent picket line and kept the mine closed for several months. Gibbs sued the national union under the federal Labor Management Relations

Act (LMRA), section 303 of which authorizes any person to recover damages for losses to his business or property suffered as a result of an unlawful secondary boycott. Gibbs also sought damages for intentional interference with advantageous commercial relations under Tennessee state law. The LMRA had preempted most state tort law grounds for relief, and substituted a comprehensive federal scheme regulating labor-management relations. But tort claims for violent activity survived. In the absence of diversity of citizenship, there was no independent basis for jurisdiction over the state law claims. Jurisdiction thus depended on a finding that the state claims were so related to the federal secondary boycott claim under section 303 as to satisfy the standard for pendent claim jurisdiction. Under the old standard, as articulated in Hurn v. Oursler, 289 U.S. 238 (1933), pendent jurisdiction would attach only if one could conclude that the state and federal claims did little more than use different labels to "characterize the same group of circumstances."]

This limited approach is unnecessarily grudging. Pendent jurisdiction, in the sense of judicial power, exists whenever there is a [federal question] claim, and the relationship between that claim and the state claim permits the conclusion that the entire action before the court comprises but one constitutional "case." The federal claim must have substance sufficient to confer subject matter jurisdiction on the court. The state and federal claims must derive from a common nucleus of operative fact. But if, considered without regard to their federal or state character, a plaintiff's claims are such that he would ordinarily be expected to try them all in one judicial proceeding, then, assuming substantiality of the federal issues, there is power in federal courts to hear the whole.

That power need not be exercised in every case in which it is found to exist. It has consistently been recognized that pendent jurisdiction is a doctrine of discretion, not of plaintiff's right. Its justification lies in considerations of judicial economy, convenience and fairness to litigants; if these are not present a federal court should hesitate to exercise jurisdiction over state claims, even though bound to apply state law to them. Needless decisions of state law should be avoided both as a matter of comity and to promote justice between the parties, by procuring for them a surer-footed reading of applicable law. Certainly, if the federal claims are dismissed before trial, even though not insubstantial in a jurisdictional sense, the state claims should be dismissed as well. Similarly, if it appears that the state issues substantially predominate, whether in terms of proof, of the scope of the issues raised, or of the comprehensiveness of the remedy sought, the state claims may be dismissed without prejudice and left for resolution to state tribunals. There may, on the other hand, be situations in which the state claim is so closely tied to questions of federal policy that the argument for exercise of pendent jurisdiction is particularly strong. In the present case, for example, the allowable scope of the state claim implicates the federal doctrine of pre-emption; while this interrelationship does not create statutory federal question jurisdiction, its existence is relevant to the exercise of discretion. Finally, there may be reasons independent of jurisdictional considerations, such as the likelihood of jury confusion in treating divergent legal theories of relief, that would justify separating state and federal claims for trial, Fed. Rule Civ. Proc. 42 (b). If so, jurisdiction should ordinarily be refused.

The question of power will ordinarily be resolved on the pleadings. But the issue whether pendent jurisdiction has been properly assumed is one which remains open throughout the litigation. Pretrial procedures or even the trial itself may reveal a substantial hegemony of state law claims, or likelihood of jury confusion, which could not have been anticipated at the pleading stage. Although it will of course be appropriate to take account in this circumstance of the already completed course of the litigation, dismissal of the state claim might even then be merited. For example, it may appear that the plaintiff was well aware of the nature of his proofs and the relative importance of his claims; recognition of a federal court's wide latitude to decide ancillary questions of state law does not imply that it must tolerate a litigant's effort to impose upon it what is in effect only a state law case. Once it appears that a state claim constitutes the real body of a case, to which the federal claim is only an appendage, the state claim may fairly be dismissed.

[Finally, the Court evaluated the district court's decision to enter judgment solely on the claims under state law. Although it had submitted both the federal section 303 claim and the state law claims to the jury, the district court granted the union's motion for judgment as a matter of law on the federal claim. The union argued that this disposition deprived the district court of jurisdiction to enter judgment on the state law claims. The Supreme Court disagreed. Power to adjudicate the whole case had attached at the outset; the decision to submit both the federal and state law claims to the jury served the interests of convenience and efficiency and did not constitute an abuse of discretion.]

OWEN EQUIPMENT & ERECTION CO. V. KROGER

Supreme Court of the United States, 1978
437 U.S. 365

JUSTICE STEWART delivered the opinion of the Court.

[Kroger, a citizen of Iowa, filed suit for the wrongful death of her husband, naming the Omaha Public Power District (OPPD), a citizen of Nebraska, as defendant and invoking diversity jurisdiction. OPPD, in turn, impleaded Owen Equipment & Erection Company under Rule 14 on the theory that Owen owned the crane on which the decedent was working at the time of his death. Kroger amended her complaint to allege claims directly against Owen, a Nebraska corporation. During trial, it became clear that Owen, like the plaintiff, was also a citizen of Iowa. Owen's headquarters were in Iowa, even though the office was located on what would have appeared to be the Nebraska side of the Missouri River. By the time this problem became clear, the Iowa statute of limitation would have apparently barred a new suit against Owen in state court. The district court retained jurisdiction and entered judgment against Owen on a verdict for Kroger. The court of appeals affirmed.]

In affirming the District Court's judgment, the Court of Appeals relied upon the doctrine of ancillary jurisdiction, whose contours it believed were defined by this Court's holding in Mine Workers v. Gibbs, supra. The *Gibbs* case differed from this one in that it involved pendent jurisdiction, which concerns the resolution of a plaintiff's federal-and state-law claims against a single defendant in one action. By contrast, in this case there was no claim based upon substantive federal law, but rather state-law tort claims against two different defendants. [W]e believe that the Court of Appeals failed to understand the scope of the doctrine of the *Gibbs* case. * * *

It is apparent that *Gibbs* delineated the constitutional limits of federal judicial power. But even if it be assumed that the District Court in the present case had constitutional power to decide the respondent's lawsuit against the petitioner,[10] it does not follow that the decision of the Court of Appeals was correct. Constitutional power is merely the first hurdle that must be overcome in determining that a federal court has jurisdiction over a particular controversy. For the jurisdiction of the federal courts is limited not only by the provisions of Art. III of the Constitution, but also by Acts of Congress.

That statutory law as well as the Constitution may limit a federal court's jurisdiction over nonfederal claims is well illustrated by two recent decisions of this Court, Aldinger v. Howard, [427 U.S. 1 (1976)] and Zahn v. International Paper Co., 414 U.S. 291 (1973). In *Aldinger* the Court held that a Federal District Court lacked jurisdiction over a state-law claim against a county, even if that claim was alleged to be pendent to one against county officials under 42 U.S.C. 1983. In *Zahn* the Court held that in a diversity class action under Fed. Rule Civ. Proc. 23 (b) (3), the claim of each member of the plaintiff class must independently satisfy the minimum jurisdictional amount set by 28 U.S.C. 1332 (a), and rejected the argument that jurisdiction existed over those claims that involved less [that the statutory amount] as ancillary to those that involved more. In each case, despite the fact that federal and nonfederal claims arose from a "common nucleus of operative fact," the Court held that the statute conferring jurisdiction over the federal claim did not allow the exercise of jurisdiction over the nonfederal claims.

---

[10] Federal jurisdiction in *Gibbs* was based upon the existence of a question of federal law. The Court of Appeals in the present case believed that the "common nucleus of operative fact" test also determines the outer boundaries of constitutionally permissible federal jurisdiction when that jurisdiction is based upon diversity of citizenship. We may assume without deciding that the Court of Appeals was correct in this regard.

The *Aldinger* and *Zahn* cases thus make clear that a finding that federal and nonfederal claims arise from a "common nucleus of operative fact," the test of *Gibbs,* does not end the inquiry into whether a federal court has power to hear the nonfederal claims along with the federal ones. Beyond this constitutional minimum, there must be an examination of the posture in which the nonfederal claim is asserted and of the specific statute that confers jurisdiction over the federal claim, in order to determine whether "Congress in [that statute] has . . . expressly or by implication negated" the exercise of jurisdiction over the particular nonfederal claim.

III

[The diversity statute has been interpreted to require complete diversity.] Thus it is clear that the respondent could not originally have brought suit in federal court naming Owen and OPPD as codefendants, since citizens of Iowa would have been on both sides of the litigation. Yet the identical lawsuit resulted when she amended her complaint. Complete diversity was destroyed just as surely as if she had sued Owen initially. * * *

It is true, as the Court of Appeals noted, that the exercise of ancillary jurisdiction over nonfederal claims has often been upheld in situations involving impleader, cross-claims or counterclaims. [But] the context in which the nonfederal claim is asserted is crucial. And the claim here arises in a setting quite different from the kinds of nonfederal claims that have been viewed in other cases as falling within the ancillary jurisdiction of the federal courts.

First, the nonfederal claim in this case was simply not ancillary to the federal one in the same sense that, for example, the impleader by a defendant of a third-party defendant always is. A third-party complaint depends at least in part upon the resolution of the primary lawsuit. Its relation to the original complaint is thus not mere factual similarity but logical dependence. Respondent's claim against the petitioner, however, was entirely separate from her original claim against OPPD, since the petitioner's liability to her depended not at all upon whether or not OPPD was also liable. Far from being an ancillary and dependent claim, it was a new and independent one.

Second, the nonfederal claim here was asserted by the plaintiff, who voluntarily chose to bring suit upon a state-law claim in a federal court. By contrast, ancillary jurisdiction typically involves claims by a defending party haled into court against his will, or by another person whose rights might be irretrievably lost unless he could assert them in an ongoing action in a federal court. A plaintiff cannot complain if ancillary jurisdiction does not encompass all of his possible claims in a case such as this one, since it is he who has chosen the federal rather than the state forum and must thus accept its limitations.

* * * [N]either the convenience of litigants nor considerations of judicial economy can suffice to justify extension of the doctrine of ancillary jurisdiction to a plaintiff's cause of action against a citizen of the same State in a diversity case.

Accordingly, the judgment of the Court of Appeals is reversed.

[The dissenting opinion of Justices White and Brennan is omitted.]

NOTES AND QUESTIONS

1.   As these cases suggest, the doctrines of pendent and ancillary jurisdiction evolved differently, depending in part on whether jurisdiction was based on a federal question or on diversity of citizenship. Thus, in *UMW v. Gibbs,* the federal secondary boycott claim anchored the jurisdiction; "pendent claim" jurisdiction extended to related state law claims. "Pendent party" jurisdiction, was thought to arise, if at all, in the context of federal question proceedings. For example, in Aldinger v. Howard, 427 U.S. 1 (1976), the plaintiff brought suit against the county and its officials, alleging that she had been fired from her county job unconstitutionally. At the time, section 1983 did not permit suit against the county (although the Court later reversed course and allowed such suits in Monell v. Department of Social Services, 436 U.S. 658 (1978)). The plaintiff thus asserted constitutional claims against the officers and state-law pendent party claims against the county. The Court found that because Congress had excluded counties from liability under 1983, it had "by implication negated [the] existence" of pendent-party jurisdiction over the county. Aldinger v. Howard, 427 U.S. at 18. The Court did not rule out pendent-party jurisdiction altogether; indeed, it appeared to acknowledge that strong efficiency arguments would support the addition of pendent parties in cases where Congress had conferred exclusive federal court jurisdiction over federal question claims.

2.   On the diversity side of the docket, by contrast, pendent claim and pendent party jurisdiction had little relevance. Pendent claims are unnecessary: Once diversity has been established, the plaintiff can join all extant claims against a particular defendant, even if the claims bear no relationship to one another. See Rule 18. Indeed, plaintiff could cumulate unrelated claims to satisfy the amount-in-controversy requirement. See supra p. 882 n. 7. Pendent parties were jurisdictional apostasy: the complete diversity rule would foreclose the joinder of claims by plaintiffs against non-diverse parties even where they derive from the same common nucleus of operative fact as properly joined claims between diverse parties. As a result, on the diversity side, the focus was on the exercise of various forms of ancillary jurisdiction, often jurisdiction over claims raised by defendants once they had been properly joined as such. In *Kroger,* the Court signaled its acceptance of these forms of ancillary jurisdiction, speaking approvingly of claims *by defendants* against non-diverse parties added by way of impleader, cross-claim, and counterclaim, even as it sought to prevent erosion of the complete diversity rule by limiting authority over claims by plaintiffs.

The Court's hostility towards any sort of pendent party jurisdiction in diversity was also reflected in its handling of the amount-in-controversy requirement. The Court consistently refused to permit the aggregation of the value of the claims of multiple plaintiffs to satisfy that requirement, holding instead that each plaintiff must individually assert a sufficient claim. See Clark v. Paul Gray, Inc., 306 U.S. 583 (1939). In a state-law class action, the Court ruled that the requirement could not be satisfied by aggregating the claims of all the class members. See Snyder v. Harris, 394 U.S. 332 (1969). Extending that conclusion in Zahn v. International Paper Co., 414 U.S. 291 (1973), the Court held that, even if the named class representative in a state-law class action had a sufficient claim, jurisdiction would not extend to the related claims of the other class members, each of whom also had to satisfy the requirement. For a summary, see Pfander, Supplemental Jurisdiction and Section 1367: The Case for a Sympathetic Textualism, 148 U.Pa.L.Rev. 109 (1999).

3.   In Finley v. United States, 490 U.S. 545 (1989), the Supreme Court ended the era of judge-made pendent-party and ancillary jurisdiction, holding that the absence of a statutory underpinning was fatal to the exercise of jurisdiction over claims by plaintiffs against non-diverse parties added to the litigation. The case arose from a plane crash at the airport in San Diego, California. The plaintiff sued the federal government under the Federal Tort Claims Act, 28 U.S.C. § 1346, seeking damages for the negligence of the Federal Aviation Administration in its handling of air traffic control and its upkeep of runway lights. The plaintiff also proposed to name two additional defendants on state law negligence claims in connection with the same plane crash. The Court explained the importance of statutory support for the joinder of additional parties as follows:

> As we noted at the outset, our cases do not display an entirely consistent approach with respect to the necessity that jurisdiction be explicitly conferred. The *Gibbs* line of cases was a departure from prior practice, and a departure that we have no intent to limit or impair. But *Aldinger* indicated that the *Gibbs* approach would not be extended to the pendent-party field, and we decide today to retain that line. Whatever we say regarding the scope of jurisdiction conferred by a particular statute can of course be changed by Congress. What is of paramount importance is that Congress be able to legislate against a background of clear interpretive rules, so that it may know the effect of the language it adopts. All our cases—*Zahn, Aldinger* and *Kroger*—have held that a grant of jurisdiction over claims involving particular parties does not itself confer jurisdiction over additional claims by or against different parties. Our decision today reaffirms that interpretive rule; the opposite would sow confusion.

4.   Congress responded to this invitation a short time later by enacting 28 U.S.C. § 1367. Read the statute. It does not refer to pendent or ancillary

jurisdiction, but instead uses the term supplemental jurisdiction to embrace both concepts.

(a)   Section 1367(a) broadly defines the supplemental jurisdiction of the district courts, extending it to all claims that are "so related" to the claims in the civil action of which the court has original jurisdiction as to form part of the same "case or controversy" within the meaning of Article III. By extending supplemental jurisdiction to the constitutional limit, section 1367(a) reaches at least as broadly as the common nucleus test of UMW v. Gibbs. The provision may reach even more broadly to encompass permissive counter-claims and set-offs raised by defendants under Rule 13. While permissive counterclaims do not arise from the same transaction or occurrence as the claims of the plaintiff, defendants may have a fairly strong interest in asserting them, particularly if the plaintiff has sizable debts. Without a set-off, defendant might be obliged to pay a judgment to the plaintiff and be unable to recover those funds in the event that defendant later succeeds in a suit against the plaintiff in a separate proceeding. See Jones v. Ford Motor Credit Company, 358 F.3d 205 (2d Cir. 2004) (upholding supplemental jurisdiction over permissive counterclaim) (citing Fletcher, "Common Nucleus of Operative Fact" and Defensive Set-Off: Beyond the Gibbs Test, 74 Ind. L.J. 171 (1998)); Global Naps, Inc. v. Verizon of New England, Inc., 603 F.3d 71 (1st Cir. 2010) (concluding that the *Gibbs* common nucleus test no longer controls and upholding supplemental jurisdiction over permissive counterclaims).

To the extent that the "common nucleus of operative fact" test remains relevant, it may not offer much guidance. Consider the following argument that there has been "a good deal of circularity and question-begging" in the courts' approach:

> Cases delineating the scope of a constitutional "case" for purposes of ancillary jurisdiction offer little help. Here courts speak of the "same transaction or occurrence." This phrase, too, is ambiguous. For example, assume a traffic accident, followed by a fist fight between the drivers. Driver A sues driver B for negligence in causing the accident; driver B counterclaims for battery arising out of the post-accident fight. On a purely linguistic or conceptual level, these two incidents could be characterized as either being part of the same occurrence or not. Courts that define the phrase in terms of evidentiary overlap would probably decline to find these incidents to be part of the same occurrence, because there likely will be little, if any, evidentiary overlap. Yet courts that define the phrase in terms of the broader concept of "logical relationship" would quite probably find that the incidents are, in fact, part of the same occurrence.

Redish, Reassessing the Allocation of Judicial Business Between State and Federal Courts: Federal Jurisdiction and "the Martian Chronicles," 78 Va. L. Rev. 1769, 1822–23 (1992).

Section 1367(a) includes language declaring that supplemental jurisdiction shall include claims that involve the joinder or intervention of additional parties. This language responds directly to *Finley,* providing the statutory foundation needed for the exercise of pendent party and ancillary jurisdiction.

(b) Section 1367(b) has been the source of much confusion. The provision's stated goal was to implement the "principal rationale" of *Kroger.* H.R. Rep. No. 101–734 at 28–29 n. 16 (1990). In cases where the district court obtains original jurisdiction on the basis of section 1332, subsection (b) sets forth a series of exceptions that qualify the broad grant of supplemental jurisdiction in subsection (a). Notably, the exceptions apply only to claims made by plaintiffs, thus allowing the assertion of supplemental jurisdiction over claims by defendants in keeping with the *Kroger* Court's view of the scope of ancillary jurisdiction. The statute defines exceptions by reference to the joinder rules of the Federal Rules of Civil Procedure. Thus, it forbids the assertion of supplemental jurisdiction over claims *by plaintiffs* against *other parties* joined under Rules 14, 19, 20, and 24, when exercising such jurisdiction would be inconsistent with the requirements of section 1332. The confusion has stemmed in good measure, though not entirely, from subsection (b)'s failure to create an explicit exception for claims by plaintiffs who were *themselves* joined under Rule 20 and Rule 23. We will consider this problem at greater length below.

(c) Section 1367(c) provides the bases on which the district court may decline to exercise supplemental jurisdiction. While the statute borrows the language and conceptual apparatus of UMW v. Gibbs, some courts have taken a narrower view of the statute. In Executive Software North America, Inc. v. United States District Court, 24 F.3d 1545 (9th Cir.1994), the court explained: "once it is determined that the assertion of supplemental jurisdiction is permissible under section 1367(a) and (b), section 1367(c) provides the only valid basis upon which the district court may decline jurisdiction." Thus, a court may only decline jurisdiction if it identifies a factual predicate in the case that corresponds to one of those enumerated in the statute. Other courts have recognized limits to authority under § 1367(c) to dismiss. See Montano v. City of Chicago, 375 F.3d 593 (7th Cir.2004) (holding that failure to exercise supplemental jurisdiction over state-law claims was an abuse of discretion). But the fact that § 1367(c) might apply in a case does not require dismissal. See Motorola Credit Corp. v. Uzan, 388 F.3d 39 (2d Cir.2004) (district court was not required to decline to exercise supplemental jurisdiction over state-law claims after dismissing all federal claims because the court was fully conversant with the facts and had conducted a trial on the merits).

(d) For a party that has unsuccessfully invoked supplemental jurisdiction, section 1367(d) tolls the running of the limitations period during the time the federal case is pending and for 30 days thereafter, permitting the party to file all the claims in state court if proceeding in federal court becomes impossible. This provision should solve limitations problems like that in Owen Equipment & Erection Co. v. Kroger, supra p. 911. As the Supreme Court explained in Jinks v. Richland County, 538 U.S. 456 (2003):

Prior to the enactment of § 1367(d), [prospective plaintiffs] had the following unattractive options: (1) They could file a single federal-court action, which would run the risk that the federal court would dismiss the state-law claims after the limitations period had expired; (2) they could file a single state-law action, which would abandon their right to a federal forum; (3) they could file separate, timely actions in federal and state court and ask that the state-court litigation be stayed pending resolution of the federal case, which would increase litigation costs with no guarantee that the state court would oblige. Section 1367(d) replaces this selection of inadequate choices with the assurance that state-law claims asserted under § 1367(a) will not become time barred while pending in federal court.

5.   Test your knowledge of the operation of section 1367 by reviewing each of the preceding cases, *Gibbs, Aldinger, Kroger,* and *Finley.* Would a district court, applying section 1367 today to the facts of those cases, reach the same conclusion that the Supreme Court did before the statute was enacted?

2.   INTERPRETING THE SUPPLEMENTAL JURISDICTION STATUTE

EXXON MOBIL CORP. v. ALLAPATTAH SERVICES, INC., ROSARIO ORTEGA v. STAR-KIST FOODS, INC.

Supreme Court of the United States, 2005
545 U.S. 546

JUSTICE KENNEDY delivered the opinion of the Court.

These consolidated cases present the question whether a federal court in a diversity action may exercise supplemental jurisdiction over additional plaintiffs whose claims do not satisfy the minimum amount-in-controversy requirement, provided the claims are part of the same case or controversy as the claims of plaintiffs who do allege a sufficient amount in controversy. Our decision turns on the correct interpretation of 28 U.S.C. § 1367. The question has divided the Courts of Appeals, and we granted certiorari to resolve the conflict.

We hold that, where the other elements of jurisdiction are present and at least one named plaintiff in the action satisfies the amount-in-controversy requirement, § 1367 does authorize supplemental jurisdiction over the claims of other plaintiffs in the same Article III case or controversy, even if those claims are for less than the jurisdictional amount specified in the statute setting forth the requirements for diversity jurisdiction. We affirm the judgment of the Court of Appeals for the Eleventh Circuit in No. 04–70, and we reverse the judgment of the Court of Appeals for the First Circuit in No. 04–79.

I

In 1991, about 10,000 Exxon dealers filed a class-action suit against the Exxon Corporation in the United States District Court for the Northern District of Florida. The dealers alleged an intentional and systematic scheme by Exxon under which they were overcharged for fuel purchased from Exxon. The plaintiffs invoked the District Court's § 1332(a) diversity jurisdiction. After a unanimous jury verdict in favor of the plaintiffs, the District Court certified the case for interlocutory review, asking whether it had properly exercised § 1367 supplemental jurisdiction over the claims of class members who did not meet the jurisdictional minimum amount in controversy.

The Court of Appeals for the Eleventh Circuit upheld the District Court's extension of supplemental jurisdiction to these class members. * * * This decision accords with the views of the Courts of Appeals for the Fourth, Sixth, and Seventh Circuits. * * *

In the other case now before us the Court of Appeals for the First Circuit took a different position on the meaning of § 1367(a). [*Rosario Ortega v. Star-Kist Foods, Inc.,*] 370 F.3d 124 (2004). In that case, a 9-year-old girl sued Star-Kist in a diversity action in the United States District Court for the District of Puerto Rico, seeking damages for unusually severe injuries she received when she sliced her finger on a tuna can. Her family joined in the suit, seeking damages for emotional distress and certain medical expenses. The District Court granted summary judgment to Star-Kist, finding that none of the plaintiffs met the minimum amount-in-controversy requirement. The Court of Appeals for the First Circuit, however, ruled that the injured girl, but not her family members, had made allegations of damages in the requisite amount.

The Court of Appeals then addressed whether, in light of the fact that one plaintiff met the requirements for original jurisdiction, supplemental jurisdiction over the remaining plaintiffs' claims was proper under § 1367. The court held that § 1367 authorizes supplemental jurisdiction only when the district court has original jurisdiction over the action, and that in a diversity case original jurisdiction is lacking if one plaintiff fails to satisfy the amount-in-controversy requirement. Although the Court of Appeals claimed to "express no view" on whether the result would be the same in a class action, its analysis is inconsistent with that of the Court of Appeals for the Eleventh Circuit. The Court of Appeals for the First Circuit's view of § 1367 is, however, shared by the Courts of Appeal for the Third, Eighth, and Tenth Circuits, and the latter two Courts of Appeals have expressly applied this rule to class actions.

II

A

The district courts of the United States, as we have said many times, are "courts of limited jurisdiction. They possess only that power authorized by Constitution and statute." * * *

Although the district courts may not exercise jurisdiction absent a statutory basis, it is well established—in certain classes of cases—that, once a court has original jurisdiction over some claims in the action, it may exercise supplemental jurisdiction over additional claims that are part of the same case or controversy. The leading modern case for this principle is *Mine Workers v. Gibbs.*

* * *

We have not, however, applied *Gibbs'* expansive interpretive approach to other aspects of the jurisdictional statutes. For instance, we have consistently interpreted § 1332 as requiring complete diversity: In a case with multiple plaintiffs and multiple defendants, the presence in the action of a single plaintiff from the same State as a single defendant deprives the district court of original diversity jurisdiction over the entire action. * * * The specific purpose of the complete diversity rule explains both why we have not adopted *Gibbs'* expansive interpretive approach to this aspect of the jurisdictional statute and why *Gibbs* does not undermine the complete diversity rule. In order for a federal court to invoke supplemental jurisdiction under *Gibbs,* it must first have original jurisdiction over at least one claim in the action. Incomplete diversity destroys original jurisdiction with respect to all claims, so there is nothing to which supplemental jurisdiction can adhere.

In contrast to the diversity requirement, most of the other statutory prerequisites for federal jurisdiction, including the federal-question and amount-in-controversy requirements, can be analyzed claim by claim. True, it does not follow by necessity from this that a district court has authority to exercise supplemental jurisdiction over all claims provided there is original jurisdiction over just one. Before the enactment of § 1367, the Court declined in contexts other than the pendent-claim instance to follow *Gibbs'* expansive approach to interpretation of the jurisdictional statutes. The Court took a more restrictive view of the proper interpretation of these statutes in so-called pendent-party cases involving supplemental jurisdiction over claims involving additional parties— plaintiffs or defendants—where the district courts would lack original jurisdiction over claims by each of the parties standing alone.

Thus, with respect to plaintiff-specific jurisdictional requirements, the Court held in *Clark v. Paul Gray, Inc.,* 306 U.S. 583 (1939), that every plaintiff must separately satisfy the amount-in-controversy requirement. * * * The Court reaffirmed this rule, in the context of a class action brought invoking § 1332(a) diversity jurisdiction, in *Zahn v. International Paper Co.,* 414 U.S. 291 (1973). It follows "inescapably" from *Clark,* the Court held in *Zahn,* that "any plaintiff without the jurisdictional amount must be dismissed from the case, even though others allege jurisdictionally sufficient claims."

The Court took a similar approach with respect to supplemental jurisdiction over claims against additional defendants that fall outside the district courts' original jurisdiction. [Here, the Court discussed *Aldinger* and *Finley.*]

As the jurisdictional statutes existed in 1989, then, here is how matters stood: First, the diversity requirement in § 1332(a) required complete diversity; absent complete diversity, the district court lacked original jurisdiction over all of the claims in the action. *Strawbridge, Kroger.* Second, if the district court had original jurisdiction over at least one claim, the jurisdictional statutes implicitly authorized supplemental jurisdiction over all other claims between the same parties arising out of the same Article III case or controversy. *Gibbs.* Third, even when the district court had original jurisdiction over one or more claims between particular parties, the jurisdictional statutes did not authorize supplemental jurisdiction over additional claims involving other parties. *Clark; Zahn; Finley.*

B

[Here, the Court quoted section 1367(a)–(b).] All parties to this litigation and all courts to consider the question agree that § 1367 overturned the result in *Finley.* There is no warrant, however, for assuming that § 1367 did no more than to overrule *Finley* and otherwise to codify the existing state of the law of supplemental jurisdiction. * * *

Section 1367(a) is a broad grant of supplemental jurisdiction over other claims within the same case or controversy, as long as the action is one in which the district courts would have original jurisdiction. The last sentence of § 1367(a) makes it clear that the grant of supplemental jurisdiction extends to claims involving joinder or intervention of additional parties. The single question before us, therefore, is whether a diversity case in which the claims of some plaintiffs satisfy the amount-in-controversy requirement, but the claims of other plaintiffs do not, presents a "civil action of which the district courts have original jurisdiction." If the answer is yes, § 1367(a) confers supplemental jurisdiction over all claims, including those that do not independently satisfy the amount-in-controversy requirement, if the claims are part of the same Article III case or controversy. If the answer is no, § 1367(a) is inapplicable and, in light of our holdings in *Clark* and *Zahn,* the district court has no statutory basis for exercising supplemental jurisdiction over the additional claims.

We now conclude the answer must be yes. When the well-pleaded complaint contains at least one claim that satisfies the amount-in-controversy requirement, and there are no other relevant jurisdictional defects, the district court, beyond all question, has original jurisdiction over that claim. The presence of other claims in the complaint, over which the district court may lack original jurisdiction, is of no moment. If the court has original jurisdiction over a single claim in the complaint, it has original jurisdiction over a "civil action" within the meaning of § 1367(a), even if the civil action over which it has jurisdiction comprises fewer claims than were included in the complaint. Once the court determines it has original jurisdiction over the civil action, it can turn to the question whether it has a constitutional and statutory basis for exercising supplemental jurisdiction over the other claims in the action.

* * *

If § 1367(a) were the sum total of the relevant statutory language, our holding would rest on that language alone. The statute, of course, instructs us to examine § 1367(b) to determine if any of its exceptions apply, so we proceed to that section. While § 1367(b) qualifies the broad rule of § 1367(a), it does not withdraw supplemental jurisdiction over the claims of the additional parties at issue here. The specific exceptions to § 1367(a) contained in § 1367(b), moreover, provide additional support for our conclusion that § 1367(a) confers supplemental jurisdiction over these claims. Section 1367(b), which applies only to diversity cases, withholds supplemental jurisdiction over the claims of plaintiffs proposed to be joined as indispensable parties under Federal Rule of Civil Procedure 19, or who seek to intervene pursuant to Rule 24. Nothing in the text of § 1367(b), however, withholds supplemental jurisdiction over the claims of plaintiffs permissibly joined under Rule 20 (like the additional plaintiffs in [*Rosario-Ortega*]) or certified as class-action members pursuant to Rule 23 (like the additional plaintiffs in [*Allapattah*]). The natural, indeed the necessary, inference is that § 1367 confers supplemental jurisdiction over claims by Rule 20 and Rule 23 plaintiffs. This inference, at least with respect to Rule 20 plaintiffs, is strengthened by the fact that § 1367(b) explicitly excludes supplemental jurisdiction over claims against defendants joined under Rule 20.

We cannot accept the view, urged by some of the parties, commentators, and Courts of Appeals, that a district court lacks original jurisdiction over a civil action unless the court has original jurisdiction over every claim in the complaint. As we understand this position, it requires assuming either that all claims in the complaint must stand or fall as a single, indivisible "civil action" as a matter of definitional necessity—what we will refer to as the "indivisibility theory"—or else that the inclusion of a claim or party falling outside the district court's original jurisdiction somehow contaminates every other claim in the complaint, depriving the court of original jurisdiction over any of these claims—what we will refer to as the "contamination theory."

The indivisibility theory is easily dismissed, as it is inconsistent with the whole notion of supplemental jurisdiction. If a district court must have original jurisdiction over every claim in the complaint in order to have "original jurisdiction" over a "civil action," then in *Gibbs* there was no civil action of which the district court could assume original jurisdiction under § 1331, and so no basis for exercising supplemental jurisdiction over any of the claims. The indivisibility theory is further belied by our practice—in both federal-question and diversity cases—of allowing federal courts to cure jurisdictional defects by dismissing the offending parties rather than dismissing the entire action. *Clark,* for example, makes clear that claims that are jurisdictionally defective as to amount in controversy do not destroy original jurisdiction over other claims. 306 U.S., at 590 (dismissing parties who failed to meet the amount-in-controversy requirement but retaining jurisdiction over the remaining party). If the presence of jurisdictionally problematic claims in the complaint meant the district court was without original jurisdiction over the single, indivisible civil action before it, then the district court would have to dismiss the whole action rather than particular parties.

We also find it unconvincing to say that the definitional indivisibility theory applies in the context of diversity cases but not in the context of federal-question cases. The broad and general language of the statute does not permit this result. The contention is premised on the notion that the phrase "original jurisdiction of all civil actions" means different things in § 1331 and § 1332. It is implausible, however, to say that the identical phrase means one thing (original jurisdiction in all actions where at least one claim in the complaint meets the following requirements) in § 1331 and something else (original jurisdiction in all actions where every claim in the complaint meets the following requirements) in § 1332.

The contamination theory, as we have noted, can make some sense in the special context of the complete diversity requirement because the presence of nondiverse parties on both sides of a lawsuit eliminates the justification for providing a federal forum. The theory, however, makes little sense with respect to the amount-in-controversy requirement, which is meant to ensure that a dispute is sufficiently important to warrant federal-court attention. The presence of a single nondiverse party may eliminate the fear of bias with respect to all claims, but the presence of a claim that falls short of the minimum amount in controversy does nothing to reduce the importance of the claims that do meet this requirement.

It is fallacious to suppose, simply from the proposition that § 1332 imposes both the diversity requirement and the amount-in-controversy requirement, that the contamination theory germane to the former is also relevant to the latter. There is no inherent logical connection between the amount-in-controversy requirement and § 1332 diversity jurisdiction. After all, federal-question jurisdiction once had an amount-in-controversy requirement as well. If such a requirement were revived under § 1331, it is clear beyond peradventure that § 1367(a) provides supplemental jurisdiction over federal-question cases where some, but not all, of the federal-law claims involve a sufficient amount in controversy. In other words, § 1367(a) unambiguously overrules the holding and the result in *Clark.* If that is so, however, it would be quite extraordinary to say that § 1367 did not also overrule *Zahn,* a case that was premised in substantial part on the holding in *Clark.*

* * *

We also reject the argument * * * that while the presence of additional claims over which the district court lacks jurisdiction does not mean the civil action is outside the purview of § 1367(a), the presence of additional parties does. * * * [That argument] also would mean that § 1367 left the *Finley* result undisturbed. *Finley,* after all, involved a Federal Tort Claims Act suit against a federal defendant and state-law claims against additional defendants not otherwise subject to federal jurisdiction. Yet all concede that one purpose of § 1367 was to change the result reached in *Finley.*

Finally, it is suggested that our interpretation of § 1367(a) creates an anomaly regarding the exceptions listed in § 1367(b): It is not immediately obvious why Congress would withhold supplemental jurisdiction over plaintiffs joined as parties "needed for just adjudication" under Rule 19 but would allow supplemental jurisdiction over plaintiffs permissively joined under Rule 20. The omission of Rule 20 plaintiffs from the list of exceptions in § 1367(b) may have been an "unintentional drafting gap." If that is the case, it is up to Congress rather than the courts to fix it. The omission may seem odd, but it is not absurd. An alternative explanation for the different treatment of Rule 19 and Rule 20 is that Congress was concerned that extending supplemental jurisdiction to Rule 19 plaintiffs would allow circumvention of the complete diversity rule: A nondiverse plaintiff might be omitted intentionally from the original action, but joined later under Rule 19 as a necessary party. The contamination theory described above, if applicable, means this ruse would fail, but Congress may have wanted to make assurance double sure. More generally, Congress may have concluded that federal jurisdiction is only appropriate if the district court would have original jurisdiction over the claims of all those plaintiffs who are so essential to the action that they could be joined under Rule 19.

To the extent that the omission of Rule 20 plaintiffs from the list of § 1367(b) exceptions is anomalous, moreover, it is no more anomalous than the inclusion of Rule 19 plaintiffs in that list would be if the alternative view of § 1367(a) were to prevail. If the district court lacks original jurisdiction over a civil diversity action where any plaintiff's claims fail to comply with all the requirements of § 1332, there is no need for a special § 1367(b) exception for Rule 19 plaintiffs who do not meet these requirements. Though the omission of Rule 20 plaintiffs from § 1367(b) presents something of a puzzle on our view of the statute, the inclusion of Rule 19 plaintiffs in this section is at least as difficult to explain under the alternative view.

And so we circle back to the original question. When the well-pleaded complaint in [the] district court includes multiple claims, all part of the same case or controversy, and some, but not all, of the claims are within the court's original jurisdiction, does the court have before it "any civil action of which the district courts have original jurisdiction"? It does. Under § 1367, the court has original jurisdiction over the civil action comprising the claims for which there is no jurisdictional defect. No other reading of § 1367 is plausible in light of the text and structure of the jurisdictional statute. Though the special nature and purpose of the diversity requirement mean that a single nondiverse party can contaminate every other claim in the lawsuit, the contamination does not occur with respect to jurisdictional defects that go only to the substantive importance of individual claims.

It follows from this conclusion that the threshold requirement of § 1367(a) is satisfied in cases, like those now before us, where some, but not all, of the plaintiffs in a diversity action allege a sufficient amount in controversy. We hold that § 1367 by its plain text overruled *Clark* and *Zahn* and authorized supplemental jurisdiction over all claims by diverse parties arising out of the same Article III case or controversy, subject only to enumerated exceptions not applicable in the cases now before us.

C

The proponents of the alternative view of § 1367 insist that the statute is at least ambiguous and that we should look to other interpretive tools, including the legislative history of § 1367, which supposedly demonstrate Congress did not intend § 1367 to overrule *Zahn*. We can reject this argument at the very outset simply because § 1367 is not ambiguous. * * * Even if we were to stipulate, however, that the reading these proponents urge upon us is textually plausible, the legislative history cited to support it would not alter our view as to the best interpretation of § 1367.

* * *

[The Court concluded that the legislative history did not shed useful light on the question before it. It noted that the proposal to adopt a supplemental jurisdiction statute emanated from a subcommittee of the Federal Courts Study Committee which explicitly favored overruling *Zahn* by statute, although the full Committee never took that position. Nonetheless, in the Court's view, the House Report was "no more authoritative" on this question than the working paper of the Federal

Courts Study Committee subcommittee that endorsed overruling *Zahn*. Moreover, three law professors who were involved in drafting the statute later acknowledged that the plain text of § 1367 overruled *Zahn,* and that the language in the House Report was a post hoc attempt to alter that result—"a deliberate effort to amend a statute through a committee report." And there was no reason, the Court felt, for concluding that members of Congress would have voted differently had they been squarely presented with the conclusion that their statute overruled *Zahn*.]

D

Finally, we note that the Class Action Fairness Act (CAFA), Pub.L. 109–2, 119 Stat. 4, enacted this year, has no bearing on our analysis of these cases. * * *

JUSTICE STEVENS, with whom JUSTICE BREYER joins, dissenting.

[Justice Stevens agreed that Justice Ginsburg's dissent showed that the Court's view of the supplemental jurisdiction statute was overly ambitious given the ambiguity of the statute. He wrote to show that the legislative history "provides powerful confirmation" of Justice Ginsburg's interpretation of the statute, stressing that the House Report said that the objective of § 1367 was essentially to restore the pre *Finley* understanding of the limits of supplemental jurisdiction.]

JUSTICE GINSBURG, with whom JUSTICE STEVENS, JUSTICE O'CONNOR, and JUSTICE BREYER join, dissenting.

* * *

The Court adopts a plausibly broad reading of § 1367, a measure that is hardly a model of the careful drafter's art. There is another plausible reading, however, one less disruptive of our jurisprudence regarding supplemental jurisdiction. If one reads § 1367(a) to instruct, as the statute's text suggests, that the district court must first have "original jurisdiction" over a "civil action" before supplemental jurisdiction can attach, then *Clark [v. Paul Gray, Inc.,* 306 U.S. 583 (1939)] and *Zahn [v. International Paper Co.,* 414 U.S. 291 (1973)] are preserved, and supplemental jurisdiction does not open the way for joinder of plaintiffs, or inclusion of class members, who do not independently meet the amount-in-controversy requirement. For the reasons that follow, I conclude that this narrower construction is the better reading of § 1367.

* * *

II

A

Section 1367, by its terms, operates only in civil actions "of which the district courts have original jurisdiction." The "original jurisdiction" relevant here is diversity-of-citizenship jurisdiction, conferred by § 1332.

The character of that jurisdiction is the essential backdrop for comprehension of § 1367.

* * *

The statute today governing federal court exercise of diversity jurisdiction in the generality of cases, § 1332, like all its predecessors, incorporates both a diverse-citizenship requirement and an amount-in-controversy specification.[5] As to the latter, the statute reads: "The district courts shall have original jurisdiction [in diversity-of-citizenship cases] where the matter in controversy exceeds the sum ... of $75,000." § 1332(a). * * *

This Court most recently addressed "[t]he meaning of [§ 1332's] 'matter in controversy' language" in *Zahn. Zahn,* like *Snyder [v. Harris,* 394 U.S. 332 (1969),] decided four years earlier, was a class action. In *Snyder,* no class member had a claim large enough to satisfy the jurisdictional amount. But in *Zahn,* the named plaintiffs had such claims. Nevertheless, the Court declined to depart from its "longstanding construction of the 'matter in controversy' requirement of § 1332." * * * The rule that each plaintiff must independently satisfy the amount-in-controversy requirement, unless Congress expressly orders otherwise, was thus the solidly established reading of § 1332 when Congress enacted the Judicial Improvements Act of 1990, which added § 1367 to Title 28.

B

These cases present the question whether Congress abrogated the nonaggregation rule long tied to § 1332 when it enacted § 1367. In answering that question, "context [should provide] a crucial guide." The Court should assume, as it ordinarily does, that Congress legislated against a background of law already in place and the historical development of that law. Here, that background is the statutory grant of diversity jurisdiction, the amount-in-controversy condition that Congress, from the start, has tied to the grant, and the nonaggregation rule this Court has long applied to the determination of the "matter in controversy."

---

[5]   Endeavoring to preserve the "complete diversity" rule first stated in *Strawbridge v. Curtiss,* 3 Cranch 267 (1806), the Court's opinion drives a wedge between the two components of 28 U.S.C. § 1332, treating the diversity-of-citizenship requirement as essential, the amount-in-controversy requirement as more readily disposable. Section 1332 itself, however, does not rank order the two requirements. What "[o]rdinary principl[e] of statutory construction" or "sound canon of interpretation," allows the Court to slice up § 1332 this way? In partial explanation, the Court asserts that amount in controversy can be analyzed claim-by-claim, but the diversity requirement cannot. It is not altogether clear why that should be so. The cure for improper joinder of a nondiverse party is the same as the cure for improper joinder of a plaintiff who does not satisfy the jurisdictional amount. In both cases, original jurisdiction can be preserved by dismissing the nonqualifying party.

* * * The Court is unanimous in reading § 1367(a) to permit pendent-party jurisdiction in federal-question cases, and thus, to overrule *Finley*. * * *

The Court divides, however, on the impact of § 1367(a) on diversity cases controlled by § 1332. Under the majority's reading, § 1367(a) permits the joinder of related claims cut loose from the nonaggregation rule that has long attended actions under § 1332. Only the claims specified in § 1367(b) would be excluded from § 1367(a)'s expansion of § 1332's grant of diversity jurisdiction. And because § 1367(b) contains no exception for joinder of plaintiffs under Rule 20 or class actions under Rule 23, the Court concludes, *Clark* and *Zahn* have been overruled.[8]

The Court's reading is surely plausible. * * *

[But an alternative would read § 1367(a)'s reference to "civil action[s] of which the district courts have original jurisdiction,"] to incorporate the rules on joinder and aggregation tightly tied to § 1332 at the time of § 1367's enactment. On this reading, a complaint must first meet that "original jurisdiction" measurement. If it does not, no supplemental jurisdiction is authorized. If it does, § 1367(a) authorizes "supplemental jurisdiction" over related claims. In other words, § 1367(a) would preserve undiminished, as part and parcel of § 1332 "original jurisdiction" determinations, both the "complete diversity" rule and the decisions restricting aggregation to arrive at the amount in controversy. Section 1367(b)'s office, then, would be "to prevent the erosion of the complete diversity [and amount-in-controversy] requirement[s] that might otherwise result from an expansive application of what was once termed the doctrine of ancillary jurisdiction." See Pfander, Supplemental Jurisdiction and Section 1367: The Case for a Sympathetic Textualism, 148 U.Pa.L.Rev. 109, 114 (1999). In contrast to the Court's construction of § 1367, which draws a sharp line between the diversity and amount-in-controversy components of § 1332, the interpretation presented here does not sever the two jurisdictional requirements.

The more restrained reading of § 1367 just outlined * * * would not discard entirely, as the Court does, the judicially developed doctrines of pendent and ancillary jurisdiction as they existed when *Finley* was decided. Instead, it would recognize § 1367 essentially as a codification of those doctrines, placing them under a single heading, but largely retaining their substance, with overriding *Finley* the only basic change: Supplemental jurisdiction, once the district court has original jurisdiction, would now

---

8   Under the Court's construction of § 1367, Beatriz Ortega's family members can remain in the action because their joinder is merely permissive, see Fed. Rule Civ. Proc. 20. If, however, their presence was "needed for just adjudication," Rule 19, their dismissal would be required. The inclusion of those who may join, and exclusion of those who should or must join, defies rational explanation * * *.

include "claims that involve the joinder or intervention of additional parties." § 1367(a).

* * *

The less disruptive view I take of § 1367 also accounts for the omission of Rule 20 plaintiffs and Rule 23 class actions in § 1367(b)'s text. If one * * * recognizes that the nonaggregation rule delineated in *Clark* and *Zahn* forms part of the determination whether "original jurisdiction" exists in a diversity case, then plaintiffs who do not meet the amount-in-controversy requirement would fail at the § 1367(a) threshold. Congress would have no reason to resort to a § 1367(b) exception to turn such plaintiffs away from federal court, given that their claims, from the start, would fall outside the court's § 1332 jurisdiction.

Nor does the more moderate reading assign different meanings to "original jurisdiction" in diversity and federal-question cases. As the First Circuit stated:

> " '[O]riginal jurisdiction' in § 1367(a) has the same meaning in every case: [An] underlying statutory grant of original jurisdiction must be satisfied. What differs between federal question and diversity cases is not the meaning of 'original jurisdiction' but rather the [discrete] requirements of sections 1331 and 1332. Under § 1331, the sole issue is whether a federal question appears on the face of the plaintiff's well-pleaded complaint; the [citizenship] of the parties and the amounts they stand to recover [do not bear on that determination]. Section 1332, by contrast, predicates original jurisdiction on the identity of the parties (*i.e.,* [their] complete diversity) and their [satisfaction of the amount-in-controversy specification]. [In short,] the 'original jurisdiction' language in § 1367 operates differently in federal-question and diversity cases not because the meaning of that term varies, but because the [jurisdiction-granting] statutes are different."

What is the utility of § 1367(b) under my reading of § 1367(a)? Section 1367(a) allows parties other than the plaintiff to assert *reactive* claims once entertained under the heading ancillary jurisdiction. As earlier observed, § 1367(b) stops plaintiffs from circumventing § 1332's jurisdictional requirements by using another's claim as a hook to add a claim that the plaintiff could not have brought in the first instance. *Kroger* is the paradigm case. There, the Court held that ancillary jurisdiction did not extend to a plaintiff's claim against a nondiverse party who had been impleaded by the defendant under Rule 14. Section 1367(b), then, is corroborative of § 1367(a)'s coverage of claims formerly called ancillary, but provides exceptions to assure that accommodation of added claims would not fundamentally alter "the jurisdictional requirements of section 1332."

* * *

NOTES AND QUESTIONS

1.   On one level, the question before the Court was to determine whether Congress meant to make aggressive changes in federal-court jurisdiction when it adopted § 1367. The proposal to adopt a supplemental jurisdiction statute emerged from the report of the Federal Courts Study Committee, which made a great many proposals. See Report of the Federal Courts Study Committee (1990). Another proposal was to amend the venue statute to remove the troublesome phrase "where the claim arose." See Bates v. C & S Adjusters, supra p. 843. Congress chose not to pursue many of the recommendations made by the committee, however, adopting instead only the "noncontroversial" ones, including supplemental jurisdiction. That would seem to counsel a cautious reading of the statute. It may be that the failure to mention plaintiffs joined under Rule 20 in § 1367(b) was a drafting mistake. Would the fact that the House Report said that § 1367(b) was intended "to implement the principal rationale of Owen Equipment v. Kroger" (supra p. 911) support that view? And the failure of § 1367(b) to mention Rule 23 stands in stark contrast to the statement in the House Report that the legislation was not intended to overturn the requirements of *Zahn.*

How should the courts approach a statute that appears to include a "mistake" by Congress? Certainly the courts should not take it upon themselves to determine that Congress has made a "mistake" of policy in adopting legislation and interpret the statute in accord with their own view of good policy. But should courts attempt to stretch statutory language to accomplish what Congress clearly intended to do even though it was maladroit in its choice of statutory language? The majority in *Allapattah* appears to conclude that Congress must correct its own mistake if it made one in § 1367. The dissenters urge that the "context" should affect the Court's attitude toward the statutory language. Which side has the better argument? Was this debate effectively resolved when the Court decided in *Finley* to require clear statutory authority for the exercise of supplemental jurisdiction? Note that the *Finley* Court relied on the absence of legislative authority to *narrow* federal jurisdiction, whereas *Allapattah* worked to *expand* it.

2.   The *Allapattah* majority says that the statute is unambiguous. Is its argument persuasive? Should the Court be concerned with whether its reading of the statute makes practical sense? For example, Justice Ginsburg asserts that the mention in § 1367(b) of Rule 19 plaintiffs but not Rule 20 plaintiffs defies rational explanation. Is the majority's explanation of § 1367(b) satisfactory on that point? The majority points out that if Justice Ginsburg's reading of § 1367(a) is correct, then some provisions of § 1367(b) defy explanation. Toward the end of her opinion (in a passage omitted from the casebook), Justice Ginsburg responds that the "enigmatic text" of the statute "defies flawless interpretation." Should that affect a determination whether the statute is ambiguous, which would warrant reliance on legislative intent?

For many, the big concern about the seeming "mistake" in § 1367(b) was that it could undermine the complete diversity rule. Law professors involved in drafting the statute observed that "[w]e can only hope that the federal courts will plug that potentially gaping hole in the complete diversity requirement." Rowe, Burbank & Mengler, Compounding or Creating Confusion about Supplemental Jurisdiction? A Reply to Professor Freer, 40 Emory L.J. 943, 961 n. *l* (1991). Early on, some courts did. See Ware v. Jolly Roger Rides, Inc., 857 F.Supp. 462, 464 (D.Md.1994) ("§ 1367 does not change the complete diversity requirement."). Is there a basis in the statutory text for treating the diversity requirement differently from the amount in controversy requirement?

The majority in *Allapattah* goes to some length to explain that the complete diversity requirement is different because it responds to the "contamination theory." For a broad critique of the Court's use of the "contamination" theory to define a civil action, see Steinman, Claims, Civil Actions, Congress, and the Court: Limiting the Reasoning of Cases Construing Poorly Drawn Statutes, 65 Wash. & Lee L.Rev. 1593 (2008). Justice Ginsburg objects in dissent that there is no way to "rank order" the diversity and amount-in-controversy requirements, both of which appear in the diversity jurisdiction statute (although the complete diversity requirement is not explicitly included in the statute and resulted instead from judicial interpretation). Actually, the Court's earlier class action decisions might be treated as doing so. In *Zahn,* it held that the fact the named class representative can satisfy the amount in controversy requirement is not sufficient; all class members must meet the requirement as well. But in Supreme Tribe of Ben-Hur v. Cauble, 255 U.S. 356 (1921), the Court held that the diversity requirement was satisfied if the named plaintiffs were diverse from defendants even though unnamed class members were not. Does that indicate that the Court previously "rank ordered" amount in controversy as more important than diversity in state-law class actions? Should the Court reconsider *Ben-Hur* in light of *Allapattah's* "contamination" analysis? Or should the Court simply decline to extend the citizenship rule in *Ben-Hur* (which involved what would today be regarded as a Rule 23(b)(1) class action) to the Rule 23(b)(3) context? The Court did not reach the citizenship issue in *Allapattah* and has never squarely held that *Ben-Hur* defines the citizenship of parties who join their separate claims for convenience under Rule 23(b)(3).

Lower courts have since *Allapattah* continued to adhere to the complete diversity rule. See, e.g., Merrill Lynch & Co. v. Allegheny Energy, Inc., 500 F.3d 171, 179 (2d Cir. 2007) (reasoning that *Allapattah* "makes clear that its expansive interpretation of § 1367 does not extend to additional parties whose presence defeats diversity").

3.   Although its interpretation of § 1367 was overturned, the First Circuit's decision in Rosario Ortega v. Star-Kist provides an illustration of the application of the amount-in-controversy requirement, see supra at p. 877. Plaintiff Beatriz, a nine year old girl in Puerto Rico, cut her right pinky finger on a can of Star-Kist tuna. Unfortunately, she injured nerves and tendons in her finger, requiring surgery and eight months of physical therapy. She had to wear a cast during the entire eight-month period and afterwards had a small scar and a 3% partial permanent impairment of the functioning of her hand, with the possibility of needing more surgery. In a portion of the opinion the

Supreme Court did not question, the First Circuit held that it could not say to a legal certainty that Beatriz could not recover more than $75,000.

Beatriz' mother, father, and sister did not have sufficient claims, however. The mother had paid nearly $5,000 in medical expenses for treatment of Beatriz. She asserted that she anticipated $25,000 in future medical expenses but offered no evidence to support that anticipation. Although the mother also claimed to have suffered emotional distress, the court found that dealing with her daughter's problem was "one of the normal responsibilities of parenthood," noting that she sought no counseling and did not witness the accident or its immediate aftermath. Altogether, this would not suffice to cover the gap between the medical expenses and $75,000. Beatriz' older sister was a student in Washington, D.C., when Beatriz suffered her injury in Puerto Rico. She did not return home due to the accident, but did take Beatriz to some physical therapy sessions during her summer vacation. Like her sister and mother, she received no counseling. Beatriz' father, finally, was divorced from her mother and did not live with her. He did spend half a day at the hospital when Beatriz had surgery, but did not bring her to any medical appointments. The First Circuit found no basis for an emotional distress award exceeding $75,000 to either the sister or the father. Given that the complaint claimed emotional distress damages in excess of $150,000 for each family member, was this a proper application of the amount in controversy requirement?

4.   Assuming as the First Circuit held that the claims of the mother, father, and sister in *Rosario Ortega* did not satisfy the amount in controversy requirement, is there a reason for excluding them from federal-court jurisdiction once Beatriz' claim is properly before the federal court? In a portion that was omitted earlier, the *Gibbs* Court stressed that federal courts favor joinder of related claims. See UMW v. Gibbs, 383 U.S. 715, 724 (1966) ("Under the Rules, the impulse is toward entertaining the broadest possible scope of action consistent with fairness to the parties; joinder of claims, parties and remedies is strongly encouraged."). Assume that Beatriz also had a claim against the company that made the can for Star-Kist. *Allapattah* suggests that the complete diversity rule would apply to such a claim and to any claims by other family members. What about the amount-in-controversy requirement? Should the policy justifications for joinder of the other family members still apply if Beatriz also sued the can manufacturer in this case? As the Court notes, section 1367(b) explicitly excludes supplemental jurisdiction over claims by plaintiffs against multiple defendants joined under Rule 20. Would it make sense to permit joinder of diverse plaintiffs, with below-threshold claims, only in suits against a single defendant? Could plaintiffs solve that problem by filing separate suits against each defendant? How should those separate suits be handled? See Rule 42 (dealing with consolidated cases).

5.   If § 1367(a) permits supplemental jurisdiction over related claims by additional plaintiffs whenever one claim satisfies federal-court jurisdiction, how should the following situation be handled? A bus operated by the City Bus Line crashes, injuring 50 passengers. All are local but one, who is from out of state. Assuming that nonresident passenger was seriously injured, she could

sue the bus company in federal court, invoking diversity jurisdiction. Could the other 49 passengers also join as plaintiffs in the suit? Under *Allapattah,* it would not matter whether the other passengers were seriously injured; like the members of Beatriz' family they could join even though they had small claims. Should it matter that they are not diverse? Recall Mas v. Perry, supra p. 866, which argued that, once jurisdiction was established over the husband's claim, sound judicial administration called for the assertion of jurisdiction over the wife's claim as well, even if her citizenship were doubtful.

6.   The Court mentions the Class Action Fairness Act of 2005 (CAFA) in *Allapattah.* As noted above, that statute added 28 U.S.C. § 1332(d), which gives the federal courts jurisdiction over certain state-law class actions that seek over $5 million in the aggregate on behalf of the class, without regard to the size of individual claims. The Act explicitly invokes minimal diversity jurisdiction, providing that such a case may be in federal court so long as any member of the class is a citizen of a state different from any defendant. When the Act applies, it thus overrides Snyder v. Harris, 394 U.S. 332 (1969), which said that class members' claims could not be aggregated to satisfy the amount in controversy requirement. In passing this legislation, Congress indicated that it viewed large state-law class actions as a significant national concern. Can you argue that this policy judgment was relevant to the *Allapattah* decision, notwithstanding the majority's disclaimer? Given the decision in *Allapattah* and the rule in *Ben-Hur,* how often would this new legislation be necessary to get cases into federal court? (Think about the importance of the value of the lead plaintiff's claim.) Could plaintiffs who wanted to stay in state court configure their suits to frustrate removal under *Allapattah?* Does CAFA provide any clues about whether Congress (at least in 2005) was in favor of forceful application of the amount-in-controversy or complete diversity requirements?

7.   For years, the district courts took the position that ancillary jurisdiction extended to the claims of those intervening as plaintiffs under Rule 24. The language of section 1367(b) raises doubts about the exercise of such jurisdiction. It declares that supplemental jurisdiction shall not extend to the claims of Rule 24 intervening plaintiffs when exercising such jurisdiction would erode the complete diversity rule (just as it forecloses the exercise of supplemental jurisdiction over claims involving plaintiffs or defendants joined under Rule 19). The drafters of the statute described it as ending the so-called Rule 19/24 anomaly by treating both forms of joinder the same way for supplemental jurisdiction purposes. See Rowe, Burbank & Mengler, Compounding or Creating Confusion about Supplemental Jurisdiction? A Reply to Professor Freer, 40 Emory L.J. 943, 955–59, 966–78 (1991).

GRIFFIN V. LEE
United States Court of Appeals for the Fifth Circuit, 2010
621 F.3d 380

Before JONES, CHIEF JUDGE, PRADO, CIRCUIT JUDGE, and OZERDEN, DISTRICT JUDGE of the Southern District of Mississippi, sitting by designation.

PER CURIAM:

[Robert A. Lee, an attorney, represented Sylvester Griffin in litigation relating to a trust. Griffin's complaint alleged a variety of state law claims in Louisiana state court, seeking reformation of the trust and the recovery of monies lost due to fraud. Defendants, including the corporate trustee (J.P. Morgan Chase) and Chase's officers, removed the case to the United States District Court for the Western District of Louisiana on the basis of diversity. After Lee was allowed to withdraw from his representation of Griffin, he filed a motion to intervene as a party under Federal Rule of Civil Procedure 24(a)(2), seeking recovery of attorney's fees. After allowing intervention, the district court held a bench trial and awarded Lee some $16,000 in attorney's fees. The question whether the district court could exercise supplemental jurisdiction over Lee's claim against Griffin was one the Fifth Circuit raised itself on appeal.]

For reasons not germane to the district court's jurisdiction, neither Griffin nor his new attorney appeared at the bench trial. The district court . . . directed that the Trustee "shall hold and conserve said monies as a debit item upon the [Trust] and pay said monies from the [Trust] to Mr. Lee out of the funds ultimately determined to be available for distribution to Mr. Griffin upon finality of Mr. Griffin's appeal." * * * Though he does not dispute that Lee is owed some fees for his work in successfully having the Trust reformed, Griffin disputes the amount awarded, and that any award should exist as a lien or encumbrance on the Trust.

* * *

III. ANALYSIS

At the time this case was removed from state court, original jurisdiction in the underlying lawsuit was founded solely upon diversity. * * * Plaintiff Griffin was a Mississippi citizen. Defendant JPMorgan Chase & Co. was a citizen of both Delaware and New York. Defendant JP Morgan Chase Bank, N.A., was a citizen of Ohio, as was Defendant Bank One Trust Co., N.A. The individual Defendants, Walter E. Busby, Drew C. Detraz, and Charlotte Ray, were Louisiana citizens. There was complete diversity of citizenship, and the record is clear that the amount in controversy exceeded $75,000.00, fulfilling the requirements of § 1332(a). [After intervention, Lee was aligned as a plaintiff], as he asserted claims for attorney's fees against his former client Griffin, and further sought to impose a lien upon the Trust. The record reflects that Lee was a citizen of Louisiana, and that the amount in controversy on his claim was clearly less than $75,000.00, as his initial pleadings sought only $54,087.51. * * * Complete diversity of citizenship was lacking between Lee and [the Louisiana] defendants, and the amount in controversy was less than $75,000. The question presented is whether there was supplemental jurisdiction over Lee's claim. We conclude that there was not.

A. Applicability of § 1367 to Lee's Claim

If a district court has original jurisdiction over at least one claim in a case, it must look to what was traditionally known as "pendent" or "ancillary" jurisdiction to assess whether it has jurisdiction over any remaining claims over which it would otherwise lack original jurisdiction. See, e.g., City of Chi. v. Int'l Coll. of Surgeons, 522 U.S. 156, 164–65 (1997) (federal question context). Congress has codified the concepts of pendent and ancillary jurisdiction in the supplemental jurisdiction statute. Id. at 165. ("Congress has codified those principles in the supplemental jurisdiction statute, which combines the doctrines of pendent and ancillary jurisdiction under a common heading); Walter Fuller Aircraft Sales, Inc. v. Republic of Phil., 965 F.2d 1375, 1389 n. 13 (5th Cir.1992) ("[T]he intent of § 1367(a) was to codify the doctrines of pendent and ancillary jurisdiction.").

Lee argues in his supplemental brief that § 1367(b) is not applicable to his claim, because the suit was removed to the district court pursuant to 28 U.S.C. § 1441(a), and not directly pursuant to § 1332(a). We are not persuaded by this argument. 28 U.S.C. § 1441(a) provides for removal of certain actions, but it does not confer subject matter jurisdiction upon the district court. It is, at bottom, a procedural statute. Even though this action was removed pursuant to § 1441(a), the district court's original jurisdiction was founded solely on § 1332. Moreover, the Supreme Court has explicitly stated that § 1367(a) "applies with equal force to cases removed to federal court as to cases initially filed there; a removed case is necessarily one 'of which the district courts . . . have original jurisdiction.'" City of Chi., 522 U.S. at 165.

B. Supplemental Jurisdiction under § 1367

1.   Statutory Framework

* * *

It is clear that Lee's Petition satisfied the requirements of § 1367(a). This does not end the inquiry, however. "If § 1367(a) were the sum total of the relevant statutory language, our holding would rest on that language alone. The statute, of course, instructs us to examine § 1367(b) to determine if any of its exceptions apply, so we proceed to that section." *Exxon Mobil*, 545 U.S. at 559–60.

Lee, who intervened as a plaintiff, was a Louisiana citizen. While Griffin, who was the original plaintiff, was a Mississippi citizen, there were defendants in the underlying case who were, like Lee, citizens of Louisiana. The record reflects that individual defendants Walter E. Busby, Drew C. Detraz, and Charlotte Ray, who were Trustee bank officers, were Louisiana citizens. Lee was not completely diverse from defendants in the underlying action.

It was also facially apparent from Lee's petition that the amount in controversy, Lee's claim for attorney's fees, fell below $75,000.00. Thus, Lee's intervention was clearly inconsistent with the jurisdictional requirements of § 1332, diversity of citizenship and the requisite amount in controversy, excluding it from the court's supplemental jurisdiction under the clear language of the supplemental jurisdiction statute.

2.   Application of § 1367

Commentators have recognized that the difficult

question has been whether, if the court has proper jurisdiction of the original action, it may allow an intervenor to come in and present a claim or defense although there would be no basis for federal jurisdiction if the intervenor were suing or being sued alone. This problem arises primarily in diversity cases, in which the would-be intervenor is a citizen of the same state as a party against whom the intervenor would be aligned if intervention is allowed or in which the controversy with regard to the intervenor is for less than the requisite jurisdictional amount.

7C C. Wright, A. Miller & M. Kane, FEDERAL PRACTICE AND PROCEDURE § 1917 (3d ed.2007).

Congress's enactment of the supplemental jurisdiction statute addressed these issues. Congress excepted from the statute's reach certain claims in cases in which original jurisdiction is founded solely upon diversity, such as claims by persons seeking to intervene as plaintiffs under Rule 24, when exercising supplemental jurisdiction over such claims would be inconsistent with the jurisdictional requirements of § 1332. See 28 U.S.C. § 1367(b); *Exxon Mobil*, 545 U.S. at 560 ("Section 1367(b), which applies only to diversity cases, withholds supplemental jurisdiction over the claims of plaintiffs proposed to be joined as indispensable parties under Federal Rule of Civil Procedure 19, or who seek to intervene pursuant to Rule 24.").

This change can be criticized as contrary to the objectives of encouraging efficient joinder and some commentators have noted that it goes beyond the "modest but significant" alterations stated by the drafters. Nonetheless, it remains the law and it now is clear that in diversity cases, ancillary (now supplemental) jurisdiction cannot be invoked for plaintiff intervenors, whether they are of right or permissive. 7C WRIGHT, MILLER & KANE, supra, § 1917. In other words, while Congress codified the concepts of pendent and ancillary jurisdiction in § 1367(a), it apparently chose to circumscribe such jurisdiction in § 1367(b) with respect to plaintiff intervenors. Despite commentators' criticism of the manner in which the statute was drafted, the Supreme Court has held that "§ 1367 is not ambiguous." *Exxon Mobil*, 545 U.S. at 567; see State Nat. Ins. Co. v. Yates, 391 F.3d 577, 581 (5th Cir.2004). Accordingly, the Supreme Court has rejected the view that it should look to other interpretive tools, including the legislative history of § 1367, to interpret the statute. Exxon Mobil, 545 U.S. at 567. As this Court has stated, "the statute is the sole repository of congressional intent where the statute is clear and does not demand an absurd result." In re Abbott Laboratories, 51 F.3d 524, 529 (5th Cir.1995).

In this case, the lack of complete diversity and the presence of an amount in controversy less than $75,000.00 are both inconsistent with the jurisdictional requirements of 28 U.S.C. § 1332. Under a plain reading of 28 U.S.C. § 1367(b), there was no supplemental jurisdiction over Lee's claim in intervention, as it was a claim by a person seeking to intervene as a plaintiff under Rule 24. Other circuits have reached similar conclusions. In Development Finance Corp. v. Alpha Housing & Health Care, Inc., 54 F.3d 156

(3d Cir.1995), the Third Circuit acknowledged that § 1367(b) eliminates supplemental jurisdiction over claims of plaintiff intervenors who share citizenship with a defendant. Id. at 159. Ultimately, the Third Circuit decided that the intervenor in that case was more properly aligned as a defendant, which cured the jurisdictional defect. Id. In TIG Insurance Co. v. Reliable Research Co., 334 F.3d 630 (7th Cir.2003), the Seventh Circuit dismissed a plaintiff intervenor's claim for want of jurisdiction, because its citizenship was not diverse from the party against whom it was asserting the claim. Id. at 634. In Baker v. Minnesota Mining and Manufacturing Co., 99 Fed.Appx. 718 (6th Cir.2004), abrogated on other grounds by Blackburn v. Oaktree Capital Management, LLC, 511 F.3d 633 (6th Cir.2008), the Sixth Circuit held that the Rule 24 intervention as a plaintiff by a party which was an arm of the Commonwealth of Kentucky, and not a "citizen" for diversity purposes, deprived the district court of jurisdiction under § 1367(b). Id. at 723. Thus, the Court concluded that the district court should have denied the non-diverse party's motion to intervene as a plaintiff.

Federal courts are courts of limited jurisdiction. They possess only that power authorized by the Constitution and statute, which is not to be expanded by judicial decree." Kokkonen v. Guardian Life Ins. Co. of Am., 511 U.S. 375, 378 (1994). "Unless a dispute falls within the confines of the jurisdiction conferred by Congress, such courts do not have authority to issue orders regarding its resolution." Giannakos v. M/V Bravo Trader, 762 F.2d 1295, 1297 (5th Cir.1985). "Such jurisdiction goes to the core of the court's power to act, not merely to the rights of the particular parties." Id. Based on the foregoing, neither the Constitution nor Congress has authorized the exercise of supplemental jurisdiction over Lee's claim here.

C. Party Alignment

We note that the issue of party alignment has not been addressed by the parties. The district court characterized Lee as an "intervenor plaintiff" and Griffin as an "intervenor defendant." Because § 1367(b) speaks only to plaintiff intervenors, we consider whether Lee was properly aligned as a plaintiff. In ascertaining the proper alignment of parties for jurisdictional purposes, courts have a "duty" to "look beyond the pleadings, and arrange the parties according to their sides in the dispute." City of Indianapolis v. Chase Nat'l Bank of City of N.Y., 314 U.S. 63, 69 (1941). "Whether the necessary 'collision of interest' exists must be ascertained from the 'principal purpose of the suit' and the 'primary and controlling matter in dispute.' " Id. As previously noted, the Third Circuit has held that if an intervenor is realigned as a defendant, § 1367(b) does not deprive the district court of supplemental jurisdiction over a counterclaim raised by the intervening defendant, even where the requirements of § 1332 are not met.

In this Circuit, "[t]he generally accepted test of proper alignment is whether the parties with the same 'ultimate interests' in the outcome of the action are on the same side." Lowe v. Ingalls Shipbuilding, A Div. of Litton Sys., Inc., 723 F.2d 1173, 1178 (5th Cir.1984). "[W]hen it relates to jurisdiction, it is [this court's] duty to notice party alignment and apply proper realignment sua sponte on appeal, and that such realignment is to be determined according to 'the principal purpose of the suit and the primary and controlling matter in dispute.' " Id. at 1178.

Based on the nature of Lee's claim, we are of the opinion that it is more appropriate to align him as a plaintiff with a claim against co-plaintiff Griffin as to the amount of attorney's fees owed, and with a direct claim against Trustee for a lien on the Trust. As a plaintiff intervening under Rule 24, § 1367(b)'s exclusion would apply, and there is no supplemental jurisdiction over Lee's claim.

D. Lee's Arguments in Support of Supplemental Jurisdiction

In his supplemental brief, Lee cites a number of cases for the proposition that a claim for, or award of, attorney's fees in a case is collateral to the case's merits, such that federal courts possess ancillary or supplemental jurisdiction over such claims. None of those cases, however, involve a Rule 24 intervention. Lee quotes heavily from In re Private Counsel Agreement, No. 5:98-CV-270, 1999 WL 1022131 (W.D.Tex. Nov. 5, 1999), which did involve a Rule 24 intervention, for the proposition that attorney's fee disputes meet the relatedness test of supplemental jurisdiction. What Lee apparently does not appreciate, however, is that In re Private Counsel Agreement was a federal question case, as were many of the other cases he cites. See id.; see also, e.g., Joseph Brenner Assoc., Inc. v. Starmaker Entm't, Inc., 82 F.3d 55 (2d Cir.1996); Baer v. First Options of Chi., Inc., 72 F.3d 1294 (7th Cir.1995). Because original jurisdiction in those cases was not founded solely on § 1332, § 1367(b)'s exclusions were inapplicable, even to Rule 24 interventions.

Lee next contends that under § 1367, the jurisdictional amount in controversy is not a requirement which must be satisfied. Even assuming that there were complete diversity of citizenship here, this argument is not compelling. The Supreme Court has concluded that in a diversity case in which some original plaintiffs satisfy the amount in controversy requirement, but others do not, § 1367(a) confers supplemental jurisdiction over all claims that are part of the same Article III case or controversy, including those that do not independently satisfy the amount in controversy requirement. *Exxon Mobil*, 545 U.S. at 558–59. Lee is not an original plaintiff.

As the *Exxon Mobil* Court also noted, "§§ 1367(b) and (c), or other relevant statutes, may provide specific exceptions" to § 1367(a)'s broad jurisdictional grant. Id. at 559. Such is the case with respect to Lee's claim, which is clearly excepted from supplemental jurisdiction by § 1367(b). In other words, what § 1367(a) giveth, § 1367(b) may taketh away. Moreover, the expansive interpretation for which Lee argues, even if accepted, would not remedy the lack of complete diversity of citizenship occasioned by his intervention. Id. at 554.

Lee next maintains that his intervention was the assertion of a state law right to intervene, and not one pursuant to the Federal Rules of Civil Procedure. He asserts that his was an "intervention of right," but not under Rule 24(a). Lee's contention that this case does not come within the purview of

§ 1367(b)'s exceptions because his right arises under state law is not persuasive. State law clearly confers upon Lee whatever substantive right he may have at issue in this case, but it was the Federal Rules of Civil Procedure, specifically Rule 24(a)(2), which the district court applied to permit his intervention. In a diversity case, the substantive right giving rise to intervention will likely originate from state law, but federal procedural rules will dictate whether the party is allowed to intervene.

Finally, Lee points out that the district court was the most convenient forum for handling the subject matter then before it. This is no doubt true, but convenience cannot supplant the unambiguous language of a jurisdictional statute. We are sympathetic to the added expense and potential waste of judicial resources Lee will likely face in pursuing his claim for legal fees in a separate action and forum. However, efficiency and economy cannot confer jurisdiction upon the courts where Congress has, according to the Supreme Court, unambiguously chosen to limit such jurisdiction. See id. at 567.

IV. CONCLUSION

Although we are sympathetic to Lee and the inconvenience he faces, because there was no supplemental jurisdiction over Lee's claim in intervention pursuant to 28 U.S.C. § 1367(b), we VACATE and REMAND with instructions that the district court DISMISS Lee's Petition of Intervention for lack of subject matter jurisdiction.

NOTES AND QUESTIONS

1.   For the most part, the lower courts have given effect to the language prohibiting the exercise of supplemental jurisdiction over claims by Rule 24 plaintiff intervenors. But cf. In re Olympic Mills Corp., 477 F.3d 1, 11–12 (1st Cir. 2007) (upholding the exercise of jurisdiction over nondiverse intervening plaintiffs without considering the language of section 1367). Given the phrasing of section 1367(b), does anything depend on whether a new party proposes to intervene as a plaintiff or as a defendant? The statute prohibits claims by plaintiffs against non-diverse intervening defendants under Rule 24 as well as claims by non-diverse intervening plaintiffs under Rule 24. As explained in Griffin v. Lee, courts do not necessarily accept the parties' own description of their status as plaintiff or defendant, but align new parties in accordance with their interests. Given that Lee, from Louisiana, was aligned as plaintiff and was asserting a claim against co-plaintiff Griffin, from Mississippi, and against the trustee, Chase, what threat to complete diversity did the claim pose? True, Griffin had joined the local officials of Chase, citizens of Louisiana, as defendants at an earlier stage of the litigation. But does the presence of those parties threaten the complete diversity rule, even where Lee asserted no claim against them?

Consider in this connection Price v. Wolford, 608 F.3d 698 (10th Cir. 2010). Plaintiffs, from Oklahoma, sought damages for medical malpractice against a physician who was a citizen of Maryland (thereby satisfying diversity). A nondiverse intervenor, the Oklahoma Health Care Authority (OHCA) sought to impress a lien on any proceeds of the litigation as reimbursement for Medicaid payments it had made to the plaintiffs. The Tenth Circuit upheld the assertion of supplemental jurisdiction over the lien claim of the OHCA, which had proposed to intervene as a defendant. As an arm of the state of Oklahoma, the OHCA is not a citizen of any state within the meaning of the diversity statute. But the court did not view the diversity-destroying quality of the OHCA's lack of state citizenship as relevant inasmuch as OHCA sought to intervene as a defendant. The court explained that the outcome may have been different had the OHCA been properly regarded as a plaintiff, but the court assessed the rules governing realignment of parties and concluded that they did not require realignment here.

Two tests for realignment were identified. Under the primary-purpose test, "the parties must be realigned if there is no adversity with regard to the primary issue in dispute." Price v. Wolford, 608 F.3d at 704 (quoting City of Indianapolis v. Chase Nat. Bank of New York, 314 U.S. 63, 69 (1941) for proposition that alignment "must be ascertained from the principal purpose of the suit"). Under the substantial-conflict test, a party need not be realigned so long as it has an "actual and substantial conflict" with a party on the other side. Price v. Wolford, 608 F.3d at 705 (quoting City of Indianapolis, 314 U.S. at 69). Applying the substantial-conflict test as law of the circuit, the court found the conflict between the plaintiffs and the intervenor OHCA sufficient to sustain OHCA's alignment as a defendant.

Was there a conflict between Lee and the non-diverse officials of Chase as to the primary issue in dispute, Lee's claim for attorney's fees? Assuming any amount Lee recovered would reduce the amount Chase paid to Griffin but would not increase Chase's obligation, could one argue that Lee and Chase and its officials were not properly regarded as antagonistic? How best can we account for the different result in the two cases, both of which involved litigation initially based on diversity jurisdiction that resulted in the creation of a fund in which a non-diverse third party claimed an interest?

2.   Before the codification of supplemental jurisdiction, district courts were thought to have "ancillary" jurisdiction over claims by non-diverse parties like those of Lee and the OHCA to the proceeds of a trust or fund that had been created or controlled by judicial decree in the course of litigation founded on diversity. Consider the broad language of the Supreme Court's decision in Julian v. Central Trust Co.,193 U.S. 93 (1904): "A bill filed to continue a former litigation in the same court . . . to obtain and secure the fruits, benefits and advantages of the proceedings and judgment in a former suit in the same court by the same or additional parties . . . or to obtain any equitable relief in regard to, or connected with, or growing out of, any judgment or proceeding at law rendered in the same court, . . . is an ancillary suit." Id. at 113–114 (citing 1 C. Bates, Federal Equity Procedure § 97 (1901)).

Does this form of ancillary jurisdiction survive the adoption of section 1367(b). Consider Kokkonen v. Guardian Life Ins. Co., 511 U.S. 375 (1994), an action brought in federal court to enforce a contract that the parties had agreed to in the course of settling prior federal litigation. Lacking any independent basis of federal jurisdiction over the breach of contract claim, the plaintiff invoked the federal court's ancillary jurisdiction. The Court found that such jurisdiction was unavailable:

> Generally speaking, we have asserted ancillary jurisdiction (in the very broad sense in which that term is sometimes used) for two separate, though sometimes related, purposes: (1) to permit disposition by a single court of claims that are, in varying respects and degrees, factually interdependent, see, *e.g., Baker v. Gold Seal Liquors, Inc.,* 417 U.S. 467, 469, n. 1 (1974); *Moore v. New York Cotton Exchange,* 270 U.S. 593, 610 (1926); and (2) to enable a court to function successfully, that is, to manage its proceedings, vindicate its authority, and effectuate its decrees, see, *e.g., Chambers v. NASCO, Inc.,* 501 U.S. 32 (1991) (power to compel payment of opposing party's attorney's fees as sanction for misconduct); *United States v. Hudson,* 11 U.S. (7 Cranch) 32, 34 (1812) (contempt power to maintain order during proceedings).

Kokkonen, 511 U.S. at 379–80. The first form of ancillary jurisdiction was unavailable in light of the factual independence of the initial federal lawsuit and the subsequent breach of contract claim; as the Court explained, "it would neither be necessary nor even particularly efficient that they be adjudicated together." Nor could the district court exercise ancillary enforcement jurisdiction:

> The facts to be determined with regard to such alleged breaches of contract are quite separate from the facts to be determined in the principal suit, and automatic jurisdiction over such contracts is in no way essential to the conduct of federal-court business. If the parties *wish* to provide for the court's enforcement of a dismissal-producing settlement agreement, they can seek to do so. When the dismissal is pursuant to Federal Rule of Civil Procedure 41(a)(2), which specifies that the action "shall not be dismissed at the plaintiff's instance save upon order of the court and upon such terms and conditions as the court deems proper," the parties' compliance with the terms of the settlement contract (or the court's "retention of jurisdiction" over the settlement contract) may, in the court's discretion, be one of the terms set forth in the order.

Kokkonen, 511 U.S. at 381. The Court did not frame its analysis in terms of section 1367, but referred to the statute only as a point of comparison.

In Peacock v. Thomas, 516 U.S. 349 (1996), the Court again considered the scope of ancillary enforcement jurisdiction. Thomas had secured a judgment in federal court against Tru-Tech for breach of duty under the Employee Retirement Income Security Act of 1974 (ERISA). Peacock, a principal of Tru-Tech, sought to defeat the judgment by making transfers to preferred creditors, including himself. Thomas brought suit in federal court, seeking to pierce the corporate veil and impose liability on Peacock for the amount of the Tru-Tech judgment. Although the lower courts granted the requested relief, the Court reversed for want of federal jurisdiction. The subsequent action against Peacock set out new facts and legal theories not presented in the first proceeding and thus lay beyond the district court's ancillary jurisdiction. Similarly, the action did not fit within the federal court's ancillary enforcement jurisdiction; it did not seek the assistance of the federal court in enforcing the first judgment but sought to impose an independent legal duty on a new party who had not appeared as such in the prior litigation. Again, the Court failed to analyze the problem in terms of section 1367, noting only that the statute had codified "much" of the common-law doctrine of ancillary jurisdiction. See *Peacock*, 516 U.S. at 354 n. 5.

In Griffin v. Lee and Price v. Wolford, the intervenor sought to recover proceeds not by bringing a separate action against a non-diverse party but by intervening in a pending action to which the district court's diversity jurisdiction plainly extended. The Court in *Kokkonen* appeared to assume that *Julian* was still good law, but found that it did not apply to an independent breach of contract suit. If *Julian* remains valid, does the existence of jurisdiction turn on an evaluation of section 1367(b) or on an assessment of the traditional scope of ancillary jurisdiction. In both *Griffin* and *Price*, the courts assumed that the claim for proceeds satisfied section 1367(a) in that they arose from the same case or controversy within the meaning of Article III of the Constitution.

3.   What weight should be ascribed to the last provision of section 1367(b), which bars supplemental jurisdiction only where its exercise "would be inconsistent with the jurisdictional requirements of section 1332." The apparent purpose of the proviso was to codify the approach taken in Owen Equipment v. Kroger, 437 U.S. 365 (1978), refusing to extend ancillary jurisdiction to claims by plaintiffs against a party brought into the litigation as a third-party defendant under Rule 14. To be sure, the *Owen* Court had approved of the exercise of supplemental jurisdiction over the Rule 14 impleader claim, allowing a new party to be joined as a defendant in the litigation without any independent jurisdictional basis. But the Court reasoned that supplemental jurisdiction should not extend to subsequent claims (contemplated in Rule 14) brought by the plaintiff against the third-party defendant in the wake of such impleader. It would be too easy, the Court believed, for plaintiffs to work around the requirements of complete diversity by omitting claims against a non-diverse third party, awaiting the predictable impleader of that party, and then amending the complaint to assert the omitted claims. Fearing an end-run around the complete diversity rule, the Court refused to permit supplemental jurisdiction.

Some courts have relied on the proviso as the basis for allowing the exercise of ancillary jurisdiction over claims by intervening plaintiffs. *See, e.g.,* Mattel Inc. v. Bryant, 446 F.3d 1011, 1014 (9th Cir. 2006) (allowing district court to exercise jurisdiction over claims of non-diverse intervening plaintiff); Westra, Inc. v. U.S. Fidelity & Guar. Co., 546 F. Supp. 2d 194, 198 (M.D. Pa. 2008) (same). Similarly, in an opinion by Judge Posner, the Seventh Circuit ruled in favor of supplemental jurisdiction over claims by a non-diverse intervening plaintiff in circumstances where the plaintiff's interests were not evident at the time the litigation was initiated. See Aurora Loan Servs. Inc. v. Craddieth, 442 F.3d 1018 (7th Cir. 2006). For Judge Posner, the plaintiff's lack of knowledge as to the identity of the proposed intervenor reduced the threat that the plaintiff was gaming the jurisdictional system in the way that the *Owen* Court feared. *Id.* at 1025.

4.   Suppose an inventor (Voda) brings suit in Oklahoma federal district court against a medical device manufacturer (Cordis Corporation), alleging infringement of a patent on a catheter used in cardiology treatments. The district courts have exclusive jurisdiction over patent claims under 28 U.S.C. § 1338. Suppose the plaintiff alleged that Cordis also infringed patents he had obtained in Great Britain, France, Canada, and Germany. While Congress has never assigned the federal courts jurisdiction over such foreign patent infringement claims, Voda urged that the state courts could exercise general subject matter jurisdiction over them. Assuming that the foreign patent claims satisfy the common-nucleus/same-case test of 1367(a), are there reasons why the district court should decline to exercise supplemental jurisdiction? In Voda v. Cordis Corp., 476 F.3d 887 (Fed. Cir. 2007), the court of appeals blocked the assertion of supplemental jurisdiction. Partly its argument was territorial: the court viewed patent rights as typically extending only through the territory of the sovereign that conferred those rights. Partly its argument was prudential: the court feared that the assertion of jurisdiction over the claims would interfere with the sovereign right of other nations to control their patent regulatory system. Should such factors inform jurisdictional analysis or should they be evaluated in connection with such discretionary doctrines as forum non conveniens?

5.   Section 1367(d) presented an interpretive difficulty —what period of time does it permit for a substitute action to be filed in state court after the federal court declines to exercise jurisdiction over supplemental claims? It's clearly at least 30 days, but it might be longer. Federal district courts had nohave occasion to resolve this question; they decide only whether to exercise supplemental jurisdiction. The state courts, meanwhile, variously embraced one of three approaches: (1) the "suspension" approach, under which the statute stops the running of the limitations period and, following dismissal, permits filing in state court within the time remaining on the limitations period when the federal suit was filed plus 30 days; (2) the "grace period" approach, which ensures the dismissed claimant can file in state court within 30 days of dismissal; or (3) the "substitution" approach, which would direct that refiling occur within 30 days no matter how much time might remain on the limitations period.

In Artis v. District of Columbia, 138 S.Ct. 594 (2018), the Supreme Court resolved the interpretive uncertainty by opting for the "suspension" approach, or what it termed stopping the clock. There, the plaintiff brought suit in federal court, alleging a federal workplace discrimination claim and certain supplemental state law claims. At the time of filing, a little more than one year of the three-year limitation period applicable to the state claims had elapsed.

Artis litigated in federal court for two and half years, at which point the district court granted the defendant's motion for summary judgment on the federal claim and declined to retain supplemental jurisdiction over the state claims. Fifty-nine days later, Artis refiled the state law claims in state court. The lower court dismissed the state law claims as untimely, reasoning that more than three years had elapsed since the alleged discrimination occurred (thus exhausting the state period) and that Artis had failed to re-file within the thirty-day grace period supplied by section 1367(d). Rejecting this characterization of subsection (d) as a grace period, the Supreme Court found that the tolling provision stopped the state limitation clock from running during the pendency of the federal proceeding, and allowed it to run again only upon dismissal of the federal action. Under the Court's reading, Artis still had nearly two years (plus thirty days) to file her state court claims after federal dismissal because the state limitation period had been tolled throughout the period of federal litigation.

6.   Section 1367 has received much scholarly attention; "it is difficult to think of another topic in civil procedure that has commanded more scholarly attention in the past thirteen years." Freer, The Cauldron Boils: Supplemental Jurisdiction, Amount in Controversy, and Diversity of Citizenship Class Actions, 53 Emory L.J. 55, 57–58 (2004). For further reading on § 1367, see Symposium, A Reappraisal of the Supplemental Jurisdiction Statute, 74 Ind.L.J. 1–250 (1998); an exchange of articles between law professors critical of the statute and others involved in drafting it, 40 Emory L.J. 943–1014 (1991), and a colloquy among five other law professors on the same topic, 41 Emory L.J. 1–113 (1992). See also Floyd, Three Faces of Supplemental Jurisdiction After the Demise of United Mine Workers v. Gibbs, 60 Fla. L. Rev. 277 (2008).

D. REMOVAL

Plaintiffs who could sue in federal court sometimes choose to sue in state court instead. Sometimes they do so because federal court does not offer jurisdiction for all the claims or parties they wish to include in the suit. But often the suit filed in state court could have readily been filed in federal court. Should defendants then be permitted to overrule plaintiff's choice to litigate in state court and take the case to federal court? That is what removal allows. As a general rule, defendants have thirty days to remove an action from state to federal court. They may do so if the state court proceeding was within the original jurisdiction of the district court, either on the basis of diversity of citizenship or as a case arising under federal law.

Removal jurisdiction is "quite an anomalous jurisdiction, giving a defendant sued in a court of competent jurisdiction, the right to elect a forum of its own choosing." C. Wright & M. Kane, Law of Federal Courts 225 (7th ed. 2011). Removal was unknown to the common law by that name and was not mentioned in the Constitution (although the common law writ of certiorari operated to remove an action to a superior court for determination). "Nevertheless there has been provision for removal of cases from state courts to federal courts from the First Judiciary Act, in 1789, to the present day, and the constitutionality of removal is entirely settled." Id. In a sense, the addition of removal jurisdiction to the original jurisdiction provided by 28 U.S.C. §§ 1331 and 1332 means that there is a de facto preference for litigation in federal court in cases where federal jurisdictional requirements are satisfied. Plaintiff may initially file there without consulting defendant, and defendant may remove to federal court without the assent of plaintiff. So if either plaintiff or defendant wants the case in federal court, it will (with few exceptions) be heard there.

Even though federal court offers many advantages, plaintiffs often strongly prefer the state court option. Walker, Keep Your Case in State Court, Trial, Sept., 2004, at 22 explains why:

> Plaintiff attorneys' preference for state courts is undisputed and understandable. Reasons for avoiding federal court range from the mundane (greater familiarity with state procedure) to the strategic (greater likelihood of securing justice for clients).

> In most cases, local judges are elected by the very people whose disputes they will hear, motivating speedy and fair adjudication. Federal judges are appointed for life, and their courts are clogged with criminal cases. The so-called war on drugs has so overburdened the federal judiciary that getting a civil case tried at all in many federal courts is nearly impossible.

> To reduce their burgeoning dockets, federal courts have increasingly engaged in stringent control of discovery, aggressive encouragement of settlement, and more frequent granting of summary judgment. As a result, litigation in federal court is more expensive and time-consuming. Moreover, plaintiffs whose cases are removed to federal court are substantially less successful than those who originally filed there. Finally, but significantly, lawsuits in federal court are increasingly being consolidated into multidistrict, pretrial litigation proceedings, where they often languish for years.

> Defense attorneys are not oblivious to these facts; upon receiving a state court complaint, they frequently search for any conceivable basis to remove the lawsuit to federal court.

Consider also the judicial views in Kilgore v. Academy Ltd., 86 F.Supp.3d 1367, 1373–74 (M.D. Ga. 2015):

> [C]orporate defendants believe they generally fare better in a federal court. This is particularly true with regard to corporate defendants defending tort claims and it is almost universally true for defendants with large retail operations. It is only necessary to

search Pacer for Wal-Mart to confirm this. As [defendant] Academy's counsel here repeatedly said, he wants and likes to be in federal court when defending companies like Academy.

In the Court's experience, there are several reasons defendants believe the ability to remove to federal court is an effective weapon. There seems to be a belief among many civil defense attorneys that plaintiffs' attorneys would rather not be in federal court. In many districts, federal juries are thought to be more financially conservative, particularly where, as in this District, jurors are summoned from well beyond the county in which the Court sits. * * * Many civil defense attorneys seem to believe that they stand a better chance of securing summary judgment in federal court than in state court. * * *

A plaintiff's lawyer who wishes to remain in state court may configure her suit in a way that will make it nonremovable, and may question whether defendant has used the proper procedure in removing if it attempts to do so. Perhaps not surprisingly, a study of case outcomes reveals that the plaintiffs' prospects for success decline after removal of the case to federal court. See Clermont & Eisenberg, Do Case Outcomes Really Reveal Anything about the Legal System? Win Rates and Removal Jurisdiction, 83 Cornell L. Rev. 581, 605–06 (1998) (concluding that removal lowers plaintiff win rates).

One more prefatory note: the existence of federal question removal suggests that the state and federal courts enjoy concurrent jurisdiction over claims based upon federal law. That, indeed, has been the presumptive rule for well over a century (or longer). See Tafflin v. Levitt, 493 U.S. 455 (1990) (reaffirming the rule in Claflin v. Houseman, 93 U.S. 130 (1876) that state courts may hear federal question claims unless Congress clearly indicates its intention to exclude them). (A separate line of cases addresses the duty of state courts to entertain such claims. See Haywood v. Drown, 556 U.S. 729 (2009); Testa v. Katt, 330 U.S. 386 (1947)). Like other canons of statutory interpretation, the presumption that state courts enjoy concurrent jurisdiction over federal claims remains subject to congressional override. Congress can confer exclusive federal jurisdiction over federal law claims, thus foreclosing state court adjudication. Such cases, if wrongly filed in state court, can still almost invariably be removed to federal court, the only forum that can entertain them. See 28 U.S.C. § 1441(f). Congress might also give the *state* courts exclusive jurisdiction over federal claims, although that would be a curious choice. Consider Mims v. Arrow Finan. Serv., LLC, 132 S.Ct. 740 (2012), which rejected the argument that the Telephone Consumer Protection Act barred *federal* courts from hearing federal question claims under the Act. The Act declared that claimants could sue "in an appropriate state court of

[a] state," but the Court saw no reason to interpret that language as forbidding federal-court jurisdiction.

NOTES AND QUESTIONS

Read 28 U.S.C. §§ 1441, 1446, and 1447, and consider the following questions:

1. Suppose your client, a Californian, is injured in a single-car crash in California while driving a new car manufactured by Ford Motor Co., a citizen of Delaware and Michigan. There is good reason to believe that the crash was caused by a defect in the car's steering.

(a) If it were urgently important that your client's case remain in state court, but not necessary that it be a California state court, how would you assure that Ford could not remove? See 28 U.S.C. § 1441(b) and recall Merrell Dow Pharmaceuticals v. Thompson, supra p. 899 n. 3(b). Why should in-state defendants be forbidden to remove on grounds of diversity? Recall that diversity jurisdiction is said to exist to protect out-of-state parties from local prejudice. If it should not be available to in-state defendants, should in-state plaintiffs similarly be forbidden to file in federal courts on grounds of diversity? What if they simply go to another state and sue there in federal court? While diversity jurisdiction (if not venue and personal jurisdiction) would be proper in the federal courts of such a state today, the Judiciary Act of 1789 did not allow diversity jurisdiction unless one of the parties was a citizen of the state in which suit was brought. Why not?

(b) If it were important to bring the case in a California state court, would there be any way to prevent Ford from removing? How about initially requesting less than $75,000 in damages? Should this suffice to defeat removal if California state-court procedure permits a plaintiff to increase the amount sought later in the suit? In Hollenbeck v. Outboard Marine Corp., 201 F.Supp.2d 990 (E.D. Mo. 2001), the complaint attempted to limit the damages claim to less than $75,000 for "as long as removal potential exists." State law allowed plaintiff to amend to increase the damage claim later, and the body of the complaint alleged present damages of at least $160,000. Removal was allowed.

(c) If the plaintiff had the car serviced and tires rotated at a local garage two weeks before the accident, there might be a claim against the garage in connection with the failure of the car's steering. If plaintiff sues the local garage as well, should that affect removability? Jurists and practitioners often refer to such defendants as "jurisdictional spoilers" inasmuch as their joinder may preclude the assertion of jurisdiction on the basis of diversity. Under settled law, the joinder of a jurisdictional spoiler can be ignored as fraudulent when " 'there is no reasonable basis in fact or colorable ground supporting the claim against the joined defendant, or no real intention in good faith to prosecute the action against the defendant.' " In re Briscoe, 448 F.3d 201, 217 (3d Cir. 2006) (quoting Abels v. State Farm Fire & Cas. Co., 770 F.2d 26, 32 (3d Cir.1985)). See also Smallwood v. Illinois Central R.R. Co., 385 F.3d 568

(5th Cir.2004) (referring to fraudulent joinder doctrine as "improper joinder"). Fraudulent or improper joinder analysis focuses strictly on the legal and factual justification for the claim against the nondiverse defendant; the motive of the plaintiff in seeking to avoid removal does not make the joinder fraudulent.

Can the federal court determine whether a defendant has been fraudulently joined without passing on the merits of the claim against that defendant? Consider Shapiro v. McManus, 136 S.Ct. 450, 455 (2015), supra p. 906 n. 7, where the Court distinguished between failing to raise a substantial question for jurisdictional purposes and failing to state a claim for relief on the merits. Unless the claim can be considered "wholly insubstantial and frivolous," the failure to state a proper cause of action "calls for a judgment on the merits and not for a dismissal for want of jurisdiction." Id. Such an approach requires the district courts to remand cases where the claim against the jurisdictional spoiler passes the test as not wholly insubstantial. As a consequence, it leaves the evaluation of the merits of the claim to the state court.

For pointers about how to anticipate and defeat fraudulent joinder arguments by bolstering the pleading of the claim against the nondiverse party, see Wilson, Mix & Match, Trial, March 2011, at 38:

> The importance of a well-drafted complaint—which adequately identifies the parties, their respective states of residence, and their liability under state law—cannot be overstated. * * * A complaint that can be dismissed only after an intricate analysis of state law is not so wholly insubstantial and frivolous that it may be disregarded for diversity jurisdiction purposes. [Although some courts look beyond the allegations of the complaint,] [t]he lesson to be learned from these decisions is that a plaintiff may need discovery to support a motion to remand. When confronted with matters outside the record, you should seek permission to conduct discovery on the issue of fraudulent joinder.

Id. at 40–41.

On the human costs of naming jurisdictional spoilers, consider the testimony of Hilda Bankston, wife of Mitch Bankston. The Bankstons ran Bankston Drugstore in Fayette, Mississippi, a favorite venue for class actions against national pharmaceutical firms. Ms. Bankston testified before the US House of Representatives in February 2002 that her husband's drugstore had been named in countless pharmaceutical class actions, including Fen-phen, Propulsid, Baycol, and Rezulin. See Hilda Bankston, Testimony, Hearing Before the Committee on the Judiciary, U.S. House of Representatives. 107th Congress, Second Sess., Feb. 6, 2002. A subsequent search of courthouse records revealed only one such lawsuit against Bankston Drugstore, and investigative journalists reported that the drug companies fully indemnified the Bankstons for the costs of defending that lawsuit. S. Mencimer, Blocking the Courthouse Door 165 (2006).

(d)   Assume that plaintiff does sue the garage, asserts a legally justifiable claim, and thus defeats removal. Six months later the garage files a motion for summary judgment on the ground that there is no evidence that it was responsible for any fault in the car's steering. If the court grants the motion, can Ford, the remaining defendant, now remove? See American Car & Foundry Co. v. Kettelhake, 236 U.S. 311, 316 (1915) (indicating that, to make the case removable, it must appear that the discontinuance of the claims against the jurisdictional spoiler "was voluntary on the part of the plaintiff"); Whitcomb v. Smithson, 175 U.S. 635, 638 (1900) (same). On the current vitality of rule barring removal after the involuntary dismissal of a jurisdictional spoiler, see Vogel v. Merck & Co., Inc., 476 F. Supp. 2d. 996 (S.D. Ill. 2007). Generally, dismissal on the basis of defendant's summary judgment motion would not be voluntary from the plaintiff's perspective and removal would be unavailable. For a criticism and suggested reform, see Underwood, From Proxy to Principle: Fraudulent Joinder Reconsidered, 69 Albany L. Rev. 1013 (2006) (arguing for abolition of the involuntary dismissal rule). What would happen if the rule were otherwise and the involuntary dismissal by the state court resulted in a prompt removal? Could the plaintiff seek to have the dismissal overturned on appeal in the state system? If so, would a successful appeal result in a subsequent remand of the action to state court?

(e)   Suppose instead that, after the garage files the summary judgment motion, plaintiff and the garage reach a settlement under which plaintiff consents to dismissal of her claim against the garage in return for payment of a sum of money. In general, the voluntary dismissal of the garage would clear the way for removal by the manufacturer, assuming it occurs within the one-year time limit specified in the statute. See 28 U.S.C. § 1446(b).

Would it matter if the garage agreed to defer the dismissal until a year and a day after plaintiff filed the suit? In Tedford v. Warner-Lambert Co., 327 F.3d 423 (5th Cir. 2003), plaintiff orchestrated the addition of a non-diverse defendant but executed a postdated notice of nonsuit as to that defendant that became effective one day after the time to remove had expired. Reasoning that "[s]trict application of the one-year limit would encourage plaintiffs to join nondiverse defendants for 366 days simply to avoid federal court," the court concluded that "Tedford's forum manipulation justifies application of an equitable exception" to the one-year limitation on removal. In 2011, Congress amended the statute to provide for tolling in cases where the plaintiff acts in "bad faith" to prevent removal. In a world where both parties seek strategic advantage through forum selection, does it make sense to include a subjective element in a jurisdictional provision?

(f)   Assume that plaintiff does not sue the garage, and Ford removes the case. A week later, plaintiff amends the complaint to reduce the prayer for damages below the jurisdictional minimum. May plaintiff then obtain a remand to state court? See St. Paul Mercury Indem. Co. v. Red Cab Co., 303 U.S. 283 (1938) (plaintiff's reduction of the amount sought below the jurisdictional minimum did not deprive the court of removal jurisdiction, for that is determined by the circumstances in the case at the time of removal and not by later events).

(g)   Assume that plaintiff does not sue the garage, and Ford removes the case. Six months later, plaintiff learns through discovery that the steering was significantly damaged during the tire rotation at the garage. Can plaintiff add a claim against the garage at that point? The removal statute now formally authorizes the district court to exercise discretion when confronted by a proposed amendment that would add non-diverse parties; it can accept the amendment and remand or deny joinder and retain the litigation. See 28 U.S.C. § 1447(e). How should the court decide whether to permit addition of the garage? Should it matter that, due to the statute of limitations, it is too late to file a separate suit against the garage in state court? Compare Spencer v. U.S. District Court, 393 F.3d 867 (9th Cir.2004) (amendment to add local, diverse, defendant after removal does not mandate remand even though case would not have been removable if the local defendant had originally been sued).

Consider also Schur v. L.A. Weight Loss Centers, Inc., 577 F.3d 752 (7th Cir. 2009), in which L.A. Weight Loss invoked diversity in removing an action that alleged it was responsible for urging the use of diet supplements that may have caused the decedent's death. After learning during discovery that two employees of the firm had given the advice in question, lawyers for the decedent's estate amended the complaint to add them as non-diverse defendants. No one objected. Later, the plaintiff sought a remand of the action to state court under section 1447(e). Because it was too late for the district court to deny the proposed amendment to the complaint, the Seventh Circuit concluded that section 1447(e) left the lower court no choice but to remand. L.A. Weight Loss's interest in avoiding the potential biases of local courts did not outweigh plaintiff's interest in avoiding the cost and inconvenience of parallel lawsuits in state and federal courts.

(h)   As discussed in note 1(a) above, section 1441(b)(2) provides that an action removable on the basis of diversity shall not be removed "if any of the parties in interest properly joined and served as defendants is a citizen of the State in which such action is brought." This forum-defendant rule does not necessarily deprive the federal court of jurisdiction if diversity otherwise obtains but has been seen as an important procedural barrier to removal. Recently, defendants have engaged in a practice of "snap removal," in which the lead defendant removes a state court proceeding immediately after it was filed and before it has been served on one or more of the parties. (Private data-collection companies monitor state dockets and report to law firms on new filings, thereby enabling firms to take action on behalf of their clients before the plaintiff can perfect service on the parties.) If the case otherwise meets the requirements of diversity, the forum defendant rule may represent the only barrier to removal. Some district courts have found removal proper in these "snap removal" scenarios, reasoning that the forum defendant was not, at the time of removal, properly "joined and served" within the literal meaning of the statute. See Frick v. Novartis Pharmaceuticals Corp., No. Civ. 05–5429 (DRD), 2006 WL 454360, at *2–3 (D.N.J. Feb. 23, 2006). Other courts, though recognizing the argument from plain meaning, have rejected the snap removal stratagem as inconsistent with the evident purpose of the statute. See Holmstrom v. Harad, 2005 WL 1950672 (N.D. Ill. Aug. 11, 2005). For an overview and suggested statutory fix, see Hellman et al., Neutralizing the Stratagem of "Snap Removal": A Proposed Amendment to the Judicial Code, 9 Federal Courts L. Rev. 103 (2016). Is there some reason why this question cannot be settled through the usual processes of appellate review? See 28 U.S.C. § 1447(d) (limiting appellate review of remand orders); Holmstrom v. Peterson, 492 F.3d 833 (7th Cir. 2007) (holding that remand order for noncompliance with forum defendant rule was not subject to appellate review).

2. The introduction of federal question claims will alter the removal analysis in various ways. For starters, the federal question claim will trigger the availability of removal without regard to the citizenship of the parties and the amount in controversy. Indeed, a federal question claim renders inapplicable the bar to removal of claims brought against defendants in their own state of citizenship. See 28 U.S.C. § 1441(b)(2). Moreover, a substantial federal-question claim will anchor the assertion of supplemental jurisdiction, potentially allowing the assertion of removal jurisdiction over all claims and parties that satisfy the relatedness test of section 1367(a). Finally, the bar to removal of claims pending more than one year does not apply to federal-question claims.

(a) Suppose the plaintiff sues Ford in state court on state law theories of liability and later amends the complaint to include a claim against Ford under federal auto-safety law. Defendants would ordinarily have thirty days to remove.

(b) Suppose that, following removal, the plaintiff decides to drop the federal-question claim and return to state court. When, in contrast to the diversity-based claim against Ford, removal is based on the assertion of a federal question claim, courts have generally been willing to order a remand following a post-removal amendment in which the plaintiff forgoes the federal question claim(s). See Carnegie-Melon University v. Cohill, 484 U.S. 343 (1988) (upholding remand following amendment that dropped the only federal question claim). Can one justify these results by observing that the plaintiff could voluntarily dismiss all the claims in federal court and, assuming no timeliness problems, re-file the case in state court without the federal claims? One advantage of a remand: It preserves the plaintiff's commencement date for limitations purposes. Would the tolling provision in 28 U.S.C. § 1367(c) also apply?

3. Congress has decreed that certain types of cases are not removable even though plaintiff could file initially in federal court. See, e.g., 28 U.S.C. § 1445(a) (Federal Employers' Liability Act and Jones Act cases); 1445(c) (worker's compensation proceedings); compare Breuer v. Jim's Concrete of Brevard, Inc., 538 U.S. 691 (2003) (action under the Fair Labor Standards Act may be removed; nothing in that statute forbids removal). Why would Congress want to guarantee plaintiffs a right to pursue certain claims in state court by denying the defendant a right to remove?

4.   The Supreme Court has emphasized that removal is limited to the grounds authorized in § 1441. Owing to concerns about mass torts, the lower federal courts began in the 1990s to permit removal of state-court cases that overlapped with federal-court proceedings under the All Writs Act, 28 U.S.C. § 1651, which authorizes federal courts to issue "all writs necessary or appropriate in aid of their respective jurisdictions." In Syngenta Crop Protection, Inc. v. Henson, 537 U.S. 28 (2002), the Supreme Court rejected this practice. In that case, the state-court plaintiff had intervened in the federal-court case, participated in settlement negotiations, and stipulated to dismissal with prejudice in federal court. Then, evidently at a hearing defendant was not notified would occur, plaintiff's lawyer told the state-court judge that only certain claims were included in the settlement of the federal action, and the state-court judge said that the state-court case could proceed. On learning of this development, defendant removed to the federal court, which had retained jurisdiction over its case, on the ground that plaintiff's actions threatened to disrupt the proceedings in federal court. The Supreme Court ruled that this was improper because "[t]he right to removal is entirely a creature of statute," and "the All Writs Act does not confer jurisdiction on the federal courts."

The challenge of coordinating related proceedings in state and federal court has grown in importance. Thus, the Multiparty Multiforum Trial Jurisdiction Act of 2002, 28 U.S.C. § 1369, conferred original federal-court jurisdiction for multiparty, multiforum situations in which the minimal diversity requirement is satisfied and there is litigation resulting from an incident that led to the death of 75 people. 28 U.S.C. § 1441(e) contains removal provisions to handle that situation. In early 2005, Congress passed the Class Action Fairness Act of 2005, which responded to perceived improprieties in the handling of some state-court class actions. The Act added 28 U.S.C. § 1453, which authorizes removal on the basis of minimal diversity of state-law class actions in which more than $5 million is sought on behalf of the class as a whole unless more than two-thirds of the class members and all the "primary defendants" are citizens of the state in which the action was filed.

5.   To remove, a defendant must file a notice of removal in the federal court, signed pursuant to Rule 11, containing a "short and plain" statement of the grounds for removal. What must the notice of removal say?

(a) In Dart Cherokee Basin Operating Co. v. Owens, 135 S.Ct. 547 (2014), the Court held that, under 28 U.S.C. § 1446(a), the "short and plain statement" required to support a notice of removal does not have to include evidence supporting the asserted ground for federal-court jurisdiction. In this class action filed in a Kansas state court, plaintiff sued on behalf of a class for allegedly underpaid royalties on oil and gas leases. Defendant filed a notice of removal, stating that the purported underpayments to putative class members totaled more than $8.2 million. Plaintiff moved to remand on the ground that defendant included "no evidence" proving that the amount in controversy exceeded the $5 million amount specified in CAFA. The district judge, applying Tenth Circuit precedent requiring proof of the amount in controversy in the notice of removal itself, granted the motion to remand. By a 5–4 margin, the

Court held that the statutory requirement that the notice be "short and plain" meant that evidence did not have to be included. Writing for the Court, Justice Ginsburg noted that plaintiffs' assertions that the amount in controversy is satisfied under Rule 8(a)(1) need not supply evidence, and suggested that it would be "anomalous" to have different requirements for a defendant invoking federal court jurisdiction. Id. at 553.

Dart Cherokee Basin also relied on amendments in the JVCA in rejecting the Tenth Circuit's evidence rule. In section 1446(c), as amended, addresses situations in which the amount claimed in the complaint reveals little about the true amount in controversy and it allows the defendant in such situations to base removal on its own assertion of the true amount, subject to a hearing on the matter in the context of a motion to remand the case. The statute specifies a preponderance of the evidence standard for ascertaining whether the amount exceeds the jurisdictional threshold. The *Dart* Court reasoned that these provisions contemplate the presentation of evidence at a post-removal hearing, rather than in the removal petition.

(b)   What if defendant can't tell whether there is diversity of citizenship from the complaint? In Lovern v. General Motors Corp., 121 F.3d 160 (4th Cir.1997), plaintiff sued in a Virginia state court claiming that his injuries in an auto accident were magnified by defects in the seatbelt, and the complaint did not allege plaintiff's citizenship. Thereafter G.M. obtained the police report about the accident, which stated that plaintiff was a resident of Virginia, and later it received his interrogatory answers, which said the same thing. Twenty-eight days after it got the police report, and eight days after receipt of the interrogatory answers, G.M. removed. By then, 88 days had passed since the complaint was served.

The appellate court held that the removal was timely under the portion of 28 U.S.C. § 1446(b) that permits removal in cases not originally removable on defendant's later receipt of a paper from which "it may first be ascertained that the case is one which is removable." Although it would seem that the case was originally removable, whether or not G.M. realized it, the court said the clock starts running only "where an initial pleading reveals a ground for removal," or at least that it does not start running if "such details are obscured or omitted." The court also said that it would not "require courts to inquire into the subjective knowledge of the defendant, an inquiry that could degenerate into a mini-trial regarding who knew what and when," and added that the court could instead "rely on the face of the initial pleading" and that the time to remove would start running only when the right to remove was "apparent within the four corners of the initial pleading." Does this make sense? Would it mean that plaintiffs who want protection against belated removal must include in their pleadings material not required by state-court pleading rules? Must the complaint say "This case is removable"?

Can you argue that the *Dart* Court's approach, by easing the defendant's ability to allege grounds for removal in the face of uncertainty, should narrow defendant's ability to initiate belated removals?

6.   *Timing for removal:* As note 5 above suggests, the defendant is under tight time pressures in deciding whether to remove. 28 U.S.C. § 1446(b) permits a defendant 30 days to file a petition to remove.

(a)   Suppose plaintiff faxes a copy of the complaint to defendant but takes no further action for 30 days. Has defendant's 30 days to remove expired? The statute says the time to remove starts running from the date of "receipt by the defendant, through service or otherwise, of a copy of the initial pleading." In Murphy Brothers, Inc. v. Michetti Pipe Stringing, Inc., 526 U.S. 344 (1999), the plaintiff faxed a file-stamped copy of the complaint to defendant but did not serve defendant for some time thereafter. When defendant removed within 30 days of formal service, plaintiff contended it was too late because more than 30 days had passed since it faxed the complaint to defendant. The Supreme Court held that the time for removal cannot start running until the defendant is formally served with summons, relying on "a bedrock principle: An individual or entity named as a defendant is not obliged to engage in litigation unless notified of the action, and brought under a court's authority, by formal process."

(b)   What if the plaintiff names two defendants and serves them at different times? Under a well-established rule of unanimity, all of the defendants must join in or consent to the removal of the action in order for it to be effective. See, e.g., Russell Corp. v. Am. Home Assur. Co., 264 F.3d 1040, 1050 (11th Cir. 2001). The 2011 amendments codified the rule of unanimity. See 28 U.S.C. § 1446(b)(2)(A).

Does the thirty-day window to remove run from the date of the first defendant's service? That would seem inconsistent with *Murphy Brothers,* supra, which suggests that a second defendant would have no duty to take action in the litigation until formally served with process. In the run-up to the adoption of the JVCA, a consensus emerged that the time should run from the date of the second defendant's service. See Bailey v. Janssen Pharmaceutica, Inc., 536 F.3d 1202 (11th Cir. 2008) (emphasizing the implications of *Murphy Brothers*). The JVCA codified the last-served rule. See 28 U.S.C. 1446(b)(2)(C). What steps can plaintiff take to mitigate the delays associated with the last-served rule?

How must co-defendants manifest their unanimous consent to removal? Some older cases required each defendant to express individual consent to removal in writing. See Roe v. O'Donohue, 38 F.3d 298, 301 (7th Cir. 1994) (each codefendant must submit their consent in writing) (abrogated on other grounds by Murphy Bros. v. Michetti Pipe Stringing, Inc., 526 U.S. 344 (1999)); Getty Oil Corp. v. Ins. Co. of North America, 841 F.2d 1254, 1262 n. 11 (5th Cir. 1988) (requiring written indication of consent from each served defendant). More recent decisions allow one defendant to represent to the district court, in the removal petition, that all defendants have consented to removal. See Griffioen v. Cedar Rapids & Iowa City Ry. Co., 785 F.3d 1182, 1188 (8th Cir. 2015) (accepting notice of removal in which attorney for one defendant represented that other defendants consented to removal); Mayo v. Bd. of Education, 713 F.3d 735, 742 (4th Cir. 2013) (same);Proctor v. Vishay

Intertechnology Inc., 584 F.3d 1208, 1225 (9th Cir. 2009) (same). Given the obligation of counsel to comply with Rule 11 in making representations as to consent in a removal notice, what does formal evidence of individualized consent add to the process?

(c) Suppose defendant does not remove within 30 days. Ordinarily that would prevent any later removal. However, 28 U.S.C. § 1446(b) permits removal after the 30-day period has elapsed based on later developments in the state-court case that make it removable "[i]f the case stated by the initial pleading is not removable." But what if it was not clear initially whether the case was removable, and defendant was wrong to conclude that it was not? Consider, for example, the defendant who only later discovers that one of his co-defendants was fraudulently joined to defeat diversity. If that mistake precludes later removal based on developments in the state-court case, should the risk of losing their removal opportunity prompt defendants to file removal notices whenever they can consistent with Rule 11?

(d) If the case was removable as originally filed, should any later development in the state-court case revive the right to remove after the 30 days has elapsed? Suppose plaintiff amends the prayer to seek 100 times as much in damages. If there was diversity and the amount-in-controversy requirement was satisfied in the original complaint is defendant forever barred from removing? A leading treatise reports that courts usually do revive the right to remove where the development "changes the character of the litigation so as to make it substantially a new suit" and concludes that this result is fair because "a willingness on the part of the defendant to remain in a state court to litigate a particular claim should not be interpreted as a willingness on his part to remain in a state court to adjudicate a completely different claim." 14C C. Wright, A. Miller, E. Cooper & J. Steinman, Federal Practice & Procedure § 3731 at 568 (4th ed. 2009).

Suppose plaintiff amends the complaint to add several federal-law claims. Section 1446(b)(3) permits removal within thirty days. Suppose, by contrast, that the initial complaint had included a federal question claim. Does the addition of more such claims re-open the removal window for a defendant that failed to remove initially? Note that the statute treats the addition of new claims as creating a new removal window only if the case stated in the initial complaint was not removable.

(e) Why impose such time pressures on defendants? What is the effect on the state-court case of the filing of a notice of removal? See 28 U.S.C. § 1446(d).

7. Courts often say that removal jurisdiction should be strictly construed and apply a presumption against its availability. The Supreme Court rejected one manifestation of the presumption against removal in Dart Cherokee Basin Operating Co. LLC v. Owens, 135 S.Ct. 547, 554 (2014) (holding that no antiremoval presumption attends cases invoking CAFA, but declining to decide "whether such a presumption is proper in mine-run diversity cases"). Does the presumption make more sense in "mine-run" cases?

Congress has made certain claims nonremovable in order to assure plaintiffs an absolute choice between state and federal court. See note 2 above. If Congress has not done so more generally, should the courts nevertheless incline against exercising removal jurisdiction? Would it be proper to construe §§ 1331 and 1332 narrowly to limit exercise of jurisdiction when the plaintiff wants to be in federal court? Has the Court effectively adopted such limits through the complete diversity rule, the well-pleaded complaint rule, and the Gunn v. Minton approach to embedded federal ingredients?

8.   What should be the scope of supplemental jurisdiction in removed actions? Professor Steinman concludes that supplemental jurisdiction should be available even though 28 U.S.C. § 1367(a) speaks only of actions commenced in federal court. She sees § 1367(b), which curtails supplemental jurisdiction in diversity cases, as having a more limited application in removed cases, however, because it speaks only of claims by or against parties added pursuant to the Federal Rules of Civil Procedure, not state analogues. "Consequently, § 1367(b)'s limitations can apply only to claims asserted or proposed to be asserted post-removal; it does not govern claims (such as counterclaims, cross-claims or third-party claims) asserted in a state court action prior to removal." Steinman, Supplemental Jurisdiction in § 1441 Removed Cases: An Unsurveyed Frontier of Congress' Handiwork, 35 Ariz. L.Rev. 305, 330 (1993). If this is correct, would a case be removable on the basis of minimum diversity where the nondiverse parties are joined pursuant to state joinder rules? Professor Steinman concludes that would not satisfy the requirement of §§ 1441(a) and (b) that removal will be allowed only in a "civil action" of which the district courts have original jurisdiction. Id. at 332. Does *Allapattah* clarify these matters?

9.   If plaintiff knows the case will be removable, should that sometimes incline plaintiff toward filing in federal court? Consider the following advice for lawyers seeking a temporary restraining order or preliminary injunction: "A removal petition by the defendant will take the case to federal court and will eat up irreplaceable time doing so. The safest course is to file in federal court if there is a reasonable basis to be there." Gohn & Oliver, In Pursuit of the Elusive TRO, 19 Litigation 25, 25–26 (Summer 1993).

10. *Joinder of federal law and state law claims:* 28 U.S.C. § 1441(c) permits defendant to remove an entire state court proceeding if it includes both a federal question claim under section 1331 and a claim not within the original, supplemental, or removal jurisdiction of district court. Upon removal, section 1441(c) directs that the district court shall sever and remand the claims that do not fall within its original jurisdiction. The sever-and-remand directive attempts to address concerns that an earlier version of section 1441(c) authorized the assertion of federal jurisdiction over matters that might exceed the bounds of Article III. For a defense of the retention of such removal authority, see Hartnett, A New Trick From an Old and Abused Dog: Section 1441(c) Lives and Now Permits the Remand of Federal Question Cases, 63 Fordham L. Rev. 1099, 1106–29 (1995) (state court joinder rules may permit plaintiff to join state and federal claims so unrelated that they would defy

removal as a single constitutional case within section 1367(a); in such a setting, 1441(c) permits removal to protect defendant's right to a federal forum and requires remand of the unrelated state law claims).

11. *Remand:* 28 U.S.C. § 1447(c) permits plaintiff to move to remand a case that was not properly removed. Ordinarily the federal court may not remand unless the removal itself was improper. See Thermtron Products, Inc. v. Hermansdorfer, 423 U.S. 336 (1976) (remand due to docket congestion in federal court not authorized); compare Carnegie-Mellon University v. Cohill, 484 U.S. 343 (1988) (federal court that has dismissed federal claim in removed case and determined not to exercise supplemental jurisdiction over state-law claims under *Gibbs* may remand those claims rather than dismiss them). The new multiparty, multiforum jurisdiction provided by 28 U.S.C. § 1369, however, permits a federal court to remand the damages part of a case after it has determined liability. See 28 U.S.C. § 1441(e)(2).

Appellate review of a decision to remand is difficult to obtain. 28 U.S.C. § 1447(d) provides that an order remanding a case "is not reviewable on appeal or otherwise." In *Thermtron,* supra, the Supreme Court justified overlooking the barrier to review on the ground that the district court there did not invoke the grounds for remand listed in the statute. In Things Remembered, Inc. v. Petrarca, 516 U.S. 124 (1995), the Court explained that "[a]s long as a district court's remand is based on a timely raised defect in removal procedure or on lack of subject-matter jurisdiction—the grounds for removal recognized in § 1447(c)—a court of appeals lacks jurisdiction to entertain an appeal of the remand order under § 1447(d)." More recent decisions appear to contemplate some scrutiny of the purported jurisdictional basis of remand orders. In Kircher v. Putnam Funds Trust, 547 U.S. 633 (2006), the Court ruled that the district court had correctly characterized its remand decision as jurisdictional and had thus reached a conclusion that foreclosed appellate review. The Court's approach suggests that the appellate courts may at least consider the plausibility of a district court order remanding on jurisdictional grounds, and may review the remand order if it concludes that the district court wrongly characterized its disposition as jurisdictional. Such a regime will invite appellate litigation over the proper characterization of district court remand orders. See also Powerex Corp. v. Reliant Energy Services, Inc., 551 U.S. 224 (2007) (barring appellate review when the district court's remand order rested on a colorable assertion of lack of subject matter jurisdiction and noting a division within the Court on the proper handling of such jurisdictional issues); Carlsbad Technology, Inc. v. HIF Bio, Inc., 556 U.S. 635 (2009) (allowing appellate review of discretionary Cohill remand orders). For a critique of the Court's approach and suggested alternative mode of review, see Pfander, Collateral Review of Remand Orders: Reasserting the Supervisory Role of the Supreme Court, 159 U. Pa. L. Rev. 493 (2011).

If remand is denied, review is not immediately available under 28 U.S.C. § 1291, limiting appeals to "final decisions." See Chapter 12. Sometimes later developments in the federal-court case may preclude review even then. In Caterpillar Inc. v. Lewis, 519 U.S. 61 (1996), the Court held that an erroneous denial of a motion to remand is not ground for reversal after trial if the defect in federal jurisdiction is cured before trial. When the case was initially removed there was incomplete diversity, but the district court denied a motion to remand. Thereafter, all claims involving the non-diverse defendant were settled and dismissed. At trial, the remaining defendant prevailed. Seeing the problem as a "statutory flaw" that was cured by the time trial began, the Court concluded that it was insufficient to invalidate the result at trial when balanced against an "overriding consideration" that "[o]nce a diversity case has been tried in federal court, * * * considerations of finality, efficiency, and economy become overwhelming." To wipe out a verdict where there is no objection to the conduct of the trial "would impose an exorbitant cost on our dual court system." What of the rule that jurisdictional determinations are to be made at the threshold of the litigation based on the situation as it then exists, rather than on post-filing developments?

CHAPTER 11

CHOOSING THE LAW TO BE APPLIED IN FEDERAL COURT

∎ ∎ ∎

A. CHOOSING BETWEEN STATE AND FEDERAL LAW

SWIFT V. TYSON

Supreme Court of the United States, 1842
41 U.S. (16 Pet.) 1

JUSTICE STORY delivered the opinion of the Court.

[Plaintiff sued in federal court in New York, jurisdiction premised on diversity of citizenship, to enforce a bill of exchange. The issue in the case was whether a pre-existing debt constituted consideration for an endorsement of the bill, making the endorsee a "holder in due course." This issue, in turn, depended largely on whether the applicable substantive common law applied was based on general principles derived by the federal court (in which event valid consideration would be found) or was to be determined on the basis of New York decisions (in which event it was assumed that consideration would be rejected).

Defendant argued that the federal court had to apply the New York decisions because of the Rules of Decision Act, originally section 34 of the Judiciary Act of 1789, 1 Stat. 92 (now codified, in slightly modified form, in 28 U.S.C.A. § 1652), which provided that "the laws of the several states, except where the constitution, treaties, or statutes of the United States shall otherwise require or provide, shall be regarded as rules of decision in trials at common law in the courts of the United States in cases where they apply." There was no doubt that the Act required federal courts to apply state statutes. The question for the Court to decide in this case was whether state common law also constituted "laws" for purposes of the Rules of Decision Act.

Justice Story concluded that, with certain exceptions, state judge-made common law did not fall within the concept of "laws" in the Rules of Decision Act.]

* * *

[T]he courts of New York do not found their decisions upon this point upon any local statute, or positive, fixed, or ancient local usage: but they deduced the doctrine from the general principles of commercial law. * * * In the ordinary use of language it will hardly be contended that the decisions of Courts constitute laws. They are, at most, only evidence of what the laws are, and are not themselves laws. They are often reexamined, reversed, and qualified by the Courts themselves, wherever they are found to be either defective, or ill-founded, or otherwise incorrect. The laws of a state are more usually understood to mean the rules and enactments promulgated by the legislative authority thereof, or long established local customs having the force of laws. In all the various cases, which have hitherto come before us for decision, this Court have uniformly supposed, that the true interpretation of the thirty-fourth section limited its application to state laws strictly local, that is to say, to the positive statutes of the state, and the construction thereof adopted by the local tribunals, and to rights and titles to things having a permanent locality, such as the rights and titles to real estate, and other matters immovable and intraterritorial in their nature and character. It never has been supposed by us, that the section did apply, or was designed to apply, to questions of a more general nature, not at all dependent upon local statutes or local usages of a fixed and permanent operation, as for example, to the construction of ordinary contracts or other written instruments and especially to questions of general commercial law, where the state tribunals are called upon to perform the like functions as ourselves, that is, to ascertain upon general reasoning and legal analogies, what is the true exposition of the contract or instruments, or what is the just rule furnished by the principles of commercial law to govern the case. And we have not now the slightest difficulty in holding, that this section, upon its true intendment and construction, is strictly limited to local statutes and local usages of the character before stated, and does not extend to contracts and other instruments of a commercial nature, the true interpretation and effect whereof are to be sought, not in the decisions of local tribunals, but in the general principles and doctrines of commercial jurisprudence.

Examples? (margin note)

 (margin note)

ERIE RAILROAD CO. v. TOMPKINS

Supreme Court of the United States, 1938
304 U.S. 64

JUSTICE BRANDEIS delivered the opinion of the Court.

The question for decision is whether the oft-challenged doctrine of Swift v. Tyson shall now be disapproved.

Tompkins, a citizen of Pennsylvania, was injured on a dark night by a passing freight train of the Erie Railroad Company while walking along its right of way at Hughestown in that state. He claimed that the accident occurred through negligence in the operation, or maintenance, of the train;

that he was rightfully on the premises as licensee because on a commonly used beaten footpath which ran for a short distance alongside the tracks; and that he was struck by something which looked like a door projecting from one of the moving cars. To enforce that claim he brought an action in the federal court for Southern New York, which had jurisdiction because the company is a corporation of that state. It denied liability; and the case was tried by a jury.

The Erie insisted that its duty to Tompkins was no greater than that owed to a trespasser. It contended, among other things, that its duty to Tompkins, and hence its liability, should be determined in accordance with the Pennsylvania law; that under the law of Pennsylvania, as declared by its highest court, persons who use pathways along the railroad right of way—that is, a longitudinal pathway as distinguished from a crossing—are to be deemed trespassers; and that the railroad is not liable for injuries to undiscovered trespassers resulting from its negligence, unless it be wanton or willful. Tompkins denied that any such rule had been established by the decisions of the Pennsylvania courts; and contended that, since there was no statute of the state on the subject, the railroad's duty and liability is to be determined in federal courts as a matter of general law.

The trial judge refused to rule that the applicable law precluded recovery. The jury brought in a verdict of $30,000; and the judgment entered thereon was affirmed by the Circuit Court of Appeals, which held that it was unnecessary to consider whether the law of Pennsylvania was as contended, because the question was one not of local, but of general, law, and that "upon questions of general law the federal courts are free, in absence of a local statute, to exercise their independent judgment as to what the law is; and it is well settled that the question of the responsibility of a railroad for injuries caused by its servants is one of general law. . . . Where the public has made open and notorious use of a railroad right of way for a long period of time and without objection, the company owes to persons on such permissive pathway a duty of care in the operation of its trains. . . . It is likewise generally recognized law that a jury may find that negligence exists toward a pedestrian using a permissive path on the railroad right of way if he is hit by some object projecting from the side of the train."

The Erie had contended that application of the Pennsylvania rule was required, among other things, by section 34 of the Federal Judiciary Act of September 24, 1789, c. 20, 28 U.S.C. § 725, 28 U.S.C.A. § 725, which provides:

> "The laws of the several States, except where the Constitution, treaties, or statutes of the United States otherwise require or provide, shall be regarded as rules of decision in trials at common law, in the courts of the United States, in cases where they apply."

Because of the importance of the question whether the federal court was free to disregard the alleged rule of the Pennsylvania common law, we granted certiorari.

First. Swift v. Tyson, 16 Pet. 1, 18, held that federal courts exercising jurisdiction on the ground of diversity of citizenship need not, in matters of general jurisprudence, apply the unwritten law of the state as declared by its highest court; that they are free to exercise an independent judgment as to what the common law of the state is—or should be * * *.

The federal courts assumed, in the broad field of "general law," the power to declare rules of decision which Congress was confessedly without power to enact as statutes. Doubt was repeatedly expressed as to the correctness of the construction given section 34, and as to the soundness of the rule which it introduced. But it was the more recent research of a competent scholar, who examined the original document, which established that the construction given to it by the Court was erroneous; and that the purpose of the section was merely to make certain that, in all matters except those in which some federal law is controlling, the federal courts exercising jurisdiction in diversity of citizenship cases would apply as their rules of decision the law of the state, unwritten as well as written.[5]

Criticism of the doctrine became widespread after the decision of Black & White Taxicab & Transfer Co. v. Brown & Yellow Taxicab & Transfer Co., 276 U.S. 518. There, Brown & Yellow, a Kentucky corporation owned by Kentuckians, and the Louisville & Nashville Railroad, also a Kentucky corporation, wished that the former should have the exclusive privilege of soliciting passenger and baggage transportation at the Bowling Green, Kentucky, railroad station; and that the Black & White, a competing Kentucky corporation, should be prevented from interfering with that privilege. Knowing that such a contract would be void under the common law of Kentucky, it was arranged that the Brown & Yellow reincorporate under the law of Tennessee, and that the contract with the railroad should be executed there. The suit was then brought by the Tennessee corporation in the federal court for Western Kentucky to enjoin competition by the Black & White; an injunction issued by the District Court was sustained by the Court of Appeals; and this Court, citing many decisions in which the doctrine of Swift & Tyson had been applied, affirmed the decree.

Second. Experience in applying the doctrine of Swift v. Tyson, had revealed its defects, political and social; and the benefits expected to flow from the rule did not accrue. Persistence of state courts in their own opinions on questions of common law prevented uniformity; and the impossibility of discovering a satisfactory line of demarcation between the

---

[5] Charles Warren, New Light on the History of the Federal Judiciary Act of 1789 (1923) 37 Harv. L. Rev. 49, 51–52, 81–88, 108.

province of general law and that of local law developed a new well of uncertainties.

On the other hand, the mischievous results of the doctrine had become apparent. Diversity of citizenship jurisdiction was conferred in order to prevent apprehended discrimination in state courts against those not citizens of the state. Swift v. Tyson introduced grave discrimination by noncitizens against citizens. It made rights enjoyed under the unwritten "general law" vary according to whether enforcement was sought in the state or in the federal court; and the privilege of selecting the court in which the right should be determined was conferred upon the noncitizen.[9] Thus, the doctrine rendered impossible equal protection of the law. In attempting to promote uniformity of law throughout the United States, the doctrine had prevented uniformity in the administration of the law of the state.

The discrimination resulting became in practice far-reaching. This resulted in part from the broad province accorded to the so-called "general law" as to which federal courts exercised an independent judgment. In addition to questions of purely commercial law, "general law" was held to include the obligations under contracts entered into and to be performed within the state, the extent to which a carrier operating within a state may stipulate for exemption from liability for his own negligence or that of his employee; the liability for torts committed within the state upon persons resident or property located there, even where the question of liability depended upon the scope of a property right conferred by the state; and the right to exemplary or punitive damages. * * *

In part the discrimination resulted from the wide range of persons held entitled to avail themselves of the federal rule by resort to the diversity of citizenship jurisdiction. Through this jurisdiction individual citizens willing to remove from their own state and become citizens of another might avail themselves of the federal rule. And, without even change of residence, a corporate citizen of the state could avail itself of the federal rule by reincorporating under the laws of another state, as was done in the *Taxicab* Case.

The injustice and confusion incident to the doctrine of Swift v. Tyson have been repeatedly urged as reasons for abolishing or limiting diversity of citizenship jurisdiction. Other legislative relief has been proposed. If only a question of statutory construction were involved, we should not be prepared to abandon a doctrine so widely applied throughout nearly a century. But the unconstitutionality of the course pursued has now been made clear, and compels us to do so.

Third. Except in matters governed by the Federal Constitution or by acts of Congress, the law to be applied in any case is the law of the state.

---

[9] It was even possible for a nonresident plaintiff defeated on a point of law in the highest court of a State nevertheless to win out by taking a nonsuit and renewing the controversy in the federal court.

And whether the law of the state shall be declared by its Legislature in a statute or by its highest court in a decision is not a matter of federal concern. There is no federal general common law. Congress has no power to declare substantive rules of common law applicable in a state whether they be local in their nature or "general," be they commercial law or a part of the law of torts. And no clause in the Constitution purports to confer such a power upon the federal courts. * * *

The fallacy underlying the rule declared in Swift v. Tyson is made clear by Mr. Justice Holmes.[23] The doctrine rests upon the assumption that there is "a transcendental body of law outside of any particular State but obligatory within it unless and until changed by statute," that federal courts have the power to use their judgment as to what the rules of common law are; and that in the federal courts "the parties are entitled to an independent judgment on matters of general law":

> "but law in the sense in which courts speak of it today does not exist without some definite authority behind it. The common law so far as it is enforced in a State, whether called common law or not, is not the common law generally but the law of that State existing by the authority of that State without regard to what it may have been in England or anywhere else. . . .

> "the authority and only authority is the State, and if that be so, the voice adopted by the State as its own [whether it be of its Legislature or of its Supreme Court] should utter the last word."

Thus the doctrine of Swift v. Tyson is, as Mr. Justice Holmes said, "an unconstitutional assumption of powers by the Courts of the United States which no lapse of time or respectable array of opinion should make us hesitate to correct." In disapproving that doctrine we do not hold unconstitutional section 34 of the Federal Judiciary Act of 1789 or any other act of Congress. We merely declare that in applying the doctrine this Court and the lower courts have invaded rights which in our opinion are reserved by the Constitution to the several States.

Fourth. The defendant contended that by the common law of Pennsylvania as declared by its highest court in Falchetti v. Pennsylvania R. Co., 160 A. 859, the only duty owed to the plaintiff was to refrain from willful or wanton injury. The plaintiff denied that such is the Pennsylvania law. In support of their respective contentions the parties discussed and cited many decisions of the Supreme Court of the state. The Circuit Court of Appeals ruled that the question of liability is one of general law; and on that ground declined to decide the issue of state law. As we hold this was error, the judgment is reversed and the case remanded to it for further proceedings in conformity with our opinion.

---

[23] Kuhn v. Fairmont Coal Co., 215 U.S. 349, 370–372; Black & White Taxicab, etc., Co. v. Brown & Yellow Taxicab, etc., Co., 276 U.S. 518, 532–536.

Reversed.

JUSTICE CARDOZO took no part in the consideration or decision of this case.

JUSTICE BUTLER (dissenting).

* * *

No constitutional question was suggested or argued below or here. And as a general rule, this Court will not consider any question not raised below and presented by the petition. Here it does not decide either of the questions presented, but, changing the rule of decision in force since the foundation of the government, remands the case to be adjudged according to a standard never before deemed permissible.

* * *

This Court has often emphasized its reluctance to consider constitutional questions and that legislation will not be held invalid as repugnant to the fundamental law if the case may be decided upon any other ground. In view of grave consequences liable to result from erroneous exertion of its power to set aside legislation, the Court should move cautiously, seek assistance of counsel, act only after ample deliberation, show that the question is before the Court, that its decision cannot be avoided by construction of the statute assailed or otherwise, indicate precisely the principle or provision of the Constitution held to have been transgressed, and fully disclose the reasons and authorities found to warrant the conclusion of invalidity. * * *

So far as appears, no litigant has ever challenged the power of Congress to establish the rule as construed. It has so long endured that its destruction now without appropriate deliberation cannot be justified. There is nothing in the opinion to suggest that consideration of any constitutional question is necessary to a decision of the case. By way of reasoning, it contains nothing that requires the conclusion reached. Admittedly, there is no authority to support that conclusion. Against the protest of those joining in this opinion, the Court declines to assign the case for reargument. It may not justly be assumed that the labor and argument of counsel for the parties would not disclose the right conclusion and aid the Court in the statement of reasons to support it. Indeed, it would have been appropriate to give Congress opportunity to be heard before divesting it of power to prescribe rules of decision to be followed in the courts of the United States.

* * *

JUSTICE MCREYNOLDS, concurs in this opinion.

JUSTICE REED (concurring in part).

I concur in the conclusion reached in this case, in the disapproval of the doctrine of Swift v. Tyson, and in the reasoning of the majority opinion, except in so far as it relies upon the unconstitutionality of the "course pursued" by the federal courts.

* * *

To decide the case now before us and to "disapprove" the doctrine of Swift v. Tyson requires only that we say that the words "the laws" include in their meaning the decisions of the local tribunals. As the majority opinion shows, by its reference to Mr. Warren's researches and the first quotation from Mr. Justice Holmes, that this Court is now of the view that "laws" includes "decisions," it is unnecessary to go further and declare that the "course pursued" was "unconstitutional," instead of merely erroneous.

The "unconstitutional" course referred to in the majority opinion is apparently the ruling in Swift v. Tyson that the supposed omission of Congress to legislate as to the effect of decisions leaves federal courts free to interpret general law for themselves. (I am not at all sure whether, in the absence of federal statutory direction, federal courts would be compelled to follow state decisions. There was sufficient doubt about the matter in 1789 to induce the first Congress to legislate.) No former opinions of this Court have passed upon it. * * * If the opinion commits this Court to the position that the Congress is without power to declare what rules of substantive law shall govern the federal courts, that conclusion also seems questionable. The line between procedural and substantive law is hazy but no one doubts federal power over procedure. The Judiciary Article and the "necessary and proper" clause of Article One may fully authorize legislation, such as this section of the Judiciary Act.

In this Court, stare decisis, in statutory construction, is a useful rule, not an inexorable command. It seems preferable to overturn an established construction of an Act of Congress, rather than, in the circumstances of this case, to interpret the Constitution.

NOTES AND QUESTIONS

1.   One of the interesting aspects of the *Erie* decision is that neither party had at any point argued that the doctrine of Swift v. Tyson should be overruled. Is it appropriate for the Court to resolve a case on the basis of a ground not raised by either party? See Friendly, In Praise of *Erie*—and of the New Federal Common Law, 39 N.Y.U. L. Rev. 383, 399 n. 71 (1964) (arguing that both sides were sufficiently aware of the possibility the Court would abandon *Swift*). Is it appropriate for the Court to reach an issue of this import when a narrower basis of decision was available? As a practical matter, *was* a narrower basis of decision available? Why do you suppose the Court chose to resolve the broad question of the *Swift* doctrine's validity?

2.   According to one scholar, corporations were significantly benefited by the federal courts' interpretation of the common law as authorized by *Swift*. E. Purcell, Brandeis and the Progressive Constitution 66 (2000). "In two common types of cases—for example, tort suits brought by injured employees and insurance actions brought by individual claimants—the federal common law grew distinctly more favorable toward business in the late nineteenth century and was far more favorable than the common law of many states." Id.

3.   According to Professor Purcell, "[t]he federal general common law resonated broadly as a political issue because) it implicated one of the fundamental divisions that separated Populists and Progressives from their conservative opponents." This was because the former "saw Swift as a license for judicial subjectivism and biased decision making," while the latter "saw it as a guarantor of security and the reign of common law principles." Hostility towards *Swift* also "grew from the states' rights tradition that rejected both diversity jurisdiction and the federal common law as intrusions on state sovereignty." E. Purcell, Brandeis and the Progressive Constitution 67 (2000).

4.   Justice Brandeis asserts that if it were not for the constitutional difficulties caused by *Swift,* he would have been reluctant to overturn that decision. What, according to Brandeis, were the constitutional problems with the *Swift* doctrine? Are these concerns legitimate? See Keefe, Gilhooley, Bailey & Day, Weary *Erie,* 34 Cornell L.Q. 494, 497 (1949): "It is difficult to determine exactly what was unconstitutional about the *Tyson* doctrine. Unquestionably Article III of the Constitution designates the federal courts as proper forums to litigate suits between 'Citizens of different States.' Given jurisdiction, it would logically follow that a federal court would have the constitutional power to determine the controversy by any reasonable method. The choice of 'federal common law' rather than the law of a particular state is clearly not so unreasonable as to be unconstitutional."

According to Professor Borchers, "the drafting and ratification history [of the Constitution] supports the conclusion that diversity was intended at least in part as a protection against aberrational state laws, particularly those regarding commercial transactions." Borchers, The Origins of Diversity Jurisdiction, the Rise of Legal Positivism, and a Brave New World for *Erie* and *Klaxon,* 72 Tex. L. Rev. 79, 81 (1993). For a defense of *Swift* against *Erie's* attack, see Corr, Thoughts on the Vitality of *Erie,* 41 Am. U. L. Rev. 1087 (1992). Professor Corr describes what he refers to as "the fragility of the *Erie* majority's position." Id. at 1091.

5.   Has *Erie's* constitutional predicate been eroded by subsequent developments? Consider the comments of Professor Thomas Merrill:

Although the framers may have intended that the federal government would be a government of limited powers, in the years since *Erie* the Supreme Court has permitted those powers to expand so much that the federal government has authority to regulate in virtually any area it chooses. * * * The Court's acquiescence in the transformation of the federal government from one of limited powers to one of plenary authority might be illustrated with the facts of *Erie* itself. The issue there—the standard of care that a railroad owes to a pedestrian walking on a railroad right of way—is one that Congress today could clearly resolve by legislation enacted pursuant to its power to regulate interstate commerce. Since the issue therefore falls within the enumerated powers of the federal government (now viewed as plenary rather than limited), there would seem to be no reason for objecting *on the grounds of federalism* if a federal court decided to formulate a rule of decision governing the issue.

The answer to this objection is that the federalism principle identified by *Erie* still exists but has been silently transformed from a general constraint on the powers of the federal government into an attenuated constraint that applies principally to one branch of that government—the federal judiciary. * * * With respect to judicial power, however, the federalism principle still has force.

Merrill, The Common Law Powers of Federal Courts, 52 U.Chi.L.Rev. 1, 14–15 (1985); see also Clark, *Erie's* Constitutional Source, 95 Cal. L. Rev. 1289 (2007); Mishkin, Some Further Last Words on *Erie*—The Thread, 87 Harv. L.Rev. 1682 (1974) (suggesting that *Erie's* principal concern was to eliminate undue judicial policy making). But see Green, Repressing *Erie's* Myth, 96 Cal. L. Rev. 595 (2008), refuting this position.

Is there any textual or theoretical basis for drawing the constitutional distinction suggested by Professor Merrill? Is there any policy argument to support the distinction? On the constitutional basis of *Erie,* see also Green, *Erie* and Problems of Constitutional Structure, 96 Cal. L. Rev. 661 (2008).

6.   If one were to reject the constitutional basis of *Erie,* might one nevertheless support the doctrine, purely as a matter of political philosophy or social policy?

7.   What weight should have been given to the newly discovered historical evidence cited by Brandeis concerning the intent of the drafters of the Rules of Decision Act? Historian Charles Warren had discovered an earlier draft of the Rules of Decision Act, never adopted, which provided that "the statute law of the several states in force for the time being and their unwritten or common law now in use, whether by adoption from the common law of England, the ancient statutes of the same or otherwise" would serve as rules of decision in federal court. On the basis of this draft (and solely on that basis), Warren concluded that the change in the final version of the statute to "laws of the several states" was intended as merely a shorthand for what had been contained in the earlier draft. Warren, New Light on the History of the Federal Judiciary Act of 1789, 37 Harv.L.Rev. 49, 84–88 (1923). Is this the only conceivable explanation for the change in statutory wording?

For an argument that the drafters of section 34 of the Judiciary Act of 1789 did not intend to require use of state law in diversity cases, see W. Ritz, Rewriting the History of the Judiciary Act of 1789, 134 (1990). See also Holt,

To Establish Justice: Politics, the Judiciary Act of 1789, and the Invention of the Federal Courts, 1989 Duke L.J. 1421, 1506–07.

One modern commentator has criticized the "bias" that Professor Warren "brought to the issue of the proper authority of federal courts hearing diversity cases to deviate from state common law." Corr, Thoughts on the Vitality of *Erie,* 41 Am. U. L. Rev. 1087, 1093 (1992). According to Professor Corr, "[i]t is an understatement to say that Warren's general view of federalism was that federal courts, below the level of the Supreme Court, should have almost no role to play." Id.

8.   What were Justice Brandeis's concerns about the unfairness of the *Swift* doctrine? Note that he states that the *Swift* doctrine "rendered impossible equal protection of the law." It is clear, however, that by this reference he did not intend to invoke the constitutional requirement of equal protection, for at that time no one had seriously suggested that a guarantee of equal protection was included within the Fifth Amendment. Boiling v. Sharpe, 347 U.S. 497 (1954), reaching this conclusion, was not decided until 16 years later. See Clark, *Erie*'s Constitutional Source, 95 Cal. L. Rev. 1289, 1299 (2007) ("*Erie*'s reference to 'equal protection' appears in a preliminary section of the opinion describing the 'political and social' defects of the *Swift* doctrine rather than the section specifically addressing 'the unconstitutionality of the course pursued.' ") What Brandeis was undoubtedly referring to was the unfairness inherent in the unequal treatment that is said to result from the evil of forum shopping. What is so bad about forum shopping? For example, what was so terrible about the *Black & White Taxicab* case? Might the injustice caused by that decision have been avoided by means short of the abolition of the *Swift* doctrine?

9.   Examine Justice Brandeis' attack on what he considered to be Story's legal philosophy underlying the *Swift* doctrine. In what way is it thought that Story's philosophy manifests itself in the *Swift* doctrine? Is it accurate to infer this legal philosophy from *Swift?* Recall that in *Swift* Story recognized certain exceptions, where state common law *would* be followed. Does the existence of these exceptions cast doubt on the inference of a particular philosophy of law from Story's adoption of the *Swift* doctrine? For a discussion of the *Erie* Court's attack on the legal philosophy underlying *Swift,* see Rutherglen, Reconstructing *Erie:* A Comment on the Perils of Legal Positivism, 10 Const. Comm. 285 (1993).

10.   Whatever philosophical assumptions underlay Justice Story's reasoning, was *Swift* an unreasonable interpretation of the Rules of Decision Act? As of 1789, when the statute was originally adopted, where would judges look to find authority to decide questions not governed by statute or "local" law? Judge Fletcher argues that "[i]n such cases, depending on the nature of the dispute, a number of different kinds of law could provide the relevant rules for decision. The general common law was by far the most important of these nonlocal and nonfederal laws. That it was not explicitly referred to in section 34 does not prove that it was not expected to be applied. Rather, the fact that it was not mentioned probably suggests quite the opposite—that its

applicability was so obvious as to go without saying." Fletcher, The General Common Law and Section 34 of the Judiciary Act of 1789: The Example of Marine Insurance, 97 Harv.L.Rev. 1513, 1517 (1984). But the hegemony of the general common law was fragmented during the 19th century, and the concept of law changed to one in which legal rules had force only by virtue of the governmental authority behind them, a view now known as "positivism." Was this development inevitable? Was it undesirable? Should this 19th century development have an impact on the interpretation of a statute enacted in 1789?

11.   There is one piece of background that should be added. Before 1938, the federal courts were generally directed to follow state procedure under a series of statutes called the Process Acts and the Conformity Act. See generally Burbank, The Rules Enabling Act of 1934, 130 U.Pa.L.Rev. 1015, 1036–42 (1982). The objective was to make sure that the procedure employed in a state was the same, whether the case was in state or federal court. In 1934 Congress passed the Rules Enabling Act, which authorized the Supreme Court to promulgate rules of practice and procedure for use in all federal courts to supplant the former requirement that federal courts use state procedure. Thus Justice Reed could observe that "no one doubts federal power over procedure." These rules were drafted by a committee headed by Dean Charles Clark of Yale Law School and became effective in 1938. After 1938, many states chose to model their procedural rules after the Federal Rules. See Oakley & Coon, The Federal Rules in State Courts: A Survey of State Court Systems of Civil Procedure, 61 Wash.L.Rev. 1367 (1986).

12.   One modern scholar has challenged the *Erie* doctrine as an "anomaly" and a "fluke of history." Sherry, Normalizing *Erie*, 69 Vand.L.Rev. 1161 (2016). In a number of other contexts, Professor Sherry argues, "federal courts are free to protect federal interests that Congress has not protected or articulated. It is only the *Erie* doctrine that dreads a sharp and unjustified distinction between codified and uncodified 'federal interests'." See also Erbsen, Erie's Four Functions: Reframing Choice of Law in Federal Courts, 89 Notre Dame L.Rev. 579 (2013).

GUARANTY TRUST CO. V. YORK
Supreme Court of the United States, 1945
326 U.S. 99

JUSTICE FRANKFURTER delivered the opinion of the Court.

* * *

In May, 1930, Van Sweringen Corporation issued notes to the amount of $30,000,000. Under an indenture of the same date, petitioner, Guaranty Trust Co., was named trustee with power and obligations to enforce the rights of the noteholders in the assets of the Corporation and of the Van Sweringen brothers. In October, 1930, petitioner, with other banks, made large advances to companies affiliated with the Corporation and wholly controlled by the Van Sweringens. In October, 1931, when it was apparent that the Corporation could not meet its obligations, Guaranty co-operated in a plan for the purchase of the outstanding notes on the basis of cash for 50% of the face value of the notes and twenty shares of Van Sweringen Corporation's stock for each $1,000 note. This exchange offer remained open until December 15, 1931.

Respondent York received $6,000 of the notes as a gift in 1934, her donor not having accepted the offer of exchange. In April, 1940, three accepting noteholders began suit against petitioner, charging fraud and misrepresentation. Respondent's application to intervene in that suit was denied, and summary judgment in favor of Guaranty was affirmed. Hackner v. Morgan, 130 F.2d 300. After her dismissal from the *Hackner* litigation, respondent, on January 22, 1942, began the present proceedings.

The suit, instituted as a class action on behalf of non-accepting noteholders and brought in a federal court solely because of diversity of citizenship, is based on an alleged breach of trust by Guaranty in that it failed to protect the interests of the noteholders in assenting to the exchange offer and failed to disclose its self-interest when sponsoring the offer. Petitioner moved for summary judgment, which was granted, upon the authority of the *Hackner* case. On appeal, the Circuit Court of Appeals, one Judge dissenting, found that the *Hackner* decision did not foreclose this suit, and held that in a suit brought on the equity side of a federal district court that court is not required to apply the State statute of limitations that would govern like suits in the courts of a State where the federal court is sitting even though the exclusive basis of federal jurisdiction is diversity of citizenship. * * *

In view of the basis of the decision below, it is not for us to consider whether the New York statute would actually bar this suit were it brought in a State court. Our only concern is with the holding that the federal courts in a suit like this are not bound by local law.

We put to one side the considerations relevant in disposing of questions that arise when a federal court is adjudicating a claim based on a federal law. Our problem only touches transactions for which rights and obligations are created by one of the States, and for the assertion of which, in case of diversity of the citizenship of the parties, Congress has made a federal court another available forum.

Our starting point must be the policy of federal jurisdiction which Erie R. Co. v. Tompkins embodies. In overruling Swift v. Tyson, 16 Pet. 1, 10 L.Ed. 865, Erie R. Co. v. Tompkins did not merely overrule a venerable case. It overruled a particular way of looking at law which dominated the judicial process long after its inadequacies had been laid bare. Law was conceived as a "brooding omnipresence" of Reason, of which decisions were merely evidence and not themselves the controlling formulations. Accordingly, federal courts deemed themselves free to ascertain what Reason, and therefore Law, required wholly independent of authoritatively declared State law, even in cases where a legal right as the basis for relief was created by State authority and could not be created by federal authority and the case got into a federal court merely because it was "between Citizens of different States" under Art. III, § 2 of the Constitution of the United States.

* * *

In exercising their jurisdiction on the ground of diversity of citizenship, the federal courts, in the long course of their history, have not differentiated in their regard for State law between actions at law and suits in equity. Although § 34 of the Judiciary Act of 1789 directed that the "laws of the several States . . . shall be regarded as rules of decision in trials of common law . . .", this was deemed, consistently for over a hundred years, to be merely declaratory of what would in any event have governed the federal courts and therefore was equally applicable to equity suits. Indeed, it may fairly be said that the federal courts gave greater respect to State-created "substantive rights" in equity than they gave them on the law side, because rights at law were usually declared by State courts and as such increasingly flouted by extension of the doctrine of Swift v. Tyson, while rights in equity were frequently defined by legislative enactment and as such known and respected by the federal courts.

Partly because the States in the early days varied greatly in the manner in which equitable relief was afforded and in the extent to which it was available, Congress provided that "the forms and modes of proceeding in suits . . . of equity" would conform to the settled uses of courts of equity. But this enactment gave the federal courts no power that they would not have had in any event when courts were given "cognizance," by the first Judiciary Act, of suits in "equity". From the beginning there has been a good deal of talk in the cases that federal equity is a separate legal system. And so it is, properly understood. The suits in equity of which the federal courts have had "cognizance" ever since 1789 constituted the body of law which had been transplanted to this country from the English Court of Chancery. But this system of equity "derived its doctrines, as well as its powers, from its mode of giving relief." Langdell, Summary of Equity Pleading (1877) xxvii. In giving federal courts "cognizance" of equity suits in cases of diversity jurisdiction, Congress never gave, nor did the federal courts ever claim, the power to deny substantive rights created by State law or to create substantive rights denied by State law.

This does not mean that whatever equitable remedy is available in a State court must be available in a diversity suit in a federal court, or conversely, that a federal court may not afford an equitable remedy not available in a State court. Equitable relief in a federal court is of course subject to restrictions: the suit must be within the traditional scope of equity as historically evolved in the English Court of Chancery, a plain, adequate and complete remedy at law must be wanting, explicit

Congressional curtailment of equity powers must be respected, see, e.g., Norris-LaGuardia Act, 47 Stat. 70, 29 U.S.C.A. § 101 et seq.; the constitutional right to trial by jury cannot be evaded. That a State may authorize its courts to give equitable relief unhampered by any or all such restrictions cannot remove these fetters from the federal courts. State law cannot define the remedies which a federal court must give simply because a federal court in diversity jurisdiction is available as an alternative tribunal to the State's courts. Contrariwise, a federal court may afford an equitable remedy for a substantive right recognized by a State even though a State court cannot give it. Whatever contradiction or confusion may be produced by a medley of judicial phrases severed from their environment, the body of adjudications concerning equitable relief in diversity cases leaves no doubt that the federal courts enforced State-created substantive rights if the mode of proceeding and remedy were consonant with the traditional body of equitable remedies, practice and procedure, and in so doing they were enforcing rights created by the States and not arising under any inherent or statutory federal law.

And so this case reduces itself to the narrow question whether, when no recovery could be had in a State court because the action is barred by the statute of limitations, a federal court in equity can take cognizance of the suit because there is diversity of citizenship between the parties. Is the outlawry, according to State law, of a claim created by the States a matter of "substantive rights" to be respected by a federal court of equity when that court's jurisdiction is dependent on the fact that there is a State-created right, or is such statute of "a mere remedial character," which a federal court may disregard?

Matters of "substance" and matters of "procedure" are much talked about in the books as though they defined a great divide cutting across the whole domain of law. But, of course, "substance" and "procedure" are the same key-words to very different problems. Neither "substance" nor "procedure" represents the same invariants. Each implies different variables depending upon the particular problem for which it is used. And the different problems are only distantly related at best, for the terms are in common use in connection with situations turning on such different considerations as those that are relevant to questions pertaining to ex post facto legislation, the impairment of the obligations of contract, the enforcement of federal rights in the State courts and the multitudinous phases of the conflict of laws.

Here we are dealing with a right to recover derived not from the United States but from one of the States. When, because the plaintiff happens to be a nonresident, such a right is enforceable in a federal as well as in a State court, the forms and mode of enforcing the right may at times, naturally enough, vary because the two judicial systems are not identical. But since a federal court adjudicating a state-created right solely because of the diversity of citizenship of the parties is for that purpose, in effect, only another court of the State, it cannot afford recovery if the right to recover is made unavailable by the State nor can it substantially affect the enforcement of the right as given by the State.

And so the question is not whether a statute of limitations is deemed a matter of "procedure" in some sense. The question is whether such a statute concerns merely the manner and the means by which a right to recover, as recognized by the State, is enforced, or whether such statutory limitation is a matter of substance in the aspect that alone is relevant to our problem, namely, does it significantly affect the result of a litigation for a federal court to disregard a law of a State that would be controlling in an action upon the same claim by the same parties in a State court?

It is therefore immaterial whether statutes of limitation are characterized either as "substantive" or "procedural" in State court opinions in any use of those terms unrelated to the specific issue before us. Erie R. Co. v. Tompkins was not an endeavor to formulate scientific legal terminology. It expressed a policy that touches vitally the proper distribution of judicial power between State and federal courts. In essence, the intent of that decision was to insure that, in all cases where a federal court is exercising jurisdiction solely because of the diversity of citizenship of the parties, the outcome of the litigation in the federal court should be substantially the same, so far as legal rules determine the outcome of a litigation, as it would be if tried in a State court. The nub of the policy that underlies Erie R. Co. v. Tompkins is that for the same transaction the accident of a suit by a non-resident litigant in a federal court instead of in a State court a block away, should not lead to a substantially different result. And so, putting to one side abstractions regarding "substance" and "procedure", we have held that in diversity cases the federal courts must follow the law of the State as to burden of proof, Cities Service Oil Co. v. Dunlap, 308 U.S. 208, as to conflict of laws, Klaxon Co. v. Stentor Co., 313 U.S. 487, as to contributory negligence, Palmer v. Hoffman, 318 U.S. 109, 117. And see Sampson v. Channell, 1 Cir., 110 F.2d 754. Erie R. Co. v. Tompkins has been applied with an eye alert to essentials in avoiding disregard of State law in diversity cases in the federal courts. A policy so important to our federalism must be kept free from entanglements with analytical or terminological niceties.

Plainly enough, a statute that would completely bar recovery in a suit if brought in a State court bears on a State created right vitally and not merely formally or negligibly. As to consequences that so intimately affect recovery or non-recovery a federal court in a diversity case should follow State law. The fact that under New York law a statute of limitations might be lengthened or shortened, that a security may be foreclosed though the debt be barred, that a barred debt may be used as a set-off, are all matters of local law properly to be respected by federal courts sitting in New York when their incidence comes into play there. Such particular rules of local law, however, do not in the slightest change the crucial consideration that if a plea of the statute of limitations would bar recovery in a State court, a federal court ought not to afford recovery.

* * *

To make an exception to Erie R. Co. v. Tompkins on the equity side of a federal court is to reject the considerations of policy which, after long travail, led to that decision. * * *

Diversity jurisdiction is founded on assurance to non-resident litigants of courts free from susceptibility to potential local bias. The Framers of the Constitution, according to Marshall, entertained "apprehensions" lest distant suitors be subjected to local bias in State courts, or, at least, viewed with "indulgence the possible fears and apprehensions" of such suitors. Bank of the United States v. Deveaux, 5 Cranch 61, 87. And so Congress afforded out-of-State litigants another tribunal, not another body of law. The operation of a double system of conflicting laws in the same State is plainly hostile to the reign of law. Certainly, the fortuitous circumstance of residence out of a State of one of the parties to a litigation ought not to give rise to a discrimination against others equally concerned but locally resident. The source of substantive rights enforced by a federal court under diversity jurisdiction, it cannot be said too often, is the law of the States. Whenever that law is authoritatively declared by a State, whether its voice be the legislature or its highest court, such law ought to govern in litigation founded on that law, whether the forum of application is a State or a federal court and whether the remedies be sought at law or may be had in equity.

* * *

The judgment is reversed and the case is remanded for proceedings not inconsistent with this opinion.

JUSTICE ROBERTS and JUSTICE DOUGLAS took no part in the consideration or decision of this case.

[Dissenting opinion of JUSTICE RUTLEDGE, joined by JUSTICE MURPHY, omitted.]

NOTES AND QUESTIONS

1.   Note that in deciding whether federal or state law is to be applied, Justice Frankfurter draws a distinction between matters of "substance" and matters of "procedure." Why is this distinction important for purposes of the choice between state and federal law? To what extent was the distinction a part of the *Erie* decision itself?

2.   What standard does Justice Frankfurter adopt in order to determine whether a legal rule is substantive or procedural for purposes of the *Erie* doctrine? What policy or policies mentioned in *Erie* is he attempting to foster?

How does he apply this standard to the facts of *York?* Professor Henry Hart noted what he considered "the triviality of the [*Erie*] principle" emphasized in *York,* and argued that "[t]he more faithfully it is carried out the more completely the constitutional and statutory grants of diversity jurisdiction are emptied of intelligible meaning." Hart, The Relations Between State and Federal Law, 54 Colum.L.Rev. 489, 512 (1954). What do you think this means? He also contended that "[t]he principle passes over the essential rationale of the *Erie* opinion—the need of recognizing the state courts as organs of coordinate authority with other branches of the state government in the discharge of the constitutional functions of the states * * *." Do you agree that this concern, rather than the policy emphasized in *York,* constituted "the essential rationale of the *Erie* opinion"?

3.   Note that Justice Frankfurter indicates that adoption of the *Erie* test he employs "does not mean that whatever equitable remedy is available in a State court must be available in a diversity suit in a federal court, or conversely, that a federal court may not afford an equitable remedy not available in a State court." Is this conclusion consistent with the case's test?

More generally, what significance should be attributed to Justice Frankfurter's recognition that federal equity is a separate system? Consider the views of Professors Wright and Kane. C. Wright & M. Kane, The Law of Federal Courts 399–400 (7th ed. 2011):

> [T]here is language in the opinion that seems to suggest that the doctrine of "equitable remedial rights" persists, and that a federal court sitting in equity is free to grant or withhold remedies without regard to what a state court would do in a similar case. Probably this is true where an Act of Congress has taken away jurisdiction to grant an injunction in particular cases [as with the Norris-La Guardia Act] or where the constitutional right to trial by jury might be abridged. It seems equally true that federal courts are free to use procedural devices made available by statutes or the Federal Rules despite the absence of similar procedures in the states. Beyond those situations it is difficult to believe that the federal court is free to fashion an independent law of remedies in equitable actions.

For a discussion of the application of the *Erie* doctrine to the availability of equitable remedies in diversity cases, see Crump, The Twilight Zone of the *Erie* Doctrine: Is There Really a Different Choice of Equitable Remedies in the "Court a Block Away"?, 1991 Wis. L. Rev. 1233.

4.   Professors Wright and Kane have suggested that the *York* test was plagued with "inevitable difficulties," because "[a]pplied literally, very little would remain of the Federal Rules of Civil Procedure in diversity cases, for almost every procedural rule may have a substantial effect on the outcome of a case. If the test was not to be carried to its literal limits, however, there was confusion as to how far it was to go." C. Wright & M. Kane, The Law of Federal Courts 379 (7th ed. 2011). Cf. Fed.R.Civ.P. 61. Are Professors Wright and Kane correct in their assertion that application of *York* to the Federal Rules of Civil

Procedure would leave very little of the Federal Rules in diversity cases? Examine, for example, Rules 15(c) and 35(a). Under the *York* test, could a federal court in a diversity case apply these rules when the state in which it sits does not do so?

Note that *York* itself did not involve a conflict between state law and a Federal Rule of Civil Procedure. Does the opinion provide some basis on which to determine whether the test of that case was intended to be applied to Federal Rules? If it were, what harm would result? Is there a logical basis on which not to extend the case's test to the Federal Rules of Civil Procedure?

5.   How would the *York* test apply to the following hypothetical case: The federal court requires that all movants' briefs be filed with a red brief cover; no brief with a cover any color other than red will be accepted. The state court, on the other hand, has a similar rule, but the required color is blue. A defendant, moving for summary judgment in federal court, employs a blue brief cover, and argues that, on the basis of *York,* the federal court sitting in diversity is required to follow the state practice of employing blue covers. Cf. Loya v. Desert Sands Unified School Dist., 721 F.2d 279 (9th Cir.1983) (for purposes of statute of limitations, complaint on long paper should be considered filed on date received though district court rejected it because of local rule requiring use of short paper); Cintron v. Union Pacific R.R., 813 F.2d 917 (9th Cir.1987) (complaint timely filed even though rejected by clerk because it lacked two holes in the top as required by local rules).

EFFORTS TO APPLY *YORK*

In post-*York* decisions decided on the same day in 1949, the Court applied that case's principle to different situations:

Cohen v. Beneficial Industrial Loan Corp., 337 U.S. 541 (1949): In a stockholders' derivative action, defendants contended that a state statute, which required that plaintiffs in stockholder derivative actions owning less than a specified percentage of the corporation's stock were required to post a bond, should be applied to the plaintiffs. The district court held the New Jersey statute inapplicable, and the court of appeals reversed. The Supreme Court, relying on *York,* found the New Jersey statute applicable. Was this a proper application of *York?* The plaintiffs had argued that Rule 23 of the Federal Rules of Civil Procedure, which imposed no bond requirement, "deals with plaintiff's right to maintain such an action in federal court and that therefore the subject is recognized as procedural and the federal rule alone prevails." (Stockholder derivative actions are today more specifically regulated by Rule 23.1.) The Supreme Court, however, held that none of the provisions of Rule 23 conflicted with the state statute.

Ragan v. Merchants Transfer & Warehouse Co., Inc., 337 U.S. 530 (1949): In a personal injury action in federal district court in Kansas, the complaint was filed in federal court within Kansas' two-year statute of limitations, but service was not made on the defendant until after the statutory period had run. Rule 3 of the Federal Rules of Civil Procedure provides that "[a] civil action is commenced by filing a complaint with the court." Kansas law, however, stated that the statute of limitations was not tolled until actual service of the summons on the defendant, rather than when the complaint was filed. Defendant argued, on the basis of Kansas law, that the statute of limitations had run. The Supreme Court, relying on both *Erie* and *York,* held state law applicable:

> Erie R. Co. v. Tompkins was premised on the theory that in diversity cases the rights enjoyed under local law should not vary because enforcement of those rights was sought in the federal court rather than in the state court. If recovery could not be had in the state court, it should be denied in the federal court. Otherwise, those authorized to invoke the diversity jurisdiction would gain advantages over those confined to state court. Guaranty Trust Co. v. York applied that principle to statutes of limitations on the theory that, where one is barred from recovery in the state court, he should likewise be barred in the federal court.

> It is conceded that if the present case were in a Kansas court it would be barred. The theory of Guaranty Trust Co. v. York would therefore seem to bar it in the federal court * * *. The force of that argument is sought to be avoided by the argument that the Federal Rules of Civil Procedure determine the manner in which an action is commenced in the federal courts—a matter of procedure which the principle of Erie R. Co. v. Tompkins does not control. It is accordingly argued that since the suit was properly commenced in the federal court before the Kansas statute of limitations ran, it tolled the statute.

> * * * [Here] there can be no doubt that the suit was properly commenced in the federal court. But in the present case we look to local law to find the cause of action on which suit is brought. Since that cause of action is created by local law, the measure of it is to be found only in local law. It carries the same burden and is subject to the same defenses in the federal court as in the state court. * * * Otherwise there is a different measure of the cause of action in one court than in the other, and the principle of Erie R. Co. v. Tompkins is transgressed.

For many years, it was widely thought that *Ragan* stood for the proposition that the Federal Rules of Civil Procedure were just as subject to the *Erie* doctrine as were purely judge-made rules. On the basis of the quoted excerpt, do you agree? In Walker v. Armco Steel Corp., 446 U.S. 740 (1980), the Court held that *Ragan* had done no such thing. *Walker* is examined in detail, infra at p. 1011.

Justice Rutledge dissented:

> I think the these decisions taken together demonstrate the extreme extent to which the Court is going in submitting the control of diversity litigation in the federal courts to the states rather than to Congress, where it properly belongs. This is done in the guise of applying the rule of Erie R. Co. v. Tompkins * * *. But in my opinion it was never the purpose of that decision to put such matters as those involved here outside the power of Congress to regulate and to confer that authority exclusively upon the states.

Is Justice Rutledge correct in suggesting that the three decisions put such matters "outside the power of Congress to regulate"? What if Congress amended the Rules of Decision Act to exempt these areas from state control, or simply passed new statutes dealing with these areas? Recall that the Rules of Decision Act requires the application of state law, except where an Act of Congress, among other things, otherwise provides. To answer these questions we must first determine exactly what it was that the Court in *York* was interpreting and applying when it established its rule. Reexamine Justice Frankfurter's opinion in *York*. Was he interpreting the Rules of Decision Act? The Constitution? What difference, if any, would it make if he had been interpreting the latter, rather than the former? Could a persuasive argument be fashioned that Justice Frankfurter appears to be interpreting neither? If so, from where does he derive the legal principle he ultimately establishes?

How, under the test of *York,* should one determine whether use of a different rule in federal court would "significantly affect the result of a litigation"? Must it be clear, *a priori,* that the plaintiff will win if one standard is employed and lose if the other standard is used? How would *York* itself have been decided under that approach? Should we say instead that the test is that state law must be employed if under one standard a party will definitely lose while the other standard would at least give that party a chance to win? How would *York* be decided under this approach?

On this issue, consider Bernhardt v. Polygraphic Co. of America, Inc., 350 U.S. 198 (1956), in which the question was whether a federal court could enforce an arbitration provision in a contract even though under Vermont law the arbitration clause could be revoked at any time before an award was made. The Supreme Court initially held that the United States Arbitration Act did not control the case. The court of appeals had held that federal common law, rather than Vermont law, controlled the issue of whether the case would go to arbitration, because "[a]rbitration is merely a form of trial * * *." The Supreme Court disagreed, holding that Vermont law had to be used:*

> If the federal court allows arbitration where the state court would disallow it, the outcome of litigation might depend on the courthouse where suit is brought. For the remedy by arbitration, whatever its merits or shortcomings, substantially affects the cause of action created by the State. The nature of the tribunal where suits are tried is an important part of the parcel of rights behind a cause of action. The change from a court of law to an arbitration panel may make a radical difference in ultimate result. Arbitration carries no right to trial by jury that is guaranteed both by the Seventh Amendment and by * * * the Vermont Constitution. Arbitrators do not have the benefit of judicial instruction on the law; they need not give their reasons for their results; the record of their proceedings is not as complete as it is in a court trial; and judicial review of an award is more limited than judicial review of a trial * * *. We said in the *York* case that "The nub of the policy that underlies *Erie R. Co. v. Tompkins* is that for the same transaction the accident of a suit by a non-resident litigant in a federal court instead of in a State court a block away should not lead to a substantially different result." There would in our judgment be a resultant discrimination if the parties suing on a Vermont cause of action in the federal court were remitted to arbitration, while those suing in the Vermont court could not be.

Is *Bernhardt* a proper application of the *York* test? Is it clear, *a priori,* whether plaintiff or defendant would be helped by resort to arbitration, rather than to judicial procedure? Should that matter, in light of the *Erie* policies *York* was designed to foster? Was it clear in *York* itself whether plaintiff or defendant would be helped by use of a different standard in federal court? How about in *Cohen or Ragan?* Should those cases be distinguished from *Bernhardt* on this basis?

ERIE AND CONFLICT OF LAWS

As we saw in the discussion of choice of law in Chapter 9, state courts do not always apply the law of their own state. Under certain circumstances, a court may decide that the law of another state is to be applied. States have employed a variety of criteria to determine which state's law is to be invoked. See Choice of Law, supra p. 809.

---

* Note that *Bernhardt* is no longer good law on this point because the Federal Arbitration Act, 9 U.S.C.A. §§ 1 et seq., has been held to preempt state-law limitations on the enforcement of agreements to arbitrate if they are included in agreements affecting commerce. See Southland Corp. v. Keating, 465 U.S. 1 (1984).

A federal court, sitting in diversity, knows, after *Erie,* that in most cases it must apply substantive state law, rather than "general" common law. However, because a diversity case always involves citizens of at least two states, the federal court will be required to determine *which* state's law to apply. May a federal court, as a matter of federal common law, choose its own conflict of laws rule to decide which state's law to apply, or, under *Erie,* must it employ the conflict of laws rule of the state in which it sits?

The Supreme Court decided this question in the post-*Erie,* pre-*York* decision of Klaxon Co. v. Stentor Electric Manufacturing Co., 313 U.S. 487 (1941):

> We are of opinion that the prohibition declared in Erie R. Co. v. Tompkins, against * * * independent determinations by the federal courts, extends to the field of conflict of laws. The conflict of laws rule to be applied by the federal court in [a particular state] must conform to those prevailing in [that state's] courts. Otherwise, the accident of diversity of citizenship would constantly disturb equal administration of justice in coordinate state and federal courts sitting side by side. * * * Any other ruling would do violence to the principle of uniformity within a state, upon which the *Tompkins* decision is based.

Is *Klaxon* a proper application of *Erie?* Would it have been decided the same way following *York?*

Consider the following criticism of *Klaxon* by Professor Hart: "In [its holding in *Klaxon*] the Court has paralyzed the capacities of the federal courts to further one of the central desiderata of a federal system. Uniformity throughout the * * * states is occasionally desirable, and where that is so a uniform federal substantive law provides the best means of securing it. But uniformity of obligation as between particular individuals, regardless of the laws of litigation, is almost invariably desirable; and the essence of this can be achieved without enacting uniform substantive laws. The promotion of this kind of uniformity, so far as this can be done without sacrifice of greater values, is one of the functions of the principles of the conflict of laws." Hart, The Relations Between State and Federal Law, 54 Colum.L.Rev. 489, 513–14 (1954).

Is Professor Hart's criticism persuasive? Consider the following language from the *Klaxon* opinion: "Whatever lack of uniformity this [decision] may produce between federal courts in different states is attributable to our federal system, which leaves to a state, within the limits permitted by the Constitution, the right to pursue local policies diverging from those of its neighbors. It is not for the federal courts to thwart such local policies by enforcing an independent 'general law' of conflict of laws." Is this statement, though written thirteen years prior to Professor Hart's article, nevertheless responsive to his criticism? Does it suggest other forum-shopping concerns by enabling plaintiffs to seek a state with favorable law?

The Court continues to adhere to the *Klaxon* holding. See, e.g., Keeton v. Hustler Magazine, Inc., 465 U.S. 770 (1984) (discussed p. 759 n. 2); Day & Zimmermann, Inc. v. Challoner, 423 U.S. 3 (1975). On the validity of *Klaxon,* see generally Horowitz, Toward a Federal Common Law of Choice of Law, 14 U.C.L.A. L.Rev. 1191 (1967); Weintraub, The *Erie* Doctrine and State Conflict of Laws Rules, 39 Ind.L.J. 228 (1964); Baxter, Choice of Law and the Federal System, 16 Stan.L.Rev. 1 (1963). For an argument that *Klaxon* "should be replaced with an approach that calls on diversity courts to apply an independent choice-of-law approach focusing on substantive values," see Borchers, The Origins of Diversity Jurisdiction, the Rise of Legal Positivism, and a Brave New World for *Erie* and *Klaxon,* 72 Tex. L. Rev. 79, 132 (1993).

The American Law Institute has recommended adoption of a "coherent and uniform federal choice of law code" for complex federal court litigation, in contravention of *Klaxon*. American Law Institute, Complex Litigation Project, ch. 6 Introductory Note (1994). The ALI argued that "[t]he rationale for developing federal choice of law standards for complex litigation is to decrease forum shopping and to reduce the extremely complicated inquiry now needed to ascertain and apply the numerous state choice of law rules that may be relevant in a consolidated action." Id. See also Lowenfeld, Mass Torts and the Conflict of Laws: The Airline Disaster, 1989 U. Ill. L. Rev. 157; Mullenix, Federalizing Choice of Law for Mass-Tort Litigation, 70 Tex. L. Rev. 1623 (1992); Mullenix, Class Resolution of the Mass-Tort Case: A Proposed Federal Procedure Act, 64 Tex. L. Rev. 1039 (1986); Vairo, Multi-Tort Cases: Cause for More Darkness on the Subject, Or a New Role for Federal Common Law?, 54 Ford. L. Rev. 167 (1985); Weintraub, Methods for Resolving Conflict-of-Laws Problems in Mass Tort Litigation, 1989 U. Ill. L. Rev. 129. Can complex cases, which often involve numerous parties from a number of states, properly be distinguished from more traditional litigation for purposes of choice of law? Is the rationale of *Klaxon* any less relevant in this context?

BYRD v. BLUE RIDGE RURAL ELECTRIC COOPERATIVE, INC.

Supreme Court of the United States, 1958
356 U.S. 525

JUSTICE BRENNAN delivered the opinion of the Court.

[Plaintiff filed a diversity suit in federal district court in South Carolina for injuries allegedly caused by defendant's negligence. Plaintiff was a lineman in a construction crew of a contractor who had contracted to build power lines for the defendant, an electric company. Plaintiff was injured while connecting power lines on the job. The trial court denied defendant's motion to dismiss, and plaintiff won a jury verdict.]

One of respondent's affirmative defenses was that under the South Carolina Workmen's Compensation Act [§ 72–111], the petitioner— because the work contracted to be done by his employer was work of the kind also done by the respondent's own construction and maintenance crews—had the status of a statutory employee of the respondent and was therefore barred from suing the respondent at law because obliged to accept statutory compensation benefits as the exclusive remedy for his injuries. Two questions concerning this defense are before us: (1) whether the Court of Appeals erred in directing judgment for respondent without a remand to give petitioner an opportunity to introduce further evidence; and (2) whether petitioner, state practice notwithstanding, is entitled to a jury determination of the factual issues raised by this defense.

I.

* * *

Relying on the decisions of the Supreme Court of South Carolina, * * * the Court of Appeals held that the statute granted respondent immunity from the action if the proofs established that the respondent's own crews had constructed lines and substations which, like the work contracted to the petitioner's employer, were necessary for the distribution of the electric power which the respondent was in the business of selling. * * *

However, instead of ordering a new trial at which the petitioner might offer his own proof pertinent to a determination according to the correct interpretation, the Court of Appeals made its own determination on the record and directed a judgment for the respondent.

* * *

We believe that the Court of Appeals erred. We do not agree with the petitioner's argument in this Court that the respondent's evidence was insufficient to withstand the motion to strike the defense and that he is entitled to our judgment reinstating the judgment of the District Court. But the petitioner is entitled to have the question determined in the trial court. This would be necessary even if petitioner offered no proof of his own. Although the respondent's evidence was sufficient to withstand the motion under the meaning given the statute by the Court of Appeals, it presented a fact question, which, in the circumstances of this case to be discussed infra, is properly to be decided by a jury. This is clear not only because of the issue of the credibility of the [respondent's] manager's vital testimony [concerning use of respondent's employees on construction projects], but also because, even should the jury resolve that issue as did the Court of Appeals, the jury on the entire record—consistent with the view of the South Carolina cases that this question is in each case largely one of degree and of fact—might reasonably reach an opposite conclusion from the Court of Appeals as to the ultimate fact whether the respondent was a statutory employer.

At all events, the petitioner is plainly entitled to have an opportunity to try the issue under the Court of Appeals' interpretation. * * *

II.

A question is also presented as to whether on remand the factual issue is to be decided by the judge or by the jury. The respondent argues on the basis of the decision of the Supreme Court of South Carolina in Adams v. Davison-Paxon Co., 96 S.E.2d 566, that the issue of immunity should be decided by the judge and not by the jury. That was a negligence action brought in the state trial court against a store owner by an employee of an independent contractor who operated the store's millinery department. The trial judge denied the store owner's motion for a directed verdict made upon the ground that § 72–111 barred the plaintiff's action. The jury returned a verdict for the plaintiff. The South Carolina Supreme Court reversed, holding that it was for the judge and not the jury to decide on the evidence whether the owner was a statutory employer, and that the store owner had sustained his defense. * * *

The respondent argues that this state-court decision governs the present diversity case and "divests the jury of its normal function" to decide the disputed fact question of the respondent's immunity under § 72–111. This is to contend that the federal court is bound under Erie R. Co. v. Tompkins, 304 U.S. 64, to follow the state court's holding to secure uniform enforcement of the immunity created by the State.

First. It was decided in Erie R. Co. v. Tompkins that the federal courts in diversity cases must respect the definition of state-created rights and obligations by the state courts. We must, therefore, first examine the rule in Adams v. Davison-Paxon Co. to determine whether it is bound up with these rights and obligations in such a way that its application in the federal court is required.

The Workmen's Compensation Act is administered in South Carolina by its Industrial Commission. The South Carolina courts hold that, on judicial review of actions of the Commission under § 72–111, the question whether the claim of an injured workman is within the Commission's jurisdiction is a matter of law for decision by the court, which makes its own findings of fact relating to that jurisdiction. The South Carolina Supreme Court states no reasons in Adams v. Davison-Paxon Co. why, although the jury decides all other factual issues raised by the cause of action and defenses, the jury is displaced as to the factual issue raised by the affirmative defense under § 72–111. A State may, of course, distribute the functions of its judicial machinery as it sees fit. The decisions relied upon, however, furnish no reason for selecting the judge rather than the jury to decide this single affirmative defense in the negligence action. They simply reflect a policy that administrative determination of "jurisdictional facts" should not be final but subject to judicial review. The conclusion is inescapable that the *Adams* holding is grounded in the practical consideration that the question had theretofore come before the South Carolina courts from the Industrial Commission and the courts had become accustomed to deciding the factual issue of immunity without the aid of juries. We find nothing to suggest that this rule was announced as an integral part of the special relationship created by the statute. Thus the requirement appears to be merely a form and mode of enforcing the immunity, Guaranty Trust Co. of New York v. York, and not a rule intended to be bound up with the definition of the rights and obligations of the parties. * * *

Second. But cases following *Erie* have evinced a broader policy to the effect that the federal courts should conform as near as may be—in the absence of other considerations—to state rules even of form and mode where the state rules may bear substantially on the question whether the litigation would come out one way in the federal court and another way in the state court if the federal court failed to apply a particular local rule. E.g., Guaranty Trust Co. of New York v. York, supra; Bernhardt v. Polygraphic Co., 350 U.S. 198. Concededly the nature of the tribunal which tries issues may be important in the enforcement of the parcel of rights making up a cause of action or defense, and bear significantly upon achievement of uniform enforcement of the right. It may well be that in the instant personal-injury case the outcome would be substantially affected by whether the issue of immunity is decided by a judge or a jury. Therefore, were "outcome" the only consideration, a strong case might appear for saying that the federal court should follow the state practice.

But there are affirmative countervailing considerations at work here. The federal system is an independent system for administering justice to litigants who properly invoke its jurisdiction. An essential characteristic of that system is the manner in which, in civil common-law actions, it distributes trial functions between judge and jury and, under the influence—if not the command[10]—of the Seventh Amendment, assigns the decisions of disputed questions of fact to the jury. The policy of uniform enforcement of state-created rights and obligations, see, e.g., Guaranty Trust Co. of New York v. York, supra, cannot in every case exact compliance with a state rule—not bound up with rights and obligations-which disrupts the federal system of allocating functions between judge and jury. Herron v. Southern Pacific Co., 283 U.S. 91. Thus the inquiry here is whether the federal policy favoring jury decisions of disputed fact questions should yield to the state rule in the interest of furthering the

---

[10] Our conclusion makes unnecessary the consideration of—and we intimate no view upon—the constitutional question whether the right of jury trial protected in federal courts by the Seventh Amendment embraces the factual issue of statutory immunity when asserted, as here, as an affirmative defense in a common-law negligence action.

objective that the litigation should not come out one way in the federal court and another way in the state court.

We think that in the circumstances of this case the federal court should not follow the state rule. It cannot be gainsaid that there is a strong federal policy against allowing state rules to disrupt the judge-jury relationship in the federal courts. In Herron v. Southern Pacific Co., supra, the trial judge in a personal-injury negligence action brought in the District Court for Arizona on diversity grounds directed a verdict for the defendant when it appeared as a matter of law that the plaintiff was guilty of contributory negligence. The federal judge refused to be bound by a provision of the Arizona Constitution which made the jury the sole arbiter of the question of contributory negligence. This Court sustained the action of the trial judge, holding that "state laws cannot alter the essential character or function of a federal court" because that function "is not in any sense a local matter, and state statutes which would interfere with the appropriate performance of that function are not binding upon the federal court under either the Conformity Act or the 'Rules of Decision' Act." Perhaps even more clearly in light of the influence of the Seventh Amendment, the function assigned to the jury "is an essential factor in the process for which the Federal Constitution provides." Concededly the *Herron* case was decided before Erie R. Co. v. Tompkins, but even when Swift v. Tyson was governing law and allowed federal courts sitting in diversity cases to disregard state decisional law, it was never thought that state statutes or constitutions were similarly to be disregarded. Yet *Herron* held that state statutes and constitutional provisions could not disrupt or alter the essential character or function of a federal court.

Third. We have discussed the problem upon the assumption that the outcome of the litigation may be substantially affected by whether the issue of immunity is decided by a judge or a jury. But clearly there is not present here the certainty that a different result would follow, cf. Guaranty Trust Co. of New York v. York, supra, or even the strong possibility that this would be the case, cf. Bernhardt v. Polygraphic Co., [supra p. 979]. There are factors present here which might reduce that possibility. The trial judge in the federal system has powers denied the judges of many States to comment on the weight of evidence and credibility of witnesses, and discretion to grant a new trial if the verdict appears to him to be against the weight of the evidence. We do not think the likelihood of a different result is so strong as to require the federal practice of jury determination of disputed factual issues to yield to the state rule in the interest of uniformity of outcome.

The Court of Appeals did not consider other grounds of appeal raised by the respondent because the ground taken disposed of the case. We accordingly remand the case to the Court of Appeals for the decision of the other questions, with instructions that, if not made unnecessary by the decision of such questions, the Court of Appeals shall remand the case to the District Court for a new trial of such issues as the Court of Appeals may direct.

Reversed and remanded.

[The opinions of Justice Whitaker, concurring in part and dissenting in part, and of Justices Frankfurter and Harlan, dissenting, are omitted.]

NOTES AND QUESTIONS

1.   In what way does the test of *Byrd* differ from that of *York*? To what extent does the alteration in the test to be applied reflect a change in the particular underlying policies intended to be fostered? See Redish & Phillips, *Erie* and the Rules of Decision Act: In Search of the Appropriate Dilemma, 91 Harv.L.Rev. 356, 365 (1977): "The most striking departure from [*York*] was the *Byrd* Court's significant emphasis on the relationship between the federal and state system, coupled with a relative disregard of more litigant-oriented concerns." Does the *Byrd* test reflect such a change?

2.   It has been suggested that "[t]he Court's approach [in *Byrd*] recognized the relevance of three distinct interests in applying *Erie:* The state's interest in not having its substantive policies undermined in diversity cases, the federal courts' interest in administering justice in accord with the dictates of significant federal principles, and the litigants' interest in not having the outcome of the case turn exclusively on the forum in which the case was brought." Redish & Phillips, supra, 91 Harv.L.Rev. at 364.

3.   What potential problems do you see with application of the *Byrd* balancing test? Professors Wright and Kane have noted that "there was considerable difficulty in applying the *Byrd* test. Able courts—and judges within a single court—were divided in situations that were distinguishable but perhaps not really different. * * * The difficulty in applying the *Byrd* test probably stemmed from the fact that there is no scale to say with assurance in a particular case that the federal interest asserted is more or less important than the interest in preserving uniformity of result with the state court. Even if there were such a scale, the weights to be put in it must be whatever the judges say they are." C. Wright & M. Kane, The Law of Federal Courts 379 (7th ed. 2011). According to Professor John Ely, "[t]he [*Byrd*] opinion exhibits a confusion that exceeds even that normally surrounding a balancing test, and lower courts understandably experienced considerable difficulty in applying it." Ely, The Irrepressible Myth of Erie, 87 Harv.L.Rev. 693, 709 (1974). For an attempt to develop a more "refined," structured and predictable balancing test, see generally Redish & Phillips, supra, 91 Harv.L.Rev. 356.

4.   What are the competing federal and state interests in *Byrd* itself? Note that the Court cites the federal interest in "distribut[ing] trial functions between judge and jury and, under the influence—if not the command—of the Seventh Amendment, assign[ing] the decisions of disputed questions of fact to the jury." The Seventh Amendment provides in relevant part that "[i]n suits at common law, where the value in controversy shall exceed twenty dollars, the

START 988–1002

right of trial by jury shall be preserved * * *." See discussion in Chapter 8, supra pp. 547–613. Thus, while apparently federal practice in this case would have assigned the disputed issue to the jury, rather than the judge, the Court at no point decides that this allocation is in fact dictated by the Seventh Amendment. If the Court had resolved that question in the affirmative, what role, if any, would have remained for the Court's balancing test? The Court apparently believed that it need not resolve the constitutional question, because even if the Seventh Amendment did not "command" the result, its "influence" was sufficiently great to weigh heavily on the federal side of the balance. How can a constitutional provision that does not dictate a particular result nevertheless "influence" the outcome? The Seventh Amendment, for example, requires that certain matters be resolved by a jury, and says absolutely nothing about the method of resolving other issues. If the Court in *Byrd* had held that the Seventh Amendment did not require use of a jury on the disputed issue, how could it have had any residual "influence" toward that end?

If one were to exclude the Seventh Amendment's "influence," what remains on the federal side of the balance? The Court notes that "[t]he federal system is an independent system for administering justice to litigants who properly invoke its jurisdiction." Is this a distinct federal interest for purposes of balancing? At various times, lower federal courts relied on this statement to reject use of state law in favor of a distinct federal standard in diversity cases. See, e.g., Monarch Insurance Co. v. Spach, 281 F.2d 401 (5th Cir.1960). It has been suggested that this interest "might be thought to prove too much; its logic would authorize federal court rejection of purely substantive state standards where, in the federal court's opinion, to apply them would cause an injustice." Redish & Phillips, supra, 91 Harv.L.Rev. at 390. The same authors also articulated the counter-argument: "A court's integrity is to a degree dependent upon its authority to control matters that are intimately bound up with its daily internal operations. In this sense, a court's power to determine the fairest procedures is qualitatively different from its authority to develop principles of substantive law." Id. at 391. Which of these two positions do you accept? In employing the interest as part of a balancing test, must one accept one view or the other? See id. at 391–92.

5. In developing the balancing test, what was the Court in *Byrd* interpreting? The Rules of Decision Act? The Constitution? Something else?

Q. Vid

HANNA V. PLUMER
Supreme Court of the United States, 1965
380 U.S. 460

CHIEF JUSTICE WARREN delivered the opinion of the Court.

The question to be decided is whether, in a civil action where the jurisdiction of the United States district court is based upon diversity of citizenship between the parties, service of process shall be made in the manner prescribed by state law or that set forth in Rule 4(d)(1) of the Federal Rules of Civil Procedure.

On February 6, 1963, petitioner, a citizen of Ohio, filed her complaint in the District Court for the District of Massachusetts, claiming damages in excess of $10,000 for personal injuries resulting from an automobile accident in South Carolina, allegedly caused by the negligence of one Louise Plumer Osgood, a Massachusetts citizen deceased at the time of the filing of the complaint. Respondent, Mrs. Osgood's executor and also a Massachusetts citizen, was named as defendant. On February 8, service was made by leaving copies of the summons and the complaint with respondent's wife at his residence, concededly in compliance with Rule 4(d)(1),* which provides:

"The summons and complaint shall be served together. The plaintiff shall furnish the person making service with such copies as are necessary. Service shall be made as follows:

"(1) Upon an individual other than an infant or an incompetent person, by delivering a copy of the summons and of the complaint to him personally or by leaving copies thereof at his dwelling house or usual place of abode with some person of suitable age and discretion then residing therein. . . ."

Respondent filed his answer on February 26, alleging, inter alia, that the action could not be maintained because it had been brought "contrary to and in violation of the provisions of Massachusetts General Laws (Ter.Ed.) Chapter 197, Section 9." That section provides:

"Except as provided in this chapter, an executor or administrator shall not be held to answer to an action by a creditor of the deceased which is not commenced within one year from the time of his giving bond for the performance of his trust, or to such an action which is commenced within said year unless before the expiration thereof the writ in such action has been served by delivery in hand upon such executor or administrator or service thereof accepted by him or a notice stating the name of the estate, the name and address of the creditor, the amount of the claim and the court in which the action has been brought has been filed in the proper registry of probate. . . ." Mass.Gen.Laws Ann., c. 197, § 9 (1958).

On October 17, 1963, the District Court granted respondent's motion for summary judgment, citing Ragan v. Merchants Transfer & Warehouse Co., 337 U.S. 530, [supra p. 977], and Guaranty Trust Co. of New York v. York, 326 U.S. 99 [supra p. 970 in support of its conclusion that the adequacy of the service was to be measured by § 9, with which, the court held, petitioner had not complied. On appeal, petitioner admitted

---

* The parallel provisions now appear in Rule 4(e)(2).—Eds.

noncompliance with § 9, but argued that Rule 4(d)(1) defines the method by which service of process is to be effected in diversity actions. The Court of Appeals for the First Circuit, finding that "[r]elatively recent amendments [to § 9] evince a clear legislative purpose to require personal notification within the year,"[1] concluded that the conflict of state and federal rules was over "substantive rather than a procedural matter," and unanimously affirmed. * * *

We conclude that the adoption of Rule 4(d)(1), designed to control service of process in diversity actions, neither exceeded the congressional mandate embodied in the Rules Enabling Act nor transgressed constitutional bounds, and that the Rule is therefore the standard against which the District Court should have measured the adequacy of the service. Accordingly, we reverse the decision of the Court of Appeals.

The Rules Enabling Act, 28 U.S.C. § 2072 provides, in pertinent part:

> "The Supreme Court shall have the power to prescribe, by general rules, the forms of process, writs, pleadings, and motions, and the practice and procedure of the district courts of the United States in civil actions.

> "Such rules shall not abridge, enlarge or modify any substantive right and shall preserve the right of trial by jury. . . ."

Under the cases construing the scope of the Enabling Act, Rule 4(d)(1) clearly passes muster. Prescribing the manner in which a defendant is to be notified that a suit has been instituted against him, it relates to the "practice and procedure of the district courts."

> "The test must be whether a rule really regulates procedure,—the judicial process for enforcing rights and duties recognized by substantive law and for justly administering remedy and redress for disregard or infraction of them." Sibbach v. Wilson & Co., 312 U.S. 1, 14. . . .

* * *

---

[1] Section 9 is in part a statute of limitations, providing that an executor need not "answer to an action . . . which is not commenced within one year from the time of his giving bond. . . ." This part of the statute, the purpose of which is to speed the settlement of estates, is not involved in this case, since the action clearly was timely commenced. Cf. Guaranty Trust Co. v. York, supra; Ragan v. Merchants Transfer Co., supra.

Section 9 also provides for the manner of service. Generally, service of process must be made by "delivery in hand," although there are two alternatives: acceptance of service by the executor, or filing of a notice of claim the components of which are set out in the statute, in the appropriate probate court. The purpose of this part of the statute, which is involved here, is, as the court below noted, to insure that executors will receive actual notice of claims. Actual notice is or course also the goal of Rule 4(d)(1); however, the Federal Rule reflects a determination that this goal can be achieved by a method less cumbersome than that prescribed in § 9. In this case the goal seems to have been achieved; although the affidavit filed by respondent in the District Court asserts that he had not been serviced in hand nor had he accepted service, it does not allege lack of actual notice.

Thus were there no conflicting state procedure, Rule 4(d)(1) would clearly control. However, respondent, focusing on the contrary Massachusetts rule, calls to the Court's attention another line of cases, a line which—like the Federal Rules—had its birth in 1938. Erie R. Co. v. Tompkins, overruling Swift v. Tyson, held that federal courts sitting in diversity cases, when deciding questions of "substantive" law, are bound by state court decisions as well as state statutes. The broad command of *Erie* was therefore identical to that of the Enabling Act: federal courts are to apply state substantive law and federal procedural law. However, as subsequent cases sharpened the distinction between substance and procedure, the line of cases following *Erie* diverged markedly from the line construing the Enabling Act. Guaranty Trust Co. of New York v. York made it clear that *Erie*-type problems were not to be solved by reference to any traditional or common-sense substance-procedure distinction:

> "And so the question is not whether a statute of limitations is deemed a matter of 'procedure' in some sense. The question is . . . does it significantly affect the result of a litigation for a federal court to disregard a law of a State that would be controlling in an action upon the same claim by the same parties in a State court?"

Respondent, by placing primary reliance on *York* and *Ragan,* suggests that the *Erie* doctrine acts as a check on the Federal Rules of Civil Procedure, that despite the clear command of Rule 4(d)(1), *Erie* and its progeny demand the application of the Massachusetts rule. Reduced to essentials, the argument is: (1) *Erie,* as refined in *York,* demands that federal courts apply state law whenever application of federal law in its stead will alter the outcome of the case. (2) In this case, a determination that the Massachusetts service requirements obtain will result in immediate victory for respondent. If, on the other hand, it should be held that Rule 4(d)(1) is applicable, the litigation will continue, with possible victory for petitioner. (3) Therefore, *Erie* demands application of the Massachusetts rule. The syllogism possesses an appealing simplicity, but is for several reasons invalid.

In the first place, it is doubtful that, even if there were no Federal Rule making it clear that in-hand service is not required in diversity actions, the *Erie* rule would have obligated the District Court to follow the Massachusetts procedure. "Outcome-determination" analysis was never intended to serve as a talisman. Byrd v. Blue Ridge Rural Elec. Cooperative. Indeed, the message of *York* itself is that choices between state and federal law are to be made not by application of any automatic, "litmus paper" criterion, but rather by reference to the policies underlying the *Erie* rule.

The *Erie* rule is rooted in part in a realization that it would be unfair for the character or result of a litigation materially to differ because the suit had been brought in a federal court. * * * The decision was also in part a reaction to the practice of "forum-shopping" which had grown up in response to the rule of Swift v. Tyson. That the *York* test was an attempt to effectuate these policies is demonstrated by the fact that the opinion framed the inquiry in terms of "substantial" variations between state and federal litigation. Not only are nonsubstantial, or trivial, variations not likely to raise the sort of equal protection problems which troubled the Court in *Erie:* they are also unlikely to influence the choice of a forum. The "outcome-determination" test therefore cannot be read without reference to the twin aims of the *Erie* rule: discouragement of forum-shopping and avoidance of inequitable administration of the laws.[9]

The difference between the conclusion that the Massachusetts rule is applicable, and the conclusion that it is not, is of course at this point "outcome-determinative" in the sense that if we hold the state rule to apply, respondent prevails, whereas if we hold that Rule 4(d)(1) governs, the litigation will continue. But in this sense every procedural variation is "outcome-determinative." For example, having brought suit in a federal court, a plaintiff cannot then insist on the right to file subsequent pleadings in accord with the time limits applicable in state courts, even though enforcement of the federal timetable will, if he continues to insist that he must meet only the state time limit, result in determination of the controversy against him. So it is here. Though choice of the federal or state rule will at this point have a marked effect upon the outcome of the litigation, the difference between the two rules would be of scant, if any, relevance to the choice of a forum. Petitioner, in choosing her forum, was not presented with a situation where application of the state rule would wholly bar recovery;[10] rather, adherence to the state rule would have resulted only in altering the way in which process was served.[11] Moreover,

---

[9] The Court of Appeals seemed to frame the inquiry in terms of how "important" § 9 is to the State. In support of its suggestion that § 9 serves some interest the State regards as vital to its citizens, the court noted that something like § 9 has been on the books in Massachusetts a long time, that § 9 has been amended a number of times and that § 9 is designed to make sure that executors receive actual notice. See note 1, supra. The apparent lack of relation among these three observations is not surprising, because it is not clear to what sort of question the Court of Appeals was addressing itself. One cannot meaningfully ask how important something is without first asking important for what purpose? *Erie* and its progeny make clear that when a federal court sitting in a diversity case is faced with a question of whether or not to apply state law, the importance of a state rule is indeed relevant, but only in the context of asking whether application of the rule would make so important a difference to the character or result of the litigation that failure to enforce it would unfairly discriminate against citizens of the forum State, or whether application of the rule would have so important an effect upon the fortunes of one or both of the litigants that failure to enforce it would be likely to cause a plaintiff to choose the federal court.

[10] See Guaranty Trust Co. of New York v. York, supra, 326 U.S. at 108–109; Ragan v. Merchants Transfer & Warehouse Co., supra, 337 U.S. at 532; Woods v. Interstate Realty Co., 337 U.S. at 538. Similarly, a federal court's refusal to enforce the New Jersey rule involved in Cohen v. Beneficial Indus. Loan Corp., 337 U.S. 541, requiring the posting of security by plaintiffs in stockholders' derivative actions, might well impel a stockholder to choose to bring suit in the federal, rather than the state, court.

[11] Cf. Monarch Insurance Co. of Ohio v. Spach, 281 F.2d 401, 412 (C.A.5th Cir. 1960). We cannot seriously entertain the thought that one suing an estate would be led to choose the federal court because of a belief that adherence to Rule 4(d)(1) is less likely to give the executor actual

it is difficult to argue that permitting service of defendant's wife to take the place of in hand service of defendant himself alters the mode of enforcement of state-created rights in a fashion sufficiently "substantial" to raise the sort of equal protection problems to which the *Erie* opinion alluded.

There is, however, a more fundamental flaw in respondent's syllogism: the incorrect assumption that the rule of Erie R. Co. v. Tompkins constitutes the appropriate test of the validity and therefore the applicability of a Federal Rule of Civil Procedure. The *Erie* rule has never been invoked to void a Federal Rule. It is true that there have been cases where this Court has held applicable a state rule in the face of an argument that the situation was governed by one of the Federal Rules. But the holding of each such case was not that *Erie* commanded displacement of a Federal Rule by an inconsistent state rule, but rather that the scope of the Federal Rule was not as broad as the losing party urged, and therefore, there being no Federal Rule which covered the point in dispute, *Erie* commanded the enforcement of state law. * * * Here, of course, the clash is unavoidable; Rule 4(d)(1) says—implicitly, but with unmistakable clarity— that in-hand service is not required in federal courts. At the same time, in cases adjudicating the validity of Federal Rules, we have not applied the *York* rule or other refinements of *Erie,* but have to this day continued to decide questions concerning the scope of the Enabling Act and the constitutionality of specific Federal Rules in light of the distinction set forth in *Sibbach.*

Nor has the development of two separate lines of cases been inadvertent. The line between "substance" and "procedure" shifts as the legal context changes. "Each implies different variables depending upon the particular problem for which it is used." Guaranty Trust Co. of New York v. York. It is true that both the Enabling Act and the *Erie* rule say, roughly, that federal courts are to apply state "substantive" law and federal "procedural" law, but from that it need not follow that the tests are identical. For they were designed to control very different sorts of decisions. When a situation is covered by one of the Federal Rules, the question facing the court is a far cry from the typical, relatively unguided *Erie* choice: the court has been instructed to apply the Federal Rule, and can refuse to do so only if the Advisory Committee, this Court, and Congress erred in their prima facie judgment that the Rule in question transgresses neither the terms of the Enabling Act nor constitutional restrictions.[13]

We are reminded by the *Erie* opinion that neither Congress nor the federal courts can, under the guise of formulating rules of decision for federal courts, fashion rules which are not supported by a grant of federal

---

notice than § 9, and therefore more likely to produce a default judgment. Rule 4(d)(1) is well designed to give actual notice, as it did in this case.

[13]   Sibbach v. Wilson & Co., supra, 312 U.S. at 13–15.

authority contained in Article I or some other section of the Constitution; in such areas state law must govern because there can be no other law. But the opinion in *Erie,* which involved no Federal Rule and dealt with a question which was "substantive" in every traditional sense (whether the railroad owed a duty of care to Tompkins as a trespasser or a licensee), surely neither said nor implied that measures like Rule 4(d)(1) are unconstitutional. For the constitutional provision for a federal court system (augmented by the Necessary and Proper Clause) carries with it congressional power to make rules governing the practice and pleading in those courts, which in turn includes a power to regulate matters which, though falling within the uncertain area between substance and procedure, are rationally capable of classification as either. Neither *York* nor the cases following it ever suggested that the rule there laid down for coping with situations where no Federal Rule applies is coextensive with the limitation on Congress to which *Erie* had adverted. Although this Court has never before been confronted with a case where the applicable Federal Rule is in direct collision with the law of the relevant State, courts of appeals faced with such clashes have rightly discerned the implications of our decisions.

> "One of the shaping purposes of the Federal Rules is to bring about uniformity in the federal courts by getting away from local rules. This is especially true of matters which relate to the administration of legal proceedings, an area in which federal courts have traditionally exerted strong inherent power, completely aside from the powers Congress expressly conferred in the Rules. The purpose of the *Erie* doctrine, even as extended in *York* and *Ragan,* was never to bottle up federal courts with 'outcome-determinative' and 'integral-relations' stoppers—when there are 'affirmative countervailing [federal] considerations' and when there is a Congressional mandate (the Rules) supported by constitutional authority." Lumbermen's Mutual Casualty Co. v. Wright, 322 F.2d 759, 764 (C.A.5th Cir.1963).

Erie and its offspring cast no doubt on the long-recognized power of Congress to prescribe housekeeping rules for federal courts even though some of those rules will inevitably differ from comparable state rules. * * * Thus, though a court, in measuring a Federal Rule against the standards contained in the Enabling Act and the Constitution, need not wholly blind itself to the degree to which the Rule makes the character and result of the federal litigation stray from the course it would follow in state courts, Sibbach v. Wilson & Co., it cannot be forgotten that the *Erie* rule, and the guidelines suggested in *York,* were created to serve another purpose altogether. To hold that a Federal Rule of Civil Procedure must cease to function whenever it alters the mode of enforcing state-created rights would be to disembowel either the Constitution's grant of power over federal procedure or Congress' attempt to exercise that power in the Enabling Act. Rule 4(d)(1) is valid and controls the instant case.

Reversed.

JUSTICE BLACK concurs in the result.

JUSTICE HARLAN, concurring.

Best opinion of what we want if there is no Fed R. on Point.

It is unquestionably true that up to now *Erie* and the cases following it have not succeeded in articulating a workable doctrine governing choice of law in diversity actions. I respect the Court's effort to clarify the situation in today's opinion. However, in doing so I think it has misconceived the constitutional premises of *Erie* and has failed to deal adequately with those past decisions upon which the courts below relied.

Erie was something more than an opinion which worried about "forum-shopping and avoidance of inequitable administration of the laws," although to be sure these were important elements of the decision. I have always regarded that decision as one of the modern cornerstones of our federalism, expressing policies that profoundly touch the allocation of judicial power between the state and federal systems. *Erie* recognized that there should not be two conflicting systems of law controlling the primary activity of citizens, for such alternative governing authority must necessarily give rise to a debilitating uncertainty in the planning of everyday affairs. And it recognized that the scheme of our Constitution envisions an allocation of law-making functions between state and federal legislative processes which is undercut if the federal judiciary can make substantive law affecting state affairs beyond the bounds of congressional legislative powers in this regard. Thus, in diversity cases *Erie* commands that it be the state law governing primary private activity which prevails.

The shorthand formulations which have appeared in some past decisions are prone to carry untoward results that frequently arise from oversimplification. The Court is quite right in stating that the "outcome-determinative" test of Guaranty Trust Co. of New York v. York, if taken literally, proves too much, for any rule, no matter how clearly "procedural," can affect the outcome of litigation if it is not obeyed. In turning from the "outcome" test of *York* back to the unadorned forum-shopping rationale of *Erie,* however, the Court falls prey to like oversimplification, for a simple forum-shopping rule also proves too much; litigants often choose a federal forum merely to obtain what they consider the advantages of the Federal Rules of Civil Procedure or to try their cases before a supposedly more favorable judge. To my mind the proper line of approach in determining whether to apply a state or a federal rule, whether "substantive" or "procedural," is to stay close to basic principles by inquiring if the choice of rule would substantially affect those primary decisions respecting human conduct which our constitutional system leaves to state regulation. If so, *Erie* and the Constitution require that the state rule prevail, even in the face of a conflicting federal rule.

The Court weakens, if indeed it does not submerge, this basic principle by finding, in effect, a grant of substantive legislative power in the constitutional provision for a federal court system (compare Swift v. Tyson), and through it, setting up the Federal Rules as a body of law inviolate. * * * So long as a reasonable man could characterize any duly adopted federal rule as "procedural," the Court, unless I misapprehend what is said, would have it apply no matter how seriously it frustrated a State's substantive regulation of the primary conduct and affairs of its citizens. Since the members of the Advisory Committee, the Judicial Conference, and this Court who formulated the Federal Rules are presumably reasonable men, it follows that the integrity of the Federal Rules is absolute. Whereas the unadulterated outcome and forum-shopping tests may err too far toward honoring state rules, I submit that the Court's "arguably procedural, ergo constitutional" test moves too fast and far in the other direction.

The courts below relied upon this Court's decisions in Ragan v. Merchants Transfer & Warehouse Co., and Cohen v. Beneficial Indus. Loan Corp. Those cases deserve more attention than this Court has given them, particularly *Ragan* which, if still good law, would in my opinion call for affirmance of the result reached by the Court of Appeals. Further, a discussion of these two cases will serve to illuminate the "diversity" thesis I am advocating.

In *Ragan,* a Kansas statute of limitations provided that an action was deemed commenced when service was made on the defendant. Despite Federal Rule 3 which provides that an action commences with the filing of the complaint, the Court held that for purposes of the Kansas statute of limitations a diversity tort action commenced only when service was made upon the defendant. The effect of this holding was that although the plaintiff had filed his federal complaint within the state period of limitations, his action was barred because the federal marshal did not serve a summons on the defendant until after the limitations period had run. I think that the decision was wrong. At most, application of the Federal Rule would have meant that potential Kansas tort defendants would have to defer for a few days the satisfaction of knowing that they had not been sued within the limitations period. The choice of the Federal Rule would have had no effect on the primary stages of private activity from which torts arise, and only the most minimal effect on behavior following the commission of the tort. In such circumstances the interest of the federal system in proceeding under its own rules should have prevailed.

Cohen v. Beneficial Indus. Loan Corp. held that a federal diversity court must apply a state statute requiring a small stockholder in a stockholder derivative suit to post a bond securing payment of defense costs as a condition to prosecuting an action. Such a statute is not "outcome determinative"; the plaintiff can win with or without it. The Court now rationalizes the case on the ground that the statute might affect the plaintiff's choice of forum but as has been pointed out, a simple forum-shopping test proves too much. The proper view of *Cohen* is in my opinion, that the statute was meant to inhibit small stockholders from instituting "strike suits," and thus it was designed and could be expected to have a substantial impact on private primary activity. Anyone who was at the trial bar during the period when *Cohen* arose can appreciate the strong state policy reflected in the statute.* I think it wholly legitimate to view Federal Rule 23 as not purporting to deal with the problem. But even had the Federal Rules purported to do so, and in so doing provided a substantially less effective deterrent to strike suits, I think the state rule should still have prevailed. That is where I believe the Court's view differs from mine; for the Court attributes such overriding force to the Federal Rules that it is hard to think of a case where a conflicting state rule would be allowed to operate, even though the state rule reflected policy considerations which, under *Erie,* would lie within the realm of state legislative authority.

It remains to apply what has been said to the present case. The Massachusetts rule provides that an executor need not answer suits unless in-hand service was made upon him or notice of the action was filed in the proper registry of probate within one year of his giving bond. The evident intent of this statute is to permit an executor to distribute the estate which he is administering without fear that further liabilities may be outstanding for which he could be held personally liable. If the Federal District Court in Massachusetts applies Rule 4(d)(1) of the Federal Rules of Civil Procedure instead of the Massachusetts service rule, what effect would that have on the speed and assurance with which estates are distributed? As I see it, the effect would not be substantial. It would mean simply that an executor would have to check at his own house or the federal courthouse as well as the registry of probate before he could distribute the estate with impunity. As this does not seem enough to give rise to any real impingement on the vitality of the state policy which the Massachusetts rule is intended to serve, I concur in the judgment of the Court.

JOHN H. ELY, THE IRREPRESSIBLE MYTH OF *ERIE*
87 Harvard Law Review 693, 697–98; 699; 710; 712–14; 717–18 (1974)

My suggestion in this Article will be that the indiscriminate admixture of all questions respecting choices between federal and state law in diversity cases, under the single rubric of "the *Erie* doctrine" or "the *Erie* problem," has served to make a major mystery out of what are really three distinct and rather ordinary problems of statutory and constitutional interpretation. Of course there will be occasions with respect to all three on which reasonable persons will differ, but that does not make the problems mysterious or even very unusual. The United States

---

* Justice Harlan, as a practicing lawyer, argued *Cohen* for defendants.—Eds.

Constitution, I shall argue, constitutes the relevant text only where Congress has passed a statute creating law for diversity actions, and it is in this situation alone that *Hanna*'s "arguably procedural" test controls. Where a nonstatutory rule is involved, the Constitution necessarily remains in the background, but is functionally irrelevant because the applicable statutes are significantly more protective of the prerogatives of state law. Thus, where there is no relevant Federal Rule of Civil Procedure or other Rule promulgated pursuant to the Enabling Act and the federal rule in issue is therefore wholly judge-made, whether state or federal law should be applied is controlled by the Rules of Decision Act, the statute construed in *Erie* and *York*. Where the matter in issue is covered by a Federal Rule, however, the Enabling Act—and not the Rules of Decision Act itself or the line of cases construing it—constitutes the relevant standard. To say that, however, and that is one of the things *Hanna* said, is by no means to concede the validity of all Federal Rules, for the Enabling Act contains significant limiting language of its own. The Court has correctly sensed that language cannot be construed to protect state prerogatives as strenuously as the Rules of Decision Act protects them in the absence of a Federal Rule. However, the Court's recent appreciation that the Enabling Act constitutes the only check on the Rules—that "Erie" does not stand there as a backstop—should lead it in an appropriate case to take the Act's limiting language more seriously than it has in the past.

* * *

[W]hatever *Hanna*'s other merits or demerits, the major point of the Court's opinion was its separation for purposes of analysis of the Rules of Decision Act, the Enabling Act, and the constitutional demands to which the *Erie* opinion had alluded.

* * *

The majority's main point, that the Rules Enabling Act alone was the appropriate measure of a Federal Rule of Civil Procedure, was sufficient to decide the case. It saw fit, however, to add a considered dictum on the question of what law would have been applicable had there been no such Rule and thus had a genuine *Erie* problem been presented.

Since "rules of decision" is hardly self-defining and the legislative history is sparse, the Court approached this issue by seeking "the policies underlying the *Erie* rule." It noted that the *Erie* opinion had evidenced concern with federal-state forum shopping, and went on to lay considerable stress on that concern in construing the Rules of Decision Act. But while the likelihood of forum shopping may turn out to be a handy touchstone for identifying those situations exhibiting the evils against which the Act was directed, forum shopping is not an evil per se. It is evil only if something evil flows from it; indeed, the very idea of the diversity jurisdiction was to provide an alternative to state court. Thus, unless the Rules of Decision Act was a pointless exercise, the First Congress must have seen something else wrong with allowing federal courts to formulate their own rules of decision and thereby to create a separate regime for those nonresident plaintiffs who wish to avail themselves of it.

* * *

What *Erie* mentioned, and *Hanna* picked up, was simple unfairness. The Court was referring to the unfairness of affording a nonresident plaintiff suing a resident defendant a unilateral choice of the rules by which the lawsuit was to be determined. But there is another unfairness, one not tied to the vicissitudes of the removal provisions—the unfairness of subjecting a person involved in litigation with a citizen of a different state of a body of law different from that which applies when his next door neighbor is involved in similar litigation with a citizen. The *Erie* opinion suggested a denial of equal protection was involved, but surely that was a metaphor. It would not be irrational to fight bias against out-of-staters by giving them access to a body of law, developed by persons beholden to no particular state, unavailable in suits between cocitizens. Not irrational, but the founders of our Republic—by not including any such power in the Constitution, and even more clearly by enacting the Rules of Decision Act— refused to do it. Bias against out-of-staters was to be resisted, but only by providing an unbiased tribunal. To provide more, or at least so it was felt, would create an unfairness in the other direction.

The point of the *Hanna* dictum is that it is difficult to find unfairness of a sort that would have troubled the framers of the Rules of Decision Act, or of a sort whose elimination would justify disrupting a federal court's routine, when the difference between the federal and state rules is trivial, when their requirements are essentially fungible. The problem with the previously prevailing rhetoric was that it is possible to speak of enforcing a rule in either of two senses—exacting compliance on the one hand, or sanctioning a noncomplying party on the other. Thus, whenever the sanction for noncompliance is dismissal, there is a sense in which "enforcement" of the rule can be outcome determinative. But it is a backhanded sense, and one that implicates the concerns that gave rise to the Rules of Decision Act only when the underlying mandate thus enforced is sufficiently more or less burdensome than its state counterpart to support a plausible claim of unfairness. The Court therefore suggested by its examples that a federal court may adhere to its own rules in diversity cases insofar, but only insofar, as they are neither materially more or less difficult for the burdened party to comply with than their state counterparts, nor likely to generate an outcome different from that which would result were the case litigated in the state court system and the state rules followed.

* * *

[I]n the context of the Rules of Decision Act, a rejuvenated outcome determination test—augmented a little and clipped a little, so as to intercept the more preposterous implications of its earlier formulations—was just what was called for. And that is what *Hanna* provided.

Hanna's main point, however, was that when the application of a Federal Rule is at issue, the Rules Enabling Act—and not the Rules of Decision Act as construed by Erie R.R. v. Tompkins and other cases—should determine whether federal or state law is to be applied. Although it is a different question how closely the two statutes should be read to track each other, this point seems plainly correct. The Enabling Act provides that "[a]ll laws in conflict with" Rules promulgated under its authority "shall be of no further force or effect," and the Rules of Decision Act is a law. But even if that language were not there, the Enabling Act is much more recent; it is specifically designed to control the validity of the Rules; and it contains language directed to the same general concern—protection of the prerogatives of state law—as the Rules of Decision Act. It indicates it is the only statutory test of a Federal Rule, and there is every reason to believe it means it.

NOTES AND QUESTIONS

1.   Consider Professor Ely's explication of *Hanna*. Is his interpretation of the decision accurate? What is the Court's test for determining the constitutional scope of *Erie?* What is the rationale for this approach?

2.   When will the Court's constitutional test be relevant? Under what circumstances, according to the Court, is the test of the Rules of Decision Act to be used?

3.   What is the actual holding in *Hanna?* Need the Court have examined the proper standard under the Rules of Decision Act in order to decide the case?

4.   The Court in *Hanna* does not expressly overrule *Byrd*. What, if anything, is left of *Byrd* after *Hanna?* In answering, consider specifically footnote 9 in the Court's opinion. Does this reveal anything about the continued vitality of the *Byrd* test? Consider the following argument: *Byrd* and *Hanna* are incompatible in their perspectives on the interpretation of the Rules of Decision Act, because they focus on fundamentally different interests and concerns.

5.   In the years after *Hanna,* lower federal courts often continued to employ the *Byrd* balancing tests, particularly on issues concerning the relationship between judge and jury. See, e.g., Mayer v. Gary Partners and Co., Ltd., 29 F.3d 330 (7th Cir.1994). Other federal courts attempted to combine *Byrd* and *Hanna.* For example, in Szantay v. Beech Aircraft Corp., 349 F.2d 60 (4th Cir.1965), the court, in holding that a South Carolina door-closing statute did not deprive the federal court of diversity jurisdiction, inquired "whether the [state] rule embodies important policies that would be frustrated by the application of a different federal jurisdictional rule and, if so, is this policy to

be overridden because of a stronger federal policy?" The Court, however, also made mention of *Hanna*'s redefinition of outcome determination.

6.   In what way does *Hanna*'s approach to the Rules of Decision Act differ from *York?* How would the *York* test have resolved the *Hanna* case? Does your answer reveal how the two differ? Is *Hanna* closer to *York* than it is to *Byrd?*

7.   Note that in its explication of the Rules of Decision Act test, the Court in *Hanna* referred to "discouragement of forum-shopping and the avoidance of inequitable administration of the laws." Are these distinct concerns, or do they simply represent different means of characterizing the same interest? See McCoid, Hanna v. Plumer: The *Erie* Doctrine Takes Shape, 51 Va.L.Rev. 884, 889 (1965): "Opposition to forum shopping was based solely on the unfairness which resulted from the opportunity of some litigants to choose advantageously between two court systems applying different law. * * * The real aim of the uniformity policy, then, is what the Chief Justice describes as 'evidence of inequitable administration of the laws' and lack of 'equal protection.'" In this regard, consider also the *Walker* decision, infra p. 1011.

8.   The *Hanna* Court's approach to the Rules of Decision Act focuses on the dangers of forum-shopping. Exactly what are those dangers? How significant are they? Consider Redish & Phillips, *Erie* and the Rules of Decision Act: In Search of the Appropriate Dilemma, 91 Harv.L.Rev. 356, 375 (1977):

> [T]here is serious doubt about the severity of the discrimination the test is attempting to avoid, since similar disparities between litigants go unquestioned in other contexts. * * * The existence of an option afforded plaintiff and denied defendant * * * is a commonly accepted litigation phenomenon. For example, a plaintiff invariably has the choice of timing in bringing a suit (within the confines established by the applicable statute of limitations), and often, in light of relaxed due process limits on personal jurisdiction, a wide choice of locale. It can generally be expected that a plaintiff will choose the timing and locale simultaneously most convenient to him and most inconvenient to the defendant.

In his separate opinion, Justice Harlan argues that the forum-shopping approach proves too much, since it logically would lead to the end of the Federal Rules of Civil Procedure in situations when the state did not provide the same rule. Is his point valid?

9.   How would Justice Harlan resolve *Erie* issues? Is he interpreting the Constitution, the Rules of Decision Act, the Rules Enabling Act, or something else? Why does he concur, rather than dissent, in *Hanna?*

10.   How should the following case be resolved after *Hanna:* State law requires that prior to actual litigation of medical malpractice claims, the plaintiff's claim be presented to a malpractice screening panel, consisting of selected attorneys and judges. The panel presents a recommendation, admissible at trial, concerning the merits of the claim. The rule reflects a state policy interest in providing a measure of protection for physicians and in

encouraging reduction in malpractice insurance rates and health care costs, thought to be increased by unduly large jury verdicts in malpractice suits. Federal practice makes no provision for the use of such a screening panel procedure. In a diversity malpractice suit in federal court, defendant seeks dismissal because plaintiff failed to follow the screening panel procedure as prescribed by state law. See, e.g., Edelson v. Soricelli, 610 F.2d 131 (3d Cir.1979) (divided court holds that state requirement of arbitration should be applied in medical malpractice case).

Federal Procedural Statutes and *Hanna-Erie*

Under the logic of *Hanna,* how should the Court resolve a difference between federal and state procedural standards when the federal standard is neither embodied in a Federal Rule of Civil Procedure nor merely a judge-made product, but rather is embodied in a distinct federal statute? Should the standard of the Rules of Decision Act control? How would Professor Ely suggest such cases should be decided?

On this question, consider the Supreme Court's decision in Stewart Organization, Inc. v. Ricoh Corp., 487 U.S. 22 (1988). This diversity suit involved a contract that contained a forum-selection clause, providing that any dispute arising out of the contract could be brought only in a court located in Manhattan. The suit, however, was filed in the Northern District of Alabama. Relying on the contractual forum-selection clause, defendant moved, pursuant to the venue transfer statute, 28 U.S.C. § 1404(a) [see supra p. 857 n. 1], to transfer the case to the Southern District of New York, or to dismiss for improper venue under 28 U.S.C.A. § 1406. The district court denied the motion, reasoning that the motion was controlled by Alabama law and that Alabama looks unfavorably upon contractual forum-selection clauses. The court of appeals reversed.

The Supreme Court, in an opinion by Justice Marshall, held that federal, not state, law controlled:

> A District Court's decision whether to apply a federal statute such as § 1404(a) in a diversity action * * * involves a considerably less intricate analysis than that which governs the "relatively unguided *Erie* choice." Hanna v. Plumer. Our cases indicate that when the federal law sought to be applied is a congressional statute, the first and chief question for the District Court's determination is whether the statute is "sufficiently broad to control the issue before the Court." This question involves a straightforward exercise in statutory interpretation to determine if the statute covers the point in dispute.
>
> If the District Court determines that a federal statute covers the point in dispute, it proceeds to inquire whether the statute represents a valid exercise of Congress' authority under the Constitution. If Congress intended to reach the issue before the

Court, and if it enacted its intention into law in a manner that abides with the Constitution, that is the end of the matter * * *. Thus, a District Court sitting in diversity must apply a federal statute that controls the issue before the court and that represents a valid exercise of Congress' constitutional power.

On the basis of this analysis, the Court held that § 1404(a) controlled.

Would Professor Ely agree with the Court's analysis? For an examination of the problems raised by Stewart Organization, Inc. v. Ricoh Corp., see Freer, Erie's Mid-Life Crisis, 63 Tulane L.Rev. 1087 (1989). Professor Freer argues that in *Stewart,* the Court was "interpreting federal legislation too broadly, employing it in [a] situation[ ] in which Congress did not clearly intend it to apply." Id. at 1090. Such an overextension, he asserts, "raises obvious separation of powers concerns," and illustrates how the federal courts are "stacking the deck against the application of state law." Id. On the general subject, see also Heiser, Forum Selection Clauses in State Courts: Limitations on Enforcement After *Stewart* and *Carnival Cruise,* 45 Fla. L. Rev. 361 (1993); Maltz, Choice of Forum and Choice of Law in the Federal Courts: A Reconsideration of *Erie* Principles, 79 Ky. L.J. 231, 245–52 (1991).

In Jinks v. Richland County, 538 U.S. 456 (2003), the Court addressed a challenge to 28 U.S.C. § 1367(d)'s tolling provision for cases in which the federal court declines to exercise supplemental jurisdiction. Defendant argued that Congress had no constitutional power to toll limitations for state-law claims asserted in state court. The Court disagreed, holding that this legislation could be viewed as "necessary" within the Necessary and Proper Clause:

> As to the "necessity": The federal Courts can assuredly exist and function in the absence of § 1367(d), but we long ago rejected the view that the Necessary and Proper Clause demands that an Act of Congress be "absolutely necessary" to the exercise of an enumerated power. Rather, it suffices that § 1367(d) is "conducive to the due administration of justice" in federal court, and is "plainly adapted" to that end. Section 1367(d) is conducive to the administration of justice because it provides an alternative to the unsatisfactory options that federal judges faced when they decided whether to retain jurisdiction over supplemental state-law claims that might be time barred in state court. [The court summarized the alternatives that existed before adoption of the statute.] By providing a straightforward tolling rule in place of this regime, § 1367(d) unquestionably promotes fair and efficient operation of the federal courts and is therefore conducive the administration of justice.

> And it is conducive to the administration of justice for another reason: It eliminates a serious impediment to access to the federal

courts on the part of plaintiffs pursuing federal and state-law claims that "derive from a common nucleus of operative fact." * * *

"We are also persuaded * * * that § 1367(d) is plainly adapted" to the power of Congress to establish the lower federal courts and provide for the fair and efficient exercise of their Article III powers. There is no suggestion by either of the parties that Congress enacted § 1367(d) as a "pretext" for "the accomplishment of objects not entrusted to the [federal] government," nor is the connection between § 1367(d) and Congress's authority over the federal courts so attenuated as to undermine the enumeration of powers set forth in Article I § 8.

Burlington Northern Railroad Co. v. Woods, 480 U.S. 1 (1987):

JUSTICE MARSHALL delivered the opinion of the Court.

[A tort action for personal injuries was removed to federal district court in Alabama on the basis of diversity of citizenship. Based on a jury verdict, the court entered judgment of over $300,000 in favor of plaintiffs, and defendant posted bond to stay the judgment pending appeal. The Court of Appeals for the Eleventh Circuit affirmed and granted plaintiff's request to impose, under Alabama's mandatory affirmance penalty statute, a penalty of 10% of the amount of the judgment. The purpose of the Alabama rule was to penalize frivolous appeals and appeals interposed for delay. The Supreme Court held the Alabama statute to be inapplicable because it was in conflict with Rule 38 of the Federal Rules of Appellate Procedure, which provided: "If the court of appeals shall determine that an appeal is frivolous, it may award just damages and single or double costs to the appellee."]

The Rule must * * * be applied if it represents a valid exercise of Congress' rule-making authority, which originates in the Constitution and has been bestowed on this Court by the Rules Enabling Act, 28 U.S.C.A. § 2072.

The constitutional constraints on the exercise of this rulemaking authority define a test of reasonableness. Rules regulating matters indisputably procedural are *a priori* constitutional. Rules regulating matters "which, though falling within the uncertain area between substance and procedure, are rationally capable of classification as either," also satisfy this constitutional standard [citing *Hanna*]. The Rules Enabling Act, however, contains an additional requirement. The Federal Rule must not "abridge, enlarge or modify any substantive right. . . ." The cardinal purpose of Congress in authorizing the development of a uniform and consistent system of rules governing federal practice and procedure suggests that Rules which incidentally affect litigants' substantive rights do not violate this provision if reasonably necessary to maintain the integrity of that system of rules. Moreover, the study and approval given each proposed Rule by the Advisory Committee, the Judicial Conference, and this Court, and the statutory requirement that the Rule be reported to Congress for a period of review before taking effect give the Rules presumptive validity under both the constitutional and statutory constraints.

* * *

[Rule 38's] discretionary mode of operation unmistakably conflicts with the mandatory provision of Alabama's affirmance penalty statute. Moreover, the purposes underlying the Rule are sufficiently co-extensive with the asserted purposes of the Alabama statute to indicate that the Rule occupies the statute's field of operation so as to preclude its application in federal diversity actions.

Petitioner nevertheless argues that, because Alabama has a similar Appellate Rule which may be applied in state court alongside the affirmance penalty statute, see Ala.Rule App.Pro. 38, a federal court sitting in diversity could impose the mandatory penalty and likewise remain free to exercise its discretionary authority under Federal Rule 38. This argument, however, ignores the significant possibility that a Court of Appeals may, in any given case, find a limited justification for imposing penalties in an amount *less than* 10% of the lower court's judgment. Federal Rule 38 adopts a case-by-case approach to identifying and deterring frivolous appeals; the Alabama statute precludes any exercise of discretion within its scope of operation. * * *

Federal Rule 38 regulates matters which can reasonably be classified as procedural, thereby satisfying the constitutional standard for validity. Its displacement of the Alabama statute also satisfies the statutory constraints of the Rules Enabling Act. The choice made by the drafters of the Federal Rules in favor of a discretionary procedure affects only the process of enforcing litigants' rights and not the rights themselves.

NOTES AND QUESTIONS

1.   In 1988, Congress amended the Rules Enabling Act. As amended, 28 U.S.C.A. § 2072 provides as follows:

(a) The Supreme Court shall have the power to prescribe general rules of practice and procedure and rules of evidence for cases in the United States district courts (including proceedings before magistrates thereof) and courts of appeals.

(b) Such rules shall not abridge, enlarge or modify any substantive right. All laws in conflict with such rules shall be of no further force or effect after such rules have taken effect.

In other new provisions, Congress spelled out procedures for the amendment of the rules and their submission to Congress before they become effective. See 28 U.S.C.A. §§ 2073; 2074. It is unlikely that these changes will have a significant effect on the issues decided in *Hanna* and *Burlington Northern*. But see note 3 infra.

Note that § 2072(b) contains what is known as the Supersession Clause, which nullifies laws in conflict with rules adopted pursuant to the Rules Enabling Act. In Henderson v. United States, 517 U.S. 654 (1996), the Court applied the Supersession Clause to override the requirement of the Suits in Admiralty Act, 46 U.S.C.A. § 742, that suits be served on the United States "forthwith." The Court's reasoning was that Fed. R. Civ. P. 4(m) guarantees plaintiffs 120 days to serve the complaint, while the "forthwith" requirement of the statute, although not precise in number of days, calls for service good deal sooner. Accordingly, the rule and the statute conflict irreconcilably. The government took the position that the service requirement of the statute was jurisdictional because it dealt with waiver of sovereign immunity, but the Court did not accept this argument, viewing service as separate from the court's jurisdiction. Justice Thomas, joined by Chief Justice Rehnquist and Justice O'Connor, dissented on the ground that prompt service is a condition for waiver of sovereign immunity.

2.   Contrast the approach of both *Hanna* and *Burlington Northern* to the Rules Enabling Act with the interpretation adopted by the Supreme Court in Sibbach v. Wilson & Co., 312 U.S. 1 (1941). In a personal injury suit in federal court defendant moved, pursuant to Rule 35(a) of the Federal Rules of Civil Procedure, for an order requiring plaintiff to submit to a physical examination by court-appointed physicians. Plaintiff refused, and was judged to be in contempt pursuant to Rule 37. The issue was whether, in a diversity case, Rule 35 or possibly contrary state law controlled on the availability of a physical examination.

Plaintiff argued that the applicable Rules violated the limits imposed by the Rules Enabling Act, since they violated a state substantive right not to be forced to submit to a physical examination. The Supreme Court rejected the argument. The Court noted that the plaintiff "admits, and, we think, correctly, that Rules 35 and 37 are rules of procedure." This admission proved fatal to plaintiff's argument, for according to the Court "[t]he test [of the Enabling Act] must be whether a rule really regulates procedure,—the judicial process for enforcing rights and duties recognized by substantive law and for justly administering remedy and redress for disregard or infraction of them." This much, the Court said, plaintiff had admitted.

3.   Professor Ely has suggested the following construction of the Enabling Act (Ely, supra, 87 Harv.L.Rev. at 718–19; 724–27):

> In thus delegating authority to the Court, the Act begins with a checklist approach—anything that relates to process, writs, pleadings, motions, or to practice and procedure generally, is authorized; anything else is not. Thus far, no limitation is imposed

that was not imposed by the Constitution. The second sentence, however, provides that "Such rules shall not abridge, enlarge or modify any substantive right. . . ." The Act therefore contains, as the Court used to say the Constitution contained, limitations of both the checklist and enclave variety. Not only must a Rule be procedural; it must in addition abridge, enlarge or modify no substantive right.

* * *

We were all brought up on sophisticated talk about the fluidity of the line between substance and procedure. But the realization that the terms carry no monolithic meaning at once appropriate to all the contexts in which courts have seen fit to employ them need not imply that they can have no meaning at all. And they are the terms the Enabling Act uses. We have, I think, some moderately clear notion of what a procedural rule is—one designed to make the process of litigation a fair and efficient mechanism for the resolution of disputes. Thus, one way of doing things may be chosen over another because it is thought to be more likely to get at the truth, or better calculated to give the parties a fair opportunity to present their sides of the story, or because, and this may point quite the other way, it is a means of promoting the efficiency of the process. Or the protection of the process may proceed at wholesale, as by keeping the size of the docket at a level consistent with giving those cases that are heard the attention they deserve. The most helpful way, it seems to me, of defining a substantive rule—or more particularly a substantive right, which is what the Act refers to—is as a right granted for one or more nonprocedural reasons, for some purpose or purposes not having to do with the fairness or efficiency of the litigation process.

* * *

Of course it is not at all unlikely that with respect to a given rule the legislature or other rulemaker will have had two (or more) goals in mind—one relating to the management of litigation and one relating to some other concern. Under the definitions suggested above, such a rule would be both procedural and substantive. This conclusion strikes me as not at all troublesome, however, and indeed fits precisely what I am suggesting is the proper interpretation of the Enabling Act. Thus, statutes of limitations are passed not simply for the substantive purpose of relieving people's minds after the passage of the designated period, but also for procedural purposes to keep down the size of the docket and to ensure that cases will not be tried on evidence so stale as to cast doubt on its trustworthiness. They are therefore procedural, which means * * * that a Federal Rule prescribing such a limitation would satisfy the Enabling Act's first sentence. It should not get by the second sentence, however, for the substantive rights established by state statutes of limitations would be abridged by applying such a Federal Rule.

How does Professor Ely's suggested interpretation of the Rules Enabling Act compare to the interpretation employed in *Hanna?* In *Sibbach?* How persuasive is Ely's suggested interpretation? Does it make sense to assume that, by insertion of the second sentence precluding a Federal Rule from abridging a "substantive" right, Congress intended to protect *state-created* substantive rights, in light of the fact that the Enabling Act was adopted in 1934, four years prior to *Erie?* See generally Burbank, The Rules Enabling Act of 1934, 130 U.Pa.L.Rev. 1015 (1982). If Professor Ely's reading of "substantive right" is anachronistic, does the recent reenactment of the Enabling Act (see note 1 supra) have a bearing on its current force?

Assuming that Congress sought to insulate substantive interests it had created against dilution through procedural rules, could the scope of rulemaking authority shift as Congress becomes more active in adopting legislation dealing with procedural issues? Legislation such as the Private Securities Litigation Reform Act of 1995 includes provisions regulating matters previously covered by the Federal Rules of Civil Procedure. See supra pp. 161–177 (regarding the requirements of the Private Securities Litigation Reform Act). For an argument that "the increasing reach of Congress' procedural legislation * * * expand[s] the scope of matters to be considered 'substantive' within the meaning of the REA," see Kelleher, Taking "Substantive Rights" (In the Rules Enabling Act) More Seriously, 74 Notre Dame L. Rev. 47 (1998).

4. Professor Perdue has suggested that "[t]he Rules Enabling Act may constrain courts, even where they are not directly interpreting a Federal Rule of Civil Procedure but are instead creating a federal common law rule of 'practice and procedure.'" Thus, she concludes, "[t]he constraints of the Rules Enabling Act should apply regardless of whether courts are interpreting a promulgated Federal Rule of Civil Procedure or creating a common law rule of procedure." Perdue, The Sources and Scope of Federal Procedural Common Law: Some Reflections on *Erie* and *Gasperini*, 46 U. Kan. L. Rev. 751, 760 (1998). She acknowledges that "[s]ome might recoil at this argument that jumbles Rules Enabling Act cases with Rules of Decision Act cases," but argues that if the source of authority to create a common law procedural rule "is the general power to create rules for the court's operation, then such a common law rule should be constrained by the Rules Enabling Act." How persuasive is this analysis?

5. After *Burlington Northern,* to what extent are the Federal Rules of Civil Procedure likely to be superseded in diversity cases by contrary state law? Consider Douglas v. NCNB Texas National Bank, 979 F.2d 1128 (5th Cir.1992). A state court suit, brought by a borrower to recover for prime rate fraud, was removed to federal court by the defendant lender. The lender filed an answer but no counterclaims. The action was later dismissed. The lender's assignee subsequently sued in federal court to collect on the notes, and the borrower defended on the grounds that these claims had been compulsory counterclaims under Rule 13(a) in the borrower's prior suit. The court rejected the borrower's argument, finding Rule 13(a) inapplicable because it conflicted

with a lender's "substantive right" under Texas law "to elect judicial or nonjudicial foreclosure in the event of a default." The court noted that "the state's compulsory counterclaim rule * * * does not require the secured party to counterclaim to collect on the debt if the creditor has a contractual right to pursue a nonjudicial foreclosure." 979 F.2d at 1129. Was the court correct in characterizing the state right as "substantive"? If so, should it have concluded that, under *Burlington Northern,* the Federal Rule's impact on the state right was merely "incidental"?

6.   Was the Court in *Burlington Northern* correct in finding a conflict between the Alabama statute and Rule 38? See generally, Whitten, *Erie* and the Federal Rules: A Review and Reappraisal After *Burlington Northern Railroad v. Woods,* 21 Creighton L.Rev. 1 (1987). Professor Whitten suggests that "the one constant in the Court's decisions dealing with Federal Rules-state law conflicts from *Sibbach* through *Burlington Northern* has been its refusal to provide significant content to the Act's substantive rights restriction." Id. Is *Burlington Northern* an appropriate case for application of the Enabling Act's "substantive rights" restriction?

7.   Consider the possible impact of the Court's subsequent decision in Shady Grove Orthopedic Associates, P.A. v. Allstate Ins. Co., 559 U.S. 393 (2010). Plaintiff sued in federal court on the basis of diversity of citizenship, seeking damages for unpaid statutory interest penalties on overdue insurance payments. The plaintiff sought certification of a class action pursuant to Rule 23 of the Federal Rules of Civil Procedure. Defendant argued that the class proceeding was precluded by § 901(b) of New York State's Civil Practice Law, which prohibits a class action in state court seeking to recover a penalty, such as statutory interest. Finding a direct conflict between Rule 23 and the state law, Justice Scalia, announcing the judgment of the Court and writing for four justices, stated: "it is not the substantive or procedural nature or purpose of the affected state law that matters, but the substantive or procedural nature of the Federal Rule. We held since *Sibbach,* and reaffirmed repeatedly, that the validity of a Federal Rule depends entirely upon whether it regulates procedure. If it does, it is authorized by [the Rules Enabling Act] and is valid in all jurisdictions, with respect to all claims, regardless of its incidental effect upon state-created rights." Justice Scalia therefore rejected Allstate's argument that Rule 23 abridged a state substantive right and as a result was inapplicable.

In his opinion concurring in part and concurring in the judgment, Justice Stevens rejected Justice Scalia's interpretation of the Rules Enabling Act. According to Stevens, the Enabling Act's limiting sentence "means only that federal rules cannot displace a State's definition of its own rights or remedies." However, Justice Stevens concluded that the New York statute was procedural, rather than substantive.

With which position do you agree? What are the implications of Justice Stevens's approach for the uniform application of the Federal Rules?

One commentator recently noted that after *Shady Grove,* "state law continues to cast a long shadow over the Federal Rules." Woolley, The Role of State Law in Determining the Construction and Validity of Federal Rules of Civil Procedure, 35 Rev. Litig. 207, 210 (2016). Professor Woolley concludes that "[t]he deference state law has enjoyed is inconsistent with the fundamental purpose of the REA, which is to provide federal rule makers with the authority to prescribe 'uniform and consistent' Federal Rules. The validity of a Federal Rule should depend on what the Rule regulates, not on whether it interferes with state law enacted for a substantive purpose." Id.

The scholarship on *Shady Grove* is extensive. Among the leading works are Roosevelt, Choice of Law in Federal Courts: From *Erie* and *Klaxon* to CAFA and *Shady Grove,* 106 Nw. U. L. Rev. 1 (2012); Brown, For Lack of a Better Rule: Using the Concept of Transsubstantivity to Solve the *Erie* Problem in *Shady Grove,* 80 U. Cinn. L. Rev. 1 (2011); Bauer, Shedding Light on *Shady Grove*: Further Reflections on the *Erie* Doctrine From a Conflicts Perspective, 86 Notre Dame L. Rev. 939 (2011); Ides, The Standard for Measuring the Validity of a Federal Rule of Civil Procedure: The *Shady Grove* Debate Between Justices Scalia and Stevens, 86 Notre Dame L. Rev. 1041 (2011).

For a decision applying *Shady Grove* to find an Alabama statute limiting the availability of class actions superseded by Federal Rule 23 in federal court, see Lisk v. Lumber One Wood Preserving, LLC, 792 F.3d 1331 (11th Circuit 2015).

Consider the application of *Shady Grove* to procedural contexts other than class actions. For example, in Hahn v. Walsh, 762 F.3d 617 7th Cir. (2014), the court considered whether a federal court sitting in diversity was obligated to use an Illinois statute requiring medical malpractice claims be accompanied by an affidavit confirming the claim's merits. Plaintiff argued that the requirement conflicted with Rules 8 and 11. The court disagreed, finding that the statute simply requires an attachment to the complaint, without altering the requirements of Rules 8 or 11. Do you agree? See also Schmigel v. Uchal, 800 F.3d 113 (3d Cir. 2015) (finding that a medical malpractice affidavit requirement could coexist with the Federal Rules).

8. In Business Guides, Inc. v. Chromatic Communications Enterprises, Inc., 498 U.S. 533 (1991), the Supreme Court, in an opinion by Justice O'Connor, upheld imposition of sanctions against a party under Rule 11 of the Federal Rules of Civil Procedure. Rule 11 then provided that signature on a paper filed in court is a certification, made after reasonable inquiry, that the paper is well grounded in fact and warranted by existing law or a good faith argument for its extension or modification. See the discussion of Rule 11 in Chapter 3, supra pp. 146–159. In *Business Guides,* the Court held that Rule 11 applies to represented parties who themselves sign the certification, and that as so construed the Rule does not violate the Rules Enabling Act. The Court first noted "that any Rules Enabling Act challenge to Rule 11 has a large hurdle to get over," because "the Rules do not go into effect until Congress has had at least seven months to look them over." 498 U.S. at 550. Moreover, the Court held that the Enabling Act challenge to Rule 11 failed under the *Burlington*

Northern standard: "There is little doubt that Rule 11 is reasonably necessary to maintain the integrity of the system of federal practice and procedure, and that any effect on substantive rights is incidental." Id. at 552. In rejecting the argument that Rule 11 represents "impermissible feeshifting" and as a result affects substantive rights, the Court reasoned that "Rule 11 sanctions are not tied to the outcome of litigation; the relevant inquiry is whether a specific filing was, if not successful, at least well founded. Nor do sanctions shift the entire cost of litigation; they shift only the cost of a discrete event." Id. The Court ultimately concluded that "[i]mposing monetary sanctions on parties that violate the Rule may confer a benefit on other litigants, but the Rules Enabling Act is not violated by such incidental effects on substantive rights."

In dissent, Justice Kennedy argued that, as construed by the majority, Rule 11 constitutes a "potential incursion into matters reserved to the States * * *." The majority's application of Rule 11 to a represented party, as opposed to its attorney, he argued, "creates a new tort of 'negligent prosecution' or 'accidental abuse of process,' applicable to any represented party ignorant enough to sign a pleading or other Rule 11 paper." He concluded that "[w]hether or not Rule 11 as construed by the majority exceeds our rulemaking authority, these concerns weigh in favor of a reasonable, alternative interpretation * * *."

9.   One commentator has argued that "the Federal Rules of Civil Procedure do not, by and large, contain preclusion law and * * * they cannot validly prescribe such law." Burbank, *Semtek,* Forum Shopping, and Federal Common Law, 77 Notre Dame L. Rev. 1027 (2002). Is this accurate? Consider Rule 13(a), concerning compulsory counterclaims. Does that rule have a preclusive effect beyond the court in which the rule has been invoked? Does Rule 13(a) violate the Rules Enabling Act's directive that the Rules not abridge, enlarge or modify a substantive right? What would the test adopted in *Burlington Northern* say about Rule 13(a)? Reconsider this question in connection with Semtek, Inc. v. Lockheed Martin Corp., infra p. 1201. For criticism of Professor Burbank's approach and a defense of *Burlington Northern*'s interpretation of the Enabling Act, see Redish & Murashko, The Rules Enabling Act and the Procedural-Substantive Tension: A Lesson in Statutory Interpretation, 93 Minn.L.Rev. 26 (2008).

Walker v. Armco Steel Corp., 446 U.S. 740 (1980):

JUSTICE MARSHALL delivered the opinion of the Court.

[Plaintiff, a carpenter, was injured on August 22, 1975, when an allegedly defective nail manufactured by defendant shattered. The complaint in this diversity case was filed in federal district court in Oklahoma on August 19, 1977, but service of process was not made on respondent's authorized service agent until December 1, 1977. Defendant moved to dismiss on the ground that the action was barred by the applicable Oklahoma statute of limitations. Although the complaint had been filed within the 2-year Oklahoma statute of limitations, state law did not deem the action "commenced" for purposes of the statute of limitations until service of the summons on the defendant. In response to defendant's motion to dismiss, plaintiff admitted that his case would be foreclosed in state court, but argued that Rule 3 of the Federal Rules of Civil Procedure governs the manner in which an action is commenced for all purposes, including the tolling of the state statute of limitations. The Supreme Court unanimously held that state law controlled, finding the case indistinguishable from *Ragan,* supra p. 977, and therefore upheld dismissal of plaintiff's case.]

There is no indication that [Rule 3] was intended to toll a state statute of limitations, much less that it purported to displace state tolling rules for purposes of state statutes of limitations. In our view, in diversity actions Rule 3 governs the date from which various timing requirements of the Federal Rules begin to run, but does not affect state statutes of limitations.

In contrast to Rule 3, the Oklahoma statute is a statement of a substantive decision by that State that actual service on, and accordingly actual notice by, the defendant is an integral part of the several policies served by the statute of limitations. * * * The statute of limitations establishes a deadline after which the defendant may legitimately have peace of mind; it also recognizes that after a certain period of time it is unfair to require the defendant to attempt to piece together his defense to an old claim. A requirement of actual service promotes both of those functions of the statute. * * * It is these policy aspects which make the service requirement an "integral" part of the statute of limitations both in this case and in *Ragan.* * * * Rule 3 does not replace such policy determinations found in state law. Rule 3 and [state law] can exist side by side, therefore, each controlling its own intended sphere of coverage without conflict.

Since there is no direct conflict between the Federal Rule and the state law, the *Hanna* analysis does not apply. Instead, the policies behind *Erie* and *Ragan* control the issue whether, in the absence of a federal rule directly on point, state service requirements which are an integral part of the statute of limitations should control in an action based on state law which is filed in federal court under diversity jurisdiction. * * * It is sufficient to note that although in this case failure to apply the state service law might not create any problem of forum shopping, the result would be an "inequitable administration of the law." Hanna v. Plumer. There is simply no reason why, in the absence of a controlling federal rule, an action based on state law which concededly would be barred in the state courts by the state statute of limitations should proceed through litigation to judgment in federal court solely because of the fortuity that there is diversity of citizenship between the litigants.

NOTES AND QUESTIONS

1. The Court in *Walker* rejected the argument that *Hanna* had overruled *Ragan*. Do you agree?

2. Note the Court's emphasis on how "integral" the state's commencement rule is to the statute of limitations. Does the Court in *Walker* return to *Byrd*, in lieu of *Hanna?* Reconsider the effect on *Byrd* of footnote 9 in *Hanna*. Would the *Hanna* Court have given any weight to the importance of the state policy in the manner that the *Walker* Court did?

3. How different is the Court's analysis from that in *York?* Note that the Court in *Walker* found no likelihood of forum shopping as the result of the use of a separate federal standard, yet nevertheless held that state law must be applied. How do you think the *Hanna* Court would have decided *Walker* under the Rules of Decision Act?

4. The Court in *Walker* found Rule 3 inapplicable to the statute of limitations issue. If the Rule were amended to provide explicitly that an action commenced for purposes of the tolling of the statute of limitations when it was filed, rather than when service was made, how do you think the Court would have held? How would the test of *Sibbach* apply?

5. In Chambers v. NASCO, Inc., 501 U.S. 32 (1991), the Court held that a district judge in a diversity case possessed "inherent power" to impose sanctions—unauthorized by rule or statute—on a party for acting in bad faith, despite a contrary rule in state court in which the district court sat. Plaintiff in that case sued for specific performance of a contract to buy defendant's television station. Defendant responded with a variety of dishonest devices to defeat the suit, including lying to the judge. After entering judgment for plaintiff, the district court imposed plaintiff's entire attorney's fees and litigation expenses—nearly $1 million—on defendant as a sanction even though there was no statute or federal rule to support such action.

The Supreme Court affirmed. Justice White, speaking for the majority, reasoned:

> Only when there is a conflict between state and federal substantive law are the concerns of Erie R. Co. v. Tompkins at issue. As we explained in Hanna v. Plumer, the "outcome determinative" test of *Erie* and Guaranty Trust Co. v. York "cannot be read without reference to the twin aims of the *Erie* rule: discouragement of forum-shopping and avoidance of inequitable administration of the laws." * * * [N]either of these twin aims is implicated by the assessment of attorney's fees as a sanction for bad-faith conduct before the court which involved disobedience of the court's orders and the attempt to defraud the court itself. * * * [T]he imposition of sanctions under the bad-faith exception depends not on which party wins the lawsuit, but on how the parties conduct themselves during the litigation. Consequently, there is no risk that the exception will lead to forum-shopping. Nor is it inequitable to apply the exception to citizens and

noncitizens alike, when the party, by controlling his or her conduct in litigation, has the power to determine whether sanctions will be assessed.

Justice Kennedy, joined by the Chief Justice and Justice Souter, dissented. He argued that "the Court upholds the wholesale shift of respondent's attorney's fees to petitioner, even though the District Court opinion reveals that petitioner was sanctioned at least in part for his so-called breach of contract. The extension of inherent authority to sanction a party's prelitigation conduct * * * turns the *Erie* doctrine upside down by punishing petitioner's primary conduct contrary to [state] law." Justice Kennedy viewed the district court's opinion as penalizing pre-litigation conduct, even though the majority rejected such an interpretation. "The inherent power exercised here," Justice Kennedy concluded, "violates the fundamental tenet of federalism announced in *Erie* by regulating primary behavior that the Constitution leaves to the exclusive province of States." Justice Scalia dissented on an unrelated issue.

Is *Chambers* consistent with the approach to the Rules of Decision Act employed in *Walker?* Is Justice White correct in asserting that *Erie* concerns are implicated "[o]nly when there is a conflict between state and federal substantive law"? Do you agree with him that when the outcome of a case is not likely to be affected by the use of different rules in state and federal court, forum-shopping is not likely to be encouraged? For example, would plaintiff's choice of forum likely be influenced by different sanction rules for bad faith conduct in a case such as *Chambers,* where the defendant was ultimately found to have acted in blatantly bad faith? Should it matter?

What approach to *Erie* is Justice Kennedy advocating?

GASPERINI V. CENTER FOR HUMANITIES, INC.

Supreme Court of the United States, 1996
518 U.S. 415

JUSTICE GINSBURG delivered the opinion of the Court.

Under the law of New York, appellate courts are empowered to review the size of jury verdicts and to order new trials when the jury's award "deviates materially from what would be reasonable compensation." N.Y. Civ. Prac. Law and Rules (CPLR) § 5501(c) (McKinney 1995). Under the Seventh Amendment, which governs proceedings in federal court, but not in state court, "the right of trial by jury shall be preserved, and no fact tried by a jury, shall be otherwise re-examined in any Court of the United States, than according to the rules of the common law." U.S. Const., Amdt. 7. The compatibility of these provisions, in an action based on New York law but tried in federal court by reason of the parties' diverse citizenship, is the issue we confront in this case. We hold that New York's law controlling compensation awards for excessiveness or inadequacy can be given effect, without detriment to the Seventh Amendment, if the review standard set out in CPLR § 5501(c) is applied by the federal trial court judge, with appellate control of the trial court's ruling limited to review for "abuse of discretion."

I

Petitioner William Gasperini, a journalist for CBS News and the Christian Science Monitor, began reporting on events in Central America in 1984. He earned his living primarily in radio and print media and only occasionally sold his photographic work. During the course of his seven-year stint in Central America, Gasperini took over 5,000 slide transparencies, depicting active war zones, political leaders, and scenes from daily life. In 1990, Gasperini agreed to supply his original color transparencies to The Center for Humanities, Inc. (Center) for use in an educational videotape, *Conflict in Central America.* Gasperini selected 300 of his slides for the Center; its videotape included 110 of them. The Center agreed to return the original transparencies, but upon the completion of the project, it could not find them.

Gasperini commenced suit in the United States District Court for the Southern District of New York, invoking the court's diversity jurisdiction pursuant to 28 U.S.C. § 1332. He alleged several state-law claims for relief, including breach of contract, conversion, and negligence. The Center conceded liability for the lost transparencies and the issue of damages was tried before a jury.

At trial, Gasperini's expert witness testified that the "industry standard" within the photographic publishing community valued a lost transparency at $1,500. This industry standard, the expert explained, represented the average license fee a commercial photograph could earn over the full course of the photographer's copyright, i.e., in Gasperini's case, his lifetime plus 50 years. Gasperini estimated that his earnings from photography totaled just over $10,000 for the period from 1984 through 1993. He also testified that he intended to produce a book containing his best photographs from Central America.

After a three-day trial, the jury awarded Gasperini $450,000 in compensatory damages. This sum, the jury foreperson announced, "is [$]1500 each, for 300 slides." Moving for a new trial under Federal Rule of Civil Procedure 59, the Center attacked the verdict on various grounds, including excessiveness. Without comment, the District Court denied the motion.

The Court of Appeals for the Second Circuit vacated the judgment entered on the jury's verdict. 66 F.3d 427 (1995). Mindful that New York law governed the controversy, the Court of Appeals endeavored to apply CPLR § 5501(c), which instructs that, when a jury returns an itemized verdict, as the jury did in this case, the New York Appellate Division "shall determine that an award is excessive or inadequate if it deviates materially from what would be reasonable compensation." * * * Surveying Appellate Division decisions that reviewed damage awards for lost transparencies, the Second Circuit concluded that testimony on industry standard alone was insufficient to justify a verdict; prime among other factors warranting consideration were the uniqueness of the slides' subject matter and the photographer's earning level.

Guided by Appellate Division rulings, the Second Circuit held that the $450,000 verdict "materially deviates from what is reasonable compensation." Some of Gasperini's transparencies, the Second Circuit recognized, were unique, notably those capturing combat situations in which Gasperini was the only photographer present. But others "depicted either generic scenes or events at which other professional photojournalists were present." No more than 50 slides merited a $1,500 award, the court concluded, after "[g]iving Gasperini every benefit of the doubt." Absent evidence showing significant earnings from photographic endeavors or concrete plans to publish a book, the court further determined, any damage award above $100 each for the remaining slides would be excessive. Remittiturs "presen[t] difficult problems for appellate courts," the Second Circuit acknowledged, for court of appeals judges review the evidence from "a cold paper record." Nevertheless, the Second Circuit set aside the $450,000 verdict and ordered a new trial, unless Gasperini agreed to an award of $100,000.

This case presents an important question regarding the standard a federal court uses to measure the alleged excessiveness of a jury's verdict in an action for damages based on state law. We therefore granted certiorari.

II

Before 1986, state and federal courts in New York generally invoked the same judge-made formulation in responding to excessiveness attacks on jury verdicts: courts would not disturb an award unless the amount was so exorbitant that it "shocked the conscience of the court." As described by the Second Circuit: "The standard for determining excessiveness and the appropriateness of remittitur in New York is somewhat ambiguous. Prior to 1986, New York law employed the same standard as the federal courts, which authorized remittitur only if the jury's verdict was so excessive that it 'shocked the conscience of the court.' "

In both state and federal courts, trial judges made the excessiveness assessment in the first instance, and appellate judges ordinarily deferred to the trial court's judgment.

In 1986, as part of a series of tort reform measures, New York codified a standard for judicial review of the size of jury awards. Placed in CPLR § 5501(c), the prescription reads:

"In reviewing a money judgment . . . in which it is contended that the award is excessive or inadequate and that a new trial should have been granted unless a stipulation is entered to a different award, the appellate division shall determine that an award is excessive or inadequate if it deviates materially from what would be reasonable compensation."

As stated in Legislative Findings and Declarations accompanying New York's adoption of the "deviates materially" formulation, the lawmakers found the "shock the conscience" test an insufficient check on damage awards; the legislature therefore installed a standard "invit[ing] more careful appellate scrutiny." At the same time, the legislature instructed the Appellate Division, in amended § 5522, to state the reasons for the court's rulings on the size of verdicts, and the factors the court considered in complying with § 5501(c). In his signing statement, then-Governor Mario Cuomo emphasized that the CPLR amendments were meant to ratchet up the review standard: "This will assure greater scrutiny of the amount of verdicts and promote greater stability in the tort system and greater fairness for similarly situated defendants throughout the State."

New York state-court opinions confirm that § 5501(c)'s "deviates materially" standard calls for closer surveillance than "shock the conscience" oversight.

Although phrased as a direction to New York's intermediate appellate courts, § 5501(c)'s "deviates materially" standard, as construed by New York's courts, instructs state trial judges as well. Application of § 5501(c) at the trial level is key to this case.

To determine whether an award "deviates materially from what would be reasonable compensation," New York state courts look to awards approved in similar cases. * * * The "deviates materially" standard, however, in design and operation, influences outcomes by tightening the range of tolerable awards.

III

In cases like Gasperini's, in which New York law governs the claims for relief, does New York law also supply the test for federal court review of the size of the verdict? The Center answers yes. The "deviates materially" standard, it argues, is a substantive standard that must be applied by federal appellate courts in diversity cases. The Second Circuit agreed. Gasperini, emphasizing that § 5501(c) trains on the New York Appellate Division, characterizes the provision as procedural, an allocation of decisionmaking authority regarding damages, not a hard cap on the amount recoverable. Correctly comprehended, Gasperini urges, § 5501(c)'s direction to the Appellate Division cannot be given effect by federal appellate courts without violating the Seventh Amendment's re-examination clause.

As the parties' arguments suggest, CPLR § 5501(c), appraised under Erie R. Co. v. Tompkins, 304 U.S. 64 (1938), and decisions in *Erie*'s path, is both "substantive" and "procedural": "substantive" in that § 5501(c)'s "deviates materially" standard controls how much a plaintiff can be awarded; "procedural" in that § 5501(c) assigns decisionmaking authority to New York's Appellate Division. Parallel application of § 5501(c) at the federal appellate level would be out of sync with the federal system's division of trial and appellate court functions, an allocation weighted by the Seventh Amendment. The dispositive question, therefore, is whether federal courts can give effect to the substantive thrust of § 5501(c) without untoward alteration of the federal scheme for the trial and decision of civil cases.

A

Federal diversity jurisdiction provides an alternative forum for the adjudication of state-created rights, but it does not carry with it generation of rules of substantive law. As *Erie* read the Rules of Decision Act: "Except in matters governed by the Federal Constitution or by Acts of Congress, the law to be applied in any case is the law of the State." 304 U.S., at 78. Under the *Erie* doctrine, federal courts sitting in diversity apply state substantive law and federal procedural law.

Classification of a law as "substantive" or "procedural" for Erie purposes is sometimes a challenging endeavor.[7] Guaranty Trust Co. v. York, 326 U.S. 99 (1945), an early interpretation of *Erie,* propounded an "outcome-determination" test. * * * A later pathmarking case, qualifying *Guaranty Trust,* explained that the "outcome-determination" test must not be applied mechanically to sweep in all manner of variations; instead, its application must be guided by "the twin aims of the *Erie* rule: discouragement of forum-shopping and avoidance of inequitable administration of the laws." Hanna v. Plumer, 380 U.S. 460, 468 (1965).

Informed by these decisions, we address the question whether New York's "deviates materially" standard, codified in CPLR § 5501(c), is outcome-affective in this sense: Would "application of the [standard] . . . have so important an effect upon the fortunes of one or both of the litigants that failure to [apply] it would [unfairly discriminate against citizens of the

---

[7]   Concerning matters covered by the Federal Rules of Civil Procedure, the characterization question is usually unproblematic: It is settled that if the Rule in point is consonant with the Rules Enabling Act, 28 U.S.C. § 2072, and the Constitution, the Federal Rule applies regardless of contrary state law. Federal courts have interpreted the Federal Rules, however, with sensitivity to important state interests and regulatory policies. See, e.g., Walker v. Armco Steel Corp., 446 U.S. 740, 750–752 (1980) (reaffirming decision in Ragan v. Merchants Transfer & Warehouse Co., 337 U.S. 530 (1949)), that state law rather than Rule 3 determines when a diversity action commences for the purposes of tolling the state statute of limitations; Rule 3 makes no reference to the tolling of state limitations, the Court observed, and accordingly found no direct conflict; S.A. Healy Co. v. Milwaukee Metropolitan Sewerage Dist., 60 F.3d 305, 310–312 (C.A.7 1995) (state provision for offers of settlement by plaintiffs is compatible with Federal Rule 68, which is limited to offers by defendants).

forum state, or] be likely to cause a plaintiff to choose the federal court"? Id., at 468, n. 9.

We start from a point the parties do not debate. Gasperini acknowledges that a statutory cap on damages would supply substantive law for *Erie* purposes. Although CPLR § 5501(c) is less readily classified, it was designed to provide an analogous control.

New York's Legislature codified in § 5501(c) a new standard, one that requires closer court review than the common law "shock the conscience" test. More rigorous comparative evaluations attend application of § 5501(c)'s "deviates materially" standard. To foster predictability, the legislature required the reviewing court, when overturning a verdict under § 5501(c), to state its reasons, including the factors it considered relevant. See CPLR § 5522(b). We think it a fair conclusion that CPLR § 5501(c) differs from a statutory cap principally "in that the maximum amount recoverable is not set by statute, but rather is determined by case law." In sum, § 5501(c) contains a procedural instruction, but the State's objective is manifestly substantive. Cf. S.A. Healy Co. v. Milwaukee Metropolitan Sewerage Dist., 60 F.3d 305, 310 (C.A.7 1995).

It thus appears that if federal courts ignore the change in the New York standard and persist in applying the "shock the conscience" test to damage awards on claims governed by New York law, " 'substantial' variations between state and federal [money judgments]" may be expected. See *Hanna,* 380 U.S., at 467–68. We therefore agree with the Second Circuit that New York's check on excessive damages implicates what we have called *Erie*'s "twin aims."[12] Just as the *Erie* principle precludes a federal court from giving a state-created claim "longer life . . . than [the claim] would have had in the state court," *Ragan,* 337 U.S., at 533–534, so *Erie* precludes a recovery in federal court significantly larger than the recovery that would have been tolerated in state court.

B

CPLR § 5501(c), as earlier noted, is phrased as a direction to the New York Appellate Division. Acting essentially as a surrogate for a New York appellate forum, the Court of Appeals reviewed Gasperini's award to determine if it "deviate[d] materially" from damage awards the Appellate Division permitted in similar circumstances. The Court of Appeals performed this task without benefit of an opinion from the District Court, which had denied "without comment" the Center's Rule 59 motion. Concentrating on the authority § 5501(c) gives to the Appellate Division, Gasperini urges that the provision shifts fact-finding responsibility from the jury and the trial judge to the appellate court. Assigning such

---

[12] For rights that are state-created, state law governs the amount properly awarded as punitive damages, subject to an ultimate federal constitutional check for exorbitancy. An evenhanded approach would require federal court deference to endeavors like New York to control compensatory damages for excessiveness.

responsibility to an appellate court, he maintains, is incompatible with the Seventh Amendment's re-examination clause, and therefore, Gasperini concludes, § 5501(c) cannot be given effect in federal court. Although we reach a different conclusion than Gasperini, we agree that the Second Circuit did not attend to "[a]n essential characteristic of [the federal-court] system," Byrd v. Blue Ridge Rural Elec. Cooperative, Inc., 356 U.S. 525, 537 (1958), when it used § 5501(c) as "the standard for [federal] appellate review."

That "essential characteristic" was described in *Byrd,* a diversity suit for negligence in which a pivotal issue of fact would have been tried by a judge were the case in state court. The *Byrd* Court held that, despite the state practice, the plaintiff was entitled to a jury trial in federal court. In so ruling, the Court said that the *Guaranty Trust* "outcome-determination" test was an insufficient guide in cases presenting countervailing federal interests [such as what *Byrd* described as "the manner in which, in civil common-law actions, [the federal system] distributes trial functions between judge and jury and, under the influence—if not the command—of the Seventh Amendment, assigns the decisions of disputed questions of fact to the jury."]

The Seventh Amendment, which governs proceedings in federal court, but not in state court, bears not only on the allocation of trial functions between judge and jury, the issue in *Byrd;* it also controls the allocation of authority to review verdicts, the issue of concern here. The Amendment reads:

> "In suits at common law, where the value in controversy shall exceed twenty dollars, the right of trial by jury shall be preserved, and no fact tried by a jury, shall be otherwise re-examined in any Court of the United States, than according to the rules of the common law."

Byrd involved the first clause of the Amendment, the "trial by jury" clause. This case involves the second, the "re-examination" clause. In keeping with the historic understanding, the re-examination clause does not inhibit the authority of trial judges to grant new trials "for any of the reasons for which new trials have heretofore been granted in actions at law in the courts of the United States." Fed. Rule Civ. Proc. 59(a). That authority is large. "The trial judge in the federal system," we have reaffirmed, "has . . . discretion to grant a new trial if the verdict appears to [the judge] to be against the weight of the evidence." *Byrd,* 356 U.S., at 540. This discretion includes overturning verdicts for excessiveness and ordering a new trial without qualification, or conditioned on the verdict winner's refusal to agree to a reduction (remittitur). See Dimick v. Schiedt, 293 U.S. 474, 486–487 (1935) [supra p. 669] (recognizing that remittitur withstands Seventh Amendment attack, but rejecting additur as unconstitutional).

In contrast, appellate review of a federal trial court's denial of a motion to set aside a jury's verdict as excessive is a relatively late, and less secure, development. Such review was once deemed inconsonant with the Seventh Amendment's re-examination clause. * * *

Before today, we have not "expressly [held] that the Seventh Amendment allows appellate review of a district court's denial of a motion to set aside an award as excessive." Browning-Ferris Industries of Vt., Inc. v. Kelco Disposal, Inc., 492 U.S. 257, 279, n. 25 (1989). [The Court held that the Seventh Amendment does not preclude such appellate review.]

* * *

C

In *Byrd,* the Court faced a one-or-the-other choice: trial by judge as in state court, or trial by jury according to the federal practice.[21] In the case before us, a choice of that order is not required, for the principal state and federal interests can be accommodated. The Second Circuit correctly recognized that when New York substantive law governs a claim for relief, New York law and decisions guide the allowable damages. But that court did not take into account the characteristic of the federal-court system that caused us to reaffirm: "The proper role of the trial and appellate courts in the federal system in reviewing the size of jury verdicts is . . . a matter of federal law." Donovan v. Penn Shipping Co., 429 U.S. 648, 649 (1977).

New York's dominant interest can be respected, without disrupting the federal system, once it is recognized that the federal district court is capable of performing the checking function, i.e., that court can apply the State's "deviates materially" standard in line with New York case law evolving under CPLR § 5501(c).[22] We recall, in this regard, that the "deviates materially" standard serves as the guide to be applied in trial as well as appellate courts in New York.

Within the federal system, practical reasons combine with Seventh Amendment constraints to lodge in the district court, not the court of appeals, primary responsibility for application of § 5501(c)'s "deviates materially" check. Trial judges have the "unique opportunity to consider

---

[21] The two-trial rule posited by Justice Scalia surely would be incompatible with the existence of the federal system [as] an independent system for administering justice, Byrd v. Blue Ridge Rural Elec. Coop., Incorporated, 356 U.S. 525, 537 (1958).

[22] Justice Scalia finds in Federal Rule of Civil Procedure 59 a federal standard for new trial motions in direct collision with, and leaving no room for the operation of, a state law like CPLR § 5501(c). The relevant prescription, Rule 59(a), has remained unchanged since the adoption of the Federal Rules by this Court in 1937. [Since this decision, the rule language has been revised slightly.—Eds.] Rule 59(a) is as encompassing as it is uncontroversial. It is indeed hornbook law that a most usual ground for a Rule 59 motion is that the damages are excessive. See C. Wright, Law of Federal Courts 676–677 (5th ed. 1994). Whether damages are excessive for the claim-in-suit must be governed by some law. And there is no candidate for that governance other than the law that gives rise to the claim for relief there, the law of New York.

the evidence in the living courtroom context," while appellate judges see only "the cold paper record."

District court applications of the "deviates materially" standard would be subject to appellate review under the standard the Circuits now employ when inadequacy or excessiveness is asserted on appeal: abuse of discretion. In light of *Erie*'s doctrine, the federal appeals court must be guided by the damage-control standard state law supplies, but as the Second Circuit itself has said: "If we reverse, it must be because of an abuse of discretion. . . . The very nature of the problem counsels restraint. . . . We must give the benefit of every doubt to the judgment of the trial judge."

IV

It does not appear that the District Court checked the jury's verdict against the relevant New York decisions demanding more than "industry standard" testimony to support an award of the size the jury returned in this case. * * * Accordingly, we vacate the judgment of the Court of Appeals and instruct that court to remand the case to the District Court so that the trial judge, revisiting his ruling on the new trial motion, may test the jury's verdict against CPLR § 5501(c)'s "deviates materially" standard.

JUSTICE STEVENS, dissenting.

[Justice Stevens explained that he essentially agreed with the Court's *Erie* analysis. Thus, he felt that "[a] state-law ceiling on allowable damages, whether fixed by dollar limit or by a standard that forbids any award that 'deviates materially from what would be reasonable compensation,' is a substantive rule of decision that federal courts must apply in diversity cases governed by New York law." He also concluded that "there is no conceivable conflict between Federal Rule of Civil Procedure 59 and the application of the New York damages limit [since Rule 59's directive] that new trials could be granted 'for any of the reasons for which trials have heretofore been granted in actions at law in courts of the United States' * * *" hardly constitutes a command that federal courts must always substitute federal limits on the size of judgments for those set by the several States." Justice Stevens disagreed, however, on the need to vacate the Second Circuit's decision and remand to the district court for it to apply the New York standard. He felt that the appellate court could do so without violating the Seventh Amendment, and that "there is no reason to suppose that the Court of Appeals has reached a conclusion with which the District Court could permissibly disagree on remand." Accordingly, he would affirm the decision of the Second Circuit.]

JUSTICE SCALIA, with whom the CHIEF JUSTICE and JUSTICE THOMAS join, dissenting.

Today the Court overrules a longstanding and well-reasoned line of precedent that has for years prohibited federal appellate courts from reviewing refusals by district courts to set aside civil jury awards as contrary to the weight of the evidence. [Justice Scalia concludes that such review is not permitted.]

* * *

II

The Court's holding that federal courts of appeals may review district court denials of motions for new trials for error of fact is not the only novel aspect of today's decision. The Court also directs that the case be remanded to the District Court, so that it may "test the jury's verdict against CPLR § 5501(c)'s 'deviates materially' standard." This disposition contradicts the principle that "[t]he proper role of the trial and appellate courts in the federal system in reviewing the size of jury verdicts is . . . a matter of federal law." Donovan v. Penn Shipping Co., 429 U.S. 648, 649 (1977) (per curiam).

The Court acknowledges that state procedural rules cannot, as a general matter, be permitted to interfere with the allocation of functions in the federal court system. Indeed, it is at least partly for this reason that the Court rejects direct application of § 5501(c) at the appellate level as inconsistent with an " 'essential characteristic' " of the federal court system—by which the Court presumably means abuse-of-discretion review of denials of motions for new trials. But the scope of the Court's concern is oddly circumscribed. The "essential characteristic" of the federal jury, and, more specifically, the role of the federal trial court in reviewing jury judgments, apparently counts for little. The Court approves the "accommodat[ion]" achieved by having district courts review jury verdicts under the "deviates materially" standard, because it regards that as a means of giving effect to the state's purposes "without disrupting the federal system." But changing the standard by which trial judges review jury verdicts does disrupt the federal system, and is plainly inconsistent with "the strong federal policy against allowing state rules to disrupt the judge-jury relationship in federal court." Byrd v. Blue Ridge Rural Elec. Co-op., Incorporated, 356 U.S. 525, 538 (1958). The Court's opinion does not even acknowledge, let alone address, this dislocation.

We discussed precisely the point at issue here in Browning-Ferris Industries of Vt., Inc. v. Kelco Disposal, Inc., 492 U.S. 257 (1989), and gave an answer altogether contrary to the one provided today. *Browning-Ferris* rejected a request to fashion a federal common-law rule limiting the size of punitive-damages awards in federal courts, reaffirming the principle of Erie R. Co. v. Tompkins, 304 U.S. 64 (1938), that "[i]n a diversity action, or in any other lawsuit where state law provides the basis of decision, the propriety of an award of punitive damages . . . and the factors the jury may consider in determining their amount, are questions of state law." But the opinion expressly stated that "[f]ederal law . . . will control on those issues involving the proper review of the jury award by a federal district court and court of appeals." "In reviewing an award of punitive damages," it said, "the role of the district court is to determine whether the jury's verdict is within the confines of state law, and to determine, by reference to federal standards developed under Rule 59, whether a new trial or remittitur should be ordered." The same distinction necessarily applies where the judgment under review is for compensatory damages: State substantive law controls what injuries are compensable and in what amount; but federal standards determine whether the award exceeds what is lawful to such degree that it may be set aside by order for new trial or remittitur.

The Court does not disavow those statements in *Browning-Ferris* (indeed, it does not even discuss them), but it presumably overrules them, at least where the state rule that governs "whether a new trial or remittitur should be ordered" is characterized as "substantive" in nature. That, at any rate, is the reason the Court asserts for giving § 5501(c) dispositive effect. The objective of that provision, the Court states, "is manifestly substantive" since it operates to "contro[l] how much a plaintiff can be awarded" by "tightening the range of tolerable awards." Although "less readily classified" as substantive than "a statutory cap on damages," it nonetheless "was designed to provide an analogous control," by making a new trial mandatory when the award "deviat[es] materially" from what is reasonable.

I do not see how this can be so. It seems to me quite wrong to regard this provision as a "substantive" rule for *Erie* purposes. The "analog[y]" to "a statutory cap on damages" fails utterly. There is an absolutely fundamental distinction between a *rule of law* such as that, which would ordinarily be imposed upon the jury in the trial court's instructions, and a *rule of review,* which simply determines how closely the jury verdict will be scrutinized for compliance with the instructions. A tighter standard for reviewing jury determinations can no more plausibly be called a "substantive" disposition than can a tighter appellate standard for reviewing trial-court determinations. The one, like the other, provides additional assurance *that the law has been complied with;* but the other, like the one, *leaves the law unchanged.*

The Court commits the classic *Erie* mistake of regarding whatever changes the outcome as substantive. That is not the only factor to be considered. Outcome-determination "was never intended to serve as a talisman," Hanna v. Plumer, 380 U.S. 460, 466–467 (1965), and does not have the power to convert the most classic elements of the *process* of assuring that the law is observed into the substantive law itself. The right to have a jury make the findings of fact, for example, is generally thought to favor plaintiffs, and that advantage is often thought significant enough to be the basis for forum selection. But no one would argue that *Erie* confers a right to a jury in federal court wherever state courts would provide it; or that, were it not for the Seventh Amendment, *Erie* would require federal courts to dispense with the jury whenever state courts do so.

In any event, the Court exaggerates the difference that the state standard will make. It concludes that different outcomes are likely to ensue depending on whether the law being applied is the state "deviates materially" standard of § 5501(c) or the "shocks the conscience" standard. Of course it is not the federal *appellate* standard but the federal *district-court* standard for granting new trials that must be compared with the New York standard to determine whether substantially different results will obtain—and it is far from clear that the district-court standard *ought* to be "shocks the conscience." Indeed, it is not even clear (as the Court asserts) that "shocks the conscience" is the standard (erroneous or not) actually applied by the district courts of the Second Circuit. The Second Circuit's test for reversing a grant of a new trial for an excessive verdict is whether the award was "clearly within the maximum limit of a reasonable range." [Justice Scalia cited a variety of district court articulations of the standard for review of a verdict for excessiveness.] In sum, it is at least highly questionable whether the consistent outcome differential claimed by the Court even exists. What seems to me far more likely to produce forum-shopping is the consistent difference between the state and federal *appellate* standards, which the Court leaves untouched. Under the Court's disposition, the Second Circuit reviews only for abuse of discretion, whereas New York's appellate courts engage in a *de novo* review for material deviation, giving the defendant a double shot at getting the damages award set aside. The only result that would produce the conformity the Court erroneously believes *Erie* requires is the one adopted by the Second Circuit and rejected by the Court: *de novo* federal appellate review under the § 5501(c) standard.

To say that application of § 5501(c) in place of the federal standard will not consistently produce disparate results is not to suggest that the decision the Court has made today is not a momentous one. The principle that the state standard governs is of great importance, since it bears the potential to destroy the uniformity of federal practice and the integrity of the federal court system. Under the Court's view, a state rule that directed courts "to determine that an award is excessive or inadequate if it deviates *in any degree* from *the proper measure of compensation*" would have to be applied in federal courts, effectively requiring federal judges to determine the amount of damages *de novo,* and effectively taking the matter away from the jury entirely. Or consider a state rule that allowed the defendant a second trial on damages, with judgment ultimately in the amount of the lesser of two jury awards. Under the reasoning of the Court's opinion, even such a rule as that would have to be applied in the federal courts.

The foregoing describes why I think the Court's *Erie* analysis is flawed. But in my view, one does not even reach the *Erie* question in this case. The standard to be applied by a district court in ruling on a motion for a new trial is set forth in Rule 59 of the Federal Rules of Civil Procedure, which provides that "[a] new trial may be granted . . . for any of the reasons for which new trials have heretofore been granted in actions at law *in the courts of the United States"* (emphasis added). That is undeniably a federal standard.[12] Federal district courts in the Second Circuit have interpreted that standard to permit the granting of new trials where "it is quite clear that the jury has reached a seriously erroneous result" and letting the verdict stand would result in a "miscarriage of justice." Assuming (as we have no reason to question) that this is a correct interpretation of what Rule 59 requires, it is undeniable that the federal rule is " 'sufficiently broad' to cause a 'direct collision' with the state law or, implicitly, to 'control the issue' before the court, thereby leaving no room for the operation of that law." Burlington Northern R. Co. v. Woods, 480 U.S. 1, 4–5 (1987). It is simply not possible to give controlling effect both to the federal standard and the state standard in reviewing the jury's award. That being so, the court has no choice but to apply the Federal Rule, which is an exercise of what we have called Congress's "power to regulate matters which, though falling within the uncertain area between substance and procedure, are rationally capable of classification as either," *Hanna,* 380 U.S., at 472.

NOTES AND QUESTIONS

1.   *Postscript:* On remand, the district judge employed the New York standard and granted a much more modest remittitur than the reduction to $100,000 the Second Circuit had endorsed. Gasperini v. Center for Humanities, Inc., 972 F.Supp. 765 (S.D.N.Y.1997). The judge explained his new figure by pointing out that the lost slides were selected from over 5,000 for their relationship with the topics covered in the video. Accordingly, he reasoned that he "should consider what our trial jury considered, namely the actual facts of this case, rather than prior lost photograph cases essentially involving professional libraries which make photographs available without any editorial commitment on the part of the photographer, or any pre-selection except by topic." Notwithstanding the miscellaneous nature of their selection process, he noted, these libraries have pegged the liquidated sum for lost photographs at $1,500 per slide on their printed forms or receipts, which seemed to him some evidence of the value of these items. Against this background, the district judge found strong reasons to set a high value for many of Gasperini's slides:

> Included in the loss are photographs taken by Mr. Gasperini while he was held a hostage of the Contras in the Nicaraguan jungle, and

---

[12]   I agree with the Court's entire progression of reasoning in the footnote 22, leading up to the conclusion that *state* law must determine "[w]hether damages are excessive." But the question of whether damages are excessive is quite separate from the question of when a jury award may be set aside for excessiveness. It is the latter that is governed by Rule 59; as *Browning-Ferris* said, district courts are "to determine, by reference to *federal standards developed under Rule 59,* whether a new trial or remittance should be ordered," 492 U.S. at 279 (emphasis added).

while he was under fire from helicopter gun ships in El Salvador. They include major historical figures at scenes of historical interest and portray the vivid aftermath of war. Most of the photographs represent scenes and images which are impossible to recreate. The jury has a right to consider the superior quality of Mr. Gasperini's work, and the uniqueness of the lost slides as well as the fact that most of them were irreplaceable.

Accordingly, the judge found that all but 70 of the slides could reasonably be valued at $1,500, and that the remaining slides could be valued at $200 per slide, justifying a remittitur of $375,000.

That left the fact that the Court of Appeals had already set the remittitur at $100,000. The judge reasoned that "[w]hile that conclusion must be considered, it is entitled to little weight because the attorneys did not argue the issue of amount, and the exhibits in evidence, which are most critical in evaluating damages, were not even sent to the Court of Appeals, nor were they requested by that Court." When defendant appealed, the Court of Appeals essentially agreed, noting that "[t]he district court was better positioned to review the reasonableness of the jury verdict, and we owe deference to its decision," noting that its earlier decision was based on a "cold paper record," and that the Supreme Court's intervening decision had emphasized that appellate review was limited to determining whether the district judge had committed an abuse of discretion. Gasperini v. Center for Humanities, Inc., 149 F.3d 137, 142 (2d Cir.1998). It did vacate the district judge's decision for "one relatively minor error," including ten slides Gasperini claimed his mother had delivered to defendant but that the jury evidently concluded defendant had not received, and remanded for a recalculation with that mistake removed.

2.   Does *Gasperini* represent a significant shift in analysis of *Erie* issues? Consider the following thoughts:

Gasperini does suggest some changes in what the Supreme Court is saying about approaches to *Erie-Hanna* issues, but the basic framework for analysis that has prevailed since *Hanna* appears very much intact. The two differences of particular note seem to be a degree of emphasis on construing possibly applicable Federal Rules with sensitivity to important state interests to avoid "direct conflicts" with state law when possible, and more centrally the clear preservation of *Byrd* interest analysis in a subset of cases involving judge-made federal procedural rules. As best we may be able to tell on the basis of *Gasperini* itself and subsequent lower-court decisions, the *Hanna* "twin aims" approach remains applicable to such decisional-rule cases—*unless* an "essential characteristic" of the federal judicial system presenting a "countervailing federal interest" is involved.

Rowe, Not Bad for Government Work: Does Anyone Else Think the Supreme Court is Doing a Halfway Decent Job in Its *Erie-Hanna* Jurisprudence?, 73 Notre Dame L. Rev. 963, 1014 (1998).

Do you agree that the Court, in interpreting the Rules of Decision Act, continues to employ *Hanna,* "unless an 'essential characteristic' of the federal judicial system presenting a 'countervailing federal interest' is involved"? If so, is such an approach consistent with the analysis contained in either *Hanna* or *Byrd?* Can the two approaches be reconciled into a single test? See footnote 9 in *Hanna;* cf. McClain v. Owens-Corning Fiberglas Corp., 139 F.3d 1124, 1125 (7th Cir. 1998) (expressing view that *Hanna* overruled *Byrd*). Do you agree with Judge Fletcher's post-*Gasperini* assertion that the *Byrd* and *Hanna* tests "are not mutually exclusive, but rather complementary"? Kohlrautz v. Oilmen Participation Corp., 441 F.3d 827, 831 (9th Cir. 2006). What is the court to do if the two tests dictate different results?

Do you agree with Professor Doernberg's suggestion that though the Court has not explicitly acknowledged the fact, in reality its approach to *Erie* has always involved a balancing of competing state and federal interests? Doernberg, The Unseen Track of *Erie Railroad:* Why History and Jurisprudence Suggest A More Straightforward Form of Analysis, 109 W. Va. L. Rev. 611 (2007). For other discussions of *Gasperini,* see Floyd, *Erie* Awry: A Comment on Gasperini v. Center for Humanities, Inc., 1997 B.Y.U.L. Rev. 267; Freer, Some Thoughts on the State of *Erie* After *Gasperini,* 76 Tex. L. Rev. 1637 (1998); Perdue, The Sources and Scope of Federal Procedural Common Law: Some Reflections on Erie and Gasperini, 46 U. Kan. L. Rev. 751 (1998).

3.   Was the Seventh Amendment the source of the standard for new trial used in federal court? The Court concludes that applying the revised standard adopted by the New York Legislature does not violate the Seventh Amendment. At some point, however, the second clause of that constitutional provision must limit the power of the judge to alter or reject the verdict. Yet the Seventh Amendment would not apply in state court. Thus, although it might prevent a federal judge from applying a state standard that intruded too deeply into the jury's function, it would not explain the use by federal and state judges of the same standard. Did the Court in *Gasperini* deal adequately with the issue of the Seventh Amendment's relevance? Note that where the Constitution controls, conflicting state law is necessarily preempted. See Continental Trend Resources, Inc. v. OXY USA, Inc., 101 F.3d 634 (10th Cir. 1996); Hayes v. Cha, 338 F. Supp.2d 470 (D.N.J. 2004).

4.   Was the Court correct in concluding that Rule 59 did not prescribe the standard to be used by the federal courts? The rule does say that the federal court should use the rules that "heretofore" were established in the federal courts, which does not seem to include a new one adopted by New York State in 1986. Here is the explanation offered by Dean Charles Clark, who acted as Reporter of the committee that drafted the Federal Rules of Civil Procedure, at a program designed to introduce the new rules to lawyers:

> We first thought we might try to state in detail, categorically, all the reasons for new trials, but if you are familiar with the subject you know that the annotations to the federal statutes dealing with those subjects cover pages and pages. It therefore did not seem practical to attempt to state the grounds, so we listed them generally.

Proceedings of the Institute on Federal Rules 324 (1938).

Some lower courts have suggested that a distinct federal standard does exist. Thus, in Atlas Food Systems and Services, Inc. v. Crane National Vendors, 99 F.3d 587, 595 (4th Cir.1996), the court concluded that "while a jury is authorized to award punitive damages on a framework of liability and the factors supplied by state law, the judgment a jury makes as to the *amount* is reviewable by federal trial courts under Federal Rule of Civil Procedure 59 less deferentially than are factual findings which may be measured against the factual record." (emphasis in original) The court did not cite *Gasperini,* and it certainly did not seem to believe that its starting point in making this determination to be state law. See also Tormenia v. First Investors Realty Co., Inc., 251 F.3d 128, 138 (3d.Cir.2000) (employing federal "shock the conscience" standard in diversity case); Miksis v. Howard, 106 F.3d 754, 764 (7th Cir.1997) ("We use federal standards to determine excessiveness of verdicts in diversity cases").

Does Rule 59 provide sufficient detail to displace pertinent state law? Compare the Court's conclusion in Stewart Organizations, Inc. v. Ricoh Corp., supra p. 1002, that 28 U.S.C.A. § 1404(a) displaced a state-law rule denying effect to a forum selection clause in a contract because Congress intended a "flexible and multifaceted analysis" to govern transfer that would be upset were state law to apply.

5.   Does the Court hold that the standard for ruling on a new trial motion is generally derived from the law of the state that provides the substantive law used to decide the case? How should a federal court in New York handle a motion for a new trial in a case governed by Connecticut law? This could easily happen under *Klaxon,* supra p. 981, if New York choice of law rules would direct the application of Connecticut law. But a New York court might well treat the standard for granting a new trial as "procedural" within the meaning of its choice of law rules, and therefore subject to New York law, since procedural matters are usually governed by the forum's law. Should a federal court therefore apply the New York standard because a New York court would?

6.   If Rule 59 generally does prescribe some federally-controlled standard for granting new trials, is there a reason why it should not apply in *Gasperini?* Perhaps Rule 59 should be interpreted narrowly to avoid a conflict with the substantive impulse of the New York Legislature. In footnote 7, the Court points out that the Federal Rules have been "interpreted with sensitivity to important state interests and regulatory policies," citing Walker v. Armco Steel Corp., supra p. 1011. But note what the Court had said in a footnote in *Walker:*

> This is not to suggest that the Federal Rules of Civil Procedure are to be narrowly construed in order to avoid a "direct collision" with state law. The Federal Rules should be given their plain meaning. If a direct collision with state law arises from that plain meaning, then the analysis developed in Hanna v. Plumer applies.

446 U.S. at 750 n. 9. Note that the Court, in note 7, asserts that "[f]ederal courts have interpreted the Federal Rules . . . with sensitivity to important state interests and regulatory policies." Is this a wise approach? What about the interest in the uniform reach of the Federal Rules? For criticism of the Court's approach, see Dudley & Rutherglen, Deforming the Federal Rules: An Essay on What's Wrong with the Recent *Erie* Decisions, 92 Va. L. Rev. 707, 748 (2006) (noting that "[w]hile this concern is legitimate . . . it compromises the entire federal court system when the Court overreacts and distorts the Federal Rules to accommodate state law.").

The Court also cites S.A. Healy Co. v. Milwaukee Metropolitan Sewerage Dist., 60 F.3d 305 (7th Cir.1995), cert. denied, 516 U.S. 1010 (1995), as exemplifying the correct "sensitivity." Plaintiff there sought to recover double its taxable costs plus prejudgment interest on them because it had made an offer of judgment to defendant but defendant had not accepted it, and plaintiff had then obtained a judgment superior to the offer. A Wisconsin statute authorized such consequences for offers by plaintiffs, but Rule 68 does not. The court found "no direct conflict" between the state statute and Rule 68 because the federal rule is limited to offers by defendants. Could the decision by the federal rulemakers *not* to give the same consequences to offers by plaintiffs come into play here? (In this connection, is it worth noting that there were formal proposals in the mid-1980s to amend Rule 68 to make it applicable to offers by plaintiffs, but that these were not adopted?) Judge Posner concluded that "there is no inconsistency when a plaintiff's demand rather than a defendant's offer is in issue."

Finding no direct conflict, the court in *Healy* returned to "first principles," and asked whether the state-law rule is "so likely to dictate outcomes that it will cause a lot of forum shopping" and whether it is "so entwined with procedures prescribed by the federal rules that it is likely to impair the integrity of federal procedure if it is applied in diversity cases?" Finding that defendants would have an added incentive to remove were a rule so favorable to plaintiffs not applicable in federal court, and that the application of the Wisconsin statute would not "tread on the toes of Rule 68" (as it would had defendant made an offer of judgment and invoked the state provision), the court applied the state statute.

Even assuming the propriety of construing the Federal Rules narrowly to avoid a conflict with state law, is Justice Scalia nevertheless correct that state law here inescapably conflicts with Rule 59?

Since *Gasperini,* lower courts have on occasion struggled with the task of determining whether a Federal Rule of Civil Procedure actually controls a particular issue. See Cohen v. Office Depot, Inc., 184 F.3d 1292 (11th Cir. 1999) (Rule 8(a)(3), concerning the pleading of remedies, precludes use of state statute requiring leave of court to include prayer for punitive damages); Vaught v. Showa Denko K.K., 107 F.3d 1137 (5th Cir. 1997) (Rule 23 does not concern tolling of statute of limitations); Senger Brothers Nursery, Inc. v. E.I. Dupont De Nemours & Co., 184 F.R.D. 674 (M.D.Fla.1999) (Rule 23, concerning class actions, does not conflict with state statute of limitations). See also Goldberg v. Pacific Indemnity Co., 627 F.3d 752, 756–57 (9th Cir. 2010) (determining the existence of a conflict between state law and a Federal Rule of Civil Procedure by inquiring whether the purpose of the state procedure and the purpose of the Federal Rule are "sufficiently coextensive" to establish that the Federal Rule occupies the state rule's "field of operation.").

On the question of whether state practice conflicts with a Federal Rule of Civil Procedure, consider the debate between Justices Scalia and Ginsburg in Shady Grove Orthopedic Associates, P.A. v. Allstate Ins. Co., 559 U.S. 393 (2010) (discussed supra p. 1009 n. 7). A New York State law, § 901(b) of the New York Civil Practice Law, precludes a class action in state court to recover a "penalty," such as statutory interest. Shady Grove sued Allstate in federal court, on the basis of diversity of citizenship, seeking certification of a class action pursuant to Federal Rule of Civil Procedure 23. Justice Scalia, writing for a majority, found a direct conflict between New York's § 901(b) and Rule 23, and therefore held that whether the state law was to be applied in a diversity suit was controlled by the terms of the Rules Enabling Act. Speaking for four justices, Justice Ginsburg dissented. She acknowledged that "[i]f a Federal Rule controls an issue and directly conflicts with state law, the Rule, so long as it is consonant with the Rules Enabling Act, applies in diversity suits." But she noted that if "no Federal Rule or statute governs the issue, the Rules of Decision Act, as interpreted in *Erie*, controls." She found no conflict between Rule 23 and New York's § 901(b), and therefore applied the forum shopping test of the Rules of Decision Act adopted in *Hanna*, rather than the tests of the Rules Enabling Act, and found that § 901(b) barred a federal class action suit. She criticized the Court for "read[ing] rule 23 relentlessly to override New York's restriction on the availability of statutory damages" and noted that previous decisions "caution us to ask, before undermining state legislation: Is this conflict really necessary?"

Rule 23 authorizes certification of a class action when all of the four requirements of Rule 23(a) and the requirements of at least one of the three categories in Rule 23(b) are satisfied. No mention is made on the rule's face of exceptions for cases in which state law would categorically deny class treatment. Is Justice Ginsburg correct in finding no conflict between the New York statue precluding class actions in suits for penalties on the one hand and Rule 23 on the other? Note that New York's substantive law did not prohibit *individual* suits for interest or penalty damages, only class suits seeking such relief.

In finding a direct conflict between Rule 23 and § 901(b), Justice Scalia rejected Allstate's argument that Rule 23 neither explicitly nor implicitly empowers a federal court "to certify a class in each and every case" where the rule's criteria are met: "[T]hat is *exactly* what Rule 23 does." While the rule provides that if the certification criteria are met "[a] class action may be maintained, " Justice Scalia noted that "[t]he discretion suggested by Rule 23's 'may' is discretion residing in the plaintiff: He may bring his claim in a class action if he wishes."

For a post-*Shady Grove* discussion of the issue, see Garman v. Campbell County School Dist. No. 1, 630 F. 3d 977 (10th Cir. 2010) (Rule 8(a) precludes application of Wyoming pleading standard).

7.   If Rule 59 does prescribe a standard for granting new trials, is there any justification under Burlington Northern Railroad Co. v. Woods, supra, p. 1004, for refusing to apply it in *Gasperini?* Does § 5501(c) create a "substantive right" which the federal rule may not alter pursuant to 28 U.S.C.A. § 2072(b)?

8.   C.P.L.R. § 5501(c) governs determinations whether the verdict is inadequate as well as whether the verdict is excessive. If the New York Legislature directs that judges should use additur if the jury returns an inadequate verdict, should federal courts do the same? Recall Dimick v. Schiedt, supra p. 669.

B. DETERMINING STATE LAW

MASON V. AMERICAN EMERY WHEEL WORKS

United States Court of Appeals, First Circuit, 1957
241 F.2d 906

Before MAGRUDER, CHIEF JUDGE, and WOODBURY and HARTIGAN, CIRCUIT JUDGES.

MAGRUDER, CHIEF JUDGE.

[While at work in Mississippi, plaintiff was injured by an emery wheel manufactured by defendant, a Rhode Island corporation. Plaintiff sued in federal court in Rhode Island, alleging that the emery wheel was unreasonably dangerous. In its answer, defendant raised lack of privity. When evidence at trial showed that the emery wheel had passed through several owners before it was sold to plaintiff's employer, the trial court granted defendant's motion to dismiss on the ground that Mississippi still required privity to sue a manufacturer for such injuries.]

Since the injury was inflicted in Mississippi, the district court, no doubt correctly under now familiar authorities, deemed itself to be obliged to apply the Mississippi local law to determine the tort liability, if any, of a manufacturer to one not in privity of contract with him. The district court came to the conclusion "reluctantly" that it was bound by the Mississippi law as declared in Ford Motor Co. v. Myers, 1928, 151 Miss. 73, 117 So. 362; that the "harsh rule" of Mississippi as so declared, "contrary to the great weight of authority" elsewhere, was that a manufacturer was not liable for negligence in the manufacture of appliances which could and would become highly dangerous when put to the uses for which they are intended, where there is no privity of contract between the user and the manufacturer.

Ford Motor Co. v. Myers was the only Mississippi case relied upon, or even referred to, by the district court. In that case the Supreme Court of

Mississippi, in a half-page opinion, did in fact apply what was at one time the prevailing rule, in holding that Ford Motor Company as the manufacturer of a truck owed no duty of care to a remote subvendee of the truck who was injured when the truck collapsed and plunged into a ditch because of a defect which could have been detected by reasonable inspection by the manufacturer before the vehicle left the factory.

At a time when the federal courts were applying their own notions of the federal common law of torts, under Swift v. Tyson, the court in Huset v. J.I. Case Threshing Machine Co., 8 Cir., 1903, 120 F. 865, 868, 61 L.R.A. 303, declared as a general rule that "a contractor, manufacturer, or vendor is not liable to third parties who have no contractual relations with him for negligence in the construction, manufacture, or sale of the articles he handles." At this late date it is hardly necessary to spend much time on the merit or justification for that supposed general rule. * * *

MacPherson v. Buick Motor Co., [217 N.Y. 382, 111 N.E. 1050 (1916)] started a new trend in this particular field of the law, and its substantive result has found favor in § 395 of the American Law Institute Restatement of Torts. If the Supreme Court of Mississippi had recently reconsidered the rule it applied in Ford Motor Co. v. Myers, and had decided to adhere to it on the ground of stare decisis, no doubt the federal courts would have had to accept the local law as so declared. But it would be gratuitous and unwarranted to assume that the Supreme Court of Mississippi would now so hold, when we bear in mind the readiness of other courts, in conservative jurisdictions at that, to overrule their earlier holdings and to bring their jurisprudence into accord with what is now the overwhelming weight of authority. * * *

Of course it is not necessary that a case be explicitly overruled in order to lose its persuasive force as an indication of what the law is. A decision may become so overloaded with illogical exceptions that by erosion of time it may lose its persuasive or binding force even in the inferior courts of the same jurisdiction. And where, as in Ford Motor Co. v. Myers, the Supreme Court of Mississippi, twenty or thirty years ago, applied an old rule which has since been generally discredited elsewhere, it is relevant to consider what the Supreme Court of Mississippi has subsequently said on the point. We think that appellant herein rightly stresses the importance of E.I. Du Pont De Nemours & Co. v. Ladner, 1954, 221 Miss. 378, 73 So.2d 249. In that very recent case, the Supreme Court of Mississippi was able to dispose of the particular issue on another ground without the necessity of expressly overruling its earlier decision in Ford Motor Co. v. Myers. But the court did take occasion, in a long and careful opinion, to indicate its awareness of the modern trend in the area * * *; it stated that, whatever may have been the rule originally, "the principle seems now to be well established by the decisions of many courts that a person who has had no direct contractual relations with a manufacturer may nevertheless recover from such manufacturer for damages to property caused by the negligence of the manufacturer in the same manner that such a remote vendee or other third person can recover for personal injuries." And it quoted, with apparent approval, many more recent authorities in support of the "modern doctrine". We think it is fair to infer from this latest expression by the Supreme Court of Mississippi that it is prepared to reconsider and revise the rule it applied in Ford Motor Co. v. Myers whenever it may have before it a case that squarely presents the issue. We have no doubt that when this occasion does come to pass, the Supreme Court of Mississippi will declare itself in agreement with the more enlightened and generally accepted modern doctrine.

A judgment will be entered vacating the order of the District Court, dismissing the complaint and remanding the case to the District Court for further proceedings not inconsistent with this opinion.

HARTIGAN, CIRCUIT JUDGE (concurring).

I concur in the opinion of the court but I am constrained to comment briefly. We were informed in oral argument by counsel for the appellee that the district court in deciding this case had before it both the *Ford* and the *Du Pont* decisions. Moreover, the district court knew from the official Mississippi report that the *MacPherson* case, then approximately twelve years old, had been considered and rejected by the Mississippi Supreme Court sitting in the *Ford* case. Therefore, "reluctantly" Judge Day adopted the *Ford* holding since it, as the only binding and conclusive statement of Mississippi law on the issue, had not been expressly modified or overruled. * * *

We, however, have inferred from pure dicta in the *Du Pont* case and from the status of the law elsewhere on this issue that Mississippi is prepared to discard the *Ford* rule and adopt the modern rule. I believe this is a sound inference since the dicta in the *Du Pont* case, though not expressly mentioning *Ford,* is sufficiently clear and the *Ford* rule is sufficiently outdated. Yet, in doing so I realize that we present a difficult problem for district judges when they must apply the *Erie* doctrine to situations wherein the considerations as between conflicting holdings and dicta are not as clearly defined as they are here. The question of how clear dicta must be to prevail over a prior controlling decision does not lend itself to easy solution.

NOTES AND QUESTIONS

1.   Why was a federal court in Rhode Island applying the law of Mississippi in this case?

2.   If you were a practicing attorney in Mississippi in 1954 (when the accident in *Mason* occurred), and a client asked you to describe the state's law on the requirement of privity in tort cases, what would you have said?

3.   In deciding what the state law is, should a federal court, in a diversity case, deem itself bound by state lower-court decisions where there is no applicable state supreme court decision? Might such a practice lead to a type of reverse forum-shopping? Could the same be said of reliance on antiquated state supreme court decisions? In Commissioner v. Estate of Bosch, 387 U.S. 456, 465 (1967), in a context not directly involving *Erie,* the Court stated that "the State's highest court is the best authority on its own law. If there be no decision by that court then federal authorities must apply what they find to be the state law after giving 'proper regard' to relevant rulings of other courts of the State. In this respect, it may be said to be, in effect, sitting as a state court." According to Judge Jerome Frank, the test should be: "What would be the decision of reasonably intelligent lawyers, sitting as judges of the highest [state] court, and fully conversant with state 'jurisprudence?'" Cooper v. American Airlines, Inc., 149 F.2d 355, 359 (2d Cir.1945). See also Valley Forge Insurance Co. v. Jefferson, 628 F.Supp. 502, 510 (D.Del.1986): "Where a state's highest court has not spoken, a federal court sitting in diversity has a duty to decide a case as it believes the state's highest court would have done." One court of appeals concluded that the proper approach to determine state common law in the absence of an applicable decision of the state supreme court was to look "to other sources: (1) lower state court decisions and Supreme Court dicta, (2) the lower court ruling in this case, (3) the general rule on the issue, (4) the rule in other states looked to by [the state's] courts, and (5) other available legal sources, such as treatises and law review commentaries." Nicolson v. Life Insurance Co. of the Southwest, 783 F.2d 1316, 1319 (5th Cir.1986). Federal courts have often emphasized, however, that in making this determination their function is not to adopt the rule that it would choose for itself, but rather to adopt the rule that the federal court believes the state court itself would adopt. See, e.g., Nichols v. Anderson, 837 F.2d 1372, 1375 (5th Cir.1988). See generally C. Wright & M. Kane, Law of Federal Courts § 58 (7th ed. 2011).

Note that one source considered by the court in *Mason* is the Restatement of Torts. Does the pertinence of that source depend on a decision by Mississippi to be bound by decisions of the American Law Institute, which promulgates Restatements? Consider Title I, § 4 of the Virgin Islands Code:

> The rules of the common law, as expressed in the restatements of the law approved by the American Law Institute, and to the extent not so expressed, as generally understood and applied in the United States, shall be the rules of decision of the courts of the Virgin Islands in cases to which they apply, in the absence of local laws to the contrary.

4.   After *Mason,* the Fifth Circuit held that privity was not a bar under Mississippi law. Grey v. Hayes-Sammons Chemical Co., 310 F.2d 291 (5th Cir.1962). Ultimately, the Mississippi Supreme Court overruled *Ford Motor Co.* and rejected the privity requirement. State Stove Mfg. Co. v. Hodges, 189 So.2d 113 (Miss.1966), cert. denied sub nom. Yates v. Hodges, 386 U.S. 912 (1967). Does this mean the *Mason* court was right?

5.   In Clark, Ascertaining the Laws of the Several States: Positivism and Judicial Federalism After *Erie,* 145 U.Pa.L.Rev. 1459 (1997), the author reasons that "a federal court's 'prediction' of state law frequently devolves into little more than a choice among competing policy considerations. No matter how pure a federal court's intentions may be, legal indeterminacy necessarily requires courts to exercise some degree of policymaking discretion." Id. at 1499. As an example of particularly problematical activity by federal judges, he cites *Mason,* noting that "for nine years (from 1957 to 1966), federal courts recognized and applied 'substantive rules of common law' that Mississippi had yet to adopt (and might have never adopted)." Id. at 1515.

6.   In Salve Regina College v. Russell, 499 U.S. 225 (1991), the Supreme Court considered the question "whether a federal court of appeals may review a district court's determination of state law under a standard less probing than that applied to a determination of federal law." Most courts of appeals had adopted a policy of deferring to district court interpretations of state law if the district judge was interpreting the law of the state in which he sat. See, e.g., Norton v. St. Paul Fire & Marine Ins. Co., 902 F.2d 1355, 1357 (8th Cir.1990). In an opinion by Justice Blackmun, the Supreme Court decided that this rule of deference was improper:

> Independent appellate review of legal issues best serves the dual goals of doctrinal coherence and economy of judicial administration. District judges preside alone over fast-paced trials: of necessity they devote much of their energy and resources to hearing witnesses and reviewing evidence. Similarly, the logistical burdens of trial advocacy limit the extent to which trial counsel is able to supplement the district judge's legal research with memoranda and briefs. Thus, trial judges often must resolve complicated legal questions without benefit of "extended reflection [or] extensive information."
>
> Courts of appeals, on the other hand, are structurally suited to the collaborative judicial process that promotes decisional accuracy. With the record having been constructed below and settled for purposes of the appeal, appellate judges are able to devote their primary attention to legal issues.
>
> * * *
>
> Independent appellate review necessarily entails a careful consideration of the district court's legal analysis, and an efficient and sensitive appellate court at least will naturally consider this analysis in undertaking its review. * * * Any expertise possessed by the district court will inform the structure and content of its conclusions of law and thereby become evident to the reviewing court. * * * Independent review, however, does not admit of unreflective reliance on a lower court's inarticulable intuitions.

The Court also concluded that "appellate deference to the district court's determination of state law is inconsistent with the principles underlying this Court's decision in *Erie,*" 499 U.S. at 233, because "deferential appellate review invites divergent development of state law among the federal trial courts even within a single state. Moreover, by denying a litigant access to meaningful review of state-law claims, appellate courts that defer to the district courts' state-law determinations create a dual system of enforcement of state-created rights, in which the substantive rule applied to a dispute may depend on the choice of forum." Id. at 234

Chief Justice Rehnquist, joined by Justices White and Stevens, dissented: "A district court's insights are particularly valuable to an appellate court in a case such as this where the state law is unsettled." Id. at 241. Consider the strength of this argument if the district judge had served on the state supreme court before appointment to the federal bench.

7.   In Yohannon v. Keene Corp., 924 F.2d 1255 (3d Cir.1991), the Third Circuit expressed the exasperation probably often felt by federal courts in attempting to discern unclear state law:

> Since [state supreme] courts often do not speak clearly or precisely to the issue in question, a federal court sitting in diversity must often take on the mantle of the soothsayers of old and predict what the supreme court of a particular state would do if it were presented with the issue that controls the case before the federal court. Such contemporary predictions are just as chancy a business as the divination of dreams that heathen kings of ancient biblical lands so often called upon their counselors to interpret in the stories of the Old Testament. Like them, in taking on the task, we hope that our prophecy will find favor in the eyes of the authority that may one day brand it true or false.

The growing popularity of unpublished opinions can make the task of determining state law even more difficult. For example, in Exxon Co. v. Banque De Paris Et Des Pays-Bas, 889 F.2d 674 (5th Cir.1989), an action on a letter of credit, the Fifth Circuit initially decided that the obligation to pay had been terminated even though the expiration date had not been reached. Five weeks after this decision, a state intermediate appellate court rendered an unreported opinion, adopting a different view of state law. On petition for rehearing, the Fifth Circuit refused to consider this decision because under Texas law an unreported opinion may not be cited as precedent. Meanwhile, the Texas Supreme Court denied a motion to publish the appellate court decision, but the state appellate court that had rendered the decision granted a similar motion and published the decision.

The Supreme Court then vacated the Fifth Circuit's judgment and remanded for reconsideration in light of the now-published state court decision. Uncertain about what the Texas Supreme Court's refusal to order the lower court opinion published meant about its attitude toward the decision itself, the Fifth Circuit certified the question to the Texas Supreme Court, which declined to answer the certified question on the ground that the answer depended on unresolved issues of fact. Thus rebuffed, the Fifth Circuit concluded that the state appellate court opinion should be followed and that it dictated a different result.

8.   *Certification:* When a state so authorizes by statute, court rule, or constitution, a federal court may refer uncertain or unsettled questions of state law to the state's highest court for decision. Under this procedure, the case itself remains in federal court. The procedure is discretionary with the federal court. "Most state high courts now offer federal courts faced with questions of state law * * * the opportunity to 'certify' those questions of state law to the state high court." Nash, Evaluating the Power of Federal Courts to Certify Questions of State Law, 88 Cornell L. Rev. 1672, 1674 (2003). Some federal courts are enthusiastic about using this opportunity: "Where there is any doubt as to the application of state law, a federal court should certify the question to the state supreme court to avoid making unnecessary Erie 'guesses' and to offer the state court the opportunity interpret or change existing law." Mosher v. Speedstar Div. of AMCA Int'l, Inc., 52 F.3d 913, 916–17 (11th Cir. 1995). The use of certification in diversity cases is somewhat controversial. See, e.g., Mattis, Certification of Questions of State Law: An Impractical Tool in the Hands of the Federal Courts, 23 U.Miami L.Rev. 717 (1969). Why might this be so?

C. THE "CONVERSE-*ERIE*" PROBLEM

DICE V. AKRON, CANTON & YOUNGSTOWN R.R.
Supreme Court of the United States, 1952
342 U.S. 359

Opinion of the Court by JUSTICE BLACK, announced by JUSTICE DOUGLAS.

Petitioner, a railroad fireman, was seriously injured when an engine in which he was riding jumped the track. Alleging that his injuries were due to respondent's negligence, he brought this action for damages under the Federal Employers' Liability Act, 35 Stat. 65, 45 U.S.C. § 51 et seq., in an Ohio court of common pleas. Respondent's defenses were (1) a denial of negligence and (2) a written document signed by petitioner purporting to release respondent in full for $924.63. Petitioner admitted that he had signed several receipts for payments made him in connection with his injuries but denied that he had made a full and complete settlement of all his claims. He alleged that the purported release was void because he had signed it relying on respondent's deliberately false statement that the document was nothing more than a mere receipt for back wages.

After both parties had introduced considerable evidence the jury found in favor of petitioner and awarded him a $25,000 verdict. The trial judge later entered judgment notwithstanding the verdict. In doing so he reappraised the evidence as to fraud, found that petitioner had been "guilty of supine negligence" in failing to read the release, and accordingly held that the facts did not "sustain either in law or equity the allegations of fraud by clear, unequivocal and convincing evidence." This judgment notwithstanding the verdict was reversed by the Court of Appeals of Summit County, Ohio, on the ground that under federal law, which controlled, the jury's verdict must stand because there was ample evidence to support its finding of fraud. The Ohio Supreme Court, one judge dissenting, reversed the Court of Appeals' judgment and sustained the trial court's action, holding that: (1) Ohio, not federal, law governed; (2) under that law petitioner, a man of ordinary intelligence who could read, was bound by the release even though he had been induced to sign it by the deliberately false statement that it was only a receipt for back wages; and (3) under controlling Ohio law factual issues as to fraud in the execution of this release were properly decided by the judge rather than by the jury. We granted certiorari because the decision of the Supreme Court of Ohio appeared to deviate from previous decisions of this Court that federal law governs cases arising under the Federal Employers' Liability Act.

First. We agree with the Court of Appeals of Summit County, Ohio, and the dissenting judge in the Ohio Supreme Court and hold that validity of releases under the Federal Employers' Liability Act raises a federal question to be determined by federal rather than state law. Congress in § 1 of the Act granted petitioner a right to recover against his employer for damages negligently inflicted. State laws are not controlling in determining what the incidents of this federal right shall be. Manifestly the federal rights affording relief to injured railroad employees under a federally declared standard could be defeated if states were permitted to have the final say as to what defenses could and could not be properly interposed to suits under the Act. Moreover, only if federal law controls can the federal Act be given that uniform application throughout the country essential to effectuate its purposes. Releases and other devices designed to liquidate or defeat injured employees' claims play an important part in the federal Act's administration. Their validity is but one of the many interrelated questions that must constantly be determined in these cases according to a uniform federal law.

Second. In effect the Supreme Court of Ohio held that an employee trusts his employer at his peril, and that the negligence of an innocent worker is sufficient to enable his employer to benefit by its deliberate fraud. Application of so harsh a rule to defeat a railroad employee's claim is wholly incongruous with the general policy of the Act to give railroad employees a right to recover just compensation for injuries negligently inflicted by their employers. And this Ohio rule is out of harmony with modern judicial and legislative practice to relieve injured persons from the effect of releases fraudulently obtained. We hold that the correct federal rule is that announced by the Court of Appeals of Summit County, Ohio, and the dissenting judge in the Ohio Supreme Court—a release of rights under the Act is void when the employee is induced to sign it by the deliberately false and material statements of the railroad's authorized representatives made to deceive the employee as to the contents of the release. The trial court's charge to the jury correctly stated this rule of law.

Third. Ohio provides and has here accorded petitioner the usual jury trial of factual issues relating to negligence. But Ohio treats factual questions of fraudulent releases differently. It permits the judge trying a negligence case to resolve all factual questions of fraud "other than fraud in the factum." The factual issue of fraud is thus split into fragments, some to be determined by the judge, others by the jury.

It is contended that since a state may consistently with the Federal Constitution provide for trial of cases under the Act by a nonunanimous verdict, Minneapolis & St. Louis R. Co. v. Bombolis, 241 U.S. 211, Ohio may lawfully eliminate trial by jury as to one phase of fraud while allowing jury trial as to all other issues raised. The *Bombolis* case might be more in point had Ohio abolished trial by jury in all negligence cases including those arising under the federal Act. But Ohio has not done this. It has provided jury trials for cases arising under the federal Act but seeks to single out one phase of the question of fraudulent releases for determination by a judge rather than by a jury.

We have previously held that "The right to trial by jury is 'a basic and fundamental feature of our system of federal jurisprudence'" and that it is "part and parcel of the remedy afforded railroad workers under the Employers' Liability Act." Bailey v. Central Vermont R. Co., 319 U.S. 350, 354. We also recognized in that case that to deprive railroad workers of the benefit of a jury trial where there is evidence to support negligence "is to take away a goodly portion of the relief which Congress has afforded them." It follows that the right to trial by jury is too substantial a part of the rights accorded by the Act to permit it to be classified as a mere "local rule of procedure" for denial in the manner that Ohio has here used. Brown v. Western R. Co., 338 U.S. 294.

The trial judge and the Ohio Supreme Court erred in holding that petitioner's rights were to be determined by Ohio law and in taking away petitioner's verdict when the issues of fraud had been submitted to the jury on conflicting evidence and determined in petitioner's favor. The judgment of the Court of Appeals of Summit County, Ohio, was correct and should not have been reversed by the Supreme Court of Ohio. The cause is reversed and remanded to the Supreme Court of Ohio for further action not inconsistent with this opinion.

JUSTICE FRANKFURTER, whom JUSTICE REED, JUSTICE JACKSON and JUSTICE BURTON join, concurring for reversal but dissenting from the Court's opinion.

Ohio, as do many other States, maintains the old division between law and equity as to the mode of trying issues, even though the same judge administers both. The Ohio Supreme Court has told us what, on one issue, is the division of functions in all negligence actions brought in the Ohio courts: "Where it is claimed that a release was induced by fraud (other than fraud in the factum) or by mistake, it is . . . necessary, before seeking to enforce a cause of action which such release purports to bar, that equitable relief from the release be secured." Thus, in all cases in Ohio, the judge is the trier of fact on this issue of fraud, rather than the jury. It is contended that the Federal Employers' Liability Act requires that Ohio courts send the fraud issue to a jury in the cases founded on that Act. To require Ohio to try a particular issue before a different fact-finder in negligence actions brought under the Employers' Liability Act from the fact-finder on the identical issue in every other negligence case disregards the settled distribution of judicial power between Federal and State courts where Congress authorizes concurrent enforcement of federally-created rights.

It has been settled ever since the Second Employers' Liability Cases (Mondou v. New York, N.H. & H.R. Co., 223 U.S. 1), that no State which gives its courts jurisdiction over common law actions for negligence may deny access to its courts for a negligence action founded on the Federal Employers' Liability Act. Nor may a State discriminate disadvantageously against actions for negligence under the Federal Act as compared with local causes of action in negligence. Conversely, however, simply because there is concurrent jurisdiction in Federal and State courts over actions under the Employers' Liability Act, a State is under no duty to treat actions arising under that Act differently from the way it adjudicates local actions for negligence, so far as the mechanics of litigation, the forms in which law is administered, are concerned. This surely covers the distribution of functions as between judge and jury in the determination of the issues in a negligence case.

In 1916 the Court decided without dissent that States in entertaining actions under the Federal Employers' Liability Act need not provide a jury system other than that established for local negligence actions. States are not compelled to provide the jury required of Federal courts by the Seventh Amendment. Minneapolis & St. L.R. Co. v. Bombolis, 241 U.S. 211. In the thirty-six years since this early decision after the enactment of the Federal Employers' Liability Act, 35 Stat. 65 (1908), the *Bombolis* case has often been cited by this Court but never questioned. Until today its significance has been to leave to States the choice of the fact-finding tribunal in all negligence actions, including those arising under the Federal Act. * * *

Although a State must entertain negligence suits brought under the Federal Employers' Liability Act if it entertains ordinary actions for negligence, it need conduct them only in the way in which it conducts the run of negligence litigation. The *Bombolis* case directly establishes that the Employers' Liability Act does not impose the jury requirements of the Seventh Amendment on the States pro tanto for Employers' Liability litigation. If its reasoning means anything, the *Bombolis* decision means that, if a State chooses not to have a jury at all, but to leave questions of fact in all negligence actions to a court, certainly the Employers' Liability Act does not require a State to have juries for negligence actions brought under the Federal Act in its courts. Or, if a State chooses to retain the old double system of courts, common law and equity—as did a good many States until the other day, and as four States still do—surely there is nothing in the Employers' Liability Act that requires traditional distribution of authority for disposing of legal issues as between common law and chancery courts to go by the board. And, if States are free to make a distribution of functions between equity and common law courts, it surely makes no rational difference whether a State chooses to provide that the same judge preside on both the common law and the chancery sides in a single litigation, instead of in separate rooms in the same building. So long as all negligence suits in a State are treated in the same way, by the same mode of disposing equitable, non-jury, and common law, jury issues, the State does not discriminate against Employers' Liability suits nor does it make any inroad upon substance.

Ohio and her sister States with a similar division of functions between law and equity are not trying to evade their duty under the Federal Employers' Liability Act; nor are they trying to make it more difficult for railroad workers to recover, than for those suing under local law. The States merely exercise a preference in adhering to historic ways of dealing with a claim of fraud; they prefer the traditional way of making unavailable through equity an otherwise valid defense. The State judges and local lawyers who must administer the Federal Employers' Liability Act in State courts are trained in the ways of local practice; it multiplies the difficulties and confuses the administration of justice to require, on purely theoretical grounds, a hybrid of State and Federal practice in the State courts as to a single class of cases. Nothing in the Employers' Liability Act or in the judicial enforcement of the Act for over forty years forces such judicial hybridization upon the States. The fact that Congress authorized actions under the Federal Employers' Liability Act to be brought in State as well as in Federal courts seems a strange basis for the inference that Congress overrode State procedural arrangements controlling all other negligence suits in a State, by imposing upon State courts to which plaintiffs choose to go the rules prevailing in the Federal courts regarding juries. Such an inference is admissible, so it seems to me, only on the theory that Congress included as part of the right created by the Employers' Liability Act an assumed likelihood that trying all issues to juries is more favorable to plaintiffs. At least, if a plaintiff's right to have all issues decided by a jury rather than the court is "part and parcel of the remedy afforded railroad workers under the Employers Liability Act," the *Bombolis* case should be overruled explicitly instead of left as a derelict bound to occasion collisions on the waters of the law. We have put the questions squarely because they seem to be precisely what will be roused in the minds of lawyers properly pressing their clients' interests and in the minds of trial and appellate judges called upon to apply this Court's opinion.

Even though the method of trying the equitable issue of fraud which the State applies in all other negligence cases governs Employers' Liability cases, two questions remain for decision: Should the validity of the release be tested by a Federal or a State standard? And if by a Federal one, did the Ohio courts in the present case correctly administer the standard? If the States afford courts for enforcing the Federal Act, they must enforce the substance of the right given by Congress. They cannot depreciate the legislative currency issued by Congress—either expressly or by local methods of enforcement that accomplish the same result. In order to prevent diminution of railroad workers' nationally-uniform right to recover, the standard for the validity of a release of contested liability must be Federal. * * * The admitted fact that the injured worker signed the release is material in tending to show the release to be valid, but presumptions must not be drawn from that fact so as to hobble the plaintiff's showing that it would be unjust to allow a formally good defense to prevail.

The judgment of the Ohio Supreme Court must be reversed for it applied the State rule as to validity of releases, and it is not for us to interpret Ohio decisions in order to be assured that on a matter of substance the State and Federal criteria coincide. Moreover, we cannot say with confidence that the Ohio trial judge applied the Federal standard correctly. * * *

NOTES AND QUESTIONS

1. In what sense is *Dice* a "converse-*Erie*" case? The doctrine is also referred to as "reverse *Erie*." See Clermont, Reverse-*Erie*, 82 Notre Dame L. Rev. 1 (2006). See also Madhany, Comment, Towards a Unified Theory of "Reverse-*Erie*", 162 U.Pa.L.Rev. 1261 (2014).

2. What did the *Dice* Court mean when it stated: "The *Bombolis* case might be more in point had Ohio abolished trial by jury in all negligence cases including those arising under the federal Act"?

3. Is there any constitutional limitation on what procedures Congress may require state courts to follow in adjudicating federal suits? Could Congress constitutionally require state judges to stand on one leg while adjudicating federal cases? If not, could it require state judges to follow the Federal Rules of Evidence in such cases?

4. What is Justice Frankfurter's reasoning to support his conclusion that the state court need not employ federal procedures? Is his reasoning persuasive? According to one commentator, "the Court should use the [converse-*Erie*] doctrine to advance, not hinder, our federalist constitutional system by upholding the use of state procedures in the adjudication of

substantive-federal rights in state courts unless such procedures would undermine the federal rights themselves." Oliveri, Converse-*Erie:* The Key to Federalism in an Increasingly Administrative State, 76 Geo. Wash. L. Rev. 1372, 1391 (2008). Is the Court's decision in *Dice* consistent with this approach?

5.   Under Georgia state practice, great factual detail was required in a complaint. This was in contrast to federal procedure where, under Rule 8(a) of the Federal Rules of Civil Procedure, a considerably more liberal pleading system is applied. Georgia state courts dismissed a complaint brought under the Federal Employers' Liability Act because it failed to meet the requirements of Georgia pleading practice. Plaintiff, in the United States Supreme Court, argued that in adjudicating this federal cause of action, the Georgia courts should be required to follow federal pleading practice. What result? See Brown v. Western Railway of Alabama, 338 U.S. 294 (1949). Noting that "[t]o what extent rules of practice and procedure may themselves dig into 'substantive rights' is a troublesome question at best," the Court held: "Strict local rules of pleading cannot be used to impose unnecessary burdens upon rights of recovery authorized by federal laws. 'Whatever springes the State may set for those who are endeavoring to assert rights that the State confers, the assertion of federal rights, when plainly and reasonably made, is not to be defeated under the name of local practice.' " What other local practices must give way in cases asserting federal rights? Must state courts permit discovery using all the devices available in federal court? Cf. Sibbach v. Wilson & Co., supra p. 1006 n. 2.

Consider Johnson v. Fankell, 520 U.S. 911 (1997), in which the Court distinguished Dice v. Akron R.R. and held that a state court did not have to follow federal law regarding the timing of an appeal. In a § 1983 civil rights suit in state court, defendants tried to appeal after the trial court denied their motion to dismiss on qualified immunity grounds. When the state supreme court dismissed their appeal, they obtained certiorari arguing that state courts should have to handle this question in the same way the federal courts would, and allow immediate review. Although there is no doubt that under Mitchell v. Forsyth, 472 U.S. 511 (1985), an immediate appeal would be allowed in federal court to protect officials against groundless suits, the Court unanimously affirmed, saying that the immediate appealability in federal court "is a federal procedural right that simply does not apply in a nonfederal forum." In *Dice,* the Court held that the F.E.L.A. implicitly required a jury trial. The federal appealability doctrine, by way of contrast, "is found in [28 U.S.C.] § 1291, which obviously has no application to state courts." The Court also noted that immediate appealability was designed in part to protect state officials in such cases, and that the state's decision to provide less protection implicated no federal interest.

6.   Is *Dice* arguably inconsistent with *Byrd,* supra, p. 982? If so, can the two be reconciled?

7.   Limitations issues can raise particularly difficult problems. These problems have surfaced in connection with federal claims for which Congress

has not specified a limitations period. For civil rights and securities fraud suits, which fall in this category, the federal courts "borrowed" limitations periods from state law. This practice of borrowing from state law raised difficulties because the limitations period could vary from state to state and because related provisions of state law (such as a requirement that service be effected within the limitations period) were sometimes different from normal federal practice. See generally Marcus, Fraudulent Concealment in Federal Court: Toward a More Disparate Standard?, 71 Geo.L.J. 829, 836–55 (1983) (discussing the difficulties in such cases where state and federal law differ regarding the events that suspend the running of limitations).

In DelCostello v. Teamsters, 462 U.S. 151 (1983), a labor case, the Supreme Court broke away from borrowing from state law in order to provide nationwide uniformity of limitations periods. Plaintiff in that case was an employee asserting a "hybrid" claim under federal labor statutes against both his employer and union. Congress had not specified a limitations period for the claim. Rather than borrow from state law for "hybrid" claims, the Court borrowed the six month limitations period from another federal labor statute. But that statute also required service within six months. In West v. Conrail, 481 U.S. 35 (1987), the Court held that this service requirement did not apply to "hybrid" suits by employees: "when the underlying cause of action is based on federal law and the absence of an express federal statute of limitations makes it necessary to borrow a limitations period from another statute, the action is not barred if it has been 'commenced' in compliance with Rule 3 within the borrowed period."

"Hybrid" labor suits can also be filed in state court, however; does this mean that Rule 3 applies to suits filed in state court as well? In Cannon v. Kroger Co., 832 F.2d 303 (4th Cir.1987), plaintiff filed such a "hybrid" claim in state court, using a state court procedure that permits a plaintiff to file an application for an extension of time to file the complaint, which is not due for another 20 days. After she filed and served her complaint, defendants removed to federal court and moved to dismiss on the ground that the action was not commenced in time. The appellate court upheld dismissal of the suit:

> After *West*, there can be no question that commencement of a "hybrid" claim brought in district court is to be assessed in accordance with the Federal Rules of Civil Procedure. Unlike appellant, we can perceive no justification for allowing a different result simply because the underlying action is initiated in a state court. The substantive rights involved remain purely federal in nature. Moreover, the choice of a forum in no way diminishes the subtle balance of interests [that prompted the Supreme Court to borrow a uniform limitations period]. The application of alternative state law procedures must inevitably intrude into the balance and threaten the goal of uniform adjudication. We conclude, therefore, that the statute of limitations applicable to "hybrid" actions runs until the action is properly commenced under the dictates of the Federal Rules of Civil Procedure.

Is this reasoning persuasive? Why wouldn't it apply equally well to federal claims with uniform congressionally set limitations periods? In this connection, it should be noted that some lower courts have read the Supreme Court's decision in DelCostello v. Teamsters, supra, as an invitation to reexamine decisions borrowing from state law for other federal claims. See In re Data Access Sys. Securities Litig., 843 F.2d 1537 (3d Cir.1988) (adopting analogous federal limitations period for federal securities fraud action). Should Rule 3 apply to all federal claims filed in state court? Recall Walker v. Armco Steel Corp., supra p. 1011 (stating that Rule 3 was not intended to toll statutes of limitations). Can *Walker* be reconciled with these decisions involving federal claims? For a criticism of this approach, see Burbank, Of Rules and Discretion: The Supreme Court, Federal Rules and Procedural Common Law, 63 Notre Dame L.Rev. 693 (1988).

For federal statutes adopted after December 1, 1990, Congress has now provided a residual statute of limitations for four years that obviates the need to fill gaps through judge-made law. See 28 U.S.C.A. § 1658. For an argument that courts should use the four-year period to fill the limitation gap in earlier statutes, see Mikva & Pfander, On the Meaning of Congressional Silence: Using Federal Common Law to Fill the Gap in Congress's Residual Statute of Limitations, 107 Yale L.J. 393 (1997).

8.   In Felder v. Casey, 487 U.S. 131 (1988), the Supreme Court held invalid the Wisconsin Supreme Court's reliance on the state's notice-of-claim statute to bar a suit brought under the federal civil rights laws, 42 U.S.C.A. § 1983. The state statute provided that before suit may be brought in state court against a state or local governmental entity or officer, the plaintiff must notify the defendant of the circumstances and amount of the claim within 120 days of the injury. Justice Brennan, writing for the Court, reasoned:

> The decision to subject state subdivisions to liability for violations of federal rights * * * was a choice that Congress, not the Wisconsin legislature, made, and it is a decision that the State has no authority to override. Thus, however understandable or laudable the State's interest in controlling liability expenses might otherwise be, it is patently incompatible with the compensatory goals of the federal legislation, as are the means the State has chosen to effectuate it.

* * *

> This burdening of a federal right, moreover, is not the natural or permissible consequence of an otherwise neutral, uniformly applicable state rule. Although it is true that the notice-of-claim statute does not discriminate between state and federal causes of action against local governments, the fact remains that the law's protection extends only to governmental defendants and thus conditions the right to bring suit against the very persons and entities Congress intended to subject to liability. We therefore cannot accept the suggestion that this requirement is simply part of "the vast body of procedural rules, rooted in policies unrelated to the definition of

any particular substantive cause of action, that forms no essential part of 'the cause of action' as applied to any given plaintiff." * * * [The] defendant-specific focus of the notice requirement serves to distinguish it, rather starkly, from rules uniformly applicable to all suits, such as rules governing service of process or substitution of parties * * *. That state courts will hear the entire § 1983 cause of action once a plaintiff complies with the notice-of-claim statute, therefore, in no way alters the fact that the statute discriminates against the precise type of claim Congress has created.

Justice O'Connor, joined by the Chief Justice, dissented.

How do you think the Court would have held had the state's notice-of-claim statute applied to every suit brought in state court? How *should* the Court have held? Assume a state judicial system provides for little or no discovery. Should the Supreme Court hold that in a § 1983 suit the state court must make available all of the discovery devices provided for in the Federal Rules of Civil Procedure?

9.   In American Dredging Co. v. Miller, 510 U.S. 443 (1994), the Court held that a Louisiana statute that precluded application of forum non conveniens only in claims for injury brought pursuant to the Jones Act, 46 U.S.C.A. § 688, was applicable despite the existence of federal forum non conveniens doctrine and an interest in uniform application of maritime law. Plaintiff, a seaman injured on the Delaware River, sued defendant, which was headquartered in New Jersey, in a Louisiana state court, for injuries under the Jones Act and general maritime law. Although the state trial court dismissed pursuant to federal forum non conveniens law, the Louisiana Supreme Court held that forum non conveniens was not available due to a Louisiana statute that requires the doctrine's application in every other type of case but forbids it in maritime injury cases.

The Supreme Court affirmed, holding that forum non conveniens is not a "characteristic feature" of admiralty or a doctrine whose application is necessary to maintain the "proper harmony" of maritime law. It concluded that the doctrine had not been unique to admiralty, although early cases invoking it were most frequently admiralty cases, and that any disuniformity would not be a matter of importance since the doctrine was basically a question of venue and therefore "a matter that goes to process rather than substantive rights." Justice Kennedy dissented, emphasizing the "undue risk" that ship owners and operators run of being sued in inconvenient venues and concluding that disuniformity on such a question could not be justified by any interest of Louisiana in view of its willingness to apply the doctrine in all other cases. He reasoned that "[t]he reverse-*Erie* metaphor, while perhaps of use in other contexts, is not a sure guide for determining when a specific state law has displaced an essential feature of the general maritime law. Procedural or substantive, the forum non conveniens defense promotes comity and trade. The States are not free to undermine those goals."

10.   For a discussion of one aspect of the "converse *Erie*" problem, see Frost, Inferiority Complex: Should State Courts Follow Lower Federal Court Precedent on the Meaning of Federal Law?, 68 Vand.L.Rev. 53 (2015). Professor Frost examines the question whether state courts are bound by lower federal court precedents in interpreting federal law. She notes that the accepted view is that they are not bound, but believes they may constitutionally be required to do so. In her words, "nothing in the Constitution would seem to prevent either Congress or the Supreme Court from establishing such a rule if they chose." Id. at 103. She reasons that while "state courts are constitutionally *adequate* for the resolution of federal claims," this fact "does not render them federal courts' *equals* when doing so. State courts lack the resources, experience, and insulation from political pressure that federal courts enjoy—problems that the Framers of the Constitution recognized and that continue to exist today." She adds that "for purely practical reasons involving the need for intrastate uniformity, a state court should not be free to disregard its own regional court of appeals when addressing the meaning of federal law." Id. Consider the implications of a state court's ability to ignore regionally applicable federal court precedent in interpreting substantive federal law on predictability in the planning of a citizen's primary conduct.

D. FEDERAL COMMON LAW

1. THE SOURCE AND LEGITIMACY OF FEDERAL COMMON LAW

In *Erie,* Justice Brandeis wrote that "[t]here is no federal general common law." However, the very same day, the Supreme Court held that federal common law controlled the issue of the apportionment of an interstate stream. Hinderlider v. La Plata River & Cherry Creek Ditch Co., 304 U.S. 92 (1938).

Justice Jackson later attempted to explain the distinction between the form of federal common law rejected in *Erie* and that which continues to exist:

> The federal Courts have no *general* common law, as in a sense they have no general or comprehensive jurisprudence of any kind, because many subjects of private law are ordinarily within the province of the states and not of the federal government. But this is not to say that whenever we have occasion to decide a federal question which cannot be answered from federal statutes alone we may not resort to all of the source materials of the common law, or that when we have fashioned an answer it does not become a part of the federal non-statutory or common law.

D'Oench, Duhme & Co. v. FDIC, 315 U.S. 447, 469 (1942) (Jackson, J., concurring). Is the distinction Justice Jackson draws persuasive? See also American Electric Power Co., v. Connecticut, 564U.S. 410, 421 (2011) (*Erie* "sparked 'the emergence of a federal decisional law in areas of national concern'") Friendly, In Praise of *Erie*—and of the New Federal Common Law, 39 N.Y.U. L. Rev. 383, 405 (1964)).

Recall that the Rules of Decision Act, 28 U.S.C.A. § 1652, provides: "The laws of the several states, except where the Constitution or treaties of the United States or Acts of Congress otherwise require or provide, shall be regarded as rules of decision in civil actions in the courts of the United States, in cases where they apply." By its terms, does this Act authorize the creation of *any* federal common law, "general" or otherwise? See M. Redish, Federal Jurisdiction: Tensions in the Allocation of Judicial Power 121–25 (2d ed. 1990). Can you fashion any arguments which allow you to construe the Rules of Decision Act to authorize the creation of federal common law? Consider this view: "Far from being a limitation on the authority of the federal courts, the Rules of Decision Act is an explicit grant of authority: It directs the federal courts to apply state law with regard to any issue that is not governed by a pertinent and valid federal rule. It reminds the federal courts that if a valid federal rule exists—whether constitutional, statutory, or judge-made—the federal rule shall govern." Westen & Lehman, Is There Life for *Erie* After the Death of Diversity?, 78 Mich.L.Rev. 311, 314 (1980). Westen and Lehman find the statute's failure to mention federal common law unimportant because "the distinction between federal common law and federal statutory law is merely a difference in emphasis." Id. at 369. Compare Redish, Continuing the *Erie* Debate: A Response to Westen and Lehman, 78 Mich.L.Rev. 959, 963–64 (1980): "[W]hat possible difference does it make that the distinction between common and statutory law is one 'in emphasis' (if indeed that is an accurate characterization)? A congressional statute is *still* an 'Act of Congress,' and federal common law is still *not* an 'Act of Congress.' "

The validity of substantive federal common law is challenged in M. Redish, The Federal Courts in the Political Order: Judicial Jurisdiction and American Political Theory 30 (1991): "[J]udicial recognition of the power to create substantive federal common law * * * violates the inescapable textual command of the [Rules of Decision] Act, and effectively renders the Act a nullity, results that are wholly unacceptable under [a] separation-of-powers analysis * * *." Federal common law, in its post-*Erie* form, is defended in Rutherglen, Reconstructing *Erie:* A Comment on the Perils of Legal Positivism, 10 Const. Comm. 285 (1993). See also Weinberg, Federal Common Law, 83 Nw.U.L.Rev. 805 (1989); Brown, Federal Common Law and the Role of the Federal Courts in Private Law Adjudication—A (New) *Erie* Problem?, 12 Pace L. Rev. 229 (1992), and Merrill, The Judicial Prerogative, 12 Pace L. Rev. 327 (1992).

On this issue, consider the relevance of one of the Supreme Court's classic "federal common law" decisions, Clearfield Trust Co. v. United States, 318 U.S. 363 (1943). The case involved a stolen check that had been mailed, but was not received by its intended recipient. An unknown person presented the check to a J.C. Penney store for cashing, and endorsed it with the name of the intended recipient. J.C. Penney endorsed the check over to Clearfield Trust, which accepted it for purposes of collection. Clearfield endorsed the check with a guaranty of all prior endorsements, collected the amount of the check from the Federal Reserve and paid it to J.C. Penney. Neither Penney nor Clearfield had suspected forgery. Federal officials did not inform any of the interested parties of the forgery until eight months after they had learned that the intended recipient had not received the check.

The United States sued Clearfield on Clearfield's express guaranty of prior endorsements. The district court held that the rights of the parties were to be determined by the law of Pennsylvania. Since the United States had unreasonably delayed giving notice of the forgery, it was barred from recovery under Pennsylvania law and the district court dismissed the complaint. The Court of Appeals for the Third Circuit reversed, and the Supreme Court affirmed the reversal, rejecting the district court's conclusion that Pennsylvania law controlled:

> The rights and duties of the United States on commercial paper which it issues are governed by federal rather than local law. When the United States disburses its funds or pays its debts, it is exercising a constitutional function or power * * *. The authority to issue the check had its origin in the Constitution and the statutes of the United States and was in no way dependent on the laws of Pennsylvania or of any other state.

Having decided that federal law applied, the Court held that "[i]f it is shown that the drawee on learning of the forgery did not give prompt notice of it and that damage resulted, recovery of the drawee is barred." By contrast, under Pennsylvania law damage arising from the delay need not have been shown before recovery could be had. Since neither Clearfield nor Penney had shown any damage caused directly by the government's delay, the Court found for the government.

Does this decision provide an arguable basis for avoiding the bar of the Rules of Decision Act? Is it persuasive? Cf. Mishkin, The Variousness of "Federal Law": Competence and Discretion in the Choice of National and State Rules for Decision, 105 U.Pa.L.Rev. 797, 800 (1957): "At the very least, effective Constitutionalism requires recognition of power in the federal courts to declare, as a matter of common law or 'judicial legislation,' rules which may be necessary to fill interstitially or otherwise effectuate the statutory patterns enacted in the large by Congress." Is this persuasive? Does it successfully circumvent the problem of the Rules of Decision Act?

Contrast with *Clearfield Trust* cases in which specific congressional delegation of power can be found. For example, in Textile Workers Union v. Lincoln Mills, 353 U.S. 448 (1957), the Supreme Court found that in suits under the Labor Management Relations Act, Congress not only created federal jurisdiction for actions to enforce collective bargaining agreements but also intended that federal courts develop rules of substantive law to decide such cases in order to achieve national uniformity:

> The Labor Management Relations Act expressly furnishes some substantive law. It points out what parties may or may not do in certain situations. Other problems will lie in the penumbra of express statutory mandates. Some will lack express statutory sanction but will be solved by looking at the policy of the legislation and fashioning a remedy that will effectuate that policy. The range of judicial inventiveness will be determined by the nature of the problem. Federal interpretation of the federal law will govern, not state law. But state law, if compatible with the purpose of [the federal act], may be resorted to in order to find the rule that will best effectuate the federal policy. Any state law applied, however, will be absorbed as federal law and will not be an independent source of private rights.

It is not uncommon for federal courts to fashion federal law where federal rights are concerned. See Clearfield Trust Co. v. United States, 318 U.S. 363, 366–67. Congress has indicated by [the federal act] the purpose to follow that course here. There is no constitutional difficulty. Article III, § 2, extends that judicial power to cases "arising under . . . the Laws of the United States. . . ." The power of Congress to regulate these labor-management controversies under the Commerce Clause is plain.

2. CATEGORIES OF FEDERAL COMMON LAW

According to one pair of commentators, federal common law should be developed in areas in which "states have such a strong self-interest in a controversy or have erected such high barriers to political participation by some groups that state law cannot be expected to provide a sufficiently detached, reliable, and neutral rule of decision for a controversy. * * * Such bias is not, in itself, a sufficient condition to create federal common law; factors noted by other commentators—especially the need to achieve uniformity in a matter of national interest—also determine the decision. But potential bias in creating state law is a necessary condition for creating federal common law." Tidmarsh & Murray, A Theory of Federal Common Law, 100 Nw. U. L. Rev. 585, 588 (2006).

Scholars have generally pointed to four areas in which substantive federal common law may be developed: Cases in which a state is a party, cases involving maritime law, cases involving federal "proprietary" interests, and cases concerning international law and foreign relations. See Hill, The Law-Making Power of the Federal Courts: Constitutional Preemption, 67 Colum.L.Rev. 1024, 1025 (1967); M. Redish, Federal

Jurisdiction: Tensions in the Allocation of Judicial Power 119–48 (2d ed. 1990).

Clearfield Trust, supra p. 1049, originated the category of federal proprietary interests. Consider the following description of the important post-*Clearfield* case of United States v. Kimbell Foods, Inc., 440 U.S. 715 (1979), from M. Redish, Federal Jurisdiction: Tensions in the Allocation of Judicial Power 130–31 (2d ed. 1990):

> The two cases combined in *Kimbell Foods* arose from loans made by the Small Business Administration and the Farmers Home Administration, respectively. The issue, not controlled by statute, was whether liens obtained by the federal agencies took precedence over private liens. In deciding whether or not to adopt a separate federal standard, the Court examined several factors. On the federal side of the balance, the Court considered both the need for uniformity and "whether application of state law would frustrate specific objectives of the federal programs." On the state side of the balance, the Court examined "the extent to which application of a federal rule would disrupt commercial relationships predicated on state law."

> After weighing these factors, the Court chose to adopt state law. . . . [T]he Court concluded that uniformity was not of great importance because of the individually negotiated nature of the loan agreements. Furthermore, the Court refused "to override intricate state laws of general applicability on which private creditors based their daily commercial transactions." The conclusion reached in *Kimbell Foods* suggested a dramatic shift in the Court's attitude towards the role of federal common law when the proprietary interests of the United States are involved. In *Clearfield,* the Court was especially solicitous of the federal interest in attaining uniformity though, as noted previously, it is questionable whether a uniform federal rule would have significantly reduced federal administrative burdens. In addition, the Court in *Clearfield* appeared generally unconcerned about the danger of disrupting "intricate state laws of general applicability on which private creditors base their daily commercial transactions." In *Kimbell Foods,* the Court's attitude on both issues appeared to be directly opposite to that expressed in *Clearfield.*

In O'Melveny & Myers v. FDIC, 512 U.S. 79 (1994), the Court held that state law, rather than federal law, governs the issue of the imputation of corporate officers' knowledge of fraud to a corporation asserting a federal cause of action. "The remote possibility that corporations may go into federal receivership," the court stated, "is no conceivable basis for adopting a special federal common-law rule divesting States of authority over the entire law of imputation." Judicial lawmaking is inappropriate, the Court held, absent a "significant conflict between some federal policy or interest and the use of state law." According to one commentator, *"O'Melveny & Myers* represents a strong statement by the Supreme Court substantially restricting courts' ability to fashion federal common law." Rosenberg, The Ultimate Independence of the Federal Courts: Defying the Supreme Court in the Exercise of Federal Common Law Powers, 36 Conn. L. Rev. 425, 451 (2004). According to Professor Rosenberg, *O'Melveny & Myers'* "significant conflict" prerequisite "strengthens the Court's prior holding in *Kimbell Foods,* and reiterates the Court's preference for legislatively-created law at either the federal or the state level." Id. See also Atherton v. FDIC, 519 U.S. 213 (1997), holding that federal common law did not control the issue of the standard of care and directors of federally issued savings institutions, because application of state law standard of care to such institutions would not conflict with or threaten federal policies of interests.

Do *Kimbell Foods* and *O'Melveny* overrule the *Clearfield Trust* principle (described supra, p. 1049)? If not, what modification, if any, do they impose?

In addition to what has been labeled the area of "proprietary" federal interests, involved in both *Clearfield* and *Kimbell Foods,* federal common law has been developed in the following types of cases: those in which the state is a party, those involving maritime law, and those having an impact on international relations. See Hill, The Law-Making Power of the Federal Courts: Constitutional Preemption, 67 Colum.L.Rev. 1024 (1967). For a discussion of these applications of federal common law, see M. Redish, Federal Jurisdiction: Tensions in the Allocation of Judicial Power 125–48 (2d ed. 1990); C. Wright & M. Kane, The Law of Federal Courts § 60 (7th ed. 2011). In addition, on occasion the Supreme Court has inferred private remedies from statutes or constitutional provisions which do not on their face provide for such remedies. These exercises could be deemed a form of federal common law.

In Boyle v. United Technologies Corp., 487 U.S. 500 (1988), the Court considered whether the "military contractor" defense, recognized under federal common law, applied in a diversity tort action, brought by the father of a military pilot killed in a crash, against the private company that had constructed his helicopter. In holding that such a defense could be utilized, Justice Scalia, writing for the Court, stated:

> In most fields of activity, to be sure, this Court has refused to find federal pre-emption of state law in the absence of either a clear statutory prescription, or a direct conflict between federal and state law. But we have held that a few areas, involving "uniquely federal interests," are so committed by the Constitution and laws of the United States to federal control that state law is preempted and replaced, where necessary, by federal law of a content

prescribed (absent explicit statutory directive) by the courts—so-called "federal common law."

The dispute in the present case borders upon two areas that we have found to involve such "uniquely federal interests." We have held that obligations to and rights of the United States under its contracts are governed exclusively by federal law. * * *

Another area that we have found to be of peculiarly federal concern, warranting the displacement of state law, is the civil liability of federal officials for actions taken in the course of their duty. * * *

We think the reasons for considering these closely related areas to be of "uniquely federal" interest apply as well to the civil liabilities arising out of the performance of federal procurement contracts. * * *

Moreover, it is plain that the Federal Government's interest in the procurement of equipment is implicated by suits such as the present one—even though the dispute is one between private parties.

In dissent, Justice Brennan, joined by Justices Marshall and Blackmun, argued: "In my view, this Court lacks both authority and expertise to fashion [a government contractor defense]. * * * I would leave that exercise of legislative power to Congress, where our Constitution places it * * *."

In its subsequent decision in Kamen v. Kemper Financial Services, Inc., 500 U.S. 90 (1991), however, the Supreme Court declined to fashion a distinct federal common law rule obliging the representative shareholder in a derivative action founded on the Investment Company Act of 1940 (ICA), 15 U.S.C.A. §§ 80a–l(a) et seq., to make a demand on the board of directors even when such a demand would be excused as futile under state law. Justice Marshall, speaking for the Court, concluded that "[b]ecause the scope of the demand requirement embodies the incorporating State's allocation of governing powers within the corporation, and because a futility exception to demand does not impede the purposes of the Investment Company Act, we decline to displace state law with a uniform rule abolishing the futility exception in federal derivative actions." He explained further:

It is clear that the contours of the demand requirement in a derivative action founded on the ICA are governed by *federal* law. Because the ICA is a federal statute, any common law rule necessary to effectuate a private cause of action under that statute is necessarily federal in character.

It does not follow, however, that the content of such a rule must be wholly the product of a federal court's own devising. Our cases indicate that a court should endeavor to fill the interstices of federal remedial schemes with uniform federal rules only when the scheme in question evidences a distinct need for nationwide legal standards, or when express provisions in analogous statutory schemes embody congressional policy choices readily applicable to the matter at hand, see, e.g., Boyle v. United Technologies Corp. Otherwise, we have indicated that federal courts should "incorporat[e] [state law] as the federal rule of decision," unless "application of [the particular] state law [in question] would frustrate specific objectives of the federal programs." United States v. Kimbell Foods, Inc. The presumption that state law should be incorporated into federal common law is particularly strong in areas in which private parties have entered legal relationships with the expectation that their rights and obligations would be governed by state-law standards.

Corporation law is one such area. * * *

Because a futility exception to demand does not impede the regulatory objectives of the ICA, a court that is entertaining a derivative action under that statute must apply the demand futility exception as it is defined by the law of the State of incorporation.

On the application of *Boyle*, See also Empire Healthchoice Assurance, Inc. v. McVeigh, 547 US 677 (2006).

On the issue of the federal common law of international relations, see Bellia & Clark, The Federal Common Law of Nations, 109 Colum. L. Rev. 1, 93 (2009): "Commentators fundamentally disagree about the status of customary international law in U.S. courts. The modern position is that such law automatically qualifies as supreme, jurisdiction-conferring federal common law. Revisionists claim it does not qualify as federal law, absent incorporation by the political branches. Both positions purport to draw support from the historical treatment of the law of nations in judicial decisions going back to the founding. Both, however, are incomplete because they fail to identify the unique role that perfect rights under the law of nations have played—and continue to play—in upholding the Constitution's allocation of powers. Courts adhere to rules based on such rights out of deference to the federal political branches, which—unlike the courts—are charged with recognizing foreign states and conducting foreign relations. As the Supreme Court has recognized, both state and federal courts must adhere to such rules—in the absence of contrary instructions from the political branches—in order to prevent the judiciary from usurping the authority of Congress and the President and making important foreign policy decisions on behalf of the nation."

CHAPTER 12

APPEALS

■ ■ ■

A. THE VALUE OF APPELLATE REVIEW

Before considering the avenues available to obtain appellate review, it is appropriate to examine the general values and costs involved in invoking the appellate process. Such an inquiry is necessary because the answer to this threshold question influences the way we will construe the various methods of obtaining appellate review.

The starting point is: why provide any appeal at all? Why not simply rely on the judgment and discretion of the trial judge to resolve the case? Consider the following defense of the value of appeal, made by Professor Paul Carrington:

> The judge responsible for making primary decisions must necessarily make a heavy investment of time and interest in particular disputes and individuals that come before him; his limited perspective and his limited opportunity for reflection makes it impossible for him to coordinate successfully with his colleagues. Vanity and pride of opinion are additional obstacles; even very sensitive, intelligent, and self-disciplined judges must be troubled at times by their own involvement of ego.

Carrington, Crowded Dockets and the Courts of Appeals: The Threat to the Function of Review and the National Law, 82 Harv.L.Rev. 542, 551 (1969). Because "[t]he trial judge is in a unique position of authority over the day-to-day actions of individuals," Carrington contends, "[m]egalomania is an occupational hazard of the judicial office." Review by a court remote "from the firing line of a trial" provides the objective supervision "essential to the goal of law." Id. at 550–51.

It has also been argued that "even if trial judges are capable of maintaining necessary objectivity, and their decisions are usually correct * * * preserving the appearance of justice in the eyes of the litigants who would otherwise view themselves as victims of arbitrary individuals is an equally important goal. A viable appellate process legitimizes the decisions of the lower courts, and thereby preserves faith in the functioning of the legal system." Redish, The Pragmatic Approach to Appealability in the Federal Courts, 75 Colum.L.Rev. 89, 97 (1975).

Institutional differences may give appellate courts a comparative advantage over district courts in the determination of disputed questions of law. Appellate courts sit in panels, often of three judges, and take a relatively deliberate approach to the task of resolving appeals. Appellate courts receive briefs and oral arguments from the parties and employ law clerks to assist with research into legal questions that district judges may have to resolve on the fly. The Supreme Court has recognized these differences in institutional setting, contrasting the "fast-paced" work of the trial judge with the more deliberative work of appellate panels devoted primarily to resolving issues of law on a full record. See Salve Regina College v. Russell, 499 U.S. 225 (1991).

Even if one is persuaded that an appeal to an independent court serves the interests of justice and promotes confidence in the judicial system, should that right be extended to all cases? It might be argued that some cases are not serious enough to warrant the expenditure of further judicial effort and the delay in finality that is incident to an appeal. But what criteria should be used for allowing an appeal—the amount in controversy, the issues at stake, the nature of the cause of action, the kind of trial court in which the case arose? The answer varies from jurisdiction to jurisdiction, depending on standards set by the legislative body, court rule, or the applicable constitution.

In many jurisdictions, as in the federal court system, "appeal as of right" is granted only to an intermediate appellate court, with a further appeal to the highest court discretionary with that court. Although some state constitutions assure a constitutional right to appeal from state court judgments, the Supreme Court of the United States has declined to find that a right to appeal is an element of due process guaranteed under the Fourteenth Amendment. See McKane v. Durston, 153 U.S. 684, 687 (1894) (no due process right to an appeal from state criminal conviction). Cf. Griffin v. Illinois, 351 U.S. 12, 18 (1956) (reaffirming *McKane* but invalidating on equal protection grounds state laws that discriminated against the poor in making appellate review available); Bankers Life & Casualty Co. v. Crenshaw, 486 U.S. 71 (1988) (state statute requiring unsuccessful appellants in certain cases to pay an additional 15% of the judgment does not violate equal protection); Halbert v. Michigan, 545 U.S. 605 (2005) (due process and equal protection require state to provide appointed counsel to indigent defendants who seek to appeal conviction after nolo plea). With appellate review guaranteed by statute, and with discretionary review of all final state-court decisions that implicate dispositive issues of federal law available (at least in theory) in the Supreme Court itself, how likely is the Court to address the continuing vitality of *McKane*?

How often do parties succeed on appeal? The answer is: it depends. In 1960, the federal appellate courts reversed the district court in roughly 25% of the cases they heard. By 2005, the overall reversal rate had dropped below 10%. See Oldfather, Defining Judicial Inactivism: Models of

Adjudication and the Duty to Decide, 94 Geo.L.J. 121, 135 n. 42 (2005). Observers have attributed the declining reversal rate to a variety of factors, including the increasingly bureaucratized process of appellate review, the growth in the number of appeals, and the growth in the number of frivolous appeals, particularly in criminal litigation. See R. Posner, The Federal Courts: Challenge and Reform 74–75 (2d ed. 1996). Certainly, the numbers suggest that reversal rates vary with the nature of the case. According to the report for twelve month period ending September 30, 2016, reversal rates in the regional circuit courts of appeals in federal criminal matters had declined to 7.4% (in contrast to an overall reversal rate of 8.2% and a reversal rate in private civil litigation of just over 15%). See Report of the Director, Administrative Office of the US Courts, Judicial Business of the United States Courts, Table B-5 (2016). Other areas of law produce higher reversal rates. For a time, in patent litigation, the U.S. Court of Appeals for the Federal Circuit reportedly reversed the district court, at least in part, in more than 50% of the appeals it heard. See Cybor Corp. v. FAS Techs., Inc., 138 F.3d 1448, 1476 (Fed. Cir. 1998) (Rader, J., dissenting). Judicial Conference statistics disclose a much lower reversal rate in recent years, although the metrics doubtless differ. See Report of the Director, Administrative Office of the US Courts, Judicial Business of the United States Courts, Table B-8 (2016) (reporting that Federal Circuit reversed in 11% of its appeals overall as compared with a reversal rate of 16% in appeals from district courts in patent cases).

One commentator, who has urged a significant cutback in the scope of appeal as of right in the federal courts, questions many of the assumptions underlying the arguments in support of appellate review. Professor Dalton argued that

> on several counts there is reason to question the intuitively appealing notion that the threat of reversal induces trial judges to self-correct. Some judges just don't take the threat seriously, because the ratio of reversal to total cases is so small, because they regard reversals as inevitable or arbitrary, or because they think it inappropriate to concern themselves with what might happen on appeal. For others, appellate review is a pressing concern, but their response to it may have little to do with improving case outcomes. Where the name of the game is to avoid reversal by toeing the appellate court line, victory will bring juster justice only if the appellate court has drawn the line in the right place * * *.

Dalton, Taking the Right to Appeal (More or Less) Seriously, 95 Yale L.J. 62, 92 (1985). He argues further that "even if appeal of right does promote self-correction by trial judges, any consequent gain in accuracy may be more than offset by harm done to the trial court as an institution. The more we underscore the fact that trial courts are hierarchically inferior to appellate courts, the more we feed the notion that they are inferior in other ways as well." Id. at 92–93. For an argument from a "liberal" judge (who was then sitting on the court of appeals) that the time has come to ration appeals, see Parker & Chapman, Accepting Reality: The Time for Adopting Discretionary Review in the Courts of Appeals Has Arrived, 50 S.M.U.L.Rev. 573 (1997).

Are these arguments persuasive? Consider the response of Professor Carrington in The Function of the Civil Appeal: A Late-Century View, 38 So.Car.L.Rev. 411, 431 (1987):

> Professor Harlan Dalton contends that the appeal of right is a disparagement of the trial judge and unlikely to make that judge more attentive to direction from higher courts. His argument rests in part on intuition and in part on the self-analysis of trial judges. My intuitions are contrary to his. * * * More important in my view, however, is the signal sent to the litigants by the recognition of the right of appeal, which does shape their perception of the fairness of the proceeding and the power or prerogative of the trial judge. We send the wrong message to a litigant when we tell him that he is dependent on the reactions of a single judge whose decisions will be reviewed by higher authority only as an act of grace. The idea of law is that the individual judge is accountable for the principled exercise of power. Discretionary accountability may look to the skeptic very much like no accountability at all.

Appellate courts have attempted to deal with the growth in their docket in a variety of ways. The Supreme Court of the United States (like many state supreme courts) has, in the large majority of cases, been given statutory discretion to select its own cases. Most intermediate appellate courts have both a mandatory and discretionary jurisdiction and have less complete control of their dockets. As a consequence, appellate courts have adopted a range of processes that seek to economize on the time and expense of appellate review. For example, federal appellate courts routinely screen incoming appeals to assign them either for disposition after full briefing and oral argument, or for disposition on the basis of more summary proceedings. Cases assigned for summary disposition are often handled by the court's staff attorneys, who draft a suggested decision for review by a panel of judges. Similarly, the judges' "elbow" law clerks, often recent law school graduates, draft memoranda that can become, with varying degrees of judicial oversight, final opinions. Do these developments amount, as a practical matter, to the replacement of the statutory right of appeal with a discretionary system of review? Are summary appellate procedures more reliable than summary trial procedures? Do changes in practice of appellate courts give us reason to doubt the institutional advantages claimed for such courts in the determination of issues of law?

Growing caseloads prompted federal appellate courts to adopt other practices to reduce the burden of full briefing and oral argument. Many courts, for example, have introduced alternative dispute resolution programs in an effort to encourage compromise where possible. In addition, many courts decide a substantial portion of their cases by unpublished opinions and orders. This practice was intended for cases raising issues that are extremely fact-specific or of insufficient general interest to warrant publication. The resulting decisions tended to be relatively brief and did not always receive the same thorough consideration as published opinions. But the practice of relying on unpublished opinions became extremely controversial. Lawyers insisted with some force that appellate courts should treat like cases alike, and cited unpublished slip opinions as authority. Some courts responded by formally denying unpublished opinions any precedential effect as law of the circuit and by forbidding counsel to cite the opinions in their briefs. Divisions arose between appellate judges, most of whom viewed unpublished opinions as a crucial docket management device, and academics who regarded non-precedential decisions with suspicion. One appellate court, agreeing with the academic critique, went so far as to declare the practice of non-publication unconstitutional. See Anastasoff v. United States, 223 F.3d 898 (8th Cir. 2000) (later vacated as moot).

After several years of controversy over publication rules and non-precedential decisions, the Supreme Court approved a change to the Federal Rules of Appellate Procedure. Rule 32.1 provides that the appellate courts cannot "prohibit or restrict the citation" of appellate opinions and orders that have been labeled as "unpublished" or "non-precedential" or the like. The rule applies only to opinions and orders issued after January 1, 2007. Furthermore, the rule provides that a party who cites an opinion or order that is not available through a "publicly accessible electronic database" must file and serve a copy of the opinion along with the brief in which it is cited. Rule 32.1 thus ensures the ability of parties to cite all appellate decisions, but it takes no position on the legitimacy or constitutionality of the practice of denying precedential effect to a particular category of non-precedential opinions. The rule thus leaves the definition of precedential effect to each of the thirteen federal circuit courts, acting through judicial decision or local court rule. See Sloan, If You Can't Beat 'Em, Join 'Em: A Pragmatic Approach to Non-Precedential Opinions in the Federal Appellate Courts, 86 Neb. L. Rev. 895 (2008).

Docket pressures have thus given rise to two tracks of appellate decisional law: the fully briefed and argued cases that produce law of the circuit and the more summary dispositions that may be given no effect at all or be regarded as only of persuasive authority. Recent statistics suggest that the federal appellate courts conducted oral hearings in only about 23% of the 39,300 cases they disposed of on the merits in the reporting year ended September 30, 2016. See Judicial Business of the United States Courts, supra, Table B-l (2016). Appellate courts dispose of the remaining 77% of their docket on the basis of written submissions. Might one predict a lower reversal rate among the cases that the appellate courts decide without argument on the basis of written submissions? Might one predict that pro se litigants often find their appeals consigned to the appellate track with fewer oral arguments and published opinions?

Whatever the impact of the two-track system of appellate review on outcomes, evidence collected in an intriguing study suggests that a spike or surge in appellate caseloads may lead to a more deferential form of appellate review. Huang, Lightened Scrutiny, 124 Harv. L. Rev. 1109 (2011), examines the behavior of appellate courts in the wake of what he describes as a "surge" in immigration appeals that primarily affected two circuits, the Second and Ninth. Huang considers the impact of the surge on reversal rates in civil appeals, both in the affected circuits and in the others. He finds that the surge was associated with a decline in civil appeal reversal rates, suggesting that deference may depend less on the formal rules governing the scope of appellate review than on the number of cases in the appellate queue. For a comparative look at appellate practice in the United States and elsewhere, see Marcus, Appellate Reviews in the Reactive Model: The Example of the American Federal Courts, in Nobody's Perfect: Comparative Essays on Appeals and Other Means of Recourse Against Judicial Decision in Civil Matters 105 (C.H. van Rhee & A. Uzelac, eds., Intersentia 2014).

At the present time, 28 U.S.C. § 1291 provides that the courts of appeals "shall have jurisdiction of appeals from all final decisions of the district courts," language that has been construed to guarantee an appeal as of right. Yet the appellate courts' reliance on written submissions and non-precedential decisions suggest that litigants no longer enjoy a right to a full-fledged appeal and oral hearing before a panel of judges. In addition, as we will see, other jurisdictional statutes, such as the Class Action Fairness Act of 2005, provide appellate courts with a measure of discretion in deciding whether to permit appellate review. Should the primary statutory right of appeal in section 1291 be more broadly transformed into a discretionary practice? What cases might best lend themselves to discretionary treatment?

The next section examines the elements of section 1291. The statute indicates that the federal appellate courts have jurisdiction only over *final* judgments. The right to appeal only from final decisions presents questions that focus on *when* an appeal is to be allowed, rather than *whether* it is to be allowed. As you consider these issues of timing, bear in mind that delaying an appeal can sometimes have the same effect as denying appellate review altogether. Parties who wish to appeal must also file a timely notice to that effect with the district court.

B. APPELLATE JURISDICTION

1. TIMELY NOTICE OF APPEAL

BOWLES V. RUSSELL
Supreme Court of the United States, 2007
551 U.S. 205

JUSTICE THOMAS delivered the opinion of the Court.

In this case, a District Court purported to extend a party's time for filing an appeal beyond the period allowed by statute. We must decide whether the Court of Appeals had jurisdiction to entertain an appeal filed after the statutory period but within the period allowed by the District Court's order. We have long and repeatedly held that the time limits for filing a notice of appeal are jurisdictional in nature. Accordingly, we hold that petitioner's untimely notice-even though filed in reliance upon a District Court's order-deprived the Court of Appeals of jurisdiction.

I

In 1999, an Ohio jury convicted petitioner Keith Bowles of murder for his involvement in the beating death of Ollie Gipson. The jury sentenced Bowles to 15 years to life imprisonment. Bowles unsuccessfully challenged his conviction and sentence on direct appeal. Bowles then filed a federal habeas corpus application on September 5, 2002. On September 9, 2003, the District Court denied Bowles habeas relief. After the entry of final judgment, Bowles had 30 days to file a notice of appeal. Fed. Rule App. Proc. 4(a)(1)(A); 28 U.S.C. § 2107(a). He failed to do so. On December 12, 2003, Bowles moved to reopen the period during which he could file his notice of appeal pursuant to Rule 4(a)(6), which allows district courts to extend the filing period for 14 days from the day the district court grants the order to reopen, provided certain conditions are met. See § 2107(c).

On February 10, 2004, the District Court granted Bowles' motion. But rather than extending the time period by 14 days, as Rule 4(a)(6) and § 2107(c) allow, the District Court inexplicably gave Bowles 17 days—until February 27—to file his notice of appeal. Bowles filed his notice on February 26—within the 17 days allowed by the District Court's order, but after the 14-day period allowed by Rule 4(a)(6) and § 2107(c).

On appeal, respondent Russell argued that Bowles' notice was untimely and that the Court of Appeals therefore lacked jurisdiction to hear the case. The Court of Appeals agreed. It first recognized that this Court has consistently held the requirement of filing a timely notice of appeal is "mandatory and jurisdictional." 432 F.3d 668, 673 (C.A.6 2005). The court also noted that courts of appeals have uniformly held that Rule 4(a)(6)'s 180-day period for filing a motion to reopen is also mandatory and not susceptible to equitable modification. 432 F.3d, at 673 (collecting cases). Concluding that "the fourteen-day period in Rule 4(a)(6) should be treated as strictly as the 180-day period in that same Rule," *id.,* at 676, the Court of Appeals held that it was without jurisdiction. We granted certiorari, and now affirm.

II

According to 28 U.S.C. § 2107(a), parties must file notices of appeal within 30 days of the entry of the judgment being appealed. District courts have limited authority to grant an extension of the 30-day time period. Relevant to this case, if certain conditions are met, district courts have the statutory authority to grant motions to reopen the time for filing an appeal for 14 additional days. § 2107(c). Rule 4 of the Federal Rules of Appellate Procedure carries § 2107 into practice. * * *

It is undisputed that the District Court's order in this case purported to reopen the filing period for more than 14 days. Thus, the question before us is whether the Court of Appeals lacked jurisdiction to entertain an appeal filed outside the 14-day window allowed by § 2107(c) but within the longer period granted by the District Court.

A

This Court has long held that the taking of an appeal within the prescribed time is "mandatory and jurisdictional." *Griggs v. Provident Consumer Discount Co.,* 459 U.S. 56, 61 (1982) *(per curiam).* Indeed, even prior to the creation of the circuit courts of appeals, this Court regarded statutory limitations on the timing of appeals as limitations on its own jurisdiction. See *Scarborough v. Pargoud,* 108 U.S. 567, 568 (1883) ("[T]he writ of error in this case was not brought within the time limited by law, and we have consequently no jurisdiction"); *United States v. Curry,* 6 How. 106, 113 (1848) ("[A]s this appeal has not been prosecuted in the manner directed, within the time limited by the acts of Congress, it must be dismissed for want of jurisdiction"). Reflecting the consistency of this Court's holdings, the courts of appeals routinely and uniformly dismiss untimely appeals for lack of jurisdiction. * * *

Although several of our recent decisions have undertaken to clarify the distinction between claims-processing rules and jurisdictional rules, none of them calls into question our longstanding treatment of statutory time limits for taking an appeal as jurisdictional. Indeed, those decisions have also recognized the jurisdictional significance of the fact that a time limitation is set forth in a statute. In *Kontrick v. Ryan,* 540 U.S. 443 (2004), we held that failure to comply with the time requirement in Federal Rule of Bankruptcy Procedure 4004 did not affect a court's subject-matter jurisdiction. Critical to our analysis was the fact that "[n]o statute . . . specifies a time limit for filing a complaint objecting to the debtor's discharge." 540 U.S., at 448. Rather, the filing deadlines in the Bankruptcy Rules are " 'procedural rules adopted by the Court for the orderly transaction of its business' " that are " 'not jurisdictional.' " *Id.,* at 454. Because "[o]nly Congress may determine a lower federal court's subject-matter jurisdiction," 540 U.S. at 452 (citing U.S. Const., Art. III, § 1), it was improper for courts to use "the term 'jurisdictional' to describe emphatic time prescriptions in rules of court," 540 U.S., at 454. See also *Eberhart v. United States,* 546 U.S. 12 (2005) *(per curiam).* As a point of contrast, we noted that § 2107 contains the type of statutory time constraints that would limit a court's jurisdiction. 540 U.S. at 453. Nor do *Arbaugh v. Y & H Corp.,* 546 U.S. 500 (2006), or *Scarborough v. Principi,* 541 U.S. 401 (2004), aid petitioner. In *Arbaugh,* the statutory limitation was an employee-numerosity requirement, not a time limit. 546 U.S. at 505. *Scarborough,* which addressed the availability of attorney's fees under the Equal Access to Justice Act, concerned "a mode of relief . . . ancillary to the judgment of a court" that already had plenary jurisdiction. 541 U.S., at 413.

This Court's treatment of its certiorari jurisdiction also demonstrates the jurisdictional distinction between court-promulgated rules and limits enacted by Congress. According to our Rules, a petition for a writ of certiorari must be filed within 90 days of the entry of the judgment sought to be reviewed. See this Court's Rule 13.1. That 90-day period applies to both civil and criminal cases. But the 90-day period for civil cases derives from both this Court's Rule 13.1 and 28 U.S.C. § 2101(c). We have repeatedly held that this statute-based filing period for civil cases is jurisdictional. * * * On the other hand, we have treated the rule-based time limit for criminal cases differently, stating that it may be waived because "[t]he procedural rules adopted by the Court for the orderly transaction of its business are not jurisdictional and can be relaxed by the Court in the exercise of its discretion. . ." [Schact v. United States, 398 U.S.] at 64 [(1970)].

Jurisdictional treatment of statutory time limits makes good sense. Within constitutional bounds, Congress decides what cases the federal courts have jurisdiction to consider. Because Congress decides whether federal courts can hear cases at all, it can also determine when, and under what conditions, federal courts can hear them. See *Curry,* 6 How., at 113. Put another way, the notion of " 'subject-matter' " jurisdiction obviously extends to " 'classes of cases . . . falling within a court's adjudicatory authority,' " *Eberhart, supra,* at 16 (quoting *Kontrick, supra,* at 455), but it is no less "jurisdictional" when Congress forbids federal courts from adjudicating an otherwise legitimate "class of cases" after a certain period has elapsed from final judgment.

The resolution of this case follows naturally from this reasoning. Like the initial 30-day period for filing a notice of appeal, the limit on how long a district court may reopen that period is set forth in a statute, 28 U.S.C. § 2107(c). Because Congress specifically limited the amount of time by which district courts can extend the notice-of-appeal period in § 2107(c), that limitation is more than a simple "claim-processing rule." As we have long held, when an "appeal has not been prosecuted in the manner directed, within the time limited by the acts of Congress, it must be dismissed for want of jurisdiction." *Curry, supra,* at 113. Bowles' failure to file his notice of appeal in accordance with the statute therefore deprived the Court of Appeals of jurisdiction. And because Bowles' error is one of jurisdictional magnitude, he cannot rely on forfeiture or waiver to excuse his lack of compliance with the statute's time limitations. See *Arbaugh, supra,* at 513–514.

B

Bowles contends that we should excuse his untimely filing because he satisfies the "unique circumstances" doctrine, which has its roots in *Harris Truck Lines, Inc. v. Cherry Meat Packers, Inc.,* 371 U.S. 215 (1962) *(per curiam).* There, pursuant to then-Rule 73(a) of the Federal Rules of Civil Procedure, a District Court entertained a timely motion to extend the time for filing a notice of appeal. The District Court found the moving party had established a showing of "excusable neglect," as required by the Rule, and granted the motion. The Court of Appeals reversed the finding of excusable neglect and, accordingly, held that the District Court lacked jurisdiction to grant the extension. *Harris Truck Lines, Inc. v. Cherry Meat Packers, Inc.,* 303 F.2d 609, 611–612 (C.A.7 1962). This Court reversed, noting "the obvious great hardship to a party who relies upon the trial judge's finding of 'excusable neglect.'" 371 U.S., at 217.

Today we make clear that the timely filing of a notice of appeal in a civil case is a jurisdictional requirement. Because this Court has no authority to create equitable exceptions to jurisdictional requirements, use of the "unique circumstances" doctrine is illegitimate. Given that this Court has applied *Harris Truck Lines* only once in the last half century, *Thompson v. INS,* 375 U.S. 384 (1964)*(per curiam),* several courts have rightly questioned its continuing validity. See, *e.g., Panhorst v. United States,* 241 F.3d 367, 371 (C.A.4 2001) (doubting "the continued viability of the unique circumstances doctrine"). We see no compelling reason to resurrect the doctrine from its 40-year slumber. Accordingly, we reject Bowles' reliance on the doctrine, and we overrule *Harris Truck Lines* and *Thompson* to the extent they purport to authorize an exception to a jurisdictional rule.

C

If rigorous rules like the one applied today are thought to be inequitable, Congress may authorize courts to promulgate rules that excuse compliance with the statutory time limits. Even narrow rules to this effect would give rise to litigation testing their reach and would no doubt detract from the clarity of the rule. However, congressionally authorized rulemaking would likely lead to less litigation than court-created exceptions without authorization. And in all events, for the reasons discussed above, we lack present authority to make the exception petitioner seeks.

III

The Court of Appeals correctly held that it lacked jurisdiction to consider Bowles' appeal. The judgment of the Court of Appeals is affirmed.

It is so ordered.

JUSTICE SOUTER, with whom JUSTICE STEVENS, JUSTICE GINSBURG, and JUSTICE BREYER join, dissenting.

The District Court told petitioner Keith Bowles that his notice of appeal was due on February 27, 2004. He filed a notice of appeal on February 26, only to be told that he was too late because his deadline had actually been February 24. It is intolerable for the judicial system to treat people this way, and there is not even a technical justification for condoning this bait and switch. I respectfully dissent.

I

" 'Jurisdiction,' " we have warned several times in the last decade, " 'is a word of many, too many, meanings.' " *Steel Co. v. Citizens for Better Environment,* 523 U.S. 83, 90 (1998). * * *

In recent years, however, we have tried to clean up our language, and until today we have been avoiding the erroneous jurisdictional conclusions that flow from indiscriminate use of the ambiguous word. Thus, although we used to call the sort of time limit at issue here "mandatory and jurisdictional," *United States v. Robinson,* 361 U.S. 220, 229 (1960), we have recently and repeatedly corrected that designation as a misuse of the "jurisdiction" label. *Arbaugh,* [546 U.S.] at 510 (2006) (citing *Robinson* as an example of improper use of the term "jurisdiction"); *Eberhart v. United States,* 546 U.S. 12, 17–18 (2005) *(per curiam)* (same); *Kontrick,* [540 U.S.] at 454 (2004) (same).

But one would never guess this from reading the Court's opinion in this case, which suddenly restores *Robinson's* indiscriminate use of the "mandatory and jurisdictional" label to good law in the face of three unanimous repudiations of *Robinson's* error. This is puzzling, the more so because our recent (and, I repeat, unanimous) efforts to confine jurisdictional rulings to jurisdiction proper were obviously sound, and the majority makes no attempt to show they were not.

The stakes are high in treating time limits as jurisdictional. While a mandatory but nonjurisdictional limit is enforceable at the insistence of a party claiming its benefit or by a judge concerned with moving the docket, it may be waived or mitigated in exercising reasonable equitable discretion. But if a limit is taken to be jurisdictional, waiver becomes impossible, meritorious excuse irrelevant (unless the statute so provides), and *sua sponte* consideration in the courts of appeals mandatory, see *Arbaugh.* As the Court recognizes, this is no way to regard time limits set out in a court rule rather than a statute, see *Kontrick* ("Only Congress may determine a lower federal court's subject-matter jurisdiction"). But neither is jurisdictional treatment automatic when a time limit is statutory, as it is in this case. Generally speaking, limits on the reach of federal statutes, even nontemporal ones, are only jurisdictional if Congress says so: "when Congress does not rank a statutory limitation on coverage as jurisdictional, courts should treat the restriction as nonjurisdictional in character." *Arbaugh,* 546 U.S. at 516. Thus, we have held "that time prescriptions," however emphatic, "are not properly typed "jurisdictional," absent some jurisdictional designation by Congress. Congress put no jurisdictional tag on the time limit here.

The doctrinal underpinning of this recently repeated view was set out in *Kontrick:* "the label 'jurisdictional' [is appropriate] not for claim-processing rules, but only for prescriptions delineating the classes of cases (subject-matter jurisdiction) and the persons (personal jurisdiction) falling within a court's adjudicatory authority." 540 U.S. at 455. A filing deadline is the paradigm of a claim-processing rule, not of a delineation of cases that federal courts may hear, and so it falls outside the class of limitations on subject matter jurisdiction unless Congress says otherwise.

The time limit at issue here, far from defining the set of cases that may be adjudicated, is much more like a statute of limitations, which provides an affirmative defense, see Fed. Rule Civ. Proc. 8(c), and is not jurisdictional. Statutes of limitations may thus be waived, or excused by rules, such as equitable tolling, that alleviate hardship and unfairness.

Consistent with the traditional view of statutes of limitations, and the carefully limited concept of jurisdiction explained in *Arbaugh, Eberhart,* and *Kontrick,* an exception to the time limit in 28 U.S.C. § 2107(c) should be available when there is a good justification for one, for reasons we recognized years ago. In *Harris Truck Lines, Inc. v. Cherry Meat Packers, Inc.,* 371 U.S. 215, 217 (1962) *(per curiam),* and *Thompson v. INS,* 375 U.S. 384, 387 (1964) *(per curiam),* we found that "unique circumstances" excused failures to comply with the time limit. In fact, much like this case, *Harris* and *Thompson* involved district court errors that misled litigants into believing they had more time to file notices of appeal than a statute actually provided. Thus, even back when we thoughtlessly called time limits jurisdictional, we did not actually treat them as beyond exemption to the point of shrugging at the inequity of penalizing a party for relying on what a federal judge had said to him. Since we did not dishonor reasonable reliance on a judge's official word back in the days when we uncritically had a jurisdictional reason to be unfair, it is unsupportable to dishonor it now, after repeatedly disavowing any such jurisdictional justification that would apply to the 14-day time limit of § 2107(c).

* * *

In ruling that Bowles cannot depend on the word of a District Court Judge, the Court demonstrates that no one may depend on the recent, repeated, and unanimous statements of all participating Justices of this Court. Yet more incongruously, all of these pronouncements by the Court, along with two of our cases, are jettisoned in a ruling for which the leading justification is *stare decisis* ("This Court has long held . . .").

II

We have the authority to recognize an equitable exception to the 14-day limit, and we should do that here, as it certainly seems reasonable to rely on an order from a federal judge. Bowles, though, does not have to convince us as a matter of first impression that his reliance was justified, for we only have to look as far as *Thompson* to know that he ought to prevail. There, the would-be appellant, Thompson, had filed post-trial motions 12 days after the District Court's final order. Although the rules said they should have been filed within 10, Fed. Rules Civ. Proc. 52(b) and 59(b) (1964), the trial court nonetheless had "specifically declared that the 'motion for a new trial' was made 'in ample time.' " *Thompson,* 375 U.S., at 385. Thompson relied on that statement in filing a notice of appeal within 60 days of the denial of the post-trial motions but not within 60 days of entry of the original judgment. Only timely post-trial motions affected the 60-day time limit for filing a notice of appeal, Rule 73(a) (1964), so the Court of Appeals held the appeal untimely. We vacated because Thompson "relied on the statement of the District Court and filed the appeal within the assumedly new deadline but beyond the old deadline." *Id.* at 387.

Thompson should control. In that case, and this one, the untimely filing of a notice of appeal resulted from reliance on an error by a district court, an error that caused no evident prejudice to the other party. Actually, there is one difference between *Thompson* and this case: Thompson filed his post-trial motions late and the District Court was mistaken when it said they were timely; here, the District Court made the error out of the blue, not on top of any mistake by Bowles, who then filed his notice of appeal by the specific date the District Court had declared timely. If anything, this distinction ought to work in Bowles's favor. Why should we have rewarded Thompson, who introduced the error, but now punish Bowles, who merely trusted the District Court's statement? * * *

I would vacate the decision of the Court of Appeals and remand for consideration of the merits.

NOTES AND QUESTIONS

1. Note that although Bowles asked the federal courts to review his state court *criminal* conviction, the Supreme Court treated the federal habeas proceeding as a *civil* proceeding governed by applicable statutes and federal rules. Such proceedings typically name the warden of the state penitentiary, here Russell, as the nominal defendant; the action tests the legality of the

state's continuing custody of the petitioner. While the Court consistently treats federal habeas proceedings as civil matters, it does not invariably regard the Federal Rules of Civil Procedure as controlling. See, e.g., Mayle v. Felix, 545 U.S. 644 (2005) (concluding that the usual transaction-based approach to relation-back analysis of the timeliness of an amended complaint under Rule 15 did not apply to federal habeas proceedings).

2.   Rule 3 of the Federal Rules of Appellate Procedure (FRAP) requires that the appellant file the notice of appeal with the clerk of the *district* court and imposes on the clerk the duty to serve the notice on other parties. Rule 3 also specifies the contents of the notice in relatively straightforward terms (names of appellants, caption of proceeding). Given the relative simplicity of filing such a notice, why would a party ever fail to act within the 30 day deadline for filing the notice set forth in Rule 4 (or as extended at the discretion of the district court)? Consider that the rules apply to all appeals, civil and criminal. Some criminal appellants, incarcerated and acting *pro se,* may have difficulty acting with dispatch. Even appellants with counsel (like Bowles) may consider a range of options (such as a motion for new trial or for relief from judgment) in addition to an appeal. For all litigants, the time limits for filing the appellate record and briefs begin to run on the date on which the appeal was filed. Finally, as we will see, there may be cases in which the parties cannot know for sure if the district court order will be regarded as a final judgment.

3.   The problem of how to characterize a particular issue crops up frequently in law. Recall for example the Court's struggle to characterize matters as substantive or procedural for purposes of the *Erie* doctrine. See Chapter 11. Here, the Court divides over whether to characterize as "jurisdictional" the time limits for filing a notice of appeal. Jurisdictional defects cannot be waived by the parties but can be raised at any time (even by the party that invoked the appellate court's jurisdiction). Moreover, the appellate court has an affirmative duty to inquire into its own jurisdiction and must raise the issue on its own motion. Finally, the court cannot forgive a time limit on equitable grounds, however reasonable the appellant's reliance or harsh the application of the strict rule. In contrast, the dissent's characterization of the rule as mandatory, rather than jurisdictional, would have meant that the rule operated somewhat like a statute of limitations; binding and dispositive if raised by opposing counsel but subject to waiver and equitable estoppel.

4.   As the *Bowles* dissent pointed out, recent decisions of the Supreme Court had refused to ascribe jurisdictional status to a range of time limits. See Eberhart v. United States, 546 U.S. 12 (2005) (time limit to file motion for new trial not jurisdictional); Kontrick v. Ryan, 540 U.S. 443 (2004) (time for filing in bankruptcy not jurisdictional); cf. Arbaugh v. Y & H Corp., 546 U.S. 500 (2006) (size-of-workforce rule to determine employment discrimination statute's application not jurisdictional). Those decisions relied on a functional analysis of the rule in question. Claim-processing rules were viewed as merely mandatory; rules that define the kinds of cases or disputing parties that fall

within federal adjudicatory power were seen as jurisdictional. How readily can lower courts apply such a functional analysis? Is such analysis consistent with the notion that Congress ultimately defines the jurisdiction of the lower federal courts and can use whatever terms it chooses in limiting that jurisdiction? One scholar observes that the dissent's approach would at most produce a canon of statutory construction that would leave Congress ultimately in charge of specifying the "jurisdictionality" of its rules. See Dane, Sad Time: Thoughts on Jurisdictionality, Legal Imagination, and Bowles v. Russell, 102 Nw. U. L. Rev. Colloq. 164 (2008).

5.   What happens after *Bowles* when a party timely invokes the district court's discretion to enlarge the time for filing the notice of appeal, but the time allowed exceeds that specified in the appellate rules (but not the statute)? That was the question in Hamer v. Neighborhood Hous. Servs., 138 S.Ct. 13 (2017), a case that arose when plaintiff sought and received a sixty-day extension of the time to appeal from the district court's final order. Under Rule 4(a)(5)(C), no extension may exceed 30 days after the prescribed time or 14 days after the date when the order granting the motion is entered, whichever is later. Hamer filed her notice of appeal within the time permitted by the district court order, but exceeded that allowable under FRAP 4(a)(5)(C). Section 2107 (discussed in *Bowles*) does not set a time limit for the period of an allowable extension of the kind Hamer sought. Noticing the problem on its own motion and asking the parties to brief the issue, the Seventh Circuit treated FRAP 4(a)(5)(C) as a rulemakers' jurisdictional gloss on the statute rather than as a claim-processing rule.

In an unanimous opinion by Justice Ginsburg, the Supreme Court reversed. Apparently setting a bright-line rule to guide future cases, the Court sharply distinguished between statutory time limits and those specified by rulemakers:

> Accordingly, a provision governing the time to appeal in a civil action qualifies as jurisdictional only if Congress sets the time. * * * A time limit not prescribed by Congress ranks as a mandatory claim-processing rule, serving "to promote the orderly progress of litigation by requiring that the parties take certain procedural steps at certain specified times."

Hamer, 138 S.Ct. at 17 (citations omitted). Having found the Rule 4 time limits non-jurisdictional, the Court remanded for further consideration of such questions as whether defendants' failure to object to the district court's extension effected a forfeiture of their right to challenge the appeal's timeliness and, if not, whether equitable factors warranted an exception to Rule 4(a)(5)(C).

The *Hamer* Court self-consciously limited its approach to what it termed the "timebound transfer of adjudicatory authority from one Article III court to another." 138 S.Ct. at 20 n. 9. Outside that setting, the Court will continue to treat as jurisdictional only those threshold limitations that the legislature "clearly states * * * shall count as [such]." Id. For examples, see note 8 infra.

6.   What other elements of the notice of appeal might be considered jurisdictional? Rule 3 requires that the notice of appeal name all of the parties to the appeal, and omission of parties can be fatal. See Torres v. Oakland Scavenger Co., 487 U.S. 312 (1988) (where one plaintiff's name was omitted from notice of appeal due to clerical error, judgment became final as to him even though it was reversed as to the other 15 plaintiffs). 28 U.S.C. § 2107 does not in terms foreclose appellate review on behalf of parties omitted due to clerical error.

7.   By its terms, FRAP Rule 4 governs the time for filing notices of appeal *as of right*. As we will see, the jurisdictional statutes also recognize a variety of modes of *discretionary* review for which the time limits may differ. For applications for discretionary review under 28 U.S.C. § 1292(b), for example, the party must seek an order first from the district court and, if successful, apply within ten days to the appellate court for an order allowing the appeal. The All Writs Act, 28 U.S.C. § 1651, which provides federal appellate courts with the power to issue writs of mandamus, does not specify a time limit for filing the petition for review. Cf. FRAP Rule 5(a)(2) (incorporating the timeliness rules of Rule 4 to govern petitions for discretionary review). In Cheney v. U.S. District Court for the District of Columbia, 542 U.S. 367 (2004), the Supreme Court concluded that the strict time limits of Rule 4 did not apply to the government's petition for mandamus review of an interlocutory District Court ruling that required the disclosure of information about the formulation of government energy policy. Instead, the Court applied a laches test to determine whether the government had "slept on its rights" or acted in ways that would prejudice the opposing party. The *Cheney* Court did not address the possibly jurisdictional nature of the time limits involved in concluding that the mandamus petition was properly before the appellate court. Note that 28 U.S.C. § 2107, the statute relied on in *Bowles v. Russell,* applies to any "appeal" from "any judgment, decree or order" in an action of a civil nature. Does the discretionary nature of mandamus review make this jurisdictional reference to review by way of an as-of-right appeal inapplicable?

8.   Compare Bowles v. Russell to Henderson v. Shinseki, 562 U.S. 428 (2011). A veteran sought to appeal a denial of benefits to the US Court of Appeals for Veteran's Benefits, an Article I tribunal. The relevant statute reads as follows:

> a person adversely affected by [the board's] decision shall file a notice of appeal with the Court within 120 days after the date on which notice of the decision is mailed pursuant to section 7104(e) of this title.

38 U.S.C. § 7266(a). The government argued that the 120-day limit operated as a jurisdictional bar to appellate review, foreclosing any tolling of the time limit and requiring dismissal of a veteran's untimely appeal. The Court rejected this argument, emphasizing a variety of factors: the placement of the time limit outside that portion of the statute that addresses the court's jurisdiction; the fact that the veterans benefit statute requires special solicitude for the rights of veterans, who often pursue benefit claims pro se; the

fact that such solicitude does not apply in the context of the ordinary run of adversarial litigation in such cases as *Bowles*, and the fact that the power in question was that of an Article I tribunal, acting as part of a complex administrative scheme, rather than an Article III court.

Consider also Gonzalez v. Thaler, 132 S.Ct. 641 (2012). There, the Court considered the jurisdictional quality of a federal statute that restricted the appellate jurisdiction of the federal circuits courts to situations in which a federal habeas petitioner had obtained a certificate of appealability (COA) from a circuit court or judge. The statute went on to limit such certificates to cases in which the petitioner has made a "substantial showing" of a constitutional violation and has indicated what particular issues provide the requisite showing. The Court found that the required indication of constitutional issues was not a jurisdictional element of the petitioner's right to appeal, and thus upheld the power of the federal appellate court to hear a habeas claim that omitted such an indication. Summarizing its analysis, the Court said (id. at 648–49):

> We accordingly have applied the following principle: A rule is jurisdictional "[i]f the Legislature clearly states that a threshold limitation on a statute's scope shall count as jurisdictional." *Arbaugh v. Y & H Corp.,* 546 U.S. 500, 515 (2006). But if "Congress does not rank a statutory limitation on coverage as jurisdictional, courts should treat the restriction as nonjurisdictional." *Id.* That clear-statement principle makes particular sense in this statute, as we consider * * * the extent to which Congress intended the COA process outlined in [the statute] to further limit the courts of appeals' jurisdiction over habeas appeals.

Among other assertions, the majority observed that its recent decisions sought to "bring some discipline" to its jurisdictional characterizations. Id. at 648 (citing Henderson v. Shinseki). See also Reed Elsevier, Inc. v. Muchnick, 559 U.S. 154 (2010) (statutory requirement that a party register a copyright before suing for infringement was not jurisdictional; expressing view that more recent decisions seek to curtail what it characterized as "drive-by" jurisdictional rulings).

9.   Scholars have been largely, though not uniformly, critical of the Court's approach in *Bowles*. See Dodson, Hybridizing Jurisdiction, 99 Cal. L. Rev. 1439 (2011); Dodson, The Failure of Bowles v. Russell, 43 Tulsa L. Rev. 631 (2008) (acknowledging that the result in Bowles may have been correct, even if wrongly based on a jurisdictional characterization); Wasserman, Jurisdiction, Merits, and Procedure: Thoughts on a Trichotomy, 102 Nw. U. L. Rev. 1547 (2008).

2. AS-OF-RIGHT APPELLATE REVIEW AND THE FINAL JUDGMENT RULE

A. The Final Judgment Rule

BULLARD V. BLUE HILLS BANK

Supreme Court of the United States, 2015
135 S.Ct. 1686

CHIEF JUSTICE ROBERTS delivered the opinion of the Court.

Chapter 13 of the Bankruptcy Code affords individuals receiving regular income an opportunity to obtain some relief from their debts while retaining their property. To proceed under Chapter 13, a debtor must propose a plan to use future income to repay a portion (or in the rare case all) of his debts over the next three to five years. If the bankruptcy court confirms the plan and the debtor successfully carries it out, he receives a discharge of his debts according to the plan.

The bankruptcy court may, however, decline to confirm a proposed repayment plan because it is inconsistent with the Code. Although the debtor is usually given an opportunity to submit a revised plan, he may be convinced that the original plan complied with the Code and that the bankruptcy court was wrong to deny confirmation. The question presented is whether such an order denying confirmation is a "final" order that the debtor can immediately appeal. We hold that it is not.

I

In December 2010, Louis Bullard filed a petition for Chapter 13 bankruptcy in Federal Bankruptcy Court in Massachusetts. A week later he filed a proposed repayment plan listing the various claims he anticipated creditors would file and the monthly amounts he planned to pay on each claim over the five-year life of his plan. See 11 U.S.C. §§ 1321, 1322. Chief among Bullard's debts was the roughly $346,000 he owed to Blue Hills Bank, which held a mortgage on a multifamily house Bullard owned. Bullard's plan indicated that the mortgage was significantly "underwater": that is, the house was worth substantially less than the amount Bullard owed the Bank.

Before submitting his plan for court approval, Bullard amended it three times over the course of a year to more accurately reflect the value of the house, the terms of the mortgage, the amounts of creditors' claims, and his proposed payments. See § 1323 (allowing preconfirmation modification). Bullard's third amended plan—the one at issue here— proposed a "hybrid" treatment of his debt to the Bank. He proposed splitting the debt into a secured claim in the amount of the house's then-current value (which he estimated at $245,000), and an unsecured claim for the remainder (roughly $101,000). Under the plan, Bullard would continue making his regular mortgage payments toward the secured claim, which he would eventually repay in full, long after the conclusion of his bankruptcy case. He would treat the unsecured claim, however, the same as any other unsecured debt, paying only as much on it as his income would allow over the course of his five-year plan. At the end of this period the remaining balance on the unsecured portion of the loan would be discharged. In total, Bullard's plan called for him to pay only about $5,000 of the $101,000 unsecured claim.

The Bank (no surprise) objected to the plan and, after a hearing, the Bankruptcy Court declined to confirm it. *In re Bullard,* 475 B.R.304 (Bkrtcy.Ct.D.Mass.2012). The court concluded that Chapter 13 did not allow Bullard to split the Bank's claim as he proposed unless he paid the secured portion in full during the plan period. *Id.* at 314. The court acknowledged, however, that other Bankruptcy Courts in the First Circuit had approved such arrangements. *Id.* at 309. The Bankruptcy Court ordered Bullard to submit a new plan within 30 days. *Id.* at 314.

Bullard appealed to the Bankruptcy Appellate Panel (BAP) of the First Circuit. The BAP first addressed its jurisdiction under the bankruptcy appeals statute, noting that a party can immediately appeal only "final" orders of a bankruptcy court. *In re Bullard,* 494 B.R. 92, 95 (2013) (citing 28 U.S.C. § 158(a)(1)). The BAP concluded that the order denying plan confirmation was not final because Bullard was "free to propose an alternate plan." 494 B.R. at 95. The BAP nonetheless exercised its discretion to hear the appeal under a provision that allows interlocutory appeals "with leave of the court." § 158(a)(3). The BAP granted such leave because the confirmation dispute involved a "controlling question of law . . . as to which there is substantial ground for difference of opinion," and "an immediate appeal [would] materially advance the ultimate termination of the litigation." 494 B.R. at 95 & n. 5. On the merits, the BAP agreed with the Bankruptcy Court that Bullard's proposed treatment of the Bank's claim was not allowed. *Id.* at 96–101.

Bullard sought review in the Court of Appeals for the First Circuit, but that court dismissed his appeal for lack of jurisdiction. *In re Bullard,* 752 F.3d 483 (2014). The First Circuit noted that because the BAP had not certified the appeal under § 158(d)(2), the only possible source of Court of Appeals jurisdiction was § 158(d)(1), which allowed appeal of only a final order of the BAP. *Id.* at 485 & n. 3. And under First Circuit precedent "an order of the BAP cannot be final unless the underlying bankruptcy court order is final." *Id.* at 485. The Court of Appeals accordingly examined whether a bankruptcy court's denial of plan confirmation is a final order, a question that it recognized had divided the Circuits. Adopting the majority view, the First Circuit concluded that an order denying confirmation is not final so long as the debtor remains free to propose another plan.

II

In ordinary civil litigation, a case in federal district court culminates in a "final decisio[n]," 28 U.S.C. § 1291, a ruling "by which a district court disassociates itself from a case," *Swint v. Chambers County Comm'n,* 514 U.S. 35, 42 (1995). A party can typically appeal as of right only from that final decision. This rule reflects the conclusion that "[p]ermitting piecemeal, prejudgment appeals . . . undermines 'efficient judicial administration' and encroaches upon the prerogatives of district court judges, who play a 'special role' in managing ongoing litigation." *Mohawk Industries, Inc. v. Carpenter,* 558 U.S. 100, 106 (2009) (quoting *Firestone Tire & Rubber Co. v. Risjord,* 449 U.S. 368, 374 (1981)).

The rules are different in bankruptcy. A bankruptcy case involves "an aggregation of individual controversies," many of which would exist as stand-alone lawsuits but for the bankrupt status of the debtor. 1 Collier on Bankruptcy ¶ 5.08[1][b], p. 5–42 (16th ed. 2014). Accordingly, "Congress has long provided that orders in bankruptcy cases may be immediately appealed if they finally dispose of discrete disputes within the larger case." *Howard Delivery Service, Inc. v. Zurich American Ins. Co.,* 547 U.S. 651, 657, n. 3 (2006) (internal quotation marks and emphasis omitted). The current bankruptcy appeals statute reflects this approach: It authorizes appeals as of right not only from final judgments in cases but from "final judgments, orders, and decrees . . . in cases and proceedings." § 158(a).

The present dispute is about how to define the immediately appealable "proceeding" in the context of the consideration of Chapter 13 plans. Bullard argues for a plan-by-plan approach. Each time the bankruptcy court reviews a proposed plan, he says, it conducts a separate proceeding. On this view, an order denying confirmation and an order granting confirmation both terminate that proceeding, and both are therefore final and appealable.

In the Bank's view Bullard is slicing the case too thin. The relevant "proceeding," it argues, is the entire process of considering plans, which terminates only when a plan is confirmed or—if the debtor fails to offer any confirmable plan—when the case is dismissed. An order denying confirmation is not final, so long as it leaves the debtor free to propose another plan.

We agree with the Bank: The relevant proceeding is the process of attempting to arrive at an approved plan that would allow the bankruptcy to move forward. This is so, first and foremost, because only plan confirmation—or case dismissal—alters the status quo and fixes the rights and obligations of the parties. When the bankruptcy court confirms a plan, its terms become binding on debtor and creditor alike. 11 U.S.C. § 1327(a). Confirmation has preclusive effect, foreclosing relitigation of "any issue actually litigated by the parties and any issue necessarily determined by the confirmation order." 8 Collier ¶ 1327.02[1][c], at 1327–6; see also

United Student Aid Funds, Inc. v. Espinosa, 559 U.S. 260, 275 (2010) (finding a confirmation order "enforceable and binding" on a creditor notwithstanding legal error when the creditor "had notice of the error and failed to object or timely appeal"). Subject to certain exceptions, confirmation "vests all of the property of the [bankruptcy] estate in the debtor," and renders that property "free and clear of any claim or interest of any creditor provided for by the plan." §§ 1327(b), (c). Confirmation also triggers the Chapter 13 trustee's duty to distribute to creditors those funds already received from the debtor. § 1326(a)(2).

When confirmation is denied *and the case is dismissed as a result,* the consequences are similarly significant. Dismissal of course dooms the possibility of a discharge and the other benefits available to a debtor under Chapter 13. Dismissal lifts the automatic stay entered at the start of bankruptcy, exposing the debtor to creditors' legal actions and collection efforts. § 362(c)(2). And it can limit the availability of an automatic stay in a subsequent bankruptcy case. § 362(c)(3).

Denial of confirmation with leave to amend, by contrast, changes little. The automatic stay persists. The parties' rights and obligations remain unsettled. The trustee continues to collect funds from the debtor in anticipation of a different plan's eventual confirmation. The possibility of discharge lives on. "Final" does not describe this state of affairs. An order denying confirmation does rule out the specific arrangement of relief embodied in a particular plan. But that alone does not make the denial final any more than, say, a car buyer's declining to pay the sticker price is viewed as a "final" purchasing decision by either the buyer or seller. "It ain't over till it's over."

Several additional considerations bolster our conclusion that the relevant "proceeding" is the entire process culminating in confirmation or dismissal. First is a textual clue. Among the list of "core proceedings" statutorily entrusted to bankruptcy judges are "confirmations of plans." 28 U.S.C. § 157(b)(2)(L). Although this item hardly clinches the matter for the Bank—the provision's purpose is not to explain appealability—it does cut in the Bank's favor. The presence of the phrase "confirmations of plans," combined with the absence of any reference to denials, suggests that Congress viewed the larger confirmation process as the "proceeding," not the ruling on each specific plan.

In Bullard's view the debtor can appeal the denial of the first plan he submits to the bankruptcy court. If the court of appeals affirms the denial, the debtor can then revise the plan. If the new plan is also denied confirmation, another appeal can ensue. And so on. As Bullard's case shows, each climb up the appellate ladder and slide down the chute can take more than a year. Avoiding such delays and inefficiencies is precisely the reason for a rule of finality. It does not make much sense to define the pertinent proceeding so narrowly that the requirement of finality would do little work as a meaningful constraint on the availability of appellate review.

Bullard responds that concerns about frequent piecemeal appeals are misplaced in this context. Debtors do not typically have the money or incentives to take appeals over small beer issues. They will only appeal the relatively rare denials based on significant legal rulings—precisely the cases that should proceed promptly to the courts of appeals.

Bullard's assurance notwithstanding, debtors may often view, in good faith or bad, the prospect of appeals as important leverage in dealing with creditors. An appeal extends the automatic stay that comes with bankruptcy, which can cost creditors money and allow a debtor to retain property he might lose if the Chapter 13 proceeding turns out not to be viable. These concerns are heightened if the same rule applies in Chapter 11, as the parties assume. Chapter 11 debtors, often business entities, are more likely to have the resources to appeal and may do so on narrow issues. But even if Bullard is correct that such appeals will be rare, that does not much support his broader point that an appeal of right should be allowed in every case. It is odd, after all, to argue in favor of allowing more appeals by emphasizing that almost nobody will take them.

We think that in the ordinary case treating only confirmation or dismissal as final will not unfairly burden a debtor. He retains the valuable exclusive right to propose plans, which he can modify freely. 11 U.S.C. §§ 1321, 1323. The knowledge that he will have no guaranteed appeal from a denial should encourage the debtor to work with creditors and the trustee to develop a confirmable plan as promptly as possible. And expedition is always an important consideration in bankruptcy.

III

The Solicitor General [as amicus curiae] notes that disputes in bankruptcy are generally classified as either "adversary proceedings," essentially full civil lawsuits carried out under the umbrella of the bankruptcy case, or "contested matters," an undefined catchall for other issues the parties dispute. See Fed. Rule Bkrtcy. Proc. 7001 (listing ten adversary proceedings); Rule 9014 (addressing "contested matter[s] not otherwise governed by these rules"). An objection to a plan initiates a contested matter. See Rule 3015(f). Everyone agrees that an order resolving that matter by overruling the objection and confirming the plan is final. As the Solicitor General sees it, an order denying confirmation would also resolve that contested matter, so such an order should also be considered final.

The scope of the Solicitor General's argument is unclear. At points his brief appears to argue that an order resolving *any* contested matter is final and immediately appealable. That version of the argument has the virtue of resting on a general principle—but the vice of being implausible. As a leading treatise notes, the list of contested matters is "endless" and covers all sorts of minor disagreements. 10 Collier ¶ 9014.01, at 9014–3. The concept of finality cannot stretch to cover, for example, an order resolving a disputed request for an extension of time.

At other points, the Solicitor General appears to argue that because one possible resolution of this particular contested matter (confirmation) is final, the other (denial) must be as well. But this argument begs the question. It simply assumes that confirmation is appealable because it resolves a contested matter, and that therefore anything else that resolves the contested matter must also be appealable. But one can just as easily contend that confirmation is appealable because it resolves the entire plan consideration process, and that therefore the entire process is the "proceeding." A decision that does not resolve the entire plan consideration process—denial—is therefore not appealable.

Perhaps the Solicitor General's suggestion is that a separately appealable "proceeding" must coincide precisely with a particular "adversary proceeding" or "contested matter" under the Bankruptcy Rules. He does not, however, provide any support for such a suggestion. More broadly, it is of course quite common for the finality of a decision to depend on which way the decision goes. An order granting a motion for summary judgment is final; an order denying such a motion is not.

Bullard and the Solicitor General also contend that our rule creates an unfair asymmetry: If the bankruptcy court sustains an objection and denies confirmation, the debtor (always the plan proponent in Chapter 13) must go back to the drafting table and try again; but if the bankruptcy court overrules an objection and grants confirmation, a creditor can appeal without delay. But any asymmetry in this regard simply reflects the fact that confirmation allows the bankruptcy to go forward and alters the legal relationships among the parties, while denial does not have such significant consequences.

Moreover, it is not clear that this asymmetry will always advantage creditors. Consider a creditor who strongly supports a proposed plan because it treats him well. If the bankruptcy court sustains an objection from another creditor—perhaps because the plan treats the first creditor too well—the first creditor might have as keen an interest in a prompt appeal as the debtor. And yet, under the rule we adopt, that creditor too would have to await further developments.

Bullard also raises a more practical objection. If denial orders are not final, he says, there will be no effective means of obtaining appellate review of the denied proposal. The debtor's only two options would be to seek or accept dismissal of his case and then appeal, or to propose an amended plan and appeal its confirmation.

The first option is not realistic, Bullard contends, because dismissal means the end of the automatic stay against creditors' collection efforts. Without the stay, the debtor might lose the very property at issue in the rejected plan. Even if a bankruptcy court agrees to maintain the stay pending appeal, the debtor is still risking his entire bankruptcy case on the appeal.

The second option is no better, says Bullard. An acceptable, confirmable alternative may not exist. Even if one does, its confirmation might have immediate and irreversible effects—such as the sale or transfer of property—and a court is unlikely to stay its execution. Moreover, it simply wastes time and money to place the debtor in the position of seeking approval of a plan he does not want.

All good points. We do not doubt that in many cases these options may be, as the court below put it, "unappealing." But our litigation system has long accepted that certain burdensome rulings will be "only imperfectly reparable" by the appellate process. *Digital Equipment Corp. v. Desktop Direct, Inc.*, 511 U.S. 863, 872 (1994). This prospect is made tolerable in part by our confidence that bankruptcy courts, like trial courts in ordinary litigation, rule correctly most of the time. And even when they slip, many of their errors—wrongly concluding, say, that a debtor should pay unsecured creditors $400 a month rather than $300—will not be of a sort that justifies the costs entailed by a system of universal immediate appeals.

Sometimes, of course, a question will be important enough that it should be addressed immediately. Bullard's case could well fit the bill: The confirmability of his hybrid plan presented a pure question of law that had divided bankruptcy courts in the First Circuit and would make a substantial financial difference to the parties. But there are several mechanisms for interlocutory review to address such cases. First, a district court or BAP can (as the BAP did in this case) grant leave to hear such an appeal. 28 U.S.C. § 158(a)(3). A debtor who appeals to the district court and loses there can seek certification to the court of appeals under the general interlocutory appeals statute, § 1292(b). See *Connecticut Nat. Bank v. Germain,* 503 U.S. 249 (1992).

Another interlocutory mechanism is provided in § 158(d)(2). That provision allows a bankruptcy court, district court, BAP, or the parties acting jointly to certify a bankruptcy court's order to the court of appeals, which then has discretion to hear the matter. Unlike § 1292(b), which permits certification only when three enumerated factors suggesting importance are all present, § 158(d)(2) permits certification when any one of several such factors exists, a distinction that allows a broader range of interlocutory decisions to make their way to the courts of appeals. While discretionary review mechanisms such as these "do not provide relief in every case, they serve as useful safety valves for promptly correcting serious errors" and addressing important legal questions. *Mohawk,* 558 U.S. at 111.

Bullard maintains that interlocutory appeals are ineffective because lower courts have been too reticent in granting them. But Bullard did, after all, obtain one layer of interlocutory review when the BAP granted him leave to appeal under § 158(a)(3). He also sought certification to the Court of Appeals under § 158(d)(2), but the BAP denied his request for reasons that are not entirely clear. The fact that Bullard was not able to obtain further merits review in the First Circuit in this particular instance does not undermine our expectation that lower courts will certify and accept interlocutory appeals from plan denials in appropriate cases.

Because the Court of Appeals correctly held that the order denying confirmation was not final, its judgment is

Affirmed.

NOTES AND QUESTIONS

1.   Under 28 U.S.C. § 1291, the federal courts of appeals have jurisdiction over "appeals from all final decisions" of the district courts. This limitation of appeals to final decisions reflects a long-held policy of requiring that the appeal of any issues in a case be reserved until there is a final decision in the lower court. What is meant by a "final decision"? The Supreme Court has defined it as a judgment that "ends the litigation on the merits and leaves nothing for the court to do but execute the judgment." Catlin v. United States, 324 U.S. 229, 233 (1945). Two such examples are the granting of a Rule 12(b)(6) motion to dismiss and the granting of a Rule 12(c) motion for judgment on the pleadings where the answer admitted all the essential allegations of the claim made in the complaint. In these situations, there would be nothing further for the court to do but to execute the judgment (unless, of course, it also granted the losing party leave to amend the pleading).

Some orders clearly do not satisfy the test—for example, grant of a request that a party be ordered to produce materials through discovery, Alexander v. United States, 201 U.S. 117 (1906); and an order disqualifying counsel, Firestone Tire & Rubber Co. v. Risjord, 449 U.S. 368 (1981). Rule 54(a) of the Federal Rules of Civil Procedure defines as final "any order from which an appeal lies." Does that help?

Justice Frankfurter commented on the policy underlying the final decision rule:

> Finality as a condition of review is an historical characteristic of federal appellate procedure. It was written into the first Judiciary Act and has been departed from only when observance of it would practically defeat the right to any review at all. Since the right to a judgment from more than one court is a matter of grace and not

a necessary ingredient of justice, Congress from the very beginning has, by forbidding piecemeal disposition on appeal of what for practical purposes is a single controversy, set itself against enfeebling judicial administration.

Cobbledick v. United States, 309 U.S. 323, 324–25 (1940).

2.   As noted in the introduction to this chapter, the federal courts have treated the grant of appellate jurisdiction in 28 U.S.C. § 1291 as entitling the losing party to appellate review as a matter of right. (To be sure, the losing party must properly preserve the issue for appeal by raising it in the lower court and the lower court's resolution of the issue must have affected the outcome.) Appellate courts thus have no power to refrain from hearing properly filed appeals, but as noted, supra p. 1060, they often resolve them on the briefs without oral argument and decline to publish the resulting opinion. Read 28 U.S.C. § 1291. Would you characterize finality as a claims-processing rule or a jurisdictional rule within the framework set out in Bowles v. Russell, supra p. 1063. See Microsoft Corp. v. Baker, infra p. 1132 (treating finality as a jurisdictional question).

3.   Despite the efficiency arguments in favor of the finality rule, situations arise in which an appellate court can clarify issues of law that will help advance the speedy resolution of the dispute. Was *Bullard* such a case? The decision rejecting the debtor's proposed repayment plan was driven by the bankruptcy court's perception that applicable law did not authorize splitting a mortgage (secured credit) into secured and unsecured components and providing for less than full repayment of the unsecured portion. How were the parties and bankruptcy court to confirm a repayment plan without knowing the answer to that question? On the other hand, an ad hoc approach to the definition of finality that took account of the importance of the legal issue could tempt litigants to seek review of any number of questions, crowding appellate dockets. Appellate finality thus implicates the familiar debate over rules versus standards.

4.   Bankruptcy, as the Court emphasized in *Bullard*, presents special problems (most of which lie beyond the scope of this chapter). In general, the bankruptcy statute encourages creditors and debtors to seek the protection of bankruptcy when a debtor's assets and future income cannot meet her obligations. The filing of a bankruptcy petition stays all litigation and forces contending parties to litigate their claims in a single proceeding (something like a big interpleader action). Sometimes, as in the case of corporations, the bankruptcy court will order a liquidation and distribute assets to the creditors; secured creditors may get more, having bargained for an interest in the specific property of the debtor as a condition of extending credit. Often, the court will write down existing debt of unsecured creditors, wipe the slate clean, and provide a fresh start. Individual debtors, like Bullard, file for bankruptcy to obtain the stay, the consolidation of proceedings, the write down, and the fresh start.

Consider what happens in a complex bankruptcy proceeding in which the bankruptcy court confirms a reorganization plan and the parties begin to carry out the plan. When such actions to implement the plan have gotten well underway, they create reliance interests that may make the confirmation order very difficult to unwind on appeal. Such cases may trigger the application of what the federal appellate courts have termed "equitable mootness." Resembling waiver or forfeiture, the doctrine of equitable mootness ultimately rests on "the notion that, with the passage of time after a judgment in equity and implementation of that judgment, effective relief on appeal becomes impractical, imprudent, and therefore inequitable." In re City of Detroit, 838 F.3d 792, 798 (6th Cir. 2016). In that case, the Sixth Circuit explained the test as follows:

> We analyze equitable mootness under a three-part test: (1) whether a stay has been obtained; (2) whether the plan has been "substantially consummated"; and (3) whether the relief requested would significantly and irrevocably disrupt the implementation of the plan or disproportionately harm the reliance interests of other parties not before the court.

Applying the test, the court found that equitable mootness barred appellate review of the bankruptcy order confirming a plan that was to end the Detroit city bankruptcy. Id. *See also* In re United Producers, 526 F.3d 942, 947–48 (6th Cir. 2008) (applying the doctrine to corporate reorganizations under Chapter 11); In re Grimland, Inc., 243 F.3d 228, 231 (5th Cir. 2001) (same). Courts have applied the doctrine to municipal bankruptcies, as in the Detroit case, as well as to corporate reorganizations under chapter 11 and to individual bankruptcy plans under chapter 13 (the chapter at issue in *Bullard*). Does the prospect that equitable mootness will block review of orders that *approve* confirmation argue for a more flexible approach to finality when parties seek to appeal as in *Bullard* from orders that *deny* confirmation?

5.   The Court in *Bullard* described bankruptcy as an aggregation of individual disputes. It suggested that the rules of appellate finality apply to the individualized disputes themselves, rather than to the bankruptcy as a whole. Why didn't the dispute over the proper treatment of the bank's mortgage qualify as such an individual dispute?

Other proceedings in federal court represent an aggregation of individual disputes. In Gelboim v. Bank of America Corp., 135 S.Ct. 897 (2015), the Court considered the application of the final judgment rule in the context of proceedings consolidated for multi-district litigation in a single district court under 28 U.S.C. § 1407 (allowing transfer of cases "involving one or more common questions of fact . . . to any district for coordinated or consolidated pretrial proceedings"). The *Gelboim* action, a suit for damages under the antitrust laws, was joined with a variety of other challenges to the way banks had allegedly depressed the so-called

LIBOR rate to lower the amount of interest they were obliged to pay on a variety of financial instruments). While the great bulk of the LIBOR rate-depression actions remained pending, the district court dismissed all of the antitrust claims in this action on the ground that the Gelboim plaintiffs lacked antitrust standing. The Gelboim plaintiffs appealed from dismissal and the banks argued that the ongoing MDL proceeding meant that there was no final judgment. The Supreme Court found that the *Gelboim* order met the definition of finality:

> The District Court's order dismissing the Gelboim-Zacher complaint for lack of antitrust injury, without leave to amend, had the hallmarks of a final decision. Ruling on the merits of the case, the District Court completed its adjudication of petitioners' complaint and terminated their action. As a result of the District Court's disposition, petitioners are no longer participants in the consolidated proceedings. Nothing about the initial consolidation of their civil action with other cases in the LIBOR MDL renders the dismissal of their complaint in any way tentative or incomplete. As is ordinarily the case, the § 1407 consolidation offered convenience for the parties and promoted efficient judicial administration, but did not meld the Gelboim-Zacher action and others in the MDL into a single unit.

> The banks' view that, in a § 1407 consolidation, no appeal of right accrues until the consolidation ends would leave plaintiffs like Gelboim and Zacher in a quandary about the proper timing of their appeals. Under Federal Rule of Appellate Procedure 4, which this Court has called "jurisdictional," *Bowles v. Russell,* 551 U.S. 205, 209 (2007), a notice of appeal in a civil case must be filed "within 30 days after entry of the judgment or order appealed from," Rule 4(a)(1)(A). If plaintiffs whose actions have been dismissed with prejudice by a district court must await the termination of pretrial proceedings in all consolidated cases, what event or order would start the 30-day clock? When pretrial consolidation concludes, there may be no occasion for the entry of any judgment. Orders may issue returning cases to their originating courts, but an order of that genre would not qualify as the dispositive ruling Gelboim and Zacher seek to overturn on appeal. And surely would-be appellants need not await final disposition of all cases in their originating districts, long after pretrial consolidation under § 1407 could even arguably justify treating the cases as a judicial unit.

> The sensible solution to the appeal-clock trigger is evident: When the transferee court overseeing pretrial proceedings in multidistrict litigation grants a defendant's dispositive motion "on all issues in some transferred cases, [those cases] become

immediately appealable ... while cases where other issues remain would not be appealable at that time" (citation omitted).

Gelboim, 135 S.Ct. at 905–06.

6.   Does the Gelboim rule apply to civil actions joined or consolidated under other procedural rules?   The Supreme Court furnished an affirmative answer in Hall v. Hall, 138 S. Ct. 1118 (2018), concluding that proceedings consolidated pursuant to Fed. R. Civ. P. 42 retained their separate identity for finality purposes.   The case arose from a family dispute between daughter Elsa and son Samuel over Samuel's handling of their mother's assets.   Simplifying somewhat, Elsa sued brother Samuel on behalf of the trust to which the mother's assets had been transferred.   In addition to defending the trust claim, Samuel later brought suit against Elsa in her personal capacity, seeking damages in tort.   After the two actions were consolidated, the jury returned two verdicts for Samuel, one that led to entry of a final judgment rejecting the trust's claims in the trust action and a second awarding Samuel damages in the personal action, a verdict that was rendered non-final when the trial court granted Elsa's motion for a new trial.   On review, the Court held that Elsa could appeal on behalf of the trust from the judgment in the trust action without awaiting a second trial of the personal action.

B.   Exceptions to the Final Judgment Rule: Practical Finality

Two cases illustrate the application of a rule of practical finality. In Moses H. Cone Memorial Hospital v. Mercury Construction Corporation, 460 U.S. 1 (1983), a hospital and a contractor had entered into a contract for the construction of additions to the hospital. The contract included provisions for binding arbitration of certain claims. After a dispute arose, the hospital filed an action in state court, seeking declarations that the contractor had lost the right to arbitration and that the hospital was not liable to the contractor. It also sought a stay of arbitration. The contractor filed suit in federal court, seeking an order compelling arbitration under § 4 of the Federal Arbitration Act. On the hospital's motion, the federal court stayed the contractor's federal suit, pending resolution of the hospital's state court suit, under one of the abstention doctrines that allows a stay of federal suit in deference to parallel litigation pending in state court in the interests of "wise judicial administration"). The Court of Appeals, after finding that it had jurisdiction under § 1291 to review the stay, reversed the stay and remanded the case for further proceedings on the contractor's suit to compel arbitration.

A majority of the Supreme Court, in an opinion by Justice Brennan, found the stay order appealable under § 1291:

[T]he District Court predicated its stay order on its conclusion that the federal and state actions involved "the identical issue of arbitrability of the claims * * *." That issue of arbitrability was the only substantive issue present in the federal suit. Hence, stay of the federal suit pending resolution of the state suit meant that there would be no further litigation in the federal forum; the state court's judgment on the issue would be res judicata. Thus, * * * Mercury [Construction Corp.] was "effectively out of court." Hence, as the Court of Appeals held, this stay order amounts to a dismissal of the suit.

Obviously, a stay is in no sense a technically final order, a fact acknowledged by the Court. But this fact alone did not prevent the stay order from being deemed "final" for purposes of § 1291; the test was whether the losing party was *effectively* out of court" (emphasis added).

In a second case, Quackenbush v. Allstate Insurance Co., 517 U.S. 706 (1996), the Court considered what it viewed as a replay of the Moses Cone scenario. The California insurance commissioner brought suit against Allstate in state court, demanding contract and tort damages as well as insurance proceeds on behalf of recently defunct family of insurance companies. Allstate removed the action and filed a motion to compel arbitration under the Federal Arbitration Act. The district court concluded, instead, that the matter fell within the scope of an abstention doctrine and ordered the proceeding remanded to state court. Allstate appealed and the Ninth Circuit upheld its appellate jurisdiction on the basis of *Moses Cone*.

On further review, the Supreme Court affirmed. Reciting the history of the Moses Cone litigation, the Court explained (517 U.S. at 714):

> We first concluded that the abstention-based stay order was appealable as a "final decision" under § 1291 because it put the litigants "effectively out of court," and because its effect was "precisely to surrender jurisdiction of a federal suit to a state court." These standards do not reflect our oft-repeated definition of finality, but in *Moses H. Cone* we found their application to be compelled by precedent.

* * *

> The District Court's order remanding on grounds of * * * abstention is in all relevant respects indistinguishable from the stay order we found to be appealable in *Moses H. Cone*. No less than an order staying a federal court action pending adjudication of the dispute in state court, it puts the litigants in this case " 'effectively out of court,' " *Moses H. Cone* supra, and its effect is "precisely to surrender jurisdiction of a federal suit to a state court." Indeed, the remand order is clearly more "final" than a stay order in this sense. When a district court remands a case to a state court, the district court disassociates itself from the case entirely, retaining nothing of the matter on the federal court's docket.

NOTES AND QUESTIONS

1.   The Federal Arbitration Act, 9 U.S.C. §§ 1 et seq., governs the enforcement of contracts for the arbitration of disputes affecting interstate commerce. The Act empowers the district court to order the parties to arbitration, if their contract so provides, and to stay proceedings in a related federal-court proceeding pending arbitration. See supra p. 115 for a discussion of arbitration. Amended in 1988, section 16 of the FAA governs appellate review of orders relating to arbitration. Why did the *Quackenbush* Court (in 1996) choose to analyze the problem of appellate finality in terms of 28 U.S.C. § 1291 rather than under the more specific terms of the FAA? Does the fact that *Moses Cone* came down in 1983, before the amendment to section 16, explain the Court's (path-dependent) approach? Or did the *Quackenbush* Court simply conceive of the case as presenting an abstention problem rather than an arbitration problem?

In Arthur Andersen LLP v. Carlisle, 556 U.S. 624 (2009), the Court took a broad view of the integrated provisions of the FAA dealing with stays pending arbitration and appellate review of orders granting or denying such stays. Carlisle brought suit against Arthur Andersen, as well as a group of lawyers and investment advisors, for fraud and breach of fiduciary duty in connection with a tax avoidance scheme gone awry. Although it was not a party to an arbitration agreement with its former client, Carlisle, Arthur Andersen sought a stay of Carlisle's fraud suit pending arbitration of Carlisle's claims against other defendants. When the district court refused the stay, Andersen appealed under section 16 of the FAA, which authorizes interlocutory review of orders denying arbitral stay orders. The Sixth Circuit dismissed for want of appellate jurisdiction on that ground that non-parties have no right to seek a stay or to appeal from its denial. The Supreme Court reversed, relying on the plain terms of the FAA's interlocutory review provision and the fact that some states have permitted non-signatories, such as Andersen, to enforce arbitral agreements as third-party beneficiaries.

2.   The Supreme Court's decision in Gillespie v. United States Steel Corp., 379 U.S. 148 (1964), appeared to invite an ad hoc balancing approach to the determination of finality. The district court decision was not technically final; it held that federal law excluded state law remedies for wrongful death claims on behalf of seamen working in maritime commerce and ordered that the trial be limited to remedies available under federal law. Nonetheless, the Sixth Circuit agreed to hear an appeal from the district court order, citing the need to avoid the unnecessary expense and time associated with piecemeal litigation. The Supreme Court, in an opinion by Justice Black, affirmed. Justice Black's opinion emphasized that the requirement of finality is to be given a "practical rather than a technical construction." The case has come to be known for setting forth a test of "practical" or "pragmatic" finality. For a discussion of the concept of practical, as opposed to technical, finality, see Redish, The Pragmatic Approach to Appealability in the Federal Courts, 75 Colum.L.Rev. 89 (1975).

Is Justice Black's decision an *interpretation* of the finality requirement of 28 U.S.C. § 1291, or is it an *exception* to it? If the latter, is it appropriate, as an institutional matter, for the Court to establish such an exception to a congressional directive? Is the decision consistent with the strict approach to appellate jurisdiction taken in Bowles v. Russell, supra p. 1063? In Bullard v. Blue Hills Bank, supra p. 1074? Cf. Swint v. Chambers County Comm'n, 514 U.S. 35 (1995) (pendent appellate jurisdiction not permitted, despite economies it would produce, because such a practice "drift[s] away from the statutory instructions Congress has given to control the timing of appellate proceedings"). Wholly apart from institutional considerations, how advisable is the use of a pragmatic balancing approach to determine appealability? Consider whether such a concept as pragmatic finality can survive the Court's approach to the collateral order doctrine in Mohawk Industries, Inc. v. Carpenter, infra p. 1090. Can it survive the definition of finality in Bullard v. Blue Hills Bank?

3.   When a district court order contemplates some further action, as in determining the nature of injunctive relief, finality is more difficult to determine. In Brown Shoe Co. v. United States, 370 U.S. 294 (1962), the district court ordered the parties to submit a detailed plan for divestiture in a suit challenging a merger under the antitrust laws. The Court found the order final because the divestiture disposed of all issues in the complaint, and the fact that the detailed plan involved further negotiation in light of market conditions did not prevent its appealability. Similarly, in Budinich v. Becton Dickinson & Co., 486 U.S. 196 (1988), the Court held that a district court order was final for purposes of § 1291, even though the recoverability or amount of attorney's fees for the litigation remained to be determined. See also Forgay v. Conrad, 47 U.S. (6 How.) 201 (1848), where Chief Justice Taney held that a judgment directing immediate delivery of physical property to the opposing party is appealable, even though the lower court had also ordered an accounting that had not yet taken place. Key to the decision in *Forgay* and cases that have followed it was "the fact that there had been a conclusive adjudication of the rights and liabilities of the parties with immediate delivery of possession of the subject matter of the suit." Radio Station WOW, Inc. v. Johnson, 326 U.S. 120, 125 n. 2 (1945).

Where damages are sought, a similar situation can arise. Thus an order, such as a summary judgment or a default judgment, may be entered in plaintiff's favor on liability, but the issue of damages will still have to be determined by trial. Such an order is not final until an order as to damages has been entered. See Guarantee Co. of North America v. Mechanics' Sav. Bank & Trust Co., 173 U.S. 582 (1899).

C. Exceptions to the Final Judgment Rule: Collateral Orders

COHEN V. BENEFICIAL INDUSTRIAL LOAN CORPORATION

Supreme Court of the United States, 1949
337 U.S. 541

JUSTICE JACKSON delivered the opinion of the Court.

[Petitioner's decedent was one of Beneficial's 16,000 shareholders, owning 100 shares which were worth less than $9,000. In 1943 he filed a derivative action in U.S. District Court in New Jersey against the corporation and certain of its managers and directors, claiming that they had violated their duties to the corporation by enriching themselves at the corporation's expense. In 1945 New Jersey enacted a statute that made derivative-action plaintiffs owning less than a specified percentage of the corporation's stock liable for defendants' costs, including attorney's fees, if defendants won the suit. The new statute also required such plaintiffs to post a bond to cover these costs as a condition for proceeding with a derivative action, and was explicitly made applicable to pending actions. Beneficial moved to require petitioner to post a $125,000 bond, but the district court held that the state law did not apply to suits in federal court. Eventually the Supreme Court held that the security-for-expenses requirement did apply in federal court, see supra p. 977, but first it had to deal with objections to appealability.]

At the threshold we are met with the question whether the District Court's order refusing to [require posting of a bond] was an appealable one. * * * It is obvious that, if Congress had allowed appeals only from those final judgments which terminate an action, this order would not be appealable.

The effect of the statute [conferring appellate jurisdiction] is to disallow appeal from any decision which is tentative, informal or incomplete. Appeal gives the upper court a power of review, not one of intervention. So long as the matter remains open, unfinished or inconclusive, there may be no intrusion by appeal. But the District Court's action upon this application was concluded and closed and its decision final in that sense before the appeal was taken.

Nor does the statute permit appeals, even from fully consummated decisions, where they are but steps towards final judgment in which they will merge. The purpose is to combine in one review all stages of the proceeding that effectively may be reviewed and corrected if and when final judgment results. But this order of the District Court did not make any step toward final disposition of the merits of the case and will not be merged in final judgment. When that time comes, it will be too late effectively to review the present order and the rights conferred by the statute, if it is applicable, will have been lost, probably irreparably. We conclude that the matters embraced in the decision appealed from are not of such an interlocutory nature as to affect, or to be affected by, decision of the merits of this case.

This decision appears to fall in that small class which finally determine claims of right separable from, and collateral to, rights asserted in the action, too important to be denied review and too independent of the cause itself to require that appellate consideration be deferred until the whole case is adjudicated. The Court has long given this provision of the statute this practical rather than a technical construction.

We hold this order appealable because it is a final disposition of a claimed right which is not an ingredient of the cause of action and does not require consideration with it. But we do not mean that every order fixing security is subject to appeal. Here it is the right to security that presents a serious and unsettled question. If the right were admitted or clear and the order involved only an exercise of discretion as to the amount of security, a matter the statute makes subject to reconsideration from time to time, appealability would present a different question.

MOHAWK INDUSTRIES, INC. v. CARPENTER
Supreme Court of the United States, 2009
558 U.S. 100

JUSTICE SOTOMAYOR delivered the opinion of the Court.

Section 1291 of the Judicial Code confers on federal courts of appeals jurisdiction to review "final decisions of the district courts." 28 U.S.C. § 1291. Although "final decisions" typically are ones that trigger the entry of judgment, they also include a small set of prejudgment orders that are "collateral to" the merits of an action and "too important" to be denied immediate review. *Cohen v. Beneficial Industrial Loan Corp.*, 337 U.S. 541, 546 (1949). In this case, petitioner Mohawk Industries, Inc., attempted to bring a collateral order appeal after the District Court ordered it to disclose certain confidential materials on the ground that Mohawk had waived the attorney-client privilege. The Court of Appeals dismissed the appeal for want of jurisdiction.

The question before us is whether disclosure orders adverse to the attorney-client privilege qualify for immediate appeal under the collateral order doctrine. Agreeing with the Court of Appeals, we hold that they do not. Postjudgment appeals, together with other review mechanisms, suffice to protect the rights of litigants and preserve the vitality of the attorney-client privilege.

I

In 2007, respondent Norman Carpenter, a former shift supervisor at a Mohawk manufacturing facility, filed suit in the United States District Court for the Northern District of Georgia, alleging that Mohawk had terminated him in violation of 42 U.S.C. § 1985(2) and various Georgia laws. According to Carpenter's complaint, his termination came after he informed a member of Mohawk's human resources department in an e-mail that the company was employing undocumented immigrants. At the time, unbeknownst to Carpenter, Mohawk stood accused in a pending class-action lawsuit of conspiring to drive down the wages of its legal employees by knowingly hiring undocumented workers in violation of federal and state racketeering laws. Company officials directed Carpenter to meet with the company's retained counsel in the *Williams* case, and counsel allegedly pressured Carpenter to recant his statements. When he refused, Carpenter alleges, Mohawk fired him under false pretenses.

After learning of Carpenter's complaint, the plaintiffs in the *Williams* case sought an evidentiary hearing to explore Carpenter's allegations. In its response to their motion, Mohawk described Carpenter's accusations as "pure fantasy" and recounted the "true facts" of Carpenter's dismissal. According to Mohawk, Carpenter himself had "engaged in blatant and illegal misconduct" by attempting to have Mohawk hire an undocumented worker. The company "commenced an immediate investigation," during which retained counsel interviewed Carpenter. Because Carpenter's "efforts to cause Mohawk to circumvent federal immigration law" "blatantly violated Mohawk policy," the company terminated him.

As these events were unfolding in the *Williams* case, discovery was underway in Carpenter's case. Carpenter filed a motion to compel Mohawk to produce information concerning his meeting with retained counsel and the company's termination decision. Mohawk maintained that the requested information was protected by the attorney-client privilege.

The District Court agreed that the privilege applied to the requested information, but it granted Carpenter's motion to compel disclosure after concluding that Mohawk had implicitly waived the privilege through its representations in the *Williams* case. The court declined to certify its order for interlocutory appeal under 28 U.S.C. § 1292(b). But, recognizing "the seriousness of its [waiver] finding," it stayed its ruling to allow Mohawk to explore other potential "avenues to appeal . . ., such as a petition for mandamus or appealing this Order under the collateral order doctrine."

Mohawk filed a notice of appeal and a petition for a writ of mandamus to the Eleventh Circuit. The Court of Appeals dismissed the appeal for lack of jurisdiction under 28 U.S.C. § 1291, holding that the District Court's ruling did not qualify as an immediately appealable collateral order within the meaning of *Cohen*. * * * The Court of Appeals also rejected Mohawk's mandamus petition. * * *

II

A

By statute, Courts of Appeals "have jurisdiction of appeals from all final decisions of the district courts of the United States, . . . except where a direct review may be had in the Supreme Court." 28 U.S.C. § 1291. A "final decisio[n]" is typically one "by which a district court disassociates itself from a case." *Swint v. Chambers County Comm'n,* 514 U.S. 35, 42 (1995). This Court, however, "has long given" § 1291 a "practical rather than a technical construction." *Cohen,* 337 U.S. at 546. As we held in *Cohen,* the statute encompasses not only judgments that "terminate an action," but also a "small class" of collateral rulings that, although they do not end the litigation, are appropriately deemed "final." *Id.* at 545–546. "That small category includes only decisions that are conclusive, that resolve important questions separate from the merits, and that are effectively unreviewable on appeal from the final judgment in the underlying action." *Swint,* 514 U.S. at 42.

In applying *Cohen*'s collateral order doctrine, we have stressed that it must "never be allowed to swallow the general rule that a party is entitled to a single appeal, to be deferred until final judgment has been entered." *Digital Equipment Corp. v. Desktop Direct, Inc.,* 511 U.S. 863, 868 (1994) (citation omitted); see also *Will v. Hallock,* 546 U.S. 345, 350 (2006) ("emphasizing [the doctrine's] modest scope"). Our admonition reflects a healthy respect for the virtues of the final-judgment rule. Permitting piecemeal, prejudgment appeals, we have recognized, undermines "efficient judicial administration" and encroaches upon the prerogatives of district court judges, who play a "special role" in managing ongoing litigation. *Firestone Tire & Rubber Co. v. Risjord,* 449 U.S. 368, 374 (1981); see also *Richardson-Merrell Inc. v. Koller,* 472 U.S. 424, 436 (1985) ("[T]he district judge can better exercise [his or her] responsibility [to police the prejudgment tactics of litigants] if the appellate courts do not repeatedly intervene to second-guess prejudgment rulings").

The justification for immediate appeal must therefore be sufficiently strong to overcome usual benefits of deferring appeal until litigation concludes. This requirement finds expression in two of the three traditional *Cohen* conditions. The second condition insists upon "*important* questions separate from the merits." *Swint,* 514 U.S. at 42 (emphasis added). More significantly, "the third *Cohen* question, whether a right is 'adequately vindicable' or 'effectively reviewable,' simply cannot be answered without a judgment about the value of the interests that would be lost through rigorous application of a final judgment requirement." *Digital Equipment,* 511 U.S. at 878–879. That a ruling "may burden litigants in ways that are only imperfectly reparable by appellate reversal of a final district court judgment . . . has never sufficed." *Id.,* at 872. Instead, the decisive consideration is whether delaying review until the entry of final judgment "would imperil a substantial public interest" or "some particular value of a high order." *Will,* 546 U.S. at 352–353.

In making this determination, we do not engage in an "individualized jurisdictional inquiry." *Coopers & Lybrand v. Livesay,* 437 U.S. 463, 473 (1978). Rather, our focus is on "the entire category to which a claim belongs." *Digital Equipment,* 511 U.S. at 868. As long as the class of claims, taken as a whole, can be adequately vindicated by other means, "the chance that the litigation at hand might be speeded, or a 'particular injustic[e]' averted," does not provide a basis for jurisdiction under § 1291 (citation omitted).

B

In the present case, the Court of Appeals concluded that the District Court's privilege-waiver order satisfied the first two conditions of the collateral order doctrine—conclusiveness and separateness—but not the third—effective unreviewability. Because we agree with the Court of Appeals that collateral order appeals are not necessary to ensure effective review of orders adverse to the attorney-client privilege, we do not decide whether the other *Cohen* requirements are met.

Mohawk does not dispute that "we have generally denied review of pretrial discovery orders." *Firestone,* 449 U.S. at 377, see also 15B C. Wright, A. Miller, & E. Cooper, Federal Practice and Procedure § 3914.23 (2d ed.1992) (hereinafter Wright & Miller) ("[T]he rule remains settled that most discovery rulings are not final"). Mohawk contends, however, that rulings implicating the attorney-client privilege differ in kind from run-of-the-mill discovery orders because of the important institutional interests at stake. According to Mohawk, the right to maintain attorney-client confidences—the *sine qua non* of a meaningful attorney-client relationship—is "irreparably destroyed absent immediate appeal" of adverse privilege rulings

We readily acknowledge the importance of the attorney-client privilege, which "is one of the oldest recognized privileges for confidential communications." *Swidler & Berlin v. United States,* 524 U.S. 399, 403 (1998). By assuring confidentiality, the privilege encourages clients to make "full and frank" disclosures to their attorneys, who are then better able to provide candid advice and effective representation. *Upjohn Co. v. United States,* 449 U.S. 383, 389 (1981). This, in turn, serves "broader public interests in the observance of law and administration of justice." *Ibid.*

The crucial question, however, is not whether an interest is important in the abstract; it is whether deferring review until final judgment so imperils the interest as to justify the cost of allowing immediate appeal of the entire class of relevant orders. We routinely require litigants to wait until after final judgment to vindicate valuable rights, including rights central to our adversarial system. See, *e.g., Richardson-Merrell,* 472 U.S., at 426 (holding an order disqualifying counsel in a civil case did not qualify for immediate appeal under the collateral order doctrine); *Flanagan v. United States,* 465 U.S. 259, 260 (1984) (reaching the same result in a criminal case, notwithstanding the Sixth Amendment rights at stake). In *Digital Equipment,* we rejected an assertion that collateral order review was necessary to promote "the public policy favoring voluntary resolution of disputes." 511 U.S. at 881. "It defies common sense," we explained, "to maintain that parties' readiness to settle will be significantly dampened (or the corresponding public interest impaired) by a rule that a district court's decision to let allegedly barred litigation go forward may be challenged as a matter of right only on appeal from a judgment for the plaintiff's favor."

We reach a similar conclusion here. In our estimation, postjudgment appeals generally suffice to protect the rights of litigants and assure the vitality of the attorney-client privilege. Appellate courts can remedy the improper disclosure of privileged material in the same way they remedy a host of other erroneous evidentiary rulings: by vacating an adverse judgment and remanding for a new trial in which the protected material and its fruits are excluded from evidence.

Dismissing such relief as inadequate, Mohawk emphasizes that the attorney-client privilege does not merely "prohibi[t] use of protected information at trial"; it provides a "right not to disclose the privileged information in the first place." Mohawk is undoubtedly correct that an order to disclose privileged information intrudes on the confidentiality of attorney-client communications. But deferring review until final judgment does not meaningfully reduce the *ex ante* incentives for full and frank consultations between clients and counsel.

One reason for the lack of a discernible chill is that, in deciding how freely to speak, clients and counsel are unlikely to focus on the remote prospect of an erroneous disclosure order, let alone on the timing of a possible appeal. Whether or not immediate collateral order appeals are available, clients and counsel must account for the possibility that they will later be required by law to disclose their communications for a variety of reasons—for example, because they misjudged the scope of the privilege, because they waived the privilege, or because their communications fell within the privilege's crime-fraud exception. Most district court rulings on these matters involve the routine application of settled legal principles. They are unlikely to be reversed on appeal, particularly when they rest on factual determinations for which appellate deference is the norm. See, *e.g., Richardson-Merrell,* 472 U.S. at 434 ("Most pretrial orders of district judges are ultimately affirmed by appellate courts."); *Reise v. Board of Regents,* 957 F.2d 293, 295 (C.A.7 1992) (noting that "almost all interlocutory appeals from discovery orders would end in affirmance" because "the district court possesses discretion, and review is deferential"). The breadth of the privilege and the narrowness of its exceptions will thus tend to exert a much greater influence on the conduct of clients and counsel than the small risk that the law will be misapplied.

Moreover, were attorneys and clients to reflect upon their appellate options, they would find that litigants confronted with a particularly injurious or novel privilege ruling have several potential avenues of review apart from collateral order appeal. First, a party may ask the district court to certify, and the court of appeals to accept, an interlocutory appeal pursuant to 28 U.S.C. § 1292(b). The preconditions for § 1292(b) review— "a controlling question of law," the prompt resolution of which "may materially advance the ultimate termination of the litigation"—are most likely to be satisfied when a privilege ruling involves a new legal question or is of special consequence, and district courts should not hesitate to certify an interlocutory appeal in such cases. Second, in extraordinary circumstances—*i.e.,* when a disclosure order "amount[s] to a judicial usurpation of power or a clear abuse of discretion," or otherwise works a manifest injustice—a party may petition the court of appeals for a writ of mandamus. *Cheney v. United States Dist. Court for D. C.,* 542 U.S. 367, 390 (2004) (citation and internal quotation marks omitted); see also *Firestone,* 449 U.S., at 378–379, n. 13. While these discretionary review mechanisms do not provide relief in every case, they serve as useful "safety valve[s]" for promptly correcting serious errors. *Digital Equipment,* 511 U.S. at 883.

Another long-recognized option is for a party to defy a disclosure order and incur court-imposed sanctions. District courts have a range of sanctions from which to choose, including "directing that the matters embraced in the order or other designated facts be taken as established for purposes of the action," "prohibiting the disobedient party from supporting or opposing designated claims or defenses," or "striking pleadings in whole or in part." Fed. Rule Civ. Proc. 37(b)(2)(i)–(iii). Such sanctions allow a party to obtain postjudgment review without having to reveal its privileged information. Alternatively, when the circumstances warrant it, a district court may hold a noncomplying party in contempt. The party can then appeal directly from that ruling, at least when the contempt citation can be characterized as a criminal punishment. *See, e.g., Church of Scientology of Cal. v. United States,* 506 U.S. 9, 18, n. 11 (1992); *Firestone,* 449 U.S. at 377; *Cobbledick v. United States,* 309 U.S. 323, 328 (1940); see also Wright & Miller § 3914.23.

These established mechanisms for appellate review not only provide assurances to clients and counsel about the security of their confidential communications; they also go a long way toward addressing Mohawk's concern that, absent collateral order appeals of adverse attorney-client privilege rulings, some litigants may experience severe hardship. Mohawk is no doubt right that an order to disclose privileged material may, in some situations, have implications beyond the case at hand. But the same can be said about many categories of pretrial discovery orders for which collateral order appeals are unavailable. As with these other orders, rulings adverse to the privilege vary in their significance; some may be momentous, but others are more mundane. Section 1292(b) appeals, mandamus, and appeals from contempt citations facilitate immediate review of some of the more consequential attorney-client privilege rulings. Moreover, protective orders are available to limit the spillover effects of disclosing sensitive information. That a fraction of orders adverse to the attorney-client privilege may nevertheless harm individual litigants in ways that are "only imperfectly reparable" does not justify making all such orders immediately appealable as of right under § 1291. *Digital Equipment,* 511 U.S. at 872.

In short, the limited benefits of applying "the blunt, categorical instrument of § 1291 collateral order appeal" to privilege-related disclosure orders simply cannot justify the likely institutional costs. *Id.* at 883. Permitting parties to undertake successive, piecemeal appeals of all adverse attorney-client rulings would unduly delay the resolution of district court litigation and needlessly burden the Courts of Appeals. See Wright & Miller § 3914.23, at 123 ("Routine appeal from disputed discovery orders would disrupt the orderly progress of the litigation, swamp the courts of appeals, and substantially reduce the district court's ability to control the discovery process."); cf. *Cunningham v. Hamilton County,* 527 U.S. 198, 209 (1999) (expressing concern that allowing immediate appeal as of right from orders fining attorneys for discovery violations would result in "the very sorts of piecemeal appeals and concomitant delays that the final judgment rule was designed to prevent"). Attempting to downplay such concerns, Mohawk asserts that the three Circuits in which the collateral order doctrine currently applies to adverse privilege rulings have seen only a trickle of appeals. But this may be due to the fact that the practice in all three Circuits is relatively new and not yet widely known. Were this Court to approve collateral order appeals in the attorney-client privilege context, many more litigants would likely choose that route. They would also likely seek to extend such a ruling to disclosure orders implicating many other categories of sensitive information, raising an array of line-drawing difficulties.

C

In concluding that sufficiently effective review of adverse attorney-client privilege rulings can be had without resort to the *Cohen* doctrine, we reiterate that the class of collaterally appealable orders must remain "narrow and selective in its membership." *Will,* 546 U.S. at 350. This admonition has acquired special force in recent years with the enactment of legislation designating rulemaking, "not expansion by court decision," as the preferred means for determining whether and when prejudgment orders should be immediately appealable. *Swint,* 514 U.S. at 48.

Specifically, Congress in 1990 amended the Rules Enabling Act, 28 U.S.C. § 2071 *et seq.*, to authorize this Court to adopt rules "defin[ing] when a ruling of a district court is final for the purposes of appeal under section 1291." § 2072(c). Shortly thereafter, and along similar lines, Congress empowered this Court to "prescribe rules, in accordance with [§ 2072], to provide for an appeal of an interlocutory decision to the courts of appeals that is not otherwise provided for under [§ 1292]." § 1292(e). These provisions, we have recognized, "warran[t] the Judiciary's full respect." *Swint,* 514 U.S. at 48; see also *Cunningham,* 527 U.S. at 210.

Indeed, the rulemaking process has important virtues. It draws on the collective experience of bench and bar, see 28 U.S.C. § 2073, and it facilitates the adoption of measured, practical solutions. We expect that the combination of standard postjudgment appeals, § 1292(b) appeals, mandamus, and contempt appeals will continue to provide adequate protection to litigants ordered to disclose materials purportedly subject to the attorney-client privilege. Any further avenue for immediate appeal of such rulings should be furnished, if at all, through rulemaking, with the opportunity for full airing it provides.

* * *

In sum, we conclude that the collateral order doctrine does not extend to disclosure orders adverse to the attorney-client privilege. Effective appellate review can be had by other means. Accordingly, we affirm the judgment of the Court of Appeals for the Eleventh Circuit.

It is so ordered.

The opinion of JUSTICE THOMAS, concurring in part and concurring in the judgment.

* * * The Court concedes that Congress, which holds the constitutional reins in this area, has determined that such value judgments are better left to the "collective experience of bench and bar" and the "opportunity for full airing" that rulemaking provides. This determination is entitled to our full respect, in deed as well as in word. Accordingly, I would leave the value judgments the Court makes in its opinion to the rulemaking process, and in so doing take this opportunity to limit—effectively, predictably, and in a way we should have done long ago—the doctrine that, with a sweep of the Court's pen, subordinated what the appellate jurisdiction statute says to what the Court thinks is a good idea.

NOTES AND QUESTIONS

1.   In 1990, after the Court's decision in Cohen v. Beneficial Industrial Loan Corp., but before its decision in Mohawk v. Carpenter, Congress amended the Rules Enabling Act to provide that the rules "shall define when a ruling of a district court is final for the purposes of appeal under section 1291 of this title." 28 U.S.C. § 2072(c). In 1992, Congress enacted a statute giving the

Supreme Court power to prescribe rules to provide for an appeal from an interlocutory decision not already provided for in existing provisions. 28 U.S.C. § 1292(e). With the power thus lodged in the judiciary to fashion generally applicable definitions of finality and to allow interlocutory appeals, why would the Court continue to recognize judge-made exceptions to the final judgment rule? Does it make sense to narrow the *Cohen* collateral order doctrine and rely on the rulemaking process instead? Which approach, judicial decision or rule making, would give the Court greater control over the content of the rule? Do you see any indication that the majority now prefers the rulemaking option? Consider the treatment of Fed.R.Civ.P. 23(f) by the Supreme Court in Microsoft Corp. v. Baker, infra p. 1132.

2.   The collateral order doctrine of Cohen v. Beneficial Industrial Loan Corp., 337 U.S. 541 (1949), applied in *Mohawk,* was restated in Coopers & Lybrand v. Livesay, 437 U.S. 463 (1978), in the following manner: "[T]he order must conclusively determine the disputed question, resolve an important issue completely separate from the merits of the action, and be effectively unreviewable on appeal from a final judgment." Courts conventionally refer to the three prongs of the collateral order doctrine: conclusiveness, separability, and unreviewability.

3.   *Conclusiveness*: In a leading analysis of the first prong, *Moses H. Cone,* supra p. 1085, the Supreme Court held that a district court's stay of its own proceedings in deference to parallel state court proceedings was immediately appealable both as a final order and under the collateral order doctrine. The *second* prong of the collateral order doctrine—that the order resolved an important issue completely separate from the merits of the action—was obviously satisfied. The *third* prong—that it was effectively unreviewable on appeal from a final judgment—was deemed satisfied because "[o]nce the state court decided the issue of arbitrability, the federal court would be bound to honor that determination as res judicata."

As for the *first* prong—whether the order conclusively determined the disputed question—the Court contrasted two kinds of nonfinal orders: those that are "inherently tentative" and those that, although technically amendable, are "made with the expectation that they will be the final word on the subject addressed." It found this stay order to be of the latter type, over a dissent that characterized the decision as pure speculation. Should the right to appeal depend on the particular circumstances of a stay or on more general considerations, such as the type of the stay at issue?

In Gulfstream Aerospace Corp. v. Mayacamas Corp., 485 U.S. 271 (1988), the Supreme Court provided a partial answer in a case (unlike *Moses Cone*) where the district court refused to grant a requested stay of federal proceedings. Gulfstream sued Mayacamas in state court in Georgia for breach of contract regarding its failure to purchase aircraft as agreed upon. A month later, Mayacamas sued Gulfstream in federal district court in California, alleging breach of the same contract. Gulfstream moved for a stay or dismissal of the federal action, citing *Colorado River* and *Moses Cone*. The district court denied the stay, and the circuit court dismissed the appeal, finding no right to immediate appeal. The Supreme Court affirmed. It found that the first prong of the collateral order doctrine was not satisfied:

> The order fails to meet the initial requirement of a conclusive determination of the disputed question. A district court that denies [an abstention] motion does not "necessarily contemplate" that the decision will close the matter for all time. In denying such a motion, the district court may well have determined only that it should await further developments before concluding that the balance of factors to be considered under [the abstention doctrine] warrants a dismissal or stay. * * * Because an order denying [an abstention] motion is "inherently tentative" in this critical sense—because it is not "made with the expectation that it will be the final word on the subject addressed"—the order is not a conclusive determination within the meaning of the collateral-order doctrine and therefore is not appealable under § 1291.

The Court's ruling that the denial of the stay was also not appealable under § 1292(a) is discussed infra, p. 1110 n. 4.

4. *Separateness*: As for the second prong of the collateral order doctrine, the Court indicated in Van Cauwenberghe v. Biard, 486 U.S. 517 (1988), that the denial of a motion to dismiss on the basis of forum non conveniens is not sufficiently separate from the merits to come within the collateral order doctrine. As noted supra p. 849, the doctrine of forum non conveniens vests the district court with discretion to dismiss an action on the basis of a variety of private and public interest factors. These factors include the relative convenience of the available forums in light of the location of the evidence, witnesses and parties and the interest of the governments in providing a forum for the adjudication of claims involving local conduct. The *Van Cauwenberghe* Court acknowledged that these matters could often be resolved on affidavits and would not necessarily entail detailed factual exploration. Nevertheless, the Court held that the determination was sufficiently enmeshed with the factual and legal merits to deprive it of the separateness needed for the collateral order doctrine.

Contrast the Court's analysis of forum non conveniens with its handling of the doctrine of official immunity in a suit for tort damages against government officials. In Harlow v. Fitzgerald, 457 U.S. 800 (1982), the Supreme Court held that federal officials are entitled to a defense of qualified immunity unless their conduct violates "clearly established statutory or constitutional rights of which a reasonable person would have known." Qualified immunity has become a standard defense in civil rights cases, with the defendant state or federal official (for example, a policeman or prison guard charged with excessive use of force) moving for dismissal or summary judgment on the ground that he could not reasonably have known that his conduct violated clearly established constitutional rights. Historically, if the trial court denied the motion, the defendant would have had to proceed with the case and could only appeal the denial if a final judgment were entered against him.

In Mitchell v. Forsyth, 472 U.S. 511 (1985), the Court held that a trial court's denial of summary judgment sought on the basis of qualified immunity is appealable under the collateral order doctrine. *Forsyth* analogized qualified immunity to absolute immunity where, for example, a defendant who asserts that he is immune on double jeopardy grounds may immediately appeal a refusal to dismiss because "such a right cannot be effectively vindicated after the trial has occurred." The Court concluded that the essence of qualified immunity is "an entitlement not to stand trial under certain circumstances" and thus that a defendant should be entitled to immediate appellate review of his qualified immunity claim.

Note that the second prong of the collateral order doctrine presented a significant hurdle in *Mitchell:* under *Harlow,* the qualified immunity decision depends almost entirely on whether the plaintiff has presented a claim of official misconduct that violates clearly established law. In finding the separateness prong satisfied, the *Mitchell* Court emphasized that the inquiries (liability on the merits and immunity) were conceptually distinct. Yet the Court conceded that the immunity inquiry will entail consideration of the factual allegations of misconduct and whether they state a violation of the law. Is it fair to say that the Court's conviction as to the importance of defendant's right not to stand trial persuaded it to discount the significance of the second prong of the analysis?

5. *Unreviewability*: The effectively unreviewable prong of the collateral order doctrine, decisive in *Mohawk*, has been the subject of much analysis in the cases.

(a) In Firestone Tire & Rubber Co. v. Risjord, 449 U.S. 571 (1981), the Supreme Court relied on this factor in holding that the collateral order doctrine is inapplicable to an appeal from an order denying a motion to disqualify counsel. The Court reasoned:

> An order denying a disqualification motion meets the first part of the "collateral order" test. It "conclusively determine[s] the disputed question," because the only issue is whether challenged counsel will be permitted to continue his representation. In addition, we will assume, although we do not decide, that the disqualification question "resolve[s] an important issue completely separate from the merits of the action," the second part of the test. Nevertheless, petitioner is unable to demonstrate that an order denying disqualification is "effectively unreviewable on appeal form a final judgment" within the meaning of our cases.

> * * *

> An order refusing to disqualify counsel plainly falls within the large class of orders that are indeed reviewable on appeal after final judgment, and not within the much smaller class of those that are not. The propriety of the district court's denial of a disqualification motion will often be difficult to assess until its impact on the underlying litigation may be evaluated, which is normally only after

final judgment. The decision whether to disqualify an attorney ordinarily turns on the peculiar factual situation of the case then at hand, and the order embodying such a decision will rarely, if ever, represent a final rejection of a claim of fundamental right that cannot effectively be reviewed following judgment on the merits.

(b) In Lauro Lines S.R.L. v. Chasser, 490 U.S. 495 (1989), plaintiffs filed suit in the Southern District of New York against the shipping line to recover damages for injuries sustained as a result of the hijacking of the Achille Lauro and subsequent wrongful death. A forum-selection clause, printed on the passenger ticket, provided that any suit must be filed in Naples, Italy. The defendant sought to appeal the district court's denial of its motion to dismiss on the basis on the forum-selection clause, relying on the collateral order doctrine. The Supreme Court rejected the defendant's argument:

> We recently reiterated the "general rule" that an order is "effectively unreviewable" only "where the order at issue involves 'an asserted right the legal and practical value of which would be destroyed if it were not vindicated before trial.'"
>
> Cost associated with unnecessary litigation is not enough to set aside the finality requirement. Instead, we have insisted that the right asserted be one that is essentially destroyed if its vindication must be postponed until trial is completed.

490 U.S. at 498–99. The Court distinguished the asserted right, under the forum-selection clause, not to be haled into a courtroom outside the selected forum, from a right not to be subjected to suit altogether: "[Defendant's] claim that it may be sued only in Naples, while not perfectly secured by appeal after final judgment, is adequately vindicable at that stage—surely as effectively vindicable as a claim that the trial court lacked personal jurisdiction over the defendant—and hence does not fall within the third prong of the collateral order doctrine."

Justice Scalia, concurring, wrote (id. at 502):

> The reason we say that the right not to be sued elsewhere than in Naples is "adequately vindicable" * * * by merely reversing any judgment obtained in violation of it is, quite simply, that the law does not deem the right *important enough* to be vindicated by, as it were, an injunction against its violation obtained through interlocutory appeal. The importance of the right asserted has always been a significant part of our collateral order doctrine.

(c) The Court held in Puerto Rico Aqueduct and Sewer Authority v. Metcalf & Eddy, Inc., 506 U.S. 139 (1993), that appeal is permitted under the collateral order doctrine from an order denying a claim of state sovereign immunity pursuant to the Eleventh Amendment:

> Once it is acknowledged that a State and its "arms" are, in effect, immune from federal-court suit under the [Eleventh] Amendment * * * it follows that the elements of the collateral order doctrine

necessary to bring an order within *Cohen*'s "small class" * * * are satisfied. First, denials of Eleventh Amendment immunity claims purport to be conclusive determinations that States and their entities have no right not to be sued in federal court. Second, a motion to dismiss on Eleventh Amendment grounds involves a claim to a fundamental constitutional protection whose resolution generally will have no bearing on the merits of the underlying action. Third, the value to the States of their constitutional immunity—like the benefits conferred by qualified immunity to individual officials * * *— is for the most part lost as litigation proceeds past motion practice, such that the denial order will be effectively unreviewable on appeal from a final judgment.

(d)   In Digital Equipment Corporation v. Desktop Direct, Inc., 511 U.S. 863 (1994), the Court focused again on the third element. The dispute arose over the use of a trade name and corresponding trademark. After suit was filed in the district court in Utah, the parties negotiated a settlement agreement and asked the district court to dismiss the action. Several months later, Desktop moved to vacate the dismissal and rescind the settlement agreement, alleging misrepresentation of material facts in the negotiations. The district court agreed, and vacated the settlement and dismissal. Digital sought reconsideration from the district court and then filed a notice of appeal. Acknowledging the absence of technical finality, Digital argued that the district court's order came within the collateral order doctrine. The Supreme Court assumed that the district court's order was conclusive and resolved an issue separate from the merits, although it observed that those points were arguable.

In concluding that the third prong was not satisfied, the Court emphasized the right not to stand trial invoked by Digital was based on the terms of a private contract and not on the public interests that underlie such doctrines as official immunity. In addition, the Court noted that Digital's contractual rights could be vindicated in a variety of ways, including through the prosecution of a breach of contract action. In the end, the Court found that Digital's "right" not to stand trial more closely resembled defenses based on personal jurisdiction, the statute of limitations, and claim preclusion—all of which it assumed would not support collateral review.

(e)   In Will v. Hallock, 546 U.S. 345 (2005), the Court relied on this aspect of *Digital Equipment* in refusing to permit collateral order review of a federal officer's judgment bar defense. The judgment bar, 28 U.S.C. § 2676, was adopted as part of the Federal Tort Claims Act in 1946 to prohibit a claimant who has first pursued a claim to judgment against the federal government from bringing a second proceeding against the employee whose actions had given rise to the claim. The judgment bar arose at common law as an early exception to the rule of strict mutuality of estoppel; as codified, the judgment bar allows the federal employee, even though a non-party to the first proceeding, to raise the judgment in the first proceeding as a defense. In concluding that the federal officials named as defendants in an action for damages could not mount an appeal from the denial of their judgment bar defense, the Court drew an analogy to the defense of claim preclusion. Both the claim preclusion defense in *Digital Equipment* and the judgment bar defense in *Will* were viewed as lacking the degree of public importance necessary to justify collateral review. Can the Court justifiably distinguish what it sees as run-of-the-mill defenses from the more important defense of qualified immunity identified in Mitchell v. Forsyth? Does the comment of Justice Scalia in *Lauro Lines* suggest that the Court has embarked on a process of ad hoc balancing that focuses on the Court's perception of the importance of the interest in avoiding trial?

CIVIL RIGHTS CASES

The collateral order doctrine of Mitchell v. Forsyth, supra p. 1100, was limited by Johnson v. Jones, 515 U.S. 304 (1995), which limited appeals on grounds of qualified immunity to those in which there is no dispute about the facts. Plaintiff there claimed that police had beaten him after they found him suffering an insulin seizure on a street, but the officers argued that he had no evidence they had done so. The district court denied their motion for summary judgment on the ground there was a genuine issue for trial, and the Supreme Court held that their appeal was properly dismissed for lack of jurisdiction. It explained its earlier decision that denial of summary judgment is immediately appealable in qualified immunity cases as premised on the assumption that there is no dispute regarding the facts. In *Forsyth,* the Court said that the appellate court "need not consider the correctness of plaintiff's version of the facts." 472 U.S. at 528. Where there is a dispute about the facts, an immediate appeal is not allowed.

In Behrens v. Pelletier, 516 U.S. 299 (1996), the Court held that defendants entitled to an immediate appeal of rejection of a qualified immunity defense may be allowed more than one such immediate appeal as a matter of right. After denial of a Rule 12(b)(6) motion, defendant appealed and lost. Then defendant moved for summary judgment, and when that was denied he appealed again. The Court held that he had a right to a second interlocutory appeal because "an order rejecting the defense of qualified immunity at either the dismissal stage or the summary-judgment stage is a 'final' judgment subject to immediate appeal." Id. at 306.

The effect of the *Forsyth* rule on the strategic positions of parties in civil rights suits is substantial. A defendant, no matter how weak his claim to qualified immunity, can bring the suit to a halt while a time-consuming and expensive appeal takes place on the issue of qualified immunity. This provides an opportunity for defendants (who are often represented by city or county attorneys or state attorney general offices) to raise the ante for continuing the case and thus to out-resource the plaintiff. Are there other situations in which an interlocutory appeal can also have this effect? Should that be a factor in applying the collateral order doctrine? Should defendants with weak claims of qualified immunity be sanctioned for taking an immediate appeal?

In Johnson v. Fankell, 520 U.S. 911 (1997), the Court held that the federal doctrine of immediate appealability does not apply to § 1983 suits against state officials in state court. The ruling was based on the inapplicability of "converse *Erie*" reasoning to state court procedure. See supra pp. 1038–1044. Will this ruling affect the strategic positions of the parties in regard to removing to federal court?

Consider the application of the collateral order doctrine in Doe v. Village of Deerfield, 819 F.3d 372 (7th Cir. 2016). Doe's complaint alleged that village officials had wrongfully prosecuted him in violation of his civil rights. Although he had obtained an order expunging his conviction, Doe nonetheless sought to proceed anonymously so he could litigate the matter without disclosing his identity as a person previously convicted of a crime. The district court denied his application to proceed anonymously. The Seventh Circuit found that all three elements of the collateral order doctrine were satisfied and allowed interlocutory review.

DISCOVERY ORDERS

Many discovery orders might appear at first glance to be suited to immediate appeal under the collateral order doctrine. They can conclusively determine a disputed question that is separate from the merits of the action, and often the order will be effectively unreviewable after final judgment. For example, a discovery order requiring the production of documents containing what a party deems trade secrets cannot effectively be reviewed after final judgment: once the secret information is revealed (absent a protective order), the damage is done. See, e.g., Diamond Ventures, LLC v. Barreto, 452 F.3d 892 (D.C. Cir. 2006) (denial of motion for protective order to prevent disclosure of trade secrets was subject to review under the collateral order doctrine); Smith v. BIC Corp., 869 F.2d 194 (3d Cir. 1989) (same); cf. In re Carco Electronics, Inc., 536 F.3d 211 (3d Cir. 2008) (district court order, which accorded trade secrets limited protection against disclosure, not subject to appellate review). Similar threatened loss of confidentiality protections may arise in other discovery contexts. See Truckstop.net, LLC v. Sprint Corp., 547 F.3d 1065 (9th Cir. 2008) (district court's order to reveal attorney-client privileged material a proper subject for review under collateral order doctrine, but not where the party seeking protection had inadvertently disclosed the material).

As the *Mohawk* Court (supra p. 1090) emphasized, the availability of review by way of contempt sanctions has often undercut the argument for collateral review of pretrial discovery orders. An illustration of the contempt citation route to immediate review is United States v. Ryan, 402 U.S. 530 (1971). There the Court held that an order denying a motion to quash a grand jury subpoena duces tecum was not appealable. The Court indicated that if the subpoena were unlawful or unduly burdensome, the party "may refuse to comply and litigate those questions in the event that contempt or similar proceedings are brought against him. Should his contentions be rejected at that time by the trial court they will then be ripe for appellate review." As a practical matter, how viable is this "contempt" alternative likely to be? Put yourself in the position of the party who wishes to seek appellate review of a discovery order. If you were to take this "contempt" avenue, what are likely to be the consequences if you are wrong in your belief that the discovery order is improper?

The "contempt" approach endorsed in *Mohawk* and *Ryan* presents another difficulty as well. Recall that generally a person who disobeys a court order is not allowed to attack the legality of that order when prosecuted for contempt under the collateral-bar rule. See supra p. 97 n. 4. Thus, in Walker v. City of Birmingham, 388 U.S. 307 (1967), the Court reasoned that this rule was necessary because "in the fair administration of justice no man can be judge in his own case, however exalted his station, however righteous his motives, and irrespective of his race, color, politics, or religion." The proper method to obtain appellate review, said the Court, was to seek it *prior* to violating the order. Is this doctrine inconsistent with the practice authorized in *Ryan?* In a footnote the Court in *Ryan* distinguished *Walker,* because "[o]ur holding that the claims there sought to be asserted were not open on review of petitioners' contempt convictions was based upon the availability of review of those claims at an earlier stage." 402 U.S. at 532 n. 4. Does this logic beg the question about the applicability of the collateral order doctrine to appeal of discovery orders? Isn't the Court simply making it harder to get appellate review of discovery orders?

There are two important qualifications to the general reluctance to employ the collateral order doctrine for discovery appeals. First, the contempt alternative is of course not available when it is an order *denying* discovery from which appeal is sought. While normally such a denial may be appealed following a final judgment in the underlying suit, this option is not available when the denial of discovery takes place in an ancillary discovery proceeding in another court, such as may occur when a nonparty served with a Rule 45 subpoena resists enforcement. In this situation, such an order has been deemed appealable as a collateral order. Nicholas v. Wyndham International, Inc., 373 F.3d 537 (4th Cir. 2004). Second, the collateral order doctrine may be employed when it is the party, rather than the witness, who seeks immediate appeal. In such a situation, the contempt alternative is of course unavailable. FDIC v. Ogden Corp., 202 F.3d 454 (1st Cir. 2000). See also Nguyen v. Excel Corp., 197 F.3d 200, 204 (5th Cir. 1999) ("When a subpoenaed third party does not have a direct and personal interest in suppression of the requested information . . . the third party is not likely to risk a contempt citation.")

In Cunningham v. Hamilton County, 527 U.S. 198 (1999), the Court held that the discovery sanctions imposed on a lawyer under Rule 37 are not immediately appealable under 28 U.S.C. § 1291. The lawyer was ordered to pay nearly $4,000 in costs and fees in connection with discovery violations, and sought immediate review. Finding that an inquiry into the sanctions order "would differ only marginally from an inquiry into the merits," the Court concluded that review could not be justified under the collateral order doctrine. It also reasoned that "[t]o permit an immediate appeal from such a sanctions order would undermine the very purposes of Rule 37(a), which was designed to protect courts and opposing parties from delaying or harassing tactics during the discovery process." Thus, although it "candidly recognize[d] the hardship that a sanctions order may sometimes impose on an attorney," the Court held that the solution to these problems lay in new legislation or rulemaking, not interpretation of existing statutes and rules.

On occasion, review of discovery orders has been authorized via mandamus pursuant to the All Writs Act, 28 U.S.C. § 1651, discussed infra p. 1126. For an ambitious attempt to rethink interlocutory review through the collateral order and mandamus doctrines, see Steinman, Reinventing Appellate Jurisdiction, 48 B.C.L. Rev. 1237 (2007).

D. Section 1292 and Interlocutory Injunctions

CARSON V. AMERICAN BRANDS, INC.
Supreme Court of the United States, 1981
450 U.S. 79

JUSTICE BRENNAN delivered the opinion of the Court.

The question presented in this Title VII class action is whether an interlocutory order of the District Court denying a joint motion of the parties to enter a consent decree containing injunctive relief is an appealable order.

I

Petitioners, representing a class of present and former black seasonal employees and applicants for employment at the Richmond Leaf Department of the American Tobacco Co., brought this suit in the United States District Court for the Eastern District of Virginia under 42 U.S.C. § 1981 and Title VII of the Civil Rights Act of 1964, 42 U.S.C. § 2000e *et seq.* Alleging that respondents had discriminated against them in hiring, promotion, transfer, and training opportunities, petitioners sought a declaratory judgment, preliminary and permanent injunctive relief, and money damages.

After extensive discovery had been conducted and the plaintiff class had been certified, the parties negotiated a settlement and jointly moved the District Court to approve and enter their proposed consent decree. See Fed. Rule Civ.Proc. 23(e). The decree would have required respondents to give hiring and seniority preferences to black employees and to fill one-third of all supervisory positions in the Richmond Leaf Department with qualified blacks. While agreeing to the terms of the decree, respondents "expressly den[ied] any violation of . . . any . . . equal employment law, regulation, or order."

The District Court denied the motion to enter the proposed decree. Concluding that preferential treatment on the basis of race violated Title VII and the Constitution absent a showing of past or present discrimination, and that the facts submitted in support of the decree demonstrated no "vestiges of racial discrimination," the court held that the proposed decree illegally granted racial preferences to the petitioner class. It further declared that even if present or past discrimination had been shown, the decree would be illegal in that it would extend relief to *all* present and future black employees of the Richmond Leaf Department, not just to *actual* victims of the alleged discrimination.

The United States Court of Appeals for the Fourth Circuit, sitting en banc, dismissed petitioners' appeal for want of jurisdiction. It held that the District Court's refusal to enter the consent decree was neither a "collateral order" under 28 U.S.C. § 1291, nor an interlocutory order "refusing" an "injunctio[n]" under 28 U.S.C. § 1292(a)(1). Three judges dissented, concluding that the order refusing to approve the consent decree was appealable under 28 U.S.C. § 1292(a)(1).

Noting a conflict in the Circuits, we granted certiorari. We hold that the order is appealable under 28 U.S.C. § 1292(a)(1), and accordingly reverse the Court of Appeals.

II

* * *

Although the District Court's order declining to enter the proposed consent decree did not in terms "refus[e]" an "injunctio[n]," it nonetheless had the practical effect of doing so. This is because the proposed decree would have permanently enjoined respondents from discriminating against black employees at the Richmond Leaf Department, and would have directed changes in seniority and benefit systems, established hiring goals for qualified blacks in certain supervisory positions, and granted job-bidding preferences for seasonal employees. Indeed, prospective relief was at the very core of the disapproved settlement.[9]

---

[9]   Neither the parties nor the Court of Appeals dispute that the predominant effect of the proposed decree would have been injunctive. The parties entitled the major part of the decree, "Injunctive Relief for the Class," and expressly agreed that respondents would be *permanently enjoined* from discriminating against black employees at the facilities of the Richmond Leaf Department."

For an interlocutory order to be immediately appealable under
§ 1292(a)(1), however, a litigant must show more than that the order has
the practical effect of refusing an injunction. Because § 1292(a)(1) was
intended to carve out only a limited exception to the final-judgment rule,
we have construed the statute narrowly to ensure that appeal as of right
under § 1292(a)(1) will be available only in circumstances where an appeal
will further the statutory purpose of "permit[ting] litigants to effectually
challenge interlocutory orders of serious, perhaps irreparable,
consequence." *Baltimore Contractors, Inc.,* [348 U.S. 176 (1955)]. Unless a
litigant can show that an interlocutory order of the district court might
have a "serious, perhaps irreparable, consequence," and that the order can
be "effectually challenged" only by immediate appeal, the general
congressional policy against piecemeal review will preclude interlocutory
appeal.

* * *

III

In the instant case, unless the District Court order denying the motion
to enter the consent decree is immediately appealable, petitioners will lose
their opportunity to "effectually challenge" an interlocutory order that
denies them injunctive relief and that plainly has a "serious, perhaps
irreparable, consequence." First, petitioners might lose their opportunity
to settle their case on the negotiated terms. As *United States v. Armour &
Co.,* 402 U.S. 673, 681 (1971), stated:

> Consent decrees are entered into by parties to a case after careful
> negotiation has produced agreement on their precise terms. The
> parties waive their right to litigate the issues involved in the case
> and thus save themselves the time, expense, and inevitable risk
> of litigation. Naturally, the agreement reached normally embodies
> a compromise; in exchange for the saving of cost and elimination
> of risk, the parties each give up something they might have won
> had they proceeded with the litigation.

Settlement agreements may thus be predicated on an express or implied
condition that the parties would, by their agreement, be able to avoid the
costs and uncertainties of litigation. In this case, that condition of
settlement has been radically affected by the District Court. By refusing to
enter the proposed consent decree, the District Court effectively ordered
the parties to proceed to trial and to have their respective rights and
liabilities established within limits laid down by that court. Because a
party to a pending settlement might be legally justified in withdrawing its
consent to the agreement once trial is held and final judgment entered, the
District Court's order might thus have the "serious, perhaps irreparable,
consequence" of denying the parties their right to compromise their dispute
on mutually agreeable terms.

There is a second "serious, perhaps irreparable, consequence" of the District Court order that justifies our conclusion that the order is immediately appealable under § 1292 (a)(1). In seeking entry of the proposed consent decree, petitioners sought an immediate restructuring of respondents' transfer and promotional policies. They asserted in their complaint that they would suffer irreparable injury unless they obtained that injunctive relief at the earliest opportunity. Because petitioners cannot obtain that relief until the proposed consent decree is entered, any further delay in reviewing the propriety of the District Court's refusal to enter the decree might cause them serious or irreparable harm.

In sum, in refusing to approve the parties' negotiated consent decree, the District Court denied petitioners the opportunity to compromise their claim and to obtain the injunctive benefits of the settlement agreement they negotiated. These constitute "serious, perhaps irreparable, consequences" that petitioners can "effectually challenge" only by an immediate appeal. It follows that the order is an order "refusing" an "injunctio[n]" and is therefore appealable under § 1292(a)(1).

Reversed.

NOTES AND QUESTIONS

1.   Examine the language of § 1292(a)(1), which was added to the judicial code in the late nineteenth century and later broadened to include orders both granting and denying applications for injunctive relief. Given the well-established policy against piecemeal appeals, why would Congress create this exception to the finality rule? According to Judge Friendly, "although the language is broader, * * * it seems rather plain that Congress was thinking primarily of the case where erroneous denial of a temporary injunction may cause injury quite as irreparable as an erroneous grant of one." Stewart-Warner Corp. v. Westinghouse Elec. Corp., 325 F.2d 822, 829–30 (2d Cir.1963) (Friendly, J., dissenting). What, if anything, does this logic say concerning the debate over the value of the right to appeal, discussed in section A of this chapter?

2.   In light of the judicial assumptions about congressional intent in § 1292(a)(1), should the Court limit applicability of the statute to interlocutory appeals from rulings on *preliminary* injunctions and not include appeals from interlocutory rulings on *permanent* injunctions? In Switzerland Cheese Association, Inc. v. E. Horne's Market, Inc., 385 U.S. 23 (1966), the district court had denied plaintiffs' motion for summary judgment granting a permanent injunction and damages, on the grounds that the court could not conclude that there was "no genuine issue as to any material fact." Plaintiffs appealed, claiming that the order denying its summary judgment motion was an "interlocutory" order "refusing" an injunction within the meaning of § 1292(a)(1).

In rejecting this argument, the Supreme Court stated that "we approach this statute somewhat gingerly lest a floodgate be opened that brings into the exception many pretrial orders." However, the Court refused to hold that denials of requests for permanent injunctive relief could *never* fall within the terms of § 1292(a)(1). It reached this view, "not because 'interlocutory' or preliminary orders may not at times embrace denials of permanent injunctions, but for the reason that the denial of a motion for a summary judgment because of unresolved issues of fact does not settle or even tentatively decide anything about the merits of the claim. It is strictly a pretrial order that decides only one thing, that the case should go to trial. Orders that in no way touch on the merits of the claim but only relate to pretrial procedures are not in our view 'interlocutory' within the meaning of § 1292(a)(1). We see no other way to protect the integrity of the congressional policy against piecemeal appeals."

Was the Court correct to conclude that a ruling on a summary judgment motion does not "even tentatively decide anything about the merits of the claim?" Does the fact that such a ruling does not "settle" the merits mean that it cannot fall within the terms of a statute authorizing review of *interlocutory* orders? In any event, is there anything in the text or apparent policy of § 1292(a)(1) that limits the statute's reach to rulings on the merits? Would the Court have been on sounder ground had it construed § 1292(a)(1) to have no applicability to permanent injunctions? Won't many decisions to grant or deny a permanent injunction, coming well along in the litigation, qualify as final judgments under section 1291?

3.   It is widely held that § 1292(a)(1) has no applicability to appeal of rulings on motions seeking temporary restraining orders, as opposed to those seeking preliminary injunctions. See Service Employees Intern. Union v. National Union of Healthcare Workers, 598 F.3d 1061, 1067–1068 (9th Cir. 2010) (acknowledging the general rule, but observing that TROs with the functional effect of preliminary injunctions may give rise to a right of appeal). Some commentators suggest the propriety of allowing review when a TRO threatens a potentially irreparable injury. 16 C. Wright, A. Miller & E. Cooper, Federal Practice and Procedure § 3922.1 (3d ed. 2012) Is this a good idea? Why not simply include *all* temporary restraining orders?

In considering the appealability of temporary restraining orders, keep in mind that the appellate court has the power under Federal Rule of Appellate Procedure 8 to stay a district court decision and to grant an injunction or restraining order that the district court refused to allow. These appellate stays issue only in cases of irreparable injury and only in the appellate court's discretion. Does the appellate court's discretionary stay authority lessen the importance of providing for as-of-right appellate review of district court decisions granting or denying temporary restraining orders?

4.   In Gulfstream Aerospace Corp. v. Mayacamas Corp., 485 U.S. 271 (1988), the parties filed overlapping actions in state and federal court for breach of the same contract. The state court plaintiff and federal court defendant, Gulfstream, moved to stay the federal proceeding, and then filed an appeal from the district court's denial of the stay. While the denial of a stay would not ordinarily be considered a final order, the so-called *Enelow-Ettelson*

doctrine permitted immediate review of certain stay orders on the theory that they were functionally equivalent to the grant or denial of preliminary injunctive relief within section 1292(a)(1). A product of the old division between law and equity, the *Enelow-Ettelson* doctrine characterized stay orders as injunctions when they were traditionally available only in a court of equity to stay proceedings at law. After summarizing the scholarly and judicial criticisms of the doctrine that had accumulated over the years, the *Gulfstream* Court overruled the "sterile and antiquated" *Enelow-Ettelson* doctrine. Accordingly, orders granting or denying stays of legal proceedings are no longer automatically subject to appellate review as preliminary injunctions under section 1292(a)(1). Other forms of review were, of course, to remain available, including as of right review of final judgments under section 1291 and discretionary modes of review. [As discussed above at pp. 1098–1099, the *Gulfstream* Court also ruled out one alternative mode of review: it concluded that review of the denial of a stay order was not available under the collateral order doctrine.]

Eight months after the Supreme Court's decision in *Gulfstream,* Congress in 1988 amended the Federal Arbitration Act, 9 U.S.C. §§ 1 et seq., allowing an immediate appeal from orders that refuse to compel arbitration or that deny a motion to stay litigation pending arbitration. Section 16(a)(1) specifically provides that an appeal may be taken from an "order refusing" a stay of arbitration, and from a denial of an application seeking to compel arbitration; it makes no provision for interlocutory review of an order *granting* a stay of arbitration. Some appellate courts had refused to permit appellate review of orders granting a stay, reasoning that the FAA allows interlocutory appellate review only when the order in question *declines* to issue a stay or otherwise evinces hostility to arbitration.

The Supreme Court rejected that approach in Green Tree Financial Corp.-Alabama v. Randolph, 531 U.S. 79 (2000). The Court acknowledged the one-sided thrust of section 16(a)(1), but noted that section 16(a)(3) provides for an appeal of any "final decision" with respect to an arbitration. The Court found that this language meant to incorporate the well-established meaning of finality that had developed in other contexts. Analyzing the judgment at hand, the Court found that the stay and dismissal of the action satisfied the requirements of a final decision in that the dismissal ended the litigation on the merits and left nothing pending in federal court. At least in the arbitration context, then, the basic rules of appellate review dictated by the *Enelow-Ettelson* doctrine have been restored by statute. Does this new statutory foundation for appellate review call into doubt the wisdom of the Court's decision to overturn the *Enelow-Ettelson* doctrine?

5.   Other orders, though not operating as a formal grant or denial of injunctive relief, might be characterized as injunctive for purposes of interlocutory review. For example, one commentator has argued that the doctrine of qualified immunity, where applicable, operates as the functional equivalent of an injunction against any further proceedings against the official in question. See Steinman, Reinventing Appellate Jurisdiction, 48 B.C.L. Rev.

1237 (2007). Professor Steinman draws on the analogy to defend collateral order review of qualified immunity decisions but argues that the doctrine would rest more firmly on 28 U.S.C. § 1292(a). Id. at 1277. Would the Court's recognition of such an injunction analogy invite other applications for review of quasi-injunctive decrees?

3. DISCRETIONARY FORMS OF APPELLATE REVIEW

In contrast to as-of-right review of final decisions under sections 1291 and 1292(a)(1), litigants may invoke a variety of discretionary modes of appellate review. Such discretionary modes of review typically begin with an application, either to the district court or to the appellate court, or both, for permission to seek interlocutory review or for the entry of a judgment that will trigger immediate review. In doubtful cases, parties may file both a notice of appeal and one or more applications for discretionary review.

A. Discretionary Review and the Role of the District Court

NYSTROM V. TREX CO., INC.
United State Court of Appeals, Federal Circuit, 2003
339 F.3d 1347

Before MAYER, CHIEF JUDGE, GAJARSA, and LINN, CIRCUIT JUDGES. LINN, CIRCUIT JUDGE.

Ron Nystrom ("Nystrom") appeals from a judgment of invalidity of certain claims and non-infringement of all claims of his U.S. Patent No. 5,474,831 ("the '831 patent") and an order denying sanctions under 28 U.S.C. § 1927, entered by the United States District Court for the Eastern District of Virginia on October 17, 2002, in favor of the defendants (collectively, "TREX"). Because TREX's invalidity and unenforceability counterclaim as to claims 1–17 remains pending at the district court, the judgment appealed is not final within the meaning of 28 U.S.C. § 1295(a)(1). Therefore, the court dismisses the appeal for lack of jurisdiction.

I. BACKGROUND

On December 5, 2001, Nystrom filed suit in the Eastern District of Virginia against TREX alleging infringement of the '831 patent. TREX counterclaimed, seeking a declaratory judgment of non-infringement, invalidity and unenforceability, and alleging antitrust violations on the part of Nystrom, his company, and his attorneys. Nystrom then filed a motion to dismiss the antitrust counterclaim. In response, TREX voluntarily dismissed the antitrust counterclaim, but then filed an amended counterclaim alleging many of the same antitrust violations against Nystrom alone. Soon after the amended counterclaim was filed, TREX again dismissed its antitrust counterclaim, prompting Nystrom to move for sanctions on the ground that TREX's attorneys "multiplie[d] the proceedings . . . unreasonably and vexatiously." 28 U.S.C. § 1927 (2000). The district court denied the motion for sanctions.

In due course, the district court held a *Markman* hearing [defined in note 1 after this case] and issued a claim construction ruling on the construction of three disputed claim terms of the'831 patent. Based on the district court's claim construction ruling, Nystrom conceded that he could not prove his infringement case against TREX. Therefore, Nystrom asked the district court to enter judgment of non-infringement in favor of TREX and to dismiss TREX's invalidity and unenforceability counterclaim without prejudice. TREX then moved for summary judgment of non-infringement and for summary judgment of invalidity of claims 18–20. On September 11, 2002, the district court entered judgment of non-infringement of all claims and deferred its rulings on the outstanding motion for summary judgment of invalidity of claims 18–20.

On September 18, 2002, the district court held a conference call with the parties to determine how best to proceed with the pending motion and the action as a whole. The parties discussed three possibilities: (1) entering a judgment on the decided issues under Federal Rule of Civil Procedure 54(b); (2) dismissing TREX's counterclaim without prejudice; or (3) certifying an interlocutory order under 28 U.S.C. § 1292(c). The parties also recognized a fourth possibility: that the district court could proceed to trial on the counterclaim remaining after a ruling on the fully briefed motion for partial summary judgment of invalidity of claims 18–20. The district court took the parties' suggestions under advisement. On October 17, 2002, the district court granted TREX's motion for summary judgment of invalidity of claims 18–20, noting that the motion was ripe for decision. The challenge to the validity and enforceability of claims 1–17 was not addressed on the merits. The district court expressly entered a final judgment with respect to claims 18–20 and ruled that "[t]he remainder of the Defendants' Counterclaim seeking declaratory judgment of invalidity and unenforceability of the'831 patent is hereby STAYED pending appeal."

Nystrom appealed the claim construction rulings, the grant of summary judgment of non-infringement based thereon, the grant of summary judgment of invalidity of claims 18–20, and the district court's denial of sanctions. Prior to the commencement of oral argument before this court, the court raised the issue of the finality of the district court's judgment and asked both parties to comment on whether this court had jurisdiction over the appeal in light of the presence in the case of the stayed counterclaim. Both parties verified that the counterclaim had not been dismissed and remained stayed pending appeal, but stated that they considered the district court's actions to have finally disposed of the case for purposes of appeal. The parties also confirmed that the district court had not made any determination or entered any direction under Rule 54(b). The court, after a brief caucus, announced that because the counterclaim remained pending, the judgment of the district court was not final, leaving this court without jurisdiction to hear the appeal. The court then ruled that the case was dismissed and adjourned the proceeding without entertaining argument on the merits.

II. DISCUSSION

"[E]very federal appellate court has a special obligation to satisfy itself . . . of its own jurisdiction . . . even though the parties are prepared to concede it." Thus, even though the parties raised no objection to our jurisdiction over this appeal, we are obligated to consider whether there is a final judgment of the district court, 28 U.S.C. § 1295(a)(1), or a basis for jurisdiction over an interlocutory order, 28 U.S.C. § 1292(c). On matters relating to this court's jurisdiction, we apply Federal Circuit law, not that of the regional circuit from which the case arose.

This court's "final judgment rule," as applied to patent disputes arising under 28 U.S.C. § 1338, is set forth at 28 U.S.C. § 1295. Section 1295's final judgment rule mirrors that of its counterpart found at 28 U.S.C. § 1291. Under the rule, parties may only appeal a "final decision of a district court." 28 U.S.C. § 1295 (2000). * * * If a case is not fully adjudicated as to all claims for all parties and there is no express determination that there is no just reason for delay or express direction for entry of judgment as to fewer than all of the parties or claims, there is no "final decision" under 28 U.S.C. § 1295(a)(1) and therefore no jurisdiction.

Determinations of claim construction made as an interlocutory matter by a district court are frequently determinative of either infringement or invalidity, but seldom both. The consequence of this is that after a claim construction ruling, the parties and the district court often find one of the infringement and validity sides of the case resolved and the other either moot or unresolved. Because claim construction is subject to de novo review as a matter of law, immediate appeal of an interlocutory claim construction ruling without a resolution of all of the factual issues of infringement or validity dependent thereon is often desired by one or both of the parties for strategic or other reasons. But, other than the accommodation for deferred accounting in 28 U.S.C. § 1292(c)(2), the rules of finality that define the jurisdiction of this court do not contain special provisions for patent cases or admit to exceptions for strategic reasons or otherwise, short of meeting the conditions specified in Rule 54(b) or 28 U.S.C. § 1292(b), (c)(1). Thus, piecemeal litigation is as strictly precluded by the rule of finality for patent cases as it is for any other case. Until the rules are changed, the parties and the district courts are obliged to conclude patent cases in strict compliance with the finality rule to avoid unnecessary litigation over jurisdictional issues in perfecting an appeal.

In the present case, the parties correctly identified for the district court three possible avenues of appeal as a matter of right. First, the district court could have considered proceeding to trial with the remaining invalidity and unenforceability counterclaim or otherwise disposing of the issue on the merits, thus "end[ing] the litigation on the merits and leav[ing] nothing for the court to do but execute the judgment." *Catlin*, 324 U.S. at 233.

Second, the district court could have dismissed the counterclaim without prejudice (either with or without a finding that the counterclaim was moot) following the grant of summary judgment of non-infringement.[1]

Third, the district court could have considered whether there was a proper basis to make "an express determination that there is no just reason for delay" and then to expressly direct the entry of final judgment on fewer than all of the claims under Federal Rule of Civil Procedure 54(b). The finality of a judgment under Rule 54(b) is subject to de novo review by this court.

A fourth avenue would have been for Nystrom to seek permission to immediately appeal the interlocutory judgments and orders of the district court under 28 U.S.C. § 1292(b), (c)(1). Such an appeal may only proceed if the district court, in its discretion, first certifies that each ruling presented for appeal "involves a controlling question of law as to which there is substantial ground for difference of opinion and that an immediate appeal from the order may materially advance the ultimate termination of the litigation. . ." 28 U.S.C. § 1292(b) (2000). Acceptance of such appeal is also subject to the absolute discretion of this court, "which may refuse to entertain such an appeal [even when certified by the district court] in much the same manner that the Supreme Court today refuses to entertain applications for writs of certiorari." Such appeals are rarely granted.

The district court chose none of these approaches. Instead, the district court kept the invalidity and unenforceability counterclaim as to claims 1–17 in the case pending appeal, expressly reserving the counterclaim as a stayed claim. Stay orders generally are not final for purposes of 28 U.S.C. § 1295. *Cf. Moses H. Cone Mem'l Hosp. v. Mercury Constr. Corp.,* 460 U.S. 1, 10 n. 11 (1983) ("[A] stay is not ordinarily a final decision for purposes of § 1291. . ."). Moreover, a "judgment that does not dispose of pending counterclaims is not a final judgment." Without finality at the district court, this court declines to entertain the present appeal. Accordingly, the appeal is dismissed for lack of jurisdiction. [Chief Justice Mayer concurred in the judgment.]

Dismissed.

---

[1] "We have previously held that a district court has discretion to dismiss a counterclaim alleging that a patent is invalid as moot where it finds no infringement." *Phonometrics, Inc. v. N. Telecom Inc.,* 133 F.3d 1459, 1468 (Fed.Cir.1998). We note that the Supreme Court's decision in *Cardinal Chemical Co. v. Morton International, Inc.,* 508 U.S. 83 (1993), which prohibits us, as an intermediate court, from vacating a judgment of invalidity when we conclude that a patent is not infringed, does not preclude the discretionary action of a district court, in an appropriate case, in dismissing an invalidity counterclaim without prejudice when it concludes a patent is not infringed.

NOTES AND QUESTIONS

1.   *Patent litigation*: The process of filing and defending patents in the
United States can be intensively litigious. It all begins with an invention—a
non-obvious contribution to any field of scientific endeavor. Next, the inventor
files a patent application with the US Patent and Trademark Office (PTO),
identifying the new invention, describing the prior art, and staking "claims"
that describe the invention's contribution to the field. If the PTO approves the
claims and grants the patent, federal law gives the patent-holder a 20-year
property right in the exclusive use of the patented item or process. Sometimes,
the patent-holder will manufacture the better mousetrap herself; sometimes,
she will wait until the world beats a path to her door and ask users of her
concept to enter into license agreements that call for royalty payments. Much
patent litigation grows out of the user's refusal to enter into or honor a license
agreement. When this happens, patent holders may sue, seeking damages and
injunctive relief; federal courts have exclusive jurisdiction of such claims. See
28 U.S.C. § 1338.

Litigation frequently begins, as it did in Nystrom v. TREX with a claim of
infringement. Defendants often respond with counterclaims, seeking either a
declaration of non-infringement or a declaration of invalidity or both. These
legal issues overlap to some degree, but differ in important respects. The issue
of infringement depends on the scope of the patent's claim: a patent might
validly apply in limited circumstances but not reach broadly enough to
encompass the use of the particular defendant. (Thus, a patent on the use of
electricity to power a mousetrap would not necessarily be infringed by a
mousetrap that relies on springs.) Issues of validity differ from those of
infringement; a patent may be declared invalid because it makes no real
contribution to the field (or for other reasons). In making decisions about
validity, federal courts do not regard the PTO's determination to grant the
patent as dispositive.

In many cases, a finding of non-infringement can provide a narrower
ground on which to resolve patent litigation. (Such narrow rulings may leave
the validity issue unresolved.) But issues of infringement and validity can both
turn on how broadly or narrowly one construes the scope of the patent claim.
At one time, the construction of patent claims was viewed as a factual issue for
the jury to resolve. But the Supreme Court ruled in Markman v. Westview
Instruments, 517 U.S. 370 (1996), that the construction of patent claims
presents a question of law for the court to resolve. Claim construction under
Markman plays a central role in patent litigation: a narrowly construed claim
may eliminate the alleged infringement; a broadly construed claim may raise
doubts as to the validity of the patent.

One can see the importance of the *Markman* ruling in Nystrom v. TREX.
Nystrom's complaint was that TREX infringed his patent; the *Markman* ruling
of the district court construed the claims in the patent in a way that made
Nystrom's infringement theory untenable. Hence, the district court granted
summary judgment on that issue. But TREX had counterclaimed, arguing that
the patent was invalid and unenforceable. These counterclaims remained

pending after the grant of summary judgment. Despite this lack of technical finality, the parties and the district court recognized the importance of securing relatively expeditious appellate review of the summary judgment order. Recall, as noted supra p. 1059, that the Federal Circuit reversal rate in patent cases reportedly once approached 50%. In such a world, it may be impossible to settle a case without first securing the appellate court's *Markman* determination. (Note that in contrast to the usual method of review of district court decisions by the regional courts of appeals, the Federal Circuit enjoys exclusive appellate jurisdiction over patent cases. See 28 U.S.C. § 1295(a)(1).)

Now consider the action of the district court in *Nystrom,* granting a stay in an attempt to facilitate appellate review. Although the Federal Circuit ruled that the stay order was non-final, the court identified three ways, apart from issuing a final judgment, that the district court could help the parties secure expeditious review: by issuing a Rule 54(b) certification; by granting certification under 28 U.S.C. 1292(b); and by issuing a dismissal of the counterclaims without prejudice. These notes explore these three options.

2.   *Rule 54(b)*: To see how Rule 54(b) operates, consider the leading case, Curtiss-Wright Corp. v. General Electric Co., 446 U.S. 1 (1980). Under contracts worth some $215 million, Curtiss-Wright agreed to supply GE with components for use in building nuclear naval vessels. Curtiss-Wright brought suit on the contracts, seeking damages and reformation of the contracts. In addition, Curtiss-Wright added a claim for $19 million, representing the balance due on work already performed. The district court ruled that Curtiss-Wright was entitled to judgment on the relatively straightforward $19 million balance due, while the more complicated claims for damages and reformation remained pending. Following this grant of summary judgment, Curtiss-Wright moved for certification of the order as a final judgment under Rule 54(b). The district court entered the requested order, along with a determination that there was no just reason for delay. (One factor particularly supporting entry of judgment was the spread between the prevailing interest rate in the market, some 16–18% in the late 1970s, and the statutory rate for pre-judgment interest of only 6%. Assuming a ten point difference in rates, GE would make $2 million for each year it succeeded in delaying entry of judgment for the undisputed balance due.) On appeal, the Third Circuit reversed the entry of partial final judgment under Rule 54(b). The court of appeals had previously announced a rule forbidding such judgments in cases involving counterclaims or set-offs. Because GE had counterclaimed in response to the contract breach claims of Curtiss-Wright, no partial final judgment (and accompanying transfer of funds) was appropriate.

On review, the Supreme Court reversed. The Court first recounted the steps that a district court must follow in making a Rule 54(b) determination:

A district court must first determine that it is dealing with a "final judgment." It must be a "judgment" in the sense that it is a decision upon a cognizable claim for relief, and it must be "final" in the sense that it is "an ultimate disposition of an individual claim entered in the course of a multiple claims action."

> Once having found finality, the district court must go on to determine whether there is any just reason for delay. Not all final judgments on individual claims should be immediately appealable, even if they are in some sense separable from the remaining unresolved claims. The function of the district court under the Rule is to act as a "dispatcher." It is left to the sound judicial discretion of the district court to determine the "appropriate time" when each final decision in a multiple claims action is ready for appeal. This discretion is to be exercised "in the interest of sound judicial administration."

Having established that the decision was entrusted to the district court's discretion, the Court faulted the court of appeals for conducting its own assessment of the factors underlying the district court's decision.

> There are thus two aspects to the proper function of a reviewing court in Rule 54(b) cases. The court of appeals must, of course, scrutinize the district court's evaluation of such factors as the interrelationship of the claims so as to prevent piecemeal appeals in cases which should be reviewed only as single units. But once such juridical concerns have been met, the discretionary judgment of the district court should be given substantial deference, for that court is "the one most likely to be familiar with the case and with any justifiable reasons for delay." The reviewing court should disturb the trial court's assessment of the equities only if it can say that the judge's conclusion was clearly unreasonable.

In the end, the Court recognized that the question of which party, Curtiss-Wright or GE was to have the benefit of the difference between the statutory and market rates of interest was a matter within the district court's discretion.

3. Why is Rule 54(b) necessary? A Rule 54(b) determination can set the stage for appellate review, but that is not its only function. As *Curtiss-Wright* illustrates, the Rule 54(b) determination facilitates the entry of a final judgment to which the usual rules of execution and appellate review apply. Thus, a Rule 54(b) judgment for money damages, unless stayed, may be collected through the usual processes of law (thus giving the judgment the finality it needs to support appellate review). Cf. Dickinson v. Petroleum Conversion Corp., 338 U.S. 507 (1950): "The liberalization of our practice to allow more issues and parties to be joined in one action and to expand the privilege of intervention by those not originally parties has increased the danger of hardship and denial of justice through delay if each issue must await the determination of all issues as to all parties before a final judgment can be had." On that score, consider the plight of a plaintiff in a multi-party litigation when one defendant prevails on a 12(b)(6) motion at the beginning of the case. Should the plaintiff have to await the resolution of all the other claims involving all of the other parties before taking an appeal from that dismissal?

Does this situation differ from that in Gelboim v. Bank of America, supra p. 1083?

4. *Curtiss-Wright* emphasizes the importance of district court discretion in issuing partial final judgments under Rule 54(b), a view the Federal Circuit echoes in *Nystrom*. This recognition of a discretionary role at the district court level might predictably trigger some hostility from appellate courts concerned with loss of control over their appellate dockets. Indeed, such a message comes through in decisions that qualify district court discretion. In Gerardi v. Pelullo, 16 F.3d 1363 (3d Cir.1994), the court held that "the district court abused its discretion when it concluded that [the judgments] were ready for appeal" pursuant to Rule 54(b). The appellate court expressed the view "that a district court should be conservative in invoking Rule 54(b) to certify a judgment as final because if an aggrieved party appeals following the certification, the district court effectively will be electing to control the docket of a court of appeals." In addition, the district court's discretion extends only to the determination that there exists no just reason for delay. The district court's determination of the ruling's finality for purposes of Rule 54(b) is reviewed de novo.

5. Rule 54(b) requires "an express determination" by the district court "that there is no just reason for delay." It has been held that a court of appeals should "not require a mechanical recitation of the rule's requirements," but instead merely "that the district court manifest 'unmistakable intent' to make its judgment final." Swope v. Columbian Chemicals Co., 281 F.3d 185, 191 n. 5 (5th Cir. 2002). If no magic words are required, why did the appellate court in *Nystrom* decline to view the district court's stay order, which was clearly designed to facilitate appellate review, as the functional equivalent of a Rule 54(b) certification? Was *Nystrom* an otherwise appropriate candidate for Rule 54(b) certification?

6. Apart from Rule 54(b) certifications, the Federal Circuit in *Nystrom* indicated that district courts may play a role in facilitating appellate review through 28 U.S.C. § 1292(b). Added in 1958, the provision seeks to "expedite the ultimate termination of litigation and thereby some unnecessary expense and delay" by allowing appeal of certain nonfinal orders. H.R.Rep.No. 1667, 85th Cong., 2d Sess. 1 (1958). See also Note, Section 1292(b): Eight Years of Undefined Discretion, 54 Geo.L.J. 940, 941 (1966): "The [final judgment] rule caused a manifest waste of time and money for both litigants and the court whenever the parties were forced to await final judgment in a lengthy trial only to have a ruling, made at the outset of the trial, reversed." Recall, however, that one of the primary purposes of the final judgment rule was to accomplish precisely the same goal. Could they both logically be designed to achieve the same end? Note that 28 U.S.C. § 1292(c)(1) extends the same model of discretionary appellate review to the Federal Circuit.

(a) Professor Michael Solimine has noted that "[d]espite the [Supreme] Court's frequent reference to section 1292(b) commentators generally discount its effectiveness as a safety valve for interlocutory appeals, since it has been historically utilized infrequently." Solimine, Revitalizing Interlocutory

Appeals in the Federal Courts, 58 Geo. Wash. L. Rev. 1165, 1193 (1990). He suggests that "[m]uch of the blame is attributable to the narrow construction given the statute by some courts, as well as the fear that relaxing the use of the statute will open the floodgates to appeals," and argues that "[t]hese fears have been greatly exaggerated." One can see these fears reflected in the *Nystrom* court's candid admission that such appeals will be rarely approved.

(b) Section 1292(b) effectively requires dual certification, both by the district and appellate courts. Both are deemed to be wholly discretionary, in the appellate court explicitly by the terms of the law and in the district court by judicial practice. See, e.g., In re Convertible Rowing Exerciser Patent Litigation, 903 F.2d 822 (Fed.Cir.1990); D'Ippolito v. Cities Service Co., 374 F.2d 643, 649 (2d Cir.1967). The appellate court may deny the appeal for any reason, including docket congestion. Not surprisingly, these certification requirements have limited use of the procedure; over the years, it has had relatively little impact on the total number of appeals taken. See Carrington, Crowded Dockets and the Courts of Appeals: The Threat to the Function of Review and the National Law, 82 Harv.L.Rev. 542, 546–47 (1969); C. Wright & M. Kane, Law of Federal Courts 759 (7th ed. 2011) (§ 1292(b) generally reserved for the "exceptional" case).

(c) Consider the twin requirements of the statute: that immediate review of the order "materially advance" the litigation's termination and that the order involve "a controlling issue of law." Views may differ about both questions. For example, in *Nystrom,* both the district court and the parties evidently viewed the *Markman* ruling as a controlling issue that would advance the termination of the litigation, although the comment of court of appeals suggests it may have disagreed. Controlling issues of law include more than just rulings on the substantive law applicable to the case. Orders denying a motion to dismiss for lack of personal jurisdiction have been granted § 1292(b) interlocutory appeal. How can they be said to constitute controlling issues of law? Orders rejecting challenges to venue, subject matter jurisdiction, justiciability, and removal have also come under § 1292(b). See 16 C. Wright, A. Miller, & E. Cooper, Federal Practice & Procedure § 3931 (2d ed. 1996). Would an order to comply with a discovery request be "controlling"? Would an order denying discovery?

(d) In Yamaha Motor Corp. v. Calhoun, 516 U.S. 199 (1996), the Court held that an appellate court which accepts a certification under § 1292(b) can address a question different from the one certified by the district court so long as it is included within the order on which the appeal is based. Plaintiffs there sued after their daughter was killed in a jet-ski accident. Defendant moved for partial summary judgment, arguing that federal maritime law displaced state law remedies. The district court agreed, but concluded also that maritime law permitted recovery for loss of society, and the district court certified the question whether such recoveries are allowed under maritime law to the court of appeals. Rather than answer this question, the court of appeals held that state law remedies remained available. In affirming, the Supreme Court said that "[t]he court of appeals may not reach beyond the certified order to address other orders made in the case," but that it may address "any issue fairly included within the certified order" whether or not that was the question posed by the district judge.

7.   The *Nystrom* court identified dismissal without prejudice as one additional mechanism by which the district court and the parties can take steps to ripen the case for appellate review. On this view, the district court's dismissal would finally conclude the litigation and set the stage for appellate review. But dismissals without prejudice do not ordinarily operate as final dispositions of the claims at issue; the contemplated order assumes that TREX could later re-file its invalidity counterclaim if circumstances changed. For example, if Nystrom were successful in securing a decision that overturned the district court's *Markman* ruling and reinstated its infringement case, TREX could presumably re-assert the counterclaims. Dismissal without prejudice would thus operate more to facilitate appellate review of the *Markman* claim than to finally dispose of all claims in the litigation. Indeed, the without-prejudice dismissal looks quite similar to the course the district chose in staying the counterclaims pending appeal.

One measure of the non-finality of a dismissal without prejudice can be found in the ongoing dispute between the parties over the patent's validity, an issue conceptually separate from that of infringement (and one that continued to divide the parties). A finding of invalidity makes the patent unenforceable; a finding of non-infringement leaves the patent intact (and presumptively valid) and holds that it was not infringed by the defendant's particular conduct. Parties in an ongoing dispute over the enforcement of particular patents may want answers to both questions. As the *Nystrom* court noted in footnote *, the Supreme Court rejected the Federal Circuit's practice of routinely dismissing counterclaims seeking a declaration of invalidity in cases where it has affirmed a finding of non-infringement. See Cardinal Chemical Co. v. Morton International, Inc., 508 U.S. 83 (1993). The Court took the view that a non-infringement ruling did not necessarily moot the parties' dispute over the patent's validity. Does the Federal Circuit's recognition of without-prejudice dismissal as a mode of securing appellate review operate, as a practical matter, to undercut the Supreme Court's decision in *Cardinal Chemical?*

Some characterize the finality that results from without-prejudice dismissals as "manufactured finality." For a general review and defense of the practice, see Cochran, Gaining Appellate Review by "Manufacturing" a Final Judgment Through Voluntary Dismissal of Peripheral Claims, 48 Mercer L. Rev. 979 (1997). Appellate courts have divided over the extent to which without-prejudice dismissals can "manufacture" a final judgment for purposes of appellate review. For example, in Chappelle v. Beacon Communications Corp., 84 F.3d 652 (2d Cir. 1996), the court held that a party could not facilitate appellate review through the voluntary dismissal of his claims. Such voluntary dismissals typically operate without prejudice under Rule 41 and leave the party free to re-file. On the other hand, in Manez v. Bridgestone Firestone Corp., 533 F.3d 578 (7th Cir. 2008), the court treated a dismissal without prejudice as a final judgment. There, the district court dismissed under the doctrine of forum non conveniens; the without-prejudice disposition was meant to recognize the ability of the plaintiff to re-file the litigation in a more convenient forum. The appellate court reasoned that the possibility of further litigation in a foreign tribunal did not deprive the district court order of finality for purposes of assessing the merits of the forum non conveniens determination. Like other non-merits decisions, such as those dismissing for lack of personal or subject matter jurisdiction, the without-prejudice denomination looks to further litigation in a different judicial system without compromising the finality of the order in the district court.

Does the suggested without-prejudice dismissal in *Nystrom* more closely resemble appellate manipulation condemned in *Chappelle* or practical finality recognized in *Manez?* In any event, following dismissal of the appeal in *Nystrom,* the district court dismissed the counterclaims without prejudice, and the case went back up on appeal to the Federal Circuit, this time without incident. See Nystrom v. TREX Co., Inc., 424 F.3d 1136, 1141 (Fed. Cir. 2005) (recounting action taken by the district court to manufacture finality and agreeing to decide the appeal on the merits). In assessing the vitality of manufactured finality, consider Microsoft Corp. v. Baker, infra at p. 1132. There, the Court found that dismissal of individual claims, with prejudice (but with a contested right to revive), did not produce a final judgment such that the representatives of a plaintiff class were free to appeal from the district court's denial of their motion to certify a class.

8.   If the parties and the district court judge agree that the ultimate resolution of the case would benefit from immediate review of potentially dispositive or influential decisions (such as the *Markman* claim construction ruling), why not allow review? As noted above, 28 U.S.C. § 1292(b) allows the district court to certify controlling issues of law for interlocutory review but requires the appellate court to agree to hear the appeal. Appellate courts have been reluctant to encourage such discretionary appeals, apparently in an effort to maintain control over their dockets. For an argument that the rules governing appellate review should be amended to allow interlocutory review by agreement of the parties and the district court, see Pfander & Pekarek Krohn, Interlocutory Review by Agreement of the Parties: A Preliminary Analysis, 105 Nw.U.L.Rev. 1043 (2011).

B. Discretionary Review by Writ of Mandamus

WILL v. UNITED STATES
Supreme Court of the United States, 1967
389 U.S. 90

CHIEF JUSTICE WARREN delivered the opinion of the Court.

The question in this case is the propriety of a writ of mandamus issued by the Court of Appeals for the Seventh Circuit to compel the petitioner, a United States District Judge, to vacate a portion of a pretrial order in a criminal case.

Simmie Horwitz, the defendant in a criminal tax evasion case pending before petitioner in the Northern District of Illinois, filed a motion for a bill of particulars, which contained thirty requests for information. The Government resisted a number of the requests, and over the course of several hearings most of these objections were either withdrawn by the Government or satisfied by an appropriate narrowing of the scope of the bill of particulars by petitioner. Ultimately the dispute centered solely on defendant's request number 25. This request sought certain information concerning any oral statements of the defendant relied upon by the Government to support the charge in the indictment. It asked the names and addresses of the persons to whom such statements were made, the times and places at which they were made, whether the witnesses to the statements were government agents and whether any transcripts or memoranda of the statements had been prepared by the witnesses and given to the Government. After considerable discussion with counsel for both sides, petitioner ordered the Government to furnish the information. The United States Attorney declined to comply with the order on the grounds that request number 25 constituted a demand for a list of prosecution witnesses and that petitioner had no power under Rule 7(f) of the Federal Rules of Criminal Procedure to require the Government to produce such a list.

Petitioner indicated his intention to dismiss the indictments against Horwitz because of the Government's refusal to comply with his order for a bill of particulars. * * * The Court of Appeals * * * granted the Government leave to file a petition for a writ of mandamus and issued a rule to show cause why such a writ should not issue to compel petitioner to strike request number 25 from his bill of particulars order. * * * The Court of Appeals at first denied the writ. The Government petitioned for reconsideration, however, and the Court of Appeals * * * reversed itself and without opinion issued a writ of mandamus directing petitioner "to vacate his order directing the Government to answer question 25 in defendant's motion for bill of particulars." * * * We vacate the writ and remand the case to the Court of Appeals for further proceedings.

Both parties have devoted substantial argument in this Court to the propriety of petitioner's order. In our view of the case, however, it is unnecessary to reach this question. The peremptory writ of mandamus has traditionally been used in the federal courts only "to confine an inferior court to a lawful exercise of its prescribed jurisdiction or to compel it to exercise its authority when it is its duty to do so." Roche v. Evaporated Milk Assn., 319 U.S. 21, 26 (1943). While the courts have never confined themselves to an arbitrary and technical definition of "jurisdiction," it is clear that only exceptional circumstances amounting to a judicial "usurpation of power" will justify the invocation of this extraordinary remedy. Thus the writ has been invoked where unwarranted judicial action threatened "to embarrass the executive arm of the government in conducting foreign relations," where it was the only means of forestalling intrusion by the federal judiciary on a delicate area of federal-state relations, where it was necessary to confine a lower court to the terms of an appellate tribunal's mandate, and where a district judge displayed a persistent disregard of the Rules of Civil Procedure promulgated by this Court. And the party seeking mandamus has "the burden of showing that its right to issuance of the writ is clear and indisputable." Bankers Life & Cas. Co. v. Holland, 346 U.S. 379, 384 (1953).

We also approach this case with an awareness of additional considerations which flow from the fact that the underlying proceeding is a criminal prosecution. All our jurisprudence is strongly colored by the notion that appellate review should be postponed, except in certain narrowly defined circumstances, until after final judgment has been rendered by the trial court. This general policy against piecemeal appeals takes on added weight in criminal cases, where the defendant is entitled to a speedy resolution of the charges against him. Moreover, "in the federal jurisprudence, at least, appeals by the Government in criminal cases are something unusual, exceptional, not favored," Carroll v. United States, 354 U.S. 394, 400 (1957), at least in part because they always threaten to offend the policies behind the double-jeopardy prohibition. * * * Mandamus, of course, may never be employed as a substitute for appeal in derogation of these clear policies. * * * This is not to say that mandamus may never be used to review procedural orders in criminal cases. * * * We need not decide under what circumstances, if any, such a use of mandamus would be appropriate. It is enough to note that we approach the decision in this case with an awareness of the constitutional precepts that a man is entitled to a speedy trial and that he may not be placed twice in jeopardy for the same offense.

In light of these considerations and criteria, neither the record before us nor the cryptic order of the Court of Appeals justifies the invocation of the extraordinary writ in this case.

* * *

The Government seeks * * * to justify the employment of the writ in this instance on the ground that petitioner's conduct displays a "pattern of manifest noncompliance with the rules governing federal criminal trials." It argues that the federal rules place settled limitations upon pretrial discovery in criminal cases, and that a trial court may not, in the absence of compelling justification, order the Government to produce a list of its witnesses in advance of trial. * * * The Government concludes that since petitioner obviously had no power to adopt such a rule, mandamus will lie under this Court's decision in La Buy v. Howes Leather Co., 352 U.S. 249 (1957), to correct this studied disregard of the limitations placed upon the district courts by the federal rules.

The action of the Court of Appeals cannot, on the record before us, bear the weight of this justification. There is absolutely no foundation in this record for the Government's assertions concerning petitioner's practice. The legal proposition that mandamus will lie in appropriate cases to correct willful disobedience of the rules laid down by this Court is not controverted. But the position of the Government rests on two central factual premises: (1) that petitioner in effect ordered it to produce a list of witnesses in advance of trial; and (2) that petitioner took this action pursuant to a deliberately adopted policy in disregard of the rules of criminal procedure. Neither of these premises finds support in the record.

* * *

Even more important in our view, however, than these deficiencies in the record is the failure of the Court of Appeals to attempt to supply any reasoned justification of its action. Had the Government in fact shown that petitioner adopted a policy in deliberate disregard of the criminal discovery rules and that this policy had proved seriously disruptive of the efficient administration of criminal justice in the Northern District of Illinois, it would have raised serious questions under this Court's decision in La Buy v. Howes Leather Co.[14] In *La Buy,* however, we specifically relied upon evidence in the record which showed a pattern of improper references of cases to special masters by the District Judge. There is no evidence in this record concerning petitioner's practice in other cases, aside from his own remark that the Government was generally dissatisfied with it, and his statements do not reveal any intent to evade or disregard the rules. We do not know what he ordered the Government to reveal under what circumstances in other cases. This state of the record renders the silence of the Court of Appeals all the more critical. We recognized in *La Buy* that the familiarity of a court of appeals with the practice of the individual district courts within its circuit was relevant to an assessment of the need for mandamus as a corrective measure. But without an opinion from the Court of Appeals we do not know what role, if any, this factor played in the decision below. * * *

Due regard, not merely for the reviewing functions of this Court, but for the "drastic and extraordinary" nature of the mandamus remedy, and for the extremely awkward position in which it places the District Judge, demands that a court issuing the writ give a reasoned exposition of the basis for its action.

---

[14] The Government also places reliance on Schlagenhauf v. Holder, arguing that it reaffirmed *La Buy.* Insofar as it did so, the case does not help the Government here, since we have no quarrel with *La Buy,* which is simply inappropriate where there is no showing of a persistent disregard of the federal rules. And it cannot be contended that *Schlagenhauf on* its facts supports an invocation of mandamus in this case. The Court these did note that the various questions concerning the construction of Rule 35 were new and substantial, but it rested the existence of mandamus jurisdiction squarely on the fact that there was real doubt whether the District Court had any power at all to order a defendant to submit to a physical examination.

Mandamus is not a punitive remedy. The entire thrust of the Government's justification for mandamus in this case, moreover, is that the writ serves a vital corrective and didactic function. While these aims lay at the core of this Court's decisions in *La Buy* and Schlagenhauf v. Holder, 379 U.S. 104 (1964), we fail to see how they can be served here without findings of fact by the issuing court and some statement of the court's legal reasoning. A mandamus from the blue without rationale is tantamount to an abdication of the very expository and supervisory functions of an appellate court upon which the Government rests its attempt to justify the action below.

The peremptory common-law writs are among the most potent weapons in the judicial arsenal. "As extraordinary remedies, they are reserved for really extraordinary causes." Ex parte Fahey, 332 U.S. 258, 260 (1947). There is nothing in the record here to demonstrate that this case falls into that category, and thus the judgment below cannot stand. What might be the proper decision upon a more complete record, supplemented by the findings and conclusions of the Court of Appeals, we cannot and do not say. Hence the writ is vacated and the cause is remanded to the Court of Appeals for the Seventh Circuit for further proceedings not inconsistent with this opinion.

JUSTICE MARSHALL took no part in the consideration or decision of this case.

[The concurring opinion of JUSTICE BLACK is omitted.]

NOTES AND QUESTIONS

1.   The All Writs Act, 28 U.S.C. § 1651, authorizes federal courts "to issue all writs necessary or appropriate in aid of their respective jurisdiction and agreeable to the usages and principles of law." Pursuant to this provision, the circuit courts of appeals may issue writs of mandamus to the district courts, requiring those courts to take certain actions. Traditionally, such writs have been reserved for extraordinary situations.

2.   Mandamus is traditionally employed as a means of protecting a right to jury trial claimed to have been improperly denied in the district court. See, e.g., Dairy Queen, Inc. v. Wood, 369 U.S. 469 (1962), supra p. 557; Beacon Theatres, Inc. v. Westover, 359 U.S. 500 (1959), supra p.550. Is there a rational way to distinguish this interlocutory ruling from any other?

In First National Bank of Waukesha v. Warren, 796 F.2d 999 (7th Cir.1986), Judge Easterbrook criticized this use of mandamus:

> Neither *Beacon Theatres* nor *Dairy Queen* answers the question: Why mandamus? * * * Surely the answer is not * * * that there is a constitutional right at stake. Much federal litigation involves constitutional rights, but the nature of the right does not dictate whether review comes in mid-course or at the end of the district

court's proceedings. Jury trial is not the most essential of rights, either.

He suggested that *Will* has significantly confined the approval of mandamus in *Beacon Theatres* and *Dairy Queen*. Other courts disagree. See In re Lockheed Martin Corp., 503 F.3d 351 (4th Cir. 2007) (reaffirming the use of mandamus to review denial of jury trial).

3. Prior to *Will,* the Court had utilized mandamus as a means of providing interlocutory review of a discovery order in a civil case, Schlagenhauf v. Holder, 379 U.S. 104 (1964). The case involved the validity and construction of Rule 35(a), providing for court-ordered mental and physical examinations of parties, see supra p. 367, as applied to a defendant in a negligence action. Rule 35 had generally been used only against plaintiffs—the individuals who undertook the action in the first place—even though by its terms Rule 35 is not so limited.

In response to the claim that use of mandamus was inappropriate to review the interlocutory discovery order, Justice Goldberg, speaking for the Court, stated:

> It is, of course, well settled, that the writ is not to be used as a substitute for appeal, even though hardship may result from delay and perhaps unnecessary trial. The writ is appropriately issued, however, when there is "usurpation of judicial power" or a clear abuse of discretion.

> Here petitioner's basic allegation was lack of power in a district court to order a mental and physical examination of a defendant. That this issue was substantial is underscored by the fact that the challenged order requiring examination of a defendant appears to be the first of its kind in any reported decision in the federal courts under Rule 35, and we have found only one such modern case in the state courts. The Court of Appeals recognized that it had the power to review on a petition for mandamus the basic, undecided question of whether a district court could order the mental or physical examination of a defendant. We agree that, under these unusual circumstances and in light of the authorities, the Court of Appeals had such power.

Does *Schlagenhauf,* on its face, provide a foundation for widespread use of mandamus as a basis for obtaining interlocutory review of discovery orders? Recall the discussion concerning appeal of discovery orders following *Cohen* and *Mohawk Corp. v. Carpenter* [supra p. 1090]. The Court has chosen not to use the collateral order doctrine in appeals from discovery orders, in part due to the availability of the "contempt" method sanctioned in United States v. Ryan [supra p. 1104]. It should be noted that the "contempt" avenue was unavailable in *Schlagenhauf,* because Rule 37 expressly exempts Rule 35 orders from enforcement by means of contempt. Attempting to synthesize these developments, one appellate court has indicated that mandamus may be available today where a discovery issue is of "extraordinary significance" or where there is an extreme need for reversal of the district court's mandate before the case goes to judgment. In re Security and Exchange Commission, 374 F.3d 184 (2d Cir. 2004). The court reasoned that under "unusual circumstances," the contempt avenue may not be adequate, and in such situations mandamus may be available.

In United States v. Jicarilla Apache Nation, 564 U.S. 162 (2011), the Supreme Court seemingly approved the government's use of mandamus to challenge a lower court order compelling disclosure of material it claimed was protected by the attorney-client privilege. Following an order by the Court of Federal Claims (CFC) requiring it to disclose the materials in question, the government sought review by way of a petition for a writ of mandamus. In rejecting mandamus relief, the Federal Circuit agreed with the CFC that the attorney-client privilege did not apply. On review of that order (by certiorari), the Court agreed with the government that the special trust relationship between the United States and Indian tribes did not trigger the so-called fiduciary exception to the attorney-client privilege. On that basis, the Court reversed the order approving the disclosure of attorney-client material. While the Court did not expressly rule on the availability of mandamus, instead remanding to the appellate court to decide the mandamus question in the first instance, it did assume that the trial court "will follow our holding here" as to the applicability of the attorney-client privilege. Id. at 2331 n. 12.

4.   Discovery was also at the center of another mandamus decision, but the special separation-of-powers context in which it arose may deprive the decision of broader impact. The Court explained the background of the litigation in Cheney v. United States District Court for the District of Columbia, 542 U.S. 367 (2004), as follows:

> The United States District Court for the District of Columbia entered discovery orders directing the Vice President and other senior officials in the Executive Branch to produce information about a task force established to give advice and make policy recommendations to the President. This case requires us to consider the circumstances under which a court of appeals may exercise its power to issue a writ of mandamus to modify or dissolve the orders when, by virtue of their overbreadth, enforcement might interfere with the officials in the discharge of their duties and impinge upon the President's constitutional prerogatives.

The case began when the Sierra Club and Judicial Watch brought suit under the Federal Advisory Committee Act, seeking information about the role of industry leaders in providing advice to President Bush's National Energy Policy Development Group (NPEDG). The government broadly opposed any disclosure of the role of non-government officials on separation of powers grounds. After the NPEDG disbanded, the plaintiffs continued to press their claims against Vice President Cheney and other high ranking officials and agencies. The district court formulated a discovery plan that would require the government to disclose information about NPEDG meetings and identity of participants.

The government asked the district court to certify the issue for interlocutory review under 28 U.S.C. 1292(b). Failing that, the government sought mandamus review in the court of appeals, unsuccessfully. The appellate court relied on United States v. Nixon, 418 U.S. 683 (1974), which ordered the President to produce evidence in response to a government subpoena in a criminal proceeding. The *Nixon* Court had held that the President cannot simply invoke executive privilege as a bar to the production of pertinent evidence, but must make a detailed submission as to particular items and explain how their production would interfere with the proper functioning of the executive branch. Because Vice President Cheney did not make a particularized showing in opposition to the requested discovery, the appellate court declined to intervene, despite its recognition of the breadth of the discovery order.

The Supreme Court vacated and remanded for further proceedings, rejecting the suggested application of United States v. Nixon, and directing the appellate court to reconsider its rejection of mandamus. [On the *Cheney* Court's treatment of the timeliness of the government's mandamus petition, see supra p. 1072 n. 6.] *Nixon* did not control for three reasons. First, it was a criminal proceeding, where the need for disclosure of information was "much weightier" due to the nation's historic commitment to the rule of law. Second, in criminal proceedings the government, through the Department of Justice, plays a filtering role in deciding what cases to bring. Notwithstanding Rule 11, the Court viewed the risk of frivolous litigation as greater in the private civil context. Third, the request for production of materials at issue in *Nixon* was more targeted and more clearly relevant than the more sweeping discovery order under review.

Regarding the availability of mandamus, the Court emphasized the special context of the case:

> Were the Vice President not a party in the case, the argument that the Court of Appeals should have entertained an action in mandamus, notwithstanding the District Court's denial of the motion for certification, might present different considerations. Here, however, the Vice President and his comembers on the NEPDG are the subjects of the discovery orders. The mandamus petition alleges that the orders threaten "substantial intrusions on the process by which those in closest operational proximity to the President advise the President." These facts and allegations remove this case from the category of ordinary discovery orders where interlocutory appellate review is unavailable, through mandamus or otherwise. It is well established that "a President's communications and activities encompass a vastly wider range of sensitive material than would be true of any 'ordinary individual.'" *United States v. Nixon,* 418 U.S. at 715. Chief Justice Marshall, sitting as a trial judge, recognized the unique position of the Executive Branch when he stated that "[i]n no case . . . would a court be required to proceed against the president as against an ordinary individual." *United States v. Burr,* 25 F. Cas.

187, 192 (No. 14,694) (CC Va. 1807). See also *Clinton v. Jones,* 520 U.S. 681, 698–699 (1997) ("We have, in short, long recognized the 'unique position in the constitutional scheme' that [the Office of the President] occupies.") As *United States v. Nixon* explained, these principles do not mean that the "President is above the law." Rather, they simply acknowledge that the public interest requires that a coequal branch of Government "afford Presidential confidentiality the greatest protection consistent with the fair administration of justice," and give recognition to the paramount necessity of protecting the Executive Branch from vexatious litigation that might distract it from the energetic performance of its constitutional duties.

These separation-of-powers considerations should inform a court of appeals' evaluation of a mandamus petition involving the President or the Vice President. Accepted mandamus standards are broad enough to allow a court of appeals to prevent a lower court from interfering with a coequal branch's ability to discharge its constitutional responsibilities. See *Ex parte Peru, supra,* at 587 (recognizing jurisdiction to issue the writ because "the action of the political arm of the Government taken within its appropriate sphere [must] be promptly recognized, and . . . delay and inconvenience of a prolonged litigation [must] be avoided by prompt termination of the proceedings in the district court"); see also *Clinton v. Jones, supra,* at 701 ("We have recognized that '[e]ven when a branch does not arrogate power to itself . . . the separation-of-powers doctrine requires that a branch not impair another in the performance of its constitutional duties' ").

On remand the en banc appellate court issued the writ of mandamus, after finding that the NPEDG was not an advisory committee within the meaning of federal disclosure laws. See In re Cheney, 406 F.3d 723 (D.C. Cir. 2005).

5.   In other cases decided since *Will v. United States,* the Court has generally continued to emphasize the limited nature of mandamus review. See Will v. Calvert Fire Insurance Co., 437 U.S. 655 (1978); Kerr v. United States District Court, 426 U.S. 394 (1976); see generally Allied Chemical Corp. v. Daiflon, Inc., 449 U.S. 33 (1980) (per curiam) (describing the cases as defining the availability of mandamus with the refrain: "What never? Well, *hardly ever!* "). But see Mallard v. United States District Court for the Southern District of Iowa, 490 U.S. 296 (1989) (holding that that an attorney who wished to challenge the denial of his motion to withdraw from a mandatory appointment to represent an indigent civil litigant could obtain mandamus in the court of appeals). Similarly, it is well established that "a writ of mandamus may be used to review the disqualification of counsel." This is "because the harm of such disqualification cannot be corrected with an ordinary appeal." Whether the writ will, in fact, be used in such cases depends upon a case-by-case synthesis of a variety of factors, including whether a direct appeal is available, uncorrectable damage is caused, the order is clear legal error or is oft-repeated, and whether the order raises new and important issue. Cole v.

United States District Court for the District of Idaho, 366 F.3d 813, 816–17 (9th Cir. 2004). Cf. Firestone Tire & Rubber Co. v. Risjord, supra p. 1100 (declining to permit collateral order review of an order *denying* a motion to disqualify counsel).

C. Discretionary Review of Class Action Litigation

Class certification decisions are not final decisions that end the case on the merits. If the district court grants certification, the case will proceed to trial and review of the certification decision could, at least in some cases, follow the trial court's disposition. If the district court denies certification, the claims of the individual named plaintiffs remain pending. But in many cases involving claims of modest size, individual plaintiffs may choose not to pursue the litigation other than through a class action. For modest claims, then, the denial of certification was sometimes seen as the "death knell" of the action and regarded as appealable under the practical finality doctrine.

The "death knell" doctrine was first employed in Eisen v. Carlisle & Jacquelin, 370 F.2d 119 (2d Cir. 1966) ("*Eisen I*"). Eisen I allowed an appeal from an order of the district court dismissing a class action, but permitting plaintiff to litigate his individual claims. Because plaintiff's individual claims amounted to $70, the court reasoned that "[t]he alternatives are to appeal now or to end the lawsuit for all practical purposes * * * [for] [w]e can safely assume that no lawyer of competence is going to undertake this complex and costly case to recover $70 for Mr. Eisen." The court therefore concluded that "[i]f the appeal is dismissed, not only will Eisen's claim never be adjudicated, but no appellate court will be given the chance to decide if this class action was proper * * *." The court stated the governing rule: "Where the effect of a district court's order, if not reviewed, is the death knell of the action, review should be allowed."

In Coopers & Lybrand v. Livesay, 437 U.S. 463 (1978), the Supreme Court rejected the death knell doctrine. "A threshold inquiry of this kind may, it is true, identify some orders that would truly end the litigation prior to final judgment; allowing an immediate appeal from those orders may enhance the quality of justice afforded a few litigants. But this incremental benefit is outweighed by the impact of such an individualized jurisdictional inquiry on the judicial system's overall capacity to administer justice."

In 1998, the Supreme Court amended Fed. R. Civ. P. 23 by adding subdivision (f), which authorizes immediate an appeal from the district court's ruling on class certification, at the discretion of the court of appeals. Rule 23(f) provides for discretionary review of orders either "granting or denying" certification and calls for the filing of a petition for leave to appeal with the clerk of the appellate court within 10 days of the certification order. See generally Solimine & Hines, Deciding to Decide: Class Action Certification and Interlocutory Review by the United States Court of Appeals Under Rule 23(f), 41 Will. & Mary L. Rev. 1531 (2000).

MICROSOFT CORP. V. BAKER

Supreme Court of the United States, 2017
137 S.Ct. 1702

JUSTICE GINSBURG delivered the opinion of the Court.

This case concerns options open to plaintiffs, when denied class-action certification by a district court, to gain appellate review of the district court's order. Orders granting or denying class certification, this Court has held, are "inherently interlocutory," *Coopers & Lybrand v. Livesay,* 437 U.S. 463, 470 (1978), hence not immediately reviewable under 28 U.S.C. § 1291, which provides for appeals from "final decisions." Pursuant to Federal Rule of Civil Procedure 23(f), promulgated in 1998, however, orders denying or granting class certification may be appealed immediately if the court of appeals so permits. Absent such permission, plaintiffs may pursue their individual claims on the merits to final judgment, at which point the denial of class-action certification becomes ripe for review.

The plaintiffs in the instant case, respondents here, were denied Rule 23(f) permission to appeal the District Court's refusal to grant class certification. Instead of pursuing their individual claims to final judgment on the merits, respondents stipulated to a voluntary dismissal of their claims "with prejudice," but reserved the right to revive their claims should the Court of Appeals reverse the District Court's certification denial.

We hold that the voluntary dismissal essayed by respondents does not qualify as a "final decision" within the compass of § 1291. The tactic would undermine § 1291's firm finality principle, designed to guard against piecemeal appeals, and subvert the balanced solution Rule 23(f) put in place for immediate review of class-action orders.

I

[The Court summarized its decision in *Coopers & Lybrand v. Livesay,* 437 U.S. 463 (1978) and Rule 23(f) of the Federal Rules.]

B

With this background in mind, we turn to the putative class action underlying our jurisdictional inquiry. The lawsuit is not the first of its kind. A few years after petitioner Microsoft Corporation released its popular videogame console, the Xbox 360, a group of Xbox owners brought a putative class action against Microsoft based on an alleged design defect in the device. The named plaintiffs, advised by some of the same counsel representing respondents in this case, asserted that the Xbox scratched (and thus destroyed) game discs during normal game-playing conditions. The District Court denied class certification, holding that individual issues of damages and causation predominated over common issues. The plaintiffs petitioned the Ninth Circuit under Rule 23(f) for leave to appeal the class-certification denial, but the Ninth Circuit denied the request.

Two years later, in 2011, respondents filed this lawsuit in the same Federal District Court. They proposed a nationwide class of Xbox owners based on the same design defect alleged [earlier]. The class-certification analysis in the earlier case did not control, respondents urged, because an intervening Ninth Circuit decision constituted a change in law sufficient to overcome the deference ordinarily due, as a matter of comity, the previous certification denial. The District Court disagreed. Concluding that the relevant Circuit decision had not undermined [earlier] causation analysis, the court determined that comity required adherence to the earlier certification denial and therefore struck respondents' class allegations.

Invoking Rule 23(f), respondents petitioned the Ninth Circuit for permission to appeal that ruling. Interlocutory review was appropriate in this case, they argued, because the District Court's order striking the class allegations created a "death-knell situation": The "small size of [their] claims ma[de] it economically irrational to bear the cost of litigating th[e] case to final judgment," they asserted, so the order would "effectively kil[l] the case."

Respondents then had several options. They could have settled their individual claims like their predecessors or petitioned the District Court, pursuant to § 1292(b), to certify the interlocutory order for appeal. They could also have proceeded to litigate their case, mindful that the District Court could later reverse course and certify the proposed class. Or, in the event the District Court did not change course, respondents could have litigated the case to final judgment and then appealed.

Instead of taking one of those routes, respondents moved to dismiss their case with prejudice. "After the [c]ourt has entered a final order and judgment," respondents explained, they would "appeal the . . . order striking [their] class allegations." In respondents' view, the voluntary dismissal enabled them "to pursue their individual claims or to pursue relief solely on behalf of the class, should the certification decision be reversed." Microsoft stipulated to the dismissal, but maintained that respondents would have "no right to appeal" the order striking the class allegations after thus dismissing their claims. The District Court granted the stipulated motion to dismiss and respondents appealed. They challenged only the District Court's interlocutory order striking their class allegations, not the dismissal order which they invited.

The Ninth Circuit held it had jurisdiction to entertain the appeal. The Court of Appeals rejected Microsoft's argument that respondents' voluntary dismissal, explicitly engineered to appeal the District Court's interlocutory order striking the class allegations, impermissibly circumvented Rule 23(f). Because the stipulated dismissal "did not involve a settlement," the court reasoned, it was a sufficiently adverse—and thus appealable—final decision under § 1291.

* * *

We granted certiorari to resolve a Circuit conflict over this question: Do federal courts of appeals have jurisdiction under § 1291 and Article III of the Constitution to review an order denying class certification (or, as here, an order striking class allegations) after the named plaintiffs have voluntarily dismissed their claims with prejudice? Because we hold that § 1291 does not countenance jurisdiction by these means, we do not reach the constitutional question, and therefore do not address the arguments and analysis discussed in the opinion concurring in the judgment.

II

From the very foundation of our judicial system," the general rule has been that "the whole case and every matter in controversy in it [must be] decided in a single appeal." *McLish v. Roff,* 141 U.S. 661, 665–666 (1891). This final-judgment rule, now codified in § 1291, preserves the proper balance between trial and appellate courts, minimizes the harassment and delay that would result from repeated interlocutory appeals, and promotes the efficient administration of justice.

Construing § 1291 in line with these reasons for the rule, we have recognized that "finality is to be given a practical rather than a technical construction." Repeatedly we have resisted efforts to stretch § 1291 to permit appeals of right that would erode the finality principle and disserve its objectives. Attempts to secure appeal as of right from adverse class-certification orders fit that bill. Because respondents' dismissal device subverts the final-judgment rule and the process Congress has established for refining that rule and for determining when nonfinal orders may be immediately appealed, see §§ 2072(c) and 1292(e), the tactic does not give rise to a "final decisio[n]" under § 1291.

A

Respondents' voluntary-dismissal tactic, even more than the death-knell theory, invites protracted litigation and piecemeal appeals. Under the death-knell doctrine, a court of appeals could decline to hear an appeal if it determined that the plaintiff "ha[d] adequate incentive to continue" despite the denial of class certification. Appellate courts lack even that authority under respondents' theory. Instead, the decision whether an immediate appeal will lie resides exclusively with the plaintiff; she need only dismiss her claims with prejudice, whereupon she may appeal the district court's order denying class certification. And, as under the death-knell doctrine, she may exercise that option more than once, stopping and starting the district court proceedings with repeated interlocutory appeals.

Consider this case. The Ninth Circuit reviewed and rejected only the District Court's application of comity as a basis for striking respondents' class allegations. The appeals court declined to reach Microsoft's other arguments against class certification. It remained open to the District Court, in the Court of Appeals' view, to deny class certification on a different ground, and respondents would be free, under their theory, to force appellate review of any new order denying certification by again dismissing their claims. In designing Rule 23(f)'s provision for discretionary review, the Rules Committee sought to prevent such disruption and delay.

Respondents nevertheless maintain that their position promotes efficiency, observing that after dismissal with prejudice the case is over if the plaintiff loses on appeal. Their way, they say, means prompt resolution of many lawsuits and infrequent use of the voluntary-dismissal tactic, for "most appeals lose" and few plaintiffs will "take th[e] risk" of losing their claims for good. Respondents overlook the prospect that plaintiffs with weak merits claims may readily assume that risk, mindful that class certification often leads to a hefty settlement. Indeed, the same argument—that the case was over if the plaintiff lost on appeal—was evident in the death-knell context, yet this Court determined that the potential for piecemeal litigation was "apparent and serious." And that potential is greater still under respondents' theory, where plaintiffs alone determine whether and when to appeal an adverse certification ruling.

B

Another vice respondents' theory shares with the death-knell doctrine, both allow indiscriminate appellate review of interlocutory orders. Beyond disturbing the "appropriate relationship between the respective courts," respondents' dismissal tactic undercuts Rule 23(f)'s discretionary regime. This consideration is "[o]f prime significance to the jurisdictional issue before us." *Swint v. Chambers County Comm'n,* 514 U.S. 35, 46 (1995).

In the Rules Enabling Act, as earlier recounted, Congress authorized this Court to determine when a decision is final for purposes of § 1291, and to provide for appellate review of interlocutory orders not covered by statute. These changes are to come from rulemaking, however, not judicial decisions in particular controversies or inventive litigation ploys. In this case, the rulemaking process has dealt with the matter, yielding a "measured, practical solutio[n]" to the questions whether and when adverse certification orders may be immediately appealed. *Mohawk Industries,* 558 U.S., at 114. Over years the Advisory Committee on the Federal Rules of Civil Procedure studied the data on class-certification rulings and appeals, weighed various proposals, received public comment, and refined the draft rule and Committee Note.

Here, however, the Ninth Circuit, after denying respondents permission to appeal under Rule 23(f), nevertheless assumed jurisdiction of their appeal challenging only the District Court's order striking the class allegations. According to respondents, even plaintiffs who altogether bypass Rule 23(f) may force an appeal by dismissing their claims with prejudice.

We are not persuaded. If respondents' voluntary-dismissal tactic could yield an appeal of right, Rule 23(f)'s careful calibration—as well as Congress' designation of rulemaking "as the preferred means for determining whether and when prejudgment orders should be immediately appealable," *Mohawk Industries,* 558 U.S., at 113—"would be severely undermined." Respondents, after all, "[sought] review of only the [inherently interlocutory] orde[r]" striking their class allegations; they "d[id] not complain of the 'final' orde[r] that dismissed their cas[e]."

Plaintiffs in putative class actions cannot transform a tentative interlocutory order into a final judgment within the meaning of § 1291 simply by dismissing their claims with prejudice—subject, no less, to the right to "revive" those claims if the denial of class certification is reversed on appeal.

* * * Contrary to respondents' argument, § 1291's firm final-judgment rule is not satisfied whenever a litigant persuades a district court to issue an order purporting to end the litigation. Finality, we have long cautioned, "is not a technical concept of temporal or physical termination." *Cobbledick,* 309 U.S., at 326. It is one "means [geared to] achieving a healthy legal system," and its contours are determined accordingly.

C

The one-sidedness of respondents' voluntary-dismissal device "reinforce[s] our conclusion that [it] does not support appellate jurisdiction of prejudgment orders denying class certification." Respondents' theory permits plaintiffs only, never defendants, to force an immediate appeal of an adverse certification ruling. Yet the "class issue" may be just as important to defendants, for "[a]n order granting certification . . . may force a defendant to settle rather than . . . run the risk of potentially ruinous liability." Committee Note on Rule 23(f) (defendants may face a "reverse death knell"). Accordingly, we recognized that "[w]hatever similarities or differences there are between plaintiffs and defendants in this context involve questions of policy for Congress." 437 U.S., at 476. Congress chose the rulemaking process to settle the matter, and the rulemakers did so by adopting Rule 23(f)'s evenhanded prescription. It is not the prerogative of litigants or federal courts to disturb that settlement.

* * *

For the reasons stated, the judgment of the Court of Appeals for the Ninth Circuit is reversed, and the case is remanded for further proceedings consistent with this opinion.

It is so ordered.

Justice GORSUCH took no part in the consideration or decision of this case.

Justice THOMAS, with whom THE CHIEF JUSTICE and Justice ALITO join, concurring in the judgment.

I agree with the Court that the Court of Appeals lacked jurisdiction over respondents' appeal, but I would ground that conclusion in Article III of the Constitution instead of 28 U.S.C. § 1291. I therefore concur only in the judgment.

* * *

The Court today holds that the Court of Appeals lacked jurisdiction under § 1291 because the voluntary dismissal with prejudice did not result in a "final decision." I disagree with that holding. . . . The order here dismissed all of the plaintiffs' claims with prejudice and left nothing for the District Court to do but execute the judgment.

The Court reaches the opposite conclusion, relying not on the text of § 1291 or this Court's precedents about finality, but on Rule 23(f). Rule 23(f) makes interlocutory orders regarding class certification appealable only with the permission of the court of appeals. The Court concludes that the plaintiffs' "voluntary dismissal" "does not qualify as a 'final decision' " because allowing the plaintiffs' appeal would "subvert the balanced solution Rule 23(f) put in place for immediate review of class-action orders."

The Court's conclusion does not follow from its reasoning. Whether a dismissal with prejudice is "final" depends on the meaning of § 1291, not Rule 23(f). Rule 23(f) says nothing about finality, much less about the finality of an order dismissing individual claims with prejudice. I agree with the Court that the plaintiffs are trying to avoid the requirements for interlocutory appeals under Rule 23(f), but our view of the balance struck in that rule should not warp our understanding of finality under § 1291.

Although I disagree with the Court's reading of § 1291, I agree that the plaintiffs could not appeal in these circumstances. In my view, they could not appeal because the Court of Appeals lacked jurisdiction under Article III of the Constitution. The "judicial Power" of the United States extends only to "Cases" and "Controversies." Art. III, § 2. This requirement limits the jurisdiction of the federal courts to issues presented "in an adversary context," *Flast v. Cohen,* 392 U.S. 83, 95 (1968), in which the parties maintain an "actual" and "concrete" interest. Put another way, "Article III denies federal courts the power to decide questions that cannot affect the rights of litigants in the case before them, and confines them to resolving real and substantial controversies admitting of specific relief through a decree of a conclusive character." *Lewis v. Continental Bank Corp.,* 494 U.S. 472, 477 (1990).

The plaintiffs' appeal from their voluntary dismissal did not satisfy this jurisdictional requirement. When the plaintiffs asked the District Court to dismiss their claims, they consented to the judgment against them and disavowed any right to relief from Microsoft. The parties thus were no longer adverse to each other on any claims, and the Court of Appeals could not "affect the[ir] rights" in any legally cognizable manner. Indeed, it has long been the rule that a party may not appeal from the voluntary dismissal of a claim, since the party consented to the judgment against it.

The plaintiffs contend that their interest in reversing the order striking their class allegations is sufficient to satisfy Article III's case-or-controversy requirement, but they misunderstand the status of putative class actions. Class allegations, without an underlying individual claim, do not give rise to a "case" or "controversy." Those allegations are simply the means of invoking a procedural mechanism that enables a plaintiff to litigate his individual claims on behalf of a class. Thus, because the Court of Appeals lacked Article III jurisdiction to adjudicate the individual claims, it could not hear the plaintiffs' appeal of the order striking their class allegations.

Plaintiffs' representation that they hope to "revive their [individual] claims should they prevail" on the appeal of the order striking their class allegations does not undermine this conclusion. This Court has interpreted Article III "to demand that an actual controversy be extant at all stages of review, not merely at the time the complaint is filed." *Campbell-Ewald Co. v. Gomez,* 136 S.Ct. 633, 669 (2016). And in any event, a favorable ruling on class certification would not "revive" their individual claims: A court's decision about class allegations "in no way touch[es] the merits" of those claims. *Gardner v. Westinghouse Broadcasting Co.*, 437 U.S. 478, 482 (1978).

* * *

Because I would hold that the Court of Appeals lacked jurisdiction under Article III to consider respondents' appeal, I concur in the judgment.

NOTES AND QUESTIONS

1. The majority in Microsoft Corp v. Baker viewed Rule 23(f) as central to its assessment, and continued a modern trend (noted in connection with Mohawk Industries v. Carpenter, supra p. 1090) of treating the creation of exceptions to finality as a matter for rulemaking rather than judicial decree. In light of Microsoft Corp. v. Baker, what, if anything, remains of the idea of "manufactured finality" in such cases as Nystrom v. TREX, supra p. 1112?

2. Note the majority's emphasis on symmetric access to appellate review and its perception that a one-sided mode of review, available only to plaintiffs, was inconsistent with even-handed case management. Can this comment be limited to appeals taken in the shadow of Rule 23(f), which authorizes both parties to seek discretionary review? Or does it apply more broadly? If so, can it be squared with the rejection of arguments from symmetry in Bullard v. Blue Hills Bank, supra p. 1074?

3. Turning to the operation of Rule 23(f), consider In re Sumitomo Copper Litigation, 262 F.3d 134 (2d Cir. 2001), a complex class action relating to investments in copper futures in which the Second Circuit considered a petition for interlocutory review under Rule 23(f). The district court had certified a class action, naming the Credit Lyonnais group as defendants. The Credit Lyonnais defendants sought discretionary review. The Second Circuit viewed Rule 23(f) as reviving the death knell doctrine, but nonetheless denied the petition for leave to appeal.

> In line with our sister circuits, we hold that petitioners seeking leave to appeal pursuant to Rule 23(f) must demonstrate either (1) that the certification order will effectively terminate the litigation and there has been a substantial showing that the district court's decision is questionable, or (2) that the certification order implicates a legal question about which there is a compelling need for immediate resolution.

> We accept, for the purposes of this case, [defendants'] assertion that class certification will effectively terminate the litigation because it will force them to settle the case rather than risk trial. We nevertheless find that a death knell review is not warranted because petitioners have failed to make a substantial showing that the district court's decision to grant certification is questionable.

The Second Circuit also rejected the defendants' contention that unresolved questions of law established a compelling need for immediate resolution. In doing so, the court carefully reviewed certain of the defendants' legal arguments and eventually concluded that none of them were sufficiently "compelling" to warrant intervention. As a result, the court invested a substantial amount of time and energy without ultimately resolving the merits of defendants' legal contentions. Is that a wise investment of appellate judicial resources? Is some evaluation of the degree of legal error below inherent in the notion of discretionary appellate review?

4.   Other courts agree that Rule 23(f) revives the death knell doctrine. See Blair v. Equifax Check Services Inc., 181 F.3d 832 (7th Cir. 1999) (viewing Rule 23(f) as allowing death knell appeals in appropriate circumstances). But the death knell inquiry will differ, depending on whether the district court grants or denies class certification. On plaintiffs' petition for review of an order *denying* class certification, the appellate court will examine the incentives of the individual plaintiffs and evaluate their willingness to pursue claims of modest value. What sorts of considerations should inform the appellate court's evaluation of incentives? In Blair v. Equifax, supra, the Seventh Circuit noted that law firms specializing in class litigation may have good reason to litigate on behalf of individual plaintiffs, at the firm's expense, with a view toward seeking review of a class certification decision that would accompany review of a decision on the merits of the individual claim. If the death knell calculus takes account of law firm finances and incentives, what will remain of the doctrine as it applies to orders denying class certification?

Death knell calculus will focus on different considerations in a case like *Sumitomo Copper,* where the defendants seek review of a decision *granting* class certification. The death knell doctrine then operates on the assumption that defendants cannot risk taking the case to trial but will be forced to settle. The Second Circuit assumed the viability of this death knell contention without deciding the question. How should a court proceed in evaluating the incentives of class action defendants who confront the prospect of a trial involving thousands of claims worth millions of dollars? Can defendants afford not to settle? Does the Court's acceptance of the concern in Microsoft Corp. v. Baker lend greater weight to "reverse death knell" arguments?

5.   Does Rule 23(f) allow review of orders that modify class certification decisions? For an affirmative answer, see Matz v. Household International Tax Reduction Investment Plan, 627 F.3d 824 (7th Cir. 2012). There, the district court reconsidered its certification order and decided to exclude roughly 3000 individuals from the certified class, a number that represented well over half of the previously certified plaintiff class. On petition for review, the Seventh Circuit concluded that an order that materially alters the scope of the class falls within Rule 23(f). Can that conclusion be squared with the language of the Rule itself, which refers only to orders that grant or deny class certification?

6.   As noted supra pp. 870–933, Congress enacted the Class Action Fairness Act of 2005 to provide for federal jurisdiction of a wide range of state law contract and consumer class actions. Among other provisions, CAFA liberalizes the provisions for removal of class actions from state to federal

court. In addition, CAFA includes a special provision for appellate review of orders "granting or denying" a motion to remand a class action to state court:

> [N]otwithstanding section 1447(d), a court of appeals may accept an appeal from an order of a district court granting or denying a motion to remand a class action to the State court from which it was removed if application is made to the court of appeals not more than 10 days after the entry of the order.

28 U.S.C. § 1453(c)(1). In providing that the court "may accept" an appeal, the statute apparently confers discretion on the appellate courts to accept or reject a petition for review. See Estate of Pew v. Cardarelli, 527 F.3d 25, 29 (2d Cir. 2008) (court will consider the importance and novelty of the issues in considering whether to exercise discretion to allow an appeal).

4. SUPREME COURT APPELLATE JURISDICTION

Traditionally, the Supreme Court exercised two distinct forms of appellate jurisdiction: appeal and certiorari. Appeals could be taken by a party relying on a state statute held by the federal court of appeals to be repugnant to either the Constitution, treaties or laws of the United States and from the state's highest court where that court had ruled against the validity of a treaty or statute of the United States or where the state court has upheld a state statute which had been challenged on federal constitutional or statutory grounds. Certiorari was available to secure review of the courts of appeals "upon the petition of any party to any civil or criminal case, before or after rendition of judgment or decree" and from the state's highest court where that court had invalidated a state statute on federal constitutional or statutory grounds "or where any title, right, privilege or immunity is generally set up or claimed" under federal law.

Technically, the primary distinction between the two was that appeal, where applicable, was of right while certiorari lay purely within the Court's discretion. As a practical matter, however, the Court treated its appeal jurisdiction as if it were discretionary. In administering its appellate docket, moreover, the Court appeared to give cases within its mandatory appeal jurisdiction no more attention than cases in which a writ of certiorari was sought. The problem was that while a denial of certiorari in no way constituted a decision on the merits and therefore had absolutely no precedential impact, dismissal of a mandatory appeal, at least as a technical matter, did constitute a decision on the merits and therefore a precedent. Cf. Edelman v. Jordan, 415 U.S. 651, 670 (1974) (refusing to accord weight to summary dispositions that did not address the merits of the issue presented).

This situation gave rise to considerable confusion. See generally Kurland, Jurisdiction of the United States Supreme Court: Time for a Change?, 59 Cornell L.Rev. 616 (1974). In response, Congress amended the relevant statutes, 28 U.S.C. § 1254 and § 1257, effectively doing away with most of the Court's mandatory jurisdiction. For a critical summary of the shift to a largely discretionary docket, see Hartnett, Questioning Certiorari: Some Reflections Seventy-Five Years After the Judges' Bill, 100 Colum. L. Rev. 1643 (2000).

Supreme Court jurisdiction over state court judgments is limited to issues of federal law. Thus, the Court may not review state court interpretations of state law, unless those interpretations somehow implicate issues of federal law. Moreover, pursuant to what is known as the "adequate state ground" doctrine, the Court will not even review state court interpretations of federal law, if the decision also rests on a ground of state law that would independently support the decision. Murdock v. City of Memphis, 87 U.S. (20 Wall.) 590 (1874). See generally Redish, Supreme Court Review of State Court "Federal" Decisions: A Study in Interactive Federalism, 19 Ga.L.Rev. 861 (1985).

Whether or not there is an independent state ground, the Court will not review a state court decision that is interlocutory even if subject to immediate appellate review under state law. In Jefferson v. City of Tarrant, 522 U.S. 75 (1997), the state trial court certified the question whether the Alabama wrongful death act controlled the recovery in a claim under 42 U.S.C. § 1983 for immediate appellate review pursuant to state procedure, and the Alabama Supreme Court decided it. Although the Supreme Court initially granted certiorari to decide this question, it determined that it lacked jurisdiction under 28 U.S.C. § 1257(a) because further proceedings in state court that could include a full trial were required. However, in Cox Broadcasting Corp. v. Cohn, 420 U.S. 469 (1975), the Court recognized four categories of cases in which appeal could be allowed despite the absence of technical finality. The first two included cases in which the federal issue would not be mooted or otherwise affected by the proceedings yet to be had because those proceedings have little substance, their outcome is certain, or they are wholly unrelated to the federal question." In the third category were cases where, "if the party seeking interim review ultimately prevails on the merits, the federal issue will be mooted; if he were to lose on the merits, however, the governing state law would not permit him again to present his federal claim for review." The final category—considered the most controversial—included "those situations where the federal issue has been finally decided in the state courts with further proceedings pending in which the party seeking review ... might prevail on the merits on nonfederal grounds, thus rendering unnecessary review of the federal issue by this Court ..." For a detailed analysis and critique of Cohn, see M. Redish, Federal Jurisdiction: Tensions in the Allocation of Judicial Power 247–60 (2d ed. 1990).

In evaluating the Court's motive for relaxing the final judgment rule, consider the consequences of a congressional switch from a largely mandatory docket made up of appeals of right to a docket that the Court can control through the exercise of discretion about when to grant certiorari. A Supreme Court facing docket pressures with a largely mandatory docket might adopt strict rules of finality as a form of self-defense. Once Congress ended mandatory appeals and gave the Court control of its docket, it may have subtly encouraged the Court to redefine its finality rule in a way that would broaden the range of possible cases from which it can select cases for full review. See Pfander, Principles of Federal Jurisdiction 114 (3d ed. 2017).

C. APPELLATE REVIEW OF JUDICIAL FINDINGS OF FACT

BOSE CORP. v. CONSUMERS UNION OF UNITED STATES, INC.

Supreme Court of the United States, 1984
466 U.S. 485

JUSTICE STEVENS delivered the opinion of the Court.

[In the May 1970 issue of its magazine, "Consumer Reports," respondent published an article evaluating the quality of numerous brands of medium-priced loudspeakers. After describing the Bose 901 system and some of its virtues, the article made the following statement: "[I]ndividual instruments heard through the Bose system seemed to grow to gigantic proportions and tended to wander about the room. For instance, a violin appeared to be 10 feet wide and a piano stretched from wall to wall. With orchestral music, such effects seemed inconsequential. But we think they might become annoying when listening to soloists."

Petitioner took exception to certain statements contained in the article, and brought a product disparagement action in the District Court for the District of Massachusetts. Following a bench trial on the issue of liability, the trial court issued a detailed opinion in respondent's favor on most issues. Finding that petitioner was a "public figure" for purposes of the doctrine of New York Times Co. v. Sullivan, 376 U.S. 254 (1964), it held petitioner could recover only if it proved by clear and convincing evidence that respondent made a false disparaging statement with "actual malice," defined as knowledge of falsity or reckless disregard of the truth.

On three key points, however, the court agreed with petitioner: It found that one sentence in the article contained a "false" statement of "fact" concerning the tendency of the instrument to wander; it found that the statement was disparaging, and it concluded "on the basis of proof which it considers clear and convincing, that the plaintiff has sustained its burden of proving that the defendant published a false statement of material fact" with knowledge that it was false or with reckless disregard of the truth. The court rendered this conclusion because it found that at the time of the article's publication the researcher for Consumer Reports knew that the words "individual instruments . . . tended to wander about the room" did not accurately describe the effects he had heard when testing the system. On this point, the trial court received testimony from Arnold Seligson, the engineer who supervised the testing of the product for respondent and wrote the report on which the article was based. As the Supreme Court concluded, "since there was no evidence that the editors were aware of the inaccuracy in the original report, the actual malice determination rests entirely on an evaluation of Seligson's state of mind when he wrote his initial report, or when he checked the article against that report."

On appeal, the First Circuit held that its review of the "actual malice" determination was not limited to the "clearly erroneous" standard of Rule 52(a), but rather that it "must perform a de novo review, independently examining the record to ensure that the district court has applied properly the governing constitutional law and that the plaintiff has indeed satisfied its burden of proof, though it acknowledged its inability to consider issues of witness credibility. On the basis of this standard, the court of appeals held that it was "unable to find clear and convincing evidence that CU published the statement that individual instruments tended to wander about the room with knowledge that it was false or with reckless disregard * * *."]

II

This is a case in which two well settled and respected rules of law point in opposite directions.

Petitioner correctly reminds us that Rule 52(a) provides:

"Findings of fact shall not be set aside unless clearly erroneous, and due regard shall be given to the opportunity of the trial court to judge of the credibility of the witnesses."[*]

We have repeatedly held that the rule means what it says. United States v. United States Gypsum Co., 333 U.S. 364, 394–396 (1948). It surely does not stretch the language of the rule to characterize an inquiry into what a person knew at a given point in time as a question of "fact." In this case, since the trial judge expressly commented on Seligson's credibility, petitioner argues that the Court of Appeals plainly erred when it refused to uphold the District Court's actual malice "finding" under the clearly erroneous standard of Rule 52(a).

On the other hand, respondent correctly reminds us that in cases raising First Amendment issues we have repeatedly held that an appellate court has an obligation to "make an independent examination of the whole record" in order to make sure "that the judgment does not constitute a forbidden intrusion on the field of free expression." New York Times v.

---

[*] This provision, now Rule 52(a)(6), has been slightly revised.—Eds.

Sullivan, 376 U.S. at 284–286. Although such statements have been made most frequently in cases to which Rule 52(a) does not apply because they arose in state courts, respondent argues that the constitutional principle is equally applicable to federal litigation. We quite agree; surely it would pervert the concept of federalism for this Court to lay claim to a broader power of review over state court judgments than it exercises in reviewing the judgments of intermediate federal courts.

Our standard of review must be faithful to both Rule 52(a) and the rule of independent review applied in New York Times v. Sullivan. The conflict between the two rules is in some respects more apparent than real. The *New York Times* rule emphasizes the need for an appellate court to make an independent examination of the entire record; Rule 52(a) never forbids such an examination, and indeed our seminal decision on the rule expressly contemplated a review of the entire record, stating that a "finding is 'clearly erroneous' when although there is evidence to support it, the reviewing court on the entire evidence is left with the definite and firm conviction that a mistake has been committed." United States v. Gypsum Co., 333 U.S. at 395. Moreover, Rule 52(a) commands that "due regard" shall be given to the trial judge's opportunity to observe the demeanor of the witnesses; the constitutionally-based rule of independent review permits this opportunity to be given its due. Indeed, as we previously observed, the Court of Appeals in this case expressly declined to second-guess the district judge on the credibility of the witnesses.

The requirement that special deference be given to a trial judge's credibility determinations is itself a recognition of the broader proposition that the presumption of correctness that attaches to factual findings is stronger in some cases than in others. The same "clearly erroneous" standard applies to findings based on documentary evidence as to those based entirely on oral testimony, but the presumption has lesser force in the former situation than in the latter. Similarly, the standard does not change as the trial becomes longer and more complex, but the likelihood that the appellate court will rely on the presumption tends to increase when trial judges have lived with the controversy for weeks or months instead of just a few hours. One might therefore assume that the cases in which the appellate courts have a duty to exercise independent review are merely those in which the presumption that the trial court's ruling is correct is particularly weak. The difference between the two rules, however, is much more than a mere matter of degree. For the rule of independent review assigns to judges a constitutional responsibility that cannot be delegated to the trier of fact, whether the factfinding function be performed in the particular case by a jury or by a trial judge.

Rule 52(a) applies to findings of fact, including those described as "ultimate facts" because they may determine the outcome of litigation. But Rule 52(a) does not inhibit an appellate court's power to correct errors of law, including those that may infect a so-called mixed finding of law and fact, or a finding of fact that is predicated on a misunderstanding of the governing rule of law. Nor does Rule 52(a) "furnish particular guidance with respect to distinguishing law from fact." Pullman-Standard v. Swint, 456 U.S. at 288. What we have characterized as "the vexing nature" of that distinction does not, however, diminish its importance, or the importance of the principles that require the distinction to be drawn in certain cases.

* * *

The First Amendment presupposes that the freedom to speak one's mind is not only an aspect of individual liberty—and thus a good unto itself * * * but also is essential to the common quest for truth and the vitality of society as a whole. * * * Nevertheless, there are categories of communication and certain special utterances to which the majestic protection of the First Amendment does not extend because they "are no essential part of any exposition of ideas, and are of such slight social value as a step to truth that any benefit that may be derived from them is clearly outweighed by the social interest in order and morality." Chaplinsky v. New Hampshire, 315 U.S. 568, 572 (1942).

Libelous speech has been held to constitute one such category; others that have been held to be outside the scope of the freedom of speech are fighting words, incitement to riot, obscenity, and child pornography. In each of these areas, the limits of the unprotected category, as well as the unprotected character of particular communications, have been determined by the judicial evaluation of special facts that have been deemed to have constitutional significance. In such cases, the Court has regularly conducted an independent review of the record both to be sure that the speech in question actually falls within the unprotected category and to confine the perimeters of any unprotected category within acceptably narrow limits in an effort to ensure that protected expression will not be inhibited. Providing triers of fact with a general description of the type of communication whose content is unworthy of protection has not, in and of itself, served sufficiently to narrow the category, nor served to eliminate the danger that decisions by triers of fact may inhibit the expression of protected ideas. * * *

Hence, in New York Times v. Sullivan, after announcing the constitutional requirement for a finding of "actual malice" in certain types of defamation actions, it was only natural that we should conduct an independent review of the evidence on the dispositive constitutional issue.* * *

In Time, Inc. v. Pape, 401 U.S. 279 (1971), a case in which the federal District Court had entered a directed verdict, we again conducted an independent examination of the evidence on the question of actual malice, labeling our definition of "actual malice" as a "constitutional rule" and stating that the question before us was whether that rule had been correctly applied to the facts of the case. Again we stated that independent inquiries "of this kind are familiar under the settled principle that '[i]n cases in which there is a claim of denial of rights under the Federal Constitution, this Court is not bound by the conclusions of lower courts, but will re-examine the evidentiary basis on which those conclusions are founded,' " noting that "in cases involving the area of tension between the First and Fourteenth Amendments on the one hand and state defamation laws on the other, we have frequently had occasion to review 'the evidence in the . . . record to determine whether it could constitutionally support a judgment' for the plaintiff."

The requirement of independent appellate review reiterated in New York Times v. Sullivan is a rule of federal constitutional law. It emerged from the exigency of deciding concrete cases; it is law in its purest form under our common law heritage. It reflects a deeply held conviction that judges, and particularly members of this Court, must exercise such review in order to preserve the precious liberties established and ordained by the Constitution. The question whether the evidence in the record in a defamation case is of the convincing clarity required to strip the utterance of First Amendment protection is not merely a question for the trier of fact. Judges, as expositors of the Constitution, must independently decide whether the evidence in the record is sufficient to cross the constitutional threshold that bars the entry of any judgment that is not supported by clear and convincing proof of "actual malice."

III

The Court of Appeals was correct in its conclusions (1) that there is a significant difference between proof of actual malice and mere proof of falsity, and (2) that such additional proof is lacking in this case.

THE CHIEF JUSTICE concurs in the judgment.

[The dissenting opinion of JUSTICE WHITE is omitted.]

JUSTICE REHNQUIST, with whom JUSTICE O'CONNOR joins, dissenting.

It is * * * ironic that, in the interest of protecting the First Amendment, the Court rejects the "clearly erroneous" standard of review mandated by Fed.Rule of Civ.Proc. 52(a) in favor of a "de novo" standard of review for the "constitutional facts" surrounding the "actual malice" determination.

But the facts dispositive of that determination, actual knowledge or subjective reckless disregard for truth, involve no more than findings about the mens rea of an author, findings which appellate courts are simply ill-prepared to make in any context, including the First Amendment context. Unless "actual malice" now means something different from the definition given to the term 20 years ago by this Court in *New York Times,* I do not think that the constitutional requirement of "actual malice" properly can bring into play any standard of factual review other than the "clearly erroneous" standard.

In this case the District Court concluded by what it found to be clear and convincing evidence that respondent's engineer Arnold Seligson had written the defamatory statement about Bose's product with actual knowledge that it was false. It reached that conclusion expressly relying on its determination about the credibility of Seligson's testimony. On appeal there was no issue as to whether the District Court had properly understood what findings were legally sufficient to establish "actual malice" nor was there any issue as to the necessary quantum of proof nor the proper allocation of the burden of proof of "actual malice." The issue on appeal thus was only the propriety of the District Court's factual conclusion that Bose had actually proven "actual malice" in this case. Yet the Court of Appeals never rebutted the District Court's conclusion that Seligson had actual knowledge that what he printed was false. Instead it concluded after de novo review that Seligson's language was merely "imprecise" and that as such, it would not "support an inference of actual malice."

It is unclear to me just what that determination by the Court of Appeals has to do with the mens rea conclusion necessary to the finding of "actual malice" and with the District Court's finding of actual knowledge here. In approving the Court of Appeals' de novo judgment on the "actual malice" question, for all the factual detail and rehearsal of testimony with which the majority's opinion is adorned, the Court never quite comes to grips with what factual finding it must focus on. * * *

In my view the problem results from the Court's attempt to treat what is here and in other contexts always has been, a pure question of fact, as something more than a fact—a so-called "constitutional fact." The Court correctly points out that independent appellate review of facts underlying constitutional claims has been sanctioned by previous decisions of this Court where "a conclusion of law as to a Federal right and a finding of fact are so intermingled as to make it necessary, in order to pass upon the Federal question, to analyze the facts." Fiske v. Kansas, 274 U.S. 380, 385–386. But in other contexts we have always felt perfectly at ease leaving state of mind determinations, such as the actual knowledge and recklessness determinations involved here, to triers of fact with only deferential appellate review—for example, in criminal cases where the burden of proving those facts is even greater than the "clear and convincing" standard applicable under New York Times.

Presumably any doctrine of "independent review" of facts exists, not so that an appellate court may inexorably place its thumb on the scales in favor of the party claiming the constitutional right, but so that perceived shortcomings of the trier of fact by way of bias or some other factor may be compensated for. But to me, the only shortcoming here is an appellate court's inability to make the determination which the Court mandates today—the de novo determination about the state of mind of a particular author at a particular time. Although there well may be cases where the "actual malice" determination can be made on the basis of objectively reviewable facts in the record, it seems to me that just as often it is made, as here, on the basis of an evaluation of the credibility of the testimony of the author of the defamatory statement. I am at a loss to see how appellate courts can even begin to make such determinations. In any event, surely such determinations are best left to the trial judge.

It is of course true as the Court recognizes that "where particular speech falls close to the line separating the lawful and the unlawful, the possibility of mistaken fact-finding inherent in all litigation will create the danger that the legitimate utterance will be penalized." Speiser v. Randall, 357 U.S. 513, 526 (1958). But the *New York Times* rule adequately addresses the need to shield protected speech from the risk of erroneous fact-finding by placing the burden of proving "actual malice" on the party seeking to penalize expression. * * *

I think that the issues of "falsity" and "actual malice" in this case may be close questions, but I am convinced that the District Court, which heard the principal witness for the respondent testify for almost six days during the trial, fully understood both the applicable law and its role as a finder of fact. Because it is not clear to me that the de novo findings of appellate courts, with only bare records before them, are likely to be any more reliable than the findings reached by trial judges, I cannot join the majority's sanctioning of factual second guessing by appellate courts. I believe that the primary result of the Court's holding today will not be greater protection for First Amendment values, but rather only lessened confidence in the judgments of lower courts and more entirely factbound appeals.

I continue to adhere to the view expressed in Pullman-Standard v. Swint, 456 U.S. 273, 287 (1982), that Rule 52(a) "does not make exceptions or purport to exclude certain categories of factual findings from the obligation of a court of appeals to accept a district court's findings unless clearly erroneous." There is no reason to depart from that rule here, and I would therefore reverse and remand this case to the Court of Appeals so that it may apply the "clearly erroneous" standard of review to the factual findings of the District Court.

Notes and Questions

1. Rule 52(a)(1) commands that the trial judge, sitting as the finder of fact, "find the facts specially." This is different, of course, from the "general verdict" practice usually used in jury trials. What purposes are served by requiring the trial court to list factual findings specially? Would the same purposes be served by requiring a jury to make findings of fact? One reason for

not requiring a jury to do so is the difficulty of getting a group of people to draw up detailed findings of fact. Special verdicts and interrogatories can serve as a substitute for findings of fact by a jury. But are there countervailing reasons for not requiring a jury to justify its verdict with specific factfinding?

2. When judgment is entered on a jury verdict, the Rule 52(a) "clearly erroneous" standard obviously does not apply. Nevertheless, the *Bose* requirement that, in libel cases involving a public figure, the appellate court must make a *de novo* review to determine whether the record presents clear and convincing proof of actual malice also applies when the factfinder is a jury. Levine v. CMP Publications, Inc., 738 F.2d 660, 674 (5th Cir.1984). If the jury finds that actual malice was not proved, should the *Bose* standard apply on appeal? Bartimo v. Horsemen's Benevolent and Protective Ass'n, 771 F.2d 894, 897–98 (5th Cir.1985), suggests that it should. Does this make sense?

3. *Bose* viewed the de novo appellate review requirement as arising from the constitutional limitation imposed by the First Amendment on libel actions. A similar limitation has been imposed on libel actions arising out of labor disputes. The Court has held that the federal labor laws contemplate vigorous and even overblown and pejorative speech, and that, as a statutory matter, proof of actual malice is required in a libel action by a public figure (which includes unions and companies) arising out of a labor dispute. Letter Carriers v. Austin, 418 U.S. 264, 272 (1974); National Labor Relations Act § 8(c), 29 U.S.C. § 158(c). In such cases, must actual malice be proven by "clear and convincing evidence" rather than just a "preponderance of the evidence," and does the *Bose* requirement of *de novo* appellate review apply? National Ass'n of Government Employees v. National Federation of Fed. Employees, 844 F.2d 216 (5th Cir.1988), a libel action brought by a union against a rival union in a collective bargaining certification election, indicated in *dictum* that *Bose* should be so extended.

4. What does "clearly erroneous" mean, as used in Rule 52(a)? In United States v. U.S. Gypsum Co., 333 U.S. 364, 395 (1948), the Supreme Court stated that a finding is "clearly erroneous" when "although there is evidence to support it, the reviewing court on the entire evidence is left with the definite and firm conviction that a mistake has been committed." See also Cooper v. Harris, 137 S.Ct. 1455, 1474 (2017), where the Supreme Court provided the following explanation of its application of the clear error standard of review to fact findings reached in the context of litigation over redistricting:

> [W]e review a district court's finding as to racial predominance only for clear error, except when the court made a legal mistake. Under that standard of review, we affirm the court's finding so long as it is "plausible"; we reverse only when "left with the definite and firm conviction that a mistake has been committed." And in deciding which side of that line to come down on, we give singular deference to a trial court's judgments about the credibility of witnesses.

5. In Teva Pharmaceuticals USA v. Sandoz, Inc., 135 S.Ct. 831 (2015), the Court held that a court of appeals reviewing the construction of a term used

in a patent should use a clear error, not de novo, standard of review. (For a description of the role of claim construction in patent litigation, see pp. 1116–1117 supra.) The patent in question used the term "molecular weight," but there was a dispute about whether that term was fatally indefinite, making the patent invalid. The district court, after taking evidence from experts, concluded that the term was sufficiently definite and held the patent valid. The Federal Circuit disagreed after reviewing de novo. The Supreme Court reversed the Federal Circuit, holding that Rule 52(a)(6) should be applied in this situation. Drawing on its earlier decision in Markman v. Westview Instruments, 517 U.S. 370 (1996), the *Teva* Court acknowledged that construction of a patent is a question of law in the same sense that document construction is a question of law. But the *Teva* Court explained the words used in such a document "may give rise to a factual dispute. If so, extrinsic evidence may help to 'establish a usage of trade or locality.'" Id. at 837. The judge may have to resolve such factual disputes to interpret the patent. But "when we held in Markman that the ultimate question of claim construction is for the judge and not the jury, we did not create an exception from the ordinary rule governing appellate review of factual matters. * * * A conclusion that an issue is for the judge does not indicate that Rule 52(a) is inapplicable." Id. at 838.

6.   In what way does the standard of Rule 52(a) for appellate review of a trial court's factual findings differ from the standard of review a trial court may employ in deciding whether to overturn a jury's verdict on a motion for judgment as a matter of law after trial? Why is this distinction drawn? In what way does appellate review of a trial court's factual findings differ from the standard of review of a trial court's conclusions of law? What is the reason for this distinction?

7.   Many decisions, including numerous procedural decisions, are not reviewed under either the clearly erroneous or the full plenary review standards. Some, including the entry of a partial final judgment under Rule 54(b), are reversed only for an "abuse of discretion." See Curtiss-Wright Corp. v. General Electric Co., supra p. 574 (requiring deference to the district court's discretionary judgment under Rule 54(b), except where the district court abused its discretion by reaching a conclusion that was "clearly unreasonable"). What does this mean? The abuse of discretion standard affords the appellate court a chance to overturn rulings it views as seriously wrong while allowing the trial court substantial latitude in a variety of areas such as discovery, amendment to pleadings, and mode of conducting the trial. As to whether the choice of a clear-error or abuse of discretion standard has any impact on appellate outcomes, see Anderson, Law, Fact, and Discretion in the Federal Courts: An Empirical Study, 2012 Utah L. Rev. 1 (reporting based on a statistical analysis that standards of review influence reversal and affirmance rates).

8.   In *Bose,* was the Court correct in requiring more searching appellate review on the question of actual malice? Was the Court creating a First Amendment exception to Rule 52(a), or was it merely characterizing the question of actual malice as a conclusion of law? If the former, is such an

exception legitimate? Compare the Court's summary judgment decision in Anderson v. Liberty Lobby, Inc., supra p. 483. If the latter, is this a legitimate characterization? See D. Faigman, Constitutional Fictions: A Unified Theory of Constitutional Facts 127 (2008) (defending independent review of the facts in free speech cases).

Contrast with *Bose* the decision in Pullman-Standard v. Swint, 456 U.S. 273 (1982). Plaintiffs there, minority workers at a Pullman-Standard plant, claimed that the seniority system at the plant violated Title VII because it had the effect of discriminating against them. Under the applicable employment discrimination law, to prevail plaintiffs had to prove that the seniority system was negotiated or maintained with actual intent to discriminate. The trial court entered findings that defendants did not have this intent, but the appellate court reversed, concluding that "[a]lthough discrimination vel non is essentially a question of fact it is, at the same time, the ultimate issue for resolution in this case, being expressly proscribed by [the statute]. As such, a finding of discrimination or non-discrimination is a finding of ultimate fact." Based on what the Supreme Court found to be an independent evaluation of the record, the court of appeals reversed.

The Supreme Court held that this review violated Rule 52(a). It reasoned that "[t]reating issues of intent as factual matters for the trier of fact is commonplace" and that the intent issue in the case "appears to us to be a pure question of fact." The appellate court's approach was therefore wrong:

> Rule 52(a) broadly requires that findings of fact not be set aside unless clearly erroneous. It does not make exceptions or purport to exclude certain categories of factual findings from the obligation of a court of appeals to accept a district court's findings unless clearly erroneous. It does not divide facts into categories; in particular, it does not divide findings of fact into those that deal with "ultimate" and those that deal with "subsidiary" facts.

> The Rule does not apply to conclusions of law. The Court of Appeals, therefore, was quite right in saying that if a district court's findings rest on an erroneous view of the law, they may be set aside on that basis. But here the District Court was not faulted for misunderstanding or applying an erroneous definition of intentional discrimination. It was reversed for arriving at what the Court of Appeals thought was an erroneous finding as to whether the differential impact of the seniority system reflected an intent to discriminate on account of race. That question, as we see it, is a pure question of fact, subject to Rule 52(a)'s clearly-erroneous standard. It is not a question of law and not a mixed question of law and fact.

456 U.S. at 287–88. Can this case be reconciled with *Bose?* If not, which expresses the proper rule for cases not involving the First Amendment?

Compare Easley v. Cromartie, 532 U.S. 234 (2001), an equal protection challenge to the way the North Carolina state legislature drew the boundary lines for one of the election districts in the state. In reviewing the finding of a constitutional violation, the Supreme Court focused on the district court's conclusion that the legislature's predominant motive in drawing the boundary was race rather than politics. In a factually rich record, the question was whether the state legislature had acted to create a safe Democratic seat or impermissibly to create a predominantly African-American seat. Among the factors that the district court considered were the snake-like shape of the voting district; the fact that several contiguous and predominantly Democratic precincts were excluded from the district; and the comments of some participants in the line-drawing process, which tended to characterize the district in racial terms. Dividing 5–4, the Court downplayed these factors, viewing the expert testimony and other evidence as failing to support a finding that race was the predominant motive. The Court notably refrained from treating predominant motive as an issue of constitutional fact that would trigger de novo review. But the dissent argued that the majority had failed to observe the limits of "clear error" review and had conducted the effective equivalent of de novo review instead. Can the majority's approach be squared with that taken in Cooper v. Harris, supra note 4?

9. Who actually writes the findings? Suppose that the trial judge, *before* finding for either party, seeks and obtains proposed findings from *both* sides, and, after reaching a decision, adopts the proposed findings of the victorious party. Should this practice be deemed invalid? Consider the view of one appellate court:

> Findings of fact that have been taken verbatim from those proposed by counsel have been criticized, see Anderson v. City of Bessemer City, 470 U.S. 564, 572 (1985); nonetheless, "they are not to be rejected out-of-hand, and they will stand if supported by evidence." United States v. El Paso Natural Gas Co., 376 U.S. 651, 656 (1964). When a district judge does more than merely adopt a party's proposed findings, "the findings issued by the District Court represent the judge's own considered conclusions," Philbrook v. Ansonia Bd. of Educ., 925 F.2d 47, 53 (2d Cir.1991) (internal quotation omitted), which may not be set aside unless clearly erroneous. See Fed.R.Civ.P. 52(a). Here, the district court did not adopt the government's proposed findings in haec verba but revised them in certain respects and not in others, demonstrating that its findings were based on its own perspective. We therefore review the findings under the clearly erroneous standard.

Counihan v. Allstate Ins. Co., 194 F.3d 357, 363 (2d Cir. 1999). Reviewing courts have taken a much dimmer view of the practice of having findings prepared by the side already identified as victorious. See Roberts v. Ross, 344 F.2d 747, 752 (3d Cir.1965): "Findings and conclusions prepared ex post facto by counsel, even though signed by the judge, do not serve adequately the function contemplated by the rule." What justifies this difference in treatment?

D. PROBLEMS OF APPELLATE PROCEDURE

STANDING ON APPEAL

In order to sue in federal court, the plaintiff must have standing. The requirement flows in part from the case-or-controversy requirement embodied in Article III of the Constitution and in part from judge-made prudential doctrines. That a party had standing to bring suit, however, does not automatically imply that an unsuccessful party will necessarily have standing to appeal. In Bender v. Williamsport Area School District, 475 U.S. 534 (1986), the issue before the Court was "[w]hether one member of a School Board has standing to appeal from a declaratory judgment against the Board." The Court concluded that "although the School Board itself had a sufficient stake in the outcome of the litigation to appeal, an individual Board member cannot invoke the Board's interest in the case to confer standing upon himself."

Students had filed suit in federal court against the Williamsport Area School District, the nine members of the School Board, the Superintendent of the District, and the high school principal. They alleged that that the defendants' refusal to recognize their religiously oriented group and to allow it to meet on the same basis as other student groups violated their First Amendment rights. The district court granted summary judgment for the plaintiff students, though no injunction was issued, and no other form of relief was granted against any defendant in his individual capacity. Although the School District did not challenge the judgment in any way, one member of the Board, John C. Youngman, Jr., did file a timely notice of appeal.

No one raised any question about Youngman's standing in the court of appeals. That court reversed on the merits of the First Amendment challenge. The Supreme Court, recognizing that only Youngman had challenged the district court's order, held that the court of appeals was without jurisdiction. "As a member of the School Board sued in his official capacity," the Court reasoned, "Mr. Youngman had no personal stake in the outcome of the litigation and therefore did not have standing to file the notice of appeal." His status as a school board member, the Court found, "does not permit him to 'step into the shoes of the Board' and invoke its right to appeal." As a general matter, "members of collegial bodies do not have standing to perfect an appeal the body itself has declined to take." Though Youngman claimed at oral argument that he was the parent of at least one student attending the high school and that as a matter of conscience he opposed prayer activities on school premises during regular school hours, the Court found nothing in the record about his status as a parent.

Chief Justice Burger, dissenting, found that Youngman did have standing to appeal: "Mr. Youngman is a parent of a student at Williamsport

High School; as a matter of conscience he is opposed to prayer activities on school premises during school hours. As this Court has repeatedly held, parents have standing to challenge conditions in public schools that their children attend." While he agreed with the Court that a plaintiff has the burden to plead facts showing his standing, these burdens "need not be placed upon a properly named defendant, like Mr. Youngman, who seeks to invoke the jurisdiction of the Court of Appeals."

NOTES AND QUESTIONS

1. Should it *ever* be deemed improper for a named party, who is on the losing side of a case in the trial court, to appeal? Would the policies underlying the requirement of standing have been undermined by allowing Youngman's appeal? In his dissent, the Chief Justice argued that standing rules, normally employed to determine whether a party may initiate an action, should be relaxed when the issue is whether an appeal may be taken. Do you agree? Compare Devlin v. Scardelletti, 536 U.S. 1 (2002) (dissident class members who object to a settlement presented to the court for its approval under Rule 23(e) may appeal approval over their objections even though they do not intervene in the class action) with Diamond v. Charles, 476 U.S. 54 (1986) (physician who intervened to support the state in defending a constitutional challenge to a state statute limiting abortion rights lacked standing to appeal once the state failed to prosecute an appeal). In Stringfellow v. Concerned Neighbors in Action, 480 U.S. 370 (1987), the Court ruled that a district court order, denying intervention as of right but allowing permissive intervention, was not subject to immediate appellate review. Such an order was neither final nor was it subject to review under the collateral order doctrine or as the effective denial of injunctive relief.

2. Should a party who *won* in the court below ever be allowed to take an appeal? Consider Camreta v. Greene, 131 S.Ct. 2020 (2011). Greene brought suit under section 1983 against Camreta, a child services worker, and a deputy sheriff, challenging the constitutionality of a school-house interview the defendants conducted with her nine-year old daughter about sex abuse at the hands of the child's father. Following dismissal of the claim by the district court, the Ninth Circuit affirmed, essentially on the ground that the defendants were entitled to qualified immunity because the law did not clearly forbid the sort of interrogation at issue. (Recall the discussion of qualified immunity in connection with the collateral order doctrine, supra pp. 1099–1110.) But en route to that determination, the Ninth Circuit also held that special needs attendant to child sex abuse investigations do not automatically justify an exception to traditional Fourth Amendment protections. (Settled law empowers appellate courts to reach the constitutional merits, as the Ninth Circuit did, in a case where the court nonetheless recognizes a qualified immunity defense on grounds of unsettled law. See Pearson v. Callahan, 555 U.S. 223 (2009).) The plaintiff, Greene, did not challenge the Ninth Circuit's ruling on qualified immunity, but Camreta sought review in the Supreme

Court of the Ninth Circuit's conclusion that the Fourth Amendment could apply to school-house child sex abuse investigations.

Despite the fact that Camreta had prevailed on qualified immunity grounds, the Court held that he had standing to seek review of the Ninth Circuit's Fourth Amendment interpretation. As the Court saw matters, Camreta was still employed as a child sex abuse investigator and had a continuing interest in the constitutional rules governing such investigations. His freedom, in the future, to conduct interviews at the school-house could be affected by the Ninth Circuit decision and he thus had standing to challenge it. In the end, though, the Court found that the appeal had been mooted by the passage of time; the plaintiff's daughter had since grown up, graduated from high school, and would no longer face the prospect of school-house interrogations.

Justice Kennedy dissented, arguing that appellate review should be available only for those who seek to challenge judgments and not for those who seek to revise the language of an appellate court opinion. Justice Kennedy also questioned the wisdom of the Court's decision to allow lower courts to reach the merits first, before disposing of a claim on qualified immunity grounds. He suggested, as an alternative, that the Court might encourage merits adjudication and the clarification of legal norms by allowing immunity-free claims for nominal damages in cases of legal uncertainty. For an analysis of the viability of such claims, along somewhat the same lines as Justice Kennedy's suggestion, see Pfander, Resolving the Qualified Immunity Dilemma: Constitutional Tort Claims for Nominal Damages, 111 Colum. L. Rev. 1601 (2011).

One final feature of the Camreta majority decision deserves attention. The Court explained that its power to review the Ninth Circuit, on appeal by a prevailing party, did not necessarily imply that a federal appellate court could entertain an appeal by a party who had prevailed in the district court. District court opinions lacked the precedential weight of appellate court opinions and thus would not impinge as significantly on future official discretion. See also Midland-Guardian of Pensacola, Inc. v. Carr, 425 F.2d 793 (5th Cir.1970) (refusing to permit a prevailing party to appeal from a district court opinion on the basis that there was no Article III case or controversy).

3.   ClearOne Communications, Inc. v. Biamp Systems, 653 F.3d 1163 (10th Cir. 2011), presents a variant of the problem of the appellant who *won* below. In this case, defendant moved to dismiss for failure to state a claim, but the motion was denied in an order that was not subject to appellate review at the time. Following discovery, the plaintiff won at trial. While the evidence was presumably sufficient to sustain a trial verdict, defendant continued to argue that the complaint was legally insufficient and should have been dismissed. The Tenth Circuit relied on an earlier Fifth Circuit decision that "[w]hen a plaintiff has prevailed after a full trial on the merits, a district court's denial of a [motion to dismiss] becomes moot." Id. at 1172 (quoting Bennett v. Pipin, 74 F.3d 578, 585 (5th Cir. 1996)). The Tenth Circuit agreed with the Fifth Circuit that "[a]fter a trial on the merits, the sufficiency of the allegations of

the complaint is irrelevant" because plaintiff "has proved, not merely alleged, facts sufficient to support relief." Does this result comport with Fed. R. Civ. P. 15(b) and its provision for the amendment of the pleadings to conform to the evidence? How does the decision affect the "plausibility" requirement of Bell Atlantic Corp. v. Twombly (supra p. 184)? Should the decision affect the notion that rulings on motions to dismiss can be reviewed after final judgment, and therefore are not appealable under the collateral order doctrine? Even an order denying a motion to dismiss could satisfy the effectively unreviewable prong of the collateral order doctrine, could such an order ever be regarded as sufficiently separate from the merits as to warrant interlocutory review?

Note also that Ortiz v. Jordan, 562 U.S. 180 (2011), seems to rule that denial of defendant's motion for summary judgment—even on qualified immunity grounds—cannot be challenged on appeal after the case goes to trial. Technically the Court's ruling was that defendants could not argue for entry of judgment in their favor because they did not make a Rule 50(a) motion at trial. But they did make a summary judgment motion, which was denied. Do you see a difference between the *failure* of the defendant in Ortiz v. Jordan to renew the issue of evidentiary sufficiency with a Rule 50(a) motion at trial and the *inability* of the defendant in Clearone Communication v. Biamp, when confronted with legally sufficient evidence at trial, to renew a motion to dismiss on the pleadings?

4.   A related concept is the notion that even where the trial judge has committed an error, the losing party is entitled to reversal only when that error was harmful. See Rule 61. This determination should depend on a consideration of the entire case and all the evidence.

THE MECHANICS OF TAKING AN APPEAL

Once an appealable order is entered, the objecting party must file a notice of appeal. This notice must be filed with the district court within the applicable time limits, 30 days in federal court unless the appealing party is the United States. See Fed.R.App.P. 4; 28 U.S.C. § 2107; Bowles v. Russell, supra p. 1063. (Note that Rule 23(f) calls for the petition for leave to appeal from decisions granting or denying class certification to be filed with the clerk of the circuit court of appeals. Mandamus applications begin at the circuit court of appeals as well.) When one party has filed a notice of appeal, other litigants have 14 more days in which to file a notice of cross appeal. See Fed.R.App.P. 4(a)(3). Why should a litigant who didn't choose to appeal in the first instance be given additional time to cross appeal after another litigant had noticed an appeal?

The filing of the appeal does not prevent the trial court's judgment from being enforced. Ordinarily, the appellant can ask the trial court to stay enforcement of the judgment, but the stay is often conditioned on the posting of a bond. See Fed.R.Civ.P. 62(d); cf. Pennzoil Co. v. Texaco, Inc., 481 U.S. 1 (1987) (state law requiring judgment debtor to file $13 billion bond to forestall execution of judgment did not so clearly violate due process as to authorize federal injunctive relief against the bond requirement).

After the notices of appeal are filed, the parties prepare their written submissions to the appellate court. In some states, this includes the process of "designating" the record, in which the litigants indicate which portions of the trial court record should be included in the record on appeal. In federal court, the entire trial court record is viewed as the record on appeal, although the parties may submit an appendix containing the pertinent materials. See Fed.R.App.P. 10; 11; 30. In any event the appellate court's review is limited to matters that are properly in the record, so that something that was overlooked at the trial level cannot be added on appeal. The issues raised by the record are argued in the parties' briefs; usually the appellant files the first brief, after which the appellee files an opposing brief and the appellant may close with a reply brief. See Fed.R.App.P. 28; 31.

After the briefing is completed, there may be an oral argument before a panel of judges. See Fed.R.App.P. 34. In some cases this is preceded by a conference that resembles the pretrial conference in the trial court. See Fed.R.App.P. 33. The case is then submitted for decision, which is usually by written opinion mailed to the parties and filed with the clerk of the appellate court. A party unhappy with the decision may petition for a rehearing by the same panel (Fed.R.App.P. 40), request rehearing by the entire court of appeals en banc (Fed.R.App.P. 35), or appeal again if a further appeal is possible.

CHAPTER 13

PRECLUSIVE EFFECTS OF JUDGMENTS

▪ ▪ ▪

Putting an end to litigation by according finality to judgments is a central objective of a modern system of civil procedure. But courts have long struggled to achieve finality without depriving parties of an opportunity to pursue in a later suit aspects of the matter that they could not reasonably have litigated (or that they had valid reasons for not litigating) in the first suit.

At common law, the writ system dictated narrow principles of finality. That the plaintiff might lose by selecting one writ and establishing a right to relief under another implied that there would be a second chance to proceed under the correct writ. Thus, finality was limited to the writ selected. With the switch to code pleading in the 19th century, courts came to favor certainty over fairness. Formalistic rules viewed preclusion of relitigating claims and issues as an inherent right flowing from the nature of a judgment. The decisions from that period "were absolute" in paying little attention to any "competing elements of decision," and "mandatory in that their controlling effect was not subject to equitable dispensation or qualification on grounds of general notions of fairness or justice in particular cases." Holland, Modernizing Res Judicata: Reflections on the *Parklane* Doctrine, 55 Ind.L.J. 615, 616–17 (1980). One focus of this chapter will be the interplay of formalistic and public policy considerations in the application of the modern counterparts of these preclusion doctrines.

A. BASIC PRECLUSION CONCEPTS

RES JUDICATA AND COLLATERAL ESTOPPEL

The term res judicata is sometimes loosely used to refer to the totality of preclusion doctrines. As a technical matter, however, it refers more appropriately to the prohibition on relitigating a claim that has already been litigated and gone to judgment. The Restatement (Second) of Judgments favors the term "claim preclusion," and this usage has been increasingly adopted by courts.

The central propositions of the doctrine of res judicata (or claim preclusion) are expressed in terms of "merger" and "bar." When a party obtains a final personal judgment in its favor, its claim is extinguished and "merged" in the judgment, thus precluding further litigation on the same claim. Likewise, when a party suffers a judgment against it, the claim is also extinguished and the party is "barred" by the judgment from relitigating the same claim. Merger and bar apply only when the second action is based on the same claim or cause of action, between the same parties or those in privity with them, and when the determination of the first action was "on the merits."

Collateral estoppel (or issue preclusion) is a doctrine applicable in situations that are not covered by res judicata (claim preclusion) because the second action is not based on the same claim or cause of action.[1] It forecloses the relitigation of issues that were actually litigated (that is, contested by the parties and submitted for determination by the court) and that were necessarily decided by the court.

One significant difference between claim and issue preclusion is that the former operates to preclude relitigation of the claim without regard to what issues were litigated in the first suit, while the latter only precludes relitigation of those issues that were actually litigated and necessarily determined in the first suit. Justice Field described this difference in Cromwell v. County of Sac, 94 U.S. (4 Otto) 351, 352–53 (1876):

> In [an action on the same claim or cause of action], the judgment, if rendered upon the merits, constitutes an absolute bar to a subsequent action. It is a finality as to the claim or demand in controversy, concluding parties and those in privity with them, not only as to every matter which was offered and received to sustain or defeat the claim or demand, but as to any other admissible matter which might have been offered for that purpose. Thus, for example, a judgment rendered upon a promissory note is conclusive as to the validity of the instrument and the amount due upon it, although it be subsequently alleged that perfect defenses actually existed, of which no proof was offered, such as forgery, want of consideration, or payment. If such defenses were not presented in the action, and established by competent evidence, the subsequent allegation of their existence is of no legal consequence. * * * [T]hat a judgment estops not only as to every ground of recovery or defense actually presented in the action, but also as to every ground which might have been presented, is strictly accurate, when applied to the demand or claim in controversy. * * *
>
> But where the second action between the same parties is upon a different claim or demand, the judgment in the prior action

---

[1]   When res judicata does not apply because, although the second suit is on the same claim or cause of action, the first suit was not decided on the merits, the doctrine of "direct estoppel" applies to preclude relitigation of the issues that were actually decided. For example, if the first action were dismissed for failure to join an indispensable party under Rule 12(b)(7), and plaintiff filed a second suit still not joining that party, he would be estopped from relitigating the issue determined in the first suit that the party was indispensable. "Direct estoppel," together with collateral estoppel, is subsumed under the broad term of "issue preclusion."

operates as an estoppel only as to those matters in issue or points controverted, upon the determination of which the finding or verdict was rendered. In all cases, therefore, where it is sought to apply the estoppel of a judgment rendered upon one cause of action to matters arising in a suit upon a different cause of action, the inquiry must always be as to the point or question actually litigated and determined in the original action, not what might have been thus litigated and determined.

The late 20th century witnessed significant changes in the preclusion doctrines. Courts moved to less absolute rules permitting a wider range of policy and fairness considerations, while at the same time extending the formal boundaries of res judicata and collateral estoppel. Thus, most courts have embraced a transactional test for defining "the same claim" requirement for res judicata and have recast the strict "mutuality" requirement for collateral estoppel. Judicial concerns with crowded dockets and impatience with certain kinds of recurring litigation have encouraged this extension of the scope of preclusion. We shall examine whether these evolving rules satisfy the needs of a modern system of procedure and how the policies of finality and judicial economy are counterbalanced against those of flexibility and fairness. For now, simply note that flexibility as to the joinder of claims and parties at the opening stage of the litigation may influence attitudes toward the fairness of preclusion after the litigation ends.

FINAL JUDGMENTS

The doctrines of claim and issue preclusion apply only to "final" judgments. In Chapter 12, we considered what a "final judgment" means for purposes of direct appeal from a district court to a U.S. Circuit Court of Appeals. Recall 28 U.S.C. § 1291. The Supreme Court has defined it as a judgment that "ends the litigation on the merits and leaves nothing for the court to do but execute the judgment." Catlin v. United States, 324 U.S. 229, 233 (1945). The policy underlying the finality requirement for purposes of preclusion resembles the policy justification for insisting on a final judgment as a prerequisite for the right to appeal. "Appeals would be wasteful, and preclusion would be folly, as to decisions that are merely tentative and contemplate further proceedings." 18A C. Wright, A. Miller, & E. Cooper, Federal Practice and Procedure § 4432 (3d ed. 2017). But the same definition of "final judgment" may not achieve both the goal of effective appellate review and the finality and economy objectives of the preclusion doctrines. For example, although a judgment on liability (but not damages) or a judgment as to some, but not all, claims or parties (Rule 54(b)) may be considered "final" for an appeal, it may be undesirable to accord it finality for purposes of precluding further litigation since other aspects of the matter are still to be settled. Id. at §§ 4432, 4434.

Trial de novo = Brand new trial (w/ possibility of new evidence)

The preclusive effect of a judgment pending on appeal raises distinctive finality issues obviously not addressed by the definition of "final judgment" for purposes of appeal. Curiously, there is no firm agreement among jurisdictions as to whether a judgment on appeal should be given preclusive effect. "On the one hand, it makes little sense to accord conclusive effect to a determination that itself may be nullified through reversal on appeal; on the other hand, it may be a waste of effort to retry an issue simply because an appeal is pending in the case where the issue was originally determined." F. James, G. Hazard & J. Leubsdorf, Civil Procedure 678 (5th ed. 2001). Some courts simply postpone consideration of the preclusive effect of a judgment until the appeal has been completed, which appears consistent with the procedural effect of Rule 62 (allowing a losing party to obtain a stay of judgment pending appeal). But see Restatement (Second) of Judgments § 13, comment f (1982) ("The better view is that a judgment otherwise final remains so despite the taking of an appeal unless what is called an appeal actually consists of a trial de novo."). The federal courts adhere to the Restatement view, although they recognize that a *successful* appeal will deprive the trial court judgment of preclusive effect. See Aurora City v. West, 74 U.S. 82, 93 (1868) (finding that when a judgment has been appealed and vacated, and has not been reentered, it has no preclusive effect); Kosinski v. Commissioner, 541 F.3d 671, 676 (6th Cir. 2008). A judgment is not deprived of finality simply because there is still time to file a motion in the trial court for a new trial or because the time for appeal has not yet expired.

Rule 62

B. CLAIM PRECLUSION (RES JUDICATA)

1. SAME CLAIM OR CAUSE OF ACTION

MANEGO V. ORLEANS BOARD OF TRADE

United States Court of Appeals, First Circuit, 1985
773 F.2d 1

Before COFFIN, RUBIN, and BOWNES, CIRCUIT JUDGES.

BOWNES, CIRCUIT JUDGE.[a]

* * *

In late 1978 and early 1979, Manego applied to the Orleans Board of Selectmen for entertainment and liquor licenses for a disco which he wanted to build on a vacant lot. The lot was located in a commercial district a few hundred feet from an ice skating rink. The rink at that time was primarily used by children for hockey and figure skating. During the winter there was also a "Disco on Ice" program for children under sixteen. As a

---

[a]   Minor changes in wording have been made throughout the opinion to excise confusing references to another earlier suit that has no bearing on this opinion.—Eds.

result of a mortgage foreclosure, the Cape Cod Five Cents Savings Bank owned the rink from 1978 until July 1979. The vice-president of the bank, David Willard, served as general manager of the rink during this period. As owner of the rink, the bank was concerned about the close proximity of an establishment serving liquor to a recreational facility primarily patronized by children and the increased likelihood of automobile accidents involving inebriated drivers and children walking to and from the rink. The bank also had more general concerns about the presence of a disco in the area.

In January of 1979, there was a meeting of the Orleans Board of Trade, a private organization which functions as the chamber of commerce for the town. At that time, Willard was also the president of the Board of Trade. Membership in this organization is open to anyone who pays the $15.00 membership fee. Willard raised the issue of the proposed disco at the meeting and after some discussion the membership voted to oppose the disco.

On January 11, 1979, a public hearing on Manego's liquor license application was held by the Orleans Board of Selectmen. Two of the selectmen, Gaston Norgeot and Thomas Nickerson, were also members of the Board of Trade. Over 100 people attended the meeting and expressed concern over the increased traffic and noise which would result from the disco as well as the effect of an establishment serving liquor in close proximity to the skating rink and the general effect of a disco on the atmosphere of the Town of Orleans. The Board of Selectmen received a petition containing 369 signatures opposing the disco and eleven letters, only two of which favored Manego's proposal. At the hearing, Willard announced that the Board of Trade had voted to oppose granting a license for the disco.

On February 8, 1979, the Selectmen denied Manego's application for a liquor license and Manego appealed this decision to the Board of Appeals, which met on February 8 and 14. Willard wrote a letter to the Board of Appeals setting forth the bank's opposition to the disco and its concern for the safety of the youngsters using the skating rink. Local counsel for the bank attended the Board of Appeals hearings. In late February, the Board of Appeals denied Manego's appeal.

On February 13, 1979, the Orleans Board of Trade held its monthly meeting and, according to the minutes, mention was made of a hearing scheduled for the next day on Manego's amusement license application and of Manego's appeal of the denial of the liquor license application by the Selectmen. At the February 14 amusement license hearing, the Selectmen requested that the Town Traffic Safety Committee study the effects of the proposed disco. On February 22, 1979, the Selectmen turned down Manego's application for an amusement license.

In spite of these license denials, the Orleans Board of Appeals granted Manego a building permit in May of 1979. The bank then filed suit in Barnstable Superior Court challenging the issuance of this permit. In July of 1979, the bank sold the rink to Paul Thibert and sometime in August withdrew its superior court suit.

In March of 1979, the entertainment license of the rink expired; no renewal was sought until July of 1979, after Thibert purchased the rink. Because the license had lapsed, the application was treated as a new application and not a renewal and a public hearing was held. During that summer, a concrete floor had been poured at the rink to allow roller skating so the new application added roller skating to the proposed activities of the facility. In addition, the rink planned to offer a ballroom dancing program for adults featuring live music from the 1940's and refreshments in the nature of soft drinks. This, too, was an addition to the rink's activities. The rink's application was granted by the Selectmen. Among the reasons cited by the Selectmen for their approval were its unique status as the only skating facility on the Lower Cape, its use by young people as safe and "noncorrupting" entertainment and the lack of noise or traffic problems created by the facility.

* * *

Manego brought a lawsuit in federal district court, naming the Board of Selectmen, the Cape Cod Five Cents Savings Bank and Willard as defendants and claiming that they had conspired to deny him the licenses because of his race in violation of 42 U.S.C. §§ 1981, 1983, 1985, 1986, 1988, 2000e et seq., § 3605 of the Fair Housing Act, and Mass.Gen.Laws Ann. ch. 151B, § 4(3B). The claims under 42 U.S.C. §§ 2000e et seq., the Fair Housing Act, and the state law claims were all dismissed by the district court for failure to state a cause of action. As to the other claims, [the district court granted summary judgment for the defendants.] * * *

The district court found that despite being given an extra ninety days to produce some concrete, factual basis for his allegation of conspiracy, which defendants had affirmatively denied in their affidavits, Manego produced only the following: two personal affidavits explaining his theory and suggesting that direct evidence of the conspiracy would emerge under cross-examination and a third affidavit of a local building contractor employed by Manego reporting that he had heard that a lumber company had been told by the Bank not to supply Manego with materials and vaguely suggesting that his own relationship with the bank had been adversely affected by his association with Manego. The district court found that since Manego had not taken advantage of an "ample opportunity" to take depositions or conduct any other form of discovery, his promise of evidence arising out of cross-examination was pure speculation, and that, furthermore, the affidavit of the building contractor could not be given any weight because it consisted primarily of hearsay.

In our opinion affirming the district court's grant of summary judgment on this ground, we said:

> In this case, plaintiff sought to infer the existence of an illegal conspiracy from the fact that the Selectmen granted a license to someone who was white but not to plaintiff, who was black. His inference is supported only by affidavit evidence of a general racial animus in the community. The fact that a group of private citizens, organized as the Orleans Board of Trade, voted unanimously to oppose his license and that members of the Board of Selectmen may have attended the meeting established nothing about the motivation of those individuals in opposing his license. The defendants countered his inference with an explanation of the difference between his disco and the skating rink which was granted a license. . .
>
> In the face of this explanation, plaintiff's promise that circumstantial evidence would emerge at trial could not withstand the defendants' motions for summary judgment.

Despite the rebuff, Manego filed another lawsuit, this time against the bank, Willard, and the Orleans Board of Trade and its members. This lawsuit, which is the subject of this appeal, differed from [the earlier suit] in two respects: it dropped the Board of Selectmen as a defendant and added the Board of Trade; and it alleged a new legal theory, antitrust violations under the Sherman Antitrust Act, 15 U.S.C. § 1. As evidence of a conspiracy between the bank and the Board of Trade to prevent the proposed disco from competing with the rink, Manego offered depositions, answers to interrogatories, affidavits, and other documents which showed: that Willard was simultaneously an officer of the bank, general manager of the rink, and President of the Board of Trade; that various members of the Board present at the January and February meetings were also Selectmen; that the Selectmen denied the licenses after the Board of Trade voted to oppose their issuance; that the Selectmen subsequently granted an entertainment license to the rink which included live music, dancing and roller disco; and that the bank brought a lawsuit challenging a construction permit granted to Manego by the Orleans Board of Appeal but dropped the lawsuit after it sold the rink. According to Manego, the Board of Trade's interest in preventing the competition between the proposed disco and the rink was derived from the interest of its president, David Willard, who managed the rink for the bank.

Willard and the Bank moved for summary judgment on the grounds that these new claims were barred by the doctrine of *res judicata* and that, in any event, its conduct was protected by the first amendment under the

Noerr-Pennington doctrine.[b] The Board of Trade also moved for summary judgment under the doctrine of *res judicata* and additionally argued that there was no genuine issue of fact concerning the alleged conspiracy.

DEFENDANTS CAPE COD FIVE CENTS SAVINGS BANK AND DAVID WILLARD

As to Willard and the bank, the district court found that this lawsuit was barred by the final judgment of the Court of Appeals in [the earlier suit] affirming the district court's grant of summary judgment to the Bank and Willard on civil rights claims. Applying a "transactional" approach to claim preclusion, the district court found that the facts forming the basis of Manego's claim of antitrust violations were the same as those which formed the basis of his earlier civil rights claims and that they were, therefore, barred by the final judgment against Manego on the civil rights claims. We agree.

While most of our previous cases have involved the preclusive effect of a previous *state* judgment on the merits and have, therefore, been based upon state *res judicata* doctrine, we have indicated that the preclusive effect given to prior judgments by various states does not differ from the preclusive effect we would give to our own judgments. In Capraro v. Tilcon Gammino, Inc., 751 F.2d 56, 58 (1st Cir.1985), we stated that "Rhode Island state law . . . ., so far as we are aware, does not in connection with the principles of res judicata differ from the Restatement (Second) of Judgments or the law of Massachusetts or federal law." We then turned, as we have in many previous cases, to § 24 of the Restatement (Second) of Judgments (1982) concerning the scope of claim preclusion. It thus appears that, *sub silentio,* we have come to view the Restatement rule as our own, even though we have never formally adopted it. We now officially embrace it.

Under the doctrine of *res judicata,* "a final judgment on the merits of an action precludes the parties or their privies from relitigating issues that were or could have been raised in that action." Allen v. McCurry, 449 U.S. 90, 94 (1980). This bar is limited, however, to cases arising out of the same cause of action or claim. E.g., Cromwell v. County of Sac, 94 U.S. 351 (1876). Our adoption of the Restatement (Second) approach commits us to a "transactional" definition of the underlying claim or cause of action:

> (1) When a valid and final judgment rendered in an action extinguishes the plaintiff's claim pursuant to the rules of merger or bar . . ., the claim extinguished includes all rights of the plaintiff to remedies against the defendant with respect to all or

---

[b] "[T]his doctrine exempts, with certain exceptions, concerted attempts to influence the passage or enforcement of laws from the sweep of anti-trust legislation regardless of anticompetitive intent." Manego v. Orleans Board of Trade, 598 F.Supp. 231, 236 (D.Mass.1984).— Eds.

any part of the transaction, or series of connected transactions, out of which the action arose.

(2)   What factual grouping constitutes a "transaction," and what groupings constitute a "series," are to be determined pragmatically, giving weight to such considerations as whether the facts are related in time, space, origin, or motivation, whether they form a convenient trial unit, and whether their treatment as a unit conforms to the parties' expectations or business understanding or usage.

Restatement (Second) of Judgments § 24 (1982).

Manego has argued that [this case] does not involve the same transaction as that which formed the basis for [the earlier case] for three reasons: the nature of the conspiracy alleged is different; the parties to the conspiracy are different, although they do share common members; and there was no allegation in [the earlier case] that the rink and disco would be offering similar entertainment and thus competing for the same customers.

As the district court pointed out, however, the mere fact that different legal theories are presented in each case does not mean that the same transaction is not behind each. Thus, the fact that one suit alleges a conspiracy with a racial animus and the other alleges a conspiracy with anticompetitive animus does not demonstrate that separate transactions are involved. Nor does it matter in this case that the named defendants are not identical. Even though the Board of Trade was not a defendant in [the earlier case], the fact that it met under the leadership of Willard and voted to oppose the disco was brought out and no new facts concerning conduct of the bank and the Board of Trade have been alleged.

We next consider whether the absence from [the earlier case] of the allegation that the bank had plans to offer live music and dancing at the rink was sufficient to prevent the application of *res judicata*. The focus of the argument below was on whether Manego reasonably could have alleged this at the time of the racial discrimination suit. Manego claimed that he did not allege the "similar entertainment" facts in [the earlier case] because he did not know of them until too late—three days before summary judgment issued. While it is the law that, if information is not reasonably discoverable, *res judicata* will not apply, see Marrapese v. State of Rhode Island, 749 F.2d 934 (1st Cir.1984), the district court found that this exception was not available here because the "entertainment" facts could have been uncovered if Manego had been diligent in his discovery efforts. The court then went on to reason that because the legal theory which rested upon the "entertainment" facts *could have been* asserted during the prior suit, *res judicata* applied to bar its assertion in a later suit. We believe, however, that, once the reasonable discovery issue is resolved, the focus of a "transactional" analysis is not on whether a second claim could have been brought in a prior suit, but whether the underlying facts of both transactions were the same or substantially similar.

There will be situations where the factual bases for separate causes of action are different but intertwined and joining them together is both possible and convenient. A failure to do so, however, will not justify the application of *res judicata*. A good illustration of this can be found in Landrigan v. City of Warwick, 628 F.2d 736 (1st Cir.1980), where we held that a law suit charging the police with covering-up an alleged use of excessive force was not precluded by a prior lawsuit based on the actual use of excessive force. The plaintiff in *Landrigan* could have pursued both causes of action in the same lawsuit and it might have been very convenient to do so, since the alleged cover-up was intimately connected to the initial police misconduct. We found, however, that because the factual basis for the cover-up was distinct from the factual basis for the misconduct, the plaintiff was not required to do so. This is to be contrasted with a situation in which the factual basis for each claim is essentially the same, so that not only *could* both claims be joined in one lawsuit, but [they] *must* be joined or be barred by *res judicata*. A good example is again provided by *Landrigan,* where we held that a prior state court suit for assault and battery precluded a later federal suit under § 1983 for excessive use of force.

The question, therefore, is whether the absence from [the earlier suit] of an allegation that the bank had plans to offer live music and dancing at the rink creates a transactional difference precluding the application of *res judicata*. Manego now argues that because an allegation that the rink and disco were competitors was essential to provide a motive for a conspiracy to restrain trade, the factual basis for such a conspiracy is distinctly different from that needed to show racial discrimination and that the antitrust action cannot be considered to arise from the same transaction or series of transactions. The answer to this question depends upon whether the underlying facts are the same regardless of the different motives, i.e., racial discrimination and restraint of trade. Aside from motive, the conduct alleged is precisely the same, i.e., the actions of the bank and Willard vis-a-vis the proposed disco. Each alleged conspiracy had the same practical end—keeping Manego from operating the disco—and each used essentially the same means—denial of the licenses, intimidation of building suppliers, and an ultimately withdrawn lawsuit challenging a building permit. This is not a case like *Landrigan* where, although the events in question are closely connected in time and space, two relatively distinct sets of facts can be separated out as the bases for separate legal wrongs. We conclude, therefore, that the difference in motive for the conspiracy does not create a separate transaction. This means that once Manego chose to allege a conspiracy involving particular specified conspiratorial acts he was required to allege all possible motives for such a conspiracy and all facts necessary to support these allegations or lose the right to do so. Whether

Choice or incompetence doesn't matter,

he took that risk by failure to discover the facts which diligent effort would have unearthed or by deliberate choice, the result is the same: the antitrust claim is barred by *res judicata* as to the bank and Willard.

DEFENDANT ORLEANS BOARD OF TRADE

The Board of Trade moved for summary judgment on the grounds that the present suit was barred by the doctrine of *res judicata* and that there was no genuine issue of material fact which would allow Manego to fall under an exception to the *Noerr-Pennington* doctrine. The district court found that *res judicata* did not apply, but that Manego had not alleged facts sufficient to overcome the protection provided by *Noerr-Pennington*,[c] and granted summary judgment for the Board of Trade. The district court's treatment of both these issues was excellent and we see no point in gilding the lily. We affirm the grant of summary judgment to the Board of Trade and its members on the basis of the district court's opinion.

NOTES AND QUESTIONS

1.   The Court of Appeals' opinion affirming summary judgment for defendants in Manego's first suit, 692 F.2d 174 (1st Cir.1982), recounted facts that put Manego in a more sympathetic light and indicate evidentiary support for both his civil rights and antitrust conspiracy claims. In February 1979, arsonists set fire to a building he owned in the area. An affidavit from the building contractor he had hired to build his disco stated that the bank had pressured one of his suppliers not to supply Manego's project and that local persons had uttered racial slurs against the contractor because of his association with Manego. A license for a similar operation was granted to a white man a year and a half after Manego's application was denied. The court noted, however:

> We recognize that, to a lay person, aggregating all of the circumstances of plaintiff's case—the denial of his license, the granting—a half year later—of a license to a white man, the fact that someone set fire to his property, and rumors that unnamed persons had uttered racial slurs—might suggest the old adage that where there is smoke, there is fire. In this case, however, the district judge invited the plaintiff to lead him to at least some glowing embers and plaintiff failed to do so. The district court recognized, properly, that smoke alone is not enough to force the defendants to a trial to prove their actions were not discriminatory.

Id. at 177. Should this information affect the res judicata issue?

---

[c]   The plaintiff had contended that two exceptions to the *Noerr-Pennington* doctrine applied: the "sham" exception, which applies where a party seeks not to influence public officials but to bar its competitor from meaningful access to adjudicatory tribunals, and the "conspiracy" exception, which applies where government officials participate with private individuals in a scheme to restrain trade.—Eds.

2. Why wasn't the Board of Trade entitled to assert the defense of res judicata in *Manego*? *Their 1st time being Sued*

3. How can it be said that the second suit in *Manego* (for violation of the antitrust act through a conspiracy among the bank, Willard, and the Board of Trade) was the same claim as the earlier suit (for violation of the civil rights statutes through a conspiracy among the bank, Willard, and the Board of Selectmen)? Since the elements of an antitrust cause of action are different from a civil rights cause of action, why aren't these different claims? Further, how can res judicata apply here when the parties are different? *Applies to where parties R the same. The underlying facts R the same*

4. Under the transactional test adopted in *Manego,* how does a court determine the "factual basis" of each suit? In *Manego,* the second suit alleged a number of facts not raised in the first suit. It gave a new account of the role of the Board of Selectmen and of the interrelationship between the bank and Willard. It also relied heavily on the claim that the bank had plans to offer live music and dancing at its rink. Wouldn't these allegations add significantly different facts to what was alleged in the first suit? How can these be called the same "factual basis" as the first suit? In a later case, the First Circuit described the transactional test as asking whether the claims derive from the "same nucleus of operative facts," with relevant factors being whether the facts are [1] related in time, space, origin, or motivation; [2] whether they form a convenient trial unit; and [3] whether treating them as a unit conforms to the parties' expectations. Apparel Art Int'l, Inc. v. Amertex Enter., 48 F.3d 576, 584 (1st Cir.1995). Does *Manego* satisfy this test?

5. Are the tests for determining the "same transaction or occurrence" for purposes of a compulsory counterclaim in Rule 13(a), supra p. 284, or for purposes of relation back of amendments under Rule 15(c), supra p. 236, applicable to the transactional test for res judicata? Recall the language in Wigglesworth v. Teamsters Local No. 592, defining transaction or occurrence for purposes of compulsory counterclaims by reference to a "same evidence" standard.

6. The plaintiff in *Manego* claimed that he learned of the bank's plans to offer live music and dancing only three days before summary judgment was entered. How could he have been expected to plead these facts in the first suit? How does the court determine what facts plaintiff should know when he files the first suit? Cf. Rule 11.

Ct. says he should have discovered it in "discovery"

Would it have made a difference if Manego had based his second suit on events that *occurred* after his first suit was filed? In Pleming v. Universal-Rundle Corp., 142 F.3d 1354 (11th Cir.1998), plaintiff claimed that defendant employer discriminated against her when it refused her request to switch from her laborer job to a clerical job after she was injured at work. Defendant asserted that it had not discriminated based on its policy against allowing employees to transfer to lower paying jobs. During discovery, plaintiff found out that, while her suit was pending, defendant had filled two more clerical positions with other applicants, and she referred to these later events in her opposition to defendant's motion for summary judgment to show that defendant's purported policy was a pretext for discrimination. The district court eventually granted defendant's motion for summary judgment on the ground plaintiff had failed to prove that defendant's explanation for its decision was a pretext.

Plaintiff then filed a second suit, alleging that defendant discriminated against her in hiring others for the later two openings, and the district court held that res judicata barred the suit. Observing that res judicata "depends upon whether the primary right and duty are the same in both cases," the court of appeals ruled that res judicata did not apply because plaintiff never formally asserted claims for the later incidents in the first suit. It noted that Rule 15(d) governs supplemental complaints and saw the issue as "whether the discussion of a related but distinct cause of action in briefs amounts to the *actual assertion* of that claim in the first proceeding." Because no supplemental complaint, amendment pursuant to Rule 15(b), or consideration of the claim in a pretrial order pursuant to Rule 16(e) had occurred, the court viewed the "isolated reference" to the later events in a decision in the first case as insufficient to show that the district court "actually adjudicated an unpled and unasserted claim."

7.   In *Landrigan,* which is described in *Manego,* why was the factual basis for the first suit (based on assault and battery) considered different from that in the second suit (based on the police cover-up of the use of excessive force)? Are they really "two relatively distinct sets of facts," as the *Manego* court suggests in distinguishing the case? Is it significant that the first suit was based on a state-law claim in a state court while the second was based on a federal civil rights claim in a federal court?

8.   In Whole Woman's Health v. Hellerstedt, 136 S.Ct. 2292 (2016), the Supreme Court invalidated a Texas law, H.B. 2, that (1) required abortion providers to have admitting privileges at local hospitals and (2) required abortion clinics to meet minimum standards for ambulatory surgical centers. Before reaching the merits of the claim that the two requirements imposed an undue burden on the right to choose an abortion, the Court faced the question whether claim preclusion barred the action. A prior suit, brought by some of the same abortion providers, sought to invalidate the admitting privileges portion of Texas law on its face, but was unsuccessful. See Planned Parenthood of Texas v. Abbott, 748 F.3d 583 (5th Cir. 2014). The Fifth Circuit viewed the earlier decision in *Abbott* as claim preclusive of the later litigation. The Supreme Court disagreed.

As for the challenge to the requirement of admitting privileges, the Court found that circumstances had changed and that such a change meant that the two claims were in fact different (136 S.Ct. at 2305–06):

> The Restatement of Judgments notes that development of new material facts can mean that a new case and an otherwise similar previous case do not present the same claim. See Restatement (Second) of Judgments § 24, Comment *f* (1980) ("Material operative facts occurring after the decision of an action with respect to the same

subject matter may in themselves, or taken in conjunction with the antecedent facts, comprise a transaction which may be made the basis of a second action not precluded by the first"); cf. *id.*, § 20(2) ("A valid and final personal judgment for the defendant, which rests on the prematurity of the action or on the plaintiff's failure to satisfy a precondition to suit, does not bar another action by the plaintiff instituted after the claim has matured, or the precondition has been satisfied"). The Courts of Appeals have used similar rules to determine the contours of a new claim for purposes of preclusion. The Restatement adds that, where "important human values—such as the lawfulness of continuing personal disability or restraint—are at stake, even a slight change of circumstances may afford a sufficient basis for concluding that a second action may be brought." § 24, Comment *f.*

* * *

Changed circumstances of this kind are why the claim presented in *Abbott* is not the same claim as petitioners' claim here. The claims in both *Abbott* and the present case involve "important human values." Restatement (Second) of Judgments § 24, Comment *f.* We are concerned with H.B. 2's "effect . . . on women seeking abortions." And that effect has changed dramatically since petitioners filed their first lawsuit. *Abbott* rested on facts and evidence presented to the District Court in October 2013. Petitioners' claim in this case rests in significant part upon later, concrete factual developments. Those developments matter. The *Abbott* plaintiffs brought their facial challenge to the admitting-privileges requirement *prior to its enforcement*—before many abortion clinics had closed and while it was still unclear how many clinics would be affected. Here, petitioners bring an as-applied challenge to the requirement *after its enforcement*—and after a large number of clinics have in fact closed. The post-enforcement consequences of H.B. 2 were unknowable before it went into effect. The *Abbott* court itself recognized that "[l]ater as-applied challenges can always deal with subsequent, concrete constitutional issues." And the Court of Appeals in this case properly decided that new evidence presented by petitioners had given rise to a new claim and that petitioners' as-applied challenges are not precluded.

When individuals claim that a particular statute will produce serious constitutionally relevant adverse consequences before they have occurred—and when the courts doubt their likely occurrence— the factual difference that those adverse consequences *have in fact occurred* can make all the difference. Compare the Fifth Circuit's opinion in the earlier case ("All of the major Texas cities . . . continue to have multiple clinics where many physicians will have or obtain hospital admitting privileges"), with the facts found in this case (the two provisions will leave Texas with seven or eight clinics). The challenge brought in this case and the one in *Abbott* are not the "very same claim," and the doctrine of claim preclusion consequently does not bar a new challenge to the constitutionality of the admitting-privileges requirement. In sum, the Restatement, cases from the Courts of Appeals, our own precedent, and simple logic combine to convince us that res judicata does not bar this claim.

As for the challenge to the surgical-center standards set for abortion clinics, a claim omitted from the *Abbott* litigation, the Court found that it differed from the claim challenging admitting privileges (id. at 2307–08):

> The Court of Appeals also held that claim preclusion barred petitioners from contending that the surgical-center requirement is unconstitutional. Although it recognized that petitioners did not bring this claim in *Abbott,* it believed that they should have done so. The court explained that petitioners' constitutional challenge to the surgical-center requirement and the challenge to the admitting-privileges requirement mounted in *Abbott* "arise from the same 'transactio[n] or series of connected transactions.' . . . The challenges involve the same parties and abortion facilities; the challenges are governed by the same legal standards; the provisions at issue were enacted at the same time as part of the same act; the provisions were motivated by a common purpose; the provisions are administered by the same state officials; and the challenges form a convenient trial unit because they rely on a common nucleus of operative facts." For all these reasons, the Court of Appeals held petitioners' challenge to H.B. 2's surgical-center requirement was precluded.

> The Court of Appeals failed, however, to take account of meaningful differences. The surgical-center provision and the admitting-privileges provision are separate, distinct provisions of H.B. 2. They set forth two different, independent requirements with different enforcement dates. This Court has never suggested that challenges to two different statutory provisions that serve two different functions must be brought in a single suit. And lower courts normally treat challenges to distinct regulatory requirements as "separate claims," even when they are part of one overarching "[g]overnment regulatory scheme." 18 C. Wright, A. Miller, & E. Cooper, Federal Practice and Procedure § 4408, p. 52 (2d ed. 2002, Supp. 2015).

> That approach makes sense. The opposite approach adopted by the Court of Appeals would require treating every statutory enactment as a single transaction which a given party would only be able to challenge one time, in one lawsuit, in order to avoid the effects of claim preclusion. Such a rule would encourage a kitchen-sink approach to any litigation challenging the validity of statutes. That outcome is less than optimal—not only for litigants, but for courts.

Although the Supreme Court based its definition of the scope of the claim on the Second Restatement, its application of the transactional test appears to differ from that in *Manego*. How would you characterize the claims in *Whole Woman's Health*? Do they all arise from the undue burden placed by H.B. 2 on a woman's right to an abortion? Would the new facts invoked in *Manego* give rise to a relevant change in circumstances within the meaning of *Whole Woman's Health*? What distinguishes the antitrust theory of liability identified by Manego in his second suit from the alternative theory underlying the providers' challenge to the Texas surgical-center requirement?

9.   Many older cases did not follow the transactional test endorsed by the Restatement (Second) of Judgments and adopted in *Manego*. It was often held that causes of action were different if they involved different "rights" and "wrongs." See Baltimore S.S. Co. v. Phillips, 274 U.S. 316 (1927). For example, in Smith v. Kirkpatrick, 111 N.E.2d 209 (N.Y.1953), plaintiff sued his employer for money due him under a theory of quantum meruit, after having lost a previous suit for the same sum based on an oral contract because it did not comply with the Statute of Frauds. The court declined to find the second suit barred by res judicata, stating:

> The two actions involve different "rights" and "wrongs." The requisite elements of proof and hence the evidence necessary to sustain recovery vary materially. The causes of action are different and distinct and the rights and interests established by the previous adjudication will not be impaired by a recovery, if that be the outcome, in quantum meruit.

What did the *Smith* court mean by saying the suits involved "different rights and wrongs"? Is it because they involved different proof and evidence? Would that indicate that the theories raised in the two suits would not make a convenient trial package and therefore that res judicata should not be used to prevent splitting the cause of action? If that is so, wouldn't the same rationale be applicable in *Manego* where the antitrust claim would seem to require different evidence from the civil rights claim? Does the transactional test leave room for considering whether the claims would be a convenient trial package? Is the "right-wrong" distinction a more satisfactory test?

In *Smith,* the judge in the first case noted that the defendant had clearly overreached the plaintiff, but that plaintiff could not recover on the oral contract because of the Statute of Frauds and had not pleaded quantum meruit. Should sympathy for a plaintiff who had a good cause of action but lost the first time because of faulty lawyering be a factor in deciding whether to apply res judicata? Is there a better procedural response? Compare Rule 15(b).

10. If the holder of a series of notes, all of which are due and in default, sues on only one, will the judgment constitute a merger or bar as to the others? The general answer is no, because each note is a separate liability arising out of a separate transaction. But what if all the notes were given as payment in a single commercial transaction? The traditional view is also that they are separate liabilities, and the plaintiff may choose to sue on them separately,

although under the modern transactional approach this may not be so certain, depending on the facts. What if there is a common reason for the default that will require the same evidence in each suit on any of the notes—as that they are invalid for charging usurious interest, or that the holder defaulted on the consideration that was paid for them, or that an identical clause in each of them is the center of the dispute? Should they not be considered the same transaction for purposes of res judicata? See generally F. James, G. Hazard & J. Leubsdorf, Civil Procedure § 11.11 (5th ed. 2001).

11. Under the Restatement's "transactional" test, a final judgment extinguishes all rights against the defendant with respect to "the transaction, *or series of connected transactions*, out of which the action arose." Restatement (Second) of Judgments § 24. What groupings constitute a "series" is "to be determined pragmatically" based on "such considerations as whether the facts are related in time, space, origin, or motivation, whether they form a convenient trial unit, and whether their treatment as a unit conforms to the parties' expectations or business understanding or usage." This issue can arise in employment discrimination cases where the employee, whose first suit went to judgment, files a second later suit alleging discriminatory acts of a somewhat different nature. In Havercombe v. Department of Education of the Commonwealth of Puerto Rico, 250 F.3d 1 (1st Cir. 2001), the plaintiff won a judgment based on allegations of race and age discrimination, and then filed a second suit alleging additional acts of discrimination. The court found the second suit precluded as part of a series of connected transactions based on similar allegations of discriminatory animus and of a hostile work environment "that does not turn on single acts but on an aggregation of acts over a period of time". It also found no basis for invoking the exceptions to claim-splitting in the Restatement—"where formal barriers existed against full presentation of claim in the first action or where the defendant has committed fraud on the plaintiff by concealing evidence of a part or phase of claim that the plaintiff failed to include in an earlier action." Restatement, supra, § 26.

12. Decisions of administrative agencies are entitled to preclusive effect when the agency acted in a judicial capacity. University of Tennessee v. Elliott, 478 U.S. 788 (1986). Restatement (Second) of Judgments, § 83(2) provides that an adjudicative determination by an administrative tribunal has preclusive effect only insofar as the proceeding entailed the essential elements of adjudication, including adequate notice to persons who are to be bound, right to present evidence and legal argument, formulation of issues of law and fact in terms of the application of rules to the specific transaction, a rule of finality, and such other procedural elements as may be necessary to conclusively determine the matter in question. See also B & B Hardware, Inc. v. Hargis Industries, Inc., 135 S.Ct. 1293 (2015) (discussed at p. 1233 infra) (holding that federal agency decisions in contested trademark registration proceedings are entitled to preclusive effect in subsequent federal court proceedings).

13. The doctrine of "election of remedies" can have an effect somewhat similar to the prohibition on splitting a cause of action. The doctrine, now increasingly rejected or limited, views the pleading of an action for one remedy

as an irrevocable election preventing the pleader from later seeking a different remedy. Consider Homeland Training Center LLC v. Summit Point Automotive Research Center, 594 F.3d 285 (4th Cir. 2010). Following an anticipatory breach of contract, the non-repudiating party first sought specific performance. When that came to nothing, the party sought damages instead. The district court refused to allow the switch, citing an election of remedies. But the appellate court reversed, observing that the doctrine of election of remedies no longer applied with its customary rigor to require an irrevocable choice of remedy at the outset of the litigation. Rather, the parties may pursue a range of alternative remedies simultaneously. Any modern election of remedies will be imposed only after judgment has been rendered, and will operate to prevent a windfall or double recovery.

OTHER ACTION PENDING

Parties sometimes file two or more suits on the same cause of action in different courts which are pending at the same time (referred to as repetitive or duplicative suits). Reasons for this include doubts as to jurisdiction in some of the fora, concern about missing the statute of limitations deadline if some of the suits are dismissed on non-merits grounds, desire to be able to forum-shop according to choice of law and other pre-trial determinations, and sometimes simply the urge to harass the other party.

A party subjected to repetitive suits need not wait until one goes to judgment and then raise it as a bar to prosecution of the other; the simultaneous defense of multiple suits is itself an onerous burden. It is possible instead to raise the defense of "other action pending," thus seeking a dismissal if there is another action on the same cause of action pending in the same state or federal district court. In evaluating the defense of "other action pending," the federal courts apply claim preclusion principles, essentially asking what impact a final disposition of the first proceeding would have on the second proceeding. See The Haytian Republic, 154 U.S. 118 (1894); Adams v. California Dep't of Health Services, 487 F.3d 684 (9th Cir. 2007).

Where a repetitive suit is pending in a different state court, a defendant may seek to enjoin the opposing party from prosecuting the repetitive suit or seek an order staying the repetitive suit pending completion of the first suit. See Fidelity & Deposit Co. v. Santa Monica Finance Co., 6 Cal. Rptr. 213 (Cal.App. 1960). The suit that was first-in-time is usually given priority, but other considerations may alter that priority. When the suits are pending in state and federal court, issues of federalism may complicate matters. In general, the Supreme Court has permitted parties to seek duplicative forms of *in personam* relief in state and federal court. See Kline v. Burke Construction Co., 260 U.S. 226 (1922) (duplicative actions for contract damages in state and federal court). As a consequence, courts have been reluctant to allow injunctions against such repetitive proceedings. Federal injunctions against state proceedings must comply with the Anti-Injunction Act, 28 U.S.C. § 2283, which does not so much bar such injunctions as regulate their availability. See Smith v. Bayer Corp., 564 U.S. 299 (2011) (narrowly interpreting district court authority under the relitigation, or res judicata, exception to anti-injunction act); Mitchum v. Foster, 407 U.S. 225 (1972) (reading 42 U.S.C. § 1983 as an exception to the prohibition against injunctions to stay proceedings in state court). No statute bars state courts from enjoining federal proceedings, but the Supreme Court has said that state courts should refrain from doing so unless the state-court action seeks *in rem* relief and involves title to property over which the state court first asserted control. See Donovan v. City of Dallas, 377 U.S. 408 (1964).

If a defendant faced with repetitive suits moves to dismiss or stay the second suit for "other action pending," the issue of their similarity would be resolved at that time and if the second suit were dismissed or stayed, that would not constitute a bar to the continued prosecution of the other. Thus a dismissal or stay for "other action pending" might be viewed as less harsh to the plaintiff than allowing one of the suits to go to final judgment and then bar the other under res judicata. Should a defendant be required to use remedies available under "other action pending" as a prerequisite to raising the defense of res judicata later? Would it ever be appropriate to view the dismissal of the second action as a disposition on the merits? Such a dismissal could have claim preclusive effect and might be viewed as barring the first proceeding.

2. EXCEPTIONS TO THE RULE AGAINST SPLITTING A CAUSE OF ACTION

Res judicata is often referred to as a rule for enforcing the prohibition against "splitting a cause of action," that is, not suing on all the theories arising out of the matters being litigated and then attempting to raise them in a second suit. The prohibition against splitting a cause of action reflects not only the desirability of finality in litigation but also concern for the efficient use of judicial resources. On some occasions, however, there are good reasons for withholding some aspect of the claim for future litigation, as when, due to procedural or substantive limitations, a party may be involuntarily forced to split his cause of action.

Notably, the rule applies both to plaintiffs, who choose the forum and procedural system at least initially, and to defendants. There is little problem with *defenses:* if a defendant fails to raise defenses available to it, it cannot as a general rule thereafter use them to attack the judgment. See Restatement (Second) of Judgments § 18(2). The treatment of *counterclaims* is more involved. When a defendant actually raises a counterclaim, all aspects of it are subject to the rules of claim preclusion. The only exception is the rare case when the defendant cannot obtain full recovery on his counterclaim (as in a court of limited jurisdiction from which the defendant could not remove the case). Id., §§ 21, 23. In that case, merger should not apply to prevent a second suit for the amount not recoverable. Id., § 21(2).

When the defendant does not raise a counterclaim available to it, there are further considerations. In the case of a *compulsory counterclaim* (i.e., one arising out of the same transaction or occurrence as the claim), economy concerns and the interest in consistent judgments favor requiring the defendant to raise the counterclaim or lose it. Federal Rule 13(a) contemplates such a result, as do the majority of states that have a compulsory counterclaim rule.

CAPITOL HILL GROUP, INC. v. PILLSBURY, WINTHROP, SHAW, PITTMAN, LLP

United States Court of Appeals for the D.C. Circuit, 2009
569 F.3d 485

Before BROWN, HENDERSON, and KAVANAUGH, Circuit Judges

BROWN, Circuit Judge:

Appellant Capitol Hill Group (CHG) filed suit in the Superior Court of the District of Columbia against its former counsel, Shaw Pittman (now Pillsbury Winthrop Shaw Pittman LLP) and various associated attorneys, for claims stemming from alleged legal malpractice. Appellees removed the case to federal court, asserting federal jurisdiction under 28 U.S.C. § 1334(b), so-called "arising in" bankruptcy jurisdiction. The district court denied appellant's motion to remand for lack of jurisdiction, and later granted summary judgment for appellees because CHG's claims are barred by res judicata. Finding no error, we affirm.

I.

To make a long and already well-documented story short—well, somewhat shorter—we summarize the relevant facts. CHG filed for bankruptcy in February 2002. CHG's primary asset, commercial property in the District of Columbia, was embroiled in a zoning dispute with the District's Department of Consumer and Regulatory Affairs regarding the amount of off-street parking required. The controversy continued during the bankruptcy proceedings and Shaw Pittman, CHG's court-approved bankruptcy counsel, represented CHG in the zoning process.

[The Zoning Administrator initially required CHG to provide 255 off-street parking places. That number was later reduced to 85, but a local neighborhood group appealed and the Bureau of Zoning Adjustment (BZA) settled on 177 parking places in an oral February 2004 order. In September 2004, BZA issued a written order, confirming that figure. By that point, the bankruptcy court had granted Shaw Pittman's request to terminate its representation of CHG. While Shaw Pittman returned its BZA-related files to CHG, it did not tell the BZA it had stopped representing CHG. Perhaps as a result, BZA sent its September 2004 order to Shaw Pittman but not to CHG. CHG's malpractice claims focused in part on the failure of Shaw Pittman to inform CHG of the September 2004 order.]

CHG and Shaw Pittman's post-representation relations were rocky. CHG first complained that Shaw Pittman's fees were unreasonable. After contested hearings, the bankruptcy judge granted summary judgment to Shaw Pittman and [in the district court's words] "awarded the firm fees based primarily on its conclusion that CHG had agreed not to contest the amount of the fees. The bankruptcy judge also made oral findings that Shaw Pittman's services were professional and that Shaw Pittman deserved to be compensated for those services." The district court affirmed the bankruptcy court's decision.

[The fee disputes continued before the bankruptcy court, producing four more decisions all upholding Shaw Pittman's fee applications.] On April 12, 2006, the parties made one final appearance before the bankruptcy court, after Shaw Pittman [sought to determine if] CHG was withholding further claims. The bankruptcy court specifically asked CHG whether it had any other claims against the firm. CHG's counsel stated "[t]here are concerns that CHG has about the representation that Shaw Pittman provided during its representation of Capitol Hill Group that began in 1999 or whatever. But nothing's been filed." CHG also represented it "had no outstanding claims against Shaw Pittman arising out of the bankruptcy proceedings." In addition, "[t]he bankruptcy court noted that CHG could have pursued malpractice claims against Shaw Pittman regarding the adequacy of its representation," in addition to claims CHG had made about excessive fees and related professional misconduct, "but that it had failed to do so and would therefore be barred from later asserting such claims by the doctrine of res judicata."

In this suit, CHG alleges Shaw Pittman committed malpractice in two respects: by failing to notify CHG when BZA issued the September 2004 order, and by failing to make a particular legal argument to the BZA. Shaw Pittman removed the case to federal court. The district court concluded it had jurisdiction, and granted summary judgment for appellees because CHG's claims are barred by res judicata.

We have jurisdiction under 28 U.S.C. § 1291 from the final order of the district court granting summary judgment for defendants. After such a final order, the district court's earlier denial of the motion to remand for lack of subject matter jurisdiction also is reviewable. We review the district court's legal conclusions regarding subject matter jurisdiction, including a denial of a motion to remand, *de novo*. And, of course, we review the district court's grant of summary judgment *de novo* as well.

II.

CHG insists the district court erred in exercising jurisdiction over this case under 28 U.S.C. § 1334(b), which provides "the district courts shall have original but not exclusive jurisdiction of all civil proceedings arising under title 11, or arising in or related to cases under title 11." "[P]roceedings or claims arising in Title 11 are those that are not based on any right expressly created by Title 11, but nevertheless, would have no existence outside of the bankruptcy."

* * *

In sum, we agree with our sister circuits that malpractice claims against court-appointed professionals stemming from services provided in the bankruptcy proceeding are "inseparable from the bankruptcy context," *Southmark Corp.* [*v. Coopers & Lybrand*, 163 F.3d 925, 931 (5th Cir. 1999)], and "constitute . . . a proceeding 'arising in' the bankruptcy." Such claims therefore fall within the bankruptcy jurisdiction of the federal courts.

III.

CHG argues res judicata should not bar it from pressing its malpractice claims against Shaw Pittman despite the fee litigation during the bankruptcy proceedings. "Under the doctrine of res judicata, or claim preclusion, a subsequent lawsuit will be barred if there has been prior litigation (1) involving the same claims or cause of action, (2) between the same parties or their privies, and (3) there has been a final, valid judgment on the merits, (4) by a court of competent jurisdiction." *Smalls v. United States,* 471 F.3d 186, 192 (D.C.Cir.2006).

CHG's arguments go to the first element listed, the so-called "identity" element; the existence of the other three elements is not contested. As the district court explained, "there is an identity of the causes of action when the cases are based on the 'same nucleus of facts' because 'it is the facts surrounding the transaction or occurrence which operate to constitute the cause of action, not the legal theory on which a litigant relies.'" *Capitol Hill Group,* 574 F.Supp.2d at 149 (quoting *Page v. United States,* 729 F.2d 818, 820 (D.C.Cir.1984)). Put a little more pithily, "claim preclusion precludes the litigation of *claims,* not just *arguments."*

A.

The district court relied primarily on three cases in granting summary judgment for appellees under the doctrine of res judicata: *Grausz* [*v. Englander*, 321 F.3d 467 (4th Cir. 2003)], *Iannochino v. Rodolakis (In re Iannochino),* 242 F.3d 36 (1st Cir.2001), and *Osherow v. Ernst & Young LLP (In re Intelogic Trace, Inc.),* 200 F.3d 382 (5th Cir.2000). In each, fee litigation in the bankruptcy proceeding precluded later malpractice claims against the bankruptcy professionals to whom the fees had been awarded.

CHG argues that, as in the Fourth Circuit's unpublished decision in *Kronish Lieb Weiner & Hellman, LLP v. Fort,* 197 Fed.Appx. 261 (4th Cir.2006) , this case arises from a different nucleus of operative facts than the fee litigation, and therefore *Iannochino, Osherow,* and *Grausz* are inapposite. We disagree. In *Kronish,* the Fourth Circuit held a Consent Order resolving a bankruptcy claim for fees stemming from pre-petition legal services did not bar the trustee of the bankruptcy estate from bringing a malpractice action against the law firm. Unlike in this case, there was no litigation before the bankruptcy court about the adequacy of the representation or the reasonableness of the fees; the claim was allowed and not contested by anyone. Moreover, the legal services at issue took place prior to the filing of the bankruptcy petition. Because the claim was for pre-petition services, the bankruptcy court had no basis on which to evaluate the quality of the legal services. As a result, the Fourth Circuit distinguished *Grausz,* its own precedent. In this case, however, [the disputed legal services were provided in connection with the bankruptcy proceeding,] there was an adversarial process before the bankruptcy court and the bankruptcy court was in a position to judge the quality of Shaw Pittman's services. We look to *Grausz,* rather than *Kronish*, and thus agree with the district court that the fee applications and the malpractice claim arise out of the same nucleus of facts and the identity element of res judicata is satisfied.

B.

Res judicata may not bar a later suit where the plaintiff was not aware of its claim at the time of the first litigation. CHG contends it had neither actual nor constructive knowledge of its claims during the bankruptcy fee litigation.

CHG insists it had no *actual* knowledge of Shaw Pittman's failure to forward the [September 2004] BZA order until March 2005, and became aware of Shaw Pittman's failure to make a particular legal argument on the parking issue in the "Spring of 2006." CHG quickly goes on to assert, in the next paragraph of its brief, "therefore . . . CHG had neither actual *nor constructive* knowledge." But, of course, when CHG gained actual knowledge of specific claims tells us nothing about its actual or constructive knowledge of the operative facts.

The district court found CHG's claims barred for two reasons: CHG (1) had actual knowledge of the general nature of its claims against Shaw Pittman, as evidenced by the arguments it did raise during the fee litigation, and (2) also had constructive knowledge. That is, CHG would have discovered the specifics of each of the two claims, had it acted with due diligence. In April 2006, at the last hearing during the bankruptcy court fee litigation, the bankruptcy judge asked CHG whether it had any other claims against Shaw Pittman, and CHG's counsel stated "[t]here are concerns that CHG has about the representation that Shaw Pittman provided during its representation of Capitol Hill Group that began in 1999 or whatever. But nothing's been filed." Moreover, at that same April 2006 hearing, counsel for Shaw Pittman and the bankruptcy judge each noted it was their understanding that future claims arising from the representation would be barred by res judicata. Following that warning and without objection from CHG, the bankruptcy judge announced the final conclusion of the fee litigation that same day.

"[R]es judicata . . . bars relitigation not only of matters determined in a previous litigation but also ones a party could have raised[.]" *NRDC v. Thomas,* 838 F.2d 1224, 1252 (D.C.Cir.1988). In April 2006, CHG was aware of Shaw Pittman's failure to forward the written BZA order, and could have become aware of the failure to make the historic designation legal argument. As in the *Osherow* case, here CHG "was sufficiently aware of the real possibility of there being errors by [the bankruptcy professional] such as now alleged and of their likely consequences before the fee hearing." "[R]ather than considering whether the [debtors] knew of the precise legal contours of their malpractice claim at the time of the fee application, we must instead determine whether they knew of the factual basis of that claim." *Iannochino,* 242 F.3d at 48–49. When CHG decided to litigate Shaw Pittman's fees, raising broad professional responsibility arguments questioning the representation, CHG's duty to discover the legal errors (if any) committed by Shaw Pittman was triggered. As the First Circuit observed, "the breakdown of the attorney/client relationship here is further evidence that the [debtors] should have raised their malpractice claims as objections to the fee award." *Id.* at 49. And as CHG was warned they would be, these claims are now precluded.

C.

CHG also argues its claims, which it asserts were permissive rather than compulsory counterclaims, cannot be automatically precluded. The First Circuit has described the principle: the "failure to interpose a counterclaim does not necessarily act as a bar to later actions." *Iannochino,* 242 F.3d at 41. There are two "exceptions" which lead to a later action being barred by res judicata: (1) compulsory counterclaims may be barred, and (2) permissive counterclaims too may be barred when "the relationship between the counterclaim and the plaintiff's claim is such that the successful prosecution of the second action would nullify the initial judgment or impair the rights established in the initial action." *Id.* at 42 (quoting RESTATEMENT (SECOND) OF JUDGMENTS § 22(2)(b)). That is, res judicata may generally bar compulsory counterclaims, but not always permissive ones; otherwise res judicata would swallow Rule 13. But if allowing a permissive counterclaim to go forward would nullify the earlier judgment or impair rights established in the earlier action, even a permissive counterclaim can be barred.

In this case, we need not determine whether CHG's claims against Shaw Pittman were permissive or compulsory counterclaims because they are barred under the second "exception" regardless. The bankruptcy judge repeatedly awarded fees to Shaw Pittman for the services rendered to CHG in connection with its bankruptcy proceedings, and the district court affirmed the awards. *E.g., In re Capitol Hill Group,* 313 B.R. 344, 349–51 (D.D.C.2004) (rejecting CHG's equitable breach of fiduciary duty/breach of professional conduct argument). As the district court noted in granting summary judgment, the bankruptcy judge also made oral findings that Shaw Pittman's services were professional and that Shaw Pittman deserved to be compensated for those services. At the final hearing before the bankruptcy court, the judge informed CHG it "could have pursued claims against Shaw Pittman regarding the adequacy of its representation . . . at the bankruptcy fee hearings but that it failed to do so and would therefore be barred from later asserting claims based on Shaw Pittman's representation by the doctrine of res judicata."

To allow CHG to litigate malpractice claims against Shaw Pittman now, based on the same representation, would nullify the initial judgment or impair the rights established by Shaw Pittman in the bankruptcy fee litigation. Unlike in regular civil litigation, "[i]n bankruptcy . . . a successful malpractice action could impair rights that [the bankruptcy professionals] had gained from the order awarding them fees. Under the relevant section of the bankruptcy code governing fee awards, a finding of malpractice would mean that the attorneys were not entitled to compensation for those services found to be substandard. *Iannochino,* 242 F.3d at 42–43; *see Southmark Corp.,* 163 F.3d at 931 ("Award of the professionals' fees and enforcement of the appropriate standards of conduct are inseparably related functions of bankruptcy courts.").

IV.

The judgment of the district court is *Affirmed.*

NOTES AND QUESTIONS

1.   Why did Capitol Hill Group withhold its malpractice claims from the bankruptcy proceeding and seek to assert them later in a different court? Note that the bankruptcy judge had repeatedly ruled for Shaw Pittman and that further disputation in bankruptcy could have resulted in further fee applications as the law firm attempted to defend its conduct there. In a separate malpractice action, Capital Hill Group would have a different judge, a possible right to trial by jury, and the right to litigate any non-frivolous claims without paying Shaw Pittman's fees. Is it fair to force Capitol Hill Group to proceed in a disfavored forum?

2.   Is the exception (quoted in *Capital Hill Group*) for permissive counterclaims, as provided by Restatement (Second) § 22(2)(b), good policy? Should it apply to most cases where common facts support both a defense and

a counterclaim? Is the key to the test merely whether later recovery on the counterclaim would be inconsistent with the earlier judgment, or is something more required? Would it apply to the following situation (taken from Restatement (Second) of Judgments § 22, comment f)?

> A brings an action against B for failure to pay the contract price for goods sold and delivered and recovers judgment for default. After entry of final judgment and payment of the price, B brings an action against A to rescind the contract for mutual mistake, seeking restitution of the contract price and offering to return the goods.

3. Some judicial systems have no compulsory counterclaim rule. In such systems, a defendant will sometimes decline to assert a counterclaim and sue on it later. In general, if the defendant alleges as a defense the same facts that would support a counterclaim, he is not precluded from maintaining a subsequent action on the counterclaim. Schwabe v. Chantilly, Inc., 226 N.W.2d 452 (Wis.1975); Restatement (Second) of Judgments § 22 and comments c & d. The rationale seems to be that where the jurisdiction chose not to make the counterclaim compulsory (in *Schwabe,* Wisconsin made all counterclaims permissive), the defendant should have the freedom to select its own forum for its counterclaim. This rule obviously subordinates the benefits of requiring the defendant to litigate common issues in the same suit to the defendant's right to select the forum for his permissive counterclaim. (Note, however, that the defendant may be collaterally estopped from relitigating issues that were actually decided in the first suit, as in Little v. Blue Goose Motor Coach Co., infra p. 1210.)

Even in situations where the defendant might otherwise refrain from setting up a (permissive) counterclaim, preclusion may still apply under the doctrine of "common law compulsory counterclaims." This doctrine comes into play when "the relationship between the counterclaim and the plaintiff's claim is such that successful prosecution of the second action would nullify the initial judgment or would impair rights established in the initial action." Restatement (Second) of Judgments, § 22(2)(b). How should this rule apply to cross-claims, which Rule 13(g) allows but does not require one party to assert against a coparty so long as it arises from transactions or occurrences before the court?

4. In light of the rules of federal subject matter jurisdiction in Chapter 10, was the court right to exercise removal jurisdiction over the malpractice claims on which Capitol Hill Group sued? State law normally creates the right to sue for malpractice, as the Supreme Court confirmed in Gunn v. Minton, supra p. 892. Claim preclusion ordinarily operates as an defense to such a claim, and thus fails to confer subject matter jurisdiction under the well-pleaded complaint rule. For a time, the Supreme Court allowed removal where claims were artfully couched in terms of state law. See Federated Dept. Stores, Inc. v. Moitie, 452 U.S. 394 (1981). The Court has since considerably narrowed the artful pleading doctrine. See Rivet v. Regions Bank of Louisiana, 522 U.S. 470 (1998). There, the Court held that claim preclusion was a defensive plea that provided no basis for removal of a state law action, even one said essentially to duplicate a previously dismissed federal action. Did the court in

Capitol Hill Group find that the malpractice claim arose under federal law, or was jurisdiction based on other considerations?

5.   Can the federal courts recognize an exception to claim preclusion on the basis of equitable or fairness considerations? The Supreme Court said no in Federated Dept. Stores, Inc. v. Moitie, 452 U.S. 394 (1981). There, a variety of different plaintiffs filed suit to recover damages under the federal antitrust laws for price fixing in the market for women's clothing in Northern California. Their claims were dismissed on the basis that consumers were not proper parties to bring suit under the relevant statute. One group of plaintiffs appealed from that dismissal and had their claims reinstated when the Supreme Court later held that consumers were entitled to sue. A second group (including Moitie) declined to appeal from the adverse federal judgment and refiled similar claims in state court under state antitrust law. Following removal on now doubtful artful pleading grounds, the district court dismissed the Moitie claim as precluded. The Ninth Circuit reversed, viewing the differential treatment of two similarly situated groups of plaintiffs as an affront to simple justice.

The Supreme Court reversed in turn, explaining as follows (id. at 401):

> [W]e do not see the grave injustice which would be done by the application of accepted principles of res judicata. "Simple justice" is achieved when a complex body of law developed over a period of years is evenhandedly applied. The doctrine of res judicata serves vital public interests beyond any individual judge's ad hoc determination of the equities in a particular case. There is simply "no principle of law or equity which sanctions the rejection by a federal court of the salutary principle of res judicata." Heiser v. Woodruff, 327 U.S. 726, 733 (1946). The Court of Appeals' reliance on "public policy" is similarly misplaced. This Court has long recognized that "[p]ublic policy dictates that there be an end of litigation; that those who have contested an issue shall be bound by the result of the contest, and that matters once tried shall be considered forever settled as between the parties." Baldwin v. Traveling Men's Assn., 283 U.S. 522, 525 (1931). We have stressed that "[the] doctrine of res judicata is not a mere matter of practice or procedure inherited from a more technical time than ours. It is a rule of fundamental and substantial justice, 'of public policy and of private peace,' which should be cordially regarded and enforced by the courts. . ." Hart Steel Co. v. Railroad Supply Co., 244 U.S. 294, 299 (1917).

Do at least some "fairness" exceptions survive *Moitie?* Consider Adams v. Pearson, 104 N.E.2d 267 (Ill.1952), where a prior judgment, obtained by fraud, was not given res judicata effect. Compare Rule 60(b)(3) (permitting relief from judgment on grounds of fraud).

6.   Should a change in the law ever give a litigant a second chance? Consider Alvear-Velez v. Mukasey, 540 F.3d 672 (7th Cir. 2010), in which the government instituted criminal proceedings to remove or deport a foreign

national who had been convicted of sexual assault on a minor in 1993. The foreign national, Alvear-Velez, defended on the basis of claim preclusion: the 1993 conviction had been the subject of a previous proceeding brought to remove him from the country, a proceeding that had been dismissed on the merits in 1994. In instituting a second removal or deportation proceeding, the government pointed to the fact that Congress had amended the immigration laws in 1996, defining the commission of any crime involving sexual abuse of a minor as warranting removal and making its determination retroactive. The Seventh Circuit found that the intervening change in law triggered an exception to claim preclusion. It thus upheld an agency decision that Alvear-Velez was subject to removal. Can we understand the decision as recognizing ongoing power in Congress to change the terms on which foreign nationals are permitted to reside in the United States, thereby triggering a change in circumstances comparable to that in Whole Woman's Health v. Hellerstedt, supra p. 1171 n. 8?

Compare the following case: A California court entered a final divorce decree that made a division of property but did not mention the husband's matured military retirement pension. At that time, there was uncertainty as to whether federal military pensions could, consistent with federal law, be divided as community property under California law. Three years later the California Supreme Court held that they were properly subject to California community property law. The wife then filed suit to establish her community property interest in the pension.

Is she barred by res judicata? Note that a change in law in a later case would not help her; under *Moitie,* "the res judicata consequences of a final, unappealed judgment on the merits [are not] altered by the fact that the judgment may have been wrong or rested on a legal principle subsequently overruled in another case." But was the divorce decree a ruling that she had no right to the pension? The California Supreme Court said it was not, because, under California community property law, property which is not mentioned in the pleadings as community property is left unadjudicated by the divorce decree. Thus, under its interpretation of California law, the decree did not adjudicate the ownership of the pension, and she was allowed to litigate that issue in a later suit. See Henn v. Henn, 605 P.2d 10 (Cal.1980). But doesn't the rule of res judicata apply to whatever was part of the transaction raised in the suit and not merely to what was actually adjudicated? Is the court saying that the divorce court not only did not, but could not, have adjudicated the interest in the property? This case has been referred to as "manipulat[ing] the scope of the 'cause of action' to permit a renewed claim." F. James, G. Hazard & J. Leubsdorf, Civil Procedure 698 (5th ed. 2001). Do you agree? Is it justified as a fairness exception?

7.   Reed v. Allen, 286 U.S. 191 (1932), suggests another problem that can arise in connection with res judicata where there are multiple lawsuits between the parties. Suppose res judicata is available as a defense to a second lawsuit but is not raised, or, if raised, is improperly rejected by the court in the second case. If the second case is decided the other way, so that there are two

contradictory judgments, which is entitled to be given res judicata effect thereafter? On the one hand, the earlier decision might be preferred because that would take away the incentive to relitigate. On the other hand, res judicata is merely an affirmative defense, and it would be odd to allow a party who has failed to assert it to resurrect it later. The courts' answer has been to find the second judgment is controlling because it is last in time. See Treinies v. Sunshine Mining Co., 308 U.S. 66 (1939). What are the advantages and disadvantages of such a rule? See Ginsburg, Judgments in Search of Full Faith and Credit: The Last-in-Time Rule for Conflicting Judgments, 82 Harv.L.Rev. 798 (1969).

8.   A "jurisdictional competence" exception to the rule against splitting a cause of action applies if the plaintiff was unable to assert a particular claim or theory in the original case "because of the limitations on the subject matter jurisdiction of the courts." Restatement (Second) of Judgments § 26(1)(c) (1982); see also Marrese v. American Academy of Orthopaedic Surgeons, infra p. 1192. This usually arises when the first suit is filed in a state court of limited jurisdiction in which it is not possible to bring the claim sued on in the second action.

3.   ON THE MERITS

The traditional requirement of res judicata that the first judgment have been "on the merits" has gradually undergone change until today those words cannot be taken literally. The term once meant what it said. Judgments on the merits (for example after a trial or a motion for summary judgment) were accorded res judicata effect, but judgments on non-merits grounds (such as dismissal for lack of jurisdiction or failure to join an indispensable party) were not.

Dismissal on a common law demurrer (or a Rule 12(b)(6) motion for failure to state a claim upon which relief can be granted) was viewed as a non-merits determination because it only tested the sufficiency of the complaint. Many courts, as well as the first Restatement of Judgments § 50 (1942), held that if "new and additional facts are alleged that cure the defects in the original pleading, it is settled that the former judgment is not a bar to the subsequent action whether or not plaintiff had an opportunity to amend his complaint." Keidatz v. Albany, 249 P.2d 264 (Cal.1952). Some courts deviated to the extent of according res judicata effect if the plaintiff was granted leave to amend but failed to do so. Elfman v. Glaser, 47 N.E.2d 925 (Mass.1943). The conflicting policies concerning the res judicata effect of a dismissal for failure to state a claim were described by Justice Traynor in *Keidatz:* "[T]here are forceful arguments, in view of the liberal rules relating to amendments to the pleadings, for requiring the plaintiff to set forth in one action all the facts relating to his dispute. * * * On the other hand less prejudice is suffered by a defendant who has had only to attack the pleadings, than by one who has been forced to go to trial until a nonsuit is granted, and the hardship suffered by being forced to defend against a new action, instead of against an amended complaint, is not materially greater." 249 P.2d at 266. However, today the policies favoring requiring plaintiffs to plead all their claims, and thus not to take up judicial time with repetitive suits, have won out, and many courts and the Restatement (Second) of Judgments § 19, comment d (1982), apply res judicata to a dismissal for failure to state a claim.

RINEHART V. LOCKE
United States Court of Appeals, Seventh Circuit, 1971
454 F.2d 313

Before SWYGERT, CHIEF JUDGE, and FAIRCHILD and STEVENS, CIRCUIT JUDGES.

FAIRCHILD, CIRCUIT JUDGE.

On June 17, 1970, plaintiff filed a complaint seeking damages and claiming that an arrest on November 24, 1964 deprived him of rights secured by the Constitution. As one defense, defendants asserted that the matter was res judicata by virtue of dismissal on May 15, 1969 of a complaint based on the same arrest. The district court sustained the defense of res judicata and dismissed the action. Plaintiff appealed. Defendants also raised, in the district court and here, the defense that the period of limitations had expired. The two complaints are identical in substance except that an averment that the arrest was made without probable cause was included in the second, but not the first. The 1969 complaint may be summarized as follows: on November 24, 1964, three defendants, private detectives, observed plaintiff at an intersection talking to a man on a motorcycle and caused a false report to be made to the county police that plaintiff was falsely representing himself to be a police officer. As a result of the report, four other defendants, county police officers, arrested plaintiff for impersonating a government official. They also charged him falsely with unlawful use of weapons and resisting arrest. No warrant had been issued for the arrest. Plaintiff was imprisoned at the police station and later convicted of the charges, but in 1967 the conviction was reversed on appeal for insufficient evidence.

The district court entered an order dismissing the 1969 complaint for failure to state a claim. In an oral ruling on the motion to dismiss, the court based dismissal on the failure to allege the absence of probable cause, although the court made other comments which may shed light on its subsequent refusal to permit amendment.

Plaintiff sought leave to file an amended complaint in which he included an averment that defendants had no probable cause to suspect plaintiff of committing an offense. On June 13, 1969, leave was denied. The court stated no reason. Under Rule 15(a), F.R.Civ.P., "leave shall be freely given when justice so requires."* Presumably the court felt justice did not so require in view of the court's earlier suggestion that the complaint itself showed that the arrest was based upon information given by three private detectives who said they had seen the offense and that the court thought plaintiff's failure to allege lack of probable cause was not inadvertent.

Plaintiff did not appeal from either 1969 order.

RES JUDICATA.

Plaintiff contends that the May, 1969 dismissal did not establish that defendants were not liable to him under § 1983 on account of the 1964 arrest, but established only that he had no cause of action unless he was able to plead and prove lack of probable cause.

The traditional general rule supports plaintiff's position: ". . . it is equally well settled, that, if the plaintiff fails on demurrer in his first action from the omission of an essential allegation in his declaration which is fully supplied in the second suit, the judgment in the first suit is no bar to the second, although the respective actions were instituted to enforce the same right; for the reason that the merits of the case, as disclosed in the second declaration, were not heard and decided in the first action." Gould v. Evansville and C.R.R. Co., 91 U.S. 526 (1875).

Comment c, § 50, Restatement, Judgments, supports the same proposition, illustrating as follows: "Thus, if in an action for breach of contract a demurrer to the complaint is sustained on the ground that the plaintiff failed to allege consideration, he is not precluded from bringing a new action in which the complaint contains an allegation of consideration. . ."

Arguably Rule 41(b), F.R.C.P., may have changed this rule where the earlier judgment, as in this case, was entered in a federal court. The rule provides in part: "Unless the court in its order for dismissal otherwise specifies, a dismissal under this subdivision and any dismissal not provided for in this rule, other than a dismissal for lack of jurisdiction, for improper venue, or for failure to join a party under rule 19, operates as an adjudication upon the merits."*

It has been held that the list in Rule 41(b) of types of dismissal which are not presumptively adjudications on the merits is not exclusive, and that the situations where dismissals not provided for in Rule 41 are to operate as [an] adjudication on the merits are those "in which the defendant must incur the inconvenience of preparing to meet the merits because there is no initial bar to the court's reaching them." [Costello v. United States, 365 U.S. 265, 286 (1961).] The same decision indicates that a dismissal for

---

*   This rule language has been revised slightly.—Eds.
*   This rule language has been revised slightly.—Eds.

failure to fulfill a "precondition" for consideration of the merits is not a decision on the merits.

With this gloss upon the rule, the question remains a close one, but we are persuaded that under the rule an order of a district court which dismisses a complaint for failure to state a claim, but which does not specify that the dismissal is without prejudice, is res judicata as to the then existing claim which it appears plaintiff was attempting to state. This view places upon a plaintiff in a case like the 1969 case in this instance the burden of persuading the district court either to include a specification that the dismissal is without prejudice or to permit an amendment. If plaintiff is unsuccessful, his recourse is to appeal. We think this view is consistent with the expedient purpose of the rules.

NOTES AND QUESTIONS

1.   The reliance in *Rinehart* on Rule 41(b), as opposed to preclusion doctrine, needs to be reexamined in light of the Supreme Court's decision in Semtek International, Inc. v. Lockheed Martin Corp., infra p. 1201. Note that in *Rinehart* the plaintiff's complaint was dismissed for failure to state a claim, and he filed a suit identical in substance in the *same federal district court*. The court's refusal to allow him to amend the first complaint to allege lack of probable cause for his arrest seems to have been based on the court's conclusion that there was probable cause and the failure to allege its absence was not inadvertent. Consider whether these facts warrant a different result as to the applicability of Rule 41(b) in *Semtek*. See Woolley, The Sources of Federal Preclusion Law After *Semtek*, 72 U.Cin.L.Rev. 527, 597 (2003): "Rule 41(b) * * * provides that a judgment entered on a Rule 12(b)(6) dismissal for failure to state a claim shall be treated as a judgment on the merits. The provision rejects the view of some jurisdictions that a judgment entered on a 12(b)(6) dismissal (or demurrer) need not be given claim-preclusive effect, insisting instead that a judgment entered on a 12(b)(6) dismissal is entitled to the same preclusive effect as a judgment entered after trial."

2.   Should res judicata be used to prevent the plaintiff in *Rinehart* from redressing violations of his civil rights just because his lawyer failed to allege lack of probable cause in the initial complaint? Is the justification that judicial resources were wasted because the court in the earlier case had to rule on a Rule 12(b)(6) motion? Couldn't that be remedied by awarding the defendant his costs and attorneys' fees for having to respond to the first inadequate complaint?

3.   The court in *Rinehart* relies on the Supreme Court's decision in Costello v. United States, 365 U.S. 265 (1961). *Costello* was an action by the United States to revoke an order granting American citizenship to the defendant, a naturalized citizen with reputed connections to the criminal underworld. An earlier proceeding brought by the government to accomplish the same goal had been dismissed for the government's failure to include an affidavit of good cause, although the order of dismissal had not expressly

indicated whether or not the dismissal was with prejudice. The defendant contended that "the order dismissing the earlier complaint must be construed to be with prejudice because it did not specify that it was without prejudice, and the ground of dismissal was not within one of the exceptions under Rule 41(b) of the Federal Rules of Civil Procedure." 365 U.S. at 284. However, the Court, in an opinion by Justice Brennan, held "that a dismissal for failure to file the affidavit of good cause is a dismissal 'for lack of jurisdiction' within the meaning of the exception under Rule 41(b)." Id. at 285. The Court reasoned that the exception encompasses "those dismissals which are based on a plaintiff's failure to comply with a precondition requisite to the Court's going forward to determine the merits of his claim. Failure to file the affidavit of good cause in a denaturalization proceeding falls within this category." Id. It added that

> [a]ll of the dismissals enumerated in Rule 41(b) which operate as adjudications on the merits * * * primarily involve situations in which the defendant must incur the inconvenience of preparing to meet the merits because there is no initial bar to the Court's reaching them. It is therefore logical that a dismissal on one of these grounds should, unless the Court otherwise specifies, bar a subsequent action. * * *

> In contrast, the failure of the Government to file the affidavit of good cause in a denaturalization proceeding does not present a situation calling for the application of the policy making dismissals operative as adjudications on the merits. The defendant is not put to the necessity of preparing a defense because the failure of the Government to file the affidavit with the complaint requires the dismissal of the proceeding.

Did the Court properly define the term, "jurisdiction" in Rule 41(b)? Does the jurisdictional treatment of the omitted affidavit make sense in light of such subsequent cases as *Reed Elsevier*, supra p. 1073 (treating as non-jurisdictional the statutory requirement that copyright registration precede an enforcement action). Did the court in *Rinehart* properly distinguish *Costello?*

4.   What is the justification for applying res judicata even though the plaintiff sought leave to amend and was refused it? Is there any valid reason for denying leave to amend under circumstances such as these? What should plaintiff have done if leave to amend was erroneously denied? See, e.g., EFCO v. U.W. Marx, Inc., 124 F.3d 394, 399–400 (2d Cir.1997) ("Where a plaintiff's motion to amend its complaint in the first action is denied, and plaintiff fails to appeal the denial, res judicata applies to the claims sought to be added in the proposed amended complaint").

5.   The Restatement (Second) of Judgments § 20(1) provides three exceptions to a valid and final judgment having claim preclusive effect:

(a)   When the judgment is one of dismissal for lack of jurisdiction, for improper venue, or for nonjoinder or misjoinder of parties, or

(b)   When the plaintiff agrees to or elects a nonsuit (or voluntary dismissal) without prejudice or the court directs that the plaintiff be nonsuited (or that the action be otherwise dismissed) without prejudice, or

(c)   When by statute or rule of court the judgment does not operate as a bar to another action on the same claim, or does not so operate unless the court specifies, and no such specification is made.

6.   Should preclusive effect be given to a judgment based on a ground that is not applicable to the claim raised in the second suit? In Williamson v. Columbia Gas & Electric Corp., 186 F.2d 464 (3d Cir.1950), one of two repetitive suits pending at the same time in the same court was dismissed on the ground of statute of limitations. Although the other suit was not barred by statute of limitations because it had a conspiracy count which prevented the statute of limitations from being tolled, the court found the second claim barred by res judicata.

In contrast, the Restatement (Second) of Judgments § 20(2) provides:

A valid and final personal judgment for the defendant, which rests on the prematurity of the action or on the plaintiff's failure to satisfy a precondition to suit, does not bar another action by the plaintiff instituted after the claim has matured, or the precondition has been satisfied, unless a second action is precluded by the operation of the substantive law.

7.   A default judgment is considered to be on the merits. Otherwise there would be no finality when a defendant failed to appear.

4.   PRECLUSION IN STATE-FEDERAL COURT ADJUDICATIONS

MARRESE V. AMERICAN ACADEMY OF ORTHOPAEDIC SURGEONS

Supreme Court of the United States, 1985
470 U.S. 373

JUSTICE O'CONNOR delivered the opinion of the Court.

[Two Illinois orthopedic surgeons who were denied membership in the Academy sued it in an Illinois state court, claiming that the denial of their applications without a hearing violated their common law associational rights under Illinois law. They did not assert claims under state antitrust law. The state court dismissed on the ground that they had failed to state a cause of action. They then sued in federal court, claiming that the denial of their membership applications constituted a boycott in violation of federal antitrust law. The Court of Appeals held that federal principles of claim preclusion barred the federal suit, noting that Illinois antitrust law was similar to federal antitrust law.]

The issue presented by this case is whether a state court judgment may have preclusive effect on a federal antitrust claim that could not have been raised in the state proceeding. Although federal antitrust claims are within the exclusive jurisdiction of the federal courts, the Court of Appeals ruled that the dismissal of petitioners' complaints in state court barred them from bringing a claim based on the same facts under the Sherman Act. The Court of Appeals erred by suggesting that in these circumstances a federal court should determine the preclusive effect of a state court judgment without regard to the law of the State in which judgment was rendered.

The preclusive effect of a state court judgment in a subsequent federal lawsuit generally is determined by the full faith and credit statute, which provides that state judicial proceedings "shall have the same full faith and credit in every court within the United States . . . as they have by law or usage in the courts of such State . . . from which they are taken." 28 U.S.C. § 1738.

This statute directs a federal court to refer to the preclusion law of the State in which judgment was rendered. "It has long been established that § 1738 does not allow federal courts to employ their own rules of res judicata in determining the effect of state judgments. Rather, it goes beyond the common law and commands a federal court to accept the rules chosen by the State from which the judgment is taken." Kremer v. Chemical Construction Corp., 456 U.S. 461, 481–482 (1982). Section 1738 embodies concerns of comity and federalism that allow the States to determine, subject to the requirements of the statute and the Due Process Clause, the preclusive effect of judgments in their own courts.

The fact that petitioners' antitrust claim is within the exclusive jurisdiction of the federal courts does not necessarily make § 1738 inapplicable to this case. Our decisions indicate that a state court judgment may in some circumstances have preclusive effect in a subsequent action within the exclusive jurisdiction of the federal courts. Without discussing § 1738, this Court has held that the issue preclusive effect of a state court judgment barred a subsequent patent suit that could not have been brought in state court. Becher v. Contoure Laboratories, Inc., 279 U.S. 388 (1929). Moreover, Kremer held that § 1738 applies to a claim of employment discrimination under Title VII of the Civil Rights Act of 1964, 42 U.S.C. §§ 2000e et seq., although the Court expressly declined to decide whether Title VII claims can be brought only in federal courts. 456 U.S., at 479, n. 20. Kremer implies that absent an exception to § 1738, state law determines at least the issue preclusive effect of a prior state judgment in a subsequent action involving a claim within the exclusive jurisdiction of the federal courts.

More generally, Kremer indicates that § 1738 requires a federal court to look first to state preclusion law in determining the preclusive effects of a state court judgment. The Court's analysis in *Kremer* began with the finding that state law would in fact bar relitigation of the discrimination issue decided in the earlier state proceedings. That finding implied that the plaintiff could not relitigate the same issue in federal court unless some exception to § 1738 applied. *Kremer* observed that "an exception to § 1738 will not be recognized unless a later statute contains an express or implied repeal." Title VII does not expressly repeal § 1738, and the Court concluded that the statutory provisions and legislative history do not support a finding of implied repeal. We conclude that the basic approach adopted in *Kremer* applies in a lawsuit involving a claim within the exclusive jurisdiction of the federal courts.

To be sure, a state court will not have occasion to address the specific question whether a state judgment has issue or claim preclusive effect in a later action that can be brought only in federal court. Nevertheless, a federal court may rely in the first instance on state preclusion principles to determine the extent to which an earlier state judgment bars subsequent litigation. *Kremer* illustrates that a federal court can apply state rules of issue preclusion to determine if a matter actually litigated in state court may be relitigated in a subsequent federal proceeding.

With respect to matters that were not decided in the state proceedings, we note that claim preclusion generally does not apply where "[t]he plaintiff was unable to rely on a certain theory of the case or to seek a certain remedy because of the limitations on the subject matter jurisdiction of the courts. . ." Restatement (Second) of Judgments § 26(1)(c) (1982). If state preclusion law includes this requirement of prior jurisdictional competency, which is generally true, a state judgment will not have claim preclusive effect on a cause of action within the exclusive jurisdiction of the federal courts.

Even in the event that a party asserting the affirmative defense of claim preclusion can show that state preclusion rules in some circumstances bar a claim outside the jurisdiction of the court that rendered the initial judgment, the federal court should first consider whether application of the state rules would bar the particular federal claim.[2]

Reference to state preclusion law may make it unnecessary to determine if the federal court, as an exception to § 1738, should refuse to

---

[2]   Our analysis does not necessarily suggest that the Court of Appeals for the Fourth Circuit erred in its holding in Nash County Board of Education v. Biltmore Co., 640 F.2d 484 (1981). The Court of Appeals there applied federal preclusion principles to conclude that a state judgment approving settlement of state antitrust claims barred a subsequent federal antitrust claim. Although our decision today indicates that the Court of Appeals should have looked in the first instance to state law to determine the preclusive effect of the state judgment, the same holding would result if application of state preclusion law suggests that the settlement bars the subsequent federal claim and if there is no exception to § 1738 in these circumstances. Cf. 640 F.2d, at 487, n. 2 (noting that State law gives preclusive effect to consent judgment). We, of course, do not address those issues here.

give preclusive effect to a state court judgment. The issue whether there is an exception to § 1738 arises only if state law indicates that litigation of a particular claim or issue should be barred in the subsequent federal proceeding. To the extent that state preclusion law indicates that a judgment normally does not have claim preclusive effect as to matters that the court lacked jurisdiction to entertain, lower courts and commentators have correctly concluded that a state court judgment does not bar a subsequent federal antitrust claim. Unless application of Illinois preclusion law suggests, contrary to the usual view, that petitioners' federal antitrust claim is somehow barred, there will be no need to decide in this case if there is an exception to § 1738. * * *

The Court of Appeals did not apply the approach to § 1738 that we have outlined.

* * *

If we had a single system of courts and our only concerns were efficiency and finality, it might be desirable to fashion claim preclusion rules that would require a plaintiff to bring suit initially in the forum of most general jurisdiction, thereby resolving as many issues as possible in one proceeding. See Restatement (Second) of Judgments § 24, Comment g (1982); C. Wright, A. Miller, & E. Cooper, [Federal Practice & Procedure] § 4407, p. 51; id. § 4412, p. 93. The decision of the Court of Appeals approximates such a rule inasmuch as it encourages plaintiffs to file suit initially in federal district court and to attempt to bring any state law claims pendent to their federal antitrust claims. Whether this result would reduce the overall burden of litigation is debatable, and we decline to base our interpretation of § 1738 on our opinion on this question.

More importantly, we have parallel systems of state and federal courts, and the concerns of comity reflected in § 1738 generally allow States to determine the preclusive scope of their own courts' judgments. These concerns certainly are not made less compelling because state courts lack jurisdiction over federal antitrust claims. We therefore reject a judicially created exception to § 1738 that effectively holds as a matter of federal law that a plaintiff can bring state law claims initially in state court only at the cost of forgoing subsequent federal antitrust claims. * * *

In this case the Court of Appeals should have first referred to Illinois law to determine the preclusive effect of the state judgment. Only if state law indicates that a particular claim or issue would be barred is it necessary to determine if an exception to § 1738 should apply. Although for purposes of this case, we need not decide if such an exception exists for federal antitrust claims, we observe that the more general question is whether the concerns underlying a particular grant of exclusive jurisdiction justify a finding of an implied partial repeal of § 1738. Resolution of this question will depend on the particular federal statute as well as the nature of the claim or issue involved in the subsequent federal action. Our previous decisions indicate that the primary consideration must be the intent of Congress.

CHIEF JUSTICE BURGER, concurring in the judgment.

[The Chief Justice agreed that § 1738 required that federal courts look first to state law, and that preclusion is forbidden if state law clearly would not bar a later federal action, but he criticized the Court's failure to address the possibility that Illinois law would not speak to this question.]

I cannot agree with the Court's interpretation of the jurisdictional competency requirement. If state law provides a cause of action that is virtually identical with a federal statutory cause of action, a plaintiff suing in state court is able to rely on the same theory of the case and obtain the same remedy as would be available in federal court, even when the plaintiff cannot expressly invoke the federal statute because it is within the exclusive jurisdiction of the federal courts. In this situation, the jurisdictional competency requirement is effectively satisfied. Therefore, the fact that state law recognizes the jurisdictional competency requirement does not necessarily imply that a state court judgment has no claim preclusive effect on a cause of action within exclusive federal jurisdiction.

* * *

[I]t is likely that the principles of Illinois claim preclusion law do not speak to the preclusive effect that petitioners' state court judgments should have on the present action. In this situation, it may be consistent with § 1738 for a federal court to formulate a federal rule to resolve the matter. If state law is simply indeterminate, the concerns of comity and federalism underlying § 1738 do not come into play. At the same time, the federal courts have direct interests in ensuring that their resources are used efficiently and not as a means of harassing defendants with repetitive lawsuits, as well as in ensuring that parties asserting federal rights have an adequate opportunity to litigate those rights. Given the insubstantiality of the state interests and the weight of the federal interests, a strong argument could be made that a federal rule would be more appropriate than a creative interpretation of ambiguous state law.[4]

A federal rule might be fashioned from the test, which this Court has applied in other contexts, that a party is precluded from asserting a claim that he had a "full and fair opportunity" to litigate in a prior action. Thus, if a state statute is identical in all material respects with a federal statute within exclusive federal jurisdiction, a party's ability to assert a claim under the state statute in a prior state court action might be said to have

---

[4] By contrast, when a federal court construes substantive rights and obligations under state law in the context of a diversity action, the federal interest is insignificant and the state's interest is much more direct than it is in the present situation, even if the relevant state law is ambiguous.

provided, in effect, a "full and fair opportunity" to litigate his rights under the federal statute. The Court will eventually have to face these questions; I would resolve them now.

NOTES AND QUESTIONS

1.   How can it be said that the plaintiffs in *Marrese* split their cause of action by not raising in a state-court suit a federal claim that could not be sued on there because it is subject to exclusive federal jurisdiction? Is it a sufficient answer that the plaintiffs didn't have to file in the state court, but could instead have filed both state and federal claims in federal court? This, of course, would only be possible if the federal court were willing to exercise supplemental jurisdiction over the state claims. Furthermore, must plaintiffs give up their right to a state forum for adjudication of their state claims under the threat of being barred from ever raising the exclusive federal jurisdiction claims?

In the Seventh Circuit opinion in *Marrese* that was reversed by the Supreme Court, Judge Posner responded to the contention that res judicata did not bar the federal antitrust claim because it could not have been raised in the state court as follows: "The plaintiffs could, however, have joined with their other state claims a claim under the Illinois Antitrust Act, and if that Act is materially identical to the Sherman Act their failure to do so bars this suit." 726 F.2d at 1153. Regarding § 1738, Judge Posner found plaintiffs' arguments that they would not be barred under Illinois preclusion law irrelevant. In his view, that statute was intended "to protect the authority of state courts, [so it] ought not prevent a federal court from giving a state court judgment *more* effect in a federal suit than the courts of the state would give it in state court." Id. at 1154.

2.   If the usual rule is that a state-court judgment does not preclude litigation of an exclusive federal jurisdiction claim, see Restatement (Second) of Judgments § 26(1)(c), what circumstances warrant deviation from that rule? Would those in *Marrese* justify an exception? Do you find persuasive Chief Justice Burger's arguments for preclusion when a plaintiff sues in state court on a state-law claim that is virtually identical to a statutory exclusive federal jurisdiction claim?

In Matsushita Elec. Indus. Co. v. Epstein, 516 U.S. 367 (1996), the Supreme Court said that "*Marrese* provides the analytical framework" for resolving these problems. It emphasized that *Marrese* "made clear that where § 1738 is raised as a defense in a subsequent suit, the fact that an allegedly precluded claim is within the exclusive jurisdiction of the federal courts *does not necessarily make § 1738 inapplicable.*" The appeal arose from competing class actions making claims about Matsushita's acquisition of MCA, Inc., through a tender offer. One suit, filed in Delaware state court, asserted claims of mismanagement and disloyalty under Delaware law. The other suit, filed in federal court, made claims under the Securities Exchange Act that were within exclusive federal jurisdiction. After defendants obtained summary judgment from the district court in the federal case, the Delaware court approved a settlement of the state-court class action for a very modest sum even though there had been an appeal from the summary judgment in federal court. Defendants then attempted to abort the federal appeal on the basis of the Delaware class action judgment, and the Court found that § 1738 required preclusion. There was a strong dissent contending that the lawyers for the Delaware plaintiffs had not properly represented the class.

3.   *Marrese* suggests that an exception to § 1738 might be found for exclusive federal jurisdiction claims depending on "whether the concerns underlying a particular grant of exclusive jurisdiction justify finding a partial repeal of § 1738," with the primary focus on the intent of Congress. What would one look for concerning congressional intent in an exclusive federal jurisdiction statute? In the antitrust context involved in *Marrese*, is it relevant that exclusive federal jurisdiction is not explicitly provided in the statutes, but has been inferred by the courts? In *Matsushita*, supra note 2, the Supreme Court rejected the argument that the exclusive federal jurisdiction provisions of the Securities Exchange Act created an exception to § 1738. It said that there should be a "relatively stringent standard" for finding such repeals, and that they would depend on showing an "irreconcilable conflict" between § 1738 and the statute granting exclusive federal jurisdiction. The Court held there was no exception in this case because it found no congressional intent to afford plaintiffs more than one day in court to challenge the legality of a securities transaction, or to prevent litigants who assert related state-law claims in state court from effectively releasing their federal claims as part of a state-court settlement. Will there often be cases in which § 1738 can be overcome?

4.   In San Remo Hotel, L.P. v. City of San Francisco, 545 U.S. 323 (2005), the Supreme Court rejected another proposed exception to § 1738, this one for takings claims brought pursuant to 42 U.S.C. § 1983. The litigation began in federal court, when the hotel challenged certain fees associated with its proposal to convert from mixed-use hotel space to tourist rooms. Citing federal abstention doctrines, the lower federal courts directed the parties to litigate the matter in state court with a view toward ripening the taking claim and perhaps obviating the necessity of a ruling on the federal claim under the Fourteenth Amendment. In keeping with that directive, the hotel filed an action in state court, presenting a range of state law claims (including claims under the state constitutional analog to the Due Process Clause). At the same time, the hotel notified the state court of its intention, through a so-called *England* reservation, to preserve its federal law takings claims for presentation to the federal court in the event the state court upheld the conversion fee. See England v. Louisiana Bd. of Medical Examiners, 375 U.S. 411 (1964). Sure enough, the state court ruled for the city and the hotel returned to federal court to pursue its takings claim. Despite the *England* reservation, however, the district court ruled that the doctrine of claim preclusion, as incorporated in § 1738, barred the assertion of the federal claims.

The Supreme Court affirmed. The Court acknowledged that the plaintiff hotel was required to present its claims to a state court in the first instance under long-standing decisions that compel litigants to provide state courts with the first opportunity to address takings claims and provide any needed compensation. See Williamson County Regional Planning Comm'n v. Hamilton Bank of Johnson City, 473 U.S. 172 (1985). The Court also acknowledged that the *England* reservation procedure permits a return to federal court in certain situations. But the Court found that the plaintiff hotel had submitted more than just a narrow state law challenge to the state courts. Rather, the plaintiff had pursued takings claims under the California constitution that were virtually identical to those it was later to pursue in federal court. As a result, when the California Supreme Court rejected the state taking claim, it did so in terms virtually "coextensive" with federal law. The Court viewed the plaintiff's voluntary expansion of the state court litigation to encompass the state takings claim as vitiating its right to return to federal court under the terms of its *England* reservation. More significantly, the Court denied that the plaintiff's obligation to ripen the takings claim through state court litigation was sufficiently unfair to warrant an exception to § 1738; as the Court noted, federal policy does not necessarily guarantee a litigant's right to litigate all federal issues in federal court. Four concurring Justices wrote separately to express concern with the breadth of the *Williamson* decision.

5.   There may be occasions when the law of the state that entered the judgment does not control its enforcement elsewhere. In Baker v. General Motors Corp., 522 U.S. 222 (1998), the Court held that a Missouri district court was not obligated to exclude testimony by a witness even though a Michigan court consent judgment forbade his testifying in actions against General Motors, his former employer. The injunction was issued in litigation resulting from the witness's departure from his GM job. Although the witness had testified in several other cases thereafter, GM argued that he should not be allowed to do so in the Bakers' suit. The district court disagreed on the ground that Missouri had a policy in favor of presenting evidence at trial. The witness (a former GM engineer) testified that a safer design was available than the one GM had used. Plaintiffs recovered $11.3 million, and the court of appeals reversed on the ground that it was improper to allow the witness to testify.

The Supreme Court unanimously concluded that the court of appeals was wrong, although there were three explanations why. Writing for the Court, Justice Ginsburg first rejected the public policy justification for refusing to enforce the Michigan judgment and recognized that the Michigan decree was entitled to full faith and credit although it was an equity decree. But other states need not adopt the enforcement mechanisms of the entering state, and the Court regarded GM's argument as eroding the Missouri federal court's power to administer its own proceedings. "Michigan lacks authority to control courts elsewhere by precluding them in actions brought by strangers to the Michigan litigation, from determining for themselves what witnesses are competent to testify and what evidence is relevant and admissible in their search for the truth." Justice Scalia concurred in the judgment, finding it sufficient to say that full faith and credit did not compel Missouri to execute the Michigan injunction. Justice Kennedy, also concurring in the judgment, expressed uneasiness about the possible breadth of the majority's reasoning about interference with litigation pending in the forum.

Compare Bay Area Factors v. Calvert, 105 F.3d 315 (6th Cir.1997), in which the court held that a California default judgment precluded discharge of a debt in a federal bankruptcy proceeding because the claim asserted in state court was for fraud, which could not be discharged in bankruptcy. In pre-*Marrese* cases, the court had refused to accord collateral estoppel effect to a default judgment as a matter of federal common law, but it concluded that *Marrese* compelled application of California law, which does give default judgments such effect. It then concluded that there was no ground for an exception to the requirements of the full faith and credit statute.

6.   After *Marrese,* can the federal courts ever accord more preclusive effect to a state-court judgment than the state courts would? See Note, A Doctrine of Faith and Credit, 94 Va. L. Rev. 247 (2008) (arguing that the "same effect" requirement in section 1738 forecloses such greater effect).

7.   Does the fact that federal interests may in some instances justify an exception to § 1738 suggest that preclusion law should be governed by the law that creates the claim that was decided?

8.   What law should determine the preclusive effect of *federal* judgments? Note the resolution of this issue in *Manego,* supra p. 1162 and reconsider the issue in relation to Semtek International, Inc. v. Lockheed Martin Corp., infra p. 1201.

9.   Preclusion law in interjurisdictional cases raises extremely difficult problems. For examination of these problems, see Erichson, Interjurisdictional Preclusion, 96 Mich. L. Rev. 945 (1998) (concluding that the second forum should apply the preclusion principles of the first one unless (1) there are grounds for an implied repeal of § 1738, or (2) the preclusion rules in question are explicitly linked to particular substantive rights of action). Reconsider these points in connection with Semtek International, Inc. v. Lockheed Martin Corp., below.

10.   Although American courts generally accord res judicata effect to judgments of foreign countries, they have sometimes refused to do so for policy reasons. See Hilton v. Guyot, 159 U.S. 113, 202 (1895) (merits of a foreign judgment should not be retried "where there has been opportunity for a full and fair trial abroad before a court of competent jurisdiction, conducting the trial upon regular proceedings, after due citation or voluntary appearance of the defendant, and under a system of jurisprudence likely to secure an impartial administration of justice between the citizens of its own country and those of other countries, and there is nothing to show either prejudice in the court, or in the system of laws under which it was sitting, or fraud in procuring the judgment."). What differences in procedures would warrant an American court not recognizing a foreign judgment? In *Hilton,* the American defendant objected that the plaintiff was permitted to testify not under oath and was not subjected to cross-examination, and that documents were admitted in evidence with which the defendants had no connection. Are such procedures "likely to secure an impartial administration of justice"?

SEMTEK INTERNATIONAL, INC. V.
LOCKHEED MARTIN CORP.

Supreme Court of the United States, 2001
531 U.S. 497

JUSTICE SCALIA delivered the opinion of the Court.

This case presents the question whether the claim-preclusive effect of a federal judgment dismissing a diversity action on statute-of-limitations grounds is determined by the law of the State in which the federal court sits.

I

Petitioner filed a complaint against respondent in California state court, alleging breach of contract and various business torts. Respondent removed the case to the United States District Court for the Central District of California on the basis of diversity of citizenship, see 28 U.S.C. §§ 1332, 1441, and successfully moved to dismiss petitioner's claims as barred by California's 2-year statute of limitations. In its order of dismissal, the District Court, adopting language suggested by respondent, dismissed petitioner's claims "in [their] entirety on the merits and with prejudice." Without contesting the District Court's designation of its dismissal as "on the merits," petitioner appealed to the Court of Appeals for the Ninth Circuit, which affirmed the District Court's order.

Petitioner also brought suit against respondent in the State Circuit Court for Baltimore City, Maryland, alleging the same causes of action, which were not time barred under Maryland's 3-year statute of limitations. Respondent sought injunctive relief against this action from the California federal court under the All Writs Act, 28 U.S.C. § 1651, and removed the action to the United States District Court for the District of Maryland on federal-question grounds (diversity grounds were not available because Lockheed "is a Maryland citizen," Semtek Int'l, Inc. v. Lockheed Martin Corp., 988 F.Supp. 913, 914 (1997)). The California federal court denied the relief requested, and the Maryland federal court remanded the case to state court because the federal question arose only by way of defense. Following a hearing, the Maryland state court granted respondent's motion to dismiss on the ground of res judicata. Petitioner then returned to the California federal court and the Ninth Circuit, unsuccessfully moving both courts to amend the former's earlier order so as to indicate that the dismissal was not "on the merits." Petitioner also appealed the Maryland trial court's order of dismissal to the Maryland Court of Special Appeals. The Court of Special Appeals affirmed, holding that, regardless of whether California would have accorded claim-preclusive effect to a statute-of-limitations dismissal by one of its own courts, the dismissal by the California federal court barred the complaint filed in Maryland, since the res judicata effect of federal diversity judgments is prescribed by federal law, under which the earlier dismissal was on the merits and claim preclusive. After the

Maryland Court of Appeals declined to review the case, we granted certiorari.

II

Petitioner contends that the outcome of this case is controlled by Dupasseur v. Rochereau, 21 Wall. 130, 135 (1875), which held that the res judicata effect of a federal diversity judgment "is such as would belong to judgments of the State courts rendered under similar circumstances," and may not be accorded any "higher sanctity or effect." Since, petitioner argues, the dismissal of an action on statute-of-limitations grounds by a California state court would not be claim preclusive, it follows that the similar dismissal of this diversity action by the California federal court cannot be claim preclusive. While we agree that this would be the result demanded by *Dupasseur*, the case is not dispositive because it was decided under the Conformity Act of 1872, 17 Stat. 196, which required federal courts to apply the procedural law of the forum State in nonequity cases. That arguably affected the outcome of the case. See Restatement (Second) of Judgments § 87, Comment a, p. 315 (1980) (hereinafter Restatement) ("Since procedural law largely determines the matters that may be adjudicated in an action, state law had to be considered in ascertaining the effect of a federal judgment").

Respondent, for its part, contends that the outcome of this case is controlled by Federal Rule of Civil Procedure 41(b) [which the Court quoted].

Since the dismissal here did not "otherwise specif[y]" (indeed, it specifically stated that it *was* "on the merits"), and did not pertain to the excepted subjects of jurisdiction, venue, or joinder, it follows, respondent contends, that the dismissal "is entitled to claim preclusive effect."

Implicit in this reasoning is the unstated minor premise that all judgments denominated "on the merits" are entitled to claim-preclusive effect. That premise is not necessarily valid. The original connotation of an "on the merits" adjudication is one that actually "pass[es] directly on the substance of [a particular] claim" before the court. Restatement § 19, Comment a, at 161. That connotation remains common to every jurisdiction of which we are aware. See ibid. ("The prototyp[ical] [judgment on the merits is] one in which the merits of [a party's] claim are in fact adjudicated [for or] against the [party] after trial of the substantive issues"). And it is, we think, the meaning intended in those many statements to the effect that a judgment "on the merits" triggers the doctrine of res judicata or claim preclusion.

But over the years the meaning of the term "judgment on the merits" "has gradually undergone change," R. Marcus, M. Redish, & E. Sherman, Civil Procedure: A Modern Approach 1140–1141 (3d ed. 2000), and it has come to be applied to some judgments (such as the one involved here) that do not pass upon the substantive merits of a claim and hence do not (in many jurisdictions) entail claim-preclusive effect. That is why the Restatement of Judgments has abandoned the use of the term—"because of its possibly misleading connotations," Restatement § 19, Comment a, at 161.

In short, it is no longer true that a judgment "on the merits" is necessarily a judgment entitled to claim-preclusive effect; and there are a number of reasons for believing that the phrase "adjudication upon the merits" does not bear that meaning in Rule 41(b). To begin with, Rule 41(b) sets forth nothing more than a default rule for determining the import of a dismissal (a dismissal is "upon the merits," with the three stated exceptions, unless the court "otherwise specifies"). This would be a highly peculiar context in which to announce a federally prescribed rule on the complex question of claim preclusion, saying in effect, "All federal dismissals (with three specified exceptions) preclude suit elsewhere, unless the court otherwise specifies."

And even apart from the purely default character of Rule 41(b), it would be peculiar to find a rule governing the effect that must be accorded federal judgments by other courts ensconced in rules governing the internal procedures of the rendering court itself. Indeed, such a rule would arguably violate the jurisdictional limitation of the Rules Enabling Act: that the Rules "shall not abridge, enlarge or modify any substantive right," 28 U.S.C. § 2072(b). In the present case, for example, if California law left petitioner free to sue on this claim in Maryland even after the California statute of limitations had expired, the federal court's extinguishment of that right (through Rule 41(b)'s mandated claim-preclusive effect of its judgment) would seem to violate this limitation.

Moreover, as so interpreted, the Rule would in many cases violate the federalism principle of Erie R. Co. v. Tompkins, 304 U.S. 64, 78–80 (1938), by engendering " 'substantial' variations [in outcomes] between state and federal litigation" which would "[l]ikely . . . influence the choice of a forum," Hanna v. Plumer, 380 U.S. 460, 467–468 (1965). See also Guaranty Trust Co. v. York, 326 U.S. 99, 108–110 (1945). Cf. Walker v. Armco Steel Corp., 446 U.S. 740, 748–753 (1980). With regard to the claim-preclusion issue involved in the present case, for example, the traditional rule is that expiration of the applicable statute of limitations merely bars the remedy and does not extinguish the substantive right, so that dismissal on that ground does not have claim-preclusive effect in other jurisdictions with longer, unexpired limitation periods. Out-of-state defendants sued on stale claims in California and in other States adhering to this traditional rule would systematically remove state-law suits brought against them to federal court—where, unless otherwise specified, a statute-of-limitations dismissal would bar suit everywhere.[5]

Finally, if Rule 41(b) did mean what respondent suggests, we would surely have relied upon it in our cases recognizing the claim-preclusive effect of federal judgments in federal-question cases. Yet for over half a century since the promulgation of Rule 41(b), we have not once done so.

We think the key to a more reasonable interpretation of the meaning of "operates as an adjudication upon the merits" in Rule 41(b) is to be found in Rule 41(a), which, in discussing the effect of voluntary dismissal by the plaintiff, makes clear that an "adjudication upon the merits" is the opposite of a "dismissal without prejudice":

> Unless otherwise stated in the notice of dismissal or stipulation, the dismissal is without prejudice, except that a notice of dismissal operates as an adjudication upon the merits when filed by a plaintiff who has once dismissed in any court of the United States or of any state an action based on or including the same claim.[*]

See also 18 Wright & Miller, [Federal Practice & Procedure] § 4435, at 329, n. 4 ("Both parts of Rule 41 . . . use the phrase 'without prejudice' as a contrast to adjudication on the merits"); 9 id., § 2373, at 396, n. 4 (" '[W]ith prejudice' is an acceptable form of shorthand for 'an adjudication upon the merits' "). The primary meaning of "dismissal without prejudice," we think, is dismissal without barring the plaintiff from returning later, to the same court, with the same underlying claim. That will also ordinarily (though not always) have the consequence of not barring the claim from other courts, but its primary meaning relates to the dismissing court itself. Thus, Black's Law Dictionary (7th ed.1999) defines "dismissed without prejudice" as "removed from the court's docket in such a way that the plaintiff may refile the same suit on the same claim," and defines "dismissal without prejudice" as "[a] dismissal that does not bar the plaintiff from refiling the lawsuit within the applicable limitations period."

We think, then, that the effect of the "adjudication upon the merits" default provision of Rule 41(b)—and, presumably, of the explicit order in the present case that used the language of that default provision—is simply that, unlike a dismissal "without prejudice," the dismissal in the present case barred refiling of the same claim in the United States District Court for the Central District of California. That is undoubtedly a necessary

---

[5] Rule 41(b), interpreted as a preclusion-establishing rule, would not have the two effects described in the preceding paragraphs—arguable violation of the Rules Enabling Act and incompatibility with Erie R. Co. v. Tompkins, 304 U.S. 64 (1938)—if the court's failure to specify an other-than-on-the-merits dismissal were subject to reversal on appeal whenever it would alter the rule of claim preclusion applied by the State in which the federal court sits. No one suggests that this is the rule, and we are aware of no case that applies it.

[*] This rule language has been revised slightly.—Eds.

condition, but it is not a sufficient one, for claim-preclusive effect in other courts.[6]

III

Having concluded that the claim-preclusive effect, in Maryland, of this California federal diversity judgment is dictated neither by Dupasseur v. Rochereau, as petitioner contends, nor by Rule 41(b), as respondent contends, we turn to consideration of what determines the issue. Neither the Full Faith and Credit Clause, U.S. Const., Art. IV, § 1, nor the full faith and credit statute, 28 U.S.C. § 1738, addresses the question. By their terms they govern the effects to be given only to state-court judgments (and, in the case of the statute, to judgments by courts of territories and possessions). And no other federal textual provision, neither of the Constitution nor of any statute, addresses the claim-preclusive effect of a judgment in a federal diversity action.

It is also true, however, that no federal textual provision addresses the claim-preclusive effect of a federal-court judgment in a federal-question case, yet we have long held that States cannot give those judgments merely whatever effect they would give their own judgments, but must accord them the effect that this Court prescribes. The reasoning of that line of cases suggests, moreover, that even when States are allowed to give federal judgments (notably, judgments in diversity cases) no more than the effect accorded to state judgments, that disposition is by direction of this Court, which has the last word on the claim-preclusive effect of all federal judgments:

> It is true that for some purposes and within certain limits it is only required that the judgments of the courts of the United States shall be given the same force and effect as are given the judgments of the courts of the States wherein they are rendered; but it is equally true that whether a Federal judgment has been given due force and effect in the state court is a Federal question reviewable by this court, which will determine for itself whether such judgment has been given due weight or otherwise. . .
>
> When is the state court obliged to give to Federal judgments only the force and effect it gives to state court judgments within its own jurisdiction? Such cases are distinctly pointed out in the opinion of Mr. Justice Bradley in Dupasseur v. Rochereau [which stated that the case was a diversity case, applying state law under

---

[6] We do not decide whether, in a diversity case, a federal court's "dismissal upon the merits" (in the sense we have described), under circumstances where a state court would decree only a "dismissal without prejudice," abridges a "substantive right" and thus exceeds the authorization of the Rules Enabling Act. We think the situation will present itself more rarely than would the arguable violation of the Act that would ensue from interpreting Rule 41(b) as a rule of claim preclusion; and if it is a violation, can be more easily dealt with on direct appeal.

state procedure]. Deposit Bank [v. Frankfort], 191 U.S. [499] [(1903)].

In other words, in *Dupasseur* the State was allowed (indeed, required) to give a federal diversity judgment no more effect than it would accord one of its own judgments only because reference to state law was *the federal rule that this Court deemed appropriate*. In short, federal common law governs the claim-preclusive effect of a dismissal by a federal court sitting in diversity. See generally R. Fallon, D. Meltzer, & D. Shapiro, Hart and Wechsler's The Federal Courts and the Federal System 1473 (4th ed.1996); Degnan, Federalized Res Judicata, 85 Yale L.J. 741 (1976).

It is left to us, then, to determine the appropriate federal rule. And despite the sea change that has occurred in the background law since *Dupasseur* was decided—not only repeal of the Conformity Act but also the watershed decision of this Court in *Erie*—we think the result decreed by *Dupasseur* continues to be correct for diversity cases. Since state, rather than federal, substantive law is at issue there is no need for a uniform federal rule. And indeed, nationwide uniformity in the substance of the matter is better served by having the same claim-preclusive rule (the state rule) apply whether the dismissal has been ordered by a state or a federal court. This is, it seems to us, a classic case for adopting, as the federally prescribed rule of decision, the law that would be applied by state courts in the State in which the federal diversity court sits. See Gasperini v. Center for Humanities, Inc., 518 U.S. 415, 429–431 (1996); Walker v. Armco Steel Corp., 446 U.S. at 752–753; Bernhardt v. Polygraphic Co. of America, 350 U.S. 198, 202–205 (1956). As we have alluded to above, any other rule would produce the sort of "forum-shopping . . . and . . . inequitable administration of the laws" that *Erie* seeks to avoid, Hanna, 380 U.S. at 468, since filing in, or removing to, federal court would be encouraged by the divergent effects that the litigants would anticipate from likely grounds of dismissal. See Guaranty Trust Co. v. York, 326 U.S. at 109–110.

This federal reference to state law will not obtain, of course, in situations in which the state law is incompatible with federal interests. If, for example, state law did not accord claim-preclusive effect to dismissals for willful violation of discovery orders, federal courts' interest in the integrity of their own processes might justify a contrary federal rule. No such conflict with potential federal interests exists in the present case. Dismissal of this state cause of action was decreed by the California federal court only because the California statute of limitations so required; and there is no conceivable federal interest in giving that time bar more effect in other courts than the California courts themselves would impose.

* * *

Because the claim-preclusive effect of the California federal court's dismissal "upon the merits" of petitioner's action on statute-of-limitations grounds is governed by a federal rule that in turn incorporates California's law of claim preclusion (the content of which we do not pass upon today), the Maryland Court of Special Appeals erred in holding that the dismissal necessarily precluded the bringing of this action in the Maryland courts. The judgment is reversed, and the case remanded for further proceedings not inconsistent with this opinion.

NOTES AND QUESTIONS

1. "It would be difficult for even the most adept spinner of law school hypotheticals to devise a case more challenging than *Semtek*." Burbank, *Semtek*, Forum Shopping, and Federal Common Law, 77 Notre Dame L. Rev. 1027, 1033–34 (2002). What are the parameters of *Semtek*'s statement that "it is no longer true that a judgment 'on the merits' is necessarily a judgment entitled to claim-preclusive effect" and that "the phrase 'adjudication upon the merits' does not bear that meaning in Rule 41(b)?" Is Rinehart v. Locke, supra p. 1188, still correct in its ruling that under Rule 41(b) "an order of a district court which dismisses a complaint for failure to state a claim, but which does not specify that the dismissal is without prejudice, is res judicata as to the then existing claim which it appears plaintiff was attempting to state"? Are the contrary positions in the cases based on the ground for dismissal, that is, failure to state a claim in *Rinehart* versus statute of limitations in *Semtek*?

Which is the stronger case for applying preclusion? Are the differing positions as to Rule 41(b) explainable by the fact that in *Rinehart* the suit was refiled in the same federal district court, as opposed to being filed in a state court in *Semtek*? In Styskal v. Weld County Board of County Commissioners, 365 F.3d 855 (10th Cir. 2004), the district court dismissed plaintiff's state-law claims "with prejudice" for lack of supplemental jurisdiction. The appellate court held that "the dismissal with prejudice by the district court in this case does not necessarily mean anything more than that Plaintiff cannot refile her claim in the United States District Court for the District of Colorado." Does Rule 41(b) have any further application beyond this situation? The court in *Styskal* explained as follows (id. at 859):

> For example, if the federal court's ruling is based on the substance of the claim (what has been termed "adjudication on the merits," see *Semtek*), the doctrine of claim preclusion would ordinarily prevent further proceedings on the claim in a later state action. But if the federal court's dismissal is based on a procedural ground, the federal ruling is unlikely to have any preclusive effect in state court, even though the dismissal may bar the plaintiff from returning to federal court.

Contrast Wagh v. Metris Direct, Inc., 363 F.3d 821 (9th Cir.2003), in which defendant removed a suit raising state-law claims and claims based on the federal Racketeer Influenced and Corrupt Organizations Act (RICO), 18 U.S.C. § 1862, from a California state court. The federal court dismissed the RICO claims under Rule 12(b)(6) and, declining to exercise supplemental jurisdiction over the state-law claims, remanded the case to state court. On appeal, plaintiff argued that the federal court should not have dismissed the RICO claims with prejudice because that would preclude him from proceeding with those claims in state court, where he claimed that the pleading requirements were "less stringent than are those of the federal courts." The appellate court rejected plaintiff's argument: "The district court's Rule 12(b)(6) dismissal with prejudice operates as an adjudication on the merits of the claims under Fed.R.Civ.P. 41(b). Even though the state courts have concurrent jurisdiction over RICO actions, given the pleading flaws in this case, res judicata bars Waugh from reasserting his RICO claims in state court." Id. at 832.

2.   Examine the text of Rule 41(b). At no point does the rule state explicitly that a dismissal for failure to comply with the statute of limitations constitutes a dismissal on the merits absent an express contrary statement by the court. How, then, can the rule be construed to dictate such a conclusion?

Once one reaches the conclusion that, under the terms of the rule, a dismissal for failure to comply with the statute of limitations is to be deemed a dismissal "on the merits," the next question naturally concerns the meaning of that phrase. The phrase may be construed on two levels: "applicational" (i.e., in what situations does it apply?), and "consequential" (i.e., what legal consequences flow from a finding that a dismissal was "on the merits"?). We have already discussed how Rule 41(b) interprets the phrase in the applicational sense. Because the rule by its terms fails to define the phrase "on the merits" in the consequential sense, however, one must draw upon preexisting constructions. Traditionally, what have been the legal consequences of a finding that a dismissal was on the merits? See supra pp. 1187–1188, indicating that, traditionally, dismissals on the merits "were accorded res judicata effect . . ."

How did the Supreme Court interpret the phrase, "on the merits," in Semtek? Is that construction consistent with the traditional understanding? How does the Court rely on the language of Rule 41(a) in construing "on the merits" in Rule 41(b)? Does the text of Rule 41(a) in reality support or undermine the Court's construction of Rule 41(b)? See Burbank, supra note 1, at 1042 (characterizing Semtek as a "transparently dubious interpretation" of Rule 41(b)).

To what extent do you think the Court's construction of the phrase, "on the merits," in Rule 41(b) was influenced by the federalism considerations embodied in the Erie doctrine? Cf. Gasperini (supra p. 1014) and Walker (supra p. 1018). Is the Court's use of federalism as legitimate here as it was in those decisions?

3.   If Rule 41(b) did, in fact, dictate that a dismissal for failure to comply with the statute of limitations, absent a contrary statement by the court, is to have res judicata effect, would either the Constitution or the Rules Enabling Act be violated? How would the constitutional test fashioned in Hanna (supra p. 988) apply? As to the limits imposed by the Rules Enabling Act, consider the

test developed by the Supreme Court in *Burlington Northern* (supra p. 1004). How would such a federal rule fare under that standard? Is that conclusion consistent with the attitude reflected on the question in *Semtek*?

4.   *Semtek* held that while federal law determines the preclusive effect of federal judgments on the merits of a case, the federal rule of decision in diversity cases generally should refer to the law of the state in which the rendering court sits. Does the Court persuasively downplay the need for nationwide uniformity? Is this similar to the policy justification given in *Erie* for federal courts being required to apply state substantive law? Should this ruling in *Semtek* apply in federal question cases? See Peia v. United States, 152 F.Supp.2d 226 (D.Conn. 2001): "The present case is distinguishable from *Semtek*, which dealt with state law claims under diversity jurisdiction. When claims are brought under diversity jurisdiction, the statute of limitations period may vary in districts located in different states. However, when claims are brought under RICO [as here] the statute of limitations period will not vary from district to district." Is it the length of the limitations period or the effect of a dismissal that counts for *Semtek* purposes?

In Harper Macleod Solicitors v. Keaty & Keaty, 260 F.3d 389 (5th Cir. 2001), the defendants defaulted in a suit in a federal district court in Texas, which made jurisdictional findings that it had jurisdiction and defendants had been properly served. When the plaintiffs sought to register the default judgment in a federal court in Louisiana, that court upheld the defendants' challenge to the jurisdiction of the Texas federal court. The Fifth Circuit rejected the argument that the Louisiana federal court should have followed Texas law that limited jurisdictional challenges in collateral attacks on judgments. It noted that *Semtek* did not address the role of state law in determining the preclusive effect of jurisdictional findings of a federal court in a diversity suit, and found that applying the restrictive Texas rule would undermine federal jurisdictional law.

5.   Consider whether the subsequent suit should be precluded in the following hypothetical cases:

(a)   A federal court in a diversity case dismisses plaintiff's complaint on the grounds that the substance of his complaint constituted a compulsory counterclaim in an earlier diversity suit in the same federal court pursuant to Federal Rule of Civil Procedure 13(a). Under the law of the state in which the federal court sits, all counterclaims are permissive.

(b)   A federal court in a diversity case dismisses as a sanction under Rule 37 because plaintiff disobeyed a discovery order. Under the law of the state, there is no parallel power to dismiss for discovery violations.

(c)   A federal court in a diversity case dismisses as a sanction for violation of Rule 11. State law does not permit dismissals as sanctions in analogous circumstances.

(d)   A federal court dismisses plaintiff's complaint on grounds of collateral estoppel, even though the defendant had not been a party to the first suit in which the fact in question had been decided, because under federal common law the doctrine of mutuality of estoppel (dictating that a party who could not be bound by a finding in an earlier case because he was not a party may not use a finding from the earlier case as collateral estoppel against a litigant who was a party in that action) is no longer applicable. Under the law of the state in which the federal court sits, however, the doctrine of mutuality of estoppel still controls.

(e)   A federal court dismissed plaintiff's suit alleging violation of federal constitutional rights "with prejudice" under Rule 41(b) for violating a court order when he stated he would not attend the trial after being denied a continuance. Plaintiff then filed a nearly identical complaint in a state court which dismissed it as precluded. The Alaska Supreme Court concluded that federal common law would govern the preclusive effect of the judgment, which, after *Semtek*, would incorporate the state's preclusion law if not incompatible with federal interests. It found that "federal cases unequivocally treat a punitive dismissal like [plaintiff's]—a judgment that terminates a case for failing to follow court orders—as a judgment 'on the merits' that has claim-preclusive effect." DeNardo v. Barrans, 59 P.3d 266 (Alaska 2002).

C. ISSUE PRECLUSION (COLLATERAL ESTOPPEL)

1.   SAME ISSUE LITIGATED

LITTLE v. BLUE GOOSE MOTOR COACH CO.
Supreme Court of Illinois, 1931
346 Ill. 266, 178 N.E. 496

PER CURIAM.

* * *

Dr. Robert M. Little, the deceased, while driving his automobile in the city of East St. Louis, collided with a passenger bus, owned and operated by defendant in error [Blue Goose]. Defendant in error sued Dr. Little before a justice of the peace for damage to its bus caused by that collision. Evidence was heard and a judgment entered in favor of defendant in error against Dr. Little for $139.35. He appealed from that judgment to the county court. That appeal was later dismissed for want of prosecution, and a procedendo awarded. During the pendency of the case before the justice of the peace, Dr. Little filed a suit in the city court of East St. Louis to recover damages for personal injuries alleged to have been suffered by him in the collision.

[This suit was prosecuted by his executrix who was substituted as plaintiff upon Dr. Little's death. Her declaration alleged a general charge of negligence in the first count and willful negligence in the second count. Blue Goose raised the defense of estoppel by verdict and, in support, introduced evidence including the transcript of the judgment in the JP court and testimony by the JP that he had held a trial at which witnesses testified, had found in favor of Blue Goose, and had entered a judgment in its favor for $139.35. This defense was rejected and, after trial in the City Court of East St. Louis on the two counts of Dr. Little's executrix' declaration, judgment was entered for her in the amount of $5,000.]

On appeal from this judgment to the Appellate Court, that court reversed the same with the following finding of fact: "The court finds that appellant sued Dr. Robert M. Little, appellee's testate, before a justice of the peace for damages to its bus in the collision which occurred on November 1, 1925, and recovered a judgment therefor in the sum of $139.35; that in the rendition of said judgment it was necessarily determined that the collision and damages occasioned to the bus was due to the negligence of Dr. Little, and that immediately prior to his death he could not have maintained an action for personal injuries growing out of the same collision."

The first question arises on the ruling of the Appellate Court invoking against the claim of plaintiff in error the doctrine of estoppel by verdict. It is argued on behalf of plaintiff in error that, where a former adjudication is relied on as a bar to a subsequent action, it is essential that there be identity both of the subject-matter and of the parties, and that, in the instant case, the subject-matter is not the same, as this is the action for death by wrongful act for the benefit of the widow and next of kin, while the former suit was a claim for damages for injury to personal property. The issue on which this case is bottomed was the issue of fact which lay at the base of the judgment recovered before the justice of the peace. The allegation of the special plea is that the issue there raised was one of negligence on the part of Dr. Little on one hand and the defendant in error on the other, and that issue having been determined against Dr. Little, the fact is forever settled between these parties or their privies. Estoppel by verdict arises when a material fact in any litigation has been determined in a former suit between the same parties or between parties with whom the parties to the subsequent suit are in privity, where the fact was also material to the issue. The Appellate Court found as a matter of fact that the issue tried before the justice of the peace was an issue of negligence and was the same issue, arising on the same facts as those relied upon in the action for the wrongful death of Dr. Little, and that the issue of negligence was necessarily determined in the suit by the defendant in error against Dr. Little. That question of fact was tried before the city court in this case, and on the evidence there adduced the Appellate Court made its finding of fact. That issue of fact therefore is not open here, and we are to proceed to further consideration of the cause under the established fact that the issue of negligence, at least under the first count of the declaration, is the same issue tried before the justice of the peace.

While on appeal to the county court the trial, had there been one, would have been de novo; yet, when the appeal was dismissed and a procedendo was issued to the justice of the peace, the judgment of the justice of the peace became a final determination of that issue between the parties, and is conclusive not only upon the immediate parties to that suit, but also upon all persons in privity with them, and cannot be litigated again between the parties to that case or their privies in any subsequent action in the same or other court where that question arises, whether upon the same or a different cause of action or whatever may have been the nature or purpose of the action in which the judgment was rendered or of that in which the estoppel is set up. It follows that Dr. Little could not during his lifetime maintain the action filed by him against the defendant in error, and since plaintiff in error's right to recover damages under the Injuries Act depends upon Dr. Little's right, during his lifetime, to recover damages for injuries arising out of the same collision, plaintiff in error cannot recover here. In a suit under the Injuries Act, the cause of action is the wrongful act and not merely the death itself. Plaintiff in error therefore was not entitled to recover under the first count of her declaration, and the Appellate Court did not err in so holding.

It is contended, however, that as the second count of the declaration charges wanton and willful negligence on the part of defendant in error, contributory negligence on the part of Dr. Little is not a defense, and that the judgment of the city court was therefore right. Contributory negligence is not a defense to willful and wanton conduct, but it does not follow that the judgment of the city court was right because of that fact. In all cases charging willful and wanton negligence, it is necessary to make proof of such negligence, and, where there is no such proof, no recovery under such charge can be had. The finding of the Appellate Court that the collision was caused by the negligence of Dr. Little necessarily was a finding of fact on the willful negligence count as well as the general negligence count. Thus the rule that contributory negligence on the part of the plaintiff is not a defense to a charge of willful negligence does not apply. Whether Dr. Little or the bus driver was responsible for the accident was, as we have seen, settled. The judgment for $139.35 necessarily decided that the bus driver was not guilty of willful negligence.

* * *

[T]he Appellate Court was right in reversing the judgment without remanding it, and its judgment will be affirmed.

NOTES AND QUESTIONS

1.   Dr. Little's executrix sued for "willful" or gross negligence. Contributory negligence is not a defense to gross negligence. Thus, even though Dr. Little was found negligent in the JP action, Blue Goose could not use his negligence as a defense if it were found in the second suit to have been grossly negligent. Why then did the issues determined by the JP judgment preclude the Executrix' gross negligence claim in the second suit? Would it be important

to know that at the time this case was decided plaintiffs suing for negligence had to plead and prove freedom from contributory negligence?

2.   Is it fair to Dr. Little's Executrix to accord issue preclusion to the judgment of a JP court which had limited jurisdiction, was not a court of record, was subject to *de novo* appeal, and in which the claim solely for property damage was so small that there was little incentive to litigate it?

3.   If Dr. Little had won in the JP court, would his executrix have been able to preclude Blue Goose from relitigating the issues of each party's negligence in the second suit?

4.   Is it likely that there will be uncertainty about what a judge found in resolving an earlier case? See Fed.R.Civ.P. 52 (requiring the court to make written findings of fact in cases tried to the court).

HARDY V. JOHNS-MANVILLE SALES CORPORATION

United States Court of Appeals, Fifth Circuit, 1982
681 F.2d 334

Before GEE and JOHNSON, CIRCUIT JUDGES, and VAN PELT, DISTRICT JUDGE.

GEE, CIRCUIT JUDGE.

[Persons exposed to asbestos suffering from asbestos-related diseases—insulators, pipefitters, carpenters, factory workers—sued various manufacturers, sellers, and distributors of asbestos, asserting causes of action including negligence, breach of implied warranty, and strict liability. The district court entered a collateral estoppel order that certain issues had been determined in plaintiffs' favor by a judgment for unrelated plaintiffs against six manufacturers of asbestos in Borel v. Fibreboard Paper Products Corp., 493 F.2d 1076 (5th Cir.1973). It construed *Borel* as establishing as a matter of law and/or fact that: (1) insulation products containing asbestos as a generic ingredient are "unavoidably unsafe products," (2) asbestos is a competent producing cause of mesothelioma and asbestosis, (3) no warnings were issued by any asbestos insulation manufacturers prior to 1964, and (4) the "warning standard" was not met by the *Borel* defendants in the period from 1964 through 1969.]

Appellants argue that *Borel* did not necessarily decide that asbestos-containing insulation products were unreasonably dangerous because of failure to warn. According to appellants, the general *Borel* verdict, based on general instructions and special interrogatories, permitted the jury to ground strict liability on the bases of failures to test, of unsafeness for intended use, of failures to inspect, or of unsafeness of the product. Strict liability on the basis of failure to warn, although argued to the jury by trial counsel for the plaintiff in *Borel,* was, in the view of the appellants, never formally presented in the jury instructions and therefore was not essential to the *Borel* jury verdict.

Appellants' view has some plausibility. The special interrogatories answered by the *Borel* jury were general and not specifically directed to failure to warn. Indeed, as we discussed at length in our review of the *Borel* judgment, the jury was instructed in terms of "breach of warranty." 493 F.2d at 1091. Although the jury was accurately instructed as to "strict liability in tort" as defined in section 402A of the Restatement (Second) of Torts, that phrase was never specifically mentioned in the jury's interrogatories. It is also true that the general instructions to the *Borel* jury on the plaintiff's causes of action did not charge on failure to warn, except in connection with negligence. Yet appellants' argument in its broadest form must ultimately fail. We concluded in *Borel:*

> The jury found that the unreasonably dangerous condition of the defendants' products was the proximate cause of Borel's injury. This necessarily included a finding that, had adequate warnings been provided, Borel would have chosen to avoid the danger.

As the appellants at times concede in their briefs, "if *Borel* stands for any rule at all, it is that defendants have a duty to warn the users of their products of the long-term dangers attendant upon its use, including the danger of an occupational disease." Indeed, the first sentence in our *Borel* opinion states that that case involved "the scope of an asbestos manufacturer's duty to warn industrial insulation workers of dangers associated with the use of asbestos." Id. at 1081. Our conclusion in *Borel* was grounded in that trial court's jury instructions concerning proximate cause and defective product * * *. Close reading of these instructions convinced our panel in *Borel* that a failure to warn was necessarily implicit in the jury's verdict. While the parties invite us to reconsider our holding in *Borel* that failure to warn grounded the jury's strict liability finding in that case, we cannot, even if we were so inclined, displace a prior decision of this court absent reconsideration en banc. Further, there is authority for the proposition that once an appellate court has disposed of a case on the basis of one of several alternative issues that may have grounded a trial court's judgment, the issue decided on appeal is conclusively established for purposes of issue preclusion. Nonetheless, we must ultimately conclude that the judgment in *Borel* cannot estop even the *Borel* defendants in this case for three interrelated reasons.

First, after review of the issues decided in *Borel,* we conclude that *Borel*, while conclusive as to the general matter of a duty to warn on the part of manufacturers of asbestos-containing insulation products, is ultimately ambiguous as to certain key issues. As the authors of the Restatement (Second) of Judgments § 29, comment g (1982), have noted, collateral estoppel is inappropriate where the prior judgment is ambivalent. * * * The *Borel* jury decided that Borel, an industrial insulation worker who was exposed to fibers from his employer's insulation products over a 33-year period (from 1936 to 1969), was entitled to have been given fair warning that asbestos dust may lead to asbestosis, mesothelioma, and other cancers. The jury dismissed the argument that the danger was obvious and regarded as conclusive the fact that Borel testified that he did not know that inhaling asbestos dust could cause serious injuries until his doctor so advised him in 1969. The jury necessarily found "that, had adequate warning been provided, Borel would have chosen to avoid the danger." In *Borel,* the evidence was that the industry as a whole issued no warnings at all concerning its insulation products prior to 1964, that Johns-Manville placed a warnings label on packages of its products in 1964, and that Fibreboard and Rubberoid placed warnings on their products in 1966.

Given these facts, it is impossible to determine what the *Borel* jury decided about *when* a duty to warn attached. Did the jury find the defendants liable because their warnings after 1966, when they acknowledge that they knew the dangers of asbestosis, were insufficiently explicit as to the grave risks involved? If so, as appellants here point out, the jury may have accepted the state of the art arguments provided by the defendants in *Borel,*—i.e., that the defendants were not aware of the danger of asbestosis until the 1960's. Even under this view, there is a second ambiguity: was strict liability grounded on the fact that the warnings issued, while otherwise sufficient, never reached the insulator in the field? If so, perhaps the warnings, while insufficient as to insulation workers like Borel, were sufficient to alert workers further down the production line who may have seen the warnings—such as the carpenters and pipefitters in this case. Alternatively, even if the *Borel* jury decided that failure to warn before 1966 grounded strict liability, did the duty attach in the 1930's when the "hazard of asbestosis as a pneumoconiotic dust was universally accepted," or in 1965, when documentary evidence was presented of the hazard of asbestos insulation products to the installers of these products?

As we noted in *Borel,* strict liability because of failure to warn is based on a determination of the manufacturer's reasonable knowledge. * * * Thus, the trial judge in *Borel* instructed the jury that the danger "must have been reasonably foreseen by the manufacturer." As both this instruction and the ambiguities in the *Borel* verdict demonstrate, a determination that a particular product is so unreasonably hazardous as to require a warning of its dangers is not an absolute. Such a determination is necessarily relative to the scientific knowledge generally known or available to the manufacturer at the time the product in question was sold or otherwise placed in the stream of commerce.

Not all the plaintiffs in this case were exposed to asbestos-containing insulation products over the same 30-year period as plaintiff Borel. Not all plaintiffs here are insulation workers isolated from the warning issued by some of the defendants in 1964 and 1966. Some of the products may be different from those involved in *Borel*. Our opinion in *Borel*, "limited to determining whether there [was] a conflict in substantial evidence sufficient to create a jury question," did not resolve that as a matter of fact all manufacturers of asbestos-containing insulation products had a duty to warn as of 1936, and all failed to warn adequately after 1964. Although we determined that the jury must have found a violation of the manufacturers' duty to warn, we held only that the jury could have grounded strict liability on the absence of a warning prior to 1964 or "could have concluded that the [post-1964 and post-1966] 'cautions' were not warnings in the sense that they adequately communicated to Borel and other insulation workers knowledge of the dangers to which they were exposed so as to give them a choice of working or not working with a dangerous product." * * * [O]ur opinion in *Borel* merely approved of the various ways the jury could have come to a conclusion concerning strict liability for failure to warn. We did not say that any of the specific alternatives that the jury had before it were necessary or essential to its verdict. * * * Like *stare decisis,* collateral estoppel applies only to issues of fact or law necessarily decided by a prior court. Since we cannot say that *Borel* necessarily decided, as a matter of fact, that all manufacturers of asbestos containing insulation products knew or should have known of the dangers of their particular products at all relevant times, we cannot justify the trial court's collaterally estopping the defendants from presenting evidence as to the state of the art.

NOTES AND QUESTIONS

1. Would more detailed "special verdicts" or "general verdicts accompanied by answer to interrogatories" (as provided for in Rule 49) have provided a more precise record of what the jury found in *Borel* on which issue preclusion could have been based? Are there any reasons in such a situation not to use special verdicts or interrogatories?

2. It may be of interest to you to learn something more about the way in which the *Borel* jury reached its verdict. Consider the following:

[T]he twelve members of the jury had been evenly split when they took their first vote, and had subsequently divided eleven to one in favor of the plaintiff. The lone holdout was a man who felt deeply that workers were lucky to have jobs and that no company which provided them should be judged too harshly for its actions, whatever they may be. Finally, after the other jurors had tried vainly to get him to change his mind, a face-saving deal was struck in which, in return for their finding Borel guilty of contributory negligence, he agreed to find that four of the defendants were negligent, and all six of them liable to Borel under the doctrine of strict liability.

P. Brodeur, Outrageous Misconduct 64 (1985). Should a "face-saving deal" be the basis for broad collateral estoppel effects? Although the jury processes are not usually known, when they are should they be taken into account in determining the preclusive effect of a judgment?

Should a post-trial inquiry generally be employed to determine what the earlier jury decided (and perhaps whether it acted in a responsible manner)? Would use of juror affidavits violate Fed.R.Evid. 606(b)? For an example of attempts to obtain juror information for use in connection with a collateral estoppel determination, see Milks v. Eli Lilly & Co., 97 F.R.D. 467 (S.D.N.Y. 1983). If former jurors disagree about what occurred, will the court have to hold a trial to determine who is correct?

3.   In *Hardy* the court had no reports about the actual deliberations of the *Borel* jury except the information in the record of that case. It found that the interrogatories the jury answered were not specifically directed to failure to warn. How could the appellate court in *Borel* have concluded that the jury did find a failure to warn? Why wouldn't the *Hardy* court reconsider that ruling?

4.   Different plaintiffs always have different characteristics, and obviously complete identity is not necessary for plaintiffs in a subsequent suit to obtain the benefit of issues decided against the common defendant in an earlier suit by other plaintiffs. Which characteristics of the plaintiff in *Borel* were so distinctive as to prevent issue preclusion as to the plaintiffs in *Hardy*? Which issues did those characteristics relate to?

5.   Should differences in the circumstances of individual plaintiffs prevent the use of offensive collateral estoppel in environmental, drug, and mass-injury cases? For example, in the Bendectin cases (see Lynch v. Merrell-National Laboratories, 646 F.Supp. 856 (D.Mass.1986)), in which thousands of women claimed injuries based on taking the same drug, should a prior case in which the plaintiff used the drug during her third trimester of pregnancy be given preclusive effect on causation for a plaintiff who used it in her second trimester? What would we need to know to answer that? Should special weight be given to the economy of not relitigating basic issues affecting thousands of plaintiffs in claims against the same defendant? Recall that similar issues arose in connection with mass-tort class actions in Chap. 4, supra pp. 337–340.

6.   Does *Borel* have any effect at all in *Hardy*? Recall the doctrine of stare decisis. To what extent does the decision in *Borel* foreclose the opportunity of defendants to defend in *Hardy*? Is this effect limited to "legal" issues decided in *Borel*? For discussion of the "preclusive" effect of stare decisis, see Barrett, Stare Decisis and Due Process, 74 U.Colo.L.Rev. 1011 (2003) (arguing that there are due process limits to applying stare decisis).

COMMISSIONER OF INTERNAL REVENUE V. SUNNEN
Supreme Court of the United States, 1948
333 U.S. 591

JUSTICE MURPHY delivered the opinion of the Court.

[Sunnen was an inventor-patentee who assigned a 1928 patent license contract to his wife. In 1935, the Board of Tax Appeals held that payments made to the wife during 1929–31 under this contract were not taxable to Sunnen. The Commissioner thereafter brought a second suit claiming that payments to the wife in later years under the same 1928 contract and under other contracts modeled on the 1928 contract were taxable to Sunnen. The Tax Court, relying on a series of 1940 decisions by the Supreme Court, held that the payments made under the other contracts were income to Sunnen. But as to payments under the 1928 contract, it concluded that it was bound by res judicata to follow the 1935 decision that they were not income of Sunnen.]

[The concepts of collateral estoppel] are applicable in the federal income tax field. Income taxes are levied on an annual basis. Each year is the origin of a new liability and of a separate cause of action. Thus if a claim of liability or non-liability relating to a particular tax year is litigated, a judgment on the merits is res judicata as to any subsequent proceeding involving the same claim and the same tax year. But if the later proceeding is concerned with a similar or unlike claim relating to a different tax year, the prior judgment acts as a collateral estoppel only as to those matters in the second proceeding which were actually presented and determined in the first suit. Collateral estoppel operates, in other words, to relieve the government and the taxpayer of "redundant litigation of the identical question of the statute's application to the taxpayer's status." Tait v. Western Md. R. Co., 289 U.S. 620, 624 [(1933)].

But collateral estoppel is a doctrine capable of being applied so as to avoid an undue disparity in the impact of income tax liability. A taxpayer may secure a judicial determination of a particular tax matter, a matter which may recur without substantial variation for some years thereafter. But a subsequent modification of the significant facts or a change or development in the controlling legal principles may make that determination obsolete or erroneous, at least for future purposes. If such a determination is then perpetuated each succeeding year as to the taxpayer involved in the original litigation, he is accorded a tax treatment different from that given to other taxpayers of the same class. As a result, there are inequalities in the administration of the revenue laws, discriminatory distinctions in tax liability, and a fertile basis for litigious confusion. Such consequences, however, are neither necessitated nor justified by the principle of collateral estoppel. That principle is designed to prevent repetitious lawsuits over matters which have once been decided and which have remained substantially static, factually and legally. It is not meant to create vested rights in decisions that have become obsolete or erroneous with time, thereby causing inequities among taxpayers.

And so where two cases involve income taxes in different taxable years, collateral estoppel must be used with its limitations carefully in mind so as to avoid injustice. It must be confined to situations where the matter raised in the second suit is identical in all respects with that decided in the first proceeding and where the controlling facts and applicable legal rules remain unchanged. If the legal matters determined in the earlier case differ from those raised in the second case, collateral estoppel has no bearing on the situation. And where the situation is vitally altered between the time of the first judgment and the second, the prior determination is not conclusive. * * *

It is readily apparent in this case that the royalty payments growing out of the license contracts which were not involved in the earlier action before the Board of Tax Appeals and which concerned different tax years are free from the effects of the collateral estoppel doctrine. That is true even though those contracts are identical in all important respects with the 1928 contract, the only one that was before the Board, and even though the issue as to those contracts is the same as that raised by the 1928 contract. For income tax purposes, what is decided as to one contract is not conclusive as to any other contract which is not then in issue, however similar or identical it may be. In this respect, the instant case thus differs vitally from Tait v. Western Md. R. Co., supra, where the two proceedings involved the same instruments and the same surrounding facts.

A more difficult problem is posed as to the $4,881.35 in royalties paid to the taxpayer's wife in 1937 under the 1928 contract. Here there is complete identity of facts, issues and parties as between the earlier Board proceeding and the instant one. The Commissioner claims, however, that legal principles developed in various intervening decisions of this Court have made plain the error of the Board's conclusion in the earlier proceeding. * * * This change in the legal picture is said to have been brought about by such cases as Helvering v. Clifford, 309 U.S. 331 (1940), [and] Helvering v. Horst, 311 U.S. 112 (1940). These cases all imposed income tax liability on transferors who had assigned or transferred various forms of income to others within their family groups, although none specifically related to the assignment of patent license contracts between members of the same family. It must therefore be determined whether this *Clifford-Horst* line of cases represents an intervening legal development which is pertinent to the problem raised by the assignment of the 1928 agreement and which makes manifest the error of the result reached in 1935 by the Board. If that is the situation, the doctrine of collateral estoppel becomes inapplicable. A different result is then permissible as to the royalties paid in 1937 under the agreement in question.

* * *

[T]he clarification and growth of these principles through the *Clifford-Horst* line of cases constitute, in our opinion, a sufficient change in the legal climate to render inapplicable in the instant proceeding, the doctrine of collateral estoppel relative to the assignment of the 1928 contract. True, these cases did not originate the concept that an assignor is taxable if he retains control over the assigned property or power to defeat the receipt of income by the assignee. But they gave much added emphasis and substance to that concept, making it more suited to meet the "attenuated subtleties" created by taxpayers. So substantial was the amplification of this concept as to justify a reconsideration of earlier Tax Court decisions reached without the benefit of the expanded notions, decisions which are now sought to be perpetuated regardless of their present correctness. Thus in the earlier litigation in 1935, the Board of Tax Appeals was unable to bring to bear on the assignment of the 1928 contract the full breadth of the ideas enunciated in the *Clifford-Horst* series of cases. And, as we shall see, a proper application of the principles as there developed might well have produced a different result, such as was reached by the Tax Court in this case in regard to the assignments of the other contracts. Under those circumstances collateral estoppel should not have been used by the Tax Court in the instant proceeding to perpetuate the 1935 viewpoint of the assignment.

NOTES AND QUESTIONS

1.   Collateral estoppel is said to apply only to issues of fact and not of law. "Ordinarily, the refusal to apply the rule of issue preclusion to an issue of law makes sense. There seems no reason why a party who has litigated an issue of law should be under greater disability to invite a court to depart from precedent than a party who has not litigated the issue. The law, whatever the content of its rules, governs all litigants alike and generally speaking should be applied to all." F. James, G. Hazard & J. Leubsdorf, Civil Procedure § 11.21 (5th ed. 2001). On the other hand, is there reason to grant more preclusive effect to legal rulings than to factual findings? Consider Professor Hazard's arguments:

> The epistemological grounds for preclusion as to issues of law are stronger than those for preclusion as to issues of fact. In resolving issues of fact, the court endeavors to portray for itself a historical transaction in the outside world of events. Its method is to infer an image of reality—a scenario—from conflicting evidence. (If the evidence were not in conflict, there would not be an issue to decide.) In deciding fact questions the court necessarily works through the medium of extrajudicial resources, for example, evidence from witnesses. That dependency on outside resources entails a possible discrepancy between what the court believes was the fact and what actually was the fact. By contrast, in the resolution of issues of law the court constructs a verbal formulation from materials of which the court has direct knowledge. These materials include the relevant

legal documentary sources, such as precedents and statutes. They also include the general view of reality in which those verbal materials take on meaning. Epistemologically, that general view of reality can be considered an envelope of judicially noticed legislative facts. That reality is seen and understood through direct judicial perception, not by perception through the medium of informants, which is how a court apprehends the facts of a case. Of course, different judges have different world views, which is why they often disagree on what the law is. But these differences are necessarily dissolved or composed in deciding an issue of law.

When a court retries an issue of fact, it makes the new determination on a different evidentiary predicate. When it retries an issue of law, however, it proceeds on the same verbal and circumstantial predicates that were involved in the first instance. Purely epistemological considerations offer considerable justification for a judicial change of mind regarding the decision of an issue of fact. They offer none regarding the decision of an issue of law. Moreover, institutional considerations militate more strongly against a judicial change of mind about the law as compared to a change of mind about the facts. In redeciding an issue of fact, the court can say that its previous decision had been ill-informed. In redeciding an issue of law, the court must say that its previous decision had been ill-considered. Yet paradoxically, once determined, an issue of law may be more easily reopened than an issue of fact.

Hazard, Preclusion as to Issues of Law: The Legal System's Interest, 70 Iowa L.Rev. 81, 88–89 (1984).

2.   Collateral estoppel can, however, apply to mixed issues of law and fact where general legal principles are applied in specific factual circumstances, as established in United States v. Moser, 266 U.S. 236 (1924). When Moser retired as a captain in the U.S. Navy in 1904, he sued in the Court of Claims for the retirement pay of a rear admiral under a statute providing that officers who had served in the Civil War would be retired with the benefits of the next higher rank. The issue was whether the statute applied to someone like Moser whose only Civil War service was as a cadet at the Naval Academy. The Court of Claims decided in his favor. In a later suit by another claimant, the Court of Claims discovered another statute which it found warranted denial of the benefits. However, in three later suits by Moser for further installments of his retirement pay, the court relied on its original judgment as to Moser and granted him the benefits. The government appealed the third suit to the Supreme Court, contending that collateral estoppel should not apply to an issue of law that had been wrongly decided in the first suit. The Court held that although collateral estoppel does not apply to "unmixed questions of law," it does apply to mixed law and fact questions:

Where, for example, a court in deciding a case has enunciated a rule of law, the parties in a subsequent action upon a different demand are not estopped from insisting that the law is otherwise, merely because the parties are the same in both cases. But a *fact, question* or *right* distinctly adjudged in the original action cannot be disputed in a subsequent action, even though the determination was reached upon an erroneous view or by an erroneous application of the law.

Because the Court found that Moser's case involved a fact question that had been adjudged in his first suit, it held that the government was estopped by the decision in the first suit. Can *Moser* be distinguished from *Sunnen*?

The problem after *Moser* became how to draw the line between an unmixed question of law and mixed issues of law and fact. This proved to be a difficult distinction. What a judge or jury usually finds are mixed questions of law and fact. When a rule of law has been determined in the context of a particular set of facts, there seems to be no reason to allow that issue to be relitigated. Modern cases and the Restatement (Second) of Judgments §§ 27–28 allow preclusion as to issues of law as well as fact except when (1) the result would place the party who won in a favored position in the general administration of the law, as in *Sunnen*, (2) the first determination was not fully appealed as it was in the second suit (thus trying to avoid allowing "repeat players" like the government from making every case a "test case"), id. at § 29, comment i, (3) the two actions involve claims that are substantially unrelated, id. at § 28(2)(a), (4) a new determination is warranted in order to take account of an intervening change in the applicable legal context or otherwise to avoid inequitable administration of the laws, id., or (5) the party against whom preclusion is sought had a significantly heavier burden of persuasion on the issue in the first suit than in the second, id. at § 28(4).

3. The *Sunnen* "separable facts" doctrine—"if the relevant facts in the two cases are separable, even though they be similar or identical, collateral estoppel does not govern the legal issues which recur in the second case"—has increasingly been questioned. Montana v. United States, 440 U.S. 147 (1979), limited *Sunnen* to cases where there has been a significant "change in the legal climate." Two circuits concluded that the "separable facts" doctrine is not good law after *Montana*. American Medical Int'l, Inc. v. Secretary of Health, Education and Welfare, 677 F.2d 118, 120 (D.C.Cir.1981) (per curiam); Hicks v. Quaker Oats Co., 662 F.2d 1158, 1167 (5th Cir.1981). The Ninth Circuit stated that it would not follow *Sunnen* "on the question of similarity of facts" but that its principles "are especially important in the context of agency relitigation of legal issues with substantial public policy implications." Western Oil & Gas Assoc. v. United States Environmental Protection Agency, 633 F.2d 803, 809 (9th Cir.1980); Peck v. C.I.R., 904 F.2d 525, 527 (9th Cir.1990).

4. New Hampshire sued Maine claiming a different boundary than had been confirmed in litigation in the 1970s over the states' lobster fishing rights. In New Hampshire v. Maine, 532 U.S. 742 (2001), the Supreme Court held New Hampshire was judicially estopped:

> [U]navailing is New Hampshire's reliance on this Court's recognition that the doctrine of estoppel or that part of it which precludes inconsistent positions in judicial proceedings is ordinarily not applied

to States, Illinois ex rel. Gordon v. Campbell, 329 U.S. 362, 369. 348. This is not a case where estoppel would compromise a governmental interest in enforcing the law. Cf. Heckler v. Community Health Services of Crawford Cty, Inc., 467 U.S. 51, 60. Nor is this a case where the shift in the government's position results from a change in public policy, cf. Commissioner v. Sunnen, or a change in the facts essential to the prior judgment, cf. Montana v. United States, 440 U.S. 147, 159 (1979). Instead, it is a case between two States, in which each owes the other a full measure of respect. The Court is unable to discern any substantial public policy interest allowing New Hampshire to construe "Middle of the River" differently today than it did 25 years ago.

5.   The Court in *Sunnen* noted that since the earlier suit, the 1940 *Clifford-Horst* line of cases had resulted in a change in the "legal climate." Had it not been for that change in the law, presumably Sunnen would have been entitled to collateral estoppel as to the question of law as to taxability of the payments. The Court's concern was that if collateral estoppel applied even after a change in the law, it would result in favoritism to some taxpayers by "creat[ing] vested rights in decisions that have become obsolete or erroneous with time."

6.   Can *Sunnen* rationally be confined to tax and customs cases? The rule is sometimes stated that "changes in the law after a final judgment do not prevent the application of res judicata and collateral estoppel, even though the grounds on which the decision was based are subsequently overruled." Precision Air Parts, Inc. v. Avco Corp., 736 F.2d 1499, 1503 (11th Cir.1984). The Fifth Circuit has recognized an exception in constitutional law cases: "Faced with changing law, courts hearing questions of constitutional rights cannot be limited by res judicata. If they were, the Constitution would be applied differently in different locations." Parnell v. Rapides Parish School Bd., 563 F.2d 180, 185 (5th Cir.1977).

Is this a legitimate exception? Doesn't the problem of conflict among lower and circuit courts, resulting in different applications of the law, also exist in non-constitutional cases? Why shouldn't that rationale justify a general "change of law" exception to res judicata? On the other hand, why should one federal court have to accept the resolution by a co-equal federal court of an issue of federal law? See Marcus, Conflicts Among Circuits and Transfers Within the Federal Judicial System, 93 Yale L.J. 677, 702 (1984) ("If a federal court accepts the interpretation of another circuit without addressing the merits, it is not doing its job."). Isn't the need to resolve conflicts between circuits one of the circumstances favoring a grant of certiorari by the Supreme Court, thus providing a better solution without requiring an exception to the res judicata rule?

7.   In United States v. Stauffer Chemical Co., 464 U.S. 165 (1984), the Supreme Court significantly cut back on *Sunnen*'s insistence that preclusion be limited to cases that are "identical in all respects." The issue there was whether the Environmental Protection Agency could use private contractors to

perform inspections of Stauffer's plants under the federal Clean Air Act. The EPA had been rebuffed when it tried to do so at Stauffer plants in Wyoming and Tennessee, and in each case litigation ensued. After the federal court in Wyoming decided that the EPA could not use private contractors, the EPA sought to relitigate that question in the Tennessee case. It argued that estoppel should be limited to "the very same facts or transaction," which was not present because two different plants were involved. Characterizing the two cases as involving "virtually identical facts," the Court rejected the limitation, observing that "[w]hatever applicability that interpretation may have in the tax context, see Commissioner v. Sunnen, we reject its general applicability outside that context." Note, however, that *Stauffer Chemical* may be limited to litigation between the same parties. With regard to preclusion against the government in litigation against different parties, see United States v. Mendoza, infra p. 1285.

In Burlington Northern R.R. v. Hyundai Merchant Marine Co., 63 F.3d 1227 (3d Cir.1995), the court ruled that, in the wake of *Stauffer Chemical Co.*, nonmutual collateral estoppel could be used as to an unmixed question of law. Plaintiff filed a declaratory judgment action seeking to avoid having to indemnify defendant for liability it incurred due to damages to cargo done by the railroad before it was delivered to the defendant shipping company in Seattle for eventual transport to South Korea. The railroad's position was that it was too late to make such a claim under the railroad's contract of carriage. The problem for the railroad was that the district court in Seattle had rejected this argument in a suit by another shipping company in 1992, reasoning that an indemnity claim does not mature until the primary liability is imposed, and that the time to present the claim cannot begin to run until then. Fearing probable suit in Seattle, the railroad filed a declaratory judgment action in New Jersey, and the district court refused to follow the Seattle decision and granted the railroad summary judgment.

The court of appeals reversed, relying on Restatement (Second) of Judgments § 28, which authorizes estoppel unless the two claims are "substantially unrelated" or a new determination is warranted to take account of an intervening change in the law. Although the contractual provision had a different time period and referred to the presentation of "claims" rather than "suits," as in the provision involved in the earlier litigation, the court found that "these distinctions are of no legal significance." Instead, the "substantial relationship" prong looks to "whether the two cases involve the same application of law," and the question whether the time period starts running before the claimant is required to make a payment is "identical" in application in the two cases. There was no intervening change in the law; to the contrary it appears only that the railroad took this case on the road to engage in forum shopping and avoid the certain loss on this point in the Ninth Circuit. Under these circumstances, the court saw no ground for avoiding collateral estoppel as to this pure issue of law, and directed the district court to grant preclusive effect to the earlier resolution of this legal issue.

8.   The Supreme Court in Richards v. Jefferson County, Alabama, 517 U.S. 793 (1996), distinguished between two types of actions brought by taxpayers. The first category encompasses cases in which the taxpayer is using that status to complain of an alleged misuse of funds, e.g., Massachusetts v. Mellon, 262 U.S. 447 (1923), or about other public action that has only an indirect impact on his interests, e.g., Stromberg v. Board of Ed. of Bratenahl, 64 Ohio St.2d 98, 413 N.E.2d 1184 (1980). As to these cases, states have wide latitude to establish procedures to limit the number of judicial proceedings through such means as application of res judicata. The second category involves a federal constitutional challenge to a state's attempt to levy personal funds. While states may determine the applicable adjective law, the taxpayer must be accorded due process and the tax will be struck down if there is a denial of "any practicable opportunity to contest a tax on federal constitutional grounds," see Brinkerhoff-Faris Trust & Sav. Co. v. Hill, 281 U.S. 673 (1930). In this case, the Court refused to bind the taxpayers by res judicata under a prior state court action (that had been brought by the city and three county taxpayers) as to which they had received neither notice nor sufficient representation.

2.   ALTERNATIVE GROUNDS FOR DECISION

JANET ALEXANDER COSMETICS V. L'OREAL USA, INC.

United States Court of Appeals, Third Circuit, 2006
458 F.3d 244

Before RENDELL, and VAN ANTWERPEN, CIRCUIT JUDGES, and ACKERMAN, DISTRICT JUDGE.

RENDELL, CIRCUIT JUDGE.

In proceedings before the Trademark Trial and Appeal Board ("TTAB" or "Board"), the predecessor in interest of L'Oreal USA, Inc. ("L'Oreal") argued that a registered trademark used by Jean Alexander Cosmetics, Inc. (JAC) was likely to be confused with two of its marks and that the registration should therefore be cancelled. The TTAB denied the petition to cancel, holding, among other things, that there was no likelihood of confusion as between the marks. In the instant action for trademark infringement, JAC seeks to revisit the Board's finding with respect to likelihood of confusion.

The District Court held that JAC was precluded from relitigating the TTAB's determination that there was no likelihood of confusion, and we agree. The issue was actually litigated and previously decided in the cancellation proceedings. Although the TTAB's conclusion on likelihood of confusion was not its only basis for denying the cancellation petition, it was one of two independently sufficient grounds on which the Board resolved the case. Under these circumstances, we will apply the doctrine of issue preclusion and affirm the District Court's dismissal of JAC's complaint.

I.

[The dispute arose over competing claims to trademark rights in marks on cosmetic products that use the letters "EQ." L'Oreal began using its "old" Shades EQ mark in 1988. JAC began using its "EQ System" mark in 1990 and, in 1993, it registered this mark with the Patent and Trademark Office ("PTO"). In 1996, L'Oreal attempted to register a modernized version of its "Shades EQ" mark that it had begun using in 1992. The examiner at the PTO rejected the application for registration of the modernized or "new" Shades EQ mark because it was likely to be confused with JAC's EQ System mark. L'Oreal then filed a petition to cancel JAC's registration for the EQ System mark. L'Oreal alleged that it had used its "old" Shades EQ mark prior to JAC's use of the EQ System mark and that, if there was a likelihood of confusion between the two marks, JAC's registration should be cancelled. In addition, L'Oreal alleged that the old and new versions of its Shades EQ mark were "legal equivalents," giving the modernized version priority over JAC's mark as well. JAC contested priority (which mark came first) and argued, as an affirmative defense, that there was no likely confusion.]

[After four years of proceedings, the TTAB refused to cancel JAC's registration of the EQ System trademark. The TTAB held that the original L'Oreal EQ mark had priority over JAC EQ System mark, but found that the modernized L'Oreal EQ mark was not a legal equivalent of the original version. Consequently, L'Oreal could not establish the priority of its mark over JAC's mark. Having resolved the question of priority, the TTAB examined likelihood of confusion. Because L'Oreal's original EQ mark had priority over JAC's EQ System mark, it was necessary for the Board to determine whether there was a likelihood of confusion between those two marks. But the TTAB also considered the likelihood of confusion between L'Oreal's modern EQ mark and JAC's EQ mark. The TTAB did this "in case upon further review, it is determined that [L'Oreal's] original and modernized marks are legal equivalents," a finding that would give L'Oreal's modernized version priority over JAC's mark.]

[The TTAB found no likelihood of confusion between JAC's mark and either the original or modernized versions of L'Oreal's mark. Instead of appealing the TTAB's decision, L'Oreal reasserted its request with the PTO to register its modernized EQ trademark. Relying on the TTAB's finding that there was no likelihood of confusion, the PTO allowed registration of L'Oreal's mark. JAC opposed registration of the modernized L'Oreal mark, arguing that it would likely be confused with the JAC mark. The TTAB held that the likelihood of confusion between the two marks had been fully and decisively litigated in the cancellation proceedings. Because JAC was precluded from relitigating likelihood of confusion, the TTAB granted summary judgment in favor of L'Oreal. Thereafter, JAC filed suit against L'Oreal in the district court alleging trademark infringement of its EQ

System mark and specifically averring likelihood of confusion. The district court dismissed the complaint, holding that issue preclusion prevented JAC from relitigating likelihood of confusion and foreclosed its claim for trademark infringement.]

II.

[Before turning to the merits, the appellate court determined the proper standard of review. Inasmuch as the district court had no occasion to exercise discretion, the appellate court applied de novo or plenary review.]

III.

* * *

We have identified four standard requirements for the application of collateral estoppel in our case law: (1) the identical issue was previously adjudicated; (2) the issue was actually litigated; (3) the previous determination was necessary to the decision; and (4) the party being precluded from relitigating the issue was fully represented in the prior action. We have also considered whether the party being precluded had a full and fair opportunity to litigate the issue in question in the prior action, and whether the issue was determined by a final and valid judgment (citations and quotations omitted).

The dispute in this case centers on whether the TTAB's finding on likelihood of confusion was "necessary" to its decision in the cancellation proceedings. JAC argues that once the Board concluded that the JAC mark had priority over the modernized L'Oreal mark, there was no reason for it to analyze likelihood of confusion as to these two marks. To resolve the case at that point, the TTAB needed only to consider whether the *original* L'Oreal mark, which had priority, was likely to be confused with the JAC mark. Thus, JAC contends that the Board's determination that there was no likelihood of confusion as between the EQ System mark and the modernized Shades EQ mark was unnecessary to its 2001 decision and should not be given preclusive effect.

L'Oreal argues that collateral estoppel applies here because both priority of use and likelihood of confusion figured prominently in the cancellation proceedings and both issues were potentially dispositive of the case. L'Oreal urges us to adopt a rule under which preclusive effect is given to a finding that is an alternative ground for a judgment where that finding, standing alone, would have been sufficient to support the judgment. Though an alternative finding may not be strictly necessary to the judgment in the sense that there was another stated basis for the decision, L'Oreal contends that giving such a finding preclusive effect would not compromise the objectives behind the necessity principle.

The requirement that a preclusive finding must have been necessary to a judgment is rooted in principles of fairness. "[P]arties should be estopped only on issues they actually deem important, and not on incidental matters." *Lynne Carol Fashions, Inc. v. Cranston Print Works Co.,* 453 F.2d 1177, 1183 (3d Cir.1972). Because litigants are likely to view an issue that is necessary to the resolution of a case as important and to litigate it vigorously, it is fair to give such a determination preclusive effect. *See Wickham Contracting Co., Inc. v. Bd. of Educ. of City of New York,* 715 F.2d 21, 28 (2d Cir.1983) (noting that the necessity rule ensures that "parties to litigation have sufficient notice and incentive to litigate matters in earlier proceedings which may bind them in subsequent matters"). The necessity requirement also ensures that preclusive effect is not given to determinations that did not "receive close judicial attention," *Commercial Assocs. v. Tilcon Gammino, Inc.,* 998 F.2d 1092, 1097 (1st Cir.1993), or that were unappealable by virtue of being incidental to a decision, *see* Restatement (Second) of Judgments § 27 cmt. h. * * *

There is no question that likelihood of confusion was a central issue in the cancellation proceedings. It was the focus of the parties' pleadings and had been litigated extensively over the course of four years. Reviewing its own decision from 2001, the TTAB noted that this was "not a case where the Board made incidental determinations on an issue which was not before it." Rather, the TTAB believed that likelihood of confusion was an important issue in the case and, in fact, intended its determination that there was no likelihood of confusion to be controlling if its holding on priority were overturned on appeal. Thus, L'Oreal is correct that the finding on likelihood of confusion constituted an alternative ground on which the Board dismissed its petition to cancel.

However, this conclusion does not resolve the question of whether the finding should be given preclusive effect because, as JAC notes, the case could have been resolved without the Board's determination that there was no likelihood of confusion between the JAC mark and the modernized L'Oreal mark. We must determine whether a finding that is an alternate, but independently sufficient, basis for a judgment should be deemed necessary to a decision for purposes of collateral estoppel.

"Traditional analysis has viewed [alternative holdings] as presenting a dilemma between two choices—preclusion must be available as to each of the independently sufficient findings, or it must be denied as to all." 18 Charles Alan Wright et al., *Federal Practice and Procedure* § 4421, at 564 (2d ed. 2002). Courts that apply collateral estoppel to alternative findings have sidestepped the requirement that the determination be "necessary" to the decision and focused instead on the trustworthiness and practical considerations surrounding the adjudication. Those courts that deny preclusion to independently sufficient findings do so because an alternative holding, by definition, is not "necessary" to a judgment.

The First Restatement of Judgments resolved this dilemma in favor of extending preclusion to each alternative holding. *See* Restatement of Judgments § 68 cmt. n (1942) ("Where the judgment is based upon the matters litigated as alternative grounds, the judgment is determinative on both grounds, although either alone would have been sufficient to support the judgment."). The Second Restatement, crafted forty years later, adopted the contrary position. It states that "[i]f a judgment of a court of first instance is based on determinations of two issues, either of which standing independently would be sufficient to support the result, the judgment is not conclusive with respect to either issue standing alone." Restatement (Second) of Judgments § 27 cmt. i.

There is no consensus among the courts of appeals as to whether the First or Second Restatement offers the better approach. [After surveying conflicting authority from the other circuits and examining its own prior decisions, the court found no binding authority.] We have never chosen between the positions of the First or Second Restatement under the circumstances before us. We will accordingly turn to the arguments in support of each approach.

Applying issue preclusion to independently sufficient alternative findings furthers the basic objectives of the doctrine. "Collateral estoppel ... has the dual purpose of protecting litigants from the burden of relitigating an identical issue with the same party or his privy and of promoting judicial economy by preventing needless litigation." *Parklane Hosiery [v. Shore]*, 439 U.S. [322], at 326 [(1979)]. Denying preclusive effect to a finding that would support a court's judgment merely because the case was disposed of on other grounds as well would result in the inefficient use of private and public litigation resources. Courts routinely decide cases on multiple grounds, each of which has been fully litigated and given careful consideration due to their potentially dispositive role in the case. Because the interests that the necessity principle protects are not compromised under these circumstances, it would be curious to conclude that *none* of these findings were necessary to the judgment for purposes of collateral estoppel. *See* Restatement of Judgments § 68 cmt. n ("It seems obvious that it should not be held that neither [alternative finding] is material [to a judgment], and hence both should be held to be material.").

In opposition to this position are three arguments against applying collateral estoppel to independently sufficient alternative findings. "First, a determination in the alternative may not have been as carefully or rigorously considered as it would have if it had been necessary to the result, and in that sense it has some of the characteristics of dicta." Restatement (Second) of Judgments § 27 cmt. i. Second, "[s]ince one alternative ground will support the judgment, the losing litigant has little incentive to appeal another ground, even if erroneous." *Hicks [v. Quaker Oats Co.]*, 662 F.2d 1158, 1168 (5th Cir. 1981); *see also* Restatement (Second) of Judgments

§ 27 cmt. i ("[T]he losing party, although entitled to appeal from both determinations, might be dissuaded from doing so because of the likelihood that at least one of them would be upheld and the other not even reached."). Without an "incentive to appeal, the losing litigant will be less likely to consider collateral consequences of the erroneous ground, and this may disadvantage him unfairly later, unless he is particularly prescient." *Hicks,* 662 F.2d at 1168.

Finally, to the extent that parties would file "cautionary appeals" to avoid the possible preclusive effects of an alternative holding in future litigation, this would "increas[e] the burdens of litigation on the parties and the courts rather than lightening those burdens." Restatement (Second) of Judgments § 27 cmt. i. Of course, this result is "contrary to the principles of judicial economy which motivated the doctrine of collateral estoppel in the first place." *Hicks,* 662 F.2d at 1169.

We are not persuaded by the rationale supporting the position of the Second Restatement. As a general matter, we are unconvinced that courts do, or should be assumed to, give less rigorous consideration to the alternative grounds they voice for their decisions. A determination that is independently sufficient to support a court's judgment is not "incidental, collateral, or immaterial to that judgment," *Hicks,* 662 F.2d at 1168, and it is reasonable to expect that such a finding is the product of careful judicial reasoning.

Moreover, because collateral estoppel applies only to issues that were "actually litigated" in prior proceedings, there is little risk that preclusive effect will be given to determinations that the parties did not deem important or that were not subject to evidentiary proof. For example, in the instant case, the parties focused on the likelihood of confusion in their pleadings and extensively litigated the issue for more than four years. Thus, litigants are adequately protected from the unfairness of giving preclusive effect to a finding that was not "vigorously litigated" or was not a "focus of the court's decision."

Nor do we believe that the position of the First Restatement increases the risk that preclusion will be applied unfairly against a litigant who failed to appeal a judgment because it was supportable on alternative grounds. This concern is utterly speculative and does not outweigh the systemic interest that courts and litigants have in ensuring that the identical parties receive only "one bite at the apple" on a given issue.

Adopting the Second Restatement's view that preclusive effect should be denied to findings because they are stated in the alternative would significantly weaken the principle that "later courts should honor the first actual decision of a matter that has been actually litigated." Wright et al., *supra,* at § 4416, p. 386. The doctrine of collateral estoppel protects this vital interest of the judicial system. *See S. Pac. Ry. v. United States,* 168 U.S. 1, 49 (1897) (noting that the "general rule" of issue preclusion "is demanded by the very object for which civil courts have been established"). Litigants often raise multiple issues that are potentially dispositive of a case, and courts routinely address them in the interest of providing a complete and thoroughly reasoned decision. To permit or require relitigation of all alternative findings would eviscerate a great number of judicial determinations that were the products of costly litigation and careful deliberation. Indeed, under the approach of the Second Restatement, the judicial findings in nearly any complex case would be unlikely to preclude subsequent relitigation of the same issues.

Thus, we will follow the traditional view that independently sufficient alternative findings should be given preclusive effect. We recognize that such determinations do not fulfill the necessity requirement for collateral estoppel in a strict sense but, just as we did not "'quibbl[e] about the necessity principle'" in the context of declaratory judgments, neither will we do so in the context of alternative holdings that have been actually litigated and decided. Applying collateral estoppel in such cases does not undermine the interests that the necessity principle protects. We have little difficulty promoting the objectives of the necessity rule rather than requiring its formal fulfillment in situations where those objectives are served and it is equitable to do so. * * * Accordingly, we adopt the view of the First Restatement and the other courts of appeals that permit the application of issue preclusion to alternative findings.

We note that at least one commentator has offered a variation on the First Restatement's rule, whereby independently sufficient alternative findings would be given preclusive effect only "if a second court can determine without extended inquiry that a particular finding reflects a careful process of decision." Wright et al., *supra,* at § 4421, p. 580. This approach might work well in circumstances such as those before us, where the same tribunal that made the potentially preclusive finding also concluded later that this finding was necessary to its earlier judgment. * * * Given that "the question of preclusion will almost always be a close one if each case is to rest on its own particular facts," Restatement (Second) of Judgments § 27 cmt. i, a rule that required case-by-case evaluation and second-guessing of how carefully the first tribunal considered a question would deny the parties the benefit of a "clear rule" and would likely result in a "wasteful expansion of the effort to reconstruct the initial process of decision," Wright et al., *supra,* at § 4421, p. 580. We thus believe that the First Restatement of Judgments articulates a clearer and better rule to be applied in the circumstances before us.

JAC contends that, regardless of whether we adopt the First Restatement rule, it would be unfair to apply issue preclusion here because JAC was the prevailing party in the cancellation proceedings and was therefore unable to appeal the TTAB's favorable finding on likelihood of confusion. *See* Restatement (Second) of Judgments § 28(1) (rejecting issue preclusion where "the party against whom preclusion is sought could not, as a matter of law, have obtained review of the judgment in the initial action"). We disagree. Any "party to a [TTAB] proceeding who is dissatisfied with the decision of the Board" may appeal. More generally, the Supreme Court has held that a prevailing party may appeal "for the purpose of obtaining a review of findings he deems erroneous which are not necessary to support the decree." Under this authority, JAC could have appealed the Board's finding on likelihood of confusion, even as the prevailing party.

JAC's corollary argument is that, even if it could have appealed the finding, it would have harmed its own interest to do so. "In the context of the [c]ancellation [p]roceeding before the TTAB, JAC had absolutely no interest in proving that there was likelihood of confusion," as this was a requirement for L'Oreal to prevail. We are unsympathetic to this argument. It was not necessary for JAC to resist the cancellation petition by denying the likelihood of confusion between its EQ mark and the modernized L'Oreal EQ mark and raising the issue as an affirmative defense. However, having raised and litigated this specific claim, JAC cannot now avoid the Board's determination of it because its own interests or the litigation context have changed.

IV.

We follow the rule of the First Restatement of Judgments and give preclusive effect to the TTAB's alternative holding that there is no likelihood of confusion between L'Oreal's modernized EQ mark and JAC's EQ mark. Because JAC's claim is barred by the doctrine of collateral estoppel, we will affirm the district court's order.

NOTES AND QUESTIONS

1. The common law recognized and protected the right of individual merchants and artisans to attach a distinctive brand or mark to their work, as a way to distinguish their products from those of competitors. Today, one can still acquire a trademark by usage and base infringement claims on the common law, but the protections tend to be local and variable.

Federal law attempts to provide a more nationally uniform framework for the assertion and protection of rights in trademarks that are used in commerce. Under the 1946 Lanham Act, 15 U.S.C. §§ 1051 et seq., Congress set up a system of trademark protection that features a combination of agency registration and federal court litigation. By registering their marks with the United States Patent and Trademark Office (PTO), firms provide notice to potential competitors and gain presumptive nationwide protection for the mark. Unregistered marks may also gain a measure of federal protection through first use. Federal courts have jurisdiction over federal claims for trademark infringement and dilution, but Congress has not excluded the state courts from hearing trademark claims. See 28 U.S.C. § 1338. Litigation over claims of infringement can be quite costly, and may feature surveys of consumer opinion that shed light on questions of likelihood of confusion. Federal law makes broad remedies available to successful claimants, including injunctive relief, destruction of offending articles, damages, and costs and attorney's fees for cases of willful infringement. See 28 U.S.C. §§ 1116–1125.

The nature of the rights obtained via registration may depend on the specific character of the trademark. For trademarks like the EQ marks at issue in Janet Alexander Cosmetics v. L'Oreal, commercial use prior to registration plays an important role in securing legal protection for the mark. One key finding was that L'Oreal changed its mark to the point that it could not claim first use of the modified mark. But then, the finding of lack of likelihood of confusion between the Alexander mark and L'Oreal's changed mark opened the way for L'Oreal to argue that its newer version could be registered.

2.   The Third Circuit assumed that the district court was obliged to afford issue preclusive effect to a contested trademark proceeding before the TTAB. The Supreme Court later confirmed that assumption in B & B Hardware, Inc. v. Hargis Industries, Inc., 135 S.Ct. 1293 (2015). Part of a long-running effort to protect its mark (SEALTIGHT), B & B objected when Hargis attempted to register a similar mark (SEALTITE), for use in a different market. Ruling on the basis of written submissions, the TTAB refused to accept Hargis's application for trademark protection, finding that the marks were confusingly similar. At about the same time, B & B brought suit against Hargis in federal court for trademark infringement. B & B attempted to establish likely confusion by pointing to the TTAB decision but the district court refused to accord issue preclusive effect to the agency's determination and sent the case to the jury, which found no likely confusion and rejected B & B's infringement claims.

On review, the Court reversed the lower courts' categorical refusal to accord the TTAB decision issue preclusive effect in the later action for infringement. The Court acknowledged that the agency resolves many trademark issues without formal contestation; no preclusive effect would attach to such proceedings. When contestation does occur, however, issue preclusion may attach to the agency's decision so long as the issues were "materially the same" and the other elements of preclusion were established. Id. at 1310. Two Justices dissented, arguing that the common law generally accorded preclusive effect only to the decisions of courts of competent jurisdiction. Agency proceedings did not qualify as such. The dissenters also argued that the application of issue preclusion would effectively consign the resolution of disputes over private trademark rights to an agency and thereby pose a threat to federal judicial independence under Article III. Both the majority and dissent invoked the statutory provision for de novo judicial review of TTAB decisions in support of their competing views.

3.   Granted that agency adjudications can have issue preclusive effect on subsequent court proceedings, was it proper to accord such effect to the TTAB decision in the context of this case? Note that JAC argued as an affirmative defense to the petition to cancel registration of its mark that there was no likely

confusion between the L'Oreal marks and its own EQ mark. JAC succeeded with this argument and the TTAB rejected L'Oreal's petition to cancel the registration of JAC's mark, finding no likely confusion. Later, JAC took the opposite position in court, claiming in its action for infringement that its mark had priority and that the L'Oreal mark was confusingly similar. Could the Third Circuit have based its ruling against JAC on a theory of judicial estoppel? That "controversial" doctrine holds that a "person cannot take factual positions in litigation that are directly inconsistent with positions previously taken by the person in a prior proceeding." R. Casad & K. Clermont, Res Judicata: A Handbook on its Theory, Doctrine, and Practice 18 (2001). The authors report that the doctrine varies widely among jurisdictions and most frequently applies to statements of fact made under oath. Id. at 18–19.

4.   In the early 20th century, it was generally accepted that, in Judge Learned Hand's words, "if a court decides a case on two grounds, each is a good estoppel." Irving National Bank v. Law, 10 F.2d 721 (2d Cir.1926). For a critical assessment of the problem, see Lucas, The Direct and Collateral Estoppel Effects of Alternative Holdings, 50 U.Chi.L.Rev. 701 (1983). The First Restatement, followed in *Janet Alexander Cosmetics*, tracked the approach of Hand and others.

The Second Restatement view, refusing to accord issue preclusive effect to alternative findings, drew on the reasoning of *Halpern v. Schwartz*, 426 F.2d 102 (2d Cir.1970). The alternative findings at issue there were made in a bankruptcy proceeding. Creditors filed an involuntary petition in bankruptcy, alleging that the debtor Evelyn Schwartz had committed three separate acts of bankruptcy. Although a finding as to any one act would have sufficed to support the imposition of involuntary bankruptcy, the bankruptcy court ruled in favor of the creditors on all alternative grounds, including a finding that Schwartz had transferred assets with the intent to hinder or defraud her creditors. After those three findings were upheld on appeal, the bankruptcy trustee argued that Schwartz should be denied a bankruptcy discharge (which would wipe the slate clean and give her a fresh start free from old debts). Only one of the three alternative grounds in support of bankruptcy—the act of transferring assets with the intent to hinder or defraud creditors—would provide a legal basis for denial of the discharge.

The question in Halpern v. Schwartz was whether that single alternative holding as to intent to hinder or defraud was entitled to issue preclusive effect in the dispute over the bankruptcy discharge. The Second Circuit said no (id. at 106–07):

> It would be unwise to require a losing litigant in bankruptcy to take an appeal from alleged errors in one alternative ground simply to ward off the conclusive effect of collateral estoppel on a later discharge proceeding, when on appeal the court could affirm on one of the other alternative grounds. This seems particularly so in bankruptcy litigation, when debtors particularly are often handicapped in financing litigation in the predischarge stages of the proceeding. The losing litigant may not have the foresight to see that

the allegedly erroneous ground may have unwanted collateral effects in the future, and hence if not clairvoyant, he may fall into a trap. Second, the winning litigant would not vigorously oppose the merits of the appeal as to one ground since he would simply stress the existence of alternative grounds on which to affirm. So, if the appellate court were to consider the merits of the claim of error, it might not have the benefit of adversary argument on the merits. And if the appellate court were to choose to avoid the merits of the claim of error on one ground, and affirm solely on the basis of one or several of the other alternative grounds, some courts have held that the lower court judgment is conclusive as to the allegedly erroneous ground despite the appellate court's unwillingness to rely on it. Even if the appellate court's affirmance on narrower grounds removes the conclusive effect as to grounds not relied on in the affirmance, the requirement of taking an appeal to protect issues in future collateral suits would not serve one important purpose of the doctrine of collateral estoppel, to minimize litigation and bring it to an end. Such a requirement would, in effect, require cautionary appeals litigating issues on appeal for their possible effect on future indeterminate collateral litigation, which neither party can be sure will occur. The rule at best would preclude some future trial litigation at the expense of currently creating extra appellate litigation.

We therefore hold that when a prior judgment adjudicating one a bankrupt rests on two or more independent alternative grounds, it is not conclusive as to issues in trial of objections to discharge which issues were necessarily found in order to establish only one of those grounds.

5. Was *Halpern* meant to apply outside the bankruptcy setting? The Third Circuit thought not, acknowledging *Halpern*'s influence on the drafters of the Second Restatement but questioning its generality.

[E]ven before the Second Restatement had been completed, the Court of Appeals for the Second Circuit noted that *Halpern* was limited to its facts and that the decision was "not intended to have . . . broad impact outside the specific context" in which *Halpern* arose, namely, bankruptcy proceedings. *Winters v. Lavine*, 574 F.2d 46, 67 (2d Cir.1978); *see also Williams v. Ward*, 556 F.2d 1143, 1154 (2d Cir.1977). Thus, in the Second Circuit, the view of the First Restatement still controls "in circumstances divergent from those in *Halpern*." *Winters*, 574 F.2d at 67.

Janet Alexander Cosmetics, 458 F.3d at 251 n. 4. Does the burden on pro se or relatively impecunious litigants deserve a place in the analysis? Is it possible to administer a rule of issue preclusion that depends on the setting and the sophistication of the parties? Is it fair to ask Janet Alexander Cosmetics to have considered the downstream implications before arguing before TTAB that there was no likelihood of confusion?

6.　In *Halpern* the court said that alternate findings are not likely to be reviewed carefully on appeal. The Third Circuit in *Janet Alexander Cosmetics* disagreed. Which court has the better of that argument? Consider Aetna Casualty & Surety Co. v. Cunningham, 224 F.2d 478 (5th Cir.1955). Plaintiff there sought recovery of the same sum alternatively for breach of contract and fraud. The trial court awarded judgment in the sum sought for breach of contract but found no fraud. Plaintiff appealed, contending that it had a stake in proving fraud as well in order to defeat efforts to obtain a discharge in bankruptcy. Defendant argued that plaintiff was not entitled to review of this decision because the relief it had obtained on the contract claim—a judgment for the sum demanded—was all it could obtain for fraud. The appellate court held that plaintiff could nevertheless appeal the fraud claim because the rejection of that claim affected the "quality of the judgment" since "amount is not the sole measure of the relief to which a party may be entitled. The judgment may have different qualities and legal consequences dependent on the claim on which it is based." Is this a more sensible way of approaching the problem in *Halpern*?

7.　The Third Circuit noted a division in the circuit courts' willingness to accord issue preclusive effect to alternative findings. See *Janet Alexander Cosmetics*, 458 F.3d at 251–52 (contrasting the Second, Seventh, Ninth, and Eleventh Circuits, which were said to be generally willing to give preclusive effect to alternative findings, with the Tenth and Federal Circuits, which were said to have refused to give such preclusive effect).

8.　Should an arbitration award be given the same preclusive effect as a court judgment or agency determination? The general rule is that if a party had a full opportunity to present its case in an arbitration, a confirmed arbitration award will be treated as a final judgment for purposes of res judicata and collateral estoppel. See Shell, Res Judicata and Collateral Estoppel Effects of Commercial Arbitration, 35 U.C.L.A.L. Rev. 623 (1988). To be sure, 28 U.S.C. § 1738, which obliges federal courts to give the same preclusive effect to a state-court judgment as would the court of the rendering state, does not apply to arbitration awards as such because they are not "judicial proceedings." But courts do give effect to arbitration awards that have been confirmed by a federal district court judgment (see 9 U.S.C. § 9). See Rudell v. Comprehensive Accounting Corp., 802 F.2d 926 (7th Cir. 1986); Aufderhar v. Data Dispatch, Inc., 452 N.W.2d 648, 652 (Minn. 1990) (where claimant was afforded a full opportunity to litigate concerning personal injury in an arbitration, he may be estopped from relitigating the issues in a suit). In the absence of such a confirming judgment, any preclusive effect given an arbitration award must arise from common law.

Do arbitrators face a symmetric obligation to give preclusive effect to prior judicial judgments? In general, arbitration operates as a creature of a contract between consenting parties with the support of a federal statute that provides for federal courts to compel arbitration, when the parties have so agreed, and to confirm arbitral awards, once they have been rendered. While federal law provides for highly deferential review of such awards, some courts have indicated a willingness to vacate the award of an arbitrator who refuses to give effect to claim and issue preclusion and thus proceeds in manifest disregard of law. See Collins v. D.R. Horton, Inc., 505 F.3d 874, 880 (9th Cir. 2007) (arbitrators are not free to ignore the preclusive effect of prior judgments under the doctrines of res judicata and collateral estoppel); Aircraft Braking Sys. Corp. v. Local 856, 97 F.3d 155, 159 (6th Cir. 1996) (same); Miller v. Runyon, 77 F.3d 189, 193 (7th Cir. 1996); cf. Miller Brewing Co. v. Forth Worth Distrib. Co., 781 F.2d 494, 499 (5th Cir. 1986) (reasoning that parties may be barred from seeking relief from an arbitration panel that would be inconsistent with res judicata).

To what extent does preclusive effect arise from an arbitration award entered in connection with a "court annexed arbitration" program that permits either party to appeal for a trial de novo (see pp. 511–513 supra). When there was no appeal, courts will generally accord collateral estoppel effect to the arbitration. For example, in Dorrance v. Lee, 976 P.2d 904 (Hawaii 1999), the parties in a mandatory "court-annexed arbitration" did not appeal the arbitrator's determination of who was negligent (and in what percentages) in an automobile accident. Summary judgment was then granted in a suit that had been filed by one of the parties prior to the issuance of the arbitration award on the ground that the findings of the arbitrator could not be relitigated. But cf. Flynn v. Gorton, 255 Cal.Rptr. 768 (Cal.App.1989) (refusing to accord such a "court-annexed arbitration" award collateral estoppel effect because the parties had no serious incentive to litigate).

When should an earlier arbitration award be given preclusive effect in a later arbitration? In Gonce v. Veterans Administration, 872 F.2d 995 (Fed.Cir.1989), the cases of certain co-workers discharged for alleged abuse of patients recorded on videotape reached arbitration first, and the arbitrators found their grievances arbitrable despite a 17-month delay. Other co-workers argued in their subsequent arbitrations that collateral estoppel effect must be given to the earlier arbitral awards on that point. Prior Federal Circuit decisions had given effect to labor arbitration decisions where the issue was identical. However, the *Gonce* court refused to follow that case, finding that the actions taken against the employees were based on separate instances of misconduct, and there were no transcripts of the proceedings, making it impossible to tell whether mitigating circumstances distinguished the cases. It commented that, pursuant to Supreme Court precedents, the preclusive effect to be given to prior arbitration awards is "for individual resolution, absent a provision in the governing contract that requires earlier awards to bind subsequent arbitrators." Id. at 997.

D. PERSONS BOUND BY JUDGMENT

1. NONPARTY PRECLUSION: PARTIES AND PERSONS IN PRIVITY

The traditional view of res judicata and collateral estoppel is that a judgment binds only parties and those in privity with them. The term "privity" is one of those conclusory words that provides little insight into the underlying policies. "The legal definition of a person in privity with another, is a person so identified with another that he represents the same legal right." Searle Brothers v. Searle, 588 P.2d 689, 691 (Utah 1978). Restatement (Second) of Judgments (1982) eschews use of the term "privity," instead describing the various kinds of nonparties who are deemed to have a sufficient relationship to a party to be bound by the judgment. See id. at §§ 39–41. See also Taylor v. Sturgell, below (following the Restatement in describing the problem as non-party preclusion rather than privity). Rooted in due process, the limits on non-party preclusion reflect the view that a non-party should not be bound by a judgment unless she had an opportunity to be heard or was so identified with a party that her interests were represented.

TAYLOR V. STURGELL
Supreme Court of the United States, 2008
553 U.S. 880

Claim can't be precluded if previous litigant has no legal relation to current litigants

JUSTICE GINSBURG delivered the opinion of the Court.

"It is a principle of general application in Anglo-American jurisprudence that one is not bound by a judgment *in personam* in a litigation in which he is not designated as a party or to which he has not been made a party by service of process." *Hansberry v. Lee,* 311 U.S. 32 (1940). Several exceptions, recognized in this Court's decisions, temper this basic rule. In a class action, for example, a person not named as a party may be bound by a judgment on the merits of the action, if she was adequately represented by a party who actively participated in the litigation. In this case, we consider for the first time whether there is a "virtual representation" exception to the general rule against precluding nonparties. Adopted by a number of courts, including the courts below in the case now before us, the exception so styled is broader than any we have so far approved.

The virtual representation question we examine in this opinion arises in the following context. Petitioner Brent Taylor filed a lawsuit under the Freedom of Information Act seeking certain documents from the Federal Aviation Administration. Greg Herrick, Taylor's friend, had previously brought an unsuccessful suit seeking the same records. The two men have no legal relationship, and there is no evidence that Taylor controlled, financed, participated in, or even had notice of Herrick's earlier suit. Nevertheless, the D.C. Circuit held Taylor's suit precluded by the judgment against Herrick because, in that court's assessment, Herrick qualified as Taylor's "virtual representative."

We disapprove the doctrine of preclusion by "virtual representation," and hold, based on the record as it now stands, that the judgment against Herrick does not bar Taylor from maintaining this suit.

I

The Freedom of Information Act (FOIA) accords "any person" a right to request any records held by a federal agency. 5 U.S.C. § 552(a)(3)(A) (2006 ed.). No reason need be given for a FOIA request, and unless the requested materials fall within one of the Act's enumerated exemptions, see § 552(a)(3)(E), (b), the agency must "make the records promptly available" to the requester, § 552(a)(3)(A). If an agency refuses to furnish the requested records, the requester may file suit in federal court and obtain an injunction "order[ing] the production of any agency records improperly withheld." § 552(a)(4)(B).

The courts below held the instant FOIA suit barred by the judgment in earlier litigation seeking the same records. Because the lower courts' decisions turned on the connection between the two lawsuits, we begin with a full account of each action.

A

The first suit was filed by Greg Herrick, an antique aircraft enthusiast and the owner of an F-45 airplane, a vintage model manufactured by the Fairchild Engine and Airplane Corporation (FEAC) in the 1930's. In 1997, seeking information that would help him restore his plane to its original condition, Herrick filed a FOIA request asking the Federal Aviation Administration (FAA) for copies of any technical documents about the F-45 contained in the agency's records.

To gain a certificate authorizing the manufacture and sale of the F-45, FEAC had submitted to the FAA's predecessor, the Civil Aeronautics Authority, detailed specifications and other technical data about the plane. Hundreds of pages of documents produced by FEAC in the certification process remain in the FAA's records. The FAA denied Herrick's request, however, upon finding that the documents he sought are subject to FOIA's exemption for "trade secrets and commercial or financial information obtained from a person and privileged or confidential," 5 U.S.C. § 552(b)(4) (2006 ed.). In an administrative appeal, Herrick urged that FEAC and its successors had waived any trade-secret protection. The FAA thereupon contacted FEAC's corporate successor, respondent Fairchild Corporation (Fairchild). Because Fairchild objected to release of the documents, the agency adhered to its original decision.

Herrick then filed suit in the U.S. District Court for the District of Wyoming. Challenging the FAA's invocation of the trade-secret exemption, Herrick placed heavy weight on a 1955 letter from FEAC to the Civil Aeronautics Authority. The letter authorized the agency to lend any documents in its files to the public "for use in making repairs or replacement parts for aircraft produced by Fairchild." This broad authorization, Herrick maintained, showed that the F-45 certification records held by the FAA could not be regarded as "secre[t]" or "confidential" within the meaning of § 552(b)(4).

Rejecting Herrick's argument, the District Court granted summary judgment to the FAA. The 1955 letter, the court reasoned, did not deprive the F-45 certification documents of trade-secret status, for those documents were never in fact released pursuant to the letter's blanket authorization. The court also stated that even if the 1955 letter had waived trade-secret protection, Fairchild had successfully "reversed" the waiver by objecting to the FAA's release of the records to Herrick.

On appeal, the Tenth Circuit agreed with Herrick that the 1955 letter had stripped the requested documents of trade-secret protection. But the Court of Appeals upheld the District Court's alternative determination—*i.e.,* that Fairchild had restored trade-secret status by objecting to Herrick's FOIA request. On that ground, the appeals court affirmed the entry of summary judgment for the FAA.

In so ruling, the Tenth Circuit noted that Herrick had failed to challenge two suppositions underlying the District Court's decision. First, the District Court assumed trade-secret status could be "restored" to documents that had lost protection. Second, the District Court also assumed that Fairchild had regained trade-secret status for the documents even though the company claimed that status only "*after* Herrick had initiated his request" for the F-45 records. The Court of Appeals expressed no opinion on the validity of these suppositions.

B

The Tenth Circuit's decision issued on July 24, 2002. Less than a month later, on August 22, petitioner Brent Taylor—a friend of Herrick's and an antique aircraft enthusiast in his own right—submitted a FOIA request seeking the same documents Herrick had unsuccessfully sued to obtain. When the FAA failed to respond, Taylor filed a complaint in the U.S. District Court for the District of Columbia. Like Herrick, Taylor argued that FEAC's 1955 letter had stripped the records of their trade-secret status. But Taylor also sought to litigate the two issues concerning recapture of protected status that Herrick had failed to raise in his appeal to the Tenth Circuit.

After Fairchild intervened as a defendant, the District Court in D.C. concluded that Taylor's suit was barred by claim preclusion; accordingly, it granted summary judgment to Fairchild and the FAA. The court acknowledged that Taylor was not a party to Herrick's suit. Relying on the Eighth Circuit's decision in *Tyus v. Schoemehl,* 93 F.3d 449 (8th Cir. 1996), however, it held that a nonparty may be bound by a judgment if she was "virtually represented" by a party.

* * *

The D.C. Circuit affirmed [applying a different multi-factor test for virtual representation]. * * *

We granted certiorari to resolve the disagreement among the Circuits over the permissibility and scope of preclusion based on "virtual representation."

II

The preclusive effect of a federal-court judgment is determined by federal common law. See *Semtek Int'l, Inc. v. Lockheed Martin Corp.,* 531 U.S. 497, 507–508 (2001). For judgments in federal-question cases—for example, Herrick's FOIA suit—federal courts participate in developing "uniform federal rule[s]" of res judicata, which this Court has ultimate authority to determine and declare. The federal common law of preclusion is, of course, subject to due process limitations. See *Richards v. Jefferson County,* 517 U.S. 793, 797 (1996).

Taylor's case presents an issue of first impression in this sense: Until now, we have never addressed the doctrine of "virtual representation" adopted (in varying forms) by several Circuits and relied upon by the courts below. Our inquiry, however, is guided by well-established precedent regarding the propriety of nonparty preclusion. We review that precedent before taking up directly the issue of virtual representation.

A

The preclusive effect of a judgment is defined by claim preclusion and issue preclusion, which are collectively referred to as "res judicata."[5] Under the doctrine of claim preclusion, a final judgment forecloses "successive litigation of the very same claim, whether or not relitigation of the claim raises the same issues as the earlier suit." *New Hampshire v. Maine,* 532 U.S. 742, 748 (2001). Issue preclusion, in contrast, bars "successive litigation of an issue of fact or law actually litigated and resolved in a valid court determination essential to the prior judgment," even if the issue recurs in the context of a different claim. By "preclud[ing] parties from contesting matters that they have had a full and fair opportunity to litigate," these two doctrines protect against "the expense and vexation attending multiple lawsuits, conserv[e] judicial resources, and foste[r] reliance on judicial action by minimizing the possibility of inconsistent decisions." *Montana v. United States,* 440 U.S. 147, 153–154 (1979).

[handwritten margin note: Not 100% accurate. R.J. = Claim P. + issue P.]

A person who was not a party to a suit generally has not had a "full and fair opportunity to litigate" the claims and issues settled in that suit. The application of claim and issue preclusion to nonparties thus runs up against the "deep-rooted historic tradition that everyone should have his

---

[5] These terms have replaced a more confusing lexicon. Claim preclusion describes the rules formerly known as "merger" and "bar," while issue preclusion encompasses the doctrines once known as "collateral estoppel" and "direct estoppel." See *Migra v. Warren City School Dist. Bd. of Ed.,* 465 U.S. 75, 77 n. 1 (1984).

own day in court." *Richards,* 517 U.S. at 798. Indicating the strength of that tradition, we have often repeated the general rule that "one is not bound by a judgment *in personam* in a litigation in which he is not designated as a party or to which he has not been made a party by service of process." *Hansberry,* 311 U.S. at 40.

B

Though hardly in doubt, the rule against nonparty preclusion is subject to exceptions. For present purposes, the recognized exceptions can be grouped into six categories.[6]

First, "[a] person who agrees to be bound by the determination of issues in an action between others is bound in accordance with the terms of his agreement." 1 Restatement (Second) of Judgments § 40, p. 390 (1980) (hereinafter Restatement). For example, "if separate actions involving the same transaction are brought by different plaintiffs against the same defendant, all the parties to all the actions may agree that the question of the defendant's liability will be definitely determined, one way or the other, in a 'test case.' " D. Shapiro, Civil Procedure: Preclusion in Civil Actions 77–78 (2001) (hereinafter Shapiro). See also *California v. Texas,* 459 U.S. 1096, 1097 (1983) (dismissing certain defendants from a suit based on a stipulation "that each of said defendants . . . will be bound by a final judgment of this Court" on a specified issue).[7]

Second, nonparty preclusion may be justified based on a variety of preexisting "substantive legal relationship[s]" between the person to be bound and a party to the judgment. Shapiro 78. See also *Richards,* 517 U.S. at 798. Qualifying relationships include, but are not limited to, preceding and succeeding owners of property, bailee and bailor, and assignee and assignor. See 2 Restatement §§ 43–44, 52, 55. These exceptions originated "as much from the needs of property law as from the values of preclusion by judgment." 18A C. Wright, A. Miller, & E. Cooper, Federal Practice and Procedure § 4448, p. 329 (2d ed.2002).[8]

Third, we have confirmed that, "in certain limited circumstances," a nonparty may be bound by a judgment because she was "adequately represented by someone with the same interests who [wa]s a party" to the

[handwritten margin note: Similar to legal relations]

---

[6]   The established grounds for nonparty preclusion could be organized differently. * * * The list that follows is meant only to provide a framework for our consideration of virtual representation, not to establish a definitive taxonomy.

[7]   The Restatement observes that a nonparty may be bound not only by express or implied agreement, but also through conduct inducing reliance by others. See 2 Restatement § 62. See also 18A Wright & Miller § 4453, pp. 425–429. We have never had occasion to consider this ground for nonparty preclusion, and we express no view on it here.

[8]   The substantive legal relationships justifying preclusion are sometimes collectively referred to as "privity." See, *e.g., Richards v. Jefferson County,* 517 U.S. 793, 798 (1996); 2 Restatement § 62, Comment *a.* The term "privity," however, has also come to be used more broadly, as a way to express the conclusion that nonparty preclusion is appropriate on any ground. See 18A Wright & Miller § 4449, pp. 351–353. To ward off confusion, we avoid using the term "privity" in this opinion.

suit. *Richards*. Representative suits with preclusive effect on nonparties include properly conducted class actions, and suits brought by trustees, guardians, and other fiduciaries. See also 1 Restatement § 41.

Fourth, a nonparty is bound by a judgment if she "assume[d] control" over the litigation in which that judgment was rendered. *Montana*, 440 U.S. at 154. See also *Schnell v. Peter Eckrich & Sons, Inc.*, 365 U.S. 260, 262, n. 4 (1961); 1 Restatement § 39. Because such a person has had "the opportunity to present proofs and argument," he has already "had his day in court" even though he was not a formal party to the litigation. *Id.*, Comment *a*, p. 382.

Fifth, a party bound by a judgment may not avoid its preclusive force by relitigating through a proxy. Preclusion is thus in order when a person who did not participate in a litigation later brings suit as the designated representative of a person who was a party to the prior adjudication. See *Chicago, R.I. & P.R. Co. v. Schendel*, 270 U.S. 611, 620 (1926); 18A Wright & Miller § 4454, pp. 433–434. And although our decisions have not addressed the issue directly, it also seems clear that preclusion is appropriate when a nonparty later brings suit as an agent for a party who is bound by a judgment. See *id.*, § 4449, p. 335.

Sixth, in certain circumstances a special statutory scheme may "expressly foreclos[e] successive litigation by nonlitigants . . . if the scheme is otherwise consistent with due process." *Martin*, 490 U.S., at 762, n. 2. Examples of such schemes include bankruptcy and probate proceedings, and *quo warranto* actions or other suits that, "under [the governing] law, [may] be brought only on behalf of the public at large," *Richards*, 517 U.S. at 804.

III

Reaching beyond these six established categories, some lower courts have recognized a "virtual representation" exception to the rule against nonparty preclusion. Decisions of these courts, however, have been far from consistent. See 18A Wright & Miller § 4457, p. 513 (virtual representation lacks a "clear or coherent theory"; decisions applying it have "an episodic quality"). Some Circuits use the label, but define "virtual representation" so that it is no broader than the recognized exception for adequate representation. See, *e.g.*, *Becherer v. Merrill Lynch, Pierce, Fenner & Smith, Inc.*, 193 F.3d 415, 423, 427 (6th Cir. 1999). But other courts, including the Eighth, Ninth, and D.C. Circuits, apply multifactor tests for virtual representation that permit nonparty preclusion in cases that do not fit within any of the established exceptions.

The D.C. Circuit, the FAA, and Fairchild have presented three arguments in support of an expansive doctrine of virtual representation. We find none of them persuasive.

A

The D.C. Circuit purported to ground its virtual representation doctrine in this Court's decisions stating that, in some circumstances, a person may be bound by a judgment if she was adequately represented by a party to the proceeding yielding that judgment. But the D.C. Circuit's definition of "adequate representation" strayed from the meaning our decisions have attributed to that term.

In *Richards,* we reviewed a decision by the Alabama Supreme Court holding that a challenge to a tax was barred by a judgment upholding the same tax in a suit filed by different taxpayers. The plaintiffs in the first suit "did not sue on behalf of a class," their complaint "did not purport to assert any claim against or on behalf of any nonparties," and the judgment "did not purport to bind" nonparties. There was no indication, we emphasized, that the court in the first suit "took care to protect the interests" of absent parties, or that the parties to that litigation "understood their suit to be on behalf of absent [parties]." In these circumstances, we held, the application of claim preclusion was inconsistent with "the due process of law guaranteed by the Fourteenth Amendment."

The D.C. Circuit stated, without elaboration, that it did not "read *Richards* to hold a nonparty . . . adequately represented only if special procedures were followed [to protect the nonparty] or the party to the prior suit understood it was representing the nonparty." As the D.C. Circuit saw this case, Herrick adequately represented Taylor for two principal reasons: Herrick had a strong incentive to litigate; and Taylor later hired Herrick's lawyer, suggesting Taylor's "satisfaction with the attorney's performance in the prior case."

The D.C. Circuit misapprehended *Richards.* As just recounted, our holding that the Alabama Supreme Court's application of res judicata to nonparties violated due process turned on the lack of either special procedures to protect the nonparties' interests or an understanding by the concerned parties that the first suit was brought in a representative capacity. *Richards* thus established that representation is "adequate" for purposes of nonparty preclusion only if (at a minimum) one of these two circumstances is present.

We restated *Richards'* core holding in *South Central Bell Telephone Co. v. Alabama,* 526 U.S. 160 (1999). In that case, as in *Richards,* the Alabama courts had held that a judgment rejecting a challenge to a tax by one group of taxpayers barred a subsequent suit by a different taxpayer. In *South Central Bell,* however, the nonparty had notice of the original suit and engaged one of the lawyers earlier employed by the original plaintiffs. Under the D.C. Circuit's decision in Taylor's case, these factors apparently would have sufficed to establish adequate representation. Yet *South Central Bell* held that the application of res judicata in that case violated due process. Our inquiry came to an end when we determined that the original plaintiffs had not understood themselves to be acting in a representative capacity and that there had been no special procedures to safeguard the interests of absentees.

Our decisions recognizing that a nonparty may be bound by a judgment if she was adequately represented by a party to the earlier suit thus provide no support for the D.C. Circuit's broad theory of virtual representation.

B

Fairchild and the FAA do not argue that the D.C. Circuit's virtual representation doctrine fits within any of the recognized grounds for nonparty preclusion. Rather, they ask us to abandon the attempt to delineate discrete grounds and clear rules altogether. Preclusion is in order, they contend, whenever "the relationship between a party and a nonparty is 'close enough' to bring the second litigant within the judgment." Courts should make the "close enough" determination, they urge, through a "heavily fact-driven" and "equitable" inquiry. Only this sort of diffuse balancing, Fairchild and the FAA argue, can account for all of the situations in which nonparty preclusion is appropriate.

We reject this argument for three reasons. First, our decisions emphasize the fundamental nature of the general rule that a litigant is not bound by a judgment to which she was not a party. Accordingly, we have endeavored to delineate discrete exceptions that apply in "limited circumstances." Respondents' amorphous balancing test is at odds with the constrained approach to nonparty preclusion our decisions advance.

Resisting this reading of our precedents, respondents call up three decisions they view as supportive of the approach they espouse. Fairchild quotes our statement in *Coryell v. Phipps,* 317 U.S. 406, 411 (1943), that privity "turns on the facts of particular cases." That observation, however, scarcely implies that privity is governed by a diffuse balancing test.[9] Fairchild also cites *Blonder-Tongue Laboratories, Inc. v. University of Ill. Foundation,* 402 U.S. 313, 334 (1971), which stated that estoppel questions turn on "the trial courts' sense of justice and equity." This passing statement, however, was not made with nonparty preclusion in mind; it appeared in a discussion recognizing district courts' discretion to *limit* the use of issue preclusion against persons who *were* parties to a judgment.

The FAA relies on *United States v. Des Moines Valley R. Co.,* 84 F. 40 (8th Cir. 1897), an opinion we quoted with approval in *Schendel,* 270 U.S., at 619–620. *Des Moines Valley* was a quiet title action in which the named

---

[9]   Moreover, *Coryell* interpreted the term "privity" not in the context of res judicata, but as used in a statute governing shipowner liability. And we made the statement Fairchild quotes in explaining why it was appropriate to defer to the findings of the lower courts, not as a comment on the substantive rules of privity.

plaintiff was the United States. The Government, however, had "no interest in the land" and had "simply permitted [the landowner] to use its name as the nominal plaintiff." The suit was therefore barred, the appeals court held, by an earlier judgment against the landowner. As the court explained: "[W]here the government lends its name as a plaintiff . . . to enable one private person to maintain a suit against another," the government is "subject to the same defenses which exist . . . against the real party in interest." *Des Moines Valley*, the FAA contended at oral argument, demonstrates that it is sometimes appropriate to bind a nonparty in circumstances that do not fit within any of the established grounds for nonparty preclusion. Properly understood, however, *Des Moines Valley* is simply an application of the fifth basis for nonparty preclusion described above: A party may not use a representative or agent to relitigate an adverse judgment.[10] We thus find no support in our precedents for the lax approach to nonparty preclusion advocated by respondents.

Our second reason for rejecting a broad doctrine of virtual representation rests on the limitations attending nonparty preclusion based on adequate representation. A party's representation of a nonparty is "adequate" for preclusion purposes only if, at a minimum: (1) the interests of the nonparty and her representative are aligned, see *Hansberry*; and (2) either the party understood herself to be acting in a representative capacity or the original court took care to protect the interests of the nonparty, see *Richards*. In addition, adequate representation sometimes requires (3) notice of the original suit to the persons alleged to have been represented, see *Richards*.[11] In the class-action context, these limitations are implemented by the procedural safeguards contained in Federal Rule of Civil Procedure 23.

An expansive doctrine of virtual representation, however, would "recogniz[e], in effect, a common-law kind of class action." That is, virtual representation would authorize preclusion based on identity of interests and some kind of relationship between parties and nonparties, shorn of the procedural protections prescribed in *Hansberry, Richards,* and Rule 23. These protections, grounded in due process, could be circumvented were we to approve a virtual representation doctrine that allowed courts to "create *de facto* class actions at will."

Third, a diffuse balancing approach to nonparty preclusion would likely create more headaches than it relieves. Most obviously, it could

---

[10] The FAA urges that there was no agency relationship between the landowner and the United States because the landowner did not control the U.S. Attorney's conduct of the suit. That point is debatable. But even if the FAA is correct about agency, the United States plainly litigated as the landowner's designated representative.

[11] *Richards* suggested that notice is required in some representative suits, *e.g.,* class actions seeking monetary relief. But we assumed without deciding that a lack of notice might be overcome in some circumstances.

significantly complicate the task of district courts faced in the first instance with preclusion questions. An all-things-considered balancing approach might spark wide-ranging, time-consuming, and expensive discovery tracking factors potentially relevant under seven- or five-prong tests. And after the relevant facts are established, district judges would be called upon to evaluate them under a standard that provides no firm guidance. Preclusion doctrine, it should be recalled, is intended to reduce the burden of litigation on courts and parties. "In this area of the law," we agree, " 'crisp rules with sharp corners' are preferable to a roundabout doctrine of opaque standards." *Bittinger v. Tecumseh Products Co.,* 123 F.3d 877, 881 (6th Cir. 1997).

C

Finally, relying on the Eighth Circuit's decision in *Tyus* [*v. Schoemehl*], 93 F.3d at 456 [8th Cir. 1996], the FAA maintains that nonparty preclusion should apply more broadly in "public-law" litigation than in "private-law" controversies. To support this position, the FAA offers two arguments. First, the FAA urges, our decision in *Richards* acknowledges that, in certain cases, the plaintiff has a reduced interest in controlling the litigation "because of the public nature of the right at issue." When a taxpayer challenges "an alleged misuse of public funds" or "other public action," we observed in *Richards,* the suit "has only an indirect impact on [the plaintiff's] interests." In actions of this character, the Court said, "we may assume that the States have wide latitude to establish procedures . . . to limit the number of judicial proceedings that may be entertained."

Taylor's FOIA action falls within the category described in *Richards,* the FAA contends, because "the duty to disclose under FOIA is owed to the public generally." The opening sentence of FOIA, it is true, states that agencies "shall make [information] available to the public." Equally true, we have several times said that FOIA vindicates a "public" interest. The Act, however, instructs agencies receiving FOIA requests to make the information available not to the public at large, but rather to the "person" making the request. Thus, in contrast to the public-law litigation contemplated in *Richards,* a successful FOIA action results in a grant of relief to the individual plaintiff, not a decree benefiting the public at large.

Furthermore, we said in *Richards* only that, for the type of public-law claims there envisioned, States are free to adopt procedures limiting repetitive litigation. In this regard, we referred to instances in which the first judgment foreclosed successive litigation by other plaintiffs because, "under state law, [the suit] could be brought only on behalf of the public at large." [12]*Richards* spoke of state legislation, but it appears equally evident that *Congress,* in providing for actions vindicating a public interest, may "limit the number of judicial proceedings that may be entertained." It

---

[12]   Nonparty preclusion in such cases ranks under the sixth exception described above: special statutory schemes that expressly limit subsequent suits.

hardly follows, however, that *this Court* should proscribe or confine successive FOIA suits by different requesters. Indeed, Congress' provision for FOIA suits with no statutory constraint on successive actions counsels against judicial imposition of constraints through extraordinary application of the common law of preclusion.

The FAA next argues that "the threat of vexatious litigation is heightened" in public-law cases because "the number of plaintiffs with standing is potentially limitless." FOIA does allow "any person" whose request is denied to resort to federal court for review of the agency's determination. Thus it is theoretically possible that several persons could coordinate to mount a series of repetitive lawsuits.

But we are not convinced that this risk justifies departure from the usual rules governing nonparty preclusion. First, *stare decisis* will allow courts swiftly to dispose of repetitive suits brought in the same circuit. Second, even when *stare decisis* is not dispositive, "the human tendency not to waste money will deter the bringing of suits based on claims or issues that have already been adversely determined against others." This intuition seems to be borne out by experience: The FAA has not called our attention to any instances of abusive FOIA suits in the Circuits that reject the virtual-representation theory respondents advocate here.

IV

For the foregoing reasons, we disapprove the theory of virtual representation on which the decision below rested. The preclusive effects of a judgment in a federal-question case decided by a federal court should instead be determined according to the established grounds for nonparty preclusion described in this opinion.

Although references to "virtual representation" have proliferated in the lower courts, our decision is unlikely to occasion any great shift in actual practice. Many opinions use the term "virtual representation" in reaching results at least arguably defensible on established grounds. In these cases, dropping the "virtual representation" label would lead to clearer analysis with little, if any, change in outcomes.

In some cases, however, lower courts have relied on virtual representation to extend nonparty preclusion beyond the latter doctrine's proper bounds. We now turn back to Taylor's action to determine whether his suit is such a case, or whether the result reached by the courts below can be justified on one of the recognized grounds for nonparty preclusion.

A

It is uncontested that four of the six grounds for nonparty preclusion have no application here: There is no indication that Taylor agreed to be bound by Herrick's litigation, that Taylor and Herrick have any legal relationship, that Taylor exercised any control over Herrick's suit, or that this suit implicates any special statutory scheme limiting relitigation. Neither the FAA nor Fairchild contends otherwise.

It is equally clear that preclusion cannot be justified on the theory that Taylor was adequately represented in Herrick's suit. Nothing in the record indicates that Herrick understood himself to be suing on Taylor's behalf, that Taylor even knew of Herrick's suit, or that the Wyoming District Court took special care to protect Taylor's interests. Under our pathmarking precedent, therefore, Herrick's representation was not "adequate." See *Richards.*

That leaves only the fifth category: preclusion because a nonparty to an earlier litigation has brought suit as a representative or agent of a party who is bound by the prior adjudication. Taylor is not Herrick's legal representative and he has not purported to sue in a representative capacity. He concedes, however, that preclusion would be appropriate if respondents could demonstrate that he is acting as Herrick's "undisclosed agen[t]."

Respondents argue here, as they did below, that Taylor's suit is a collusive attempt to relitigate Herrick's action. The D.C. Circuit considered a similar question in addressing the "tactical maneuvering" prong of its virtual representation test. The Court of Appeals did not, however, treat the issue as one of agency, and it expressly declined to reach any definitive conclusions due to "the ambiguity of the facts." We therefore remand to give the courts below an opportunity to determine whether Taylor, in pursuing the instant FOIA suit, is acting as Herrick's agent. Taylor concedes that such a remand is appropriate.

We have never defined the showing required to establish that a nonparty to a prior adjudication has become a litigating agent for a party to the earlier case. Because the issue has not been briefed in any detail, we do not discuss the matter elaborately here. We note, however, that courts should be cautious about finding preclusion on this basis. A mere whiff of "tactical maneuvering" will not suffice; instead, principles of agency law are suggestive. They indicate that preclusion is appropriate only if the putative agent's conduct of the suit is subject to the control of the party who is bound by the prior adjudication. See 1 Restatement (Second) of Agency § 14, p. 60 (1957) ("A principal has the right to control the conduct of the agent with respect to matters entrusted to him.").[13]

---

[13] Our decision in *Montana v. United States,* 440 U.S. 147 (1979), also suggests a "control" test for agency. In that case, we held that the United States was barred from bringing a suit because it had controlled a prior unsuccessful action filed by a federal contractor. We see no reason why preclusion based on a lesser showing would have been appropriate if the order of the two actions had been switched—that is, if the United States had brought the first suit itself, and then sought to relitigate the same claim through the contractor. See *Schendel,* 270 U.S., at 618 ("[I]f, in legal contemplation, there is identity of parties" when two suits are brought in one order, "there must be like identity" when the order is reversed.).

B

On remand, Fairchild suggests, Taylor should bear the burden of proving he is not acting as Herrick's agent. When a defendant points to evidence establishing a close relationship between successive litigants, Fairchild maintains, "the burden [should] shif[t] to the second litigant to submit evidence refuting the charge" of agency. Fairchild justifies this proposed burden-shift on the ground that "it is unlikely an opposing party will have access to direct evidence of collusion."

We reject Fairchild's suggestion. Claim preclusion, like issue preclusion, is an affirmative defense. Ordinarily, it is incumbent on the defendant to plead and prove such a defense, and we have never recognized claim preclusion as an exception to that general rule. We acknowledge that direct evidence justifying nonparty preclusion is often in the hands of plaintiffs rather than defendants. See, *e.g., Montana,* 440 U.S. at 155 (listing evidence of control over a prior suit). But "[v]ery often one must plead and prove matters as to which his adversary has superior access to the proof." In these situations, targeted interrogatories or deposition questions can reduce the information disparity. We see no greater cause here than in other matters of affirmative defense to disturb the traditional allocation of the proof burden.

* * *

For the reasons stated, the judgment of the United States Court of Appeals for the District of Columbia Circuit is vacated, and the case is remanded for further proceedings consistent with this opinion.

NOTES AND QUESTIONS

1.   *Postscript:* On remand in Taylor v. Sturgell, the district court refused discovery. See Taylor v. Babbitt, 673 F.Supp.2d 20 (D.D.C. 2009); see generally 8 C. Wright, A. Miller & R. Marcus, Federal Practice & Procedure § 2005 at 55–58 (3d ed. 2010) (discussing discovery practice in FOIA actions). The FAA Air Transportation Modernization and Safety Improvement Act of 2012 included something its primary sponsor called the "Herrick Amendment," which removes the trade secret status of vintage aircraft drawings and grants access to them through FOIA requests for all those who want access for non-commercial purposes.

2.   In rejecting virtual representation, the Court in Taylor v. Sturgell relied on fundamental principles of due process as articulated in Hansberry v. Lee, supra p. 311. Recall that Hansberry involved an attempt on the part of an all-white neighborhood association to enforce a racially restrictive agreement against the Hansberrys. Despite prior litigation on behalf of a class of plaintiffs that resulted in a judgment upholding the agreement, the Court ruled that the Hansberrys had not been represented in that proceeding and could not be bound by it. The Court emphasized both the conflicts among members of the

plaintiff class and the fact that the defendants had not been named as representatives for others seeking to resist enforcement.

Two other cases were central to the *Taylor* Court's analysis. In Richards v. Jefferson County, Alabama, 517 U.S. 793 (1996), the Supreme Court held that state-law preclusion principles could not foreclose a suit by individual taxpayers challenging the constitutionality of a tax on the basis that other litigants had asserted similar challenges in an earlier suit. In South Central Bell Tel. Co. v. Alabama, 526 U.S. 160 (1999), the Court reaffirmed that ruling even though the later litigants were represented by the same lawyer. Despite that shared representation by counsel, it reasoned, there was "no special relationship between the earlier and later plaintiffs." It added that "[t]he two relevant cases involve different plaintiffs and different tax years. Neither is a class action, and no one claims that there is 'privity' or some other special relationship between the two sets of plaintiffs; hence, the Case Two plaintiffs are strangers to Case One, and * * * they cannot be bound by the earlier judgment."

The Court has thus consistently reaffirmed the notion that each individual has a right under due process to his or her own day in court to vindicate legal rights and interests held by that individual. See Bone, Rethinking the "Day in Court" Ideal and Nonparty Preclusion, 67 N.Y.U.L.Rev. 193 (1992) (examining historical background and policy bases for binding nonparties). Does such an emphasis raise doubts about the class action device more generally? See Redish & Larsen, Class Actions, Litigant Autonomy, and the Foundations of Procedural Due Process, 95 Cal. L. Rev. 1573 (2007). Or does it simply require close attention to the procedural rules and possible conflicts associated with class certification? See Stephenson v. Dow Chemical Co., infra p. 1271. In light of the Court's consistent reluctance to permit erosion of due process norms, what explains the willingness of some lower federal courts to broaden non-party preclusion through notions of virtual representation? Factors that apparently informed the lower courts' approach were the desire to achieve a final resolution of legal issues, the perceived impact of duplicative litigation on crowded federal dockets, and the sense in some cases that the litigation was lawyer- rather than client-driven.

The Court responds to these concerns in part by emphasizing day-in-court values and in part by citing the doctrine of stare decisis and the parties' predictable reluctance to spend money on litigation that seeks to challenge established precedent. The plaintiff Taylor attempted to side-step stare decisis problems by initiating litigation in the D.C. Circuit, rather than in the Tenth Circuit, where Herrick's case had produced a ruling favorable to Fairchild and the FAA. Does that maneuver undermine the Court's view or simply exemplify the sort of forum shopping inherent in our system of regional federal appellate courts?

3.   Although the Court denies that its taxonomy should be regarded as definitive, the six-part categorization of nonparty preclusion will likely structure lower court analysis of such matters for the foreseeable future.

(a) Is it possible to infer an agreement to accept a particular disposition as binding based on a pattern of conduct, rather than an explicit contract or stipulation? All of the examples in the *Taylor* Court's first category involve explicit agreements. What of an argument that conduct by parties in later litigation reflects an attempt to skirt the effect of a prior judgment, thus implying a tacit recognition of its binding quality? The examples cited in *Taylor* involve parties *already before the court* who agree to accept the court's disposition as binding in their own case. As a result, when different parties later sue, finding a tacit agreement may be quite difficult. Compare Pollard v. Cockrell, 578 F.2d 1002 (5th Cir.1978), in which plaintiffs sued in federal court challenging the constitutionality of ordinances regulating massage parlors. Defendants claimed that they were bound by the earlier decision of a state court rejecting the same challenges in a suit brought by other massage parlors represented by the same lawyers. The court refused to bind the federal plaintiffs because there was no showing of any other relationship between the two groups of plaintiffs.

(b) The second category involves a pre-existing substantive legal relationship, such as that between bailor and bailee or assignor and assignee. The Court treats this category as reflecting values embedded in the underlying substantive law. Consider Terrell v. DeConna, 877 F.2d 1267 (5th Cir.1989), where the court held that a spouse seeking to recover for loss of consortium is barred by collateral estoppel from relitigating defendant's liability for an accident if the injured spouse has earlier failed in an action against this defendant. The court rejected a virtual representation argument, but found nonetheless upheld preclusion: "Although close family relationships will not alone suffice to establish privity between successive parties for purposes of issue or claim preclusion, the relevant considerations are different when * * * the successor plaintiff's claims are also derivative from the first plaintiff's claims." The court also cited commentary suggesting that a claim for loss of consortium should be barred, whatever the outcome of the injured spouse's litigation, unless pursued as part of that litigation.

For a contrast to *Terrell* consider the same court's earlier decision in Freeman v. Lester Coggins Trucking, Inc., 771 F.2d 860 (5th Cir. 1985). Plaintiff in that case was injured in a car crash and sued the other driver in state court, losing on a jury verdict on a finding that defendant was not negligent. Plaintiff then filed suit against the same defendant in federal court on behalf of himself as the representative of his wife and three minor children who survived the accident, and also asserting a wrongful death claim for the death of a daughter in the accident, using the same lawyer. The court held that plaintiff's personal claim was foreclosed by issue preclusion, but that preclusion did not apply to the claims asserted on behalf of the other family members because those claims belonged to the other family members and they deserved their own day in court.

The law prescribes special rules of preclusion in a number of substantive contexts. The most common example binds successors in interest by judgments concerning interests in property. See Restatement (Second) of Judgments

§§ 43; 44. Similarly, where an injured person sues and recovers for his injuries, but later dies from them, special rules apply concerning preclusion in survival and wrongful death actions. Restatement (Second) of Judgments §§ 46; 47. Where one is obligated to indemnify another against the claim asserted in a suit, there are special rules on preclusion if the indemnitor is notified of the suit and given an opportunity to participate. See id., §§ 57; 58. Finally, actions by partners on behalf of a partnership usually bind the other partners. Id. § 60.

Membership organizations often mount suits for injunctive and declaratory relief on behalf of their members. Does the entry of a judgment in such litigation preclude members who were not otherwise before the court? In Cooper v. Harris 137 S.Ct. 1455 (2017), two voters brought suit to challenge the voting map in North Carolina as an unlawful racial gerrymander. The state sought summary judgment, arguing that the voters were members of the statewide NAACP, which had previously challenged the legality of the voting map. The evidence showed that the plaintiffs had paid dues to either the national NAACP or to a local affiliate, but did not necessarily show any connection to North Carolina's statewide chapter. Citing Taylor v. Sturgell, 553, U.S. 880, 892–93 (2008), the Court acknowledged that a judgment might bind both a party and a non-party where the two share a special relationship, but found that the state had failed to prove the existence of such a relationship.

(c)   Adequate representation, the third category of nonparty preclusion, includes the familiar example of class actions as well as such fiduciary relationships as those between trustees and beneficiaries. As set out in Restatement (Second) of Judgments § 41, a nonparty is bound when "represented" by a party because that party is "(a) the trustee of an estate or interest of which the person is a beneficiary; or (b) invested by the person with authority to represent him in an action; or (c) the executor, administrator, guardian, conservator, or similar fiduciary manager of an interest of which the person is a beneficiary; or (d) an official or agency invested by law with authority to represent the person's interests; or (e) the representative of a class of persons similarly situated, designated as such with the approval of the court, of which the person is a member." What is the justification for binding "represented" persons? Consider McCoid, A Single Package for Multiparty Disputes, 28 Stan.L.Rev. 707, 716–17 (1976):

> I believe that consent and/or necessity are the principal supports of all res judicata privity categories based on representation, a concept that covers a number of quite different relationships. * * * Several relationships, such as trustee-beneficiary and agent-principal, are contractual, and the role of one party is understood to include representation in litigation. Even where there is no prearrangement there may be a subsequent assent, such as accepting the representation of a personal representative, which amounts to the same thing. In these cases representation is supported by consent. In still other cases representation flows from necessity. This factor itself is a broad one covering a variety of exigencies such as incompetency (guardian-ward), need for marketable title (unborn remaindermen),

and need for unified estate administration (administrator-estate beneficiary). The common element is the need to go forward with litigation which will be effective.

As the Restatement suggests, class members are bound by a judgment in a class action because the class representative has been designated by the court to represent them. But what if class members exercise their right to opt out? In Becherer v. Merrill Lynch, Pierce, Fenner & Smith, Inc., 193 F.3d 415 (6th Cir. 1999), a group of investors in a condominium opted out of a settlement class action that had been brought on behalf of all investors, and later filed identical claims in a separate suit. They, or at least some of them, had previously retained the same lawyer to represent them, contributed money to the class-action expense fund, and worked closely with the Association of Unit Owners which financed and controlled the class action. The district court found them bound by the judgment, noting that they had "improperly maneuvered in order to avoid the potential effects of res judicata" by having their counsel argue inconsistently in earlier proceedings concerning the effect of a class judgment. But the court of appeals found that such financing and involvement in the class action was not sufficient to demonstrate "control" and that there was no evidence that they could have held the class representatives or the Association legally "accountable" for the result. The majority "also found that 'acquiescence cannot be shown in a class action case where the nonparties opt out of the class and there is no other court approval of representation by a party.' " Does this shed light on the tacit agreement idea discussed above? We will consider preclusion in class actions in greater detail below, infra p. 1271.

(d)   The fourth category holds that anyone who "controls or substantially participates in the control of the presentation on behalf of a party" is bound by the outcome. Restatement (Second) of Judgments § 39. Montana v. United States, 440 U.S. 147 (1979), referred to in *Taylor*, illustrates control sufficient to warrant a finding of preclusion. There the contractor on a federal dam project brought suit in state court against the Montana State Board of Equalization, contending that the state's gross receipts tax upon contractors for public, but not private, construction projects was unconstitutional. The Montana Supreme Court found the tax constitutional. The United States then sued Montana in federal court, challenging the constitutionality of the tax as it affected it in its dealings with contractors. The Court held that the U.S. was bound by the state judgment because it had required that the suit be filed; reviewed and approved the complaint; paid the attorneys' fees and costs; directed the appeal; and submitted an amicus brief on appeal.

Why should it be critical that the nonparty control the conduct of the case? To what extent does a party control the actual conduct of a case? Isn't it usually more directly in the control of the lawyer? Cf. Wainwright v. Sykes, 433 U.S. 72, 93 (1977) (Burger, C.J., concurring) (in a criminal case, "[o]nce counsel is appointed, the day-to-day conduct of the defense rests with the attorney. * * * Not only do these decisions rest with the attorney, but such decisions must, as a practical matter, be made without consulting the client. The trial process simply does not permit the type of frequent and protracted interruptions which would be necessary if it were required that clients give knowing and intelligent approval to each of the myriad tactical decisions as a trial proceeds.").

(e)   The Court's fifth category, and the only one applicable to the *Taylor* case itself, involves situations in which one party acts as the designated representative of another, or litigates pursuant to an agency relationship. The Court indicated that the contours of this agency or designated representative category were to be narrowly construed. Thus, it would take more than a whiff of tactical maneuvering to trigger this exception, and the courts must apply ordinary agency principles in determining whether the party to the early proceeding (Herrick) had a right to control the conduct of the party to the subsequent proceeding (Taylor). What sorts of evidence would tend to establish control? Would Taylor's agreement to share information if he were successful in the second proceeding make him Herrick's agent?

(f)   A sixth category applies to situations in which a statute specifically forecloses subsequent litigation by non-parties. The Court identifies probate and bankruptcy proceedings as examples of such statutory non-party preclusion. In those examples, a designated party (the administrator of the decedent's estate or the trustee in bankruptcy) has power under the statute to pursue legal claims on behalf of the estate. Beneficiaries of the estate are generally bound by the result of the administrator's or trustee's litigation. This category thus overlaps to some degree with the exception for adequate representation in the third category.

4.   Could Taylor have intervened under Rule 24 as a party in the first proceeding brought by Herrick? If so, can he be bound by the earlier disposition on the theory that he bypassed an opportunity to have his interest represented in the prior action? Cf. Provident Tradesmens Bank & Trust Co. v. Patterson, 390 U.S. 102, 114 (1968) (nonparty who "purposefully bypassed an adequate opportunity to intervene" might be foreclosed by the outcome reached in his absence). Is this consistent with Rule 19 (governing "necessary parties")? Would it mean that all who have a right to intervene are necessary parties (because they may be precluded by the result reached in their absence)?

In Martin v. Wilks, 490 U.S. 755 (1989), the Court rejected arguments for a rule of mandatory intervention. Plaintiffs there were white firefighters who challenged preferences in promotion for African-American firefighters given pursuant to the decree in an earlier employment discrimination case in which these whites were not parties. The defendant city argued that plaintiffs could not attack the provisions of the earlier decree collaterally because they should have intervened. The Supreme Court held that they could not be required to intervene to protect their rights, and therefore that they could proceed with their suit.

The Civil Rights Act of 1991 contained provisions aimed at overturning certain aspects of Martin v. Wilks. It insulated employment practices implementing a litigated or consent judgment against later attack by a person who had, prior to the entry of judgment, actual notice of the proposed judgment and its possible adverse effect and a "reasonable opportunity to present objections to such judgment." It further insulated such employment practices against later attack by a person without notice or an opportunity to present objections if that person's interests "were adequately represented by another person who had previously challenged the judgment or order on the same legal grounds and with a similar factual situation." 42 U.S.C. § 2000e–2(n)(1). Did this clarify what constitutes a "purposeful bypass" of an opportunity to intervene?

Assume that the objector is allowed to intervene. Should the intervenor be bound by a judgment if not given the full rights of a party? Increasingly courts grant intervention on condition that the intervenor not file separate pleadings, or not call separate witnesses, or only communicate with the court through the counsel of the side on which it has intervened. How should a court decide whether these limitations are so incapacitating as to prevent preclusion? Note the relationship between intervention and preclusion. For intervention of right, one must demonstrate that "the disposition of the action may as a practical matter impair or impede 'his ability to protect his interest relating to the property or transaction that is the subject of the action.'" Rule 24(a). See People Who Care v. Rockford Board of Education, 68 F.3d 172, 179 (7th Cir. 1995) (finding a would-be intervenor had no risk of preclusion and "if his interests are so similar to those of the parties in this case that his concerns were fully represented, then he has no right to intervene").

2. MUTUALITY OF ESTOPPEL

The traditional view of collateral estoppel accepted the principle that estoppel must be mutual, which is referred to as the doctrine of "mutuality of estoppel." It rested on the principle that a person should not benefit from collateral estoppel unless he would also have been bound by the prior judgment. This approach was followed in the Restatement of Judgments § 99 (1942). The requirement of mutuality was viewed an as elementary aspect of fairness under due process, as well as a necessary limitation of the scope of an in personam judgment.

An exception to the mutuality doctrine arose in the area of indemnity. Assume that a person involved in an accident with the master's car, which was driven by a servant, sued the servant and lost and then sued the master. The master was not a party to the action, nor in privity with the servant, and since the master couldn't be bound by the judgment if the servant had lost, the mutuality rule would prohibit the master from benefitting from it. Nevertheless, courts allowed the master to use the judgment in favor of the servant to prevent the plaintiff from relitigating the issues of negligence decided against him in the first suit. This was viewed as a limited exception to protect the master's right of indemnity where the third party had chosen the structure of the first suit and had full opportunity to litigate the issues. Good Health Dairy Products Corp. v. Emery, 275 N.Y. 14, 9 N.E.2d 758 (1937); Restatement of Judgments § 96 (1942).

Among the earliest, and most influential, opinions to reject the mutuality requirement was Bernhard v. Bank of America, 122 P.2d 892 (Cal.1942). There Mrs. Bernhard sued the executor of an estate of which she was a beneficiary, claiming he had converted to his own use money from the deceased's bank account. Judgment was for the executor on a finding that the money was a gift to him from the deceased. Mrs. Bernhard then sued the bank for allowing the executor to withdraw the money. The critical issue was whether the executor had a right to the money. Under the mutuality doctrine, the bank was not a party to the first suit and since it would not have been bound had the executor lost, it could not take advantage of the favorable judgment in the executor's favor. Nevertheless the court allowed the bank to collaterally estop Mrs. Bernhard from relitigating the issue of the ownership of the money taken by the executor.

Justice Traynor found that while "due process of law forbids the assertion of a plea of res judicata *against* a party" unless he was a party or in privity with a party, there is no compelling reason "for requiring that the party *asserting* the plea of res judicata must have been a party, or in privity with a party, to the earlier litigation." He thus shifted the inquiry away from whether the person asserting the preclusion would have been bound by the judgment to whether the party against whom it was asserted had a full and fair opportunity to litigate the issue in the first suit.

In Blonder-Tongue Laboratories, Inc. v. University of Illinois Foundation, 402 U.S. 313 (1971), the Supreme Court abandoned mutuality as a matter of federal law, at least to the extent of permitting the "defensive use" of issue preclusion by a person not a party to the first suit against a plaintiff who was a party to the first suit. The Court questioned "whether it is any longer tenable to afford a litigant more than one full and fair opportunity for judicial resolution of the same issue." Id. at 328. It stated, however, that a judgment would not preclude a losing party from relitigating an issue if he could demonstrate that the first action failed to allow him a "fair opportunity procedurally, substantively, and evidentially to pursue his claim." Id. at 333.

PARKLANE HOSIERY CO. v. SHORE   *Issue Prcl.*

Supreme Court of the United States, 1979
439 U.S. 322

JUSTICE STEWART delivered the opinion of the Court.

This case presents the question whether a party who has had issues of fact adjudicated adversely to it in an equitable action may be collaterally estopped from relitigating the same issues before a jury in a subsequent legal action brought against it by a new party.

The respondent brought this stockholder's class action against the petitioners in a Federal District Court. The complaint alleged that the petitioners, Parklane Hosiery Co., Inc. (Parklane), and 13 of its officers, directors, and stockholders, had issued a materially false and misleading proxy statement in connection with a merger. The proxy statement, according to the complaint, had violated [federal securities laws and regulations]. The complaint sought damages, rescission of the merger, and recovery of costs.

Before this action came to trial, the SEC filed suit against the same defendants in the Federal District Court, alleging that the proxy statement that had been issued by Parklane was materially false and misleading in essentially the same respects as those that had been alleged in the respondent's complaint. Injunctive relief was requested. After a 4-day trial, the District Court found that the proxy statement was materially false and misleading in the respects alleged. The Court of Appeals for the Second Circuit affirmed this judgment.

The respondent in the present case then moved for partial summary judgment against the petitioners, asserting that the petitioners were collaterally estopped from relitigating the issues that had been resolved against them in the action brought by the SEC.[2] The District Court denied the motion on the ground that such an application of collateral estoppel would deny the petitioners their Seventh Amendment right to a jury trial. The Court of Appeals for the Second Circuit reversed, holding that a party who has had issues of fact determined against him after a full and fair opportunity to litigate in a nonjury trial is collaterally estopped from obtaining a subsequent jury trial of these same issues of fact. The appellate court concluded that "the Seventh Amendment preserves the right to jury trial only with respect to issues of fact, [and] once those issues have been fully and fairly adjudicated in a prior proceeding, nothing remains for trial, either with or without a jury." * * *

I

The threshold question to be considered is whether, quite apart from the right to a jury trial under the Seventh Amendment, the petitioners can be precluded from relitigating facts resolved adversely to them in a prior equitable proceeding with another party under the general law of collateral estoppel. Specifically, we must determine whether a litigant who was not a party to a prior judgment may nevertheless use that judgment "offensively" to prevent a defendant from relitigating issues resolved in the earlier proceeding.

---

[2]   A private plaintiff in an action under the proxy rules is not entitled to relief simply by demonstrating that the proxy solicitation was materially false and misleading. The plaintiff must also show that he was injured and prove damages. Since the SEC action was limited to a determination of whether the proxy statement contained materially false and misleading information, the respondent conceded that he would still have to prove these other elements of his prima facie case in the private action. The petitioners' right to a jury trial on those remaining issues is not contested.

A

Collateral estoppel, like the related doctrine of res judicata, has the dual purpose of protecting litigants from the burden of relitigating an identical issue with the same party or his privy and of promoting judicial economy by preventing needless litigation. Blonder-Tongue Laboratories, Inc. v. University of Illinois Foundation, 402 U.S. 313, 328–329. Until relatively recently, however, the scope of collateral estoppel was limited by the doctrine of mutuality of parties. Under this mutuality doctrine, neither party could use a prior judgment as an estoppel against the other unless both parties were bound by the judgment. Based on the premise that it is somehow unfair to allow a party to use a prior judgment when he himself would not be so bound,[7] the mutuality requirement provided a party who had litigated and lost in a previous action an opportunity to relitigate identical issues with new parties.

By failing to recognize the obvious difference in position between a party who has never litigated an issue and one who has fully litigated and lost, the mutuality requirement was criticized almost from its inception. Recognizing the validity of this criticism, the Court in Blonder-Tongue Laboratories, Inc. v. University of Illinois Foundation, supra, abandoned the mutuality requirement, at least in cases where a patentee seeks to relitigate the validity of a patent after a federal court in a previous lawsuit has already declared it invalid. The "broader question" before the Court, however, was "whether it is any longer tenable to afford a litigant more than one full and fair opportunity for judicial resolution of the same issue." 402 U.S. at 328. The Court strongly suggested a negative answer to that question:

> In any lawsuit where a defendant, because of the mutuality principle, is forced to present a complete defense on the merits to a claim which the plaintiff has fully litigated and lost in a prior action, there is an arguable misallocation of resources. To the extent the defendant in the second suit may not win by asserting, without contradiction, that the plaintiff had fully and fairly, but unsuccessfully, litigated the same claim in the prior suit, the defendant's time and money are diverted from alternative uses— productive or otherwise—to relitigation of a decided issue. And, still assuming that the issue was resolved correctly in the first suit, there is reason to be concerned about the plaintiff's allocation of resources. Permitting repeated litigation of the same issue as long as the supply of unrelated defendants holds out reflects either the aura of the gaming table or 'a lack of discipline and of disinterestedness on the part of the lower courts, hardly a worthy

---

[7] It is a violation of due process for a judgment to be binding on a litigant who was not a party or a privy and therefore has never had an opportunity to be heard. Hansberry v. Lee, 311 U.S. 32, 40.

or wise basis for fashioning rules of procedure.' Kerotest Mfg. Co. v. C-O-Two Co., 342 U.S. 180, 185 (1952). Although neither judges, the parties, nor the adversary system performs perfectly in all cases, the requirement of determining whether the party against whom an estoppel is asserted had a full and fair opportunity to litigate is a most significant safeguard. Id. at 329.

B

Prox. mentioned this case in class

The *Blonder-Tongue* case involved defensive use of collateral estoppel—a plaintiff was estopped from asserting a claim that the plaintiff had previously litigated and lost against another defendant. The present case, by contrast, involves offensive use of collateral estoppel—a plaintiff is seeking to estop a defendant from relitigating the issues which the defendant previously litigated and lost against another plaintiff. In both the offensive and defensive use situations, the party against whom estoppel is asserted has litigated and lost in an earlier action. Nevertheless, several reasons have been advanced why the two situations should be treated differently.

First, offensive use of collateral estoppel does not promote judicial economy in the same manner as defensive use does. Defensive use of collateral estoppel precludes a plaintiff from relitigating identical issues by merely "switching adversaries." Bernhard v. Bank of America Nat. Trust & Savings Assn., 19 Cal.2d, at 813, 122 P.2d, at 895. Thus defensive collateral estoppel gives a plaintiff a strong incentive to join all potential defendants in the first action if possible. Offensive use of collateral estoppel, on the other hand, creates precisely the opposite incentive. Since a plaintiff will be able to rely on a previous judgment against a defendant but will not be bound by that judgment if the defendant wins, the plaintiff has every incentive to adopt a "wait and see" attitude, in the hope that the first action by another plaintiff will result in a favorable judgment. Thus offensive use of collateral estoppel will likely increase rather than decrease the total amount of litigation, since potential plaintiffs will have everything to gain and nothing to lose by not intervening in the first action.[13]

A second argument against offensive use of collateral estoppel is that it may be unfair to a defendant. If a defendant in the first action is sued for small or nominal damages, he may have little incentive to defend vigorously, particularly if future suits are not foreseeable. Cf. Berner v. British Commonwealth Pac. Airlines, 346 F.2d 532 (CA2) (application of offensive collateral estoppel denied where defendant did not appeal an adverse judgment awarding $35,000 and defendant was later sued for over $7 million). Allowing offensive collateral estoppel may also be unfair to a

---

[13] The Restatement (Second) of Judgments (Tent. Draft No. 2, 1975) § 88(3) provides that application of collateral estoppel may be denied if the party asserting it "could have effected joinder in the first action between himself and his present adversary."

defendant if the judgment relied upon as a basis for the estoppel is itself inconsistent with one or more previous judgments in favor of the defendant.[14] Still another situation where it might be unfair to apply ← *Third* offensive estoppel is where the second action affords the defendant procedural opportunities unavailable in the first action that could readily cause a different result.[15]

We have concluded that the preferable approach for dealing with these problems in the federal courts is not to preclude the use of offensive collateral estoppel, but to grant trial courts broad discretion to determine when it should be applied. The general rule should be that in cases where a plaintiff could easily have joined in the earlier action or where, either for the reasons discussed above or for other reasons, the application of offensive estoppel would be unfair to a defendant, a trial judge should not allow the use of offensive collateral estoppel.   *Ct's have discretion*

In the present case, however, none of the circumstances that might justify reluctance to allow the offensive use of collateral estoppel is present. The application of offensive collateral estoppel will not here reward a private plaintiff who could have joined in the previous action, since the respondent probably could not have joined in the injunctive action brought by the SEC even had he so desired.[17] Similarly, there is no unfairness to the petitioners in applying offensive collateral estoppel in this case. First, in light of the serious allegations made in the SEC's complaint against the petitioners, as well as the foreseeability of subsequent private suits that typically follow a successful Government judgment, the petitioners had every incentive to litigate the SEC lawsuit fully and vigorously. Second, the judgment in the SEC action was not inconsistent with any previous decision. Finally, there will in the respondent's action be no procedural opportunities available to the petitioners that were unavailable in the first action of a kind that might be likely to cause a different result.[19]

---

[14] In Professor Currie's familiar example, a railroad collision injures 50 passengers all of whom bring separate actions against the railroad. After the railroad wins the first 25 suits, a plaintiff wins in suit 26. Professor Currie argues that offensive use of collateral estoppel should not be applied so as to allow plaintiffs 27 through 50 automatically to recover. [Currie, Mutuality of Estoppel: Limits of the *Bernhard* Doctrine, 9 Stan. L.Rev. 281 (1957)], at 304.

[15] If, for example, the defendant in the first action was forced to defend in an inconvenient forum and therefore was unable to engage in full scale discovery or call witnesses, application of offensive collateral estoppel may be unwarranted. Indeed, differences in available procedures may sometimes justify not allowing a prior judgment to have estoppel effect in a subsequent action even between the same parties, or where defensive estoppel is asserted against a plaintiff who has litigated and lost. The problem of unfairness is particularly acute in cases of offensive estoppel, however, because the defendant against whom estoppel is asserted typically will not have chosen the forum in the first action.

[17] SEC v. Everest Management Corp., 475 F.2d 1236, 1240 (CA2) ("[T]he complicating effect of the additional issues and the additional parties outweighs any advantages of a single disposition of the common issues"). Moreover, consolidation of a private action with one brought by the SEC without its consent is prohibited by statute. 15 U.S.C. § 78u(g).

[19] It is true, of course, that the petitioners in the present action would be entitled to a jury trial of the issues bearing on whether the proxy statement was materially false and misleading

We conclude, therefore, that none of the considerations that would justify a refusal to allow the use of offensive collateral estoppel is present in this case. Since the petitioners received a "full and fair" opportunity to litigate their claims in the SEC action, the contemporary law of collateral estoppel leads inescapably to the conclusion that the petitioners are collaterally estopped from relitigating the question of whether the proxy statement was materially false and misleading.

II

The question that remains is whether, notwithstanding the law of collateral estoppel, the use of offensive collateral estoppel in this case would violate the petitioners' Seventh Amendment right to a jury trial.

[The court observed that its jury-trial decisions in *Beacon Theatres* [supra p. 550] and *Katchen* [supra p. 563] assumed that relitigation of issues common to both legal and equitable claims could be foreclosed by res judicata or collateral estoppel. It found no persuasive reason why the meaning of the Seventh Amendment should depend on whether mutuality of parties is present and thus rejected the argument that non-mutual estoppel violates the Seventh Amendment.]

The judgment of the Court of Appeals is affirmed.

JUSTICE REHNQUIST, dissenting.

* * *

I think it is clear that petitioners were denied their Seventh Amendment right to a jury trial in this case. Neither respondent nor the Court doubts that at common law as it existed in 1791, petitioners would have been entitled in the private action to have a jury determine whether the proxy statement was false and misleading in the respects alleged. The reason is that at common law in 1791, collateral estoppel was permitted only where the parties in the first action were identical to, or in privity with, the parties to the subsequent action. It was not until 1971 that the doctrine of mutuality was abrogated by this Court in certain limited circumstances. Blonder-Tongue Laboratories, Inc. v. University of Illinois Foundation, 402 U.S. 313. But developments in the judge-made doctrine of collateral estoppel, however salutary, cannot, consistent with the Seventh Amendment, contract in any material fashion the right to a jury trial that a defendant would have enjoyed in 1791. In the instant case, resort to the doctrine of collateral estoppel does more than merely contract the right to a jury trial: It eliminates the right entirely and therefore contravenes the Seventh Amendment.

---

had the SEC action never been brought—a matter to be discussed in Part II of this opinion. But the presence or absence of a jury as fact finder is basically neutral, quite unlike, for example, the necessity of defending the first lawsuit in an inconvenient forum.

The Court responds, however, that at common law "a litigant was not entitled to have a jury (in a subsequent action at law between the same parties) determine issues that had been previously adjudicated by a chancellor in equity," and that "petitioners have advanced no persuasive reason . . . why the meaning of the Seventh Amendment should depend on whether or not mutuality of parties is present." But that is tantamount to saying that since a party would not be entitled to a jury trial if he brought an equitable action, there is no persuasive reason why he should receive a jury trial on virtually the same issues if instead he chooses to bring his lawsuit in the nature of a legal action. The persuasive reason is that the Seventh Amendment requires that a party's right to jury trial which existed at common law be "preserved" from incursions by the government or the judiciary. Whether this Court believes that use of a jury trial in a particular instance is necessary, or fair or repetitive is simply irrelevant. If that view is "rigid," it is the Constitution which commands that rigidity. To hold otherwise is to rewrite the Seventh Amendment so that a party is guaranteed a jury trial in civil cases unless this Court thinks that a jury trial would be inappropriate.

* * *

Relying on Galloway v. United States, 319 U.S. 372 (1943) [supra p. 614], Champlin Refining Co., [283 U.S. 494 (1931)], and Fidelity & Deposit Co. v. United States, 187 U.S. 315 (1902), the Court seems to suggest that the offensive use of collateral estoppel in this case is permissible under the limited principle that a mere procedural change that does not invade the province of the jury and a defendant's right thereto to a greater extent than authorized by the common law is permissible. But the Court's actions today constitute a far greater infringement of the defendant's rights than it ever before has sanctioned. In *Galloway,* the Court upheld the modern form of directed verdict against a Seventh Amendment challenge, but it is clear that a similar form of directed verdict existed at common law in 1791. The modern form did not materially alter the function of the jury. Similarly, the modern device of summary judgment was found not to violate the Seventh Amendment because in 1791 a demurrer to the evidence, a procedural device substantially similar to summary judgment, was a common practice. The procedural devices of summary judgment and directed verdict are direct descendants of their common-law antecedents. They accomplish nothing more than could have been done at common law, albeit by a more cumbersome procedure. * * *

By contrast, the development of nonmutual estoppel is a substantial departure from the common law and its use in this case completely deprives petitioners of their right to have a jury determine contested issues of fact. * * *

Even accepting, arguendo, the majority's position that there is no violation of the Seventh Amendment here, I nonetheless would not sanction the use of collateral estoppel in this case. * * * In my view, it is "unfair" to apply offensive collateral estoppel where the party who is sought to be estopped has not had an opportunity to have the facts of his case determined by a jury. Since in this case petitioners were not entitled to a jury trial in the Securities and Exchange Commission (SEC) lawsuit, I would not estop them from relitigating the issues determined in the SEC suit before a jury in the private action. I believe that several factors militate in favor of this result.

First, the use of offensive collateral estoppel in this case runs counter to the strong federal policy favoring jury trials, even if it does not, as the majority holds, violate the Seventh Amendment. * * *

Second, I believe that the opportunity for a jury trial in the second action could easily lead to a different result from that obtained in the first action before the court and therefore that it is unfair to estop petitioners from relitigating the issues before a jury. This is the position adopted in the Restatement (Second) of Judgments, which disapproves of the application of offensive collateral estoppel where the defendant has an opportunity for a jury trial in the second lawsuit that was not available in the first action.[22] The Court accepts the proposition that it is unfair to apply offensive collateral estoppel "where the second action affords the defendant procedural opportunities unavailable in the first action that could readily cause a different result." Differences in discovery opportunities between the two actions are cited as examples of situations where it would be unfair to permit offensive collateral estoppel. But in the Court's view, the fact that petitioners would have been entitled to a jury trial in the present action is not such a "procedural opportunit[y]" because "the presence or absence of a jury as factfinder is basically *neutral,* quite unlike, for example, the necessity of defending the first lawsuit in an inconvenient forum." Ante, n. 19 (emphasis added).

* * *

Contrary to the majority's supposition, juries can make a difference, and our cases have, before today at least, recognized this obvious fact. * * * Jurors bring to a case their common sense and community values; their "very inexperience is an asset because it secures a fresh perception of each trial, avoiding the stereotypes said to infect the judicial eye." H. Kalven & H. Zeisel, The American Jury 8 (1966).

The ultimate irony of today's decision is that its potential for significantly conserving the resources of either the litigants or the judiciary is doubtful at best. That being the case, I see absolutely no reason to frustrate so cavalierly the important federal policy favoring jury decisions

---

[22] Restatement (Second) of Judgments § 88(2), comment d (Tent. Draft No. 2, Apr. 15, 1975). * * * [T]he Reporter's note states: "The differences between the procedures available in the first and second actions, while not sufficient to deny issue preclusion between the same parties, may warrant a refusal to carry over preclusion to an action involving another party."

of disputed fact questions. The instant case is an apt example of the minimal savings that will be accomplished by the Court's decision. As the Court admits, even if petitioners are collaterally estopped from relitigating whether the proxy was materially false and misleading, they are still entitled to have a jury determine whether respondent was injured by the alleged misstatements and the amount of damages, if any, sustained by respondent. Thus, a jury must be impaneled in this case in any event. The time saved by not trying the issue of whether the proxy was materially false and misleading before the jury is likely to be insubstantial. It is just as probable that today's decision will have the result of coercing defendants to agree to consent orders or settlements in agency enforcement actions in order to preserve their right to jury trial in the private actions. In that event, the Court, for no compelling reason, will have simply added a powerful club to the administrative agencies' arsenals that even Congress was unwilling to provide them.

NOTES AND QUESTIONS

1.   For a plaintiff to be denied use of offensive collateral estoppel (arising from an earlier judgment in which he was not a party) because he could have joined the first suit, should the cost and inconvenience of joining the earlier suit be considered? Is a person required to go to another state to join a suit there in order not to be labeled a "wait and see" plaintiff who is excluded from the benefits of the judgment? Must he do so even if the other state's law is less favorable to him? Should his financial ability or legal sophistication be taken into account?

2.   Must a plaintiff who filed suit first join a later suit in order to take advantage of a judgment arising out of it? In Polk v. Montgomery County, Maryland, 782 F.2d 1196 (4th Cir.1986), Polk was arrested at her home for failure to obtain a Maryland drivers' license and related minor offenses. She was forced to disrobe and submit to a strip search by a jail matron in the presence of another female detainee. She sued the county for violation of her civil rights, and later a second plaintiff filed a similar suit that was certified as a class action. The class action came to trial first, and the county lost. Should Ms. Polk be able to use the judgment offensively?

3.   Consider the following cases concerning the "wait and see" plaintiff problem:

(a)   In Hauser v. Krupp Steel Producers, Inc., 761 F.2d 204 (5th Cir. 1985), plaintiff was the wife of a truck driver injured in a highway accident. Her husband recovered for his injuries against the owner of the other vehicle in a suit in which she did not join. She then sued for loss of consortium. The court found she was not entitled to offensive use of collateral estoppel on the finding that the other vehicle was responsible for the accident because she failed to present a valid reason for not joining her husband's earlier action. What would be a valid reason?

(b) Defendant's oil well exploded, killing two workers and injuring a third. The families of the deceased workers brought a joint wrongful death action and obtained a judgment. The injured worker then filed his own suit and invoked collateral estoppel to preclude relitigation of the liability issue. There was no procedural bar to his joining the first action. Nations v. Sun Oil Co., 695 F.2d 933 (5th Cir.1983), held he was entitled to wait until the consequences of his injuries were clear and so was not a "wait and see" plaintiff denied the preclusive effect of the judgment.

(c) Despite cases like *Nations*, the *Parklane* concern with "wait and see" parties continues to have resonance. In Dana v. E.S. Originals, Inc., 342 F.3d 1320 (Fed.Cir.2003), plaintiff sued for infringement of his patent for "flashing Discoshoes" by defendants' marketing footwear with flashing lights. He moved for summary judgment as to liability on the ground that defendants had previously been sued in a California court by a company that had purchased the patent from him. After the California court found the patent was enforceable, the parties entered a consent decree that enjoined the defendants from marketing infringing footwear, but stated that it would have no collateral estoppel effect in favor of any party. Plaintiff in the federal suit then sued for infringement that took place *before* he had assigned the patent to the plaintiff in the California suit. The district court allowed collateral estoppel because defendants were aware that plaintiff might be "a potential adversary in a future action and attempted to preclude future litigation by private agreement in lieu of joining the assignor." The Federal Circuit found this was not the right inquiry and remanded for the lower court to determine whether plaintiff "could easily have joined the earlier action." Plaintiff argued that he had not joined the California suit "for reasons of expense or because he had no right to join that action." Should failure to join because of expense protect him from being considered a "wait and see" party not entitled to invoke collateral estoppel? Would a finding that the plaintiff in the California suit was not willing to join him as a plaintiff, and that he would therefore have to intervene, protect him from being a "wait and see" party?

4. When will "tactical" considerations justify not joining the earlier suit? In Starker v. United States, 602 F.2d 1341 (9th Cir.1979), the son sued the IRS and won a $37,000 tax refund, and his father then sued for a $300,000 tax refund arising out of the same transaction. The court "decline[d] to speculate on motivation," finding there were valid tactical reasons for the father's not joining the first suit. In contrast, Richardson Oil Co. v. Cook, 617 F.Supp. 669 (W.D.Ark.1985), involved an accident between an oil company truck and another truck in which the oil company's driver was killed. The oil company sued the driver of the other truck in federal court for property damage, and its driver's widow sued the same defendant in state court for wrongful death. The widow's case went to trial first, and she received a judgment with findings that the defendant was negligent. The federal court refused to apply collateral estoppel, finding there was no reason that the oil company could not have joined the widow's suit and so, as a "wait and see" plaintiff, it was not entitled to use the earlier judgment. Is this consistent with *Starker*? What tactical reasons might the oil company have had in not joining the widow's suit?

5.   What criteria should be used to judge if a party had a sufficient "incentive to litigate" the issues sought to be precluded? In Benjamin v. Coughlin, 643 F.Supp. 351 (S.D.N.Y.1986), a class of Rastafarians sought to enjoin the N.Y. Department of Corrections from shaving their hair, alleging violation of their religious beliefs. In two prior actions by single Rastafarian plaintiffs, N.Y. state courts held that shaving violated their religious beliefs. Did the state have sufficient incentive to litigate those actions? The court allowed the plaintiffs to use the preclusive effect of the judgment.

6.   How much "inconsistency of prior judgments" will preclude offensive use of collateral estoppel? Is one prior inconsistent suit sufficient? Sometimes a number of similar suits will go to judgment before a plaintiff attempts to take advantage of one of the favorable judgments. In Hardy v. Johns-Manville Sales Co., supra p. 1213, the court, noting that of 70 prior cases defendants had won 35, refused to accord preclusive effect. Should the court have looked to the nature of the cases, including whether they were hotly contested? Even in a group of 70 prior cases, could a court determine that one was regarded by the parties, and particularly by the common defendant, as a "test case" and therefore accord it preclusive effect?

Note that Justice Rehnquist argues in his dissent in *Parklane* that a second trial could "easily" have led to a different result. Similarly, the court in Hardy v. Johns-Manville found the existence of prior defense verdicts important because "[o]ne jury's determination should not * * * bind another jury's determination of an issue over which there are equally reasonable resolutions of doubt." 681 F.2d at 346. How can a court know whether there are "equally reasonable" resolutions of the case? Recall the standard for taking the case from the jury on a motion for judgment as a matter of law. Does that standard mean that the case should not go to the jury unless it could reasonably decide either way? If so, does this mean that in any case that should go to the jury, the jury's verdict should not have collateral estoppel effect when invoked by nonparties?

7.   The court in State Farm Fire & Casualty Co. v. Century Home Components, Inc., 550 P.2d 1185 (Ore.1976), was faced with the problem of inconsistent judgments. Approximately 50 suits were filed on behalf of persons whose goods were damaged in a fire alleged to have been caused by defendant's negligence. The first case tried resulted in a judgment for the defendant, but plaintiff appealed on the ground defendant failed to produce certain critical evidence. While that appeal was pending, the second and third cases were tried; defendant won the second and lost the third. Then the initial decision in the first case was reversed and, on retrial, defendant lost. All the other plaintiffs then conformed their complaints to those in the successful suits and asserted collateral estoppel as to liability. The court refused to apply offensive collateral estoppel because, due to defendant's victory in the second case, "we are not free to disregard incongruous results when they are looking us in the face." It noted, however, that "[w]e do not mean to say that one favorable determination can never be overcome and estoppel never applied despite the number of subsequent determinations to the contrary."

Plaintiffs in *Century Home* argued that the results were not incongruous because the cases were tried differently, but the court disagreed:

We do not give much weight to variations in the wording of the pleadings, however, where essentially the same acts and omissions are alleged. To concentrate on slight discrepancies in the allegations of negligence would put defendant at a distinct disadvantage, for claimants could modify the wording after each judgment for defendant until one claimant prevailed, after which all remaining claimants could conform their complaints to that of the prevailing claimant and could then successfully claim that the prior judgments for defendant were based upon different issues.

The thrust of plaintiff's argument must be that the jury in [the third case] and the court in [the retrial of the first case] adjudicated defendant negligent in respects which were not considered by the jury in [the second case]. The records of the cases, however, do not permit such a conclusion. Since the jury in [the third case] returned a general verdict, we do not know in which respects it found defendant negligent and, given the substantial similarity of some of the allegations and the basic thrust of the negligence alleged, we are unable to conclude that it found defendant negligent on the basis of conduct not submitted to the jury in [the second case]. * * * Allegations of essentially the same conduct were submitted to the jury in [the second case] under proper instructions by the court, and the jury obviously found that defendant was not negligent in the respects specified by the court in [the retrial of the first case].

* * *

Plaintiffs maintain, however, that the circumstances of the [retrial of the first case] clearly indicate that it was the better tried of all the cases. They assert that the issues were more clearly defined, there was substantially more money at stake than in [the second case], defendant brought in additional experts to testify at considerable expense, the evidence regarding the fire, and particularly its origin, was more fully developed, and defendant was aware that the outcome might have a significant effect on the cases waiting in the wings.

The only relevant implication of plaintiffs' position is that, since [the retrial of the first case] was more fully tried, the result must be substantially better than the jury verdict in [the second case]. We decline the invitation to decide which case was the better tried, in which case the evidence more truly presented the facts, and which "full and fair opportunity" by defendant resulted in the "correct" decision. The existence of conflicting determinations of similar issues demonstrates that different bodies can legitimately draw different conclusions.

8.   Courts are generally reluctant to deny issue preclusion on grounds of "inadequate procedural opportunity" when there was a reasonable opportunity for discovery and trial in the prior forum. In United States v. $100,000 in United States Currency, 602 F.Supp. 712 (S.D.N.Y.1985), an earlier bail hearing was found not to be a full and fair proceeding so as to preclude relitigation of issues determined there.

9.   If a losing defendant, fearing the use of the judgment against him in other cases, enters into a generous settlement in exchange for an order vacating the judgment, should a later plaintiff be allowed to assert the vacated judgment as collateral estoppel? For an argument in favor of honoring such agreements, see Note, Avoiding Issue Preclusion by Settlement Conditioned Upon the Vacatur of Entered Judgments, 96 Yale L.J. 860 (1987). In Chemetron Corp. v. Business Funds, Inc., 682 F.2d 1149 (5th Cir.1982), the court held that where the final judgment entered in a prior securities fraud case was withdrawn after a settlement agreement, it would still be applied offensively against the defendant as to issues of fact adjudicated in the prior case where such application was determined not to be unfair. See also U.S. Bancorp Mortgage Co. v. Bonner Mall Partnership, 513 U.S. 18 (1994) (refusing to vacate lower court's judgment in case that settled on appeal because this "refined form of collateral attack would * * * disturb the orderly operation of the federal judicial system").

10.   Prior criminal case judgments may be given preclusive effect. In Allen v. McCurry, 449 U.S. 90 (1980), the plaintiff in a civil rights action, alleging violation of his Fourth Amendment rights by seizure of evidence, had earlier been convicted in a state court prosecution in which his motion to suppress the evidence on Fourth Amendment grounds was denied. The Supreme Court upheld a finding that the Fourth Amendment issue was precluded. Preclusive effect has been accorded to guilty pleas. Rodriguez v. Schweiger, 796 F.2d 930 (7th Cir.1986).

11.   *Parklane* found that the judgment resulting from a judge trial in a solely equitable action would collaterally estop relitigation of the same issues in a subsequent legal action despite the right to trial by jury. What if both equitable and legal claims are brought in the same action, but the legal claims are erroneously dismissed? That was the situation in Lytle v. Household Mfg., Inc., 494 U.S. 545 (1990). A fired employee sued his employer for damages and injunctive relief, alleging race discrimination under both Title VII of the Civil Rights of 1964 (which is treated as an equitable claim for purposes of trial by jury, see pp. 574–578 supra) and 42 U.S.C. § 1981. The district court dismissed the § 1981 claims on the ground that Title VII provided the exclusive remedy. Then the court conducted a bench trial on the Title VII claims and entered judgment for the defendant. The Court of Appeals found the dismissal of the § 1981 claims was erroneous because the two remedies were distinct. However, it ruled that the court's findings on the Title VII claims collaterally estopped plaintiff from relitigating the same issues in relation to his § 1981 claims.

The Supreme Court reversed, rejecting that analogy to *Parklane* and invoking right-to-jury-trial cases:

[handwritten margin note: Here he tried to do both @ drift and was denied.]

Only the district Court's erroneous dismissal of the § 1981 claims enabled that court to resolve issues common to both claims, issues that otherwise would have been resolved by a jury. But for that erroneous ruling this case would be indistinguishable from Beacon Theatres [v. Westover, supra p. 550] and Dairy Queen [v. Wood, supra p. 557]. It would be anomalous to hold that a district court may not deprive a litigant of his right to a jury trial by resolving an equitable claim before a jury hears a legal claim raising common issues, but that a court may accomplish the same result by erroneously dismissing the legal claim.

The Court also commented that "the purposes served by collateral estoppel do not justify applying the doctrine to this case." Collateral estoppel was unnecessary, it said, to prevent multiple lawsuits because the case involved only one suit and there would be no dissipation of judicial resources in "needless litigation." But wouldn't a new trial be required? Yes, said the Court, but "relitigation of factual issues before a jury is no more 'needless' in this context than in cases in which a trial court erroneously concludes that a claim is equitable rather than legal, see, e.g., *Dairy Queen*, or that the resolution of an equitable claim can precede resolution of a legal claim, see, e.g., *Beacon Theatres*."

Is *Lytle* consistent with *Parklane*? <u>Ritter v. Mount St. Mary's College</u>, 814 F.2d 986 (4th Cir.1987), reached a different conclusion: "The effect of this error, just like the 'effect' of the prior suit in *Parklane*, is the same. Issues on which the plaintiff had a right to a jury determination were tried to the court. What the appellant in this case is in reality concerned about is not the error of the district court, which was rectified, but rather the 'harm' of the denial of jury trial, which resulted from the error." Does *Lytle* just reflect the Court's unwillingness to go that far in favoring finality over the right to jury trial?

12. The concerns over fairness and a conflict with the traditional purposes of collateral estoppel expressed in *Lytle* persuaded the Texas Supreme Court not to apply the doctrine in Sysco Food Services, Inc. v. Benjamin Trapnell, 890 S.W.2d 796 (Tex.1994). That suit resulted from the death of a woman from consuming sulfites at a Navy officers' club buffet. The sulfites could have come from three foods she ate—potato whitener on the fruit salad, pie filling, or hash browns. The manufacturers of the three foods were sued in state court, and the Navy was sued in federal court under the Federal Tort Claims Act for negligence in using sulfites and failing to warn. This bifurcation was necessary because federal courts have exclusive jurisdiction over suits brought under the Federal Tort Claims Act, and at this time prior to the passage in 1990 of 28 U.S.C. § 1367, there was no supplemental jurisdiction over the additional parties (see supra p. 914 n. 2). The federal court granted summary judgment for the Navy based on its finding that no potato whitener had been added to the fruit salad. The manufacturer of the potato whitener then moved for summary judgment in the state court on the ground that the plaintiffs were collaterally estopped from relitigating the finding that potato whitener was not added to the salad.

The Texas Supreme Court held that collateral estoppel was properly refused because doing so would not promote the goals served by the doctrine, citing *Lytle*. It would not conserve judicial resources because the two other manufacturers, who were not parties to the federal suit, could still relitigate whether there was potato whitener in the salad and therefore that the whitener, and not their products, caused the death. Likewise, the goal of protecting defendants from multiple suits would not be achieved by applying collateral estoppel here because the manufacturers were the only parties to the state-court suit. Could this reasoning prevent the application of collateral estoppel wherever the parties are not identical in the two suits?

13. According to a 2009 survey of state practice, thirty-four states have adopted the doctrine of offensive non-mutual collateral estoppel; seventeen states retain the requirement of mutuality. See Note, Rebalancing Fairness and Efficiency: The Offensive Use of Collateral Estoppel in Section 1983 Actions, 89 B.U. L. Rev. 1305, 1344, Appendix B (2009). One of the mutuality states, Florida, acknowledges the move toward non-mutual estoppel even as it reaffirms its own approach. See Cook v. State, 921 So. 2d 631, 635 (Fla. Dist. Ct. App. 2005) ("Notwithstanding the federal decisions in which collateral estoppel has been applied despite the absence of mutuality . . ., [in] Florida collateral estoppel only applies when the identical issue has been litigated between the same parties or their privies"). Both Florida and Tennessee, another state that continues to insist on mutuality, permits mutual offensive collateral estoppel—that is, the plaintiff can foreclose a defendant from relitigating an issue that the defendant had previously litigated unsuccessfully in another action against the *same plaintiff*. A Tennessee court commented that this "use of mutual offensive collateral estoppel seems to provide all the benefits of the issue preclusion doctrine without any of the perceived undesirable consequences of nonmutual offensive collateral estoppel" since it "will not increase the total amount of litigation, and it will not necessarily be unfair to the defendant." Beaty v. McGraw, 15 S.W.3d 819, 826 (Tenn.Ct.App. 1998). Would you expect some expansion of the concept of privity in a state that purports to continue to adhere to mutuality?

3. COLLATERAL ATTACK ON CLASS ACTION JUDGMENTS

STEPHENSON V. DOW CHEMICAL CO.

United States Court of Appeals, Second Circuit, 2001
273 F.3d 249, aff'd, 539 U.S. 111 (2003)

Before: CARDAMONE and F.I. PARKER, CIRCUIT JUDGES, and SPATT, DISTRICT JUDGE.

PARKER, CIRCUIT JUDGE.

This appeal requires us to determine the effect of the Supreme Court's landmark class action decisions in Amchem Products, Inc. v. Windsor, 521 U.S. 591 (1997), and Ortiz v. Fibreboard Corp., 527 U.S. 815 (1999), on a previously settled class action concerning exposure to Agent Orange during the Vietnam War.

* * *

I. BACKGROUND

* * *

The first Agent Orange litigation began in the late 1970s, when individual veterans and their families filed class action suits in the Northern District of Illinois and Southern and Eastern Districts of New York, alleging that exposure to Agent Orange caused them injury. In re "Agent Orange" Prod. Liab. Litig., 635 F.2d 987, 988 (2d Cir.1980) ("Agent Orange I"). By order of the MDL Panel, these actions were transferred to the Eastern District of New York and consolidated for pretrial purposes. Plaintiffs asserted claims of negligent manufacture, strict liability, breach of warranty, intentional tort and nuisance. In re "Agent Orange" Prod. Liab. Litig., 597 F.Supp. 740, 750 (E.D.N.Y.1984) ("Agent Orange III"); aff'd 818 F.2d 145 (2d Cir.1987).

In 1983, the district court certified the following class under Federal Rule of Civil Procedure 23(b)(3):

> those persons who were in the United States, New Zealand or Australian Armed Forces at any time from 1961 to 1972 who were injured while in or near Vietnam by exposure to Agent Orange or other phenoxy herbicides, including those composed in whole or in part of 2, 4, 5-trichlorophenoxyacetic acid or containing some amount of 2, 3, 7, 8-tetrachlorodibenzo-p-dioxin. The class also includes spouses, parents, and children of the veterans born before January 1, 1984, directly or derivatively injured as a result of the exposure.

* * * The court also ordered notice by mail, print media, radio and television to be provided to class members, providing in part that persons who wished to opt out must do so by May 1, 1984.

Trial of the class claims was to begin on May 7, 1984. On the eve of trial, the parties reached a settlement. The settlement provided that defendants would pay $180 million into a settlement fund, $10 million of which would indemnify defendants against future state court actions alleging the same claims. The settlement provided that "[t]he Class specifically includes persons who have not yet manifested injury." Additionally, the settlement specifically stated that the district court would "retain jurisdiction over the Fund pending its final disposition."

The district court held fairness hearings throughout the country, and approved the settlement as fair, reasonable and adequate. The court rejected the motion to certify a subclass of those class members who objected to terms of the settlement. The court concluded that "[n]o purpose would have been served by appointing counsel for a subclass of disappointed claimants except to increase expenses to the class and delay proceedings."

Seventy-five percent of the $180 million was to be distributed directly " 'to exposed veterans who suffer from long-term total disabilities and to the surviving spouses or children of exposed veterans who have died.' " "A claimant would qualify for compensation by establishing exposure to Agent Orange and death or disability not 'predominately' caused by trauma. . ." Payments were to be made for ten years, beginning January 1, 1985 and ending December 31, 1994:

> No payment will be made for death or disability occurring after December 31, 1994. Payment will be made for compensable deaths occurring both before and after January 1, 1985. Payments will be made for compensable disability to the extent that the period of disability falls within the ten years of the program's operation.

"Most of the remaining [25%] of the settlement fund established the Agent Orange Class Assistance Program, . . . which made grants to agencies serving Vietnam veterans and their families." Explaining the creation of this kind of fund, Judge Weinstein stated that it was "[t]he most practicable and equitable method of distributing benefits to" those claimants who did not meet eligibility criteria for cash payments.

We affirmed class certification, settlement approval and much of the distribution plan. We rejected challenges to class certification, concluding that "class certification was justified under Rule 23(b)(3) due to the centrality of the military contractor defense." We specifically rejected an attack based on adequacy of representation, again based on the military contractor defense which, we reasoned, "would have precluded recovery by all plaintiffs, irrespective of the strengths, weaknesses, or idiosyncrasies of their claims." We additionally concluded that the notice scheme devised by Judge Weinstein was the "best notice practicable" under Federal Rule of Civil Procedure 23(c)(2). Finally, we affirmed the settlement as fair, reasonable and adequate, given the serious weaknesses of the plaintiffs' claims.

In 1989 and 1990, two purported class actions, Ivy v. Diamond Shamrock Chemicals Co. and Hartman v. Diamond Shamrock Chemicals Co., were filed in Texas state courts. These suits, on behalf of Vietnam veterans exposed to Agent Orange,[3] sought compensatory and punitive damages against the same companies as in the settled suit. The plaintiffs alleged that their injuries manifested only after the May 7, 1984 settlement. Additionally, the *Ivy/Hartman* plaintiffs expressly disclaimed any reliance on federal law, asserting only state law claims. Nonetheless,

---

[3]   Two plaintiffs in the *Ivy* litigation alleged injuries stemming from Agent Orange exposure while acting in a civilian capacity, and thus were not members of the class bound by the 1984 settlement. Their claims were severed from the claims of the other plaintiffs.

the defendants removed the actions to federal court on the grounds that these claims had already been asserted and litigated in federal court. The MDL Panel transferred the actions to Judge Weinstein in the Eastern District of New York.

* * *

[Plaintiffs argued] that it was unfair to bind them to the settlement when their injuries were not manifested until after the settlement had been reached. The district court rejected this argument, based on the following reasoning:

> All of the courts which considered the Agent Orange Settlement were fully cognizant of the conflict arguments now hypothesized by the plaintiffs and took steps to minimize the problem in the way they arranged for long-term administration of the Settlement Fund.
>
> In many cases the conflict between the interests of present and future claimants is more imagined than real. In the instant case, for example, the injustice wrought upon the plaintiffs is nonexistent. *These plaintiffs, like all class members who suffer death or disability before the end of 1994, are eligible for compensation from the Agent Orange Payment Fund.* The relevant latency periods and the age of the veterans ensure that almost all valid claims will be revealed before that time.
>
> Even when it is proper and necessary for the courts to be solicitous of the interests of future claimants, the courts cannot ignore the interests of presently injured plaintiffs as well as defendants in achieving a settlement. Class action settlements simply will not occur if the parties cannot set definitive limits on defendants' liability. Making settlement of Rule 23 suits too difficult will work harms upon plaintiffs, defendants, the courts, and the general public.

The district court therefore dismissed the *Ivy/Hartman* litigation.

We affirmed the district court's dismissal. *Ivy/Hartman II*, 996 F.2d 1425, 1439 [(2d Cir.1993)]. * * *

We * * * addressed plaintiffs' argument that they were not members of the prior class, because they were not "injured" as the term was used in the class definition. We concluded that, for the purposes of the Agent Orange litigation, "injury occurs when a deleterious substance enters a person's body, even though its adverse effects are not immediately apparent." We emphasized that the plaintiffs in the original suit had sought to include such "at-risk" plaintiffs, over defendants' objections, and that we had already affirmed the inclusion of these plaintiffs in the class.

We likewise rejected plaintiffs' argument that their due process rights were violated because they were denied adequate representation and adequate notice in the prior action. We reasoned that "providing individual notice and opt-out rights to persons who are unaware of an injury would probably do little good." We concluded that the plaintiffs were adequately represented in the prior action, and that a subclass of future claimants was unnecessary " 'because of the way [the settlement] was structured to cover future claimants.' "

Shortly before our decision in *Ivy/Hartman II*, the $10 million set aside for indemnification from state court Agent Orange judgments was transferred to the Class Assistance Program, because the district court deemed such a fund unnecessary. The distribution activities had begun in 1988, and concluded in June 1997. During the ten year period of the settlement, $196.5 million was distributed as cash payments to approximately 52,000 class members. The program paid approximately $52 million to "after-manifested" claimants, whose deaths or disabilities occurred after May 7, 1984. Approximately $71.3 million of the fund was distributed through the Class Assistance Program.

[In August, 1998, Joe Isaacson sued the chemical manufacturers who produced Agent Orange in New Jersey state court. Isaacson had served in Vietnam in 1968–69 in the Air Force, working on planes that sprayed Agent Orange. In 1996, he was diagnosed with non-Hodkins Lymphoma, and in his suit he alleged state-law claims that defendants were liable for his condition. In February, 1999, Daniel Stephenson sued the same defendants in federal court in Louisiana. He had served in Vietnam from 1965 to 1970 as a helicopter pilot, and was in regular contact with Agent Orange during that time. In February, 1998, he was diagnosed with multiple myeloma, a bone marrow cancer.

Defendants removed Isaacson's suit to federal court, and the federal court denied his motion to remand. The MDL Panel transferred both Stephenson's and Isaacson's suits to Judge Weinstein, who consolidated them.]

Defendants moved to dismiss under Federal Rule of Civil Procedure 12(b)(6), asserting that plaintiffs' claims were barred by the 1984 class action settlement and subsequent final judgment. Judge Weinstein granted this motion from the bench following argument, rejecting plaintiffs' argument that they were inadequately represented and concluding that plaintiffs' suit was an impermissible collateral attack on the prior settlement.

Because we disagree with this conclusion, based on the Supreme Court's holdings in *Amchem* and *Ortiz*, we must vacate the district court's dismissal and remand for further proceedings.

II. DISCUSSION

* * *

Collateral Attack

The parties devote much energy to debating the permissibility of a collateral attack in this case. Plaintiffs assert that, since the Supreme Court's decision in Hansberry v. Lee, 311 U.S. 32 (1940) [*supra* p. 311], courts have allowed collateral attacks on class action judgments based upon due process concerns. Defendants strenuously disagree and contend that to allow plaintiffs' suit to go forward, in the face of the 1984 global settlement, would "violate defendants' right to due process of law." Defendants likewise strenuously argue that the district court's injunction against future litigation prevents these appellants from maintaining their actions. While it is true that "[a]n injunction must be obeyed until modified or dissolved, and its unconstitutionality is no defense to disobedience," defendants' injunction-based argument misses the point. The injunction was part and parcel of the judgment that plaintiffs contend failed to afford them adequate representation. If plaintiffs' inadequate representation allegations prevail, as we so conclude, the judgment, which includes the injunction on which defendants rely, is not binding as to these plaintiffs.

Defendants contend that Supreme Court precedent permits a collateral attack on a class action judgment "only where there has been no prior determination of absent class members' due process rights." According to defendants, because the "due process rights of absent class members have been extensively litigated in the Agent Orange litigation," these plaintiffs cannot now attack those prior determinations. We reject defendants' arguments and conclude that plaintiffs' collateral attack, which seeks only to prevent the prior settlement from operating as res judicata to their claims, is permissible.

First, even if, as defendants contend, collateral attack is only permitted where there has been no prior determination of the absent class members' rights, plaintiffs' collateral attack is allowed. It is true that, on direct appeal and in the *Ivy/Hartman* litigation, we previously concluded that there was adequate representation of all class members in the original Agent Orange settlement. However, neither this Court nor the district court has addressed specifically the adequacy of representation for those members of the class whose injuries manifested after depletion of the settlements funds. See *Ivy/Hartman II*, 996 F.2d at 1436 (creating a subclass of future claimants was unnecessary because the settlement covered such claimants); *Ivy/Hartman I*, 781 F.Supp. at 919 ("These plaintiffs, like all class members *who suffer death or disability before the end of 1994*, are eligible for compensation from the Agent Orange Payment Fund." (emphasis added.)) Therefore, even accepting defendants' argument, plaintiffs' suit can go forward because there has been no prior adequacy of representation determination with respect to individuals whose claims arise after the depletion of the settlement fund.[6]

Second, the propriety of a collateral attack such as this is amply supported by precedent. In Hansberry v. Lee, 311 U.S. 32 (1940) [supra p. 311], the Supreme Court entertained a collateral attack on an Illinois state court class action judgment that purported to bind the plaintiffs. The Court held that class action judgments can only bind absent class members where "the interests of those not joined are of the same class as the interests of those who are, and where it is considered that the latter fairly represent the former in the prosecution of the litigation." Additionally, we have previously stated that a "[j]udgment in a class action is not secure from collateral attack unless the absentees were adequately and vigorously represented."

Allowing plaintiffs' suit would be consistent with many other circuit decisions recognizing the ability of later plaintiffs to attack the adequacy of representation in an earlier class action. For example, the Fifth Circuit holds:

> To answer the question whether the class representative adequately represented the class so that the judgment in the class suit will bind the absent members of the class requires a two-pronged inquiry: (1) Did the trial court in the first suit correctly determine, initially, that the representative would adequately represent the class? and (2) Does it appear, after the termination of the suit, that the class representative adequately protected the interest of the class? The first question involves us in a collateral review of the . . . [trial] court's determination to permit the suit to proceed as a class action with [the named plaintiff] as the representative, while the second involves a review of the class representative's conduct of the entire suit—an inquiry which is not required to be made by the trial court but which is appropriate in a collateral attack on the judgment. . . .

Gonzales v. Cassidy, 474 F.2d 67, 72 (5th Cir.1973).

---

[6] Defendants rely heavily on a recent Ninth Circuit decision, Epstein v. MCA, Inc., 179 F.3d 641 (9th Cir.1999), in support of their limited collateral review theory. *Epstein* held that a collateral attack is available only "to consider whether the procedures in the prior litigation afforded the party against whom the earlier judgment is asserted a 'full and fair opportunity' to litigate the claim or issue." According to the Ninth Circuit,

> Due process requires that an absent class member's right to adequate representation be protected by the adoption of the appropriate procedures by the certifying court and by the courts that review its determinations; due process does not require collateral second-guessing of those determinations and that review.

Here, neither the district court nor this Court has determined the adequacy of representation with respect to these plaintiffs whose injuries did not arise until after the settlement expired. Without adopting the Ninth Circuit's decision in *Epstein*, we conclude that plaintiffs' collateral attack is proper even under its standard.

Defendants' citation to Federated Department Stores, Inc. v. Moitie, 452 U.S. 394 (1981) [supra p. 892], is unavailing. According to that case, a "judgment merely voidable because based upon an erroneous view of the law is not open to collateral attack, but can be corrected only by a direct review and not by bringing another action upon the same cause [of action]." Defendants' reliance on this case misperceives plaintiffs' argument. Plaintiffs do not attack the merits or finality of the settlement itself, but instead argue that they were not proper parties to that judgment. If plaintiffs were not proper parties to that judgment, as we conclude below, res judicata cannot defeat their claims. Further, such collateral review would not, as defendants maintain, violate defendants' due process rights by exposing them to double liability. Exposure to liability here is not duplicative if plaintiffs were never proper parties to the prior judgment in the first place.

We therefore hold that a collateral attack to contest the application of res judicata is available. We turn next to the merits of this attack.

Due Process Considerations and Res Judicata

The doctrine of res judicata dictates that "a final judgment on the merits of an action precludes the parties or their privies from relitigating issues that were or could have been raised in that action." Res judicata ordinarily applies "if the earlier decision was (1) a final judgment on the merits, (2) by a court of competent jurisdiction, (3) in a case involving the same parties or their privies, and (4) involving the same cause of action."

Plaintiffs' argument focuses on element number three in the res judicata analysis: whether they are parties bound by the settlement. Plaintiffs rely primarily on the United States Supreme Court's decisions in Amchem Products, Inc. v. Windsor, 521 U.S. 591 (1997), and Ortiz v. Fibreboard Corp., 527 U.S. 815 (1999).

In *Amchem*, the Supreme Court confronted, on direct appeal, a challenge to class certification for settlement purposes in an asbestos litigation. The class defined in the complaint included both individuals who were presently injured as well as individuals who had only been exposed to asbestos. The Supreme Court held that this "sprawling" class was improperly certified under Federal Rules of Civil Procedure 23(a) and (b). Specifically, the Court held that Rule 23(a)(4)'s requirement that the named parties " 'will fairly and adequately protect the interests of the class' " had not been satisfied. The Court reasoned that

> named parties with diverse medical conditions sought to act on behalf of a single giant class rather than on behalf of discrete subclasses. In significant respects, the interests of those within the single class are not aligned. Most saliently, for the currently injured, the critical goal is generous immediate payments. That

goal tugs against the interest of exposure-only plaintiffs in ensuring an ample, inflation-protected fund for the future.

Amchem also implied, but did not decide, that the notice provided to exposure-only class members was likewise inadequate. The Court stated that, because many exposure-only individuals, may not be aware of their exposure or realize the ramifications of exposure, "those without current afflictions may not have the information or foresight needed to decide, intelligently, whether to stay in or opt out."

In *Ortiz*, the Supreme Court again addressed a settlement-only class action in the asbestos litigation context. *Ortiz*, however, involved a settlement-only limited fund class under Rule 23(b)(1)(B). The Supreme Court ultimately held that the class could not be maintained under Rule 23(b)(1)(B), because "the limit of the fund was determined by treating the settlement agreement as dispositive, an error magnified" by conflicted counsel. In so holding, *Ortiz* noted that "it is obvious after Amchem that a class divided between holders of present and future claims (some of the latter involving no physical injury and attributable to claimants not yet born) requires division into homogeneous subclasses under Rule 23(c)(4)(B), with separate representation to eliminate conflicting interests of counsel."

Res judicata generally applies to bind absent class members except where to do so would violate due process. Due process requires adequate representation "at all times" throughout the litigation, notice "reasonably calculated . . . to apprise interested parties of the pendency of the action," and an opportunity to opt out. Shutts, 472 U.S. at 811–12.

Both Stephenson and Isaacson fall within the class definition of the prior litigation: they served in the United States military, stationed in Vietnam, between 1961 and 1972, and were allegedly injured by exposure to Agent Orange. However, they both learned of their allegedly Agent Orange-related injuries only after the 1984 settlement fund had expired in 1994. Because the prior litigation purported to settle all future claims, but only provided for recovery for those whose death or disability was discovered prior to 1994, the conflict between Stephenson and Isaacson and the class representatives becomes apparent. No provision was made for post-1994 claimants, and the settlement fund was permitted to terminate in 1994. *Amchem* and *Ortiz* suggest that Stephenson and Isaacson were not adequately represented in the prior Agent Orange litigation.[8] Those cases

---

8 We also note that plaintiffs likely received inadequate notice. [Phillips Petroleum v.] Shutts [472 U.S. 797 (1985)], provides that adequate notice is necessary to bind absent class members. As described earlier, Amchem indicates that effective notice could likely not ever be given to exposure-only class members. Because we have already concluded that these plaintiffs were inadequately represented, and thus were not proper parties to the prior litigation, we need not definitively decide whether notice was adequate.

indicate that a class which purports to represent both present and future claimants may encounter internal conflicts.

Defendants contend that there was, in fact, no conflict because all class members' claims were equally meritless and would have been defeated by the "military contractor" defense. This argument misses the mark. At this stage, we are only addressing whether plaintiffs' claims should be barred by res judicata. We are therefore concerned only with whether they were afforded due process in the earlier litigation. Part of the due process inquiry (and part of the Rule 23(a) class certification requirements) involves assessing adequacy of representation and intra-class conflicts. The ultimate merits of the claims have no bearing on whether the class previously certified adequately represented these plaintiffs.

Because these plaintiffs were inadequately represented in the prior litigation, they were not proper parties and cannot be bound by the settlement. We therefore must vacate the district court's dismissal and remand for further proceedings. We, of course, express no opinion as to the ultimate merits of plaintiffs' claims.

NOTES AND QUESTIONS

1.   The Supreme Court granted certiorari in *Stephenson*, but ultimately issued a per curiam decision, affirming the judgment of the Second Circuit in Stephenson's action by an equally divided court, Justice Stevens not participating. (The Second Circuit's decision in Isaacson's action, by contrast, was vacated on the ground that it had been improperly removed from state court.) Counsel for plaintiffs characterized this result as a "fabulous total victory" because it did not vacate the Second Circuit's decision regarding Stephenson's suit, but counsel for Dow pointed out that the Supreme Court's decision had no precedential value. See Mauro, High Court Affirms 2nd Circuit in Agent Orange Case, S.F. Recorder, June 10, 2003, at 3.

2.   As an alternative to relying on state courts to give effect to res judicata, federal courts that enter class action judgments can enjoin subsequent litigation filed by class members that is covered by the preclusive effect of the judgment if they retain jurisdiction over the action for purposes of enforcing their decrees. See In the Matter of VMS Securities Litig., 103 F.3d 1317, 1324 (7th Cir.1996) ("in the context of complex class action litigation, a federal district court may appropriately use the All Writs Act to * * * enjoin the prosecution of subsequent state court claims in order to enforce its ongoing orders against relitigation and to guard the integrity of its prior rulings over which it had expressly retained jurisdiction"); compare Grimes v. Vitalink Communications Corp., 17 F.3d 1553 (3d Cir.1994) (questioning whether failure to opt out would suffice to provide personal jurisdiction for such an injunction, at least if entered by a state court). The Anti-Injunction Act, 28 U.S.C. § 2283, includes an exception for injunctions issued to protect or effectuate a judgment. See Chick Kam Choo v. Exxon Corp., 486 U.S. 140 (1988) (scope of injunctive relief under the relitigation exception to the Anti-

Injunction Act limited to matters precluded by the decision of the federal court).

In Smith v. Bayer Corp., 564 U.S. 299 (2011), the Supreme Court held that the Anti-Injunction Act bars a federal district court from granting an injunction to protect or effectuate that court's *refusal* to certify a class action. This case arose from overlapping class action litigation in the Minnesota federal court and a West Virginia state court. Acting under Rule 23 of the Federal Rules of Civil Procedure, the federal judge refused to certify a proposed class action involving the alleged victims of a prescription drug that Bayer later removed from the market. At Bayer's request, the district judge then enjoined Smith from continuing to prosecute a class action in the West Virginia state court on behalf of Baycol's alleged victims in that state. Notably, the West Virginia action began before the enactment of the Class Action Fairness Act of 2005 (CAFA), and was not subject to removal and MDL (multidistrict litigation) treatment in federal court.

The Court unanimously overturned the anti-suit injunction. Although it acknowledged that anti-suit injunctions may be appropriate to effectuate a federal judgment, such authority comes into play only where the same issues resolved in the federal action also arise in the state proceeding. Here, the Court noted that the state's procedural rules governing class certification were not necessarily the same as those the federal court applied. Although it had adopted a version of the Federal Rules of Civil Procedure, West Virginia had not interpreted its own version with the same parsimony. (Specifically, the West Virginia Supreme Court had taken a more certification-friendly view of the requirement that common issues of fact or law "predominate" for class certification purposes.) As a result, the two certification proposals did not present the same issue for preclusion purposes. The Court also noted that Smith, the lead plaintiff in the West Virginia proceeding, was not a party to, and was not represented in, the federal court proceeding in Minnesota and could not be precluded from pursuing the state court action. Having concluded that preclusion principles would not bar the second class action, the Court applied settled law under Chick Kam Choo, supra, in rejecting the injunction.

3.   Does *Stephenson* allow collateral attacks so liberally that the finality of class action judgments is threatened? That should not be the case if the *Stephenson* holding is limited to its facts. The finding that the class representatives were inadequate flowed directly from Amchem Products, Inc. v. Windsor, 521 U.S. 591 (1997), which overturned the certification of a settlement class action on behalf of persons exposed to asbestos (including both those who presently manifested injury and "futures plaintiffs" who have not). The court found an inherent conflict between the interests of these two groups since each would want a larger share of the settlement. The impact of *Amchem* was that "futures plaintiffs" should not be combined in a class action with persons who have manifested injury (unless possibly by subclasses and represented by different attorneys). Thus the combining of both groups in the Agent Orange class action could simply not stand after *Amchem*. This situation in which a clear bright-line precedent now demonstrates inadequacy of

representation in an earlier class action judgment is not likely to occur in many cases. See Hoffman, Syngenta, Stephenson and the Federal Judicial Injunctive Power, 37 Akron L. Rev. 605 (2004).

In Hospital Management Associates, Inc. v. Shell Oil Co., 591 S.E.2d 611 (S.C. 2004), the court upheld summary judgment according full faith and credit to two nationwide class action settlements in other state courts despite the assertion of opt-out class members that they were entitled to attack the judgments collaterally. Noting the inconclusive Supreme Court handling of *Stephenson*, the court commented:

> In our opinion, there are important policy considerations favoring both limited and broad collateral review. Certainly, in the specialized context of class action litigation, the significant interest in efficiency and finality favor limited review. If the due process issues are fully and fairly litigated and necessarily decided by the rendering court, then the strong interest in finality militates in favor of an extremely limited collateral review. Without limited review, a nationwide class action could be vulnerable to collateral actions in the 49 other states in which it was not litigated initially. It would seem to be a waste of judicial resources to require reviewing courts to conduct an extensive substantive review when one has already been undertaken in a sister state. As the Ohio court stated in Fine v. America Online: "To allow substantive collateral attacks would be counter intuitive to [the] procedural relief that a class-action suit is intended to afford our judicial system nationwide." 743 N.E.2d at 421–22.

> On the other hand, there is a fundamental interest in not allowing constitutionally infirm judgments to be enforced. It would be troublesome to enforce a class action settlement against parties over whom the rendering court did not have personal jurisdiction. We note, however * * * that direct appellate review of a class action is the appropriate vehicle to correct whatever errors may have been made at the trial court level.

> We hold that, in a case such as this one, only a limited collateral review is appropriate. It would run counter to the class action goals of efficiency and finality to allow successive reviews of issues that were, in fact, fully and fairly litigated in the rendering court. Moreover, second-guessing the fully litigated decisions of our sister courts would violated the spirit of full faith and credit.

> * * * [W]hat this limited review entails is "an examination of *procedural* due process and nothing more." Fine v. America Online, 743 N.E.2d at 421. More specifically, we must determine: (1) whether there were safeguards in place to guarantee sufficient notice and adequate representation; and (2) whether such safeguards were, in fact, applied.

The court then proceeded to examine the notice given (an extensive multimedia campaign which the court found to be constitutionally sufficient) and the adequacy of representation. On that score, it found that the courts, in contrast to *Amchem*, had procedures in place to ensure adequate representation and that they were implemented throughout the litigations. It therefore found that full faith and credit should be accorded the two class action settlement judgments.

4.   In *Stephenson* the court says that the original class action provided inadequate representation for those whose injuries manifested themselves after 1994. What solution could there be to such a problem? What should the original class action have provided to overcome this difficulty? Compare the way in which the settlement regimes in *Amchem* and *Ortiz* addressed the question of future claims. Keep in mind that, at the time the class-action settlement was arranged, no class member would know whether he would become sick before 1994, and some might consider the coverage for another decade reasonable protection. Consider the analysis in Nagareda, Administering Adequacy in Class Representation, 82 Tex. L. Rev. 287, 322 (2003):

> The ten-year term for cash benefits under the Agent Orange class settlement appears far from arbitrary, however, when one considers that any veteran would have had an exceedingly weak scientific case on the causation element, at least as of 1984, and that the ten-year term for cash benefits extended to more than two decades after the last alleged exposure of class members.

5.   The court in *Stephenson* also says in footnote 8 that notice may have been inadequate in the original Agent Orange litigation with regard to these plaintiffs. But it had earlier held that notice in that suit was adequate in the *Ivy/Hartman* litigation (996 F.2d at 1435):

> In the instant case, society's interest in the efficient and fair resolution of large-scale litigation outweighs the gains from individual notice and opt-out rights, whose benefits here are conjectural at best. As appellants correctly note, providing individual notice and opt-out rights to persons who are unaware of an injury would probably do little good.

Why should the *Stephenson* plaintiffs be treated differently for purposes of notice?

6.   The Class Action Fairness Act of 2005 requires defendants to give notice of proposed settlements to state and federal officials, and provides that if this notice is not given, class members may choose not to be bound. 28 U.S.C. § 1715(e)(1). Would this solve the due process problem?

7.   Besides notice and the right to opt out of the class action, is there any other way in which to protect the interests of class members? Read Rule 23(e). It requires court approval of any class action settlement, and calls for careful examination of the proposed settlement. Would such review by the court strengthen the case for binding class members?

8.   The finding of inadequate representation in *Stephenson* rested on class conflicts similar to those in *Hansberry*. What if the first class action results in a judgment for the defendant, due to the inadequate efforts of the class lawyer? In Pelt v. Utah, 539 F.3d 1271 (10th Cir. 2008), the plaintiff class, representing members of the Navajo tribe, sought to require Utah to provide an accounting of a state-run oil and gas royalty fund that had been established for the tribe's benefit by federal law. Two previous class actions, one brought in the early 1960s and a second one brought in 1970, both led to judicial decisions acknowledging the obligation of the state to provide an accounting. But both ended with a dismissal for failure to prosecute, without actually compelling the state to perform the accounting. While the appellate court in *Pelt* acknowledged that the third class action presented the same issue and involved parties that had been represented in the first two actions, it concluded that the representation in the earlier cases was so inadequate as to violate due process standards. It accordingly affirmed the district court's conclusion that claim preclusion did not bar the third class action. To what extent should a court consider, in the context of a collateral attack, the quality of class counsel's representation? The second class action was certified, meaning that the district court found class representation to be adequate. Indeed, *three* law firms represented the tribe's interest in that action, successfully pressed the tribe's claim of entitlement to the Supreme Court, and later secured an award of attorney's fees, reflecting the court's perception that the class action had been reasonably successful. Does the finding of inadequate representation make sense on these facts? Does it reflect the court's perception that the State owes an ongoing duty to account to the tribe that was not vitiated by the earlier dispositions? If so, would it make more sense to treat the State's current duty to account as a transaction or occurrence separate from those involved in the earlier proceedings?

9.   In Matsushita Elec. Indus. Co. v. Epstein, 516 U.S. 367 (1996), two class actions were filed on behalf of shareholders claiming improprieties in relation to a merger of the company. One was in federal court, and asserted claims that were subject to exclusive federal jurisdiction. The other, in a Delaware state court, asserted state-law claims. The Supreme Court ruled that a judgment entered in the Delaware state court based on a court-approved settlement of that case was entitled to enforcement under 28 U.S.C. § 1738 in the federal-court class action. In reaching this result, the Court noted that the Delaware Supreme Court had held in another case that courts called upon to approve class-action settlements had to ensure that the class members were adequately represented, and that the state-court judge had reviewed the proposed settlement before approving it. Should that review suffice? Compare Kahan & Silberman, Matsushita and Beyond: The Role of State Courts in Class Actions Involving Exclusive Federal Claims, 1996 Sup.Ct.Rev. 219 (arguing that when class members have an opportunity to object to a proposed settlement they should not be permitted to attack it in a collateral proceeding) with Woolley, The Availability of Collateral Attack for Inadequate Representation in Class Suits, 79 Tex.L.Rev. 383 (2000) (arguing that there

must be a constitutional right to litigate adequacy of representation in a later proceeding).

10. Preclusion issues arising from class action litigation have attracted a broad range of distinguished commentary. For a sampling, see Issacharoff & Nagareda, Class Settlements Under Attack, 156 U. Pa. L. Rev. 1649 (2008); Wolff, Federal Jurisdiction and Due Process in the Era of Nationwide Class Actions, 156 U. Pa. L. Rev. 2035 (2008); Wolff, Preclusion in Class Action Litigation, 105 Colum. L. Rev. 717 (2005); Monaghan, Antisuit Injunctions and Preclusion Against Absent Nonresident Class Members, 98 Colum. L. Rev. 1148 (1998).

4. COLLATERAL ESTOPPEL AGAINST THE GOVERNMENT

UNITED STATES V. MENDOZA
Supreme Court of the United States, 1984
464 U.S. 154

JUSTICE REHNQUIST delivered the opinion of the Court.

[A Filipino national residing in the U.S. petitioned in 1978 for naturalization under a World War II statute that granted foreigners who served honorably in the U.S. military during the war the right to apply for and receive U.S. citizenship. The act was repealed after the war, and only applicants applying for citizenship prior to December 31, 1946 were entitled to naturalization. The U.S. immigration office in the Philippines was closed between October 1945 and August 1946. Mendoza argued that this fact excused his delay in petitioning. He relied on a 1975 decision of a district court holding that 68 Filipino war veterans were entitled to naturalization despite delay due to the closure of the immigration office in the Philippines, which it found to violate their rights to due process. The court of appeals held that the government was estopped to relitigate this issue. The Supreme Court reversed.]

We have long recognized that "the Government is not in a position identical to that of a private litigant," INS v. Hibi, 414 U.S. 5, 8 (1973) (per curiam), both because of the geographic breadth of government litigation and also, most importantly, because of the nature of the issues the government litigates. It is not open to serious dispute that the government is a party to a far greater number of cases on a nationwide basis than even the most litigious private entity; in 1982, the United States was a party to more than 75,000 of the 206,193 filings in the United States District Courts. In the same year the United States was a party to just under 30% of the civil cases appealed from the District Courts to the Court of Appeals. Government litigation frequently involves legal questions of substantial public importance; indeed, because the proscriptions of the United States Constitution are so generally directed at governmental action, many constitutional questions can arise only in the context of litigation to which the government is a party. Because of those facts the government is more likely than any private party to be involved in lawsuits against different parties which nonetheless involve the same legal issues.

A rule allowing nonmutual collateral estoppel against the government in such cases would substantially thwart the development of important questions of law by freezing the first final decision rendered on a particular legal issue. Allowing only one final adjudication would deprive this Court of the benefit it receives from permitting several courts of appeals to explore a difficult question before this Court grants certiorari. Indeed, if nonmutual estoppel were routinely applied against the government, this Court would have to revise its practice of waiting for a conflict to develop before granting the government's petitions for certiorari.

The Solicitor General's policy for determining when to appeal an adverse decision would also require substantial revision. The Court of Appeals faulted the government in this case for failing to appeal a decision that it now contends is erroneous. But the government's litigation conduct in a case is apt to differ from that of a private litigant. Unlike a private litigant who generally does not forego an appeal if he believes that he can prevail, the Solicitor General considers a variety of factors, such as the limited resources of the government and the crowded dockets of the courts, before authorizing an appeal. The application of nonmutual estoppel against the government would force the Solicitor General to abandon those prudential concerns and to appeal every adverse decision in order to avoid foreclosing further review.

In addition to those institutional concerns traditionally considered by the Solicitor General, the panoply of important public issues raised in governmental litigation may quite properly lead successive Administrations of the Executive Branch to take differing positions with respect to the resolution of a particular issue. While the Executive Branch must of course defer to the Judicial Branch for final resolution of questions of constitutional law, the former nonetheless controls the progress of governmental litigation through the federal courts.

* * *

The Court of Appeals did not endorse a routine application of nonmutual collateral estoppel against the government, because it recognized that the government does litigate issues of far-reaching national significance which in some cases, it concluded, might warrant relitigation. But in this case it found no "record evidence" indicating that there was a "crucial need" in the administration of the immigration laws for a redetermination of the due process question. * * * The Court of Appeals did not make clear what sort of "record evidence" would have satisfied it that there *was* a "crucial need" for redetermination of the question in this case, but we pretermit further discussion of that approach; we believe that the standard announced by the Court of Appeals for determining when relitigation of a legal issue is to be permitted is so wholly subjective that it affords no guidance to the courts or to the government. Such a standard leaves the government at sea because it cannot possibly anticipate, in determining whether or not to appeal an adverse decision, whether a court will bar relitigation of the issue in a later case. * * *

We hold, therefore, that nonmutual offensive collateral estoppel simply does not apply against the government in such a way as to preclude relitigation of issues such as those involved in this case.[7] The conduct of government litigation in the courts of the United States is sufficiently different from the conduct of private civil litigation in those courts so that what might otherwise be economy interests underlying a broad application of collateral estoppel are outweighed by the constraints which peculiarly affect the government. We think that our conclusion will better allow thorough development of legal doctrine by allowing litigation in multiple forums. Indeed, a contrary result might disserve the economy interests in whose name estoppel is advanced by requiring the government to abandon virtually any exercise of discretion in seeking to review judgments unfavorable to it. The doctrine of res judicata, of course, prevents the government from relitigating the same cause of action against the parties to a prior decision,[8] but beyond that point principles of nonmutual collateral estoppel give way to the policies just stated.

Our holding in this case is consistent with each of our prior holdings to which the parties have called our attention, and which we reaffirm. Today in a companion case we hold that the government may be estopped under certain circumstances from relitigating a question when the parties to the two lawsuits are the same. United States v. Stauffer Chemical Co., 464 U.S. 165 (1984); see also Montana v. United States, [440 U.S. 147 (1979)]; United States v. Moser, 266 U.S. 236 (1924) [supra p. 1221 n. 2]. None of those cases, however, involve the effort of a party to estop the government in the absence of mutuality.

The concerns underlying our disapproval of collateral estoppel against the government are for the most part inapplicable where mutuality is present, as in *Stauffer Chemical, Montana,*[9] and *Moser.* The application of

---

[7]   The government does not base its argument on the exception to the doctrine of collateral estoppel for "unmixed questions of law" arising in "successive cases involving unrelated subject matter." Montana v. United States, supra, 440 U.S. at 162. Our holding in no way depends on that exception.

[8]   In Nevada v. United States, 463 U.S. 110 (1983), we applied principles of res judicata against the United States as to one class of claimants who had not been parties to an earlier adjudication, but we recognized that this result obtained in the unique context of "a comprehensive adjudication of water rights intended to settle once and for all the question of how much of the Truckee River each of the litigants was entitled to."

[9]   In *Montana* an individual contractor brought an initial action to challenge Montana's gross receipts tax in state court, and the federal government brought a second action in federal court

an estoppel when the government is litigating the same issue with the same party avoids the problem of freezing the development of the law because the government is still free to litigate that issue in the future with some other party. And, where the parties are the same, estopping the government spares a party that has already prevailed once from having to relitigate—a function it would not serve in the present circumstances. We accordingly hold that the Court of Appeals was wrong in applying nonmutual collateral estoppel against the government in this case.

NOTES AND QUESTIONS

1.   In a companion case to *Mendoza*, United States v. Stauffer Chemical Co., 464 U.S. 165 (1984) (supra p. 1223 n. 7), the Court held that "the doctrine of mutual defensive collateral estoppel is applicable against the government to preclude relitigation of the same issue already litigated against the same party in another case involving virtually identical facts." The issue was whether the Environmental Protection Agency could use private contractors to inspect private plants for compliance with its regulations. The government argued that collateral estoppel should not apply to this "unmixed question of law," but the Court disagreed: "we think that applying an exception to the doctrine of mutual defensive estoppel in this case would substantially frustrate the doctrine's purpose of protecting litigants from burdensome relitigation and of promoting judicial economy." Note, Nonmutual Issue Preclusion Against States, 109 Harv.L.Rev. 792 (1996), critiques *Mendoza* for its "blunt approach" and urges a presumption against, rather than a categorical ban on, estoppel against state governments. The Note chronicles the problems that *Mendoza* has wrought in the federal courts in the form of relitigation of matters thought settled in a given circuit, and the ways in which state courts have reacted to the doctrine. Concluding that since the likelihood of divergent lower court interpretations is less, and that the burden on states of allowing estoppel would also be less, the Note concludes that a flat ban is too strong.

2.   The opinion refers to issues "such as those involved in this case," in denying collateral estoppel. Is there any situation in which *Mendoza* might permit offensive collateral estoppel against the U.S.? Consider United States v. Alaska, 521 U.S. 1 (1997), where the state argued in a dispute with the government over the ownership of submerged coastal lands, that the doctrine should apply to government litigation over similar issues brought before the Supreme Court as part of its limited original jurisdiction over controversies involving the states as parties. The Court refused to consider the proposed exception after concluding that the prior decision did not necessarily decide the question at hand. Id. at 13–14.

3.   Why shouldn't *Mendoza* apply to any defendant subject to multiple litigation on the same issues, for example, automobile manufacturers? How

---

raising the same challenge. The government totally controlled and financed the state-court action; thus for all practical purposes there was mutuality of parties in the two cases. "The United States had a sufficient 'laboring oar' in the conduct of the state-court litigation," Montana v. United States, 440 U.S. at 155, to be constituted a "party" in all but a technical sense.

different is the government from other litigants? Recall Hardy v. Johns-Manville Sales Corp., supra p. 1213. That case involved problems of nonmutual collateral estoppel in the context of asbestos claims which have run into the tens of thousands. Are issues of foreseeability, or other problems of fairness, so different in holding these repeat litigants to be bound by the outcomes of earlier cases?

4.   The Eighth Circuit in United States v. Gurley, 43 F.3d 1188, 1198 n. 2 (8th Cir. 1994), viewed the government exception as an "unsettled issue of law" in light of the different results in *Mendoza* and *Stauffer Chemical Co.* It did not reach the issue, resolving the appeal on other grounds. Some courts have refused to follow the government exception. See, e.g., United States v. Butner, 2000 WL 1842410, *3 (W.D.Mo. 2000) (finding the government estopped from prosecuting defendant for testifying falsely in another case in which it had taken the contradictory position that his testimony was not material). State of Alaska v. United Cook Inlet Drift Association, 895 P.2d 947 (Alaska S.Ct. 1995), a case challenging regulations of the state board of fisheries, rejected the exception to preclude offensive use of collateral estoppel in all cases against the state. It distinguished state from federal litigation since the state attorney general litigates in a single jurisdiction and is faced with a smaller volume of litigation, and here the state had a wide variety of options even if it were collaterally estopped.

5.   Can it legitimately be argued that the government should be *more* subject to preclusion with regard to legal issues than private parties? For an argument that due to its size and power, the government should be required to adhere to decisions about the legality of its conduct, see Note, Collateral Estoppel and Nonacquiescence: Precluding Government Relitigation in the Pursuit of Litigant Equality, 99 Harv.L.Rev. 847 (1986). As this Note points out, the government currently makes conscious choices to refuse to follow judicial decisions holding its conduct illegal except with respect to a litigant who has successfully challenged its actions in court. This practice is called "nonacquiescence." After *Mendoza,* does the government have a license to pursue such a strategy? Should it?

In some instances, the lack of connection between government agencies would make preclusion a questionable policy. Where one agency litigates and loses an issue, it may be inappropriate to bind another independent agency. For an argument that, where agencies have overlapping authority, privity between them should be found, see Comment, Interagency Privity and Claim Preclusion, 57 U.Chi.L.Rev. 195 (1990).

6.   The government sometimes gains the benefit of preclusion doctrines that private litigants cannot invoke. Consider Manning v. United States, 546 F.3d 430 (7th Cir. 2008). There, the plaintiff had obtained a jury verdict of some $6.5 million against officials of the FBI, demonstrating to the jury's satisfaction that the officials had conspired to procure the plaintiff's false conviction. Plaintiff also pursued a claim against the government itself under the Federal Tort Claims Act, seeking damages for the same tortious conduct of the government's officials. A federal judge conducted a bench trial of the FTCA

claims and ruled for the government, according little weight to the prior jury verdict. What's more, the district court ruled that the subsequent FTCA "judgment" triggered a statutory bar to any action by the claimant against the FBI employees "by reason of the same subject matter." 28 U.S.C. § 2676. As a consequence, the district court found that the results of the bench trial, coupled with the statutory judgment bar, retroactively invalidated the prior jury verdict. The decision, affirmed by the Seventh Circuit, thus set aside the plaintiff's favorable constitutional tort judgment under Bivens v. Six Unknown Named Agents of the Federal Bureau of Narcotics, 403 U.S. 388 (1971).

In evaluating the decision, note that the judgment bar was part of the original FTCA, enacted in 1946 at a time when many state courts continued to apply strict rules of mutuality. As noted above, supra p. 1256, one exception to mutuality developed in connection with master-servant litigation and allowed the master facing liability under *respondeat superior* to rely upon a prior judgment in favor of a servant as a bar to suit on the same theory of liability. The statute appears to have been designed to extend the benefits of non-mutual estoppel to the situation in which the plaintiff first proceeds to judgment against the government and, if unsuccessful, brings a second proceeding on the same factual claim of negligence against the employee. For a summary of the history of the FTCA, and an argument that the judgment bar was not meant to apply to claims under Bivens, see Pfander & Aggarwal, Bivens, the Judgment Bar, and the Perils of Dynamic Textualism, 8 St. Thomas L.J. 417 (2011).

In Simmons v. Himmelreich, 136 S.Ct. 1843 (2015), the Supreme Court narrowed the reach of the judgment bar. There, the victim of a beating by a fellow inmate brought suit against both the government under the FTCA and against the relevant prison officials under *Bivens*, alleging negligence in the way prisoners were assigned to cells. The trial court dismissed the FTCA claim after concluding that it fell within the so-called "discretionary" function exception. The officials then argued that the dismissal triggered the judgment bar, blocking *Bivens* liability. Focusing on the language of the FTCA, the Court refused to apply the bar. When a case under the FTCA has been dismissed under one of the FTCA exceptions, that finding also triggers a statutory exception to the judgment bar.

The Court found this result compelled both by the language of the statute and by the common sense of claim preclusion:

> [O]ur holding that the judgment bar provision "shall not apply" to the categories of claims in the "Exceptions" section in fact allows the statute to operate in an utterly sensible manner. Ordinarily, the judgment bar provision prevents unnecessarily duplicative litigation. If the District Court in this case had issued a judgment dismissing Himmelreich's first suit because the prison employees were not negligent, because Himmelreich was not harmed, or because Himmelreich simply failed to prove his claim, it would make little sense to give Himmelreich a second bite at the money-damages apple by allowing suit against the employees: Himmelreich's first suit

> would have given him a fair chance to recover damages for his beating.

Simmons, 136 S.Ct. at 1849. Though dicta, the Court's account of the statute's "utterly sensible" operation suggests that the bar will apply most commonly to cases in which the merits of an overlapping FTCA have been first adjudicated. In a footnote with potentially important future implications, the Court acknowledged that the judgment bar was designed to fill a gap in the common-law doctrine of preclusion as defined in version of the Restatement of Judgments that was current when the FTCA was enacted. Id. at 1849 n. 5.

INDEX

References are to Pages
